MAGRITTE

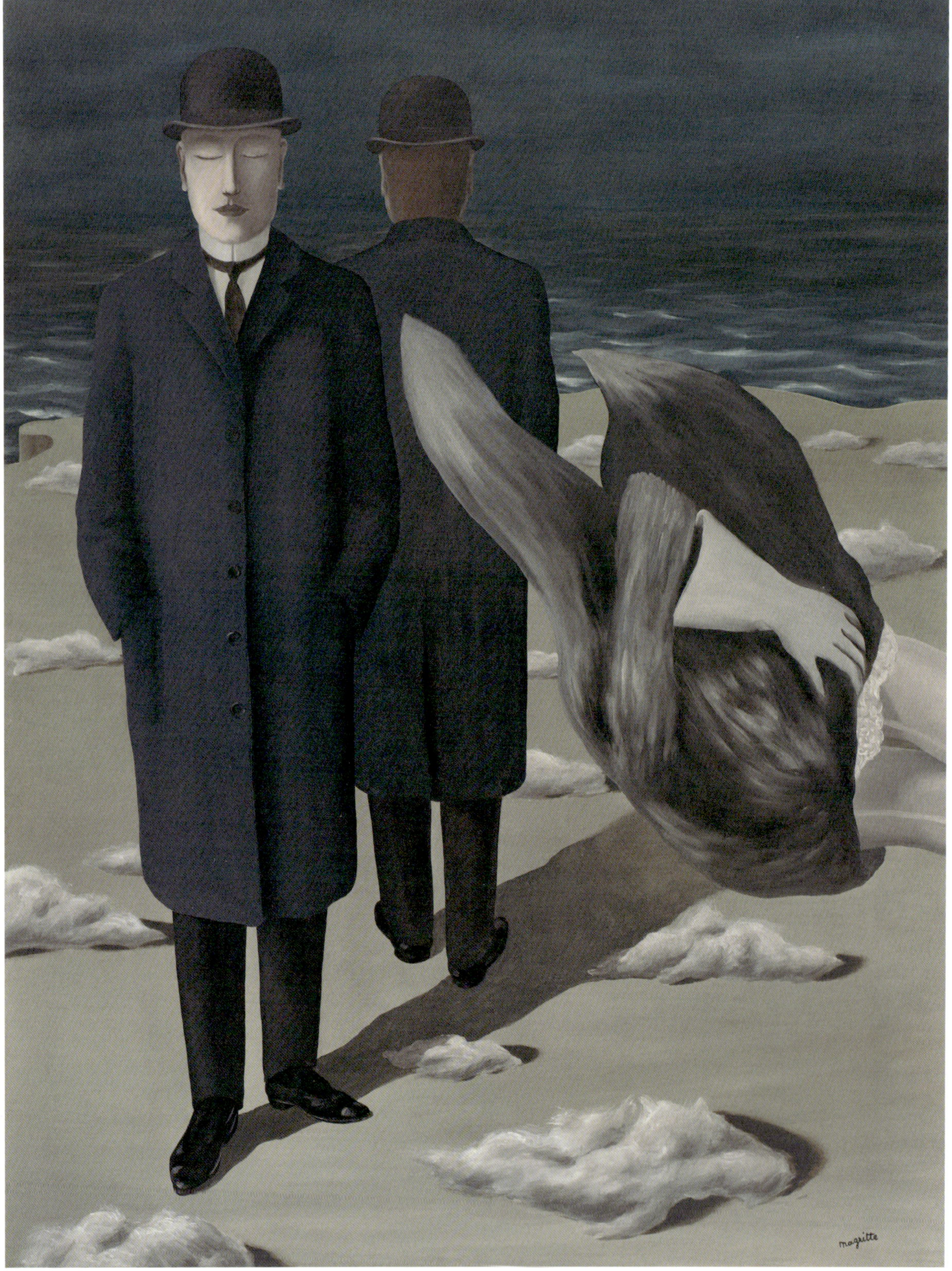
magritte

MAGRITTE

The Mystery of the Ordinary

1926–1938

Edited by **Anne Umland**

with essays by
Stephanie D'Alessandro
Michel Draguet and Claude Goormans
Josef Helfenstein with Clare Elliott
and Anne Umland

The Museum of Modern Art, New York

Published in conjunction with the exhibition *Magritte: The Mystery of the Ordinary, 1926–1938*, organized by The Museum of Modern Art, New York; The Menil Collection, Houston; and the Art Institute of Chicago. The exhibition at The Museum of Modern Art is organized by Anne Umland, The Blanchette Hooker Rockefeller Curator of Painting and Sculpture, with Danielle M. Johnson, Curatorial Assistant, Department of Painting and Sculpture; at The Menil Collection, by Josef Helfenstein, Director; and at the Art Institute of Chicago, by Stephanie D'Alessandro, the Gary C. and Frances Comer Curator of Modern Art.

The exhibition *Magritte: The Mystery of the Ordinary, 1926–1938* is presented at
The Museum of Modern Art, New York, from September 28, 2013, to January 12, 2014
The Menil Collection, Houston, from February 14 to June 1, 2014
The Art Institute of Chicago, from June 29 to October 12, 2014

Bank of America

Bank of America is the National Sponsor of *Magritte: The Mystery of the Ordinary, 1926–1938*.

Major support for the MoMA presentation is provided by the American Friends of Magritte, Inc., and by The International Council of The Museum of Modern Art.

Additional funding is provided by the MoMA Annual Exhibition Fund.

This exhibition is supported by an indemnity from the Federal Council on the Arts and the Humanities.

Support for the accompanying publication is provided by Charly Herscovici.

The presentation at The Menil Collection is generously supported by Fayez Sarofim; The Eleanor and Frank Freed Foundation; The Robert J. Kleberg, Jr. and Helen C. Kleberg Foundation; David and Anne Kirkland; Janie C. Lee and David B. Warren; The Linbeck Family Charitable Trust; The John P. McGovern Foundation; Taub Foundation: Marcy Taub Wessel, Henry J. N. Taub II, and H. Ben Taub; Clare Casademont and Michael Metz; Dedalus Foundation; Baker Botts L.L.P.; Paul and Janet Hobby; Henrietta K. Alexander; Diane and Mike Cannon; and the City of Houston.

Funding for The Art Institute of Chicago presentation is generously provided by the Auxiliary Board of the Art Institute of Chicago, the Lead Affiliate Sponsor.

Annual support for Art Institute exhibitions is provided by the Exhibitions Trust: Goldman Sachs, Kenneth and Anne Griffin, Thomas and Margot Pritzker, the Earl and Brenda Shapiro Foundation, the Trott Family Foundation, and the Woman's Board of the Art Institute of Chicago.

Additional support is provided by the Prince Charitable Trusts.

Produced by the Department of Publications, The Museum of Modern Art, New York

Edited by Diana C. Stoll
Designed by McCall Associates, New York
Production by Marc Sapir
Printed and bound by De Keure, Belgium

This book is typeset in Linotype Fairfield; Linotype Commercial Script; Fenotype Squarendon; MVB Sweet Sans; Adobe Clarendon; and Tungsten, by Hoefler & Frere-Jones. The paper is 150 gsm Perigord matt

Published by The Museum of Modern Art, 11 W. 53 Street, New York, New York 10019

Library of Congress Control Number: 2013941520

ISBN: cloth: 978-0-87070-865-7; paper: 978-0-87070-898-5

Distributed in the United States and Canada by ARTBOOK | D.A.P.
55 Sixth Avenue, 2nd floor, New York, New York 10013
www.artbook.com/www.artbook.com

Distributed outside the United States, Canada, and Belgium by Thames & Hudson Ltd
181 High Holborn, London WC1V 7QX
www.thamesandhudson.com

Published in Belgium by Ludion

Front cover: *Le Double secret* (*The Secret Double*). 1927 (detail; see plate 20). Back cover: *Le Domaine d'Arnheim* (*The Domain of Arnheim*). 1938 (detail; see plate 125). Frontispiece: *Le Sens de la nuit* (*The Meaning of Night*). 1927 (see plate 11). Page 7: *Objet peint: Œil* (*Painted Object: Eye*). 1932/35 (see plate 110)

Printed and bound in Belgium

Contents

Continuing our long tradition of support for the arts, Bank of America is pleased to be the National Sponsor of *Magritte: The Mystery of the Ordinary, 1926–1938*.

As a company serving customers and clients in more than one hundred countries, we understand how the arts create meaningful connections between people, communities, and cultures. Our Corporate Social Responsibility program provides financial and other forms of support to many programs and nonprofit institutions focused on the arts. Through these efforts we are able to help strengthen institutions that contribute to local economies, build mutual respect and understanding in our communities, and engage our customers, clients, and employees who live and work in neighborhoods around the world.

We hope you enjoy this exhibition and are able to share this special experience with your family and friends.

Brian T. Moynihan
Chief Executive Officer, Bank of America

FOREWORD

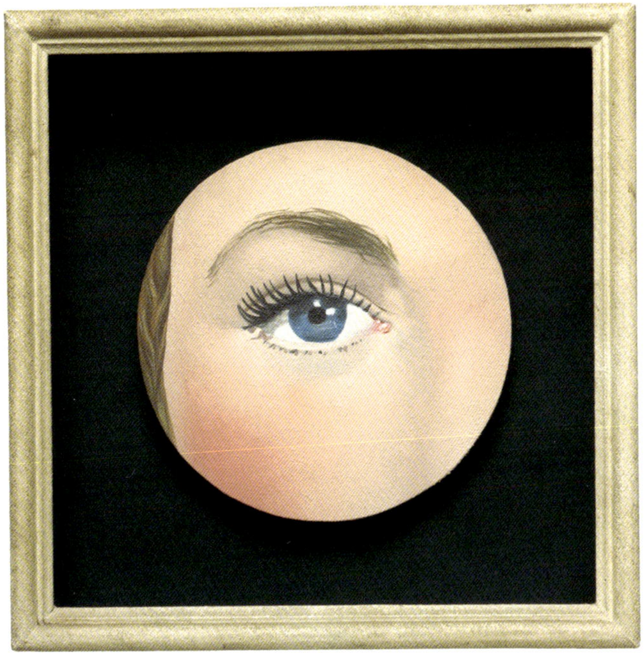

Between 1926 and 1938, René Magritte pioneered a radically new, non-academic approach to figurative painting. Earlier, he had experimented with a series of quasi-abstract styles; now, he set himself the task of making, in his words, "everyday objects shriek out loud," and of creating works that would "challenge the real world." By 1938—thirteen years into this remarkable venture—he delivered an important lecture that highlighted his own accomplishments as a Surrealist painter.

The exhibition *Magritte: The Mystery of the Ordinary, 1926–1938* explores the evolution of the artist's vision during this time. It investigates the key strategies Magritte used to *defamiliarize* the familiar, including displacement, doubling, isolation, metamorphosis, "misnaming" objects, and representing visions seen in half-waking states. In so doing, the exhibition reveals the many ways Magritte's art consistently forces us to recognize clearly legible, realistically rendered images as simply representational, and demonstrates the importance of his development during this essential period.

The Museum of Modern Art, The Menil Collection, and the Art Institute of Chicago have long been committed to the art of René Magritte. MoMA was the first major American museum to acquire works by Magritte for its collection, coincident with the artist's inclusion in Alfred H. Barr, Jr.'s landmark exhibition *Fantastic Art, Dada, Surrealism* in 1936–37. Three decades later, in 1965, MoMA presented a major Magritte retrospective, which inspired the artist to visit the United States for the first time. He attended the exhibition opening in New York and then traveled to Houston, Texas, to meet his great patrons and friends, John and Dominique de Menil. Their foundation would later generously support the Magritte catalogue raisonné project, and their personal collection of the artist's works comprises the basis of The Menil Collection's Magritte holdings, which are rivaled today only by those of the Royal Museums of Fine Arts of Belgium, Brussels. The Art Institute of Chicago has also been a strong supporter of Magritte over the years. By the 1950s Chicago was well known as a city of Surrealist collectors, and Magritte's work had featured in group exhibitions at the AIC since 1949. Building on this interest, in 1966 the museum hosted the *René Magritte* retrospective organized by MoMA. Since that time, the Art Institute of Chicago has acquired several important Magritte canvases; particularly notable are those from the celebrated Surrealist collection of Edward James. The prospect of presenting these paintings, along with those from the collections of MoMA and the Menil, inspired the present collaborative endeavor. The corpus of works from the three partner institutions provides a major touchstone within this exhibition, as does an important group of loans from the Royal Museums of Fine Arts of Belgium.

We are grateful to Anne Umland, The Blanchette Hooker Rockefeller Curator of Painting and Sculpture, for the original concept of the exhibition, and to Stephanie D'Alessandro, the Gary C. and Frances Comer Curator of Modern Art at the Art Institute of Chicago, for her incisive, collaborative contributions to the shaping of the checklist and the exhibition's catalogue. And two of the signatories below are both appreciative and a little envious of the third, Josef Helfenstein, Director of The Menil Collection, for joining Anne and Stephanie as a curatorial partner. We are also thankful to Charly Herscovici, President of the Magritte Foundation, for so generously facilitating Anne, Stephanie, and Josef's research, and for his support of this catalogue, and to Michel Draguet, Director General of the Royal Museums of Fine Arts of Belgium—which includes the Magritte Museum—for so enthusiastically supporting our institutions' endeavors. We are indebted to the many private and institutional lenders who have entrusted us with the care of their works during the course of this exhibition.

We acknowledge the generous donors who have made possible the organization of this exhibition, in particular our National Sponsor, Bank of America. In New York, major support for the exhibition was provided by the American Friends of Magritte, Inc., and by The International Council of The Museum of Modern Art. In Houston, the exhibition is generously supported by Fayez Sarofim; The Eleanor and Frank Freed Foundation; The Robert J. Kleberg, Jr. and Helen C. Kleberg Foundation; David and Anne Kirkland; Janie C. Lee and David B. Warren; The Linbeck Family Charitable Trust; The John P. McGovern Foundation; Taub Foundation: Marcy Taub Wessel, Henry J. N. Taub II, and H. Ben Taub; Clare Casademont and Michael Metz; Dedalus Foundation; Baker Botts L.L.P.; Paul and Janet Hobby; Henrietta K. Alexander; Diane and Mike Cannon; and the City of Houston. In Chicago, funding is provided by the Auxiliary Board of the Art Institute of Chicago, the Lead Affiliate Sponsor. Annual support for Art Institute exhibitions is provided by the Exhibitions Trust: Goldman Sachs, Kenneth and Anne Griffin, Thomas and Margot Pritzker, the Earl and Brenda Shapiro Foundation, the Trott Family Foundation, and the Woman's Board of the Art Institute of Chicago; and additional support is provided by the Prince Charitable Trusts. We also appreciate the support of the Federal Council on the Arts and the Humanities, which provided a generous indemnity.

Glenn D. Lowry
Director, The Museum of Modern Art

Josef Helfenstein
Director, The Menil Collection

Douglas Druick
President and Eloise W. Martin Director, The Art Institute of Chicago

ACKNOWLEDGMENTS

The organization of this first intensive exploration of René Magritte's breakthrough Surrealist period from 1926 to 1938 has involved the assistance and collaboration of many individuals. We have been extraordinarily fortunate in the generous help we have received and the goodwill with which it has been given. Our deepest gratitude must go to the many lenders listed on page 13, both public and private, without whom this exhibition could not have been realized.

The thoughtful, enthusiastic support of Charly Herscovici, President of the Magritte Foundation, has been most sincerely appreciated. Without his location of essential loans and his keen interest in our research, publication, and exhibition, we could never have succeeded. We thank him most wholeheartedly for all his efforts on our behalf. Michel Draguet, Director General of the Royal Museums of Fine Arts of Belgium, Brussels—which includes the Magritte Museum—has also been a vital ally; we are grateful for the core group of loans he has made available to the exhibition and for his constant, ongoing support.

For essential loans and assistance with research, we owe thanks to the following colleagues at public institutions, especially those who made special concessions so that crucial works could be studied and new high-resolution images made for this publication: Doreen Bolger, Jay Fisher, and Rena Hoisington, Baltimore Museum of Art; Alfred Pacquement, Brigitte Léal, Didier Schulmann, Agnès de Bretagne, Emmanuelle Etchecopar Etchart, Camille Morando, and Nécha Mamod, Centre Pompidou, Musée national d'art moderne, Paris; Maxwell Anderson, Olivier Meslay, and Heather MacDonald, Dallas Museum of Art; James Cuno and Thomas W. Gaehtgens, J. Paul Getty Museum and the Getty Research Institute, Los Angeles; Dieter Schwarz, Kunstmuseum Winterthur; Marion Ackermann and Anette Kruszynski, Kunstsammlung Nordrhein-Westfalen, Düsseldorf; Raimund Stecker, Lehmbruck Museum, Duisberg; Michael Govan and Stephanie Barron, Los Angeles County Museum of Art; Thomas P. Campbell, Jennifer Russell (who also provided essential support through the early phases of this project as Senior Deputy Director for Exhibitions, Collections, and Programs at The Museum of Modern Art), and Anna Wall, The Metropolitan Museum of Art, New York; Daniel Birnbaum and Iris Müller-Westermann, Moderna Museet, Stockholm; Claire Leblanc, Musée d'Ixelles, Brussels; Frederik Leen, Sophie Van Vliet, and Valérie Haerden, Royal Museums of Fine Arts of Belgium, Brussels; Sjarel Ex, the late Jonieke van Es, and Patty Wageman, Museum Boijmans Van Beuningen, Rotterdam; Manuel J. Borja-Villel, Museo Nacional Centro de Arte Reina Sofía, Madrid; Earl A. Powell III, National Gallery of Art, Washington D.C.; Ron Radford, Gael Newton, and Anne O'Hehir, National Gallery of Australia, Canberra; Timothy Rub, Carlos Basualdo, and Michael Taylor (now Director, Hood Museum of Art), Philadelphia Museum of Art; Klaus Schrenk, Carla Schulz-Hoffmann (former Deputy Director General and Chief Curator), and Oliver Kase, Bayerische Staatsgemäldesammlungen, Pinakothek der Moderne, Munich; David White and Gina C. Guy, Robert Rauschenberg Foundation, New York; Simon Groom and Patrick Elliott, Scottish National Gallery of Modern Art, Edinburgh; Michael Semff, Staatliche Graphische Sammlung München; Kyllikki Zacharias, Staatliche Museen zu Berlin, Nationalgalerie; Sean Rainbird (now Director, National Gallery of Ireland), Christiane Lange, and Ina Conzen, Staatsgalerie Stuttgart; Nicholas Serota, Caroline Collier, Christoph Grunenberg (now Director, Kunsthalle Bremen), and Matthew Gale, Tate; and Toshihide Yoshida, Amano Kazuo, Norie Nishizaki, and Toshiharu Suzuki, Toyota Municipal Museum of Art. We also thank Laura C. Cunningham, Assistant Indemnity Administrator, National Endowment for the Arts.

Important information and assistance with loans have been provided by many individuals: first and foremost, Emmanuel Di Donna, who gave his time and expertise with remarkable goodwill. In addition, we owe a great deal to Marcel Fleiss, who helped us with many aspects of the project, and to Daniel Abadie, William Acquavella, Agnès Bertola, Marc Blondeau, Isy Brachot, Isy Gabriel Brachot, Ivor Braka, Monique Bréhier, Dieter Brusberg, Olivier Camu, Andrea Caratsch, Jan Ceuleers, Emmanuel Clavé, Nina del Rio, Edouard Derom, Patrick Derom, Marie-Claire Destexhe, Christine Duchiron-Brachot, Catherine Duret, John Elderfield, Daniel Filipacchi, Julia Friedrich, Jon Hendricks, Avi Keitelman, Maurice Keitelman, Kasper König,

Kynaston McShine, Daniel Malingue, Édouard Malingue, Eléonore Malingue, Gilles Marquenie, Gabriella Cittone Martino, Rino Martusciello, Karla Merrifield, Adrien Meyer, Tobias Meyer, Franco Momente, Connor Monahan, Herbert Neumann, Jean-Marc Peretti, Philippe Perrin, Anne Radcliffe, Rachel Rees, Célia Rémy, Jasper Sharp, Rodica Sibleyras, Christine Sirtaine-Janlet, Stephan Slachmuylders, Anna Swinbourne, Dominique Terlinden, Phillip van den Bossche, Ronny Van De Velde, Christophe van de Weghe, Paolo Vedovi, and David Zwirner. For facilitating the study of specific objects from this period in Magritte's work, we are grateful to Hana and Nabil Akkari, Sandra Amann, Abigail Asher, Janet Briner, Martin Craig, Paul Destribats, Natasha Elkon, Mica Ertegun, Esther Grether, Amy and Ronald Guttman, Mania and Bernhard Hahnloser, Patricia Jaspers, Anna Jim, Gilbert Kaplan, Todd Levin, The Mis Family, Daniella Luxembourg, Klaus Neugebauer; David, Leslee, and Leo Rogath; Catherine Sagnier, and Emmanuel Tajan.

A project such as this could not have been realized without the indispensable research of past and present scholars. We would like to recognize most particularly David Sylvester, editor of the first five volumes of the Magritte catalogue raisonné and author of many essays, exhibition catalogues, and other publications on the artist. We also owe profound thanks to Sarah Whitfield, who, in addition to editing the recent sixth volume of the Magritte catalogue raisonné, generously served as our outside reader, bringing her extensive knowledge and sharp critical insights to bear on early drafts of all the essays. Thanks too are due to those who helped us access primary documents: Paul Cougnard, Bibliothèque littéraire Jacques Doucet, Paris; Regan Brumagen, Rakow Research Library, Corning Glass Museum; Sharon-Michi Kusunoki, the Edward James Foundation, Chichester, West Sussex; Véronique Cardon, Archives for Contemporary Art in Belgium, Royal Museums of Fine Arts of Belgium, Brussels; Peter Morris, Chicago; Susan Anderson, Archives, Philadelphia Museum of Art; and Kirstie Meehan, Archives, Scottish National Gallery of Modern Art, Edinburgh.

A primary focus of research for this project was to find what could be discovered in the paintings themselves; this endeavor was greatly facilitated by the expertise and dedication of conservators and other colleagues. We gratefully acknowledge the generous support of: Christina Currie, Institut royal du Patrimoine artistique, Brussels; Joris Dik, Delft University of Technology; Hartwig Fischer (now Director General, Staatliche Kunstsammlungen Dresden), Folkwang Museum, Essen; Charles de Mooij and Fiona Zachariasse, Het Noordbrabants Museum, 's-Hertogenbosch; Jaap Boon, JAAP Enterprise for Art Studies, Amsterdam; Takashi Suzuki, Yuuki Akamatsu, and Sumi Hayashi (former Curator), Kawamura Memorial DIC Museum of Art; Joe Fronek and Jini Rasmussen, Los Angeles County Museum of Art; Isabelle Duvernois and Sabine Rewald, Metropolitan Museum of Art; Lars Byström, Moderna Museet; Juan Antonio Sánchez Pérez, Museo Nacional Centro de Arte Reina Sofía; Oliver Fairclough and Adam Webster, National Museum Wales; Suzanne Penn, Philadelphia Museum of Art; Don H. Johnson, Rice University and co-director, Thread Count Automation Project, Houston; Kristin Parker, Rose Art Museum, Brandeis University, Waltham, Massachusetts; Christian Klemm (former Curator of the Collection) and Tobia Bezzola (now Director, Folkwang Museum, Essen), Kunsthaus Zürich; and Otto Hubacek, Kunstsammlung Nordrhein-Westfalen. For critical assistance with other aspects of research for this project, we sincerely thank: Nele Bernheim, Phillip Van den Bossche, Richard Calvocoressi, Xavier Canonne, Anouck Clissen, Rhys Conlon, Herman Daled, Patrice George, Darren Phi, Diane Maglio, Roderick Orr-Ewing, and Adrian Sudhalter.

The partnership between The Museum of Modern Art, The Menil Collection, and the Art Institute of Chicago began three years ago with The Museum of Modern Art's proposal that our institutions collaborate in the research, project planning, and securing of loans for an exhibition focused on Magritte's defining Surrealist years. We are grateful for the dedication, creativity, and consummate professionalism of our colleagues at each institution. Most particularly, we consider ourselves fortunate to be part of an outstanding collaborative team that includes a distinguished group of museum conservators. At The Museum of Modern Art, these include Michael Duffy and Anny Aviram; at The Menil Collection, Brad Epley and Katrina Bartlett; and at the Art Institute of Chicago, Allison Langley. In addition to the core research group for the project, we are grateful to a number of additional staff in our institutions' conservation departments for supporting our work: at The Museum of Modern Art, Jim Coddington, Chief Conservator; Cindy Albertson, Kress Fellow; Lee Ann Daffner, Photography Conservator; Scott Gerson, Associate Conservator; and Ana Martins, Associate Research Scientist; at The Menil Collection, Erin Stephenson, Mellon Fellow, and Adam Baker, conservation framer and photographer; and at the Art Institute of Chicago, Frank Zuccari and Kirk Vuillemot. The insights, contributions, and suggestions of Mr. Duffy, Mr. Epley, Ms. Bartlett, and Ms. Langley, as well as those from Danielle Johnson, Curatorial Assistant, Department of Painting and Sculpture, The Museum of Modern Art, have significantly enriched the catalogue.

The Museum of Modern Art administered the exhibition and produced the English-language version of this book. Our foremost thanks go to Glenn D. Lowry, Director; Ramona Bannayan, Senior Deputy Director for Exhibitions and Collections; and Peter Reed, Senior Deputy Director for Curatorial Affairs, for their steadfast support. Ann Temkin, The Marie-Josée and Henry Kravis Chief Curator of Painting and Sculpture, has been an enthusiastic advocate from the inception of the project. We also wish to thank, in the Department of Exhibition Planning and Administration, Erik Patton, Associate Director, Randolph Black, Associate Coordinator, and Maria DeMarco Beardsley (former Coordinator of Exhibitions); in General Counsel, Patty Lipshutz and Nancy Adelson; in the Office of the Registrar, Stefanii Ruta-Atkins, Allison Needle, and Corey Wyckoff; in the Department of Art Handling and Preparation, Rob Jung and Sarah Wood; in the Department of Graphic Design, Claire Corey, Sabine Dowek, Greg Hathaway, and Wendy Olson; in the Department of Exhibition Design and Production, Jerry Neuner, Betty Fisher, Peter Perez, and Michele Arms. Supporting our research from the outset were Milan Hughston and the dedicated staff of The Museum of Modern Art's Library and Archives: Jenny Tobias, Michelle Harvey, and Lori Salmon. We are especially grateful to Erik Landsberg, Robert Kastler, and Roberto Rivera in the Department of Imaging Services for facilitating the new photography requested for this publication. We are also indebted to, in the Department of Education, Wendy Woon, Sara Bodinson, Pablo Helguera, and Stephanie Pau; in the Department of External Affairs, Todd Bishop, Lauren Stakias, Heidi Speckhart, and Claire Huddleston; in the Department of Communications, Kim Mitchell, Margaret Doyle, and Paul Jackson; in Digital Media, Allegra Burnette, Chiara Bernasconi, and David Hart; and in International Programs, Jay Levenson. The assistance of Special Events, Facilities, Security, and Visitor Services is warmly appreciated.

In the Department of Painting and Sculpture, Danielle Johnson has been a partner in the truest sense. Even before joining the Museum in 2011, she generously contributed time and expertise in developing the exhibition's concept, and has worked tirelessly to ensure that this publication and the exhibition it accompanies are the very best they can be. We salute her commitment to Magritte's work, and have relied on her scholarly insight and curatorial judgment in every phase of this endeavor, in addition to her skillful handling of myriad administrative and diplomatic responsibilities. Special thanks also go to Janet Yoon, who came to the project when it was already well underway and quickly mastered its complexities of content and procedure. Former colleagues Nora Lawrence and Caitlin Kelly provided essential assistance through the early phases of this project, as did Blair Hartzell and Paulina Pobocha. Cora Rosevear and Lily Goldberg worked with exceptional attentiveness to the issues of loan arrangements. We would also like to acknowledge the kind help of Leah Dickerman, Laura Hoptman, and Danielle King. This project has benefited from the dedicated efforts of a number of interns who worked on it over the years of its preparation: Shira Backer, Helen Goldenberg, Louisa Strauss, and Jessica Womack. Special thanks go to Lee Hallman, Andrew W. Mellon Curatorial Fellow. In the Department of Prints and Drawings, we wish to thank Christophe Cherix and Katherine Alcauskas. In the Department of Photography, we wish to thank Quentin Bajac.

At the Menil Collection, we thank Clare Elliott, Assistant Curator, for her hard work on behalf of the exhibition and the catalogue, and for her support in the research and writing of the catalogue essay focused on Magritte's years in Paris. We would also like to recognize the research assistance provided by Eric Wolf, Head Librarian; Geraldine

Aramanda, Archivist; Lisa Barkely, Archival Assistant; and Mari Lozón de Cantelmi, former Menil intern. We are thankful to Joseph N. Newland, Director of Publishing, for his thoughtful comments on the Paris years essay. Special gratitude is due to Anne Adams, Chief Registrar; Melanie Crader, Budget and Project Manager; Michael Cannon, Chief Financial Officer; and Sheryl Kolasinski, Deputy Director and Chief Operating Officer, for their careful oversight of this complex project. We thank Brooke Stroud, Exhibition Designer; and Tom Walsh, Head of Art Services, for their diligence and professionalism, and also for their creativity and sensitivity in ensuring that the exhibition was installed with the utmost care. We acknowledge the Menil Collection's security and facilities staff, under the direction of Steve McConathy and Getachew Mengesha, for their role in guaranteeing the continued safety of the works in the exhibition. We extend thanks to Karl Kilian, Director of Public Programs; Amanda Shagrin, Manager of Membership Programs; and Vance Muse, Director of Communications, for helping to bring awareness of the exhibition to both the institution's members and the general public. We appreciate the important efforts on behalf of the exhibition of the Menil's development department under Acting Director Alexis Harrigan. Thanks are also due to Madeline Kelly, Assistant to the Director. Finally, we are grateful to the Menil Collection's Board of Trustees, under the leadership of President Harry C. Pinson, for their unwavering support for this ambitious exhibition.

At the Art Institute of Chicago, sincere thanks go to Douglas Druick, President and Eloise W. Martin Director; Martha Tedeschi, Deputy Director for Art and Research; and Dorothy Schroeder, Vice President for Exhibitions and Museum Administration, who steadfastly supported this project from its start. We also wish to thank David Thurm, Chief Operating Officer, and Jeanne Ladd, Vice President of Museum Finance. We also thank, in General Counsel, Julia E. Getzels, Maria Simon, Jennifer Sostaric, and Troy Klyber; in Design and Construction, Sara Urizar and Markus Dohner; in Physical Plant, William Caddick and his staff; and in Graphic Design, Jeff Wonderland and his talented team. We are especially grateful to Louis Meluso and Christopher Gallagher in Imaging for facilitating the new photography requested for this publication. We are also indebted to, in the Department of Education, Judith Kirshner; in the Department of Development, Steven Berry, Jennifer Moran, and George Martin; in the Department of Marketing and Public Affairs, Gordon Montgomery and Erin Hogan; and in the Library, Jack Brown, Melanie Emerson, and Autumn Mather, for facilitating our research. In the Department of Medieval to Modern European Painting and Sculpture, in addition to Sylvain Bellenger, Searle Chair and Curator, we are especially grateful to Jennifer Paoletti, Exhibition Manager; Jennifer Cohen, former Research Associate; Elizabeth McGoey, Research Associate; and Marie Dihu, former Assistant, who contributed to this project in numerous significant ways; additional thanks go to Adrienne Jeske, Katharine Baetjer, Robert Burnier, Aza Quinn-Brauner. We also thank Alison Fisher, Department of Architecture and Design, for her assistance with research. In the Ryerson and Burnham Library, we are grateful to Jack Brown and Christine Fabian for administering several loans to the exhibition.

Led by Christopher Hudson, The Museum of Modern Art's Department of Publications has provided expert, dedicated work in the preparation of the present volume, produced in collaboration with their Belgian partners, Ludion. Chul R. Kim, David Frankel, and Marc Sapir deserve our gratitude for their efforts and advice. We deeply appreciate Diana Stoll's clear thinking and consummate care as an editor. Mark Nelson of McCall Associates produced an elegant and sensitive design that admirably suits the subject; we sincerely thank him for his great efforts. Hannah Kim and Makiko Wholey provided critical support as well. The willingness of our lenders and their respective curators, collection managers, registrars, imaging specialists, and assistants to accommodate our requests for new imaging has been remarkable. We are tremendously grateful to be able to represent, with high quality, color-accurate reproductions, the extraordinary body of work Magritte created during his breakthrough Surrealist years.

Anne Umland
Josef Helfenstein
Stephanie D'Alessandro

LENDERS TO THE EXHIBITION

The Baltimore Museum of Art
Staatliche Museen zu Berlin, Nationalgalerie, Sammlung Scharf-Gerstenberg
Musée d'Ixelles, Brussels
Royal Museums of Fine Arts of Belgium, Brussels
Royal Museums of Fine Arts of Belgium, Brussels/ Archives for Contemporary Art in Belgium
National Gallery of Australia, Canberra
The Art Institute of Chicago
Ryerson & Burnham Libraries, The Art Institute of Chicago
Dallas Museum of Art
Lehmbruck Museum, Duisberg
Kunstsammlung Nordrhein-Westfalen, Düsseldorf
Scottish National Gallery of Modern Art, Edinburgh
The Menil Collection, Houston
Menil Collection Library, Special Collections, Houston
The Getty Research Institute, Los Angeles
Los Angeles County Museum of Art, Los Angeles
Museo Nacional Centro de Arte Reina Sofía, Madrid
Staatliche Graphische Sammlung München
Pinakothek der Moderne, Bayerische Staatsgemäldesammlungen, Munich
The Metropolitan Museum of Art, New York
The Museum of Modern Art, New York
The Museum of Modern Art Library, New York
The Robert Rauschenberg Foundation, New York
Centre Pompidou, Musée national d'art moderne/ Centre de création industrielle, Paris
Centre Pompidou, Musée national d'art moderne— Bibliothèque Kandinsky
Philadelphia Museum of Art
Museum Boijmans Van Beuningen, Rotterdam
Moderna Museet, Stockholm
Staatsgalerie Stuttgart
Tate
Toyota Municipal Museum of Art
National Gallery of Art, Washington, D.C.
Kunstmuseum Winterthur

Timothy Baum, New York
Isadora and Isy Gabriel Brachot
Irma and Norman Braman, Miami Beach, Florida
Eric Decelle, Brussels
Gale and Ira Drukier
Ruth Horwich
Jasper Johns
Daniel Malingue
Sylvio Perlstein, Antwerp
Mr. and Mrs. Wilbur Ross

Anonymous lenders
Courtesy Brachot Gallery, Belgium
Private collection, courtesy Keitelman Gallery, Brussels
Deposited with the Magritte Museum, Brussels
Private collection, Switzerland, courtesy Simon Studer Art, Geneva
Private West Coast collection, courtesy BLAIN | DI DONNA Gallery, New York
Private collection, courtesy Galerie 1900–2000, Paris
Private collection, courtesy Het Noordbrabants Museum, 's-Hertogenbosch

Galerie Vedovi, Brussels

AG Insurance

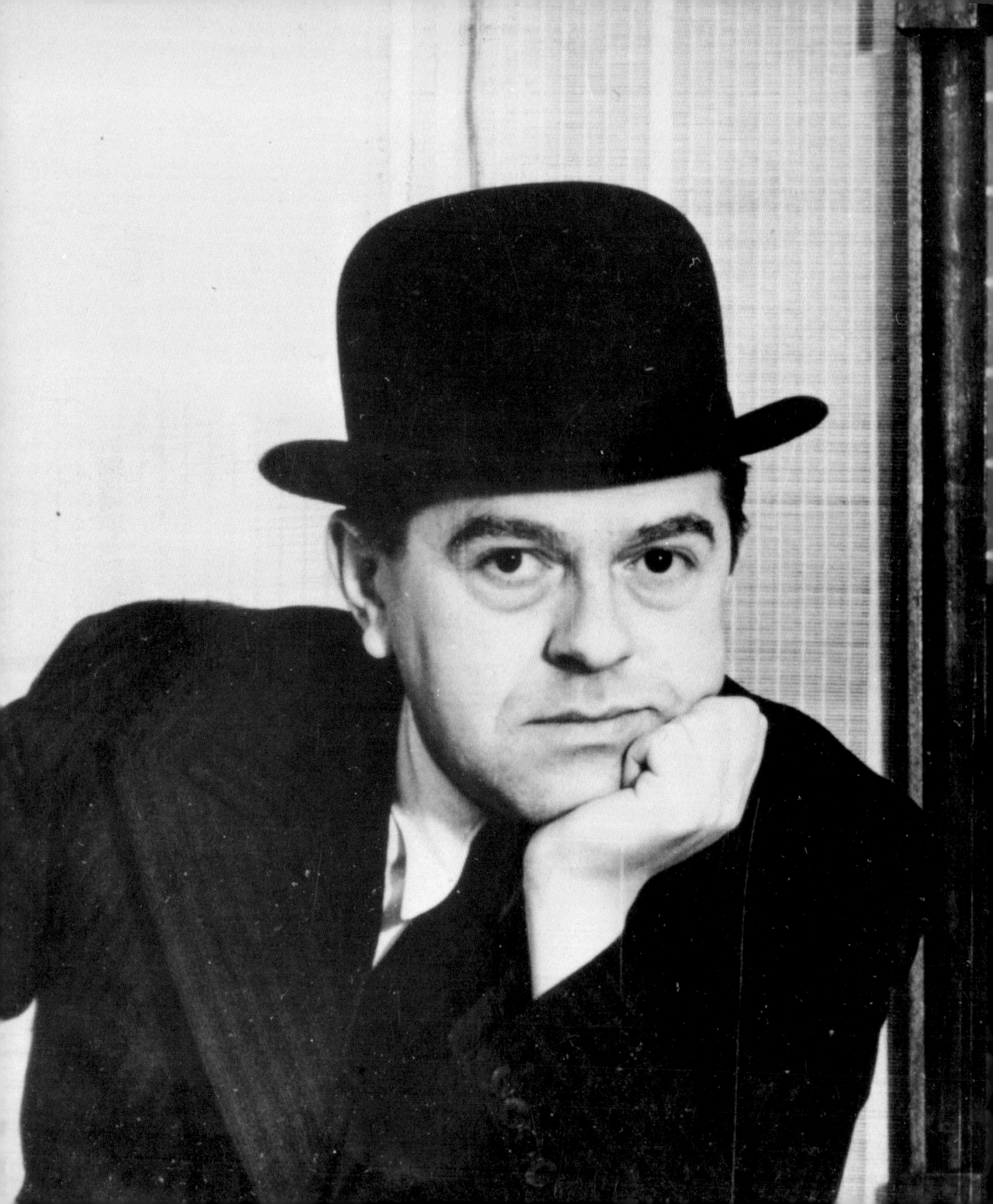

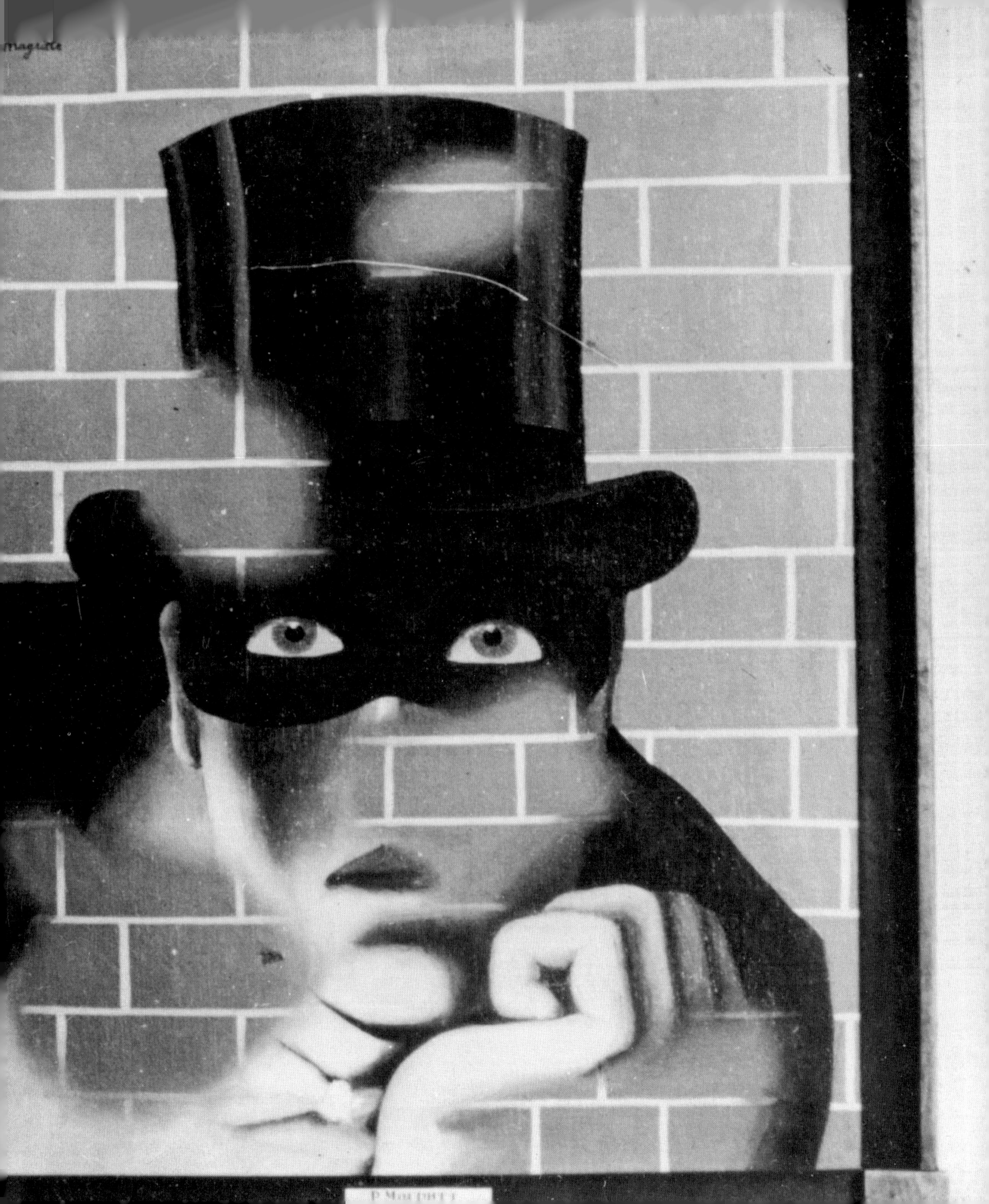
magritte

Introduction MAGRITTE'S ESSENTIAL SURREALIST YEARS 1926–1938

Anne Umland, Stephanie D'Alessandro, and Josef Helfenstein

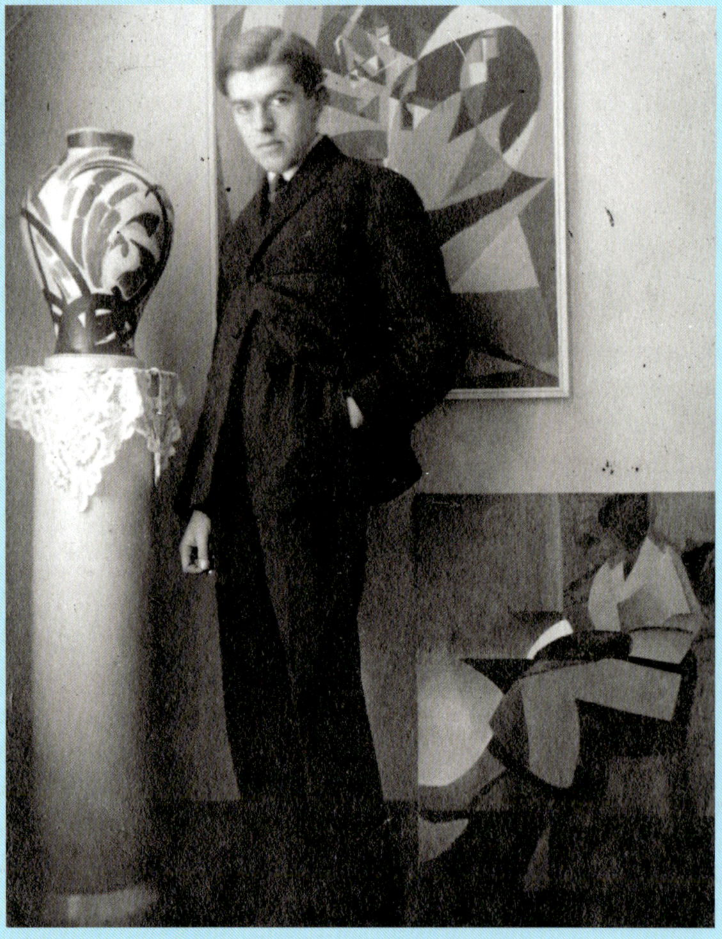

Figure 1. René Magritte at the family house, 16, avenue du Boulevard, Saint-Josse, Brussels, with [*Seated Woman*], 1920 (Sylvester 1:18), and an unidentified abstract painting. Dated on verso March 1921. Photographer unknown. 4 5/8 x 3 5/8" (11 x 8.4 cm). Menil Archives, The Menil Collection, Houston

On Sunday, November 20, 1938, René Magritte delivered an important autobiographical lecture titled "La Ligne de vie" ("Lifeline") at the Koninklijk Museum voor Schone Kunsten in Antwerp, some thirty miles north of Magritte's home on the outskirts of Brussels.[1] Falling just one day shy of his fortieth birthday and at a moment of increasing international recognition for the artist, the occasion provided him with a unique opportunity for retrospective self-assessment and an accounting of his artistic development and goals.[2] Among the most significant leitmotifs of Magritte's lecture was his own defining involvement with Surrealism, to which he referred directly and indirectly several times in "La Ligne de vie."

Despite this definitive acknowledgment of the importance of his own historical relationship with the Surrealists, Magritte's early contributions to the movement remain largely underrecognized.[3] So too do the range and distinctive character of his efforts first created under the sign of Surrealism, beginning with the body of work he produced in 1926 and 1927 for his inaugural one-person exhibition in Brussels, and concluding in 1938, the year of "La Ligne de vie."[4] The outbreak of World War II the following year marks a caesura. After the war, Magritte's relation to Surrealism took on a different character; as was the case for so many people and things, the war left him, and the movement itself, irrevocably changed.[5]

This publication and the exhibition it accompanies look back at Magritte's foundational Surrealist years, focusing with a historically specific lens on the works he produced between 1926 and 1938. The aim is to sharpen contemporary understanding of his achievement: What are the characteristics of Magritte's work that identify him as a Surrealist? How does his work of this period compare to Surrealism's other great painters, such as Joan Miró, Max Ernst, and Salvador Dalí? What is it that makes Magritte unique? Although his figurative vocabulary, along with the traditional character of his chosen materials—oil paint and canvas—and his nominally "academic" technique, have led some to dismiss Magritte's art as retrograde, the body of work he created during this intensely innovative thirteen-year period reveals that this is anything but the case. An investigation of these paintings shows that his famously deadpan style and approach to subject matter—the antithesis, in many ways, of Dalí's lustrous, richly glazed surfaces and hallucinatory imagery—were but part of a methodically deconstructive practice, aimed at casting doubt on conventional systems of representation, both verbal and visual, in ways that remain utterly distinct.

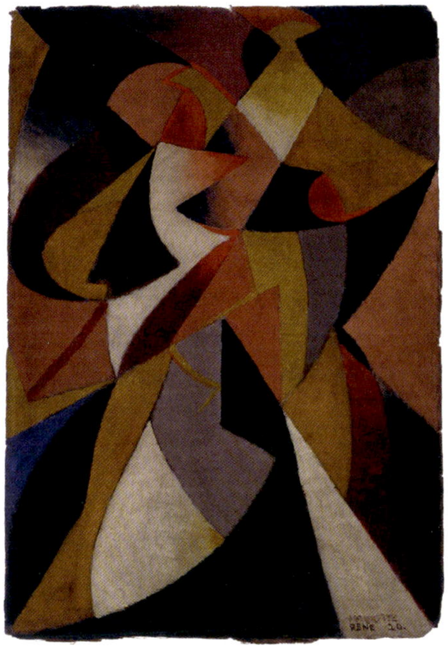

Figure 2. René Magritte. [*Head of a Man*]. 1920. Oil on canvas, 25 x 18" (63.5 x 45.2 cm). The Menil Collection, Houston. (Sylvester 1:14)

Prior to 1927 Magritte was best known (to the degree that he was known at all) as a graphic artist and a painter of stylized, post-Cubist paintings that demonstrated he had absorbed the anti-illusionistic lessons of the avant-garde (figs. 1, 2).[6] His first one-person exhibition, presented at the Galerie Le Centaure in Brussels from April 23 to May 3, 1927, introduced a dramatically different René Magritte.

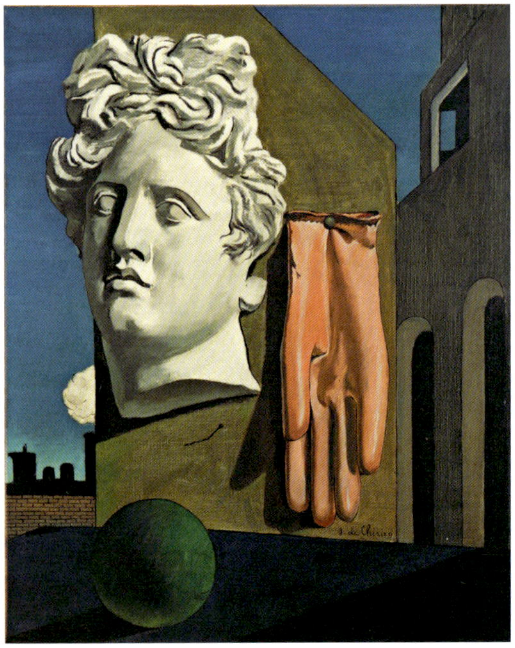

Figure 3. Giorgio de Chirico. *The Song of Love*. 1914. Oil on canvas, 28 3/4 x 23 3/8" (73 x 59.1 cm). The Museum of Modern Art, New York. Nelson A. Rockefeller Bequest

It included forty-nine paintings and twelve *papiers collés* created between January 1926 and April 1927. These works bore witness to Magritte's deliberate decision, as retrospectively described in "La Ligne de vie," to introduce into his pictures "objects with all the details they show us in reality."[7] Magritte contextualized this shift from semi-abstract to figurative painting in relation to a variety of factors: the Surrealist movement itself, which, he asserted, "claims for our waking life a freedom similar to that which we have in dreams"; the works of artists such as Giorgio de Chirico (fig. 3), Marcel Duchamp, Max Ernst, and Pablo Picasso, whom he acknowledged as key precursors of "what is now called 'Surrealist Painting'"; and Magritte's own discovery and subsequent rejection of Futurism.[8]

Magritte additionally noted that his decision to paint objects that could "be clearly apprehended" was precipitated by a specific moment of insight: the artist recalled "a prolonged contemplative experience [...] in an unpretentious Brussels brasserie [...where] I was in a frame of mind such that the moldings on a door seemed to me to be imbued with a mysterious quality of existence and for a long time I stayed in contact with their reality."[9] By the late 1930s descriptions of such catalytic visual encounters were a well-established Surrealist trope. Max Ernst's quasi-autobiographical treatise "Au delà de la peinture" ("Beyond Painting") offers an early case in point that was surely known to Magritte.[10] A portion of Ernst's text was first published in the October 1927 issue of *La Révolution surréaliste* (under the title "Visions de demi-sommeil" [Visions of half-sleep]), on the heels of Magritte's move to Paris.[11] It was published again, in expanded form, in 1936 and yet again in 1937, just one year prior to Magritte's crafting and delivery of his "La Ligne de vie" lecture.[12] The parallels between Magritte's talk and Ernst's "Au delà de la peinture" alert us to the highly constructed and selective character of "La Ligne de vie": it is by no means a transparent, straightforward, or factual account, but rather one in which the fictional and nonfictional are continuously entangled, in the artist's effort to project a logical consistency onto the narrative of his own development as a Surrealist painter up until 1938.[13] The alignments between the two texts also suggest that Magritte may have conceived his lecture, at least in part, in response to Ernst's previously published accounts.

Thus the differences, as well as the similarities, between Magritte's and Ernst's narratives provide insights into both artists' approaches.[14] Ernst memorably opens "Au delà de la peinture" with a description of a vision he had in his bedroom as a young boy, in a state of half-sleep: "I see before me a panel," he writes, using the vivid present tense, "very rudely painted with wide black lines on a red ground, representing false mahogany and calling forth associations of organic forms."[15] This verbal picture of a *faux bois* panel that provoked associative visions of new, imaginary forms is followed by another image, of Ernst's father drawing on the same panel with a "fat crayon" while "panting violently." In the lines that ensue, Ernst identifies the occasion as "the night of my conception." This associates his elliptical descriptions of artistic activity and generation with copulation. It also identifies the overall scenario as an unusual Freudian "primal scene," in which the child observes his own making.

By contrast, the detached tone of Magritte's account of his "prolonged contemplative experience" at the Brussels brasserie, along with that experience's relatively prosaic character, seem particularly marked when held up against Ernst's psychosexually overdetermined text. Magritte locates his moment of visual revelation not in the sexually charged, intimate sphere of the bedroom, but in an "unpretentious" brasserie, a place of public discourse and conviviality. Equally significant is "the mysterious quality" of the "moldings on a door"—presumably made from real wood as opposed to Ernst's "false mahogany"—that captured and rewarded Magritte's intense and extended gaze. By staring at the moldings for a "prolonged" period, he was able to apprehend their *ordinary* mystery, reinforcing his conviction to "only paint objects with all their visible details."[16] Ernst's act of looking at a painted representation of a mahogany panel, contrarily, produced visions of newly imagined things. He went on from this moment, which he described as "primal," to pursue ever more new possibilities for automatically generating images, using found materials like "floor-boards [. . .] leaves and their veins, the ragged edges of a bit of linen," and so on.[17]

In a later section of "Au delà de la peinture," Ernst cites Louis Aragon's influential essay "La Peinture au défi" ("The Challenge to Painting"), which identifies Ernst as the first to create "the two forms of collage most removed from the principle of the *papier collé*—the photographic collage and the illustration collage," as evidence of his own pioneering role as the inventor of Surrealist collage.[18] A few pages later, Ernst itemizes the various "conquests" of collage, among which, he notes, was "*surrealist painting*, in at least one of its multiple aspects, that which, between 1921 and 1924, I was the only one to develop, and in which, later, while I advanced alone, feeling my way, into the yet unexplored forests of *frottage*, others continued their researches (Magritte, for example, whose pictures are collages entirely painted by hand, and Dalí)."[19] Illustrated directly above this passage is Ernst's painting *La Belle Saison* (*The Beautiful Season*)—an enlarged 1925 version, in oil on canvas, of a small 1920 collage (fig. 4).[20] The preceding pages feature numerous large, collagelike paintings, created—according to the captions—between 1921 and 1924: *Oedipus Rex*; *Célébes* (sic); and *La Révolution la nuit* (*Revolution by Night*), to name just a few.[21] All bolstered Ernst's claim to having invented not just one important new artistic tradition but two: Surrealist collage *and* Surrealist collagelike painting.

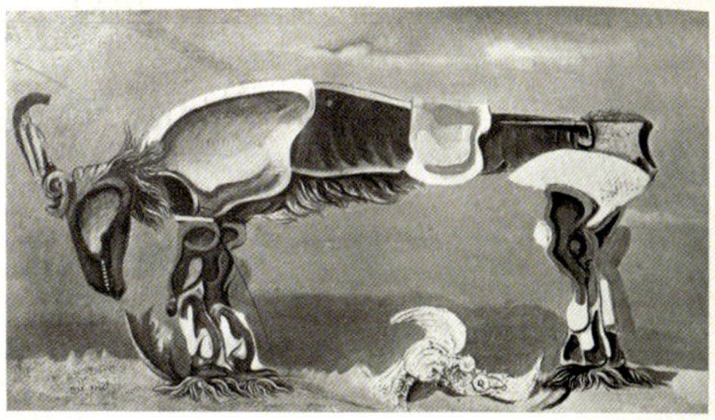

la belle saison. 1925. Coll. privée. 100 × 65

la quantité exacte des possibilité de bonheur humain à toute époque. La quantité d'humour noir contenue dans chaque collage authentique s'y trouve dans la proportion inverse des possibilités de bonheur (objectif et subjectif).

Ceci infirme l'opinion de quelques-uns qui ont voulu voir dans la prétendue absence de tout humour dans la peinture surréaliste, la différence essentielle entre celle-ci et les œuvres dadaïstes : notre époque serait-elle plus rose que les années 1917-1921 ?

QUELLE EST LA PLUS NOBLE CONQUÊTE DU COLLAGE ?

C'est l'irrationnel. C'est l'irruption magistrale de l'irrationnel dans tous les domaines de l'art, de la poésie, de la science, dans la mode, dans la vie privée des individus, dans la vie publique des peuples.*) Qui dit collage, dit l'irrationnel. Le collage s'est introduit sournoisement dans nos objets usuels. Nous avons acclamé son apparution dans les films surréalistes (je pense à l'*Age d'or* de Buñuel et Dali : la vache dans le lit, l'évêque et la girafe jetés par la fenêtre, le chariot traversant le salon du gouverneur, le ministre de l'Intérieur collé au plafond après son suicide, etc.). En faisant succéder sans choix des collages aux collages, nous fûmes surpris par la clarté de l'action irrationnelle qui en résultait : La *Femme 100 têtes*, le *Rêve d'une petite fille qui voulut entrer au Carmel*, la *Semaine de bonté*. N'oublions pas cette autre conquête du collage : la peinture surréaliste, au moins quant à l'un de ses multiples aspects, en l'espèce celui que, entre 1921 et 1924, je fus seul à élaborer*) et dont plus tard, pendant que, seul, j'avançais à tâtons dans les forêts encore inexplorées du « frottage », d'autres ont continué les recherches (Magritte, par exemple, dont les tableaux sont collages entièrement peints à la main, et Dali).

*) Je rappelle cette note parue dans le « *Oberbadisches Volksblatt* », du 12 février 1934 :

DU SUPERZELE POLITIQUE
Imagination maladive.

« Depuis quelque temps, les autorités reçoivent une certaine » quantité de cartes postales, de tableaux et d'affiches dans les» quels on flaire de la propagande communiste camouflée. Dans » la chevelure d'une tête, quoiqu'il s'agisse d'une photographie, » on a voulu découvrir la figure de Lénine, dans l'oreille de la » même tête une image obscène. On a trouvé cachés dans une » affiche, un crâne fracassé et une tête de communiste. Il est à » remarquer que, pour jouir de cette affiche-devinette, collée et » accrochée de façon habituelle, le spectateur serait obligé de » marcher sur la tête. Les lieux officiels s'opposent à un tel super» zèle politique qui pourrait alarmer inutilement la population et » nuire à des intérêts légitimes. Les lieux officiels ont reçu l'ordre » d'opprimer avec toute leur énergie ces agissements insensés qui » facilement pourraient dégénérer en psychose dangereuse. »

*) Chirico, auquel je dois de rendre hommage en passant, avait déjà pris un autre chemin, on sait lequel.

Chacun connaît cet autre aspect extrêmement important de la peinture surréaliste, celui dont les représentants les plus authentiques sont Arp, Miró, Man Ray, Picasso et Giacometti, et dont les origines remontent aux « papiers collés » de Braque et de Picasso.

42

Figure 4. Page from *Max Ernst: Œuvres de 1919 à 1936* (*Max Ernst: Works from 1919 to 1936*), showing *La Belle Saison* (*The Beautiful Season*, 1925). Paris: Éditions Cahiers d'art, 1937. The Museum of Modern Art Library, New York

Magritte protested Ernst's characterization of his own work in a letter he wrote to André Breton, the leader of the Paris Surrealists, most likely in the spring of 1937.[22] Therein Magritte asked Breton to write about him, and specifically requested that Breton correct Ernst's "too facile comment" that Magritte's paintings were "collages entirely painted by hand."[23] Magritte complained to Breton that Ernst was disparagingly implying that his work involved nothing more than a simple juxtaposition of images, discounting the very particular character of his approach to "objects," which involved what Magritte described mysteriously as a "mental operation."[24] Though he didn't mention this, Ernst's text also implied that Magritte, too, was a "conquest," passively pursuing a course of action initiated by Ernst.

Magritte acknowledged in "La Ligne de vie" that for him (as indeed for most artists associated with Surrealism) "the placing of objects out of context" was a "basic device" for defamiliarizing the familiar.[25] Juxtaposition, in other words—which Ernst broadly described as "collage"—played a fundamental role. But to suggest, as Ernst did, that Magritte's paintings were nothing more than "hand-painted collages,"[26] and as such akin to his own collagelike works, elides the substantive differences in style and strategy that make them instantly recognizable and completely unique.

Consider, for example, the relation between Ernst's *Pietà ou la révolution la nuit* (*Pietà or Revolution by Night*, 1923; fig. 5) and Magritte's *Le Sens de la nuit* (*The Meaning of Night*, 1927; plate 11). This is one of several cases in which Magritte seems to point directly at the older artist's work in order to "correct" him.[27] Magritte's painting is far simpler than Ernst's; the palette is distinctively subdued, as is the facture, and there is a degree of spatial illusionism that at first glance appears to be straightforward but on further inspection reveals itself to have been subtly manipulated. More significantly, while Ernst presents us with three distinct subjects, Magritte offers a pair of seemingly identical figures, presented back to back. While these bowler-hatted men would years later come to be seen as stand-ins for Magritte himself—the bourgeois artist, going about the business of painting in a deliberate, dispassionate way—here, at their moment of entry into the artist's œuvre, they play a different role. The reiteration of the figure forces recognition of both as purely and merely representational. Neither is "real," despite their convincingly modeled, three-dimensional forms. Masquerading as ordinary, they reveal themselves to be extraordinary, their very "normalness" a key to what makes Magritte's art so memorably strange.

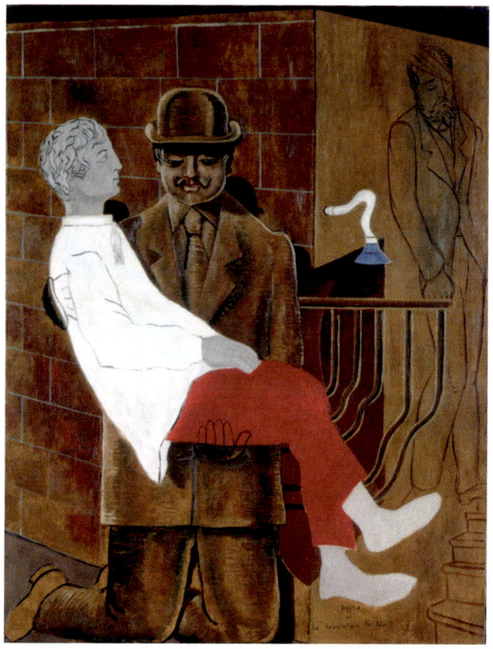

Figure 5. Max Ernst. *Pietà ou la révolution la nuit* (*Pietà or Revolution by Night*). 1923. Oil on canvas, 45 3/4 x 35" (116.2 x 88.9 cm). Tate, London

All who study the life and work of Magritte are indebted to the vast corpus of critical commentary and primary documentation assembled and published by David Sylvester, author of many essays, exhibition catalogues, and books on the artist, and editor of the definitive Magritte catalogue raisonné.[28] That multivolume reference is a model of its kind, providing an essential scholarly foundation upon which we hope to build in the present project, by bringing intense focus to specific groups of works by Magritte, made in specific places, at specific moments in time.

In the first of the four essays that comprise the core of this publication, Anne Umland investigates the body of work Magritte produced in Brussels between January 1926 and his departure for France in September 1927, a crucial period for Magritte's self-definition as a Surrealist, and a time of close, collaborative involvement with Paul Nougé, leader of the Brussels Surrealist group.[29] The second essay, by Josef Helfenstein with Clare Elliott, focuses on works created during Magritte's almost three years of living just outside Paris, in the suburb of Perreux-sur-Marne—a moment of creative growth for the artist and the most productive period in his career. Following this Michel Draguet and Claude Goormans consider the works Magritte produced after a combination of personal and financial factors forced him to leave France in June 1930 and return to Brussels, where he lived for the rest of his life. The volume's final essay, by Stephanie D'Alessandro, concentrates on the weeks Magritte spent working in London in 1937, and on the series of paintings he produced between 1937 and 1938 for the eccentric British collector and great Surrealist patron, Edward James, an opportunity that solidified the future public persona of the artist, and the perception of his work.

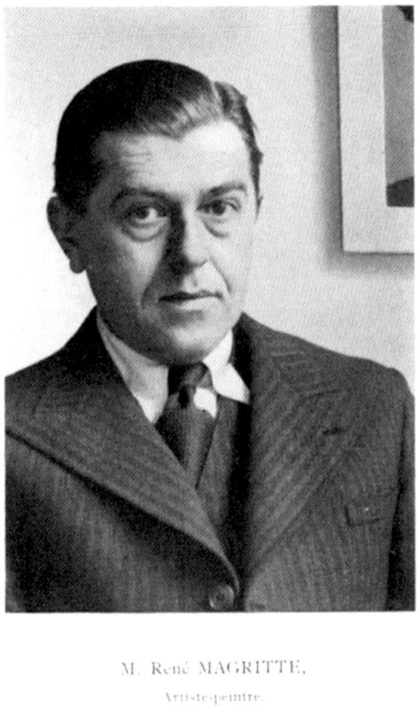

Figure 6. Photograph of Magritte, as reproduced in the program of his lecture "La Ligne de vie" ("Lifeline"), 1938. Photographer unknown. Library of the Koninklijk Museum voor Schone Kunsten, Antwerp

The overarching intent of this project is to position individual works created by Magritte between 1926 and 1938 within an expanded frame of references and relations. Throughout, the authors have aimed to make use of the insights gained by looking closely at Magritte's works with conservators, and to take into account the material qualities of individual objects, considered in themselves as primary evidence of the most important kind.

Admittedly, such tactics might not have met with Magritte's approval. To focus on the physical particularities of his work, understood materially and historically; to build, whenever possible, on insights gained by looking at individual objects with conservators; to situate individual works within the context of their times—such approaches run counter to Magritte's own post–World War II statements and practice. He repeatedly discounted the significance of what he characterized as mere "technical problems," insisting always that it is not the mode of realization but the *idea* that matters.[30] Furthermore, beginning in 1946, the number of "variants" he produced of successful compositions increased dramatically—although he began this practice as early as 1926, it became more exclusively market-driven in the postwar years.[31] As a result, works from the 1920s and 1930s and related variants from the 1940s, 1950s, and 1960s are often treated interchangeably in the Magritte literature, despite their many differences in composition and scale, and in the circumstances of their making.[32] This lack of attention to the specific historical contexts of these variants, and the substitution of one for another, tends to obscure the important weight of the artist's very intentional strategies of doubling, duplication, and replication.[33] All can be said to undermine notions of "originality" and "uniqueness" in ways consistent not only with Surrealist rhetoric, but with Duchamp's concept of the readymade, underscoring the rich complexity of Magritte's modern artistic identity.

"I don't want to belong to my own time, or, for that matter, to any other," Magritte told the artist and critic Suzi Gablik in 1966, a year before his death.[34] Nearly thirty years earlier, in "La Ligne de vie," he was in a very different frame of mind, and careful to locate himself in relation to his moment (fig. 6). His opening salvo: "Mesdames, Messieurs, Camarades"—"Ladies, Gentlemen, Comrades"—announced his left-leaning sympathies, although he was careful during the course of the lecture to distinguish himself, and the Surrealists, from political parties of every stripe.[35] His references to "that pain in the arse called Hitler,"[36] and to the Italians and Germans bent on "murder[ing] the young Spanish Republic,"[37] signal his keen awareness of the troubling political tensions that would culminate, in 1939, in the start of World War II. "Surrealism is revolutionary," Magritte told his audience, "because it is relentlessly hostile to all those bourgeois ideological values which keep the world in the appalling conditions in which it is today."[38] Between 1926 and 1938, his art shared in those revolutionary aspirations. Rooted in the commonplace, it sought to act on perceptions in ways that rendered reality disturbing and strange, and that made, in Magritte's own words, "everyday objects shriek aloud."[39] His paintings from this period are invitations to look closely and to pay careful, critical attention to what is seen, both in each image and, when turned away from them, in the surrounding world. If Magritte's work has performed as he intended, one may find that, as Nougé memorably wrote in 1931, "the world has been altered. There are no longer any ordinary things."[40]

Notes

References in the following notes in the form "Sylvester 1:8" refer to the volume and catalogue numbers of works in the six-volume Magritte catalogue raisonné. Likewise, references in the form "Sylvester 1, p. 304" refer to the volume and page numbers of corresponding texts. The first five volumes of the catalogue raisonné, published 1992–97, were edited by David Sylvester; the final volume, published 2012, was edited by Sarah Whitfield. For complete publication information for all six volumes, see the "Selected Bibliography," p. 252.

1. *Ligne de vie* (lifeline) is a term used by palmists to refer to the line or crease on the palm of a person's hand that indicates the length of his or her life. Danielle Johnson suggests that Magritte may have enjoyed his punning title's quasi-mystical connotations and the way it introduces the idea of reading meaning into abstract symbols and signs. For an invaluable discussion of the lecture's significance and its different published versions, see David Sylvester and Sarah Whitfield, "Magritte's Lost Lecture," in Gisèle Ollinger-Zinque and Frederik Leen, eds., *René Magritte, 1898–1967* (Ghent and Brussels: Ludion, Royal Museums of Fine Arts of Belgium, 1998), pp. 41–43. For a similar discussion, see Sylvester 2, pp. 67–72.

2. Between 1936 and 1938, Magritte participated in many significant one-person exhibitions and group shows of Surrealist art, including: *René Magritte* (Julien Levy Gallery, New York, 1936); *René Magritte: Peintures, objets surréalistes* (Palais des Beaux-Arts, Brussels, 1936); *Exposition surréaliste d'objets* (Galerie Charles Ratton, Paris, 1936); *The International Surrealist Exhibition* (New Burlington Galleries, London, 1936); *René Magritte* (Huize Esher Surrey, The Hague, 1936); *Fantastic Art, Dada, Surrealism* (The Museum of Modern Art, New York, 1936); *Surrealist Objects and Poems* (London Gallery, London, 1937); *René Magritte* (Julien Levy Gallery, 1938); *Exposition internationale du Surréalisme* (Galerie Beaux-Arts, Paris, 1938); *René Magritte: Surrealist Paintings and Objects* (London Gallery, 1938); and *Exposition internationale du Surréalisme* (Galerie Robert, Amsterdam, 1938).

3. The Magritte catalogue raisonné is an indispensible foundation for Magritte studies and includes essential information about his interactions with the Surrealist movement. The 1920s and 1930s are treated primarily in volumes 1, 2, and 4, with supplements and newly discovered works in volumes 5 and 6. Beyond this resource, there have been few in-depth studies of Magritte's relationship to the larger Surrealist movement of the 1920s and 1930s. Lisa Kim Lipinski suggests that being labeled a "Surrealist" helped Magritte's career but may limit our understanding of his art; she also examines his critical reception in the interwar period. See Lipinski, "René Magritte and Simulation: Effects Beyond His Wildest Dreams," Ph.D. diss., University of Texas at Austin, 2000, pp. 19–56 and 58–121. Gérard Durozoi includes Magritte in his survey of Surrealism, but does not fully address his relationship to the larger movement, instead treating him primarily in the context of the Belgian circle of artists. See Durozoi, *History of the Surrealist Movement*, trans. by Alison Anderson (Chicago: University of Chicago Press, 2002), pp. 147–59 and 271–86. On Magritte's "Les Mots et les images," see Kim Grant, *Surrealism and the Visual Arts: Theory and Reception* (Cambridge, U.K.: Cambridge University Press, 2005), pp. 255–59. For an examination of Magritte's work of the 1920s and 1930s, particularly in relation to Salvador Dalí, as well as for a discussion of how Magritte fit into the Surrealist movement and contributed to its development, see Danielle M. Johnson, "Salvador Dalí and René Magritte, 1928–1938," Ph.D. diss., New York University, 2012.

4. This is not to suggest that others have not considered this period in Magritte's work to be critical. In fact, as Michael Draguet has noted, David Sylvester believed that "the period of the development of Surrealism, in the second half of the 1920s" was "the key moment of Magritte's development." See Draguet, "Reconnaissance Without End," in Sylvester, *Magritte* (Brussels: Mercatorfonds, 2009 edition), p. VII. The 1992 Hayward Gallery exhibition selected by Sylvester and Whitfield provides a case in point: of the 168 works included in the exhibition, well over half were created between 1926 and 1938, although the exhibition itself covered Magritte's entire career (1920–67). The present project is the first to focus exclusively on this important period and body of work.

5. For an account of Magritte's unsuccessful attempts in 1946–47 to promote his conception of "sunlit Surrealism" with Paris Surrealism's leader, André Breton, see, for example, Sylvester 2, pp. 131–47.

6. Sarah Whitfield provides a useful synopsis of Magritte's entire life and career, including the years prior to his involvement with Surrealism. See "Chronology," in Daniel Abadie, ed., *Magritte* (New York: Distributed Art Publishers, 2003), pp. 275–97.

7. Magritte, "La Ligne de vie" (1938), trans. in Ollinger-Zinque and Leen, eds., *Magritte, 1898–1967*, p. 47. (All following "Ligne de vie" references and page numbers are from this volume.) This 1998 translation was adapted from that in Sylvester 5, pp. 9–22.

8. "Ligne de vie," p. 45.

9. Ibid.

10. For another discussion of the relation between Magritte and Ernst, particularly Magritte's appropriation and reconceptualization of Ernst's work, see Patricia Allmer, *René Magritte: Beyond Painting* (Manchester, U.K.: Manchester University Press, 2009), pp. 108–47.

11. Max Ernst, "Visions de demi-sommeil," in *La Révolution surréaliste*, nos. 9–10 (October 1, 1927): n.p. In a letter to Paul Nougé, written in the fall of 1927, Magritte mentions *La Révolution surréaliste*, undoubtedly referring to this October 1927 issue. He asks if Nougé has received it and notes that while this number disillusioned him a little, he has not had the chance to examine it at length. See Magritte, letter to Nougé, September 1927, in Marcel Mariën, ed., *Lettres surréalistes: 1924–1940* (Brussels: Les Lèvres nues, 1973), no. 105.

12. Max Ernst's "Au-delà de la peinture" was published in the journal *Cahiers d'art*, nos. 6–7, year 11 (1936): 149–84; and again, without changes, in the monograph *Max Ernst: Œuvres de 1919 à 1936* (Paris: Éditions Cahiers d'art, 1937), pp. 13–46. See Ernst, "Beyond Painting" (1936), trans. by Dorothea Tanning, in *Max Ernst: Beyond Painting (and Other Writings by the Artist and His Friends)* (New York: Wittenborn, Schultz, 1948), pp. 3–25.

13. A lucid discussion of autobiographical writing in relation to Max Ernst is in Julia Drost, "Biographical Notes," in Werner Spies, ed., *Max Ernst: Life and Work* (New York: Thames & Hudson, 2006), pp. 20–21. For characterization of "La Ligne de vie" as "an account of the experience of life and art that has made Magritte a surrealist painter," see Sylvester and Whitfield, "Magritte's Lost Lecture," in Ollinger-Zinque and Leen, eds., *Magritte, 1898–1967*, p. 41. A 1987 sale of contents from Magritte's studio included "a presentation copy [of Ernst's *Œuvres de 1919 à 1936*] inscribed by Max Ernst to René Magritte on the half title." See *The Remaining Contents of the Studio of René Magritte* (London: Sotheby's, July 2, 1987), lot 1012.

14. Allmer addresses "La Ligne de vie" in relation to "Au delà de la peinture," focusing more on the similarities between the texts and "Magritte's possible appropriation and adaptation of these texts for his own autobiographical writings." See Allmer, *Magritte: Beyond Painting*, p. 112.

15. Ernst, "Visions de demi-sommeil," p. 293. See also Ernst, "Beyond Painting," in *Ernst: Beyond Painting*, p. 3.

16. Magritte, "Ligne de vie," p. 45.

17. Ernst, "Beyond Painting," in *Ernst: Beyond Painting*, p. 7.

18. Louis Aragon, "The Challenge to Painting," in Pontus Hultén, ed.

and trans., *The Surrealists Look at Art* (Venice, Calif.: Lapis Press, 1990), p. 63. The essay was originally published in *La Peinture au défi* (Paris: Galerie Goemans, Librarie José Corti, 1930), p. 22. Quoted in Ernst, "Beyond Painting," in *Ernst: Beyond Painting*, p. 12.

19. Ernst, "Beyond Painting," in *Ernst: Beyond Painting*, p. 17.

20. This spread appears in both the 1936 and the 1937 publications of Ernst's "Au-delà de la peinture" (n.p. in the former; p. 42 [fig. 4] in the latter). For a color reproduction of *La Belle Saison* (1925), see William A. Camfield, *Max Ernst: Dada and the Dawn of Surrealism* (Munich: Prestel, 1993), plate 184.

21. Unlike *La Belle Saison*, none of these works have actual collage sources.

22. René Magritte, letter to André Breton, May 1937(?). (The letter itself is undated, but "20 mai 1937" is handwritten, not in Magritte's hand, on the envelope, perhaps indicating the date of receipt.) One passage from this letter has been transcribed in French, and another passage summarized and translated to English; both courtesy David Sylvester's René Magritte Catalogue Raisonné Research Papers, Menil Archives, The Menil Collection, Houston. The original letter is held in the Fonds Breton, Bibliothèque Jacques Doucet. The catalogue raisonné uses the date May 20, 1937, for this letter; see Sylvester 2:438, pp. 245–46.

23. Magritte, letter to Breton, May 1937(?).

24. Ibid.

25. Magritte, "Ligne de vie," p. 46.

26. David Sylvester titled a chapter of his 1992 monograph "Hand-painted Collage." See idem, *Magritte: The Silence of the World* (Houston and New York: Menil Foundation, Abrams, 1992), p. 110.

27. See Sylvester 1:137, p. 209 for a discussion of Magritte's *L'Assassin menacé* (1927; plate 12) and Ernst's *La Vierge corrigeant l'enfant Jésus devant trois temoins: André Breton, Paul Éluard et le peintre* (*The Virgin Chastising the Infant Jesus before Three Witnesses: André Breton, Paul Éluard, and the Painter*, 1926). See also Sylvester 1:143, p. 215 for a discussion of Magritte's *L'Importance des merveilles* (*The Importance of Marvels*, 1927) and Ernst's *Célèbes* (1921).

28. Sylvester's monograph *Magritte: The Silence of the World* appeared in 1992; in the same year, the first volume of the Magritte catalogue raisonné was published. Also in 1992 the South Bank Centre in London organized a major exhibition that traveled to the Metropolitan Museum, the Menil Collection, and the Art Institute of Chicago. Sarah Whitfield and David Sylvester selected the show and Whitfield wrote the catalogue. See Whitfield, *Magritte* (London: Hayward Gallery, 1992).

29. Sylvester and Whitfield were the first English-language scholars to consider Magritte's relationship with Nougé in any depth. In the first volume of the catalogue raisonné, they write: "As much as anyone, Magritte looked for guidance to Nougé, who by 1927 had become something of a mentor to him, as is evident in the correspondence we quote passim and in Magritte's many approving references to Nougé's writings on him." See Sylvester 1, p. 50. Similarly, Sylvester writes that, judging from the tone of their correspondence while Magritte was in Paris, "Nougé clearly saw Magritte as a budding genius; Magritte clearly saw Nougé as his guru." See *Magritte: The Silence of the World*, p. 109. On Magritte and his friends, including Nougé, as self-described "accomplices" and for Nougé as the leader of the Belgian Surrealists, see Whitfield, "Magritte and His Accomplices," in idem, *Magritte* (London: South Bank Centre, 1992). On Nougé's writing on Magritte, see Grant, *Surrealism and the Visual Arts*, pp. 301–4; and Johnson, "Salvador Dalí and René Magritte," esp. pp. 37–41, 212–29, 253–56, 269–71, and 275–77.

30. Magritte, quoted in Otto Hahn, "Le Père du pop art," *L'Express*, Paris (November 30, 1964): 60. Repr. in René Magritte, *Écrits complets*, ed. by André Blavier (Paris: Flammarion, 1979), p. 186.

31. Magritte completed variants of his works from 1926, when he produced several versions of *Le Jockey perdu* (*The Lost Jockey*). The word "variant," however, first appeared in his correspondence with New York gallerist Julien Levy in 1936, the year that Magritte sent numerous small versions of his previous paintings to be displayed at his solo exhibition. On variants in the 1936 Julien Levy exhibition, see Sylvester, *Magritte: The Silence of the World*, pp. 238–40. Magritte began to work with New York dealer Alexander Iolas around 1946 and produced many variants for him from that point on. See Sylvester 2, pp. 119–20.

32. The most notable recent example of such conflations occurred in the exhibition and catalogue produced by the Tate Liverpool in 2011, both of which are organized by themes. See Christoph Grunenberg and Darren Phi, eds., *Magritte A to Z* (London: Tate Publishing, 2011).

33. Allmer addresses Magritte's variants but focuses primarily on those done in the 1940s and later, in response to the market. See Allmer, *Magritte: Beyond Painting*, pp. 180–86. The authors of the 2004 volume *Art Since 1900* suggest that Magritte's early strategies of multiplication and his later willingness to make copies of his work may have derived from his work in advertising, from concepts current in the Surrealist movement in the 1920s and 1930s, and from the idea of what would later be called the "simulacrum," or the copy without an original. See "1927a," in Hal Foster et al., *Art Since 1900* (London and New York: Thames & Hudson, 2004), pp. 212–15.

34. Magritte died on August 15, 1967. Suzi Gablik interviewed him in Brussels during the week of July 27–August 3, 1966. See Gablik, "A Conversation with René Magritte," *Studio International* 173, no. 887 (March 1967): 129. Repr. in Magritte, *Écrits complets*, pp. 645–47.

35. It is unclear whether Magritte was an official member of the Communist Party in the 1930s although it is known that he joined briefly in 1945–46. The catalogue raisonné authors characterize his position vis-à-vis the party as "a fellow traveler" and "strong sympathizer." See Sylvester 2, pp. 33–34. Magritte, like many of the Surrealists, was disenchanted with organized politics by the end of the 1930s, noting in "La Ligne de vie" that "we [Belgian and French Surrealists] put ourselves at the service of the proletarian revolution. It was a failure. The political leaders of the workers' parties proved to be far too self-important and far too lacking in shrewdness to grasp what the Surrealists could contribute." See Magritte, "Ligne de vie," p. 45. For discussions of the complex and ever-shifting relationship between the Surrealists and the Communist Party, see Steven Harris, *Surrealist Art and Thought in the 1930s: Art, Politics, and the Psyche* (Cambridge, U.K., and New York: Cambridge University Press, 2004), pp. 2–4 and 49–55; and Helena Lewis's discussion of the years 1926–38 in *The Politics of Surrealism* (New York: Paragon House, 1988), pp. 55–160.

36. "Ligne de vie," p. 45.

37. Ibid.

38. Ibid., p. 46.

39. Ibid.

40. "L'Univers est changé, il n'y a plus de choses ordinaires," originally published in Paul Nougé's "Avertissement," in *E.L.T. Mesens & E. van Tonderen présentent seize tableaux de René Magritte* (Brussels: Salle Giso, 1931), p. 7; trans. in Sylvester 2, p. 8.

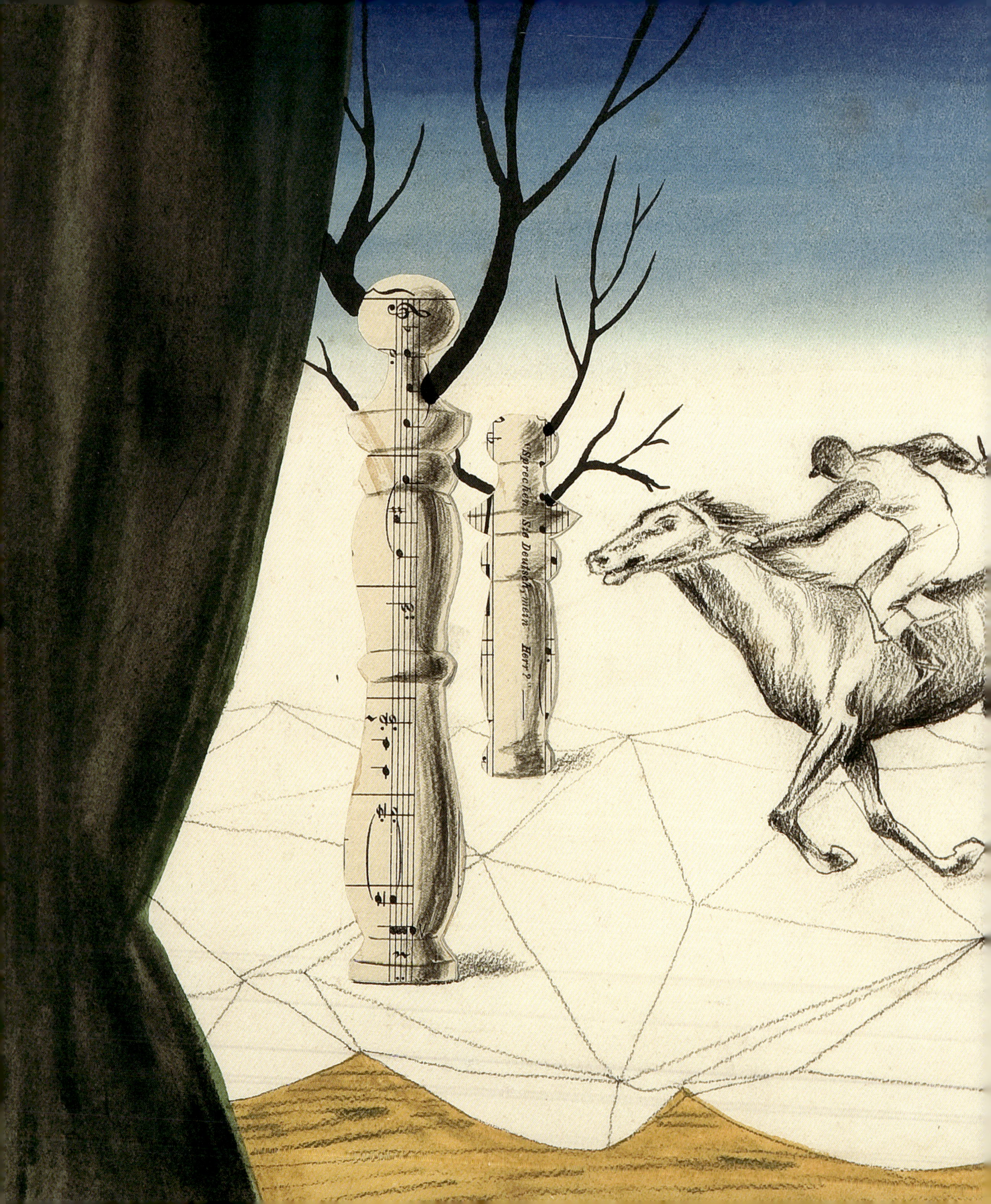
"Sprechen Sie Deutsch, mein Herr?"

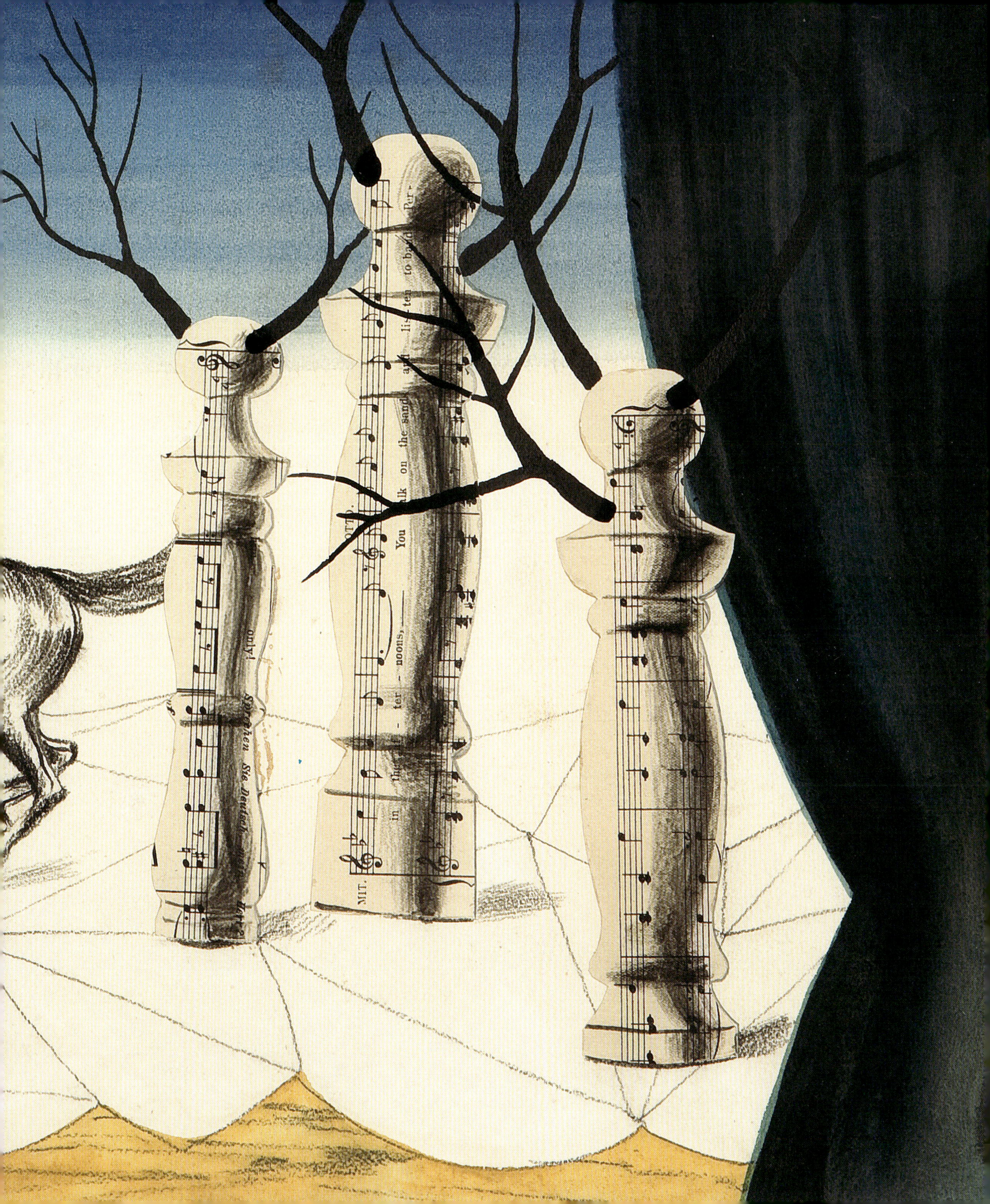

"THIS IS HOW MARVELS BEGIN" *Brussels* 1926–1927

Anne Umland

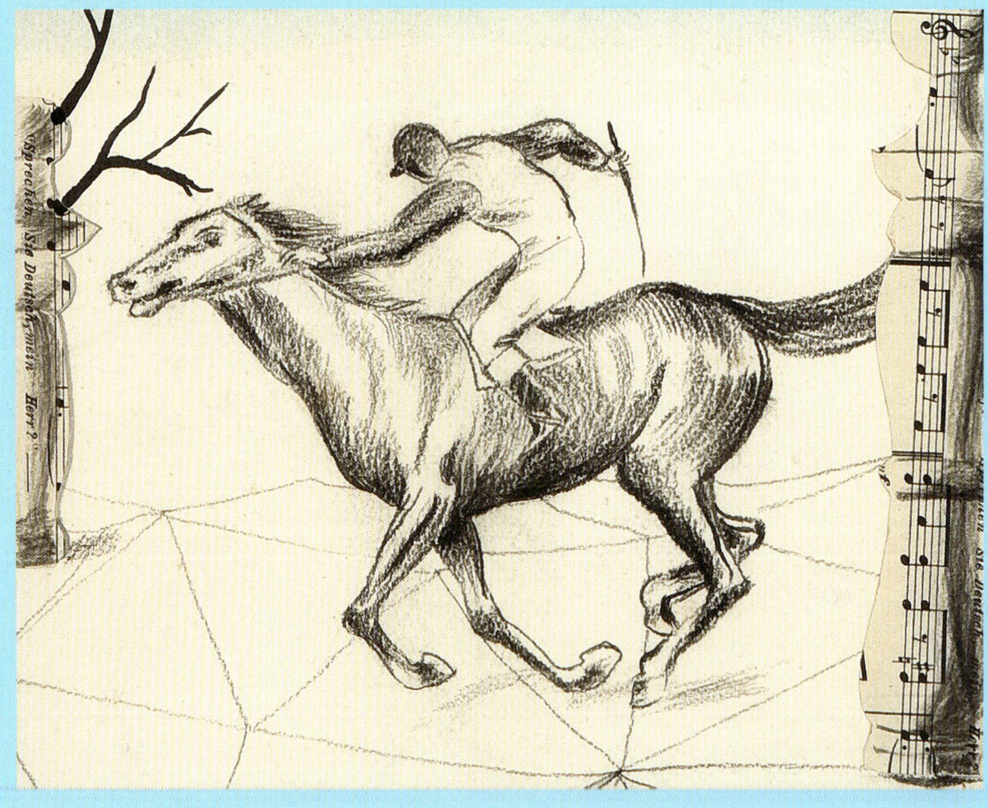

Figure 1. René Magritte. Detail of *Le Jockey perdu* (*The Lost Jockey*). 1926 (see plate 4)

On Saturday, April 23, 1927, René Magritte's first one-person exhibition opened in Brussels at the elegant, newly redesigned Galerie Le Centaure, located at 62, avenue Louise, one of the city's most fashionable streets.[1] The show featured forty-nine paintings and twelve *papiers collés*, all produced since January 1926, around the time when the artist's contract with the gallerist and avant-garde impresario Paul-Gustave Van Hecke had begun.[2] Although the local reviews were generally unfavorable, the exhibition launched Magritte's career as Brussels's leading—in fact only—Surrealist painter, in the months prior to his departure for Paris in September 1927.

The body of work Magritte created in anticipation of his Le Centaure exhibition and during the four months that followed was therefore pivotal. It was produced at a crucial moment of artistic self-definition for the artist, poised to move from the periphery of the Surrealist coterie to its center in Paris, in the circle of André Breton. To look closely at a series of key works from this foundational moment is to watch the twenty-eight-year-old Magritte reinventing himself as a figurative painter whose evolving Surrealist project was one of severing the links between surface and essence, representation and reality. In this, his works may be considered in relation not only to the specifics of his Belgian context, but to general Surrealist preoccupations with undermining rational systems, with dreams and the Freudian "uncanny," with violence, and with notions of originality.

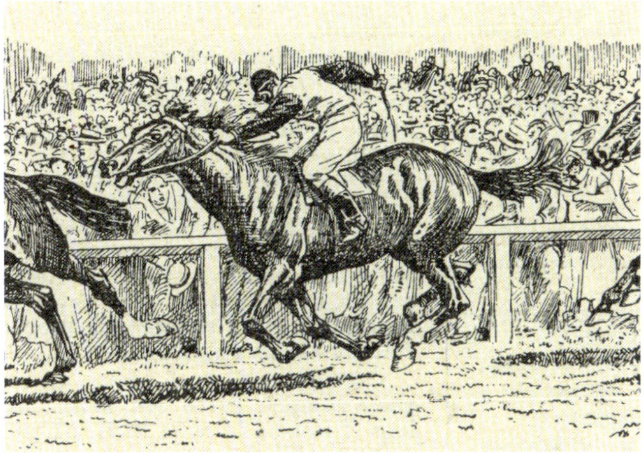

Figure 2. Detail of page from the *Larousse universel* dictionary, vol. 1, 1922 (under "courses" ["races"]), used as a source for Magritte's *Le Jockey perdu* (*The Lost Jockey*, 1926; plate 4). Courtesy Yale University Library

LE JOCKEY PERDU

Magritte's *papier collé* titled *Le Jockey perdu* (*The Lost Jockey*, 1926; plate 4) is an image of dramatically arrested motion. A jockey, with his back to us, looks over his shoulder at unseen opponents and raises his crop to urge his horse on (fig. 1). The animal's nose stretches forward; its flying mane and tail and the position of its legs all indicate that it is traveling at breakneck speed. The contrast between these signs of movement and the stasis of the image offers an early example of what Breton would later identify as "the fixed-explosive," an important category of "convulsive beauty," in which the animate is abruptly brought to a halt.[3] Magritte rendered his horse and rider using strokes of charcoal of varying length, density, and degrees of precision.[4] The black-and-white tonalities and the pronounced contrasts of light and shadow combine to create an image that is illustrational in character. The sharp outlines, particularly those of the horse's hooves and legs, create the sense of a cutout or collage. The overall impression is that the steed and its jockey have been lifted from another context, with the original surrounding circumstances—other horses and riders, racetrack, spectators—left far behind.

Magritte did, in fact, find this jockey and racehorse elsewhere: careering across a page of his treasured *Larousse universel* dictionary (figs. 2, 3),[5] among a series of line-engravings illustrating aspects of horse racing. He magnified and isolated the small *Larousse* horse and rider (possibly with the use of a pantograph—a standard graphic-arts tool used for enlarging directly). In *Larousse*, the jockey

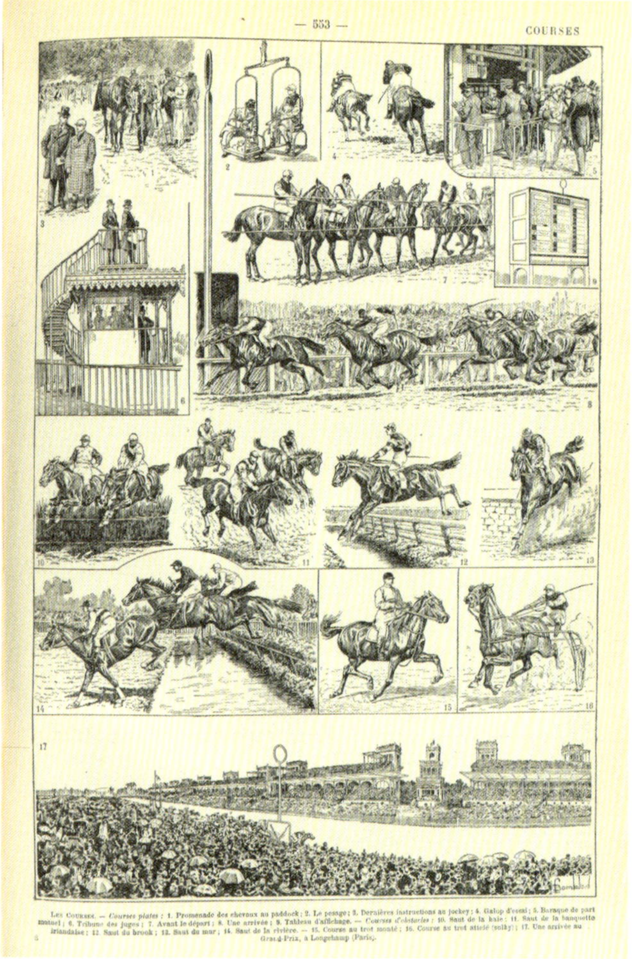

Figure 3. Page from the *Larousse universel* dictionary, vol. 1, 1922 (under "courses" ["races"]), used as a source for Magritte's *Le Jockey perdu* (*The Lost Jockey*, 1926; plate 4). Courtesy Yale University Library

and his mount can be seen to be losing by a length, accounting for the powerful impression of desperate, last-ditch, forward-thrusting movement they convey even when isolated.[6] Having delivered them from one fate (the loss of a race), Magritte consigned them to another: a lonely existence in a strangely populated forest, framed by curtains at either side that identify the space as a theatrical stage. Here, set upon an aberrant perspectival grid, horse and rider acquire a ghostly presence, an effect heightened by Magritte's strategic erasure of details found in *Larousse*: the horse's bridle is reduced to a bare minimum, saddle and girth are virtually eliminated, and the jockey's capped head is rendered as a featureless sphere. At the same time, Magritte was careful to preserve visual traces of the image's illustrational origins, which were themselves printed from an engraved translation of a drawing by a graphic artist of an actual race. This image of a "lost jockey," then, is not just one or two but at least three generations removed from the real world.[7]

Magritte spoofed the conventionally illusionistic dimensionality of the *Larousse* horse and rider by adding traces of shadows under the horse's hooves. These serve to anchor the image visually and to suggest that it occupies a physical position within this overtly artificial space. The same holds true for the five branch- or antler-sprouting *bilboquets*[8]—the lathe-turned forms that feature so prominently in Magritte's work—cut out from a score of sheet music and collaged onto the work's support paper.[9] Magritte carefully shaded each of these elements, articulating the curves of their silhouettes; he also outlined their right edges with dark pencil strokes. These additions, like the sketchy shadows behind them, have a quotational quality. They function conventionally to create the illusion of dimensionality and depth, and at the same time, this effect is countered by the sheet music's flat, nonspatial character, which draws attention to the notes' agency as conventions or signs.

Each of the five *bilboquets* in *Le Jockey perdu* is carefully individuated, not only in terms of dimensions and in the shapes and placement of their sinuous black ink branches (or antlers), but also in terms of their physical contours; they catch us up in a game of variety and sameness, uniqueness and repetition—central preoccupations for the artist at this time. Magritte's friend and "accomplice,"[10] the Belgian Surrealist Paul Nougé, acknowledged the important place the *bilboquet* held in the artist's early Surrealist works.[11] It was a form with multivalent connotations, ranging from mannequins (as seen in Magritte's contemporaneous commercial work and paintings; plates 22 and 28) to balusters or table legs to chess pieces, and it would become one of Magritte's stock elements, a distinctive "type" that could be multiplied, resized, and repositioned ad infinitum, each time slightly differently, posing a provocative challenge (as did his lifting of the *Larousse* image) to prevailing definitions of originality in art.[12]

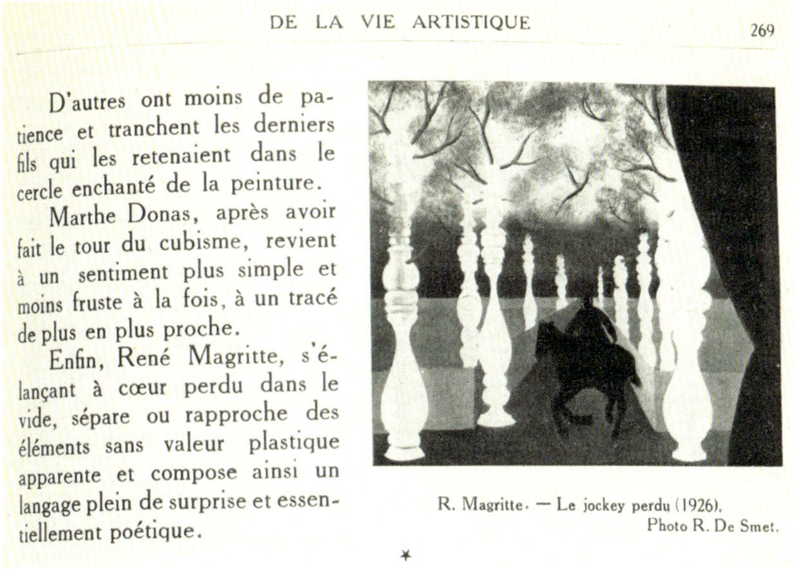

DE LA VIE ARTISTIQUE 269

D'autres ont moins de patience et tranchent les derniers fils qui les retenaient dans le cercle enchanté de la peinture.

Marthe Donas, après avoir fait le tour du cubisme, revient à un sentiment plus simple et moins fruste à la fois, à un tracé de plus en plus proche.

Enfin, René Magritte, s'élançant à cœur perdu dans le vide, sépare ou rapproche des éléments sans valeur plastique apparente et compose ainsi un langage plein de surprise et essentiellement poétique.

R. Magritte. — Le jockey perdu (1926).
Photo R. De Smet.

Figure 4. Reproduction of Magritte's *Le Jockey perdu* (*The Lost Jockey*, 1926; Sylvester 1:81), illustrating Camille Goemans's article "La Jeune Peinture belge" ("Young Belgian Painting"), in *Bulletin de la vie artistique* (Paris), September 1926. The Museum of Modern Art Library, New York

According to *Le Jockey perdu*'s first owner, the Belgian avant-garde collector Pierre Janlet, the work's original title was *Le Jockey égaré* (The jockey who lost his way)[13]—words that correspond to those used by Van Hecke to describe Magritte, in the first full-length article published on the artist's work, written to coincide with his Galerie Le Centaure exhibition.[14] A few months earlier, an oil-on-canvas version of the same subject—a mounted jockey, flanked by two rows of white *bilboquets*—was reproduced as part of an article on the state of contemporary painting in Belgium (fig. 4). The one sentence therein that was devoted to Magritte was positioned next to this image, which bore the caption "Le jockey perdu." The article's author, Camille Goemans, another Belgian Surrealist and a friend of Magritte's, described the artist as "hurtling recklessly into the void," much like the jockey, galloping off into the unknown.[15]

In the checklist for Magritte's Le Centaure exhibition, the painted version of *Le Jockey perdu* is the first entry. During the course of the exhibition, it was displayed in the gallery's street-level window—further confirmation of its early importance among Magritte's Surrealist works.[16]

According to the authors of Magritte's catalogue raisonné, *Le Jockey perdu* was also "the first image he repeated," ushering in what would become (by the mid- to late 1930s and especially after World War II) his frequent practice of producing different versions—"variants," as he called them—of successful works.[17]

Magritte's friend and legal advisor, Harry Torczyner, acquired the former *Jockey égaré* in 1960. At that time, Magritte told Torczyner that this *papier collé* should be titled *Le Jockey perdu*, aligning the work more closely not only with the 1926 oil on canvas but with the multiple versions of the subject he created in the 1940s and later.[18] He said to Torczyner that his new acquisition "announced *The Lost Jockey*," a statement that led the catalogue raisonné authors to conclude that the *papier collé* version preceded the 1926 oil painting.[19] In fact, however, Magritte might well have meant that the *papier collé* ushered in the *many* versions of the theme that would follow through the years. Each of the later paintings and gouaches is distinct, but all share the distinguishing features of the horse and rider that Magritte had positioned center-stage in the *papier collé*.[20] By contrast, in the 1926 oil on canvas (and in another early "lost jockey" *papier collé*; fig. 5), the silhouetted profiles of the horse and rider are markedly different from those in the later variants, and from those in the erstwhile *Jockey égaré*. A comparison of the three 1926 versions—one on canvas and two on paper—

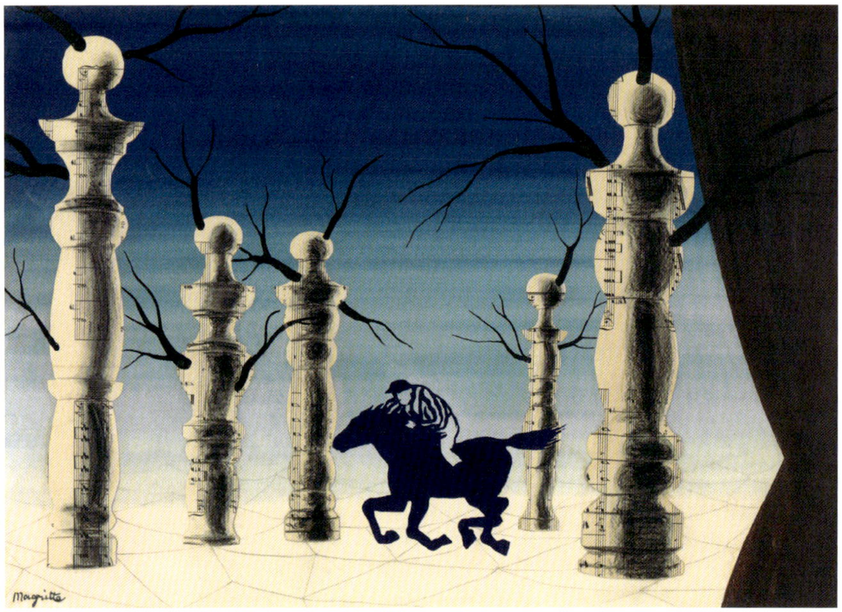

Figure 5. René Magritte. *Le Jockey perdu* (*The Lost Jockey*). 1926. Cut-and-pasted sheet music, gouache, watercolor, and pencil on paper, 15 1/4 x 21 13/16" (38.7 x 55.4 cm). Location unknown. (Sylvester 4:1606)

offers precious insight into which of the "lost jockeys" Magritte would come to judge most successful: that of the horse and rider who, in the original *Larousse* illustration, are seen to be losing the race by a length. Even when isolated and repositioned, this pair best retains its dramatic momentum, the better to contrast with its permanently fixed and frozen state.

LE SENS DE LA NUIT

In Magritte's imposing painting *Le Sens de la nuit* (*The Meaning of Night*, 1927; plate 11), a bowler-hatted man commands our first attention.[21] His eyes are closed and his face is white, only slightly warmer in shade than the stiff white collar that rises up to meet his chin. His lips, a cool, bluish-blood-red, provide the face's only note of color. The pronounced contrast between them and the man's skin recalls the exaggerated makeup worn by male actors in early films, although there is nothing animated about this particular "performer." His features are absolutely still and affectless, like those of a wax-museum figure, or a plaster death mask.[22] From the tips of his polished black leather shoes to the top of his *chapeau melon* (the hat that would come to be so closely associated with Magritte), he is impeccably turned out.[23] His long overcoat, Edwardian starched collar, and precisely knotted black cravat represent a type of conservative daywear that would have been instantly recognized by viewers in the late 1920s as a businessman's uniform, British in origin.[24] The man's closed eyes, however, signal his remove from the everyday, as does the uncanny character of his surroundings, rendered in a subdued palette of blacks, grays, beiges, and occasional luminous whites.

Behind him is another figure, identically dressed, with his back to us. Slightly smaller in size, conforming to the rules of perspective, he stands on a sand-colored beach or platform that is jagged at left like a puzzle piece. He faces ominous skies and a deep gray sea. The position of his feet mirrors those of his forward-facing counterpart, hinting—as does his pose—that this might be nothing more than a reflection, captured in an immaterial mirror, the presence of which is implied rather than seen.[25] His left foot and leg, however, cast their own distinct shadow: a visual clue to his presence as a physical entity within the stagelike perspectival structure of the scene.

The third figure in the painting, by contrast, conforms to no such spatial logic. It flies in from the right, as if out of nowhere, entering on a diagonal and disturbing the composition's otherwise straightforward, frontal harmonies. As such, it confirms what the bowler-hatted man's closed eyes suggest: this is the irrational space of a dream. The identity of this deracinated apparition is elusive. Its most clearly defined element is a prominent, disembodied hand or glove, which grasps the lower edge of what appears to be

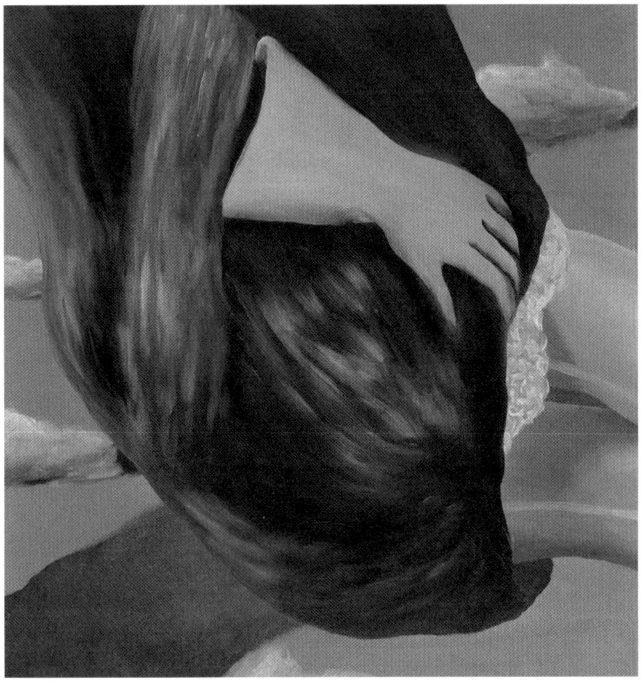

Figure 6. Detail of Magritte's *Le Sens de la nuit* (*The Meaning of Night*, 1927; plate 11)

a furry garment, pulling it up to reveal a glimpse of lace and the tops of a pair of seamed-stocking legs. Its silvery-gray tones suggest it might have photographic origins, and (as others have pointed out) it connects in a general way to the fur-related imagery found in Magritte's commercial work and *papiers collés* of the time.[26] The vaguely pincerlike shape of its two outer extremities, for example—which extend toward and perhaps even brush up against the back-facing figure—recalls the necklines of fur coats in Magritte's fashion illustrations for two Maison S. Samuel catalogues (see for example plate 30). Overall, the various components of the figure present a compendium of painterly effects and textures, all of which (as intimated by the bodyless hand or glove) evoke tactile experiences: the softness of fur, the delicacy of lace, the silkiness of stockings (fig. 6). Each is rendered with virtuoso handling that carries over to the strangely substantive clouds that litter the landscape's surface, the sheer weight of which seems to have caused them to fall to earth (although paradoxically they retain the scale of clouds seen at a distance in the sky).

Unlike everything else in the picture, including the earthbound clouds, the amorphous fur-covered figure casts no shadow. It hovers in an indeterminate space between the bowler-hatted men's world and ours, providing a visual corollary for the way irrational thoughts can suddenly intrude upon the mind. The fur shape's angle and imagery encourage us to consider what Sigmund Freud notoriously defined—in 1927, the same year as Magritte's painting—as a site of traumatic recognition and feminine "lack." Although Magritte rejected psychoanalytic interpretations of his paintings,[27] by the late 1920s, and particularly in Surrealist circles (both in Brussels and Paris), this intruding figure would have been instantly recognized as an amalgam of Freudian fetish objects—stockinged legs, a lacy undergarment, fur, each related to a castration scenario that involved notions of illicit looking and erotic displacement.[28] The fetish object, in standard Freudian interpretation, replaces "the normal sexual object" by "some part of the body [. . .] or some inanimate object which bears an assignable relation to the person whom it replaces and preferably to that person's sexuality (e.g. a piece of clothing or underlinen)."[29] Fur was identified by Freud as a fetish object owing to its "association with the hair of the *mons Veneris*."[30] Even flight, or the wish to be able to fly in dreams, was understood by Freud "as nothing else than a longing to be capable of sexual performance."[31]

To point to these relationships is not to diminish or limit the painting's mystery but rather to sharpen our historical understanding of Magritte's imagery, including his (later iconic) bowler-hatted man. Such figures, to an even greater extent than those of the "jockey perdu," multiplied in appearance in Magritte's work, particularly during the 1950s and 1960s, gradually becoming a persona adopted by the artist himself.[32] To consider the bowler-hatted man here, at his point of entry into Magritte's work, in this original context, is to recognize him not only as a standard type, or traditional everyday man, but as a revolutionary dreamer, whose ordinary exterior conceals an unfathomable inner life of desire and poetic possibility. His closed eyes, which renounce the external world for the realm of the psyche, amount to a manifesto: a sign of Surrealist solidarity.

L'ASSASSIN MENACÉ

"All this will be called: 'The murderer threatened,'" wrote Magritte's friend Nougé in 1927.[33] These words concluded a scenario he had composed (perhaps for a film), possibly in collaboration with Magritte. This text names all the protagonists in *L'Assassin menacé* (*The Menaced Assassin*, 1927; plate 12), Magritte's largest and most densely populated canvas to date. Included in the dramatis personae: a "corpse of rare perversity," a "young man of great beauty dressed with the most restrained elegance, leaning ever so slightly over a gramophone horn," "four heads [that] stare at the murderer," and "two men [...] on either side of the wide-open door."[34] Of the subjects Nougé listed, only "a meditative cat" that "observes the corpse" failed to make an appearance in the completed canvas, along with the fourth "head," or witness, whose presence may simply be concealed from us by the brown-suited young man's right shoulder.[35] Although the circumstances and nature of Magritte's collaboration with Nougé on this text remain uncertain, the relationship between the words and the image is undeniable. As a result, notions of "authorship" (as pertains to the painting) are muddied along the lines of French poet Lautréamont's dictum "Poetry must be made by all and not by one," a cri de cœur among Paris Surrealists who, like their Brussels counterparts, were advocates of group activity and communal creation.[36]

Infrared imaging used with transmitted light allows us to see that Magritte painted the background of *L'Assassin menacé* rapidly (fig. 7).[37] He used broad vertical strokes of pale lavender-white and pinkish paint to cover the interior walls, and warm, beige-brown ones to establish the floor. He reserved areas for each of his primary figures and possibly worked across the canvas from left to right, completing each character before moving on, although it is impossible to ascertain this with certainty. It is clear, though, that his process was additive and that each figure occupies a predetermined spatial zone, which helps to account for their eerie isolation and lack of interaction in the scene. Positioned within a tripartite series of architecturally defined, telescoping spaces, they are separated from one another not only physically but psychologically. The directions of their respective gazes offer a clue to their psychic

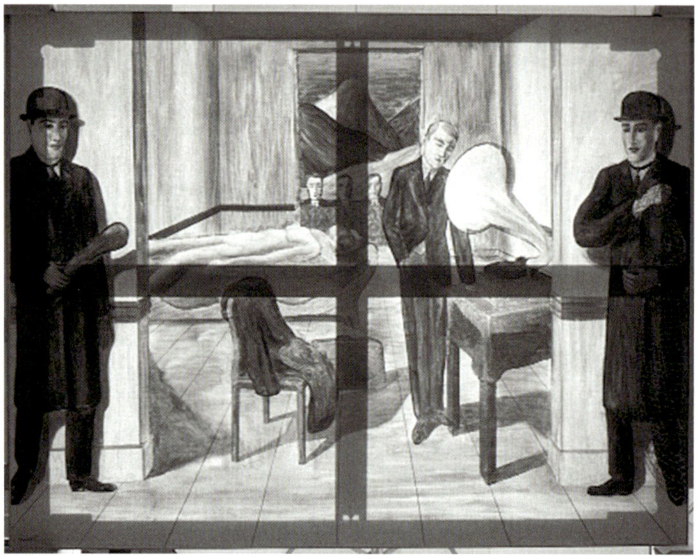

Figure 7. Infrared image in transmitted light (with the light source behind the canvas) of Magritte's *L'Assassin menacé* (*The Menaced Assassin*, 1927; plate 12). Conservation Department, The Museum of Modern Art, New York

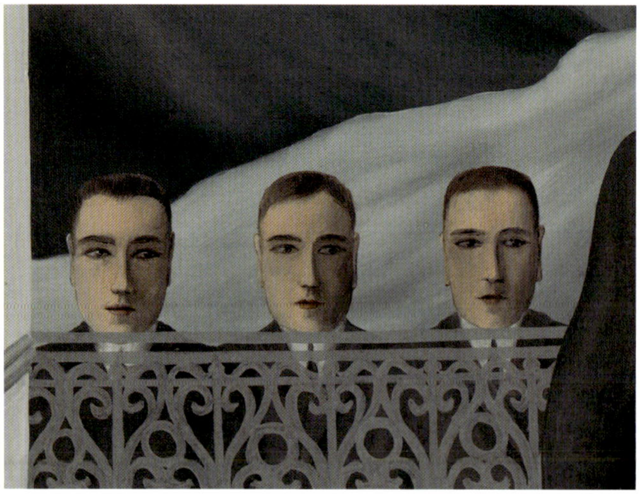

Figure 8. Detail of Magritte's *L'Assassin menacé* (*The Menaced* Assassin, 1927; see plate 12)

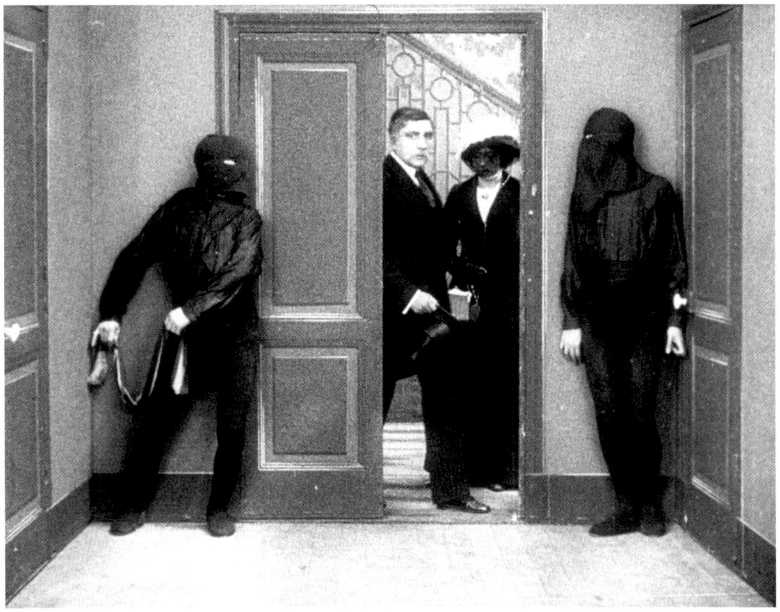

Figure 9. Still from Louis Feuillade's 1913 film *Le Mort qui tue* (*The Murderous Corpse*), showing two assassins poised to ambush Monsieur Thomery (Luitz-Morat). Production Gaumont, Neuilly-sur-Seine, France

remove. The two bowler-hatted men, for example, look not at each other, nor in the direction of the room behind them, but slightly down and out of the picture, at something unseen. The elegant young man—presumably the "menaced assassin" of the work's title—gazes down into the oversized horn of a gramophone. Even the three heads looking in on the scene from the window, described by Nougé as "star[ing] at the murderer,"[38] direct their eyes not at the young man or out at the viewer, but at something in the corner, hidden by the wall on the right, against which stands the man with the net (fig. 8). The painting thematizes the act of seeing, while inviting careful, dispassionate investigation—like that of a detective—even as it reminds us of vision's limits and blind spots, which can cause us to miss things hidden in plain sight.[39]

The gramophone's presence alerts us to the painting's deafening stillness. Each figure appears as though in a state of suspended animation. To an even greater degree than in *Le Sens de la nuit*, the effect is akin to that of a wax-museum display, or some sort of perpetual *tableau vivant*. Paradoxically, it is the cadaver, with blood coagulated around its mouth, that is the most "lively" figure in the room—partly due to the peculiarly disjunctive, offset relationship between its head and its naked body, which appear to have been severed from one another (although what we can see of the neck is bloodless).

The image is intentionally disturbing; it recalls those in four other prose pieces Nougé composed in 1927 in which women play dominant and frequently gruesome roles.[40] One of these, like the text related to *L'Assassin menacé*, corresponds to a painting of the same year by Magritte,[41] *Jeune Fille mangeant un oiseau (Le Plaisir)* (*Girl Eating a Bird [Pleasure]*, plate 15), which features a lace-collared young lady sinking her teeth into the exposed flesh of a bird. In this instance, the female plays the role of aggressor, not victim, and is seen close-up, accompanied not by other people, but by four brightly colored birds. In *L'Assassin menacé*, by contrast, a woman's body is offered up as a literal *corpus delicti*, the material evidence of a crime. However, there are no clues—a knife, overturned furniture—to indicate how she might have met her fate.

The art historian José Vovelle was the first to point to the connections between Magritte's paintings and the wildly popular, pre–World War I series of Fantômas films by the French director Louis Feuillade.[42] Echoes of one Fantômas film in particular, *Le Mort qui tue* (*The Murderous Corpse*), first released in November 1913, seem to haunt *L'Assassin menacé*, which David Sylvester describes as the "most cinematic image in Magritte's œuvre."[43] Although reticent in general about his childhood, Magritte later recalled going to the Cinéma Bleu in Charleroi, where

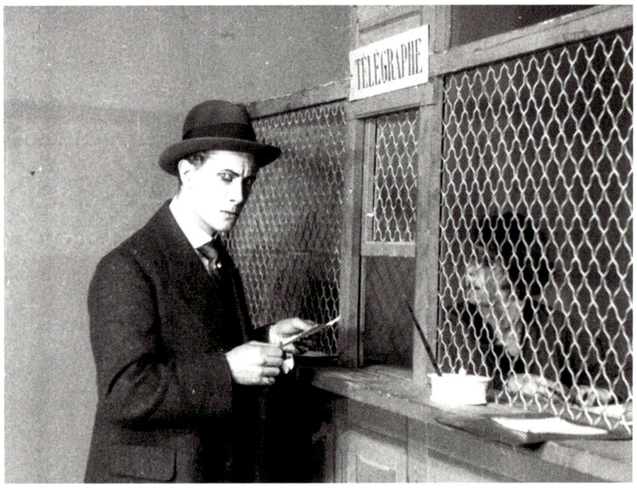

Figure 10. Still from Louis Feuillade's 1913 film *Le Mort qui tue* (*The Murderous Corpse*), showing Jérôme Fandor (George Melchior). Production Gaumont, Neuilly-sur-Seine, France

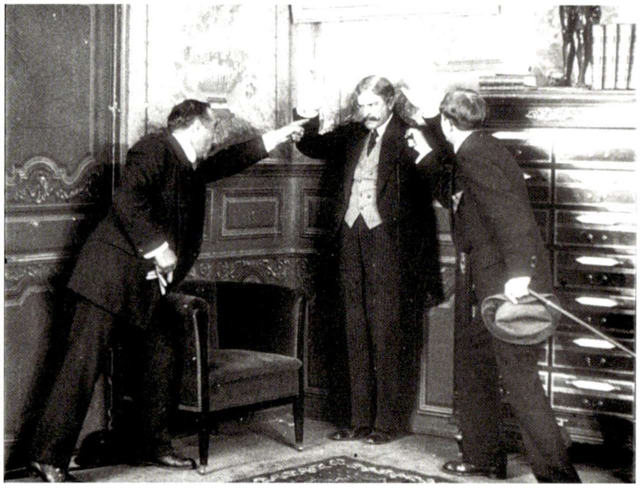

Figure 11. Still from Louis Feuillade's 1913 film *Le Mort qui tue* (*The Murderous Corpse*), showing Inspector Juve (Edmond Bréon, left) just after removing the human-skin glove from the hand of Fantômas (René Navarre, center). Production Gaumont, Neuilly-sur-Seine, France

he moved in the spring of 1913 and might well have seen *Le Mort qui tue* when it was released later that year.[44] Whether he might have seen the film at a time closer in date to realizing *L'Assassin menacé* is unknown—it is apparent, however, that it made an indelible impression. As Vovelle notes, for example, there are compelling compositional parallels between the painting and a scene in the film in which two hooded killers wait outside an open door, just before garroting the mustached Monsieur Thomery, one of *Le Mort qui tue*'s many murder victims (fig. 9).[45] Magritte replaced Feuillade's two masked criminals with a pair of anonymous men, whose bowler hats would have identified them in the context of the film as representatives of law and order.[46] Their role in Magritte's painting is, however, ambivalent. Poised like stalkers, and armed with cudgel and net, they convey a sense of frozen menace that conflicts with their respectable attire—a substitution that may be read as a subversive reversal entirely consistent with the Surrealists' determination to place all supposedly rational systems and signs of authority on trial.

Judging from the cut of his suit—and more specifically his soft-felt fedora hat, placed on the chair beside him—Magritte's "young man of great beauty" may also be linked to *Le Mort qui tue*. He resembles the film's inquisitive young reporter, Jérôme Fandor (fig. 10), a morally upright (and regularly imperiled) counterpart to the evil Fantômas. Lifted from the film and repositioned in *L'Assassin menacé*, this young man, too, becomes an anonymous type. Identified by his stylish clothes and fine leather shoes as something of a dandy or Jazz Age man, he provides a soft foil for the somber, conservatively dressed would-be killers and their stiff, hard-felt hats. As fashion historian Diane Maglio has noted, all three men are depicted with their jackets and overcoats buttoned on the "wrong" side for menswear, a subtle detail that suggests the scene might be considered a mirror image, contributing to its phantasmagoric or imaginary character.

In the final, most memorable scene in *Le Mort qui tue*, Fantômas's nemesis, Inspector Juve, accompanied by Fandor, strips a glove made of human skin from Fantômas's hand (fig. 11). Fantômas had used this glove—which, in an earlier, particularly grisly scene, he is seen flaying from a murder victim's hand—to leave behind the dead man's fingerprints instead of his own when carrying out his crimes. A fingerprint is, of course, conventionally understood to be a unique and nontransferable sign of identity, physically connected to a singular self.[47] What *Le Mort qui tue* slyly suggests, by contrast, is that this essential "proof" of identity is detachable and transferable. Several of Magritte's subsequent paintings—notably *La Fin des contemplations* (*An End to Contemplation*; plate 18) and *Le Double secret* (*The Secret Double*; plate 20), both from 1927—present images of epidural detachment, of sections of skin peeled away. In *L'Assassin menacé*, however, it is *Le Mort qui tue*'s unsettling conflation of attire with identity that resonates: Fantômas's macabre glove insists that there is no "natural" or "inherent" relationship between surface and essence, appearance and self. To equate human skin with gloves—and by implication, the human self with hats, suits, and overcoats—is to suggest that all are no more than repositionable signifiers, radically destabilizing our sense of what constitutes "identity."

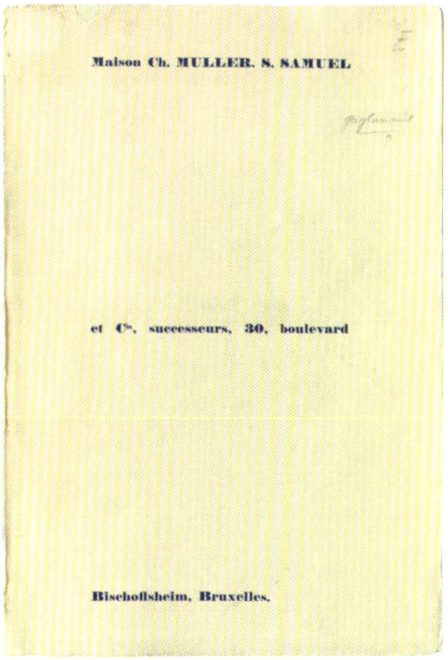

Figure 12. Cover of René Magritte and Paul Nougé's catalogue *Pour l'année 1928, la Maison Samuel nous présente quelques manteaux* (*For the Year 1928, the Maison Samuel Presents Some Coats*). 1927. The Museum of Modern Art Library, New York

THE SAMUEL CATALOGUE

Probably at some point after the close of his Galerie Le Centaure exhibition in May 1927, and certainly prior to his move to Paris in September of that same year, Magritte and Nougé collaborated on a commission from a Brussels furrier known as "Maison Ch. Müller. S. Samuel et Cie."[48] The small paperback catalogue that they produced together was not signed by either man (in keeping with the Brussels Surrealists' penchant for anonymity). Masquerading as a commercial production whose sole purpose was to promote the Maison Samuel's winter 1928 fur collection, it is in fact an insidiously subtle Surrealist manifesto, in which the worlds of fashion, fine arts, poetry, and publicity collide.

The publication has a decidedly plain cover (fig. 12).[49] It measures approximately eight by six inches, and includes only eighteen pages.[50] Nothing about its design or its material character is outstanding; if anything, the little booklet seems intended to look, from the outside, as nondescript as possible, all the better to blend in, undetected, among other small paperbacks on a shelf.[51] Magritte contributed sixteen photomechanically reproduced illustrations to the publication; all but two were printed in black and white. Nougé provided a prologue and an epilogue, along with sixteen concise texts—one for each of Magritte's illustrations—most of them consisting of a single sentence or phrase. Within the catalogue, Nougé's words appear on verso pages, centered, with large areas of empty space above and below. Magritte's images are positioned opposite them on the recto pages; all are vertical in orientation and are likewise surrounded by ample margins. The sparseness of the text pages provides an effective counterpoint to the relatively dense, visually rich detail of Magritte's illustrations, which combine hand-drawn and hand-painted elements with cutouts of photographs and photomechanically reproduced images.

No archival evidence concerning details of either the commission or the collaborative process seems to have survived.[52] It is unknown, for example, whether Magritte provided Nougé with all sixteen illustrations at once as a fait accompli, or if they had some dialogue while Magritte was creating them. We also do not know if Magritte conceived of the illustrations independently—as individual works—or if he envisioned them as the sequence in which they appear in the book. That the finished Samuel catalogue presents a narrative line seems certain, but whether Magritte was responsible for this, or Nougé, or the two of them working together, presently is unascertainable. Regardless, the final result merits consideration as a carefully thought-out composition, not just in terms of the individual relationships between the sixteen pairs of text and image, but also in terms of the order in which these pairs fall in the booklet's pages.[53]

The first eight pairs in the catalogue introduce a series of stylized yet, with one exception, naturalistically rendered and relatively interchangeable female models (see for example plates 25–27).[54] Each sports a different fur coat, and is placed in an ambiguous stagelike setting. The eyes of the women are invariably closed or otherwise obscured. Magritte included a bisected photograph of his own face, also with eyes closed, in the lower-right corner of the second illustrated spread, a subtle sign of authorship (although originally recognized, of course, only by a select few; see plate 25). The head of the model who appears to his left is partially hidden by a cutout of a car illustration (fig. 13). "What one guesses is perhaps what she is thinking," Nougé tells us. "Dressed thus, she requires no explanation."[55] His words suggest that the collage element might be read as materialized thought, while adding to the illustration's overall mood of interior reflection and silent reverie. In the pages that follow, a woman steps through a freestanding open door and, in each of the next three spreads, turns her back to us. In one particularly remarkable image her body dissolves, replaced by a polka-dotted profile and amorphous limbs (plate 26). Nougé's words repeatedly encourage readers to consider the relation between coats and concealment: "Not in the eyes, not in the hands, it is in the folds of her coat that she hides her secrets and yours."[56]

A color illustration marks the sequence's halfway point (plate 27). Exceptionally, the model's face is fully visible and turned toward us, showing that her eyes are closed. "She invents the world in complete security," Nougé tells us. "Her dreams protect her as well as her coat."[57] In the following four spreads, the female models are abruptly replaced by Magritte's characteristic *bilboquets* and strangely perforated cutouts, inanimate objects that function as mannequins, stepping into the role performed by the dreaming women in the prior pages (see for example plates 28, 29).[58] A threshold is crossed: the real is supplanted by the imagined. Nougé's words complement the images, conjuring a world of movement, reflection, and disappearance: "She advances fearlessly. The innocence of sleep and the fatality of spells precede her step by step" (plate 28).[59] "Only a reflection of her coat remains as souvenir. She is gone, used, erased."[60]

The last spread in the series of four dream images features a curtain, two fur coats, one lacking a head, but with recognizable women's legs beneath; the other supported by a flat, perforated shape (plate 29). A drawn bird swoops in from stage left, its head positioned over the neck of the "headless" coat, taking the model's place. "Here the last likeness is discarded," Nougé writes. "There are no longer any ordinary things."[61] In his prologue to the Samuel catalogue, Nougé had counseled "vigilance." The message was clear: Be careful. Stay alert. Things are not what they seem.

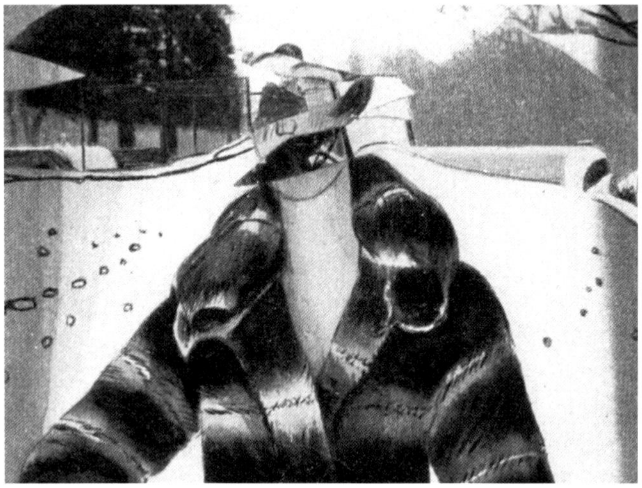

Figure 13. Detail of *Novelty* (plate 25), from René Magritte and Paul Nougé's catalogue *Pour l'année 1928, la Maison Samuel nous présente quelques manteaux* (*For the Year 1928, the Maison Samuel Presents Some Coats*). 1927. The Museum of Modern Art Library, New York

His words implicated not only the Maison Samuel's luxury products, and his and Magritte's unconventional commercial catalogue, but the world of appearances, generally speaking. Evidently their goal with the Samuel catalogue was not just to sell furs, but to advertise the uncanny power of dreams. It was a reminder of all that remains hidden beneath the surface, whether of fur coats or of the psyche.

DOUBLES AND DOUBLING

The final four word-and-image pairs in the Samuel catalogue trace a path from dream state to the real. In the first, we see a naturalistically rendered model in a fur coat, accompanied by the words: "Now she returns to the world, she can smile at all the dangers."[62] Two pages later, she is joined by her dream-double; the two walk arm in arm (plate 30). "A mirror would be useless," observes Nougé. "She divides herself without trouble. But this is how marvels begin."[63] Nougé's word choice here, as throughout the catalogue, is richly evocative. In French, "se dédoubler" translates literally as "to be divided into halves." In psychoanalytic parlance, it means "to have a split personality," inviting interpretation of Magritte's illustration in relation to Freud's concept of the uncanny, in which "doubles" and repetition play key roles.[64] For Freud, the uncanny entailed a conjoining of opposites: the familiar and agreeable with what, according to social mores, should be kept out of sight. The leering, distorted features of Magritte's mannequin figure give physical form to what the model represses: her reified, commoditized, and inanimate "other," whose appearance recalls that of a reflection in a fun-house mirror: isolated, cutout, and given thin yet solid form.

Magritte's 1927 portrait of Nougé (plate 16) raises the representational stakes. Although iconographically connected to the Samuel catalogue—with Nougé portrayed in formal evening attire, and with one of the irregularly contoured, perforated "mannequin" cutouts redeployed as a strangely situated, almost free-floating door—it introduces a different approach to the subject of the "double," reimagining it not only in psychoanalytic terms but as an image-generating strategy. In the Samuel catalogue, Magritte paired his fur model with a dream-double, a visually distinct doppelgänger, brought together on the page. In his portrait of Nougé, by contrast, there appears little, at first glance, to distinguish the image of the figure situated on the left side of the composition from its counterpart on the right. We are encouraged to consider the two figures as identical—in attire, in posture, and in the position of their heads. The implication is that they are duplicates of one another, and this duality forces us to recognize the obvious: neither image *is* Nougé; both are representations.[65]

In the portrait of Nougé it is not only duplication, or reiteration, that renders the figures mysterious or unsettling; the pronounced slenderness of their bodies is also strange. They give the impression of something seen at an oblique angle, impossibly situated within a space defined by a perforated screen that rises up behind them, and by the "door," the lower tip of which balances precariously on the edge of the painting, with its front edge seemingly pressed against the surface. At the same time, this element recedes diagonally, cutting into and/or bypassing the figure of Nougé at right in a way that differentiates what we can see of him from what we see of that at left. The two figures are also distinguished by the cropping of the right one's proper left arm by the picture's edge, and a subtle shift in lighting, which affects both figures' skin tones as well as the atmospheric background behind their heads. Both figures appear to be missing their right hands.

Some have interpreted the bifurcated, "quasi-stereographic"[66] structure of Magritte's image of Nougé biographically, suggesting it alludes to Nougé's double life as a biochemist and an avant-garde writer.[67] By contrast, in what is believed to be among the last paintings Magritte completed before his departure for Paris, *La Fin des contemplations* (plate 18)—a title alleged to have been "found" by Nougé[68]—Magritte dispensed with all clues that might encourage biographical or narrative speculation. The painting is among the most radically reductive in his entire œuvre. In the portrait of Nougé, a comparison of the painting's right and left sides gradually reveals a number of differences. Such a comparison in *La Fin des contemplations* is an exercise in frustration. The three thick black lines that border the left and right edges of the composition and mark its exact center are identical in proportion.[69] The same holds true for the two jaggedly "cutout" figures;

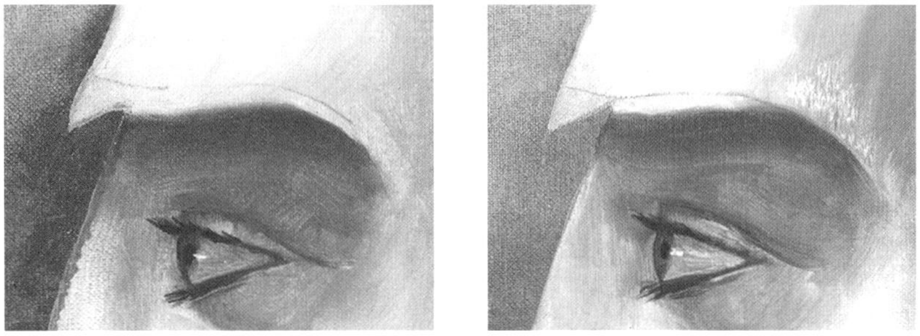

14a and b. Infrared images showing details (left and right eyes and brow lines) of Magritte's *La Fin des contemplations* (*An End to* Contemplation, 1927; plate 18). The Menil Collection, Houston

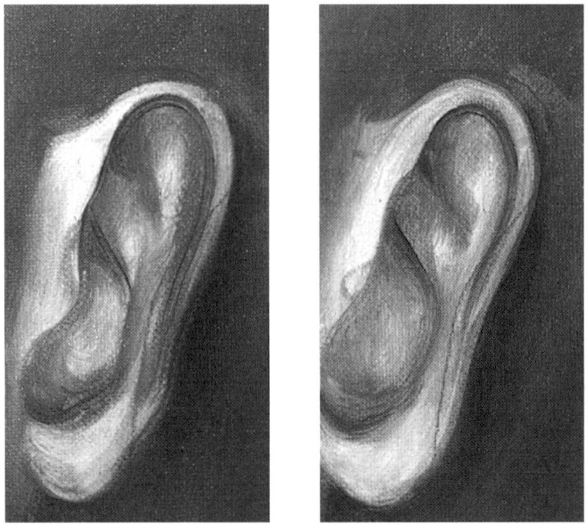

Figures 15a and b. Infrared images showing details (left and right ears) of Magritte's *La Fin des contemplations* (*An End to Contemplation*, 1927; plate 18). The Menil Collection, Houston

for the white, trompe l'œil "torn paper" (actually painted) collage pieces that rise behind them, decisively secured to the painting's surface with actual snap fasteners; and even for the faint, chalklike line that emerges from behind the white shapes in each image's lower-right corner. The position of this line and the tonalities of the figures' skin and backgrounds subtly change from left to right, as do other small details: the lines of the inner ears, for example, and the forms of the white "collage" elements. Overall, however, the relationship between the work's two sides is one of same to same.

According to Menil conservators Katrina Bartlett and Brad Epley, examination of *La Fin des contemplations* using infrared reflectography reveals underdrawing and "minor artist's changes in the brow line of the figures and in the ears" (figs. 14a,b; 15a,b). It appears that each figure "was initially planned with pencil in the same form"—possibly using "a template or cut-out"—and was then "altered in the same manner during painting." This likely indicates that Magritte painted both figures together, "instead of fully planning and finishing one figure before starting the second."[70] On one hand, this implies that the slight differences (in the detailing of the ears, for example) were deliberate, or at least that Magritte deliberately let them be. More significantly, it means that the relationship between the two figures is *not* one of copy to model but, instead, of equivalents (of same to same).

The French philosopher Michel Foucault would later define this type of relationship in Magritte's paintings as one of "similitude," which he opposed to "resemblance." "Resemblance," according to Foucault, "has a 'model,' an original element that orders and hierarchizes the increasingly less faithful copies that can be struck from it," whereas "the similar develops in series that have neither beginning nor end, [. . .] that obey no hierarchy, but propagate themselves from small differences among small differences."[71] To demonstrate his concept of similitude, Foucault turned to Magritte's 1962 painting *La Représentation* (Representation; fig. 16), instead of to 1927 paintings like the portrait of Nougé or *La Fin des contemplations*. With this, Foucault elided the earlier works' inaugural role, as well as the original context in which Magritte's engagement with issues of doubling—similitude—first emerged: that of Brussels Surrealism, on the

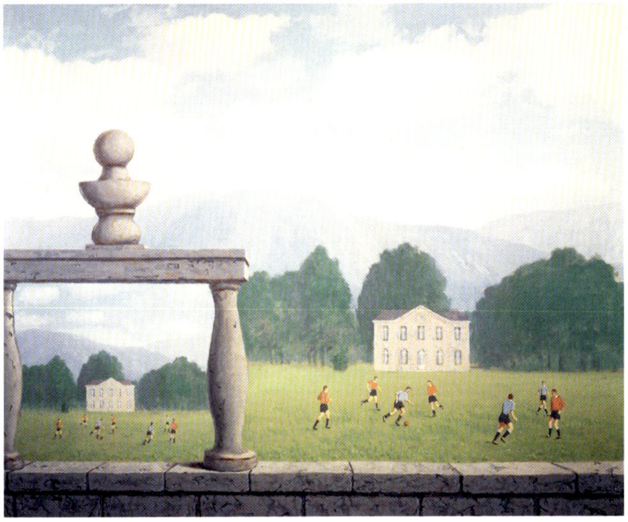

Figure 16. René Magritte. *La Représentation* (*Representation*). 1962. Oil on canvas, 31 7/8 x 39 3/8" (81 x 100 cm). Private collection

eve of Magritte's departure for Paris, a moment of richly generative collaboration with Nougé, whose interests in concealment, split-subjectivities, and violence—as demonstrated by his texts related to paintings such as *L'Assassin menacé* and *Jeune Fille mangeant un oiseau*—appear to have paralleled Magritte's own.[72]

In *La Fin des contemplations*, as distinct from *Représentation*, Magritte visibly "cut" into three-dimensionally modeled figures, revealing them to be two-dimensional, partial, and insubstantial. In so doing, he located his attempts to reinvent the image as free-floating representation at a corporeal level, associating surface—what Foucault described as the "filmy thinness" of the image—with that of the body, and in particular, of skin.[73] Although bloodless, this visual dissection has a visceral impact, one that severs the alliance of surface (the visible) with the essence of things. It helps us to recognize the degree of violence that informs Magritte's later assaults on the representational hierarchies and conventions that support fixed meanings, and on the normative association of what something looks like with what it is.

Notes

The quote that serves as this essay's title, "This Is How Marvels Begin," is from a 1927 text by Paul Nougé. For the complete bibliographic citation, see n. 54.

References in the following notes in the form "Sylvester 1:8" refer to the volume and catalogue numbers of works in the six-volume Magritte catalogue raisonné. Likewise, references in the form "Sylvester 1, p. 304" refer to the volume and page numbers where corresponding texts are located. The first five volumes of the catalogue raisonné, published 1992–97, were edited by David Sylvester; the final volume, published 2012, was edited by Sarah Whitfield. For complete publication information for all six volumes, see the "Selected Bibliography," p. 252.

Catalogue raisonné numbers are provided for works that are not reproduced as plates or figures in the present volume. Unless otherwise noted, all English translations in this essay are the author's.

1. See the "Carte d'invitation, exposition 'René Magritte,' Galerie Le Centaure, Bruxelles, 23.04-3.05.1927." Royal Museums of Fine Arts of Belgium, Brussels/Archives for Contemporary Art in Belgium, inv. no. 89858. On the redesign of the gallery, see Jean Milo, *Vie et survie du "Centaure"* (Brussels: Éditions nationales d'art, 1980), pp. 39–40.
2. For details of Magritte's contract with Van Hecke, see Sylvester 1, p. 57.
3. See Hal Foster, *Compulsive Beauty* (Cambridge, Mass.: MIT Press, 1993), pp. 23–29, for a discussion of Breton's ideas of "convulsive beauty" and "fixed-explosive."
4. I am indebted to Scott Gerson, Associate Conservator, The Museum of Modern Art, for this observation.
5. The silhouette of horse and rider in the other 1926 *papier collé* of *Le Jockey perdu* (fig. 5) is based on an illustration from the same *Larousse* page. Patricia Allmer, in *René Magritte: Beyond Painting* (Manchester, U.K.: Manchester University Press, 2009), p. 218, notes: "The jockey

can be traced back to images in charts for 'cheval,' 'équitation' and 'courses,' in *Larousse* [...]." The specific *Larousse* source (see figs. 2, 3) for *Le Jockey perdu* (plate 4) is published here for the first time.

6. The offset front leg could be explained by a slight shift in the pantograph, since the shape is otherwise the same as that in the original illustration. After establishing the outline, Magritte may have filled in the details freehand. Scott Gerson, email message to the author, August 22, 2012; and Michael Duffy, Paintings Conservator, The Museum of Modern Art, email message to the author, August 23, 2012.

7. See Allmer, *Magritte: Beyond Painting,* p. 42, for discussion of how encyclopedia imagery, "short-circuits the artwork's relations to reality."

8. See Sylvester 1, p. 161, for discussion of "what Magritte calls a bilboquet" as "something special to himself and not the wooden cup-and-ball toy the word normally means."

9. Magritte used the vocal score for *The Girls of Gottenberg*, a 1907 English musical comedy, for paper source materials for all but three of his thirty known *papiers collés* dating from 1925–27. The author is grateful to Caitlin Kelly for her identification of the exact sheets used in each collage. On Magritte's use of this score, see Sylvester 1, p. 56.

10. On Magritte's friends as "accomplices," see Sarah Whitfield, "Magritte and His Accomplices," in idem, *Magritte* (London: South Bank Centre, 1992), pp. 25–48. Eight self-designated "accomplices" ("complices") of Magritte signed the untitled catalogue essay for *René Magritte* (Brussels, Galerie L'Époque, 1928).

11. See Paul Nougé, letter to René Magritte, n.d. [November 1927], repr. in Marcel Mariën, ed., *Lettres surréalistes: 1924–1940* (Brussels: Les Lèvres nues, 1973), no. 110, p. 55. At least seventeen (and perhaps eighteen as one painting is lost) of the forty-nine paintings in the Le Centaure exhibition include *bilboquets.*

12. On the *bilboquet*'s appearances, see David Sylvester, *Magritte: The Silence of the World* (Houston and New York: Menil Foundation, Abrams, 1992), pp. 71–72. See also Peter Wollen, "Magritte and the Bowler Hat," in idem, *Paris/Manhattan: Writings on Art* (New York: Verso, 2004), p. 139.

13. Sylvester 4:1605, p. 295.

14. Paul-Gustave Van Hecke, "René Magritte: Peintre de la pensée abstraite," *Sélection* 6, no. 6 (March 1927): 442.

15. Camille Goemans, "La Jeune Peinture belge," *Bulletin de la vie artistique* (Paris), no. 1 (September 1926): 269. Trans. in Sylvester 1:81, p. 170.

16. *Exposition Magritte* (Brussels: Galerie Le Centaure, 1927); repr. in Marcel Mariën, ed., *L'Activité surréaliste en Belgique (1924–1950)* (Brussels: Lebeer Hossmann, 1979), pp. 145–46. The authors of the catalogue raisonné speculate about the importance of listing the painting as no. 1 in the catalogue. See Sylvester 1:81 and p. 68; see also Sylvester, *Magritte: The Silence of the World,* p. 91. Jean Milo, assistant director of Le Centaure from 1926 to 1931, recalled that *Le Jockey perdu* was displayed in the vitrine of the building. See Milo, *Vie et survie du "Centaure,"* p. 3.

17. See Sylvester 1:81, p. 170.

18. René Magritte, letter to Harry Torczyner, June 22, 1960; repr. in Torczyner, *L'Ami Magritte: Correspondance et souvenirs* (Antwerp: Mercator, 1992), no. 136, pp. 148–49.

19. Ibid. The catalogue raisonné authors speculate that the painting was completed in February or March 1926, which leads them to surmise that the collage version was likely completed around the beginning of the year. See Sylvester 1:8, p. 169; and Sylvester 4:1605, p. 295.

20. See Sylvester 2:504, and Sylvester 4:1178, 1180, 1253, and 1435. For other works featuring the same *Larouse* horse and jockey, see Sylvester 3:923 and 924.

21. See Wollen, "Magritte and the Bowler Hat," in idem, *Paris/Manhattan*, pp. 129–30, for a vivid reading of this painting that complements my own.

22. A number of other paintings from 1926 and 1927 include similar "death masks." See Sylvester 1:94, 101, 110, 112, 115, 124, and 129.

23. I am grateful to Professor Diane Maglio, Fashion Dept., Berkeley College, Larry L. Luing School of Business, for the analysis of menswear throughout this essay.

24. See Fred Miller Robinson, *The Man in the Bowler Hat: His History and Iconography* (Chapel Hill: University of North Carolina Press, 2011 [first published 1993]), pp. 125–48. Wollen, in "Magritte and the Bowler Hat," in idem, *Paris/Manhattan* (p. 132), discusses the hat in relation to fashion, detective fiction, the performing arts, Purism, and patriarchy.

25. The coat on the forward-facing figure buttons on the "wrong" side for menswear, a sign that *Le Sens de la nuit* may be an imaginary or "reflected" image.

26. On the correspondences between this painting and Magritte's illustrations for the 1926 Maison Samuel catalogue, see Sylvester 1:136, p. 207; Sylvester, *René Magritte: The Silence of the World*, p. 98; and Whitfield, *Magritte*, cat. no. 18. Magritte designed a second Maison Samuel catalogue in 1927, in collaboration with Paul Nougé (see plates 25–30).

27. Later in life, the artist noted: "Psychoanalysis is a very intelligent system. But it is only one interpretation among many. It gives a symbolic value to represented things, to objects chosen by the artist. Me, I think that a cloud in a painting is nothing more than a cloud." See Pierre Descargues, "René Magritte, le plus célèbre des surréalistes belges parle du mystère," *Feuille d'avis de Lausanne-Magazine* (November 1, 1961); repr. in René Magritte, *Écrits complets*, ed. by André Blavier (Paris: Flammarion, 2001 [originally 1979]), no. 162; trans. by Danielle M. Johnson. For the suggestion that Magritte used Freudian symbols to deny the efficacy of psychoanalysis or parody it, see Allmer, *Magritte: Beyond Painting*, pp. 95, 99. On Magritte's early interest in Freud and its effect on his "word-image" paintings, see Danielle M. Johnson, "Salvador Dalí and René Magritte, 1928–1938," Ph.D. diss., New York University, 2012, pp. 161–64, and 201.

28. Sigmund Freud, "Fetishism" (1927), in *The Standard Edition of the Complete Psychological Works of Sigmund Freud*, vol. 21, trans. and ed. by James Strachey (London: Hogarth, 1962), pp. 153–57.

29. Sigmund Freud, *Three Essays on the Theory of Sexuality* (1905), in *The Standard Edition of the Complete Psychological Works of Sigmund Freud*, vol. 7, trans. and ed. by James Strachey (London: Hogarth, 1953), p. 19.

30. Ibid., p. 155.

31. Sigmund Freud, "Leonardo da Vinci and a Memory of His Childhood" (1910), in *The Standard Edition of the Complete Psychological Works of Sigmund Freud*, vol. 11, trans. and ed. by James Strachey (London: Hogarth, 1957), p. 126.

32. The bowler-hatted man first appeared in Magritte's work in 1926–27 (in three paintings and two *papiers collés*), and then only occasionally in the 1930s and 1940s. The artist revisited the theme in earnest between 1950 and 1966. See Wollen, "Magritte and the Bowler Hat," in idem, *Paris/Manhattan.*

33. Paul Nougé, "Images peintes" (1927), in idem, *Histoire de ne pas rire* (Brussels: Les Lèvres nues, 1956), p. 190; trans. in Sylvester 1, p. 208.

34. Ibid, p. 189.

35. Ibid.

36. Isidore Ducasse (Comte de Lautréamont), *Poésies* (1870), facsimile repr. in idem, *Œuvres complètes* (Paris: La Table Ronde, 1970), p. 10. Louis Aragon repeated Lautréamont's phrase in *La Peinture au défi* (Paris: Galerie Goemans, Librairie José Corti, 1930), in Eng. as "The Challenge to Painting," in *The Surrealists Look at Art*, ed. and trans. by Pontus Hultén (Venice, Calif.: Lapis, 1990), p. 72.

37. Infrared imaging is traditionally used with reflected light to detect underdrawing and inscriptions; in transmitted light, paint density and Magritte's brushwork are more easily interpreted. Thanks

to Michael Duffy, along with his colleagues in The Museum of Modern Art's Department of Conservation, Anny Aviram and Jim Coddington, for their insights about this painting.
38. David Sylvester, *Magritte* (New York: Praeger, 1969), p. 13, follows Nougé in stating the three are "gazing impassively at the oblivious criminal."
39. This description draws on John Berger's statement that in *L'Assassin menacé* "we are shown everything—and nothing." Berger, "A Way to Magritte," *New Society* (March 20, 1969): 450.
40. See Sylvester 1, pp. 207–8.
41. See Sylvester 1, pp. 216–17.
42. José Vovelle, "Magritte et le cinéma," *Cahiers de l'Association Internationale pour l'étude de Dada et du Surréalisme* 4 (1970 [published 1971]): 103–13.
43. Sylvester 1:133, p. 204. For further discussion of *Le Mort qui tue* in relation to the Fântomas series, see Richard Abel, *The Ciné Goes to Town: French Cinema, 1896–1914* (Berkeley: University of California Press, 1994), pp. 376–77.
44. For Magritte's recollection of going to the Cinéma Bleu, see I[rène] H[amoir], "Notes biographiques," in *XXXme Salon [du] Cercle Royal Artistique et Littéraire de Charleroi* (Charleroi, Belgium: Salle de la Bourse, 1956), p. 4. See Vovelle, "Magritte et le cinéma," p. 104, for the suggestion—erroneously citing Scutenaire's *La Terre n'est pas une vallée de larmes* (Brussels: La Boétie, 1945), p. 42—that Magritte recalled going to watch Feuillade's Fantômas films at the Cinéma Bleu. (In fact, Scutenaire mentions Fritz Lang and Carl Theodor Dreyer, not Feuillade.) Magritte contributed a short essay, "Notes sur Fantômas" to *Distances* in 1928.
45. Vovelle, "Magritte et le cinéma," pp. 106–7.
46. Regarding the common association of bowler hats with detectives in detective films and fiction from early decades of the twentieth century up to the 1960s, see Wollen, "Magritte and the Bowler Hat," in idem, *Paris/Manhattan*, pp. 132–33.
47. For Charles Sanders Peirce's definition of an "index" in relation to an "icon" or a "symbol," see *Peirce on Signs: Writings on Semiotic by Charles Sanders Peirce*, ed. by James Hoopes (Chapel Hill: University of North Carolina Press, 1991), pp. 239–40 and 251–52.
48. This was the second of two commissions for the Maison Samuel; the first catalogue had been undertaken the previous year. See Sylvester 1, pp. 59–60, 74–75; Mariën, ed., *L'Activité surréaliste en Belgique*, p. 149; and Georges Roque, *Ceci n'est pas un Magritte* (Paris: Flammarion, 1985), pp. 176–85.
49. Its plainness is apparent especially when compared, for example, with the extravagant productions of Paris fur companies like the well-known Maison Fourrures Max.
50. The discussion that follows is indebted to conversations with Scott Gerson.
51. See Tom Gutt, "Ces Belles Fleurs du charbon," preface to the facsimile repr. of *Le Catalogue Samuel* (Brussels: Didier Devillez, 1996), p. 10, for his suggestion that the booklet's austere appearance may have been due to budgetary constraints. Sarah Whitfield proposes that the plainness of the catalogue has its origin in school textbooks, as was the case with another Magritte/Nougé publication, *Clarisse Juranville* (plates 31, 32); see Sylvester 1, p. 75, and Josef Helfenstein with Clare Elliott, "'A Lightning Flash Is Smoldering Beneath the Bowler Hats': Paris, 1927–1930," in the present volume, pp. 73–74. Whitfield, email correspondence with the author, January 17, 2013.
52. See Gutt, "Belles Fleurs du charbon," in *Le Catalogue Samuel*, pp. 9–10, on the lack of archival traces. It is unknown whether the catalogues were ever distributed to prospective clients, or what the response of their commissioner was to the highly unconventional commercial publication.
53. For comments on certain pairs, see Sylvester, *Magritte: The Silence of the World*, p.108. For a more detailed discussion of the image titled *Novelty*, see Michel Draguet, *Magritte tout en papier: Collages, dessins, gouaches* (Paris: Hazan, Fondation Dina Vierny—Musée Maillol, 2006), pp. 42–43. While Gutt pays close attention to the Samuel catalogue as a whole, he concentrates on Nougé's texts and is dismissive of Magritte's illustrations. See Gutt, "Belles Fleurs du charbon," in *Le Catalogue Samuel*, p. 12.
54. See René Magritte and Paul Nougé, *Le Catalogue Samuel* (Brussels: La Maison Ch. Müller, S. Samuel et Cie., 1927), n.p. or the 1996 facsimile edition, n.p.
55. Ibid.
56. Ibid.
57. Ibid.; trans. in Sylvester 1, p. 74.
58. For all the images, see Magritte and Nougé, *Le Catalogue Samuel*.
59. Ibid.; trans. in Sylvester 1, p. 74.
60. Magritte and Nougé, *Le Catalogue Samuel*.
61. Ibid. In the catalogue preface for Magritte's 1931 solo exhibition at the Salle Giso in Brussels, Nougé used a similar phrase, prefaced in a significantly different way: "The world has been altered, there are no longer any ordinary things." Paul Nougé, *E.L.T. Mesens & E. van Tonderen présentent seize tableaux de René Magritte* (Brussels: Salle Giso, 1931); trans. in Sylvester 2, p. 8.
62. Magritte and Nougé, *Le Catalogue Samuel*.
63. Ibid.
64. See Sigmund Freud, "The 'Uncanny'" (1919), in *The Standard Edition of the Complete Psychological Works of Sigmund Freud*, vol. 17, trans. and ed. by James Strachey (London: Hogarth, 1962), pp. 217–56. My understanding of the "uncanny" is indebted to Foster, *Compulsive Beauty*, pp. xvii–xviii, 7–8, and 20–21.
65. The authors of *Art Since 1900* write of Magritte's "repetition compulsion" and remark that "it could be said that what allows one to identify Magritte as a Surrealist is the sense that a form of doubling grips his work from the very start"; see Hal Foster et al., *Art Since 1900* (London and New York: Thames & Hudson, 2004), p. 212. For additional discussions of Magritte and doubling, see Johnson, "Salvador Dalí and René Magritte," pp. 115–21 and 151–58; Sylvester, *Magritte: The Silence of the World*, pp. 65–69; and David Lomas, "Simulacra and the Order of Mimesis in Salvador Dalí and Glenn Brown," in *Persistence and Memory: New Critical Perspectives on Dalí at the Centennial*, ed. by Charles Hine, William Jeffett, and Kelly Reynolds (St. Petersburg, Fla.: Bompiani/Salvador Dalí Museum, 2004), pp. 202–4.
66. Sylvester 1: 151, p. 221.
67. Evelyn Benesch, Ulf Küster, and Steingrim Laursen, *René Magritte: The Key to Dreams* (Vienna, Riehen, Basel, and Ghent: BA-CA Kunstforum/Fondation Beyeler/Ludion, 2005), p. 64.
68. Marcel Mariën, arguably the first historian of the Belgian Surrealist group, claimed that Nougé "found" this title. See Sylvester 1:165.
69. Brad Epley, email message to the author, September 14, 2012.
70. Katrina Bartlett and Brad Epley, "Memorandum," April 11, 2012.
71. Michel Foucault, *This Is Not a Pipe* (Berkeley and Los Angeles: University of California Press, 1983), p. 44. Early version published as "Ceci n'est pas une pipe," *Les Cahiers du chemin* 2 (January 15, 1968): 79–105. First published in book form as *Ceci n'est pas une pipe* (Montpellier, France: Fata Morgana, 1973).
72. Regarding Nougé's "notion of effacement as a subversive tool, fostering 'complicity' and unifying the Belgians," see Patricia Allmer, Jan Dirk Baetens, and Hilde Van Gelder, "Introduction: Surrealism in Belgium," in *Collective Inventions: Surrealism in Belgium*, ed. by Allmer and Van Gelder (Leuven, Belgium: Leuven University Press, 2007), p. 18. Regarding the written productions of Nougé, Goemans, and Marcel Lecomte being "deliberately depersonalized, extremely concise, and highly unsettling," see David Willinger, *Theatrical Gestures of Belgian Modernism: Dada, Surrealism, Futurism, and Pure Plastic in Twentieth-Century Belgian Theatre* (New York: Peter Lang, 2002), p. 13.
73. Foucault, *This Is Not a Pipe*, p. 41.

1. **UNTITLED.** 1926. Cut-and-pasted sheet music, gouache, and watercolor on paper, 21 5/8 x 15 3/4" (55 x 40 cm)

2. **UNTITLED.** 1926. Cut-and-pasted sheet music, watercolor, charcoal, pencil, and ink on paper, 15 3/4 x 21 5/8" (40 x 55 cm)

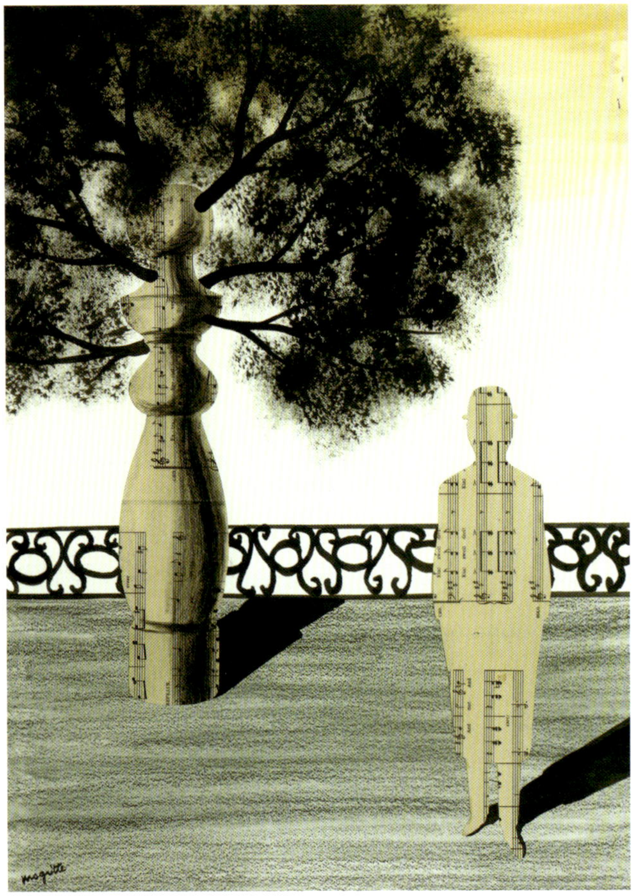

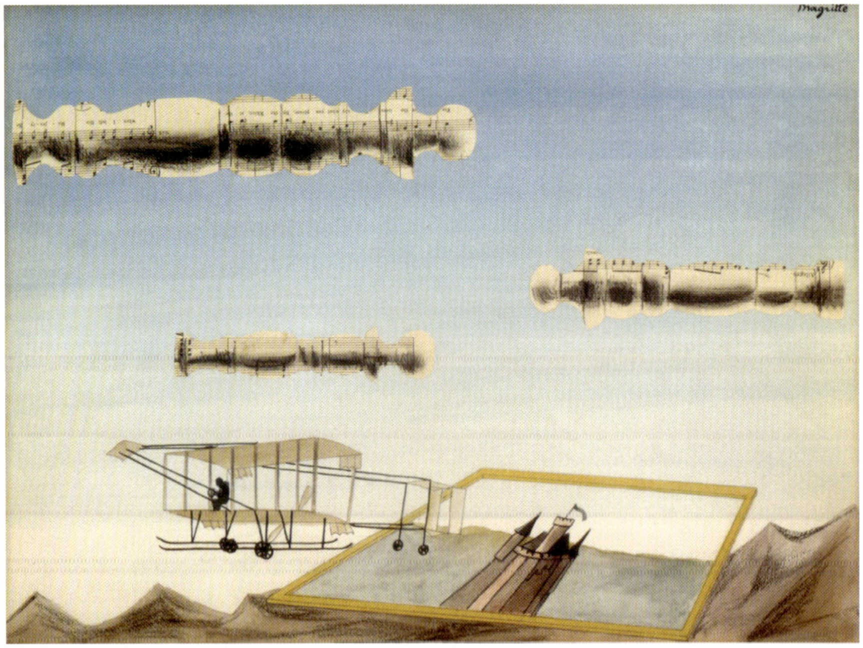

3. NOCTURNE. 1927.
Cut-and-pasted sheet music, gouache, and watercolor on paper, 16 9/16 x 22 1/16" (42 x 56 cm)

4. LE JOCKEY PERDU (THE LOST JOCKEY). 1926.
Cut-and-pasted sheet music, watercolor, pencil, and ink on paper, 15 1/2 x 21 5/16" (39.3 x 54.2 cm)

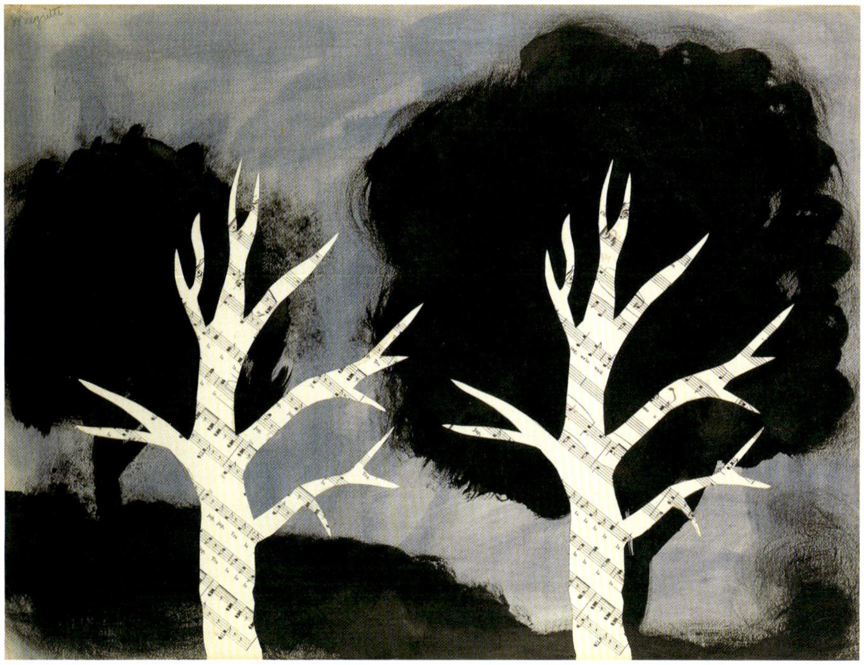

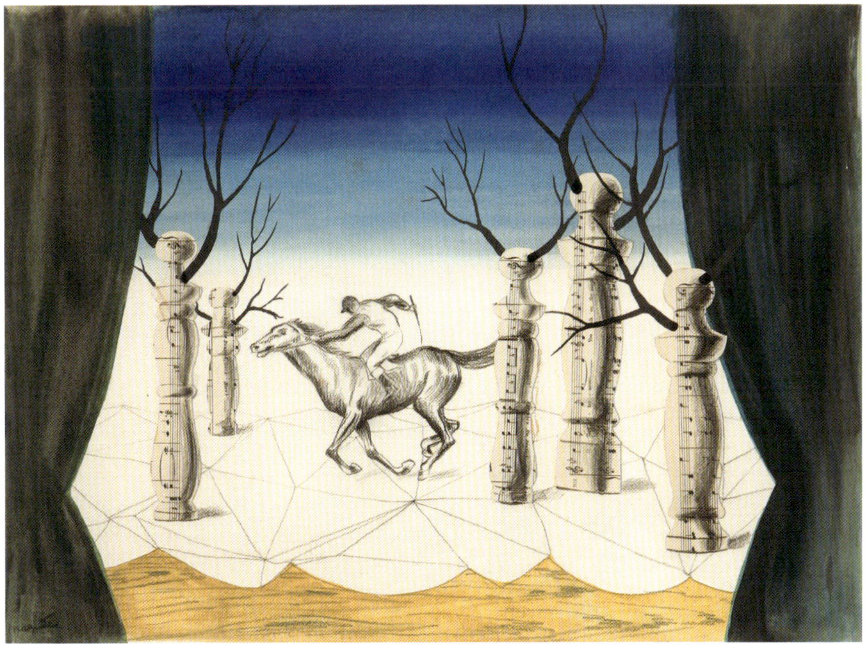

5. UNTITLED. 1926. Cut-and-pasted printed paper and sheet music and watercolor on paper, 22 7/16 x 16 1/8" (57 x 41 cm)

6. UNTITLED. 1926. Cut-and-pasted printed paper and sheet music, pencil, colored pencil, and watercolor on paper, 15 3/4 x 21 7/8" (40 x 55.5 cm)

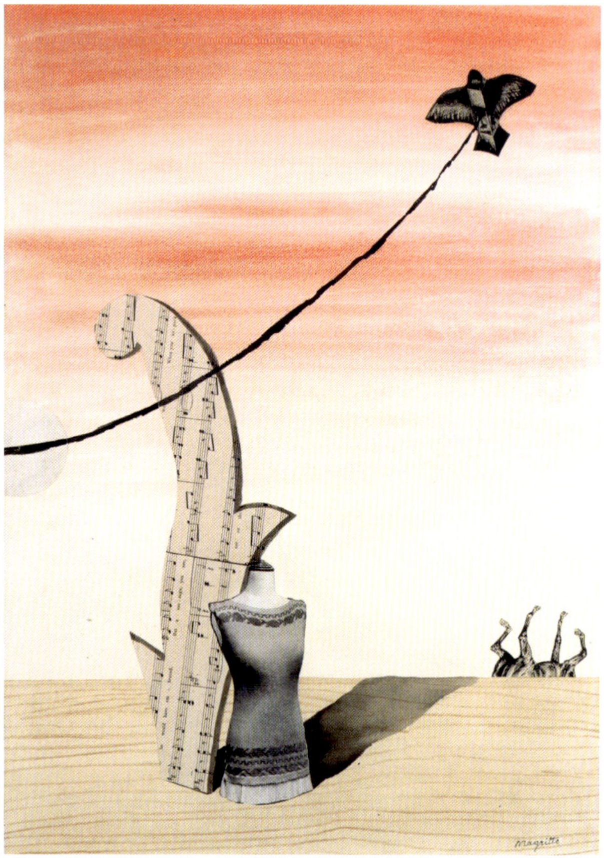

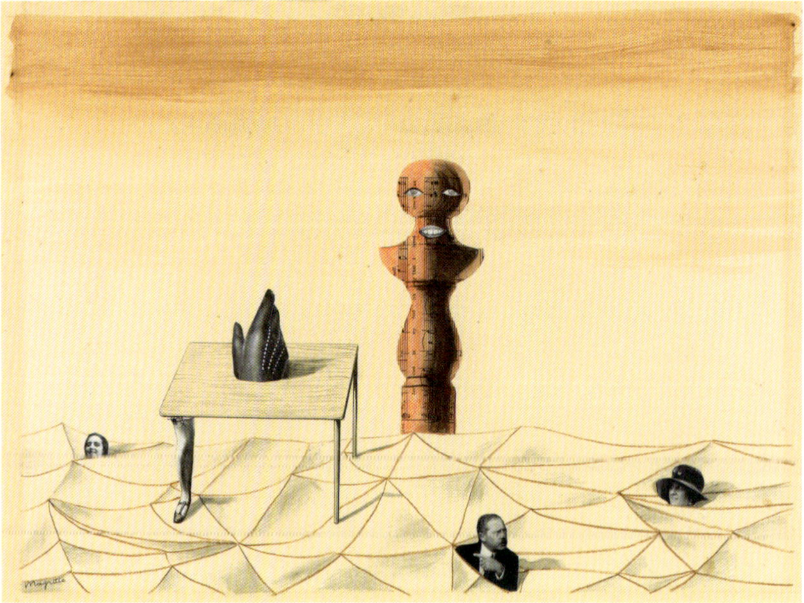

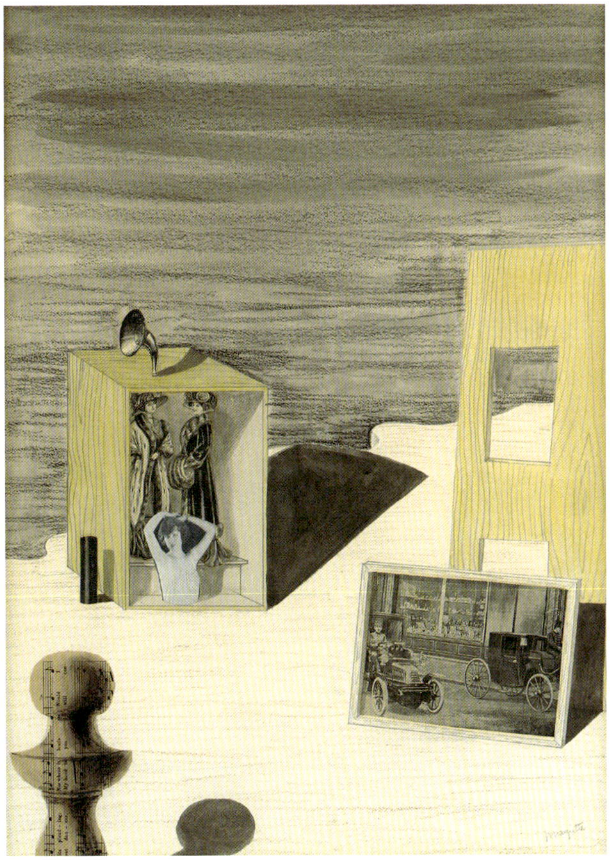

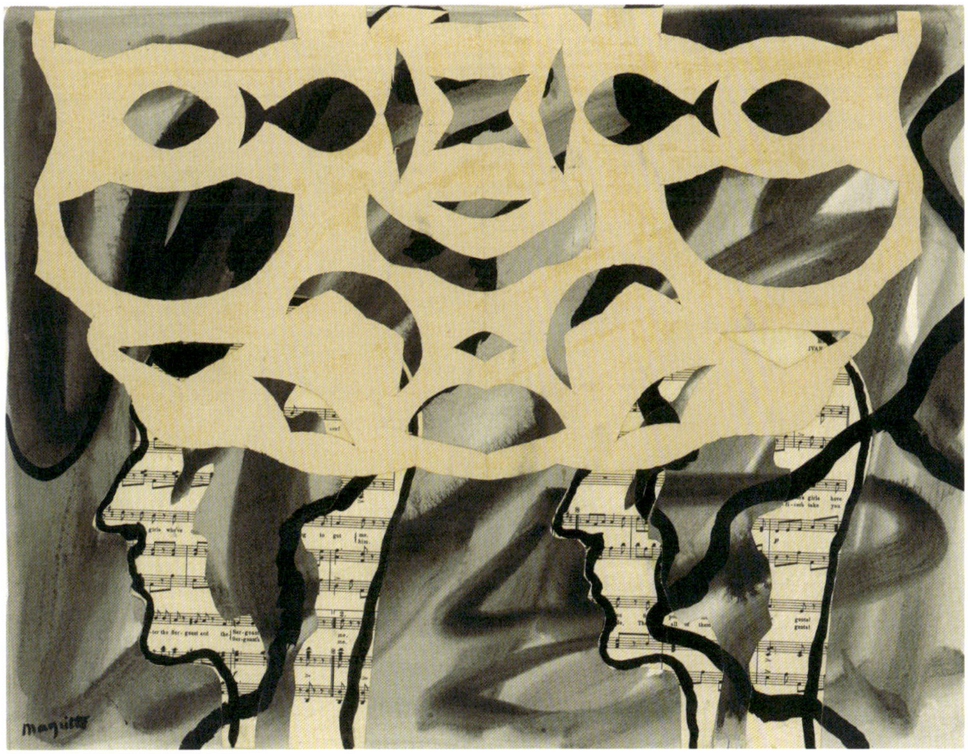

7. UNTITLED. 1926. Cut-and-pasted printed paper and sheet music, watercolor, pencil, and colored pencil on paper, 21 1/8 x 15 3/8" (53.7 x 39 cm)

8. UNTITLED. 1927. Cut-and-pasted paper and sheet music and watercolor on paper, 19 15/16 x 25 13/16" (50.7 x 65.5 cm)

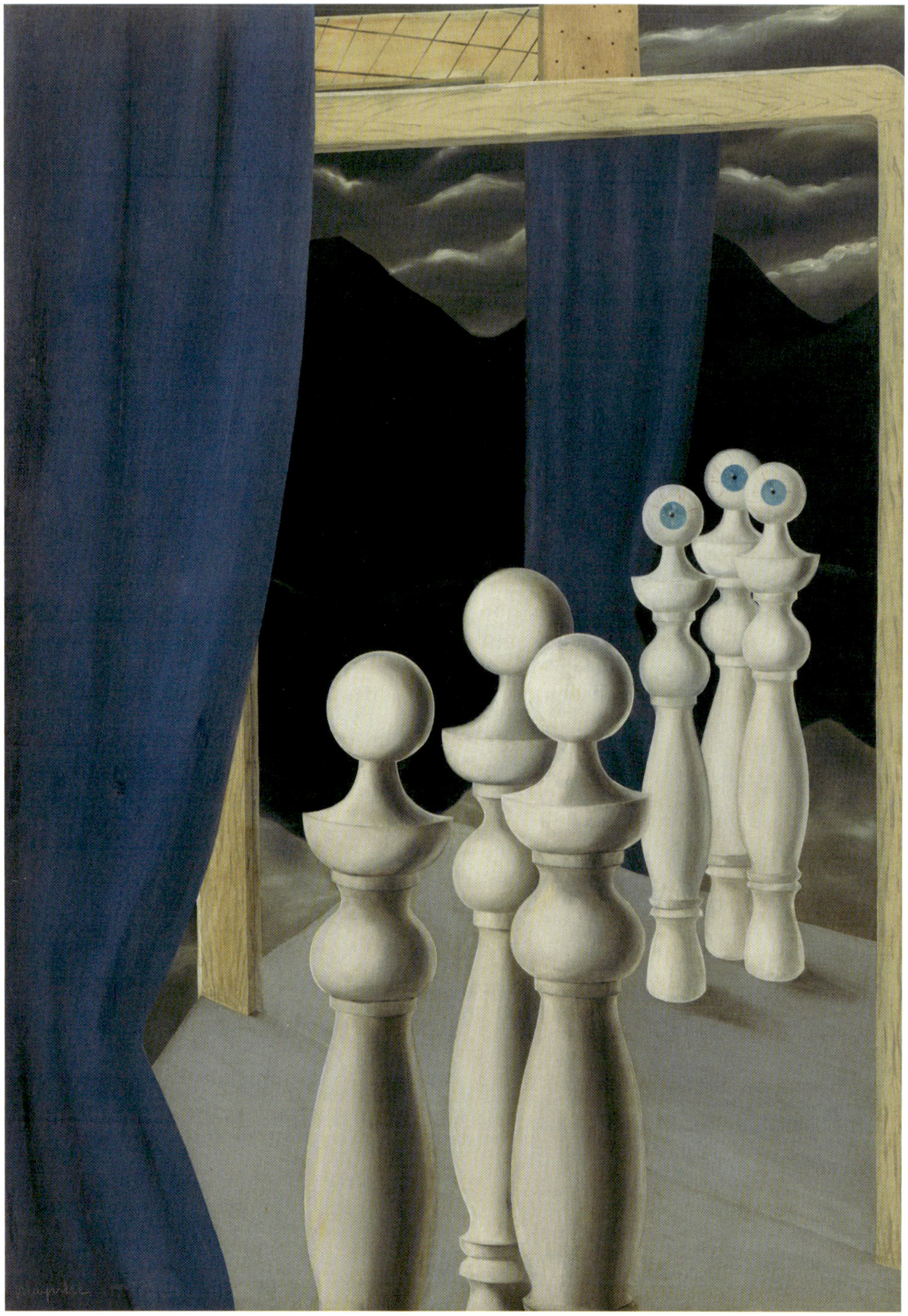

9. LE RENCONTRE (THE ENCOUNTER). 1926.

Oil on canvas, 54 15/16 x 39" (139.5 x 99 cm)

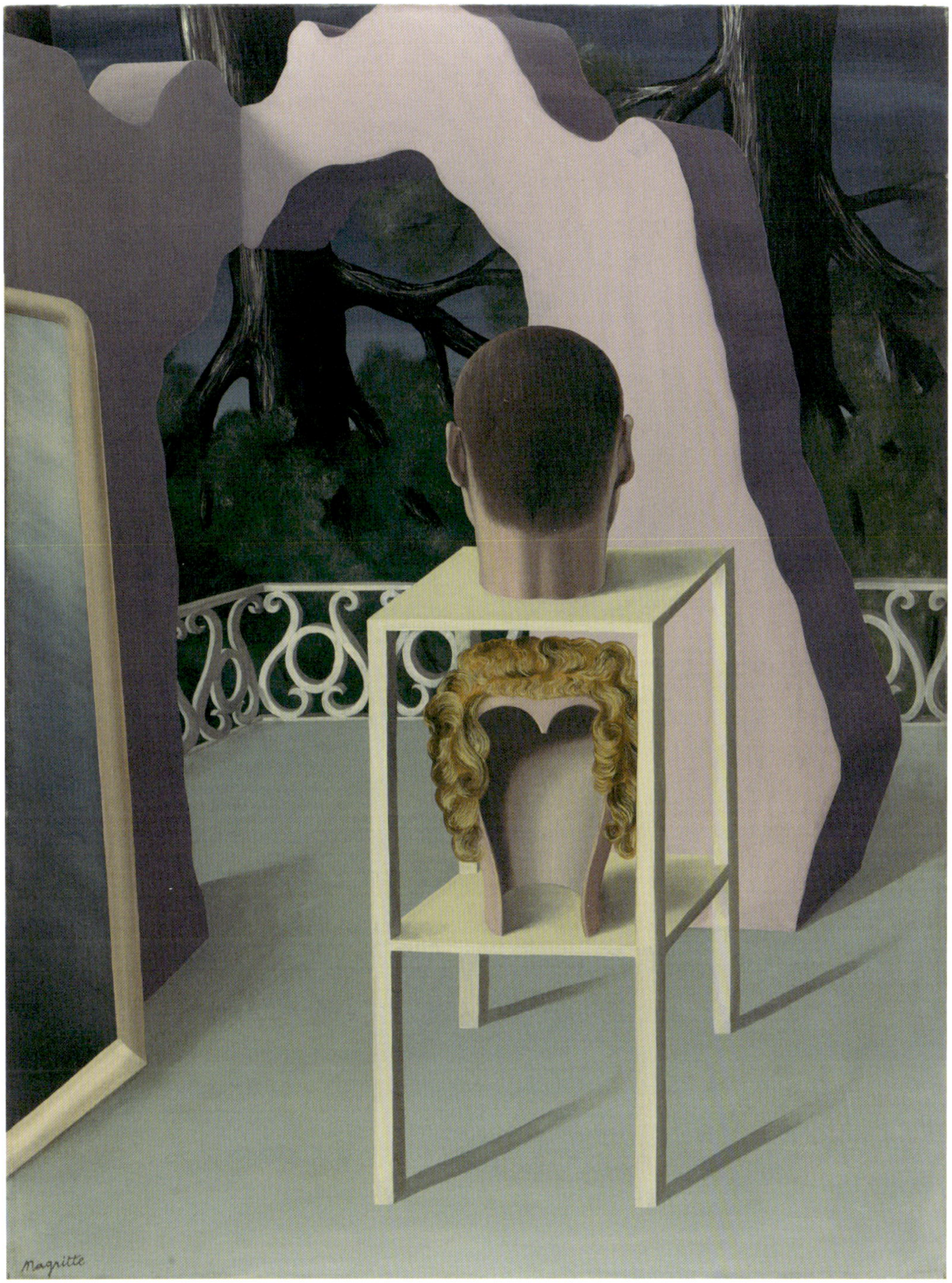

10. LE MARIAGE DE MINUIT (THE MIDNIGHT MARRIAGE). 1926.

Oil on canvas, 54 3/4 x 41 5/16" (139 x 105 cm)

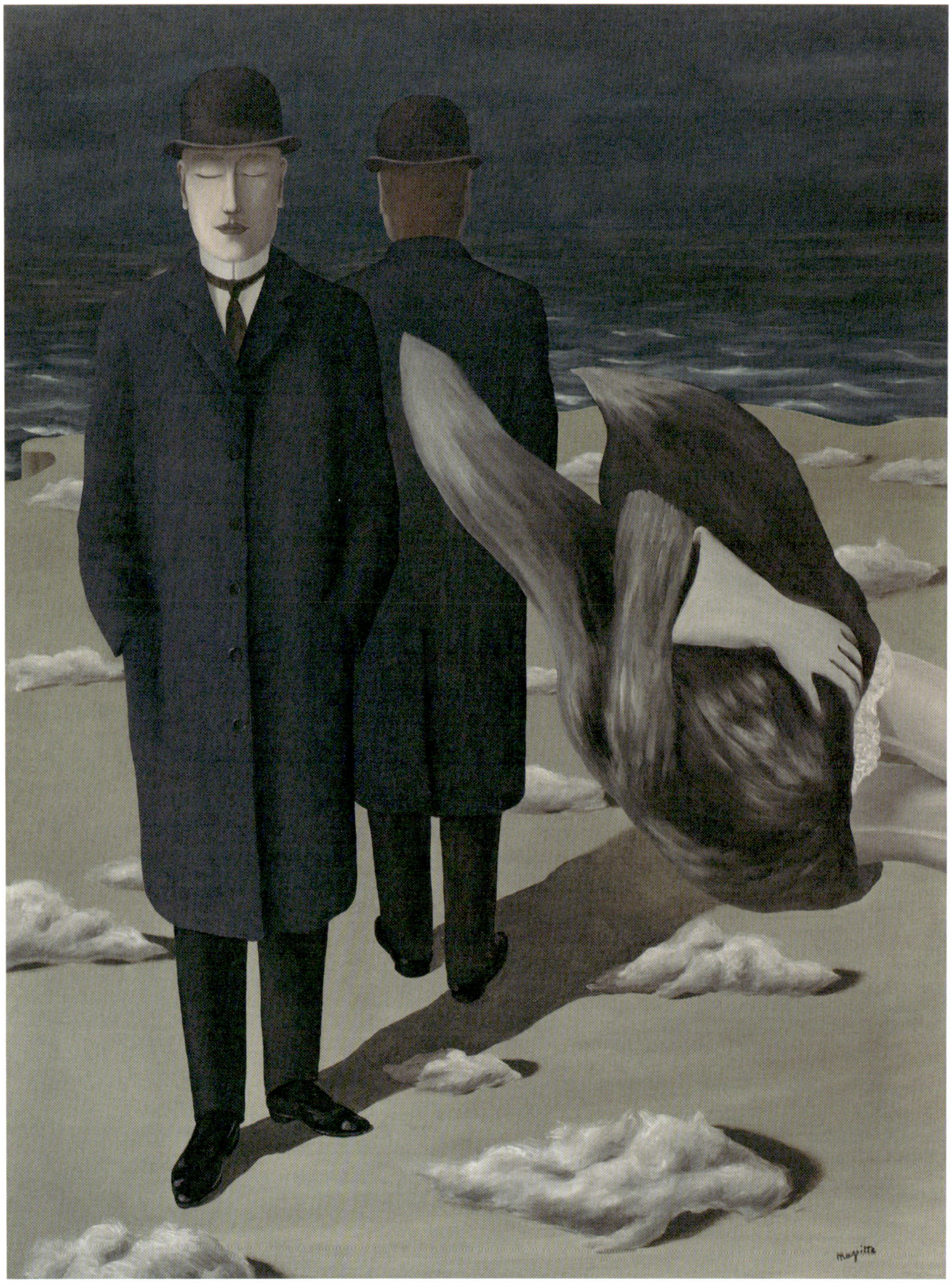

11. LE SENS DE LA NUIT (THE MEANING OF NIGHT). 1927.
Oil on canvas, 54 3/4 x 41 5/16" (139 x 105 cm)

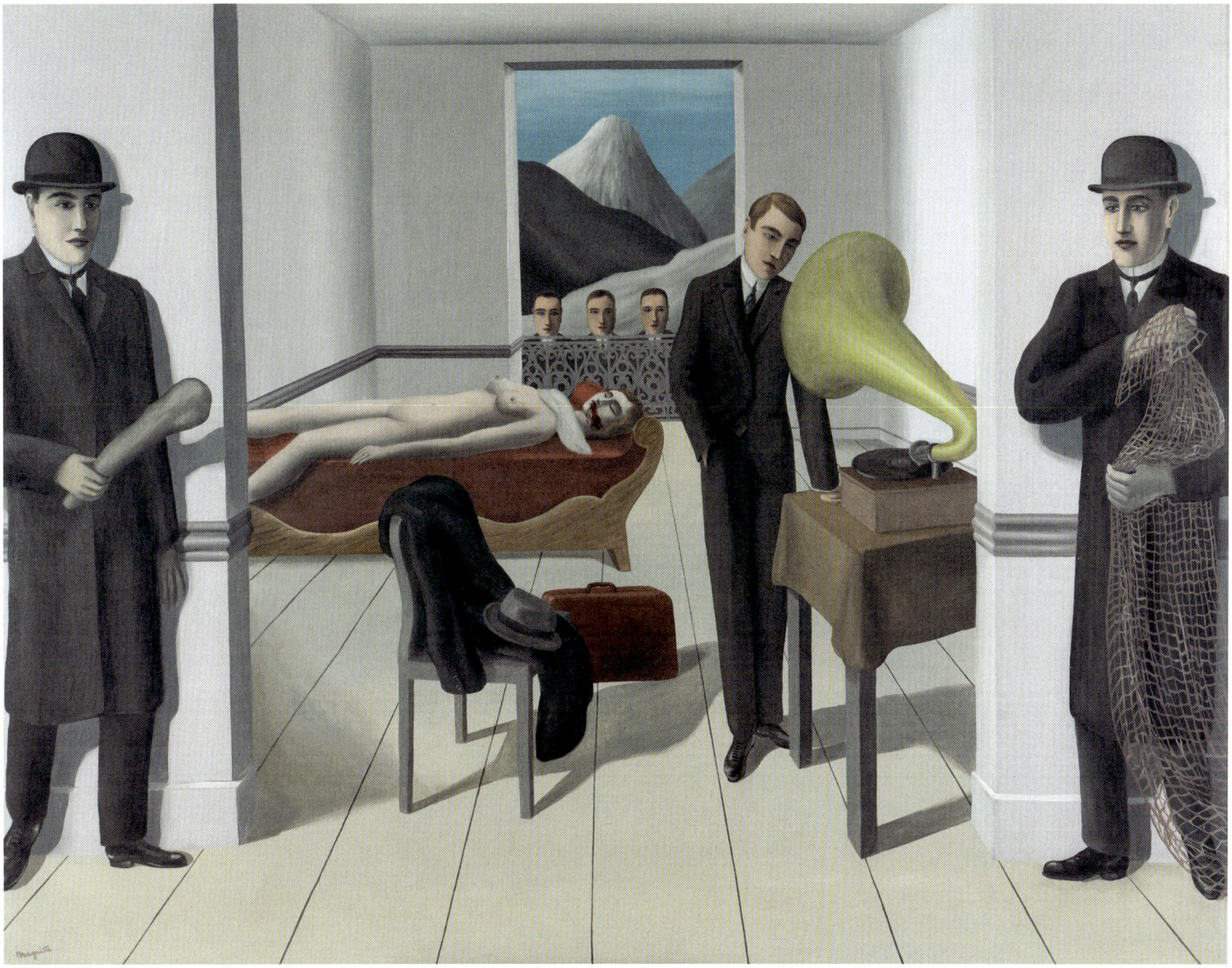

12. L'ASSASSIN MENACÉ (THE MENACED ASSASSIN). 1927.
Oil on canvas, 59 1/4" x 6' 4 7/8" (150.4 x 195.2 cm)

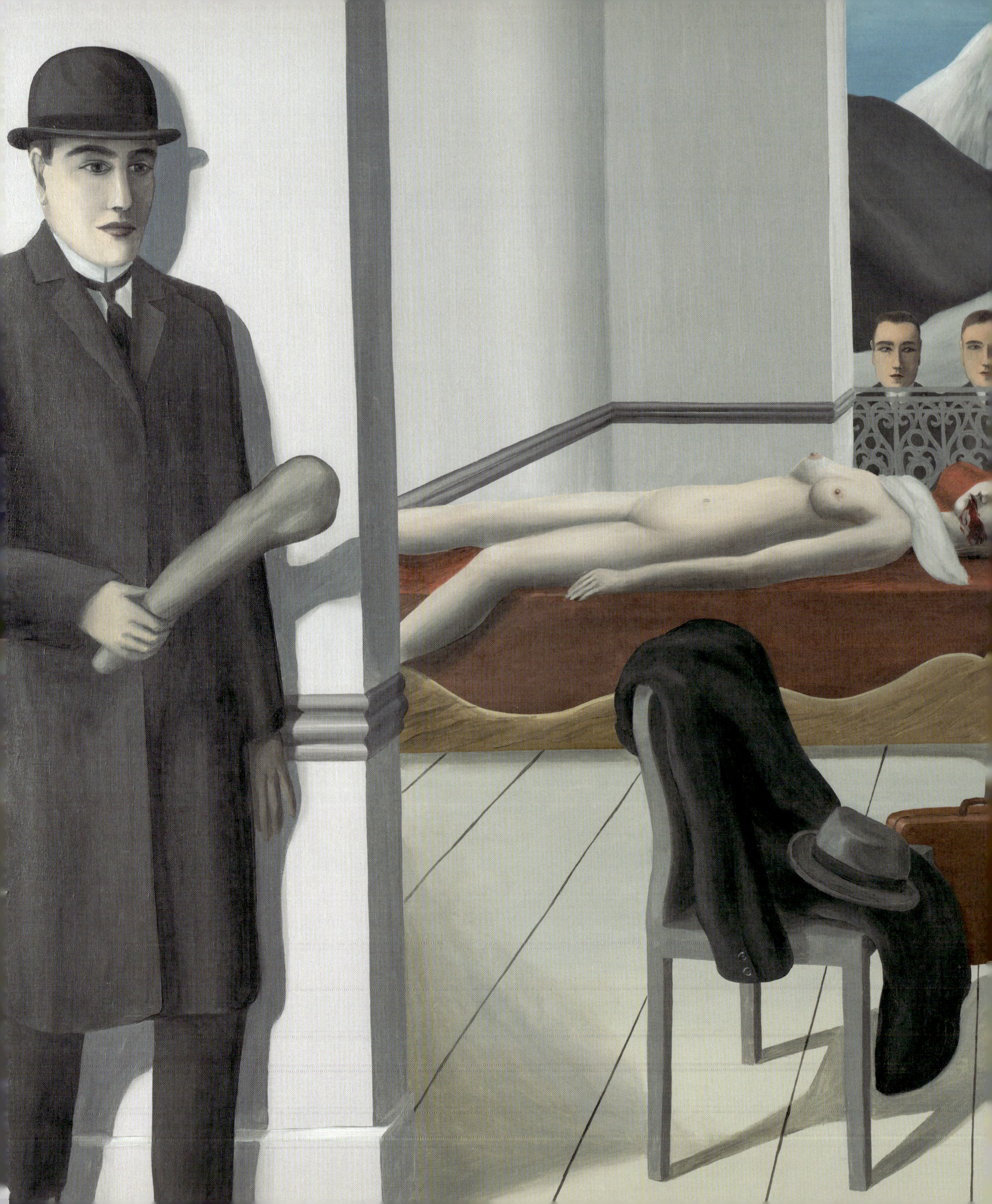

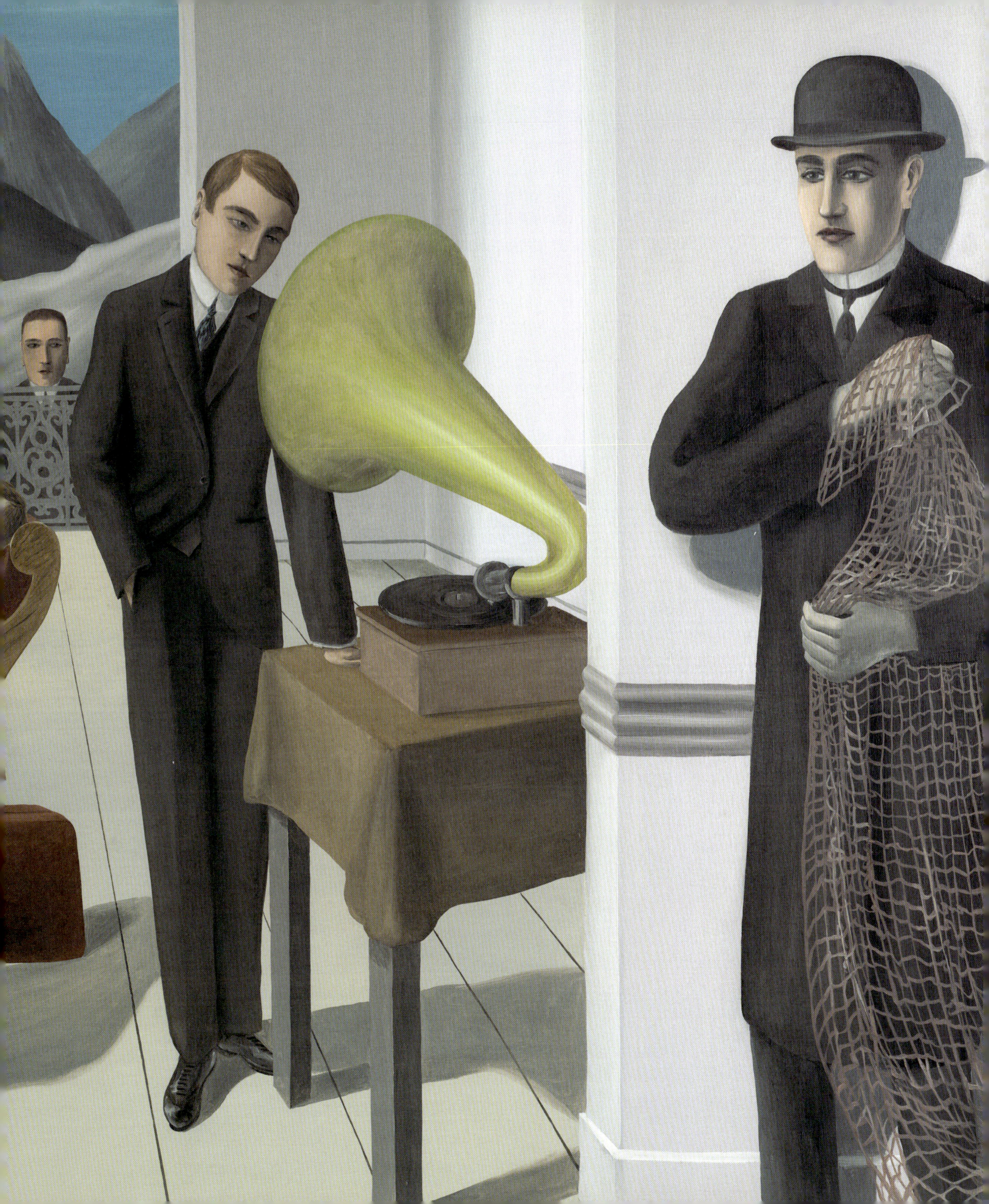

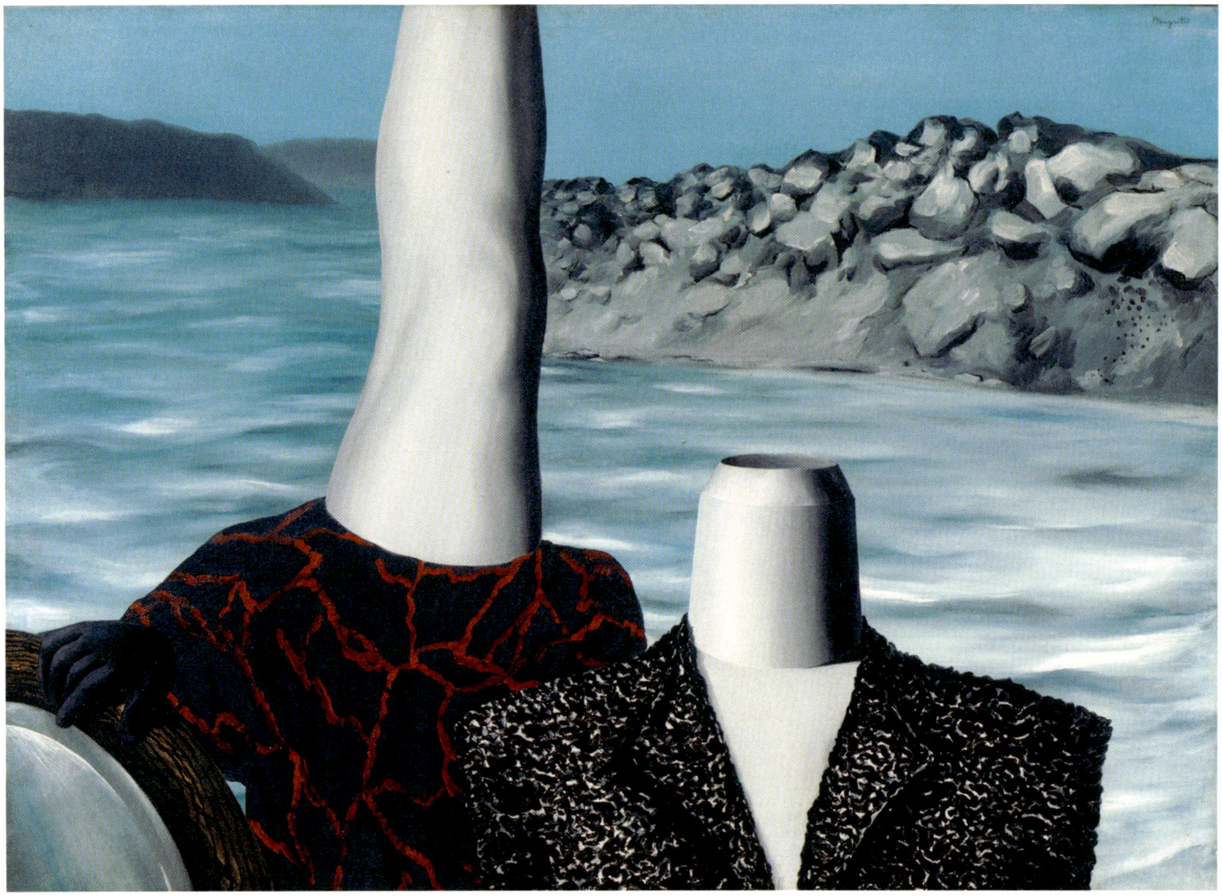

13. LES HABITANTS DU FLEUVE (THE DENIZENS OF THE RIVER). 1926.

Oil on canvas, 28 3/4 x 39 3/8" (73 x 100 cm)

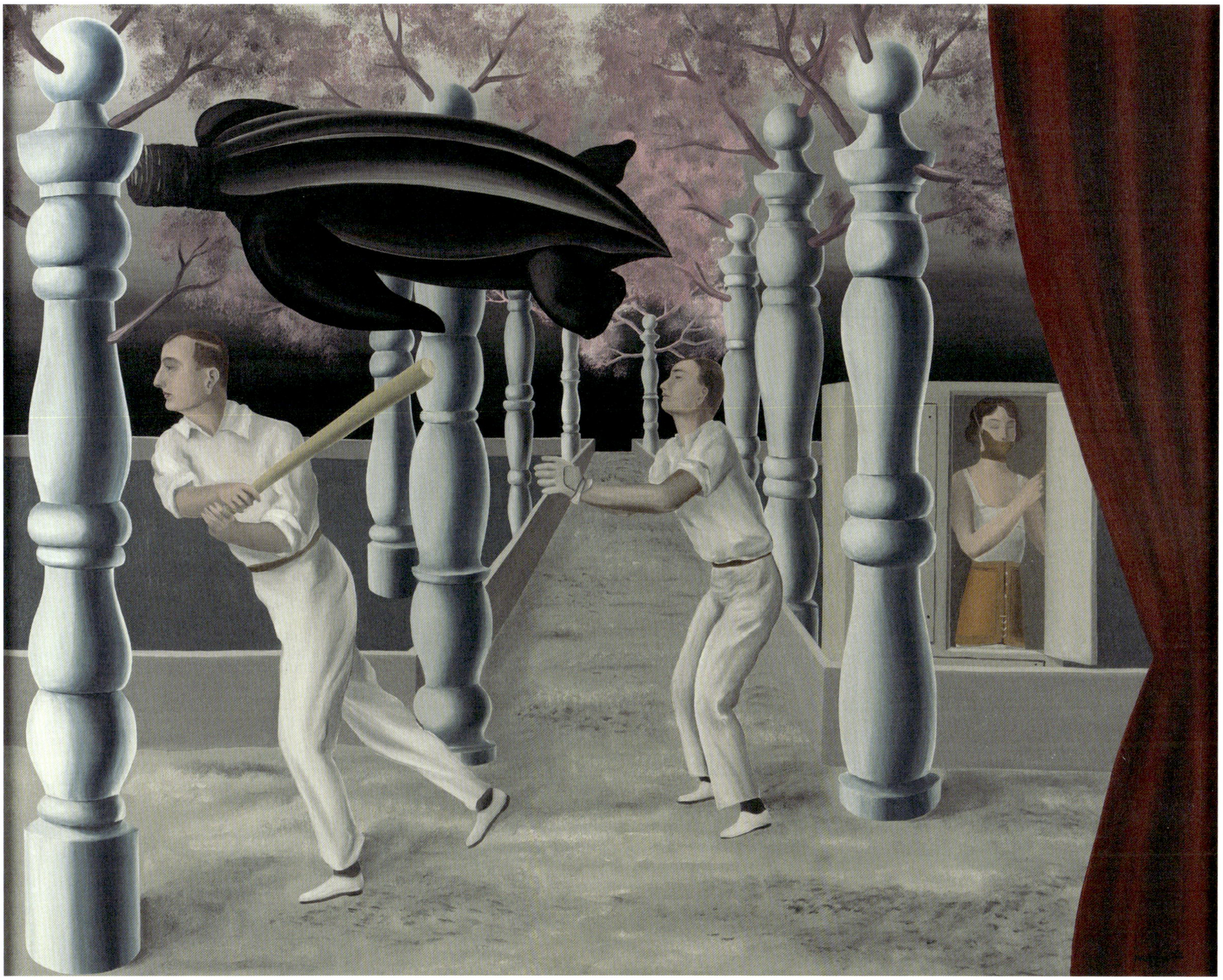

14. LE JOUEUR SECRET (THE SECRET PLAYER). 1927.

Oil on canvas, 59 13/16 x 6' 4 3/4" (152 x 195 cm)

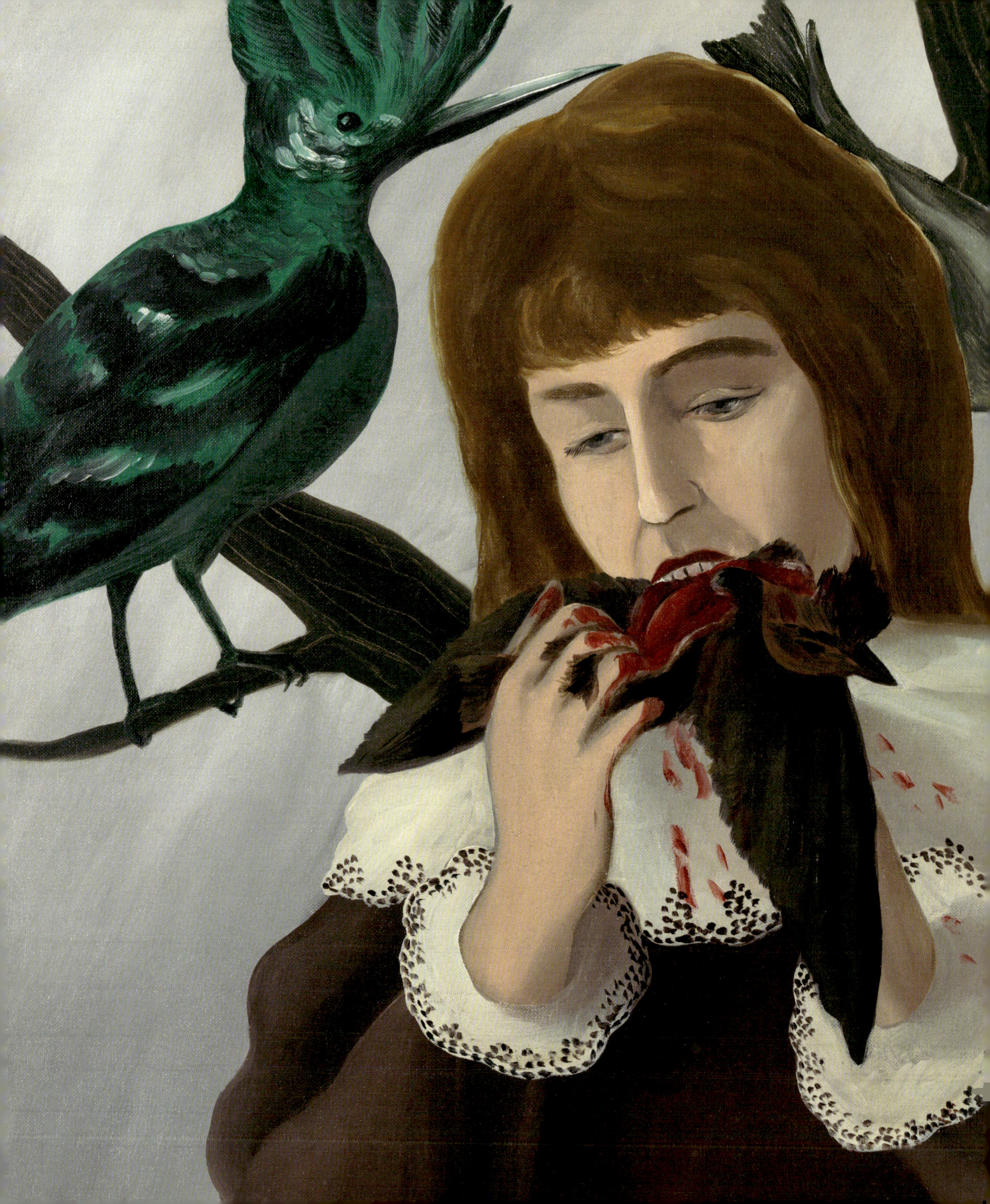

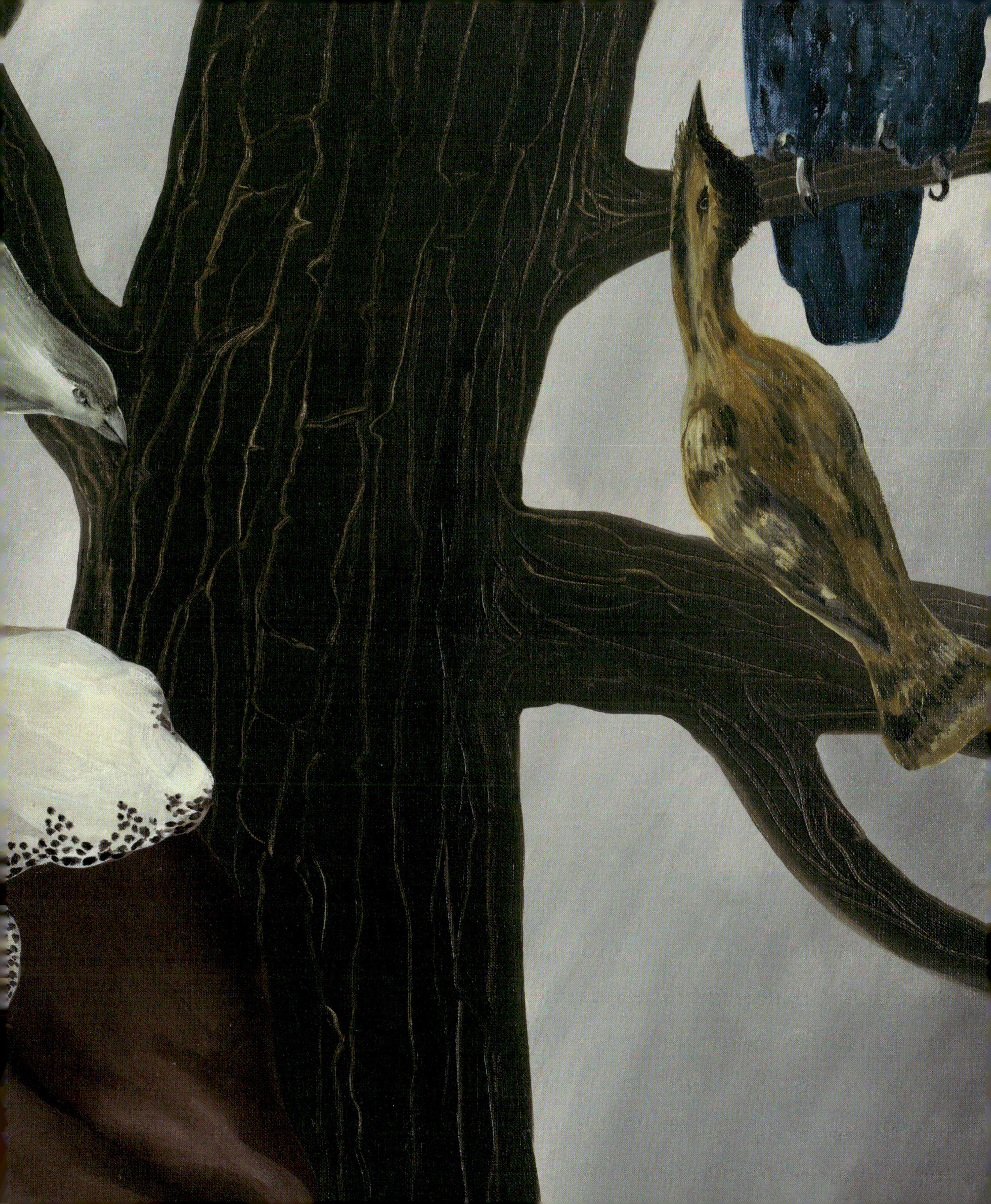

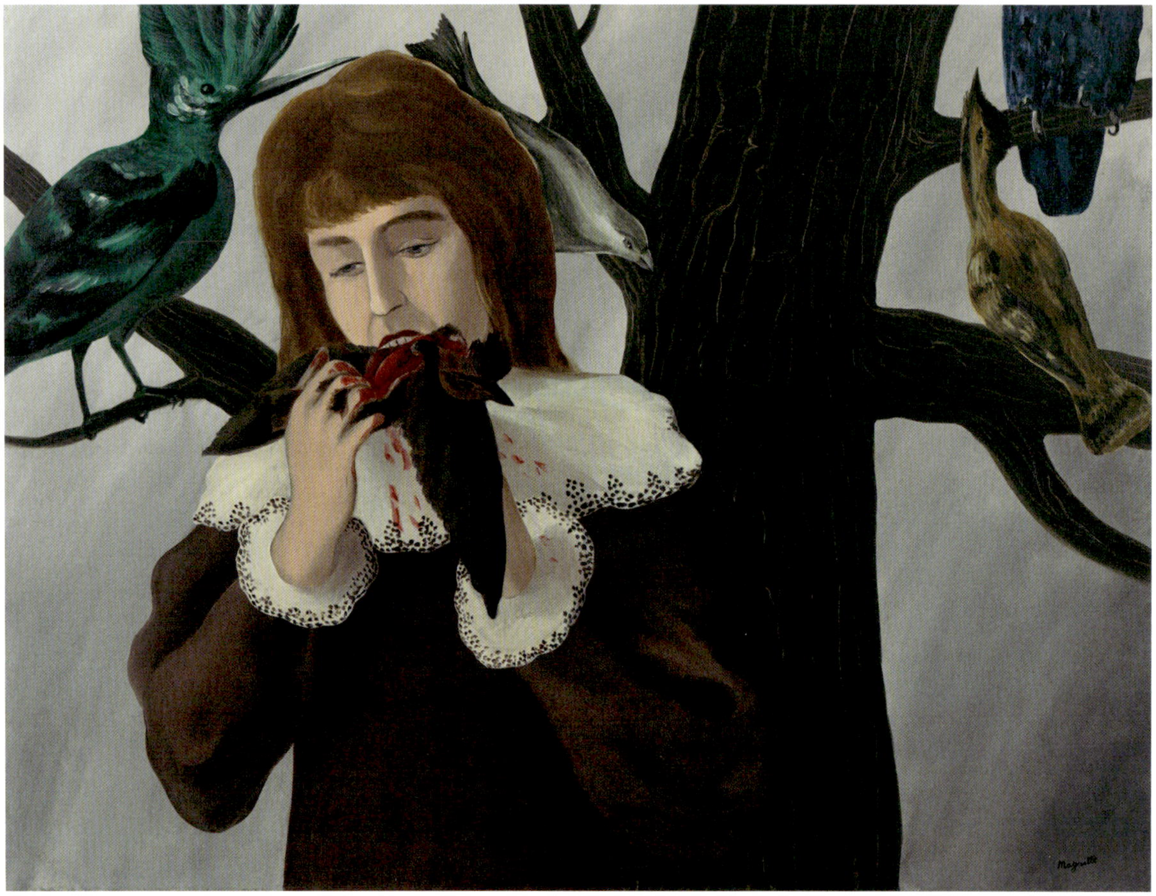

15. JEUNE FILLE MANGEANT UN OISEAU (LE PLAISIR)
(GIRL EATING A BIRD [PLEASURE]). 1927. Oil on canvas, 29 1/8 x 38 3/16" (74 x 97 cm)

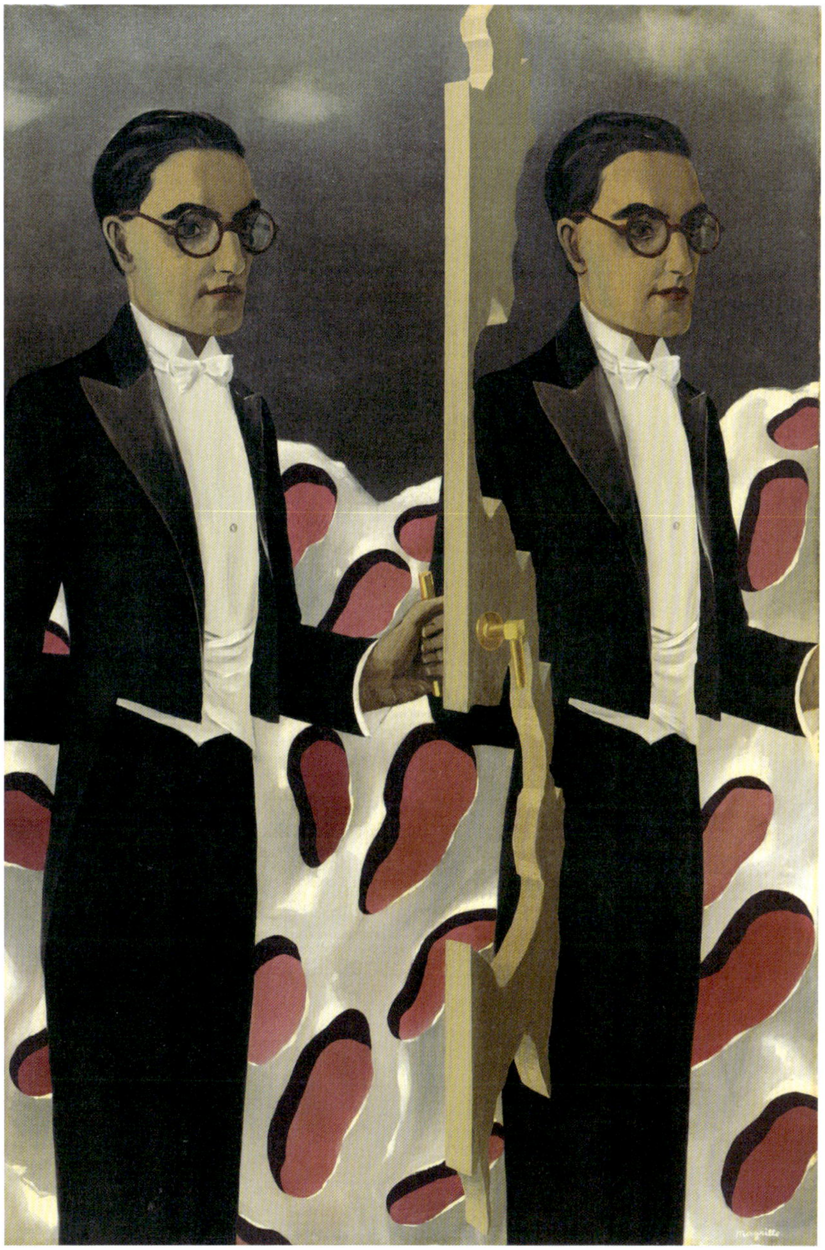

16. [PORTRAIT OF PAUL NOUGÉ]. 1927.
Oil on canvas, 37 3/8 x 25 9/16" (95 x 65 cm)

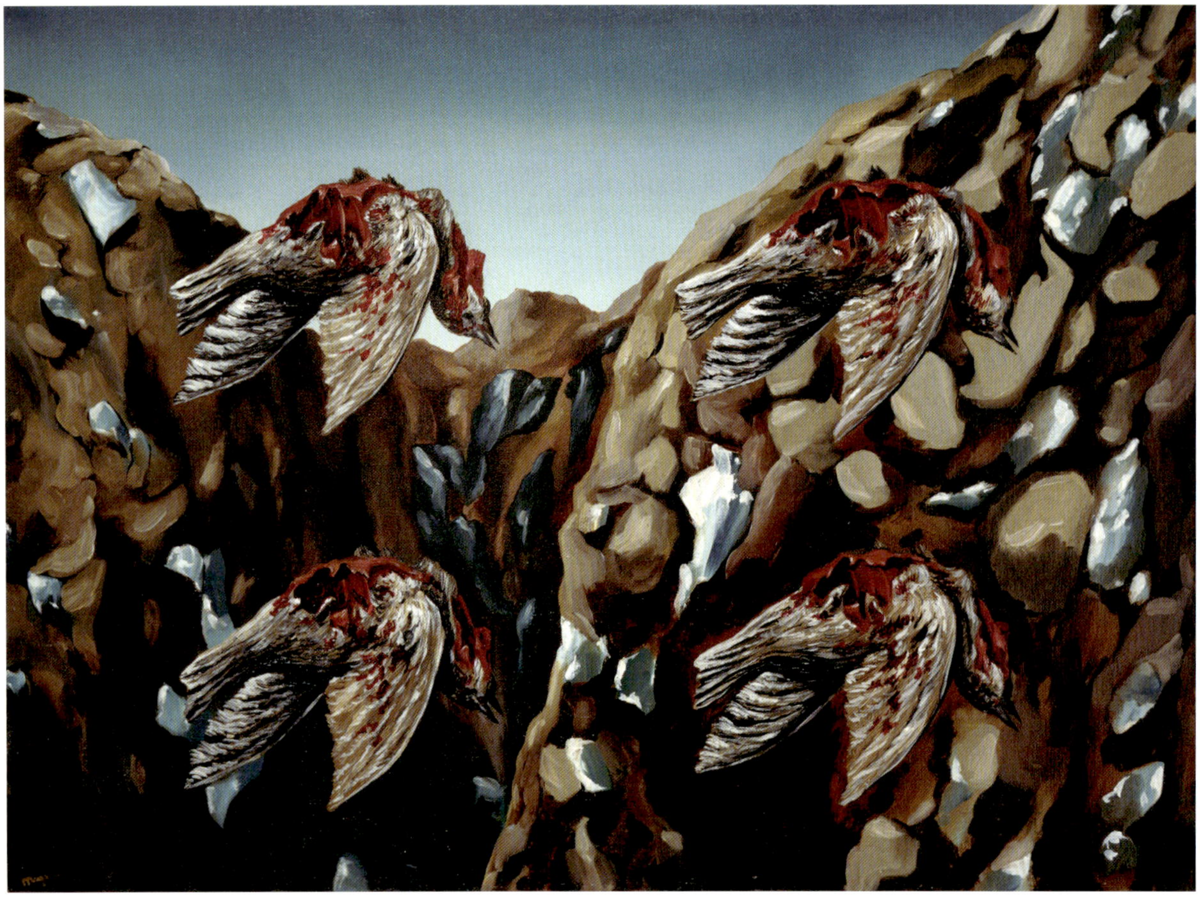

17. LE CIEL MEURTRIER (THE MURDEROUS SKY). 1927.

Oil on canvas, 28 3/4 x 39 3/8" (73 x 100 cm)

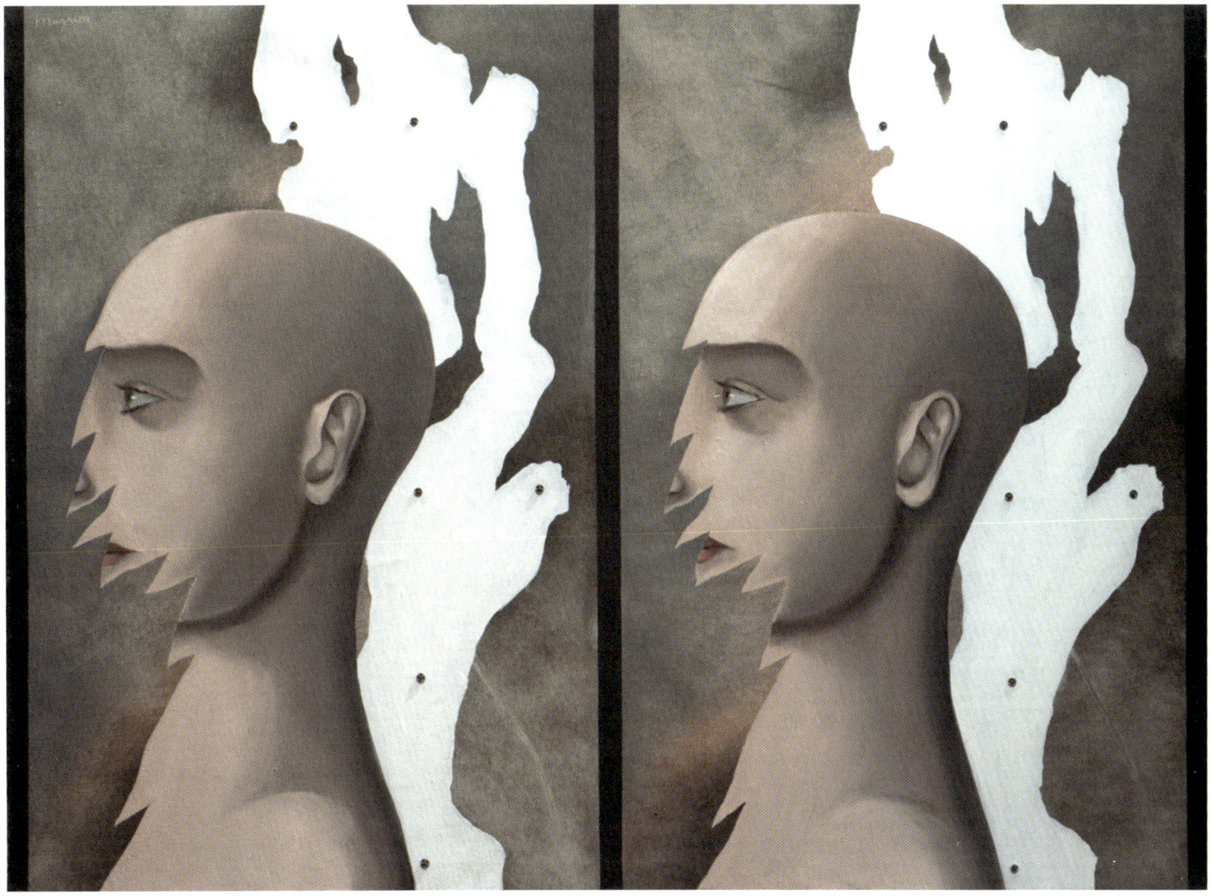

18. LA FIN DES CONTEMPLATIONS (AN END TO CONTEMPLATION). 1927.

Oil on canvas with metal snap fasteners, 28 3/4 x 39 3/8" (73 x 100 cm)

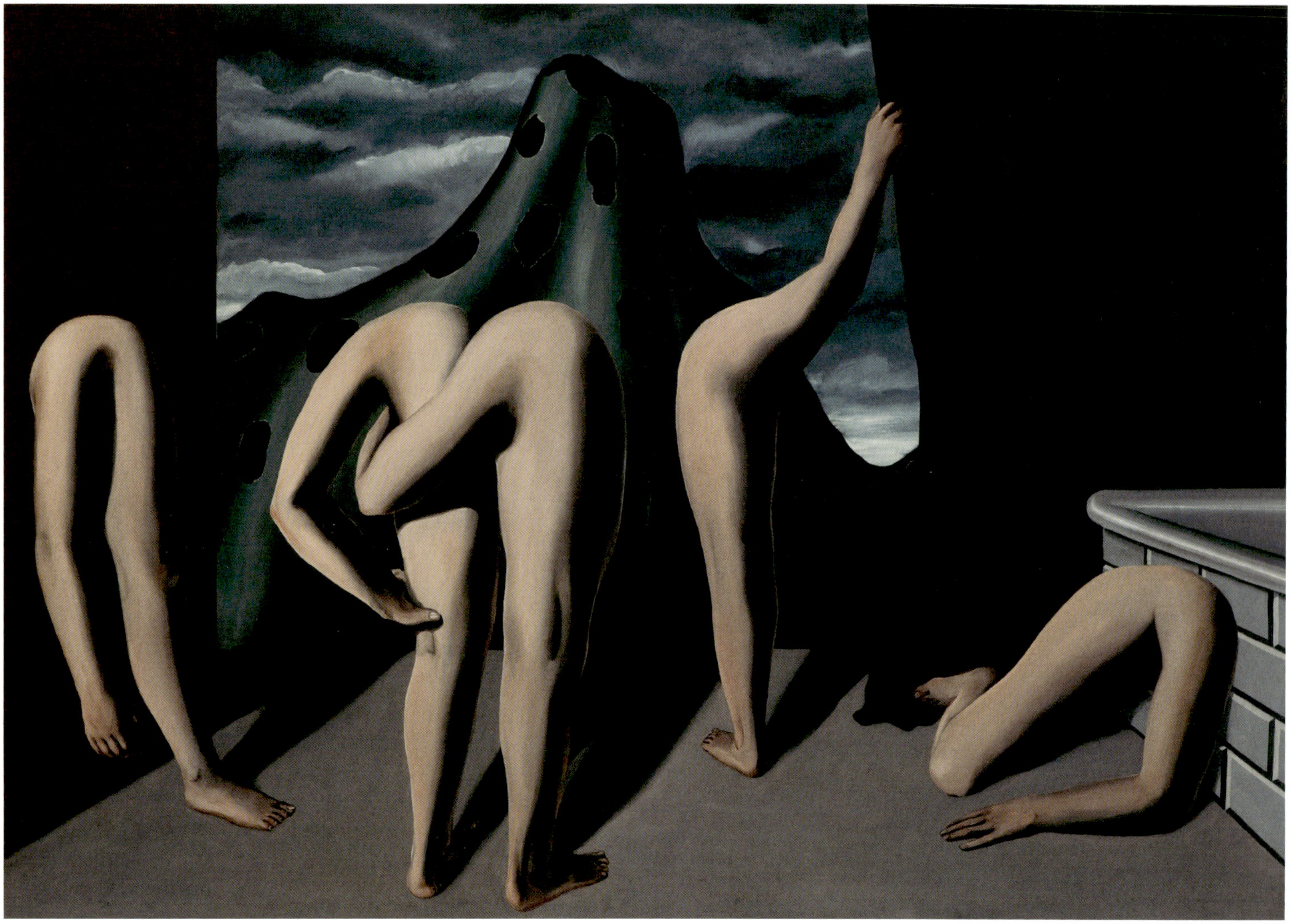

19. ENTR'ACTE. 1927.

Oil on canvas, 44 7/8 x 63 3/4" (114 x 162 cm)

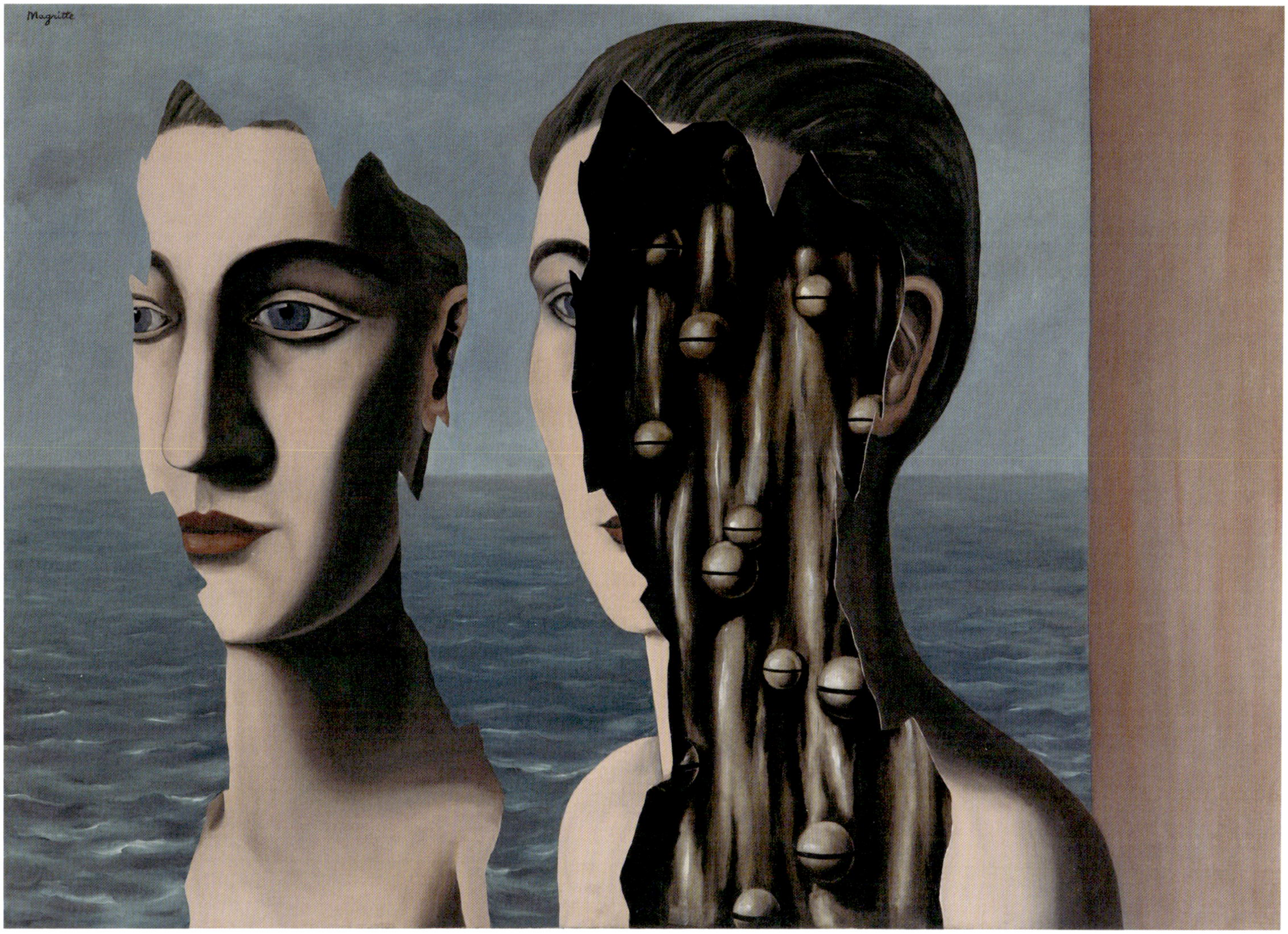

20. LE DOUBLE SECRET (THE SECRET DOUBLE). 1927.

Oil on canvas, 44 7/8 x 63 3/4" (114 x 162 cm)

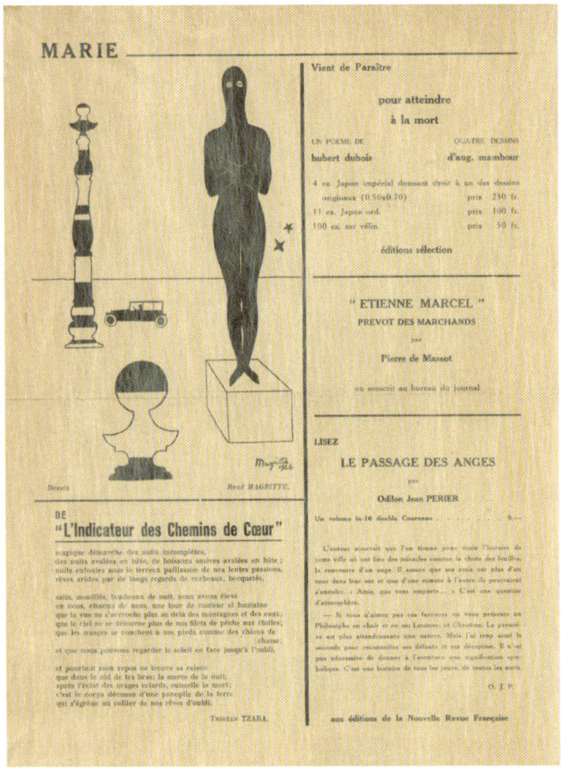

MARIE

Vient de Paraître

pour atteindre
à la mort

UN POEME DE — QUATRE DESSINS
hubert dubois — d'aug. mambour

4 ex. Japon impérial donnant droit à un des dessins originaux (0.50x0.70) prix 250 fr.
11 ex. Japon ord. prix 100 fr.
100 ex. sur vélin. prix 50 fr.

éditions sélection

" ETIENNE MARCEL "
PREVOT DES MARCHANDS
par
Pierre de Massot

on souscrit au bureau du journal

LISEZ

LE PASSAGE DES ANGES
par
Odilon Jean PERIER

Un volume in-16 double Couronne . . . . 8.—

O. J. P.

aux éditions de la Nouvelle Revue Française

Dessin — René MAGRITTE.

DE
"L'Indicateur des Chemins de Cœur"

magique démarche des nuits incomplètes,
des nuits avalées en hâte, de boissons amères avalées en hâte ;
nuits enfouies sous le terreux paillasson de nos lentes passions,
rêves arides par de longs regards de corbeaux, becquetés.

calix, mouillés, tombeaux de nuit, nous avons élevé
en nous, chacun de nous, une tour de couleur si hautaine
que la vue ne s'accroche plus au delà des montagnes et des eaux;
que le ciel ne se détourne plus de nos filets de pêche aux étoiles;
que les nuages se couchent à nos pieds comme des chiens de chasse;
et que nous pouvons regarder le soleil en face jusqu'à l'oubli.

et pourtant notre repos ne trouve sa raison
que dans le nid de tes bras; la marée de la nuit,
après l'éclat des orages criards, ruisselle la mort;
c'est le corps décousu d'une panoplie de la terre
qui s'égrène au collier de nos rêves d'oubli.

Tristan TZARA.

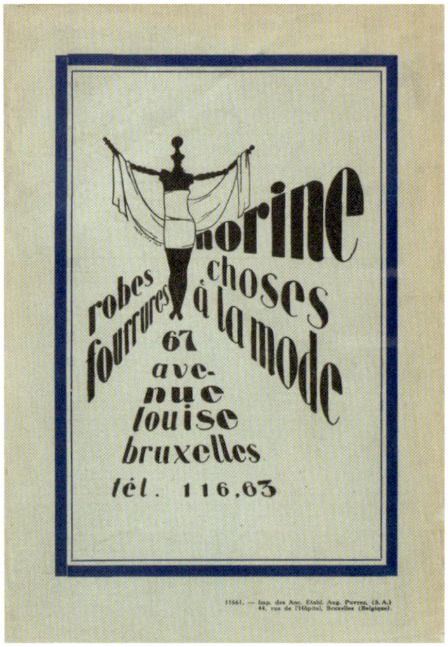

21. Illustration (upper left) in *Marie*, nos. 2 and 3 (July 8, 1926), page 5.
Periodical, 12 3/4 x 9 13/16" (32.4 x 25 cm)

22. Advertisement for Couture Norine, back cover of *Variétés* (May 1928).
Periodical, 9 15/16 x 7 1/16" (25.3 x 18 cm)

23. Advertisements for *joaillier-orfèvre* (jeweler-goldsmith) Max Kerrels,
and for *modiste* (fashion designer) Jane Brouwers, in *Le Centaure* (October 1926).
Periodical, page: 9 1/2 x 6 5/16" (24.2 x 16 cm)

24. Advertisements for *atelier d'art* (art studio) Floréal, and for Ravenstein restaurant,
in *Le Centaure* (November 1926). Periodical, page: 9 1/2 x 6 5/16" (24.2 x 16 cm)

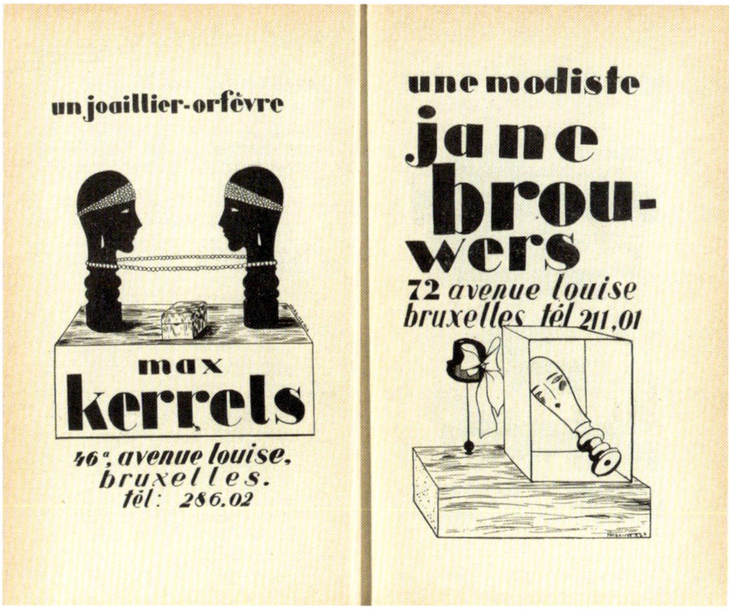
un joaillier-orfèvre
max
kerrels
46a, avenue louise,
bruxelles.
tél: 286.02
une modiste
jane
brou-
wers
72 avenue louise
bruxelles tél 211,01

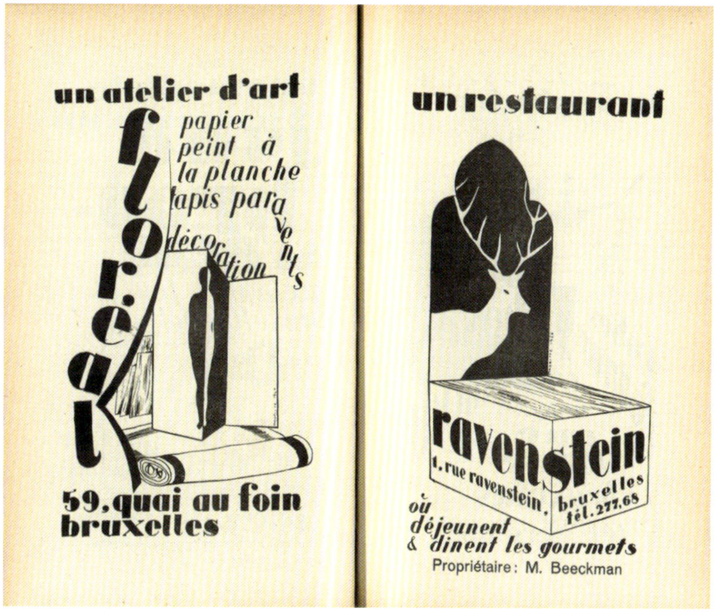
un atelier d'art
floréal
papier
peint à
la planche
tapis paravents
décoration
59, quai au foin
bruxelles
un restaurant
ravenstein
1, rue ravenstein, bruxelles
tél. 277,68
où
déjeunent
& dinent les gourmets
Propriétaire: M. Beeckman

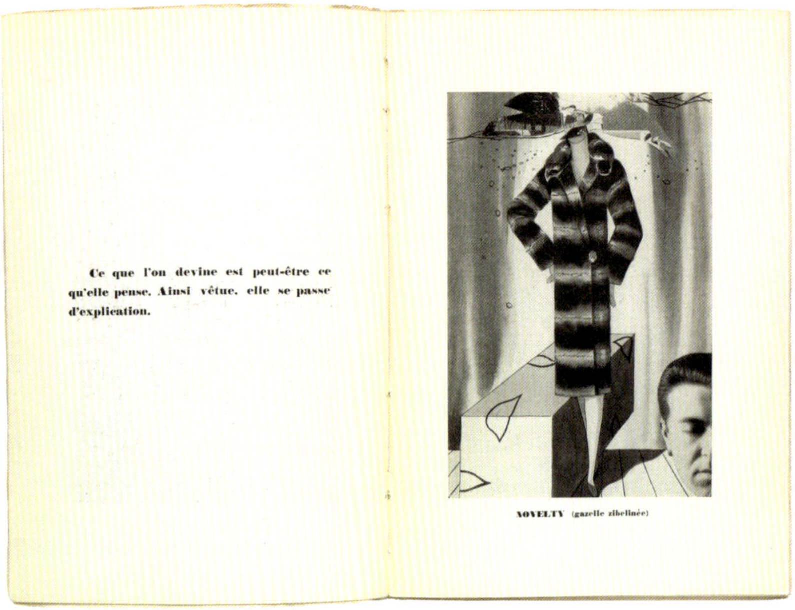
Ce que l'on devine est peut-être ce qu'elle pense. Ainsi vêtue, elle se passe d'explication.

NOVELTY (gazelle zibelinée)

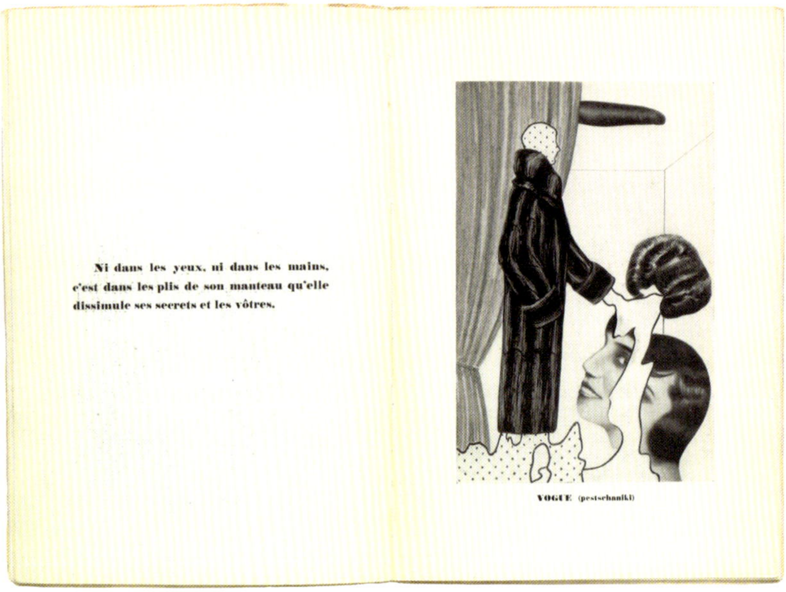
Ni dans les yeux, ni dans les mains, c'est dans les plis de son manteau qu'elle dissimule ses secrets et les vôtres.

VOGUE (pestschaniki)

25–30. In collaboration with Paul Nougé. *Pour l'année 1928, la Maison Samuel nous présente quelques manteaux (For the Year 1928, the Maison Samuel Presents Some Coats)*. 1927. Fur catalogue, page: 8 ½ x 5 ⅞" (21.6 x 14.9 cm)

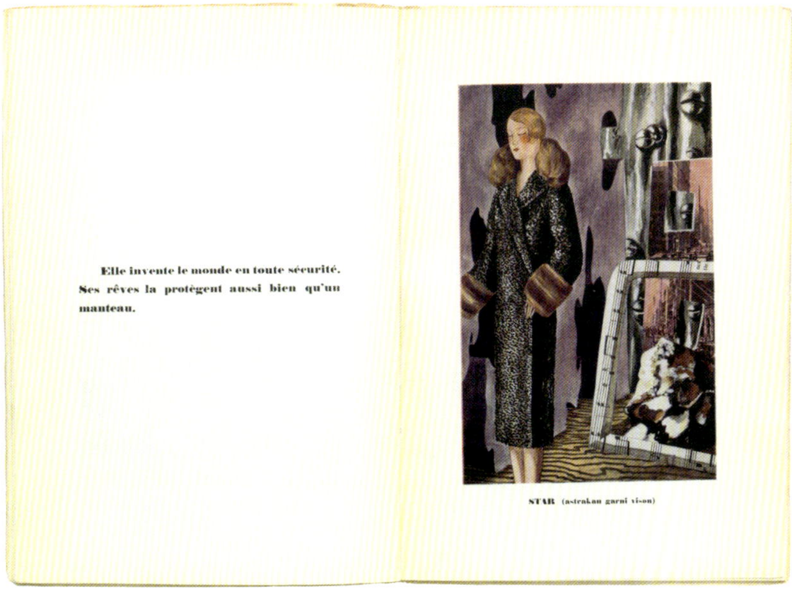

Elle invente le monde en toute sécurité. Ses rêves la protègent aussi bien qu'un manteau.

STAR (astrakan garni vison)

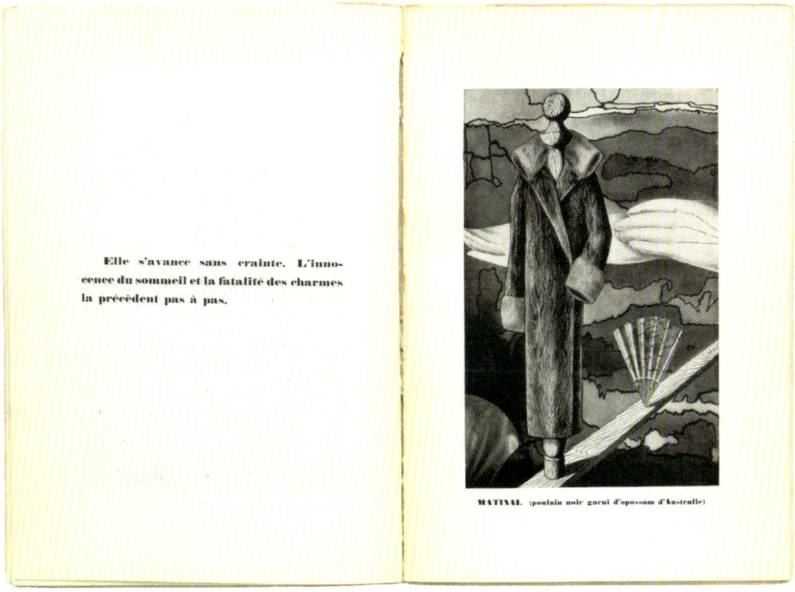

Elle s'avance sans crainte. L'innocence du sommeil et la fatalité des charmes la précèdent pas à pas.

MATINAL. (poulain noir garni d'opossum d'Australie)

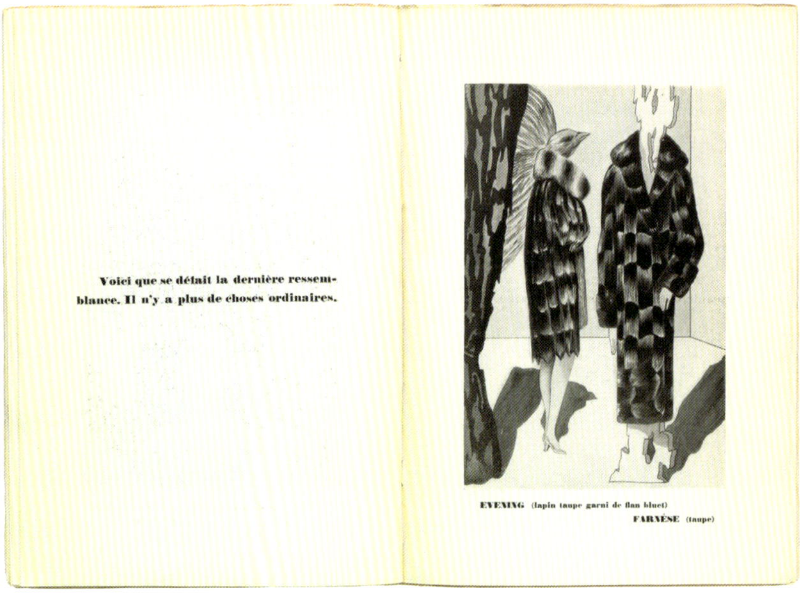

Voici que se défait la dernière ressemblance. Il n'y a plus de choses ordinaires.

EVENING (lapin taupe garni de flan bluet)

FARNÈSE (taupe)

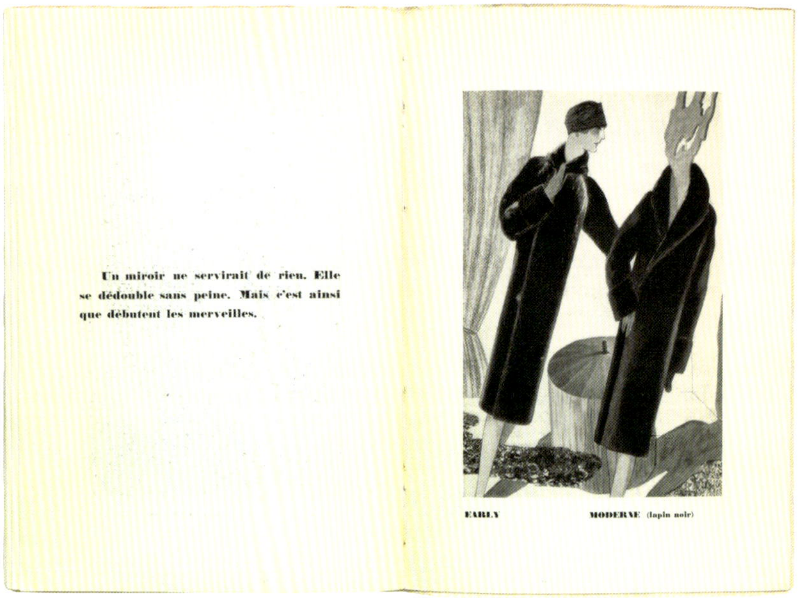

Un miroir ne servirait de rien. Elle se dédouble sans peine. Mais c'est ainsi que débutent les merveilles.

EARLY MODERNE (lapin noir)

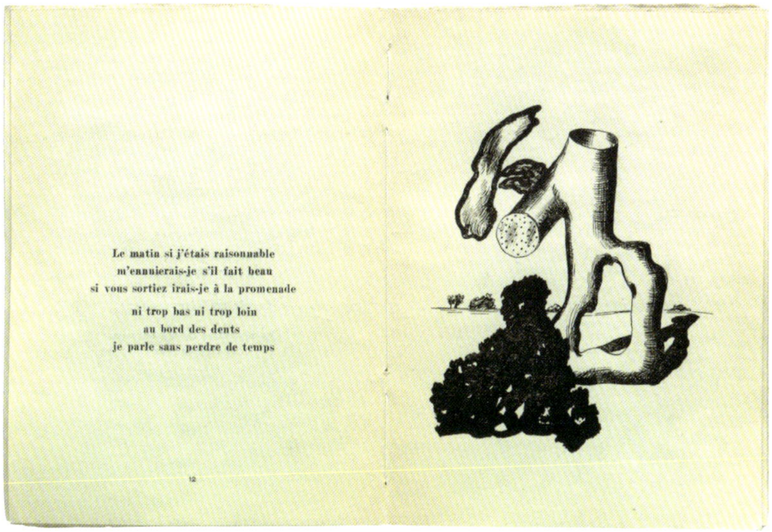
Le matin si j'étais raisonnable
m'ennuierais-je s'il fait beau
si vous sortiez irais-je à la promenade
ni trop bas ni trop loin
au bord des dents
je parle sans perdre de temps

12

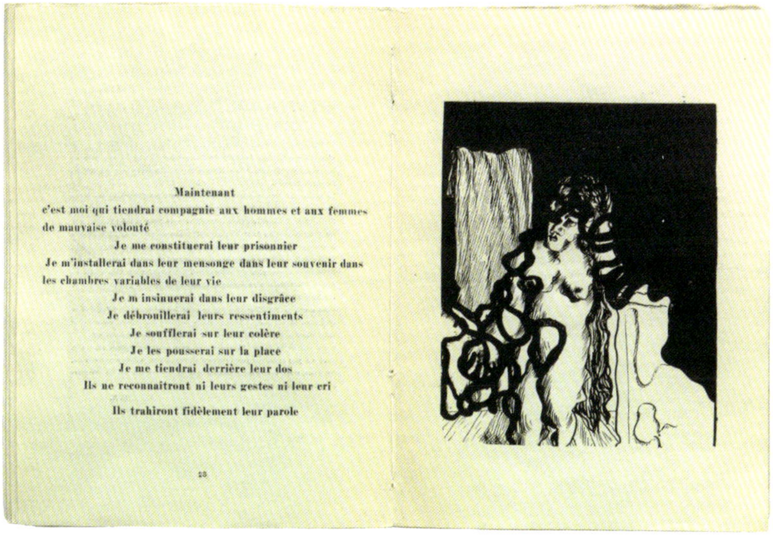
Maintenant
c'est moi qui tiendrai compagnie aux hommes et aux femmes
de mauvaise volonté
Je me constituerai leur prisonnier
Je m'installerai dans leur mensonge dans leur souvenir dans
les chambres variables de leur vie
Je m insinuerai dans leur disgrâce
Je débrouillerai leurs ressentiments
Je soufflerai sur leur colère
Je les pousserai sur la place
Je me tiendrai derrière leur dos
Ils ne reconnaitront ni leurs gestes ni leur cri
Ils trahiront fidèlement leur parole

28

31, 32. In collaboration with Paul Nougé. *Clarisse Juranville: Quelques écrits et quelques dessins* (*Clarisse Juranville: Some Writings and Some Drawings*), pages 12–13 and 28–29. 1927. Book, page: 6 1/4 x 4 7/8" (15.9 x 12.3 cm)

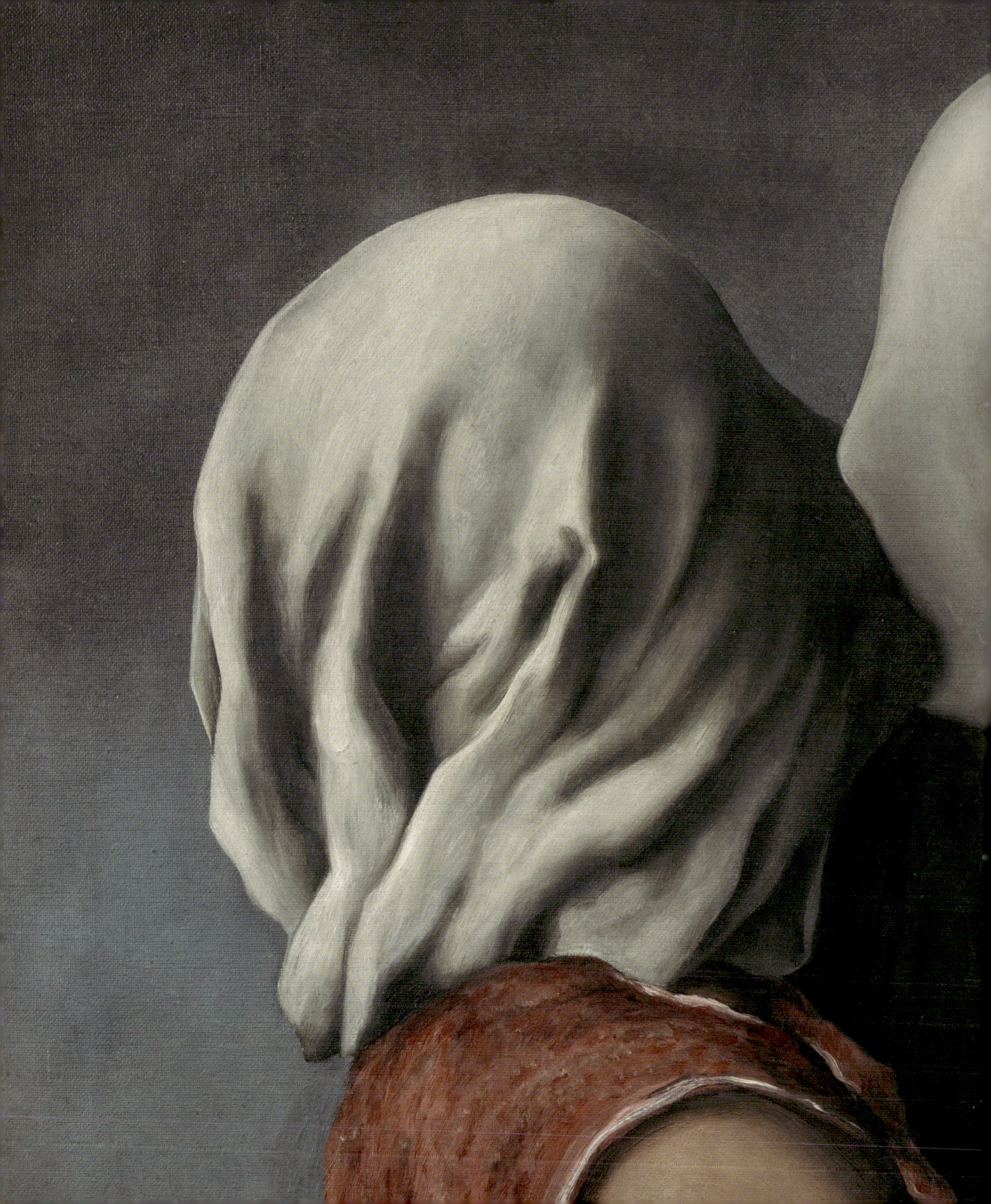

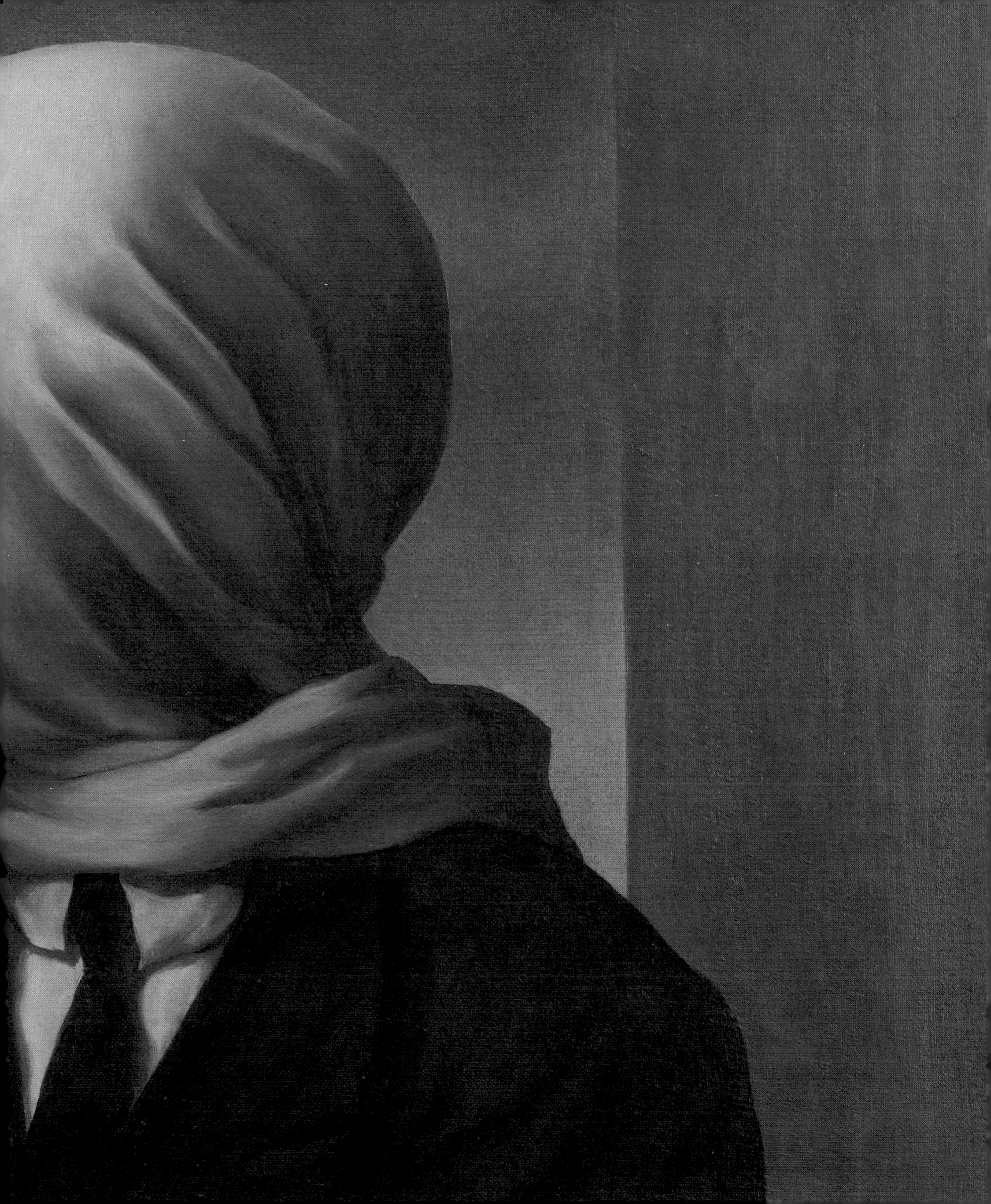

"A LIGHTNING FLASH IS SMOLDERING BENEATH THE BOWLER HATS" *Paris* 1927–1930

Josef Helfenstein with Clare Elliott

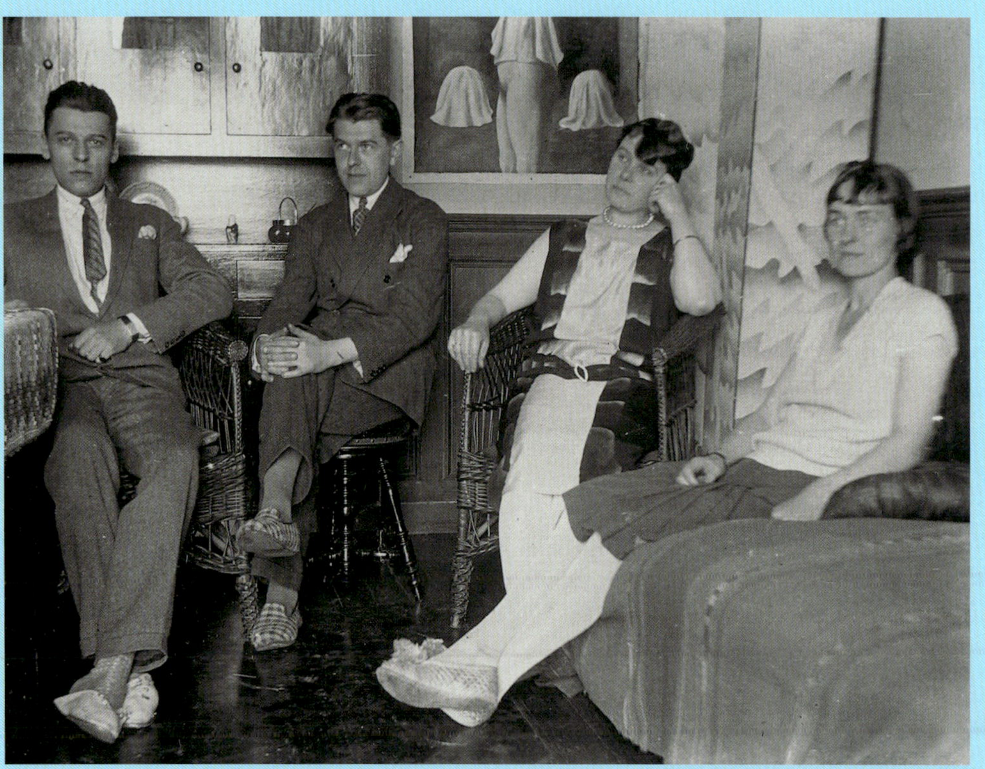

Figure 1. Paul, René, and Georgette Magritte (at right), with an unidentified friend at the apartment in Le Perreux-sur-Marne, France, 1928. Photographer and location unknown

René Magritte lived almost his entire life in Belgium, in or near the capital city of Brussels. By the mid-1920s he was active among a group of Belgian Surrealists there that included Paul Nougé, Camille Goemans, Marcel Lecomte, and, later, Louis Scutenaire.[1] With the notable exception of Magritte, the group was not made up of visual artists, but rather of poets, writers, and philosophers. Magritte's first extended stay in Paris was in early 1924, when he attempted to find work there as a commercial artist in one of the city's design ateliers. Unable to secure employment, he returned to Brussels after only a month.[2]

In 1927, a few months after his first solo exhibition at the Galerie Le Centaure in Brussels (a show that provoked a largely negative critical response), Magritte—perhaps believing he now had better career prospects in Paris—tried again to establish himself in the French capital. In doing so, the artist moved closer to the center of Surrealist activity, and was reunited with his friend Goemans, who had moved there in the summer of 1927 to establish a gallery.[3] He introduced Magritte to Jean Arp, Max Ernst, and Joan Miró—all represented at Goemans's gallery, which finally opened in the fall of 1929, and to Salvador Dalí, who arrived in Paris in the spring of 1929. Magritte's connections to André Breton and Louis Aragon, both of whom he had met earlier, either in Belgium or on previous visits to Paris,[4] deepened considerably during his almost three years in France.

Magritte's relationship with the French Surrealists, however, never grew to be very close, and his position among them remained ambivalent, even while he lived in Paris. He respected and admired a number of the artists and writers there—Aragon, Breton, Paul Éluard, Ernst—but always maintained a distance, both intellectually and geographically. Even while in Paris, Magritte was somewhat isolated; he and his wife, Georgette, lived in the suburb of Le Perreux-sur-Marne rather than in the city center.[5] The Magritte household remained thoroughly Belgian, with the artist's brother, Paul (who followed the couple to France), living nearby, and the three sharing daily meals (fig. 1).[6] Magritte was also on the outside in terms of his relationship to Paris galleries. Though he sold a few of his works discreetly through Goemans in 1927 and 1928, he was under contract with Paul-Gustave Van Hecke's Brussels gallery L'Époque until 1929.[7] Magritte's only two solo exhibitions during this period took place in Belgium.[8] He was never invited to show at the Galerie Surréaliste, nor did he participate in the important Surrealist exhibition at the Galerie au Sacre du Printemps in April 1928.[9] Although Breton (as well as Aragon and Éluard) began to collect his work,[10] he was not included in Breton's 1928 book *Le Surréalisme et la peinture* nor in the second Surrealist manifesto, published the following year.

Despite the relatively short duration of his stay (he and Georgette returned to Brussels in July 1930), Magritte's time in Paris was the most prolific chapter of his life. He completed more than thirty paintings between the end of September and mid-December 1927, and the following year more than one hundred (this in contrast to a typical average output during the rest of his life of twenty to thirty paintings per year). In total, he painted approximately one hundred seventy-five works in less than three years in Paris.[11] It was arguably also the most innovative period of his career. Many of Magritte's themes and concepts that had originated in Brussels in 1926 and 1927 matured during these years. He created entirely new groups of works that would eventually be considered among his most important and inventive paintings, among them the biomorphic images based on his discovery of metamorphosis and the melding of materials; the "word-paintings," combining language and image in unprecedented ways; and the *toiles découpées*, or cut-up canvases, perhaps his most radical attack on the tradition of painting to date. During his time in the French capital, Magritte became one of the most creative artists of the era, systematically challenging representation in painting in ways that no other artist had done before.

ENTERING THE SCENE OF THE FRENCH SURREALISTS

Prior to Magritte's arrival in Paris, Surrealism was dominated by painters who tended toward a style of biomorphic abstraction, often achieved through automatic techniques. Breton promoted "psychic automatism" in his first Surrealist manifesto (1924) as the core element of the creative process in literature.[12] By using methods such as free association, or the mysterious visual material of dreams, the goal was to unleash the creative forces of the subconscious, freeing the process from the control of the rational mind. Applied by visual artists, automatism became a general term associated with collage, *frottage*, *grattage*, *fumage*, and other techniques developed by Surrealist artists in the 1920s and 1930s. In contrast, Magritte focused on familiar, yet idiosyncratic, subject matter, and honed a painting style that was decidedly readable. At the same time, his works questioned the logic of language and meaning, and exacerbated the puzzles of representation. Magritte never fully embraced the automatist techniques that were championed by Breton and practiced, to varying degrees, by the artists surrounding him—including Arp, Ernst, André Masson, Miró, and Yves Tanguy.[13] Indeed, Magritte was suspicious of the "so-called spontaneity" and the mediumistic aspect of such techniques.[14]

While Magritte continued to pursue his distinctive style and subject matter, exchanges with his new circle of friends soon became manifest. The first canvas he completed in Paris, *Les Muscles célestes* (*The Muscles of the Sky,* 1927; plate 34) features biomorphic shapes that recall those in Arp's wooden reliefs, such as *Soulier bleu renversé à deux talons, sous une voûte noire* (*Overturned Blue Shoe with Two Heels under a Black Vault,* c. 1925; fig. 2). In Magritte's work, the sky descends in the form of sharply outlined figures composed of air and clouds onto a stagelike wooden floor extending before a scrim of trees. Magritte's painting plays with the representative elements of sky, trees, and stage, but subverts the rational relationship between image and reality. The effect is collagelike—an apparent layering of forms—and yet not, as the painting simultaneously includes signs of three-dimensionality, such as shadows and perspectival structure. Clouds and air become corporeal, casting shadows, and what should be a thicket of trees is merely a two-dimensional dividing line between earth and sky. By combining physical solidity with abstraction, Magritte creates a pictorial paradox that is possible only in painting. The impression here, of something disturbing and yet recognizable, evokes a precarious familiarity that is fundamental to Magritte's art.

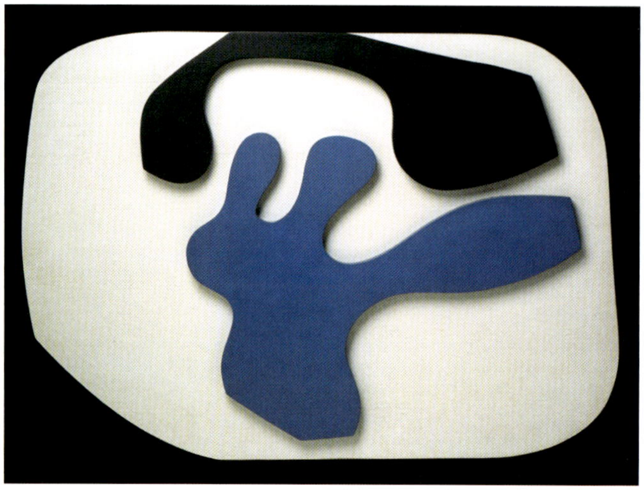

Figure 2. Jean (Hans) Arp. *Soulier bleu renversé à deux talons, sous une voûte noire* (*Overturned Blue Shoe with Two Heels under a Black Vault*). c. 1925. Painted wood, 31 1/4 x 41 1/8" (79.3 x 104.6 cm). The Solomon R. Guggenheim Foundation, Peggy Guggenheim Collection, Venice

Le Prince des objets (*The Prince of Objects*; plate 36), of the same year, shows the artist experimenting with ideas championed by the leaders of the Paris group even more directly. It is one of a few works in which Magritte uses actual collage—adding small patches of fabric to the canvas—and belongs to a group of paintings that feature a glossy, black, framelike form with irregular outlines.[15] According to David Sylvester, these oddly shaped frames "must be references to the traditional game, often used for fortune-telling, of melting lead pellets and dousing the molten mass in cold water so that it solidifies in strange and evocative forms."[16] In this example, the molten frame encloses part of the background wall, specifically an area in the process of transforming from a smooth painted surface into a textured wood grain. The work embodies a number of techniques and tropes that were of interest to the Surrealists: collage, games of chance, magic; biomorphic abstraction; the wood pattern of Ernst's *frottage*; and finally (for Magritte a breakthrough) the use of paint to depict metamorphosis of one material into another. Magritte wrote to Nougé of this and similar canvases: "I think I have made a really striking discovery in painting. Up to now I have used composite objects, or else the placing of an object was sometimes enough to make it mysterious. [...] I have found a new potential in things—their ability to become *gradually* something else, an object *merging into* an object other than itself."[17]

This "discovery" would be echoed in the title of another 1927 painting, *Découverte* (*Discovery*; plate 35),[18] which features a female nude changing gradually but dramatically into wood, in a version of the myth of Daphne, the nymph transformed into a laurel tree to escape the pursuit of Apollo. But nothing is certain here: the pattern of the wood grain, imposed onto skin, recalls the stripes of feline fur;[19] and the solidity of the figure contradicts its apparent mutability. The levels of ambiguity are representative of Magritte's aim—to challenge the viewer's perception of reality.

WORD-PAINTINGS

> The use of speech for the ordinary purposes of life imposes a limited meaning on words designating objects. It would seem that everyday language sets imaginary boundaries to the imagination.
> —Magritte, "La Ligne de vie" ("Lifeline"), 1938[20]

Painted in October 1927, within the first six weeks of his Paris stay, *La Clef des songes* (*The Interpretation of Dreams* [or more literally *The Key of Dreams*, a translation that avoids obvious Freudian innuendos]; plate 37)[21] presents four objects arranged within four trompe-l'œil frames of equal size.[22] Dividing images into discrete spaces was a strategy with which Magritte had started to experiment while still in Brussels, with *La Fin des contemplations* (*An End to Contemplation*, 1927; plate 18), and would pursue in a variety of formats during his time in Paris. *La Clef des songes* is the first of Magritte's "word-paintings" that presents itself as a kind of "key," or legend, in which four easily read images are paired with words: an image of a suitcase is labeled with the words *Le ciel* (the sky, or heaven), a knife with *L'oiseau* (the bird), and a leaf with *La table* (the table). Only a sponge bears its expected name—*L'éponge*—a resolution that reinforces the puzzlement of the other disjunctions, while simultaneously estranging the expected. Two man-made objects are placed above two objects from the natural world. A leaf or a sponge divorced from its organic environment will soon disintegrate; their vulnerability evokes the fragility of the way we construct language and the unreliable nature of representing reality. Magritte signs the work directly above the knife (perhaps an allusion to the threatening aspect of his work, in terms of both content and technique). The knife—slashing at pictorial tradition—also brings to mind the technique of collage, a new form of image outside of painterly convention. As early as 1930, Louis Aragon noted the analogy of Magritte's word-paintings to collage in a footnote to his essay "La Peinture au défi" ("The Challenge to Painting"): "Is there a connection between collage and the use of writing in painting as practiced by Magritte? I see no way to deny it."[23]

La Clef des songes borrows its form from illustrations in children's reading primers of the time. Earlier in 1927 Magritte and Nougé had collaborated on a parody publication titled *Clarisse Juranville: Quelques écrits et quelques dessins* (*Clarisse Juranville: Some Writings and Some Drawings*; plates 31, 32). Juranville was the author of a common grammar workbook, *La Conjugaison enseignée par la pratique* (Conjugation taught by practice), first published in the 1880s.[24] The cover of Magritte and Nougé's book is unassuming enough in typography and layout to resemble a real textbook, but a strange insignia between the title and the name of the publisher hints that it might be something different.[25] Indeed, rather than providing a set of rules establishing correct use of language and syntax, the booklet consists of eleven passages written by Nougé alongside five illustrations "recently discovered by Monsieur René Magritte" (as they are described in Nougé's preface).[26] The texts are composed in the simple manner of grammar lessons, but their meanings are sometimes absurd, and their themes of anonymity, displaced objects, and potential violence echo those of Magritte's paintings. One passage, for example, reads:

> They resembled everyone else
> They forced the lock
> They replaced the lost object
> They shot guns
> They mixed drinks
> They sowed handfuls of questions
> They retired modestly
> while erasing their signatures.[27]

In keeping with the intentionally confounding nature of this apparently inconspicuous booklet, Magritte's role remains unclear (as indicated by Nougé in his preface). None of the drawings is signed; none of them features Magritte's characteristic imagery. Any linear or logical relationship between text and image has been contaminated, and there seems to be no hierarchy between them. By thus removing both elements from their traditional functions, Nougé and Magritte succeeded in subverting rational conventions to liberate the mind—one of the highest overarching goals of the Surrealist movement.

Magritte's interactions with the Parisian Surrealists spurred him to build upon what he and Nougé had begun in Brussels. He became familiar with Miró's *peinture-poésie* canvases of 1925–27, which juxtapose abstract compositions with words and phrases written in a cursive hand with flourishes that distinguish it from Magritte's plain, unembellished script (fig. 3). The appropriation of grammar and vocabulary primers is analogous to Ernst's redeployment of illustrations found in *La Nature*, a popular magazine devoted to science and technology (another "objective" source whose authority the Surrealists loved to attack).[28] This subversive take on educational texts grew directly out of the Surrealists' idealization of the unregulated freedom of the child's mind, not yet trammeled by the "civilizing" influence of education. The very tools designed to educate (or, to the Surrealists' way of thinking, to rein in imaginative thinking) are here commandeered to ridicule the system. In undermining the logic and authority of these sources, the Surrealists were attacking the fundamental conventions of bourgeois society.

The investigation of the relationship between text and image would occupy Magritte throughout his stay in Paris, accounting for nearly a quarter of the works he completed there (interestingly, he would revisit the theme only occasionally after leaving the city).[29] He wryly summarized his concepts in his illustrated text "Les Mots et les images" ("Words and Images"; plates 84–89)—a playfully programmatic set of principles about the two elements—published in *La Révolution surréaliste* in 1929.[30]

Like *La Clef des songes*, subsequent word-paintings contain niches enclosing written words; however, the words are no longer paired with images of objects. *L'Apparition* (*The Apparition*, 1928; plate 56) is the earliest and most narrative of these paintings; here, abstract biomorphic shapes contain the words *nuage* (cloud), *fusil* (rifle), *horizon*, *fauteuil* (armchair), and *cheval* (horse), all incorporated into a darkened landscape, surrounding a solitary figure with his back to the viewer. The word *nuage* appears just above the man's head in the sky, where a cloud (or a speech bubble) might logically appear. *Horizon* is located where the blackened sky meets a featureless sand-colored ground. The remaining three words seem to be arranged at random, and the size and the outline of their compartments are arbitrary in relation to the meaning of the words they contain—save the cloud, which is a feasible cloud shape.[31] Also from 1928, *Le Masque vide* (*The Empty Mask*; plate 41) is divided into four sections by what would appear to be picture frames or window mullions, or possibly the supporting bars of a stretcher on the back of a large canvas. The sectors are of nonuniform sizes and shapes, and the framework as a whole occupies its own space. The words within each niche—*ciel* (sky/heaven), *corps humain (ou forêt)* (human body [or forest]), *rideau* (curtain), and *façade de maison* (house façade)—are familiar, but have no inherent

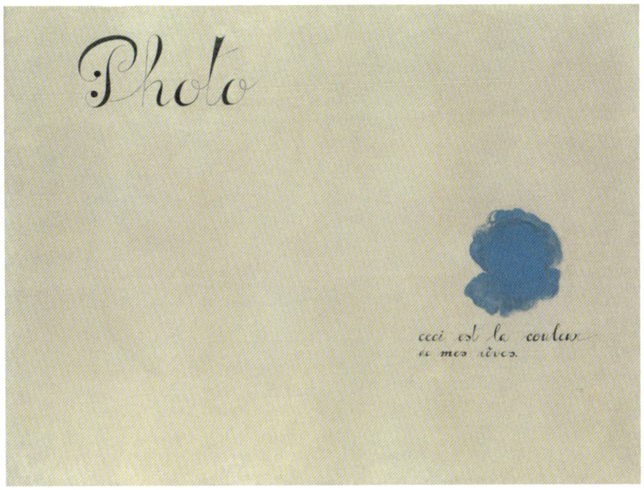

Figure 3. Joan Miró. *Photo: Ceci est la couleur de mes rêves* (*Photo: This Is the Color of My Dreams*). 1925. Oil on canvas, 38 x 51" (96.5 x 129.5 cm). The Metropolitan Museum of Art, New York, The Pierre and Maria-Gaetana Matisse Collection, 2002

connection to one another (and the alternative of "forest" for "human body" is likewise mystifying). The compartments in *Le Miroir vivant* (*The Living Mirror*, 1928; plate 55), by contrast, do not constitute a framework, but are interconnected, biomorphic abstractions (highly reminiscent of Miró's *peintures-poésies*), set against a plain black background; they contain the words *personage éclatant de rire* (person bursting with laughter), *horizon*, *cris d'oiseaux* (birdcalls), and *armoire*. In *L'Arbre de la science* (*The Tree of Knowledge*; plate 61), the words *cheval* (horse) and *sabre* (sword) suggest battle, as does the form at the lower right, which resembles the barrel of a gun. The lettering is carefully rendered, like the writing of schoolchildren learning penmanship, character by character, as forms rather than as signifiers: language is disassembled into its elementary parts and given new meaning.

Le Paysage fantôme (*The Phantom Landscape*, 1928; plate 50) shows the word *montagne* (mountain) written across the face of a woman who stares impassively at the viewer. Although the likeness is based on the photograph of a friend in Brussels,[32] Magritte neutralized the identity of the individual through his choice of dull colors and style of academic flatness, reducing the portrait to an impenetrably generic image. As is so often the case in his most successful works, Magritte instills in the viewer a spark of suspicion that the apparently familiar, painted in the most ordinary way, is actually a trap, hiding something unknown, disturbing, even threatening.

In *L'Usage de la parole* (*The Use of Speech*, 1928; plate 42)—a title Magritte used no fewer than six times in 1928[33]—the artist presents the written element as speech bubbles emerging from the mouths of two faces in profile, a convention of comic strips and cartoons. The somewhat grandiose title is another of the artist's word-traps: while it suggests a treatiselike exploration of language, the painting fails to deliver on that promise. The division between the two parts of the work echoes the disconnection between image and word. It has been suggested that the pair may be Breton (left) and Magritte (right), possibly engaged in word association,[34] an exercise the Surrealist artists frequently undertook to stimulate creativity and illogical connections. Another Surrealist activity is recalled in *La Bonne Nouvelle* (*The Good News*, 1928; plate 40): the game of Cadavre exquis (Exquisite Corpse), in which players collaborate by blindly completing each other's stories or drawings. This painting's inscription reads: "Je te passe la plume, ma pauvre amie, enchantée de tant et tant de conscience des détresses. Geert" (I hand you the pen, dear friend, enchanted by so much awareness of distress. Geert)."[35]

Magritte's investigation of language culminates in *La Trahison des images* (*The Treachery of Images*, 1929; plate 64). The previous year (according to the date given by the catalogue raisonné) he completed [*Biomorphs with Words*] (plate 39),[36] in which a roughly outlined pipelike shape is anchored with the label *la pipe*. This earlier work is one of a few in which Magritte uses heavy impasto, emphasizing the physicality of the paint used to represent form—an objective paralleled by the exploration of language to represent meaning. In contrast to the unusually experimental style of this untitled work, *La Trahison des images* presents an easily recognizable illustration of a pipe, flat and crisp as a commercial sign. The image floats against a creamy background above the seemingly contradictory declaration "Ceci n'est pas une pipe" (This is not a pipe). The confrontation between the words and the image synthesizes the lessons explored in the earlier word-paintings, for now the two appear not merely disconnected, but actually opposing each other. Paradoxically, of course, the assertion is true: a *painting* of a pipe is not a pipe, nor is the word *pipe* a pipe; finally, the word and the image denoting the object have nothing inherently in common with each other—nor with an actual pipe.

In numerous ways, Magritte incorporated the written word into the act of painting as a means of deconstructing and redefining both image and language, in an attempt to nettle the problem of representation. Refusing to confer a subordinate role to either written or visual representation, and instead using language and image to disrupt one another, to upend logic, Magritte engages the revolutionary potential of both. Painting is thus redefined as an analytical, critical instrument, challenging perception and activating the mind of the viewer.

PAINTING THE ACT OF PAINTING: *TENTATIVE DE L'IMPOSSIBLE*

In *Tentative de l'impossible* (*Attempting the Impossible*, 1928; plate 44), Magritte pushed his investigation of painting to a level not seen before. Here he depicts, in the nontemporal medium of painting, the *act* of painting in the most literal way. The painter (Magritte himself) is shown "finishing" a female nude (modeled by Georgette) by painting her left arm, the only missing part. He is represented with the traditional attributes associated with the practice of oil painting—palette, brushes, wet paint, and palette cups.[37] Part of the enigma of the work is its seeming naïveté, the literal representation of something "impossible." Like the mythical sculptor Pygmalion, the artist here—in this case a painter—creates Galatea, the nude female body. The action is taking place in real space, while simultaneously its representation is frozen in time on the surface of the canvas. But unlike the passionate Pygmalion depicted by Jean-Léon Gérôme around 1890 (fig. 4), this artist—dressed in a suit, posing stiffly—seems utterly detached from the act of creation in which he is involved.

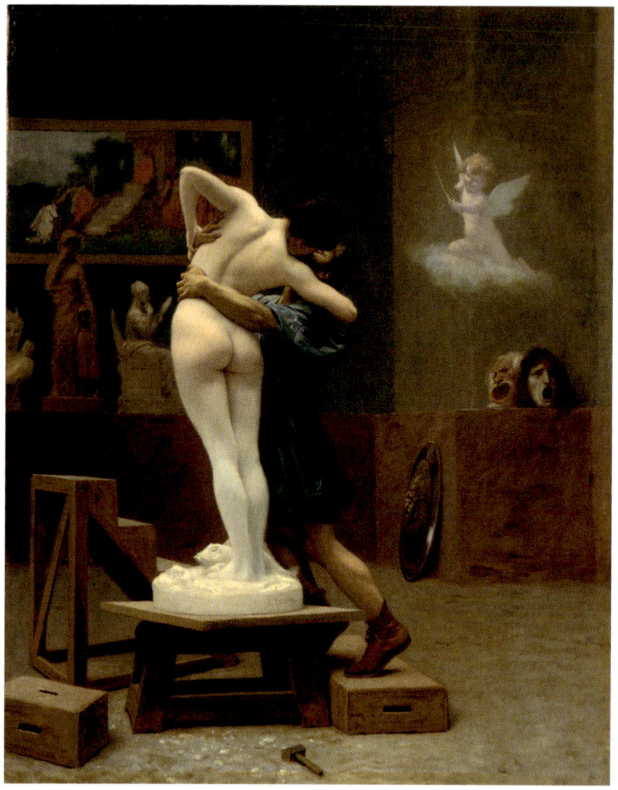

Figure 4. Jean-Léon Gérôme. *Pygmalion and Galatea*. c. 1890. Oil on canvas, 35 x 27" (88.9 x 68.6 cm). The Metropolitan Museum of Art, New York, Gift of Louis C. Raegner, 1927

Les Jours gigantesques (*The Titanic Days*, 1928; plate 48) offers an interesting comparison. Both works depict a clothed man and a nude woman; in each the female is "completed" by the male, though in radically different ways. In *Les Jours gigantesques* the two bodies are collaged onto each other, and—unlike the classically proportioned figures in *Tentative de l'impossible*—they are solid to the point of exaggeration. (The title *Les Jours gigantesques*, provided by Nougé, refers both to their massiveness and to the mythological fight of the Titans.) The woman's posture here is contorted, in contrast to Georgette's frozen contrapposto in *Tentative de l'impossible*. In place of the comfortable middle-class surroundings seen in that canvas, in *Les Jours gigantesques* we find an undefined, unfurnished space. The background—bluish, indistinguishable—may be interpreted as a flat wall, an open sky, or an abyss; it augments the threatening mystery of the scene. As violent and theatrical as *Tentative de l'impossible* is dispassionate, *Les Jours gigantesques* demonstrates the artist's ongoing fascination with the notion of negating, through painting itself, the conventions of pictorial space, as well as his continuing exploration of the visible and the hidden. It is one of the most disturbing images Magritte ever painted.

Tentative de l'impossible is likewise ambiguous in what it represents and conceals. On one hand, it is a key example of Magritte's investigations into the power of painting and the tension between object and representation. On the other, it demystifies the creative process: painting here is a rote act, nothing more than the application of medium in order to achieve likeness. The artist has been subversively redefined, from a hero with spiritual powers to a Sunday painter, acting mechanically in an uninspiring domestic setting.

Furthermore, Magritte here challenges the archetype of the female muse, a recurring Surrealist conceit. Exemplified by the title character of Breton's 1928 novel *Nadja*, described as a "veritable sphinx,"[38] the figure of the muse was celebrated by the Surrealists—mainly for her uncanny ability to inspire creativity in male artists. But in contrast to Breton's Nadja, "so pure, so free of any earthly tie,"[39] Magritte's model seems rather bland, like an unfinished statue in the living room of his apartment. In *Tentative de l'impossible* the romantic bond between painter and painting—here between artist and muse—is nonexistent; and the stakes of this particular bond are especially fraught, since it is Georgette and Magritte themselves who are represented.

In *Tentative de l'impossible*, Magritte masterfully illustrates the layers of constructing reality, exposing the tricks and traps of this endeavor.[40] A series of photographs sheds further light on Magritte's thinking and adds yet another stratum of representation. One image, made in 1928, shows him with his palette in front of the unfinished painting (plate 71). Magritte stares to the right, his hand poised in midgesture. The attributes in the photograph replicate exactly those in the painting: the large brush points conspicuously upward to the canvas, emphasizing the staged connection between the painting in progress and its producer.

This is one of the earliest known instances of Magritte confronting himself as a painter through the medium of photography.[41] By posing in front of this representation of the act of painting and mechanically reproducing its unfinished status, Magritte undermines the originality of the work, thereby increasing the conceptual complexity of what is represented. He orchestrated a second photograph (plate 74), today known as *Amour* (*Love*; a title likely given after the fact).[42] Here, in a case of medium role-reversal, the photograph is set up to resemble the painted portrait. (Along these lines, Nougé would later observe that in Magritte's work "the model tries to resemble her portrait.")[43] Again, Magritte poses here as if "painting" Georgette in real space, with his brush touching her left arm. The quasi-pictorial quality of the photograph and its lack of sharp focus counterbalance the matter-of-factness of the staged scene itself. Perhaps provoking the photograph's given title, here Georgette's gaze meets that of her husband/the painter—whereas in the painting, there seems to be no visual or emotional communication between artist and model.

Using the camera allowed Magritte to deepen the investigative process of *Tentative de l'impossible*. (As we shall see, he would employ photography in the following years to even more provocative ends.) The act of painting is here represented as both creation and reproduction. The photographs, paradoxically, emphasize *creation*, while the painting illustrates Magritte's thinking about both the attraction and abyss of representation. Photography is a medium drained of all metaphysics, no longer laden with what Aragon called painting's "carpetbag of superstitions."[44] By visualizing the act of painting with the antimodernist literalness and naïveté of a Sunday painter and choosing as a setting the prosaic surroundings of his own living room in Le Perreux-sur-Marne, Magritte succeeds in extinguishing from the very outset the metaphysical spark of what is depicted. The mystery of the creative act had long been targeted by Dada and Surrealist artists, including Marcel Duchamp and Francis Picabia starting in the 1910s, and later by Ernst, Aragon, and Breton. However, no artist before Magritte had represented the creative act with such understatement and antiheroic banality. Far from a parody, *Tentative de l'impossible* is a playful manifesto about creation, illusion, and representation in painting. It is, all at once, a self-portrait, the only known painted image of him and Georgette together, and, most importantly, an ironic portrait of the act of creation.

1929: SUCCESS AND CRISIS

Although Magritte completed fewer canvases in 1929, it was his most productive year of collaboration with the Surrealists while living in Paris. While he continued to work with his colleagues in Brussels, his involvement with the group in Paris expanded significantly. Breton and Aragon served as editors for a special issue of the Belgian periodical *Variétés*, titled "Le Surréalisme en 1929," which included two paintings and a drawing by Magritte.[45] He was also among the artists and writers invited to respond to a questionnaire issued by Breton and Aragon concerning collective political action.[46] At the end of the year, the journal *La Révolution surréaliste* published four contributions by Magritte.[47] A full-page photomontage shows portraits of sixteen contributors to the issue arranged around a female nude—a reproduction of Magritte's 1929 painting *La Femme cachée* (*The Hidden Woman*).[48] The group, all pictured with eyes closed, includes Magritte and his Belgian friends among the current members of the Surrealist group (plates 90 and 91).[49] Opposite this montage appears Magritte's reply to the question "What sort of hope do you put in love?" The issue also includes a small, unsigned collage by the artist titled *Paris en 1930* (*Paris in 1930*) and his page-and-a-half-long illustrated text "Les Mots et les images" (plate 89). Magritte had begun compiling the observations set forth in this piece shortly after he moved to Paris in the autumn of 1927; it is not known how far in advance of the publication date he completed it.[50]

The year 1929 was a tumultuous one in terms of Magritte's relationship with his dealers, all of whom were hit by the global financial crisis. In Brussels, the Galerie L'Époque and its share in Magritte's contract were taken over by the Galerie Le Centaure. Le Centaure, however, survived for only three more months, and in July its arrangement with the artist was terminated. The shifting situation allowed Goemans to deal with Magritte's work more actively from Paris, and in September he offered the artist a contract with his gallery, which opened the following month—coinciding precisely with the crash of the stock market on Wall Street and the beginning of the worldwide depression. Within a short time, the entire art market collapsed; Goemans was forced to close in early 1930, after only three exhibitions.

Dalí arrived on the Paris scene in the spring of 1929, ready to work with Luis Buñuel on their film *Un Chien andalou*. There is scant documentation about the friendship between Magritte and Dalí, but the latter's autobiography indicates that he knew Magritte by reputation before coming to France.[51] Dalí also mentions Magritte in four of the seven known "Documentals" (reports on the Surrealist activities in Paris) that he wrote for the Barcelona newspaper *La Publicitat*.[52] Dalí was several years younger and his eccentric personality differed vastly from Magritte's affect of Belgian provincial normalcy—public personas that would grow more pronounced throughout the two artists' careers. They did, however, have in common their foreignness among the French, as well as their newly discovered talents as contributors of provocative and unprecedented styles of representational painting.

In August 1929 Magritte and his wife joined Goemans and his companion, Yvonne Bernard, along with Buñuel, and Paul and Gala Éluard at the family home of Dalí in Cadaqués, Spain. Here Magritte completed an unknown number of paintings, including *Le Temps menaçant* (*Threatening Weather*; plate 65), in which three incongruous objects—a nude female torso, a tuba, and a chair—dominate a seascape. Painted in white, afloat over the brilliant blue water, the objects seem formed from the amorphous substance of clouds. The painting's title (supplied by Paul Éluard) contradicts the scene's placid sea and calm skies.[53] The painting's highly polished technique, bright palette, and rocky forms doubtlessly reflect the influence of Dalí as well as the landscape of Cadaqués.[54] At the same time, Magritte's influence on Dalí's painting is also manifest here, as seen most clearly perhaps in the latter's *L'Énigme du désir: Ma mère, ma mère, ma mère* (*The Enigma of Desire: My Mother, My Mother, My Mother,* 1929; fig. 5) in which *ma mère* is inscribed, in the cursive typical of Magritte's writing, over and over in separate compartments (reminiscent of other Magritte canvases of this period, as we have seen).

As Magritte's involvement with the French Surrealists was intensifying in the last year of the decade, the movement was facing a crisis. Tensions with the political left, especially the Communist Party, led Breton to reposition the circle of artists both intellectually and politically. In an effort to reaffirm his leadership, he condemned a number of recent developments and purged the group of dissenters in a wave of expulsions. By the end of 1929 Antonin Artaud, Georges Bataille, Robert Desnos, Michel Leiris, André Masson, Joan Miró, Pierre Naville, Philippe Soupault, and Roger Vitrac had distanced themselves from the movement,

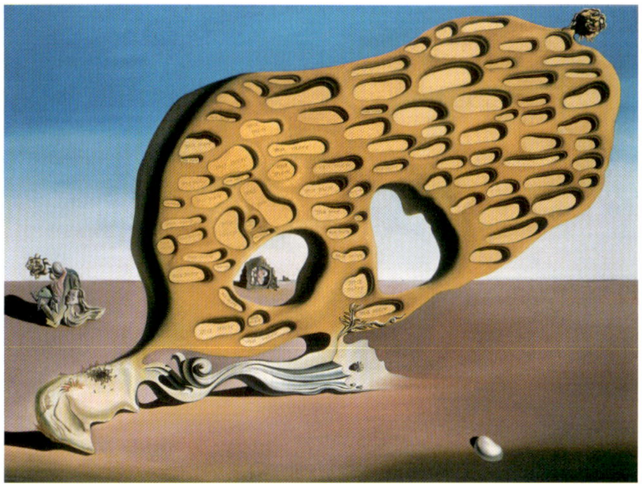

Figure 5. Salvador Dalí. *L'Énigme du désir: Ma mère, ma mère, ma mère* (*The Enigma of Desire: My Mother, My Mother, My Mother*). 1929. Oil on canvas, 43 x 59" (110 x 150.7 cm). Pinakothek der Moderne, Bayerische Staatsgemäldesammlungen, Munich

quit altogether, or been forced out.[55] Newly emerging artists compensated for the loss of several of the founding writers and painters, and Dalí—and to a lesser extent Magritte—moved to the forefront.

But just as he was being accepted to the inner circle of the Surrealist group, Magritte came to a breach in his relations with Breton. On December 14, 1929, the day before the publication of "Les Mots et les images" in *La Révolution surréaliste*—Magritte's most important contribution to the movement yet—he and Breton had a serious falling out. At a gathering at Breton's apartment, the writer demanded that Georgette remove a cross that she was wearing. Georgette refused, protesting that it was a family heirloom, and the offended Magrittes left the party immediately, despite the intervention of several friends who tried to convince them to stay.[56] As minor as the incident may seem, it represented a real rupture: Magritte and Breton did not reconcile for several years. The break with Breton affected Magritte's relationships with the other members of the French Surrealist group (with the exception of Éluard, with whom he remained close); furthermore, it had the flavor of personal defeat—Magritte had failed to establish a lasting link to a group with which, despite his ambivalent position and desire for independence, he had made such a concerted effort to connect.

PAINTING-OBJECTS FROM 1930

In the last few months of his stay in Paris, however, Magritte completed some of his most significant paintings to date. He created three *toiles découpées*[57]—*L'Évidence éternelle* (*The Eternally Obvious* [or *The Eternal Evidence*]; plate 66),[58] *Les Perfections célestes* (*Celestial Perfections*; plate 67), and *Profondeurs de la terre* (*The Depths of the Earth*; plate 68)—in the first weeks of 1930, with plans to show them at his first solo exhibition, at Goemans's Paris gallery, in April. Based on Magritte's comments in his February 1930 letter to Nougé,[59] the artist considered these to be among his most important and innovative works. They are a culmination of his far-reaching investigation into representation and illusion, and the roles of painting and object in general.[60]

L'Évidence éternelle has received far more attention than the two other *toiles découpées*, both during and after Magritte's lifetime.[61] The life-size standing nude, presumably a portrait of Georgette, is made up of five small paintings, each one radically cropped; every panel is in a gold frame, emphasizing the compactness of the enclosed images.[62] The gaze of the viewer cannot help "reconstituting" the full image of the body, by imagining the missing parts between the canvases. The familiarity of the subject matter and the anachronistically academic style in which it is painted are contradicted by the unfamiliarity of the composition.[63]

By choosing the iconographic model of the female nude, Magritte inserted himself into a distinguished and yet loaded tradition of figurative painting. It is known that the artist was familiar with Jean Auguste Dominique Ingres's 1848 *Vénus Anadyomène* (fig. 6), a masterpiece of Western mythological and academic painting celebrating the female nude.[64] Ingres's own preparatory drawings, focusing on the head, breasts, navel, and lower torso (figs. 7a–d), show a surprising similarity to Magritte's dissected painting in both study and execution. However, Magritte's "Venus" (à la Georgette) is stripped of all idealized appeal and aura

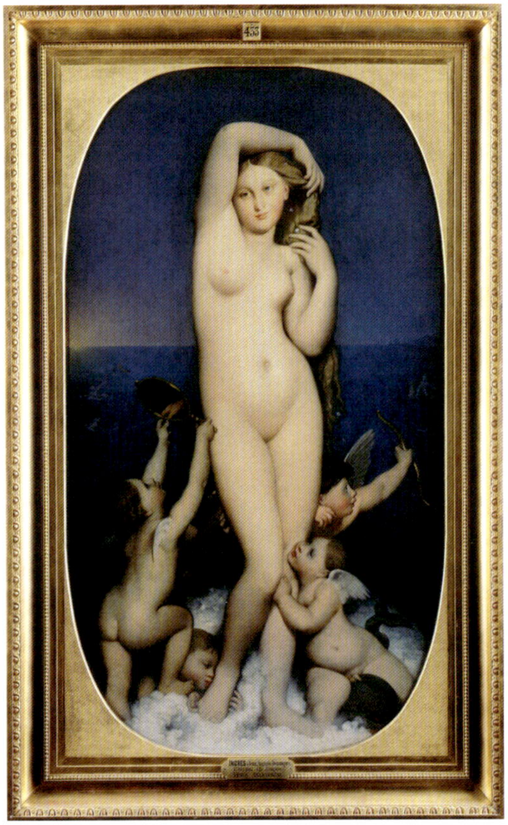

Figure 6. Jean Auguste Dominique Ingres. *Vénus Anadyomène*. 1848. Oil on canvas, 64 3/16 x 36 1/4" (163 x 92 cm). Musée Condé, Chantilly, France

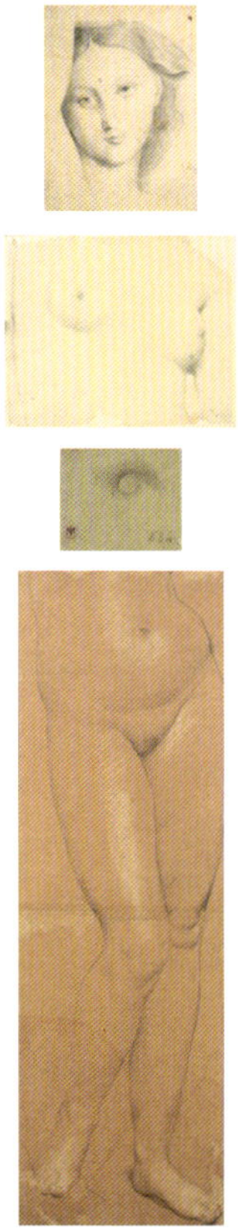

Figures 7a–d. Jean Auguste Dominique Ingres. Studies for *Vénus Anadyomène*, showing details of head, breasts, navel, and abdomen and legs. All 1808. a. Pencil on paper, 11 x 8 1/4" (28 x 21 cm); b. Pencil on tracing paper, 9 7/8 x 11 7/16" (25 x 29 cm); c. Black and white chalk on two pieces of vegetable paper, 2 3/8 x 2 3/8" (6 x 6 cm); d. Pencil on tracing paper, 40 3/16 x 13 3/4" (102 x 35 cm). Musée Ingres, Montauban, France

of classical mythology. Taking on the full weight of a canonized tradition, this work constitutes the end point of the classical era of painting, by literally deconstructing the academic ideal of the female nude.

Magritte was aware of the tension between composition (traditionally a means of aesthetic unification) and fragmentation. His painting *Les Idées de l'acrobate* (*The Acrobat's Ideas*, 1928; plate 47) may be seen as an earlier manifestation of this awareness, although here the female nude is not merely fragmented but also twisted and deformed. In his February 1930 letter to Nougé (see p. 230, fig. 1), Magritte wrote of *L'Annonciation* (*The Annunciation*, 1930; plate 70) and *Au seuil de la liberté* (*On the Threshold of Liberty*, 1930; see p. 199, fig. 6): "It may be observed that with this type of picture it becomes impossible to cut them up without destroying them completely," while simultaneously noting, perhaps with some satisfaction, "(in the case of the woman, the sky or the landscape, it seems to me they gain from being subjected to such a process)."[65] Indeed, *L'Évidence éternelle* successfully both carries on and disrupts the time-honored tradition of voyeurism and the female nude. Fragmentation here clearly invokes a feature of pornographic voyeurism, as well as the aggressive, predatory aspect of the act of seeing. It alludes to the violence of new modes of visual production and reproduction—photography, film, and the fetishizing of the female body in advertising.[66]

A comparison of *L'Évidence éternelle* to *Tentative de l'impossible* reveals striking similarities, especially with respect to the composition of the nude. It is possible that the earlier painting (and the related photograph known as *Amour*) inspired the pose and/or the deliberate cropping of the female figure in *L'Évidence éternelle*. Although the

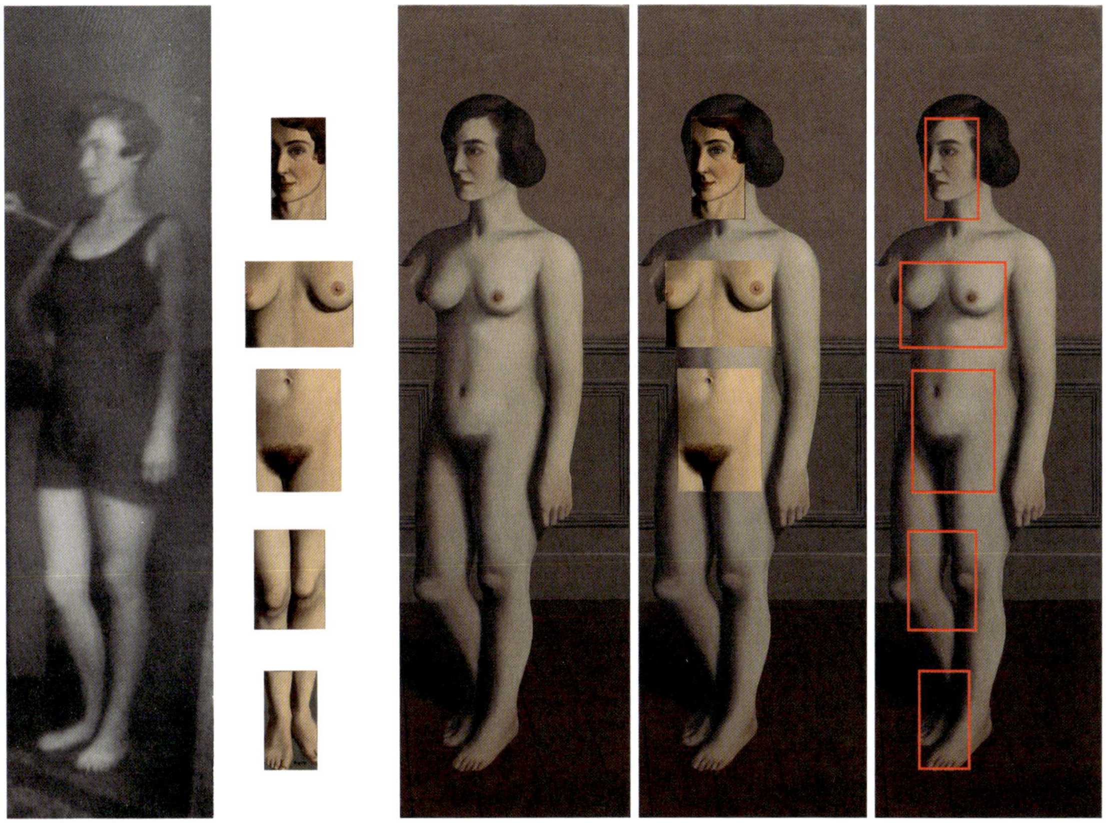

Figures 8, 9, and 10. Detail of a 1928 photograph of Georgette Magritte (known as *Amour* [*Love*]; plate 74), shown in reverse, compared with *L'Évidence éternelle* (*The Eternally Obvious*, 1930; plate 66) and with details of *Tentative de l'impossible* (*Attempting the Impossible*, 1928; plate 44), shown in reverse. Composite: The Menil Collection, Houston

figure is presented frontally in the later painting, with the head and upper body moving slightly to the right, the classical pose of Georgette in these two works is very similar, albeit a mirrored image (figs. 8, 9, and 10).[67]

The title *L'Évidence éternelle* is ambivalent in its own right: its affirmative certainty belies the fact that the image hides as much as, if not more than, it reveals. The proclamation of any "eternal" truth is of course ironic. The word *evidence* relates to different forensic realms—among them philosophy and (to the point here) criminology. In this painting, Magritte has created a symbolic connection between representation and crime: the puzzle of the fragmented female nude body replicates the mystery of misdeed.

With *L'Évidence éternelle*, Magritte moves very close to the Surrealists' notoriously anticonformist attitude toward crime. In the tradition of the Marquis de Sade (much venerated by the Surrealists), the group fundamentally opposed the Judeo-Christian idea of sin. More than once, they publicly commented on controversial legal cases,[68] extolling certain criminal acts as the ultimate form of social revolt on the one hand, and as poetic expression on the other.[69] Identifying with such antisocial behavior was part of a commitment to a broad social revolution, and to what Breton described in 1934 as "Surrealism's dedication to the 'liberation of the mind' outside the Western traditions of rationalism."[70]

Two photographs of *L'Évidence éternelle*, taken sometime between July 1930 and January 1931, add further complexity to the meaning of this work.[71] One was first reproduced in the catalogue of Magritte's 1931 solo exhibition at the Salle Giso (plate 112). The manner of the painting's presentation in the photograph is decidedly perplexing. In the image, the five canvases that make up the work are seen mounted on a glass sheet, which stands in a filthy cellar-

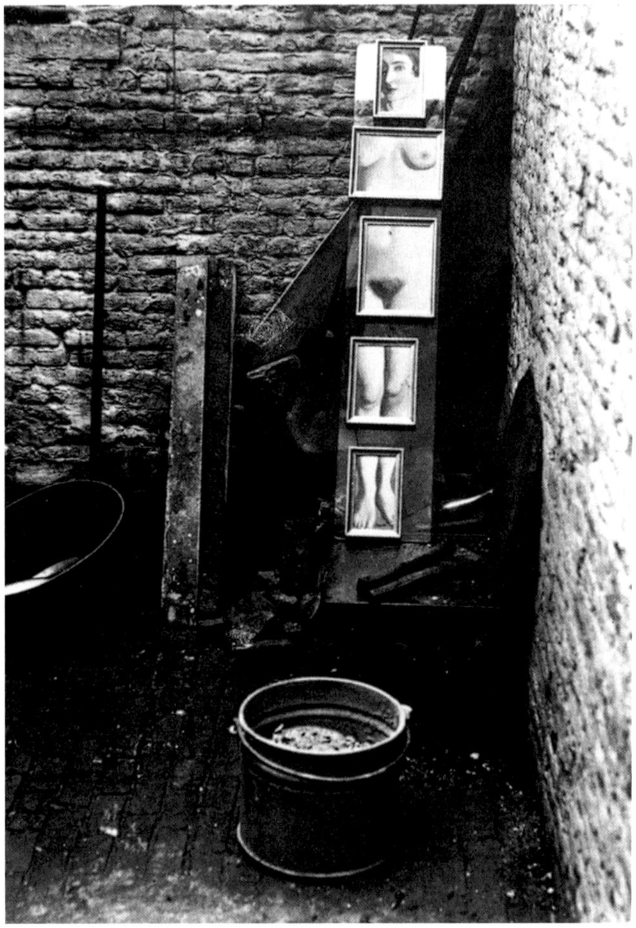

Figure 11. ***L'Évidence éternelle*** **(*The Eternally Obvious*, 1930; plate 66). 1930 or 1931. Photograph by Cami Stone. Location unknown**

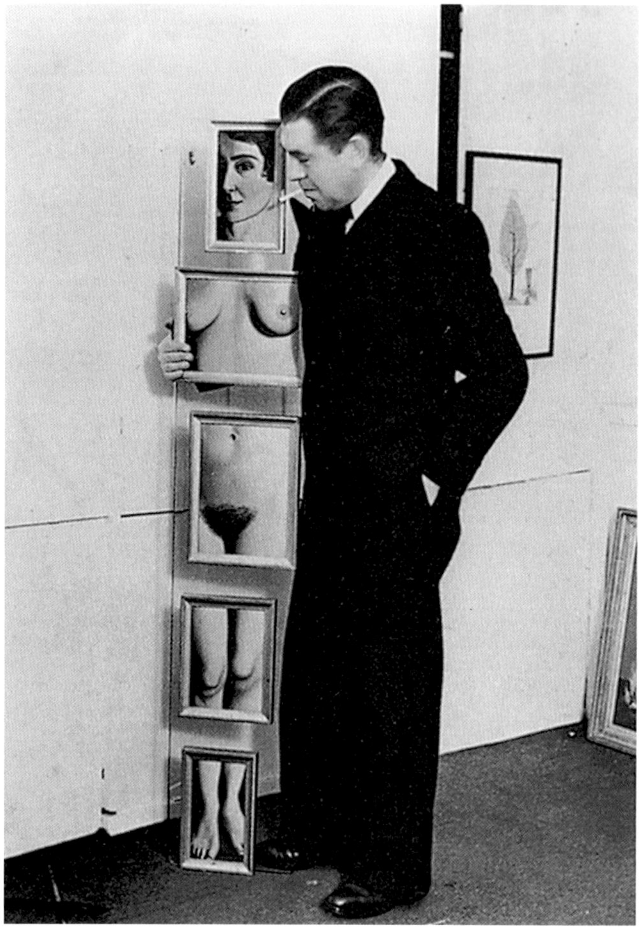

Figure 12. René Magritte with *L'Évidence éternelle* (*The Eternally Obvious*, 1930; plate 66) at the London Gallery. 1938. Photographer unknown. Location unknown

like space, in front of a washtub and surrounded by hanging laundry. In another photograph, apparently taken in the same claustrophobic space, the work leans against a brick wall, beside a bucket of coal (fig. 11). The positioning of the piece in the basement—its isolation in this crude environment—increases the sense of the vulnerability of what is represented and conveys an impression of lurking violence. The tension between the fragility of the painting and of its subject, and the distant, cold eroticism of the photograph evokes a disturbing sense that this is the scene of a sexual crime. Furthermore, by locating the painting-object in this antiaesthetic setting, Magritte fundamentally undercuts the work's perception at the abstract level of "fine art." The placement of the painted image among the objects in this basement points again to Magritte's interest in playing with the distinction between two-dimensional images and three-dimensional physical reality.

Nougé's role with regard to these photographs may have been more pivotal than has so far been noted. Magritte's correspondence with him about the creation of the *toiles découpées* is documented in the Magritte catalogue raisonné.[72] Nougé also refers to similar notions of "shock" or revelation in the experience of decontextualized objects in his 1933 essay "René Magritte ou les images défendues" (René Magritte or the forbidden [or protected] images). He mentions that such objects become isolated "in the most charming way" simply by going "into the attic."[73]

A third photograph of *L'Évidence éternelle* was made several years later, during the installation of Magritte's 1938 exhibition at the London Gallery (fig. 12). Neatly dressed

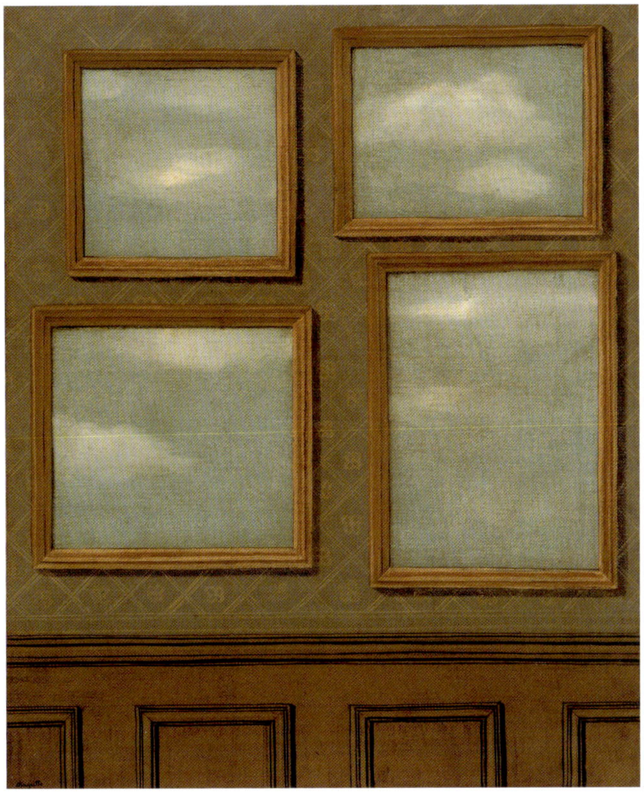

Figure 13. René Magritte. *Le Salon de Monsieur Goulden* (*Mr. Goulden's Drawing Room*). 1928 or 1929. Oil on canvas, 18 x 15" (46 x 38 cm). Location unknown. (Sylvester 1:300)

and with a cigarette in his mouth, the artist poses rakishly with his arm around the glass panel, touching with his hand the canvas that features an image of the model's breasts. It recalls the photomontage he created in 1929 for *La Révolution surréaliste*, in which the (fully clothed) male Surrealists are juxtaposed with a painted naked female figure.

The conceptual relationship between the painting-object and the photographs, however, is much deeper than Magritte's casual posture here suggests. With its five rigorous "close-ups," *L'Évidence éternelle* is the result of a subversive clash between style and technique: while the figure is painted in a conventional academic manner,[74] Magritte used means more commonly associated with photography—such as cropping and (in the most literal sense) framing—to fragment the body. Utilized like photography, here painting mimics the other medium's "predatory side" and "incongruity."[75] The photographs of *L'Évidence éternelle* in different settings further obscure the boundaries between the two mediums and increase the confusion about what is real.

In 1937, seven years after painting *L'Évidence éternelle*, Magritte created another version of the same idea. In that work, with the title *La Représentation* (*Representation*; plate 121), he developed the central canvas of *L'Évidence éternelle*, playing the same game of presence and absence, parodying the idealized female nude and deconstructing it. The frame, however, now follows the contours of the two-dimensional body; fragment and frame have become unified.[76]

No photographs exist of the original arrangements of canvases that comprise Magritte's two other object-paintings, *Les Profondeurs de la terre* and *Les Perfections célestes*, and the original glass panels upon which they were mounted have been lost. However, the artist indicated the arrangement of the four canvases of *Les Profondeurs de la terre* with a sketch in a letter to E.L.T. Mesens, who negotiated the sale of Magritte's paintings before the artist left Paris.[77] In *Les Perfections célestes*, however, the configuration can only be guessed at, and has varied in publications and exhibitions through the years. The overall layout—two canvases on top and two below—can be deduced from two earlier Magritte paintings, *La Vie secrète* (*The Secret Life*, 1928)[78] and *Le Salon de Monsieur Goulden* (*Monsieur Goulden's Drawing Room*, 1928 or 1929; fig. 13), both of which show similar arrangements of four canvases that together add up to an illustration of a cloudy sky. Magritte's signature on one of the canvases offers the only hint that the panel should perhaps occupy the lower-right position in the quartet. What may be two halves of a long, gray cloud suggest that the two upper canvases should be placed adjacent to each other (as pictured here), although none of the other cloud formations necessarily reinforces this relationship. Along with *L'Évidence éternelle*, both *Les Profondeurs de la terre* and *Les Perfections célestes* were among a group of works, then untitled, sold to Mesens in 1930 and exhibited under their current titles twice in 1931.

Magritte's *toiles découpées* marked his ingenious response to a widely perceived "crisis of painting" at the center of an ongoing theoretical dispute within the Surrealist movement. Painting as commodity and as a traditional medium of art making had been under attack throughout the 1920s, a charge led by Aragon, Breton, and Pierre Naville, and waged by such artists as Duchamp, Ernst, Miró, and Picabia. The debate about the legitimacy of painting intensified in the late 1920s and early 1930s, and Aragon's brilliant 1930 essay "La Peinture au défi" ("The Challenge to Painting")—published only weeks after Magritte had executed his group of new works—indicated an unprecedented level of urgency. With the *toiles découpées*, Magritte reached new territory in his critique of representation. By physically deconstructing the image, the artist forces the viewer to engage and "complete" the painting in his mind. With these works, Magritte succeeded in articulating the tensions between painting as image and painting as object more convincingly than ever before.

THE FINAL MONTHS IN PARIS

In March 1930 Magritte stopped painting and started looking for work as a commercial artist. He participated in a group show called *Exposition de collages* organized by Aragon and Goemans, with only one work[79] among over thirty contributions, by Arp, Georges Braque, Dalí, Duchamp, Ernst, Juan Gris, Man Ray, Miró, Picabia, Picasso, and Tanguy. Goemans's plans for Magritte's solo show that spring, which was to include his most important paintings to date, never materialized, as the Paris gallery closed its doors in April.[80] It was not until 1948—nearly twenty years later—that Magritte would have his first one-person exhibition in Paris.

Magritte's estrangement from Breton (and hence from the majority of the Surrealists); the closing of Goemans's gallery, which left the artist without a contract or a monthly stipend; and the consequences of the global economic depression that began with the stock market crash in October 1929 made Magritte's situation in Paris untenable. Spring 1930 marked the beginning of an extended artistic crisis. He left Paris in July and went back to Belgium. Forced to support himself and Georgette, he returned to commercial design work. Symbolically, this decision constitutes a fundamental break with Magritte's ambitious artistic and intellectual objectives during the years in Paris.

Living in the suburbs of the French capital put Magritte simultaneously in proximity to and at a distance from Breton's Surrealist group and those affiliated with it. The fact that he remained geographically apart, even in the three years he worked most intimately with the Parisian Surrealists, and carefully kept a distance from the consuming politics of the movement, may well have been among the conditions he needed in order to create a unique body of work. Magritte produced some of his most iconic paintings in this period—including *La Clef des songes*, *Les Jours gigantesques*, *Les Amants* (*The Lovers;* plate 54), *Tentative de l'impossible*, *La Trahison des images*, *Le Faux Miroir* (*The False Mirror;* plate 59), and *L'Évidence éternelle*. He deliberately adopted the techniques of academic representation—and then turned representation on its head. In Magritte's paintings, the familiar becomes uncanny; recognizable representation is a trap—a veritable denial of what is known. In Paris, Magritte succeeded in fundamentally questioning the connection between image and interpretation, establishing for himself a unique position in the ongoing modernist discourse about the role of art, and especially painting, in contemporary society.

Notes

We wish to thank our colleagues at The Museum of Modern Art, New York: Anne Umland, for her thoughtful advice and critical reading of this essay; and Danielle Johnson, for sharing her expertise and extensive research. We are also grateful to the following Menil staff for their support and contributions: Brad Epley, Chief Conservator; Katrina Bartlett, Assistant Paintings Conservator; Joseph Newland, Head of Publications; and Eric Wolf, Head Librarian; and to former Menil intern Marie Lozón de Cantelmi for her initial research on the project.

The title of this essay derives from Louis Aragon's text "La Peinture au défi" (Paris: Galerie Goemans, Librairie José Corti, 1930), p. 9: "Un éclair est couvé sous les chapeaux melons"; trans., as "The Challenge to Painting," in Pontus Hultén, ed., The Surrealists Look at Art *(Venice, Calif.: Lapis, 1991), p. 51. Although Aragon does not explicitly refer to Magritte in this part of his essay, the coincidence between his highly evocative, poetic sentence and the significance of the bowler-hatted figure in Magritte's work starting in 1926 is striking. It seems likely that, by the time Aragon wrote his text, he was aware of the importance of this image in Magritte's work (e.g. in* Les Rêveries du promeneur solitaire, *1926 [Sylvester 1:124];* Le Sens de la nuit, *1927 [plate 11]; and* L'Assassin menacé, *1927 [plate 12]). Aragon's poetic metaphor is all the more intriguing as it evokes the conflict between bourgeois normalcy and revolutionary energy, a tension that seems a fitting description of Magritte's persona and role within the Surrealist movement.*

References in the following notes in the form "Sylvester 1:8" or "Whitfield 6:7" refer to the volume and catalogue numbers of works in the six-volume Magritte catalogue raisonné. Likewise, references in the form "Sylvester 1, p. 304" refer to the volume and page numbers where corresponding texts are located. The first five volumes of the catalogue raisonné, published 1992–97, were edited by David Sylvester; the final volume, published 2012, was edited by Sarah Whitfield. For complete publication information for all six volumes, see the "Selected Bibliography," p. 252.

Catalogue raisonné numbers are provided for works that are not reproduced as plates or figures in the present volume. Unless otherwise noted, all English translations in this essay are by the authors.

1. Scutenaire made himself known to the group in June 1927. See Sylvester 1, p. 73; and Xavier Canonne, *Surrealism in Belgium: 1924–2000* (Brussels: Mercatorfonds, 2007), p. 21.
2. Although the exact dates are not clear, Magritte seems to have gone to Paris and returned within the month of February 1924. Sylvester 1, p. 44; and Michel Draguet, *Magritte: His Work, His Museum* (Brussels: Musée Magritte/Hazan), p. 36.
3. Goemans had had close connections in Paris since 1924. See Goemans, "Expérience du Surréalisme" (lecture given in La Louvière, Belgium, January 29, 1949), cited in Sylvester 1, p. 69.
4. André Breton visited Brussels in August 1925; Louis Aragon in January 1927. Magritte's early letters from Paris also indicate that he already knew the two men. See ibid., p. 77.
5. The Magrittes were unable to find a suitable apartment in central Paris. Le Perreux-sur-Marne is approximately seven miles (eleven kilometers) east of central Paris. At the time the Magrittes lived there, they were required to take both a bus and the métro in order to reach the city center. See ibid.
6. Ibid.
7. See ibid., p. 70.
8. The two exhibitions were *René Magritte* (Galerie L'Époque, Brussels, January 7, 1928–closing date unknown); and a one-day exhibition held in conjunction with a recital and speech (Salle de Bourse, Charleroi, January 20, 1929). See Sylvester 5, p. 103.
9. Sylvester 1, p. 92.
10. Breton acquired nine works by Magritte between 1927 and 1930 (Sylvester 1:200, 209, 219, 280, 302, 312, 321; Sylvester 4:1623 and 1628a) and another six in later years (Sylvester 3:931; Sylvester 4:1127, 1351, 1351a, 1459, and appendix 158); Aragon was given two works by Magritte in 1929 (Sylvester 1:301 and 317); and Éluard would own nine works by the artist beginning in 1928 or 1929 (Sylvester 1:233, 234, 241; Sylvester 2:434, 476; Sylvester 4:1108, 1165, 1194, and 1227).
11. Sylvester 1 dates nos. 166–331 firmly to the period of Magritte's stay in Paris, and Whitfield 6 attributes its no. 3 to this time as well. It has been noted that Magritte's rate of production decreased and his style became more technically refined toward the end of 1928 and after the Paris years; see David Sylvester, *Magritte: The Silence of the World* (Houston and New York: Menil Foundation, Abrams, 1992), pp. 181–82; see also Sylvester 1, p. 93. This is a topic that deserves further investigation.
12. André Breton, *Manifeste du Surréalisme* (Paris, 1924); in *Manifestoes of Surrealism*, trans. by Richard Seaver and Helen R. Lane (Ann Arbor: University of Michigan Press, 1969), pp. 3–47.
13. Examination of a number of Magritte's early works, using X-radiography, infrared reflectography (IRR), and microscopy, reveals pencil underdrawings and calculated changes, sometimes significant, in the final compositions. For example, in *L'Alphabet des révélations* (*The Alphabet of Revelations*, 1929; plate 63), the wooden pattern of the painted stretcher continues beneath the image of the tear in the canvas, indicating that the composition was carefully planned; IRR examination of *La Bonne Nouvelle* (*The Good News*, 1928; plate 40) reveals underdrawing and slight changes in the painting of the envelope. This evidence of careful planning and change supports the theory that Magritte utilized conscious compositional decisions as opposed to automatism. See also Anne Umland's discussion of *La Fin des contemplations* (*An End to Contemplation*, 1927; plate 18) in the present volume, pp. 37–39. We are grateful to Brad Epley and Katrina Bartlett for bringing these observations to our attention.
14. Magritte, in Suzi Gablik, *Magritte* (Greenwich, Conn.: New York Graphic Society, 1970), pp. 70–71.
15. It is possible that here Magritte is employing collage ironically. Rather than using the technique to create the kind of visual disruption of a "typical" Surrealist collage, he uses it instead to effect the illusion of repair and reconstruction: the additional pieces of fabric appear to be "patches" of either the wall or the canvas itself. We thank Anne Umland for this observation.
16. See Sylvester, *Magritte: The Silence of the World*, p. 112.
17. René Magritte, letter to Paul Nougé, November 1927, in Marcel Mariën, ed., *Lettres surréalistes: 1924–1940* (Brussels: Les Lèvres nues, 1973), no. 112; trans. in Sylvester 1, pp. 245–46 (emphasis in original).
18. The work's original title was *L'Expérience du miracle* (*Experience of the Miraculous*); this title was inscribed by Magritte on the stretcher bar, and later crossed out. Sylvester 1:187, p. 248.
19. Magritte may have had in mind Fernand Khnopff's painting *Des Caresses* (1896), which shows a figure composed of a leopard body and a woman's head. See Sylvester 1, p. 249.
20. René Magritte, "La Ligne de vie" (1938 lecture delivered at the Koninklijk Museum voor Schone Kunsten in Antwerp); trans. in Gisèle Ollinger-Zinque and Frederik Leen, eds., *René Magritte, 1898–1967* (Brussels and Ghent: Royal Museums of Fine Arts of Belgium, Ludion, 1998), pp. 46–47. This 1998 translation was adapted from that in Sylvester 5, pp. 9–22.
21. According to the authors of the catalogue raisonné, the title *La Clef des songes* comes from Henry Vidal's 1921 French translation of the *Oneirocritica* of Artemidorus. The painting's English title was based on the translation of that book, which has been known since the mid-seventeenth century as *The Interpretation of Dreams*. (See Sylvester 1, p. 239.) The more literal translation, *The Key of Dreams*,

might better serve the work because it avoids Freudian connotations that Magritte would not have intended.

22. Magritte made a second version with the same title in a vertical format after returning to Brussels in 1930, and a third in 1935 (plate 102), Sylvester 1:332 and Sylvester 2:370.

23. Aragon, "The Challenge to Painting," in Hultén, ed., *The Surrealists Look at Art*, p. 68.

24. See Sylvester 1, p. 75.

25. The cover is illustrated in Sylvester 1, p. 75.

26. Paul Nougé, *Clarisse Juranville: Quelques écrits et quelques dessins* (Brussels: René Henriquez, 1927), p. 7.

27. Ibid., p. 18.

28. Thirty-one collages assembled from illustrations in *La Nature* in 1921 were published by Ernst and Éluard in *Répétitions* (Paris: Au Sans Pareil, 1922) and *Les Malheurs des immortels* (Paris: Librairie Six, 1922). See William A. Camfield, *Max Ernst: Dada and the Dawn of Surrealism* (Houston: Menil Collection, 1993), pp. 107–10.

29. See Sylvester, *Magritte: The Silence of the World*, p. 168.

30. René Magritte "Les Mots et les images," *La Révolution surréaliste*, no. 12 (December 15, 1929): 32–33.

31. Michel Foucault has remarked of this work: "Here, shapes are so vague as to be unnamable if they did not identify themselves. And on the real painting as seen—blobs, shadows, silhouettes—there is superimposed the invisible possibility of another painting at once familiar because of the figures presented and yet bizarre because [of] the juxtaposition of horse and armchair." Foucault, *This Is Not a Pipe* (Berkeley: University of California Press, 1982), p. 40.

32. Sylvester 1, p. 272.

33. The locations of only three of these canvases are still known: Sylvester 1:275, 276, and 277.

34. See Sylvester, *Magritte: The Silence of the World*, p. 159.

35. In this painting Magritte redoubles his game of absences. He shows us what appears to be the back of a canvas. Echoing the hidden image is a closed envelope, the contents of which are likewise concealed. Both word and image are absent, save the inscription on the painted framework, supplied by his friend Geert van Bruaene. See Sylvester 1, pp. 265–66.

36. The title [*Biomorphs with Words*] was supplied by the editors of the catalogue raisonné. Sylvester 1, p. xii.

37. We thank Brad Epley for clarifying these technical details.

38. André Breton, *Nadja* (1928), trans. by Richard Howard (New York: Grove Press, 1960), p. 78.

39. Ibid, p. 90.

40. See Sylvester, *Magritte: The Silence of the World*, p. 150.

41. See Patrick Roegiers, *Magritte et la photographie* (New York and Ghent: DAP, Ludion, 2005), pp. 22–23, 55. The authors of the catalogue raisonné hold that photographs of Magritte with *Tentative de l'impossible* and with *Le Masque vide* were "manifestly taken at the same session in the autumn of 1928." See Sylvester 1, pp. 318–19. Sarah Whitfield suggests that the photographs were likely made by Paul Magritte.

42. The photograph was likely given this title at a later point by Louis Scutenaire; see Scutenaire, *La Fidélité des images René Magritte: Le Cinématographe et la photographie* (Brussels: Lebeer-Hossmann, 1976). We are grateful to Michel Draguet for pointing this out.

43. Paul Nougé, *René Magritte ou les images défendues* (Brussels: "La Boétie," 1943), p. 42. The essay was first published, in shorter form, in 1933 in the periodical *Le Surréalisme au service de la révolution*, no. 5: 24–28.

44. Aragon, "The Challenge to Painting," in Hultén, ed., *The Surrealists Look at Art*, p. 58.

45. *Variétés*, special issue, "Le Surréalisme en 1929," June 1929.

46. See Sylvester 1, p. 100.

47. For a description of Magritte's four contributions, see Sylvester 1, p. 109.

48. *La Femme cachée* is Sylvester 1:302. Athough no documentation of who assembled the photomontage is known to date, it is likely that Magritte collaborated on it. According to the catalogue raisonné, Marcel Mariën remembered that "Magritte wanted to see *La femme cachée* reproduced in the review and conceived the montage as a means of achieving this." See Sylvester 1, p. 111.

49. The group is arranged in alphabetical order from left to right and top to bottom: Maxime Alexandre, Louis Aragon, André Breton, Luis Buñuel, Jean Caupenne, Salvador Dalí, Paul Éluard, Max Ernst, Marcel Fourier, Camille Goemans, Magritte, Paul Nougé, Georges Sadoul, Yves Tanguy, André Thirion, and Albert Valentin. Ibid.

50. See Sylvester 1, pp. 109–11.

51. Dalí writes of being introduced to a woman named Marguerite and mistaking her for Magritte, whom he "considered one of the most 'mysteriously equivocal' painters of the moment." Salvador Dalí, *The Secret Life of Salvador Dalí*, trans. by Haakon M. Chevalier (New York: Dial, 1942), pp. 208–9.

52. Dalí's four "Documental-Paris-1929" articles mentioning Magritte appeared on the front pages of four issues of Barcelona's *La Publicitat* newspaper, vol. 51: May 7, May 23, June 28, and July 7, 1929. The first three are included in *The Collected Writings of Salvador Dalí*, ed. and trans. by Haim Finkelstein (Cambridge, U.K.: Cambridge University Press, 1998), pp. 111 and 113; that volume contains six of seven known "Documentals." The seventh article (that of July 7, 1929), discovered by Anne Umland in 1995, has been translated into Castilian Spanish (Dalí wrote the originals in Catalán); see Fèlix Fanés, "Un texto perdido de Salvador Dalí," *La Vanguardia* (Barcelona), January 17, 1999. For a discussion of Magritte in Dalí's "Documental-Paris-1929," see Danielle M. Johnson, "Salvador Dalí and René Magritte, 1928–1938," Ph.D. diss., New York University, 2012, pp. 173–82.

53. Éluard was the first owner of this painting; he probably purchased it from the artist while at Cadaqués. See Sylvester 1, pp. 338–39.

54. That this work reflects Magritte's time in Cadaqués is noted in ibid., and in Sylvester, *Magritte: The Silence of the World*, pp. 224–26.

55. The history of schisms within the Surrealist group is a complex issue, made more confusing by the fact that a number of artists—Duchamp, Picasso, Picabia, and Miró among them—never joined the Surrealist group to begin with. See Robert Kopp, "If Images Could Change the World," in Philippe Büttner, ed., *Surrealism in Paris* (Basel: Fondation Beyeler, 2011), pp. 24–25.

56. This incident has been recounted by various participants and observers, including Georgette Magritte, Goemans, and Claude Spaak. See Sylvester 1, pp. 111–12. See also Luis Buñuel, *Mon Dernier Soupir* (Paris: Ramsay, 1982, 2006), p. 136.

57. Magritte's term *toile découpée* (cut-up canvas) does not literally reflect the process by which the works were created. Microscopic examination of *L'Évidence éternelle* reveals that each of the five canvases was painted separately. The paint layer does not extend onto the tacking margins, as it would if the painting had been initially realized as a complete image and then cut into smaller sections before stretching. We are grateful to Epley and Bartlett for their careful study of *L'Évidence éternelle*, upon which this and subsequent observations about the painting here are based.

58. The translation provided for this work in the catalogue raisonné, *The Eternally Obvious*, seems perhaps interpretative; the more literal translation of "evidence" for *évidence* is possibly less so. It is not known who created the original title for this work, although Nougé presumably provided titles for the other two *toiles découpées*. See Sylvester 1, p. 351.

59. René Magritte, letter to Paul Nougé, first half of February 1930, in Marcel Mariën, ed., *Lettres surréalistes: 1924–1940* (Brussels: Les Lèvres nues, 1973), no. 179.

60. Magritte's classification of the *toiles découpées*, especially with regard to their status between painting and object, changed over the years. Initially, he described the works as "objects"; and in 1937 *L'Évidence éternelle* was exhibited in London in E.L.T. Mesens's exhibition *Surrealist Objects and Poems* under the category of "Surrealist objects." In the exhibition *René Magritte: Surrealist Paintings and Objects* at the London Gallery, 1938, however, it was termed a "picture object." See Sylvester 1, pp. 349–50.

61. *L'Évidence éternelle* has an extensive exhibition history, which indicates that Magritte felt it was an important work; it was exhibited no fewer than six times in the 1930s. The other two *toiles découpées*, however, were shown only twice, both in Brussels in 1931; see Sylvester 1, pp. 350, 351.

62. Magritte wrote to Mesens with the exact plan and sizes of the frames that complete the cut-up figure, indicating that he consciously sought a claustrophobic cropping of the image. The frames were built so that the aperture of each corresponds exactly to its painting's dimensions. Whereas in conventional frames the canvas would be inset and a fraction of its perimeter covered, the frame opening for each of the five paintings aligns perfectly with the edge of the canvas with no image loss. See Magritte, letter to Mesens, July 3, 1930, in Sylvester 1, p. 349.

63. X-radiographic and IRR images taken of *L'Évidence éternelle* reveal that Magritte painted the image directly on the canvas with little underdrawing and limited change from the present composition.

64. Sylvester points out that Magritte had postcards of Ingres's *Vénus Anadyomène*, and also of his *La Source* (1820–56); see Sylvester 2:546, p. 326. See also Patricia Condon with Marjorie B. Cohn and Agnes Mongan, *In Pursuit of Perfection: The Art of J.A.D. Ingres* (Louisville, Ky.: J. B. Speed Art Museum, 1983), pp. 150–53. For the assemblage of Ingres's studies gathered in fig. 7, the authors are indebted to Dimitri Salmon's *Ingres et les Modernes* (Quebec: Musée national de beaux-arts du Québec, 2009), p. 15.

65. Sylvester 1, p. 349; the original letter is also reproduced in Sylvester 1, p. 114. In transcribing and translating this passage, the authors of the catalogue raisonné overlooked the line Magritte drew connecting the phrase "Voici aussi les croquis de deux grandes tableaux" (Here are sketches of two large paintings [followed by sketches of *L'Annonciation* and *Au seuil de la liberté*]) to his remark that works such as these would be "destroy[ed . . .] completely" by being cut up; by contrast, "the woman, the sky or the landscape" (that is, works such as *L'Évidence éternelle*, *Les Profondeurs de la terre*, and *Les Perfections célestes*) "gain from being subjected to such a process."

66. Susan Sontag refers to the camera as a "predatory weapon" and to photography's "predatory side" in *On Photography* (New York: Picador, 1977), pp. 14, 64.

67. Perhaps coincidentally, the cropping that occurs by line of sight in *Tentative de l'impossible* and *Amour* (here both are reversed for the sake of comparison) is very similar to that which Magritte initiates on the left side of the top three canvases in *L'Évidence éternelle*, before the angle of the viewer alters the composition. Again, we are grateful to Epley and Bartlett for calling attention to the intriguing relationships among these three works; this observation seems nothing less than a discovery.

68. The first issue of *La Révolution surréaliste,* for example, carried a photomontage centered on a portrait of Germaine Berton, an anarchist activist who assassinated a right-wing politician in November 1924. The Surrealists were later fascinated by the sisters Christine and Léa Papin, two domestic servants who brutally murdered and disfigured their employer's wife and adult daughter in 1933. Both Éluard and René Crevel sympathized with the sisters, decrying the press's sensationalistic coverage of their trial. The same year, Magritte contributed to *Violette Nozières*, a booklet produced by a group of Surrealists in tribute to an eighteen-year-old working-class woman who poisoned her father and attempted to poison her mother, claiming to be motivated by years of sexual abuse. See Jonathan P. Eburne, *Surrealism and the Art of Crime* (Ithaca, N.Y., and London: Cornell University Press, 2008); and Sylvester 2, pp. 23–24.

69. See Robert S. Short, "The Politics of Surrealism," in *The Left-Wing Intellectuals Between the Wars, 1919–1939,* ed. by Walter Laqueur and George L. Mosse (New York: Harper Torchbooks, 1966), p. 6.

70. André Breton, "Qu'est-ce que le Surréalisme?" (1934), ed. and trans. by Franklin Rosemont, *What Is Surrealism?* (New York: Mondat, 1978), p. 113; quoted in Robin Adèle Greeley, "Image, Text and the Female Body: René Magritte and the Surrealist Publications," *Oxford Art Journal* 15, no. 2 (1992): 50.

71. The photographs were taken by Cami Stone, the professional name of the Belgian photographer Wilhelmine Schammelhout (1892–1975). Little is known about her role in composing these images. See Sylvester 1, p. 349.

72. Ibid.

73. See Nougé, *René Magritte ou les images défendues*, p. 31.

74. While many of Magritte's canvases appear at first glance to have been achieved via traditional academic painting techniques, in fact the artist only approximated such methods. Brad Epley proposes that a more precise description of his technique may be "calculated realism": paintings executed just well enough to convincingly depict form, with nothing more to convey the individuality of the artist. We are indebted to Epley and Bartlett for their observations with regard to Magritte's technical approach.

75. Sontag, *On Photography*, pp. 64, 99.

76. See Silvia Eiblmayer, *Die Frau als Bild: Der weibliche Körper in der Kunst des 20. Jahrhunderts* (Berlin: Dietrich Reimer, 1993), p. 115.

77. Magritte, letter to Mesens, June 10, 1930, repr. in Joë Bousquet, ed., *Lettres mêlées* (Brussels: Les Lèvres nues, 1979), p. 29; quoted in Sylvester 1, pp. 118–19. We are grateful to Danielle Johnson for pointing out the sketch in this letter.

78. Sylvester 1:288.

79. Untitled, 1930, oil, corrugated cardboard, and card on canvas, location unknown. Sylvester 1:325, pp. 346–47. The exhibition took place at Galerie Goemans, Paris.

80. To the very end of Magritte's stay in Paris, his and Goemans's lives remained closely linked. When Goemans had to close his gallery, he also lost his apartment, and the Magrittes allowed him to stay with them before Goemans returned to Brussels to find new work. S. Heydeman, "Ma Vie avec Camille Goemans," *Espace,* no. 1 (1973): 17. We thank Michel Draguet for bringing this to our attention.

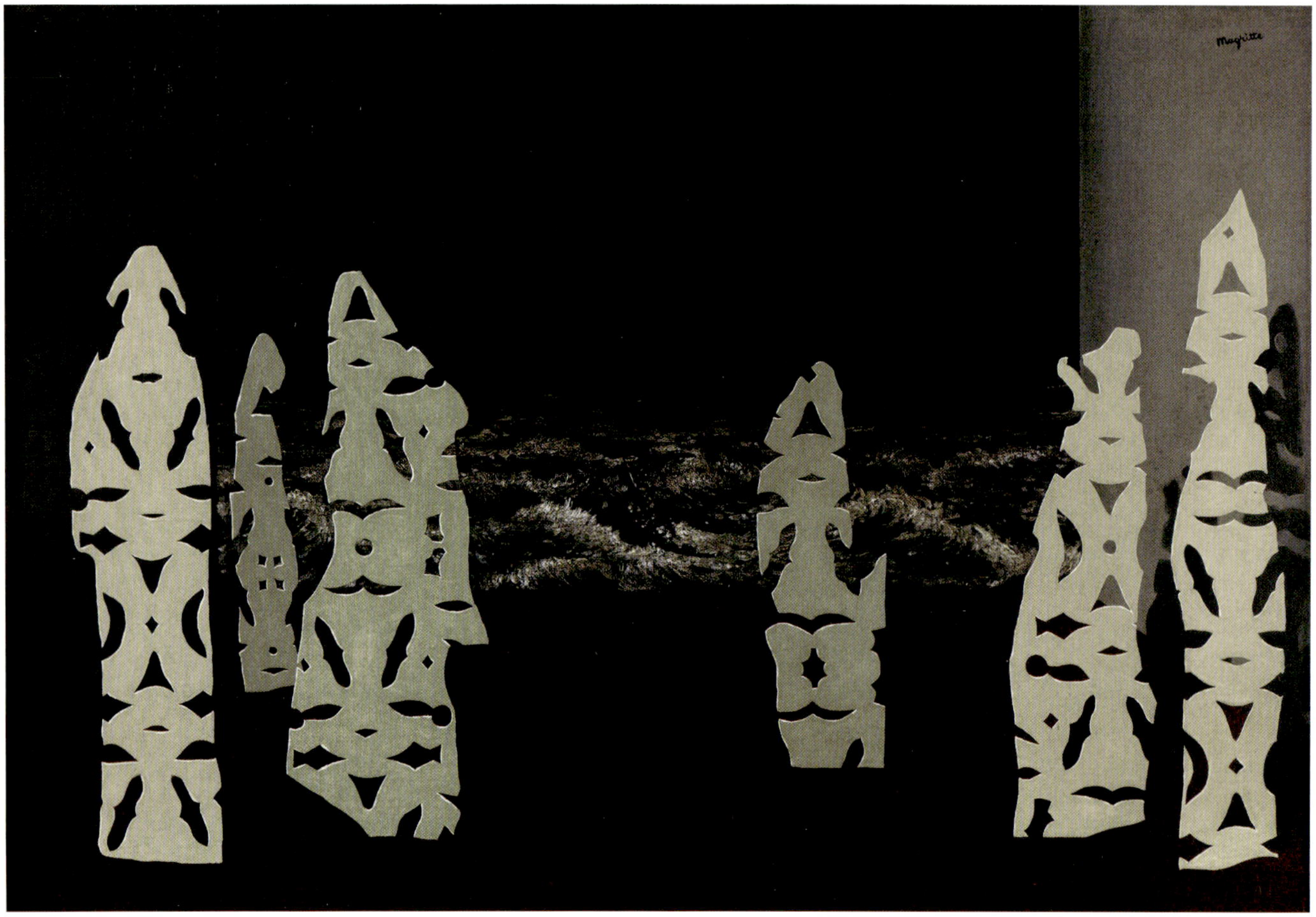

33. **LA PARURE DE L'ORAGE (THE FINERY OF THE STORM).** 1927.
Oil on canvas, 31 7/8 x 45 11/16" (81 x 116 cm)

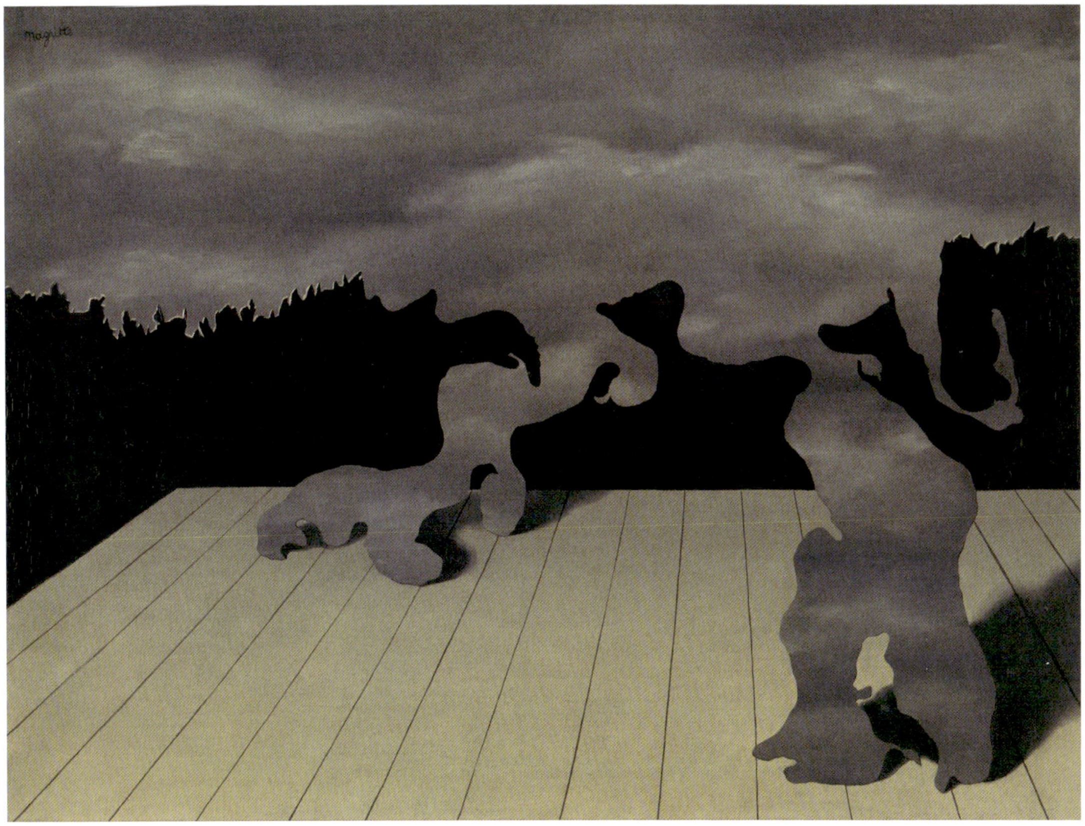

34. LES MUSCLES CÉLESTES (THE MUSCLES OF THE SKY). 1927.
Oil on canvas, 21 1/4 x 28 3/4" (54 x 73 cm)

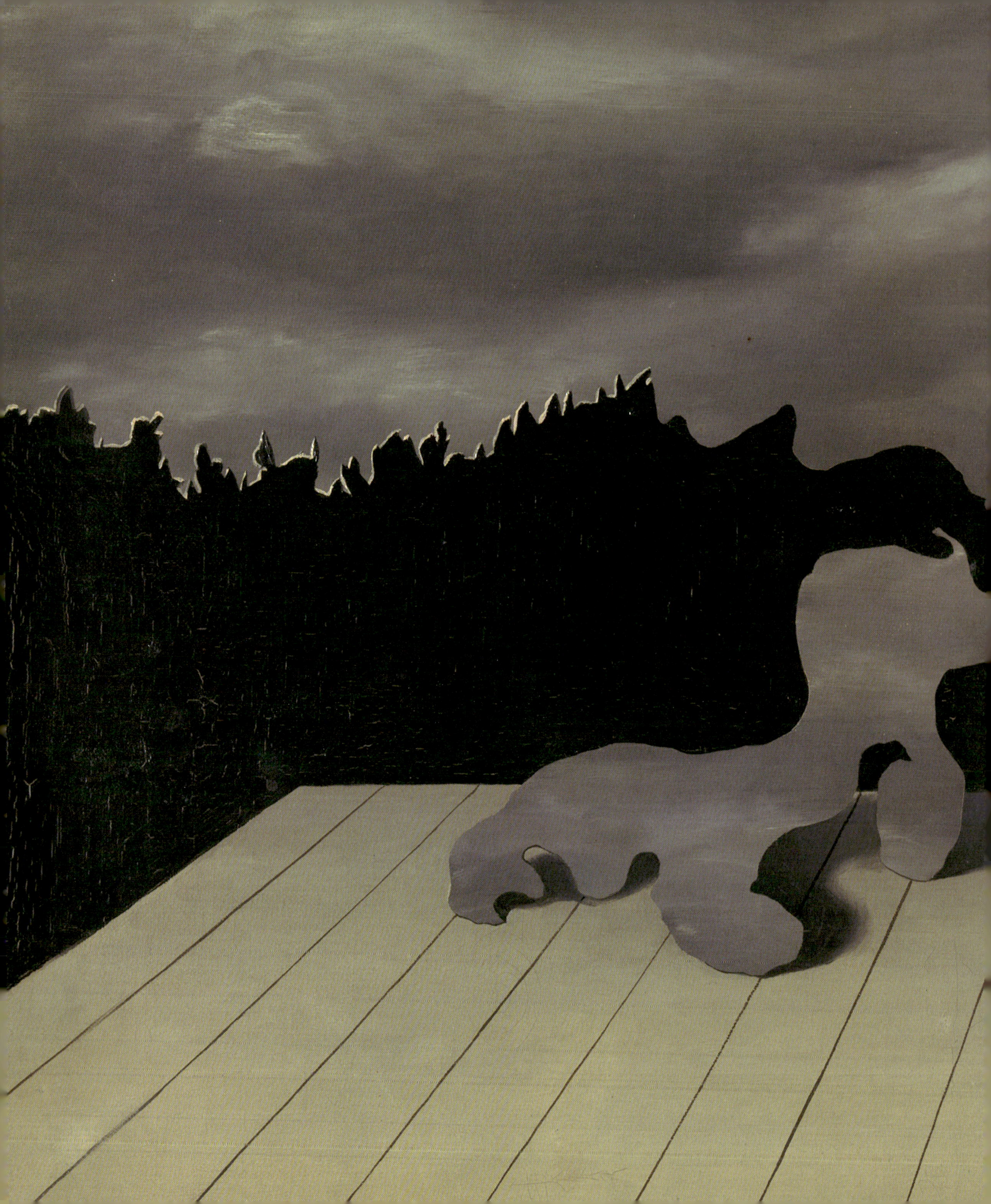

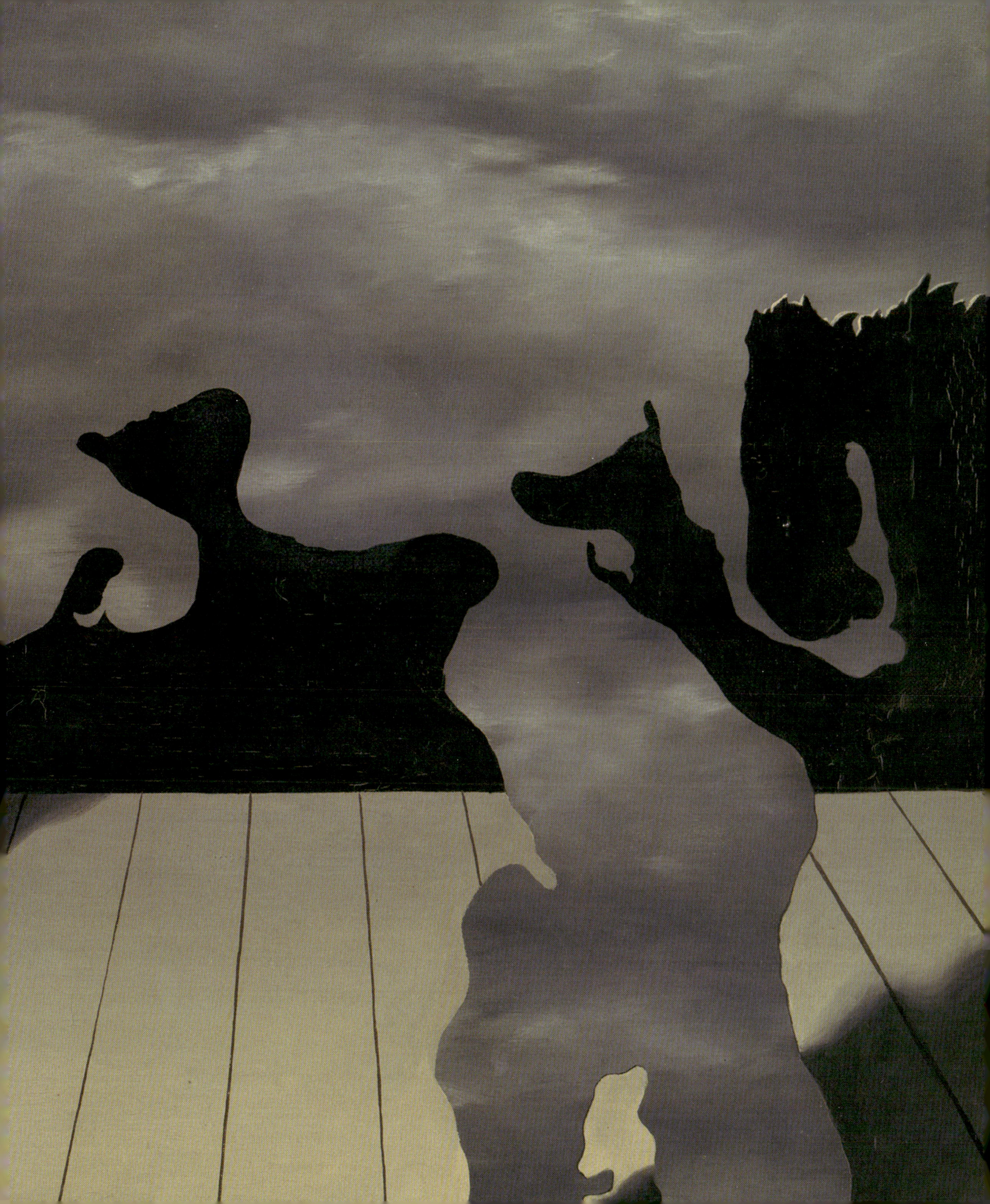

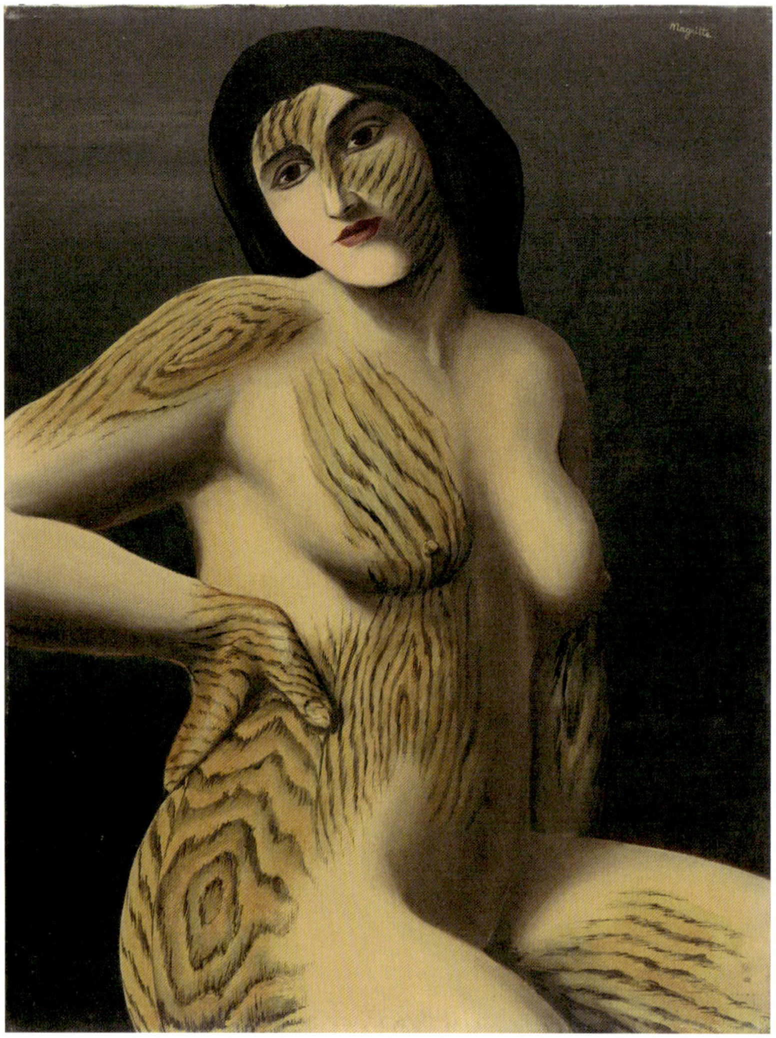

35. DÉCOUVERTE (DISCOVERY). 1927.

Oil on canvas, 25 9/16 x 19 11/16" (65 x 50 cm)

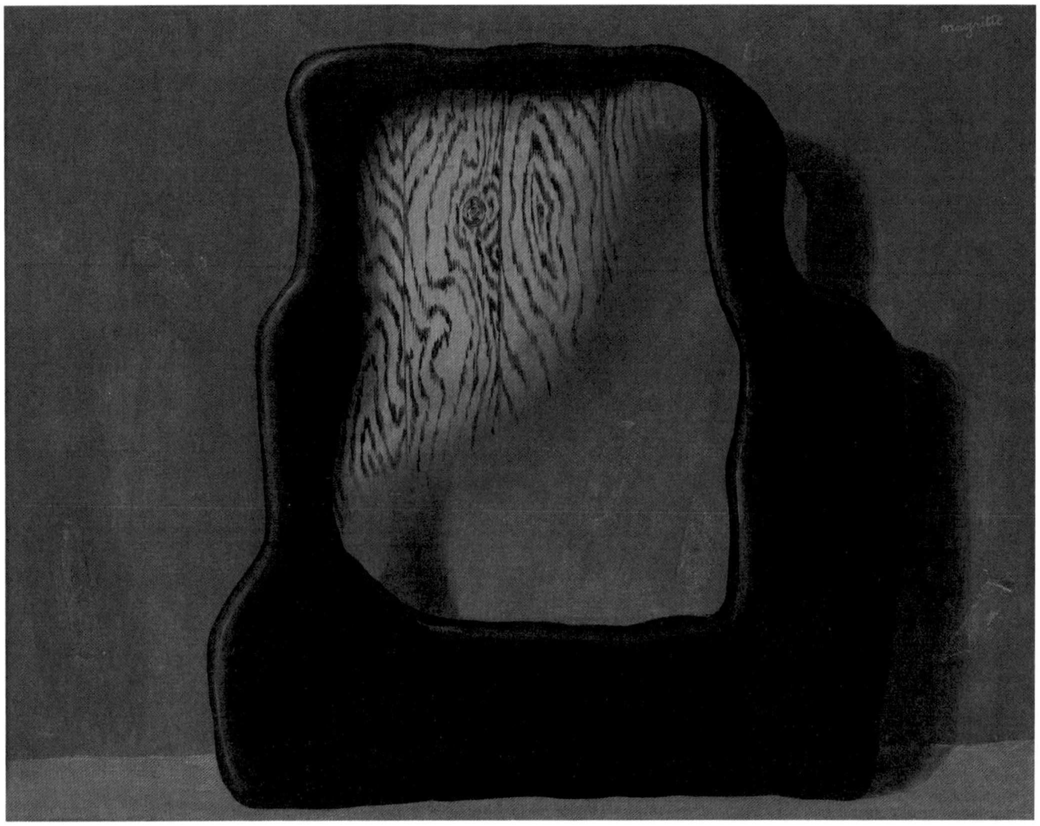

36. LE PRINCE DES OBJETS (THE PRINCE OF OBJECTS). 1927.

Oil on canvas, 19 11/16 x 25 9/16" (50 x 65 cm)

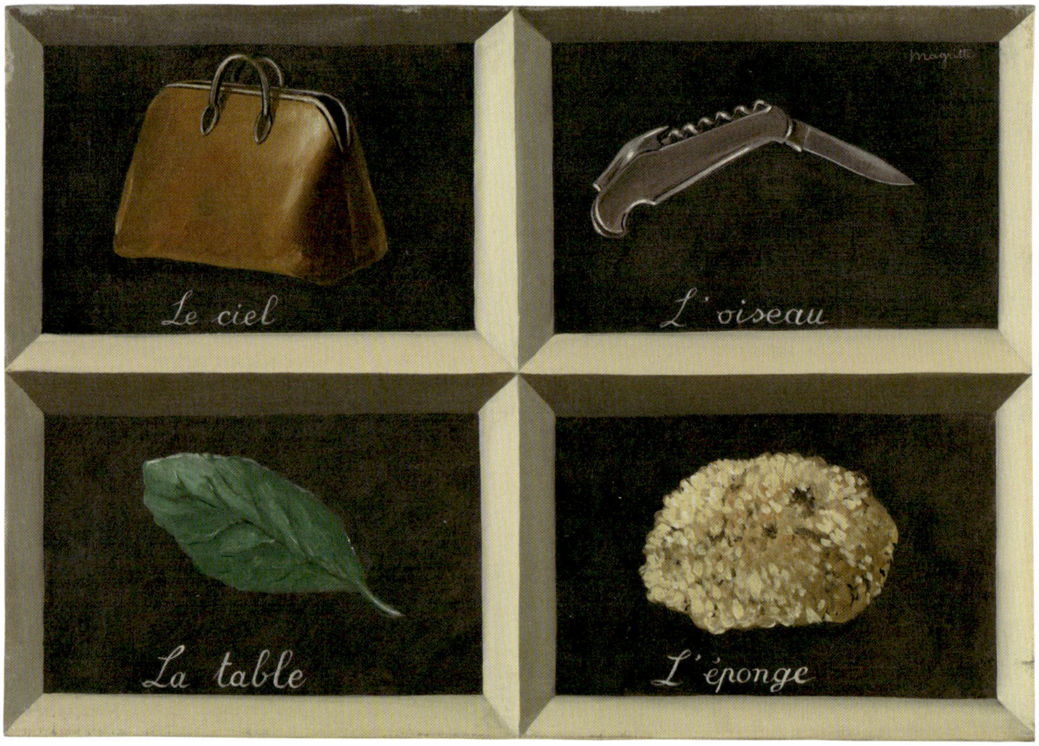

37. LA CLEF DES SONGES (THE INTERPRETATION OF DREAMS). 1927.

Oil on canvas, $14\,^{15}/_{16}$ x $21\,^{5}/_{8}$" (38 x 55 cm)

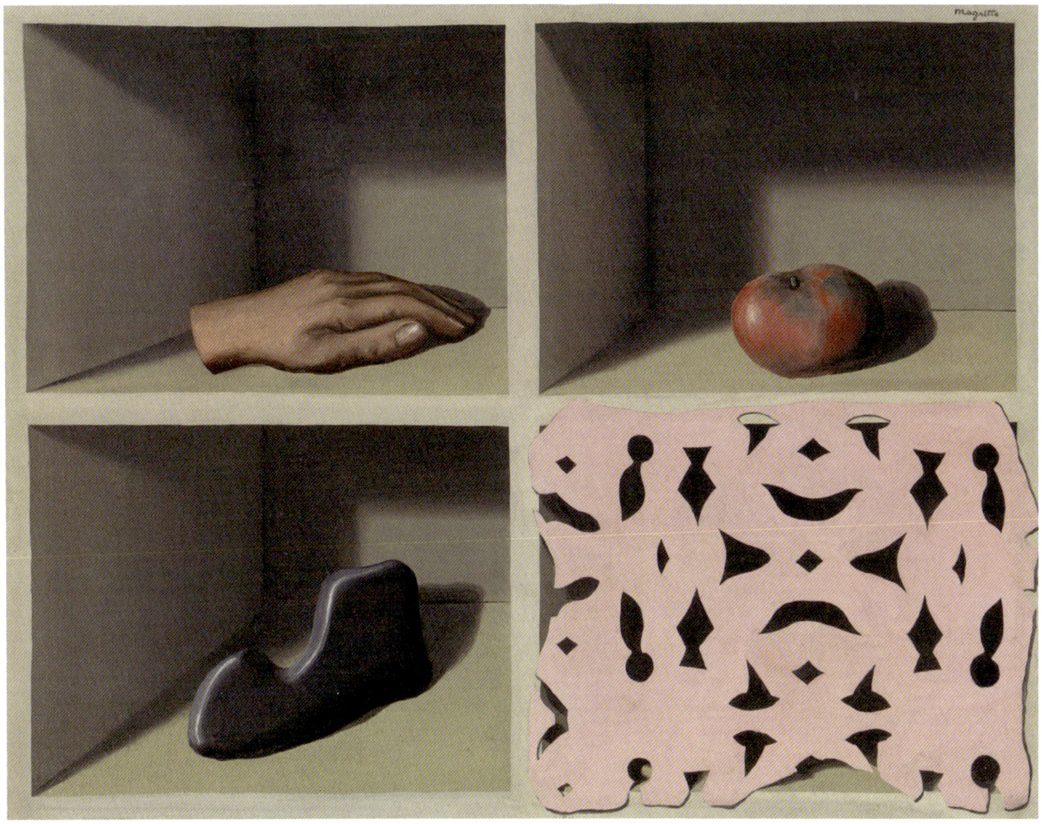

38. LE MUSÉE D'UNE NUIT (ONE-NIGHT MUSEUM). 1927.

Oil on canvas, 19 11/16 x 25 9/16" (50 x 65 cm)

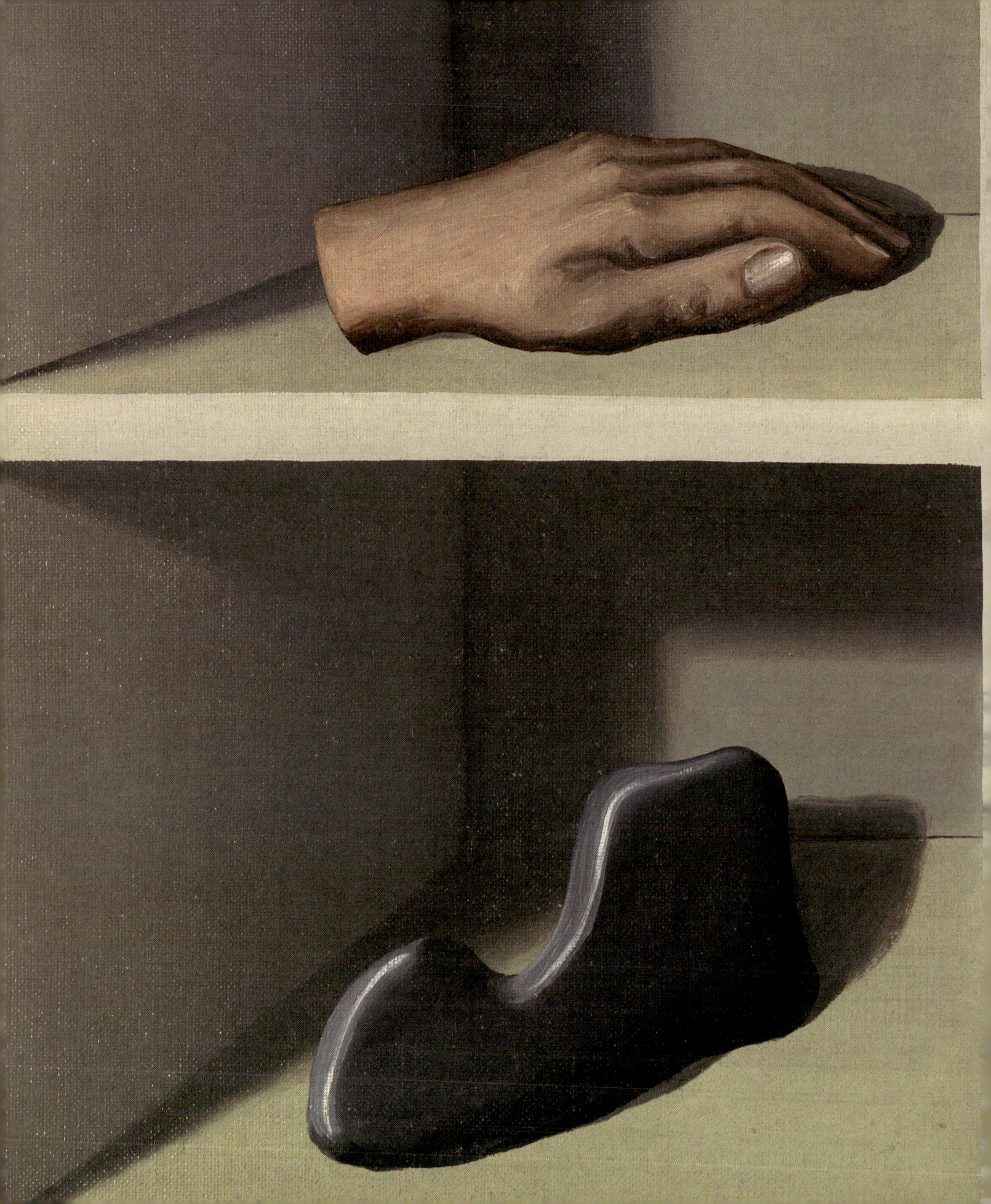

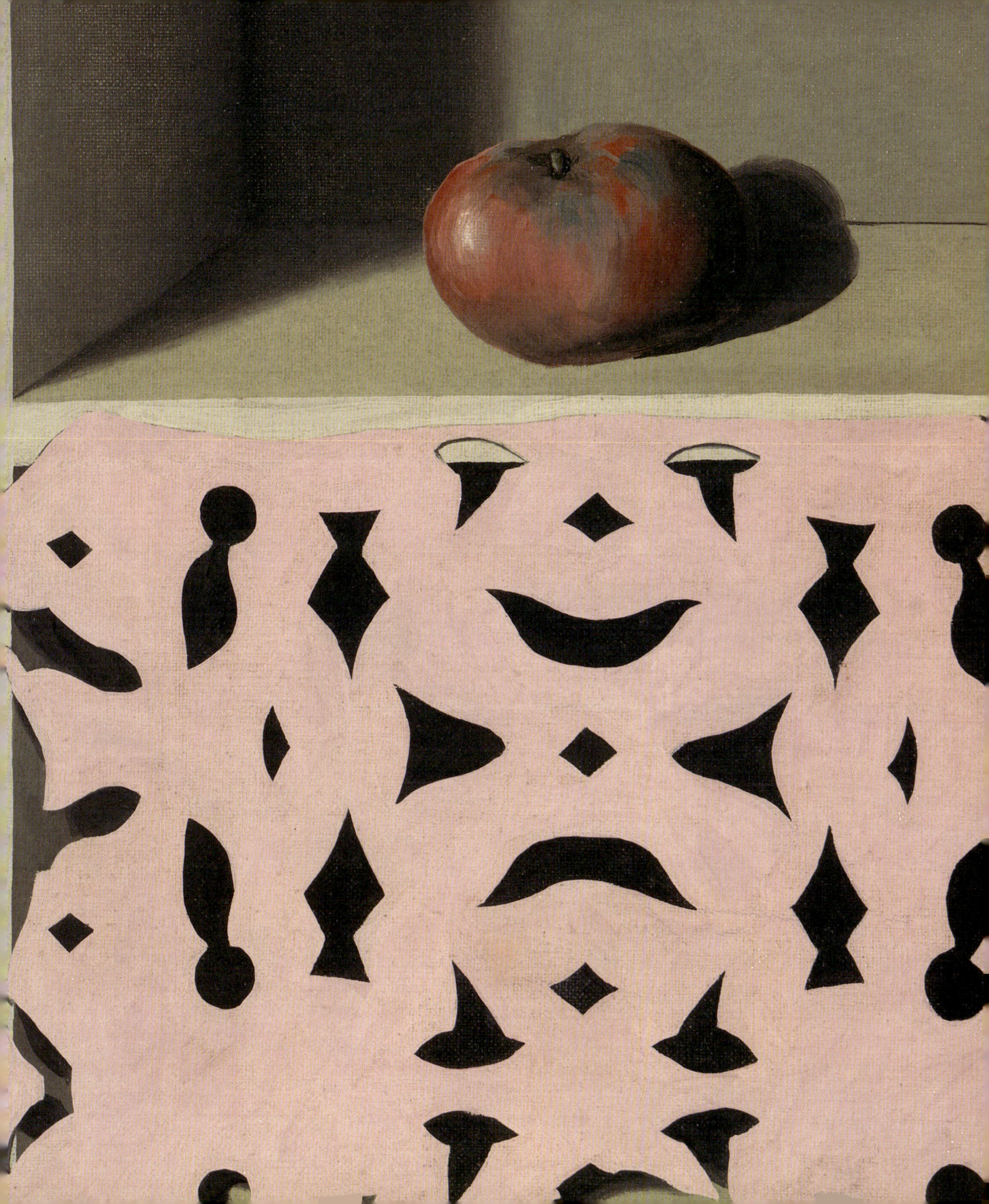

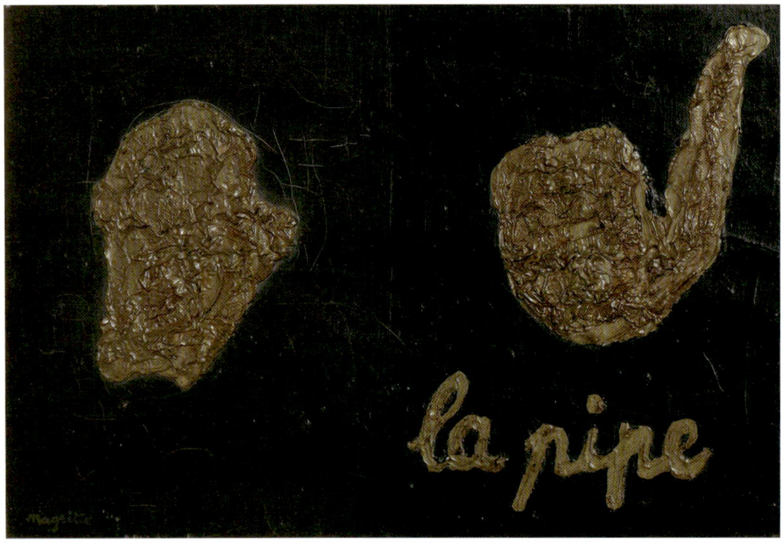

39. [BIOMORPHS WITH WORDS]. 1928.

Oil on canvas, 10 5/8 x 16 1/8" (27 x 41 cm)

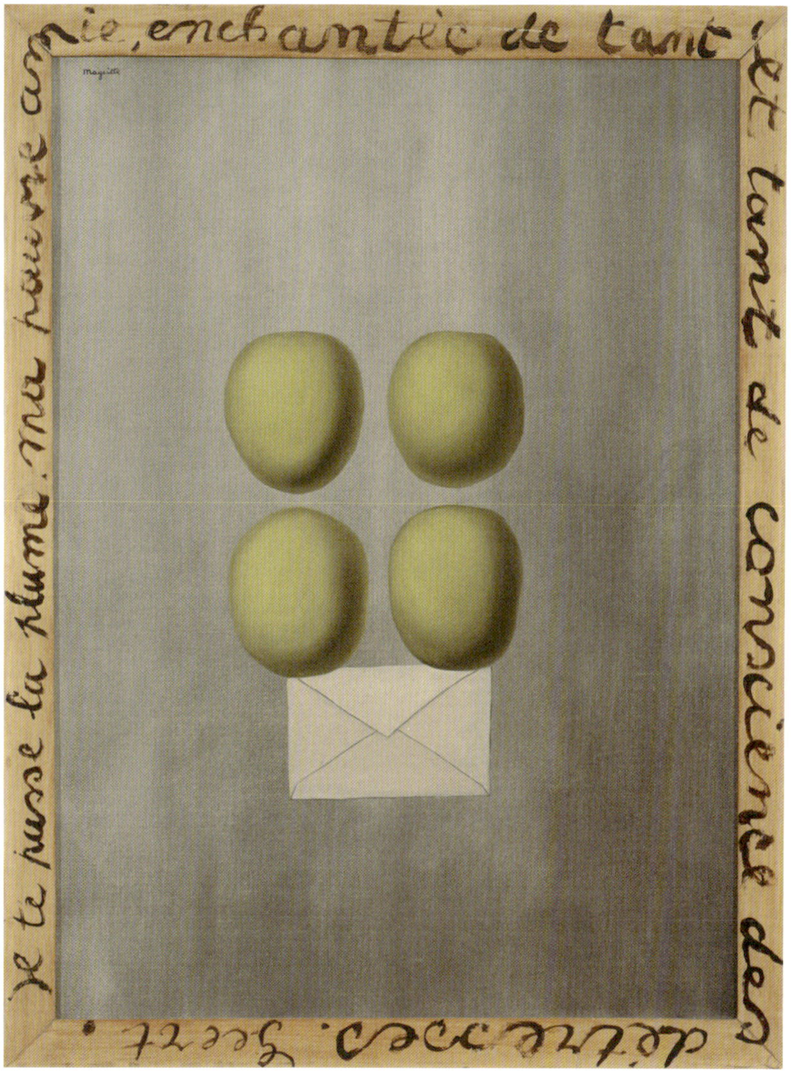

40. LA BONNE NOUVELLE (THE GOOD NEWS). 1928.

Oil on canvas, 28 3/4 x 21 1/4" (73 x 54 cm)

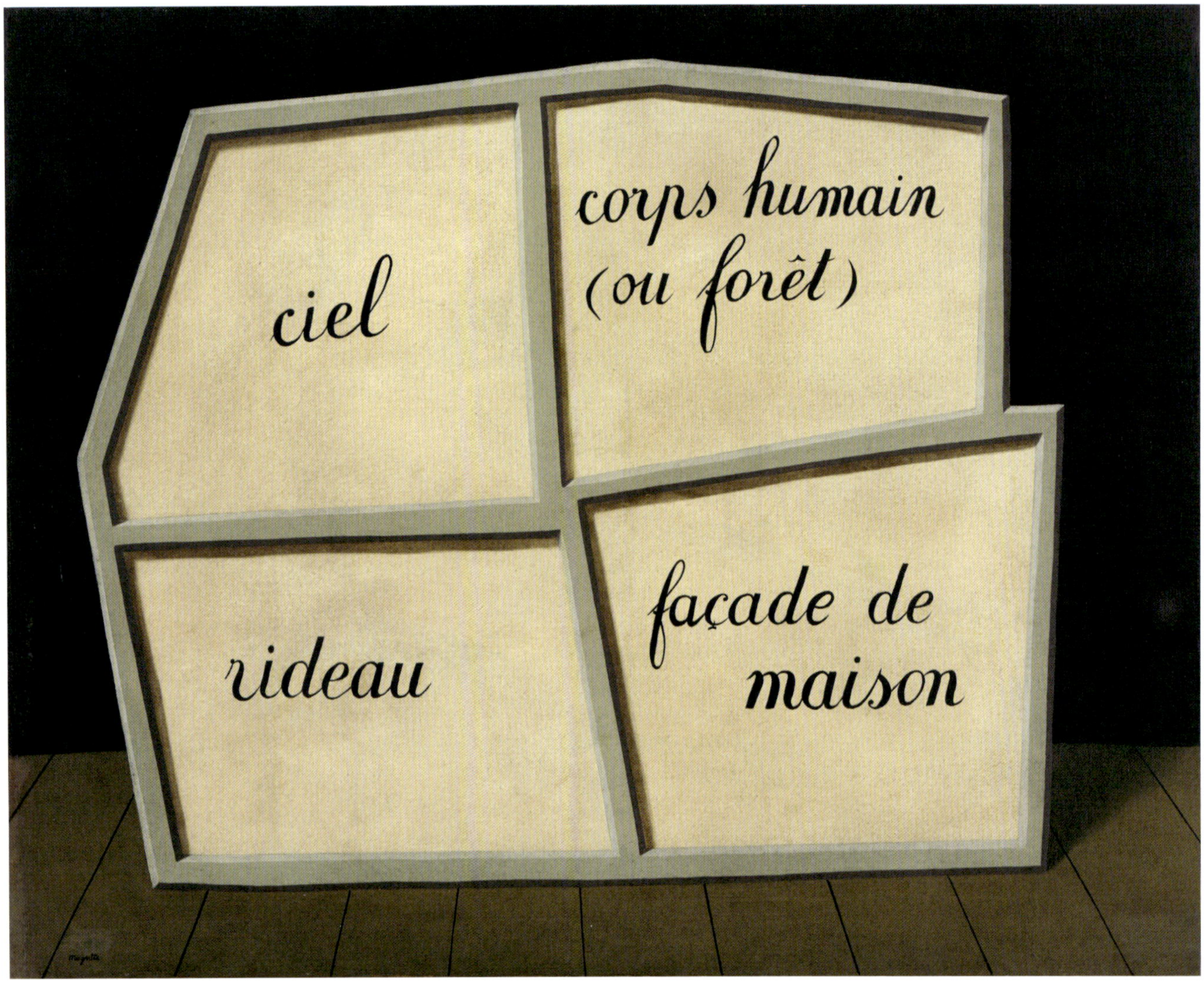

41. LE MASQUE VIDE (THE EMPTY MASK). 1928.
Oil on canvas, 28 ¾ x 36 ¼" (73 x 92 cm)

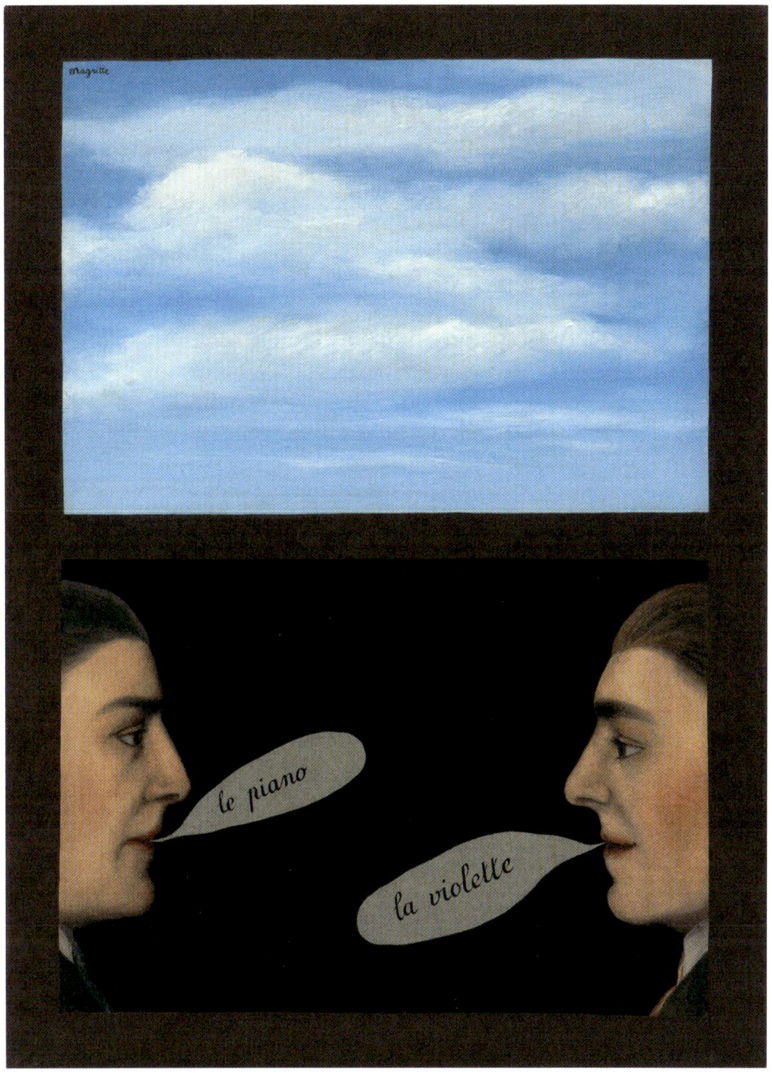

42. L'USAGE DE LA PAROLE (THE USE OF SPEECH). 1928.

Oil on canvas, 28 3/4 x 21 1/4" (73 x 54 cm)

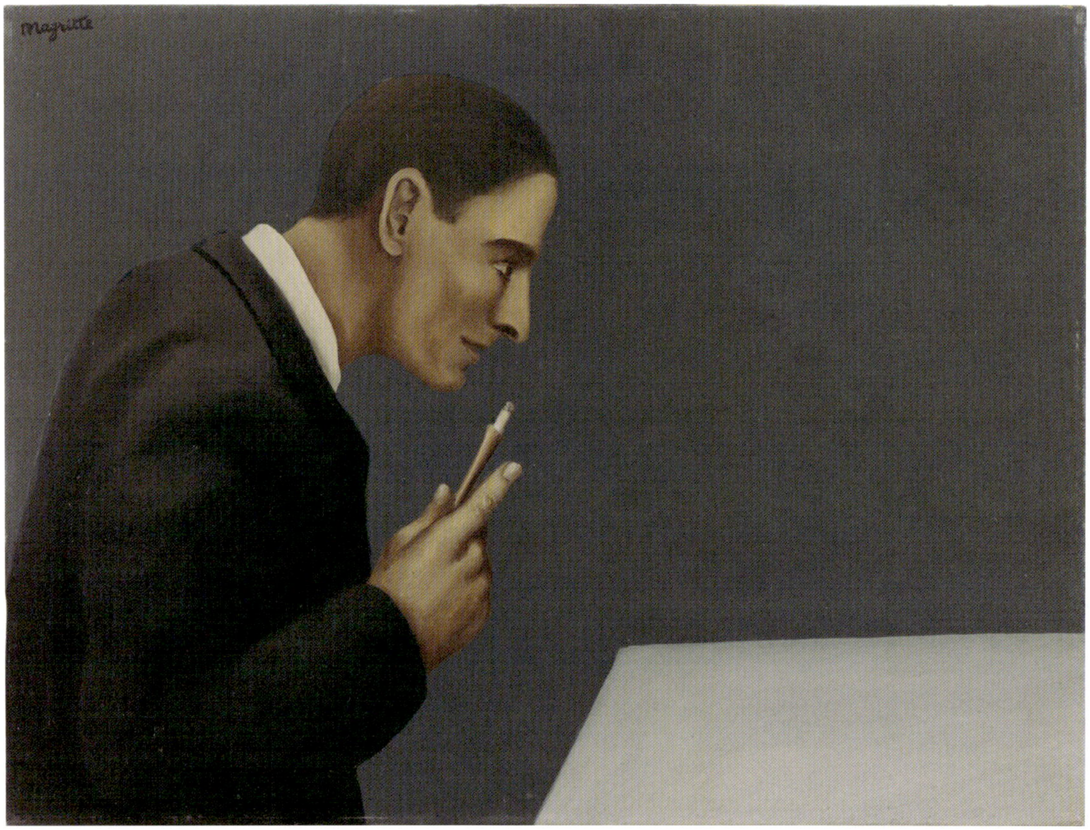

43. PERSONNAGE MÉDITANT SUR LA FOLIE (FIGURE BROODING ON MADNESS). 1928.

Oil on canvas, 21¼ x 28¾" (54 x 73 cm)

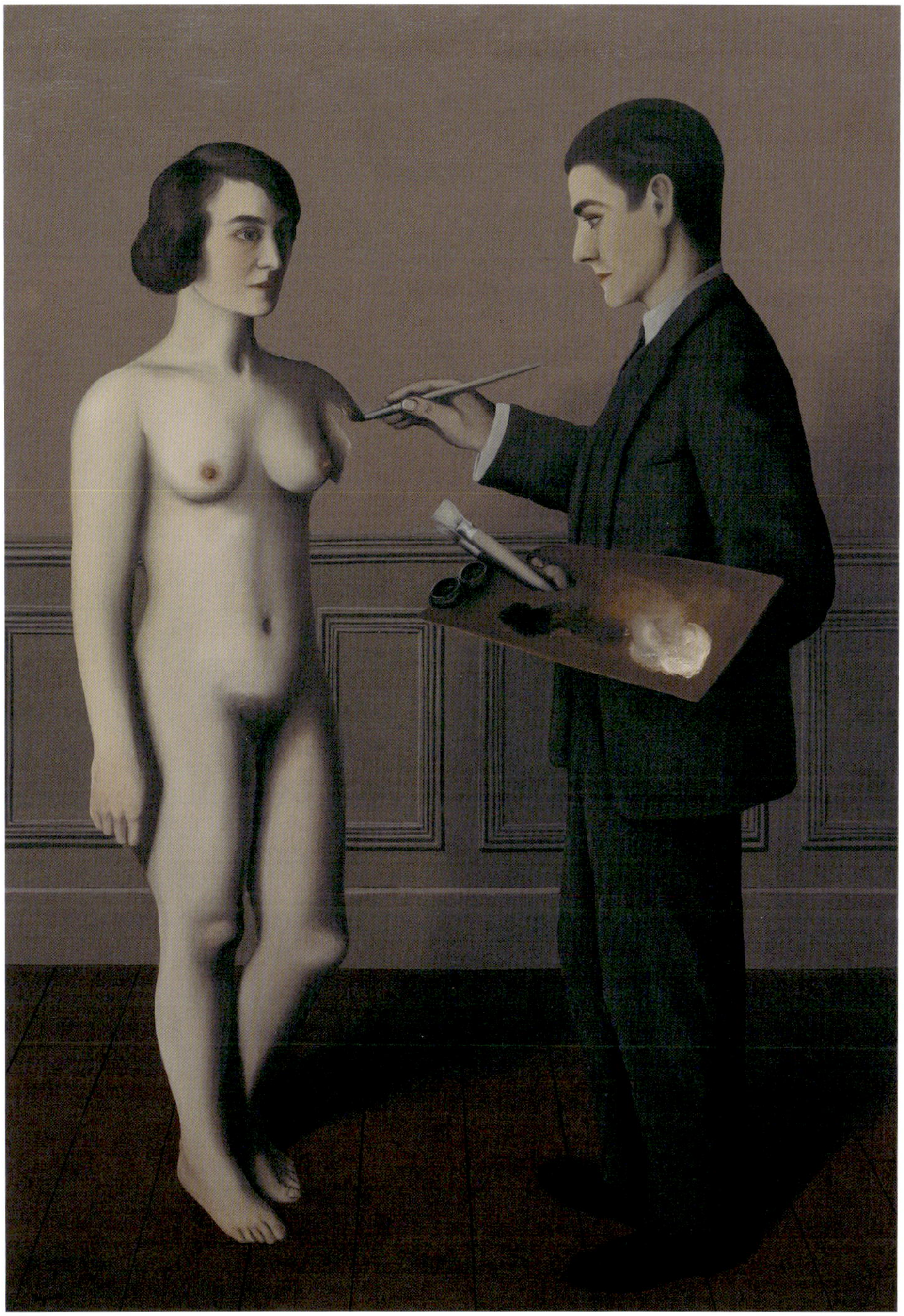

44. TENTATIVE DE L'IMPOSSIBLE (ATTEMPTING THE IMPOSSIBLE). 1928.
Oil on canvas, 45 11/16 x 31 7/8" (116 x 81 cm)

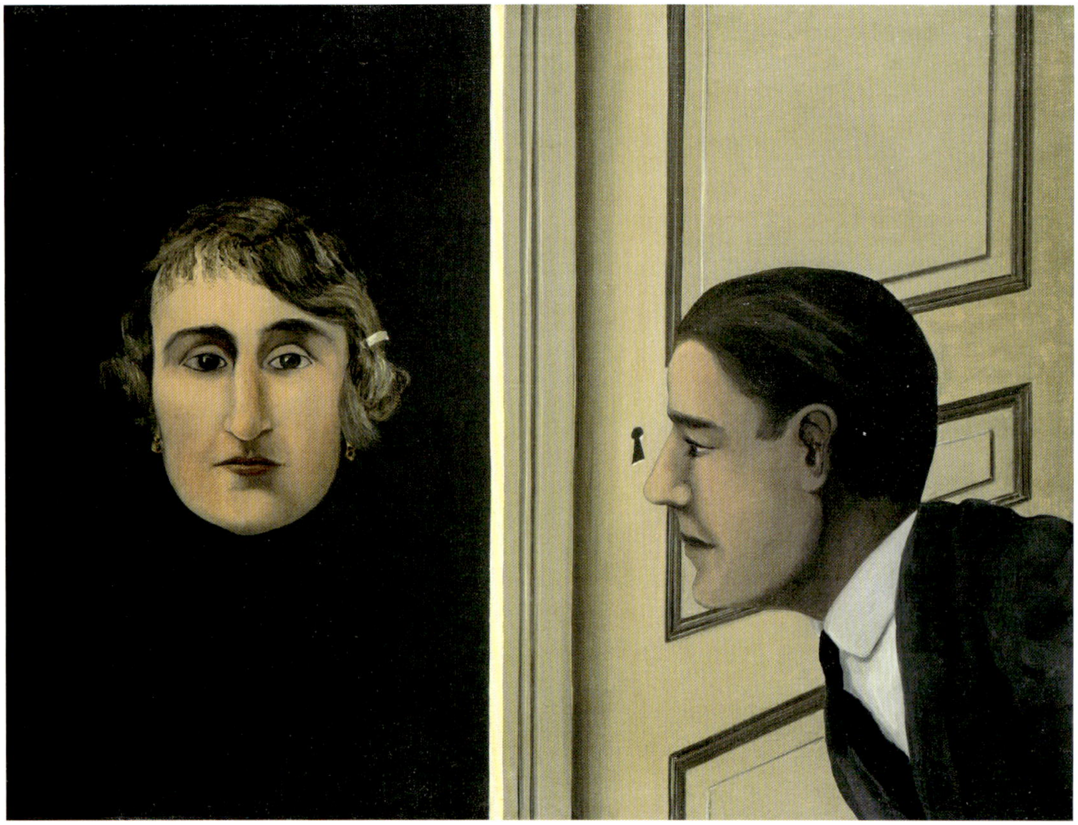

45. L'ESPION (THE SPY). 1928.

Oil on canvas, 21 1/4 x 28 3/4" (54 x 73 cm)

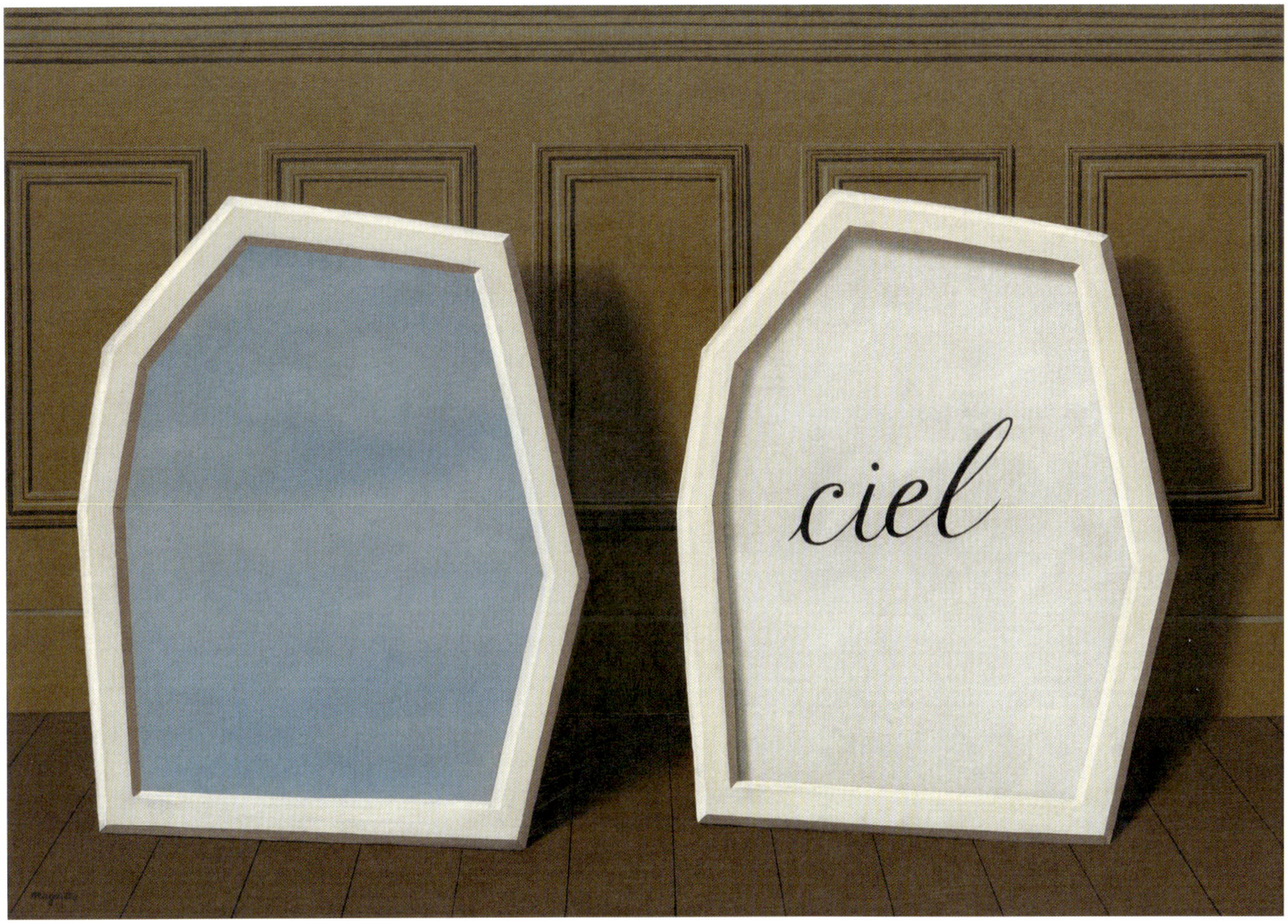

46. LE PALAIS DE RIDEAUX (III) (THE PALACE OF CURTAINS [III]). 1929.

Oil on canvas, 32 x 45 7/8" (81.2 x 116.4 cm)

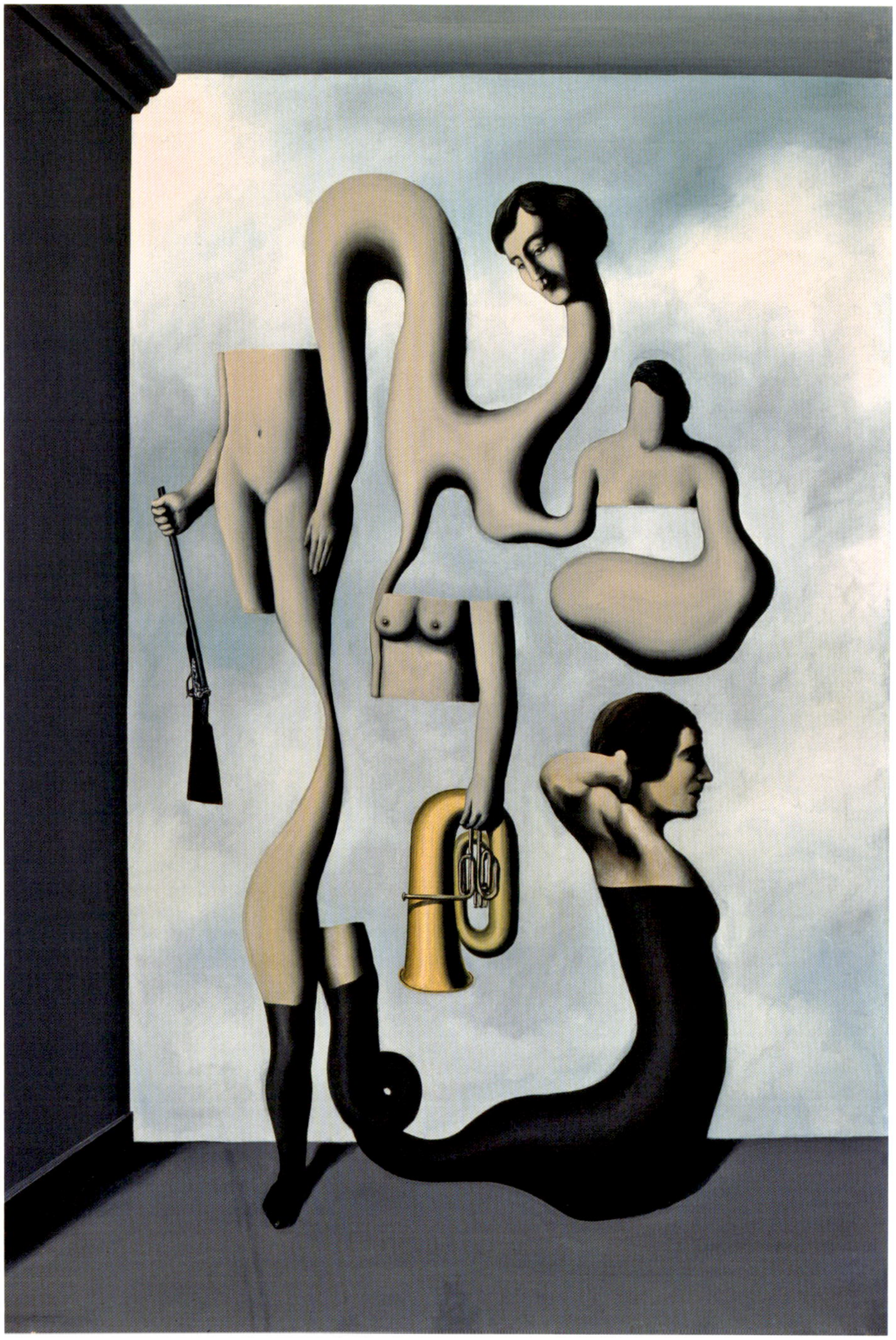

47. LES IDÉES DE L'ACROBATE (THE ACROBAT'S IDEAS). 1928.

Oil on canvas, $45\,^{11}/_{16} \times 31\,^{7}/_{8}$" (116 x 81 cm)

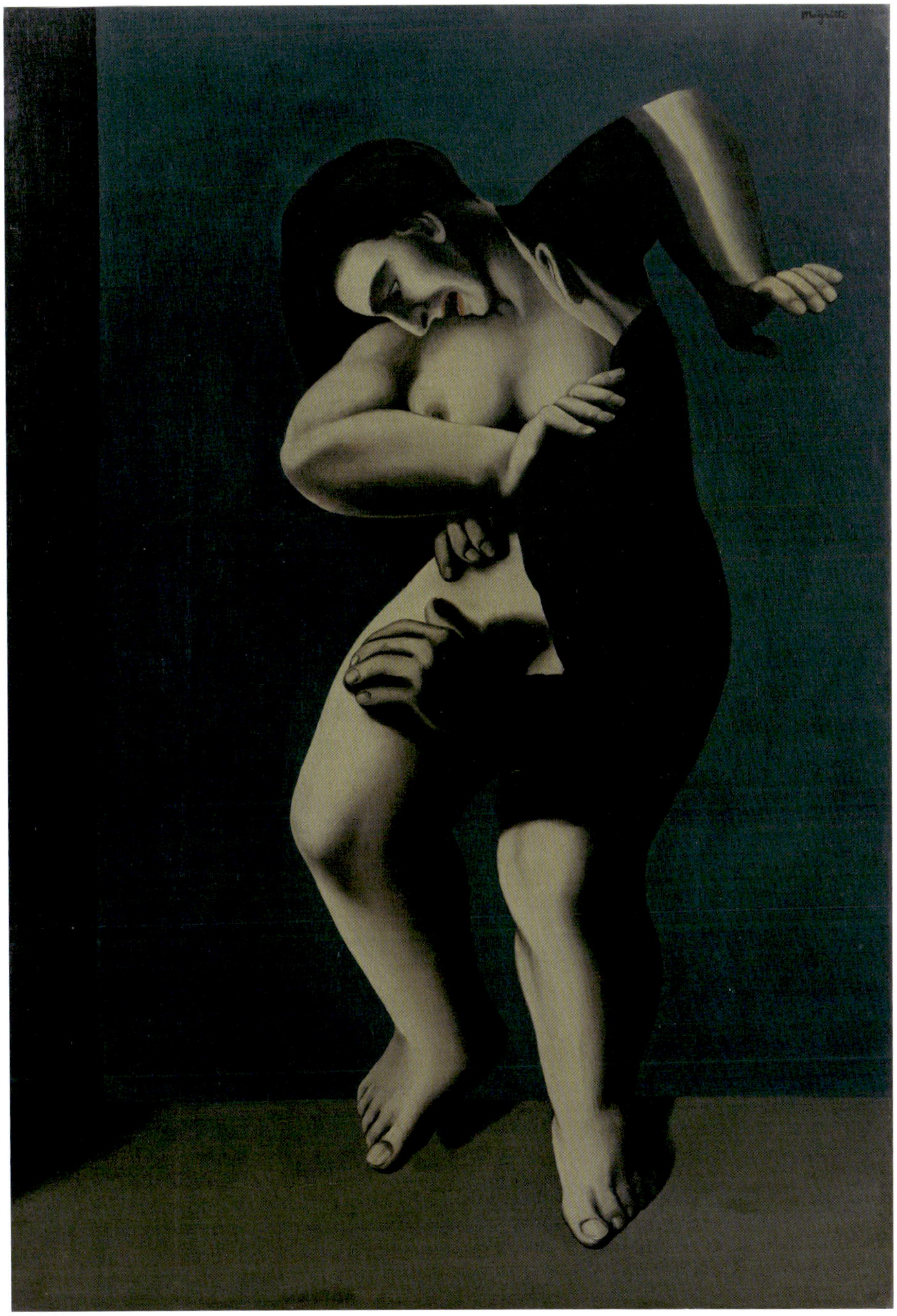

48. **LES JOURS GIGANTESQUES (THE TITANIC DAYS).** 1928.

Oil on canvas, 45 11/16 x 31 7/8" (116 x 81 cm)

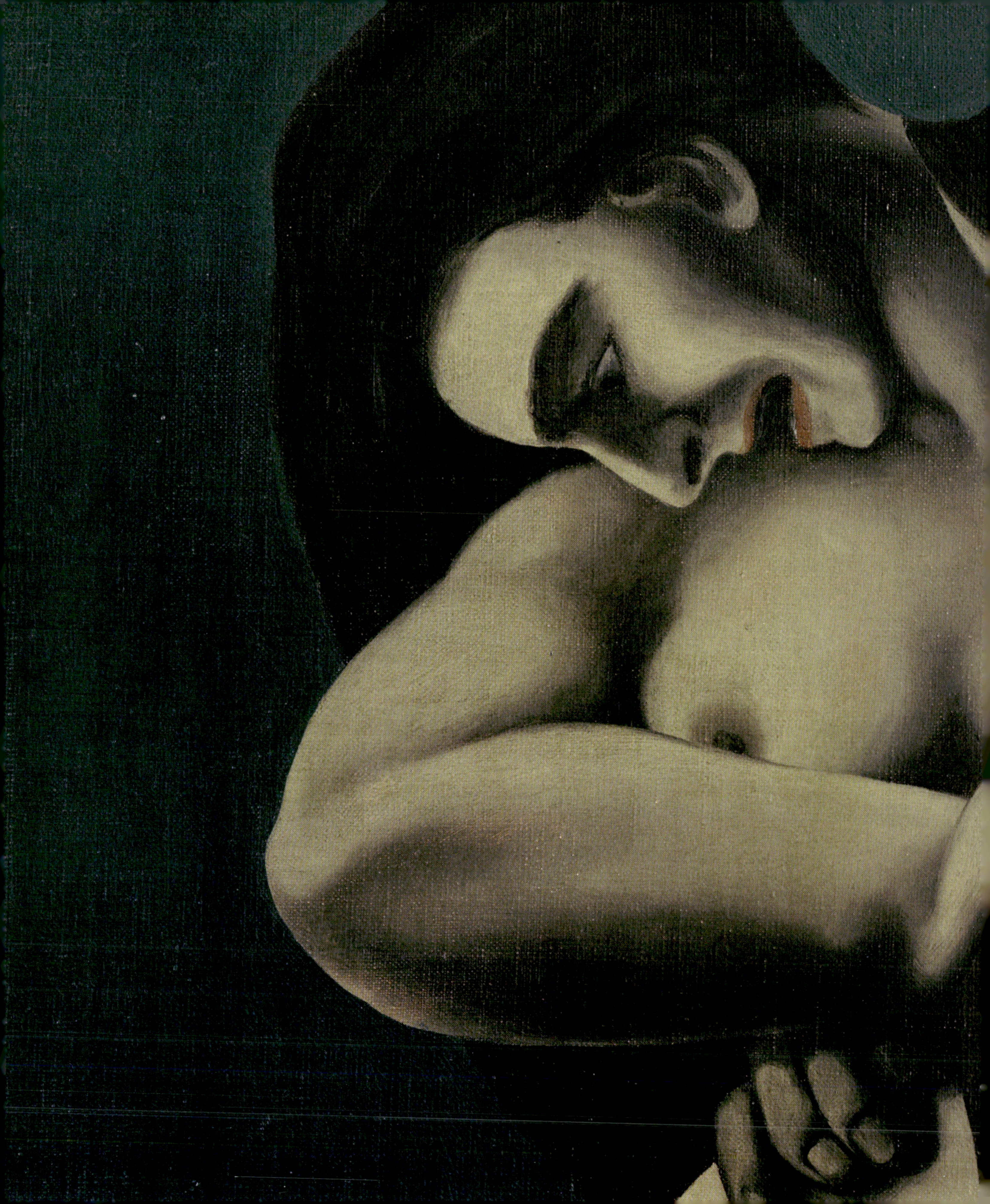

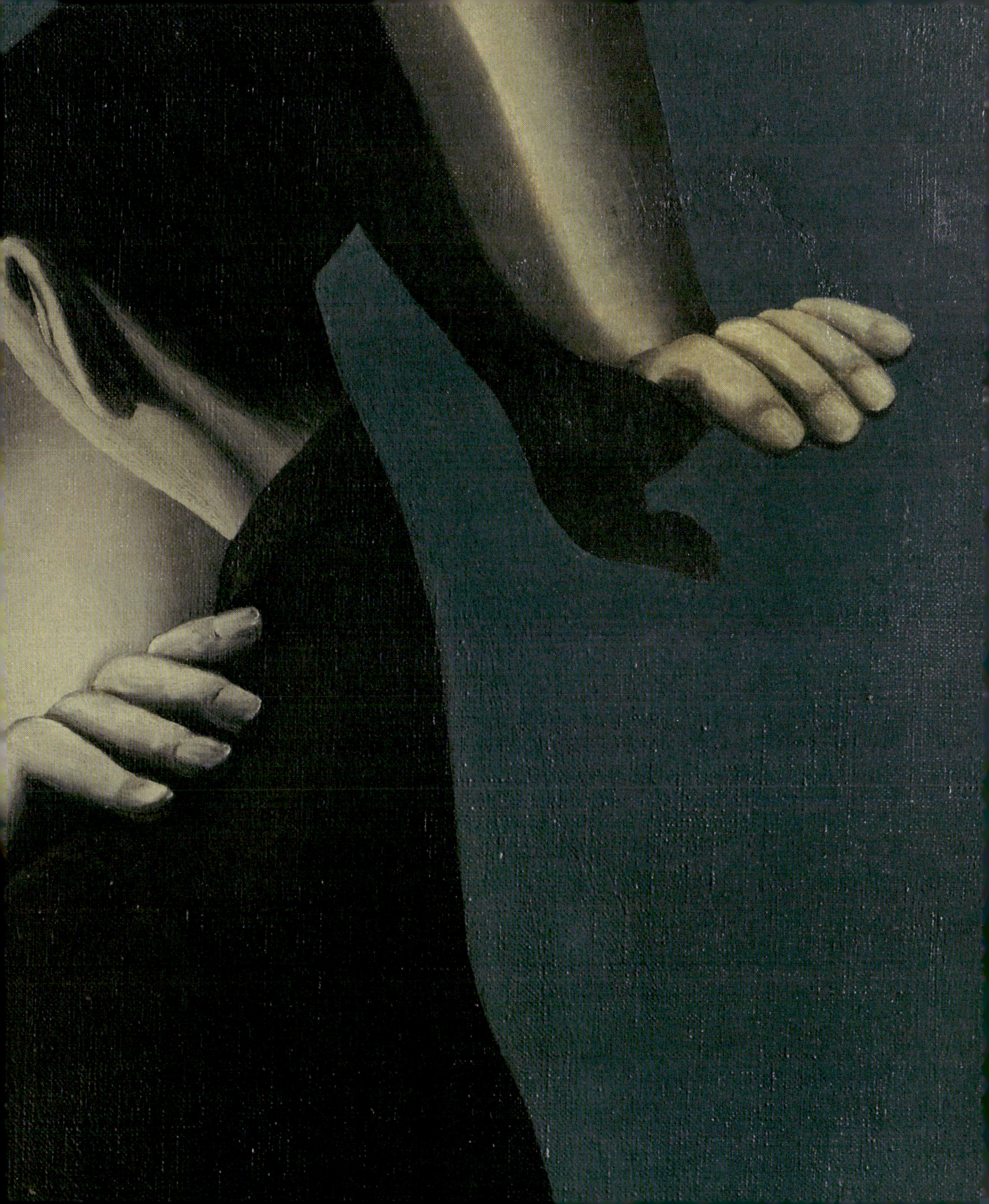

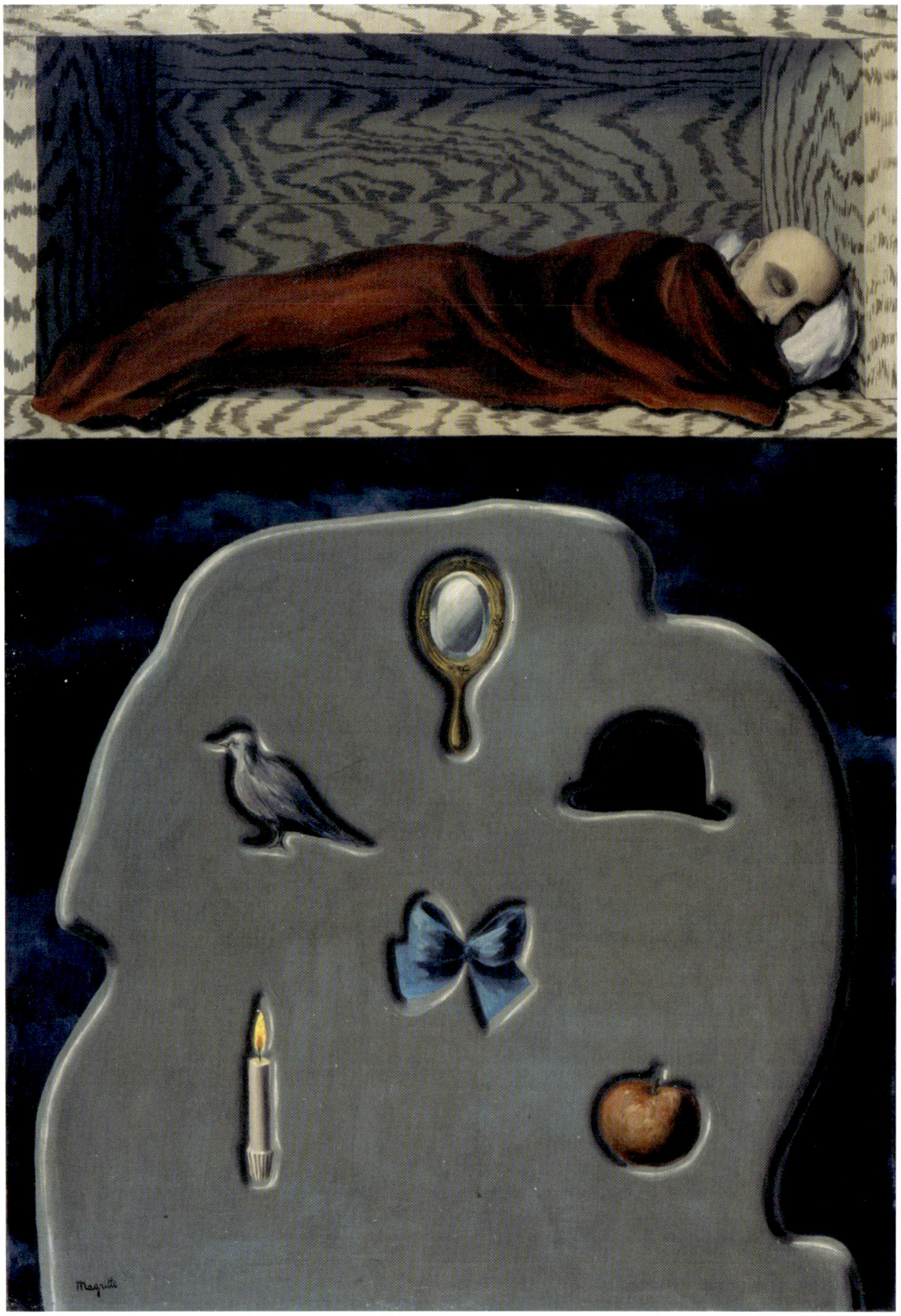

49. LE DORMEUR TÉMÉRAIRE (THE DARING SLEEPER). 1928.

Oil on canvas, 45 11/16 x 31 7/8" (116 x 81 cm)

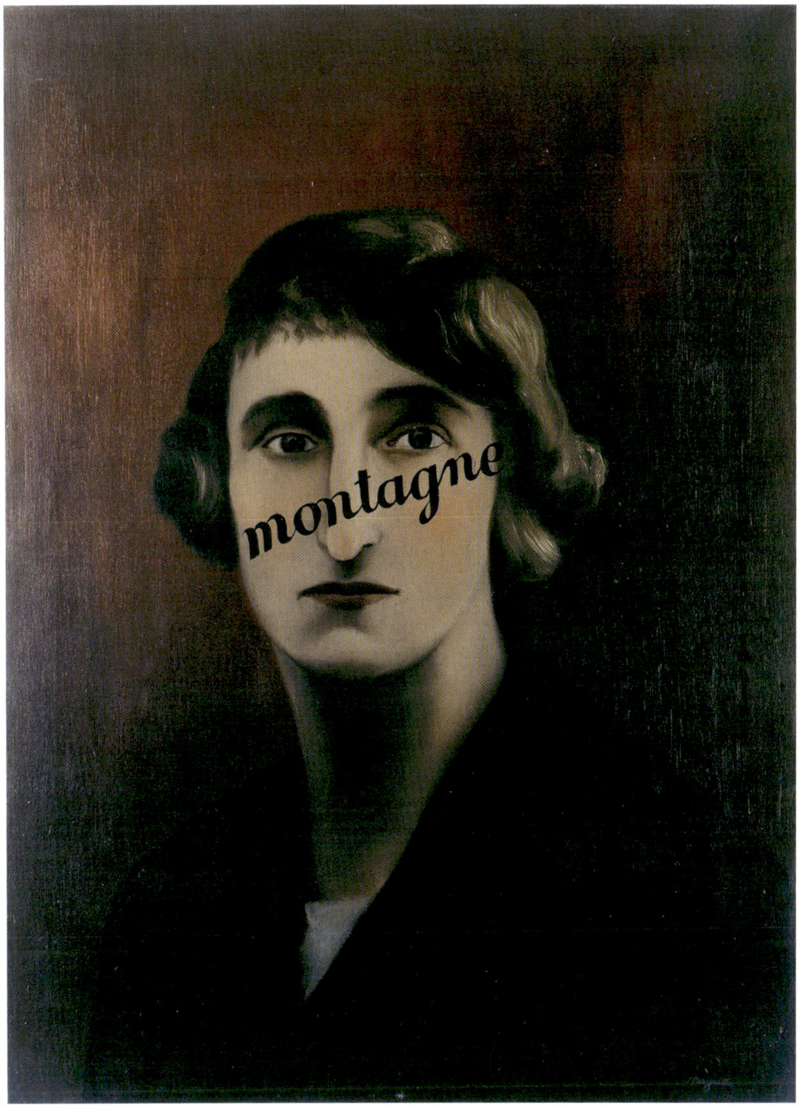

50. LE PAYSAGE FANTÔME (THE PHANTOM LANDSCAPE). 1928.
Oil on canvas, 28 3/4 x 21 1/4" (73 x 54 cm)

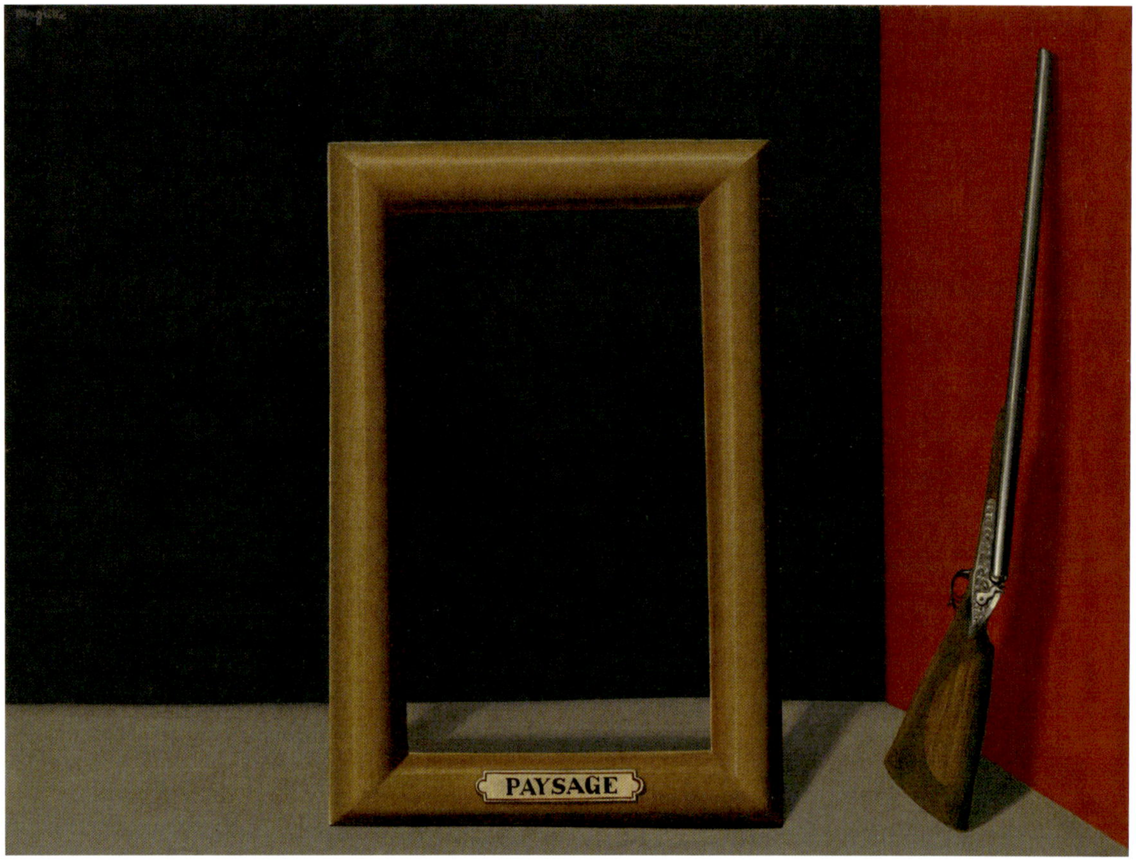

51. LES CHARMES DU PAYSAGE (THE DELIGHTS OF LANDSCAPE). 1928.

Oil on canvas, 21 1/4 x 28 3/4" (54 x 73 cm)

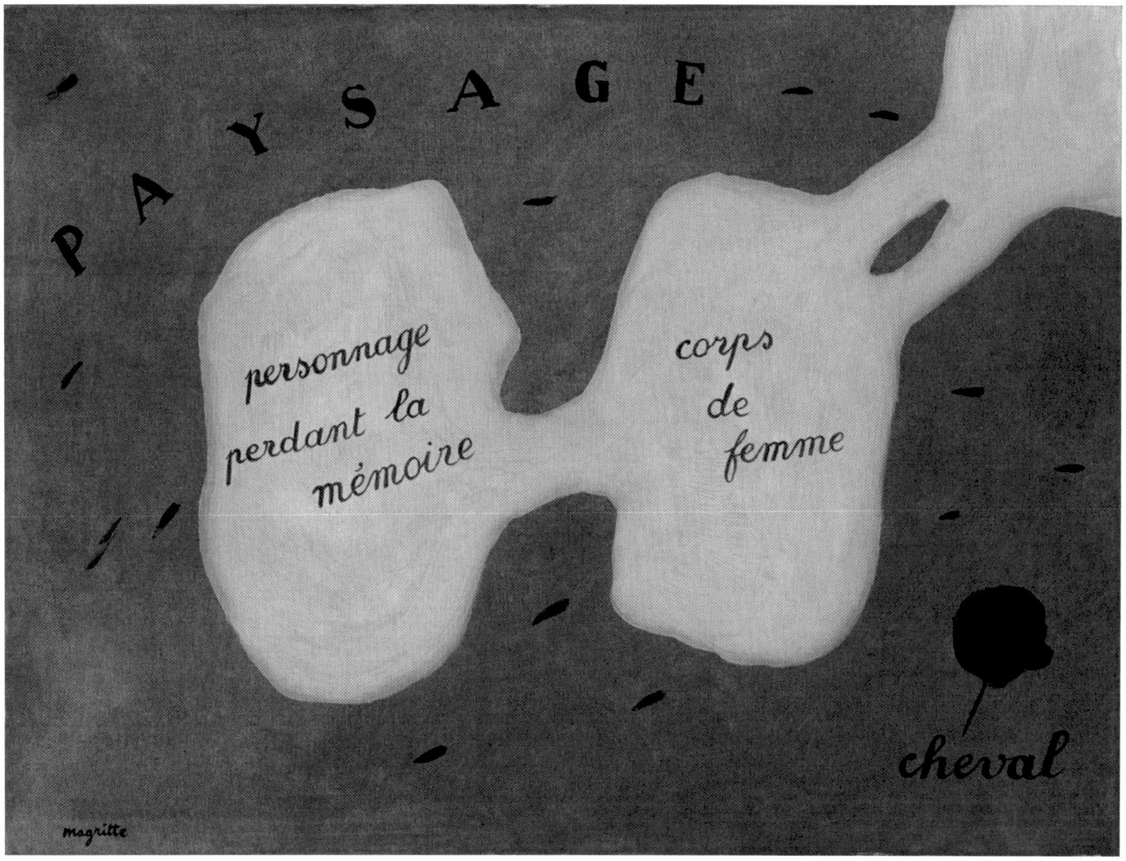

52. LE MONDE PERDU (THE LOST WORLD). 1928.

Oil on canvas, 21 1/4 x 28 3/4" (54 x 73 cm)

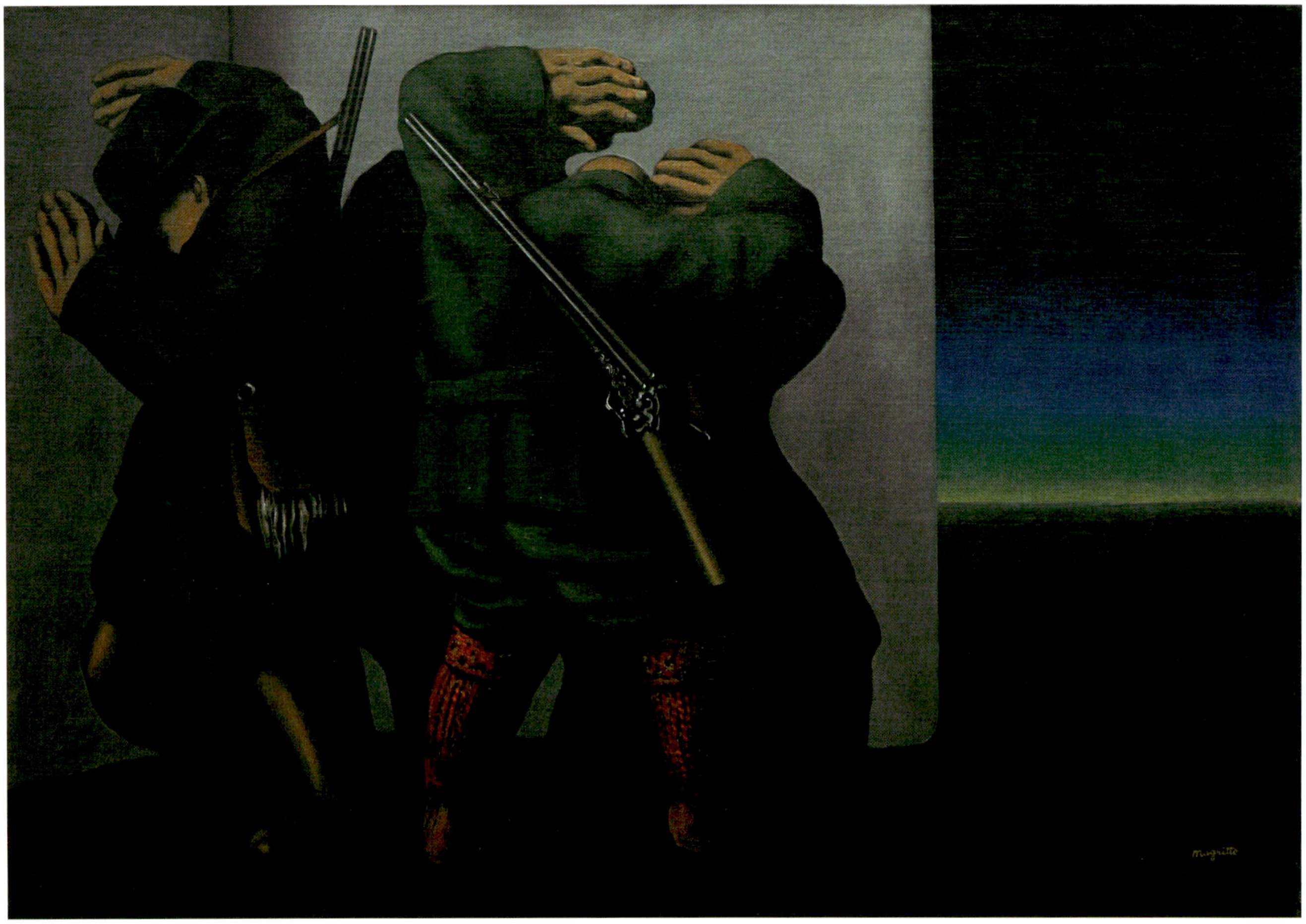

53. LES CHASSEURS AU BORD DE LA NUIT (THE HUNTERS AT THE EDGE OF NIGHT). 1928.

Oil on canvas, $31\frac{7}{8} \times 45\frac{11}{16}$" (81 x 116 cm)

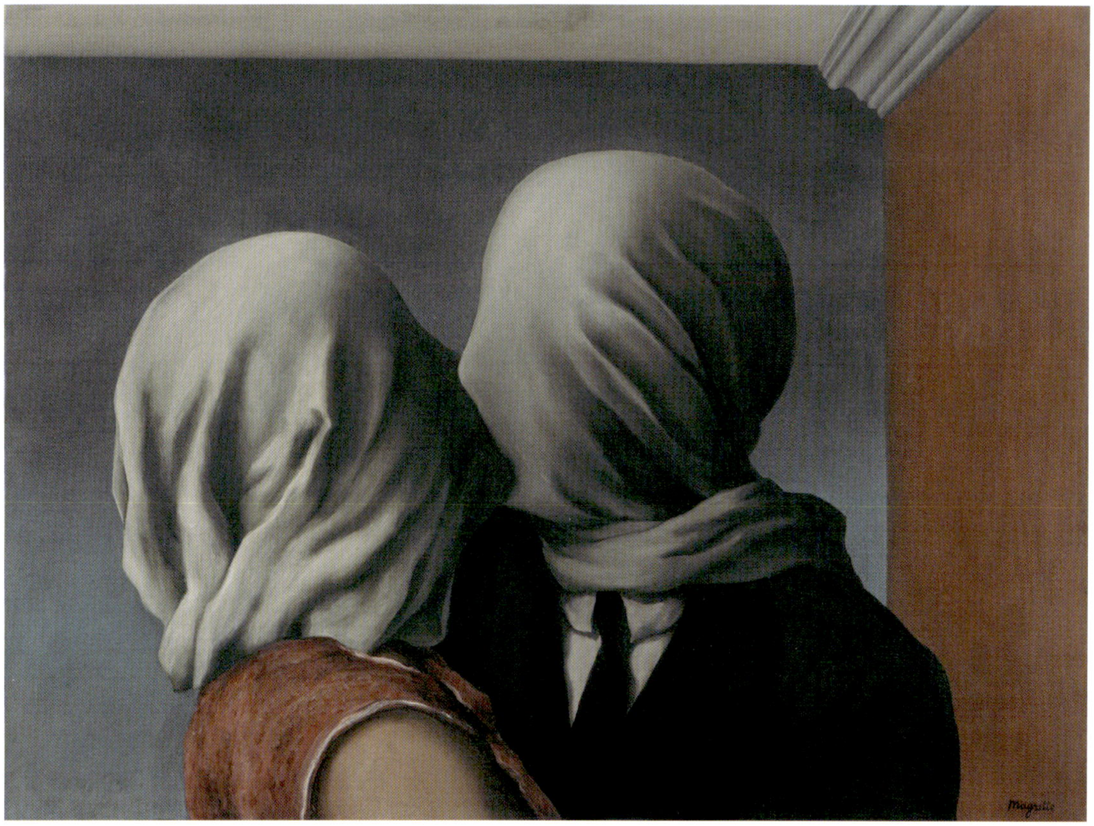

54. LES AMANTS (THE LOVERS). 1928.
Oil on canvas, 21 3/8 x 28 7/8" (54 x 73.4 cm)

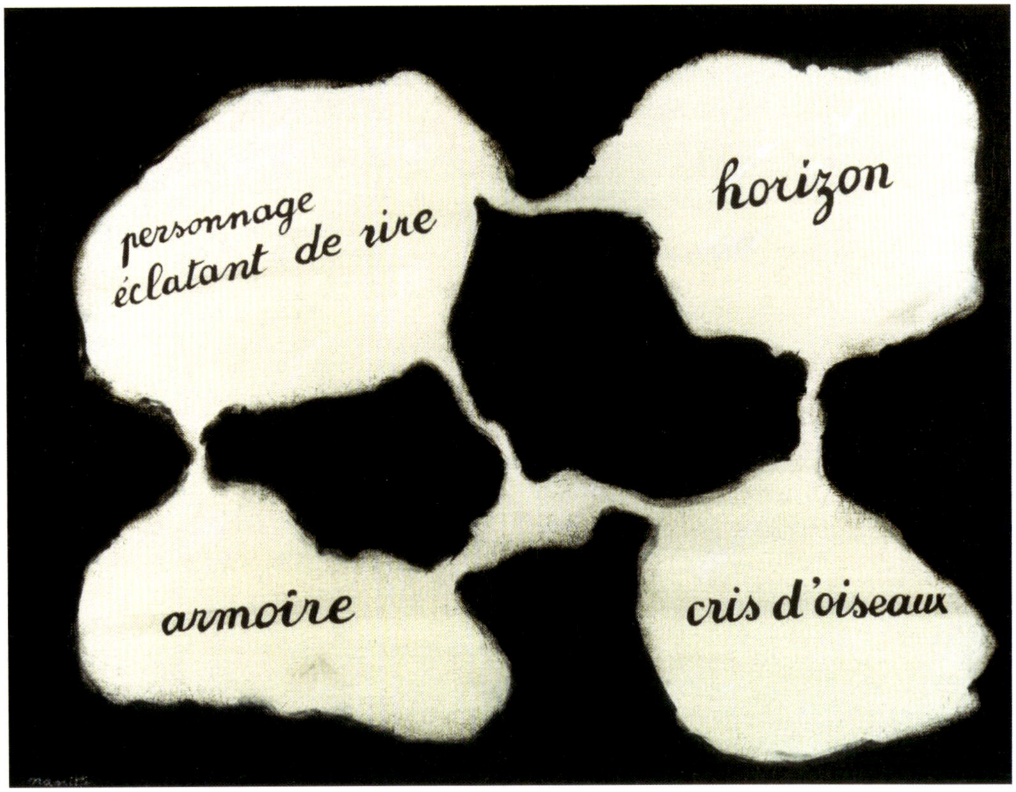

55. LE MIROIR VIVANT (THE LIVING MIRROR). 1928.

Oil on canvas, 21 1/4 x 28 3/4" (54 x 73 cm)

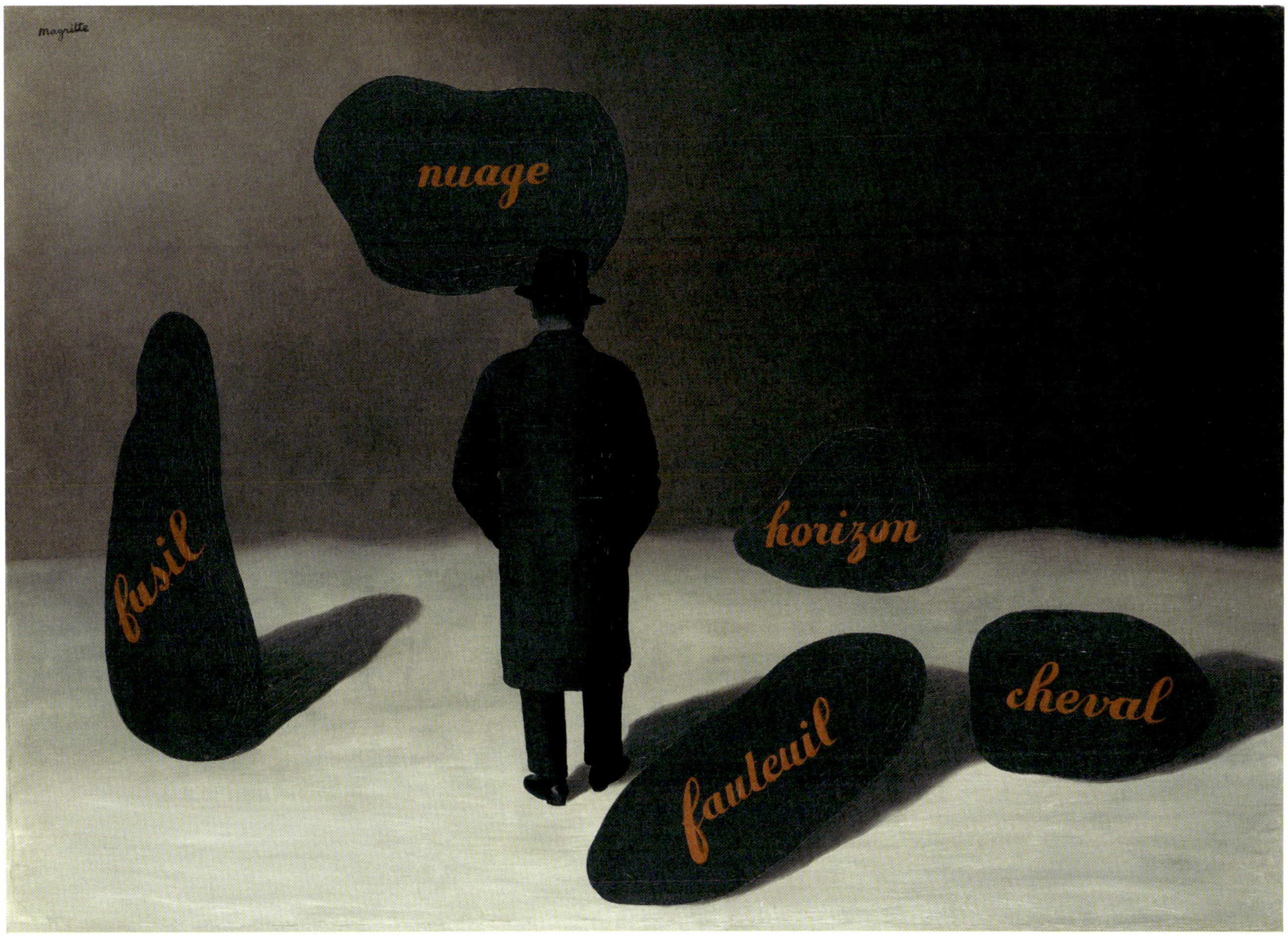

56. L'APPARITION (THE APPARITION). 1928.

Oil on canvas, $31\frac{7}{8}$ x $45\frac{11}{16}$" (81 x 116 cm)

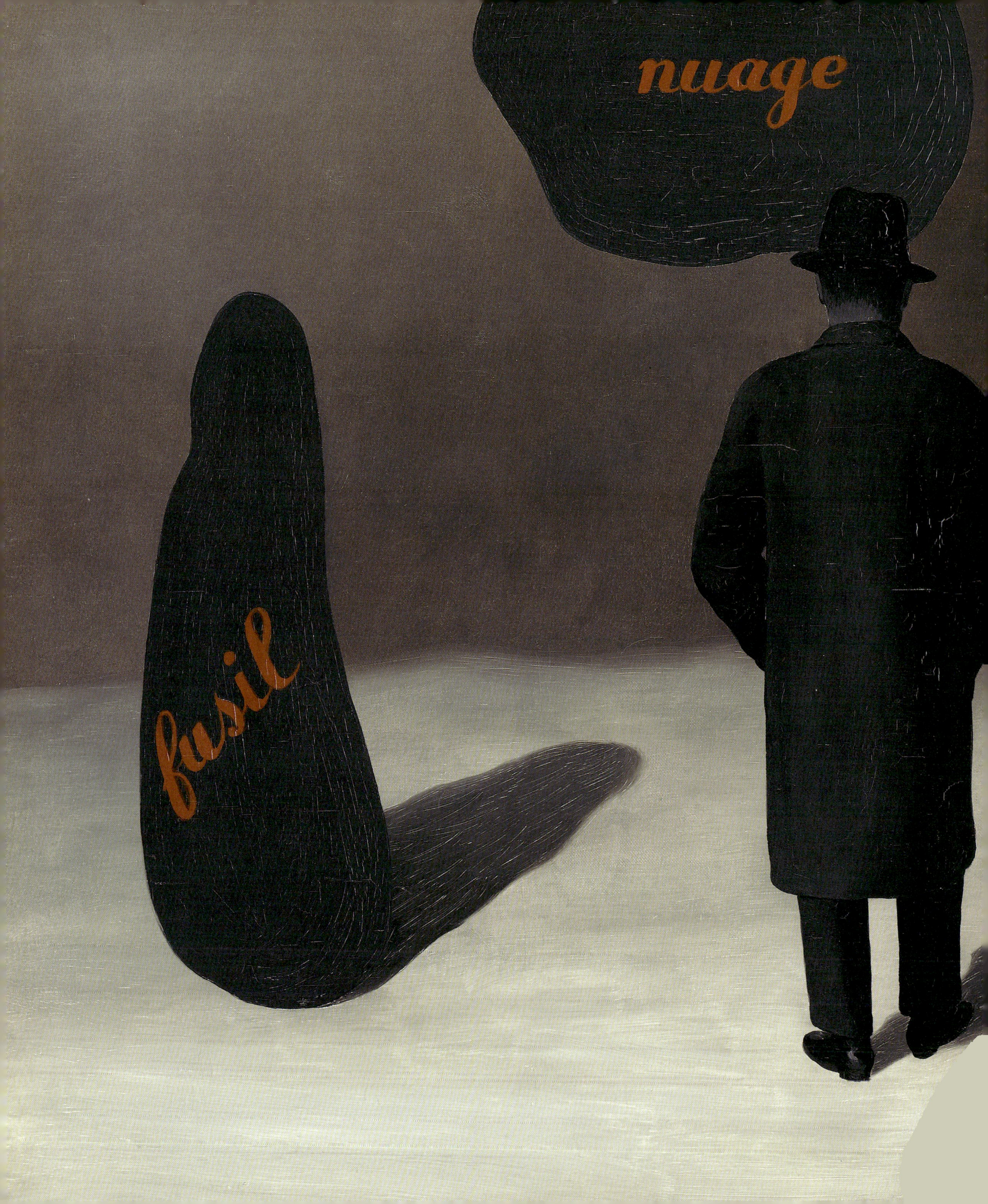
nuage
fusil

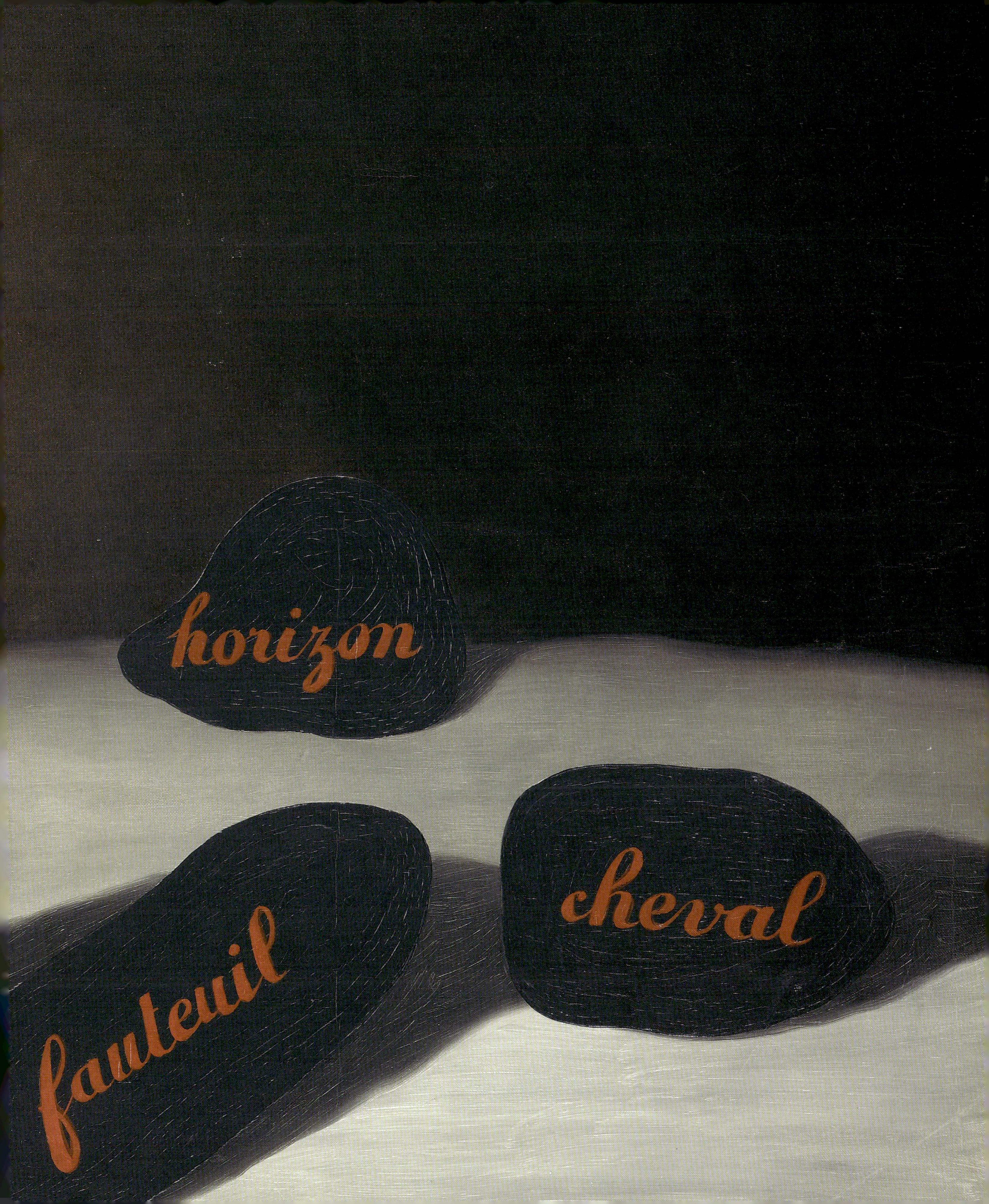
horizon
cheval
fauteuil

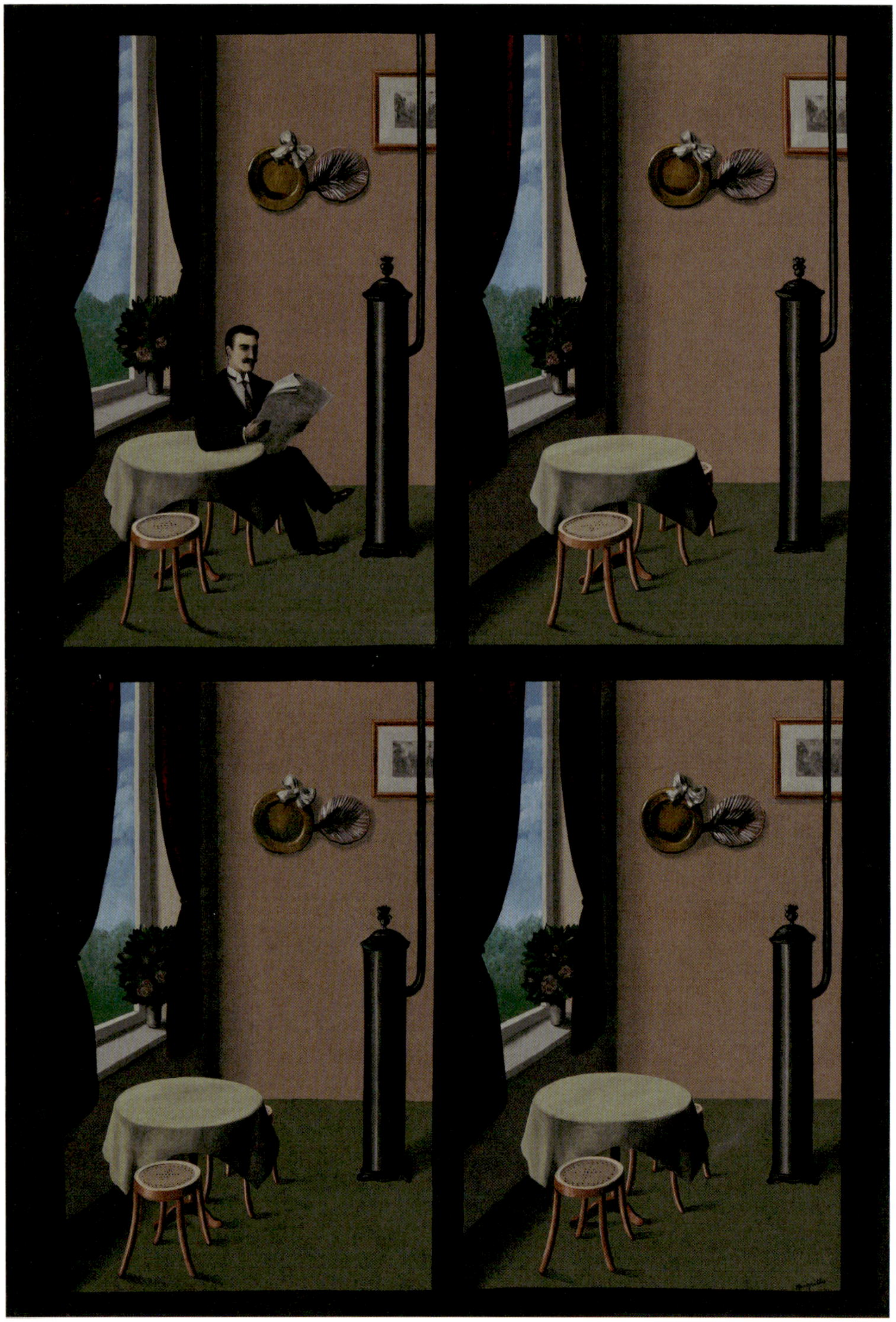

57. L'HOMME AU JOURNAL (THE MAN WITH THE NEWSPAPER). 1928.
Oil on canvas, 45 11/16 x 31 7/8" (116 x 81 cm)

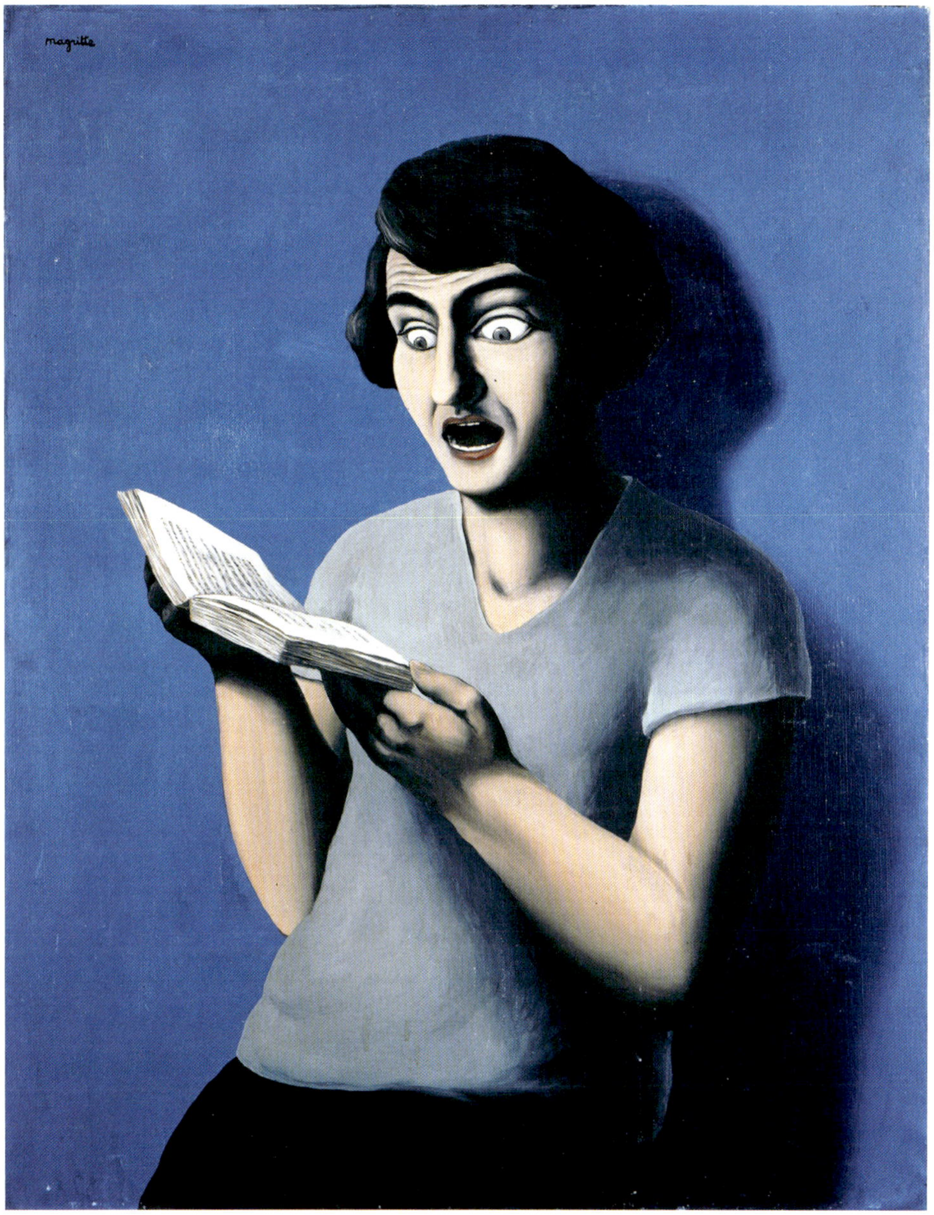

58. LA LECTRICE SOUMISE (THE SUBJUGATED READER). 1928.
Oil on canvas, 36 1/4 x 28 3/4" (92 x 73 cm)

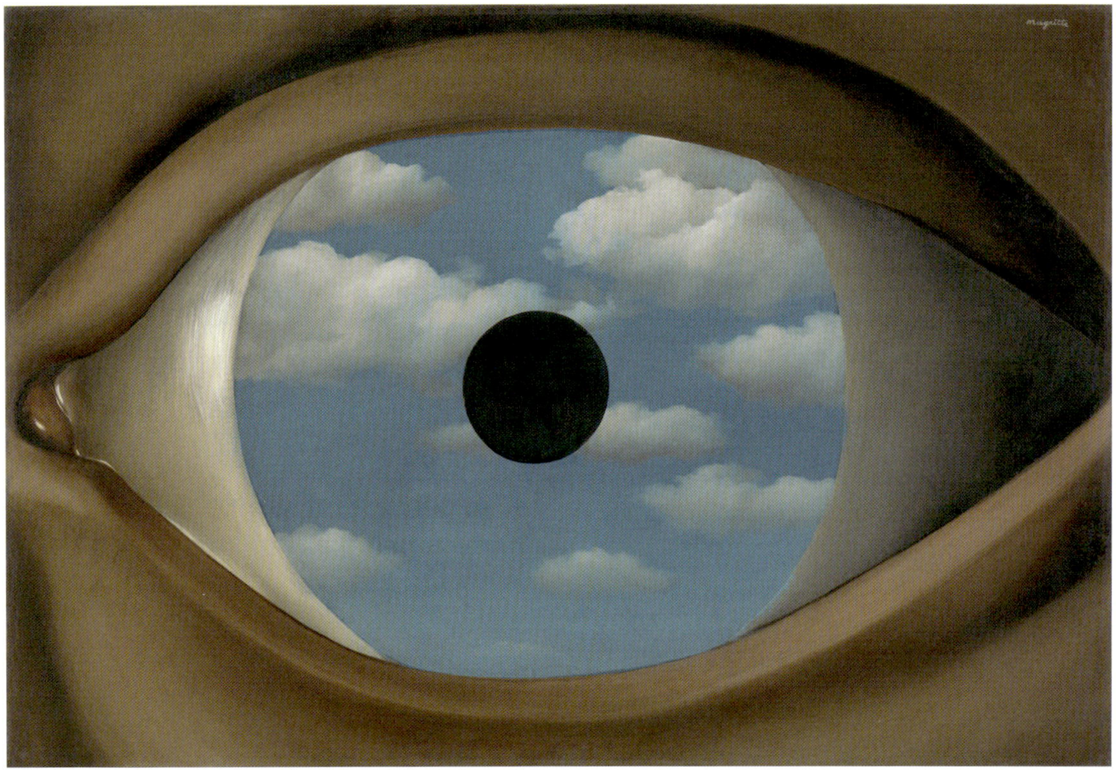

59. LE FAUX MIROIR (THE FALSE MIRROR). 1929.
Oil on canvas, 21 1/4 x 31 7/8" (54 x 80.9 cm)

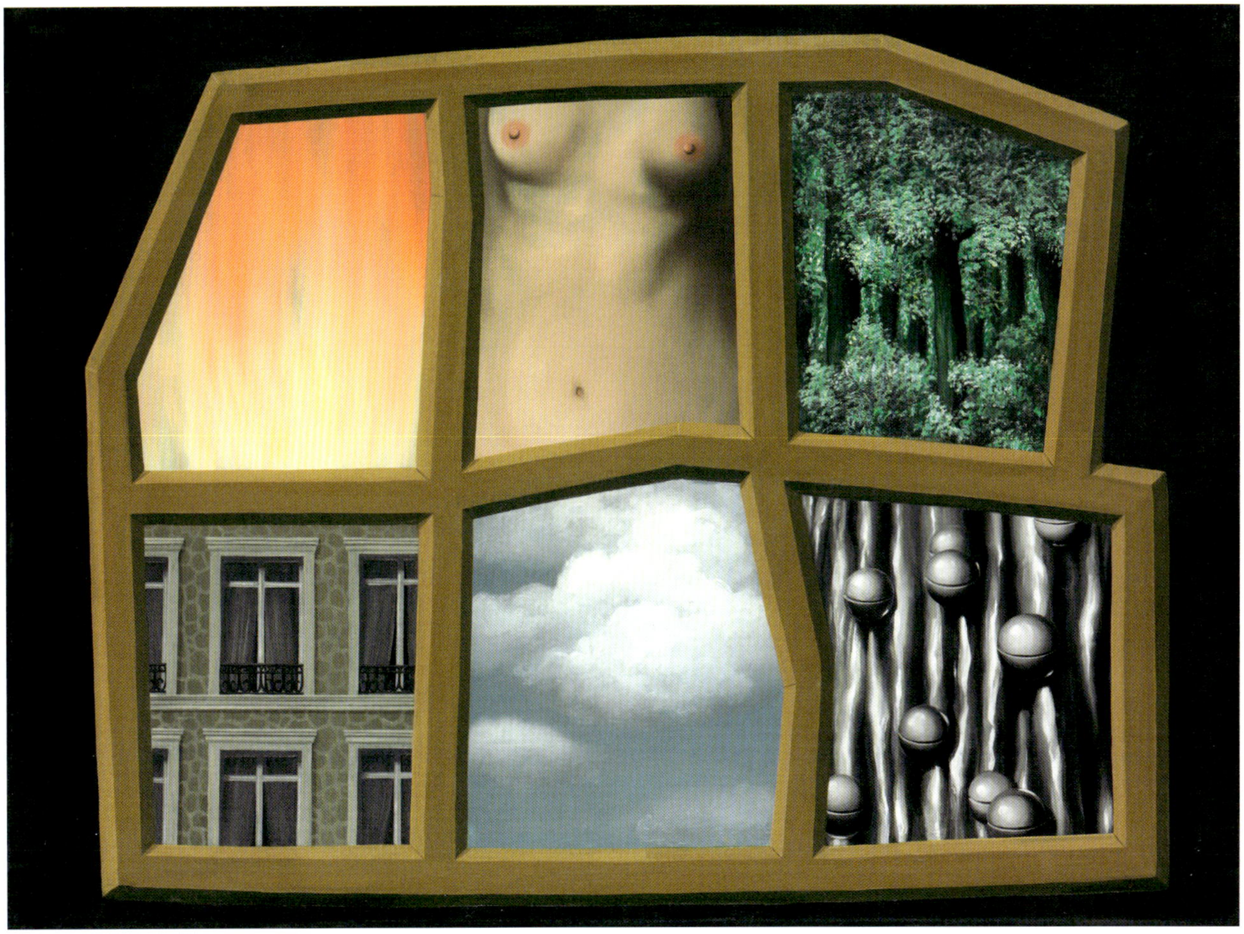

60. LES SIX ÉLÉMENTS (THE SIX ELEMENTS). 1929.
Oil on canvas, 28 3/4 x 39 3/8" (73 x 100 cm)

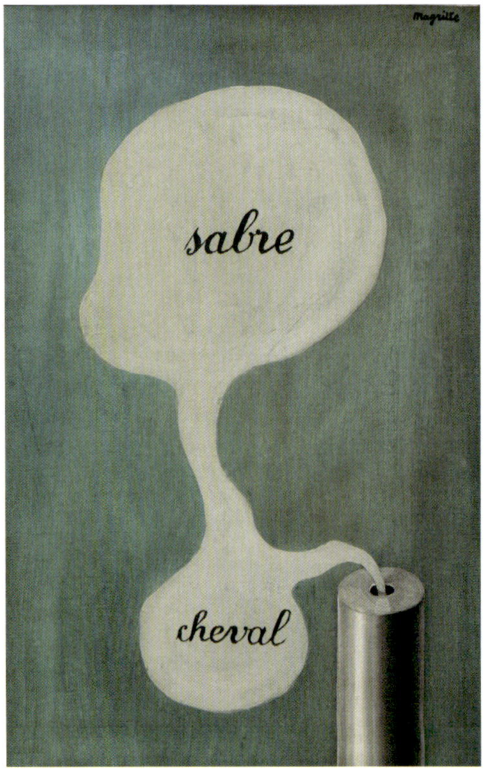

61. L'ARBRE DE LA SCIENCE (THE TREE OF KNOWLEDGE). 1929.
Oil on canvas, 16 1/8 x 10 5/8" (41 x 27 cm)

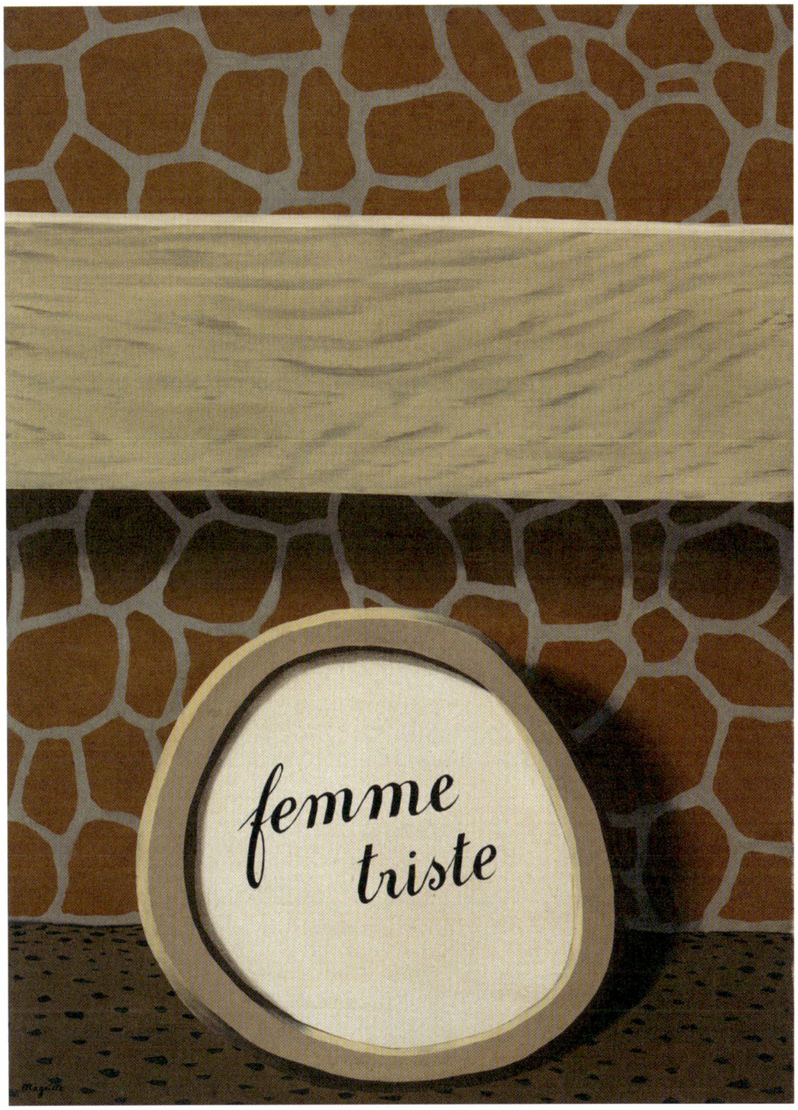

62. LE SENS PROPRE (THE LITERAL MEANING). 1929.

Oil on canvas, 28 3/4 x 21 1/4" (73 x 54 cm)

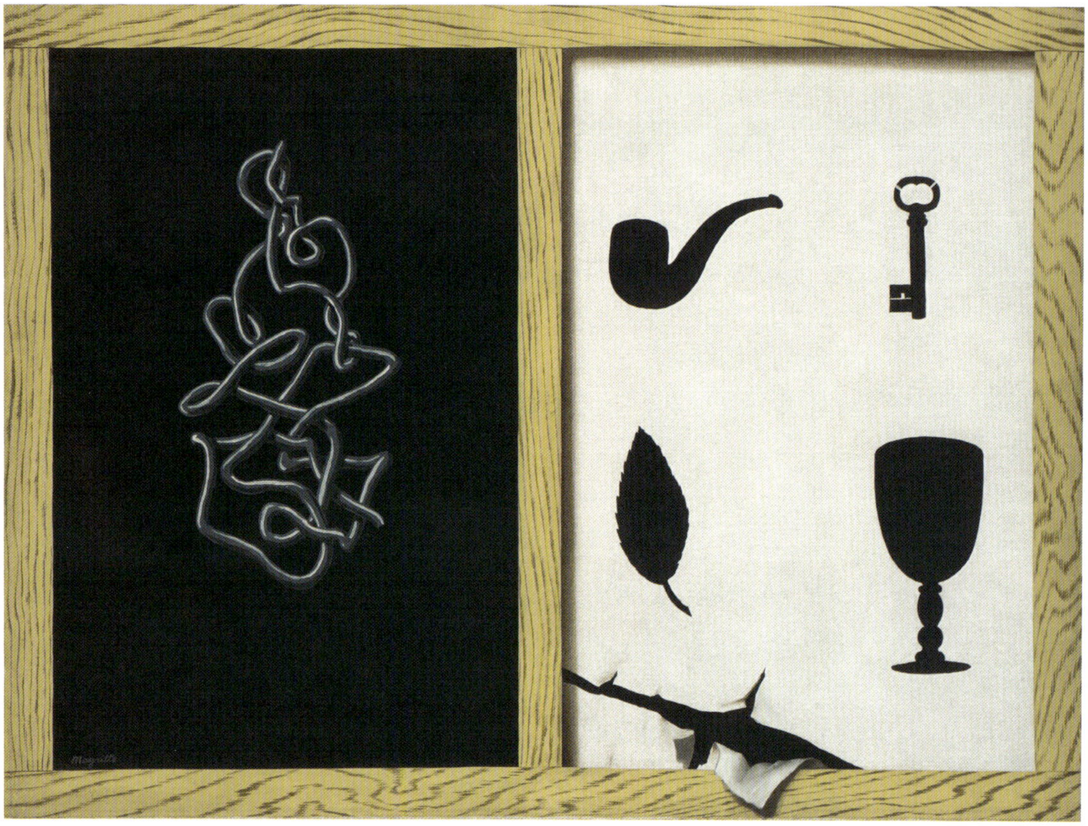

63. L'ALPHABET DES RÉVÉLATIONS (THE ALPHABET OF REVELATIONS). 1929.

Oil on canvas, 21 1/4 x 28 3/4" (54 x 73 cm)

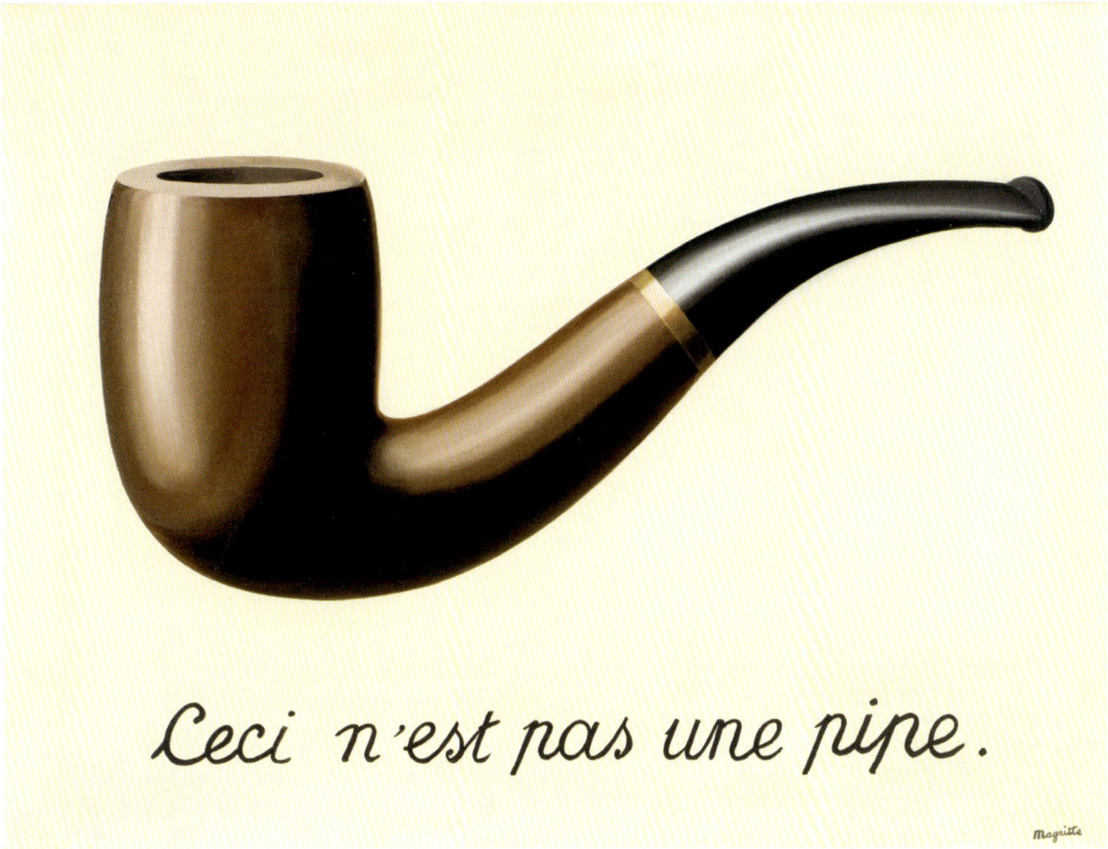

64. **LA TRAHISON DES IMAGES (THE TREACHERY OF IMAGES).** 1929.
Oil on canvas, 23 5/8 x 31 7/8" (60 x 81 cm)

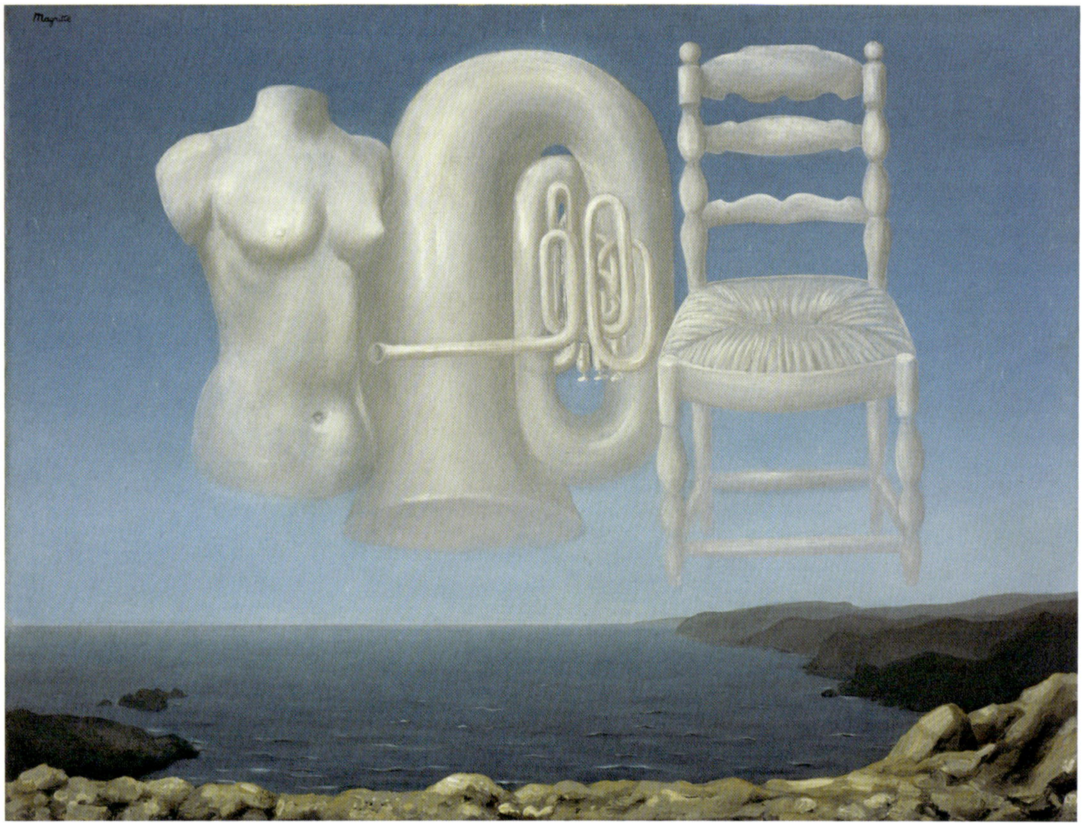

65. LE TEMPS MENAÇANT (THREATENING WEATHER). 1929.

Oil on canvas, 21 1/4 x 28 3/4" (54 x 73 cm)

66. L'ÉVIDENCE ÉTERNELLE (THE ETERNALLY OBVIOUS). 1930.

Oil on five canvases, top to bottom: 8 11/16 x 4 3/4" (22 x 12 cm); 7 1/2 x 9 7/16" (19 x 24 cm); 10 5/8 x 7 1/2" (27 x 19 cm); 8 11/16 x 6 5/16" (22 x 16 cm); 8 11/16 x 4 3/4" (22 x 12 cm)

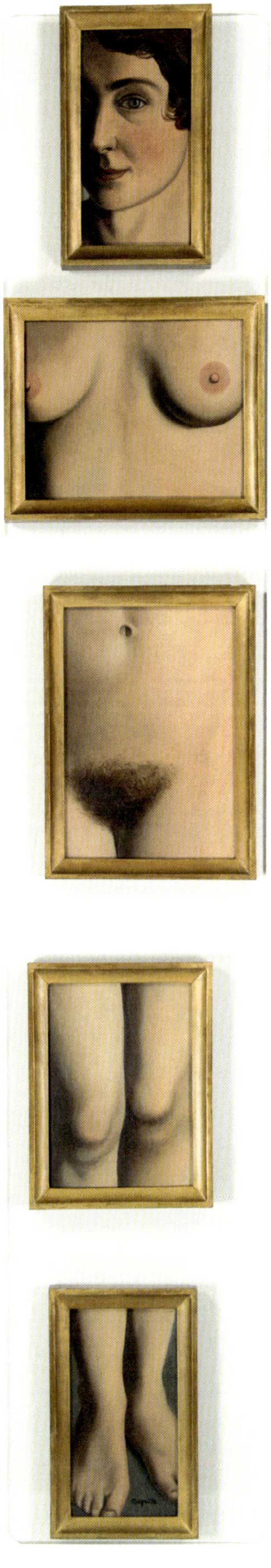

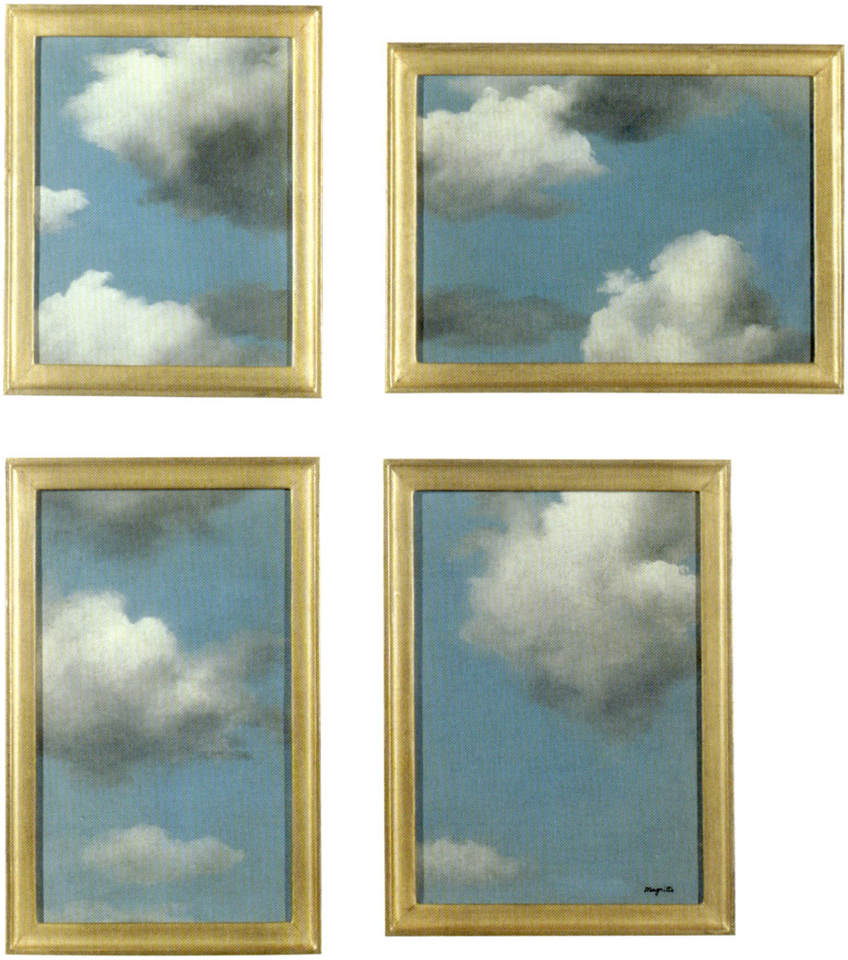

67. LES PERFECTIONS CÉLESTES (CELESTIAL PERFECTIONS). 1930.
Oil on four canvases, top left: 10 5/8 x 8 11/16" (27 x 22 cm); top right: 9 7/16 x 13" (24 x 33 cm); bottom left: 13 3/4 x 8 11/16" (35 x 22 cm); bottom right: 13 x 9 7/16" (33 x 24 cm)

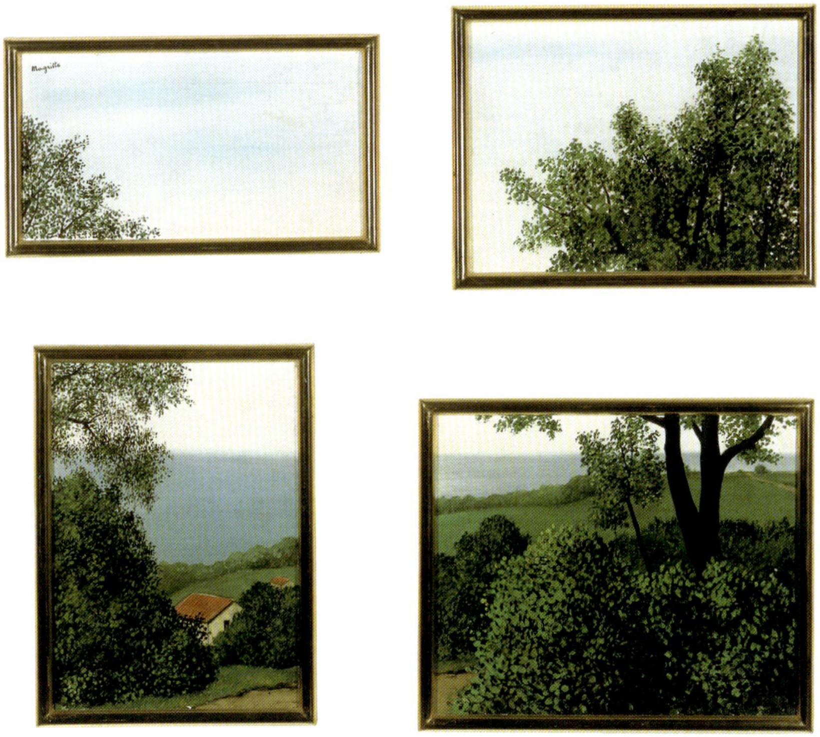

68. **PROFONDEURS DE LA TERRE (THE DEPTHS OF THE EARTH)**. 1930.

Oil on four canvases, top left: 4 3/4 x 8 11/16" (12 x 22 cm); top right: 6 5/16 x 8 11/16" (16 x 22 cm); bottom left: 8 11/16 x 6 5/16" (22 x 16 cm); bottom right: 7 1/2 x 9 7/16" (19 x 24 cm)

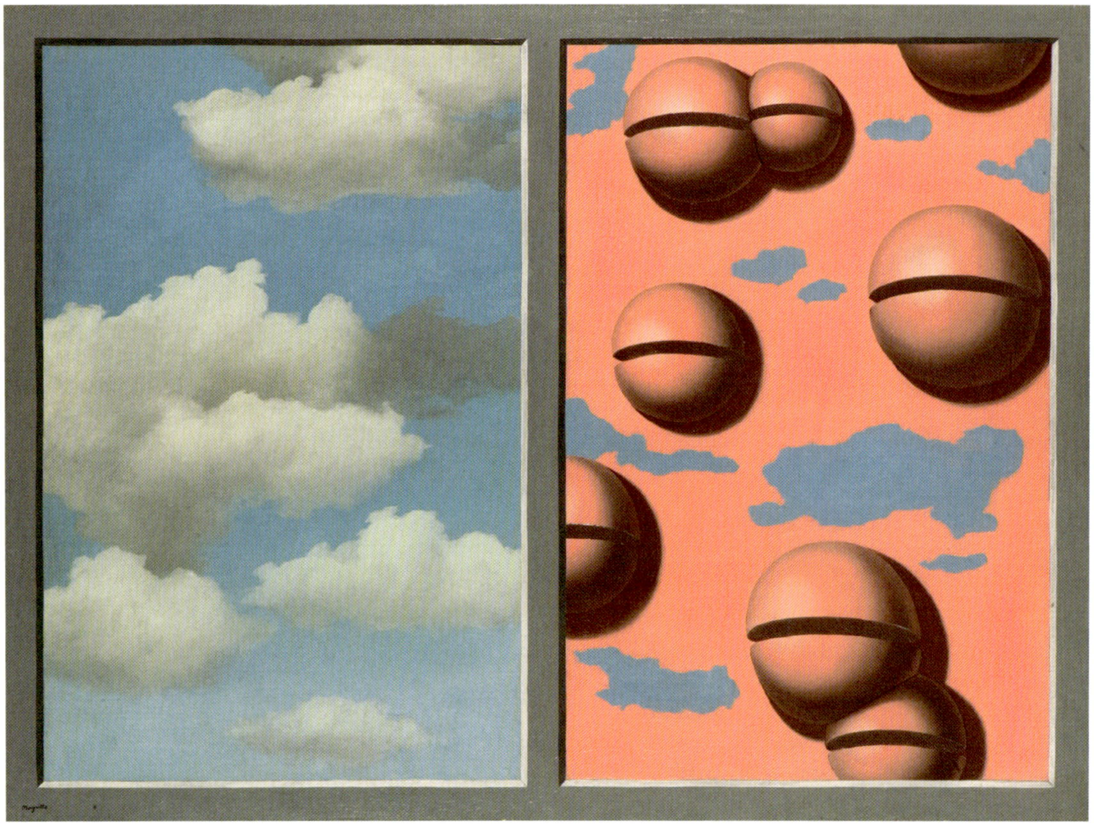

69. GRELOTS ROSES, CIELS EN LAMBEAUX (PINK BELLS, TATTERED SKIES). 1930.
Oil on canvas, 28 3/4 x 39 3/8" (73 x 100 cm)

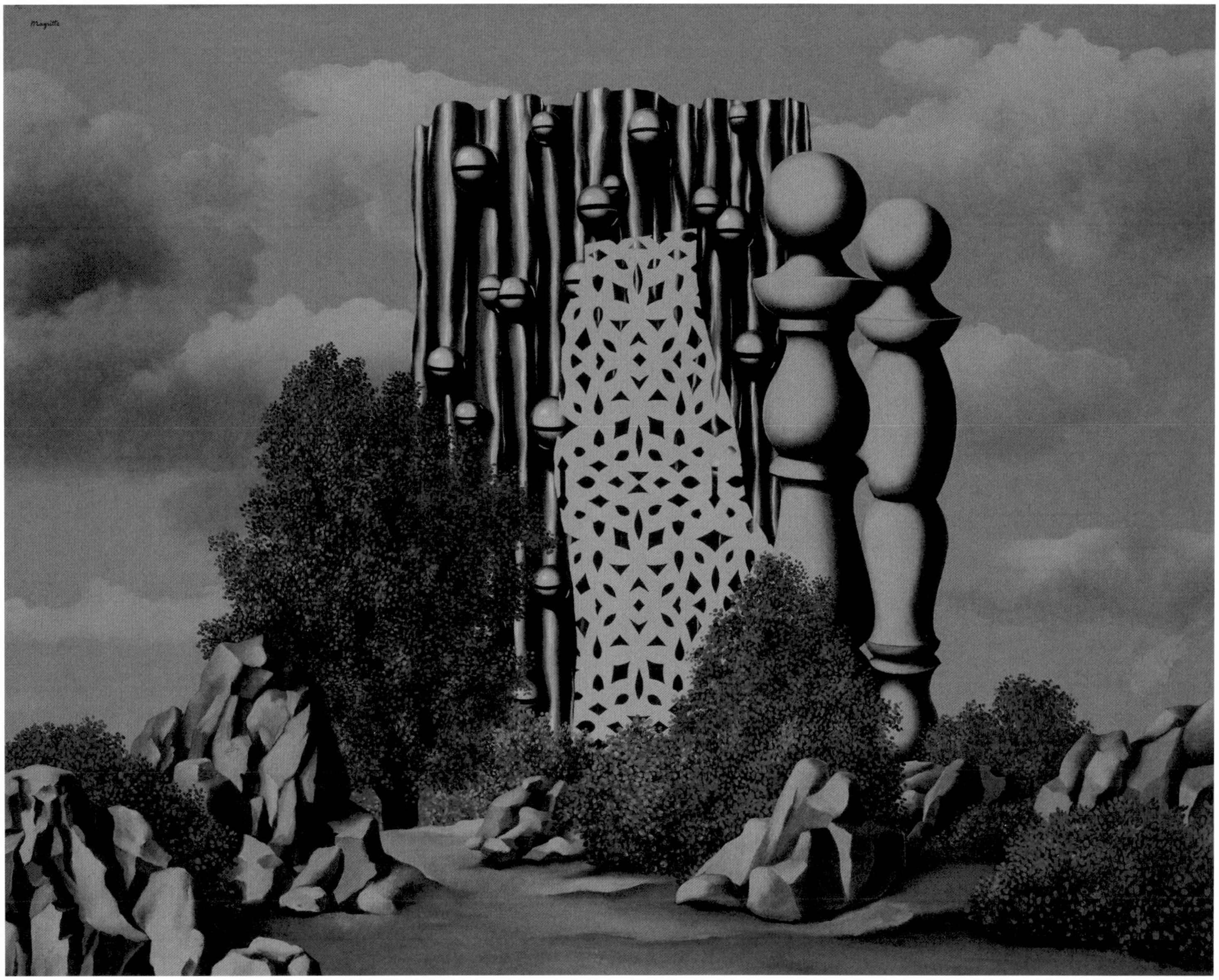

70. L'ANNONCIATION (THE ANNUNCIATION). 1930.
Oil on canvas, 44 7/8 x 57 1/2" (114 x 146 cm)

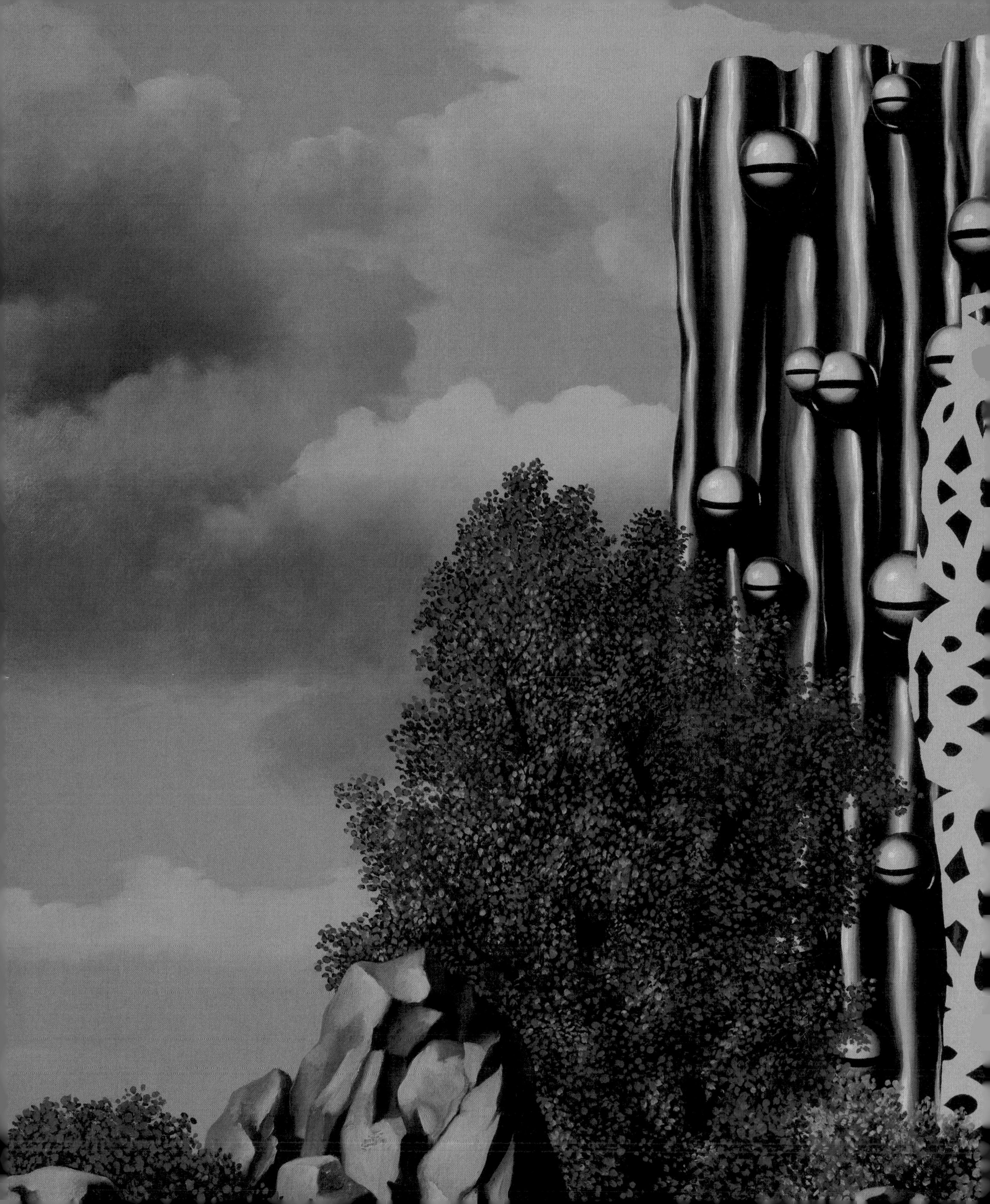

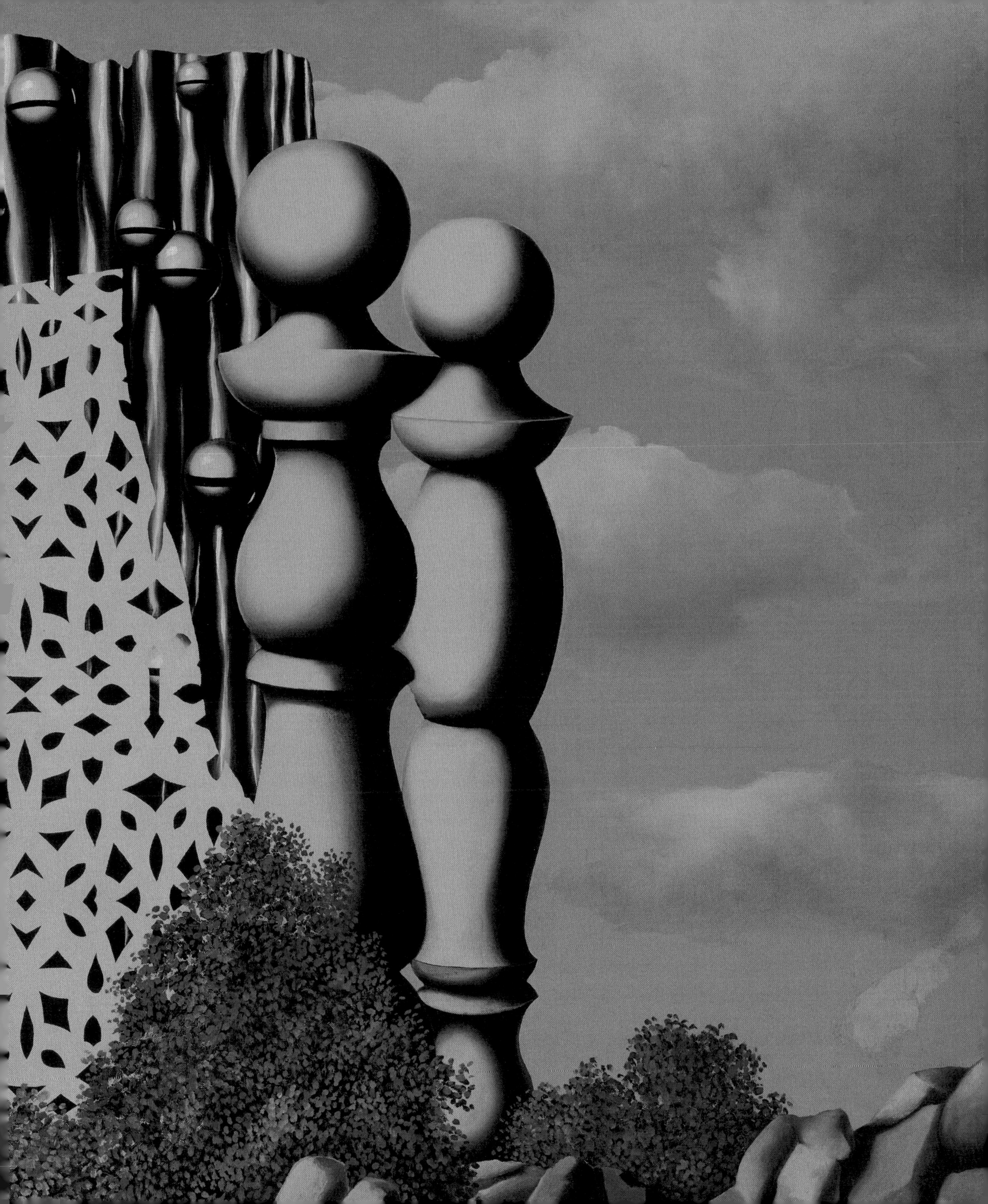

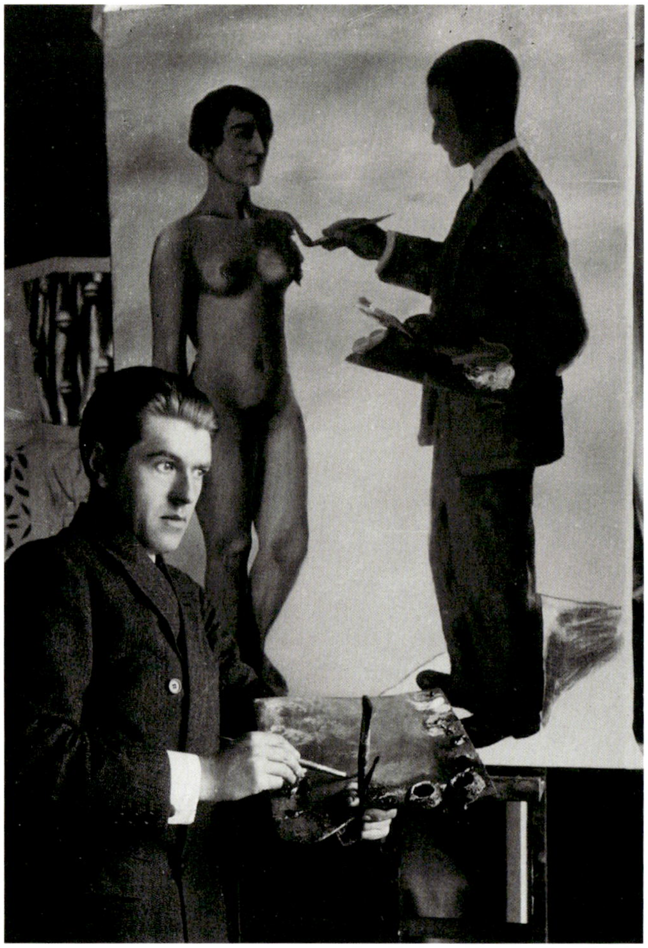

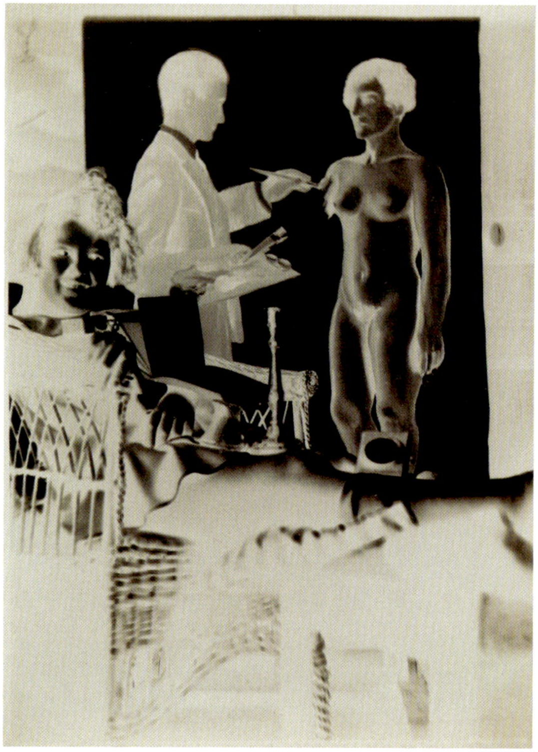

71. René Magritte and *Tentative de l'impossible* (*Attempting the Impossible*). 1928.
Photographer unknown. Gelatin silver print, 8 11/16 x 6 1/8" (22 x 15.5 cm)

72. Unidentified girl and *Tentative de l'impossible* (*Attempting the Impossible*). 1928.
Photograph by Raoul Ubac. Gelatin silver print (reversal print), 4 1/2 x 3 5/16" (11.4 x 8.4 cm)

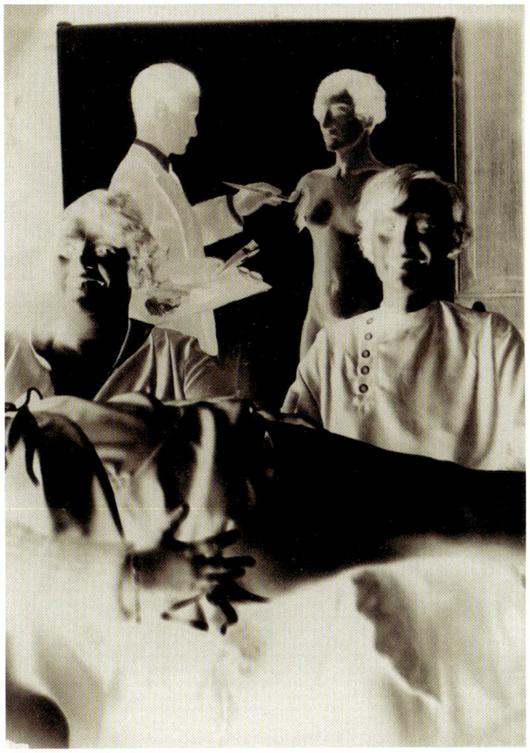

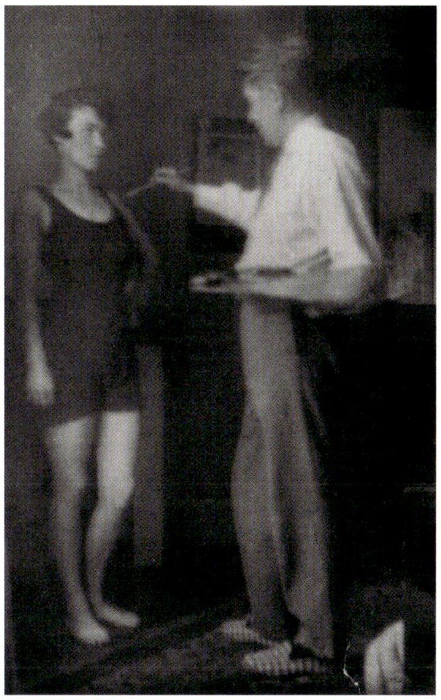

73. Georgette Magritte (right), with unidentified individuals and *Tentative de l'impossible* (*Attempting the Impossible*). 1928. Photograph by Raoul Ubac. Gelatin silver print (reversal print), 4 11/16 x 3 7/16" (11.9 x 8.8 cm)

74. AMOUR (LOVE). 1928. Photographer unknown. Gelatin silver print, 4 1/8 x 2 3/4" (10.5 x 7 cm)

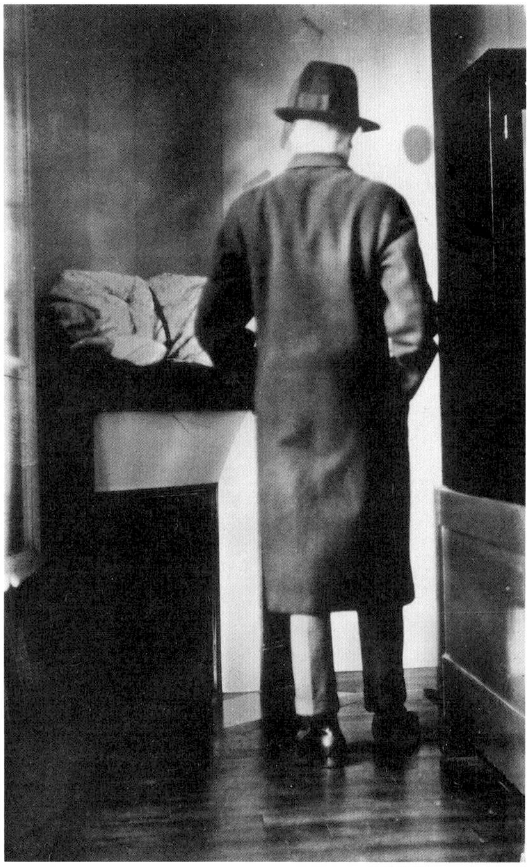

75. LA MORT DES FANTÔMES (THE DEATH OF GHOSTS). 1928.

Photographer unknown. Gelatin silver print, 5 1/2 x 3 1/2" (13.9 x 8.9 cm)

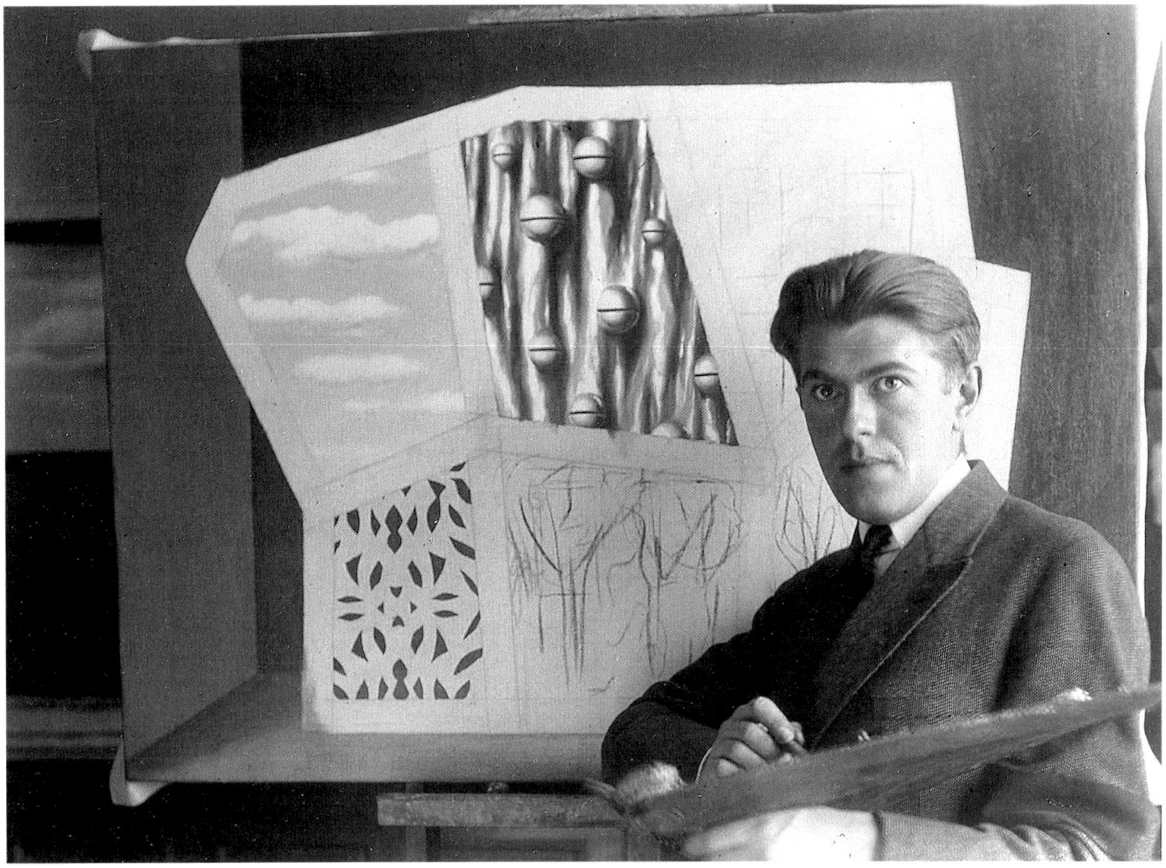

76. René Magritte and *Le Masque vide* (*The Empty Mask*). 1928.
Photographer unknown. Gelatin silver print, 12 5/8 x 15" (32 x 38 cm)

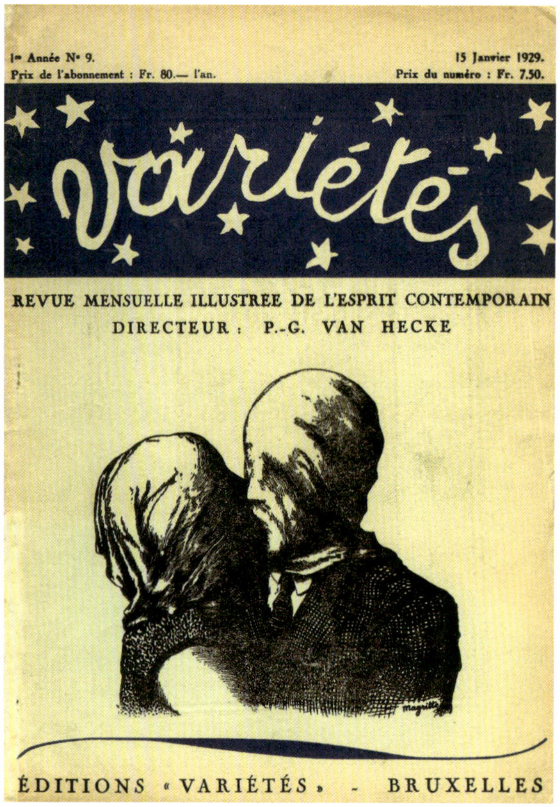

77–79. Cover and interior illustrations for *Variétés* (January 1929).

Periodical, page: 9 15/16 x 7 1/16" (25.3 x 18 cm)

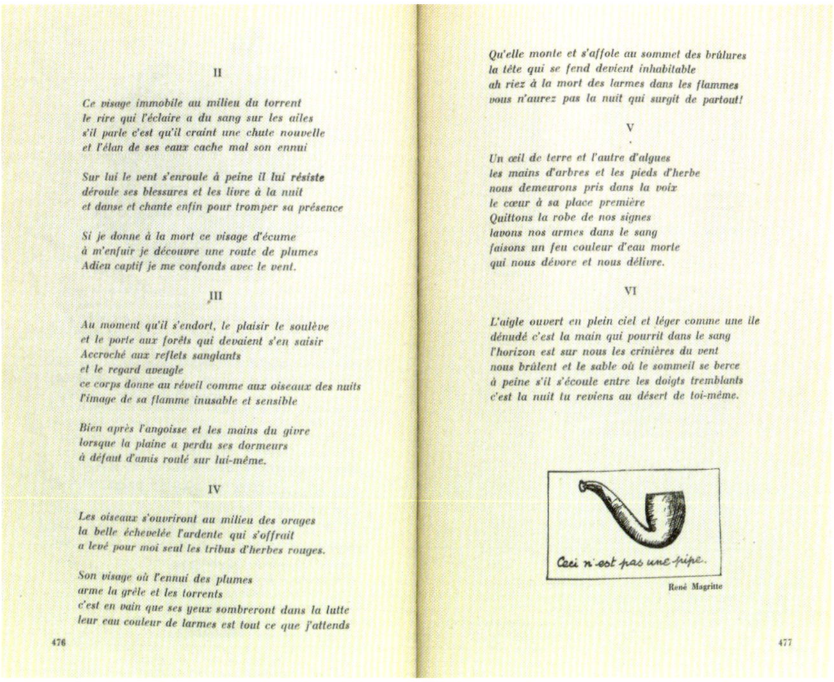

II

Ce visage immobile au milieu du torrent
le rire qui l'éclaire a du sang sur les ailes
s'il parle c'est qu'il craint une chute nouvelle
et l'élan de ses eaux cache mal son ennui

Sur lui le vent s'enroule à peine il lui résiste
déroule ses blessures et les livre à la nuit
et danse et chante enfin pour tromper sa présence

Si je donne à la mort ce visage d'écume
à m'enfuir je découvre une route de plumes
Adieu captif je me confonds avec le vent.

III

Au moment qu'il s'endort, le plaisir le soulève
et le porte aux forêts qui devaient s'en saisir
Accroché aux reflets sanglants
et le regard aveugle
ce corps donne au réveil comme aux oiseaux des nuits
l'image de sa flamme inusable et sensible

Bien après l'angoisse et les mains du givre
lorsque la plaine a perdu ses dormeurs
à défaut d'amis roulé sur lui-même.

IV

Les oiseaux s'ouvriront au milieu des orages
la belle échevelée l'ardente qui s'offrait
a levé pour moi seul les tribus d'herbes rouges.

Son visage où l'ennui des plumes
arme la grêle et les torrents
c'est en vain que ses yeux sombreront dans la lutte
leur eau couleur de larmes est tout ce que j'attends

476

Qu'elle monte et s'affole au sommet des brûlures
la tête qui se fend devient inhabitable
ah riez à la mort des larmes dans les flammes
vous n'aurez pas la nuit qui surgit de partout!

V

Un œil de terre et l'autre d'algues
les mains d'arbres et les pieds d'herbe
nous demeurons pris dans la voix
le cœur à sa place première
Quittons la robe de nos signes
lavons nos armes dans le sang
faisons un feu couleur d'eau morte
qui nous dévore et nous délivre.

VI

L'aigle ouvert en plein ciel et léger comme une île
dénudé c'est la main qui pourrit dans le sang
l'horizon est sur nous les crinières du vent
nous brûlent et le sable où le sommeil se berce
à peine s'il s'écoule entre les doigts tremblants
c'est la nuit tu reviens au désert de toi-même.

Ceci n'est pas une pipe.

René Magritte

477

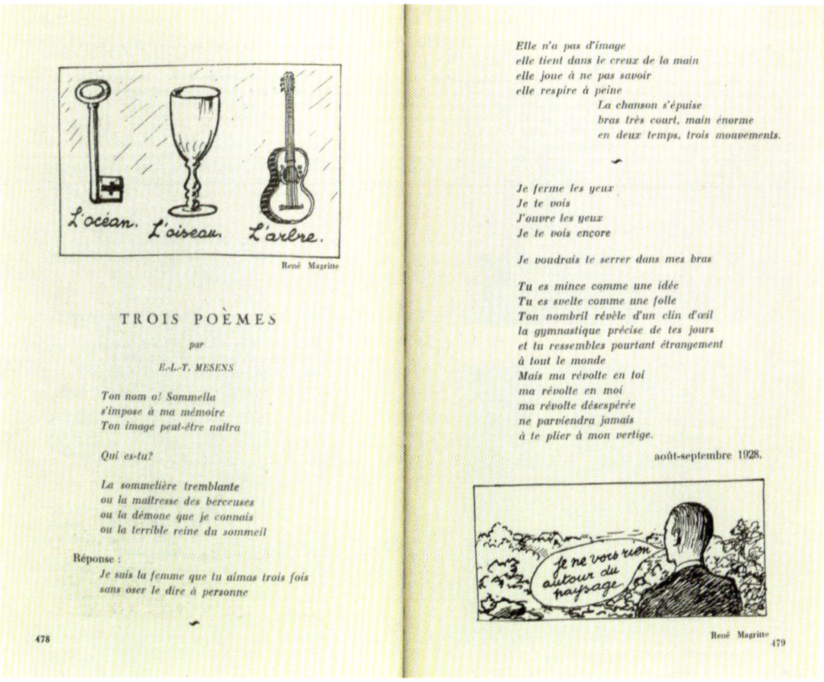

L'océan. L'oiseau. L'arbre.

René Magritte

TROIS POÈMES

par

E.-L.-T. MESENS

Ton nom o! Sommella
s'impose à ma mémoire
Ton image peut-être naîtra

Qui es-tu?

La sommelière tremblante
ou la maîtresse des berceuses
ou la démone que je connais
ou la terrible reine du sommeil

Réponse :
Je suis la femme que tu aimas trois fois
sans oser le dire à personne

478

Elle n'a pas d'image
elle tient dans le creux de la main
elle joue à ne pas savoir
elle respire à peine
La chanson s'épuise
bras très court, main énorme
en deux temps, trois mouvements.

Je ferme les yeux
Je te vois
J'ouvre les yeux
Je te vois encore

Je voudrais te serrer dans mes bras

Tu es mince comme une idée
Tu es svelte comme une folle
Ton nombril révèle d'un clin d'œil
la gymnastique précise de tes jours
et tu ressembles pourtant étrangement
à tout le monde
Mais ma révolte en toi
ma révolte en moi
ma révolte désespérée
ne parviendra jamais
à te plier à mon vertige.

août-septembre 1928.

Je ne vois rien autour du paysage

René Magritte

479

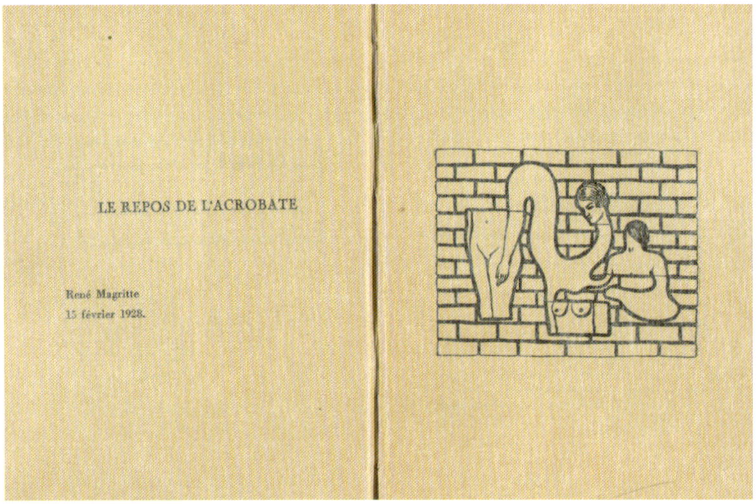

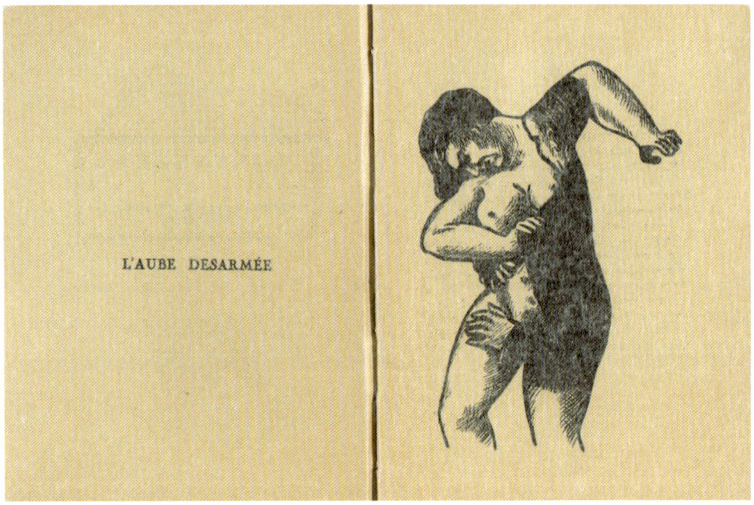

80. Illustration in *Distances*, no. 2 (March 1928).
Periodical, page: 6 x 4 1/2" (15.2 x 11.4 cm)

81. Illustration in *Distances*, no. 3 (April 1928).
Periodical, page: 6 x 4 1/2" (15.2 x 11.4 cm)

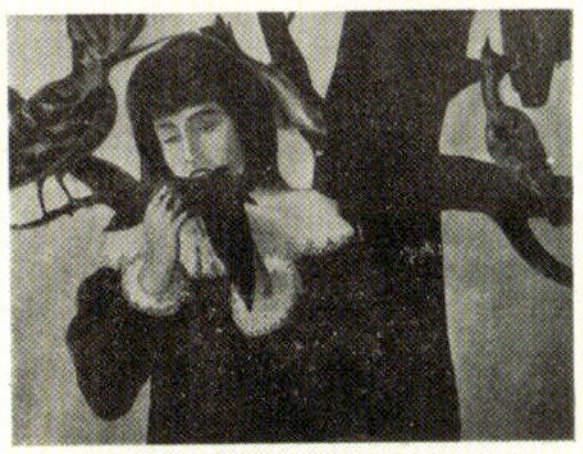

JEUNE FILLE MANGEANT UN OISEAU

LA STATUE ERRANTE. D'un long regard aveugle elle heurte l'espace, et, seule de la terre, elle tend son miroir…

Voit-elle à ses yeux morts, usés à ne rien voir, battre et se fendre la blancheur où elle passe, et glissant à ses pieds, cette ombre qui se meut parmi ses mouvements, comme une aile de feu ; voit-elle le regard qui se mêle avec elle et la suit, inquiet, et jaloux de savoir cette apparence sourde au monde se mouvoir, déprise, indifférente à sa grâce mortelle ?

On la voit, cependant, de tout son corps peser dans l'entaille profonde où sa prouesse lente recouvre, à chaque pas, la trace d'un baiser ; vivant de se sentir, à tout moment, vivante…

CAMILLE GOEMANS et RENÉ MAGRITTE
Paris, le 16 Février 1929.

« Le Sens Propre »

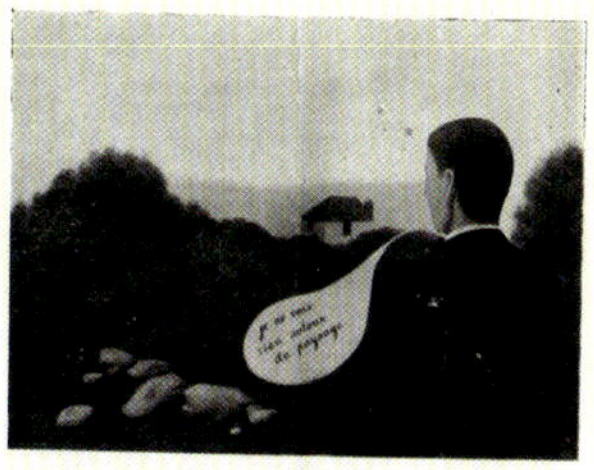

LE PAYSAGE ISOLÉ

LES DEUX STATUES. Avec la même main opposée à la main ; avec les mêmes yeux se défiant en face ; elles tendent, noué, l'invisible chemin par où, de l'une à l'autre, obscur, le secret passe.

Puis, dans la nuit semblable où chacune se va, comme un filet jeté à la glace rivale, ou perdre, ou regagner, l'apparence qu'elle a, ô mortelles de pierre, est-elle point égale ?

Ombre sur ombre, si, tels deux corps attachés et que mêle l'ardeur d'une passion unique, un double cœur résonne et ses cris étouffés une bouche contient dans cet instant panique ; si, d'année en année, au bout de son regard, chacune se répond par un même visage ; si, pour jamais lié à ce couple hagard, l'univers est fermé sur cette seule image.

CAMILLE GOEMANS et RENÉ MAGRITTE
Paris, le 2 Mars 1929.

« Le Sens Propre »

82. In collaboration with Camille Goemans. *Le Sens propre,* no. 1 (February 16, 1929). Leaflet, 10 13/16 x 8 7/16" (27.5 x 21.5 cm)

83. In collaboration with Camille Goemans. *Le Sens propre,* no. 3 (March 2, 1929). Leaflet, 10 13/16 x 8 7/16" (27.5 x 21.5 cm)

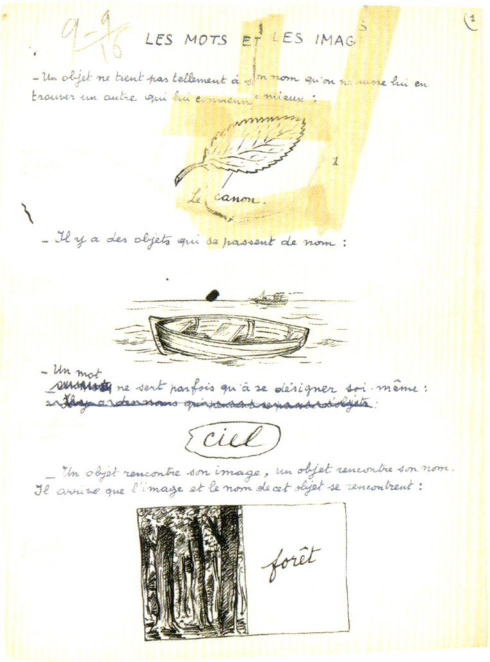

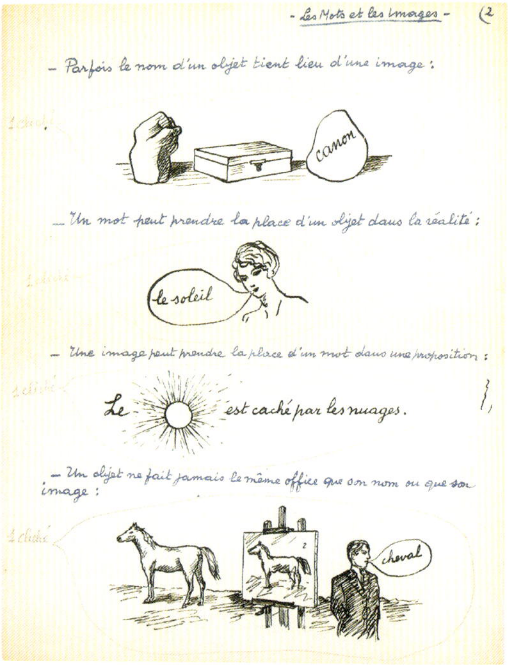

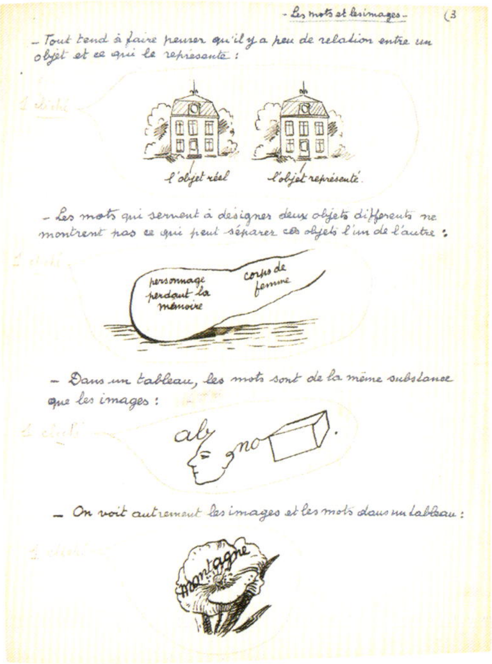

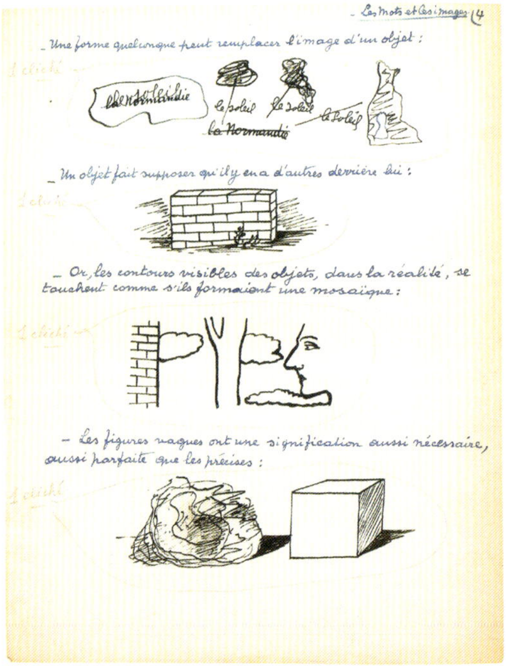

84–88. Manuscript pages for "Les Mots et les images" ("Words and Images"). 1929.
Blue ink, collage, pencil, and India ink on paper; plates 84–87: 10 11/16 x 8 3/16" (27.2 x 20.8 cm) each; plate 88: 6 1/4 x 8 3/16" (15.8 x 20.8 cm)

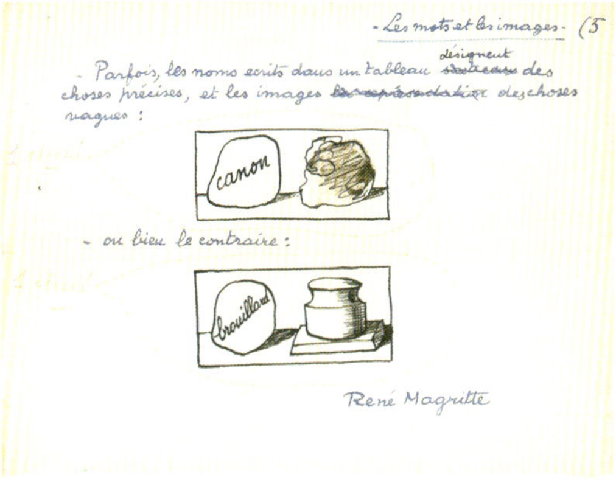

- Les mots et les images - (5

- Parfois, les noms écrits dans un tableau ~~[illegible]~~ désignent des choses précises, et les images ~~[illegible]~~ des choses vagues :

canon

- ou bien le contraire :

brouillard

René Magritte

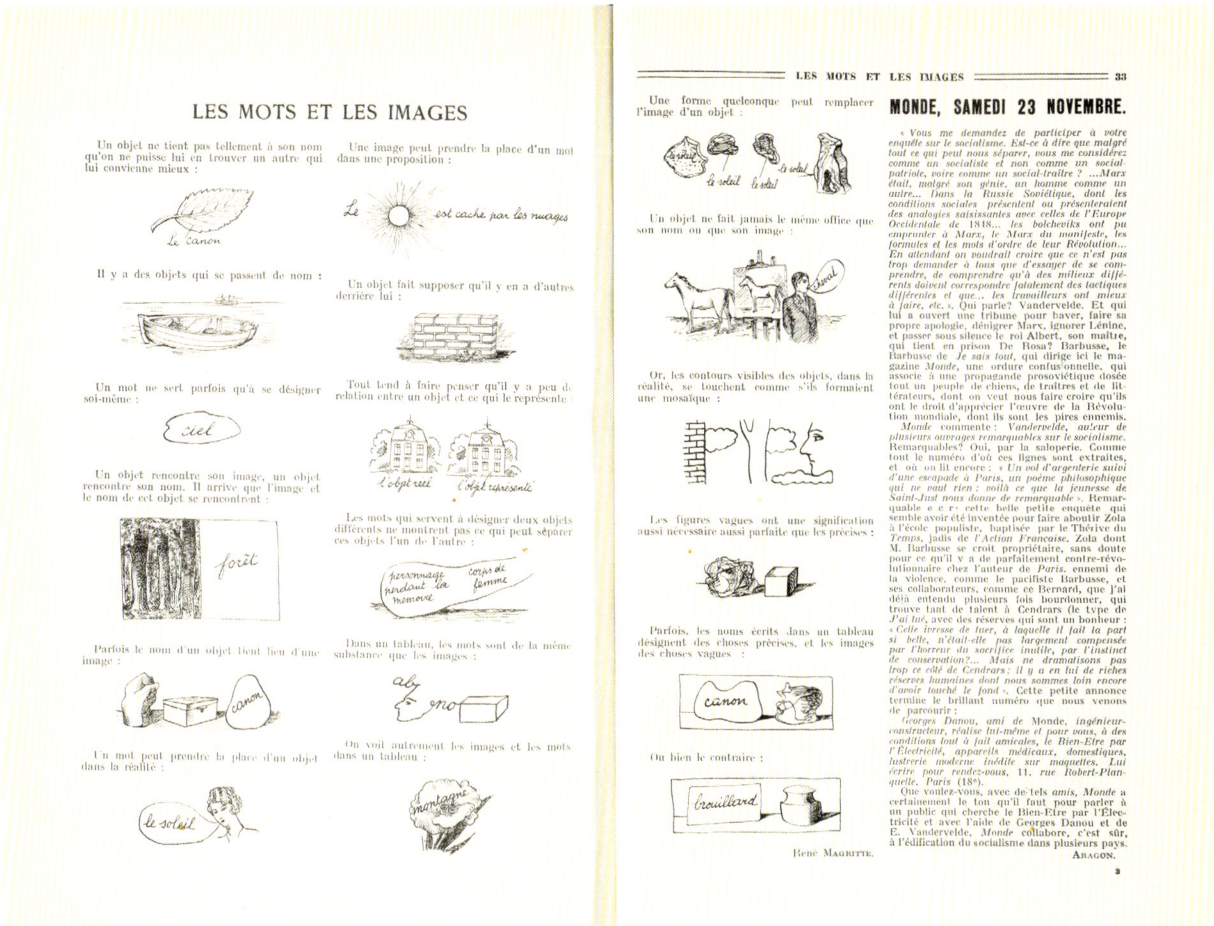

LES MOTS ET LES IMAGES

Un objet ne tient pas tellement à son nom qu'on ne puisse lui en trouver un autre qui lui convienne mieux :

Le canon

Il y a des objets qui se passent de nom :

Un mot ne sert parfois qu'à se désigner soi-même :

ciel

Un objet rencontre son image, un objet rencontre son nom. Il arrive que l'image et le nom de cet objet se rencontrent :

forêt

Parfois le nom d'un objet tient lieu d'une image :

canon

Un mot peut prendre la place d'un objet dans la réalité :

le soleil

Une image peut prendre la place d'un mot dans une proposition :

Le est caché par les nuages

Un objet fait supposer qu'il y en a d'autres derrière lui :

Tout tend à faire penser qu'il y a peu de relation entre un objet et ce qui le représente :

l'objet réel · l'objet représenté

Les mots qui servent à désigner deux objets différents ne montrent pas ce qui peut séparer ces objets l'un de l'autre :

personnage perdant la mémoire · corps de femme

Dans un tableau, les mots sont de la même substance que les images :

aby · mo

On voit autrement les images et les mots dans un tableau :

montagne

LES MOTS ET LES IMAGES 33

Une forme quelconque peut remplacer l'image d'un objet :

le soleil · le soleil · le soleil · le soleil

Un objet ne fait jamais le même office que son nom ou que son image :

cheval

Or, les contours visibles des objets, dans la réalité, se touchent comme s'ils formaient une mosaïque :

Les figures vagues ont une signification aussi nécessaire aussi parfaite que les précises :

Parfois, les noms écrits dans un tableau désignent des choses précises, et les images des choses vagues :

canon

Ou bien le contraire :

brouillard

René Magritte.

MONDE, SAMEDI 23 NOVEMBRE.

« *Vous me demandez de participer à votre enquête sur le socialisme. Est-ce à dire que malgré tout ce qui peut nous séparer, vous me considérez comme un socialiste et non comme un social-patriote, voire comme un social-traître ? ...Marx était, malgré son génie, un homme comme un autre... Dans la Russie Soviétique, dont les conditions sociales présentent ou présenteraient des analogies saisissantes avec celles de l'Europe Occidentale de 1848... les bolcheviks ont pu emprunter à Marx, le Marx du manifeste, les formules et les mots d'ordre de leur Révolution... En attendant on voudrait croire que ce n'est pas trop demander à tous que d'essayer de se comprendre, de comprendre qu'à des milieux différents doivent correspondre fatalement des tactiques différentes et que... les travailleurs ont mieux à faire, etc.* ». Qui parle? Vandervelde. Et qui lui a ouvert une tribune pour baver, faire sa propre apologie, dénigrer Marx, ignorer Lénine, et passer sous silence le roi Albert, son maître, qui tient en prison De Rosa? Barbusse, le Barbusse de *Je sais tout*, qui dirige ici le magazine *Monde*, une ordure confusionnelle, qui associe à une propagande prosoviétique dosée tout un peuple de chiens, de traîtres et de littérateurs, dont on veut nous faire croire qu'ils ont le droit d'apprécier l'œuvre de la Révolution mondiale, dont ils sont les pires ennemis.

Monde commente : *Vandervelde, auteur de plusieurs ouvrages remarquables sur le socialisme.* Remarquables? Oui, par la saloperie. Comme tout le numéro d'où ces lignes sont extraites, et où on lit encore : « *Un vol d'argenterie suivi d'une escapade à Paris, un poème philosophique qui ne vaut rien : voilà ce que la jeunesse de Saint-Just nous donne de remarquable* ». Remarquable e c r· cette belle petite enquête qui semble avoir été inventée pour faire aboutir Zola à l'école populiste, baptisée par le Thérive du *Temps*, jadis de *l'Action Française*. Zola dont M. Barbusse se croit propriétaire, sans doute pour ce qu'il y a de parfaitement contre-révolutionnaire chez l'auteur de *Paris*, ennemi de la violence, comme le pacifiste Barbusse, et ses collaborateurs, comme ce Bernard, que j'ai déjà entendu plusieurs fois bourdonner, qui trouve tant de talent à Cendrars (le type de *J'ai tué*, avec des réserves qui sont un bonheur : « *Cette ivresse de tuer, à laquelle il fait la part si belle, n'était-elle pas largement compensée par l'horreur du sacrifice inutile, par l'instinct de conservation?... Mais ne dramatisons pas trop ce côté de Cendrars ; il y a en lui de riches réserves humaines dont nous sommes loin encore d'avoir touché le fond* ». Cette petite annonce termine le brillant numéro que nous venons de parcourir :

Georges Danou, ami de Monde, *ingénieur-constructeur, réalise lui-même et pour vous, à des conditions tout à fait amicales, le Bien-Etre par l'Électricité, appareils médicaux, domestiques, lustrerie moderne inédite sur maquettes. Lui écrire pour rendez-vous, 11, rue Robert-Planquette, Paris (18e).*

Que voulez-vous, avec de tels *amis*, *Monde* a certainement le ton qu'il faut pour parler à un public qui cherche le Bien-Etre par l'Électricité et avec l'aide de Georges Danou et de E. Vandervelde, *Monde* collabore, c'est sûr, à l'édification du socialisme dans plusieurs pays.

Aragon.

3

89. "Les Mots et les images" ("Words and Images"), in *La Révolution surréaliste*, no. 12 (December 15, 1929). Periodical, page: 11 ½ x 7 ⅞" (29.2 x 20 cm)

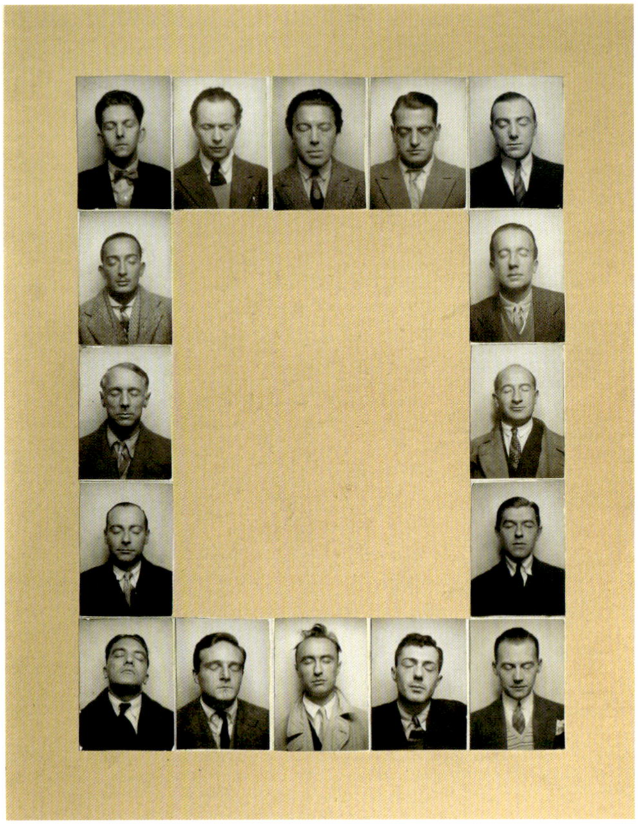

90. Untitled (photomontage). 1929. Gelatin silver prints mounted on board, 8 1/16 x 5 7/8" (20.5 x 15 cm)

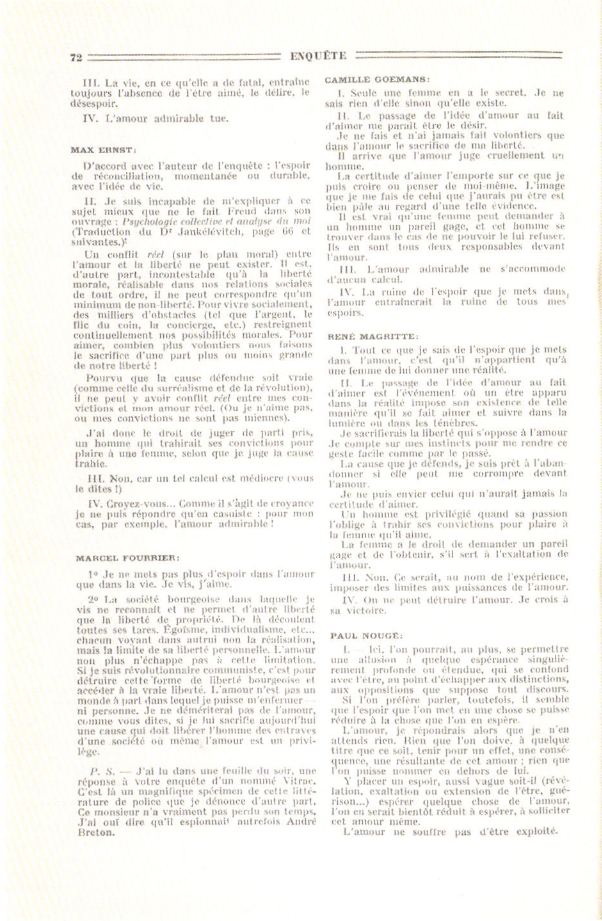

72 ENQUÊTE

III. La vie, en ce qu'elle a de fatal, entraîne toujours l'absence de l'être aimé, le délire, le désespoir.

IV. L'amour admirable tue.

MAX ERNST :

D'accord avec l'auteur de l'enquête : l'espoir de réconciliation, momentanée ou durable, avec l'idée de vie.

II. Je suis incapable de m'expliquer à ce sujet mieux que ne le fait Freud dans son ouvrage : *Psychologie collective et analyse du moi* (Traduction du Dr Jankélévitch, page 66 et suivantes.)

Un conflit *réel* (sur le plan moral) entre l'amour et la liberté ne peut exister. Il est, d'autre part, incontestable qu'à la liberté morale, réalisable dans nos relations sociales de tout ordre, il ne peut correspondre qu'un minimum de non-liberté. Pour vivre socialement, des milliers d'obstacles (tel que l'argent, le flic du coin, la concierge, etc.) restreignent continuellement nos possibilités morales. Pour aimer, combien plus volontiers nous faisons le sacrifice d'une part plus ou moins grande de notre liberté !

Pourvu que la cause défendue soit vraie (comme celle du surréalisme et de la révolution), il ne peut y avoir conflit *réel* entre mes convictions et mon amour réel. (Ou je n'aime pas, ou mes convictions ne sont pas miennes).

J'ai donc le droit de juger de parti pris, un homme qui trahirait ses convictions pour plaire à une femme, selon que je juge la cause trahie.

III. Non, car un tel calcul est médiocre (vous le dites !)

IV. Croyez-vous... Comme il s'agit de croyance je ne puis répondre qu'en casuiste : pour mon cas, par exemple, l'amour admirable !

MARCEL FOURRIER :

1° Je ne mets pas plus d'espoir dans l'amour que dans la vie. Je vis, j'aime.

2° La société bourgeoise dans laquelle je vis ne reconnaît et ne permet d'autre liberté que la liberté de propriété. De là découlent toutes ses tares. Égoïsme, individualisme, etc... chacun voyant dans autrui non la réalisation, mais la limite de sa liberté personnelle. L'amour non plus n'échappe pas à cette limitation. Si je suis révolutionnaire communiste, c'est pour détruire cette forme de liberté bourgeoise et accéder à la vraie liberté. L'amour n'est pas un monde à part dans lequel je puisse m'enfermer — ni personne. Je ne démériterai pas de l'amour, comme vous dites, si je lui sacrifie aujourd'hui une cause qui doit libérer l'homme des entraves d'une société où même l'amour est un privilège.

P. S. — J'ai lu dans une feuille du soir, une réponse à votre enquête d'un nommé Vitrac. C'est là un magnifique spécimen de cette littérature de police que je dénonce d'autre part. Ce monsieur n'a vraiment pas perdu son temps. J'ai ouï dire qu'il espionnait autrefois André Breton.

CAMILLE GOEMANS :

I. Seule une femme en a le secret. Je ne sais rien d'elle sinon qu'elle existe.

II. Le passage de l'idée d'amour au fait d'aimer me paraît être le désir.

Je ne fais et n'ai jamais fait volontiers que dans l'amour le sacrifice de ma liberté.

Il arrive que l'amour juge cruellement un homme.

La certitude d'aimer l'emporte sur ce que je puis croire ou penser de moi-même. L'image que je me fais de celui que j'aurais pu être est bien pâle au regard d'une telle évidence.

Il est vrai qu'une femme peut demander à un homme un pareil gage, et cet homme se trouver dans le cas de ne pouvoir le lui refuser. Ils en sont tous deux responsables devant l'amour.

III. L'amour admirable ne s'accommode d'aucun calcul.

IV. La ruine de l'espoir que je mets dans l'amour entraînerait la ruine de tous mes espoirs.

RENÉ MAGRITTE :

I. Tout ce que je sais de l'espoir que je mets dans l'amour, c'est qu'il n'appartient qu'à une femme de lui donner une réalité.

II. Le passage de l'idée d'amour au fait d'aimer est l'événement où un être apparu dans la réalité impose son existence de telle manière qu'il se fait aimer et suivre dans la lumière ou dans les ténèbres.

Je sacrifierais la liberté qui s'oppose à l'amour Je compte sur mes instincts pour me rendre ce geste facile comme par le passé.

La cause que je défends, je suis prêt à l'abandonner si elle peut me corrompre devant l'amour.

Je ne puis envier celui qui n'aurait jamais la certitude d'aimer.

Un homme est privilégié quand sa passion l'oblige à trahir ses convictions pour plaire à la femme qu'il aime.

La femme a le droit de demander un pareil gage et de l'obtenir, s'il sert à l'exaltation de l'amour.

III. Non. Ce serait, au nom de l'expérience, imposer des limites aux puissances de l'amour.

IV. On ne peut détruire l'amour. Je crois à sa victoire.

PAUL NOUGÉ :

I. — Ici, l'on pourrait, au plus, se permettre une allusion à quelque espérance singulièrement profonde ou étendue, qui se confond avec l'être, au point d'échapper aux distinctions, aux oppositions que suppose tout discours. Si l'on préfère parler, toutefois, il semble que l'espoir que l'on met en une chose se puisse réduire à la chose que l'on en espère.

L'amour, je répondrais alors que je n'en attends rien. Rien que l'on doive, à quelque titre que ce soit, tenir pour un effet, une conséquence, une résultante de cet amour ; rien que l'on puisse nommer en dehors de lui.

Y placer un espoir, aussi vague soit-il (révélation, exaltation ou extension de l'être, guérison...) espérer quelque chose de l'amour, l'on en serait bientôt réduit à espérer, à solliciter cet amour même.

L'amour ne souffre pas d'être exploité.

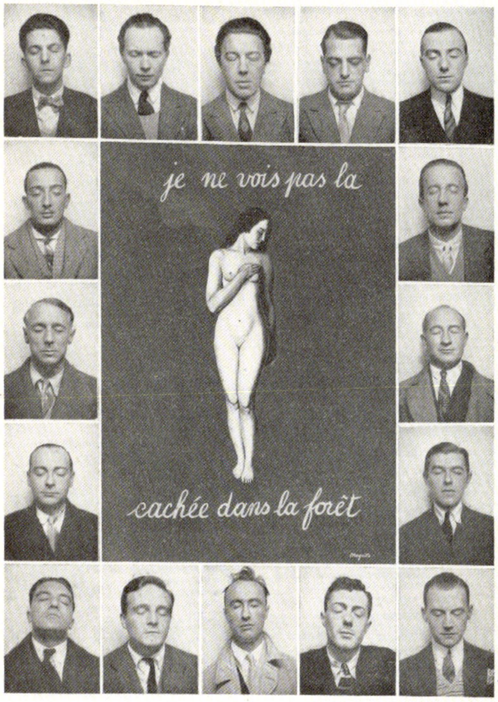

91. Photo-reproduction of gelatin silver print portraits of sixteen Surrealists surrounding a photograph of Magritte's *La Femme cachée* (*The Hidden Woman*, 1929; Sylvester 1:302) in *La Révolution surréaliste*, no. 12 (December 15, 1929). Periodical, page: 11 1/2 x 7 7/8" (29.2 x 20 cm). Pictured, from left to right and top to bottom: Maxime Alexandre, Louis Aragon, André Breton, Luis Buñuel, Jean Caupenne, Salvador Dalí, Paul Éluard, Max Ernst, Marcel Fourier, Camille Goemans, René Magritte, Paul Nougé, Georges Sadoul, Yves Tanguy, André Thirion, and Albert Valentin

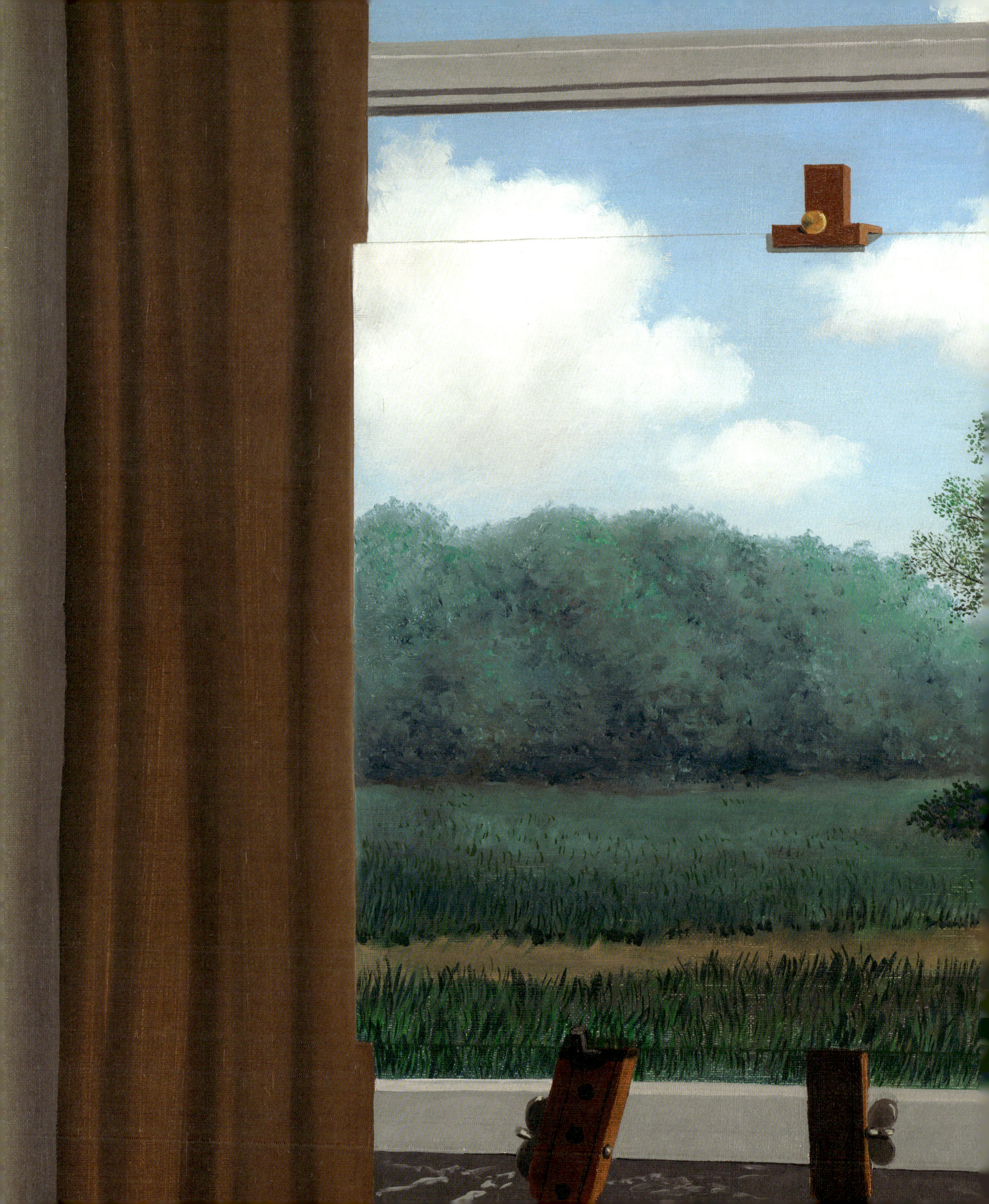

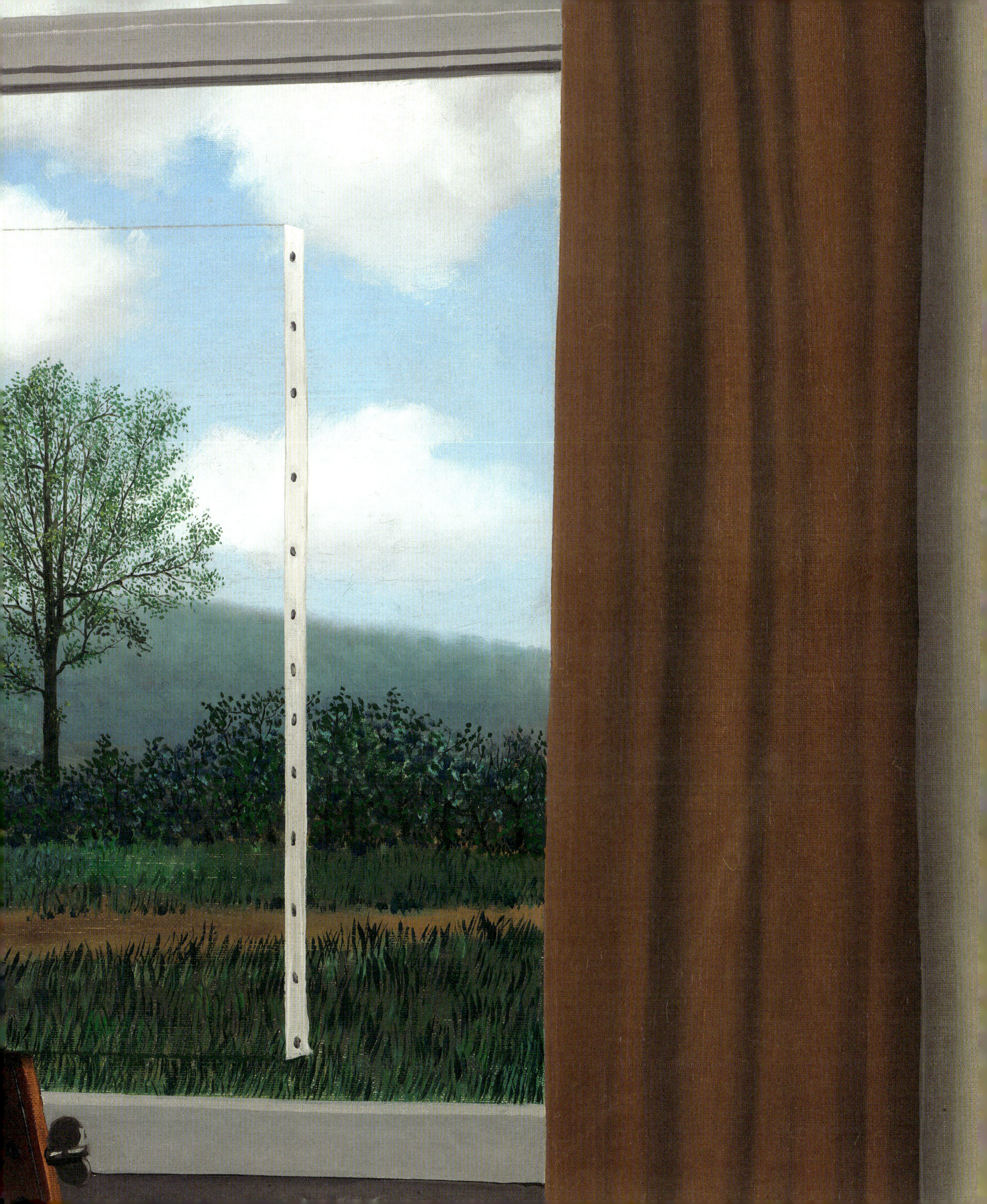

"ONCE THE IMAGE IS ISOLATED, WHAT HAPPENS TO THE MIND?" *Brussels* 1930–1936

Michel Draguet and Claude Goormans

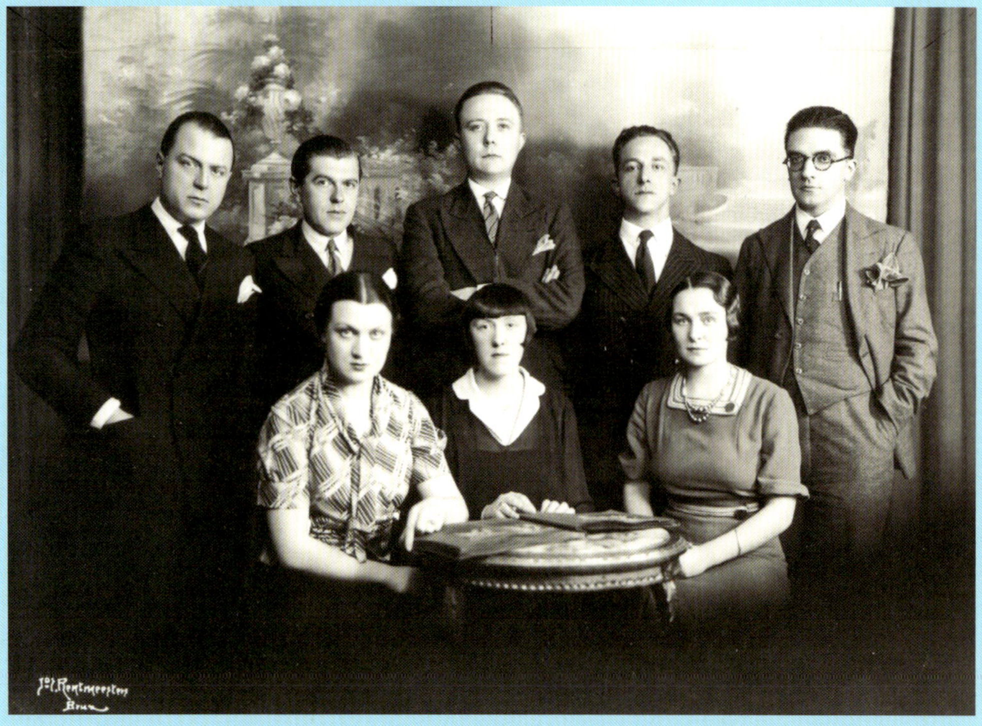

Figure 1. Jos Rentmeesters. *Le Rendez-vous de chasse: Le Group surréaliste belge* (*The Hunters' Gathering: The Belgian Surrealist Group*). Pictured, from left to right (standing): E.L.T. Mesens, René Magritte, Louis Scutenaire, André Souris, Paul Nougé; (seated): Irène Hamoir, Marthe Beauvoisin, Georgette Magritte. Brussels, 1934. Photograph, 7 1/2 x 9 7/16" (19 x 24 cm). Royal Museums of Fine Arts of Belgium, Brussels/Archives for Contemporary Art in Belgium

In July 1930, René and Georgette Magritte left Paris and returned to Brussels. Their stay in France, meant to confirm the painter's standing within the Parisian inner circle, had ended in disaster—both financial and personal. The artist's eagerly anticipated solo exhibition at Paris's Galerie Goemans had been canceled in April, and he had stopped painting, bringing to an end a period of artistic innovation that had promised new possibilities.

His search for work in Paris as a graphic designer had been unsuccessful. In the spring of 1930 the couple's survival depended upon on the sale of Magritte's library to several Paris booksellers, and additional funds from Georgette's father.[1] In June E.L.T. (Édouard Léon Théodore) Mesens, having been apprised of Magritte's desperate situation by Camille Goemans and Paul Nougé, offered to purchase outright all the works he might have.[2] Magritte accepted the offer, and wrote to Mesens describing all the canvases in his possession, several of which were still untitled.[3] After quick negotiations, Mesens bought them all—eight paintings and three *toiles découpées* (cut-up canvases)—for more money than Magritte had anticipated: eleven thousand Belgian francs.[4]

It was this windfall that allowed the Magrittes to leave Paris a month later and to find a place to live on the outskirts of Brussels. Louis Scutenaire later described their modest, working-class home, in which the artist had no proper studio and had to paint in conditions that were, to say the least, uncomfortable. "The workroom's dimensions were meager," Scutenaire reported, "[...] he was hemmed in by the table, the door, and the stove. He would bump into one, the other would roast him, and the door would open and close when people came and went, hitting his arm, sending the paintbrush veering off." Furthermore, when the sun was out it created a glare on the canvases, while when it was behind a cloud the artist could scarcely see to work. Scutenaire concluded: "With the deep reasons [Magritte] had to be resentful of painting, these material conditions were of negligible help."[5]

In his workshop at the bottom of the garden, Magritte managed his graphic-design business under the name Studio Dongo (fig. 2). That venture, which was purely commercial,

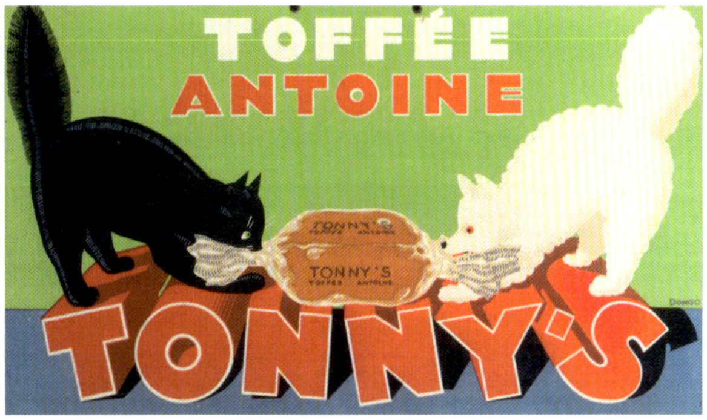

Figure 2. René Magritte. *Toffée Antoine Tonny's*. 1931. Lithograph on cardboard, 10 1/2 x 17 7/8" (26.7 x 45.4 cm). Agency: Studio Dongo, Brussels

resulted in a reduction in his painterly output: between late 1930 and 1934 he produced fewer than fifty canvases and only a dozen gouaches. His correspondence during those years reveals that his enthusiasm for the world of advertising had been noticeably dulled—as he lamented to Nougé: "The public [today demands] exclusively mediocre things."[6] Advertising no longer fed Magritte's imagination; now it was, rather, a crust of bread to which he clung for dear life.

However, the return to Brussels offered the artist a chance to reenter the solidarity of a social setting that had been his before he left for Paris (fig. 1). He participated in numerous group exhibitions that championed contemporary art in a time of economic crisis,[7] and found support among his friends, in particular Mesens. The collector now had an important stock of Magritte works, which would increase in 1932 with the liquidation of Brussels's Galerie Le Centaure, and then of Paul-Gustave Van Hecke's collection.

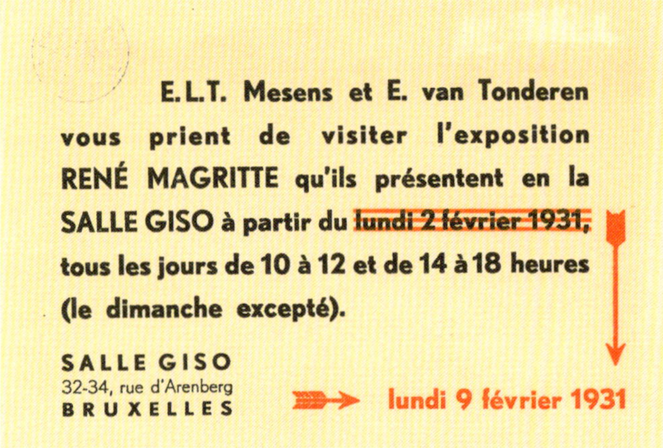
E.L.T. Mesens et E. van Tonderen
vous prient de visiter l'exposition
RENÉ MAGRITTE qu'ils présentent en la
SALLE GISO à partir du ~~lundi 2 février 1931,~~
tous les jours de 10 à 12 et de 14 à 18 heures
(le dimanche excepté).

SALLE GISO
32-34, rue d'Arenberg
BRUXELLES

lundi 9 février 1931

Figure 3. Invitation to the exhibition *René Magritte* at the Salle Giso, Brussels. 1931. Royal Museums of Fine Arts of Belgium, Brussels/ Archives for Contemporary Art in Belgium

Working with Ewold van Tonderen, Mesens managed to stage the Magritte exhibition that had been thwarted in Paris; it took place at the Salle Giso, an interior-design showroom that had been lent for the occasion (fig. 3).[8] The opening of the exhibition, which took place one or two nights prior to February 9, 1931, was a spectacular happening that combined music (composed by Mesens himself) and Magritte's paintings. Visitors entered a dark hallway lit by a single giant candle, and were then ushered to a bar by two footmen in red, with faces painted green and hair powdered. A stately pace was set by the ticking of a double metronome. Once inside, gallery-goers drank at the dimly lit bar, as four phonographs simultaneously played a military march, a waltz, and Stravinsky arias. At one in the morning, the lighting was gradually increased, dramatically bringing Magritte's paintings into view. The Dadaist concert then gave way to composer José Padilla's popular tune "New York," and the night came to a close with wild dancing.[9]

THE PATH TO OBJECTS

Of the sixteen paintings exhibited at the Salle Giso, eleven were owned by Mesens. Nougé was responsible for the catalogue text: along with his "Avertissement" ("Warning": a prefatory note dated November 10, 1930) and a text called "Les Grands Voyages" ("Great Journeys"),[10] he offered titles—presented as "an aid to conversation"—for the works shown. The publication contained only one illustration: a photograph of *L'Évidence éternelle* (*The Eternally Obvious*, 1930; plate 112) by Cami Stone.[11] With the economic crisis hitting hard all around, Nougé's catalogue text adopted a Marxist tone to underscore the revolutionary scope of painting beyond its "thin canvas rectangle," which, he wrote, "contains something capable of changing for all time the meaning of justice and love, the meaning, the style, and the tension of a human existence."[12] As Nougé saw it, Magritte was using poetic images as tools to subvert a society that was "no longer very sure of itself." The image of *L'Évidence éternelle* played out this theme; the painting highlights the notion of transformation and its effect on the banality of our existence. Indeed, this notion provided the basis that allowed Magritte to turn his back on the "psychological" implications in such paintings as *L'Assassin menacé* (*The Menaced Assassin*, 1927; plate 12) and *Le Joueur secret* (*The Secret Player*, 1927; plate 14)—both of which evoke a strange and disquieting mood. By linking himself to the banality of the everyday, the artist makes the object (such as those analyzed in his series of "word-paintings") into the premise for reality's deconstruction. "The world has been altered," Nougé observed. "There are no longer any ordinary things."[13] For the writer, Magritte's dynamic imagination was irrevocably changing man's view of his surroundings. Objects were vectors for a new relationship to reality that also greatly informed the Brussels Surrealists' commitment to the Communist Party. As Magritte would explain in 1946, the object is a prism through which we can see not only the alienating theme of meaning, but the potential of creating a new relationship to reality—thereby laying the foundations for a future society based on Marxist dialectical materialism: a materialism that would, as the Surrealists saw it, attribute a major expository role to poetry.[14] Nougé confirmed this in the conclusion of his "Avertissement": "Some of the paintings virulently attain, through paths that are their own, the most burning call to revolt. All they need is to be heard."[15] Though short, Nougé's text was pivotal, and heralded imminent changes in Magritte's work.

A lover of popular cinema, in 1932 Magritte returned to cinematographic work in collaboration with Nougé; together they created two short, untitled films.[16] (Although both were unfortunately destroyed, the screenplays of these works, published in 1968, provide much insight into them.)[17] While the films paid tribute to Luis Buñuel's 1929 *Un Chien andalou*,[18] which set the tone for the genre, they also provided a synthesis of the central themes of Magritte's recent paintings: the confusion and ambiguity of perception at night, somnambulism, mirrors, dead ends, the virtual nature of painted images. Magritte and Nougé drew on enigmatic objects, such as a black glove fallen on a table, filmed in a way that evokes an untitled collage Magritte had created six years earlier, in 1926 (plate 6). With their inscrutable narrative structures, these filmic incursions contributed to the evolution of Magritte's relationship to the object, which henceforth would be less about deconstructing the engagement with language than about contextualizing the object itself.

This is the goal toward which Magritte was working in the early 1930s. Now cut off from the Paris circles and more or less insulated within the Brussels coterie, he methodically set out to revise his painting. The ambiguous meanings of these short dramas composed with Nougé may have helped to direct Magritte toward a culture of mystery that would feed into his view of painting as an act of interrogation. In his films, as in his paintings, the artist was clearly seeking to define the mechanisms of thought.[19]

THE ART OF THE PROBLEM

His return to Brussels gave Magritte the opportunity to develop his philosophy of objects, moving away from the positive nature of representation addressed by the demonstrative character of the word *ceci*, or "this" (as in the phrase "Ceci n'est pas une pipe"/"This is not a pipe" in *La Trahison des images* [*The Treachery of Images*, 1929; plate 64]). Since the Renaissance, and Leon Battista Alberti's famous window, representation in painting had been defined as the imitation of a discrete fragment of reality. In place of this definition, beginning in late 1932, Magritte substituted what we might call an *art of the problem*, by way of which he attempted to dismantle the traps of language he had illustrated in his "word-paintings." For Magritte, painting had become a mode of resolving "problems" visually.[20] He explained some of the principles of this new approach in his 1938 lecture "La Ligne de vie" ("Lifeline"):

> One night [...] I woke up in a room where there happened to be a bird sleeping in a cage. A splendid misapprehension made me see the cage with the bird gone and replaced by an egg. I had grasped a new and astonishing poetic secret, because the shock I experienced was caused precisely by the affinity between the two objects: the cage and the egg, whereas previously I had provoked the shock by bringing together totally unrelated objects. Proceeding from this revelation, I tried to discover if objects other than the cage, thanks to the pinpointing of some element peculiar to them, and a strictly predestined part of them, could not display the same obvious poetic quality that the egg and the cage had achieved through being brought together.[21]

The artist had discussed this idea of "affinity" between certain objects earlier, in his 1937 lecture at the London Gallery. As examples of his meaning, he used two works from late 1932, *Les Affinités électives* (*Elective Affinities*; plate 92) and *La Réponse imprévue* (*The Unexpected Answer*; fig. 4),[22] and here, too, alluded to his "misapprehension" of the egg in the cage. "This is how it works," he noted: "We are familiar with a bird in a cage; our interest is quickened if the bird is replaced by a fish or a shoe; but although these images are interesting, they are unfortunately accidental, arbitrary. It is possible to arrive at a new image that will stand up to examination through its definitiveness, its rightness: the image which shows an egg in the cage."[23] The gaze, compelled to move beyond what is most obvious, may then reach a mysterious point at which are brought to light a reason for being, a primary cause, a fundamental logic as indisputable as truth, buried in the deepest heart of humanity, an evidence, an actuality that even our consciousness obscures—the image is tasked with revealing all this. Speaking of *La Réponse imprévue*, which depicts a door pierced by a large hole revealing darkness beyond, the artist noted: "Our gaze always wants to go further and to see at last the object, the reason for our existence."[24]

With works such as *La Réponse imprévue* and *La Condition humaine* (*The Human Condition*, 1933; plate 97), the painter began to tackle his work with an increasingly philosophical bent. His impetus was now not a matter

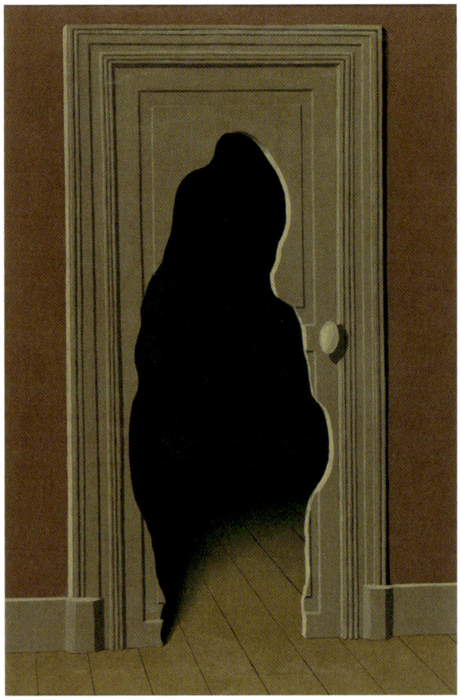

Figure 4. René Magritte. *La Réponse imprévue* (*The Unexpected Answer*). 1932. Oil on canvas, 7 x 21¼" (18 x 54 cm). Royal Museums of Fine Arts of Belgium, Brussels. (Sylvester 2:350 and Whitfield 6:52)

of deconstructing language so much as of uncovering a predetermined meaning from each object—a meaning found not in the thing itself but through the application of thought and inquiry.

Metaphor was at the heart of his philosophy. In a 1932 letter to André Souris, the painter discussed the poetic force of metaphor in relation to everyday objects: "If we accept the reality of [a] secret desire which justifies the use of metaphor, we can also understand why we are affected by the sight of an ordinary object placed in an unfamiliar and lonely setting: our secret desire is for a change in the order of things, and it is appeased by the vision of a new order (isolation) [...] the fate of an object in which we had no interest suddenly begins to disturb us."[25]

Magritte would return to this idea in his "La Ligne de vie" lecture, again touching on the notion of an "affinity" between objects that, when brought together, would reveal what he called a "new and astonishing poetic secret"—known on some profound level but hitherto unrecognized:

> In the course of my research, I became certain that the element to be discovered, the unique feature residing obscurely in each object, was always known to me in advance, but that my knowledge of it was, so to speak, hidden in the depths of my thought.
>
> As my research had necessarily to arrive at a single correct answer for each object, my investigation took the form of trying to find the solution of a problem with three points of reference: the object, the something linked to it in the obscurity of my consciousness and the light into which this something had to be brought.[26]

Magritte sought the "single correct answer for each object" persistently; discovering the solutions in the mute evidence of the image would be the running theme of his work until the end. In "La Ligne de vie," the artist specified some of the meanings he gave to his paintings devoted to the "art of the problem." They are composed as rhetorical figures. Among the "problems" he addressed were: the window, in *La Condition humaine*;[27] fire, with *L'Échelle du feu* (*The Ladder of Fire*, 1934; fig. 5);[28] the house, in *Éloge de la dialectique* (*In Praise of the Dialectic*, 1937);[29] and light, the sun,[30] and the sea in *L'Invention collective* (*Collective Invention*, 1935; plate 100). The leaf metonymically designating the tree in *La Géante* (*The Giantess*, 1935; fig. 6)[31] is echoed by the metaphor of *La Durée poignardée* (*Time Transfixed*, 1938; plate 126). Of the latter painting, Magritte explained: "As regards the railway-engine, I made it spring from the hearth of a dining-room fireplace instead of the usual stovepipe. This metamorphosis is called 'Time Transfixed.'"[32] The substitution Magritte refers to as a "metamorphosis" is in fact a metaphorical *transference*: the locomotive's furnace is analogous to the chimney. Elsewhere, the link could be "oxymoronic," as in the case of *L'Invention collective*. "'Collective Invention' is the answer to the problem of the sea," he wrote. "On the beach I laid

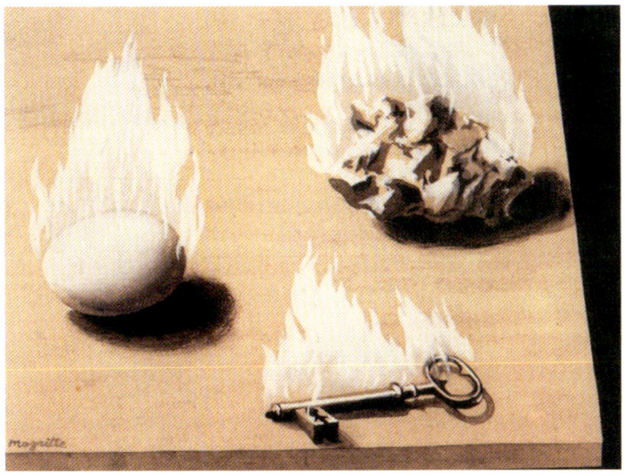

Figure 5. René Magritte. *L'Échelle du feu* (*The Ladder of Fire*). 1934. Gouache on paper, 7 1/16 x 9 7/16" (18 x 24 cm). Location unknown. (Sylvester 4:1108)

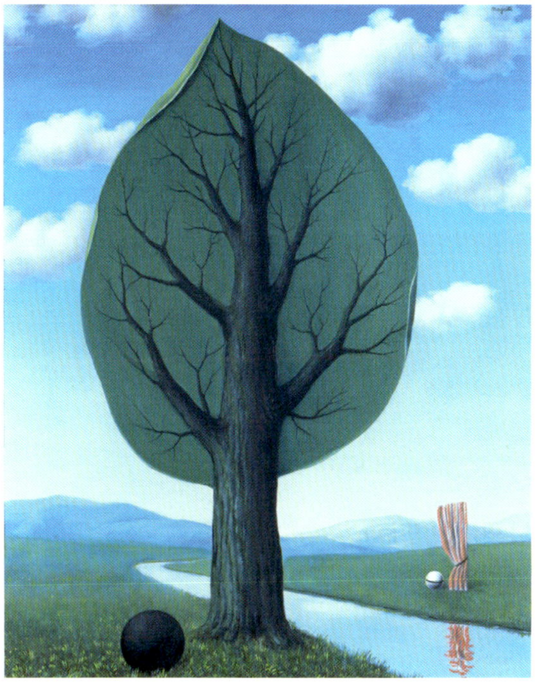

Figure 6. René Magritte. *Le Géante* (*The Giantess*). 1935. Oil on canvas, 28 3/4 x 23 5/8" (73 x 60 cm). Private collection, courtesy Guggenheim, Asher Associates. (Sylvester 2:362)

a siren [or mermaid], the top part of whose body is that of a fish, while the bottom part consists of the belly and legs of a woman."[33] By the simple inversion of the two elements that traditionally make up a mermaid—the fish and the woman—Magritte transforms her into a monster worthy of Hieronymus Bosch.[34]

Over the years 1932–39, Magritte's "problem" paintings would turn into a collective game that André Breton observed attentively. Magritte had applied to Breton in early 1933, asking for his opinion on the new approach the painter had introduced with *Les Affinités électives* and *La Réponse imprévue*. Keenly interested, Breton asked Magritte for more information, from which point the two men would gradually rebuild their broken relationship. In an undated letter, likely written in May 1937, Magritte communicated to Breton the solution he had reached to the "problem" of rain, which he had been trying to find for some time and had explored in *Le Chant de l'orage* (*The Song of the Storm*, 1937; plate 122). As Magritte put it: "Once discovered, the solution appears simple to an almost disconcerting degree. It is: a country landscape, quite a broad vista. Rain is pouring down and large clouds (bigger than the houses or the trees) are crawling over the ground."[35]

STYLISTIC FIGURES AND INVESTIGATIONS

Magritte's first monographic exhibition at the Palais des Beaux-Arts in Brussels was presented from May 27 to June 7, 1933. The show's focus was on his Paris period: forty-nine of the paintings were from 1926–29, while only eight were from the three years that had passed since 1930. However, the event (like Nougé's catalogue text) is a testament to the inventive approach to which Magritte was committed.

Two painted plaster casts were included in the exhibition: at the time, both were titled *L'Avenir des statues* (*The Future of Statues*; see plates 94 [a similar work] and 95—the former is a 1932 iteration of the original 1931 work). These pieces show that Magritte was now delving still further into the potentials of objects—an investigation that was in keeping with the general evolution of the Surrealist movement.[36] For these works, Magritte used (respectively) a copy of the Venus de Milo and a death mask of Napoleon that had earlier provided fodder for his pictorial imagination (for example, in his 1927 painting *La Forêt* [*The Forest*; fig.7]). No longer just tools for interpretive projection, objects were now utilized directly as supports for color, thus shedding the emotional burden of their status as "memorabilia."

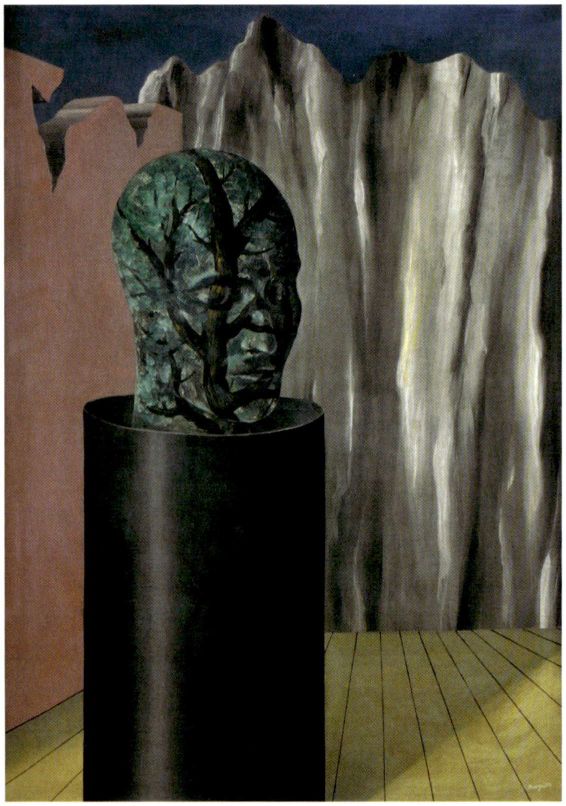

Figure 7. René Magritte. *La Forêt* (*The Forest*). 1927. Oil on canvas, 39 3/8 x 28 3/4" (100 x 73 cm). Musée des Beaux-Arts (BAL), Liège. (Sylvester 1:147)

The Venus de Milo adaptation would be given its specific title, *Les Menottes de cuivre* (*The Copper Handcuffs*), only in 1936, when Magritte invited Breton to name it. In coloring this plaster cast, Magritte transformed a testament to the classical ideal into a boldly colored "flag" (as Nougé later described it).[37] Similarly, the death mask is transformed into a sky.

Magritte was taking part in what Breton termed the *crise de l'objet* (crisis of the object).[38] This line of thinking led to the painter's participation in the *Exposition surréaliste d'objets* (*Surrealist Exhibition of Objects*), organized by Breton and the principal Surrealists at the Galerie Charles Ratton in Paris, presented May 22–29, 1936.

Magritte's artistic engagement with the female body reveals much about the painter's thought process and its evolution from 1928's *Les Jours gigantesques* (*The Titanic Days*; plate 48) and 1930's *L'Évidence éternelle*. *Le Viol* (*The Rape*; plate 96) was painted in the spring of 1934 and presented that May at the Palais des Beaux-Arts, as part of the *Minotaure* exhibition, organized by Albert Skira Editions and installed by Mesens. The painting reveals much about the psychic dimension of an unquestionably male gaze, directed at women. One reason for the representation's effectiveness is that it draws on the principle of resemblance, "which exists in the layout of the organs of the face and of the organs of a woman's body," as Magritte wrote to Breton in June 1934.[39] The rape metaphor in *Les Jours gigantesques* finds a response in the metonymic treatment of *Le Viol*: here, the fragmented female body of *L'Évidence éternelle* has been reunified, in a fantasized form. The painter has advanced, from one work to the next, along his own path of "problems" in order to unveil a reality that had been unknown though suspected. In "La Ligne de vie," Magritte would reference *Le Viol* as his answer to the question of woman.[40]

Le Viol struck Breton, who delivered a lecture in Brussels on June 1, 1934, during the *Minotaure* exhibition. Titled "Qu'est-ce que le Surréalisme?" ("What Is Surrealism?"), his talk would be published in book form in July with a rendering of *Le Viol* on the cover (plate 114).[41] (In a June 1934 letter to Breton, Magritte proudly exhorted: "I hope you will be pleased by this cover-project, I also think that it is excellent from the publicity point of view. An image of this kind is not likely to pass unnoticed in a bookshop window.")[42] Fascinated, Breton expressed his desire to devote a text entirely to this emblematic painting; with this in view he asked Magritte for documentation, including descriptions of other works and recent photographs, that would shed light on the idea of "problems" engaged via images.[43] The project, however, never came to pass.

In his spring 1937 letter to Breton, Magritte linked his poetics of questioning to "the search for metaphor" and stressed the fact that a painting such as *Le Viol* possesses "a virtue that is [its] own."[44] Furthermore, as the artist himself had asserted, the image was not likely to go unnoticed.

INTERPRETATIONS IN QUESTION

Breton's interest in Magritte's approach would bring new light to the psychic themes in the artist's work, anticipating questions about the role of psychoanalysis in Magritte's thinking.

As the artist pointed out in "La Ligne de vie," between 1925 and 1936 he established his "systematic search for a disturbing poetic effect."[45] Magritte observed that Nougé, in his 1933 essay "Les Images défendues" (meaning either "forbidden images" or "protected images"),[46] analyzed the means he had used to bring that search to fruition, and Magritte went on to list some of these strategies:

> The creation of new objects, the transformation of known objects; a change of substance in the case of certain objects: a wooden sky, for instance; the use of words in association with images; the misnaming of an object; the development of ideas suggested by friends; the use of certain visions glimpsed between sleeping and waking, such in general were the means devised to force objects out of the ordinary, to become sensational, and so establish a profound link between consciousness and the external world.[47]

Toward the end of his life Magritte would firmly disavow any connection to dreams in his work:[48] indeed, he would describe dreams as a "sous-réalité" (sub-reality), an "easily forgettable malady of thought," and denied that they had any poetic value: "Poetry [gives] inadequate 'reality' an exciting meaning, [which is] *surreality*."[49] Contrary to his later point of view, in the 1930s Magritte associated a sense of universal mystery with the actions of condensing and displacement that are characteristic of dreams; painting was the place where realities hidden in the unconscious emerged, a hall of mirrors for the gaze.[50]

We may recall Sigmund Freud's own assessment of Surrealism, as witnessed in 1938, when the famous psychoanalyst met with Salvador Dalí and critiqued his painting *Métamorphose de Narcisse* (*Metamorphosis of Narcissus*, 1937).[51] It is prudent to keep in mind Freud's skepticism toward the analysis of Surrealist works before gathering Magritte's dreamlike elements into a catalogue of Freudian symbols—in which a pipe is a sexual reference; a box, a chest, a cupboard, and a table all female symbols; a suitcase the weight of the sins we carry; a staircase or ladder a representation of sexual intercourse; wood the "female material" par excellence; an overcoat a male symbol, and so on.[52] Objects may indeed embody such symbols behind their seeming ordinariness, but their appearance in Magritte's work is not (as it was in Dalí's case) the result of a *conscious*, voluntary approach. Thus, in his refusal to consciously paint dream images, Magritte perhaps provided, albeit unwittingly, objects symbolic of his own psychic life—they may in fact be all the more revealing in that the symbols and their interpretations were denied by their author.[53]

Magritte's rejection of the purported psychological motivations ascribed to his imagery provides a possible parallel to the artist's desire to separate his work from the bourgeois order from which it derived. This was a complex position, also reflected in the staid physical appearance and presentation of the artist, who willingly defined himself as "conventional" and "conservative" in his daily life, despite his many radical artistic endeavors (see plate 130).[54] In this, Magritte's position was in keeping with the Surrealist movement's general evolution in the 1930s, as many of its proponents were concerned with whether to identify themselves as Communists, and whether, indeed, they had revolutionary aims.[55]

In the late 1930s, a particular image by Magritte became subject to an emphatic interpretation that almost veered into caricature. In *Le Modèle rouge* (*The Red Model*)—two versions of which were painted in 1935 (plate 101 and fig. 8), and another in 1937 (plate 116)—Magritte looked at the "problem" of the shoe and offered a metaphorical solution. In the painting, the foot becomes a shoe, and vice versa, demonstrating, through what Magritte termed a "monstrous custom,"[56] the mutation of skin into leather.

Magritte would sit through a detailed interpretation of this work on March 11, 1937, over the course of an evening in London, spent in the company of Dr. Vits, a German psychoanalyst who had fled the Nazis, and Dr. Matté, a South American surgeon who, as Magritte noted to Paul Colinet (in a letter written, strangely, in English), "has read

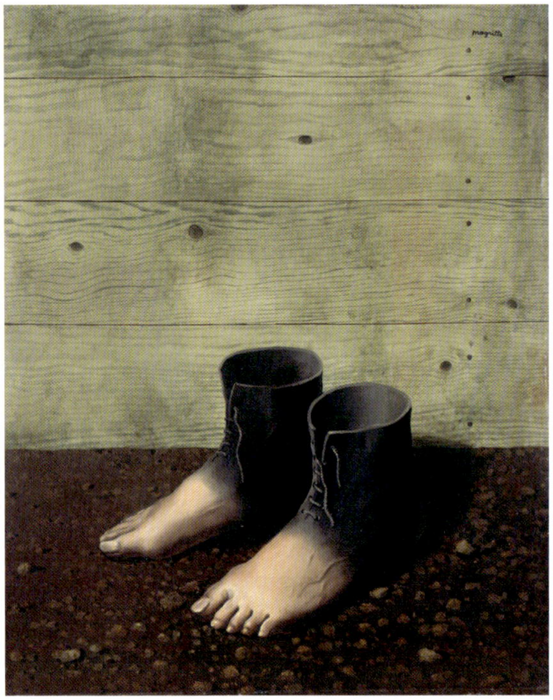

Figure 8. René Magritte. *Le Modèle rouge* (*The Red Model*). 1935. Oil on canvas, mounted on panel. 22 x 18 1/8" (56 x 46 cm). Centre Pompidou, Paris. Musée national d'art moderne/Centre de création industrielle. (Sylvester 2:382)

our friend Freud" and who treated young children with the aid of painting.[57] Magritte wrote to Colinet that Dr. Matté identified the paintbrush with the reproductive organ ("male," the artist specified helpfully). Admirers of Surrealism, the two doctors questioned the artist about the meaning of his paintings and offered their own analyses. Magritte reported to Colinet: "They think my picture 'The Red Model' is a case of castration. You will see from this how it is all becoming very simple." And he added: "After several interpretations of this kind, I made them a real psychoanalytical drawing (you know what I mean): 'canon bibital' [private gun], etc. Of course they analyzed these pictures with the same coldness. Just between ourselves, it's terrifying to see what one is exposed to in making an innocent sketch."[58] Interpretations of *Le Modèle rouge* have ranged from speculations about its revelatory proletarianism[59] to seeing the image (as Magritte notes here) as a symbol of emasculation (although, as the artist insisted in his letter, his intent was entirely "innocent").

In his 1937 version of *Le Modèle rouge* Magritte added some curious details: alongside the human boots, a cigarette butt and a few matches are scattered on the floor, giving a sense of disorderly realism and discomfort to the scene. A scrap of newspaper on the ground (see plate 116) shows an upside-down reproduction of *Les Jours gigantesques*; we can just make out the first letters of the title.[60] The disturbing and dense complexity of the image has, it would seem, little to do with the work's central interrogation, directed at the shoe itself. The introduction of these new elements into *Le Modèle rouge* would pave the way for many attempts at decoding the image. Such attempts—as Magritte lamented—did not address the objects in question so much as a predetermined "answer" produced by a gaze ever guided by preconceptions. The reference in the later version to *Les Jours gigantesques*, crumpled and thrown on the floor, invites us to connect the two representations by making *Le Modèle rouge* into a symbol of aggression and phallic power.

THE FEMININE IDEAL

In February–March 1934, Magritte participated in a large international exhibition at the Palais des Beaux-Arts in Brussels called *Le Nu dans l'art vivant* (*The Nude in Living Art*), organized by L'Art Vivant and the Palais's Société Auxiliaire des Expositions. For the event, a hundred paintings and sculptures by artists from the nineteenth and twentieth centuries were brought together. While the nude had been part of Magritte's work from the beginning of his career, by the mid-1930s he was discovering it afresh by striking up a new dialogue with the classical ideal. *Woman* remained an object of fantasy projection (as seen in 1931's *La Géante*, his visual response to a poem by Nougé, which was in turn a variation on a sonnet by Charles Baudelaire).[61] Beyond the motif of hypertrophied objects that so appealed to Magritte, *La Géante* introduced a new artistic take on the female body: from this point he began to follow an impulse toward the ideal.

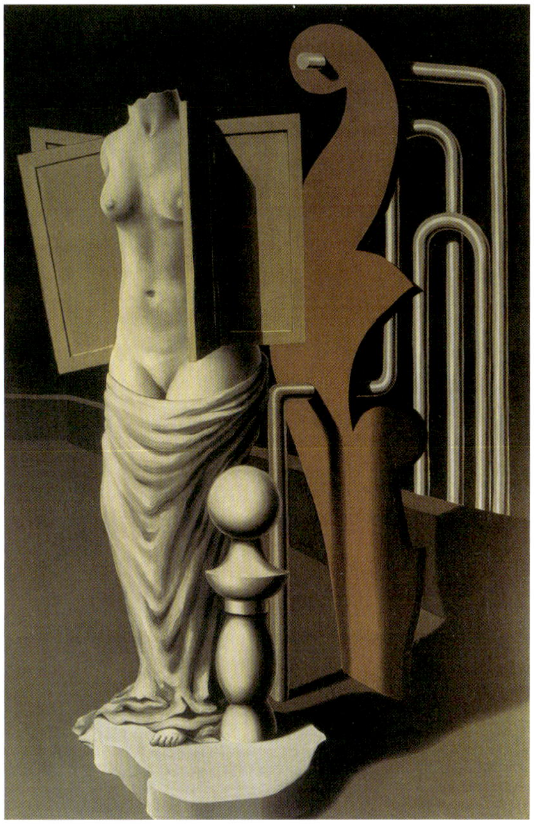

Figure 9. René Magritte. ***La Statue volante* (*The Flying Statue*). 1927. Oil on canvas, 47 3/4 x 31 1/2" (120 x 80 cm). Private collection. (Sylvester 1:132)**

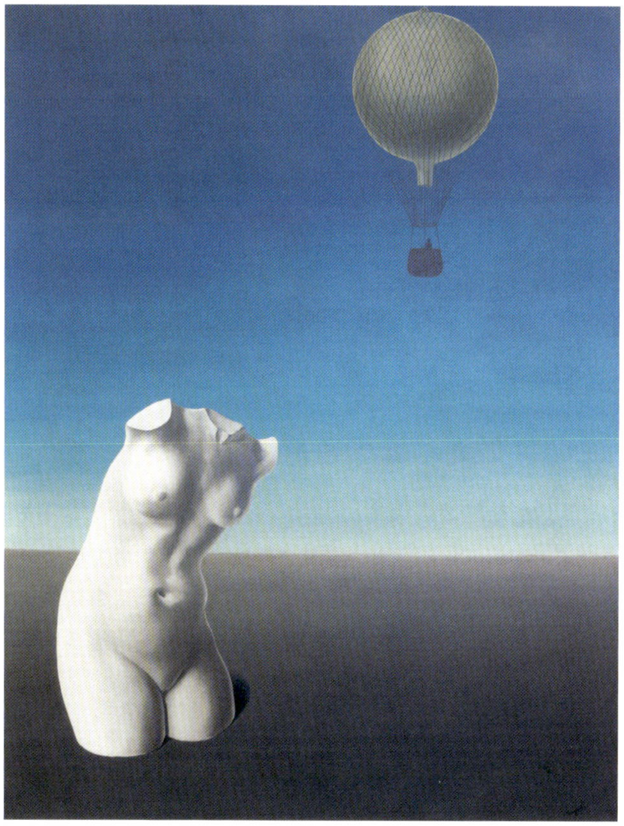

Figure 10. René Magritte. ***Quand l'heure sonnera* (*When the Time Comes*). 1932. Oil on canvas, 45 11/16 x 35" (116 x 89 cm). Mr. and Mrs. Wilbur Ross. (Sylvester 2:347)**

Magritte was drawn to the fragmented forms of classical statuary. Produced in 1927, his painting *La Statue volante* (*The Flying Statue*; fig. 9) evinced the psychic ambivalence characteristic of his paintings of the time. The sculpture in this work, originally painted a pastel-pink, seems to morph into flesh (an approach both related and opposed to that of grisaille as used in the Flemish tradition, in which the body is represented in the process of transforming into sculpture). In 1932–33, Magritte came back to *La Statue volante*; among the changes he made was a new emphasis on the classical motif—doubtless the result of his recent research with plaster casts.[62]

Such paintings as *La Belle de nuit* (*Lady of the Night*)[63] and *Quand l'heure sonnera* (*When the Time Comes*; fig. 10), both from 1932, contend with an issue that would soon be integral to Magritte's investigations: the idea of light. His manner of articulating the "problem" of light, as set forth in "La Ligne de vie," is telling: "As regards light, I reflected that while it has the power to make objects visible, its existence is manifest only on condition that it is accepted by objects. But for matter, light would be invisible. This is made obvious, I think, in 'The Light of Coincidence' [*La Lumière des coïncidences*; plate 93] where an ordinary object, a female torso, is lit by a candle. In this case, it seems that the object illuminated itself gives life to light."[64]

Magritte underscored the predominance of material over form in his understanding of light. This explains his fascination with the marmoreal coldness of ancient statuary, which, while it reveals light, leads to a perception of woman as the idealized, even divine, "Eternal Feminine."[65]

LA MAGIE NOIRE

This "Eternal Feminine" is closely examined again in *La Magie noire* (*Black Magic*; plate 98), a painting that was shown for the first time in 1934, shortly after its creation, in the *Minotaure* exhibition at the Palais des Beaux-Arts. David Sylvester has suggested, based on their similar palettes, that *La Magie noire* and *Le Viol* could have been painted at the same time, as the artist was following a new line of investigation.[66] The similarities with *Le Viol* are indeed striking; as Nougé would later observe, the earlier work—which evokes the "problem" of woman—"disturbs us, insults us, or harms us in order to awaken the spectator and lead him to 'greater awareness.'"[67] *La Magie noire* sparks a similar "awakening," but by arousing a sense of the marvelous.

La Magie noire thus engages the mysterious "alchemy"[68] that leads, as Magritte noted, to "transforming a woman's flesh into the sky"[69] by way of a poetics he had earlier explored in his painted plaster pieces. The "magic" in the title is not a reference to the supernatural, divorced from the real; rather, it evokes the experience—at the very core of Magritte's art of questioning—of each moment as a theater of the unpredictable. (As he would later put it: "Each instant manifests the absolute mystery of the present.")[70] Nougé translated such a state of mind when he evoked the "objective revelation" to which the work of art invites us: "The light is so pure and so present that the body gives itself over to the color of the sky and slips away from our sight like the darkest night. This is, however, only the transparent spell of reality and not a miracle. Suddenly, arising from the depths of the image or ourselves, one can hear a kind of solemn warning."[71]

The motif of black magic is linked to the idea of mutable materials (alchemy): sometimes flesh is transformed into sky, at other times stone changes into flesh—the artist is playing with the wonders of metamorphosis. Whether flesh or stone, with eyes open to the void or closed upon an inner world that keeps us out, here, the woman in poetic blue is seen as the ultimate resolution to the question of life: the Eternal Feminine.[72]

The impulse toward the classical that Magritte showed by paying tribute to this Eternal Feminine seems to have met with greater success than did the "art of the problem" with which he had been grappling since the early 1930s. In a June 1934 letter to Breton, Magritte wrote: "Unfortunately the people who buy my pictures are more attracted by those like *La Magie noire* for instance, which appeal to them immediately because of the pretty colours or what have you."[73] But as attested by the many variants on the theme, the idealized Woman clearly had a central position in the painter's mind.

La Magie noire also addresses the themes of the *marvelous*, about which Magritte would theorize extensively,[74] and of the mysterious. Nougé's interest in these notions was not as intense as Magritte's (and partly for this reason, the painter drew closer to Paul Éluard during this period).[75] Resistant to the idea of *mystery* developed by the painter—"The cult of mystery is not our strong suit; a mystery is only worth the revolt it elicits"—Nougé urged viewers of Magritte's works to transcend the limitations of language. He wrote: "Images sometimes help us reduce words' prestige."[76]

In Magritte's 1934 text "Le Fil d'Ariane" ("Ariadne's Thread"), he was more specific about his poetics. There he defined the space of creation as that of the mind, where, he believed, only the poetic could qualify as "real."

> Taking the poetic phenomenon *as being real*, and if we are trying to discover its *meaning*, here is a new direction leading us at once away from that sterile region in which the mind exhausts itself in trying to fertilize. The object of poetry would become a knowledge of the secrets of the world which would allow us to act upon the elements. Magic operations would become possible. They would provide real satisfaction for that profoundly human desire for the marvellous. [...][77]

The point, according to Magritte, is to isolate the mystery at work in the poetics. As he wrote in "Le Fil d'Ariane": "The reality of the element that offers up its secret is truly the place we must not leave at any price; it is a guidepost."[78]

Notes

The quotation that serves as the title for this essay: "L'image isolée, qu'advient-il de l'esprit?" ("Once the image is isolated, what happens to the mind?") is from Paul Nougé's 1933 essay "René Magritte ou les images défendues" (1933), repr. in idem, René Magritte (in extenso) *(Brussels: Didier Devillez, 1997), p. 54.*

References in the following notes in the form "Sylvester 1:8" or "Whitfield 6:7" refer to the volume and catalogue numbers in the six-volume catalogue raisonné of Magritte's works. Likewise, references in the form "Sylvester 1, p. 304" refer to the volume and page numbers. The first five volumes of the catalogue raisonné, published 1992–97, were edited by David Sylvester; the final volume, published in 2012, was edited by Sarah Whitfield. For complete publication information for all six volumes, see the "Selected Bibliography," p. 252.

Catalogue raisonné numbers are provided for works that are not reproduced as plates or figures in the present volume. Unless otherwise noted, all English translations in this essay are by Sharon Bowman.

1. See Sylvester 1, p. 117.
2. E.L.T. (Édouard Léon Théodore) Mesens, letter to Magritte, June 5, 1930, David Sylvester's René Magritte Catalogue Raisonné Research Papers, Menil Archives, The Menil Collection, Houston.
3. See Sylvester 1, p. 119.
4. Magritte himself had cited a lower estimate in his correspondence with Mesens. See ibid., p. 117.
5. Jean Émile Louis Scutenaire, *Avec Magritte* (1947), (Brussels: Lebeer-Hossmann, 1977), p. 37.
6. Magritte, letter to Paul Nougé, 1931, repr. in Marcel Mariën, ed., *Lettres surréalistes: 1924–1940* (Brussels: Les Lèvres nues, 1973), no. 193.
7. Among the exhibitions in which Magritte participated was *L'Art Vivant en Belgique, 1910–1930*, presented at the Galerie Giroux, January 17–28, 1931, through an initiative by the recently formed L'Art Vivant association. In April of the same year the association organized *L'Art Vivant en Europe*, which led to a rapprochement between Magritte and the Palais des Beaux-Arts. (Mesens, who had given up his own gallery, was now on the museum's staff.)
8. See Sylvester 2, p. 7.
9. For further description of the Salle Giso opening, see "Surréalisme," *Le Rouge et le noir* (February 18, 1931): n.p.
10. Paul Nougé, "Les Grands Voyages" (dated 1930; published 1931), repr. in *René Magritte*, p. 32.
11. Cami Stone (1892–1975, née Wilhelmine Schammelhout) was a Belgian photographer and a pioneer in the fields of photojournalism and advertising photography. She and her companion, Sasha Stone, were the subjects of a 2010 exhibition at Berlin's Galerie Berinson (no catalogue accompanied the show). See Sylvester 1, p. 349.
12. Nougé, "Avertissement" (1931), repr. in *René Magritte*, p. 27; trans. in Sylvester 2, p. 8.
13. Ibid.
14. For more on this subject, see Magritte, "Le Surréalisme en plein soleil" (1946), in idem, *Écrits complets*, ed. by André Blavier (Paris: Flammarion, 1979), pp. 210–11.
15. Nougé, "Avertissement" (1931); trans. in Sylvester 2, p. 8.
16. In the spring of 1932 Magritte collaborated with Nougé in the filming of these two short works, whose screenplays Marcel Mariën would publish in *Le Fait accompli*, no. 2 (May 1968), in Nougé's name only. Earlier, in 1929, Magritte had written the screenplay for a short film titled *Fleurs meurtries* (*Bruised Flowers*; see Maurice Rapin and Mirabelle Dors, *Magritte au cinéma* [Paris: La Tendance Populaire Surréaliste, 1961]). Directed by Robert Livet, it was filmed in a "subjective camera" style intended to locate the spectator right at the heart of a thought process that was being developed. A similar approach was used by Magritte and Nougé in their two 1932 films, which were unfortunately destroyed. Several years later—in 1936, according to Henri Storck; in 1938–39, according to David Sylvester—Magritte would develop a screenplay for his film *L'Idée fixe*, which directly recalls his pictorial world. See Magritte, "L'Idée fixe" (1936 or 1938–39), in idem, *Écrits complets,* pp. 66–67.
17. See *Le Fait accompli*, no. 2 (May 1968). José Vovelle describes both screenplays as the juxtaposition of images "which could be literary transcriptions of the painter's canvases" and sequences "so close to *Un Chien andalou* that it is easy to believe that the authors have just discovered Buñuel and Dalí's film." See Vovelle, "Magritte et le cinéma," *Cahiers dada Surréalisme*, no. 4 (1970): 106.
18. On the subject of Buñuel, in 1951 Magritte would underscore what to him characterized film's Surrealist dimension: "Surrealism is not an aesthetic. It is a state of revolt which should not be confused with the irrational, cruelty or scandal." See Magritte, *Écrits complets*, p. 502.
19. See Rapin and Dors, *Magritte au cinéma*.
20. Georges Roque discusses the links between Magritte's paintings and his work in advertising, with regard to the resolution of visual "problems." See Roque, *Ceci n'est pas un Magritte: Essai sur Magritte et la publicité* (Paris: Flammarion, 1978).
21. Magritte initially laid out these ideas in his February 1937 lecture (part of the *Pictures by Young Belgian Artists* exhibition organized by Mesens at the London Gallery [see Magritte, *Écrits complets*, pp. 96–98]), expanding upon them the following year in "La Ligne de vie" ("Lifeline"), his lecture delivered at Antwerp's Koninklijk Museum voor Schone Kunsten; trans. in Gisèle Ollinger-Zinque and Frederik Leen, eds., *René Magritte, 1898–1967* (Ghent and Brussels: Ludion, Royal Museums of Fine Arts of Belgium, 1998), p. 47. (All following "Ligne de vie" references and page numbers are from this volume.) This 1998 translation was adapted from that in Sylvester 5, pp. 9–22.
22. Both works were dated by Sylvester to early 1933. On the revised 1932 dating, see Whitfield 6:50 and p. 78.
23. Magritte, "London Lecture" (1937), in idem, *Écrits complets*,

p. 97; trans. in David Sylvester, *Magritte: The Silence of the World* (Houston and New York: Menil Foundation, Abrams, 1992), p. 222.
24. Ibid., pp. 222–23.
25. Magritte, letter to André Souris, 1932, in Mariën, ed., *Lettres surréalistes,* no. 199, p. 106; trans. in Sylvester 2, pp. 17–18.
26. Magritte, "Ligne de vie," p. 47.
27. Magritte expounded on "the problem of the window" in *La Condition humaine* in "Ligne de vie": "The problem of the window gave rise to 'The Human Condition.' In front of a window seen from the inside of a room, I placed a picture representing exactly the section of the landscape hidden by the picture. The tree represented in the picture therefore concealed the tree behind it, outside the room. For the spectator, it was both inside the room in the picture and, at the same time, conceptually outside in the real landscape. This is how we see the world, we see it outside ourselves and yet the only representation we have of it is inside us." Ibid.
28. "'The Ladder of Fire' afforded me the privilege of being acquainted with the feeling experienced by the first men who produced a flame by rubbing together two pieces of stone. In turn, from a piece of paper, an egg and a key, I caused fire to spring forth." Ibid.
29. Sylvester 2:426. "As regards the house, through an open window in the house-front I showed a room containing in its turn a house. This is 'In Praise of the Dialectic.'" Ibid.
30. "As regards the sun, I have found an answer: a grave. On the ground is a gravestone and the sun illuminates the sky, the earth and the grave. This answer is of the present moment and may become inadequate in the future. Taking the sun as the starting point of the journey we are engaged upon, taking the sun as our origin, we cannot for the time being envisage any more distant conclusion to this journey than death. This is a present certainty, and as the title of the picture, the expression 'The Beyond' recovers an emotional content." Ibid., p. 48.
31. "The tree, as the subject of a problem, became a large leaf the stem of which was a trunk directly planted in the ground. I called it 'The Giantess' in memory of a poem by Baudelaire." Ibid.
32. Ibid.
33. Ibid.
34. Magritte would revisit the idea of combining such oxymoronic elements in 1946 with his "Surréalisme en plein soleil" ("Sunlit Surrealism"), Magritte's personal concept of Surrealism's future.
35. Magritte, letter to André Breton, May 1937? (the letter is undated, but "20 mai 1937" is written in an unidentified hand on the envelope, perhaps indicating May 20 as the date of receipt). The original letter is held in the Fonds Breton, Bibliothèque Jacques Doucet. Trans. of this passage is in Sylvester 2, p. 245 (here the letter is dated May 20, 1937). Marcel Mariën later noted that Magritte's endeavor led him to "the ideal solution [to the problem of rain]: that of the object upon which the rain should fall." Mariën, "Note préalable" in René Magritte, *Croquer les idées* (Brussels: Les Lèvres nues, 1978).
36. For further discussion of the Surrealists and objects, see Max Hollein, Ingrid Pfeiffer, and Karoline Hille, *Surreal Objects: Three-Dimensional Works from Dalí to Man Ray* (Frankfurt: Schirn Kunsthalle, 2011).
37. See Paul Nougé, "L'Avenir des statues" (1933), repr. in idem, *René Magritte,* p. 68. See also Sylvester 2, pp. 21–22.
38. André Breton, "Crise de l'objet," *Cahiers d'art* 1–2 (May 1936): 21–26. Idem, "Crisis of the Object," in *Surrealism and Painting*; trans. by Simon Watson Taylor (Boston: MFA Publishing, 1965, 1972, 2002), p. 277.
39. Magritte, letter to Breton, June 22, 1934, David Sylvester's René Magritte Catalogue Raisonné Research Papers, Menil Archives, The Menil Collection, Houston (copy).
40. Magritte, "Ligne de vie," p. 48.
41. André Breton, *Qu'est-ce que le Surréalisme?* (Brussels: René Henriquez, 1934).
42. Magritte, letter to Breton, June 22, 1934, David Sylvester's René Magritte Catalogue Raisonné Research Papers, Menil Archives, The Menil Collection, Houston (copy); trans. in Sylvester 2, p. 30.
43. Breton, letter to Magritte, July 1, 1934, David Sylvester's René Magritte Catalogue Raisonné Research Papers, Menil Archives, The Menil Collection, Houston (copy).
44. Magritte, letter to Breton, May 1937?
45. Magritte, "Ligne de vie," p. 46.
46. Paul Nougé, "Les Images défendues," originally published in *Le Surréalisme au service de la révolution*, no. 5 (1933): 24–28. For the complete publication history of this text, see Sylvester 2, p. 19.
47. Magritte, "Ligne de vie," p. 46
48. See Magritte, letter to Volker Kahmen, June 29, 1967, David Sylvester's René Magritte Catalogue Raisonné Research Papers, Menil Archives, The Menil Collection, Houston (copy).
49. Magritte, interview with Carl Waï, originaly published in *Le Patriote illustré* (1966), repr. in Magritte, *Écrits complets*, p. 663.
50. On Magritte's sense of his work's relation to dreams in this period, see his letter to Paul Colinet, March 12, 1937 (written in English), repr. in *Magritte* (London: Marlborough Gallery, 1973), n.p.
51. See Fiona Bradley, *Surrealism* (London: Tate Gallery, 1997).
52. See Sigmund Freud, *The Interpretation of Dreams* (1900), trans. by James Strachey (NuVision Publications, 2004), pp. 135 and 477–90. For further discussion of Magritte and Freud, see Patricia Allmer, *René Magritte: Beyond Painting* (Manchester, U.K.: Manchester University Press, 2009), pp. 98–99.
53. Years later, Magritte would renounce extrapolative interpretations thus: "It would cost nothing to evoke some unnoticed work in my brain and say that it was what had determined the content of what I call an unexpected image. It would cost nothing either to add that, for instance, inevident memories of Baudelaire poems could have been, without my knowledge, the source of the painting *Les Fleurs du Mal*. References to unconscious activity coddle, one could say, the stubborn habit of explaining. But we are given no enlightenment about the thing being explained. Indeed, the thing being explained is lost in favor of a more or less intelligent practical explanation or hypothesis." Magritte, "Discours de réception à l'Académie Picard" (1957), in idem, *Écrits complets*, p. 440.
54. Magritte's affect as a conservative bourgeois is well known through photographs of the artist. This self-presentation was consciously and purposefully contrived. For more on this strategy, see Patrick Roegiers, *Magritte and Photography* (London: Lund Humphries, 2005).
55. For more on Magritte and Communism, see Magritte, *Écrits complets*, pp. 235–57.
56. Magritte, "Ligne de vie," p. 48.
57. Magritte, letter to Colinet, March 12, 1937. All known details about the doctors Vits and Matté are located in this letter; no further information about them has come to light.
58. Ibid.
59. The painting has been characterized as revealing "proletarian revolutionary temptations in a time of Surrealism." See *100 Œuvres nouvelles (1974–1976)* (Paris: Musée National d'Art Moderne, 1977), p. 86. In 1935 Edmond Kinds described the work and its title as showing the artist's desire to "help us understand . . . that we are all *des pieds*" (*pieds* means "feet"—slang for "idiots"). See *Documents* 35, no. 6 (November 1935): 9.
60. For further discussion of this 1937 variant of *Le Modèle rouge*, see Stephanie D'Alessandro, "'Mirrors That Become Paintings': Magritte's Commissions for Edward James, London, 1937–1938," in this volume, pp. 195–201.
61. Sylvester 2:341, pp. 175–76.
62. For further information about the changes introduced to *La Statue volante* in 1932–33, see Sylvester 2, pp. 181–82.
63. Sylvester 2:346.
64. Magritte, "Ligne de vie," p. 47.
65. The "Eternal Feminine," or *Ewig-Weibliche*—the feminine aspect of God—is an important theme in Johann Wolfgang von Goethe's *Faust, Part II*, which ends with these lines, spoken by

a Mystic Choir: "All of the transient,/Is parable, only:/The insufficient,/Here, grows to reality:/ The indescribable,/Here, is done:/ Woman, eternal,/Beckons us on."

66. Sylvester 2, p. 187.

67. Paul Nougé, "René Magritte ou la révélation objective" (1936), in idem, *René Magritte*, p. 38.

68. Ibid., p. 36.

69. Magritte, handwritten text about titles, Royal Museums of Fine Arts of Belgium, Brussels/ Archives for Contemporary Art in Belgium. See idem, *Écrits complets*, pp. 259–63.

70. Magritte, "Dans la nuit de René Magritte il y a le ciel qui flotte sur nous tous" (1958), in ibid., p. 465.

71. Nougé, "René Magritte ou la révélation objective" (1936), in idem, *René Magritte*, pp. 36–37.

72. Magritte had touched on the idea of this metaphysical transformation of woman to eternal being a few years earlier, writing in 1929: "To progress from the *idea* of love to the *fact* of loving [...] a being who has appeared in reality makes his existence so crucial that he must be loved and followed through light or darkness." Magritte, "Réponse à l'enquête sur l'amour" (1929), in idem, *Écrits complets*, p. 57.

73. Magritte, letter to André Breton, June 22, 1934, David Sylvester's René Magritte Catalogue Raisonné Research Papers, Menil Archives, The Menil Collection, Houston (copy); trans. in Sylvester 2, p. 187.

74. See, for example, Magritte, "La Peinture inutile de M." (1953), in idem, *Écrits complets*, pp. 343–44.

75. In the fall of 1935, Paul Éluard would publish his poem "René Magritte" in issue 5–6 of *Cahiers d'art*, along with a text and two paintings by Magritte. The poem, on which Éluard had been working since 1933, can be found in the collection *Les Yeux fertiles*, published in 1936, and then in an Eng. trans. by Man Ray in the catalogue for the exhibition at the Julien Levy Gallery in New York. Magritte would speak of their closeness in 1962, declaring that Éluard "was able to evoke reality unseparated from its mystery—the mystery that does not arise from any doctrine. The mystery to which nothing can be compared, and without which no thought or world would be possible." See Jan Walravens, "Rencontre avec Magritte," in Magritte, *Écrits complets*, p. 536.

76. Nougé, "René Magritte ou la révélation objective," in idem, *René Magritte*, p. 35.

77. Magritte, "Le Fil d'Ariane" (1934), in idem, *Écrits complets*, p. 82; trans. in Sylvester 2, p. 28.

78. Magritte, "Le Fil d'Ariane" (1934) in idem, *Écrits complets*, p. 82.

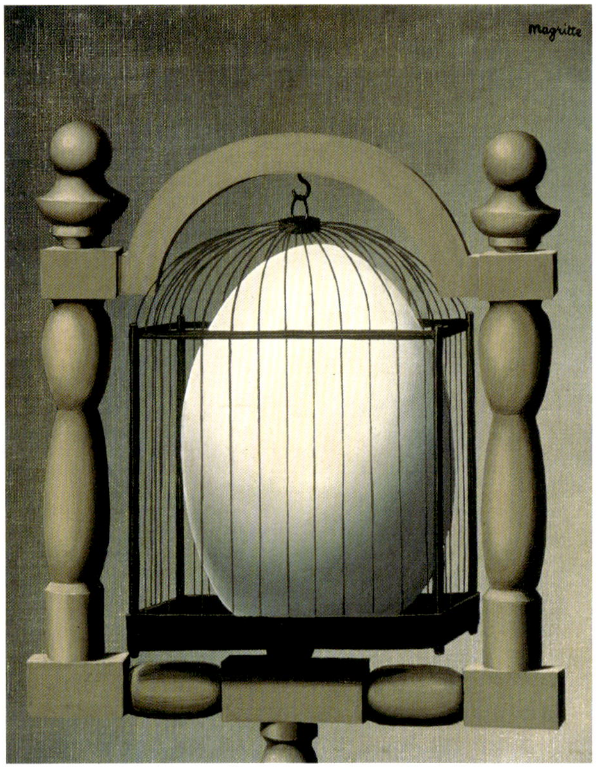

92. LES AFFINITÉS ÉLECTIVES (ELECTIVE AFFINITIES). 1932.

Oil on canvas, 16 1/8 x 13" (41 x 33 cm)

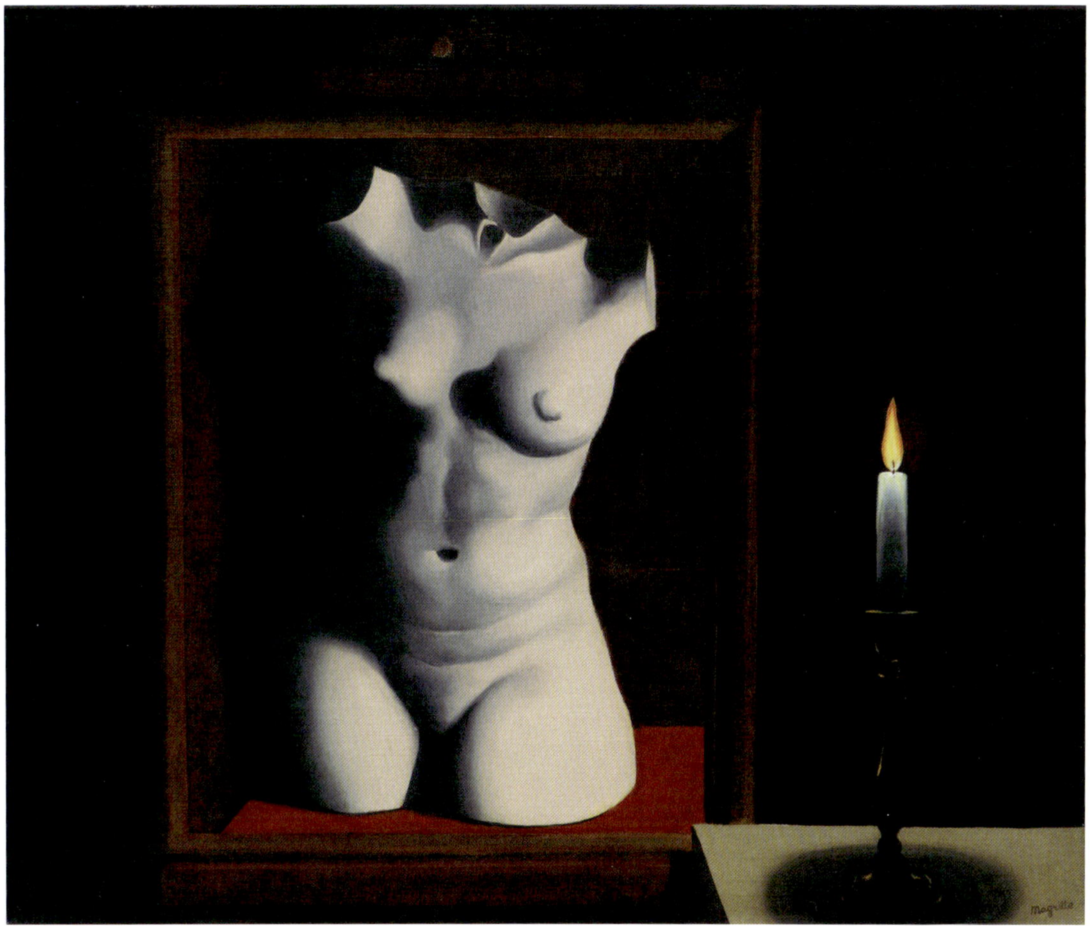

93. LA LUMIÈRE DES COÏNCIDENCES (THE LIGHT OF COINCIDENCES). 1933.
Oil on canvas, 23 5/8 x 28 3/4" (60 x 73 cm)

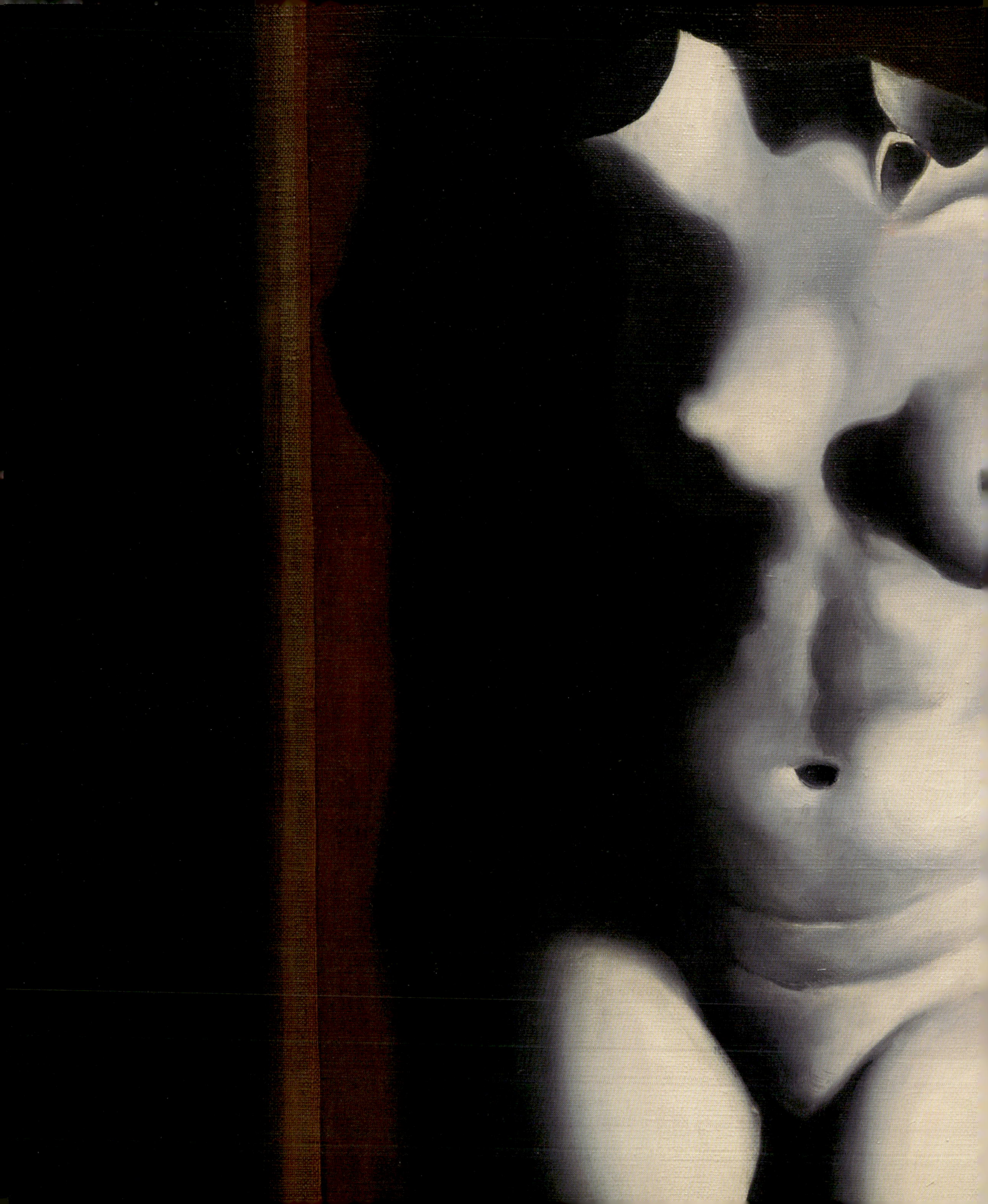

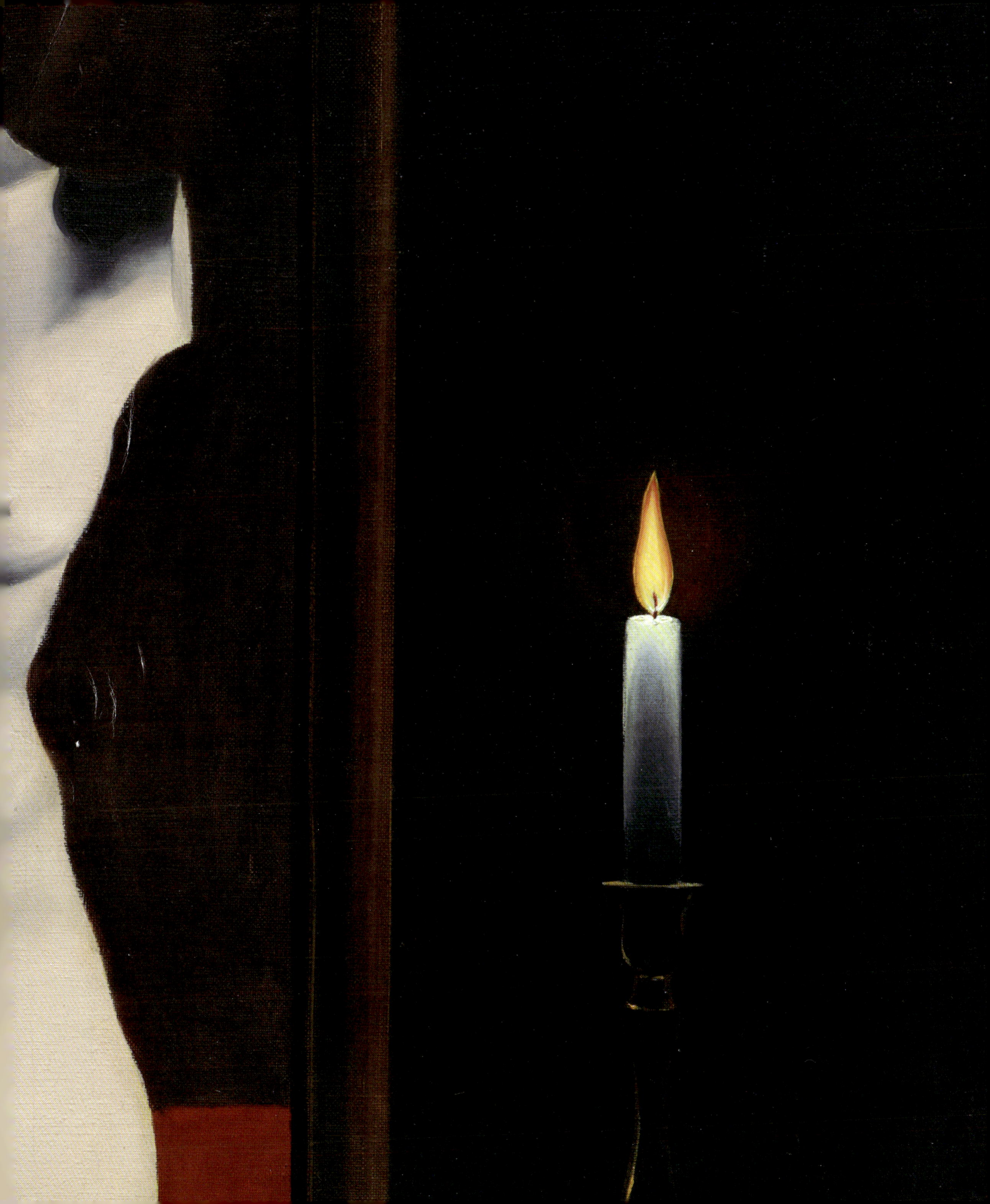

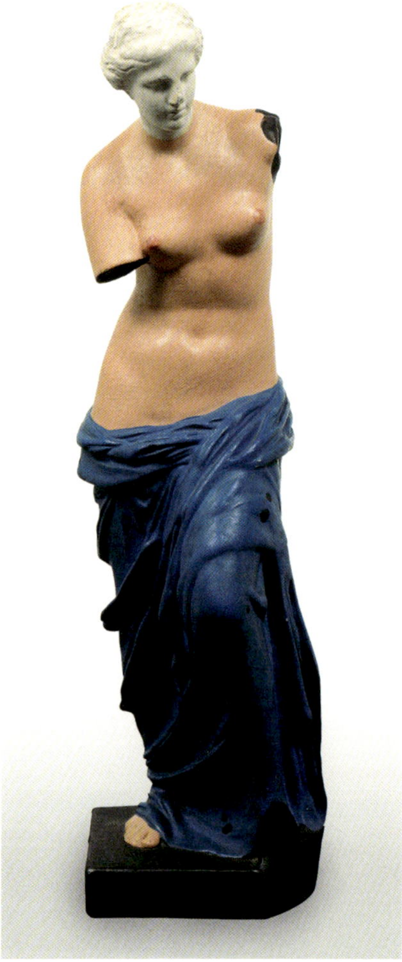

94. LES MENOTTES DE CUIVRE (THE COPPER HANDCUFFS). 1931.

Oil on plaster, 14 $^{9}/_{16}$" (37 cm) high

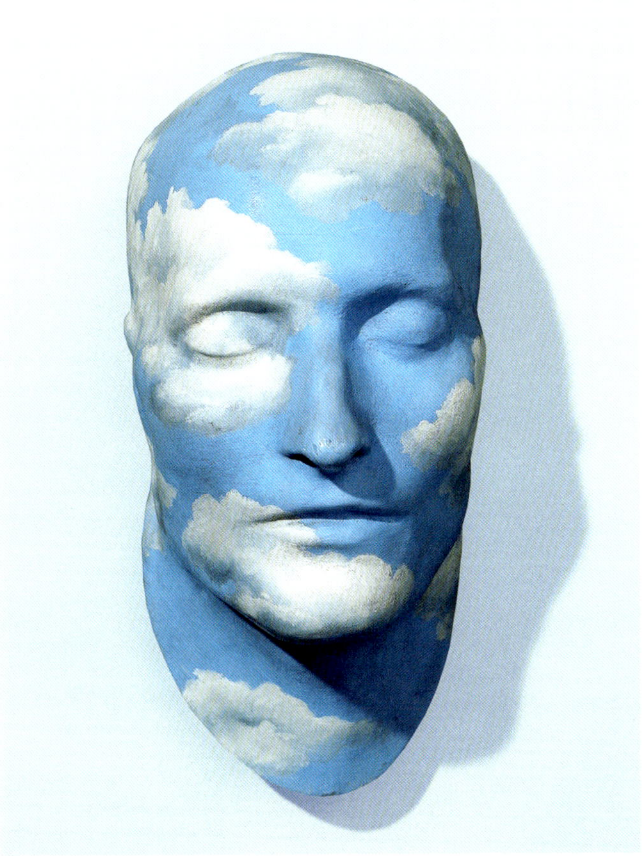

95. L'AVENIR DES STATUES (THE FUTURE OF STATUES). c. 1932.

Oil on plaster, 12 5/8" (32 cm) high

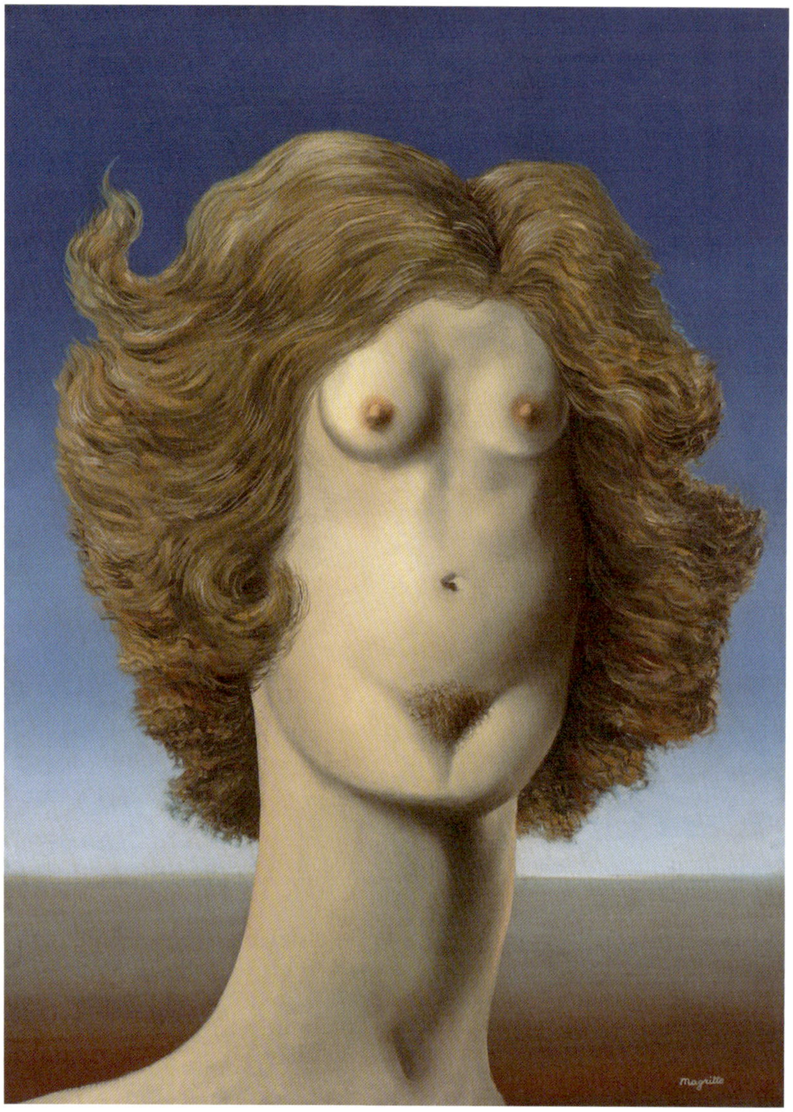

96. LE VIOL (THE RAPE). 1934.
Oil on canvas, 28 3/4 x 21 1/4" (73 x 54 cm)

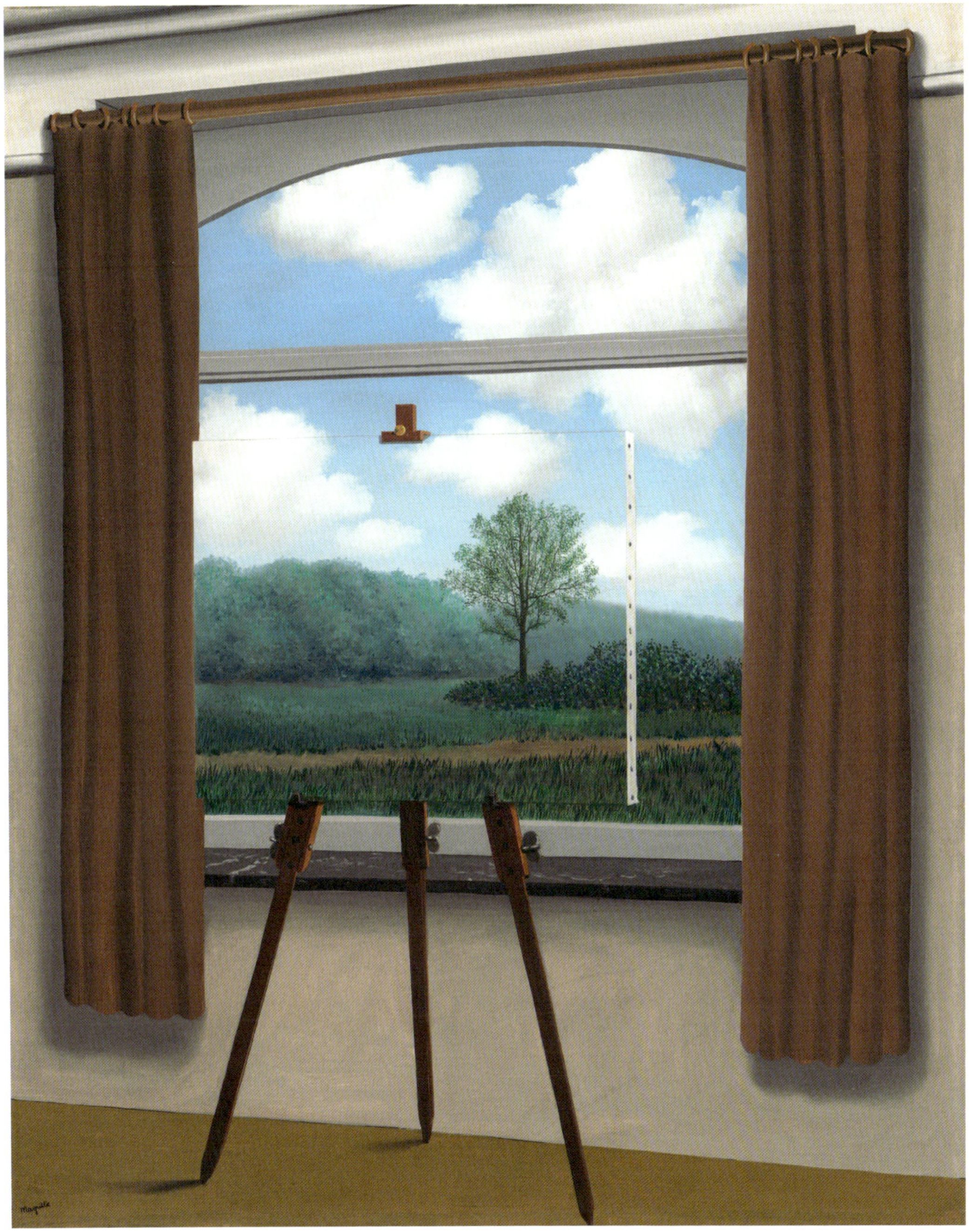

97. LA CONDITION HUMAINE (THE HUMAN CONDITION). 1933.

Oil on canvas, 39 3/8 x 31 7/8" (100 x 81 cm)

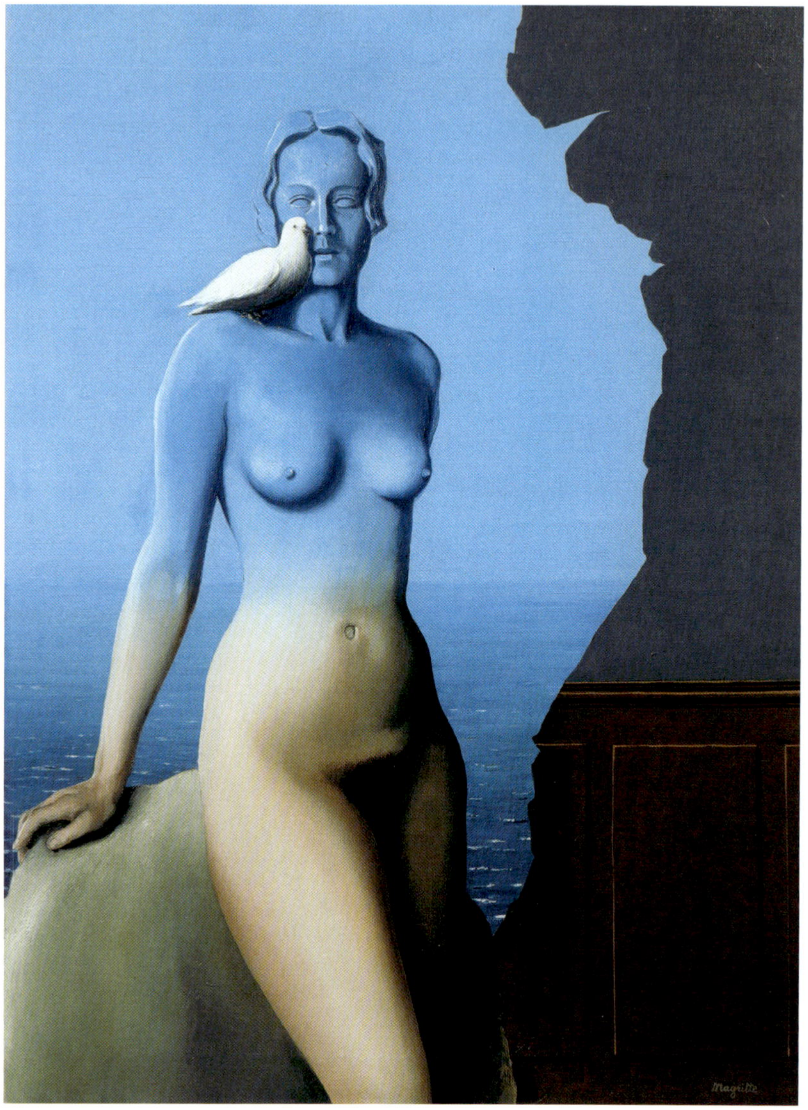

98. LA MAGIE NOIRE (BLACK MAGIC). 1934.

Oil on canvas, 28 3/4 x 21 1/4" (73 x 54 cm)

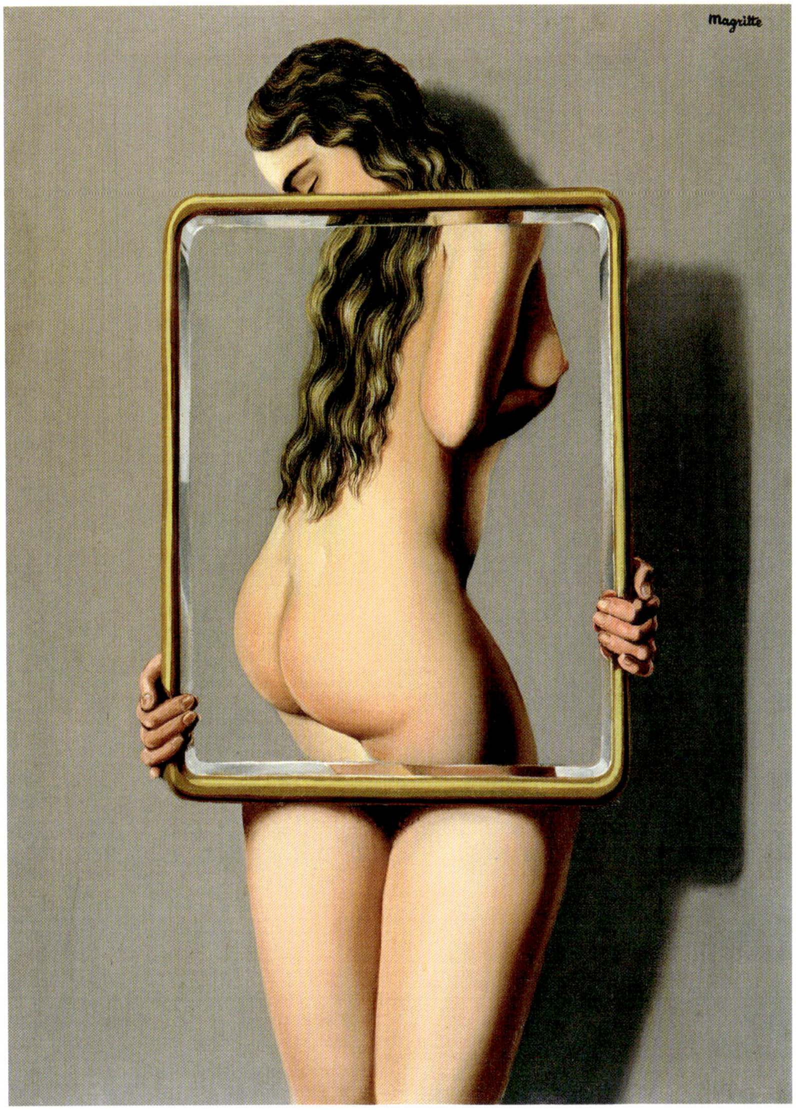

99. LES LIAISONS DANGEREUSES (DANGEROUS LIAISONS). 1935.

Oil on canvas, 28 3/4 x 21 1/4" (73 x 54 cm)

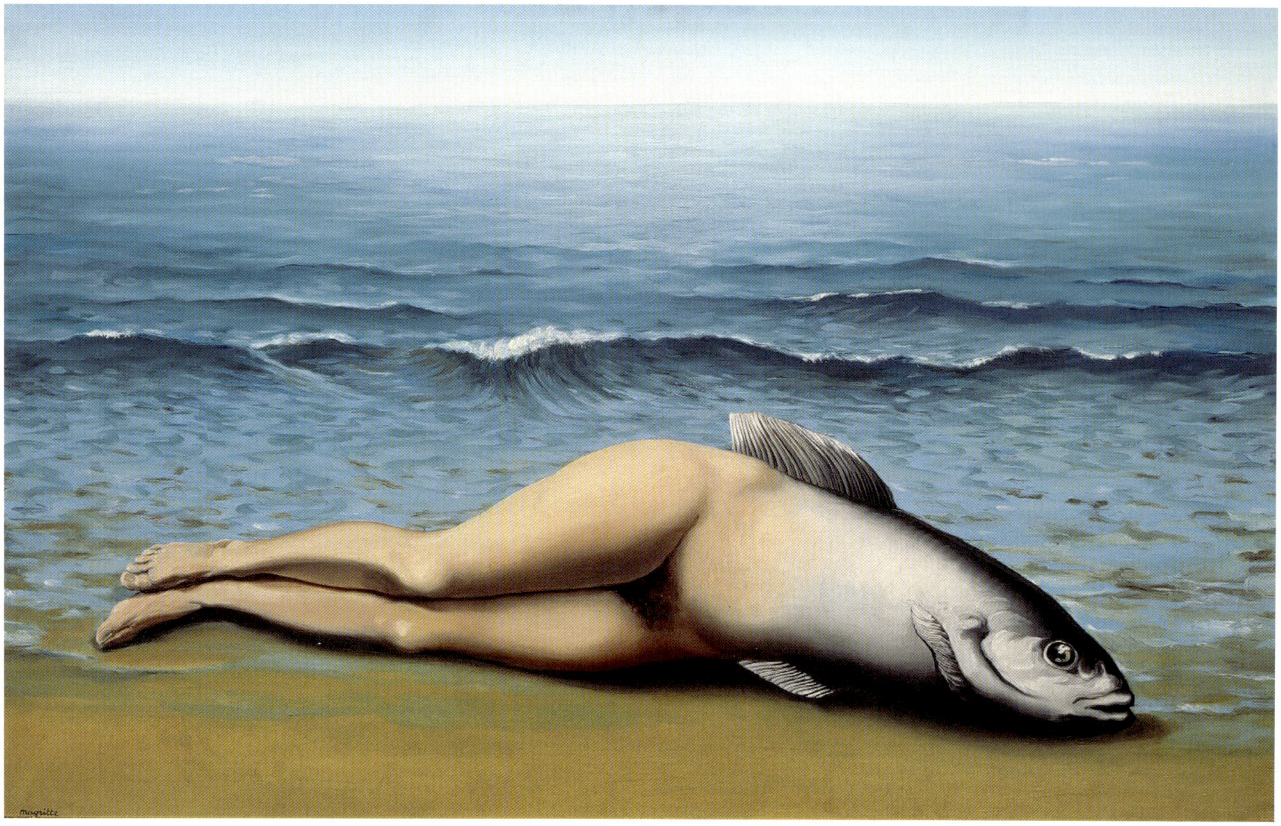

100. L'INVENTION COLLECTIVE (COLLECTIVE INVENTION). 1935.

Oil on canvas, 28 3/4 x 45 11/16" (73 x 116 cm)

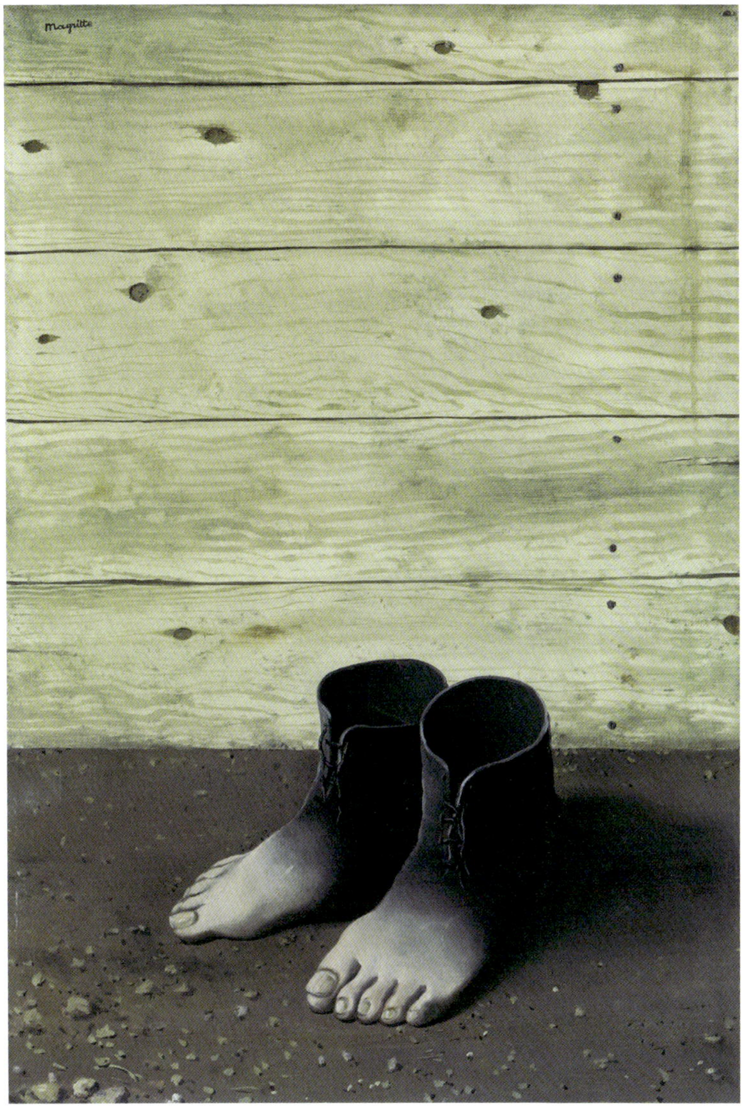

101. LE MODÈLE ROUGE (THE RED MODEL). 1935.

Oil on canvas, 29 3/8 x 19 1/16" (72 x 48.5 cm)

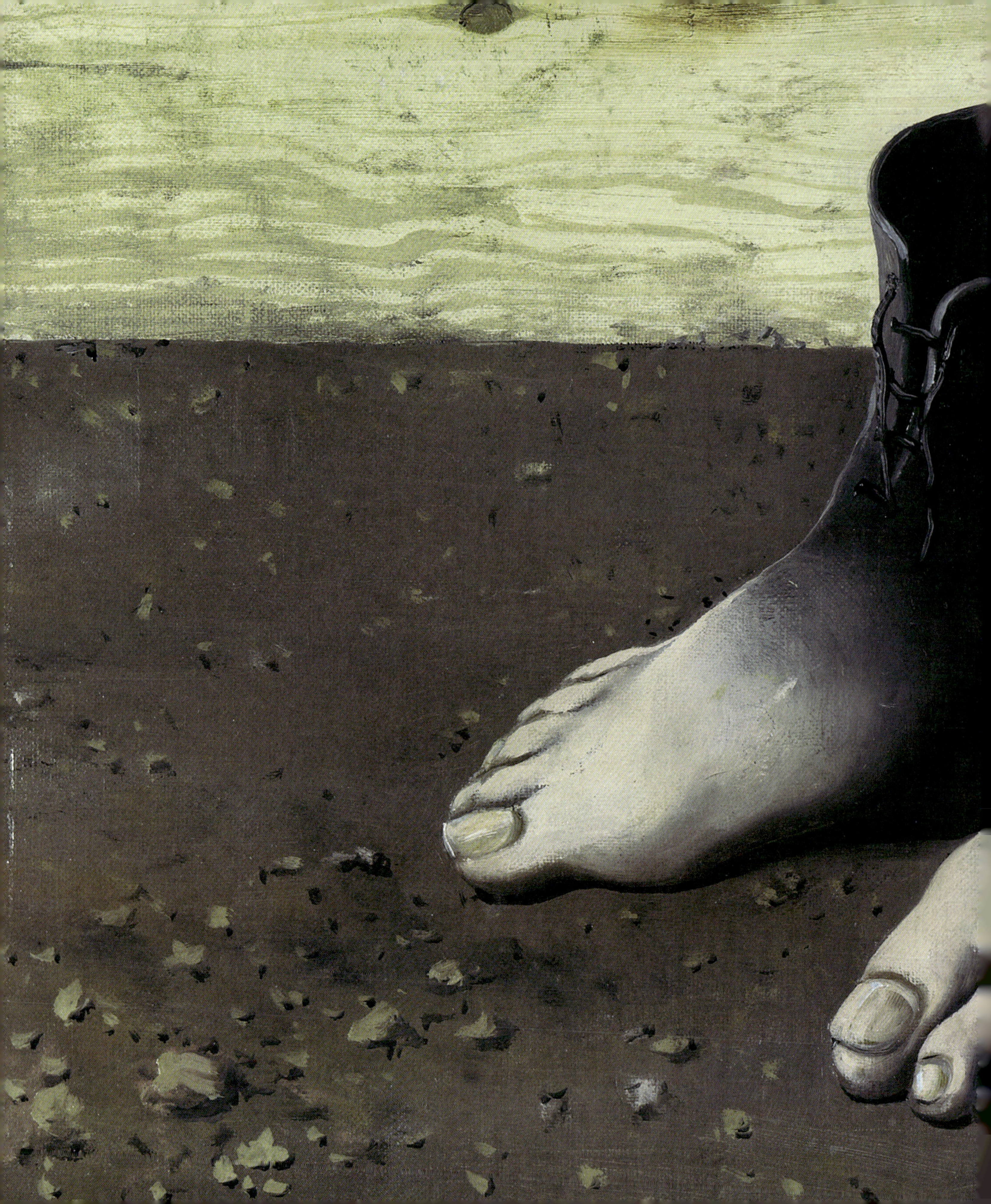

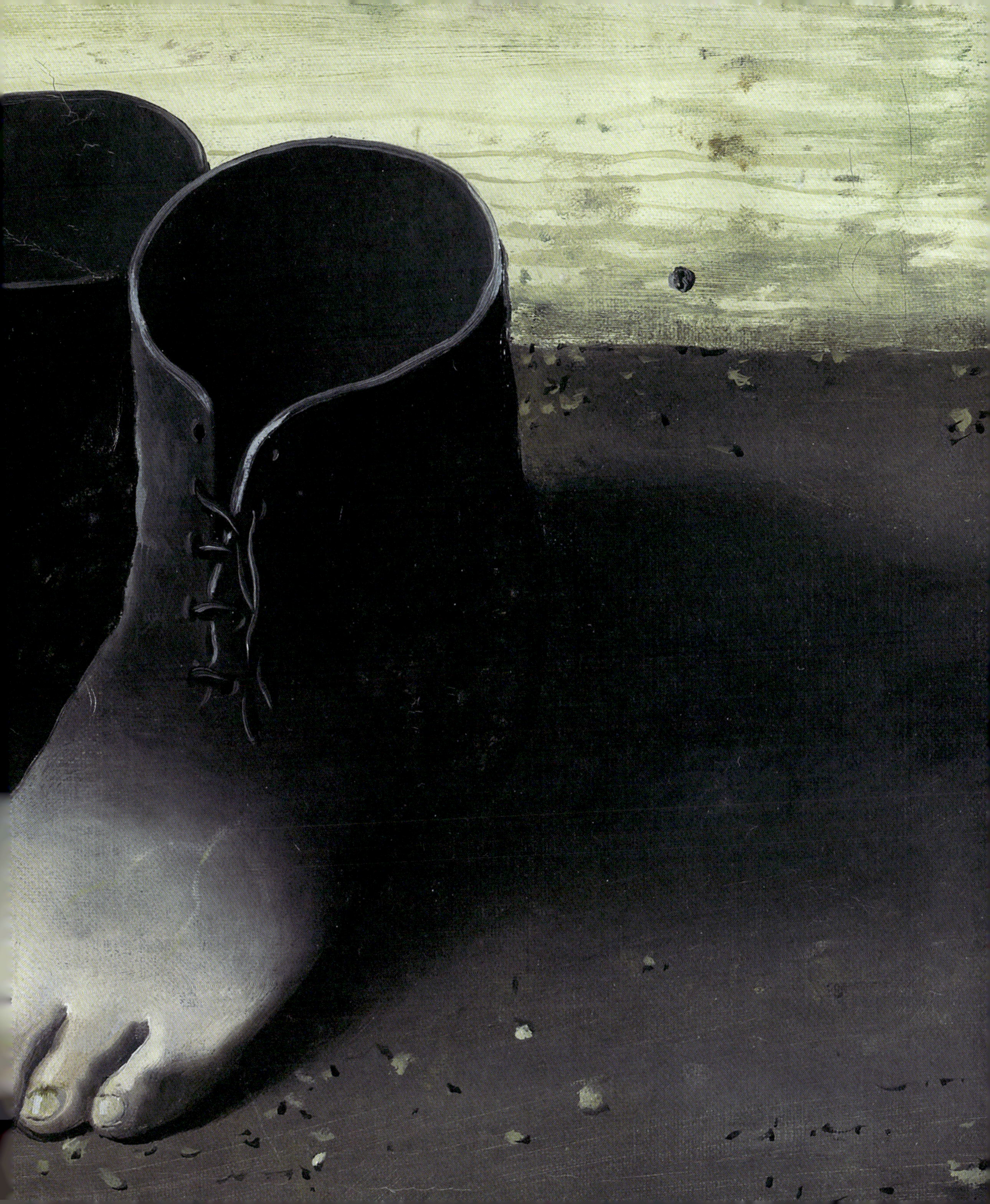

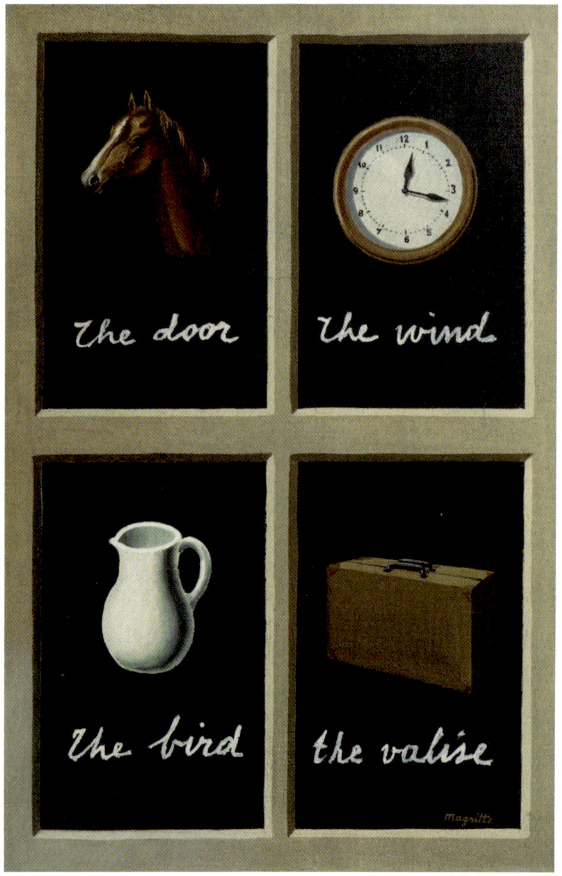

102. LA CLEF DES SONGES (THE INTERPRETATION OF DREAMS). 1935.
Oil on canvas, 16 1/8 x 10 5/8" (41 x 27 cm)

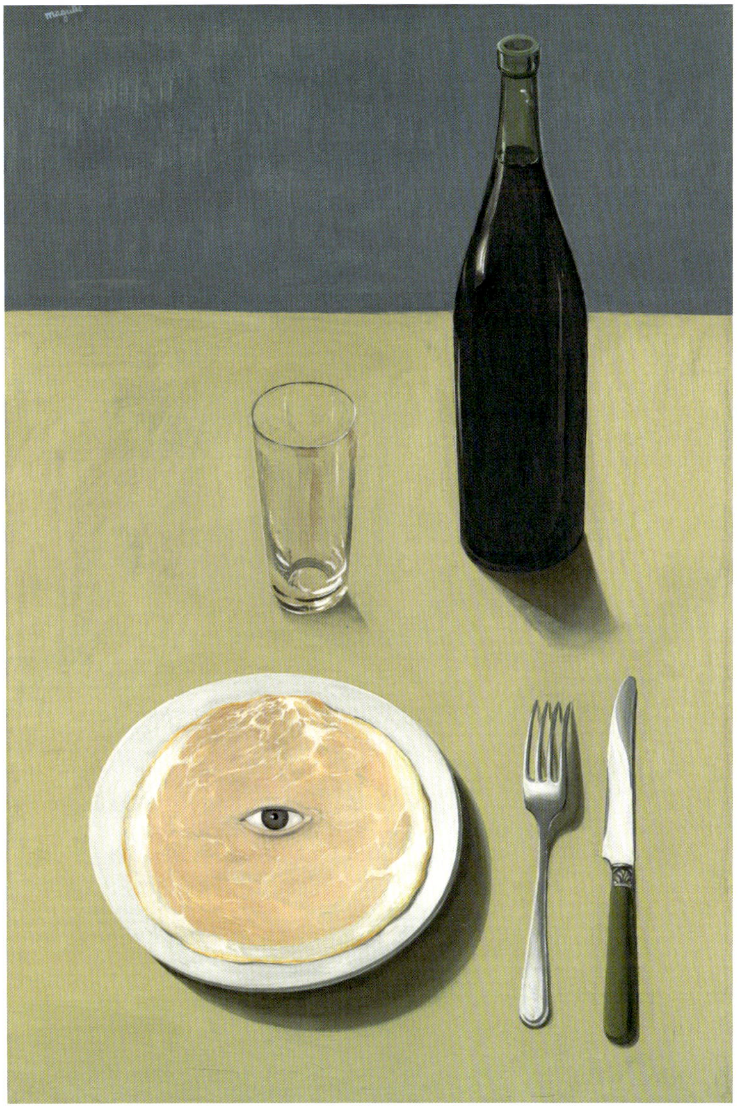

103. LE PORTRAIT (THE PORTRAIT). 1935.

Oil on canvas, 28 7/8 x 19 7/8" (73.3 x 50.2 cm)

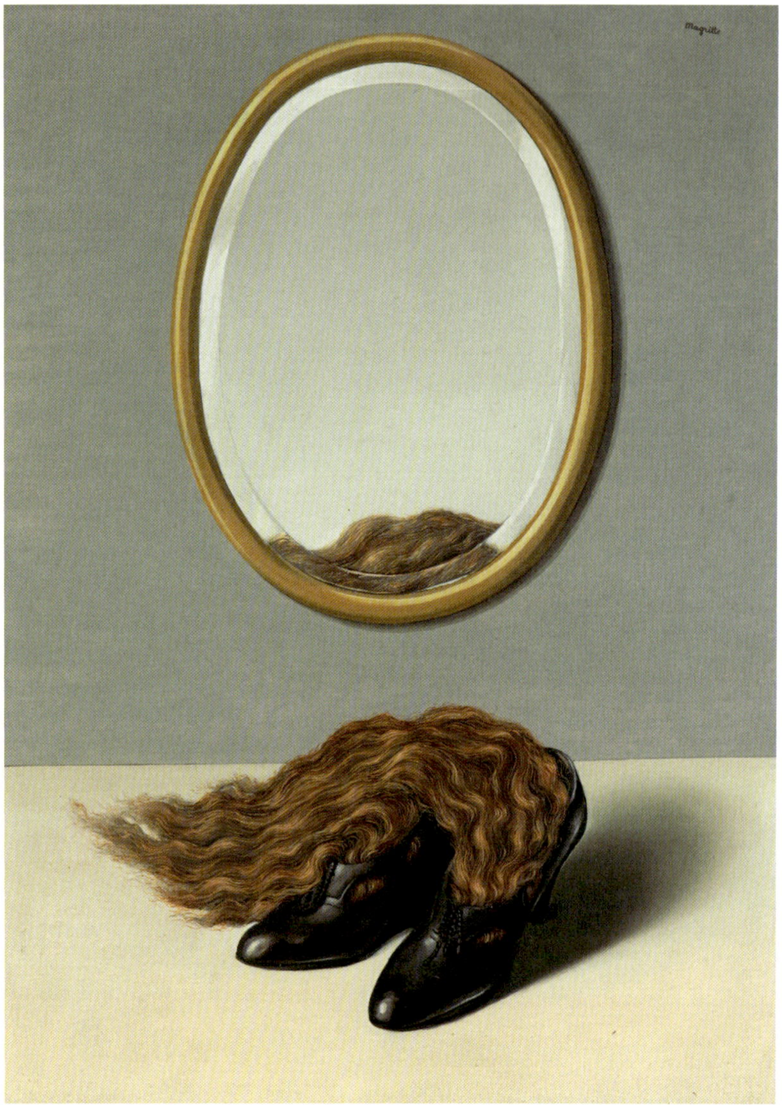

104. L'AMOUR DÉSARMÉ (LOVE DISARMED). 1935.
Oil on canvas, 28 3/8 x 21 1/4" (72 x 54 cm)

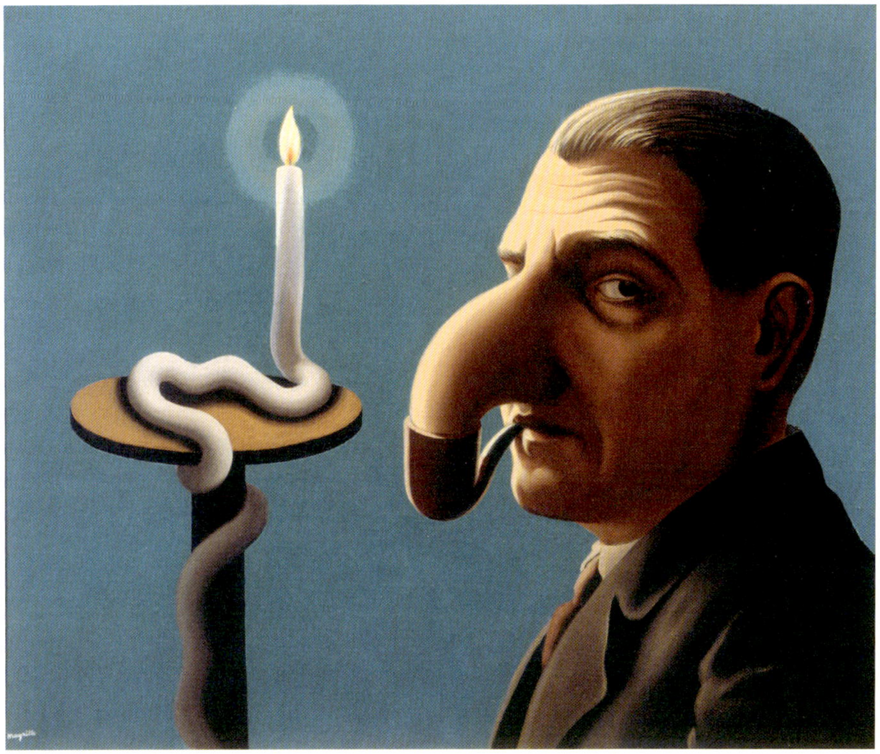

105. LA LAMPE PHILOSOPHIQUE (THE PHILOSOPHER'S LAMP). 1936.

Oil on canvas, 18 1/8 x 21 5/8" (46 x 55 cm)

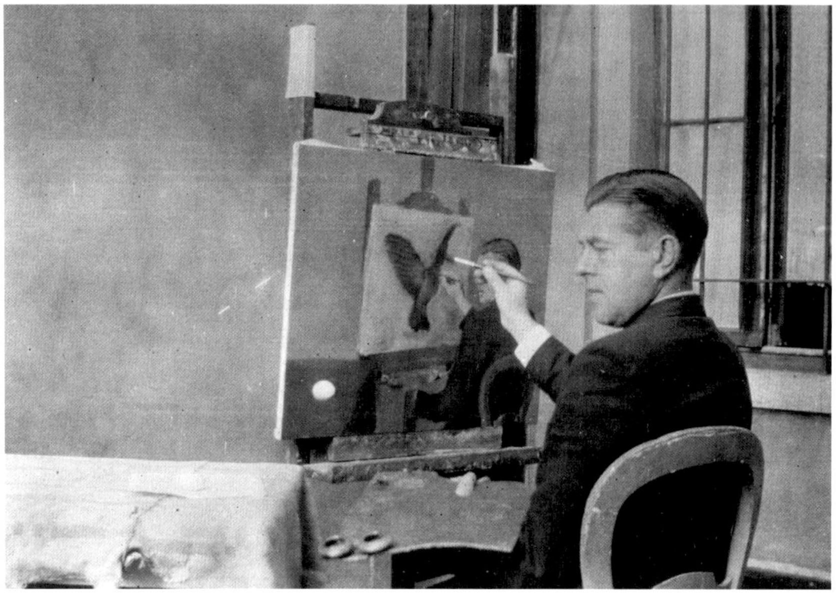

106. René Magritte and *La Clairvoyance* (*Clairvoyance*). 1936.
Photographer unknown. Gelatin silver print, 2 7/16 x 3 7/16" (6.2 x 8.7 cm)

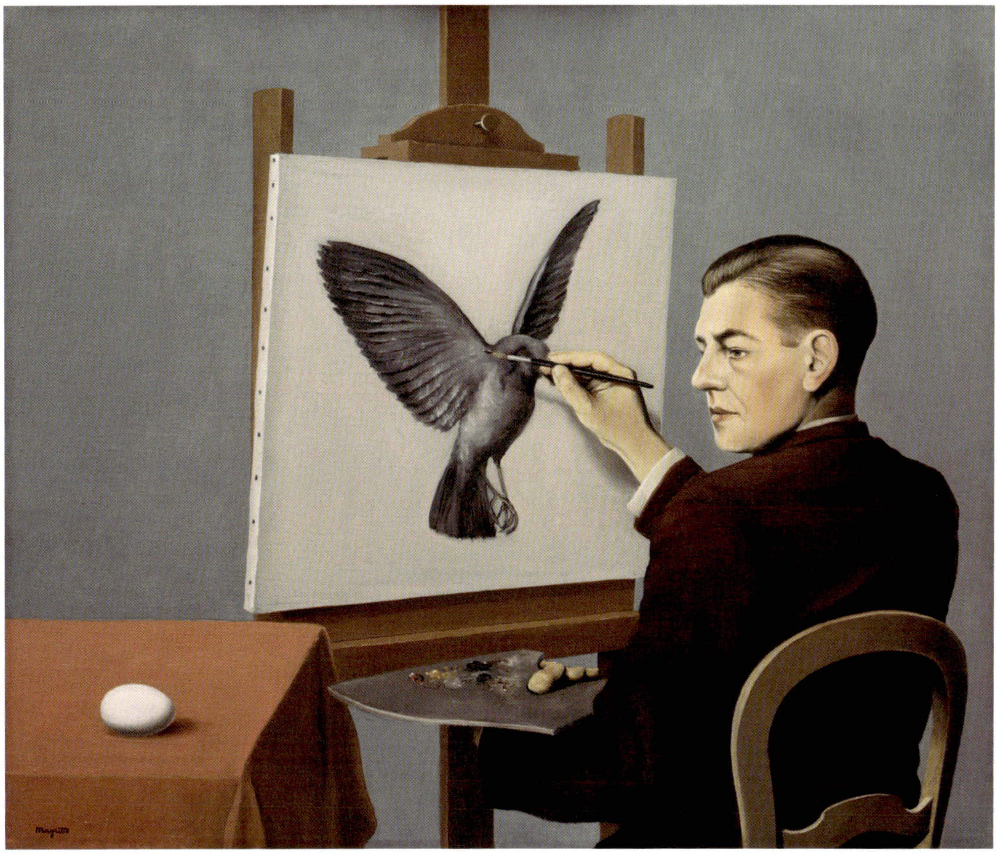

107. LA CLAIRVOYANCE (CLAIRVOYANCE). 1936.

Oil on canvas, 21¼ x 25 9/16" (54 x 65 cm)

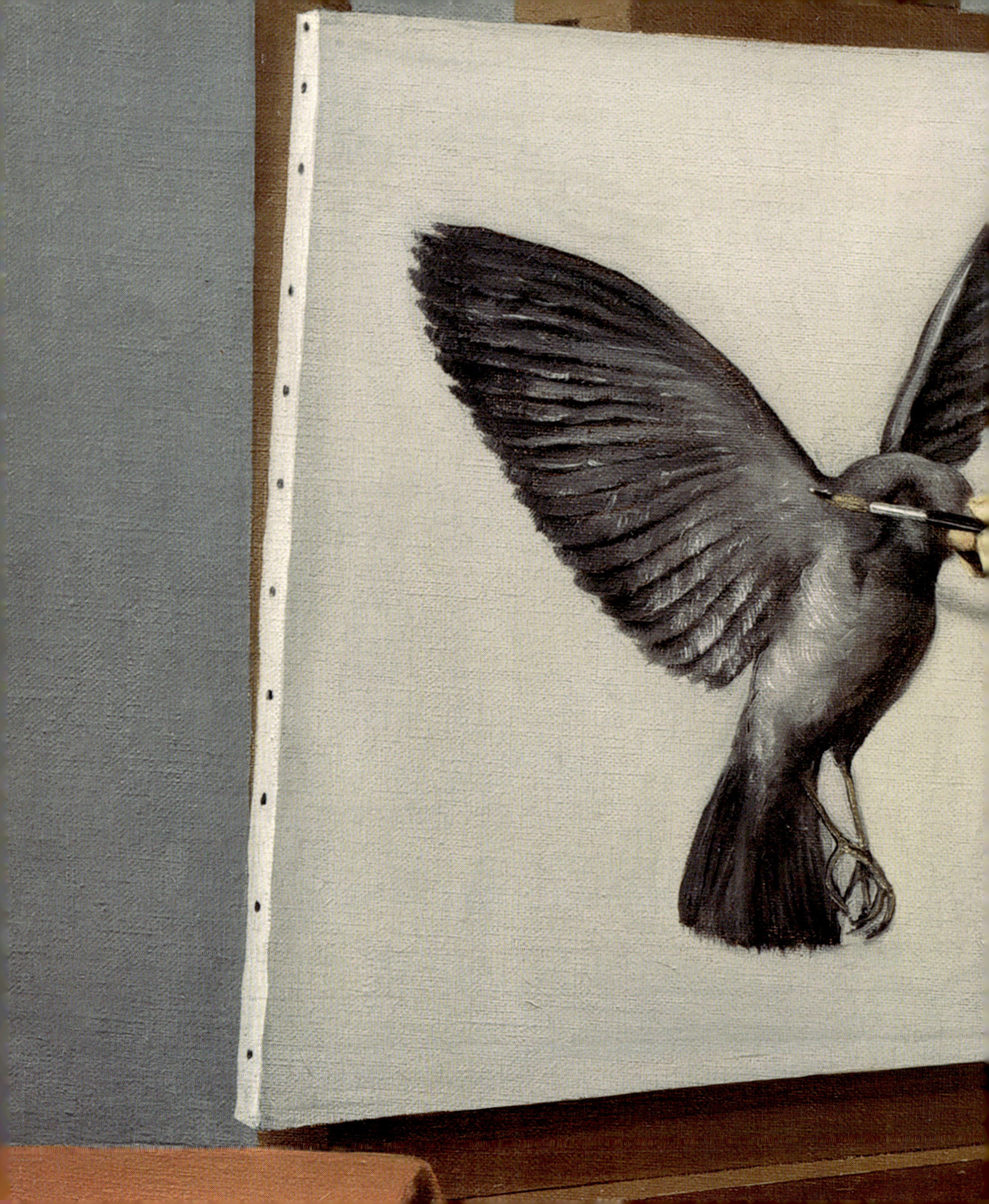

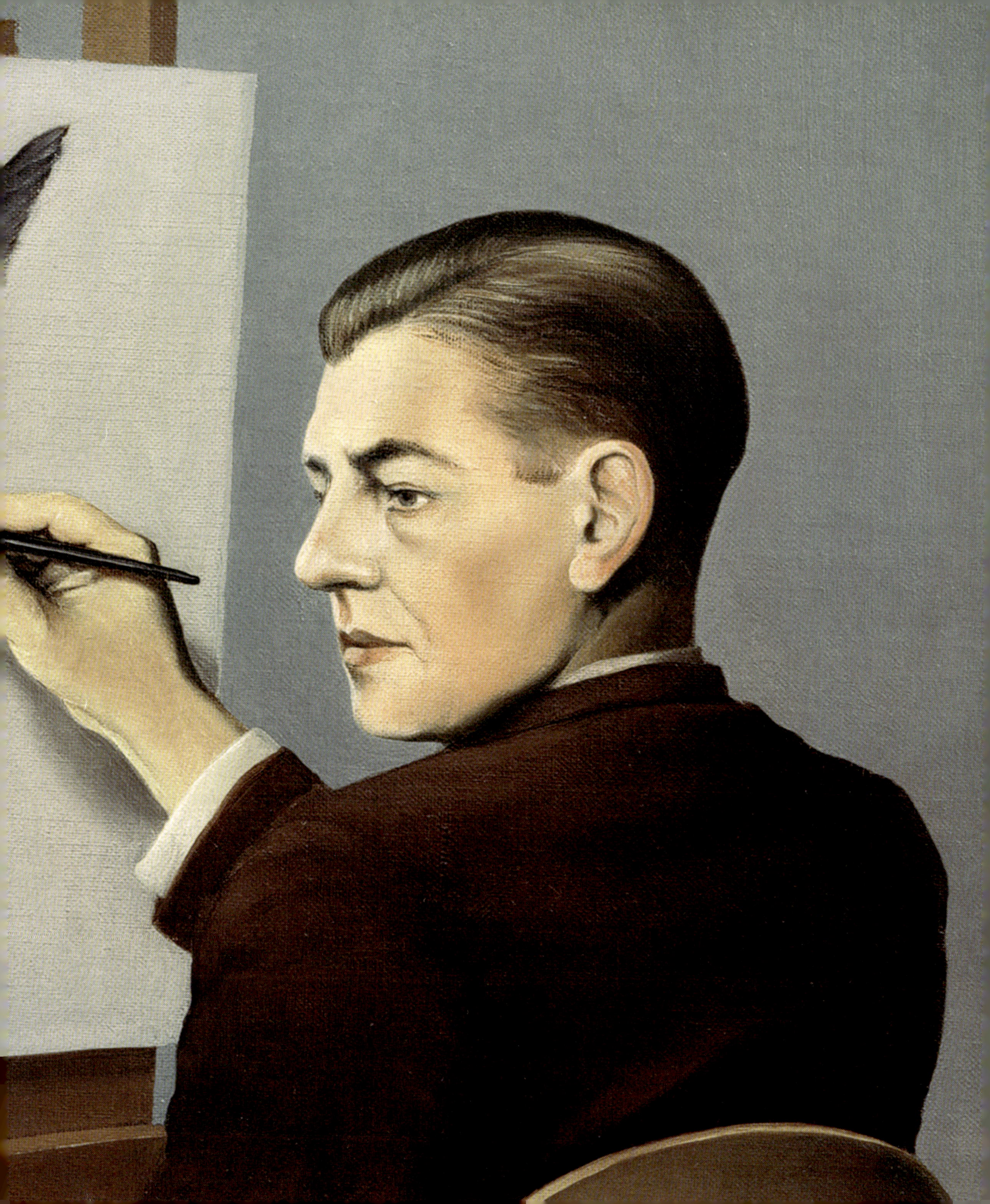

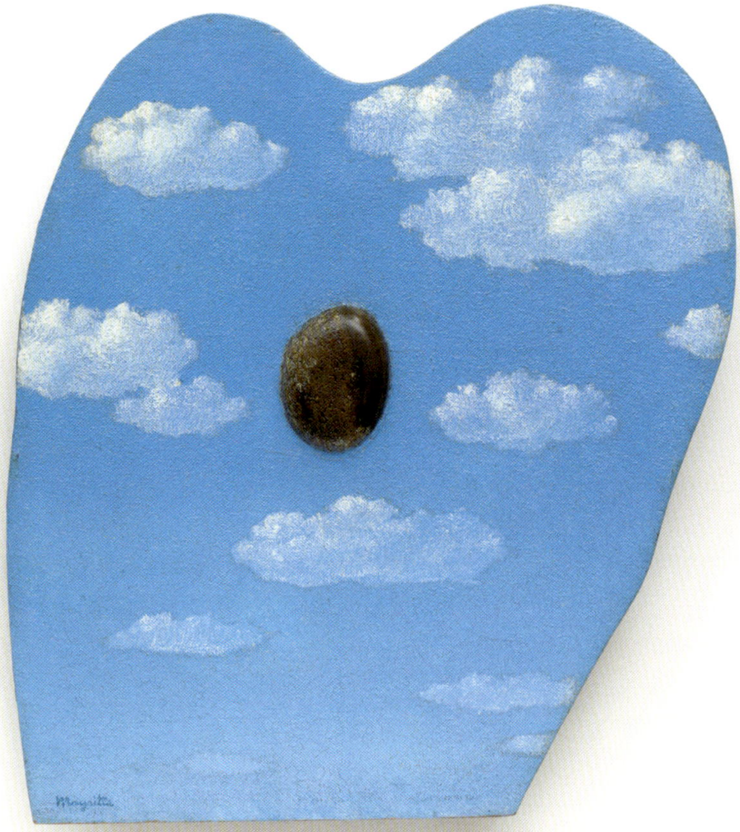

108. LE FAIT PRIMITIF (THE PRIMORDIAL FACT). 1936.
Oil on panel with pebble, 14 3/16 x 13 3/8" (36 x 34 cm)

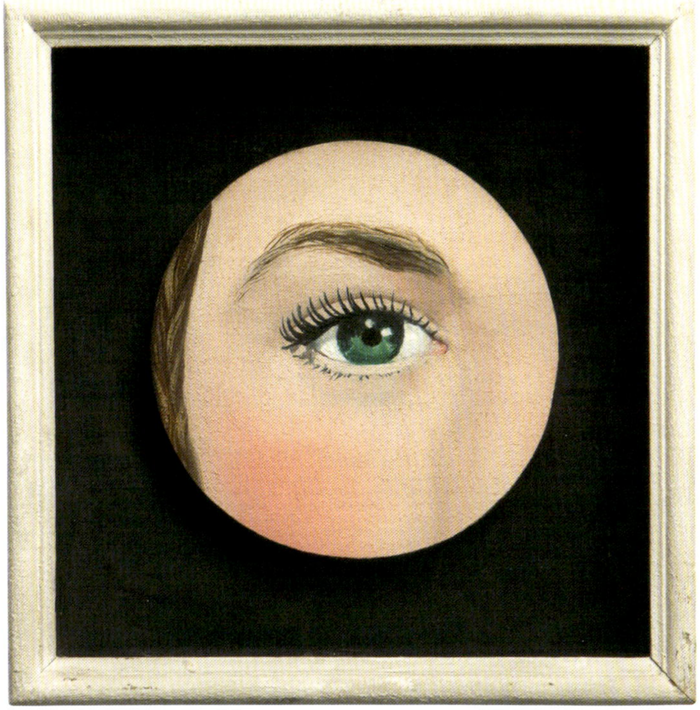

109. OBJET PEINT: ŒIL (PAINTED OBJECT: EYE). 1936 or 1937.
Oil on panel glued to wooden base, 10 x 10 x 2" (25.4 x 25.4 x 5.1 cm)

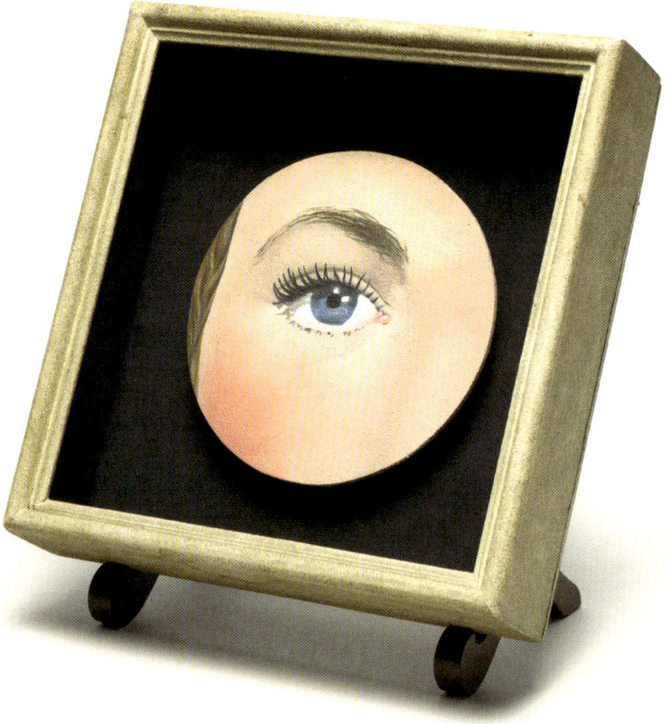

110. OBJET PEINT: ŒIL (PAINTED OBJECT: EYE). 1932/35.
Oil on panel glued to wooden base, 10 5/8 x 9 3/4 x 5 11/16" (27 x 24.8 x 14.4 cm)

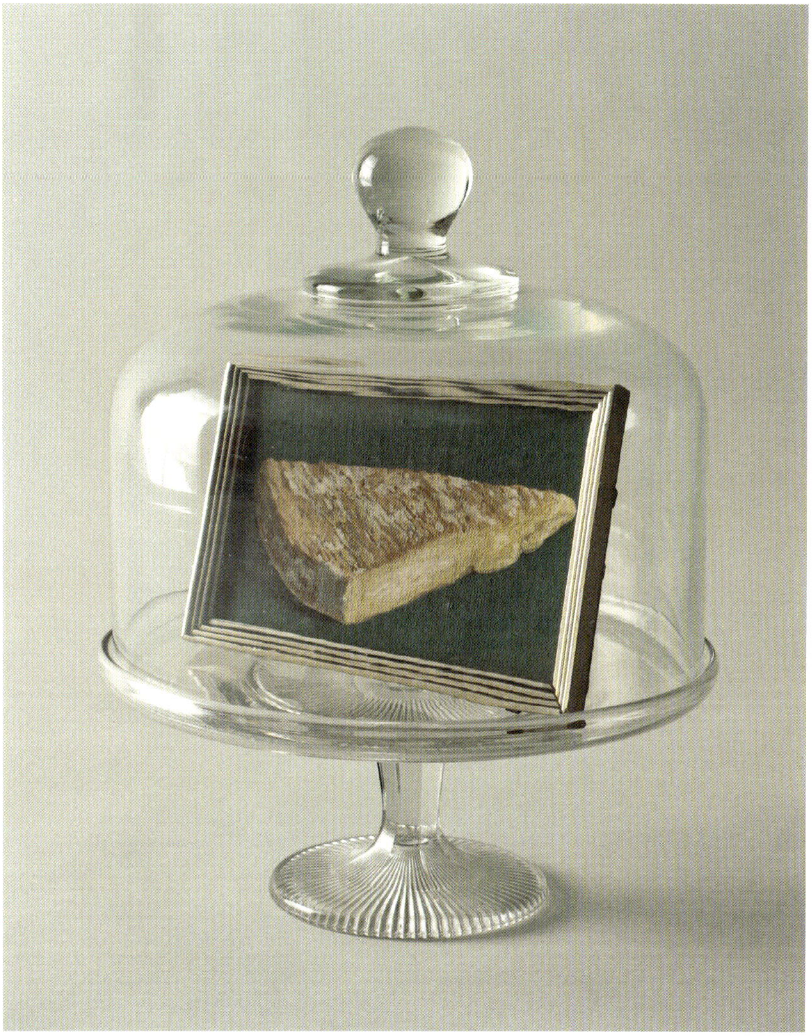

111. CECI EST UN MORCEAU DE FROMAGE (THIS IS A PIECE OF CHEESE). 1936 or 1937. Oil on canvas board in gilded wooden frame, 4 1/16 x 7 1/4" (10.3 x 18.4 cm); with glass dome and pedestal, 12" (31 cm) high, 10" (25 cm) diam.

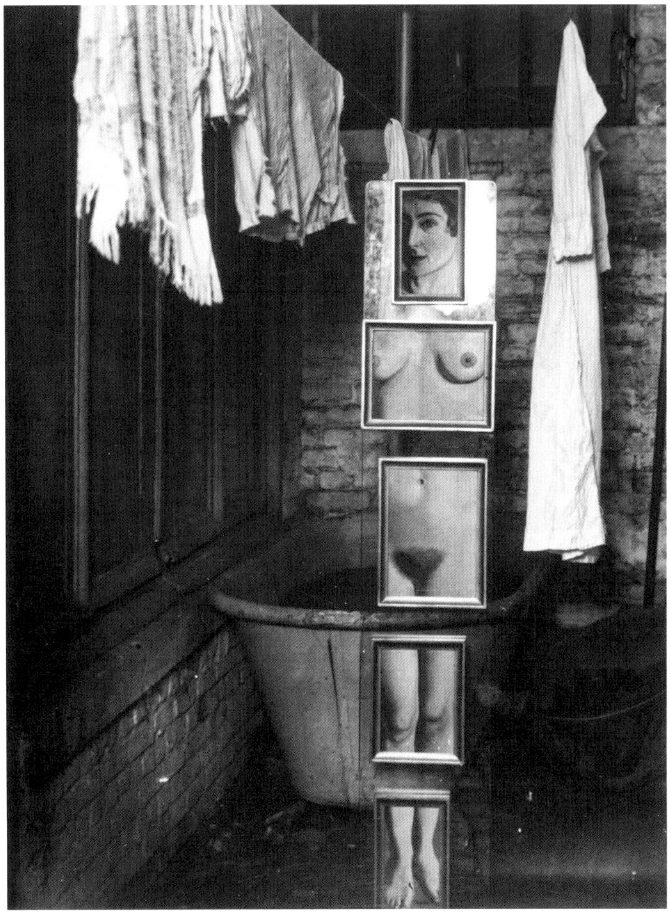

112. L'ÉVIDENCE ÉTERNELLE (THE ETERNALLY OBVIOUS). 1930 or 1931.
Photograph by Cami Stone. Gelatin silver print, 9 1/8 x 6 7/8" (23.2 x 17.4 cm)

113. Illustration in *Violette Nozières*. 1933, pages 24–25.
Book, page: 7 1/2 x 5 5/8" (19.4 x 14.3 cm)

114. Cover illustration for André Breton's *Qu'est-ce que le Surréalisme?*
(*What Is Surrealism?*). 1934. Book, 9 3/4 x 6 3/16" (24.8 x 15.7 cm)

115. Cover illustration for *Bulletin international du Surréalisme*, no. 3
(August 1935). Periodical, 11 7/16 x 8 1/8" (29 x 20.6 cm)

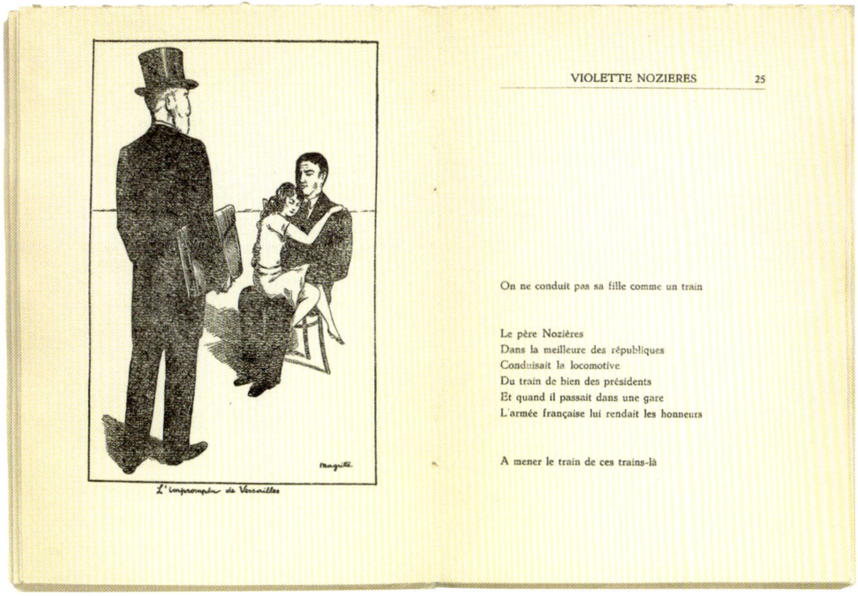

VIOLETTE NOZIERES 25

On ne conduit pas sa fille comme un train

Le père Nozières
Dans la meilleure des républiques
Conduisait la locomotive
Du train de bien des présidents
Et quand il passait dans une gare
L'armée française lui rendait les honneurs

A mener le train de ces trains-là

L'impromptu de Versailles

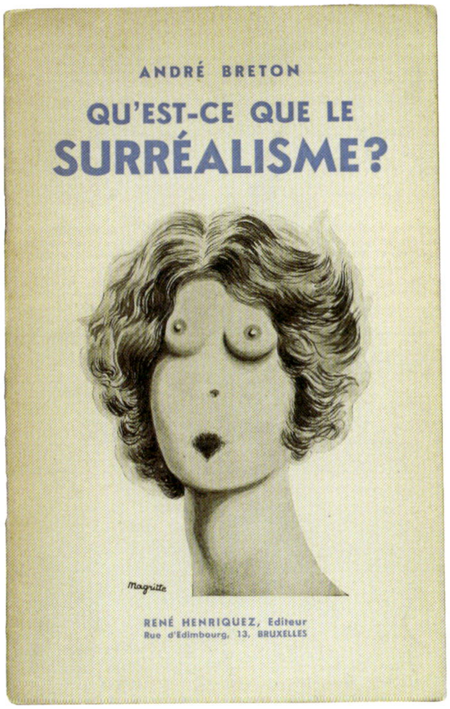

ANDRÉ BRETON

QU'EST-CE QUE LE SURRÉALISME?

RENÉ HENRIQUEZ, Editeur
Rue d'Edimbourg, 13, BRUXELLES

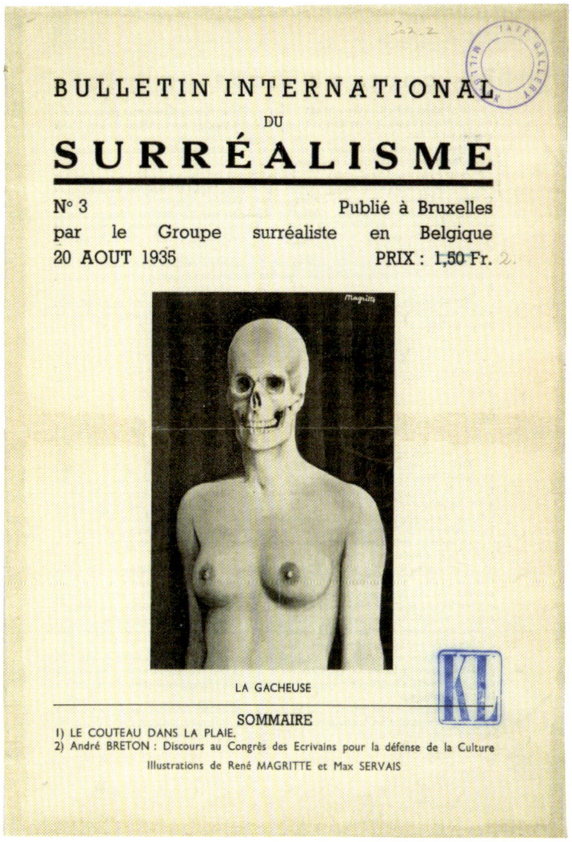

BULLETIN INTERNATIONAL DU SURRÉALISME

N° 3 Publié à Bruxelles par le Groupe surréaliste en Belgique
20 AOUT 1935 PRIX : 1,50 Fr.

LA GACHEUSE

SOMMAIRE

1) LE COUTEAU DANS LA PLAIE.
2) André BRETON : Discours au Congrès des Ecrivains pour la défense de la Culture

Illustrations de René MAGRITTE et Max SERVAIS

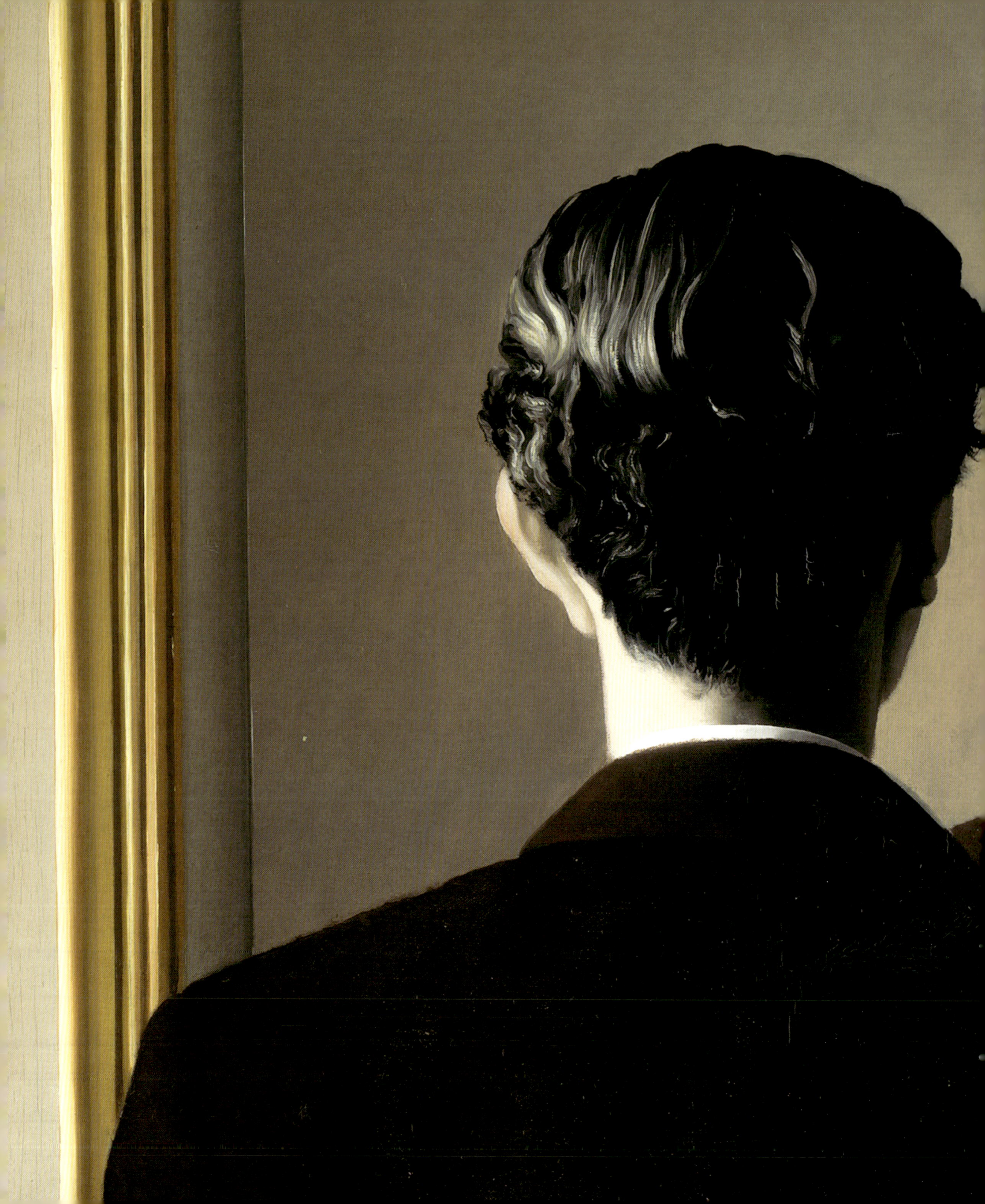

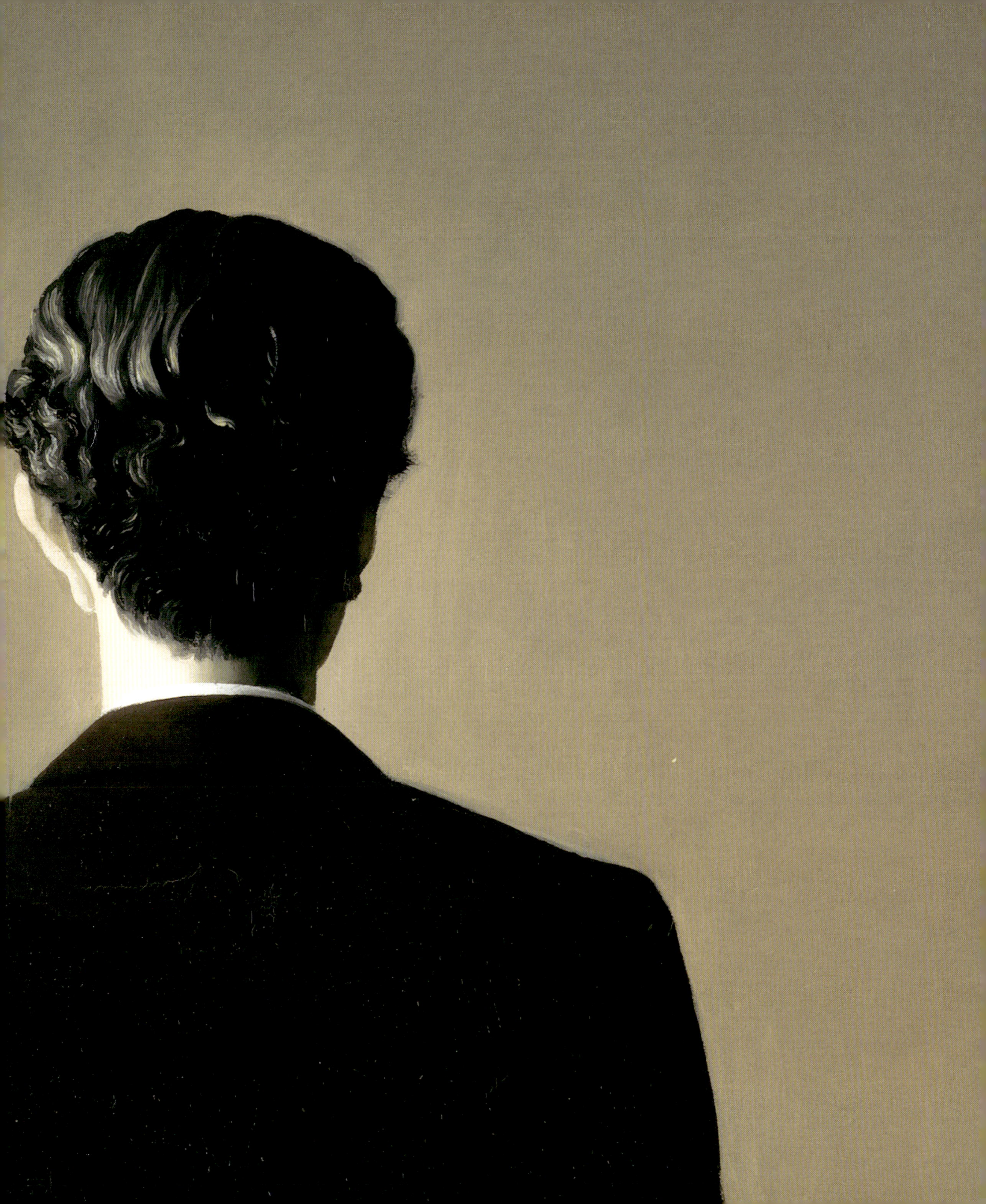

"MIRRORS THAT BECOME PAINTINGS": MAGRITTE'S COMMISSIONS FOR EDWARD JAMES *London* 1937–1938

Stephanie D'Alessandro

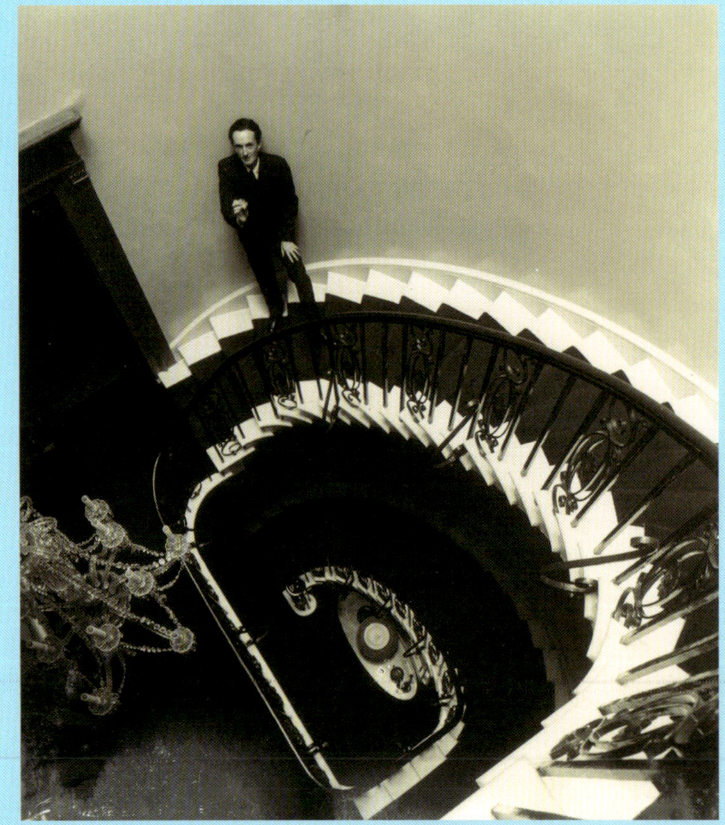

Figure 1. Norman Parkinson. Edward James on the grand staircase of 35 Wimpole Street, London, photographed for *Harper's Bazaar*. Late 1930s. Gelatin silver print, 8 11/16 x 12" (22 x 30.5 cm). © Norman Parkinson Limited/Courtesy Norman Parkinson Archive

Early in 1937 René Magritte accepted a commission for three paintings from Edward James (fig. 1), the eccentric British poet, arts patron, and collector of Surrealist art, for James's home at 35 Wimpole Street in London. The two had met just the year before, following the 1936 *International Surrealist Exhibition* at London's New Burlington Galleries, in which James would have seen Magritte's work.[1] They spent a short time together afterward in Paris visiting museums.[2]

In many ways, the project represented the promise of an artistic and professional turning point for Magritte: it was the first major art commission he had ever received. The artist had previously taken orders for works, but they were solely for portraits and generally from members of his own circle of acquaintance: the majority were done in the early years of his career (four portraits in the 1920s for one of Magritte's officers in the army, and two for his brother Raymond); others were much more recent (starting in 1936 with four portraits for such artistic supporters as Claude Spaak). The only other commission the artist had received was around 1931, for a decorative mural at Maison Norine, the fashion house of Norine (Honorine) Deschryver, who was the wife of Magritte's former dealer, Paul-Gustave Van Hecke.[3] This work, no longer extant, is recorded in a small, squared gouache; unlike his portraits, the image does not reflect Magritte's contemporaneous artistic concerns and is more in keeping with a popular Art Deco style.[4]

James's commission was thus unprecedented and represented a major artistic opportunity. The three works were large and of nonstandard sizes: *Le Modèle rouge* (*The Red Model*; plate 116) and *La Jeunesse illustrée* (*Youth Illustrated*; plate 118) each measure approximately 72 by 54 inches (183 by 136 centimeters), and *Au seuil de la liberté* (*On the Threshold of Liberty*; plate 117) is nearly 94 by 73 inches (238 by 185 centimeters). Even allowing for the vagaries of changing hands, lining, and restretching, the last of these canvases far surpasses any dimensions Magritte had ever chosen for a painting before. The next largest works he had produced were *L'Assassin menacé* (*The Menaced Assassin*; plate 12) and *Le Joueur secret* (*The Secret Player*; plate 14), each measuring nearly 60 by 77 inches (152 x 195 centimeters); these were made for his premiere at the Brussels Galerie Le Centaure in 1927, an occasion for artistic bravado and potential notice.[5] The scale of the three commissioned canvases for James represented a similar opportunity to garner attention on a grand scale for the skill and intellect with which Magritte approached his art.

The 1937 commission also offered the promise of a much-needed new market for the artist. Indeed, just a few months earlier Magritte had been unable to travel to London for the New Burlington show, financially required to stay in Brussels to complete commercial work for the Studio Dongo, his graphic design firm.[6] And while his art had been presented steadily in Paris and Brussels, he had yet to find a sustained audience outside France and Belgium. Magritte's first American exhibition, at New York's Julien Levy Gallery in 1936, had been a commercial disaster: only the dealer had purchased works from the show. Surely the idea of a commission in London—and one for the home of such a prominent collector of Surrealism, who was also a generous patron of Salvador Dalí—would have been a welcome and encouraging development.

Given the significant opportunity represented by the commission, this watershed point in Magritte's career warrants closer investigation, particularly focusing on the material details of the works themselves. A careful review of the specifics of each of the three paintings, their relationship to others before them and to each other, as well as to the context for their presentation, will provide new insight into both the commission itself and its place within Magritte's œuvre. In undertaking such a review, this essay aims to reveal how, far from an isolated event during the artist's seminal Surrealist years, Magritte's paintings for Edward James drew upon various aspects of his earlier career and would moreover have an impact on his work far beyond the five short weeks he spent in London.

AN INVITATION

"I would be delighted," wrote James to Magritte on January 28, 1937, "if you could come and spend a month or two in London, here at 35 Wimpole Street. You were so kind to me in Paris and took me to all the fine museums. So I should like, in turn, to show you London and the English countryside with all its beauties, which are many."[7] With these cordial words, James initiated a commission for three canvases for his home; the specifics were explained in a more businesslike letter eight days later to Magritte's friend E.L.T. (Édouard Léon Théodore) Mesens, who was acting as the artist's representative.[8] It must be noted from the outset that few of the letters exchanged among the three men discussing the particulars of the commission are available, and thus a number of significant details remain unknown: Did James specify the dimensions of the works? Did he identify the subjects? Did he name the location or order in which they would be installed? Did he describe a specific effect that he hoped would be produced?[9]

While these crucial details may be discovered at some point in the future, answers to certain questions may be determined by examining each work in tandem with historical information and in conversation with one another. A particular detail in the available correspondence that has, as yet, been overlooked but should not be underestimated is that both James and Magritte specifically referred to the three works as *panneaux* (panels), thus connecting the canvases to the tradition of painted *décorations*, or visually harmonious, large-scale pictures of historical or mythical subjects that were typically made to evoke tranquility and uplift.[10] Panels in that tradition—by such artists as Pierre Bonnard and Édouard Vuillard—were made for specific architectural settings within domestic interiors and share an overall synthetic appearance, usually with less depth, detail, and color contrast, and with more flattened forms. An examination of each of Magritte's works as well as their effect as a whole should be judged with this tradition in mind, especially as each commissioned work is a "variant" (as the artist called them) of a previous work. Such reiterations had been part of Magritte's working process since the 1920s but beginning in the mid-1930s they took on a more specific complexion.

Variations and series of images have been a productive mode of working throughout the history of artistic practice, and still held great creative potential for modern artists—including Henri Matisse and Pablo Picasso—in the 1930s. According to David Sylvester, Magritte's initial adoption of the practice reflected his effort to explore an image further or in a different way (such as the three 1926 variations of *Le Jockey perdu* [*The Lost Jockey*; plate 4]).[11] In 1935, however, in preparation for his exhibition at the Julien Levy Gallery, Magritte made fifteen new paintings that were variants of existing images, many on a smaller scale than their predecessors. One of these was *Le Modèle rouge* that is today in the collection of the Musée National d'Art Moderne, Paris (see p. 158, fig. 8); it is slightly smaller and has a darker palette than the first version (plate 101). Following this, the artist would more regularly make variants of his works: while repetition and reiteration were very much a part of Magritte's Surrealist working practice, their increasing use in the artist's work in this moment also coincided with his difficult financial situation.[12] While the works for James were not new ideas as such—in addition to the two 1935 versions of *Le Modèle rouge*, *Au seuil de la liberté* was first painted in 1930 and *La Jeunesse illustrée* in early 1937, just weeks before his invitation to London—Magritte made significant changes to each composition that demand our attention and suggest how they functioned together in the tradition of *décorations*.[13]

In his 1938 lecture in Antwerp titled "La Ligne de vie" ("Lifeline"), Magritte explained that the idea for the composition of *Le Modèle rouge* was devised as a solution to one of his "problems." It centers on the "monstrousness" of customs—the ease with which a "force of habit" can permit the human foot to rest undisturbed within a leather shoe (and the metamorphosis represented by the closeness of dead and living skin).[14] In his work for James, Magritte enlarged the image and used an ochre-and-brown palette closer to that of the first version. The familiar human-foot-shaped boots still rest on the earth before a similar wood-paneled wall, but the artist made a number of alterations: around the boots, we now see a cigarette butt and a used match, as well as some old English pennies and other coins. On the right there is a fragment from a French-language

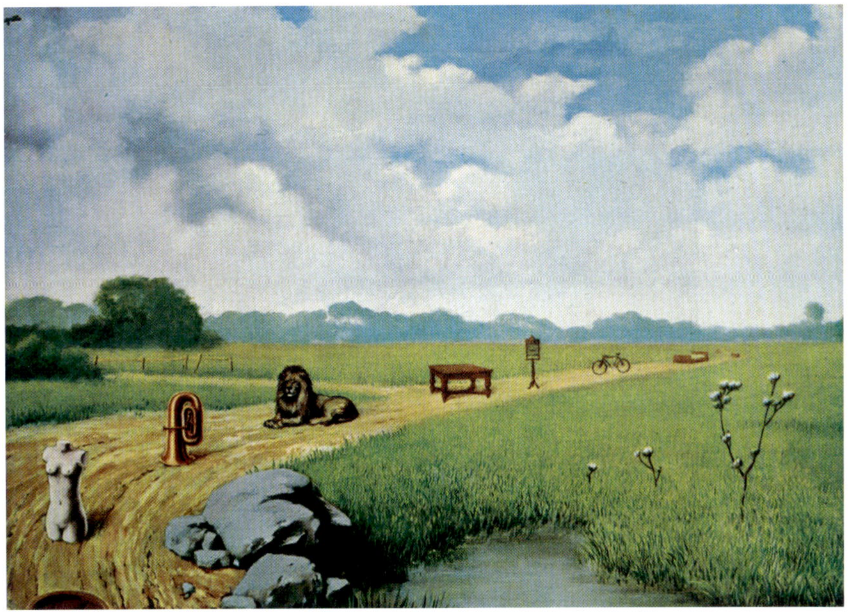

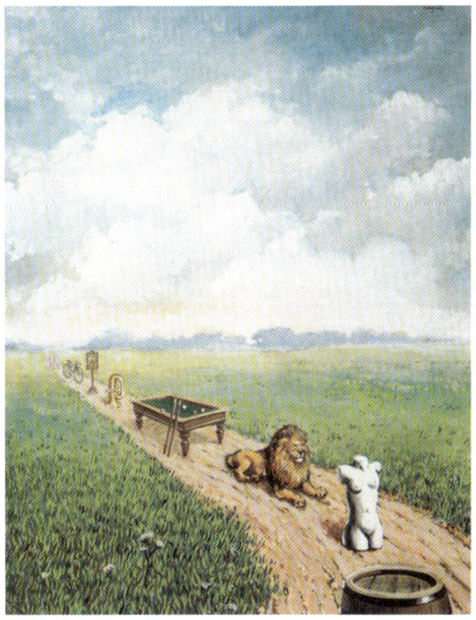

Figure 2. René Magritte. *La Jeunesse illustrée* (*Youth Illustrated*). 1937. Oil on canvas, 18 11/16 x 27" (47.5 x 68.5 cm). Location unknown. (Sylvester 2:425)

Figure 3. René Magritte. *La Jeunesse illustrée* (*Youth Illustrated*). 1937. Gouache on paper, 13 3/8 x 10 11/16" (34 x 27.5 cm). Location unknown. (Sylvester 4:1126)

newspaper that illustrates a reversed image of Magritte's variant for his 1928 painting *Les Jours gigantesques* (*The Titanic Days*; plate 48). The article is difficult to read, but certain words—such as *mutilés* (mutilated), *fumées* (smoke), and *sentencieux* (moralizing)—can be deciphered. The boots, now with a pull added at each heel, are identified with the world of work, or perhaps of military service. In previous versions, the laces are more carefully tied; in the 1937 painting, they have missed several holes. Most notable is the wood paneling: here, Magritte pushed far beyond the first version, accentuating the drips and streaks of mold, knotty holes, and weathered areas with incredible skill. In fact, he took such care in aging the wood that in order to make the drips of condensation at the top of the painting, he literally poured medium from the top of the canvas—as if the work itself had been exposed to the elements, causing its surface to corrode.[15] Magritte's additions can generally be categorized as rubbish, the detritus of society, and indeed, an overall sense of decay pervades the image. Recalling some forgotten shed or storeroom, the setting of this painted composition would be wholly inconsistent with the elegant interior of James's home.

La Jeunesse illustrée was also revisited, although the previous version (fig. 2) was still quite new.[16] From the artist's correspondence with his wife, Georgette, we know that Magritte made a gouache (fig. 3) at James's home in preparation for the painting. A study of the three works makes it clear that he executed a number of initial alterations for the commission, specifically enlarging and then changing the format from a horizontal to a vertical image. He also made other modifications: lightening the clouds (which suggest a cumulus-version of those in his 1936 *Le Précurseur* [*The Forerunner*])[17] and intensifying the blue sky; reducing the objects on the horizon; brightening and simplifying the field (removing the clumps of trees, rocks, thistles, and pond); and reversing the orientation of the path. In comparing the gouache with the final composition, it is also evident that the artist pushed this process even further, making the image more austere while heightening the illumination to such a degree that the objects on the path are in sharpened focus, suggesting their increased symbolic potential.

The everyday object was a cornerstone of Magritte's approach to Surrealism; in *La Jeunesse illustrée*, he carefully considered the exact array of items, testing a number of variations before settling on the barrel, plaster female bust, seated lion, billiard table with cue sticks and balls, trumpet, cage with bird, bicycle, armchair, globe, and ladder.[18] The appearance and reappearance of these objects is significant: some (such as the bust and the trumpet) are familiar from earlier compositions by the artist; others

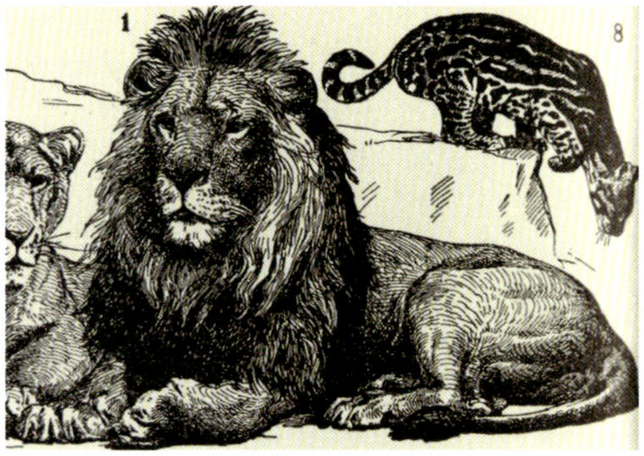

Figure 4. Detail of illustration from the "fourrures" ("furs") entry of the *Larousse universel* dictionary, vol. 1, 1922, used as a source by Magritte. Courtesy Yale University Library

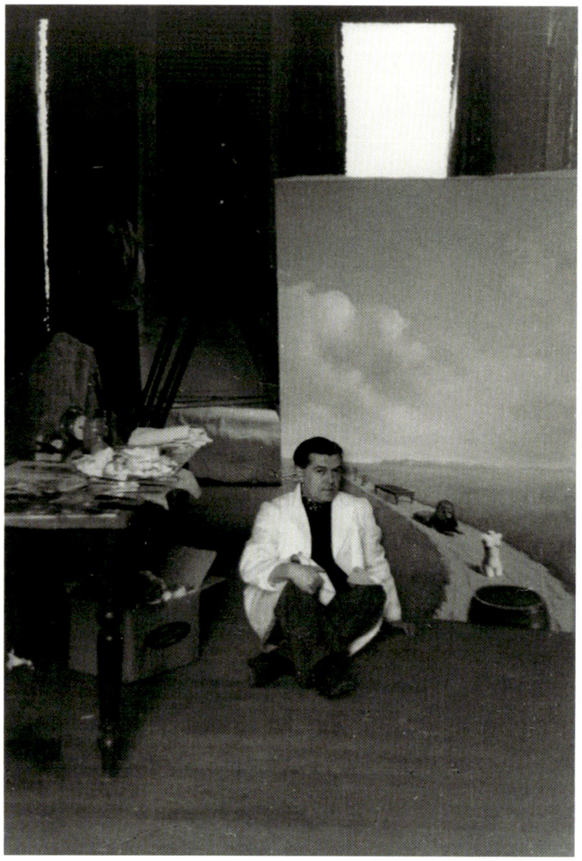

Figure 5. Magritte working in a temporary studio at 35 Wimpole Street, London. Photographer unknown. Winter 1937. Location unknown

(the barrel, the lion, and the caged bird) make their first appearance in the various versions of *La Jeunesse illustrée*. In several letters to Georgette, Magritte requested "the 'furs' page," a reference to an illustrated entry in his copy of the *Larousse* dictionary back in Brussels, which she eventually sent (fig. 4). It is clear that the artist relied on this illustration for the lion in the final image. His use of the illustrations in *Larousse* dates back to some of his earliest Surrealist works, and other items in *La Jeunesse illustrée* have similar visual corollaries in the dictionary.[19] Still more objects on the path—specifically the armchair, globe, and ladder—are completely new to James's version of *La Jeunesse illustrée* and Magritte's œuvre to date. Inventories of James's possessions at the end of his life and photographs of Magritte working in the patron's home (fig. 5) indicate that sources for these items were available to the artist on the premises. The inclusion of the objects has the effect of drawing the viewer more intimately into the scene; while their location is unfamiliar, these objects make it seem uncannily familiar.

The third work in the James commission, *Au seuil de la liberté*, was also an enlarged and revised version of an earlier canvas, a painting that was likely seen by James at the 1936 *International Surrealist Exhibition* in London.[20] Like *La Jeunesse illustrée*, its original orientation was horizontal (fig. 6). The composition derives from previous "compartmentalized" paintings—*Le Musée d'une nuit* (*One-Night Museum*, 1927; plate 38) and *Les Six Éléments* (*The Six Elements*, 1929; plate 60)—in which Magritte presented similar objects in niches or separated as framed images, gathered together in a suggestively taxonomic order. In the earlier *Au seuil de la liberté*, we are given a close-up view into one of those spaces—a "room," as Magritte described it, "with walls made up of sky, fire, a paper cutout, a house façade, a woman's breasts, planks. On the floor stands a large cannon aimed at these things."[21] In the version for James, the space is deeper, with more area for the floor and a high ceiling—suggesting a room filled with painted *décorations*. While the individual objects are the same in both compositions, Magritte did make changes: in the later iteration, the female torso has been turned in toward the corner, the trunks of trees have been straightened, the planks are more varied in intensity, the sky is darker, the bells are whiter, the building façade is more uniform in palette, the fire is more complex and animated, and the cutout is

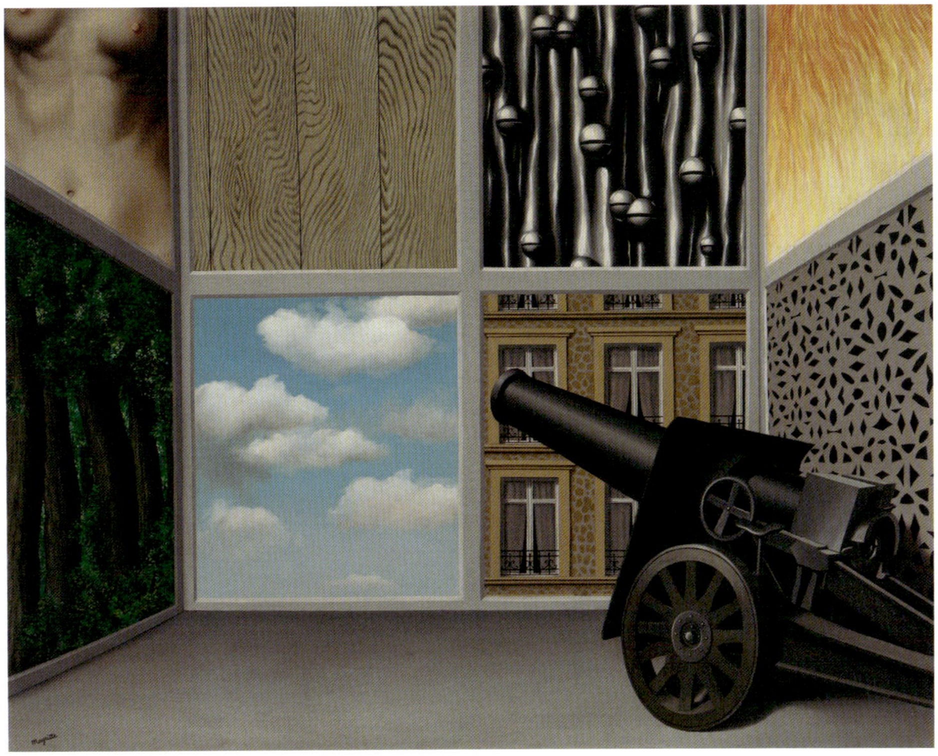

Figure 6. René Magritte. *Au seuil de la liberté* (*On the Threshold of Liberty*). 1930. Oil on canvas, 44 7/8" x 57 1/2" (114 x 146 cm). Museum Boijmans Van Beuningen, Rotterdam. (Sylvester 1:326)

more regularized with stronger horizontals in its pattern.[22] The cannon (identified as a World War I howitzer) is more closely cropped and pivoted slightly in and down, and now has more shadow at its base.[23] Another noteworthy change can be found in Magritte's signature, which appears on the lower-right area of the cannon, as if cast into the metal during the manufacturing process. The canvas is an impressive collection of painterly effects, from the brushwork used to make the soft fleshy contours of the torso to the impressionistic wet-in-wet strokes for the tree leaves to the thin washes of color layered one upon the other to produce the grainy wood.[24] As a final demonstration of his skill, Magritte painted a small trompe l'œil crack running from the molding just above the square section of wood planks and into the ceiling. It suggests decay and recalls the state of the setting of *Le Modèle rouge*; at the same time, as with *La Jeunesse illustrée*, the resulting scene is both worldly and otherworldly. Indeed, for this and other reasons we will examine, *Au seuil de la liberté* functioned in James's home as a bridge between the two other works and served as the anchor in a carefully orchestrated Surrealist experience.

A BALLROOM

On April 18, 1937, almost a month after the completion of the panels, James wrote excitedly to Magritte: "Your paintings produced a profound sensation at my ball. That evening, *Youth Illustrated* prompted many conversions to Surrealism among the British youth. But above all, the human boots struck a chord in the young dancing couples in their capitalist heels!"[25]

James's words suggest that the guests in attendance at that event (a party for his niece's society debut) experienced the three paintings as an ensemble that served as traditional *décorations*. Indeed, study of the three paintings indicates that many of Magritte's changes with regard to the works' compositions relate to making the compositions function as a programmatic whole, likely with *Au seuil de la liberté* in the middle, *Le Modèle rouge* on the left, and *La Jeunesse illustrée* on the right. For instance, he changed the overcast and gray sky from the first version of *La Jeunesse illustrée* to something brighter and bluer, bringing the sky in James's panel closer in tone to that in *Au seuil de la liberté*. Similarly, for the large composition Magritte rotated the earlier forward-facing torso toward the corner; in doing so, he echoed the orientation of the plaster bust in *La Jeunesse illustrée*. The artist made analogous changes in *Le Modèle*

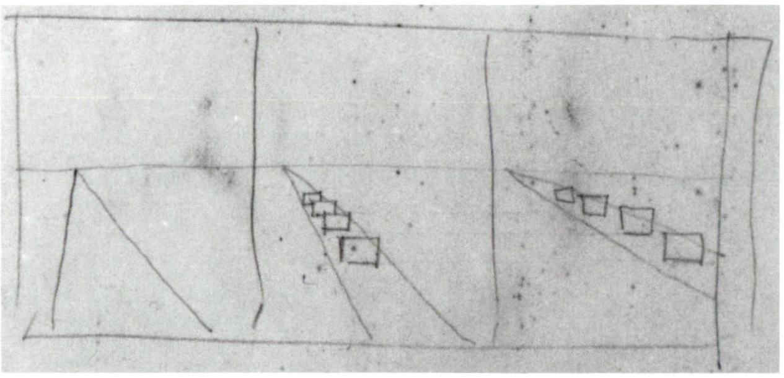

Figure 7. René Magritte. Detail of drawing on the verso of the gouache study of *La Jeunesse illustrée* (*Youth Illustrated*; see fig. 3). Menil Archives, The Menil Collection, Houston

rouge and *Au seuil de la liberté*: lightening the palette of the wood planks in the smaller canvas, bringing it in line with those depicted in *Au seuil de la liberté*. And there is another significant connection between these two pictures that does not exist between their variants: Magritte's small adjustments to the direction of the cannon's aim in the large canvas and the addition of the painted words *mutilées* and *fumées* on the newspaper scrap in *Le Modèle rouge* that seem, together, to playfully recognize their adjacency in James's home.

Magritte made numerous sketches and gouaches in preparation for these works, and when the canvases were prepared, he painted all three concurrently.[26] It is clear that he studied how each panel would engage the space around it, as well as how the three would interact with one another: a series of sketches on the verso of the gouache of *La Jeunesse illustrée* (fig. 7) shows his consideration of three different openings and vanishing points for the path, with and without objects. In the end, the artist chose something close to the middle sketch, with its vanishing point set about a quarter of the way into the scene. Magritte also altered the start of the path in the foreground to include both of its sides; in doing so, he gave the viewer a more emphatic way—quickly back and to the left—into the scene. He also changed the horizon lines in both *Le Modèle rouge* and *La Jeunesse illustrée*, thus producing square areas of similar proportion on each canvas, which he then filled with wood planks and sky, respectively. This change not only brings parity and balance to the overall grouping of paintings, but also gives the impression that the space of *Au seuil de la liberté* extends beyond itself by way of the other two compositions.[27] Most critical in this regard are the alterations Magritte made to the architectural details of the large canvas: an annotated infrared reflectograph (fig. 8) of the work shows lines drawn beneath the present layer of paint; from these lines, we can discern the earlier locations of the middle horizontal member of the "frame" on the back and wing walls, as well as the bottom edge of the left wing wall. In the process of painting the image, Magritte preserved the angle at the top of the wing walls, but changed it at the bottom and lowered the horizontal frame at the back. By doing so, he altered the work's perspective.

While suggestively drawing on such traditions of organizing space, Magritte also challenged them by using conflicting proportions and angles. Indeed, the space within

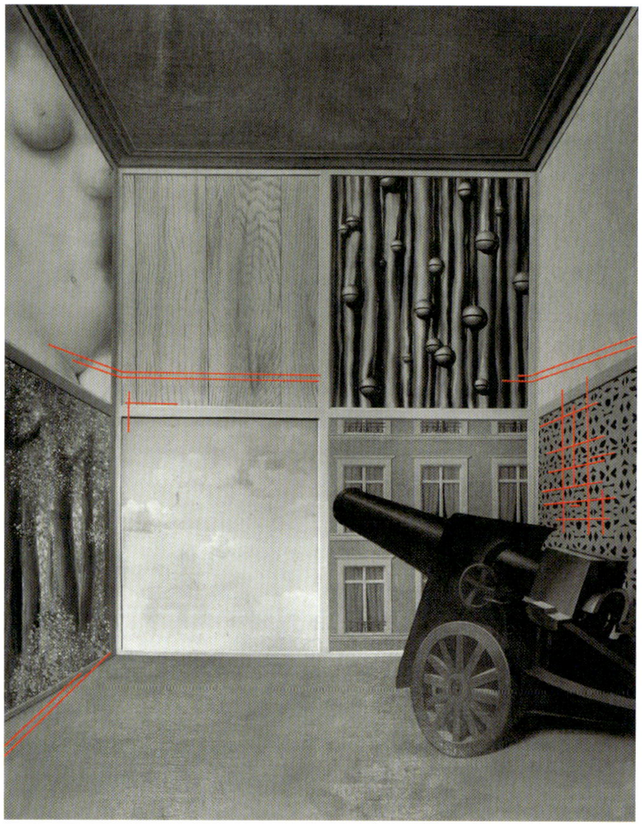

Figure 8. Infrared image of Magritte's *Au seuil de la liberté* (*On the Threshold of Liberty*, 1937; see plate 117), showing lines made by the artist. Art Institute of Chicago Conservation Department

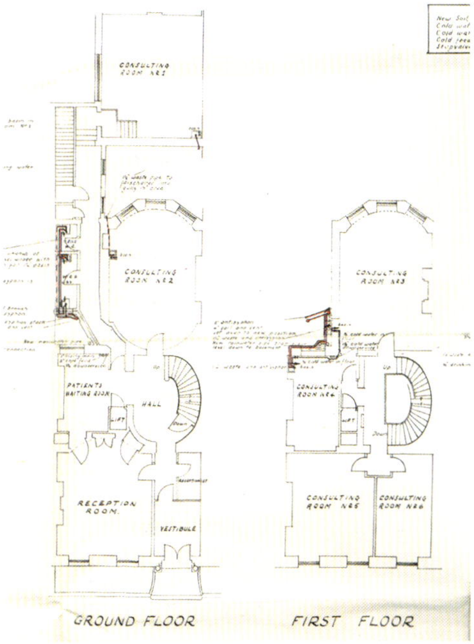

Figure 9. Floor plans for the ground and first floors of 35 Wimpole Street, London. 1949. City of Westminster Archives Centre

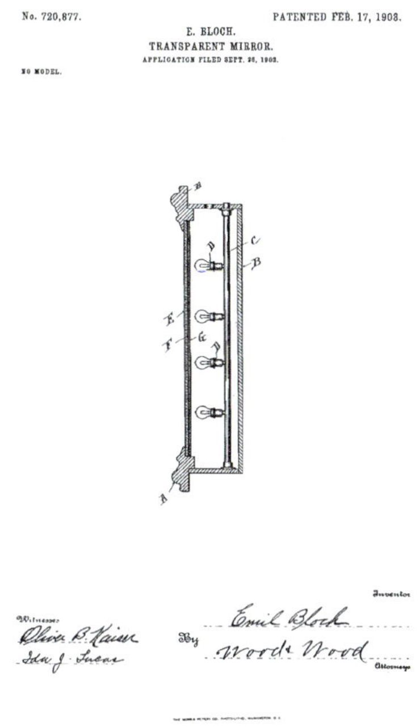

Figure 10. Emil Bloch. Diagram from patent no. 720,877 for a "transparent mirror" for illuminated advertisement display. February 2, 1903. The United States Patent and Trademark Office, Alexandria, Virginia

each of the works has been made strange: in *La Jeunesse illustrée*, we are abruptly positioned at the start of the path already upon the barrel, but the torso is far smaller than logic would dictate, judging from the short distance between them, and gives a Carrollian sense of space to the whole. Likewise in *Le Modèle rouge*, we see the planks directly before us, at eye level within an insistently shallow space, but the bits of trash are shown from different angles, making the ground seem to shift. In this consistency of strangeness, Magritte achieved an overall synthetic and "marvelous" effect.[28]

At the same time, it may also be said that Magritte's commission subverted the tradition of the *décoration* in its installation. Accounts from Roland Penrose, who spent much time with Magritte during the artist's London visit, confirm that the works were hung in the ballroom of James's home.[29] While no records have yet surfaced to delineate further details, it is possible to reconstruct the installation at least to a certain degree from documents located in the archives of the City of Westminster. A 1949 floor plan for 35 Wimpole Street (fig. 9) shows an area on the "first floor" (second floor in the American convention) that was likely the ballroom in 1937.[30] The large room has a curved end wall with three windows and a sizeable fireplace on one side; the three paintings would easily have fit in a row on either of the room's long walls. Even more remarkable, according to Penrose's recollection, is that the works were "set into the ballroom walls behind two-way mirrors so that they only became visible when lights behind the glass were switched on." Letters between Magritte and his friends back in Brussels allude to this unusual installation. A note from the author Paul Colinet, in a letter sent from a group of friends to Magritte shortly after the artist's arrival in London, describes James's home as featuring "mirrors that become paintings"; along with the letter, Colinet enclosed a collage with hidden imagery that revealed itself only when held before a light.[31]

There are several potential sources for this intriguing presentation with mirrors: illuminated displays behind reflective surfaces had existed in commercial advertising since at least the early 1900s on both sides of the Atlantic (fig. 10), and it is reasonable to think that Magritte, with his commercial work for Studio Dongo, might have seen or even used such a system before his trip to London. Another source of the presentation might have been the designer Norris Wakefield, who carried out much of the decoration at Wimpole Street (at James's behest), and of whom Magritte would have been aware from his time living with James; Wakefield had seen such glass in use earlier in Paris.[32]

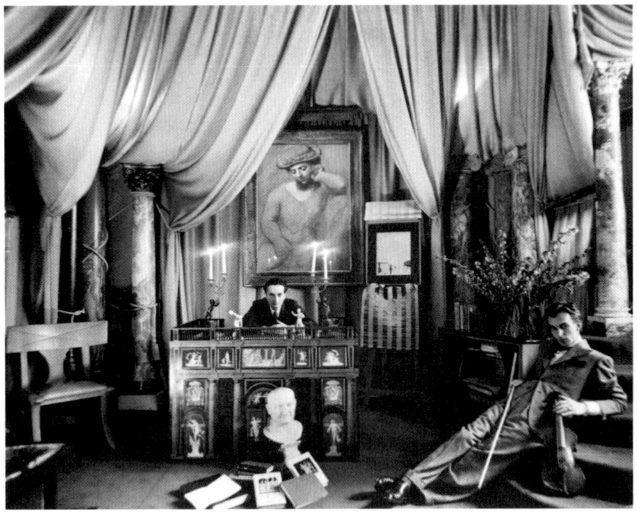

Figure 11. Norman Parkinson. Edward James with composer Igor Markevitch in the "tent room" of 35 Wimpole Street, London, sitting below Pablo Picasso's *Femme assise au chapeau* (*Seated Woman with Hat*, 1923–34) and Salvador Dalí's *Le Calme blanc* (*White Calm*, 1936). 1939. Photographed for *Harper's Bazaar*. Gelatin silver print, 9 5/8 x 6 7/8" (24.5 x 17.5 cm). © Norman Parkinson Limited/Courtesy Norman Parkinson Archive

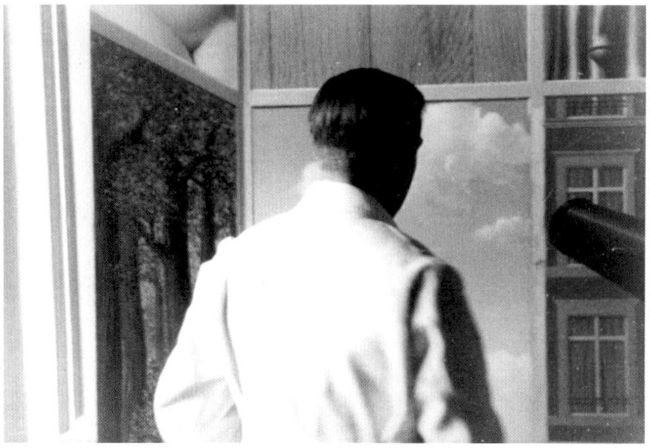

Figure 12. Magritte in front of *Au seuil de la liberté* (*On the Threshold of Liberty*, 1937; plate 117) at James's London home. Photographer unknown. Menil Archives, The Menil Collection, Houston

Indeed, Surrealist presentations had begun to take a new direction in Paris the year before, at the Galerie Charles Ratton's *Exposition surréaliste d'objets* (*Surrealist Exhibition of Objects*), in which items by Magritte (similar to plates 94 and 111) and others were installed in a manner borrowed from department-store displays. Magritte and James had also been involved in dramatic stagings of their own in the past: the artist, along with Mesens, had prepared a special presentation for his 1931 solo exhibition at the Salle Giso in Brussels. There, Magritte's *L'Assassin menacé* was displayed in the gallery's window, illuminated by white light bulbs installed across the floor. On the night of the opening, guests arrived to find the space in darkness with two men standing by a candle and a double metronome; later, the lights gradually came on to musical accompaniment, revealing Magritte's paintings.[33]

James, too, had devised innovative presentations of works in his art collection: for instance, in his London home he installed small canvases by Dalí in sliding panels that lit up when opened. Norman Parkinson's photograph of James's study, or "tent room" (fig. 11), records yet another display scheme, for Dalí's *Le Calme blanc* (*White Calm*, 1936), with a striped fabric shade on an easel. Furthermore, according to one contemporary source's report on the ball for James's niece, the host even installed a painting behind a false window in the dining room to produce a "Sahara-like effect outside [...] showing a skipping girl and a temple (or is it a hut?) in the distance." The same source reported on James's "novel idea of projecting very modernist pictures on to the white staircase wall from lantern-lighted slides."[34]

Without more documentation, however, it is difficult to confirm the origin and originator of the installation of Magritte's three paintings; we cannot even be certain on which wall or how they were hung. A photograph of Magritte standing before *Au seuil de la liberté* (fig. 12) shows molding on the left side of the painting that may be part of the work's final presentation, but little additional information is available to confirm this. Nevertheless, it is not hard to appreciate what James called the "profound sensation" elicited by the paintings, serving as part of a stage set for a surreal transformation. One can imagine the way Magritte's detailed work, illuminated within the darkened ballroom like a theater, was enhanced how the lighting source behind the frames added more confusion to the shifting shadows and intense brightness already in the scenes,

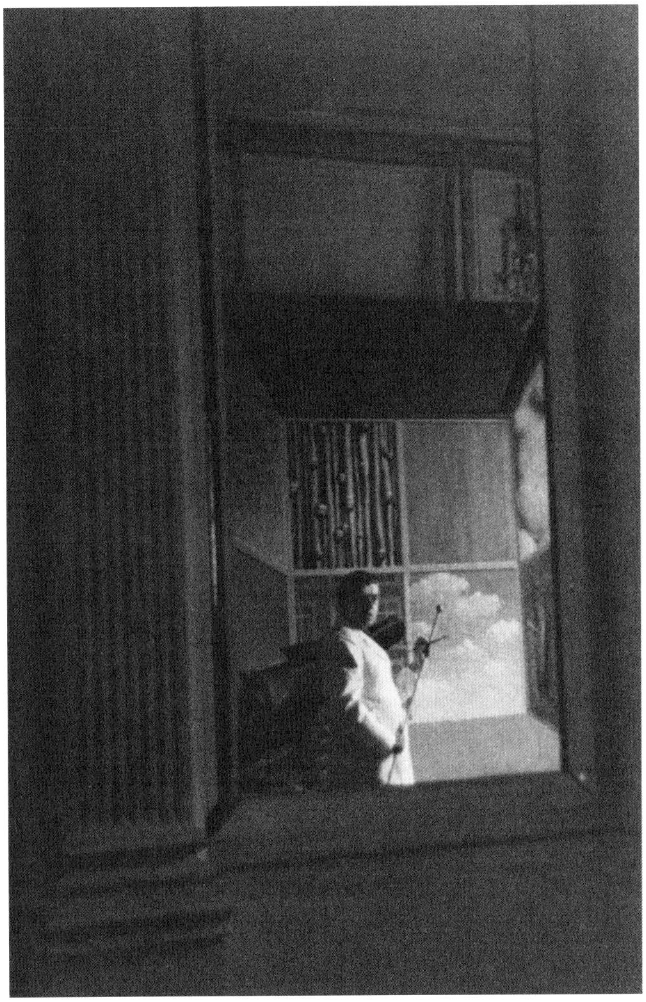

Figure 13. E.L.T. (Édouard Léon Théodore) Mesens, or Edward James(?). Magritte in the ballroom of James's London home with *Au seuil de la liberté* (*On the Threshold of Liberty*, 1937; plate 117). March 1937. Photograph. Location unknown

and even more, how the fluctuating space and perspectives further confounded the expectation of James's unsuspecting visitors that the paintings function as traditional "windows." Indeed, mirrors became windows, but those windows offered views onto a place that was familiar, strange, sensational, and disequilibrating.

James's home, to be sure, enhanced the reception of Magritte's panels, which were the apex of a decorative scheme that began at the door of the house, developed as visitors ascended the stairs, and reached its conclusion in the ballroom.[35] The potential power of this experience is evident in a photograph from Magritte's trip that stands out from the others, which typically show him working in his temporary studio over James's garage (see fig. 5). This image is more formal (fig. 13): the artist is posed with maulstick in hand before *Au seuil de la liberté*, looking out to the viewer from the reflected image of a large framed mirror. With its high ceiling, chandelier, and ornately decorated walls, the room is more formal as well. The photograph is surely staged, carefully constructed to prevent the reflection of the photographer (Mesens or James?) from being recorded in the image and possibly to gauge the effect of the paintings once installed: here, Magritte is standing in for his work, as if envisioning its marvelous impact on visitors. That experience was also potent for the artist: based on the works that followed his London trip, it is certain that as much as 35 Wimpole Street enriched the engagement with his paintings, it also continued to stir his own imagination.

A HOME

By the time of Magritte's visit to London, Edward James was well known as a passionate and generous benefactor of the arts, as well as an artist in his own right: his poetry was regularly published in the Surrealist journal *Minotaure* (which he also sponsored). Born of privilege, he had inherited his family's considerable properties and collections, and in the early 1930s began transforming his residences, including a country estate in West Dean (in West Sussex) and his mid-Georgian London townhouse on Wimpole Street. In contrast to the West Dean home (called Monkton House), the exterior of which James had painted in a surprising puce tone, the London residence was from the outside indistinguishable from the other elegant homes in the neighborhood. Once inside, however, it was like no other, merging antique and modern furnishings with art in a style known as "fantasy" or "fantastic modern."[36] James's "tent room" is a prime example, with its marble columns and gilded Corinthian capitals, decoratively knotted cords with tassels, voluminous tented swags, eighteenth-century Italian furniture, and contemporary pieces by Picasso and Dalí. James installed works by many Surrealists there, as

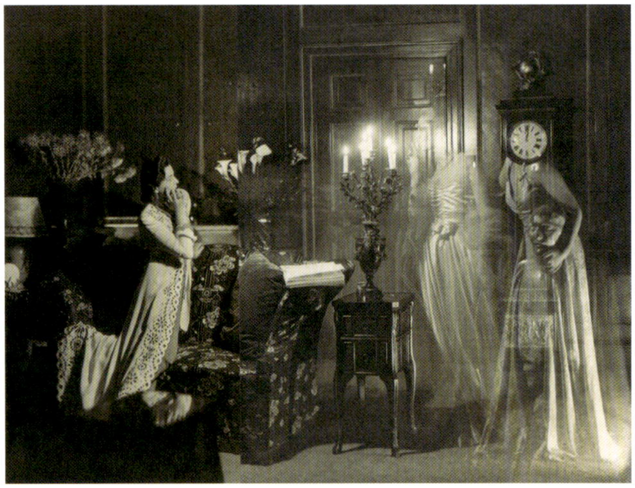

Figure 14. Norman Parkinson. Surrealist-inspired fashion shoot at 35 Wimpole Street, London, for *Harper's Bazaar*. January 1939. Vintage gelatin silver print, 16 15/16 x 13 3/8" (43 x 34 cm).

well as by such Neo-Romantic painters as Christian Bérard, Eugène Berman, and Pavel Tchelitchew, whose imaginary ruins and emotive figures complemented the mix of old furnishings and figurative Surrealism. The somber atmosphere established by these Neo-Romantic canvases also foreshadowed the sense of decay in Magritte's paintings for the ballroom. James's home was unusual enough that he was acknowledged in 1936 in the London press for his "remarkable, less orthodox ideas of interior decoration."[37] And just two years later, when *Harper's Bazaar* sought a location for a Surrealist-inspired photograph by Norman Parkinson, the editors chose Wimpole Street, noting how "insidiously [...] the surrealist influence permeated the setting" and composition (fig. 14).[38]

At the time of Magritte's commission, the artist best represented in James's home was Salvador Dalí.[39] In addition to their exchanges about works of art, the collector and the Spanish artist were engaged in a dialogue about James's residences: together in London in the fall of 1935, they were immersed in ideas and plans for an "imaginary town," as Dalí described it, "in collaboration for a suite of ideas."[40] The following year, in the Wimpole Street dining room, they began to draft a series of interior and exterior designs inspired by Dalí's paranoiac-critical theories (fig. 15). While it would be several years before these works were realized, designs for a "torso set of drawers" (1936), as well as *Mae West Lips Sofa* (1936), the enigmatic *Lobster Telephone* (1937), and pink-glove tea service (1938–39) likely all derived from this moment.[41] James offered Dalí a contract that year for the purchase of works of art but their design relationship was one of true collaboration, defined by a mutually interested alliance in which the artist drew ideas generated from their discussions and the collector supervised the work to its final execution.[42]

Most significant for this discussion are the efforts James made to execute various Surrealist-inspired decorative schemes in his home. In May 1936, for example, he attempted to re-create in plaster and mica, for his drawing room, the rock formations at Cap de Creus (in northeastern Catalonia, near Dalí's hometown of Figueres), and wrote to Dalí requesting a postcard to share with his architects.[43] Later, James pursued plans (inspired by Leonor Fini) to cover his morning room in ivy and his drawing room with images of arteries and white skeletons painted on dark wine-colored moiré silk.[44] It may also be that he commissioned interior designer Jean-Michel Frank—known for his "strange luxury of nothingness"—to strip a room of its paneling (as Frank had done for other clients) in order to reveal its cracked surfaces and, in keeping with Magritte's panels, to produce a sense of decay and neglect.[45]

James surely hired Magritte with his larger decorative program in mind, and the commission undoubtedly involved a similar form of collaboration.[46] He also likely shared with the artist his larger plans for 35 Wimpole Street as well as the designs he and Dalí had been creating. Magritte would have welcomed this collaborative environment; indeed, he envisioned James's commission as an opportunity to have a continued role in what the Wimpole Street home was to become. Soon after his arrival in London, for instance, Magritte gave his host a gift of a version of *L'Avenir des statues* (*The Future of Statues*, c. 1931; similar to plate 95).[47] The painted object delighted James to such an extent that Norman Parkinson soon photographed his portrait with it;

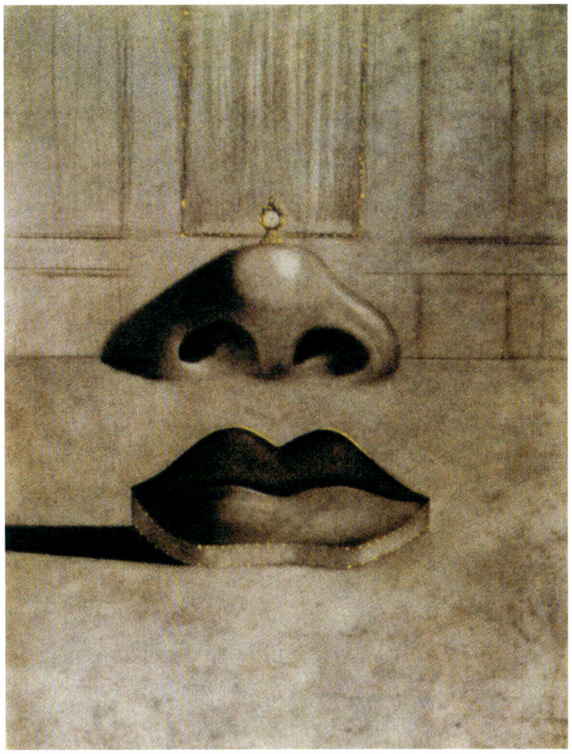

Figure 15. Salvador Dalí. *Naissance de l'ameublemnent paranoïaque* (*Birth of Paranoiac Furniture*). c. 1937. Chalk and gouache on paper, 24 1/2 x 18 1/2" (62.2 x 47 cm). Formerly in the collection of Edward James. Location unknown

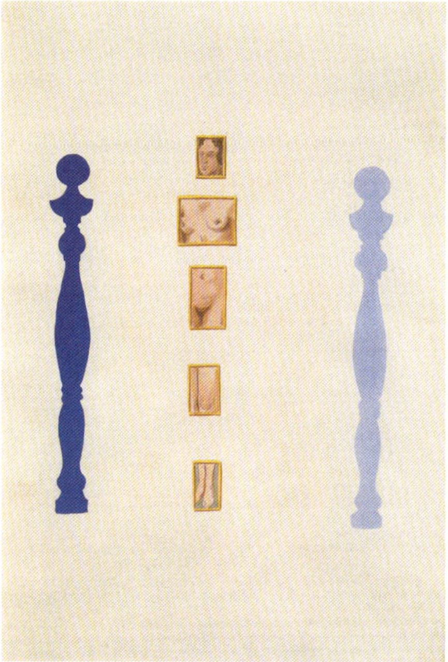

Figure 16. René Magritte. Sketch for a decorative object. c. 1937. Gouache on paper, 19 3/4 x 14 3/16" (50.2 x 36 cm). Location unknown

the work was also used as a prop in Parkinson's Surrealist-inspired fashion shoot for *Harper's Bazaar* in 1939. After his return home, Magritte sent James a version of *La Malédiction* (*The Curse*, 1937);[48] James showed the painting to Dalí and in a telegram shared with Magritte the Spaniard's enthusiastic response: "Dalí says Magritte is definitely the painter I like best."[49]

More than this, however, Magritte's works in the months following his London trip demonstrate the lasting inspiration of the environment of 35 Wimpole Street and its owner. While Magritte was in London, James commissioned additional canvases from him, including a version of *Le Monde poétique* (*The Poetic World*) as well as a portrait of James, *La Reproduction interdite* (*Not to Be Reproduced*, plate 123), both completed in 1937.[50] In making the latter, Magritte chose to present his patron standing before a fireplace mantel and large mirror in his home; this mirror—like those in the Wimpole Street ballroom—misfunctions, reflecting not James's face, but the back of his head. Months later, Magritte changed his idea for a composition of a "man whose head is a light" into another portrait of James, titled *Le Principe du plaisir* (*The Pleasure Principle*, plate 124), the composition of which he directed with the assistance of photographs made by Man Ray.[51] Correspondence reveals that Magritte proposed making *Le Principe du plaisir* the same dimensions as the earlier portrait, perhaps imagining their tandem installation in James's home. Both works reference the dramatic experiences of mirrors, lights, and tricks on perception and sensation at 35 Wimpole Street, and indicate Magritte's continued, though in the end unsuccessful, attempts to engage with James's larger decorative program.

Two other works are especially noteworthy in this regard. One is a gouache that dates from Magritte's London visit (fig. 16); it shows *L'Évidence éternelle* (*The Eternally Obvious*; plate 66) flanked by two *bilboquets*, the lathe-turned spindles or balusters that regularly appear in Magritte's paintings. David Sylvester identified this composition as a proposal for a decorative project in James's home.[52] No further documents have surfaced to contextualize this work, but the idea of another commission that played with a common everyday item (a mirror or a banister) and its transformation (into a window or a woman) is in keeping with the elements of Magritte's commission for James, as well as with James's own designs for his home in London. It also points to the expectations Magritte might have had for further collaborations in the James home. Even more significant is *La Durée poignardée* (*Time Transfixed*, 1938; plate 126), a work not commissioned by James, but purchased by him after its exhibition in Magritte's solo presentation at Brussels's Palais des Beaux-Arts in May 1939. Here, a diminutive locomotive unexpectedly appears, suspended with its puffs of smoke, in the fireplace of a domestic interior (James's home), the same pictured in *La Reproduction interdite*.[53] The setting is strangely calm, even sterile, which produces a sense of uncertainty in what we see: the fireplace shows no trace of use, the candlesticks have no candles, and the clock announces the time as 12:43, close to the midpoint of either day or night. This strange half-state relates to Magritte's own explanation of the work in his "La Ligne de vie" lecture: as an exploration of the metamorphosis of everyday vision, in which a "railway-engine [...] spring[s] from the hearth of the dining-room fireplace instead of the usual stovepipe."[54] A year later, when he learned that James had purchased the painting, Magritte was quick to write to the collector: "It is curious that I thought of you while painting *Time Transfixed* [...] I was thinking that the ideal place [...] would be at the foot of your staircase and in this way your visitors would be transfixed on the ground floor and could arrive in an interesting fashion on the first floor."[55] This, of course, was the location of his commissioned panels and the "interesting fashion" of arrival Magritte hoped to orchestrate would have boosted the reception of his ballroom works. Perhaps aiming to make the argument more convincing, Magritte included a drawing with his letter, of the painting in place at the bottom of the staircase (fig. 17).

The installation, however, was not to be. James eventually hung the canvas over a fireplace instead, and, after a few additional gouaches, acquired no further works from Magritte after 1939.[56] While this turn of events likely had little to do with the protracted interchange between James and Magritte the summer before, in which the artist acknowl-

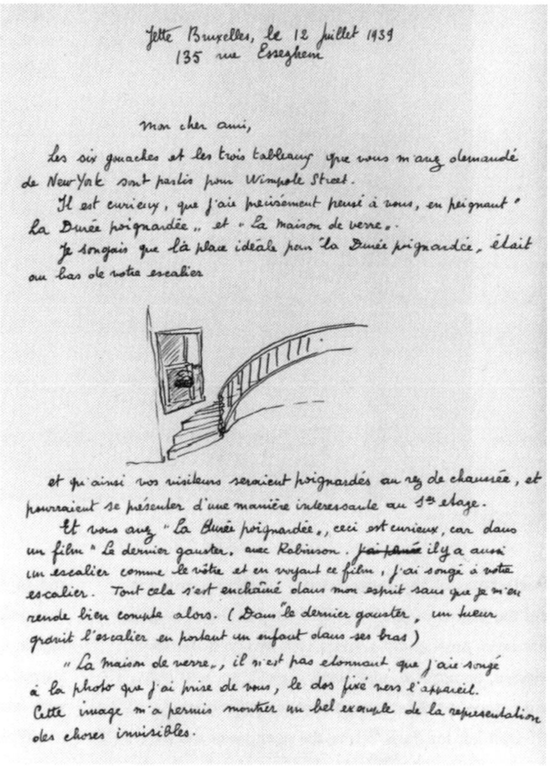
Jette Bruxelles, le 12 juillet 1939
135 rue Esseghem

Mon cher ami,

Les six gouaches et les trois tableaux que vous m'avez demandé de New York sont partis pour Wimpole Street.

Il est curieux, que j'aie précisément pensé à vous, en peignant "La Durée poignardée" et "La maison de verre".

Je songeais que la place idéale pour "La Durée poignardée" était au bas de votre escalier

et qu'ainsi vos visiteurs seraient poignardés au rez de chaussée, et pourraient se présenter d'une manière intéressante au 1er étage.

Et vous avez "La Durée poignardée", ceci est curieux, car dans un film "Le dernier gangster" avec Robinson. ~~j'ai pensé~~ il y a aussi un escalier comme le vôtre et en voyant ce film, j'ai songé à votre escalier. Tout cela s'est enchaîné dans mon esprit sans que je m'en rende bien compte alors. (Dans "le dernier gangster", un tueur gravit l'escalier en portant un enfant dans ses bras)

"La maison de verre", il n'est pas étonnant que j'aie songé à la photo que j'ai prise de vous, le dos fixé vers l'appareil. Cette image m'a permis montrer un bel exemple de la représentation des choses invisibles.

Figure 17. René Magritte, letter to Edward James, July 12, 1939, concerning a possible location at 35 Wimpole Street for *La Durée poignardée* (*Time Transfixed*, 1938; plate 126). Edward James Foundation, London

edged his desire for a contract and expressed irritation at not selling more works to the collector, the loss of such an initially promising patron in 1939 was difficult for Magritte.[57]

The 1937 commission represented a major artistic and economic opportunity in Magritte's early career; equally important was the experience of James's home as a total Surrealist environment in all its bold and marvelous theatricality. Magritte's time in London would have a stimulating effect on his art—and possibly even played a role in his presentation of himself as an artist. In April 1938 he was again in England, now preparing for a solo exhibition at Mesens's London Gallery. A series of publicity photographs for the exhibition show Magritte physically interacting—

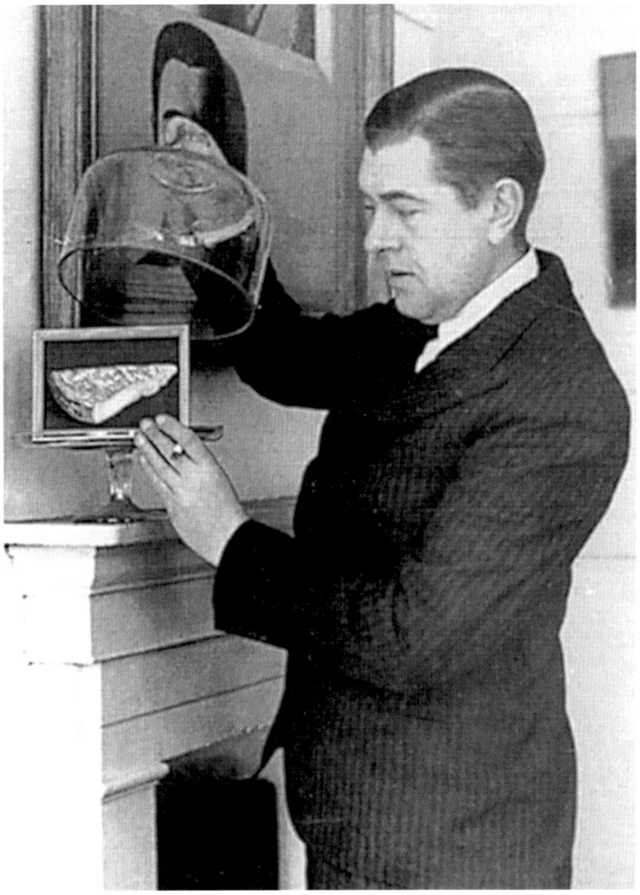

Figure 18. René Magritte lifting the glass dome of *Ceci est un morceau de fromage* (*This Is a Piece of Cheese*, 1936 or 1937; plate 111). Photographer unknown. 1938. Location unknown

literally performing—with his works: lifting the glass dome of *Ceci est un morceau de fromage* (*This Is a Piece of Cheese*; fig. 18) and putting his arm around *L'Évidence éternelle* (see p. 82, fig. 12), encouraging his audience to imagine a newly sensorial relationship with the works and a similar experience for themselves. Most telling is one photograph in which the artist—perhaps for the first time—presents himself as the world would come to know him for the rest of his long career, in the dramatic persona of the bowler-hatted man (plate 130).[58] Posing with the now-lost 1928 painting *Le Barbare* (*The Barbarian*),[59] Magritte looks out to the viewer—not unlike his paintings in James's home, beckoning from the other side of a picture frame—inviting us to enter the phantasmagorical world of his art.

Notes

The author wishes to thank Allison Langley, Associate Conservator, and Jennifer Cohen, former Research Associate in the department of Medieval to Modern European Painting and Sculpture, Art Institute of Chigaco, for their tireless research and insightful comments on this topic. Thanks also to Peter Morris, Chicago, for generously making essential documents from Magritte available for this essay.

The quote that serves as the title of this essay, "Mirrors That Become Paintings," derives from Belgian author Paul Colinet, 1937. For further information about this quote and its source, see n. 31.

References in the following notes in the form "Sylvester 1:8" refer to the volume and catalogue numbers of works in the six-volume Magritte catalogue raisonné. Likewise, references in the form "Sylvester 1, p. 304" refer to the volume and page numbers where corresponding texts are located. The first five volumes of the catalogue raisonné, published 1992–97, were edited by David Sylvester; the final volume, published 2012, was edited by Sarah Whitfield. For complete publication information for all six volumes, see the "Selected Bibliography," p. 252.

Catalogue raisonné numbers are provided for works that are not reproduced as plates or figures in the present volume. Unless otherwise noted, all English translations in this essay are the author's.

1. See David Sylvester, *Magritte: The Silence of the World* (Houston and New York: Menil Foundation, Abrams, 1992), p. 243.
2. According to David Sylvester, Magritte was unable to come to the London exhibition due to obligations for his commercial work and two commissioned portraits. See Sylvester 2, p. 49. The Paris meeting is mentioned in a letter from Edward James to Magritte, January 28, 1937. David Sylvester's René Magritte Catalogue Raisonné Research Papers, Menil Archives, The Menil Collection, Houston.

3. See Sylvester 5:342a, which documents the now-destroyed mural; and in the same volume, 1106a and 1106b, which are gouache studies; note that 1106a is squared for enlargement and transfer.
4. While it does not parallel Magritte's work as a fine artist, this mural does reflect some of the illustrations he made for Norine's fashion salon in 1928 (plate 22), and followed her tastes as the leading Brussels couturier. Magritte's relationship to decoration is a rich area yet to be fully explored; decoration is often included with commercial work, for which there are also few sustained studies. Carine Pol provides a helpful overview in "Publicity: Commercial Art According to René Magritte," in Gisèle Ollinger-Zinque and Frederik Leen, eds., *René Magritte, 1898–1967* (Ghent and Brussels: Ludion, Royal Museums of Fine Arts of Belgium, 1998), pp. 308–20. See also Georges Roque, *Ceci n'est pas un Magritte* (Paris: Flammarion, 1983).
5. Similarly, in preparation for his canceled 1930 Galerie Goemans exhibition, Magritte painted the two large canvases *Au seuil de la liberté* and *L'Annonciation* (*The Annunciation*; plate 70); see Sylvester 1, p. 347.
6. Studio Dongo produced exhibition and window displays, posters, and other related materials. For more on the firm and its founding in 1930 as a response to Magritte's financial woes, see Sylvester 1, pp. 115–21; and Sylvester 2, pp. 3–5.
7. Edward James, letter to Magritte, January 28, 1937. Edward James Foundation, London. See Sylvester 2, p. 51.
8. James wrote to Mesens on February 5, 1937, confirming conditions of the commission previously agreed upon, including the fee of £250 for the three panels. No earlier correspondence about this matter has yet been uncovered. For excerpts of James's letter to Mesens, see Sylvester 2, p. 51 (copy available at David Sylvester's René Magritte Catalogue Raisonné Research Papers, Menil Archives, The Menil Collection, Houston).
9. James was deeply involved in the decoration of his homes and it is likely that some of these details, especially the dimensions of the works and even the subjects, may have been determined before Magritte's arrival in London. Indeed, two photographs of *Le Modèle rouge* (which is located at the Moderna Museet, Stockholm) are today in the Edward James Foundation collections, perhaps the result of Magritte bringing the photographs with him to use for his work. (There is a note on the verso of one of these prints that the painting was in the collection of Claude Spaak, who acquired it soon after it was painted.) It is not known whether James requested at least one or two of the subjects of the works in advance, or whether Magritte himself made the decision to remake at least two works for the commission. Without further documentation, we have no definitive knowledge of what Magritte was asked to do.
10. Few letters between James and Magritte, or between James and Mesens, have been made available to this date, but those that have specifically use the term *panneaux*. Letters between Magritte and his wife, Georgette, during the period when the artist was in London, in the collection of Peter Morris (who kindly made them available for this study), reflect the same usage. Magritte used *panneaux* exclusively at the start of his visit but after James had ordered other pictures from him, the artist used the term *tableaux* (paintings), referring more broadly to all his works for the patron. For more on the history of decoration and its popularity in the late nineteenth and early twentieth centuries, see Gloria Groom, *Beyond the Easel: Decorative Painting by Bonnard, Vuillard, Denis, and Roussel, 1890–1930* (Chicago: Art Institute of Chicago, 2001).
11. For more on *Le Jockey perdu*, see Anne Umland, "'This Is How Marvels Begin': Brussels, 1926–1927," in the present volume, pp. 27–30.
12. David Sylvester, in *Magritte* (Brussels: in association with the Menil Foundation Mercatorfonds, 2009), p. 295, states that Magritte's decision was made in preference to doing commercial work. It is clear that the artist and Mesens were already sensitive to the complex relationship his works had to one other: in both the 1937 exhibition *Three Surrealist Painters* and the 1938 London Gallery show, the catalogues identify "states," "versions," and still other works with the same title but different roman numerals.
13. For a different approach, see Sylvester 2, p. 238; two of the works for James are referred to as "recapitulations."
14. See Magritte, "La Ligne de vie," lecture at Antwerp's Koninklijk Museum voor Schone Kunsten, November 20, 1938; trans. in Ollinger-Zinque and Leen, eds., *Magritte, 1898–1967*, p. 48. (All following "Ligne de vie" references and page numbers are from this volume.) This 1998 translation was adapted from that in Sylvester 5, pp. 9–22. See also Sylvester 3, p. 205. For more on this lecture, see the introductory essay, pp. 17–21; and Michel Draguet, "'Once the Image Is Isolated, What Happens to the Mind?': Brussels, 1930–1936," pp. 153–59, both in the present volume.
15. See Allison Langley, "Examination Report for *The Red Model*," June 2012, conservation files, Art Institute of Chicago.
16. See Magritte, letter to Paul Éluard, January 30, 1937, in Sylvester 2, p. 425 (copy available at David Sylvester's René Magritte Catalogue Raisonné Research Papers, Menil Archives, The Menil Collection, Houston).
17. *Le Précurseur* exists in two versions, both made in 1936. See Sylvester 2:417 and 418, p. 229.
18. In addition to the two compositions illustrated here, two other versions of the work existed before James's painting: a horizontal gouache (Sylvester 4:1125) and a sketch in a letter to the Scutenaires, March 1, 1937, illustrated in *Magritte: Retrospective Loan Exhibition* (New York: Marlborough Fine Art, 1973), pp. 29–30. The identification of items originates in Magritte's letter to Éluard of January 30, 1937.
19. *Larousse universel en 2 volumes: Nouveau dictionnaire encyclopédique*, ed. by Claude Augé (Paris: Librairie Larousse, 1922–23). It is also possible that Magritte used an illustration from *Larousse* for the boots in *Le Modèle rouge*. For more on this topic, see Patricia Allmer, *René Magritte: Beyond Painting* (Manchester, U.K.: Manchester University Press, 2009), esp. chap. 2.
20. The artist Humphrey Jennings purchased this work. The first version of *Le Modèle rouge* was also shown at the 1936 *International Surrealist Exhibition*.
21. Magritte, letter to Mesens, June 10, 1930, in Joë Bousquet, et al., *Lettres mêlées (1920–1966)* (Brussels: Les Lèvres nues, 1979), p. 29 (copy available at David Sylvester's René Magritte Catalogue Raisonné Research Papers, Menil Archives, The Menil Collection, Houston). Trans. in Sylvester 1, p. 348.
22. Allison Langley reports that Magritte drew a grid pattern on top of the pink paint in this section to aid in the perspectival placement of the black cutouts. See "Examination Report for *Threshold of Liberty*," October 2011, conservation files, Art Institute of Chicago.
23. According to A. M. Hammacher, the cannon is a French fifteen-centimeter howitzer of the 1914–18 type, manufactured by Scheider-Canet, operating on the De Bauge system; see Hammacher, *René Magritte*, trans. by James Brockway (New York: Abrams, 1974), p. 98. No example of such a weapon exists in the copy of *Larousse* once owned by Magritte, but a similar-looking "canon de 155 long Scheider" appears as illustration no. 21 under "Artillerie" in the *Larousse du XXe siècle*, a publication to which the artist would have had access.
24. Langley, "Examination Report for *Threshold of Liberty*."
25. The event, a dance in honor of James's niece, Rosemary Howard, occurred on April 12, 1937 (*Western Morning News* [London], April 14, 1937). James's report is in a letter to Magritte, April 18, 1937, Tate Library and Archive, London.
26. Magritte's letters to Georgette, in the collection of Peter Morris, document his work on sketches

and watercolors or gouaches while waiting for the canvases to be ready to paint; the only known work dating to this time is the gouache of *La Jeunesse illustrée* (fig. 3). Their correspondence also charts his work on the panels simultaneously, although they were finished at different times.

27. The present discussion is based on visual examination of *Le Modèle rouge* and *La Jeunesse illustrée*; it is clear that much of our understanding of Magritte's working methods would benefit greatly from a systematic and sustained study of technical information gleaned from the artist's paintings in these years.

28. The "marvelous" is an aesthetic concept dating to André Breton's first *Manifeste du Surréalisme* (1924); it incorporates the idea of a shock or surprise in the juxtaposition of two or more unrelated objects that can transform reality. For more on this concept, see Katharine Conley, *Robert Desnos, Surrealism, and the Marvelous in Everyday Life* (Lincoln: University of Nebraska Press, 2003).

29. Roland Penrose, as recounted to Sylvester (Sylvester 2, p. 53).

30. "Alterations to No. 35 Wimpole Street, W.1, Proposed Layout of New Sanitary Services, drafted 7 December 1949, approved 30 August 1950, architectural drawing, Laurence M. Gotch & Partners, Architects & Surveyors," City of Westminster Archives. Thanks to Rory Lalwan, Senior Archives & Local Studies Assistant at the archives, for bringing this document to the author's attention.

31. Paul Colinet, note in a group letter to Magritte, February 15, 1937, reproduced in *The Remaining Contents of the Studio of René Magritte* (London: Sotheby's, July 2, 1987, lot 981). The fact that this letter was written so soon after Magritte's arrival may suggest that the artist knew about the details of the installation and shared them with his friends before coming to London.

32. See Michael Pick, "Edward James in Wimpole Street," *Thirties Society Journal* 6 (1987): 46.

33. See Sylvester 2, p. 7; and discussion of this event in Draguet, "Once the Image Is Isolated," p. 152.

34. Stephan Calloway, "Edward James's Interiors," in Nicola Coleby, ed., *A Surreal Life: Edward James* (Brighton and Hove, U.K.: Royal Pavilion, Libraries & Museums, 1998), p. 98; and "An Unusual House," *Sunday Times* (London), April 18, 1937.

35. This dramatic scheme follows a similar buildup for the décor in a traditional Georgian townhome; see Rachel Stewart, *The Town House in Georgian London* (New Haven: Yale University Press, 2009).

36. See Emily Genauer, *Modern Interiors Today and Tomorrow* (New York: Illustrated Editions, 1939), pp. 200–13; and Ghislaine Wood, "The Illusory Interior," in Wood, ed., *Surreal Things: Surrealism and Design* (London: V&A Publications, 2007), pp. 39–57.

37. "These Names Make News," *Daily Express* (London), June 26, 1936, acknowledges James's style; the article also mentions a lunch party James gave in honor of Dalí's exhibition at London's Lefevre Gallery, June–July 1936.

38. *Harper's Bazaar* (London), January 1939. Thanks to Alex Anthony at the Norman Parkinson Archive for providing images of the original collaged composition of photographs from which the editorial in the publication (pp. 20–21) was trimmed.

39. According to Sharon-Michi Kusunoki, by 1939 James's collection of Surrealist art comprised more than 250 works, including 180 works by Dalí; see Kusunoki's entry on Edward James in Dawn Ades and Michael R. Taylor, *Dalí* (New York and Philadelphia: Rizzoli, Philadelphia Museum of Art, 2004), p. 439.

40. See Ian Gibson, *The Shameful Life of Salvador Dalí* (New York: Faber and Faber, 1997), p. 347; and Dalí, letter to James, October 26, 1935 (Edward James Archive, U.K.), cited in Bonnie Clearwater, *Salvador Dalí, Dream of Venus* (North Miami: Museum of Contemporary Art, 1999), p. 211.

41. See Kusunoki, in Ades and Taylor, *Dalí*, p. 284, esp. no. 4; the Royal Crown Derby tea service is discussed and illustrated in Wood, "Illusory Interior," in *Surreal Things*, pp. 49 and 282.

42. James asked his attorney to draw up an agreement with Dalí on July 1, 1936, but a final signed contract took more time; it was in force only from June 1, 1937, through June 1, 1938. For more on their collaboration, see Kusunoki, "Breaking Canons; Edward James: His Life and Work," p. 27, and Dawn Ades, "Edward James and Surrealism," p. 75, both in Coleby, ed., *A Surreal Life*.

43. James wrote to the Dalís on May 10, 1936, stating that "my architects tell me that the weight would be too great if I put pieces of real rock on the walls, and the house—which is so old and fragile—would collapse under the strain." See Jean-Louis Gaillemin, *Dalí: Master of Fantasies* (New York: Abrams, 2004), p. 106. The postcard, which was likely sent to James some time after his initial request, is in the collection of the Edward James Foundation, London.

44. Kusunoki, "Edward James: Architect of Surrealism," in Wood, ed., *Surreal Things*, p. 207, n. 5.

45. Pierre-Emmanuel Martin-Vivier, "Jean-Michel Frank: The Surrealist Interior," in ibid., p. 194.

46. Magritte, who was in a difficult financial position at the time of the commission, was eager to establish a good relationship with James, and likely even hoped that a longer-term form of patronage might develop. Magritte's apparent coarseness, unfortunately, did not appeal to the more refined James. Correspondence from the artist to his friends and family, in the collection of Peter Morris, recounts the many evenings Magritte found James already asleep or out of London during his stay.

47. Magritte, letter to Georgette Magritte, undated, [February 15] 1937, collection of Peter Morris.

48. Sylvester 2:433, p. 241.

49. James, telegram to Magritte, May 18, 1937, Tate Library and Archive, London.

50. *Le Monde poétique* is illustrated in Sylvester 2:435, p. 243, listed as "whereabouts unknown."

51. Man Ray took a number of photographs related to Magritte's request; they are in the collection of the Centre Georges Pompidou, Paris.

52. Sylvester 4, p. 61.

53. The source of the fireplace remains disputed in Magritte's literature: it is either from the Wimpole Street house (see Sylvester 2, p. 267, citing information from the Edward James Foundation) or from the coal-burning stove in Magritte's own Brussels apartment (see Sarah Whitfield, *Magritte* [London: Hayward Gallery, 1992, cat. no. 81] and Louis Scutenaire, *Avec Magritte* [Brussels: Lebeer Hossmann, 1977], p. 37).

54. Magritte, "Ligne de vie," p. 47.

55. Magritte, letter to James, July 12, 1939, Edward James Foundation, London. Magritte continues: "And you have *Time Transfixed*, this is curious because in the film *The Last Gangster* with [Edward G.] Robinson, there is also a staircase like yours, and while watching the film, I thought of your staircase."

56. The information about the final placement of *La Durée poignardée* comes from the artist George Grosz, whose work James also collected, and who made illustrations for some of James's writing. Grosz wrote in his autobiography: "Over his Victorian chimneypiece Edward had hung a painting of a railway engine, floating in the air." See Grosz, *The Autobiography of George Grosz: A Small Yes and A Big No*, trans. by Arnold J. Pomerans (London: Allison & Busby, 1982), p. 232.

57. A history of the affair between Magritte and James, as well as the subsequent related one between Magritte and Mesens, can be found in Sylvester 2, pp. 61–67.

58. See Sylvester, *Magritte: The Silence of the World*, p. 14; and Luc Sante, "Magritte the Detective," *Threepenny Review*, no. 56 (Winter 1994): 27.

59. Sylvester 1: 188, p. 249.

The following three works, *Le Modèle rouge* (*The Red Model*), *Au seuil de la liberté* (*On the Threshold of Liberty*), and *La Jeunesse illustrée* (*Youth Illustrated*), were commissioned by Edward James in 1937 for the ballroom of his London home at 35 Wimpole Street. Their sequence in the plates accords with the way these three monumental paintings were likely displayed, with *Au seuil de la liberté* flanked on the left by *Le Modèle rouge* and on the right by *La Jeunesse illustrée*.

116. LE MODÈLE ROUGE (THE RED MODEL). 1937.
Oil on canvas, 6' 1⁄16" x 53 9⁄16" (183 x 136 cm)

117. AU SEUIL DE LA LIBERTÉ (ON THE THRESHOLD OF LIBERTY). 1937.
Oil on canvas, 7'10" x 6'1" (238.8 x 185.4 cm)

118. LA JEUNESSE ILLUSTRÉE (YOUTH ILLUSTRATED). 1937.
Oil on canvas, 6' 1⁄16" x 53 9⁄16" (183 x 136 cm)

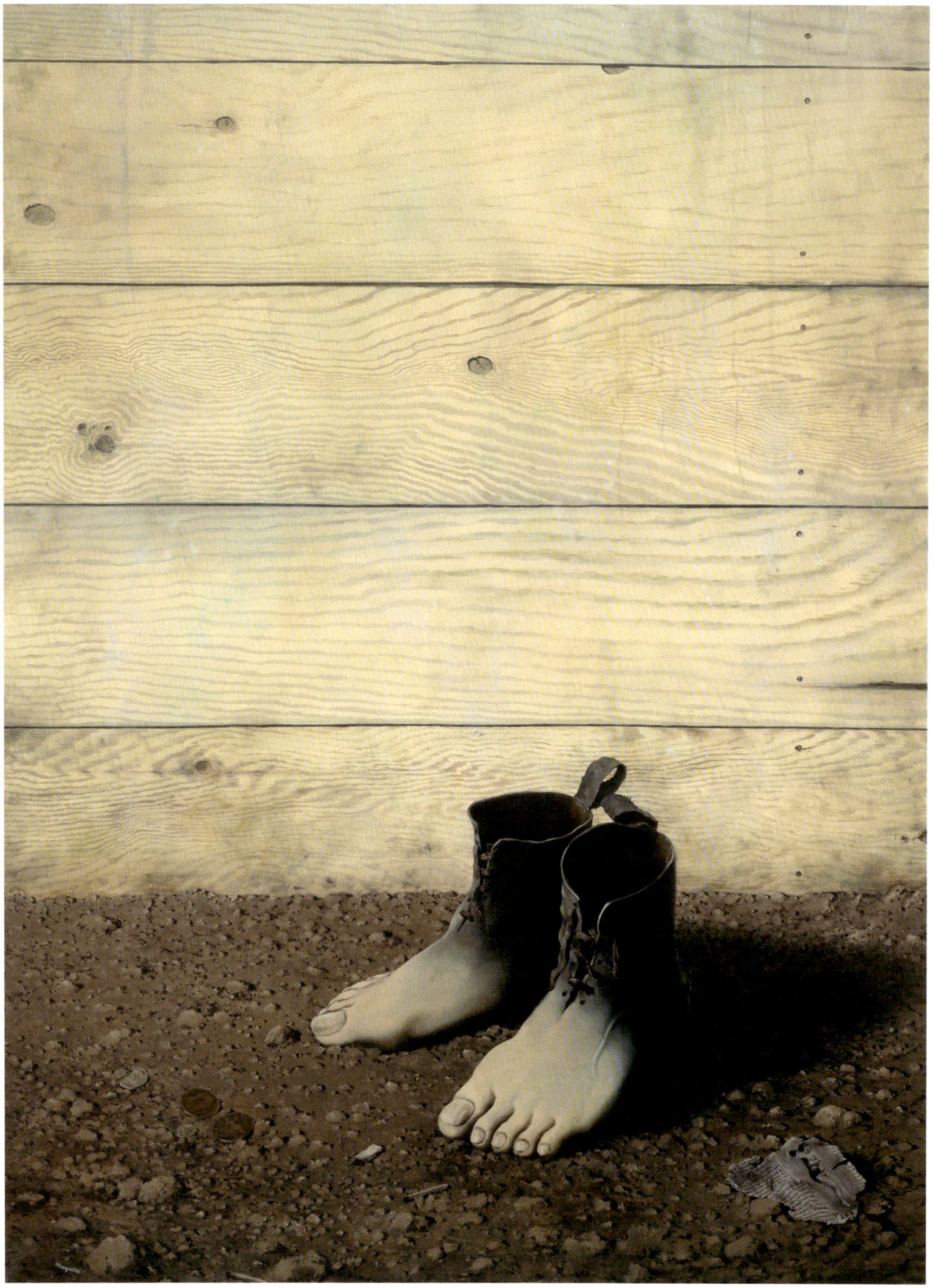

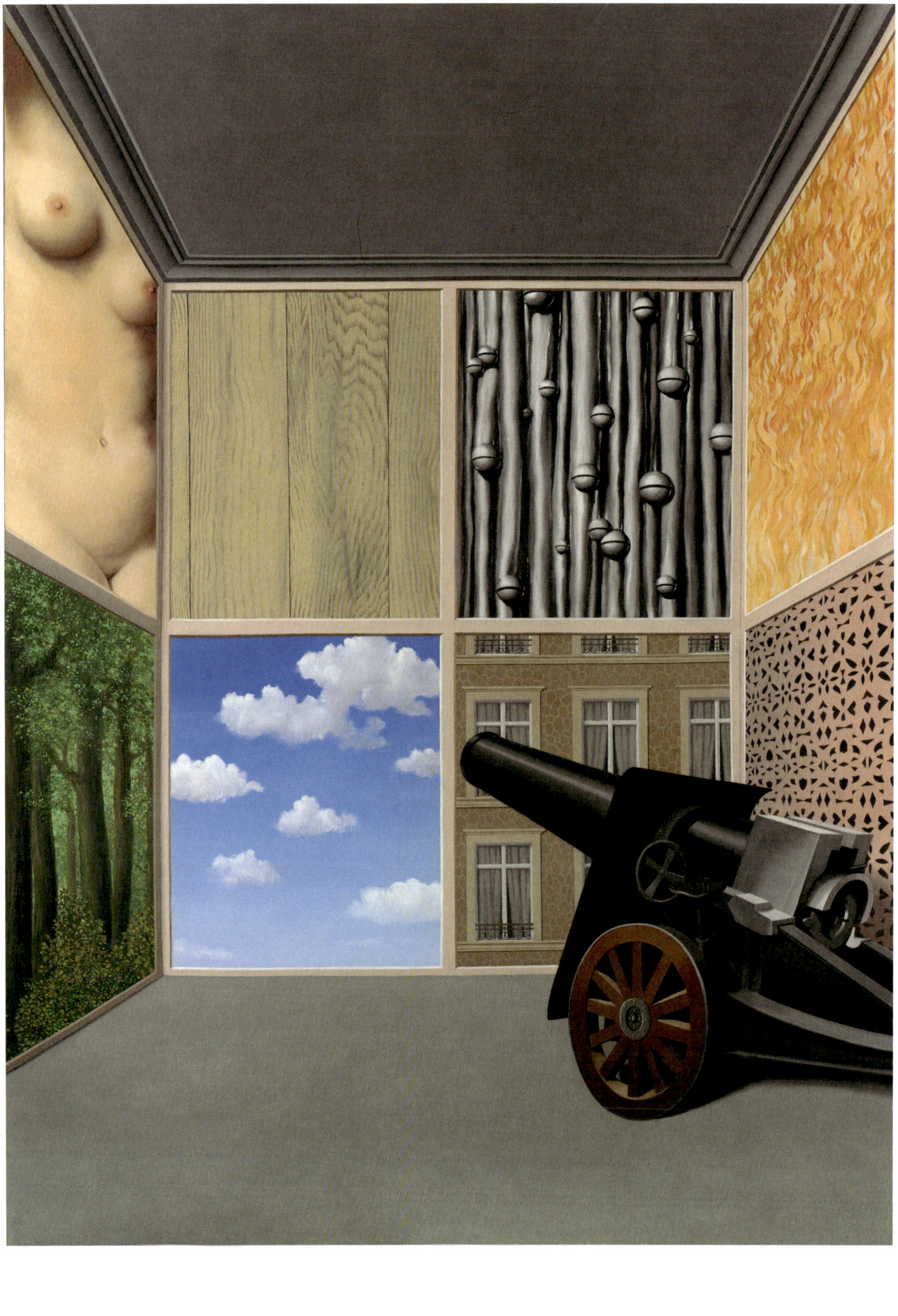

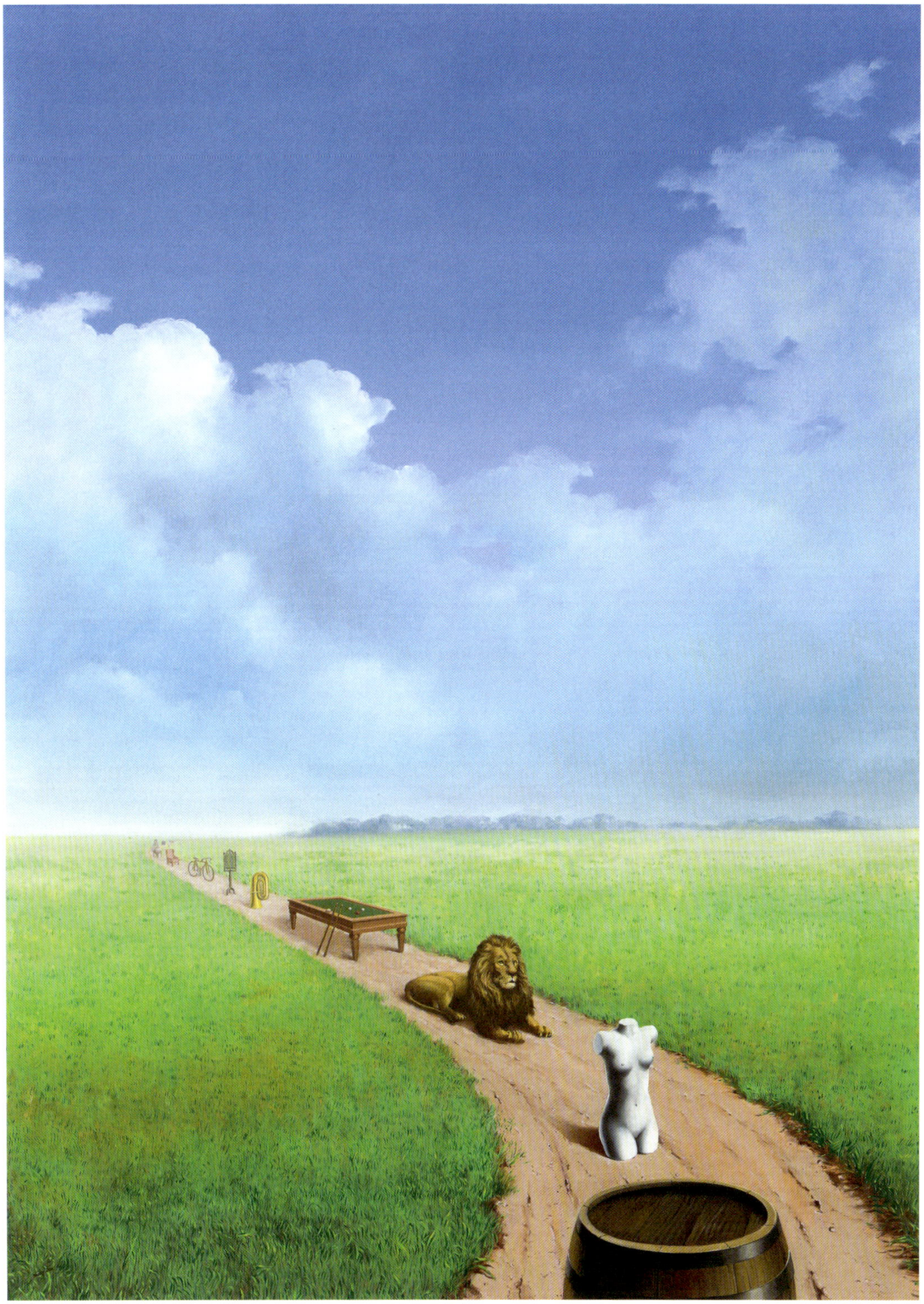

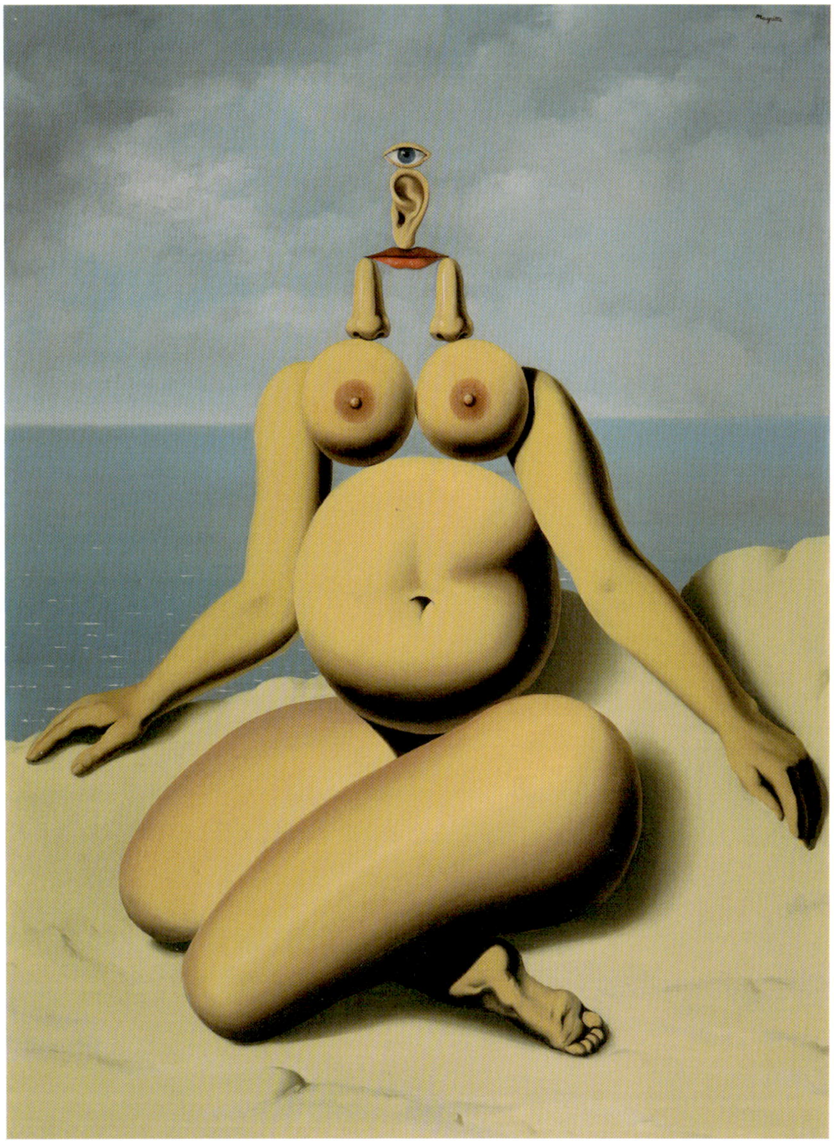

119. LA RACE BLANCHE (THE WHITE RACE). 1937.
Oil on canvas, 31 7/8 x 23 5/8" (81 x 60 cm)

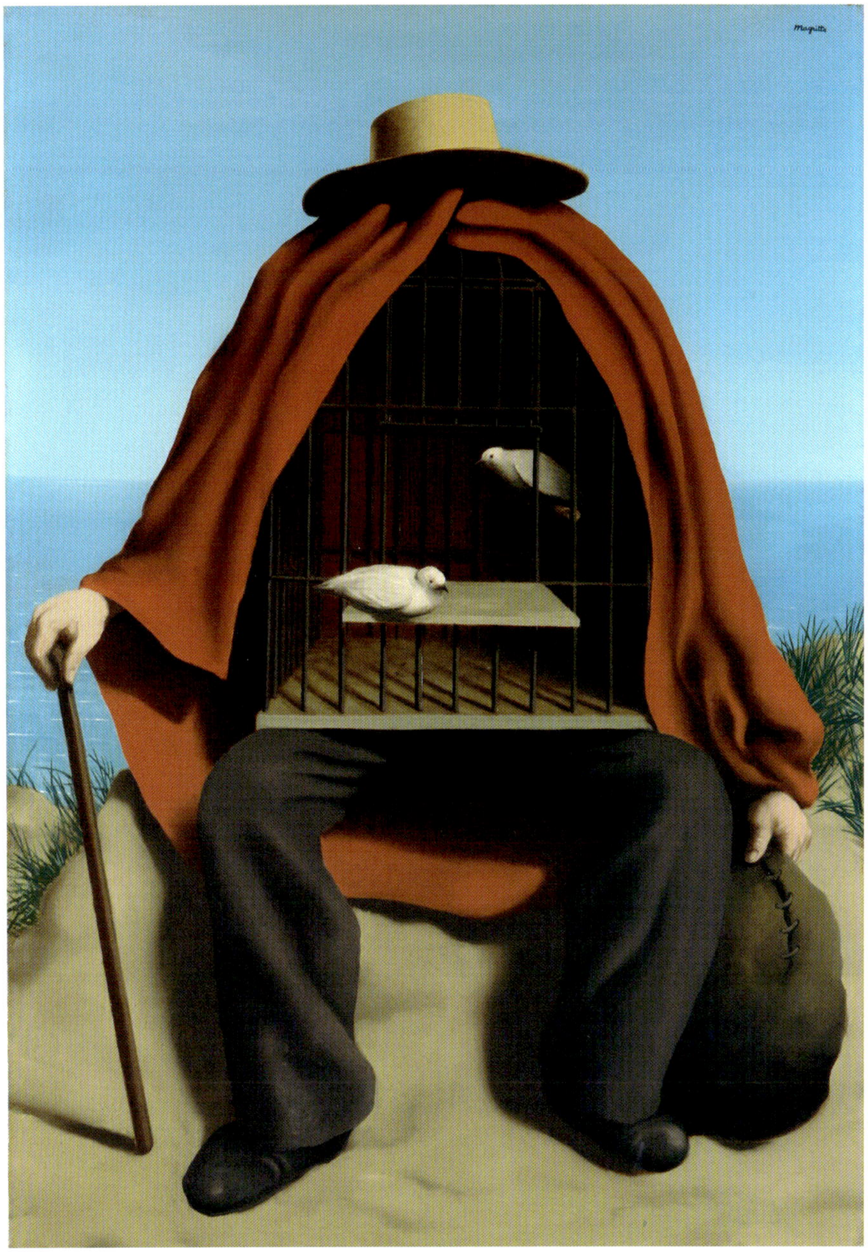

120. LE THÉRAPEUTE (THE HEALER). 1937.

Oil on canvas, 36 1/4 x 25 9/16" (92 x 65 cm)

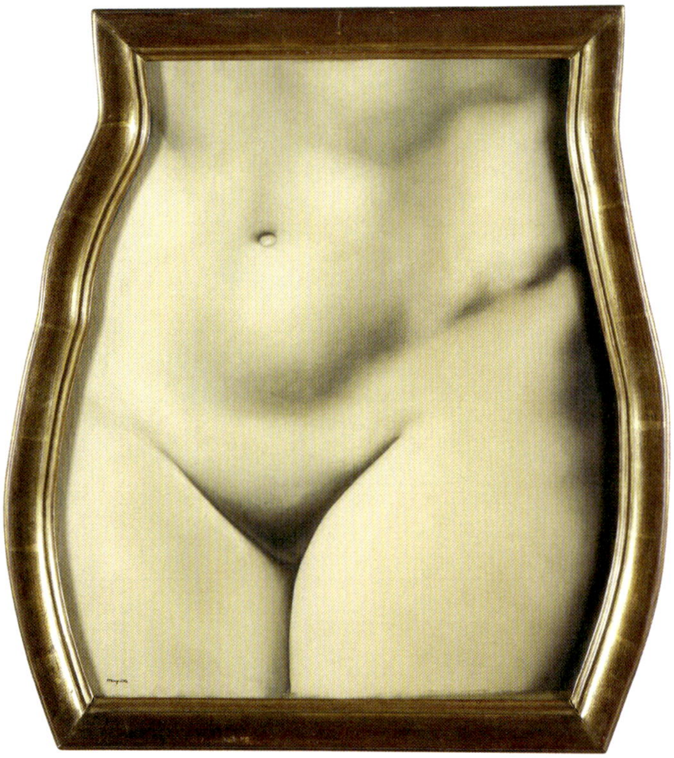

121. LA REPRÉSENTATION (REPRESENTATION). 1937.

Oil on canvas mounted on panel, 19 1/8 x 17 5/16" (48.5 x 44 cm)

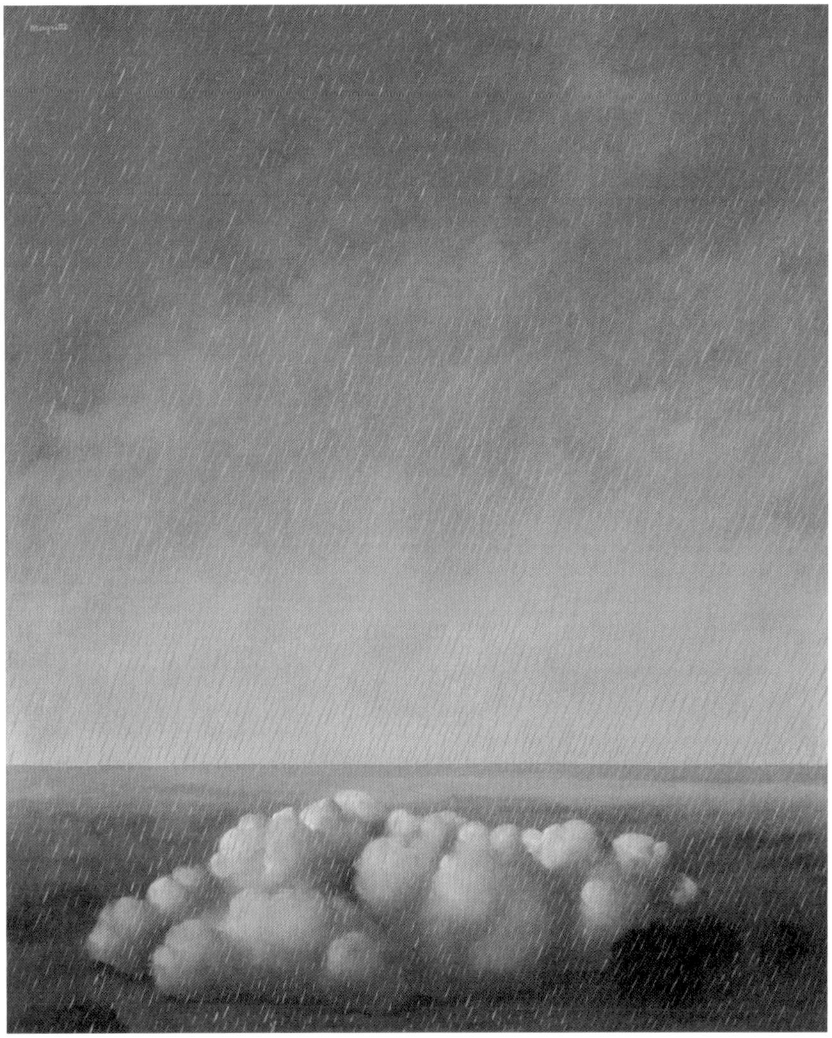

122. LE CHANT DE L'ORAGE (THE SONG OF THE STORM). 1937.

Oil on canvas, 25 9/16 x 21 1/4" (65 x 54 cm)

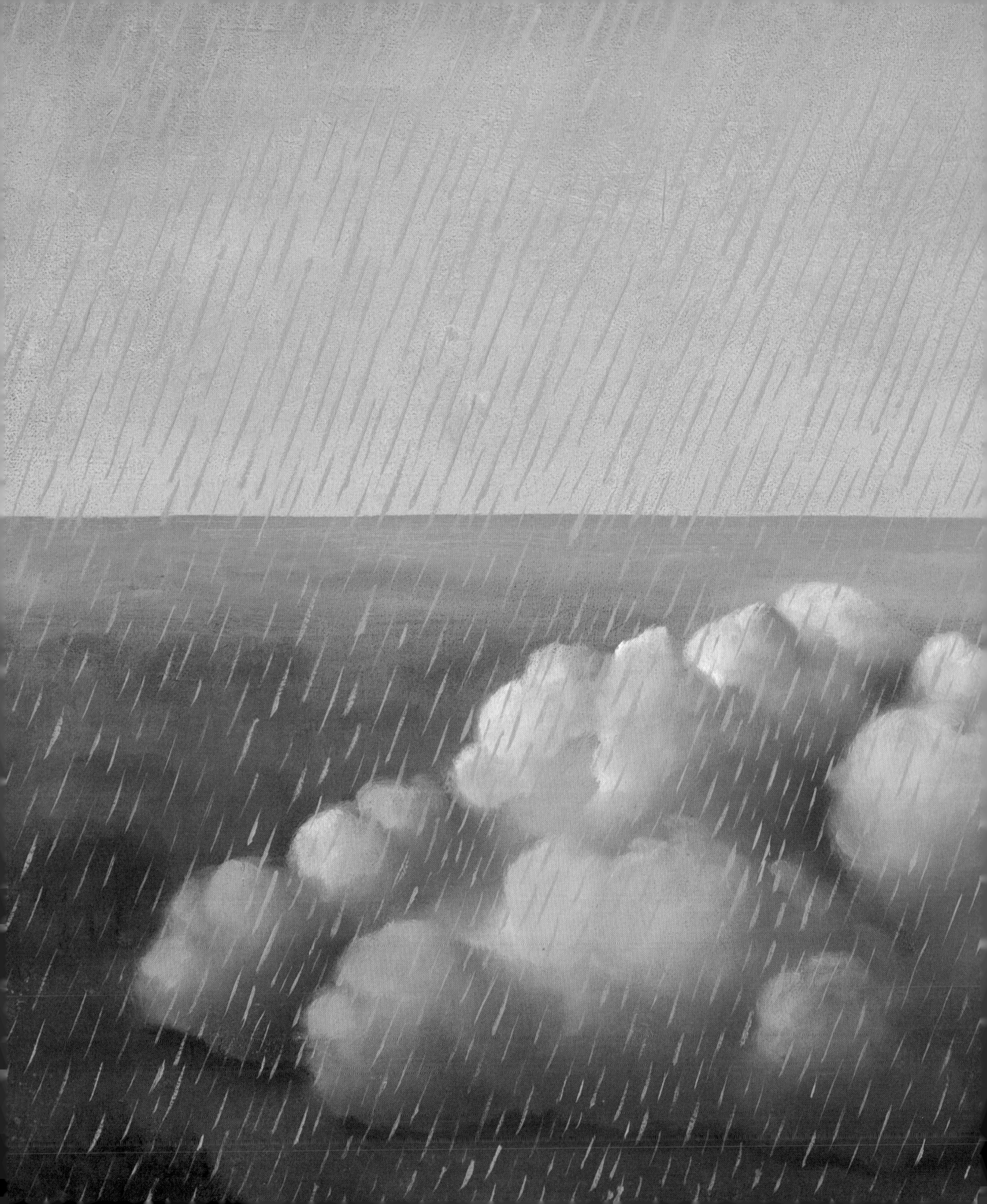

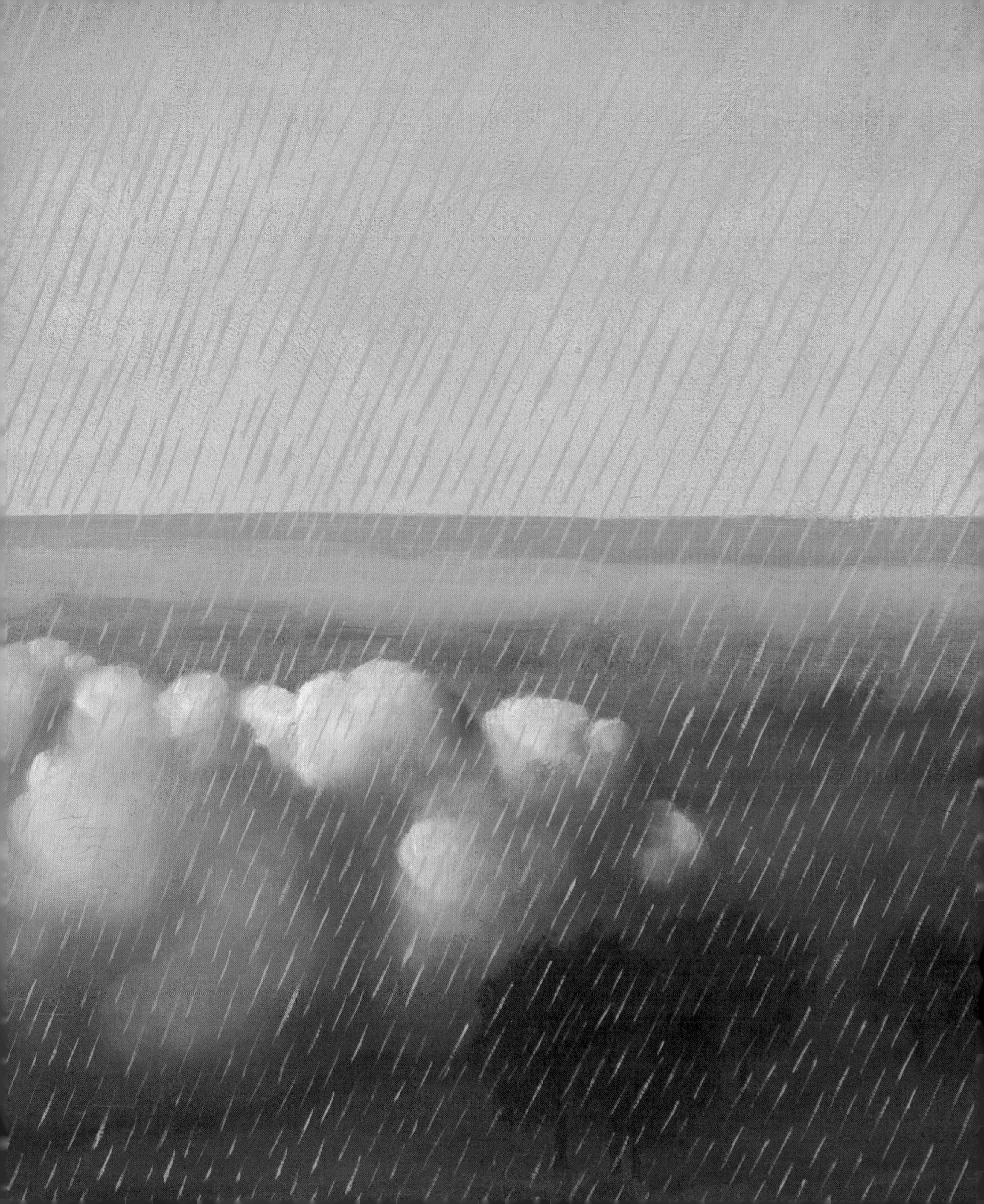

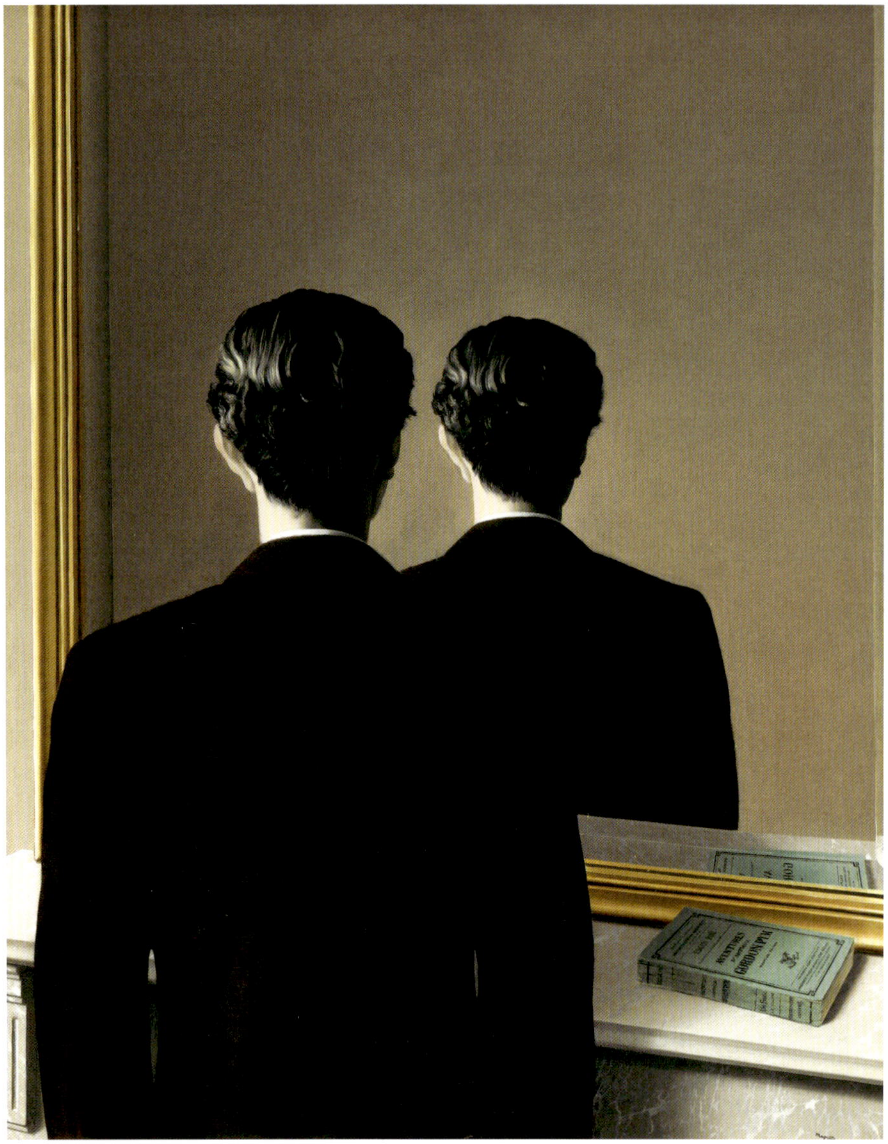

123. LA REPRODUCTION INTERDITE (NOT TO BE REPRODUCED). 1937.
Oil on canvas, 31 7/8 x 25 9/16" (81 x 65 cm)

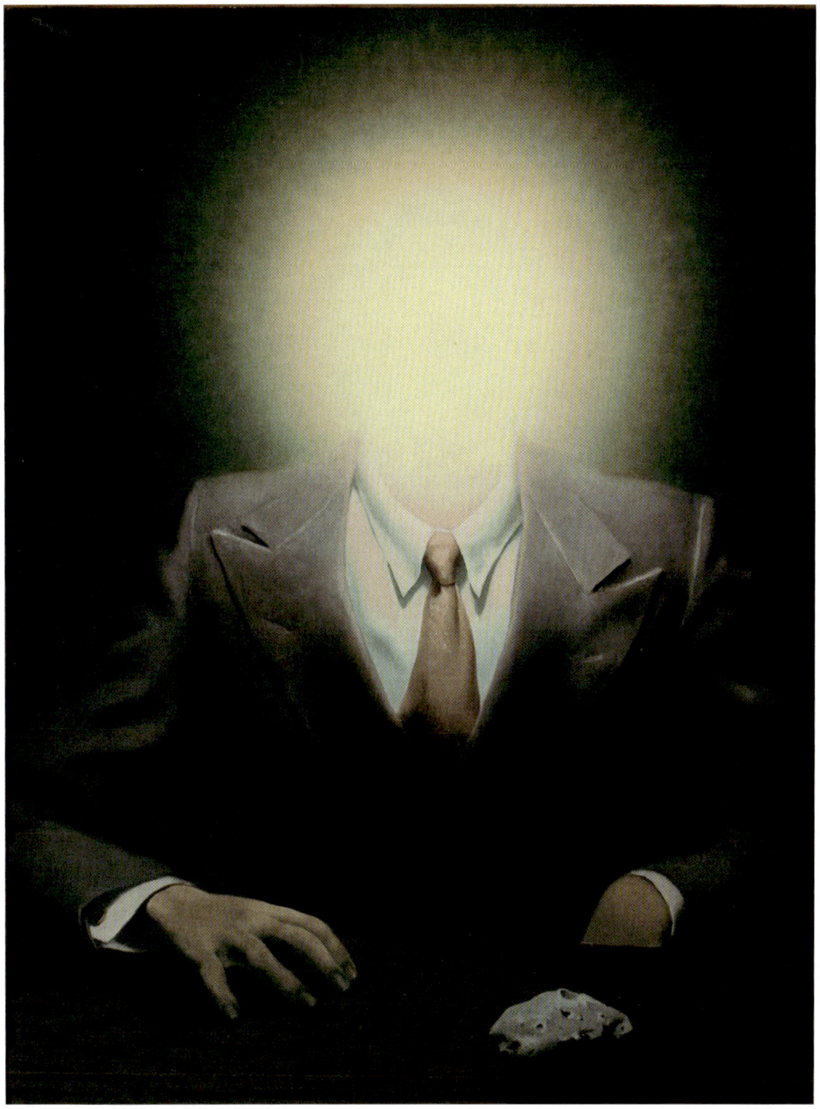

124. LE PRINCIPE DU PLAISIR (THE PLEASURE PRINCIPLE). 1937.
Oil on canvas, 28 3/4 x 21 1/4" (73 x 54 cm)

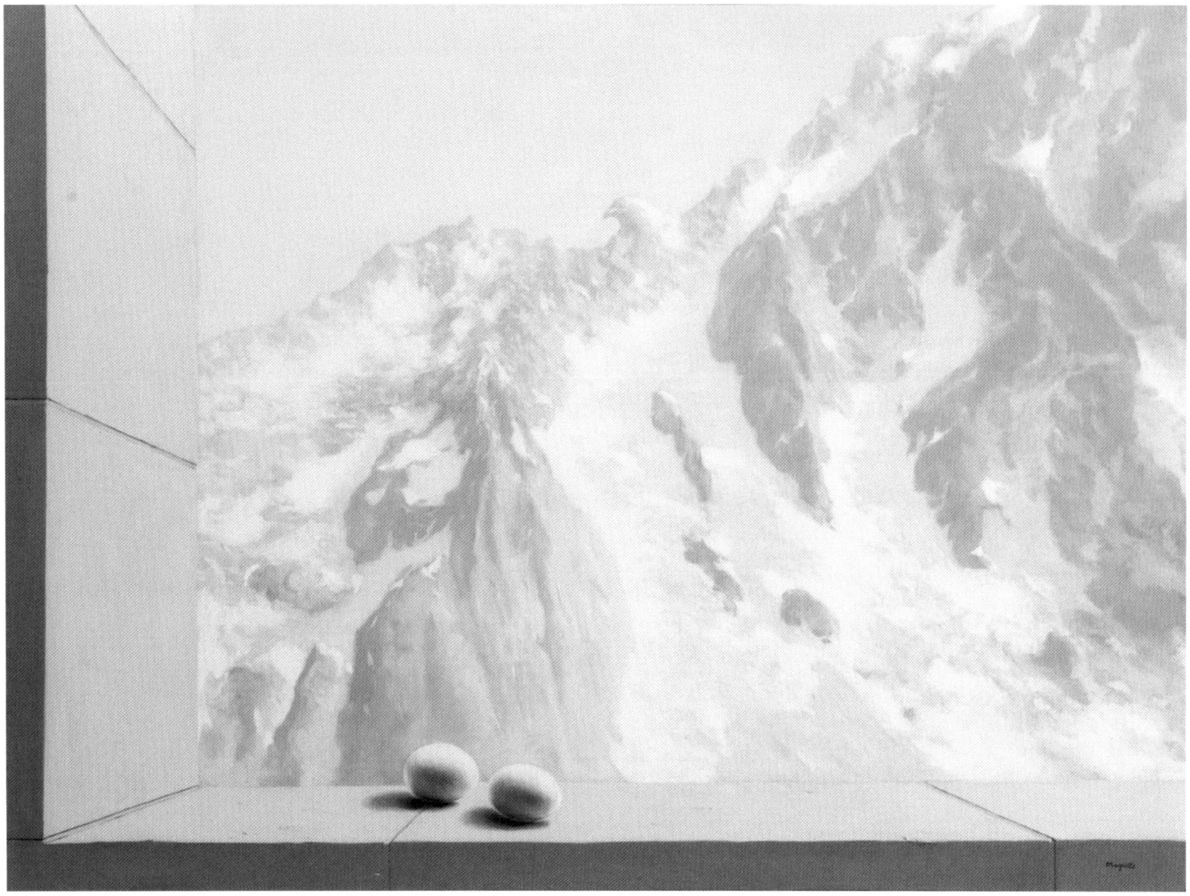

125. LE DOMAINE D'ARNHEIM (THE DOMAIN OF ARNHEIM). 1938.

Oil on canvas, 28 3/4 x 39 3/8" (73 x 100 cm)

126. LA DURÉE POIGNARDÉE (TIME TRANSFIXED). 1938.

Oil on canvas, 57 7/8 x 39" (147 x 99 cm)

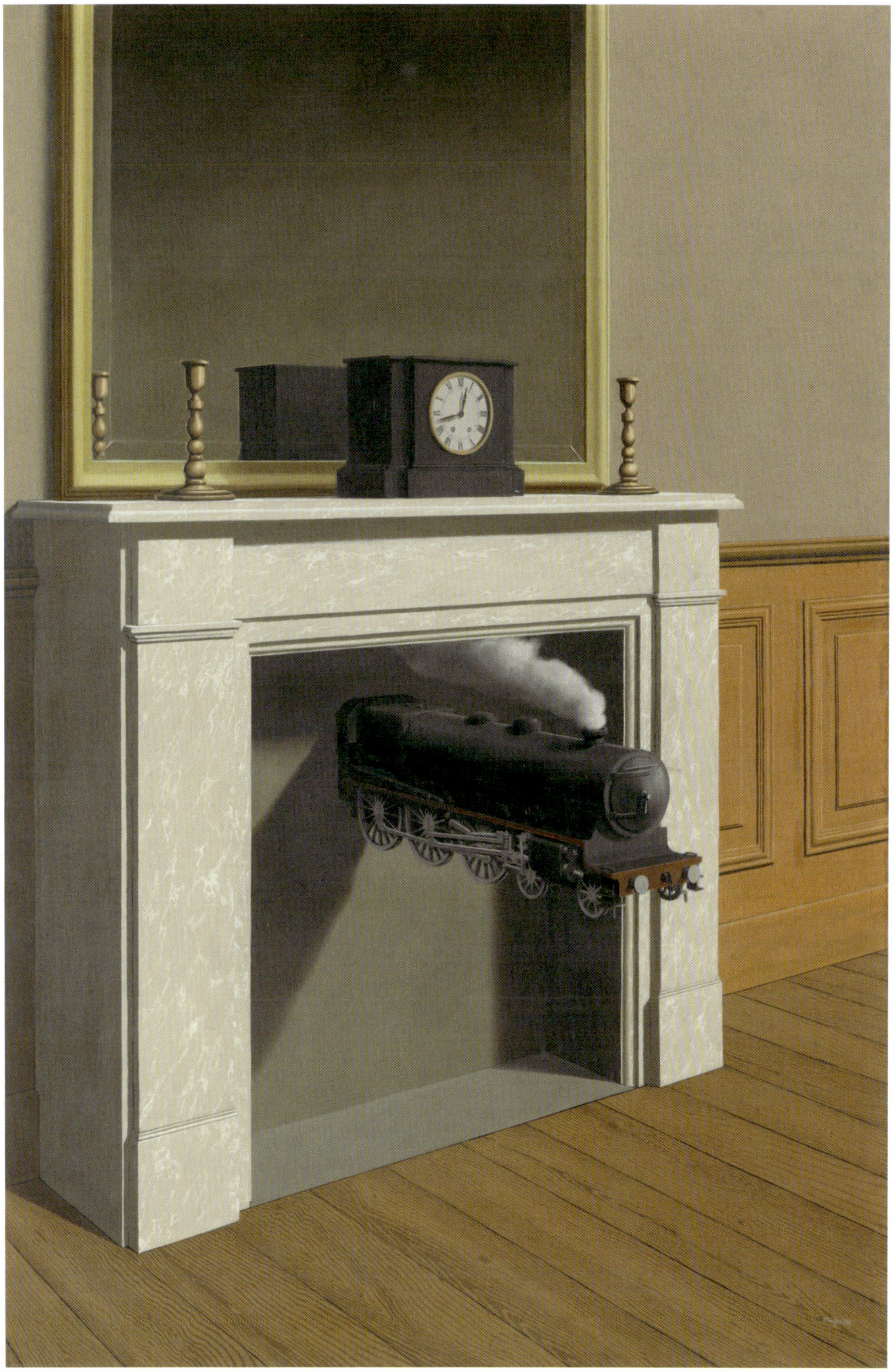

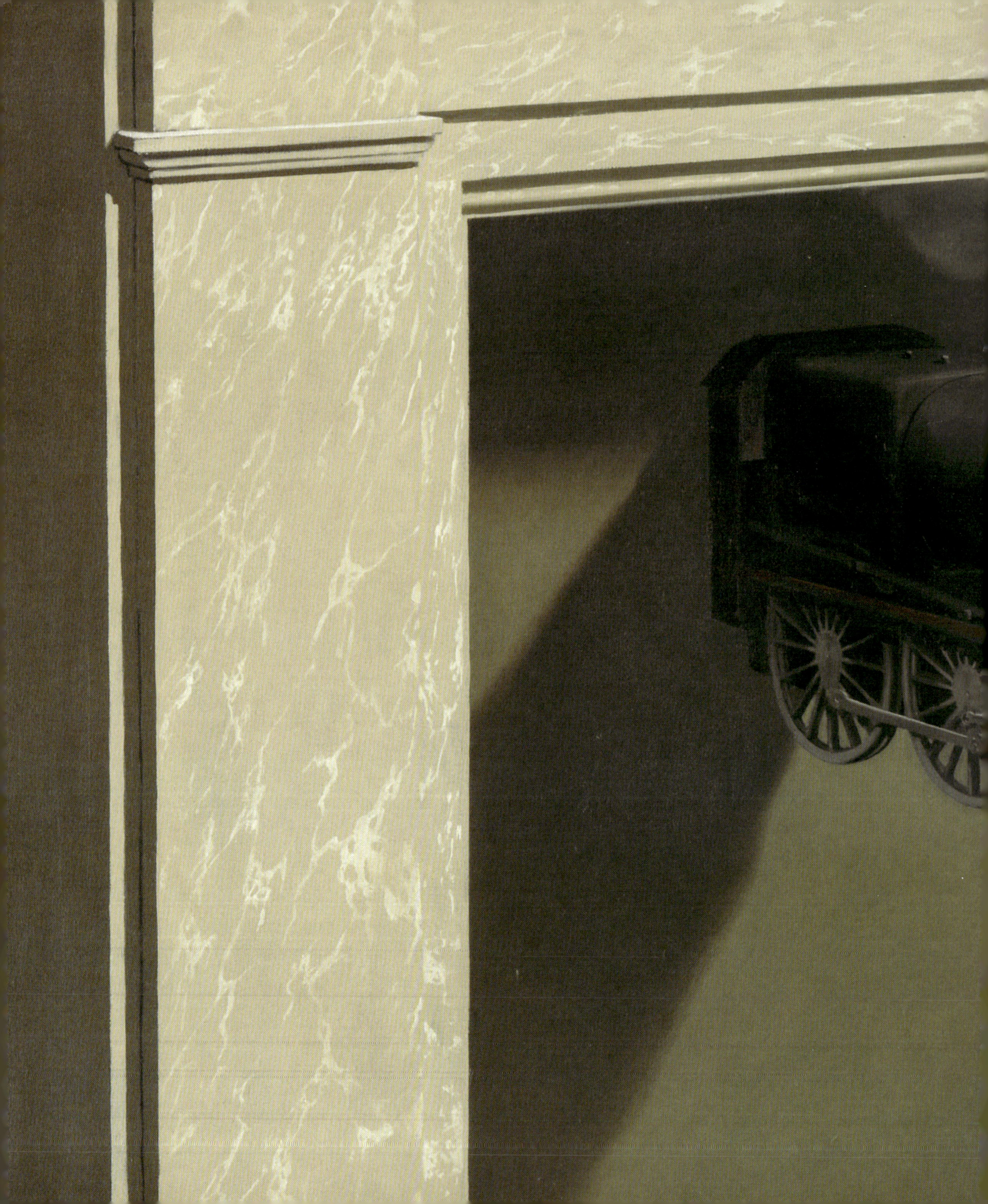

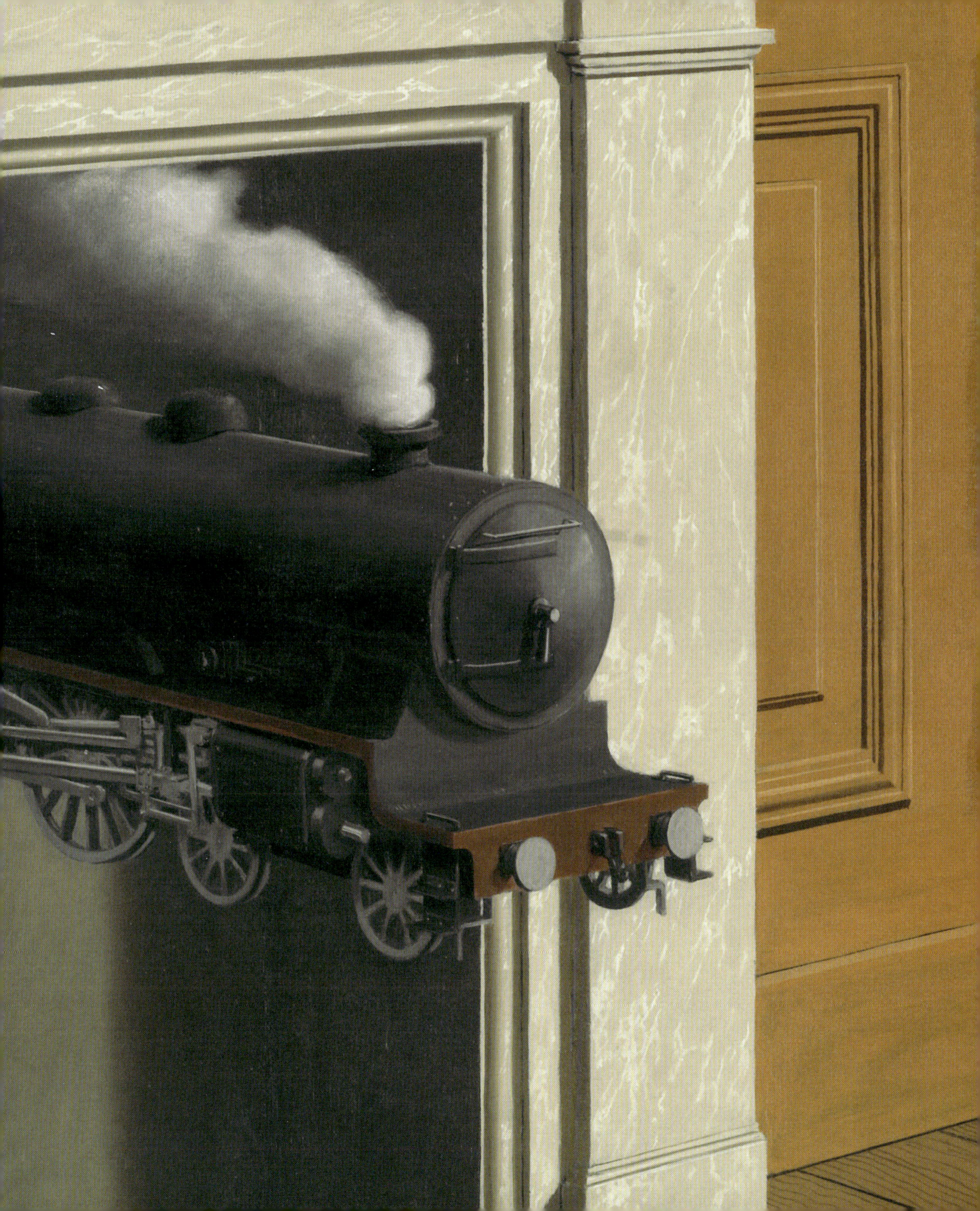

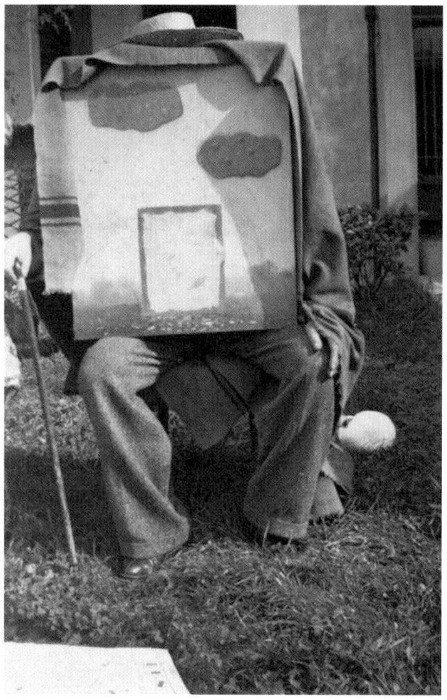

127. DIEU, LE HUITIÈME JOUR (GOD, THE EIGHTH DAY). 1937.
Photographer unknown. Gelatin silver print, 3 3/8 x 2 1/4" (8.5 x 5.7 cm)

128. Edward James in front of *Au seuil de la liberté* (*On the Threshold of Liberty*). 1937.
Photograph by René Magritte. Gelatin silver print, 4 1/4 x 6 9/16" (10.8 x 16.7 cm)

129. E.L.T. Mesens hanging *La Clairvoyance* (*Clairvoyance*) at the London Gallery. 1937.
Photographer unknown. Gelatin silver print, 5 7/16 x 7 1/16" (13.8 x 17.9 cm)

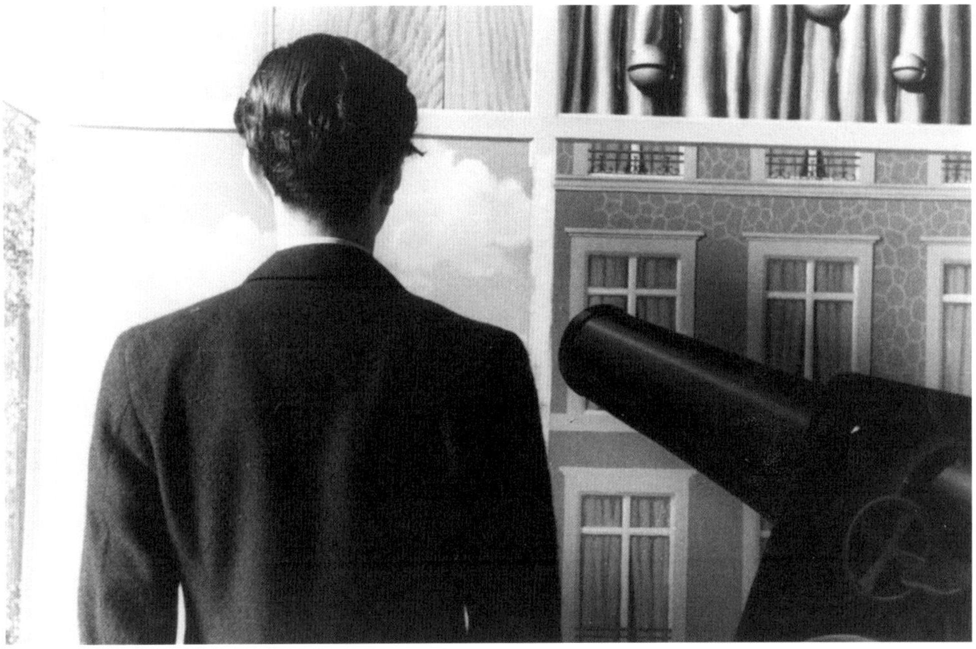

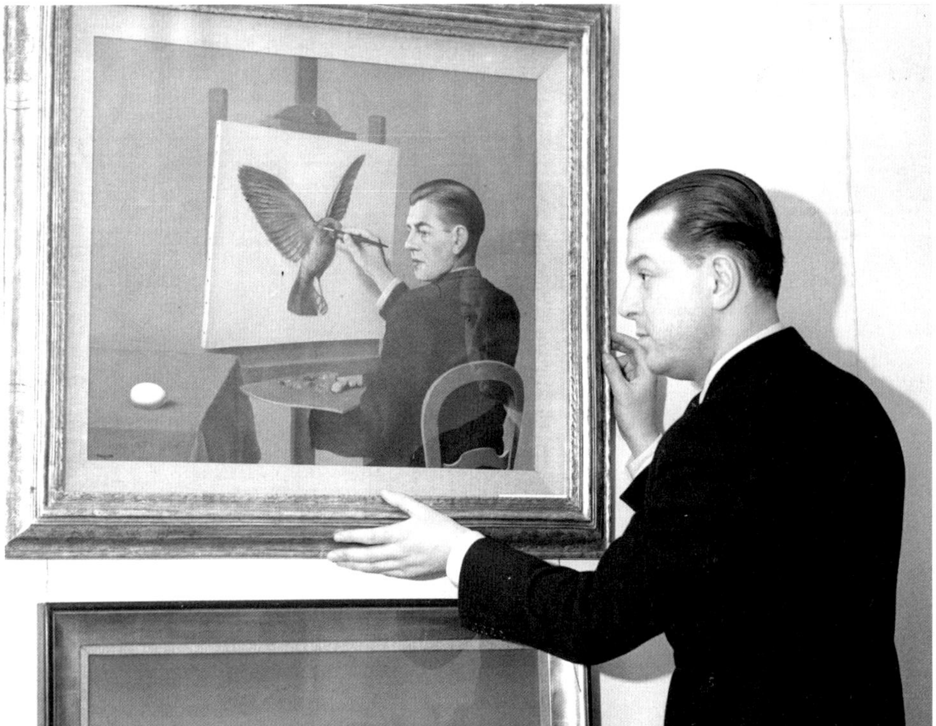

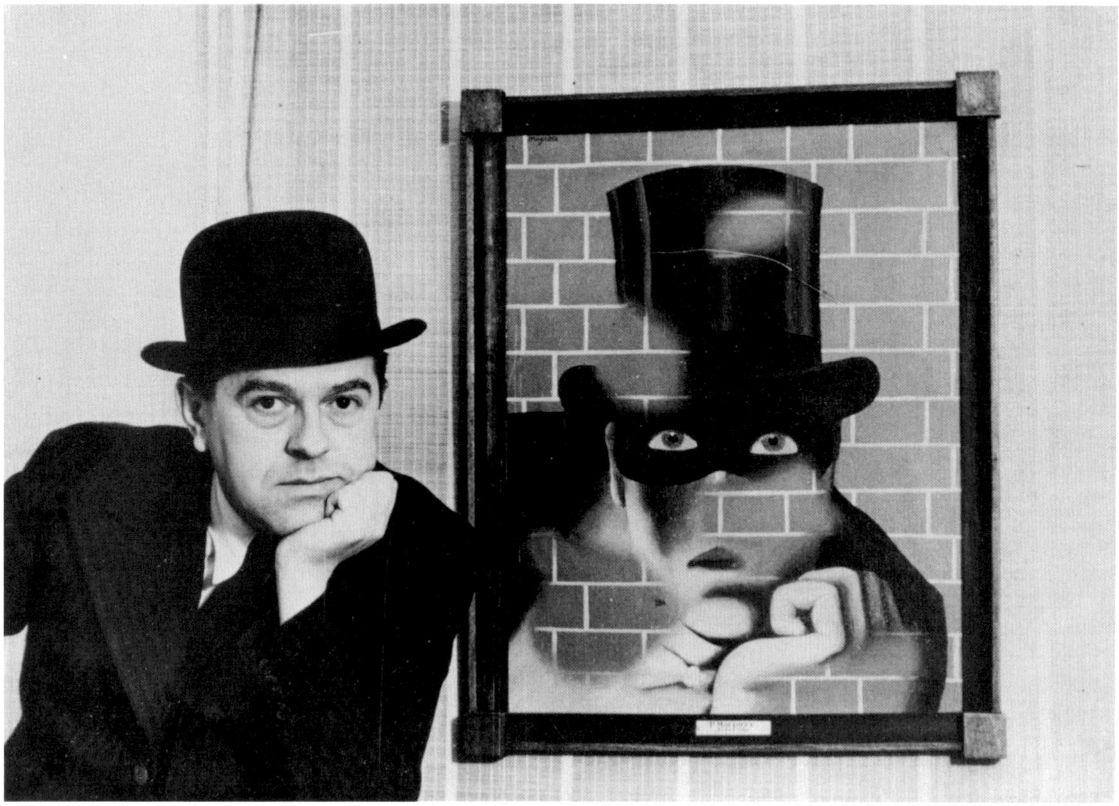

130. René Magritte and *Le Barbare* (*The Barbarian*). 1938.
Photographer unknown. Gelatin silver print, 7 3/8 x 9 7/8" (18.8 x 25 cm)

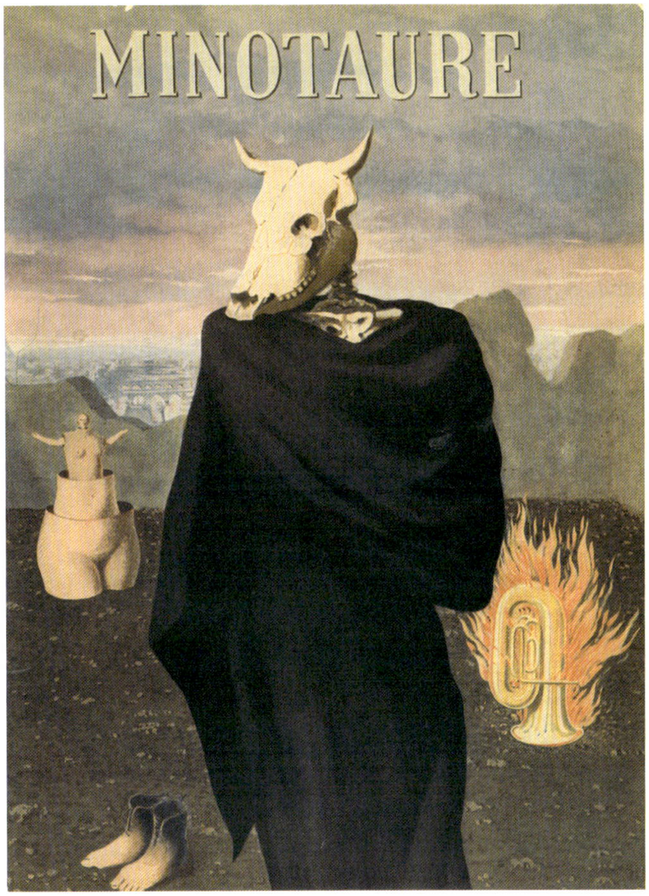

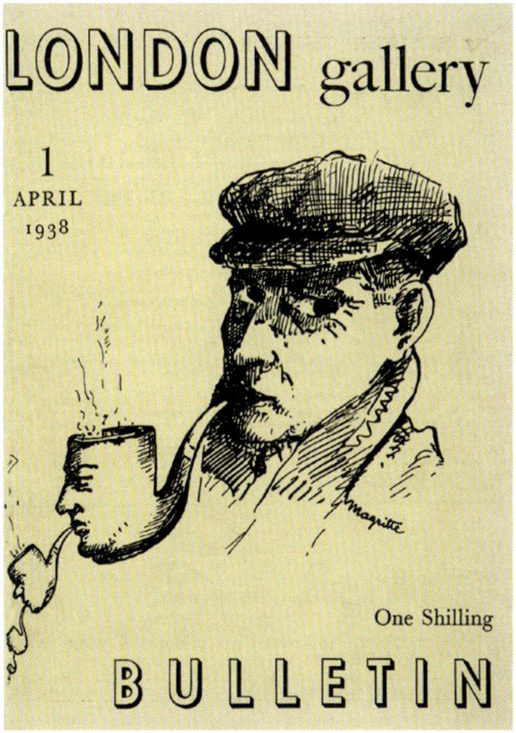

131. Cover illustration for *Minotaure*, no. 10 (Winter 1937).
Periodical, 12 3/8 x 9 5/8" (31.5 x 24.4 cm)

132. Cover illustration for *London Gallery Bulletin*, no. 1 (April 1938).
Periodical, 9 1/2 x 6 3/4" (24.1 x 17.1 cm)

CHRONOLOGY 1926–1938

Compiled by Danielle M. Johnson

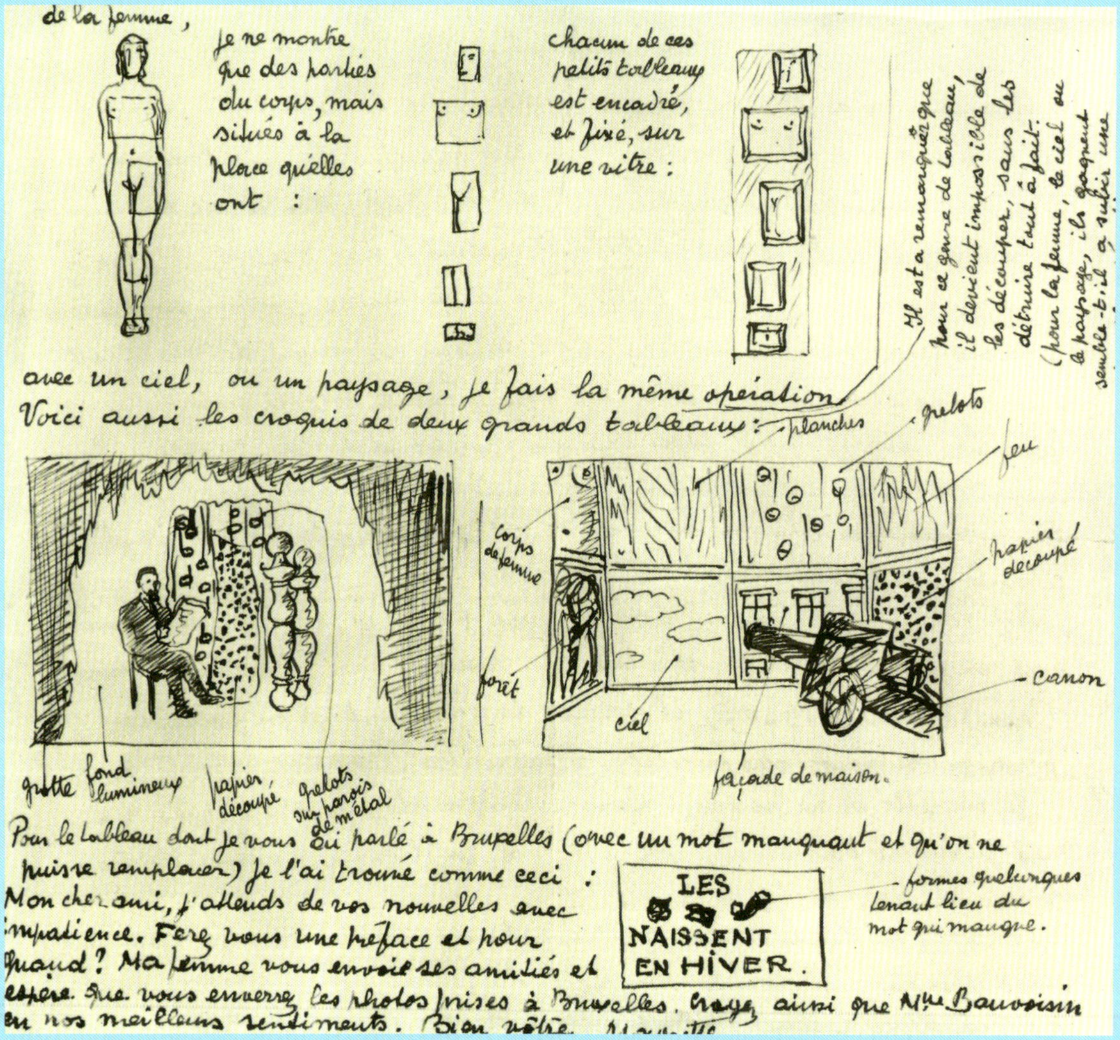

de la femme, je ne montre que des parties du corps, mais situés à la place qu'elles ont :

chacun de ces petits tableaux est encadré, et fixé, sur une vitre :

avec un ciel, ou un paysage, je fais la même opération

Il est a remarquer que pour ce genre de tableau, il devient impossible de les découper, sans les détruire tout à fait. (pour la femme, le ciel ou le paysage, ils gagnent semble-t-il a subir une

Voici aussi les croquis de deux grands tableaux :

Pour le tableau dont je vous ai parlé à Bruxelles (avec un mot manquant et qu'on ne puisse remplacer) je l'ai trouvé comme ceci :

Mon cher ami, j'attends de vos nouvelles avec impatience. Ferez vous une préface et pour quand? Ma femme vous envoie ses amitiés et espère que vous enverrez les photos prises à Bruxelles. Croyez ainsi que Mme Bourvoisin en nos meilleurs sentiments. Bien vôtre.

Figure 1. René Magritte. Detail, letter to Paul Nougé, February 1930. Location unknown

This chronology outlines significant moments in Magritte's biography from 1926 to 1938: travel, connections with other Surrealist artists and writers, contributions to journals, and important exhibitions and reviews. It is based primarily on the six volumes of the Magritte catalogue raisonné as well as on histories and chronologies of Surrealism and primary sources (some published in accessible anthologies and collections of letters). David Sylvester's René Magritte Catalogue Raisonné Research Papers, Menil Archives, The Menil Collection, Houston, collected over a period of twenty years, offer an invaluable resource for Magritte scholars. Quotations and translations not found within the catalogue raisonné are cited in the endnotes.

1926

January: René Magritte, twenty-eight years old and living at 7, rue Ledeganck, Laeken, in northwest Brussels, establishes a "gentleman's agreement" with Paul-Gustave Van Hecke, an independent dealer. Their understanding guarantees the purchase of Magritte's output.

Sometime between **January 4 and February 3:** Magritte and his wife, Georgette, move to a larger apartment, at 113, rue Steyls, Laeken.

Summer: Magritte works on illustrations for the Maison S. Samuel et Cie. autumn fur catalogue. Camille Goemans, a dealer, critic, and poet, who first met Magritte in 1923, contributes the accompanying texts.

June: First issue of *Marie*, edited by E.L.T. (Édouard Léon Théodore) Mesens, includes two epigrams by Magritte. He and Mesens, an artist, writer, musician, and dealer, had met in 1920 at an exhibition of the work of Magritte and the Belgian abstract artist Pierre Flouquet.

July: Magritte contributes a drawing to the second issue of *Marie* (plate 21).

September: André De Ridder, co-director with Van Hecke of the Belgian journal *Sélection*, writes to Goemans on September 10 and asks him to collaborate on a special issue on Surrealism. On September 19 Goemans rejects the idea: "Neither Violier [*sic*: Jean Viollier], nor Magritte, nor [Gert] Wollheim is a Surrealist. There's nothing you or I can do about it. It's a fact. SURREALISM isn't a school; up to now it has been an absolutely closed group into which nobody is admitted without the consent of the Surrealists themselves." De Ridder and Van Hecke respond to Goemans in separate letters, both on September 24, claiming that Surrealism is a universal phenomenon and should be discussed openly. Van Hecke writes: "To hell with all dictators, from Lenin to Mussolini, through Breton. What are we to do, unless perhaps [...] we were to invent a label for Magritte [...] which will express more accurately than they do what art such as his contains by way of originality."

October: Brussels's Galerie Le Centaure, first established in October 1921 by Walter Schwarzenberg, merges with Blanche Charlet's Galerie Charlet and reopens at new premises. It acquires a half-share of Van Hecke's contracts, including Magritte's. The journal *Le Centaure*, edited by Georges Marlier, is launched. Numerous advertisements by Magritte will be reproduced in it over the next two years (plates 23, 24).

1927

February or March: "Adieu à *Marie*," the final issue of *Marie*, is published, with Paul Nougé replacing Mesens as editor. The contributors to this issue—Goemans, Magritte, Mesens, and Nougé—form the Belgian Surrealist group. Magritte contributes "Vous" ("You"), five short statements on art, one of which is: "Painting excites your admiration through the likeness of things the originals of which you do not admire." Magritte and Nougé may have met around the beginning of 1925, after the launch of the periodical *Correspondance* in November 1924. Nougé's brainchild, *Correspondance* was the first manifestation of Surrealism in Belgium.

March: In *Sélection*, Van Hecke publishes the first article on Magritte. After identifying Surrealists as painters of abstract thought and Expressionists as painters of direct thought, he calls Magritte "a great young painter of abstract thought," and writes that in his paintings "the elusive dream and impalpable subconscious manifest themselves in a more direct appearance, so that they help, surround, and reinforce the most striking and most mundane reality."[1] Following the text are sixteen full-page illustrations of paintings from 1926 and 1927 (including plate 9).

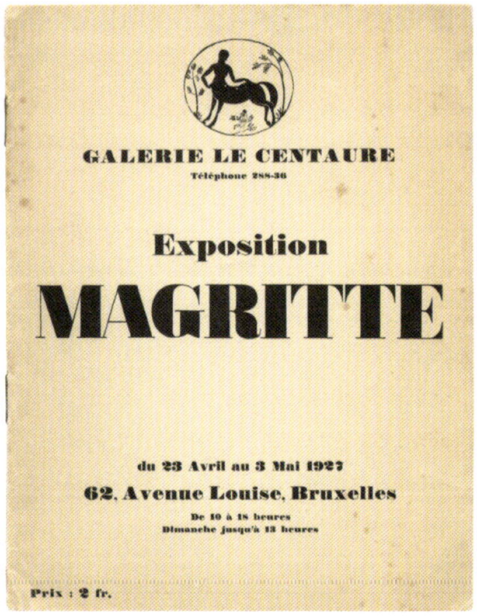

Figure 2. Cover for the *Exposition Magritte* catalogue, Galerie Le Centaure, Brussels. 1927. Royal Museums of Fine Arts of Belgium, Brussels/Library RMFAB

April 23–May 5: *Exposition Magritte*, the artist's first solo show, is presented at Galerie Le Centaure. It consists of forty-nine paintings (including plates 9, 11, 12, and 14) and twelve *papiers collés* (perhaps plates 1–8). The catalogue includes introductory texts by Van Hecke and Nougé (**fig. 2**). In a 1966 interview, Magritte will recall: "It was my first exhibition that truly represented what I consider valuable [. . .] in my work."[2]

Probably by **April 27:** Goemans moves to Paris and will gradually begin to sell Magritte's work (despite Magritte's agreement with Van Hecke and Galerie Le Centaure).

May 1: Pierre Flouquet reviews Magritte's Le Centaure exhibition, asserting that this "surrealist" work is decadent and lacks conviction. Flouquet pays particular attention to *L'Assassin menacé* (*The Menaced Assassin*, 1927; plate 12), writing that "the perfumed crowd literally threatens the murderer, so densely does it swarm around him and admire him."[3]

May 8: Armand Eggermont writes in a review: "I like a lot *Le Jockey perdu* [*The Lost Jockey*, 1926; see p. 29, fig. 4] in the world of bowling pins. [. . .] The *papiers collés* go back to outdated processes: music paper cut in the form of pins, fashion plates headless and without hands arranged on abstract surfaces."[4]

Summer: Magritte collaborates with Nougé on two publications: a second fur catalogue for the firm now under the name "Maison Ch. Müller. S. Samuel et Cie. successeurs" (see p. 35, fig. 12, plates 25–30); and *Clarisse Juranville: Quelques écrits et quelques dessins* (*Clarisse Juranville: Some Writings and Some Drawings*; plates 31, 32), a spoof on the work of a well-known nineteenth-century writer of grammar textbooks and etiquette books.

June: Magritte meets the writer Louis Scutenaire, who becomes a Surrealist colleague and lifelong friend.

Sometime between **September 10 and 15:** The Magrittes leave Belgium and move to 101, avenue de Rosny, Le Perreux-sur-Marne, a suburb of Paris. Through Goemans, Magritte becomes acquainted with Jean Arp, Max Ernst, Joan Miró, and eventually Salvador Dalí.

Late September/early October: Magritte receives copies of the second Samuel catalogue and *Clarisse Juranville*. He writes to Nougé of the catalogue: "Breton [. . .] and also Aragon thought it good." Magritte paints what may be his first word-painting, *La Clef des songes* (*The Interpretation of Dreams*; plate 37).

October 22: Galerie L'Époque, owned by Van Hecke and his wife, the couturier Norine (Honorine) Deschryver, and directed by Mesens, opens in Brussels with an exhibition of works by Surrealists and Expressionists, including one painting by Magritte, *La Pose enchantée* (*The Enchanted Pose*, 1927).[5]

November: In a letter to Nougé, Magritte writes of his "striking discovery in painting"—the capability of one object to merge or transform into another: "Things are tangible and yet a few planks of solid wood become imperceptibly transparent in certain places, or else a naked woman has parts which also change into a different substance" (for example, plates 35 and 36). In his response, Nougé briefly compares this new discovery to "the transubstantiations which the cinema sometimes effects in time and the modifications which you bring about in space."

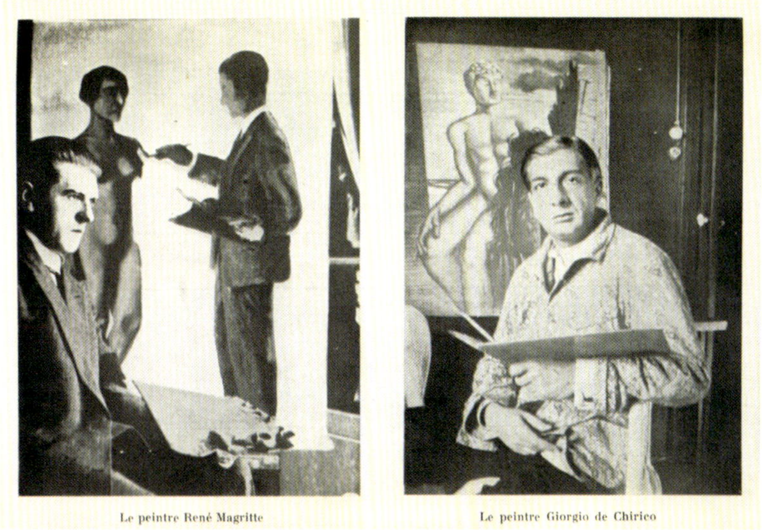

Figure 3. Page from *Variétés* (January 1929), with photographs of René Magritte in front of *Tentative de l'impossible* (*Attempting the Impossible*, 1928; plate 44), and Giorgio de Chirico in front of an unidentified painting (likely from his Gladiator series). The Museum of Modern Art Library, New York

1928

January 2: Goemans writes to Nougé: "I'm on slightly bad terms with the Galerie Surréaliste [in Paris . . .]. My only wish is that they should show Magritte. But how can one rely on them? They change their minds every day."

January 7: Magritte's second solo exhibition opens at Galerie L'Époque (it will run for approximately two weeks). All twenty-three works were completed in Brussels or Paris in 1927. Eight Belgian Surrealists, identified as "accomplices of René Magritte," sign the short catalogue text.

February: Nougé and Goemans found the review *Distances*. Magritte contributes two short texts to the first issue: "L'Homme au visage sans chemin" (The man with the impassive face) and "Théâtre en plein cœur de la vie" (Theater at the heart of life).

March: Magritte contributes a short essay, "Notes sur Fantômas" ("Notes on Fantômas"), and an illustration, *Le Repos de l'acrobate* (*The Acrobat's Rest*, 1928; plate 80), to *Distances*.

April: The third and final issue of *Distances* contains an untitled text by Magritte and an illustration, *L'Aube désarmé* (*Defenseless Dawn*, 1928; plate 81).

1929

January: An illustration after Magritte's painting *Les Amants* (*The Lovers*, 1928; plate 54) appears on the cover of the journal *Variétés* (plate 77), edited by Van Hecke; *L'Homme au journal* (*The Man with the Newspaper*, 1928; plate 57) is reproduced inside. Another page juxtaposes a photograph of Magritte with palette and brush standing in front of his unfinished painting *Tentative de l'impossible* (*Attempting the Impossible*, 1928; plate 44) with a photograph of Giorgio de Chirico, also with palette and brush in front of one of his paintings (**fig. 3**). Five word-drawings are interspersed throughout (including plates 78 and 79), the first time this aspect of Magritte's work appears in print.

January 20: At lease eighteen of Magritte's paintings from 1926–28 (including plates 13, 18, and 38) are presented for a single day at the Salle de la Bourse, Charleroi, in conjunction with a recital of modern music directed by composer André Souris. Nougé's introduction to the recital defends music against detractors (such as Breton) and outlines his aesthetic theory based on the power of language.[6]

Late January: Galerie Le Centaure takes over Galerie L'Époque and its part of Magritte's contract. Mesens leaves his position as director of Galerie L'Époque and begins to deal privately.

February 16–March 16: Magritte collaborates with Goemans on *Le Sens propre* (*The Literal Meaning*), a series of five leaflets published weekly (among them plates 82, 83). Each leaflet features a painting by Magritte and a poem written by Goemans in response to the image.

By April 28: Magritte meets Dalí, who arrived in Paris in March or early April to film *Un Chien andalou* with Luis Buñuel.[7]

May 23: Dalí is the first to write about *La Trahison des images* (*The Treachery of Images*, 1929; plate 64), in the fourth of his series of seven articles titled "Documental-Paris-1929" in the Barcelona paper *La Publicitat*: "One of the latest works by Renné Margueritte [*sic*] is a painted pipe. Underneath there is an inscription saying 'ceci n'est pas une pipe' ['this is not a pipe']."[8]

June 1: A special issue of *Variétés* is published; titled "Le Surréalisme en 1929," and edited by Breton and Paul Éluard, it includes two of Magritte's paintings and a word-drawing. Also published is Magritte's response to a questionnaire on collective political action. This is his first public participation in the French Surrealist movement.

June 24: After the preview of *Un Chien andalou* (June 6), Buñuel writes to Dalí: "There were a lot of things that Magritte liked very much [about the film] and others which bothered him. Of course this film does harm his painting a little."[9]

July 7: Dalí's final "Documental-Paris-1929" is published; it concludes: "Renée Magritt [*sic*] proposes: Shall we speak of painting? All the friends, and Renée Magritt as well, begin to laugh."[10]

July 13: Magritte ends his contract with Galerie Le Centaure, writing in a letter to Marcel Lecomte, a writer affiliated with the Belgian Surrealists, that he has more faith in Parisian dealers.

End of July–beginning of September: Magritte and Georgette vacation in Cadaqués, Spain, where Dalí's family has a vacation home. The Magrittes share a house with Buñuel; Éluard and his wife, Gala; and Goemans and his girlfriend, Yvonne Bernard. Magritte paints *Le Temps menaçant* (*Threatening Weather*; plate 65) and perhaps four small word-paintings, including *L'Arbre de la science* (*The Tree of Knowledge*; plate 61). Months later (February 1, 1930), Catalan artist Àngel Planells publishes a profile of Magritte in a Cadaqués newspaper, claiming that Magritte is not interested in technique and is a narrator rather than a painter, using painting as a vehicle to show his unconscious or "interior images."[11]

October: Galerie Goemans opens in Paris with an exhibition of artists under contract, *Hans Arp, René Magritte, Salvador Dalí, Yves Tanguy*. The U.S. stock market crashes at the end of the month.

December 14: At a gathering at his apartment, Breton asks Georgette to remove a cross she is wearing. Offended, the Magrittes abruptly leave. A few weeks later, Magritte writes to Souris: "The breach between me and the Surrealists seems pretty definite."

December 15: The twelfth and final issue of *La Révolution surréaliste* begins with Breton's "Second Manifeste du Surréalisme" ("Second Surrealist Manifesto"), officially reorienting Surrealism toward social issues and self-observation during the creative

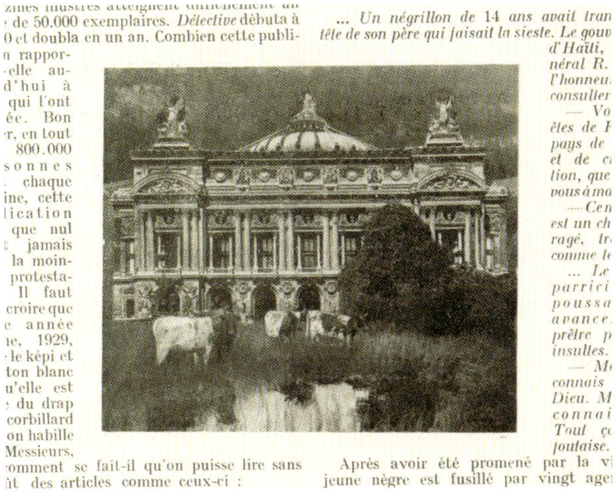

Figure 4. René Magritte. Reproduction of montage of postcards in the journal *La Révolution surréaliste*, no. 12 (December 1929). The Museum of Modern Art Library, New York

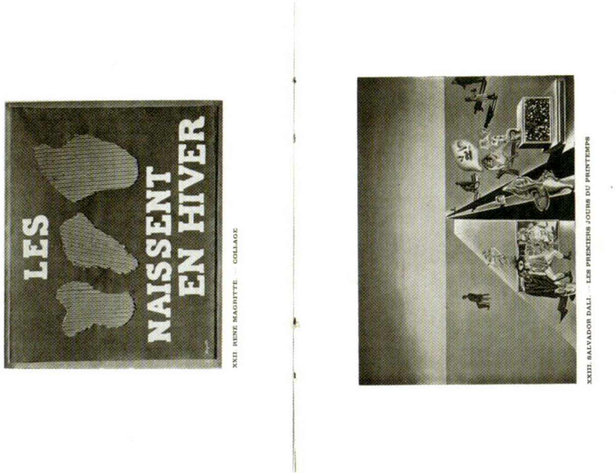

Figure 5. René Magritte. At left: "Collage," reproduced in the catalogue for *Exposition de collages*, Gallerie Goemans, Paris, 1930. The Museum of Modern Art Library, New York

process. Included in the issue is Magritte's word-image essay "Les Mots et les images" ("Words and Images"; plate 89); a montage of postcards (**fig. 4**); and a photomontage (plate 91) of portraits of Surrealists surrounding a reproduction of Magritte's 1929 painting *La Femme cachée* (*The Hidden Woman*).[12] He also contributes answers to a survey on love, observing: "All I know of the hope I place in love, it's that it is up to a woman to give it reality."

1930

Mid-February: Magritte writes to Nougé, asking him to contribute a catalogue preface for his solo exhibition at Galerie Goemans, scheduled for early March; Magritte notes that Éluard "seems to have forgotten how keen he once was to do it." The letter contains sketches (p. 230, **fig. 1**) of Magritte's "latest work," including *L'Évidence éternelle* (*The Eternally Obvious*, 1930; plate 66) and *L'Annonciation* (*The Annunciation*, 1930; plate 70).

March 28–April 12: Magritte's "word-collage" of paper and corrugated cardboard on canvas is exhibited in *Exposition de collages* at Galerie Goemans. The preface to the catalogue is Louis Aragon's polemical text "La Peinture au défi" ("The Challenge to Painting"). Now lost, Magritte's work is known only from the reproduction in the catalogue, where it is listed simply as "Collage" (**fig. 5**).

Sometime between **April 12 and 27:** After losing its backer, Galerie Goemans closes without mounting the planned Magritte exhibition. Goemans is called before Breton and other Surrealists to answer for the closing, since this leaves the Surrealists without a dedicated exhibition venue. Monthly payments from the gallery to Magritte cease. Now painting very little, he looks for work as a commercial artist.

May: Goemans returns to Brussels to seek work.

Summer?: In an undated letter, Magritte informs Nougé that he intends to return to Brussels if he doesn't find work in Paris soon, noting: "I shall have to, since there is no one here to rely on to help me here." Georgette will later report to the catalogue raisonné authors that he was offered a job in a commercial studio but turned it down because he wished to go home.

June: Magritte sells eleven paintings in his possession to Mesens (including plates 59, 66–70).

Sometime between **July 7 and 10:** Magritte and Georgette move back to Belgium, renting an apartment at 135, rue Esseghem, in the Jette district on the outskirts of Brussels. The artist will live and work here until 1954.

Late 1930: Magritte opens Studio Dongo, a commercial art business, with his younger brother Paul, who handles the business details. The artist is commissioned to create posters, advertising copy, and stands for commercial displays.

1931

February 7 or 8(?): *E.L.T. Mesens & E. van Tonderen présentent seize tableaux de René Magritte* (*E.L.T. Mesens & E. van Tonderen Present Sixteen Paintings by René Magritte*) opens with an all-night event at the Brussels showroom of the interior-decorating firm Salle Giso. The works in the exhibition are from 1927–30 (including plates 12, 15, 53, 59, 63, 66–69, and 103). The catalogue includes two texts by Nougé, "Avertissement" ("Warning") and "Les Grands Voyages" ("Great Journeys"), and a photograph of *L'Évidence éternelle* by Belgian photographer Cami Stone (plate 112).

December 19–January 6, 1932: The exhibition *Guiette, Magritte, Picard* is presented at the Palais des Beaux-Arts, featuring twenty-six paintings and three gouaches created by Magritte between 1926 and 1930 (including plates 16, 51, 57, 63, 66–68, and 70).

1932

October 17, 19, 24, 25: The Galerie Le Centaure holdings are auctioned off. The gallery had closed at the end of 1931 due to the continuing financial crisis. Before the auction, Mesens purchases at least 150 Magrittes, dated 1926–29. Between November 1932 and May 1933, Mesens will purchase more works by Magritte from Van Hecke's private collection (at least two, and possibly eighteen or more).

1933

January 3: Having resumed contact with Breton, Magritte writes to thank him for a copy of his book *Les Vases communicants* (*Communicating Vessels*, 1932): "The kind of interest you have shown in the dream phenomenon is the only one that can touch me," Magritte writes, "but I confess to not seeing the necessity of worrying about ideas like time or space. You should, it seems to me, tackle them in their turn so that they lose their abstract character."[13] He sends Breton drawings of his two latest paintings: *Les Affinités électives* (*Elective Affinities*; plate 92) and *La Réponse imprévue* (*The Unexpected Answer*; p. 154, fig. 4). This suggests that both of these paintings were completed at the end of 1932, inaugurating a new way of working based on the discovery of "affinities" between objects. Because *Les Affinités électives* was acknowledged by Magritte as a point of departure toward this new method, in later years his Surrealist colleagues regularly referenced it. For instance, Nougé observed: "The egg like the cage contains the bird. And this analogy, otherwise similar, illuminates the forgotten idea that we form of the cage, of the egg, of the bird. The cage prison but also the cage of promise, but also [. . .] from response to response to the limits of fatigue and the universe."[14]

May 15: Two final issues of *Le Surréalisme au service de la révolution*, with Breton as director, are published simultaneously, marking Magritte's first public participation in the Paris Surrealist movement since 1929. Issue 5 includes his drawing of a nun with her habit raised to expose her stocking and garters and Nougé's "Les Images défendues" (Forbidden [or protected] images). Although a footnote to the essay reads: "Extracts from a book to be published by Éditions Nicolas Flamel," the book (titled *René Magritte ou les images défendues*) will not appear until 1943. Issue 6 reproduces the first iteration of *Au seuil de la liberté* (*On the Threshold of Liberty*, 1930; see p. 199, fig. 6).

May 27–June 7: *Exposition René Magritte* is presented at Brussels's Palais des Beaux-Arts, featuring fifty-seven paintings dated 1926–32. Nougé's preface to the catalogue, "L'Avenir des statues" ("The Future of Statues"), focuses on the two objects on display: a painted Venus de Milo statue (similar to plate 94) and a painted plaster death mask (plate 95),[15] and so positions Magritte as a maker of Surrealist objects, a genre whose popularity had been growing since Dalí formally introduced the idea in 1931.

June 7–18: Two of Magritte's paintings (plates 38 and 69) appear in *Exposition surréaliste: Sculpture-objets-peintures-dessins* (*Surrealist Exhibition: Sculpture-Objects-Paintings-Drawings*), Galerie Pierre Colle, Paris.

October 27–November 26: The Surrealists show as a group at the Salon des Surindépendants, Paris. Magritte is represented with four or five paintings (including plates 59, 97, and perhaps 49).

December 1: *Violette Nozières* is published by Éditions Nicolas Flamel. This book, a project of the Paris Surrealists, supports Nozières, an eighteen-year-old who poisoned her parents, killing her father. Magritte's drawing illustrates her claim that she was sexually abused by her father; a depiction of the presiding judge of the case stands in the foreground (plate 113).

1934

May 12–June 3: *Minotaure*, an exhibition celebrating the first anniversary of the journal of the same name, is presented at the Palais des Beaux-Arts in Brussels. Mesens's installation separates the Surrealists from the rest of the eclectic group of artists associated with the journal. Magritte's scandalous painting *Le Viol* (*The Rape*, 1934; plate 96) is on display behind a velvet curtain, along with works by Balthus, Victor Brauner, and Dalí.

June: Belgian and French Surrealists collaborate on "Intervention Surréaliste," a special issue of the Brussels quarterly *Documents 34*, edited by Mesens. Magritte signs "L'Action immédiate" ("Immediate Action"), a tract by the Belgian group that supports revolutionary action, and is pictured in a group photograph of the Belgian Surrealists (see p. 150, fig. 1). He contributes several illustrations, and the issue also includes his text "Le Fil d'Ariane" ("Ariadne's Thread"), where he suggests that poetry of the real will reveal the secrets of the world.

June 1: Breton delivers his lecture "Le Surréalisme" at the Salle de la Maison des Huit Heures, Brussels, headquarters of the socialist trade unions. Breton begins his speech:

> Comrades: The activity of our surrealist comrades in Belgium is closely allied with our own activity, and I am happy to be in their company this evening. Magritte, Mesens, Nougé, Scutenaire and Souris are among those whose revolutionary will—outside of all consideration of their agreement or disagreement with us on particular points—has been for us in Paris a constant reason for thinking that the surrealist project, beyond the limitations of space and time, can contribute to the efficacious reunification of all those *who do not despair of the transformation and who wish this transformation to be as radical as possible.*[16]

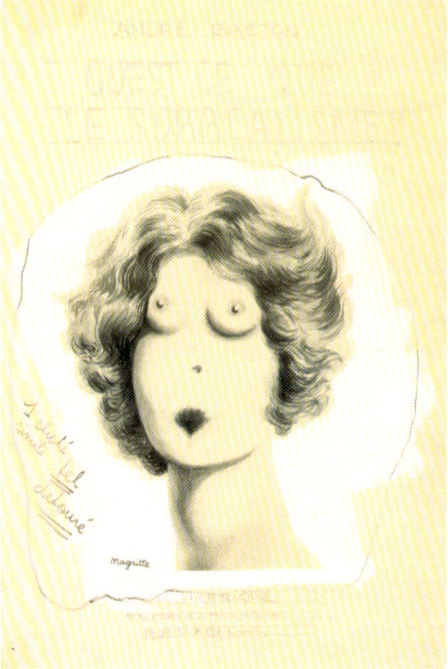

Figure 6. René Magritte. Original design for the cover of *Qu'est-ce que le Surréalisme?* (*What Is Surrealism?*). Included in René Magritte's letter to André Breton, June 22, 1934. Location unknown

June 22: Magritte writes to Breton, enclosing a cover design (**fig. 6**) for the planned publication of the June 1 lecture: "I hope you will be pleased with this cover project, I also think that it is excellent from the publicity point of view. An image of this kind is not likely to pass unnoticed in a bookshop window."

July 1: Breton responds to Magritte: "I am full of enthusiasm for your drawing, it is a marvellously vital and disturbing piece of work. [. . .]" He continues: "We absolutely must find a way to give the public a better understanding of your most recent researches, the importance of which, I repeat, seems to me to be extreme." Breton asks for descriptions and photographs of Magritte's recent works and indicates that he will write about him in an article or in the reissue of *Le Surréalisme et la peinture* (*Surrealism and Painting*, 1928)—the publication of which will ultimately be delayed until 1945.

July 15: Breton's "Le Surréalisme" speech is published as a book, *Qu'est-ce que le Surréalisme?* (*What Is Surrealism?*), with Magritte's drawing of *Le Viol* reproduced on the cover (plate 114).

November: In a single-page article in *Documents* 34, again titled "Qu'est-ce que le Surréalisme?," Breton writes that Surrealism is "the cuckoo's egg left in the nest (whose brood is lost) with the complicity of René Magritte. It's relearning to read in the star alphabet of E.L.T. Mesens. It's the great lesson in mystery of Paul Nougé"[17]

November 17: Magritte responds to a letter of August 8 from Julien Levy, the premier Surrealist dealer in the United States. Along with his letter, Magritte sends "small paintings" and "reproductions of other paintings."[18]

December 21: Levy writes again, asking Magritte to send photographs from time to time of his new, larger paintings.[19]

1935

May 11: Levy writes to Magritte: "I would like to show your paintings in February of the next season."[20]

August: Magritte is a signatory of "Du temps que les Surréalistes avaient raison" ("On the Time When the Surrealists Were Right"), a text ending the Surrealists' official involvement with the Communist Party. Arguing against conformity, the text insists upon the right to freedom of expression and to the study of "the human problem in all its forms."

August 20: Magritte's gouache *La Gâcheuse* (*The Spoiler*, 1935) is reproduced as the cover illustration for the *Bulletin international du Surréalisme*, no. 3 (plate 115). Magritte and his Belgian colleagues sign "Le Couteau dans la plaie" ("The Knife in the Wound"), a tract that condemns Joseph Stalin's growing nationalism and declares that "the liberation of the human spirit cannot be found through paths other than that of the worldwide Proletarian revolution."[21]

October 13–27: *Exposition surréaliste*, organized by Mesens, is presented at the Salle d'Exposition de la Commune de La Louvière (including plates 69, 101, 103). On the opening day, a "Manifestation Surréaliste" includes a lecture by Mesens, readings, and music. In a letter to Éluard (likely written in September), Magritte had described his vision for this event: "We shall have moving around the exhibition hall that incredible invention thought up by Dalí; the old woman in toreador costume and with an omelette on her shaven head."

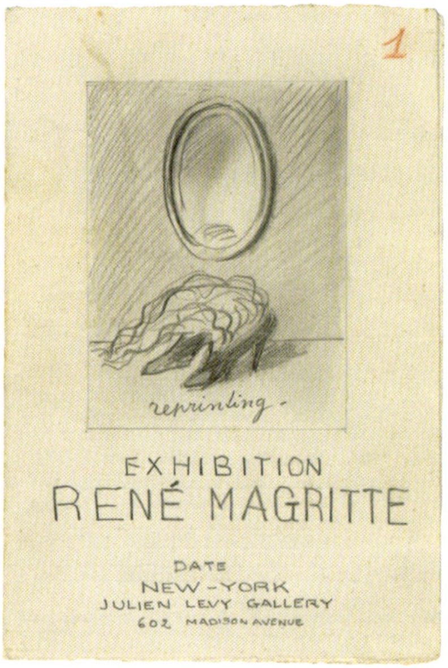

Figure 7. René Magritte. Cover mock-up of a catalogue for his exhibition at the Julien Levy Gallery, New York. 1936. Julien Levy Papers, The Philadelphia Museum of Art, Archives

November 10: Magritte writes to Levy about *La Trahison des images* (plate 64): "What happens is giving evidence of the impossibility of defining an object in a satisfying manner: 'a pipe is an object used to smoke,' is not a sufficient definition, it's too vague. But if one accepts this point of departure one sees already that my painting cannot be used to smoke."[22] He attaches texts to be included in the catalogue as well as an eight-page mock-up (**fig. 7**) featuring drawings of his recent works.

1936

January 3–20: *René Magritte*, the artist's first show in America, is presented at the Julien Levy Gallery in New York, featuring twenty-two works (including plates 63, 102, and 104). The catalogue is a scaled-down version of the maquette Magritte had sent to Levy: a flyer with a reproduction of *L'Homme au journal*; Éluard's poem "René Magritte" (translated by Man Ray); and the translation of a text by Nougé, later published as "Pour s'approcher de René Magritte" ("Getting Closer to René Magritte") in *René Magritte ou les images défendues*. One of the works displayed is an English-language version of *La Clef des songes*—titled *The Key of Dreams* in the catalogue (1935; plate 102). Many of the works in the show are smaller variants of earlier paintings.

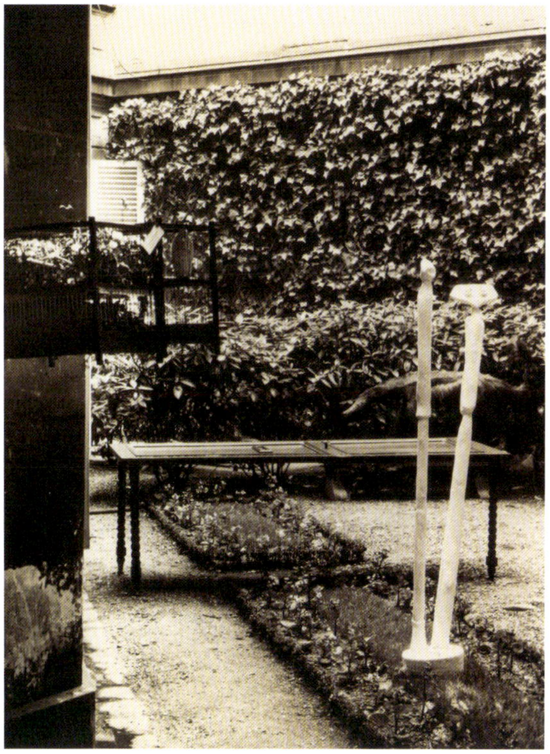

Figure 8. Man Ray. Exterior view at the *Exposition surréaliste d'objets* (*Surrealist Exhibition of Objects*), Galerie Charles Ratton, Paris, showing Magritte's *Table-porte* (*Table-Door*). 1936. Location unknown

March 10: Breton writes to Magritte that the *Exposition surréaliste d'objets* (*Surrealist Exhibition of Objects*) is scheduled for April (it will actually open in May) at the Galerie Charles Ratton, Paris, and a general Surrealist exhibition in London for June. He asks Magritte for photographs of *objets trouvés* and for advice on how to execute his "table project" (a door placed on top of table legs) for the *Exposition surréaliste d'objets*. He declares: "You know that we here are more and more captivated by your work, which is an unbroken series of discoveries (that, at least, is the opinion of Dalí, Éluard, and Picasso, I'm quite sure, and mine too)."

March 19: Magritte writes to Breton about two objects for the Ratton exhibition: a small painting of a piece of cheese displayed under a cheese dome, and a painted reproduction of a Venus de Milo (similar to plates 94 and 111). He asks Breton to find a name for the Venus figure; Breton will choose *Les Menottes de cuivre* (*The Copper Handcuffs*).[23]

April 25–May 6: *René Magritte: Peintures, objets surréalistes* (*Paintings, Surrealist Objects*), Palais des Beaux-Arts, Brussels, features thirty paintings (including plates 96, 100, 101, 103, 105, and perhaps 66), three "objects," and a unique category of *tableaux-objets* (painting-objects), including *La Découverte du feu* (*The Discovery of Fire*, 1936).[24]

May 1: An unsigned article, "René Magritte ou la révélation objective" ("René Magritte or Objective Revelation") appears in *Les Beaux-Arts* (Brussels). It reproduces seven paintings on view at the Palais des Beaux-Arts exhibition, each paired with a short, poetic passage by one of the artist's friends. (It will later be discovered that Nougé made substantial revisions to these passages.) After the commentaries, the text reads: "Thus, the painted images by René Magritte tend to wake us up, to tear us from sleep without the grandeur of automatism or habit."[25]

May 22–29: The *Exposition surréaliste d'objets* is presented at Galerie Charles Ratton, and includes three works by Magritte: *Table-porte* (*Table-door*, 1936; **fig. 8**);[26] *Les Menottes de cuivre* (1936; similar to plate 94);[27] and *Ceci est un morceau de fromage* (*This Is a Piece of Cheese*, 1936; similar to plate 111).[28]

June 11–July 4: The *International Surrealist Exhibition*, New Burlington Galleries, London, includes eight paintings by Magritte (including plates 70 and 101) and six works on paper.

November 14–December 5: *René Magritte*, at the Huize Esher Surrey, The Hague, consists of twenty paintings and six gouaches (including plates 63, 96, 104, 105, and 107).

December 7–January 17, 1937: *Fantastic Art, Dada, Surrealism* at The Museum of Modern Art, New York, features nine Magritte paintings and one gouache (including plates 13, 59, 101, and 103).

1937

January 28: Poet and arts patron Edward James writes to Magritte, inviting him to spend a month or two in London. In his letter, James indicates that he and Magritte had visited museums together previously in Paris.

January 28–February 27: *Pictures by Young Belgian Artists*, at the London Gallery, features five oil paintings and two watercolors (including plates 70 and 101) by Magritte. Organized by Mesens, the show also includes work by Paul Delvaux, Flouquet, Victor Servranckx, and Mesens himself.

February 5: James writes to Mesens about the conditions for a commission from Magritte.

February 12–March 19: Magritte stays with James at 35 Wimpole Street and completes three paintings for James's ballroom: *Le Modèle rouge* (*The Red Model*; plate 116); *Au seuil de la liberté* (*On the Threshold of Liberty*; plate 117), and *La Jeunesse illustrée* (*Youth Illustrated*; plate 118).

February 21 or 22: Magritte gives a talk at the London Gallery in which he outlines his aims "to illustrate certain features peculiar to words, images and real objects." Some days earlier, he had written to Georgette about his plans to speak for about ten minutes, with a translator present, and to make one or two drawings on a chalkboard. He mused: "There is a problem to be solved: to rapidly define my way of painting and what is special about it. I think I'll manage it."[29]

July 4: Magritte meets Marcel Mariën, a seventeen-year-old working as a photographer's assistant. In 1978, Mariën will write that, upon meeting the artist, he was immediately "invited to take part in research into what he called 'the problem,' and which aimed at the emotional enrichment of the most familiar objects of everyday life, whatever their size, from a glass of water to a chain of mountains, or from an egg to the starry sky."

November 24: The London Gallery's exhibition *Surrealist Objects and Poems* has a midnight opening. Five works by Magritte are displayed, including *L'Évidence éternelle* (plate 66); *Le Fait primitif* (*The Primordial Fact*, 1936; plate 108); and *Ceci est un morceau de fromage* (1936 or 1937; plate 111), along with versions of *L'Avenir des statues*[30] and *Les Menottes de cuivre*.[31]

December 11–22: *Trois Peintres surréalistes* [*Three Surrealist Painters*]*: René Magritte, Man Ray, Yves Tanguy*, Palais des Beaux-Arts, Brussels, includes twenty-four works by Magritte, twenty-two of them dated 1935–37 (including plates 119–122). The introduction by Scutenaire, "Trois Fenêtres" ("Three Windows"), notes: "Everyday things, shoes, egg, door, eventually become so familiar that they go to the invisible. But Magritte fights objects from the void—and the world slowly repopulates. Difficult but necessary enterprise that this illumination of an idea obscured by the mists of habit and indifference."[32]

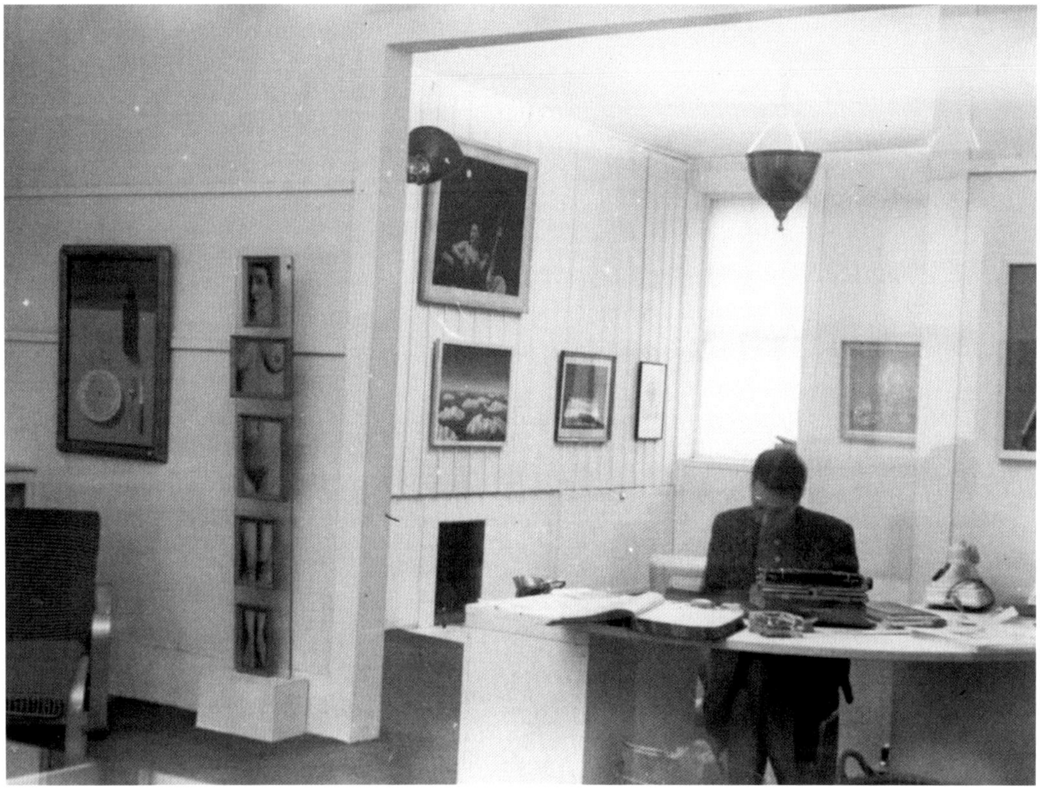

Figure 9. Installation view of *René Magritte: Surrealist Paintings and Objects*, London Gallery. 1938. Scottish National Gallery of Modern Art, Edinburgh

1938

January 4–18: *René Magritte,* the artist's second solo show at the Julien Levy Gallery, is a retrospective collection of sixteen paintings (including plates 53, 69, and 102).

January 8: Edward Alden Jewell writes a review noting the works' painterly qualities: "Apart from his mystical researches, René Magritte finds time and inclination, both, to accomplish some distinguished passages of tone and of paint texture."[33] Two years earlier, reviewing Magritte's first show at the Levy gallery, Jewell had written that the canvases were "arid with respect to esthetic content."[34]

January 17–February 24: *Exposition internationale du Surréalisme* (*International Exhibition of Surrealism*), at the Galerie Beaux-Arts, Paris, features at least nine Magritte paintings (including plates 79, 119, 120, and perhaps 65 and 98). Magritte travels to Paris for the opening. The exhibition and its simple accompanying catalogue are followed by a more substantial publication: the *Dictionnaire abrégé du Surréalisme* (*Abbreviated Dictionary of Surrealism*), to which Magritte contributes illustrations for three entries.

March: By March 1, Roland Penrose and Mesens have taken over the London Gallery from Noel (known as Peter) Norton and Marguerita Strettel. Mesens wishes to open the gallery under their ownership with a Magritte exhibition.

March 30–April 1 or 2(?): Magritte is in London for the opening of his exhibition.

April 1–May 3: *René Magritte: Surrealist Paintings and Objects* at the London Gallery (**fig. 9**). The exhibition includes works from Magritte's years as a Surrealist, 1926–38, with thirty-three paintings (including plates 9, 96, 103, and perhaps 66), four objects (including plate 108), and nine works on paper. At the opening event (which begins at midnight on the night of March 31–April 1), an "explorer" (played by Julian Trevelyan, British artist and poet) dressed in a sun-helmet, red gloves, and glasses with mirrored lenses, introduces the exhibition, announcing in part:

> At last, passing through Belgium,
> I heard voices. Loudest of all,
> the paintings of Magritte — the
> paintings that are now here.
> They explain what I heard before,
> accurately, subtly, and — above
> all — with a marvelous patience.
> For it had not been altogether easy
> to understand the putrefaction
> of the old world, or the germination of the new.

The inaugural issue of *London Gallery Bulletin* (plate 132) serves as the exhibition's catalogue. Along with essays by British writers Herbert Read and Humphrey Jennings, and Éluard's poem, it also includes an article by Nougé, "Final Advice," in which he suggests that man's unconscious and the exterior world are one dialectical entity, and that Magritte's painting results from the interaction of the two.

July 16–August 5: Magritte tries without success in letters to persuade James to provide him with a yearly stipend in return for paintings. (James's final purchase of Magritte's work will occur in 1939: three paintings and nine gouaches, including plates 125 and 126.)

November 20: Magritte delivers his lecture "La Ligne de vie" ("Lifeline"), in which he traces the history of Surrealist painting and outlines the development of his own work, at the Koninklijk Museum voor Schone Kunsten, Antwerp. Mariën's introduction is printed in an accompanying leaflet, along with a loose-leaf photograph of the artist (p. 21, fig. 6). Magritte begins his speech: "Ladies, Gentlemen, Comrades, The old question: 'Who are we?' is given a disappointing answer in the world in which we have to live." Humanity, he maintains, must work toward the proletarian revolution that will transform the world. But in the meantime humanity can defend itself against the present "mediocre reality" through nature, love, and finally, Surrealism:

> Lastly, Surrealism provides humanity with a method and mental approach favourable to the investigation of areas which have been deliberately ignored or despised, and yet of direct concern to humanity. Surrealism claims for our waking life a freedom similar to that which we have in our dreams. This freedom is a latent possession of the mind, and in practice new technicians need only to concentrate on eliminating some complex or another — the complex of the ridiculous perhaps — and on determining the slight changes in habit that would be necessary for our ability to see only what we choose to see to change into the ability to discover immediately the objects of our desires. Everyday experience, cluttered up though it is by religion, secular or military morality, permits of these possibilities up to a point.
>
> In any case, the Surrealists know how to be free. "Freedom, the colour of man," as André Breton proclaims.[35]

Notes

References in the following notes in the form "Sylvester 1:8" refer to the volume and catalogue numbers of works in the six-volume Magritte catalogue raisonné. Likewise, references in the form "Sylvester 1, p. 304" refer to the volume and page numbers where corresponding texts are located. The first five volumes of the catalogue raisonné, published 1992–97, were edited by David Sylvester; the final volume, published 2012, was edited by Sarah Whitfield. For complete publication information for all six volumes, see the "Selected Bibliography," p. 252.

Catalogue raisonné numbers are provided for works that are not reproduced as plates or figures in the present volume. Unless otherwise noted, all translations are by the author.

1. Paul-Gustave Van Hecke, "René Magritte, peintre de la pensée abstraite," *Sélection*, no. 6 (March 1927): 441–42. A shorter version of this article was published a month later: "René Magritte," *Le Centaure* 7, no. 1 (April 1927): 131–34.
2. René Magritte, interview with Jacques Goossens, January 28, 1966, transcript published in Magritte, *Écrits complets*, ed. by André Blavier (Paris: Flammarion, 1979, 2001), p. 625.
3. Pierre Flouquet,"Au Centaure: René Magritte," in *7 Arts* 5, no. 23 (May 1, 1927): 2; trans. by Janet Yoon.
4. Armand Eggermont, [Review of *Exposition Magritte*, Galerie Le Centaure, 1927], *Le Thyrse*, May 8, 1927, p. 214.
5. Sylvester 1:163.
6. Paul Nougé's introduction to the concert was published as *La Conférence de Charleroi* (Brussels: Le Miroir infidèle, 1946); and in English, as "Music Is Dangerous," in *View* 7, no. 2 (December 1946): 15–20, and no. 3 (March 1947): 23–29.
7. It is known that Magritte and Dalí were in contact by this date from a postcard dated April 28, 1929. Sent from Perreux-sur-Marne to Sebastià Gasch, it was signed by Armand and Yvonne Bernard, Luis Buñuel,

Salvador Dalí, Camille Goemans, Georgette and René Magritte. Cited in Joan M. Minguet Batllori, *Salvador Dalí, cine y surrealismo(s)* (Barcelona: Parsifal, 2003), p. 99.
8. Salvador Dalí, "Documental-Paris-1929," *La Publicitat* 51 (Barcelona), May 23, 1929, p. 1.
9. Luis Buñuel, letter to Salvador Dalí, June 24, 1929. Cited in Batllori, *Salvador Dalí, cine y surrealismo(s)*, p. 104. For the entire letter translated into English, see *Salvador Dalí, lletres i ninots: fons Dalí del Museu Abelló* (Mollet del Vallès, Spain: Museu Abelló, Fundació Municipal d'Art, 2001), pp. 273–74.
10. Dalí, "Documental-Paris-1929," *La Publicitat* 51, July 7, 1929, p. 1.
11. Àngel Planells, "Siluetes de pintors: René Magritte," *Sol Ixent* (Cadaqués, Spain), February 1, 1930.
12. Sylvester 1:302.
13. René Magritte, letter to André Breton, January 3, 1933. Repr. in Michel Draguet, *Magritte tout en papier* (Paris: Fondation Maillol, 2006), n.p.
14. Paul Nougé, *René Magritte (in extenso)* (Brussels: Didier Devillez, 1997), p. 131. Reportedly written between 1932 and 1936, these comments were not published until 1970, in the journal *Le Fait accompli* 34–35 (April 1970).
15. Sylvester 2: appendix (app.) 86.
16. André Breton, *Qu'est-ce que le Surréalisme?* (Brussels: René Henriquez, 1934); trans., as "What Is Surrealism?," in Breton, *What Is Surrealism?: Selected Writings*, ed. by Franklin Rosemont (New York: Pathfinder, 1978), p. 151.
17. André Breton, "Qu'est-ce que le Surréalisme?," *Documents 34*, no. 2 (November 1934): 19.
18. Magritte, letter to Julien Levy, November 17, 1934. Julien Levy Gallery records, Philadelphia Museum of Art, Archives.
19. Julien Levy, letter to Magritte, December 21, 1934. Julien Levy Gallery records, Philadelphia Museum of Art, Archives.
20. Levy, letter to Magritte, May 11, 1935. Julien Levy Gallery records, Philadelphia Museum of Art, Archives.
21. "Le Couteau dans la plaie," *Bulletin international du Surréalisme* (August 20, 1935): 3.
22. Magritte, letter to Levy, November 10, 1935. Julien Levy Gallery records, Philadelphia Museum of Art, Archives.
23. Magritte, letter to Breton, n.d.; Bibliothèque Doucet, Paris, item no. BRT.C.1.101 1.2/2. The catalogue raisonné dates this letter as March 19, 1936. See Sylvester 2:678 and 682, pp. 427 and 682.
24. Sylvester 2:680.
25. "René Magritte ou la révélation objective," *Beaux-Arts* (Brussels), no. 208 (May 1, 1936).
26. Sylvester 2:679.
27. Sylvester 2:678.
28. Sylvester 2:682.
29. Magritte, letter to Georgette Magritte, n.d. [mid-February? 1937], David Sylvester's René Magritte Catalogue Raisonné Research Papers, Menil Archives, The Menil Collection, Houston, folder MC [01] 1/08.
30. Sylvester 2:675.
31. Sylvester 2:677.
32. Louis Scutenaire, "Trois Fenêtres," in *Trois Peintres surréalistes: René Magritte, Man Ray, Yves Tanguy* (Brussels: Palais des Beaux-Arts, 1937), n.p.
33. Edward Alden Jewell, "Canvases Shown by René Magritte," *New York Times*, January 8, 1938, p. 13. Included in Scrapbook 1934–1938, Julien Levy Gallery records, Philadelphia Museum of Art, Archives.
34. Edward Alden Jewell, "Show Lists Works of Surrealist Art," *New York Times*, January 8, 1936, p. 17. Included in Scrapbook 1934–1938, Julien Levy Gallery records, Philadelphia Museum of Art, Archives.
35. René Magritte, "La Ligne de vie," lecture delivered November 20, 1938, at Antwerp's Koninklijk Museum voor Schone Kunsten; trans. in Gisèle Ollinger-Zinque and Frederik Leen, eds., *René Magritte, 1898–1967* (Ghent and Brussels: Ludion, Royal Museums of Fine Arts of Belgium, 1998), p. 44. This 1998 translation was adapted from that in Sylvester 5, pp. 9–22.

CATALOGUE OF THE EXHIBITION

The order of entries in the following pages corresponds to the sequence of plates in this publication.

*The six-volume René Magritte catalogue raisonné is the primary reference for the titles, locations, and dates of works cited here. In accordance with the style of the catalogue raisonné, the majority of titles are provided in the original French first, followed by an English translation: this indicates that there is clear evidence of Magritte's endorsement of the original title. The English titles are not always literal translations from the French, but represent how the works are best known in this language. In the cases where the artist deliberately left a work without a title, it is designated "Untitled." Certain works unnamed by the artist have been assigned descriptive titles in the catalogue raisonné; these are indicated in brackets (e.g. [*Portrait of Paul Nougé*]).*

The location and date following the title indicates the city of the work's execution and the year (or presumed year) of its completion. From September 1927 to July 1930, Magritte lived in Le Perreux-sur-Marne, a suburb of Paris. His intention in moving to France was to live in the city proper, in order to participate in the Surrealist movement there (indeed, in later interviews he referred to having lived "in Paris" at the time); therefore, for Magritte's works made during this period, the location is given as Paris.

Mediums and dimensions of the works have been provided by their lenders or custodians, in some cases with amendments or additions by curators and conservators at The Museum of Modern Art; The Menil Collection, Houston; and the Art Institute of Chicago. In dimensions, height precedes width, and both precede depth for three-dimensional objects.

Works marked with an asterisk are not included in the exhibition but are of great significance to this period of Magritte's career. If a work is shown in certain venues only, those venues are specified at the end of the catalogue entry. In the case of books and periodicals held in the collections of more than one of the organizing institutions, each version and its place of presentation are indicated.

The photographs in this catalogue relate directly to paintings and objects Magritte created during the period covered by the exhibition, or highlight his interest in performing for the camera in ways that parallel concerns expressed in his paintings. Although the photographers are in most cases unidentified, it is believed that Magritte participated in staging the images.

Works listed in the Magritte catalogue raisonné are identified in the form "Sylvester 1:8" or "Whitfield 6:40" indicating the volume and catalogue numbers of works in that six-volume publication. The first five volumes of the catalogue raisonné, published 1992–97, were edited by David Sylvester; the final volume, published 2012, was edited by Sarah Whitfield. For complete publication information for all six volumes, see the "Selected Bibliography," p. 252.

Plate 1
Untitled
Brussels, 1926
Cut-and-pasted sheet music, gouache, and watercolor on paper
21 5/8 x 15 3/4" (55 x 40 cm)
Private collection. Courtesy Keitelman Gallery, Brussels
(Sylvester 4:1616)

Plate 2
Untitled
Brussels, 1926
Cut-and-pasted sheet music, watercolor, charcoal, pencil, and ink on paper
15 3/4 x 21 5/8" (40 x 55 cm)
Private collection, Switzerland. Courtesy Simon Studer Art, Geneva
(Sylvester 4:1602)

Plate 3
Nocturne
Brussels, 1927
Cut-and-pasted sheet music, gouache, and watercolor on paper
16 9/16 x 22 1/16" (42 x 56 cm)
Private collection. Courtesy Galerie 1900–2000, Paris
(Sylvester 4:1623)

Plate 4
Le Jockey perdu (*The Lost Jockey*)
Brussels, 1926
Cut-and-pasted sheet music, watercolor, pencil, and ink on paper
15 1/2 x 21 5/16" (39.3 x 54.2 cm)
Gale and Ira Drukier
(Sylvester 4:1605)

Plate 5
Untitled
Brussels, 1926
Cut-and-pasted printed paper and sheet music and watercolor on paper
22 7/16 x 16 1/8" (57 x 41 cm)
Daniel Malingue
(Sylvester 4:1607)

Plate 6
Untitled
Brussels, 1926
Cut-and-pasted printed paper and sheet music, pencil, colored pencil, and watercolor on paper
15 3/4 x 21 7/8" (40 x 55.5 cm)
Staatliche Museen zu Berlin, Nationalgalerie, Sammlung Scharf-Gerstenberg
(Sylvester 4:1603)

Plate 7
Untitled
Brussels, 1926
Cut-and-pasted printed paper and sheet music, watercolor, pencil, and colored pencil on paper
21 1/8 x 15 3/8" (53.7 x 39 cm)
Musée d'Ixelles, Brussels
(Sylvester 4:1609)

Plate 8
Untitled
Brussels, 1927
Cut-and-pasted paper and sheet music and watercolor on paper
19 15/16 x 25 13/16" (50.7 x 65.5 cm)
Staatliche Graphische Sammlung München
(Sylvester 4:1627)
Menil and AIC only

Plate 9
Le Rencontre (*The Encounter*)
Brussels, 1926
Oil on canvas
54 15/16 x 39" (139.5 x 99 cm)
Kunstsammlung Nordrhein-Westfalen, Düsseldorf
(Sylvester 1:99)

Plate 10
Le Mariage de minuit (*The Midnight Marriage*)
Brussels, 1926
Oil on canvas
54 3/4 x 41 5/16" (139 x 105 cm)
Royal Museums of Fine Arts of Belgium, Brussels
(Sylvester 1:116)

Plate 11
Le Sens de la nuit (*The Meaning of Night*)
Brussels, 1927
Oil on canvas, 54 3/4 x 41 5/16" (139 x 105 cm)
The Menil Collection, Houston
(Sylvester 1:136)

Plate 12
L'Assassin menacé (*The Menaced Assassin*)
Brussels, 1927
Oil on canvas
59 1/4" x 6' 4 7/8" (150.4 x 195.2 cm)
The Museum of Modern Art, New York. Kay Sage Tanguy Fund
(Sylvester 1:137)

Plate 13
Les Habitants du fleuve (*The Denizens of the River*)
Brussels, 1926
Oil on canvas
28 3/4 x 39 3/8" (73 x 100 cm)
Private collection
(Sylvester 1:125)

Plate 14
Le Joueur secret (*The Secret Player*)
Brussels, 1927
Oil on canvas
59 13/16" x 6' 4 3/4" (152 x 195 cm)
Royal Museums of Fine Arts of Belgium, Brussels
(Sylvester 1:138)

Plate 15
Jeune Fille mangeant un oiseau (Le Plaisir) (*Girl Eating a Bird [Pleasure]*)
Brussels, 1927
Oil on canvas
29 1/8 x 38 13/16" (74 x 97 cm)
Kunstsammlung Nordrhein-Westfalen, Düsseldorf
(Sylvester 1:145)

Plate 16
[*Portrait of Paul Nougé*]
Brussels, 1927
Oil on canvas
37 3/8 x 25 9/16" (95 x 65 cm)
Royal Museums of Fine Arts of Belgium, Brussels
(Sylvester 1:151)

Plate 17
Le Ciel meurtrier (*The Murderous Sky*)
Brussels, 1927
Oil on canvas, 28 3/4 x 39 3/8" (73 x 100 cm)
Centre Pompidou, Paris. Musée national d'art moderne/Centre de création industrielle. Purchase
(Sylvester 1:153)

Plate 18
La Fin des contemplations (*An End to Contemplation*)
Brussels, 1927
Oil on canvas with metal snap fasteners
28 3/4 x 39 3/8" (73 x 100 cm)
The Menil Collection, Houston
(Sylvester 1:165)

Plate 19
Entr'acte
Brussels, 1927
Oil on canvas
44 7/8 x 63 3/4" (114 x 162 cm)
Private collection
(Sylvester 1:162)

Plate 20
Le Double secret (*The Secret Double*)
Brussels, 1927
Oil on canvas
44 7/8 x 63 3/4" (114 x 162 cm)
Centre Pompidou, Paris. Musée national d'art moderne/Centre de création industrielle. Purchase
(Sylvester 1:164)

Plate 21
Illustration in *Marie*, nos. 2 and 3 (July 8, 1926), page 5
Brussels, 1926
Periodical
Page: 12 3/4 x 9 13/16" (32.4 x 25 cm)
Ryerson & Burnham Libraries, The Art Institute of Chicago
AIC only

Plate 22
Advertisement for Couture Norine in *Variétés* (May 1928)
Brussels, 1928
Periodical
Page: 9 15/16 x 7 1/16" (25.3 x 18 cm)
Centre Pompidou, Paris. Musée national d'art moderne — Bibliothèque Kandinsky

Plate 23
Advertisements for *joaillier-orfèvre* (jeweler-goldsmith) Max Kerrels, and for *modiste* (fashion designer) Jane Brouwers in *Le Centaure* (October 1926)
Brussels, 1926
Periodical
Page: 9 1/2 x 6 5/16" (24.2 x 16 cm)
Centre Pompidou, Paris. Musée national d'art moderne — Bibliothèque Kandinsky

Plate 24
Advertisements for *atelier d'art* (art studio) Floréal, and for Ravenstein restaurant, in *Le Centaure* (November 1926)
Brussels, 1926
Periodical
Page: 9 1/2 x 6 5/16" (24.2 x 16 cm)
Centre Pompidou, Paris. Musée national d'art moderne — Bibliothèque Kandinsky

Plates 25–30
(In collaboration with Paul Nougé)
Pour l'année 1928, la Maison Samuel nous présente quelques manteaux (*For the Year 1928, the Maison Samuel Presents Some Coats*)
Brussels, 1927
Fur catalogue
Page: 8 1/2 x 11 3/4" (21.6 x 29.8 cm)
The Museum of Modern Art Library, New York
MoMA only
–
Menil Collection Library, Special Collections
Menil and AIC only

Plates 31 and 32*
(In collaboration with Paul Nougé)
Clarisse Juranville: Quelques écrits et quelques dessins (*Clarisse Juranville: Some Writings and Some Drawings*), pages 12–13, 28–29
Brussels, 1927
Book
Page: 6 1/4 x 9 1/4" (15.9 x 23.5 cm)
The Museum of Modern Art Library, New York
MoMA only
–
Menil Collection Library, Special Collections
Menil only
–
Mary Reynolds Collection, Ryerson & Burnham Libraries, The Art Institute of Chicago
AIC only

Plate 33
La Parure de l'orage (*The Finery of the Storm*)
Paris, 1927
Oil on canvas
31 7/8 x 45 11/16" (81 x 116 cm)
Mr. and Mrs. Wilbur Ross
(Sylvester 1:170)

Plate 34
Les Muscles célestes (*The Muscles of the Sky*)
Paris, 1927
Oil on canvas
21 1/4 x 28 3/4" (54 x 73 cm)
Deposited with the Magritte Museum, Brussels
(Sylvester 1:166)

Plate 35
Découverte (*Discovery*)
Paris, 1927
Oil on canvas
25 9/16 x 19 11/16" (65 x 50 cm)
Royal Museums of Fine Arts of Belgium, Brussels
(Sylvester 1:187)

Plate 36
Le Prince des objets (*The Prince of Objects*)
Paris, 1927
Oil on canvas
19 11/16 x 25 9/16" (50 x 65 cm)
Galerie Vedovi, Brussels
(Sylvester 1:183)

Plate 37
La Clef des songes (*The Interpretation of Dreams*)
Paris, 1927
Oil on canvas
14 15/16 x 21 5/8" (38 x 55 cm)
Pinakothek der Moderne, Bayerische Staatsgemäldesammlungen, Munich
(Sylvester 1:172)
Menil and AIC only

Plate 38
Le Musée d'une nuit (*One-Night Museum*)
Paris, 1927
Oil on canvas
19 11/16 x 25 9/16" (50 x 65 cm)
Private collection, London
(Sylvester 1:171)

Plate 39
[*Biomorphs with Words*]
Paris, 1928
Oil on canvas
10 5/8 x 16 1/8" (27 x 41 cm)
Collection Sylvio Perlstein, Antwerp
(Sylvester 1:279)

Plate 40
La Bonne Nouvelle (*The Good News*)
Paris, 1928
Oil on canvas
28 3/4 x 21 1/4" (73 x 54 cm)
The Menil Collection, Houston
(Sylvester 1:210)
Menil and AIC only

Plate 41
Le Masque vide (*The Empty Mask*)
Paris, 1928
Oil on canvas
28 3/4 x 36 1/4" (73 x 92 cm)
Kunstsammlung Nordrhein-Westfalen, Düsseldorf
(Sylvester 1:296)

Plate 42
L'Usage de la parole (*The Use of Speech*)
Paris, 1928
Oil on canvas
28 3/4 x 21 1/4" (73 x 54 cm)
Private collection, Los Angeles
(Sylvester 1:275)

Plate 43
Personnage méditant sur la folie (*Figure Brooding on Madness*)
Paris, 1928
Oil on canvas
21 1/4 x 28 3/4" (54 x 73 cm)
Royal Museums of Fine Arts of Belgium, Brussels
(Sylvester 1:283)

Plate 44
Tentative de l'impossible (*Attempting the Impossible*)
Paris, 1928
Oil on canvas
45 11/16 x 31 7/8" (116 x 81 cm)
Toyota Municipal Museum of Art, Japan
(Sylvester 1:284)

Plate 45
L'Espion (*The Spy*)
Paris, 1928
Oil on canvas
21 1/4 x 28 3/4" (54 x 73 cm)
Collection of Irma and Norman Braman,
Miami Beach, Florida
(Sylvester 1:215)
MoMA only

Plate 46
Le Palais de rideaux (III)
(*The Palace of Curtains [III]*)
Paris, 1929
Oil on canvas
32 x 45 7/8" (81.2 x 116.4 cm)
The Museum of Modern Art, New York.
The Sidney and Harriet Janis Collection
(Sylvester 1:305)

Plate 47
Les Idées de l'acrobate (*The Acrobat's Ideas*)
Paris, 1928
Oil on canvas
45 11/16 x 31 7/8" (116 x 81 cm)
Pinakothek der Moderne, Bayerische
Staatsgemäldesammlungen, Munich
(Sylvester 1:224)

Plate 48
Les Jours gigantesques (*The Titanic Days*)
Paris, 1928
Oil on canvas
45 11/16 x 31 7/8" (116 x 81 cm)
Kunstsammlung Nordrhein-Westfalen,
Düsseldorf
(Sylvester 1:247)

Plate 49
Le Dormeur téméraire (*The Daring Sleeper*)
Paris, 1928
Oil on canvas
45 11/16 x 31 7/8" (116 x 81 cm)
Tate. Purchase 1969
(Sylvester 1:217)

Plate 50
Le Paysage fantôme (*The Phantom Landscape*)
Paris, 1928
Oil on canvas
28 3/4 x 21 1/4" (73 x 54 cm)
Private collection
(Sylvester 1:218)

Plate 51
Les Charmes du paysage
(*The Delights of Landscape*)
Paris, 1928
Oil on canvas
21 1/4 x 28 3/4" (54 x 73 cm)
Private collection, London
(Sylvester 1:273)

Plate 52
Le Monde perdu (*The Lost World*)
Paris, 1928
Oil on canvas
21 1/4 x 28 3/4" (54 x 73 cm)
Kunstmuseum Winterthur. Purchase 1984
(Sylvester 1:256)

Plate 53
Les Chasseurs au bord de la nuit
(*The Hunters at the Edge of Night*)
Paris, 1928
Oil on canvas
31 7/8 x 45 11/16" (81 x 116 cm)
Private collection
(Sylvester 1:228)
MoMA only

Plate 54
Les Amants (*The Lovers*)
Paris, 1928
Oil on canvas
21 3/8 x 28 7/8" (54 x 73.4 cm)
The Museum of Modern Art, New York.
Gift of Richard S. Zeisler
(Sylvester 1:250)

Plate 55
Le Miroir vivant (*The Living Mirror*)
Paris, 1928
Oil on canvas
21 1/4 x 28 3/4" (54 x 73 cm)
Private collection
(Sylvester 1:295)

Plate 56
L'Apparition (*The Apparition*)
Paris, 1928
Oil on canvas
31 7/8 x 45 11/16" (81 x 116 cm)
Staatsgalerie Stuttgart
(Sylvester 1:220)

Plate 57
L'Homme au journal
(*The Man with the Newspaper*)
Paris, 1928
Oil on canvas, 45 11/16 x 31 7/8" (116 x 81 cm).
Tate. Presented by the Friends of the Tate
Gallery, 1964
(Sylvester 1:270)

Plate 58*
La Lectrice soumise (*The Subjugated Reader*)
Paris, 1928
Oil on canvas
36 1/4 x 28 3/4" (92 x 73 cm)
Louvre Abu Dhabi
(Sylvester 1:230)

Plate 59
Le Faux Miroir (*The False Mirror*)
Paris, 1929
Oil on canvas
21 1/4 x 31 7/8" (54 x 80.9 cm)
The Museum of Modern Art, New York.
Purchase
(Sylvester 1:319)

Plate 60
Les Six Éléments (*The Six Elements*)
Paris, 1929
Oil on canvas
28 3/4 x 39 3/8" (73 x 100 cm)
Philadelphia Museum of Art. The Louise
and Walter Arensberg Collection, 1950
(Sylvester 1:321)

Plate 61
L'Arbre de la science (*The Tree of Knowledge*)
Paris, 1929
Oil on canvas
16 1/8 x 10 5/8" (41 x 27 cm)
Patronage AG Insurance
(Sylvester 1:317)

Plate 62
Le Sens propre (*The Literal Meaning*)
Paris, 1929
Oil on canvas
28 3/4 x 21 1/4" (73 x 54 cm)
The Robert Rauschenberg Foundation,
New York
(Sylvester 1:309)

Plate 63
L'Alphabet des révélations
(*The Alphabet of Revelations*)
Paris, 1929
Oil on canvas
21 1/4 x 28 3/4" (54 x 73 cm)
The Menil Collection, Houston
(Sylvester 1:304)

Plate 64
La Trahison des images
(*The Treachery of Images*)
Paris, 1929
Oil on canvas
23 5/8 x 31 7/8" (60 x 81 cm)
Los Angeles County Museum of Art, Los Angeles. Purchased with funds provided by the Mr. and Mrs. William Preston Harrison Collection
(Sylvester 1:303)

Plate 65
Le Temps menaçant (*Threatening Weather*)
Paris, 1929
Oil on canvas
21 1/4 x 28 3/4" (54 x 73 cm)
Scottish National Gallery of Modern Art, Edinburgh
(Sylvester 1:313)

Plate 66
L'Évidence éternelle (*The Eternally Obvious*)
Paris, 1930
Oil on five canvases
Top to bottom: 8 11/16 x 4 3/4" (22 x 12 cm); 7 1/2 x 9 7/16" (19 x 24 cm); 10 5/8 x 7 1/2" (27 x 19 cm); 8 11/16 x 6 5/16" (22 x 16 cm); 8 11/16 x 4 3/4" (22 x 12 cm)
The Menil Collection, Houston
(Sylvester 1:327)

Plate 67
Les Perfections célestes
(*Celestial Perfections*)
Paris, 1930
Oil on four canvases
Top left: 10 5/8 x 8 11/16" (27 x 22 cm); top right: 9 7/16 x 13" (24 x 33 cm); bottom left: 13 3/4 x 8 11/16" (35 x 22 cm); bottom right: 13 x 9 7/16" (33 x 24 cm)
Courtesy Brachot Gallery, Belgium
(Sylvester 1:329)

Plate 68
Profondeurs de la terre
(*The Depths of the Earth*)
Paris, 1930
Oil on four canvases
Top left: 4 3/4 x 8 11/16" (12 x 22 cm); top right: 6 5/16 x 8 11/16" (16 x 22 cm); bottom left: 8 11/16 x 6 5/16" (22 x 16 cm); bottom right: 7 1/2 x 9 7/16" (19 x 24 cm)
Property of a West Coast collector
(Sylvester 1:328)

Plate 69
Grelots roses, ciels en lambeaux
(*Pink Bells, Tattered Skies*)
Paris, 1930
Oil on canvas
28 3/4 x 39 3/8" (73 x 100 cm)
Museo Nacional Centro de Arte Reina Sofía, Madrid
(Sylvester 1:331)

Plate 70
L'Annonciation (*The Annunciation*)
Paris, 1930
Oil on canvas
44 7/8 x 57 1/2" (114 x 146 cm)
Tate. Purchased with assistance from the Friends of the Tate Gallery, 1986
(Sylvester 1:330)

Plate 71
René Magritte and *Tentative de l'impossible* (*Attempting the Impossible*)
Paris, 1928 (photographer unknown)
Gelatin silver print
8 11/16 x 6 1/8" (22 x 15.5 cm)
Private collection of Isadora and Isy Gabriel Brachot

Plate 72
Unidentified girl and *Tentative de l'impossible* (*Attempting the Impossible*)
Paris, 1928 (photograph by Raoul Ubac)
Gelatin silver print (reversal print)
4 1/2 x 3 5/16" (11.4 x 8.4 cm)
Private collection

Plate 73
Georgette Magritte (right), with unidentified individuals, and *Tentative de l'impossible* (*Attempting the Impossible*)
Paris, 1928 (photograph by Raoul Ubac)
Gelatin silver print (reversal print)
4 11/16 x 3 7/16" (11.9 x 8.8 cm)
Private collection of Isadora and Isy Gabriel Brachot

Plate 74
Amour (*Love*)
Paris, 1928 (photographer unknown)
Gelatin silver print
4 1/8 x 2 3/4" (10.5 x 7 cm)
Private collection of Isadora and Isy Gabriel Brachot

Plate 75
La Mort des fantômes (*The Death of Ghosts*)
Paris, 1928 (photographer unknown)
Gelatin silver print
5 1/2 x 3 1/2" (13.9 x 8.9 cm)
Private collection of Isadora and Isy Gabriel Brachot

Plate 76
René Magritte and *Le Masque vide* (*The Empty Mask*)
Paris, 1928 (photographer unknown)
Gelatin silver print
12 5/8 x 15" (32 x 38 cm)
Private collection, Belgium

Plates 77, 78*, 79
Cover and interior illustrations for *Variétés* (January 1929)
Paris, 1929
Periodical
Page: 9 15/16 x 7 1/16" (25.3 x 18 cm)
Plate 77: Private collection
Plate 78: The Museum of Modern Art Library, New York
Plate 79: Scottish National Gallery of Modern Art, Edinburgh

Plate 80
Illustration in *Distances*, no. 2 (March 1928)
Paris, 1928
Periodical
Page: 6 x 9" (15.2 x 22.9 cm)
Centre Pompidou, Paris. Musée national d'art moderne — Fonds Destribats. Trésor national (National treasure), acquired thanks to the Lagardère Group

Plate 81
Illustration in *Distances*, no. 3 (April 1928)
Paris, 1928
Periodical
Page: 6 x 9" (15.2 x 22.9 cm)
Centre Pompidou, Paris. Musée national d'art moderne — Bibliothèque Kandinsky

Plate 82
(In collaboration with Camille Goemans)
Le Sens propre, no. 1 (February 16, 1929)
Paris, 1929
Leaflet
10 13/16 x 8 7/16" (27.5 x 21.5 cm)
The Getty Research Institute, Los Angeles (2601-283)
MoMA only

Plate 83
(In collaboration with Camille Goemans)
Le Sens propre, no. 3 (March 2, 1929)
Paris, 1929
Leaflet
10 13/16 x 8 7/16" (27.5 x 21.5 cm)
The Getty Research Institute, Los Angeles (2661-350)
Menil only

Plates 84–88
Manuscript pages for "Les Mots et les images" ("Words and Images")
Paris, 1929
Blue ink, collage, pencil, and India ink on paper
Plates 84–87: 10 11/16 x 8 3/16" (27.2 x 20.8 cm) each
Plate 88: 6 1/4 x 8 3/16" (15.8 x 20.8 cm)
Eric Decelle, Brussels
(Whitfield 6:47)

Plate 89
"Les Mots et les images" ("Words and Images"), in *La Révolution surréaliste*, no. 12 (December 15, 1929)
Paris, 1929
Periodical
Page: 11 1/2 x 7 7/8" (29.2 x 20 cm)
Centre Pompidou, Paris. Musée national d'art moderne — Bibliothèque Kandinsky

Plate 90
Untitled (photomontage)
Paris, 1929
Gelatin silver prints mounted on board
8 1/16 x 5 7/8" (20.5 x 15 cm)
Collection Sylvio Perlstein, Antwerp

Plate 91
Photo-reproduction of gelatin silver print portraits of sixteen Surrealists surrounding a photograph of Magritte's *La Femme cachée* (*The Hidden Woman*, 1929) in *La Révolution surréaliste*, no. 12 (December 15, 1929)
Paris, 1929
Periodical
Page: 11 1/2 x 7 7/8" (29.2 x 20 cm)
The Metropolitan Museum of Art, New York, The Joyce F. Menschel Photography Library

Plate 92
Les Affinités électives (*Elective Affinities*)
Brussels, 1932
Oil on canvas
16 1/8 x 13" (41 x 33 cm)
Private collection
(Sylvester 2:349 and Whitfield 6:50 and 51)
MoMA only

Plate 93
La Lumière des coïncidences (*The Light of Coincidences*)
Brussels, 1933
Oil on canvas
23 5/8 x 28 3/4" (60 x 73 cm)
Dallas Museum of Art. Gift of Mr. and Mrs. Jake L. Hamon
(Sylvester 2:352)

Plate 94
Les Menottes de cuivre (*The Copper Handcuffs*)
Brussels, 1931
Oil on plaster
14 9/16" (37 cm) high
Royal Museums of Fine Arts of Belgium, Brussels
(Sylvester 2:673)

Plate 95
L'Avenir des statues (*The Future of Statues*)
Brussels, c. 1932
Oil on plaster
12 5/8" (32 cm) high
Lehmbruck Museum, Duisberg, Germany
(Sylvester 2:674)

Plate 96
Le Viol (*The Rape*)
Brussels, 1934
Oil on canvas
28 3/4 x 21 1/4" (73 x 54 cm)
The Menil Collection, Houston
(Sylvester 2:356)

Plate 97
La Condition humaine (*The Human Condition*)
Brussels, 1933
Oil on canvas
39 3/8 x 31 7/8" (100 x 81 cm)
National Gallery of Art, Washington, D.C. Gift of the Collector's Committee 1987.55.1
(Sylvester 2:351)

Plate 98
La Magie noire (*Black Magic*)
Brussels, 1934
Oil on canvas
28 3/4 x 21 1/4" (73 x 54 cm)
Private collection
(Sylvester 2:355)

Plate 99*
Les Liaisons dangereuses (*Dangerous Liaisons*)
Brussels, 1935
Oil on canvas
28 3/4 x 21 1/4" (73 x 54 cm)
Private collection, courtesy BLAIN|DI DONNA Gallery, New York
(Sylvester 2:364)

Plate 100*
L'Invention collective (*Collective Invention*)
Brussels, 1935
Oil on canvas
28 3/4 x 45 11/16" (73 x 116 cm)
Daniel Filipacchi
(Sylvester 2:360)

Plate 101
Le Modèle rouge (*The Red Model*)
Brussels, 1935
Oil on canvas
28 3/8 x 19 1/16" (72 x 48.5 cm)
Moderna Museet, Stockholm
(Sylvester 2:380)

Plate 102
La Clef des songes
(*The Interpretation of Dreams*)
Brussels, 1935
Oil on canvas
16 1/8 x 10 5/8" (41 x 27 cm)
Collection of Jasper Johns
(Sylvester 2:370)

Plate 103
Le Portrait (*The Portrait*)
Brussels, 1935
Oil on canvas
28 7/8 x 19 7/8" (73.3 x 50.2 cm)
The Museum of Modern Art, New York. Gift of Kay Sage Tanguy
(Sylvester 2:379)

Plate 104
L'Amour désarmé (*Love Disarmed*)
Brussels, 1935
Oil on canvas
28 3/8 x 21 1/4" (72 x 54 cm)
Private collection
(Sylvester 2:381)
MoMA only

Plate 105
La Lampe philosophique
(*The Philosopher's Lamp*)
Brussels, 1936
Oil on canvas
18 1/8 x 21 5/8" (46 x 55 cm)
Private collection
(Sylvester 2:399)

Plate 106
René Magritte and
La Clairvoyance (*Clairvoyance*)
Brussels, 1936 (photographer unknown)
Gelatin silver print
2 7/16 x 3 7/16" (6.2 x 8.7 cm)
Private collection, Belgium

Platc 107
La Clairvoyance (*Clairvoyance*)
Brussels, 1936
Oil on canvas
21 1/4 x 25 9/16" (54 x 65 cm)
Mr. and Mrs. Wilbur Ross
(Sylvester 2:419)

Plate 108
Le Fait primitif (*The Primordial Fact*)
Brussels, 1936
Oil on panel with pebble
14 3/16 x 13 3/8" (36 x 34 cm)
Private collection, courtesy Het Noordbrabants Museum, 's-Hertogenbosch, Netherlands
(Sylvester 2:680)

Plate 109
Objet peint: Œil (*Painted Object: Eye*)
Brussels, 1936 or 1937
Oil on panel glued to wooden base
10 x 10 x 2" (25.4 x 25.4 x 5.1 cm)
Collection Timothy Baum, New York
(Sylvester 2:685)

Plate 110
Objet peint: Œil (*Painted Object: Eye*)
Brussels, 1932/35
Oil on panel glued to wooden base
10 5/8 x 9 3/4 x 5 11/16" (27 x 24.8 x 14.4 cm)
The Art Institute of Chicago, through prior gift of Arthur Keating, 1989.53
(Sylvester 2:686)

Plate 111
Ceci est un morceau de fromage
(*This Is a Piece of Cheese*)
Brussels, 1936 or 1937
Oil on canvas board in gilded wooden frame 4 1/16 x 7 1/4" (10.3 x 18.4 cm); with glass dome and pedestal, 12" (31 cm) high, 10" (25 cm) diam.
The Menil Collection, Houston
(Sylvester 2:683)

Plate 112
L'Évidence éternelle (*The Eternally Obvious*)
Brussels, 1930 or 1931 (photograph by Cami Stone)
Gelatin silver print
9 1/8 x 6 7/8" (23.2 x 17.4 cm)
National Gallery of Australia, Canberra, Purchase 1989

Plate 113
Illustration in *Violette Nozières*, pages 24–25
Brussels, 1933
Book
Page: 7 1/2 x 5 5/8" (19.4 x 14.3 cm)
The Museum of Modern Art Library, New York
MoMA only
–
Menil Collection Library, Special Collections
Menil only
–
Mary Reynolds Collection, Ryerson & Burnham Libraries, The Art Institute of Chicago
AIC only

Plate 114
Cover illustration for André Breton's *Qu'est-ce que le Surréalisme?* (*What Is Surrealism?*)
Brussels, 1934
Book
9 3/4 x 6 3/16" (24.8 x 15.7 cm)
The Museum of Modern Art Library, New York
MoMA only
–
Menil Collection Library, Special Collections
Menil only
–
Mary Reynolds Collection, Ryerson & Burnham Libraries, The Art Institute of Chicago
AIC only

Plate 115
Cover illustration for *Bulletin international du Surréalisme*, no. 3 (August 1935)
Brussels, 1935
Periodical
11 7/16 x 8 1/8" (29 x 20.6 cm)
David Sylvester's René Magritte Catalogue Raisonné Papers, Menil Archive, The Menil Collection, Houston
MoMA and Menil only
–
Mary Reynolds Collection, Ryerson & Burnham Libraries, The Art Institute of Chicago
AIC only

Plate 116
Le Modèle rouge (*The Red Model*)
London, 1937
Oil on canvas
6' 1/16" x 53 9/16" (183 x 136 cm)
Museum Boijmans Van Beuningen, Rotterdam
(Sylvester 2:428)

Plate 117
Au seuil de la liberté
(*On the Threshold of Liberty*)
London, 1937
Oil on canvas
7' 10" x 6' 1" (238.8 x 185.4 cm)
The Art Institute of Chicago. Gift of Mary and Leigh Block, 1988.141.10
(Sylvester 2:430)

Plate 118
La Jeunesse illustrée (*Youth Illustrated*)
London, 1937
Oil on canvas
6' 1/16" x 53 9/16" (183 x 136 cm)
Museum Boijmans Van Beuningen, Rotterdam
(Sylvester 2:429)
AIC only

Plate 119
La Race blanche (*The White Race*)
Brussels, 1937
Oil on canvas
31 7/8 x 23 5/8" (81 x 60 cm)
The Art Institute of Chicago. Promised gift of Ruth Horwich
(Sylvester 2:445)
AIC only

Plate 120
Le Thérapeute (*The Healer*)
Brussels, 1937
Oil on canvas
36 1/4 x 25 9/16" (92 x 65 cm)
Private collection
(Sylvester 2:427)

Plate 121
La Représentation (*Representation*)
Brussels, 1937
Oil on canvas mounted on panel
19 1/8 x 17 5/16" (48.5 x 44 cm)
Scottish National Gallery of Modern Art, Edinburgh
(Sylvester 2:434)

Plate 122
Le Chant de l'orage (*The Song of the Storm*)
Brussels, 1937
Oil on canvas
25 9/16 x 21 1/4" (65 x 54 cm)
The Menil Collection, Houston
(Sylvester 2:448)

Plate 123
La Reproduction interdite
(*Not to be Reproduced*)
Brussels, 1937
Oil on canvas
31 7/8 x 25 9/16" (81 x 65 cm)
Museum Boijmans Van Beuningen, Rotterdam
(Sylvester 2:436)

Plate 124
Le Principe du plaisir
(*The Pleasure Principle*)
Brussels, 1937
Oil on canvas
28 3/4 x 21 1/4" (73 x 54 cm)
Private West Coast collection, courtesy BLAIN|DI DONNA Gallery, New York
(Sylvester 2:443)

Plate 125
Le Domaine d'Arnheim
(*The Domain of Arnheim*)
Brussels, 1938
Oil on canvas
28 3/4 x 39 3/8" (73 x 100 cm)
Private collection
(Sylvester 2:456)
MoMA only

Plate 126
La Durée poignardée (*Time Transfixed*)
Brussels, 1938
Oil on canvas
57 7/8 x 39" (147 x 99 cm)
The Art Institute of Chicago, Joseph Winterbotham Collection, 1970.426
(Sylvester 2:460)

Plate 127
Dieu, le huitième jour (*God, the Eighth Day*)
Brussels, 1937 (photographer unknown)
Gelatin silver print
3 3/8 x 2 1/4" (8.5 x 5.7 cm).
The Metropolitan Museum of Art, New York, Ford Motor Company Collection, Gift of the Ford Motor Company and John C. Waddell, 1987 (1987.1100.157)

Plate 128
Edward James in front of *Au seuil de la liberté*
(*On the Threshold of Liberty*)
London, 1937 (photograph by René Magritte)
Gelatin silver print
4 1/4 x 6 9/16" (10.8 x 16.7 cm)
The Metropolitan Museum of Art, New York, Ford Motor Company Collection, Gift of the Ford Motor Company and John C. Waddell, 1987 (1987.1100.157)

Plate 129
E.L.T. Mesens hanging *La Clairvoyance*
(*Clairvoyance*) at the London Gallery
London, 1937 (photographer unknown)
Gelatin silver print
5 7/16 x 7 1/16" (13.8 x 17.9 cm)
Royal Museums of Fine Arts of Belgium, Brussels/Archives for Contemporary Art in Belgium

Plate 130
René Magritte and *Le Barbare*
(*The Barbarian*)
London, 1938 (photographer unknown)
Gelatin silver print
7 3/8 x 9 7/8" (18.8 x 25 cm)
The Baltimore Museum of Art. Purchase with exchange funds from the Edward Joseph Gallagher III Memorial Collection; and partial gift of George H. Dalsheimer, Baltimore (BMA.1988.440)

Plate 131
Cover illustration for *Minotaure*, no. 10
(Winter 1937)
Brussels, 1937
Periodical
12 3/8 x 9 5/8" (31.5 x 24.4 cm)
Centre Pompidou, Paris. Musée national d'art moderne — Bibliothèque Kandinsky

Plate 132
Cover illustration for *London Gallery Bulletin*, no. 1 (April 1938)
Brussels, 1938
Periodical
9 1/2 x 6 3/4" (24.1 x 17.1 cm)
Scottish National Gallery of Modern Art, Edinburgh

SELECTED BIBLIOGRAPHY

This selected bibliography focuses on sources recommended for the study of Magritte's work of the 1920s and 1930s; many of these publications relate specifically to Surrealism. For a comprehensive bibliography dedicated to Magritte, see David Sylvester's René Magritte Catalogue Raisonné, *vol. 5,* Supplement, Exhibition Lists, Bibliography, Cumulative Index *(reference below), pp. 143–282. For a supplement to this bibliography that includes books and articles published between 1992 and 2007, see Michel Draguet, Virginie Devillez, and Ingrid Goddeeris,* Magritte, His Work, His Museum *(Brussels: Hazan, Musée Magritte Museum, 2009), pp. 253–59. The endnotes in the present volume include additional bibliographic references.*

Abadie, Daniel, ed. *Magritte*. Ghent and Paris: Ludion, Galerie nationale du Jeu de Paume, 2003.

Allmer, Patricia. *René Magritte: Beyond Painting*. Manchester, U.K.: Manchester University Press, 2009.

Allmer, Patricia, and Hilde Van Gelder, eds. *Collective Inventions: Surrealism in Belgium*. Leuven, Belgium: Leuven University Press, 2007.

Canonne, Xavier. *Surrealism in Belgium, 1920–2004*. Brussels: Mercatorfonds, 2006.

Draguet, Michel. *Magritte tout en papier*. Paris: Hazan and Fondation Dina Vierny/Musée Maillol, 2006.

Durozoi, Gérard. *History of the Surrealist Movement*. Translated by Alison Anderson. Chicago: University of Chicago Press, 2002.

Foucault, Michel. *This Is Not a Pipe*. Translated by James Harkness. Berkeley: University of California Press, 1983.

Grant, Kim. *Surrealism and the Visual Arts: Theory and Reception*. Cambridge, U.K.: Cambridge University Press, 2005.

Gablik, Suzi. *Magritte*. Greenwich, Conn.: New York Graphic Society, 2000 (1st ed. 1970).

Johnson, Danielle M. "Salvador Dalí and René Magritte, 1928–1938." Ph.D. diss., New York University, 2012.

Lipinski, Lisa Kim. "René Magritte and Simulation: Effects Beyond His Wildest Dreams." Ph.D. diss., University of Texas at Austin, 2000.

Magritte, René, *Écrits complets*. Edited by André Blavier. Paris: Flammarion, 2001 (1st ed. 1979).

———. "Lettres à Paul Nougé." *Le Fait accompli*, nos. 127–29. Brussels: Les Lèvres nues, 1973.

———. "La Ligne de vie" (1938). Translation in Ollinger-Zinque and Leen, eds., *René Magritte, 1898–1967* (reference below), pp. 44–48. This 1998 translation was adapted from that in Sylvester, ed., *René Magritte: Catalogue Raisonné*, vol. 5, *Supplement, Exhibition Lists, Bibliography, Cumulative Index* (reference below), pp. 9–22.

———. "Les Mots et les images." *La Révolution Surréaliste* 12 (December 15, 1929): 32–33. Translation in Gablik, *Magritte* (reference above, 1970 edition), pp. 138–40.

Mariën, Marcel. *Apologies de Magritte, 1938–1993*. Brussels: Didier Devillez, 1994.

———, ed. "Lettres surréalistes: 1924–1940." In *Le Fait accompli*, nos. 81–95. Brussels: Les Lèvres nues, 1973.

———. *L'Activité surréaliste en Belgique (1924–1950)*. Brussels: Lebeer Hossmann, 1979.

Nougé, Paul. *Histoire de ne pas rire*. Lausanne: L'Age d'Homme, 1980. (Collection includes *René Magritte ou les images défendues* [Brussels: Les Auteurs Associés, 1943].)

———. *René Magritte (in extenso)*. Edited by Virginie Devillez. Foreword by Olivier Smolders. Brussels: Didier Devillez, 1997. (Collection includes *René Magritte ou les images défendues* [Brussels: Les Auteurs Associés, 1943].)

Ollinger-Zinque, Gisèle, and Frederik Leen, eds. *René Magritte, 1898–1967*. Ghent and Brussels: Ludion, Royal Museums of Fine Arts of Belgium, 1998.

Scutenaire, Louis. *Magritte*. Antwerp: De Sikkel for Ministère de l'Instruction publique, 1948.

———. *Avec Magritte*. Brussels: Lebeer Hossmann, 1977.

Sylvester, David. *Magritte: The Silence of the World*. New York: Abrams, 1992.

———, ed. *René Magritte: Catalogue Raisonné*, vol. 1, *Oil Paintings, 1916–1930*, by David Sylvester and Sarah Whitfield. Houston: Menil Foundation, in association with Mercatorfonds, Antwerp, and Philip Wilson Publishers, London, 1992.

———, ed. *René Magritte: Catalogue Raisonné*, vol. 2, *Oil Paintings and Objects, 1931–1948*, by David Sylvester and Sarah Whitfield. Houston: Menil Foundation, in association with Mercatorfonds, Antwerp, and Philip Wilson Publishers, London, 1993.

———, ed. *René Magritte: Catalogue Raisonné*, vol. 3, *Oil Paintings, Objects, and Sculptures, 1949–1967*, by Sarah Whitfield and Michael Raeburn. Houston: Menil Foundation, in association with Mercatorfonds, Antwerp, and Philip Wilson Publishers, London, 1993.

———, ed. *René Magritte Catalogue Raisonné*, vol. 4, *Gouaches, Temperas, Watercolours and Papiers Collés, 1918–1967*, by Sarah Whitfield and Michael Raeburn. Houston: Menil Foundation, in association with Mercatorfonds, Antwerp, and Philip Wilson Publishers, London, 1994.

———, ed. *René Magritte Catalogue Raisonné*, vol. 5, *Supplement, Exhibition Lists, Bibliography, Cumulative Index*, by David Sylvester, Sarah Whitfield, and Michael Raeburn. Houston: Menil Foundation, in association with Mercatorfonds, Antwerp, and Philip Wilson Publishers, London, 1997.

Sylvester, David, and Sarah Whitfield, "Magritte's Lost Lecture." In Ollinger-Zinque and Leen, eds., *René Magritte, 1898–1967* (reference above), pp. 41–43. (This essay was adapted from Sylvester, ed., *René Magritte: Catalogue Raisonné*, vol. 2, *Oil Paintings and Objects, 1931–1948*, pp. 67–72.)

Vovelle, José. *Le Surréalisme en Belgique*. Brussels: André de Rache, 1972.

Whitfield, Sarah. *Magritte*. London: South Bank Centre, 1992.

———, ed. *René Magritte: Catalogue Raisonné*, vol. 6, *Newly Discovered Works: Oil Paintings, Gouaches, Drawings*. Brussels: Mercatorfonds, in association with the Menil Foundation, Houston, and the Magritte Foundation, Brussels, 2012.

INDEX OF PLATES AND FIGURES

Paintings, Papiers Collés, and Objects by René Magritte

Illustrated Letters, Illustrations, and Original Designs for Publications by René Magritte

Photographs

Unless otherwise noted, photographers are unknown.

Related Documents

Works by Other Artists

ILLUSTRATION CREDITS

Unless otherwise noted, all images of and by René Magritte © 2013 Charly Herscovici

Photographs by David Allison: plates 19, 42, 104, 109.
The Art Institute of Chicago: plates 89, 91, 110, 117, 126, p. 7, pp. 224–25 (detail); Department of Conservation: p. 200 fig. 8; photograph by Jamie M. Stukenberg/Professional Graphics Inc., Rockford, Illinois: plate 119.
© Artists Rights Society (ARS), New York/ADAGP, Paris: plate 60.
The Baltimore Museum of Art, photograph by Mitro Hood: plate 130, pp. 14–15.
Banque d'Images, ADAGP/Art Resource, N.Y.: plates 55, 58, p. 39 fig. 16, p. 151 fig. 2, p.155 fig. 6, p. 198 fig. 5.
BLAIN|DI DONNA, New York: plates 99, 124.
© bpk, Berlin/Sammlung Scharf-Gerstenberg, Nationalgalerie, Staatliche Museen, Berlin/Art Resource, N.Y., photograph by Joerg P. Anders: plate 6.
© bpk, Berlin/Pinakothek der Moderne, Bayerische Staatsgemäldesammlungen, Munich/Art Resource, N.Y.: p. 79 fig. 5, plates 37, 47.
Collection of Irma and Norman Braman, Miami Beach, Florida: plate 45.
© CNAC/MNAM/Dist. RMN-Grand Palais/Art Resource, N.Y.: photograph by Georges Meguerditchian: front cover, plate 20; photograph by Jacques Faujour, plate 17; photograph by Adam Rzepka, p.158 fig. 8.
Community Museum of Ixelles, Brussels: plate 7.
Dallas Museum of Art: plate 93, pp.166–67 (detail).
Gale and Ira Drukier, photograph by David Allison: plate 4, pp. 24–25 (detail).
Galerie 1900–2000, Paris: plate 3.
Production Gaumont, Neuilly-sur-Seine: p.33 fig. 9, p. 34 fig. 10, p. 34 fig. 11.
Photographs by Xavier Grandsart: plates 39, 90.
The Solomon R. Guggenheim Foundation, Peggy Guggenheim Collection, Venice, 1976: p. 72 fig. 2.
Herscovici/Art Resource, N.Y.: plate 2.
Het Noordbrabants Museum, 's-Hertogenbosch, photograph by Petr Cox: plate 108.
Collection of Jasper Johns, photograph by Jerry Thompson: plate 102.
Bibliotheek, Koninklijk Museum voor Schone Kunsten, Antwerp: p. 21 fig. 6.
Kunstsammlung Nordrhein-Westfalen, Düsseldorf, photographs by Achim Kukulies, Düsseldorf: plates 9, 15, 41, 48, details pp. 54–55 (detail), pp.108–9 (detail).
Lehmbruck Museum, Duisburg/© ADAGP, Paris: photograph by Bernd Kirtz: plate 95.
Museum Associates/Los Angeles County Museum of Art, © 2013, Licensed by Art Resource, N.Y.: plate 64.
Ludion, 2013: plates 1, 50, 67, 68, 71, 73, 74, 75, 84, 85, 86, 87, 88, 98, 114, 115, p. 70 fig. 1, p. 82 fig. 11, p. 82 fig. 12, p. 83 fig. 13.
The Menil Archives, The Menil Collection, Houston: p. 16 fig. 1, p. 200 fig. 7, p. 202 fig. 12.
The Menil Conservation Department, The Menil Collection, Houston: p. 38 figs. 14a, 14b, p. 38 figs. 15a, 15b, p. 81 fig. 8, p. 81 fig. 9, p. 81 fig. 10.
The Menil Collection, Houston, photographs by Paul Hester: frontispiece, plates 11, 18, 40, 63, 66, 96, 111, 122, p. 17 fig. 2, p. 31 fig. 6 (detail), pp. 218–19 (detail).
© The Metropolitan Museum of Art, New York/Art Resource, N.Y.: plates 127, 128, p. 75 fig. 3, p. 76 fig. 4.
Moderna Museet, Stockholm, photograph by Maria Winsö: plate 101, pp. 176–77 (detail).
© Musée Ingres, Montauban, photographs by Guy Roumagnac: p. 80 figs. 7a–7d.
Musée des Beaux-Arts de Liège: p. 156 fig. 7.
Archivo fotografico Museo Nacional Centro de Arte Reina Sofía, Madrid: plate 69.
Museum Boijmans Van Beuningen, Rotterdam, photographs by Studio Tromp, Rotterdam: plates 116, 118, 123, p. 199 fig. 6, pp. 192–93 (detail).
© The Museum of Modern Art, New York: Conservation Department: p. 32 fig. 7; Department of Imaging Services: p. 28 fig. 3, p. 198 fig. 4; photographs by Thomas Griesel: plates 25, 26, 27, 28, 29, 30, 31, 32, 54, 78, 79, 113, p. 19 fig. 4, p. 29 fig. 4, p. 35 fig. 12, p. 36 fig. 13, p. 233 fig. 3, pp. 68–69 (detail); photograph by Kate Keller: p. 18 fig. 3; photographs by Jonathan Muzikar: plates 21, 23, 24, 80, 81, 131, p. 155 fig. 5, p. 159 fig. 10, p. 197 fig. 2, p. 197 fig. 3, p. 205 fig. 15, p. 205 fig. 16, p. 206 fig. 17, p. 235 fig. 4, p. 237 fig. 6, p. 239 fig. 8; photographs by John Wronn: plates 12, 46, 59, 103, p. 32 fig. 8, pp. 50–51 (detail).
National Gallery of Art, Washington, D.C.: plate 97, pp. 148–49 (detail).
National Gallery of Australia, Canberra: plate 112.
© Norman Parkinson Limited/Courtesy Norman Parkinson Archive: p. 194 fig. 1, p. 202 fig. 11, p. 204 fig. 14.
Philadelphia Museum of Art, Archives: p. 238 fig. 7.
© RMN–Grand Palais/Art Resource, N.Y., photograph by Harry Bréjat: p. 80 fig. 6.
The Robert Rauschenberg Foundation: plate 62.
Mr. and Mrs. Wilbur Ross: plate 107; photograph by Peter Harholdt, 2013: plate 33, pp. 184–85 (detail).
© Royal Museums of Fine Arts of Belgium, Brussels/Archives for Contemporary Art in Belgium: plates 82, 83, p. 150 fig. 1, p. 152 fig. 3; Keystone Press, London: plate 129.
© Royal Museums of Fine Arts of Belgium, Brussels, photographs by J. Geleyns/Ro scan: plates 10, 14, 16, 34, 35, 38, 43, 51, 94, p. 154 fig. 4, pp. 90–91 (detail), pp. 96–97 (detail); Patronage AG Insurance: plate 61; Paolo Vedovi: plate 36; Library: p. 232 fig. 2.
© Schweizerisches Institut für Kunstwissenschaft, Zurich, photograph by Lutz Hartmann: plate 52.
Scottish National Gallery of Modern Art, Edinburgh: plates 65, 121; p. 241 fig. 9.
Staatliche Graphische Sammlung München: plate 8.
© Staatsgalerie, Stuttgart: plate 56, pp. 118–19 (detail).
Tate, 2013: plates 49, 57, 70, pp. 134–35 (detail).
© Tate/Art Resource: p. 20 fig. 5.
Toyota Municipal Museum of Art, photograph by Hayashi Tatsuo: plate 44.
Photograph by Michael Tropea: plate 72.
The United States Patent and Trademark Office: p. 201 fig. 10.
City of Westminster Archives Centre, p. 201 fig. 9.

TRUSTEES OF THE MUSEUM OF MODERN ART

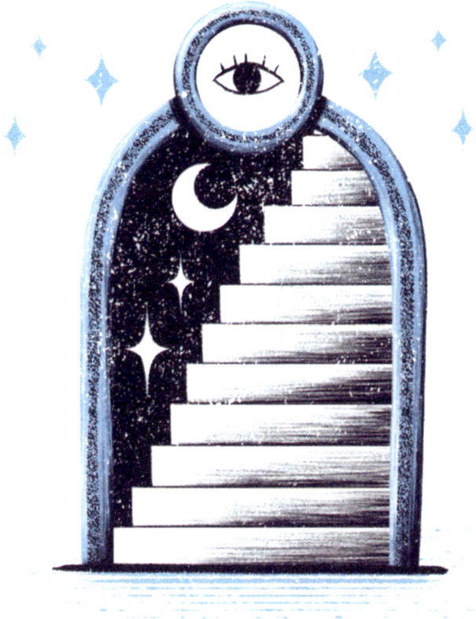

EL FOLLETÍN ILUSTRADO

Lunwerg es un sello editorial de Editorial Planeta, S. A.
Avenida Diagonal, 662-664 - 08034 Barcelona
Calle Josefa Valcárcel, 42 - 28027 Madrid
lunwerg@lunwerg.com
www.lunwerg.com
www.facebook.com/lunwerg
http://twitter.com/Lunwergfoto

Primera edición: septiembre de 2019
ISBN: 978-84-17858-24-7
Depósito legal: B. 14.122-2019
Imprime: Talleres Gráficos Soler

Impreso en España

El papel utilizado para la impresión de este libro es cien por cien libre de cloro y está calificado como papel ecológico.

EL FOLLETÍN ILUSTRADO

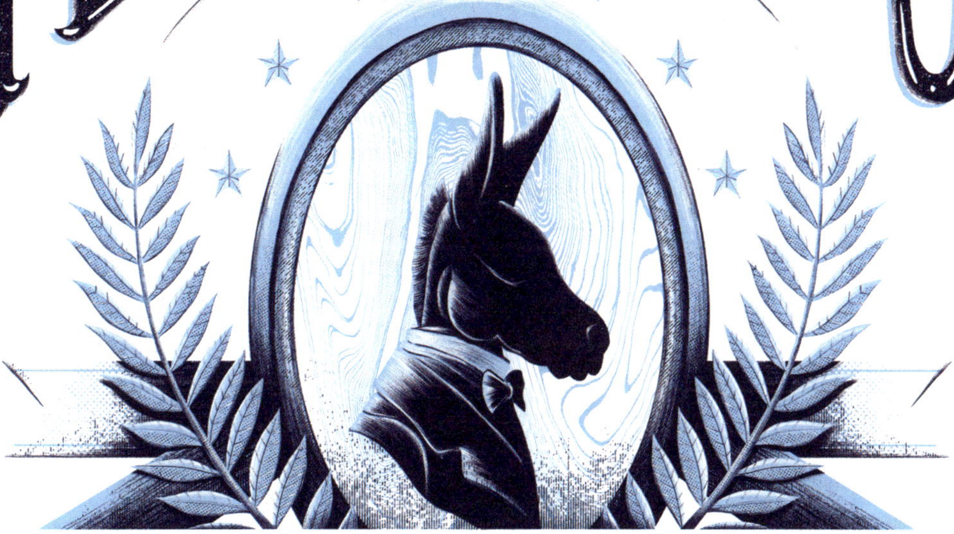

PERSONAJES ESTELARES (Y ALGÚN ESPERPENTO) DE LA ESPAÑA RECIENTE

MAR ABAD & BUBA VIEDMA

LUNWERG
EDITORES

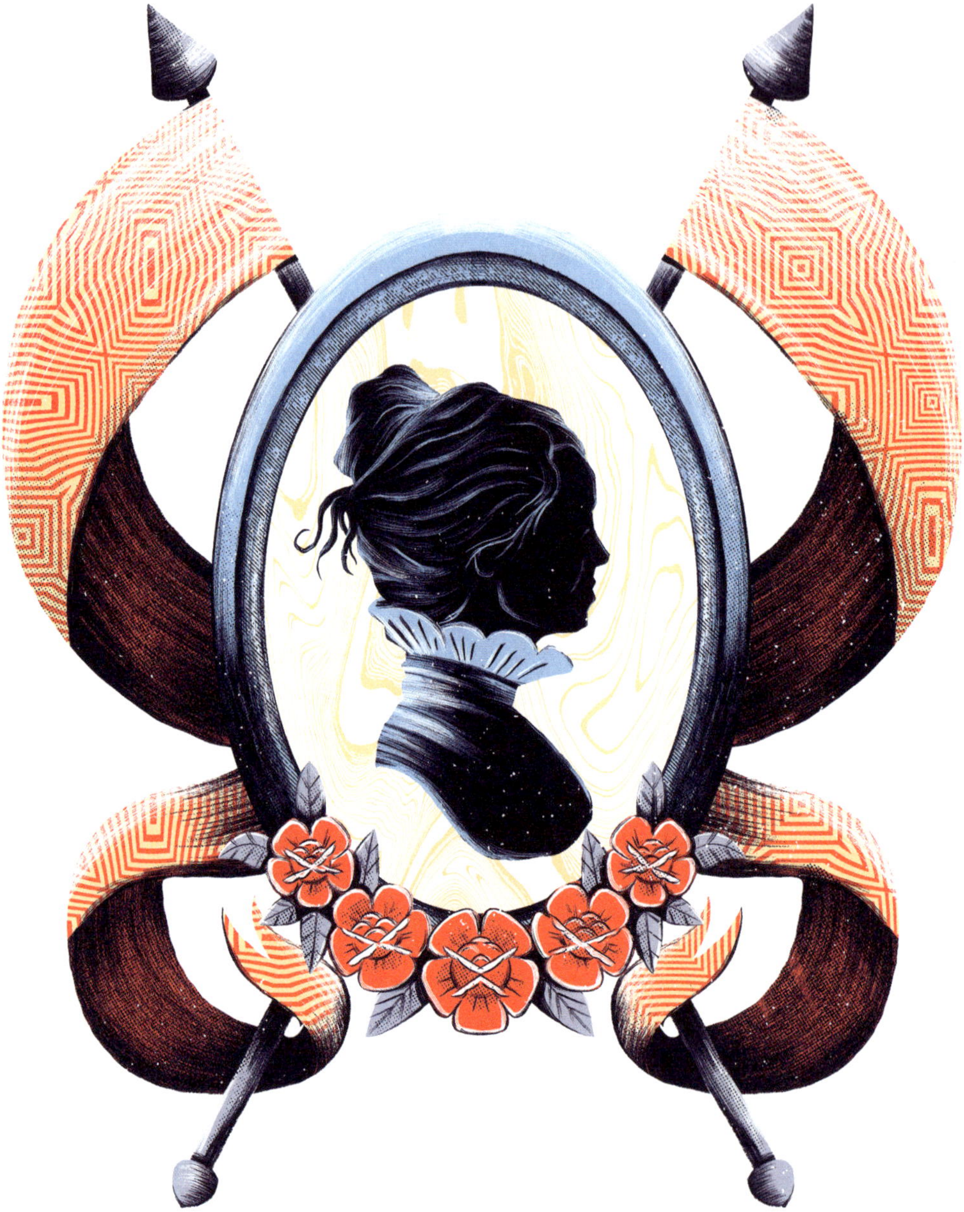

A mi rubillo Marcus.

A Javi y Vicen, para que descubran que en los libros
hay tanta emoción como en los videojuegos.

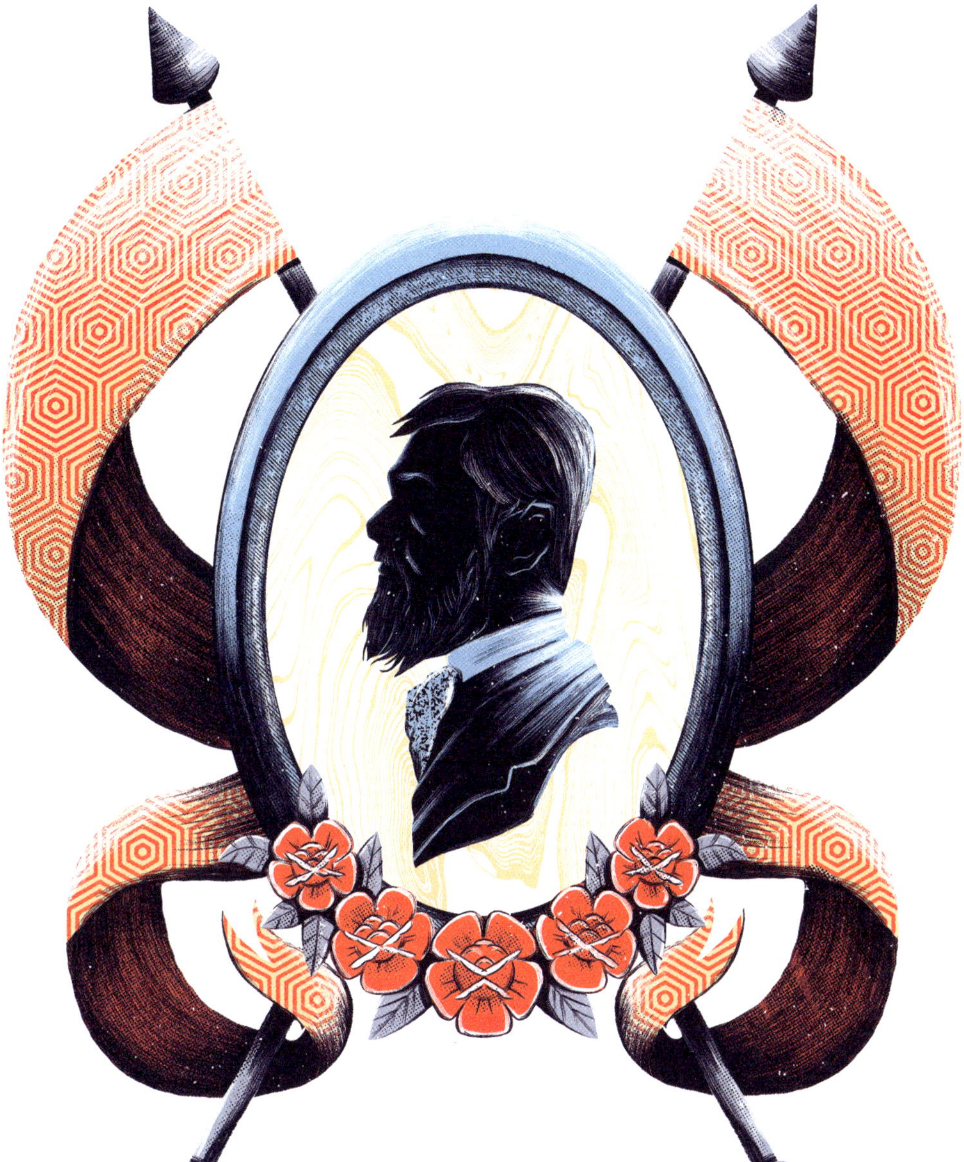

A Laura, por acompañarme en el camino.

A mi padre, que sin saberlo empezó todo este lío leyéndome «La historia interminable» antes de dormir.

A Candela, mi Niña de Fuego.
Estoy deseando leerte cuentos tal y como hacía tu abuelo.

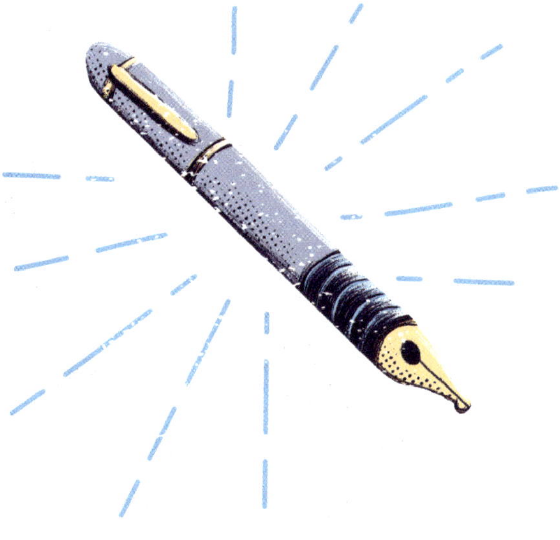

TODOS los DOMINGOS IBA al ATENEO de MADRID a LEER PERIÓDICOS ANTIGUOS. ERA UN RITUAL: RELLENAR la FICHA, ESPERAR a que TRAJERAN los TOMOS, LEERLOS en el SILENCIO de la BIBLIOTECA. Las TARDES SE ESCURRÍAN entre PÁGINAS CENTENARIAS que a VECES TENÍA que MIRAR con GAFAS y MASCARILLA, PORQUE el PASADO PUEDE PICAR en los OJOS.

ME FASCINABAN las NOTICIAS de FINALES del SIGLO XIX y PRINCIPIOS del XX. ESOS RELATOS LLENOS de SUSPENSE, SORPRESA, SUSTO, EMOCIÓN. ESAS PALABRAS... ¡QUÉ RIMBOMBANCIA! ¡QUÉ GRANDILOCUENCIA! ¡QUÉ INSULTOS MÁS BIEN PUESTOS!

VISTAS desde HOY, ESAS NOTICIAS PARECÍAN CHISTES y CARICATURAS. PERO DETRÁS de NARRATIVAS TAN CURIOSAS LATÍA UN PASADO DESCONOCIDO y FASCINANTE. ERA COMO SI ESTUVIERA DORMIDO, SOLO DORMIDO; Y CUANDO lo LEÍAS VOLVÍA a HACERSE PRESENTE y los PERSONAJES VOLVÍAN a VIVIR.

ENTENDÍ ENTONCES que ENCERRARSE en el PRESENTE es UN PRECIPICIO hacia la IGNORANCIA. QUE es IMPOSIBLE ENTENDER el PRESENTE SIN CONOCER el PASADO. QUE NO PODEMOS PREVER el FUTURO SIN COMPRENDER el AYER.

DESCUBRÍ que DESPUÉS de TANTOS AÑOS de ESTUDIO NO CONOCÍA MIS RAÍCES. NI SIQUIERA en la FACULTAD de PERIODISMO ME HABÍAN HABLADO de los PERIODISTAS y de las NARRATIVAS que, MARAVILLADA, ENCONTRABA CADA DOMINGO en el ATENEO.

ENAMORADA de CADA UNO de los ARTÍCULOS de MANUEL CHAVES NOGALES, PENSÉ en CREAR UNA SECCIÓN en la REVISTA «YOROKOBU» que DIERA a CONOCER a MUCHOS de los PERSONAJES FABULOSOS que IBA ENCONTRANDO. LO HABLÉ con el ILUSTRADOR BUBA VIEDMA PORQUE QUERÍA que FUESE UN PROYECTO CONJUNTO: ÉL DIBUJABA y YO ESCRIBÍA.

Y lo LLAMARÍAMOS «EL FOLLETÍN ILUSTRADO» por DOS MOTIVOS de CAJÓN: «FOLLETÍN» en HOMENAJE al MODO de CONTAR las HISTORIAS de PRINCIPIOS del XX e «ILUSTRADO» porque los DIBUJOS HABLARÍAN TANTO como los TEXTOS.

En la PRIMAVERA de 2015 PUBLICAMOS la PRIMERA ENTREGA en la REVISTA «YOROKOBU». Y en el PROPIO ESTRENO NOS SALTAMOS a la TORERA UNO de los PUNTALES del PROYECTO: ESCOGIMOS a UN ESCRITOR de CHICAGO. ACABABA de LEER «YO ESTOY VIVO y VOSOTROS ESTÁIS MUERTOS», el LIBRO de EMMANUEL CARRÈRE sobre PHILIP K. DICK, y DECIDIMOS MEZCLAR las FANTASÍAS LISÉRGICAS de ESTE AUTOR con LAS NARRATIVAS CASTIZAS del FOLLETÍN.

DESDE ENTONCES, CADA MES, BUBA y YO ESCOGEMOS un PERSONAJE, lo ESTUDIAMOS y MOSTRAMOS UNA ESCENA de SU VIDA.

En ESTE LIBRO HEMOS CREADO NUEVOS FOLLETINES de PERSONAJES y ESCENAS de la ESPAÑA RECIENTE. DE NUESTRA HISTORIA, que, AUNQUE ESTÉ a la VUELTA de la ESQUINA, es MUY DESCONOCIDA. HEMOS BUSCADO PERSONALIDADES DESLUMBRANTES (Y ALGUNA FIGURA MACABRA), MOMENTOS ESTELARES y HECHOS ESPERPÉNTICOS.

SON HISTORIAS MUY CORTAS, UNA ESPECIE de FLASH, que TRAEN al PRESENTE a HEROÍNAS, ILUSTRES y ALGÚN que OTRO ANIMAL. SON HISTORIAS que NO QUEREMOS PERDER NUNCA. Y es UNA FORMA de DAR las GRACIAS a la SABIDURÍA que NOS DEJARON y al EJEMPLO que AÚN NOS DAN.

MAR ABAD

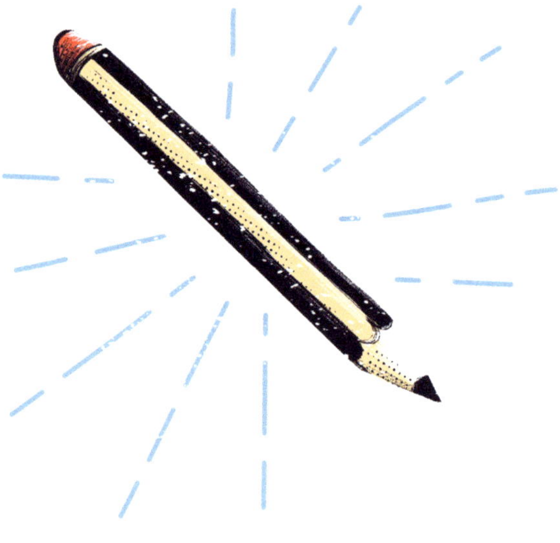

HACE UNOS AÑOS, LUIS B HERNÁNDEZ, el DIRECTOR de ARTE de «YOROKOBU», ME LLAMÓ para HABLARME de UNA NUEVA SECCIÓN FIJA que MAR ABAD QUERÍA HACER DENTRO de la REVISTA.

Las PREMISAS NO ERAN MUCHAS (de HECHO, NI SIQUIERA SABÍAMOS SI SERÍA UNA DOBLE PÁGINA o UNA SIMPLE). SOLO SABÍAN que SERÍAN PERFILES de PERSONAJES UN TANTO ESPECIALES, que QUERÍAN que HUBIESE un TITULAR DIBUJADO, que el TEXTO ESTUVIESE ROTULADO a MANO y que SE CERRASE con UN RETRATO del PERSONAJE en CUESTIÓN. ESO y que MAR QUERÍA que lo HICIESE YO. PARA MÍ, que en AQUEL ENTONCES CASI ACABABA de EMPEZAR a DEDICARME a la ILUSTRACIÓN de FORMA PROFESIONAL, UNA SECCIÓN FIJA ERA UNA GRAN RESPONSABILIDAD a la VEZ que UN HONOR.

El PRIMER PERSONAJE FUE PHILIP K. DICK, con UN TEXTO AMBIENTADO en SU NOVELA «UBIK». ME DOCUMENTÉ GRÁFICA y BIOGRÁFICAMENTE. INTENTÉ RAMIFICAR MI ESTILO HACIA UNA NUEVA DIRECCIÓN, PUESTO que TAMBIÉN ILUSTRABA ARTÍCULOS SUELTOS en la REVISTA y QUERÍA que ESTO FUESE DIFERENTE. DECIDÍ AÑADIR un PAR de PEQUEÑAS ILUSTRACIONES ACCESORIAS, le DI UNA VUELTA CONCEPTUAL al RETRATO FINAL de K. DICK y... LISTO. HABÍA NACIDO «El FOLLETÍN ILUSTRADO».

PERO HAY MÁS. CUANDO ACABÉ el ENCARGO, SALÍ de CASA HACIA la BIBLIOTECA de MI BARRIO, ME HICE con UN EJEMPLAR de «UBIK» y lo DEVORÉ. Y ESO es lo que ME SUCEDE CADA VEZ que ILUSTRO UN TEXTO de «El FOLLETÍN». ES COMO UN APERITIVO, UN «TEASER» de ALGO MÁS GORDO que DESPIERTA TU CURIOSIDAD y TE INVITA a SABER MÁS. ES la PRIMERA MUESTRA GRATIS de un CAMELLO de CAÑADA REAL.

CREO que PODRÍA DECIR MUCHAS COSAS BUENAS de «El FOLLETÍN», de MI TRABAJO con MAR ABAD DURANTE ESTOS AÑOS y, MÁS CONCRETAMENTE, del LIBRO que NOS OCUPA, pero para MÍ ESTE DETALLE es ESENCIAL: CADA VEZ que ENTREGO UN ARTE FINAL de «El FOLLETÍN ILUSTRADO» SOY UN POCO MÁS CULTO, UN POCO MÁS CURIOSO, UN POCO MÁS CRÍTICO... EN DEFINITIVA, UN POCO MEJOR. PARA ESTE LIBRO he ENTREGADO CINCUENTA de GOLPE. YA ESTOY UN POCO MÁS CERCA del NOBEL.

BUBA VIEDMA

ÍNDICE

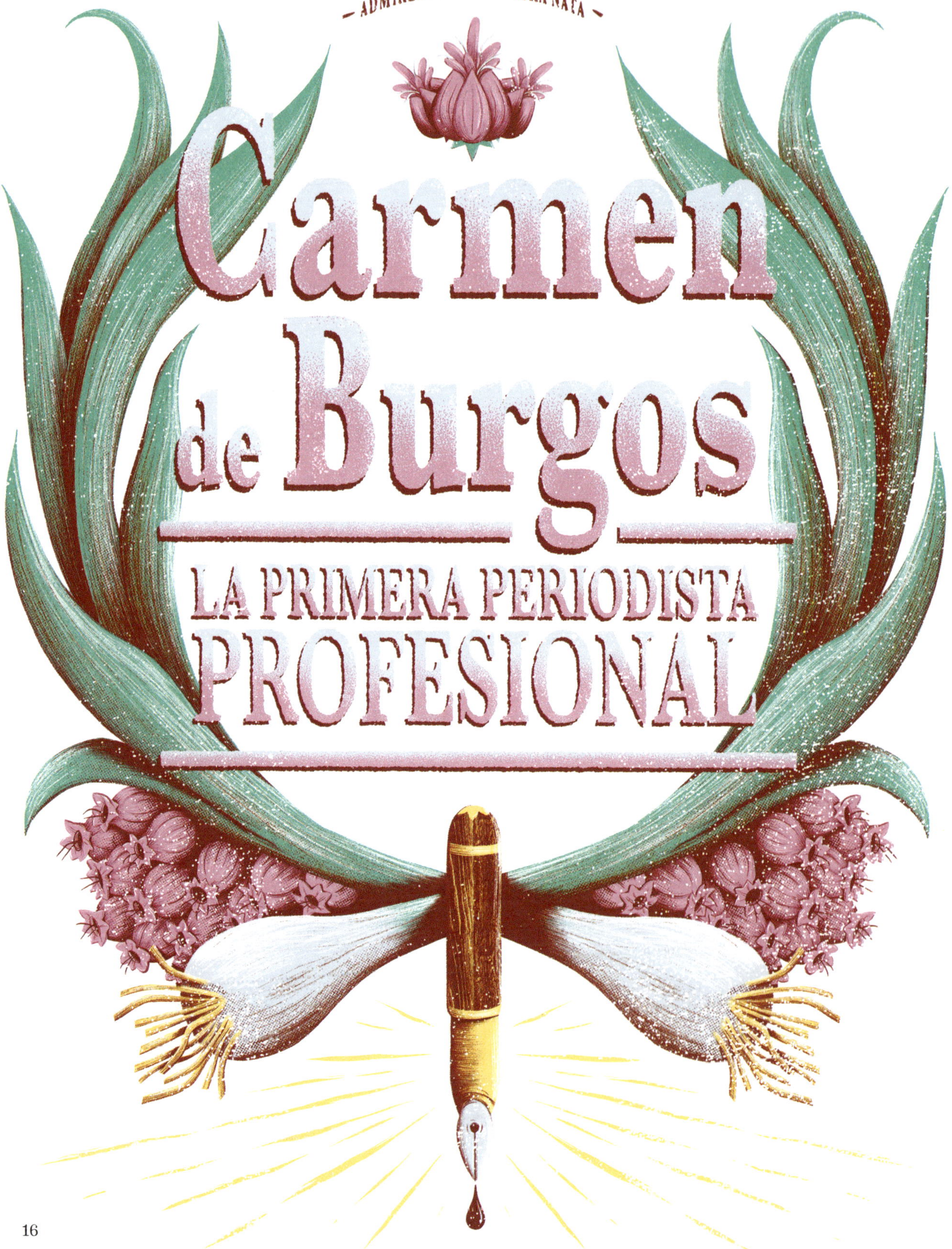
ADMIREN A ESTA PIONERA NATA
Carmen de Burgos
LA PRIMERA PERIODISTA PROFESIONAL

EL 1 de ENERO de 1903 se PRODUCE un HECHO INSÓLITO: POR PRIMERA VEZ un PERIÓDICO CONTRATA a UNA MUJER. AUGUSTO DE FIGUEROA NO PIDE una COLABORACIÓN. QUIERE a CARMEN de BURGOS (1867-1932) COMO «REPORTERO» en la REDACCIÓN del «DIARIO UNIVERSAL».

DE las PERIODISTAS se ESPERAN NOTAS de MODA y TOILETTE, PERO ELLA HABLA de la OPRESIÓN («LAS OBRERAS de MODISTA»...), del CIVISMO («CÓMO se SIRVE un TÉ»...) y de la LIBERTAD CONQUISTADA en OTROS PAÍSES.

«ME VEO OBLIGADA a HACER ESCARCEOS por PERIÓDICOS EXTRANJEROS para TENEROS INFORMADAS de los PROGRESOS de la MUJER», ESCRIBE a sus LECTORAS.

EL 2 de ENERO de 1904 OCURRE ALGO IMPENSABLE: POR PRIMERA VEZ un DIARIO ORGANIZA un PLEBISCITO para QUE los ILUSTRES y los LECTORES den su OPINIÓN SOBRE el DIVORCIO.

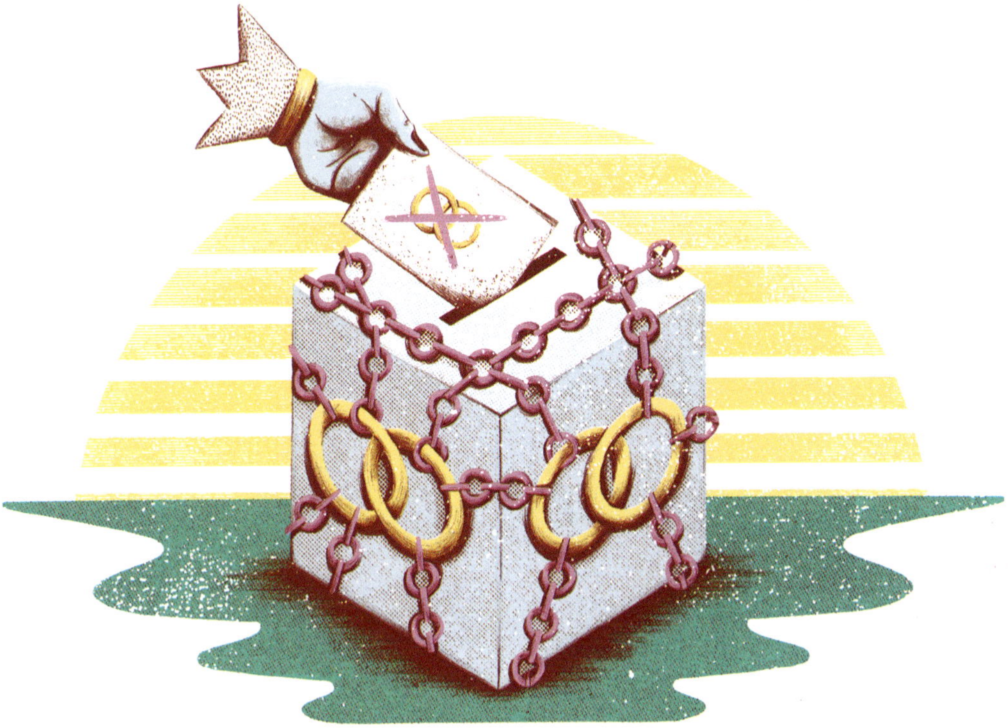

LOS CURAS, los CARLISTAS y la BEATERÍA AMBIENTE TRINAN de HORROR. LA INSULTAN, la PERSIGUEN. PERO los INTELECTUALES (BLASCO IBÁÑEZ, BAROJA, UNAMUNO...) ADMIRAN la VALENTÍA de ESTA PERIODISTA que FIRMA con el SEUDÓNIMO de COLOMBINE.

RESULTADO: 1.462 VOTOS a FAVOR y 320 en CONTRA. Y en CONCLUSIÓN ESCRIBE: «ES INDUDABLE que SE ESTABLECERÁ ENTRE NOSOTROS ESTA CONQUISTA de la CIVILIZACIÓN».

En 1906 EMPRENDE OTRA CAMPAÑA en PRENSA. ESTA VEZ por el VOTO FEMENINO. PERO a la MAYORÍA le ESPANTA: 922 a FAVOR y 3.640 en CONTRA.

COMO COROLARIO DICE: «EL PUEBLO ESPAÑOL, COMPARADO con el de OTRAS NACIONES, SUFRE un NOTABLE ATRASO. La MUJER AÚN TIENE que CONQUISTAR su CULTURA, sus DERECHOS CIVILES y CAMBIAR sus COSTUMBRES».

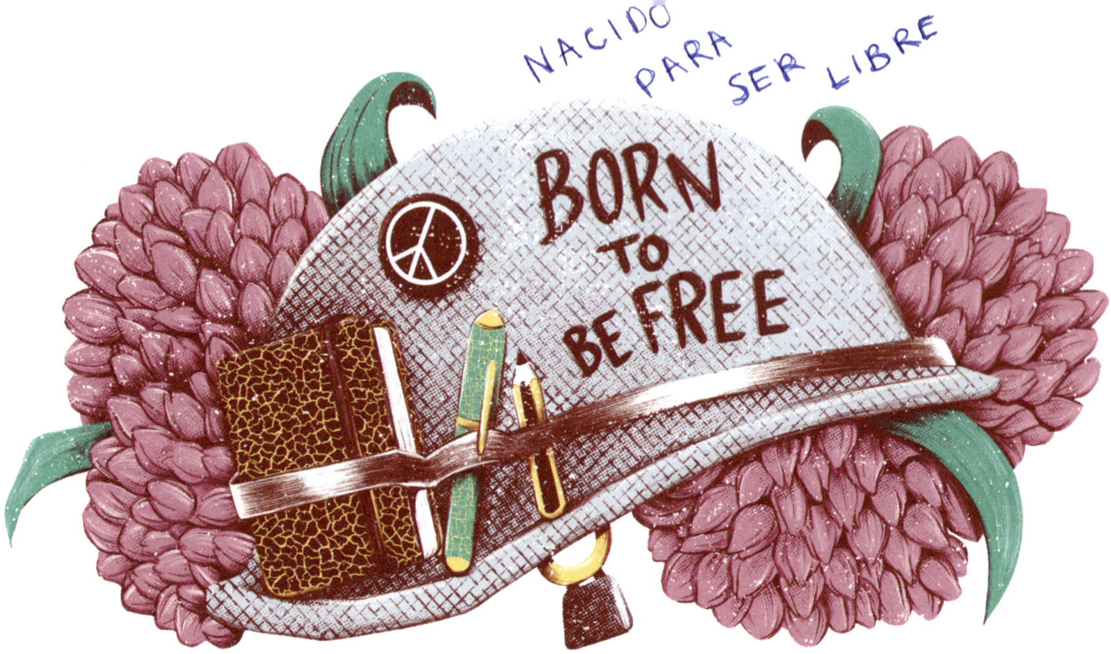

En el VERANO de 1909 VUELVE a OCURRIR ALGO INÉDITO. LOS LECTORES del «HERALDO de MADRID» VEN, OJIPLÁTICOS, que UNA MUJER HA IDO al FRENTE de MELILLA para INFORMAR SOBRE los HERIDOS y las TROPAS. ¡ES la PRIMERA CORRESPONSAL de GUERRA!

Y a su VUELTA, SIN la CENSURA MILITAR SOBRE la CHEPA, EMPRENDE OTRA CAMPAÑA:

¡GUERRA A LA GUERRA!

RECLAMA la OBJECIÓN de CONCIENCIA y AÚN MÁS: «LO que HAY que PEDIR es la SUPRESIÓN de los EJÉRCITOS, el DESARME. QUE ACABEN de una VEZ PARA SIEMPRE las ODIOSAS GUERRAS».

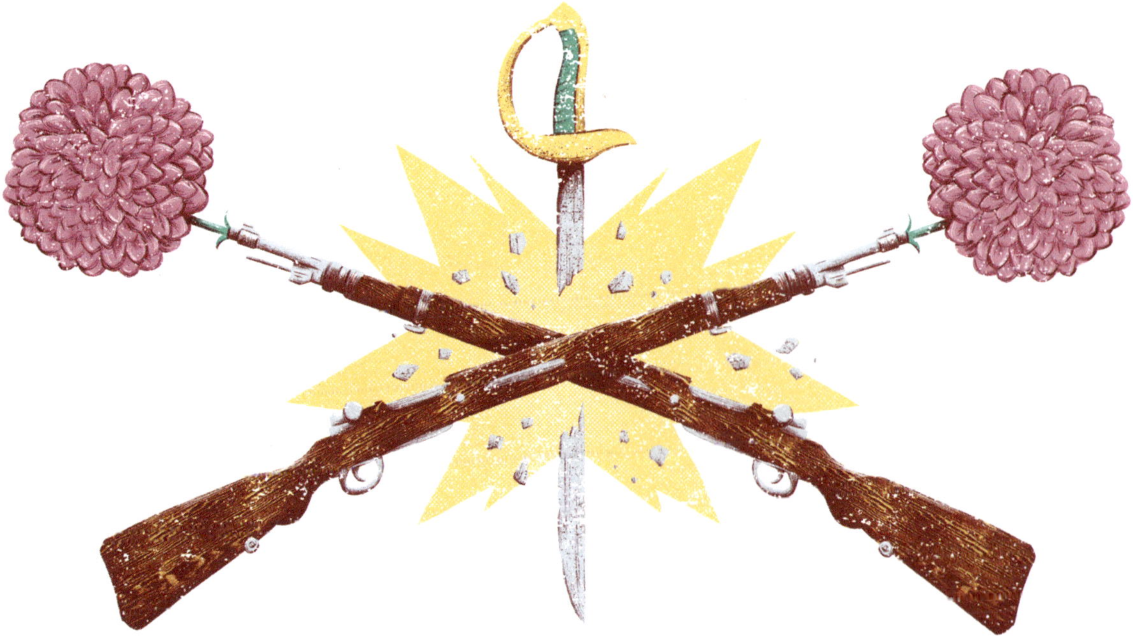

COLOMBINE ESCRIBE en PERIÓDICOS ESPAÑOLES, PORTUGUESES y AMERICANOS. PUBLICA NOVELAS CORTAS y LARGAS. ES MAESTRA. Y a la VEZ SE DEJA el PELLEJO y su CORAZÓN ACHACOSO en CONSEGUIR que las MUJERES DEJEN de VIVIR APLASTADAS por el CÓDIGO CIVIL y el QUÉ DIRÁN.

LO HACE en sus TEXTOS, en sus CONFERENCIAS y en 1921, CUANDO se PLANTA en las PUERTAS del CONGRESO para LIDERAR una MANIFESTACIÓN FEMINISTA de la CRUZADA de MUJERES ESPAÑOLAS. ¡ES la PRIMERA VEZ que OCURRE ALGO ASÍ! Y LLEVAN un MANIFIESTO que PIDE la IGUALDAD de HOMBRES y MUJERES.

-EMPIECE USTED por SU INFANCIA -le INDICA el PERIODISTA de «LA ESFERA», en el GABINETE de TRABAJO de COLOMBINE, MIENTRAS le HACE una ENTREVISTA un DÍA de 1922.

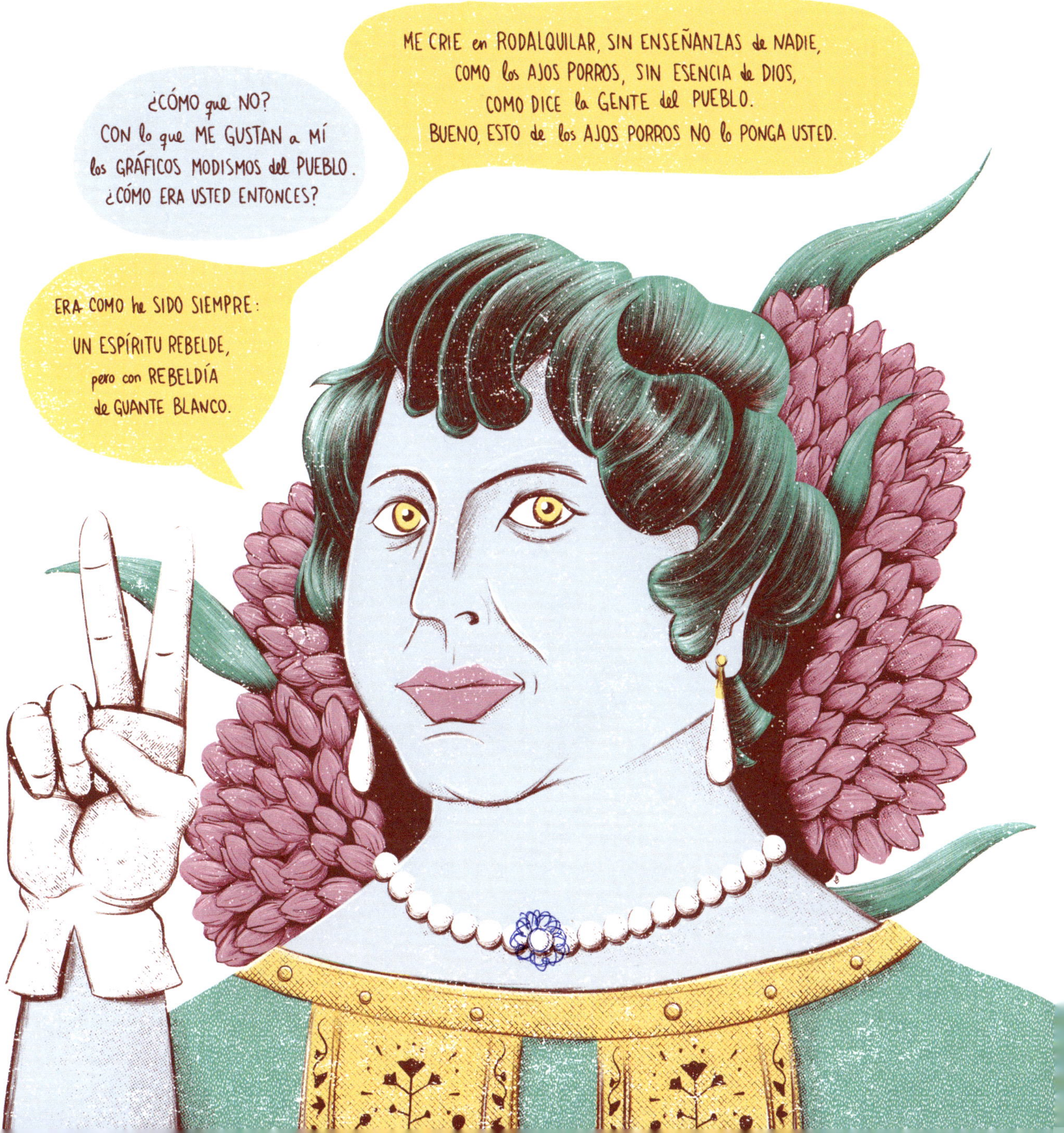

DÉJENSE ENVOLVER POR LOS COLORES Y LAS FORMAS DE...

MARÍA BLANCHARD

LA VANGUARDISTA INCOMPRENDIDA

Un TRASPIÉ TORCIÓ el DESTINO de **MARÍA BLANCHARD** (1881-1932). NO HABÍA NACIDO AÚN y SU COLUMNA YA TOMÓ una EXTRAÑA DESVIACIÓN CUBISTA. OCURRIÓ CUANDO SU MADRE, EMBARAZADA, CAYÓ al BAJAR de un COCHE de CABALLOS.

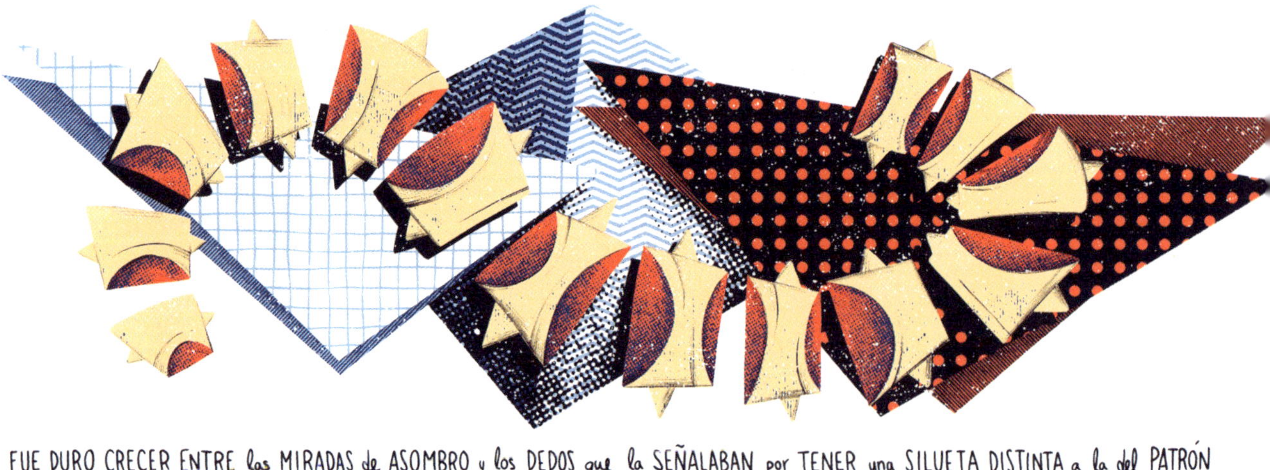

FUE DURO CRECER ENTRE las MIRADAS de ASOMBRO y los DEDOS que la SEÑALABAN por TENER una SILUETA DISTINTA a la del PATRÓN CLÁSICO. LOS NIÑOS, con OSCURA CRUELDAD, la LLAMABAN «BRUJA». PERO se EQUIVOCABAN. ERA una PERSONA MENUDITA, con el PELO CASTAÑO DESPEINADO en FLOTANTES ABUELOS y UNA MIRADA SUSURRANTE de PÁJARO con TRISTE ALEGRÍA. ASÍ la RETRATÓ con sus PALABRAS **RAMÓN GÓMEZ de la SERNA**.

MARÍA PINTABA; BUSCABA la BELLEZA que NUNCA ENCONTRÓ en su CUERPO. PINTABA, y su PADRE la CONVENCIÓ para que FUERA a MADRID a ESTUDIAR con los MEJORES MAESTROS. PERO ENTONCES la EFERVESCENCIA del ARTE ESTABA en PARÍS. En 1909 CONSIGUIÓ una BECA para ESTUDIAR en ESA CIUDAD y ALLÍ DESCUBRIÓ la LIBERTAD y las VANGUARDIAS. NUNCA MÁS le INTERESÓ la PINTURA CLÁSICA.

En PARÍS GANÓ su PRIMERA MEDALLA. Se HIZO AMIGA de **JUAN GRIS**. VIVIÓ con **ANGELINA BELOFF** y **DIEGO RIVERA**.

«NINGÚN COLORISTA de NUESTRO TIEMPO la SOBREPASA», ASEGURÓ el PINTOR MEXICANO.

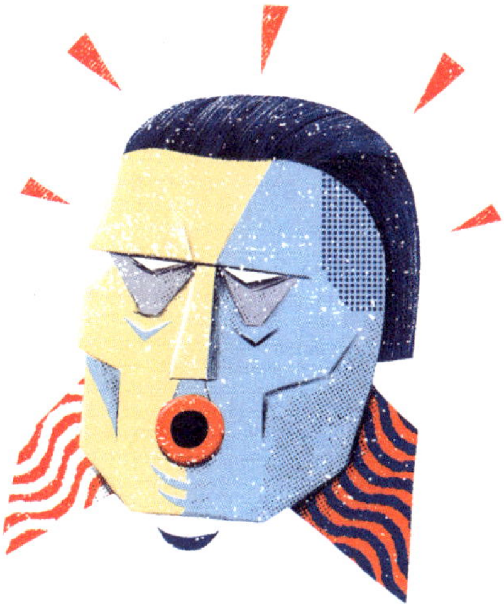

En 1915 EXPUSO en MADRID JUNTO a RIVERA y LUIS BAGARÍA. NADIE ENTENDIÓ un ARTE que NO COPIABA la REALIDAD TAL CUAL. El PÚBLICO y la CRÍTICA se BURLARON de ELLOS. MARÍA FUE a SALAMANCA a ENSEÑAR PINTURA y sus ALUMNOS se QUEDARON PERPLEJOS. QUERÍAN APRENDER a PINTAR COMO se HABÍA HECHO TODA la VIDA de DIOS.

HARTA, DECEPCIONADA, HIZO BORRÓN y CUENTA NUEVA. SE FUE a PARÍS para SIEMPRE. ALLÍ VALORABAN su OBRA. EXPUSO en GALERÍAS de RENOMBRE. LLEVARON sus CUADROS a OTROS PAÍSES. Y CUANDO MURIÓ, ABATIDA por la TUBERCULOSIS, el PERIÓDICO «L'INTRANSIGEANT» PUBLICÓ:

«El SITIO que OCUPABA en el ARTE CONTEMPORÁNEO ERA PREPONDERANTE. SU ARTE ERA PODEROSO, HECHO de MISTICISMO y de un AMOR APASIONADO por la PROFESIÓN. BLANCHARD QUEDARÁ COMO UNA de las ARTISTAS MÁS SIGNIFICATIVAS de NUESTRA ÉPOCA. SU VIDA de RECLUSA y ENFERMA HABÍA AGUDIZADO una de las MÁS BELLAS INTELIGENCIAS de ESTE TIEMPO».

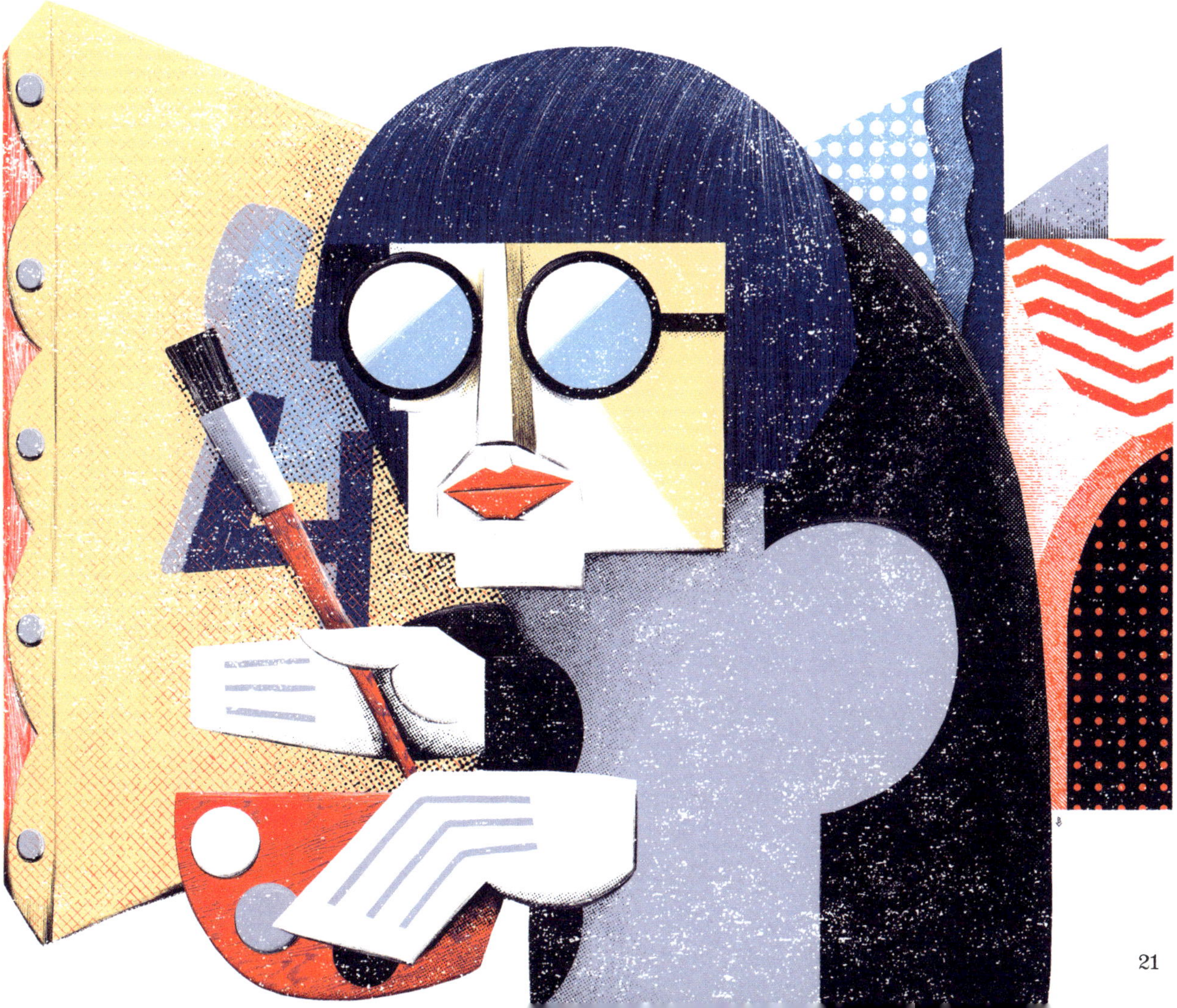

PROTÉJANSE DE LAS LLAMAS Y ATIENDAN A LO QUE CUENTA EL SIN PAR...

GALDÓS ATÓNITO ANTE EL CRIMEN DE FUENCARRAL

ES UNA NOCHE de VERANO de 1888. EN la CALLE FUENCARRAL HUELE a QUEMADO. DE UNA VENTANA SALE HUMO NEGRO a BORBOTONES. LOS VECINOS LLAMAN a la POLICÍA.

«¡FUEGO, FUEGO!»

VARIOS HOMBRES INTENTAN ABRIR la PUERTA de la CASA en LLAMAS con UNA PALANQUETA. NO HAY MANERA. AVISAN a UN CERRAJERO y la PUERTA, al FIN, CEDE.

«GUARDIAS, ¡MUCHO CUIDADO, que HAY UN PERRO MUY MALO!», GRITA UN VECINO.

YA NO HAY FLAMA. QUEDAN SOLO CENIZAS, HUMO y... ¡UN CADÁVER! EL CUERPO de la MARQUESA VIUDA de VARELA YACE MEDIO CARBONIZADO a los PIES de SU CAMA.

ENTRAN DESPUÉS en la COCINA y VEN OTRO CUERPO en el SUELO. ES UNA MUJER DELGADA, QUEBRADA de COLOR y con UN LUNAR de PELO en la CARA. ALGUIEN la RECONOCE: ES HIGINIA, la CRIADA. EL ENORME PERRO de PRESA ESTÁ a SU LADO.

-LEVÁNTESE USTED -LE PIDE el SUBINSPECTOR de POLICÍA.

-NO PUEDO, ESTOY BALDADA -CONTESTA la MUJER.

-ENTONCES YO la AYUDARÉ.

UN VECINO SE METE por MEDIO. TEME que el PERRO MUERDA al SUBINSPECTOR.

-NO TENGA USTED MIEDO. EL PERRO NO SE MOVERÁ -TRANQUILIZA la MUJER.

LOS AGENTES la INTERROGAN. DICE que ESTABA en SU DORMITORIO CUANDO la DESPERTÓ el INCENDIO. NO SABE QUÉ HA PODIDO PASAR

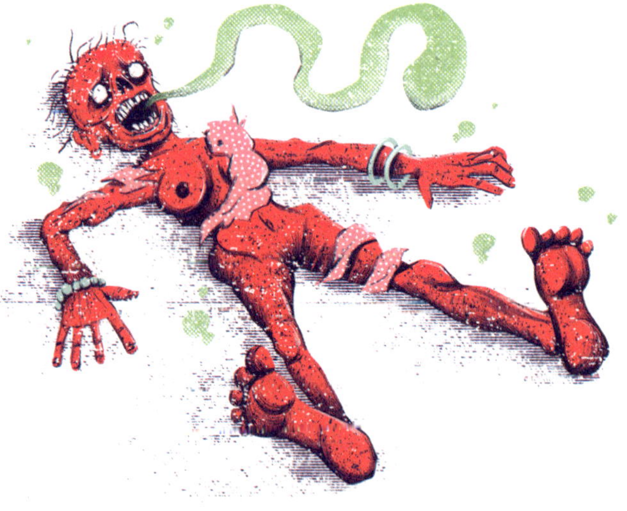

BENITO PÉREZ GALDÓS ESTÁ HORRORIZADO con lo que LEE, y ESCRIBE:

«LA PRENSA BUSCA en PRIMER LUGAR EMOCIONES con que SACIAR la VORACIDAD de SUS LECTORES, PROCURA DAR a ESTOS CADA DÍA NOTICIAS ESTUPENDAS. EN CUANTO SE INDICA que TAL PERSONA VA a SER INTERROGADA por el JUEZ, los PERIODISTAS BUSCAN SU DOMICILIO, lo ACOSAN a PREGUNTAS y NO VUELVEN a la REDACCIÓN SIN UN CAUDAL MÁS o MENOS AUTÉNTICO de NOTICIAS».

UN DÍA CUENTAN que la MARQUESA TENÍA HERIDAS en el PECHO: SOSPECHOSO. OTRO, que HIGINA ACABABA de ENTRAR a SERVIR: MMM... DICEN que FUE el HIJO, UN JOVEN de MAL VIVIR, QUIEN CONTRATÓ a la CRIADA. CUENTAN que EN el BARRIO ERAN FAMOSOS los GRITOS que SE PEGABAN la MADRE y el HIJO.

Y LLEGA el DÍA en que los PERIÓDICOS, en UNA ESPIRAL del MORBO, DAN el FINAL del NOVELÓN: JOSÉ VÁZQUEZ ENCARGÓ a la CRIADA que MATARA a SU MADRE para RECIBIR la HERENCIA.

GALDÓS, en «LA PRENSA» de BUENOS AIRES, LAMENTA el GIRO que ESTÁN TOMANDO los DIARIOS:

LOS GRANDES CRÍMENES MENUDEAN. EN VANO SE BUSCARÍAN en la PRENSA ACONTECIMIENTOS POLÍTICOS o LITERARIOS. LOS PERIÓDICOS LLENAN las COLUMNAS CON RELATOS del «CRIMEN de la CALLE de FUENCARRAL», del «CRIMEN de VALENCIA», del «CRIMEN de MÁLAGA». LOS «REPORTERS» y NOTICIEROS, en VEZ de PASARSE la VIDA en el SALÓN de CONFERENCIAS, VISITAN los JUZGADOS a TODAS HORAS, ACOMETEN a los CURIALES, ATOSIGÁNDOLES a PREGUNTAS, y CON los DATOS que ADQUIEREN, CONSTRUYEN LUEGO la HISTORIA MÁS o MENOS FANTASEADA y NOVELESCA del ESPANTOSO DRAMA.

NO PODÍA IMAGINAR GALDÓS que el DELIRIO MÁS GRANDE de la PRENSA ESTABA AÚN por VENIR: ¡ESAS NOTICIAS de GATITOS que CAUSARÍAN FUROR en el HIPERTECNOLÓGICO SIGLO XXI!

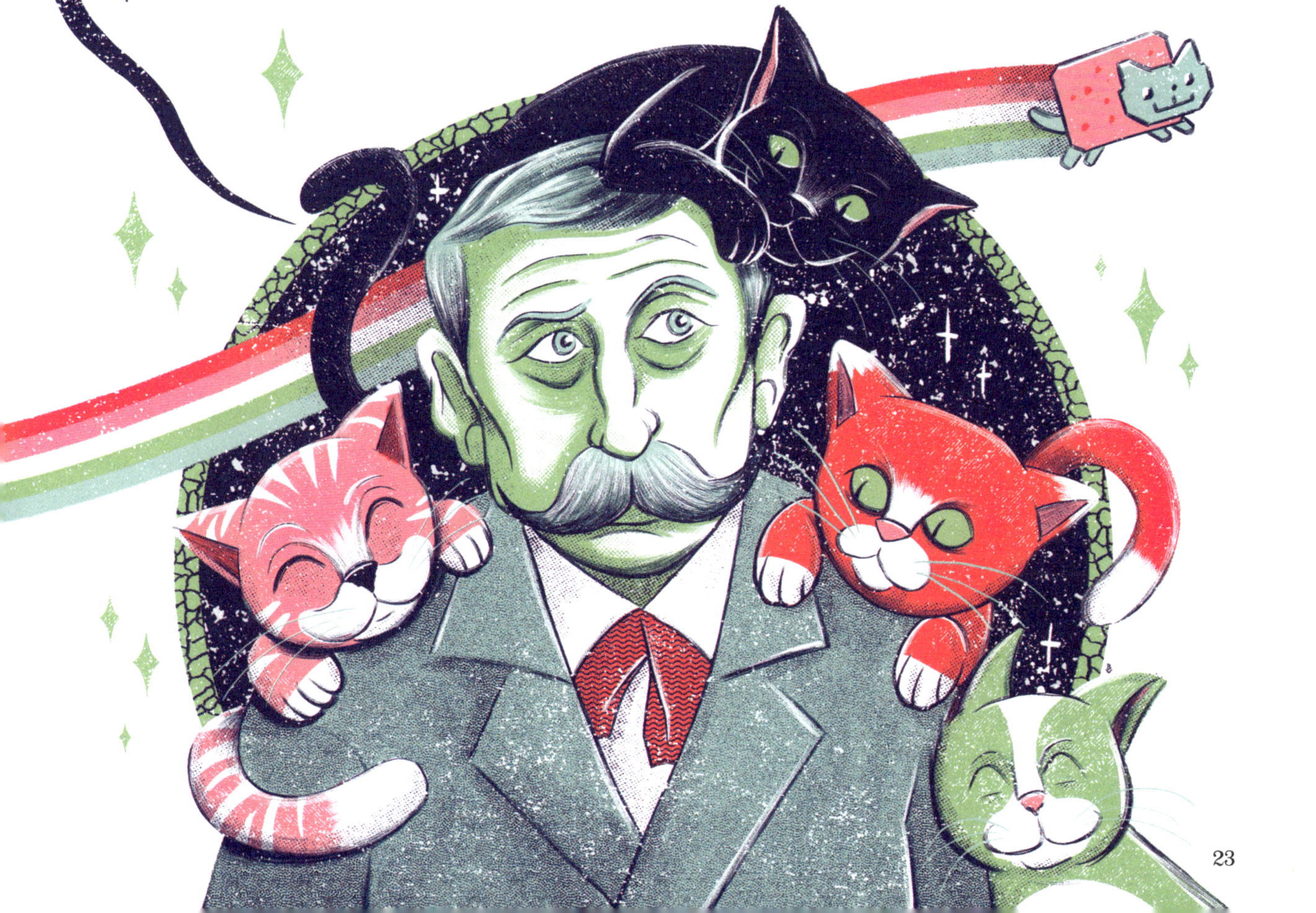

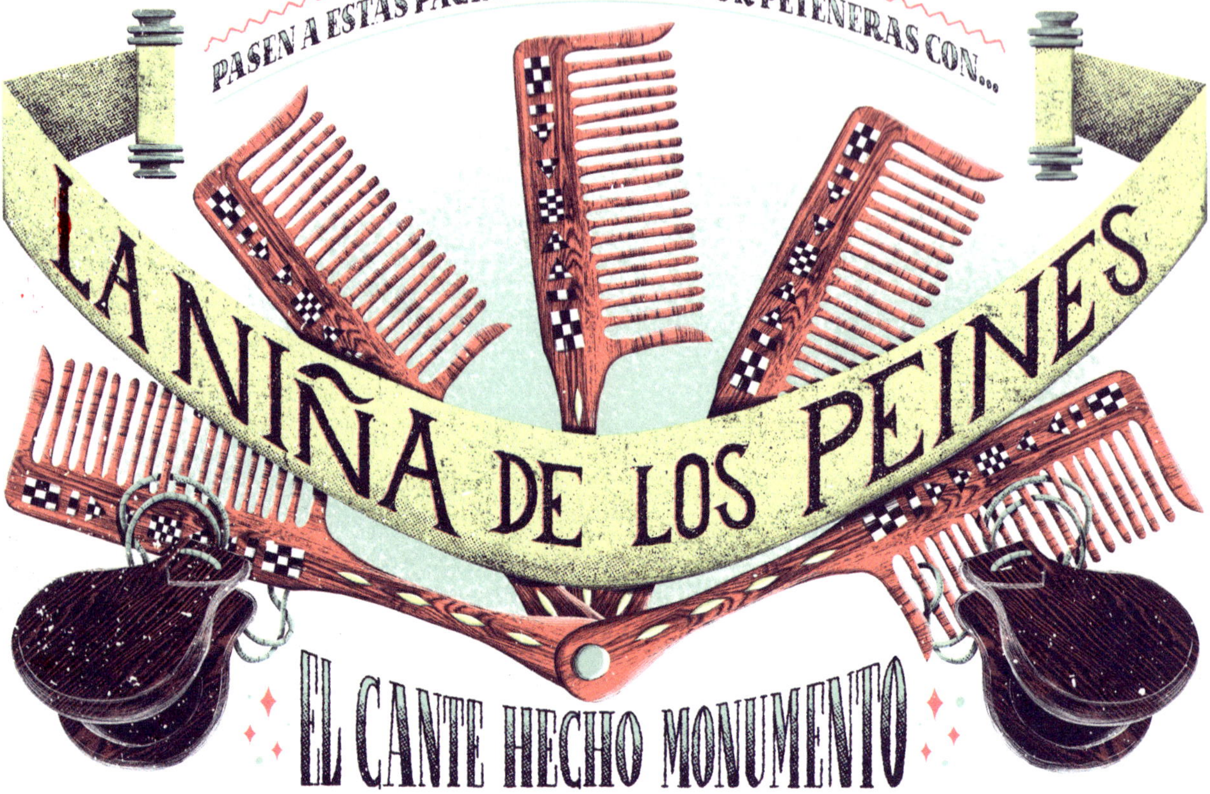

PASEN A ESTAS PÁGINAS Y SALGAN POR PETENERAS CON...

LA NIÑA DE LOS PEINES

EL CANTE HECHO MONUMENTO

DE CUNA GITANA SALIÓ una VOZ de PLATA FUNDIDA. FUE un DÍA de INVIERNO. En la CALLE BUTRÓN de SEVILLA NACIÓ una NIÑA de PADRE CANTAOR y MADRE ABNEGADA. QUISO el DESTINO que PASTORA MARÍA PAVÓN CRUZ (1890-1969) HEREDARA el ARTE del PADRE y, en SUS LABIOS de MUJER, lo LLEVARA a LO MÁS GRANDE.

Al CANTE se ECHARON TAMBIÉN sus HERMANOS. Y OCURRIÓ que un DÍA TENÍA que ACTUAR el MAYOR, TOMÁS PAVÓN, en la FERIA de SEVILLA, pero el AZAR HIZO un VOLTEO y, en su LUGAR, SALIÓ la NIÑA. TENÍA OCHO AÑOS. Y TRIUNFÓ. OLES y APLAUSOS COMO BURBUJAS.

En 1901 DEBUTÓ en el CAFÉ del BRILLANTE de MADRID y el ÉXITO la LLEVÓ por CAFÉS CANTANTES de «TOA» la PIEL de TORO. UNOS DICEN que FUE un TANGO que ENAMORÓ al MUNDO el que DIO NOMBRE a la ARTISTA:

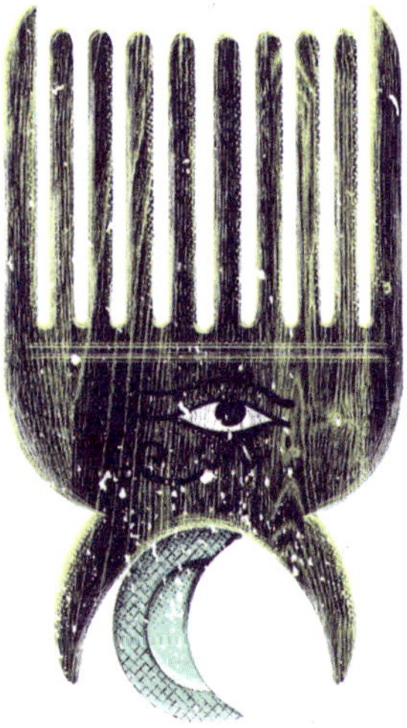

PÉINATE TÚ con MIS PEINES,
que MIS PEINES son de AZÚCAR,
QUIEN con MIS PEINES se PEINA
HASTA los DEDOS se CHUPA.

PÉINATE TÚ con MIS PEINES,
MIS PEINES son de CANELA,
LA GACHÍ que se PEINA
con MIS PEINES
CANELA LLEVA de VERAS.

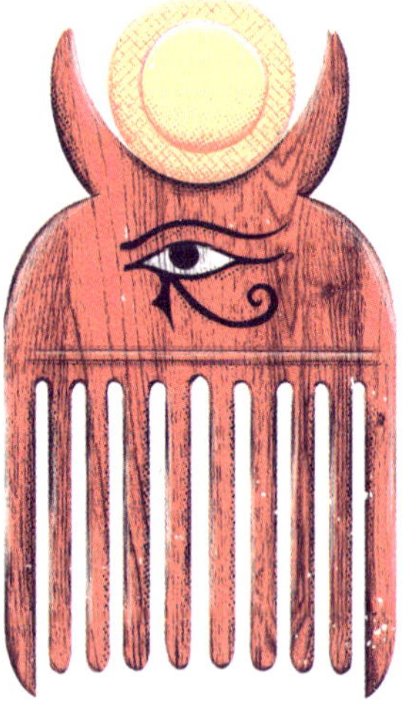

OTROS CUENTAN que el REMOQUETE NACIÓ una NOCHE que, AHÍ en lo ALTO, ENTRE las ONDAS NEGRAS del CABELLO, en VEZ de PEINETA, LUCÍAN DOS PEINES.

FARAONA se HIZO del TANGO y la SEGUIRIYA. DEL SALIR por PETENERAS, BULERÍAS y SOLEÁS. DEL HACER MAGIA de la LÓGICA. DEL ESCANDALIZAR a GITANOS y PAYOS.

Y LLEGÓ el AMOR «PA» la GITANA. PASTORA PAVÓN se CASÓ con PEPE PINTO y, ENTRE tanta P, VOLARON PALMAS. OLE con OLE y OLÉ. DOS CANTAORES de LUNA de MIEL.

«TIENE una VOZ REDONDA, un BAJO que LLORA, un COMPÁS, un CANTE PERFECTO. Y LUEGO una ENORME EXTENSIÓN de CANTES DISTINTOS. ELLA FUE en REALIDAD QUIEN METIÓ el CUPLÉ por BULERÍAS», DECÍA PEPE PINTO de su MUJER.

MÁS POÉTICO FUE **LORCA** HABLANDO de su CANTE JONDO: «JUGABA con su VOZ de SOMBRA, con su VOZ de ESTAÑO FUNDIDO, con su VOZ CUBIERTA de MUSGO».

HOY, unos DISCOS de PIZARRA GUARDAN sus TANGOS y BULERÍAS. HOY, ANDALUCÍA ENTERA PRESUME de su CANTAR. ALLÍ, en su TIERRA de CUNA, han HECHO de su VOZ un MONUMENTO. Y DICEN los DOCUMENTOS que es «BIEN de INTERÉS CULTURAL».

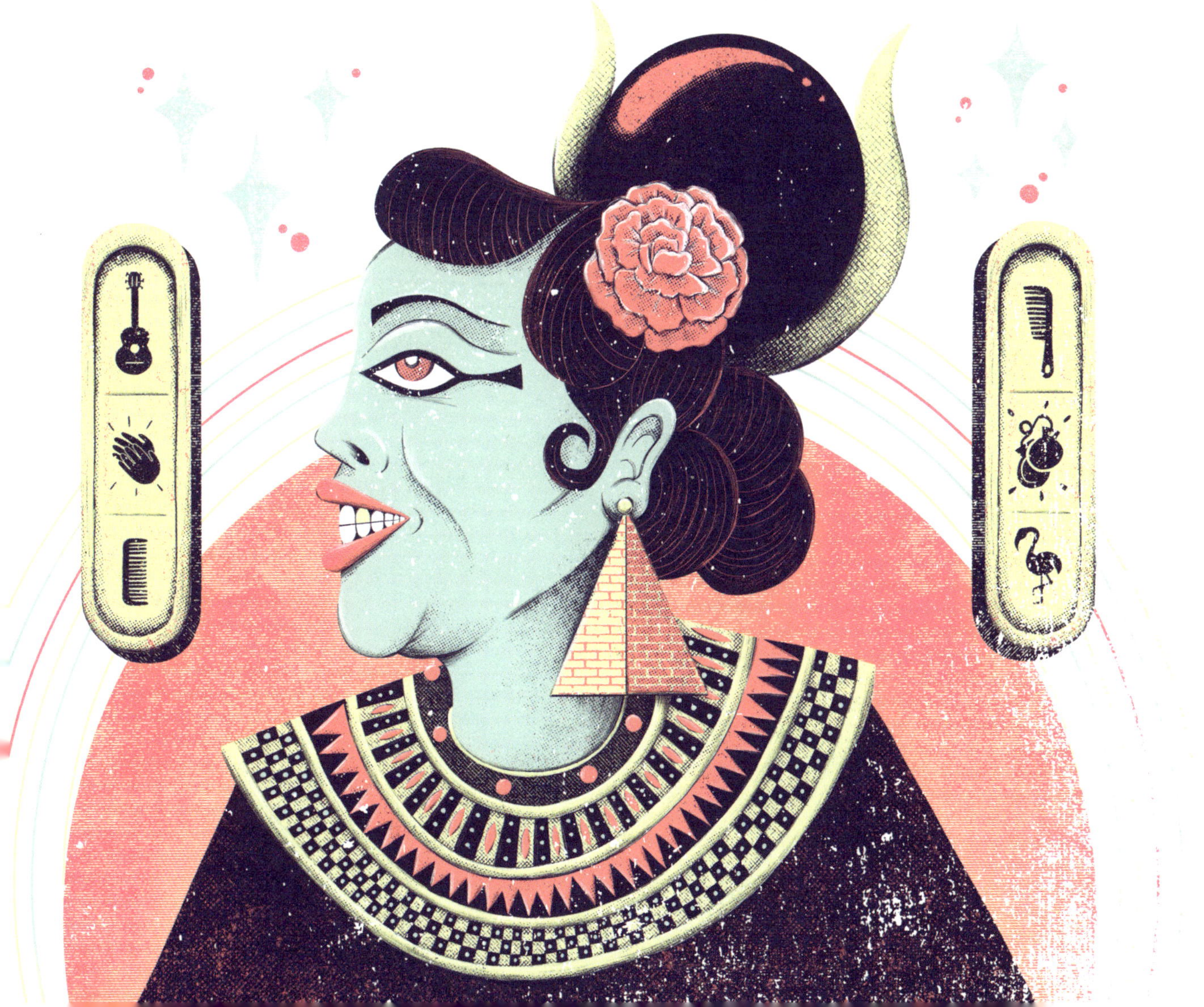

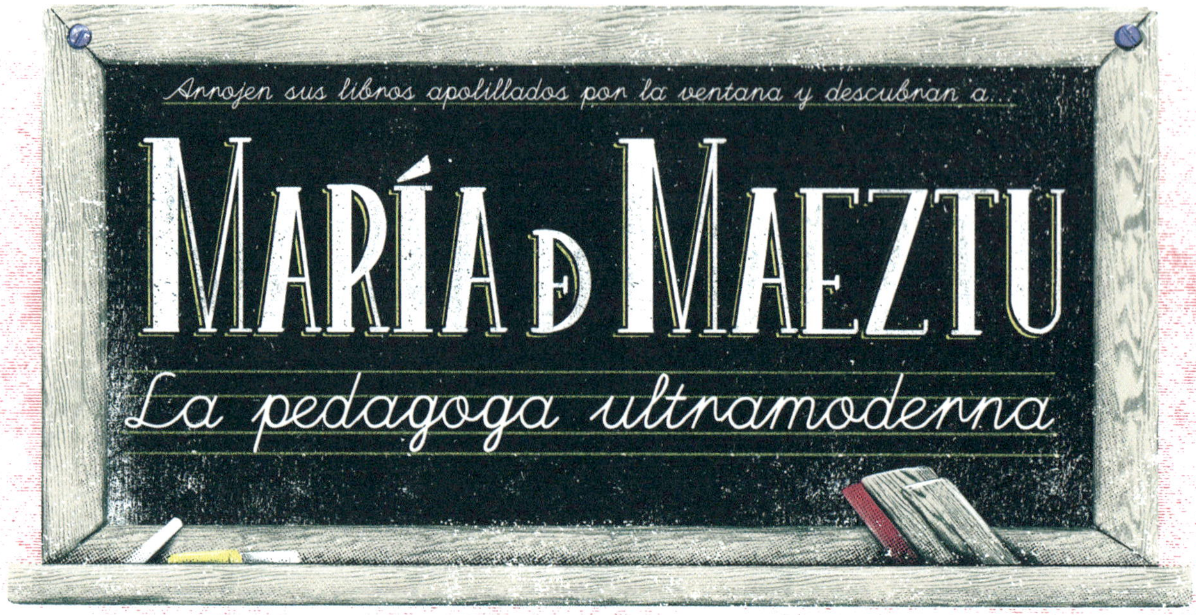

ENTONCES PENSABAN que las ENTENDEDERAS DURAS se ABLANDABAN a PALOS. A FUERZA de REGLAZOS en la MANO y COCOTAZOS en el COGOTE, los NIÑOS ACABARÍAN APRENDIENDO la LECCIÓN.

«¡LA LETRA con SANGRE ENTRA!», DECÍAN, ILUSTRES, los PROFESORES.

PERO, en 1909, **MARÍA de MAEZTU** (1881-1948) FUE a la UNIVERSIDAD de OVIEDO y ALLÍ SENTENCIÓ con VALENTÍA:

«ES VERDAD el DICHO ANTIGUO de que la LETRA con SANGRE ENTRA, PERO NO HA de SER con la del NIÑO, SINO con la del MAESTRO».

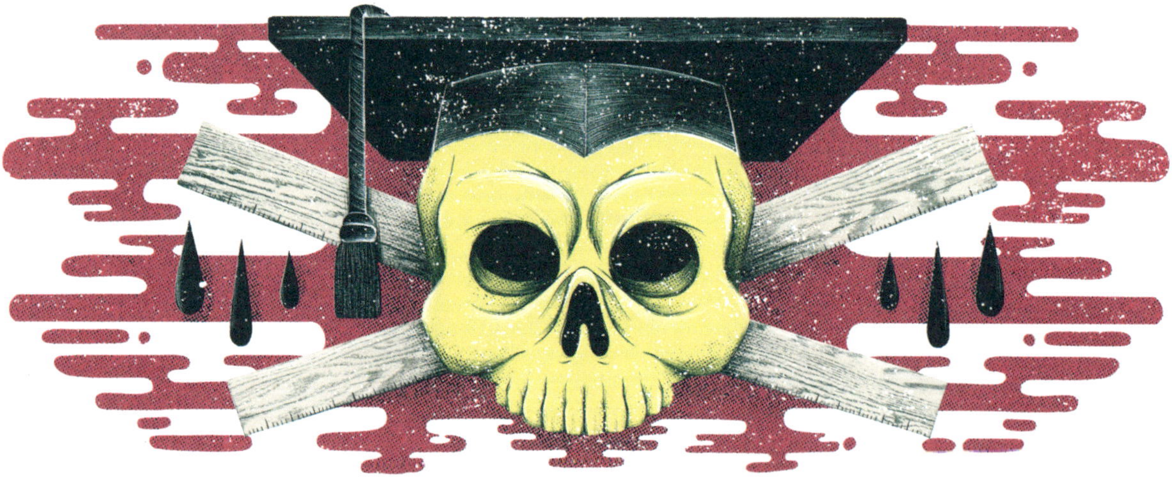

EN SUS VIAJES por EUROPA, y en sus INCANSABLES ESTUDIOS, la PEDAGOGA HABÍA DESCUBIERTO que APRENDER PODÍA y DEBÍA SER un GOZO. DIVERTIRSE MEJOR que SACRIFICARSE.

ESTA LICENCIADA en DERECHO y FILOSOFÍA y LETRAS, MENUDA y VIBRANTE, con VERBO SEGURO y PERSUASIVO, ENCANDILABA a TODO el que la OÍA. En ESE CHORRO de PALABRAS ELOCUENTES DEFENDÍA SIEMPRE la CULTURA y HACÍA HINCAPIÉ en un PUNTO: La EDUCACIÓN de las MUJERES. ¿CÓMO, SI NO, PODRÍAN TENER los MISMOS DERECHOS y OPORTUNIDADES que los HOMBRES?

ESTAS IDEAS TAN INNOVADORAS la LLEVARON a DIRIGIR DOS CENTROS ANSIOSOS de ESTRENAR la ESPAÑA del FUTURO: LA RESIDENCIA de SEÑORITAS y el INSTITUTO-ESCUELA. Y en los DOS ARMÓ su REVOLUCIÓN PEDAGÓGICA.

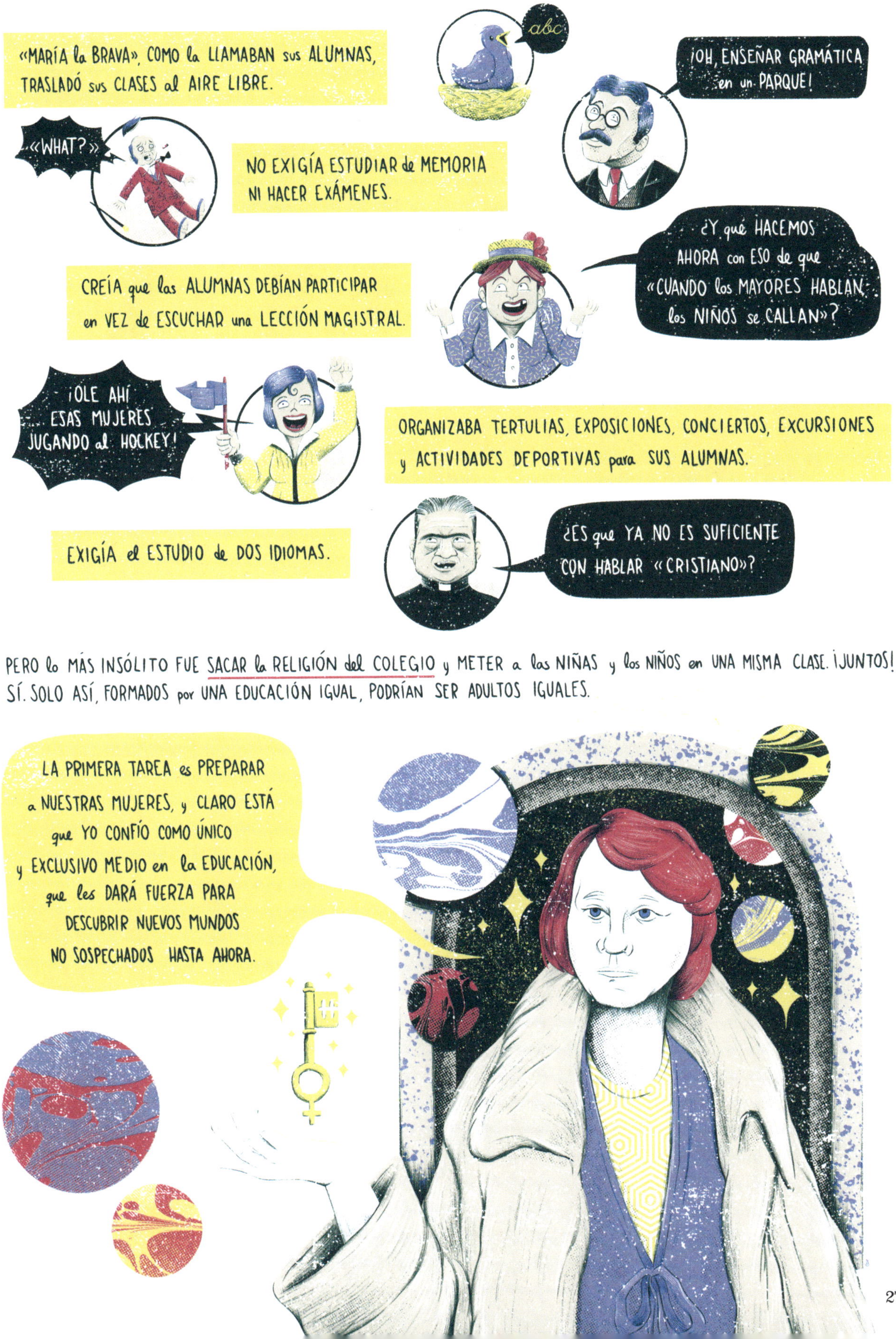
«MARÍA la BRAVA», COMO la LLAMABAN sus ALUMNAS, TRASLADÓ sus CLASES al AIRE LIBRE.
abc
¡OH, ENSEÑAR GRAMÁTICA en un PARQUE!
«WHAT?»
NO EXIGÍA ESTUDIAR de MEMORIA NI HACER EXÁMENES.
¿Y qué HACEMOS AHORA con ESO de que «CUANDO los MAYORES HABLAN los NIÑOS se CALLAN»?
CREÍA que las ALUMNAS DEBÍAN PARTICIPAR en VEZ de ESCUCHAR una LECCIÓN MAGISTRAL.
¡OLE AHÍ ESAS MUJERES JUGANDO al HOCKEY!
ORGANIZABA TERTULIAS, EXPOSICIONES, CONCIERTOS, EXCURSIONES y ACTIVIDADES DEPORTIVAS para SUS ALUMNAS.
EXIGÍA el ESTUDIO de DOS IDIOMAS.
¿ES que YA NO ES SUFICIENTE CON HABLAR «CRISTIANO»?
PERO lo MÁS INSÓLITO FUE SACAR la RELIGIÓN del COLEGIO y METER a las NIÑAS y los NIÑOS en UNA MISMA CLASE. ¡JUNTOS! SÍ. SOLO ASÍ, FORMADOS por UNA EDUCACIÓN IGUAL, PODRÍAN SER ADULTOS IGUALES.
LA PRIMERA TAREA es PREPARAR a NUESTRAS MUJERES, y CLARO ESTÁ que YO CONFÍO COMO ÚNICO y EXCLUSIVO MEDIO en la EDUCACIÓN, que les DARÁ FUERZA PARA DESCUBRIR NUEVOS MUNDOS NO SOSPECHADOS HASTA AHORA.

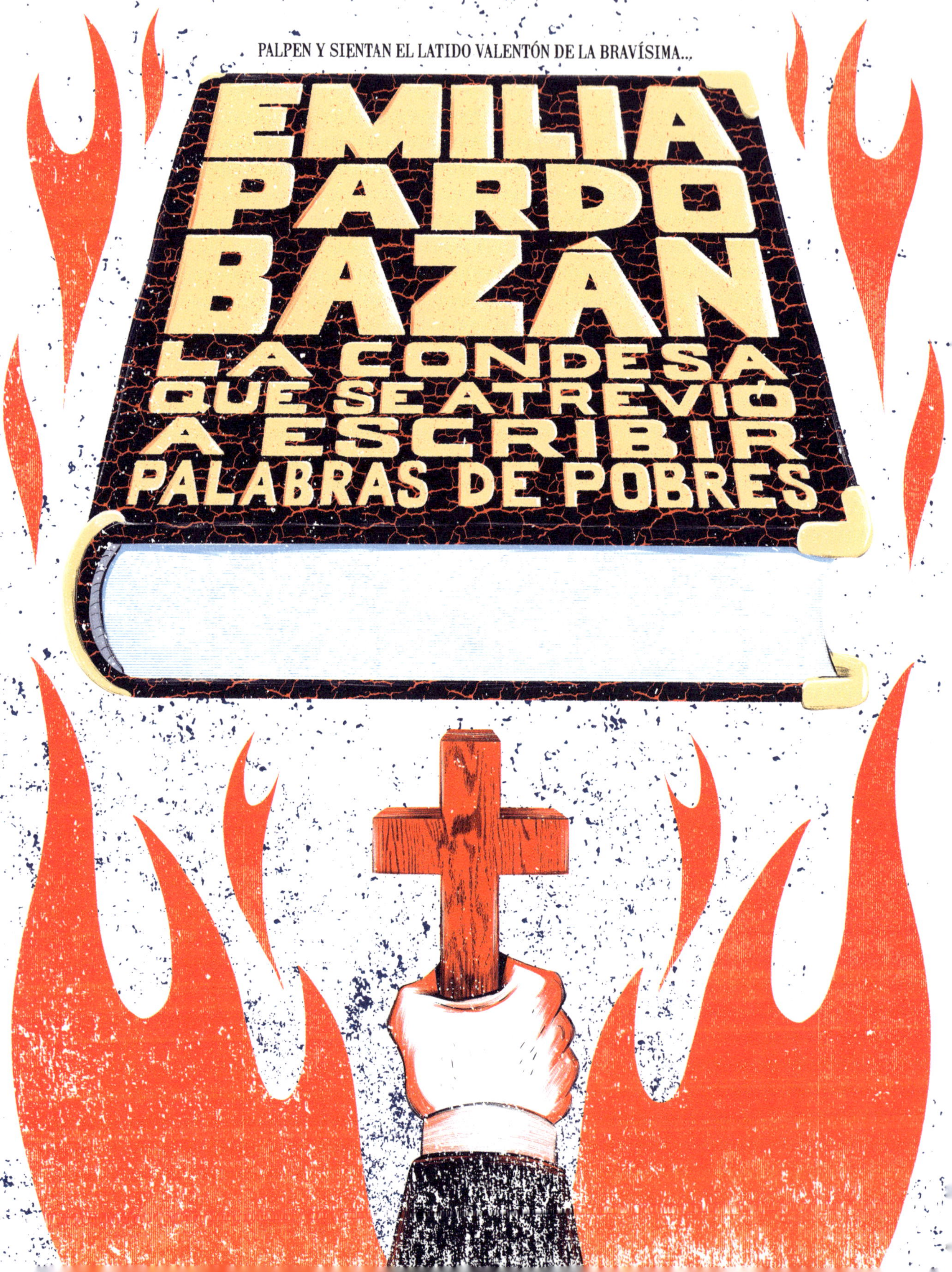
PALPEN Y SIENTAN EL LATIDO VALENTÓN DE LA BRAVÍSIMA...
EMILIA
PARDO
BAZÁN
LA CONDESA
QUE SE ATREVIÓ
A ESCRIBIR
PALABRAS DE POBRES

En la ESPAÑA de LEY y ORDEN de 1880, la **CONDESA PARDO BAZÁN** ESCRIBE ARTÍCULOS SOBRE una LITERATURA que SE HA PUESTO en BOGA en FRANCIA: el NATURALISMO. NADIE se RASGA las VESTIDURAS MIENTRAS SUS TEXTOS VAN DEJÁNDOSE LEER en el DIARIO «LA ÉPOCA», PERO el DÍA que APARECEN ATADOS por el LOMO de un LIBRO, SE MONTA la ZAPATIESTA.

¡CÓMO PUEDE HABLAR una MUJER CATÓLICA, una ESPOSA y una BUENA MADRE de FAMILIA de un ESTILO LITERARIO que CREE en el PROGRESO CIENTÍFICO y USA PALABRAS de POBRES! Los CRÍTICOS DERRAMARON RÍOS de TINTA para CRITICAR «LA CUESTIÓN PALPITANTE». ¡ESCÁNDALO! ¡CONTROVERSIA!

NO ES una PALPITACIÓN lo que PROVOCA ESTE LIBRO en que DOÑA EMILIA HABLA del NATURALISMO de ZOLA y FLAUBERT. SON FIERAS CONVULSIONES en la SOCIEDAD.

-¡ENTRE las PÁGINAS del LIBRO HAY CONTRABANDO de DOCTRINAS ATEAS! -CLAMA la GAZMOÑERÍA.

-EL NATURALISMO NO ES COMO SUS ENEMIGOS SE lo FIGURAN NI SE PARECE a la IDEA que SUS PARTIDARIOS TIENEN de ÉL -CONTESTA PARDO BAZÁN.

La CONDESA y los CRÍTICOS AFILAN sus PLUMAS y, COMO ESPADACHINES, EMPIEZAN a SOLTAR ESPADAZOS en las PÁGINAS de los PERIÓDICOS.

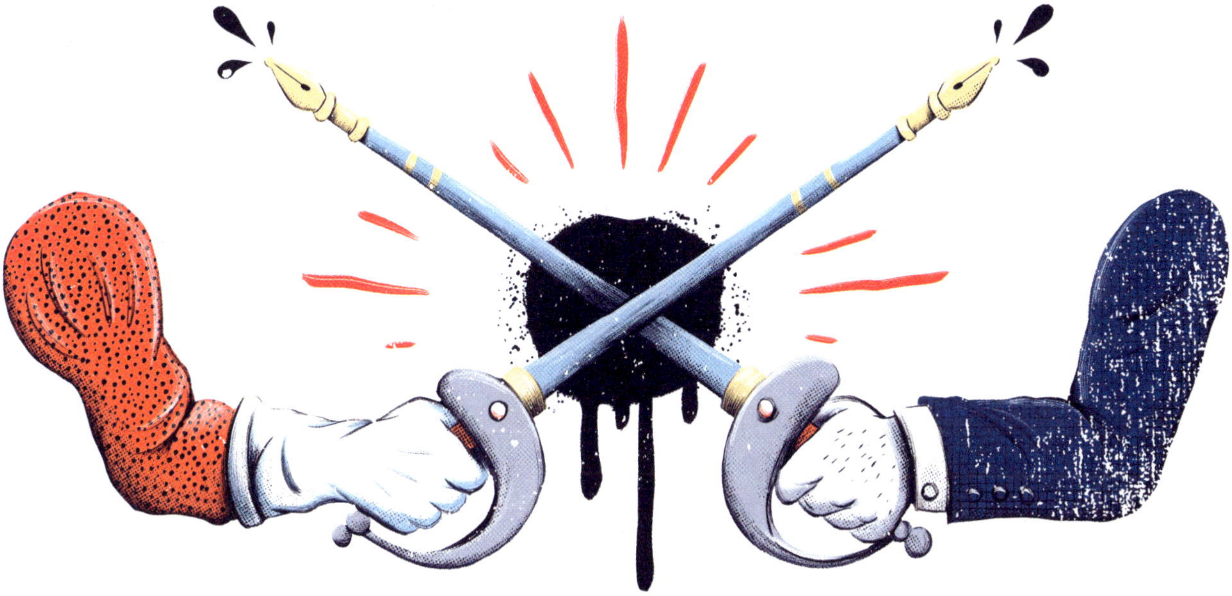

-PERO, SEÑORA, ¿CÓMO SE ATREVE USTED a POLEMIZAR CON un CABALLERO TAN IMPORTANTE COMO el ESCRITOR y POLÍTICO DON EDUARDO CALCAÑO? -PREGUNTA ASOMBRADO el CRÍTICO LUIS ALFONSO.

-Y ¿ACASO NO SOY YO TAN IMPORTANTE COMO ÉL o MÁS? -RESPONDE DOÑA EMILIA.

-PERO, SEÑORA, RECAPACITE USTED y PIENSE que TIENE HIJOS y HONOR FAMILIAR.

-CÁLLESE USTED, que NO ES para TANTO, y el que YO DIVULGUE una TEORÍA NO COMPROMETE MI HONRA.

-RECUERDE USTED, SEÑORA, que es RELIGIOSA.

-NATURALMENTE que lo SOY. POR ESO ESTOY a SALVO de SUS ATAQUES, y LIMPIA de MANCHA.

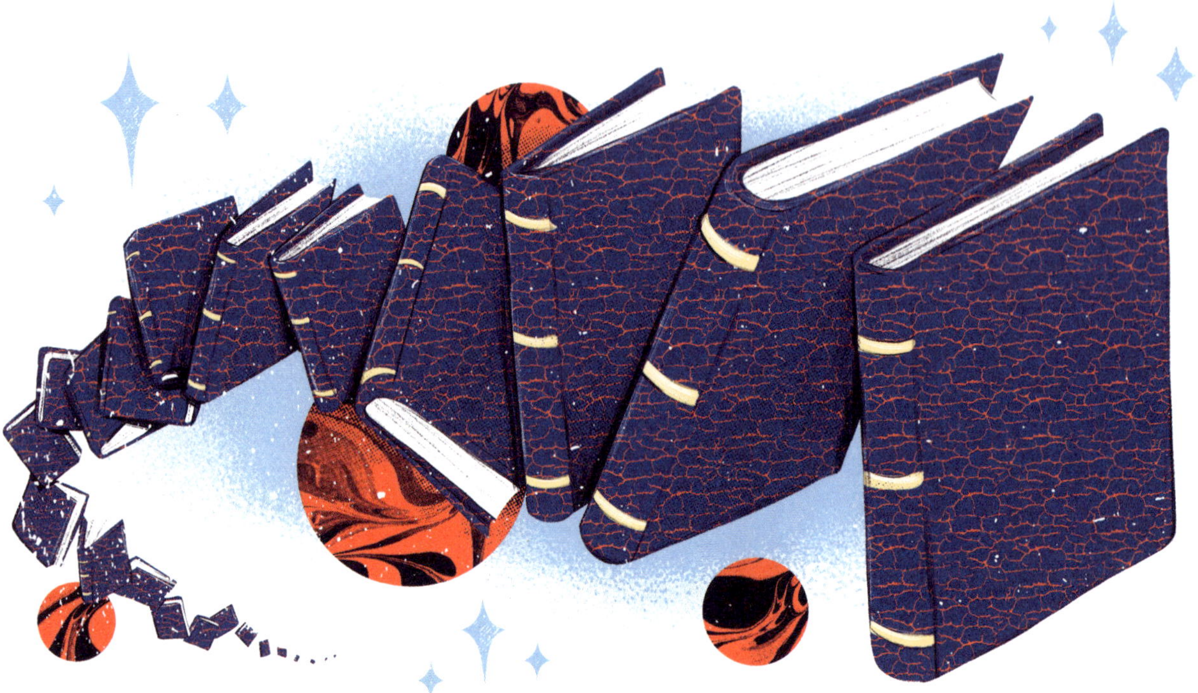

EL PÚBLICO se AGITA. EL LIBRO se AGOTA. Y HA de REEDITARSE VARIAS VECES PORQUE CLARÍN, MENÉNDEZ PELAYO y TODA la INTELECTUALIDAD SE BAMBOLEAN en ESTE OLEAJE de DISCUSIÓN.

EL ESCÁNDALO y los CUCHICHEOS RECORREN las ESQUINAS del CASINO y del CÍRCULO de HOMBRES INSIGNES que FRECUENTA SU MARIDO, DON JOSÉ QUIROGA.

«¿CÓMO HAS PERMITIDO a TU MUJER que ESCRIBA ESO?», LE PREGUNTAN los CONTERTULIOS. ¡HEREJÍA! ¡EXCOMUNIÓN!

ASUSTADO, HORRORIZADO, ESTE HOMBRE HIDALGO, de FAMILIA PÍA, CORRE a su CASA. SUBE al ESTUDIO de su ESPOSA a TODA VELOCIDAD y le EXIGE que DEJE de ESCRIBIR. ¡SE lo PROHÍBE! DEBE RETIRAR ESA OBRA IMPÍA y PEDIR PERDÓN al BUEN SENTIR.

¿RETIRAR SU LIBRO? ¡LO ÚNICO que VA a RETIRAR es a ESTE MARIDO de SU VISTA!

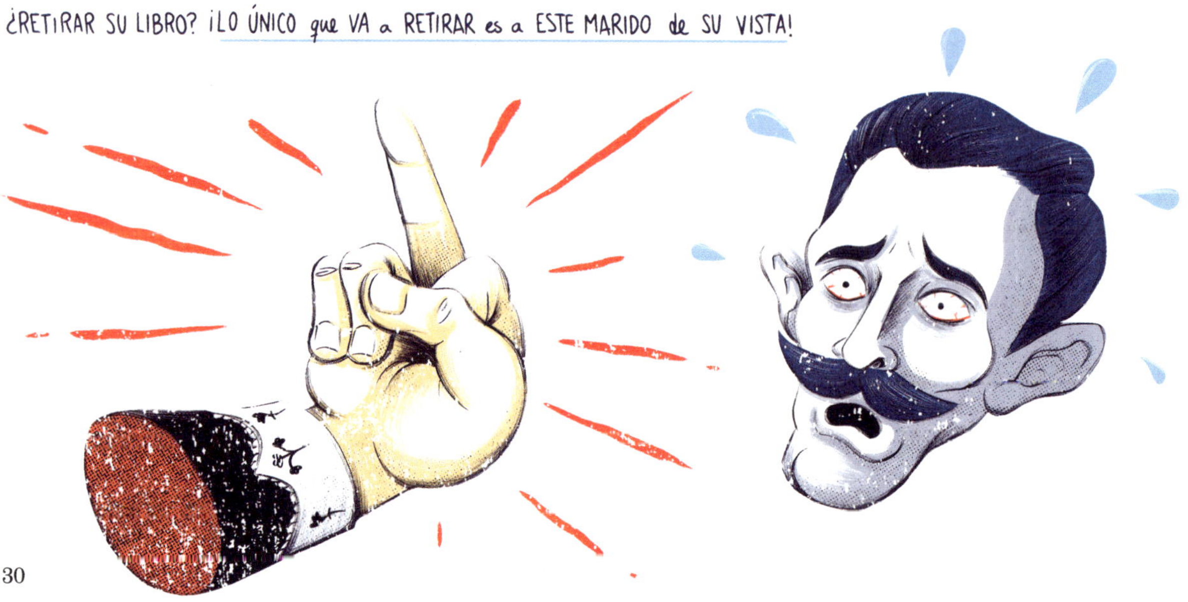

A DOÑA EMILIA le DA un PÁLPITO y, CON la OBRA BAJO el BRAZO, EMPRENDE un VIAJE a ROMA. AHÍ MUESTRA a un CARDENAL del VATICANO su «CUESTIÓN PALPITANTE» y, DESPUÉS de LEERLO CON LUPA, SENTENCIA el NUNCIO:

«PUEDES ESTAR TRANQUILA, HIJA MÍA. TU LIBRO es BUENO, NO TIENE NADA CONTRA el DOGMA NI CONTRA las DOCTRINAS de NUESTRA SANTA MADRE IGLESIA».

¿QUÉ HABÍA ESCRITO DOÑA EMILIA para LEVANTAR AQUELLAS IRAS PUDIBUNDAS y ESOS PASMOS de TERROR?

«La POESÍA se MODIFICA y ADMITE la REALIDAD VULGAR COMO ELEMENTO de BELLEZA: FÁCIL es PROBARLO CON SOLO NOMBRAR a CAMPOAMOR. La HISTORIA se APOYA CADA VEZ MÁS en la CIENCIA y en el CONOCIMIENTO ANALÍTICO de las SOCIEDADES. La CRÍTICA DEJÓ de SER MAGISTERIO y PONTIFICADO, CONVIRTIÉNDOSE en ESTUDIO y OBSERVACIÓN INCESANTE.»

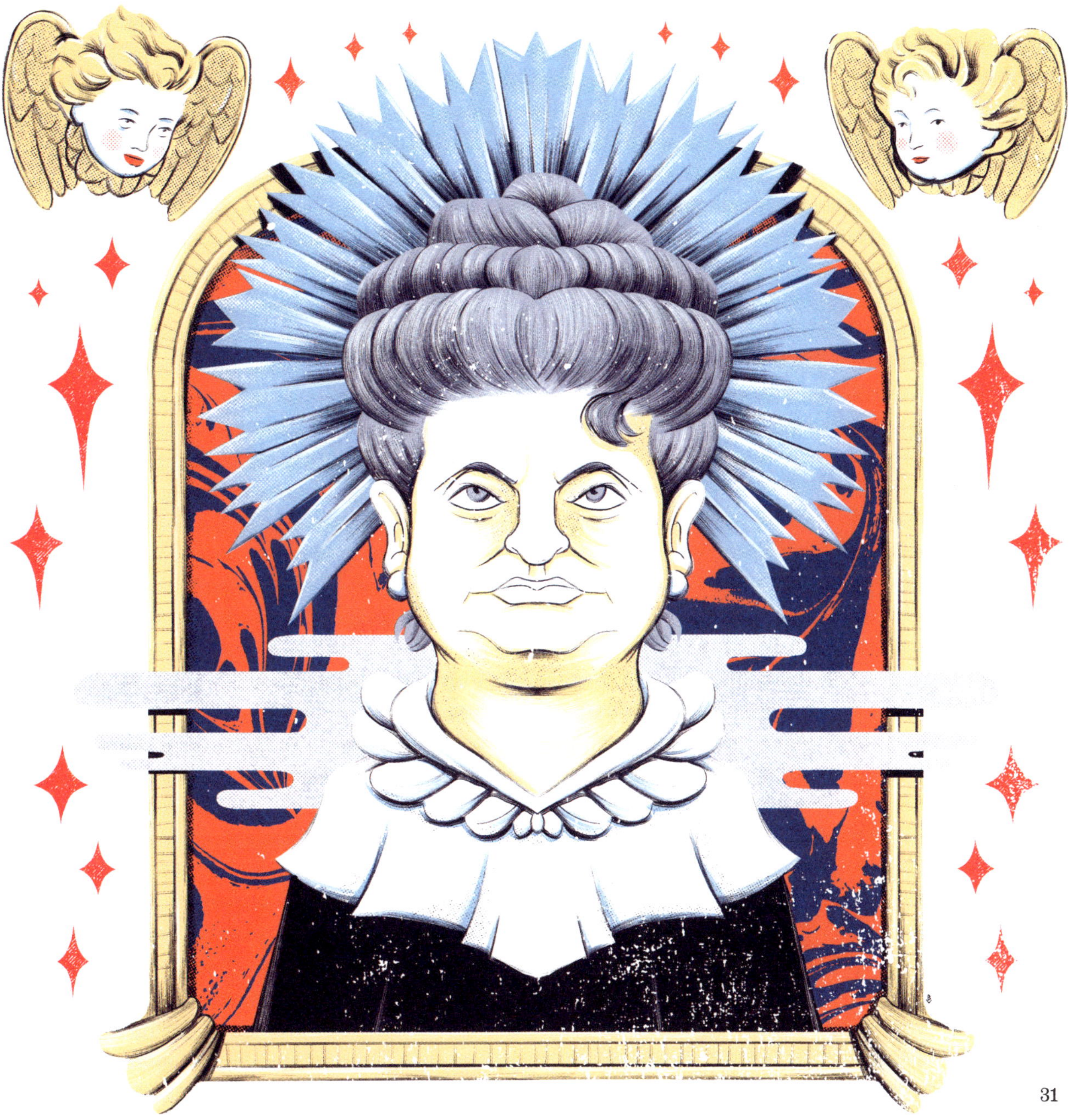

DESCUBRAN, CON LOS PELOS DE PUNTA, A...

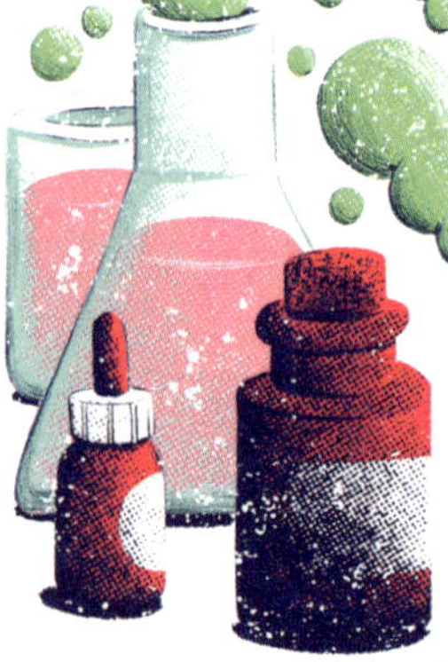

MARÍA TERESA TORAL

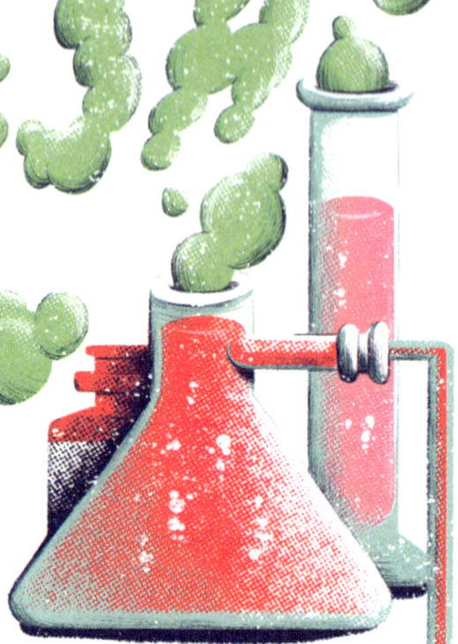

LA QUÍMICA ANTIFASCISTA

ERA EXTRAÑO ENCONTRAR a UNA MUJER ENTRE los SIGNOS del HELIO, el LITIO y el BERILIO. PERO el REPUTADO FÍSICO y QUÍMICO ENRIQUE MOLES QUERÍA a ESTA ALUMNA EXCEPCIONAL en su LABORATORIO. **MARÍA TERESA TORAL** (1911-1994) HABÍA ESTUDIADO FARMACIA y QUÍMICA. A LA VEZ. Y FUE PREMIO EXTRAORDINARIO.

En la ESCUELA de MADRID INVESTIGABAN JUNTOS el PESO ATÓMICO de los ELEMENTOS QUÍMICOS. Y ELLOS MISMOS CONSTRUÍAN el INSTRUMENTAL para que las MEDICIONES FUERAN EXACTAS. Los CIENTÍFICOS de TODO el MUNDO los MIRABAN con ADMIRACIÓN.

ERA 1936 y MARÍA TERESA ESTABA a PUNTO de MARCHAR al REINO UNIDO para AMPLIAR sus ESTUDIOS. PERO, de PRONTO, ¡BUM!, ESE VERANO se PRODUJO el ESTALLIDO MÁS FIERO de su VIDA. NO PROCEDÍA de UNA MOLÉCULA EXTRAVIADA en el LABORATORIO: ERA la GUERRA que DINAMITARÍA la CARRERA de ESTA RECONOCIDA CIENTÍFICA.

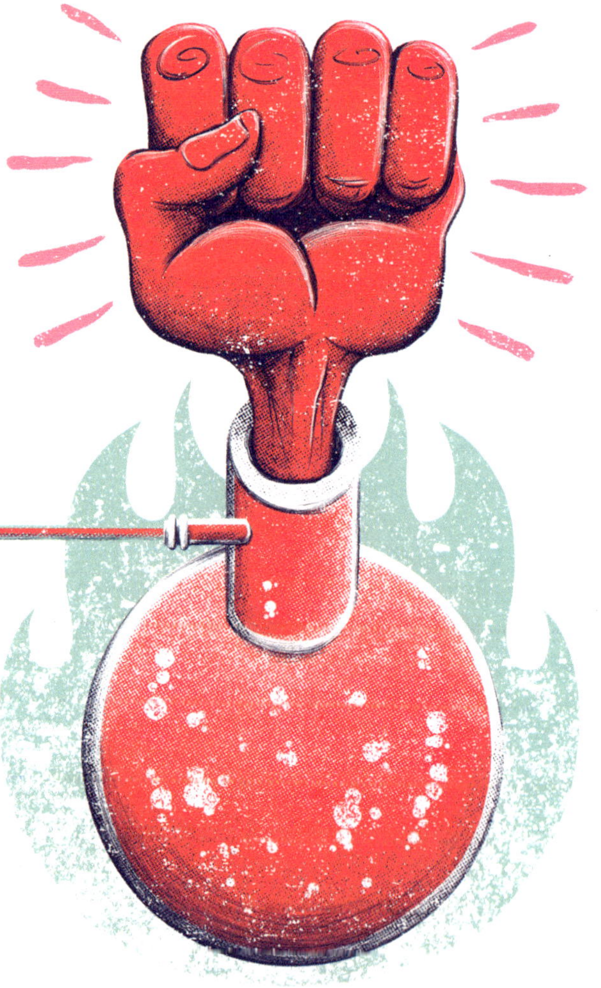

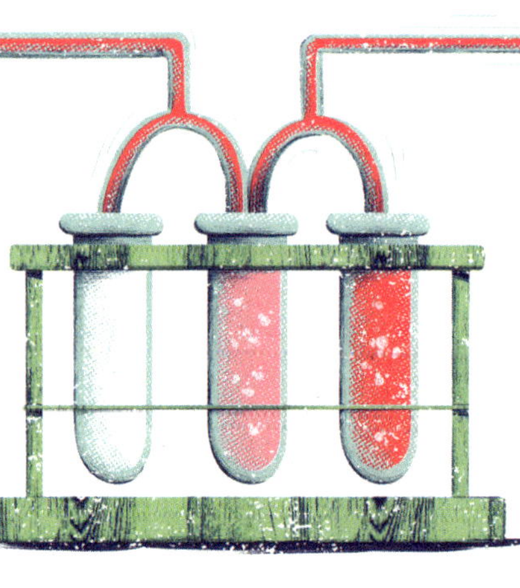

La JOVEN de VEINTICINCO AÑOS, HORRORIZADA por la AMENAZA FASCISTA, PASÓ de la INVESTIGACIÓN a la «FABRICACIÓN de MATERIAL de GUERRA». ESO DECÍA el EXPEDIENTE que en 1939 la LLEVÓ a la CÁRCEL. ALLÍ ORGANIZÓ UNA FARMACIA para CUIDAR a MILES de PRESAS HACINADAS y FALSIFICÓ FICHAS MÉDICAS para QUE las MADRES PUDIERAN ESTAR MÁS TIEMPO con SUS HIJOS.

La LIBERTAD CONDICIONAL TENÍA CASI TODAS las PUERTAS CERRADAS. TAN SOLO PUDO VOLVER a TRABAJAR en UNA FARMACIA que le CEDIÓ SU MADRE. PERO ENTONCES a MARÍA TERESA le IMPORTABA MÁS EXPLOSIONAR la DICTADURA que IMAGINAR CHISPITAS en TABLAS PERIÓDICAS. El LOCAL se CONVIRTIÓ en un CENTRO de DISIDENCIA y, un DÍA, SU AMOR GUERRILLERO la DELATÓ.

ENTRÓ de NUEVO en la CÁRCEL y ESTA VEZ QUISIERON FUSILARLA. PERIÓDICOS de TODO el MUNDO PEDÍAN su LIBERTAD. HASTA el «NEW YORK TIMES» SOLICITÓ a FRANCO que NO EJECUTARA a «la LISE MEITNER de ESPAÑA». Al JUICIO ACUDIÓ IRENE JOLIOT-CURIE, HIJA de MARIE CURIE y PREMIO NOBEL de QUÍMICA, para EVITAR SU MUERTE.

Lo CONSIGUIERON, y MARÍA TERESA se EXILIÓ a MÉXICO. ALLÍ se DEDICÓ a ENSEÑAR QUÍMICA y a HACER GRABADOS que DENUNCIABAN el SUFRIMIENTO.

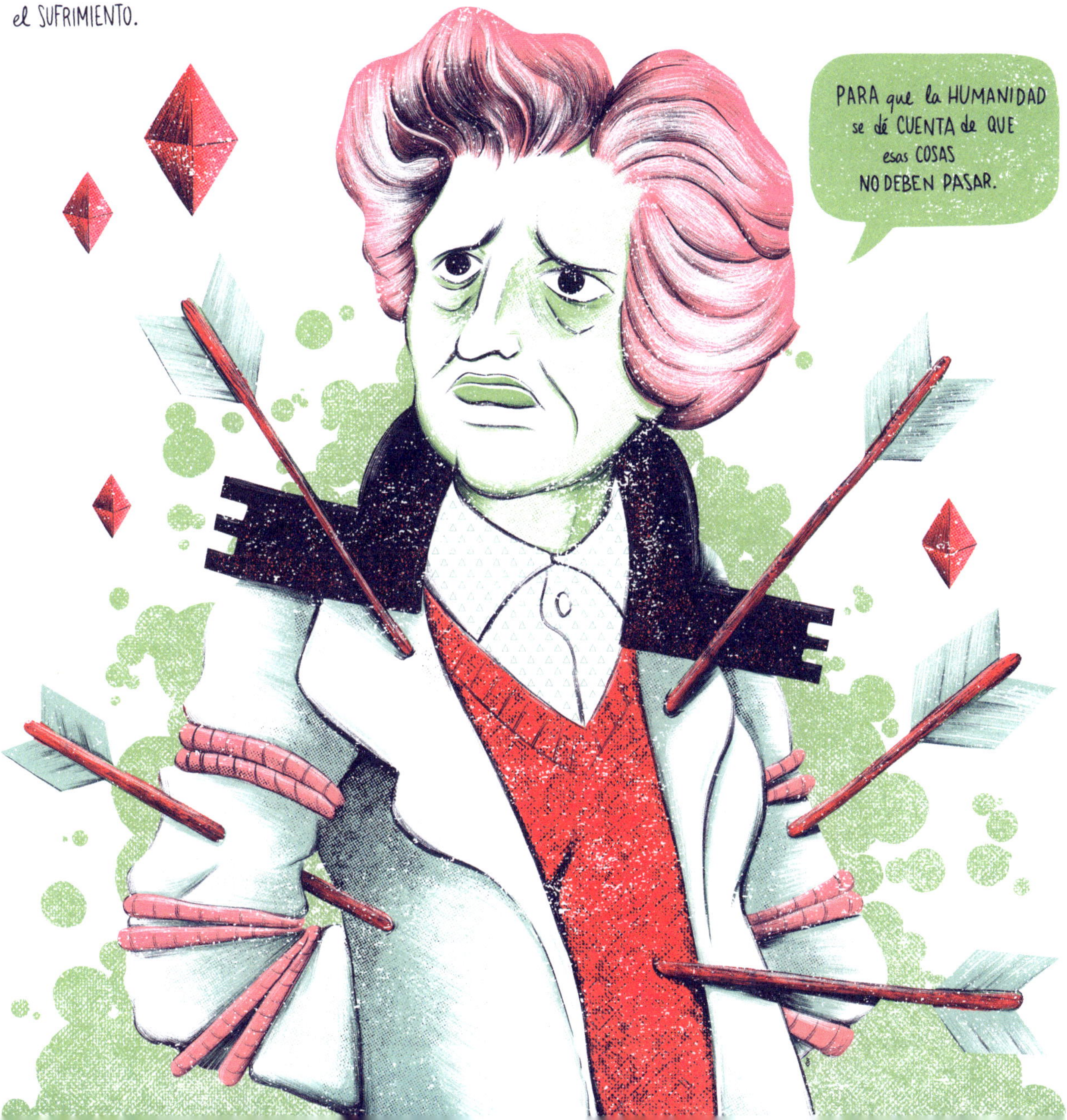

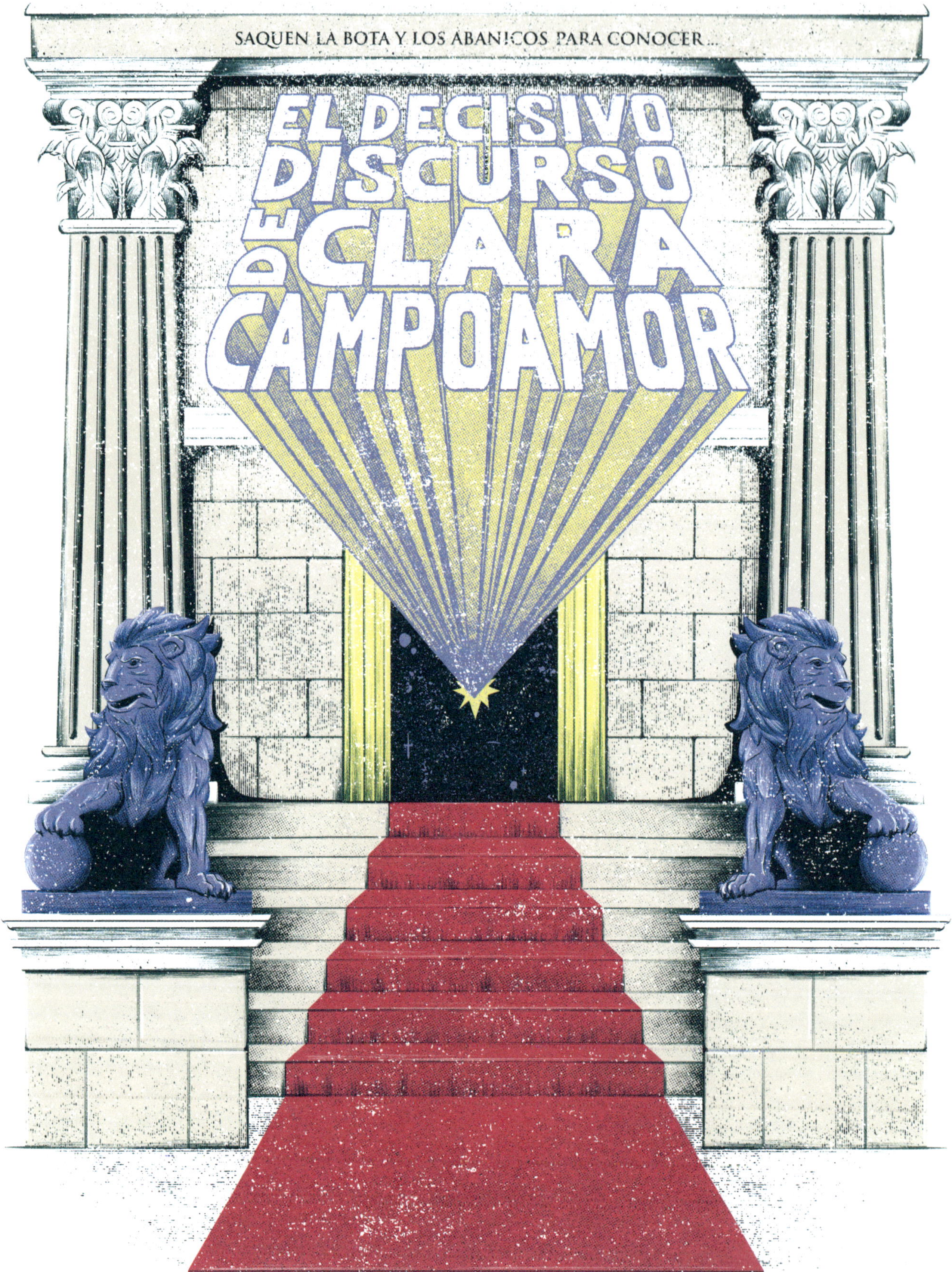
SAQUEN LA BOTA Y LOS ABANICOS PARA CONOCER...
EL DECISIVO
DISCURSO
DE CLARA
CAMPOAMOR

LA «NIÑA BONITA» ABRIÓ las PUERTAS del PARLAMENTO a las MUJERES. La SEGUNDA REPÚBLICA ROMPIÓ el CANDADO PUESTO a las DAMAS en los ASUNTOS de GOBIERNO y, por PRIMERA VEZ, los LEONES del CONGRESO DABAN los BUENOS DÍAS a DOS ABOGADAS: CLARA CAMPOAMOR y VICTORIA KENT.

PERO HABÍA ALGO DESCONCERTANTE que NO ENCAJABA con el ESPÍRITU DEMOCRÁTICO de la ESPERADA, la BONITA, la FLAMANTE REPÚBLICA que TANTO CIVISMO IBA a TRAER: Las MUJERES PODÍAN SER VOTADAS PERO NO PODÍAN VOTAR.

HACÍA AÑOS que el DEBATE SOBRE el SUFRAGIO FEMENINO DABA ZARPAZOS por los PERIÓDICOS, por las TRIBUNAS, por MANIFIESTOS... Y al FIN, el 1 de OCTUBRE de 1931, LLEGÓ al EPICENTRO del HEMICICLO.

LA MAÑANA AMANECIÓ NERVIOSA. LOS SEÑORES DIPUTADOS TENÍAN que DAR el SÍ o el NO a UNA ENMIENDA de LEY que DICTABA que los CIUDADANOS de AMBOS SEXOS MAYORES de VEINTITRÉS AÑOS TENÍAN IDÉNTICOS DERECHOS ELECTORALES.

La DECISIÓN ESTABA en MANOS de 470 HOMBRES y SOLO 2 MUJERES: KENT, en CONTRA, y CAMPOAMOR, a FAVOR.

FUE NOTA MUY COMENTADA que MUCHAS DAMAS, a las PUERTAS de la CÁMARA, REPARTIERON a los DIPUTADOS UNAS HOJAS que DECÍAN: «SEÑORES DIPUTADOS: NO MANCHEN USTEDES la CONSTITUCIÓN ESTABLECIENDO en ELLA PRIVILEGIOS. QUEREMOS la IGUALDAD de los DERECHOS ELECTORALES. ¡VIVA la REPÚBLICA!».

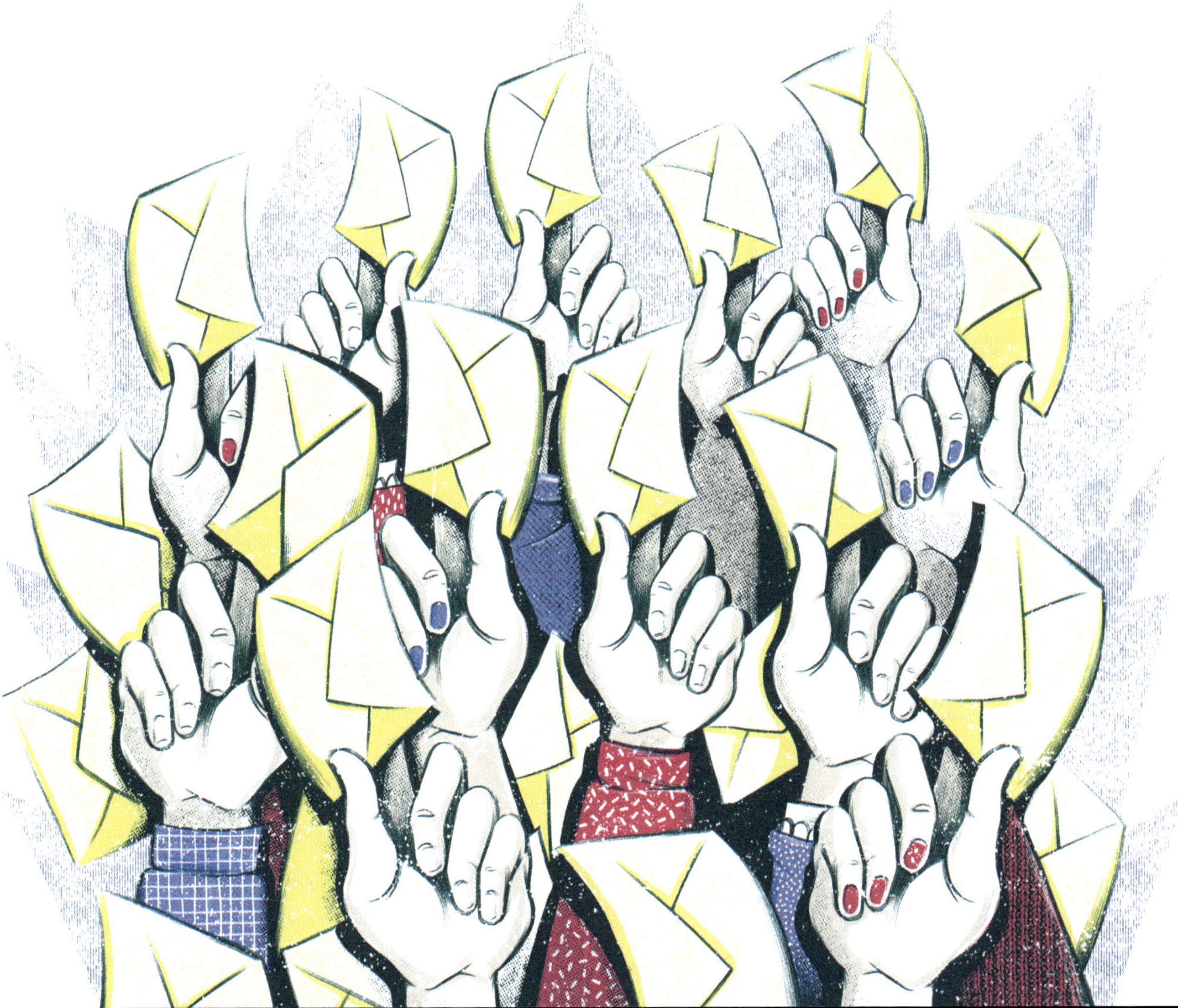

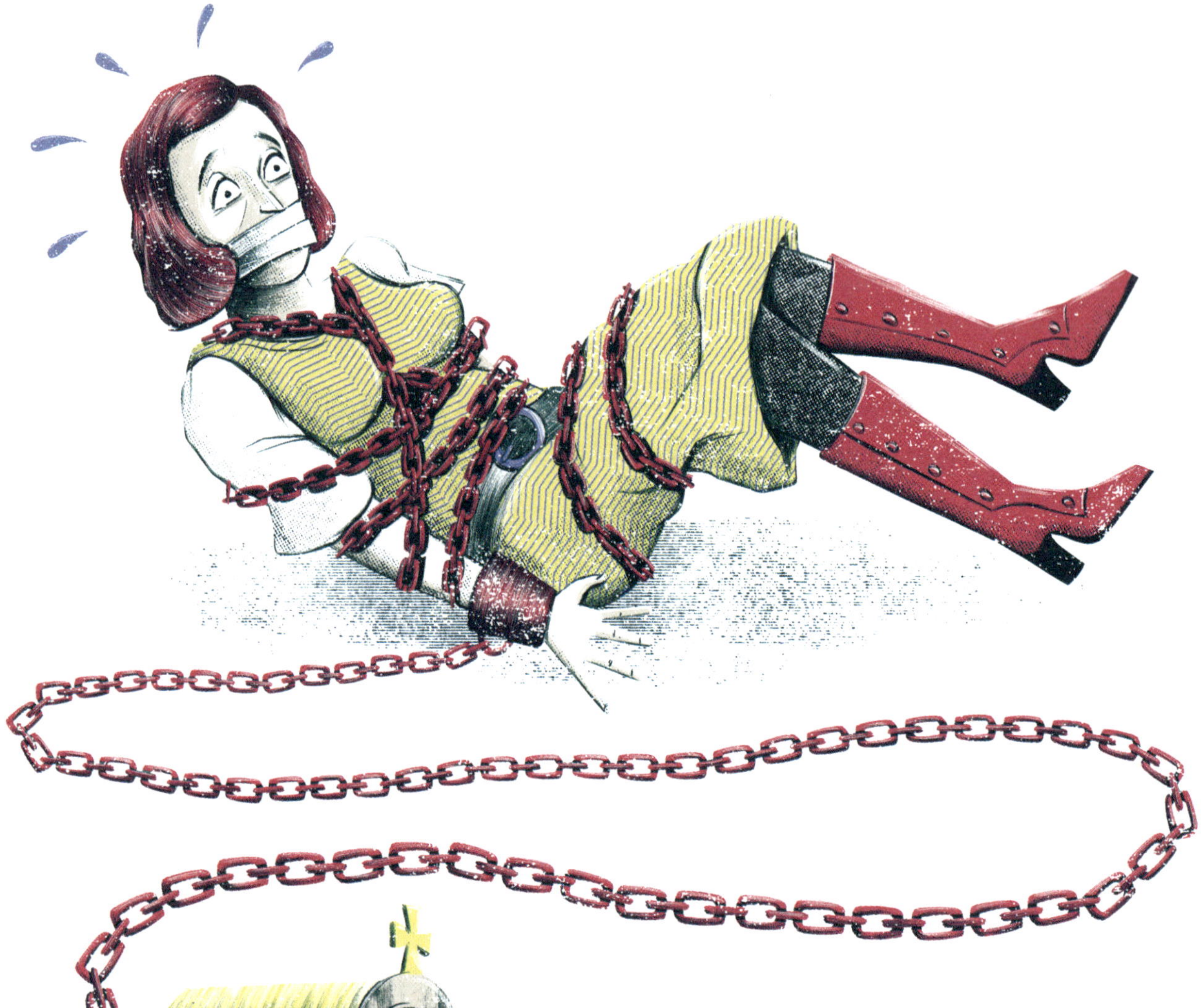

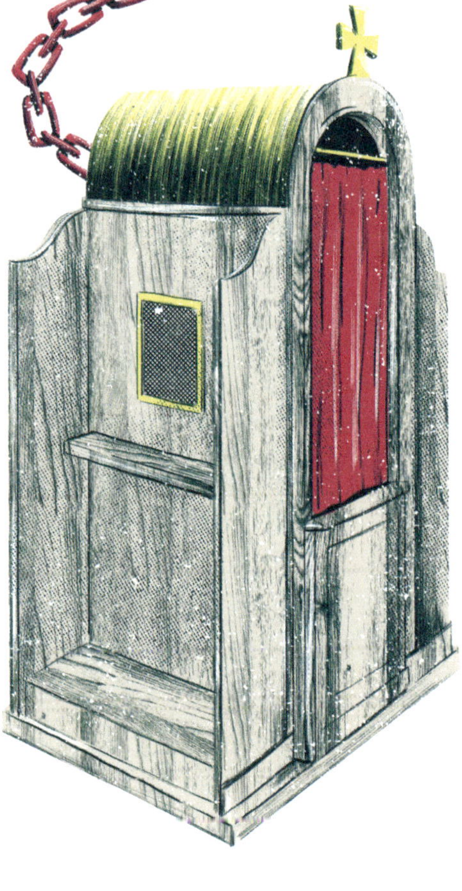

TRANSITABA la MAÑANA, PALPITANTE, ENTRE DISCURSOS, INTRIGAS, CAMBIOS de OPINIÓN...

«LA MUJER NO PUEDE VOTAR PORQUE es UNA CRIATURA ESENCIALMENTE HISTÉRICA y SUMISA –CLAMABAN ALGUNOS IMPERTINENTES–. QUIZÁ a PARTIR de los CUARENTA y CINCO AÑOS, la EDAD CRÍTICA, YA TENDRÁ la SUFICIENTE SERENIDAD de ESPÍRITU para PODER EJERCER ESTE DERECHO.»

«¡LA MUJER DEBERÍA VOTAR CUANDO ESTÉ EMANCIPADA de los CONFESIONARIOS!», PEDÍAN OTROS.

La DIPUTADA del PARTIDO RADICAL CLARA CAMPOAMOR SE LEVANTÓ de su ASIENTO. HABLÓ y REBATIÓ a TODOS. A los que ACUSABAN a las MUJERES de ANALFABETAS. A los que las DESPRECIABAN COMO MERAS MARIONETAS de sus INSTINTOS y a los que LES ATRIBUÍAN una SUPUESTA INFERIORIDAD BIOLÓGICA.

«NO COMETÁIS un ERROR HISTÓRICO que NO TENDRÉIS NUNCA BASTANTE TIEMPO para LLORAR; que NO TENDRÉIS NUNCA BASTANTE TIEMPO PARA LLORAR al DEJAR al MARGEN de la REPÚBLICA a la MUJER, que REPRESENTA a UNA FUERZA NUEVA, una FUERZA JOVEN», ALENTÓ la ABOGADA.

LOS DIPUTADOS EMITIERON su VOTO. ENTRE TANTO REVUELO, TANTA CONFUSIÓN ENTRE IDEALISMO y PRAGMATISMO, NADIE SABÍA QUIÉN VOTARÍA QUÉ. Y ENTONCES, de PRONTO, el ACONTECER de TODO AQUEL DÍA se CONCENTRÓ en DOS FRASES PRONUNCIADAS por UNA VOZ MASCULINA:

«PUESTA a VOTACIÓN la ENMIENDA, HA SIDO APROBADA por 161 VOTOS a FAVOR FRENTE a 121 en CONTRA.
LAS MUJERES, por TANTO, TIENEN el VOTO».

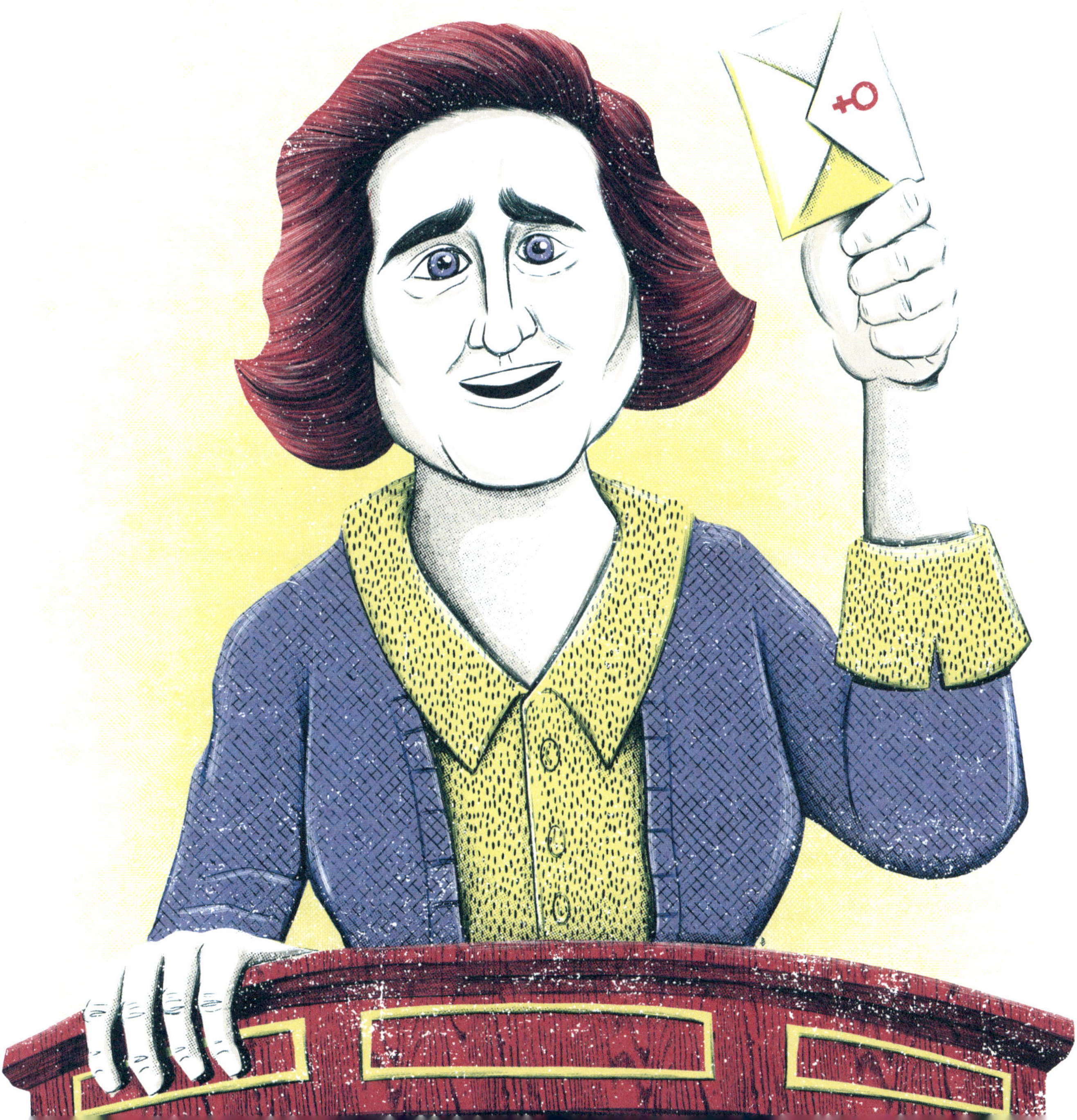

DEJEN CORRER SUS LÁGRIMAS ANTE LA HORRIBLE PÉRDIDA DE...

AUGUSTO DE FIGUEROA

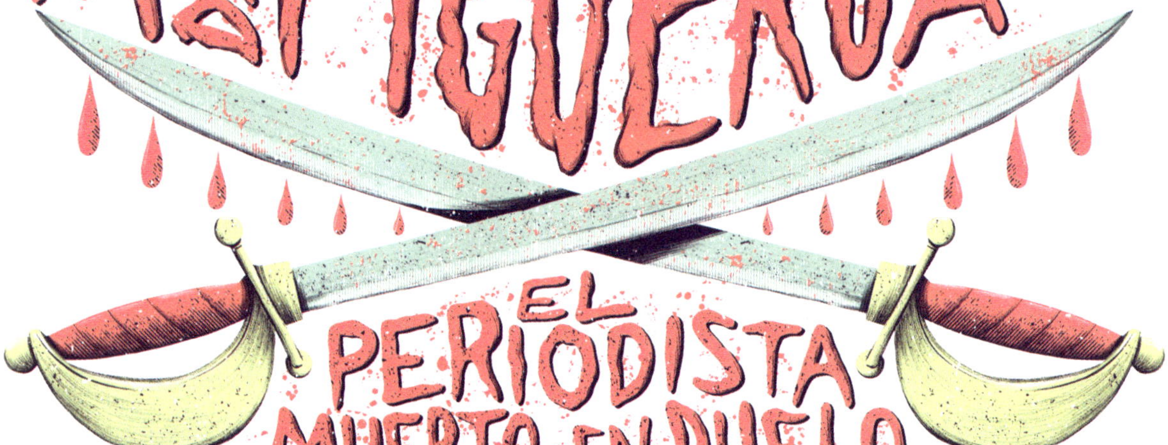

EL PERIODISTA MUERTO EN DUELO

EL 1 de ENERO de 1904 DOS HOMBRES ESTÁN CITADOS en MÁLAGA. ACUDEN con SUS ESPADAS. VAN a TRATAR un ASUNTO de HONOR.

EL HIJO del GENERAL MANUEL SALAMANCA HA RETADO en DUELO al REPUTADO PERIODISTA AUGUSTO SUÁREZ de FIGUEROA. QUIERE RESTABLECER el HONOR de SU PADRE a ESPADAZOS. EN ESTOS DÍAS de PRINCIPIOS del XX AÚN es COMÚN DEJAR la RAZÓN a UN LADO y RESOLVER las DISPUTAS desde el HÍGADO.

EL HOMBRE que RETA NO PERDONA a FIGUEROA. NO OLVIDA que el PERIODISTA PUBLICÓ en «EL HERALDO» que SU PADRE FUE un DESASTRE COMO GOBERNADOR de CUBA en 1890.

LLEGA la HORA.

SACAN las ESPADAS.

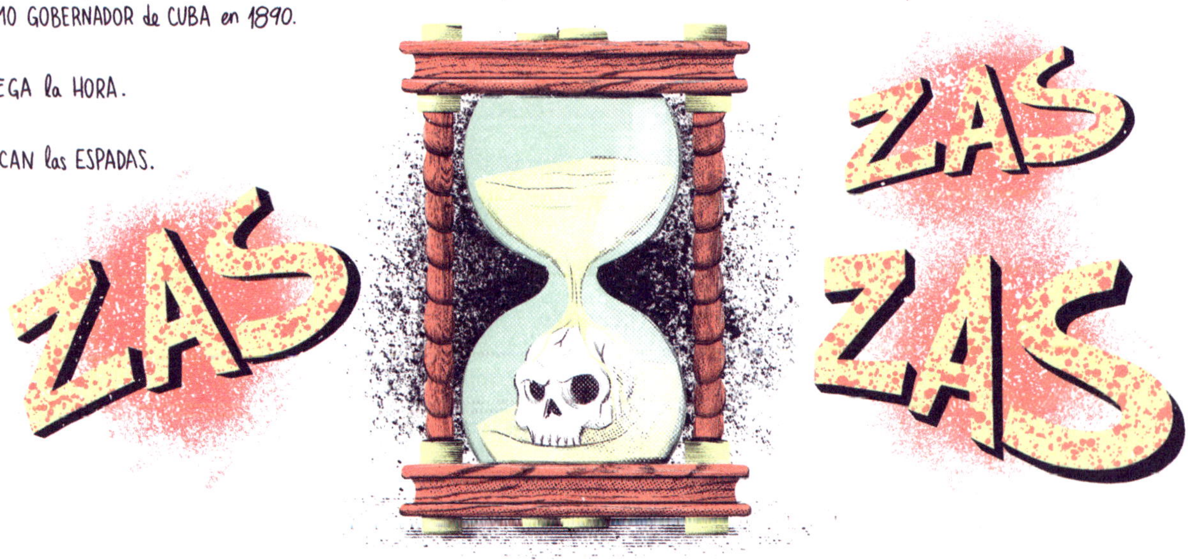

FIGUEROA, el ESGRIMIDOR de IDEAS, ACABA TIRADO en el SUELO. SE ESTÁ DESANGRANDO. MUCHO. LAS HERIDAS SON PROFUNDAS. VENDAS y MÁS VENDAS. NO HAY NADA que HACER. El GRAN BATALLADOR de IDEAS MUERE.

LLORA la PRENSA al DÍA SIGUIENTE.

«El de HOY es DÍA de LUTO para el PERIODISMO ESPAÑOL, que PIERDE, al MORIR AUGUSTO SUÁREZ de FIGUEROA, un ESCRITOR ILUSTRE, VERDADERO MAESTRO en el ÁSPERO, INGRATO y DESGASTADOR OFICIO de ESCRIBIR ESTAS HOJAS», DICE «El HERALDO».

NI UN DIARIO INFORMA del DUELO. ACASO CUELAN UNA ALUSIÓN a lo que NADIE CUENTA. DESCRIBEN el DOLOR COMO «DUELO» SIN CITAR que UN «DUELO» lo MATÓ. DICEN, APENADOS, que el HOMBRE «SE HA ROTO COMO UNA NOBLE ESPADA de TOLEDO».

A los CINCUENTA y CINCO AÑOS, MUERE ESTE ROMÁNTICO del PERIODISMO. «AÚN CUANDO PODÍA ENSEÑAR a los que NECESITAMOS de LECCIONES —CLAMA "El HERALDO"—, CUANDO AÚN PODÍA SER ÚTIL a su PATRIA, PRODIGÁNDOLE ADVERTENCIAS, SUGIRIÉNDOLE OPINIONES, INFUNDIÉNDOLE ÁNIMOS en HORAS de PELIGRO, en MOMENTOS de DESMAYO.»

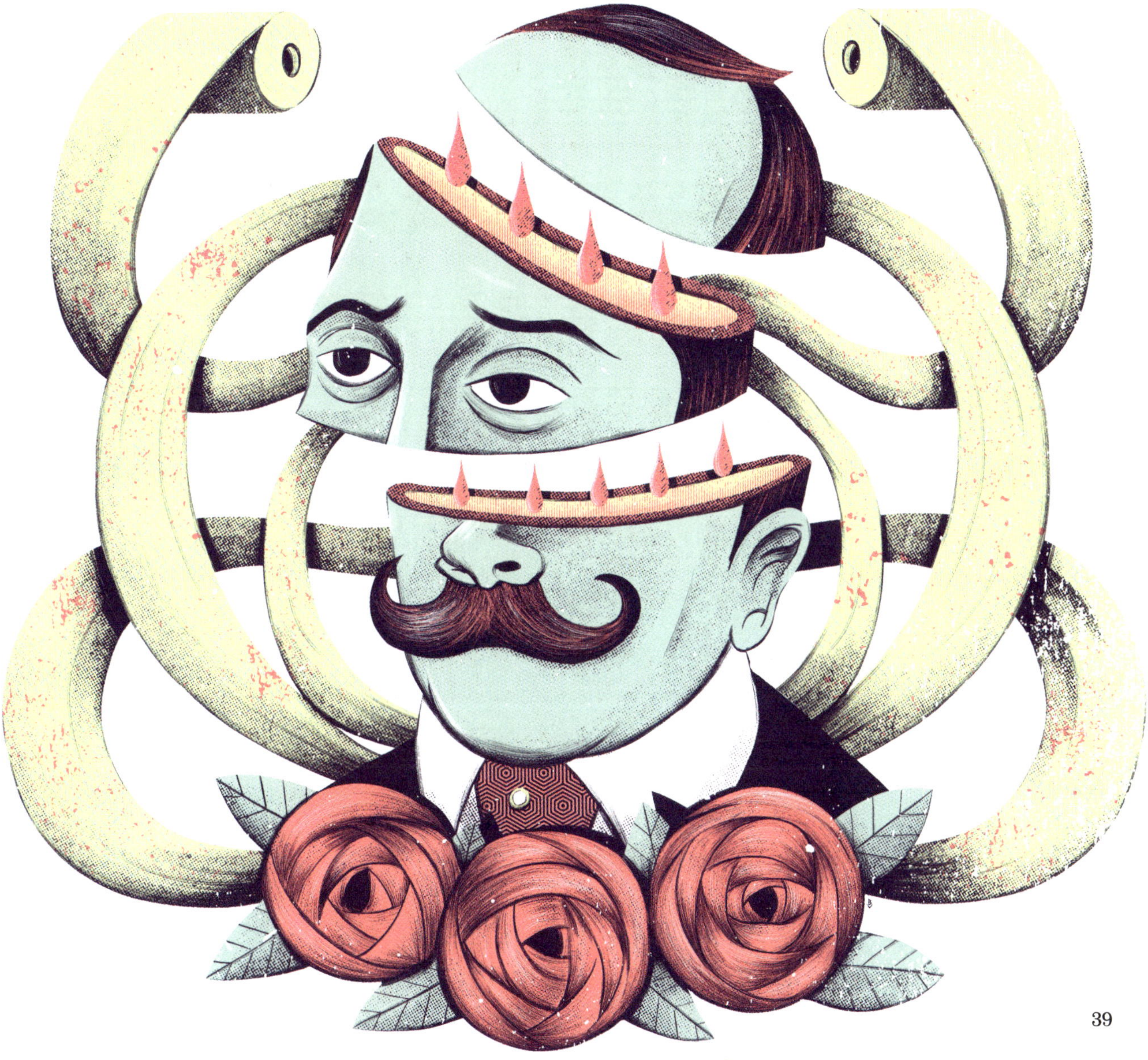

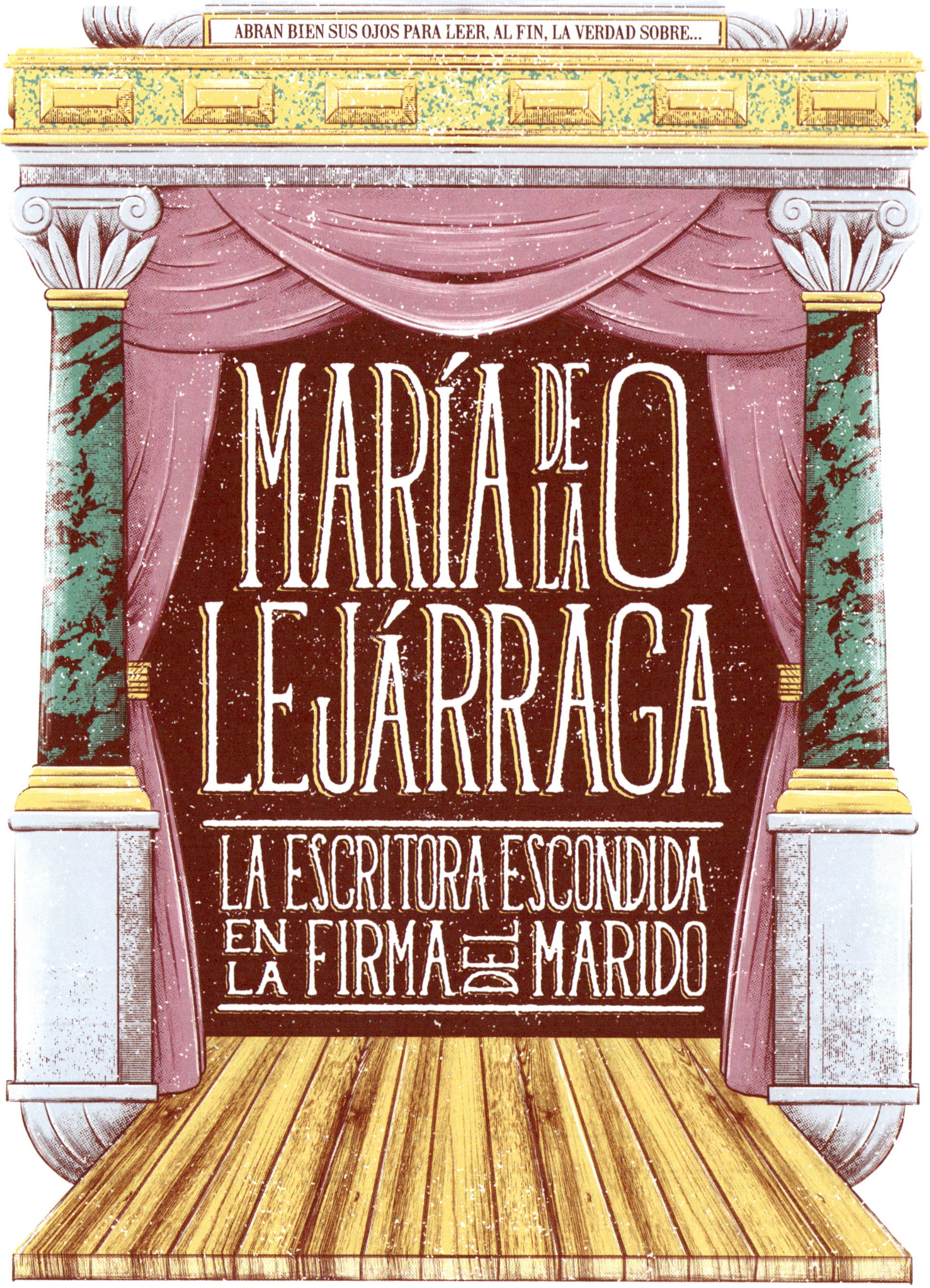
ABRAN BIEN SUS OJOS PARA LEER, AL FIN, LA VERDAD SOBRE...
MARÍA DE LA O
LEJÁRRAGA
LA ESCRITORA ESCONDIDA
EN LA FIRMA DEL MARIDO

Ella ERA el GENIO ETÉREO.

Él, la GLORIA CORPÓREA.

MARÍA de la O LEJÁRRAGA ESCRIBÍA las OBRAS de TEATRO.

GREGORIO MARTÍNEZ SIERRA FIRMABA y RECIBÍA el APLAUSO.

ESTA INJUSTICIA SE ORIGINÓ en UN DISGUSTO. EN 1899, ESTA MAESTRA de INGLÉS, CULTA y MODERNA, PUBLICÓ «CUENTOS BREVES». A la CRÍTICA le PARECIÓ un ACIERTO, pero a SU FAMILIA NO le GUSTÓ. UNA MUJER NO DEBÍA EXPONERSE ASÍ, CON ESA FRESCURA, en la PORTADA de UN LIBRO.

Al AÑO SIGUIENTE, MARÍA (1874-1974) SE CASÓ CON UN JOVEN SEIS AÑOS MENOR. NO ERA TAN BRILLANTE COMO ELLA (NI SIQUIERA ACABÓ SUS ESTUDIOS), PERO el AMOR que SENTÍAN por el TEATRO los LLEVÓ al AMOR del COLCHÓN.

A las CINCO de la MAÑANA, TODOS los DÍAS, SONABA el RELOJ. MARÍA PREPARABA las CLASES y LIMPIABA la CASA. A las OCHO IBA al COLEGIO y VOLVÍA a las DOCE a COCINAR para los DOS. A las CUATRO, de NUEVO a la ESCUELA, y, TRAS RECOGER la CENA, ESCRIBÍA las NOVELAS y LIBRETOS que GREGORIO FIRMABA DESPUÉS.

Ella ESCONDÍA SU AUTORÍA. NO QUERÍA DISGUSTAR a SUS PADRES. Y el ESPOSO, ENCANTADO: TODOS los ÉXITOS LLEVABAN SU NOMBRE, AUNQUE, en REALIDAD, SOLO ERA el DIRECTOR de ESCENA.

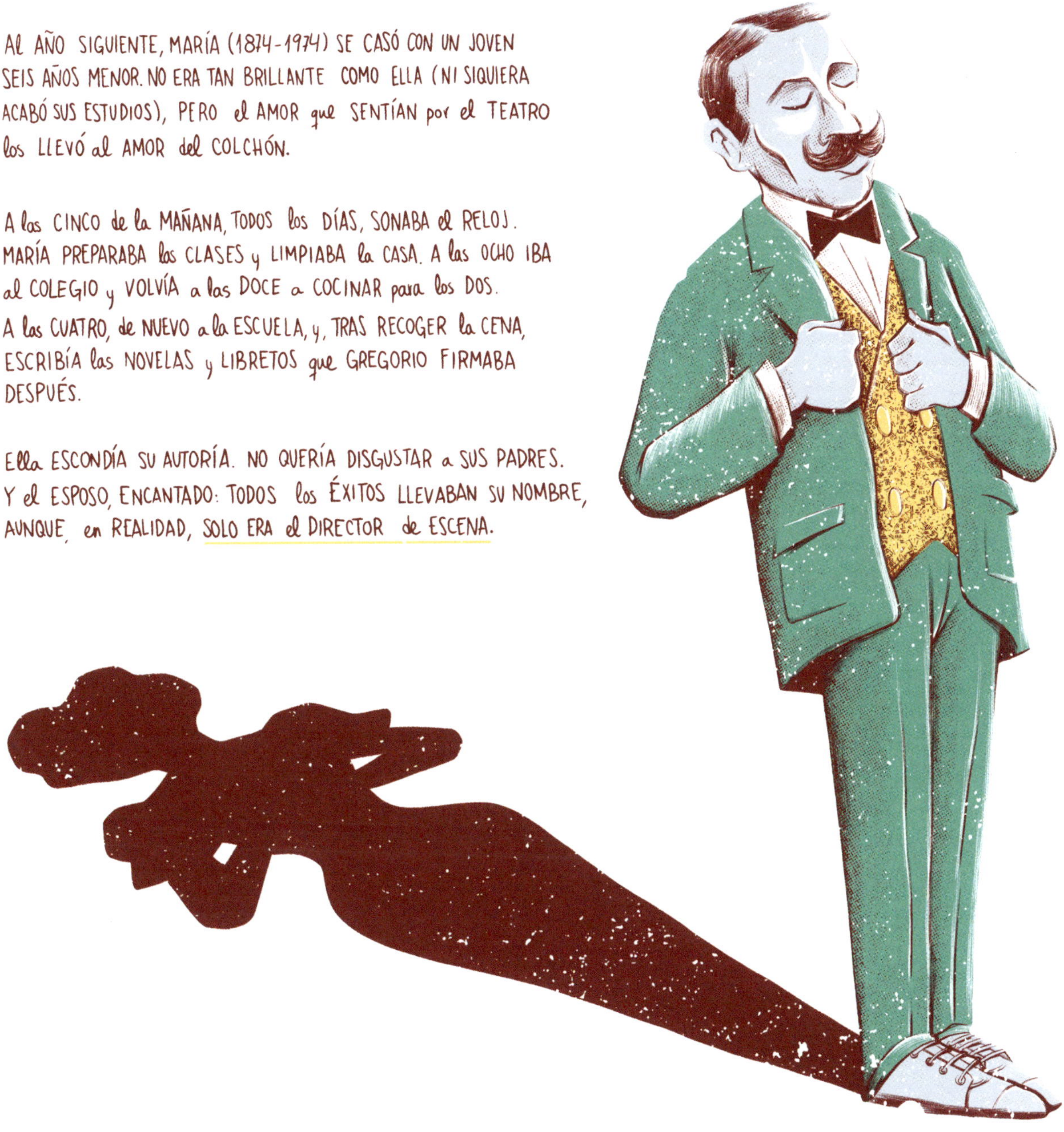

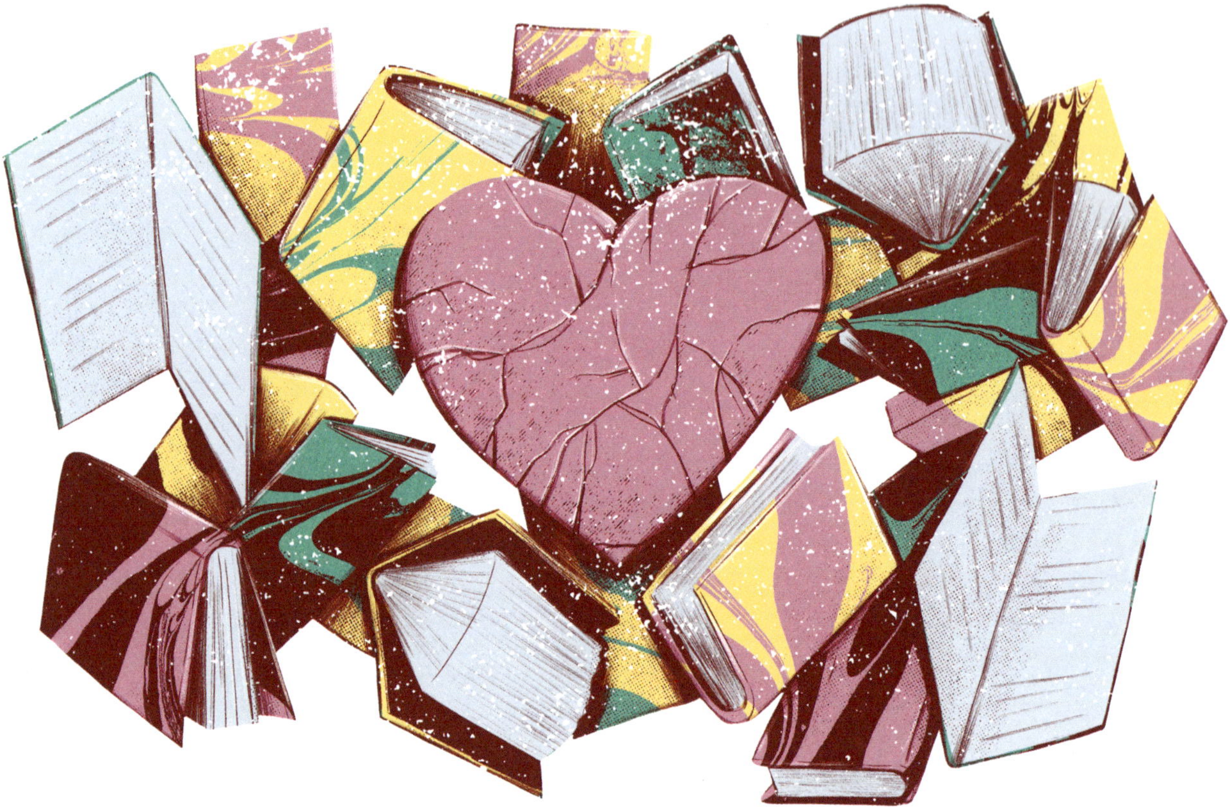

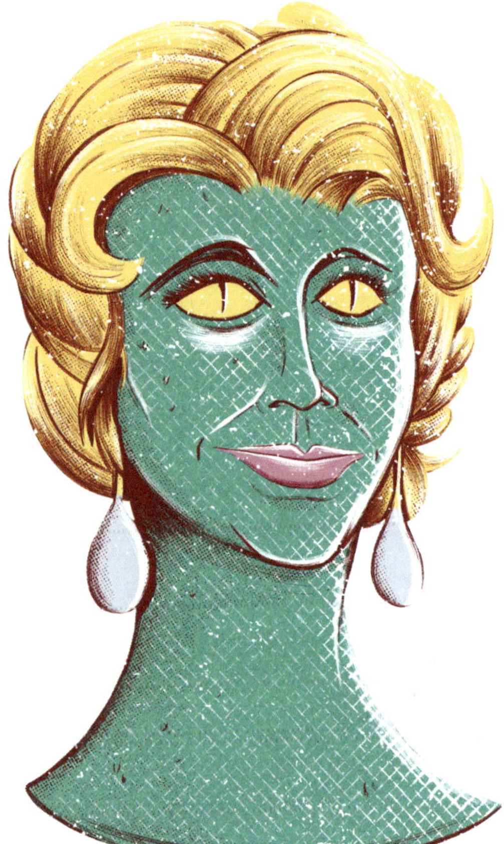

ENTRE NOVELAS y LIBRETOS, MARÍA SE VIO ENVUELTA en el GRAN DRAMA de su VIDA. Y ESTA VEZ NO SERÍA AUTORA, SINO PROTAGONISTA.

GREGORIO, el LITERATO IMPOSTOR, PRONTO HIZO de SU MATRIMONIO UNA IMPOSTURA. TODOS SABÍAN de SUS AMORÍOS CON la ACTRIZ PRINCIPAL de SU COMPAÑÍA de TEATRO, CATALINA BÁRCENA.

PASARON AÑOS en los que MARÍA ESCRIBÍA, GREGORIO DIRIGÍA y CATALINA RECIBÍA los APLAUSOS en el ESCENARIO. A VECES, en las OBRAS, AULLABA DOLORIDO el SILENCIO de la AUTORA: El DIRECTOR y la ACTRIZ SE VEÍAN REPRESENTANDO HISTORIAS SOBRE la DECEPCIÓN del AMOR y la PERFIDIA de UNA MUJER que ROMPE UN MATRIMONIO.

La GRAN MENTIRA HIZO que MARÍA EXPANDIERA SUS IDEAS FEMINISTAS en la VOZ de su ESPOSO. ÉL LEÍA y FIRMABA SUS «CARTAS a las MUJERES de ESPAÑA» COMO SI HUBIESEN SIDO PARIDAS de SUS PROPIAS ENTRAÑAS.

HASTA que, EN 1922, el TRIÁNGULO DRAMÁTICO ESTALLÓ por UN PARTO de VERDAD. CATALINA y GREGORIO TUVIERON una HIJA. MARÍA SE SEPARÓ. Y NI SIQUIERA ENTONCES DEJÓ de ESCRIBIR para la GLORIA del ADÚLTERO.

LA PROCLAMACIÓN de la SEGUNDA REPÚBLICA LLEVÓ a MARÍA a la POLÍTICA. EN 1933, a PUNTO de CUMPLIR los SESENTA AÑOS, FUE DIPUTADA en el CONGRESO. PERO la GUERRA la CONDENÓ al EXILIO.

HUYÓ a ARGENTINA CON SU SECRETO y AHÍ QUEDÓ GUARDADO HASTA que, al MORIR GREGORIO, SU HIJA RECLAMÓ los DERECHOS de AUTOR. A MARÍA, PAUPÉRRIMA, NO le QUEDÓ OTRA. PUBLICÓ UNAS MEMORIAS que DESCUBRÍAN el PASTEL.

«AHORA, ANCIANA y VIUDA, VÉOME OBLIGADA a PROCLAMAR MI MATERNIDAD para COBRAR MIS DERECHOS de AUTORA.»

LA IGNORARON. TODOS. INCLUSO los que SABÍAN la VERDAD.

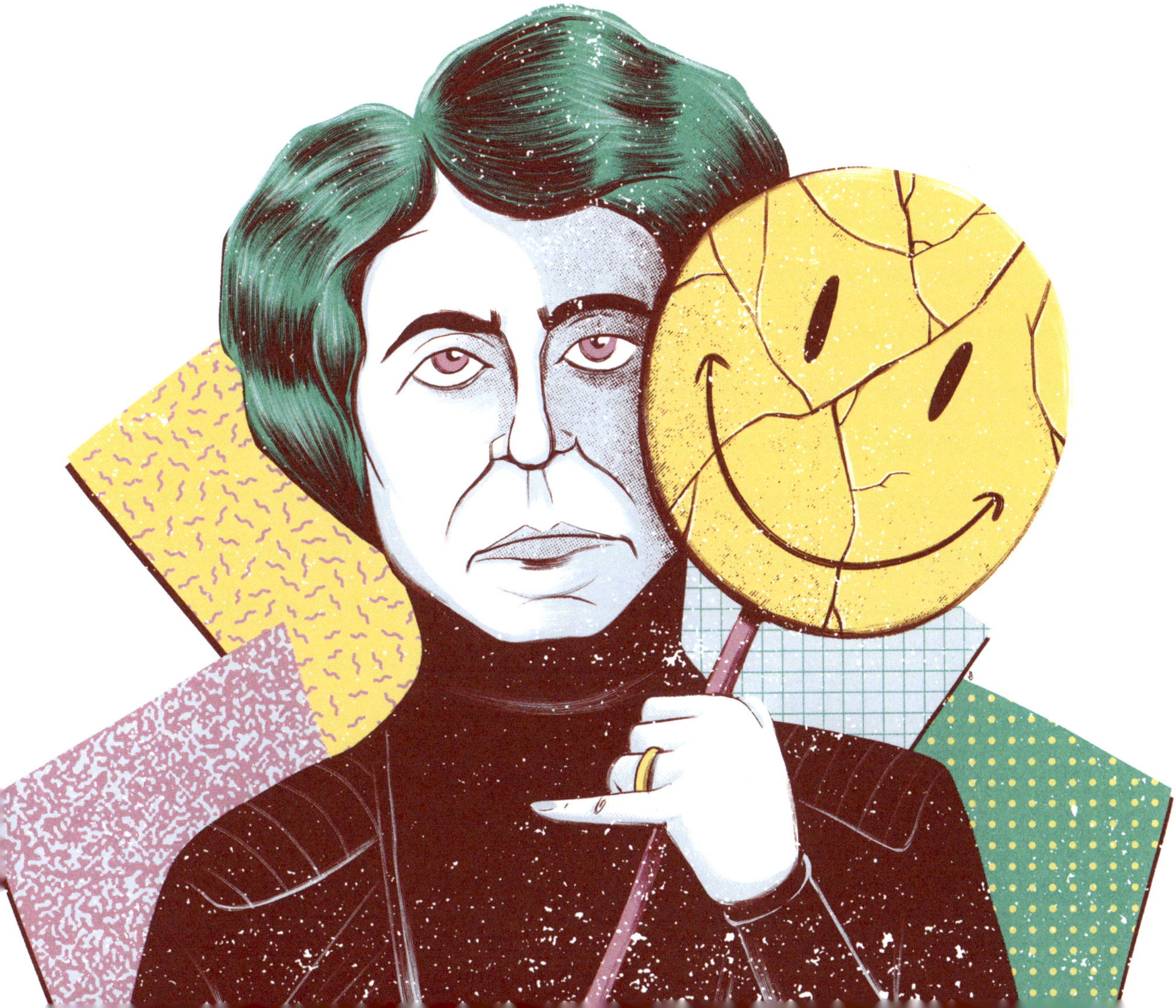

ASISTAN AL ESPECTÁCULO SANGRIENTO DEL CHUCHO MÁS ILUSTRE DE MADRID

EL PERRO PACO

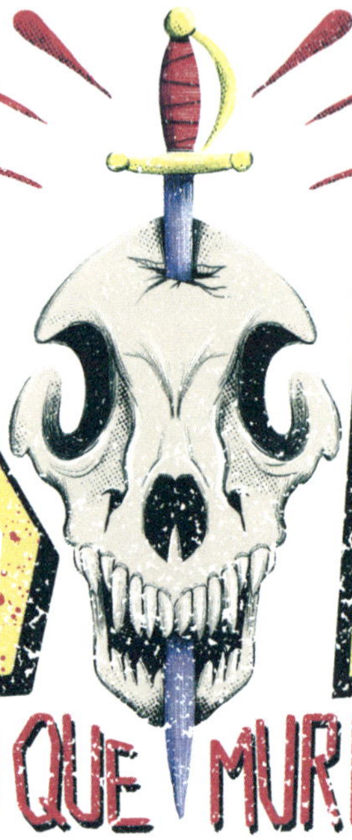

EL CRÍTICO TAURINO QUE MURIÓ DE UNA ESTOCADA

ERA el CAFÉ de FORNOS UNO de los LUGARES DISTINGUIDOS del MADRID del SIGLO XIX. A SUS PUERTAS QUEDABAN las CALLES POLVORIENTAS, LAS BOÑIGAS de los CABALLOS y los CHUCHOS CALLEJEROS.

PERO un DÍA de 1881 un PERRO LOGRÓ TRASPASAR el PORTÓN del LOCAL y se ACERCÓ a UNO de los COMENSALES. El MARQUÉS BOGARAYA le ECHÓ ALGO de SU PLATO y el PERRO, AGRADECIDO, DIO UNAS VOLTERETAS.

El NOBLE, ENTUSIASMADO, ORDENÓ al CAMARERO que a PARTIR de ENTONCES PUSIERA COMIDA a PACO TODOS los DÍAS. ASÍ BAUTIZÓ al CHUCHO, que en POCO TIEMPO ADOPTÓ la VIDA de un MARQUÉS. ACUDÍA al TEATRO, a CONCIERTOS y a los CLUBES MÁS EXCLUSIVOS.

TODOS le ABRÍAN la PUERTA. Y TANTO SE REFINÓ SU CULTURA que lo CONVIRTIERON en CRÍTICO de ESPECTÁCULOS. LOS PERIODISTAS ESCRIBÍAN la OPINIÓN del PERRO PACO DESPUÉS de CADA FUNCIÓN. La CONOCÍAN por SUS LADRIDOS y SUS GESTOS CANINOS.

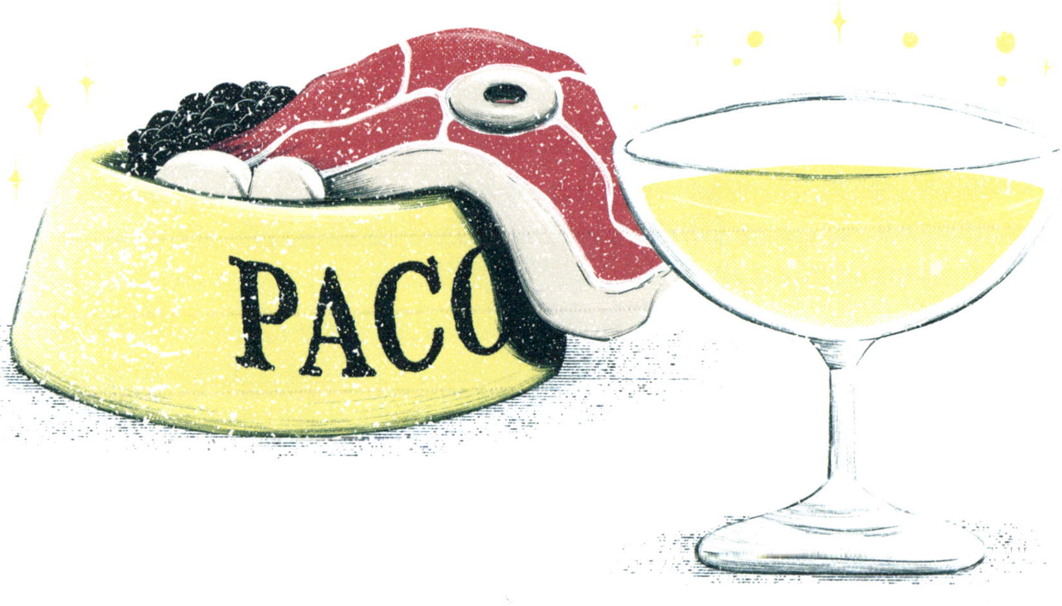

ERA «La FIGURA MÁS INTERESANTE de ESTA CORTE, el HÉROE FAVORITO de los MADRILEÑOS», SEGÚN el PERIÓDICO «El IMPARCIAL».

PRONTO SE AFICIONÓ a los TOROS. LOS REVISTEROS MÁS CÉLEBRES DECÍAN que su INSTINTO TAURINO ERA «INCREÍBLE» y en SUS CRÓNICAS COMENTABAN el JUICIO que el ANIMAL HACÍA de las CORRIDAS.

El 21 de JUNIO de 1882 FUE a VER TOREAR a PEPE el de los GALÁPAGOS. El NOVILLERO NO ESTUVO FINO y PACO, INDIGNADO, SALTÓ al RUEDO. El CRÍTICO TAURINO SE ENREDÓ con los PIES del MATADOR y lo HIZO CAER al SUELO. ENFADADO, el TORERO SE LEVANTÓ y le METIÓ UNA ESTOCADA al PERRO que lo DEJÓ CUAJADO.

El PÚBLICO SE LEVANTÓ en UNA MAREA de IRA y PEPE el de los GALÁPAGOS SALIÓ HUYENDO de la PLAZA para que NO lo LINCHARAN. SEIS DÍAS DESPUÉS MURIÓ el PERRO PACO y en UN PERIÓDICO ESCRIBIERON:

«PACO DEJA un VACÍO DIFÍCIL de LLENAR COMO FUNDADOR de la CLASE de BOHEMIOS de la RAZA CANINA. ACOMPAÑAMOS a SUS ADMIRADORES en SU JUSTO DOLOR y PEDIMOS un CASTIGO para el ASESINO».

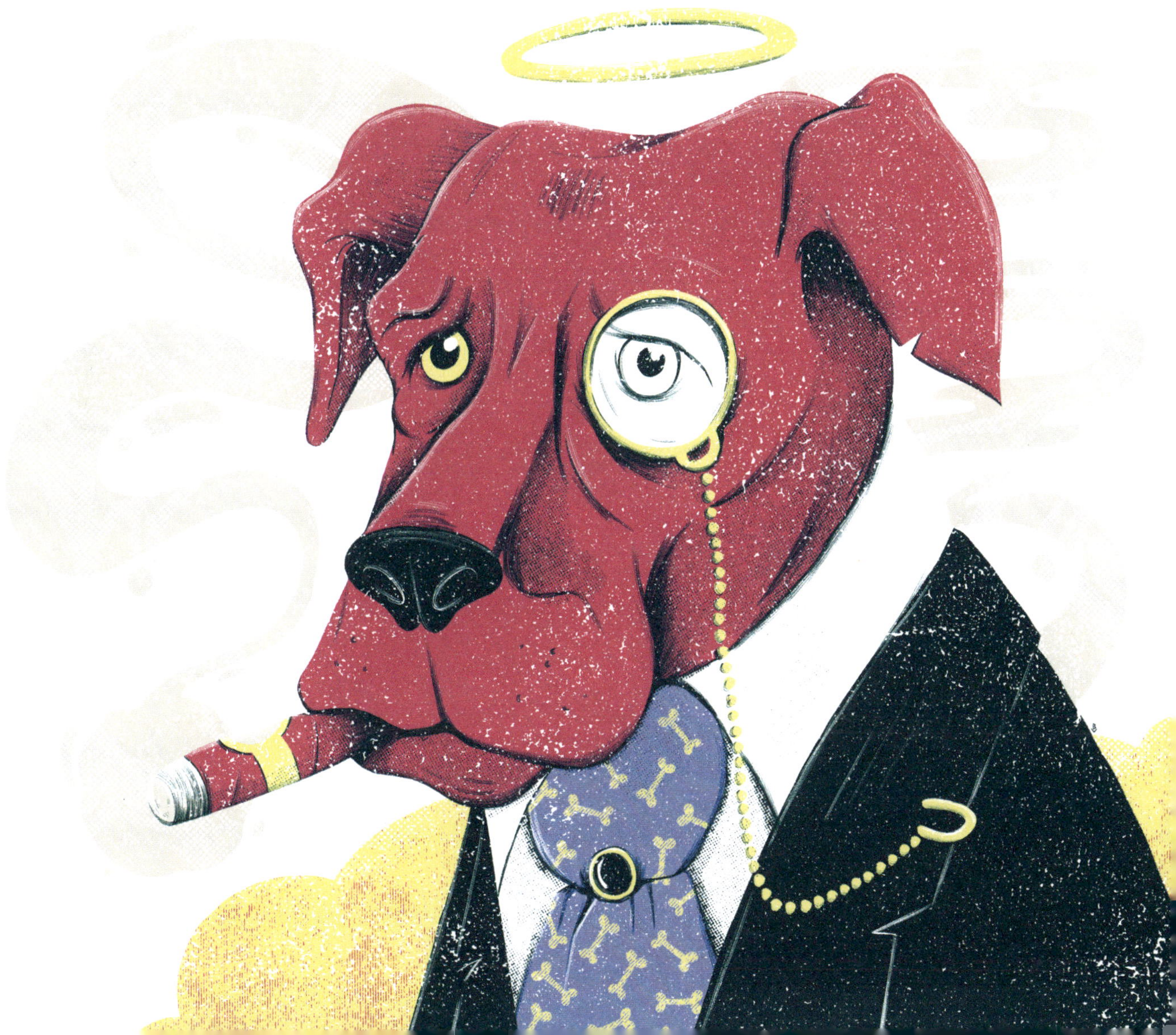

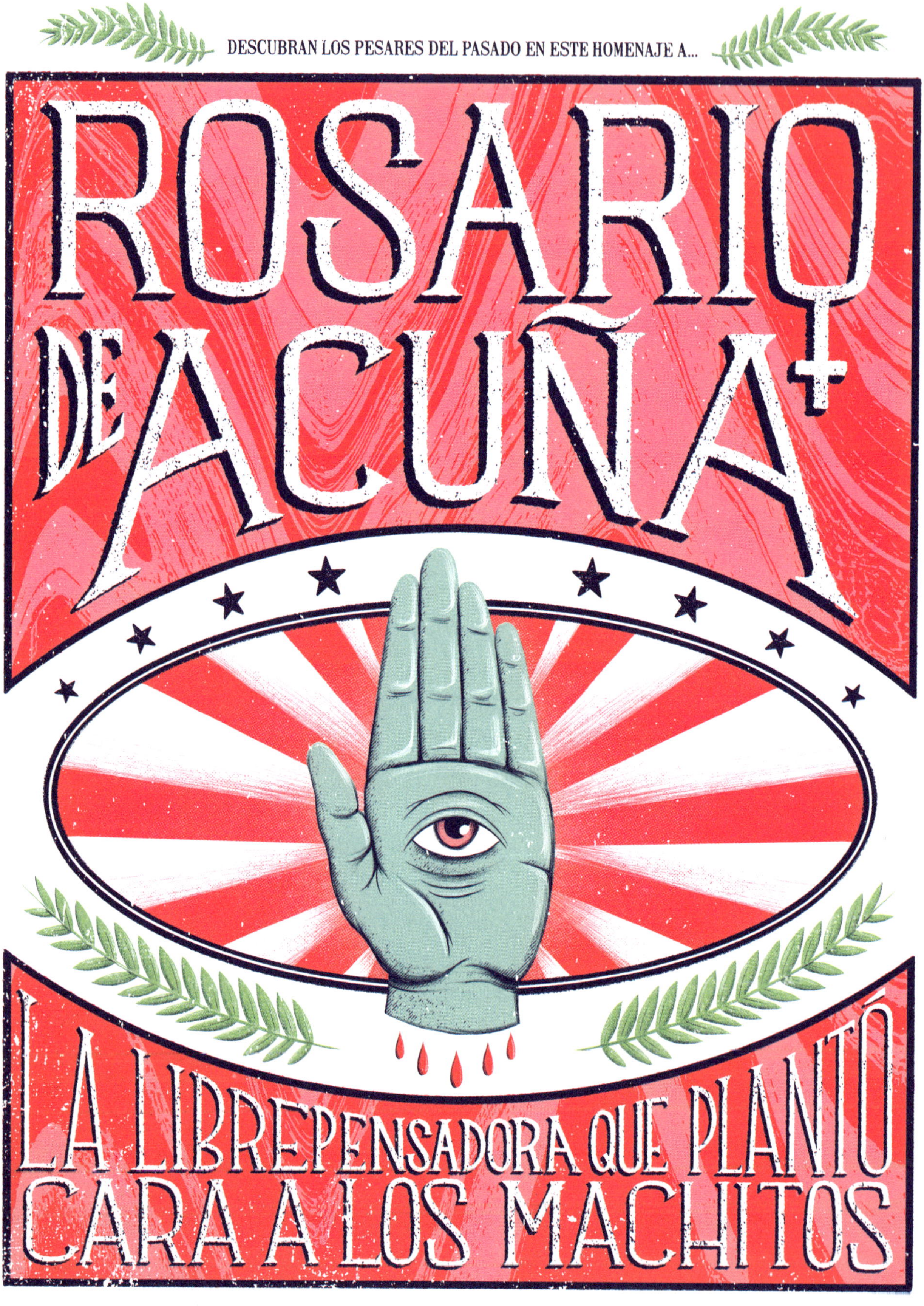
DESCUBRAN LOS PESARES DEL PASADO EN ESTE HOMENAJE A...
ROSARIO DE ACUÑA
LA LIBREPENSADORA QUE PLANTÓ CARA A LOS MACHITOS

NACIÓ BURGUESA. DAMA ESPAÑOLA con CUATROCIENTOS AÑOS de ASCENDENCIA de REINAS, OBISPOS, CONQUISTADORES y SANTOS, SEGÚN EXPLICABA ELLA MISMA. PERO ANTES de CUMPLIR los CUARENTA RENUNCIÓ a SUS ORÍGENES: A ESE GRUPO SELECTO de la ARISTOCRACIA, la MONARQUÍA y la IGLESIA.

ROSARIO de ACUÑA (1851-1923) ABOMINABA de la SUPERSTICIÓN y, en SUS ARTÍCULOS y CONFERENCIAS, PROMOVÍA la CIENCIA, la EDUCACIÓN y el PROGRESO. En 1884 se PROCLAMÓ LIBREPENSADORA y DOS AÑOS DESPUÉS INGRESÓ en la MASONERÍA.

FUE una AFAMADA DRAMATURGA, una EMPRESARIA PREMIADA, una EXITOSA PERIODISTA, una MONTAÑERA INSÓLITA, una PIONERA del FEMINISMO y, ANTE TODO, una VALIENTE. MUY VALIENTE. MUCHO MÁS de lo que AQUELLA SOCIEDAD PODÍA SOPORTAR.

UN DÍA de OTOÑO de 1911 VARIOS UNIVERSITARIOS ATACARON a una ESTUDIANTE. «LA RODEARON, VEJÁNDOLA con un VOCABULARIO de BURDEL e INTENTANDO OFENDERLA de OBRA», CONTÓ el «HERALDO de MADRID». POR FORTUNA, PASABA un ARRIERO con su CARRO y, a CODAZOS y EMPUJONES, se METIÓ en el CORRO de DESVERGONZADOS para LIBRAR a la MUCHACHA de AQUELLAS INDECENCIAS.

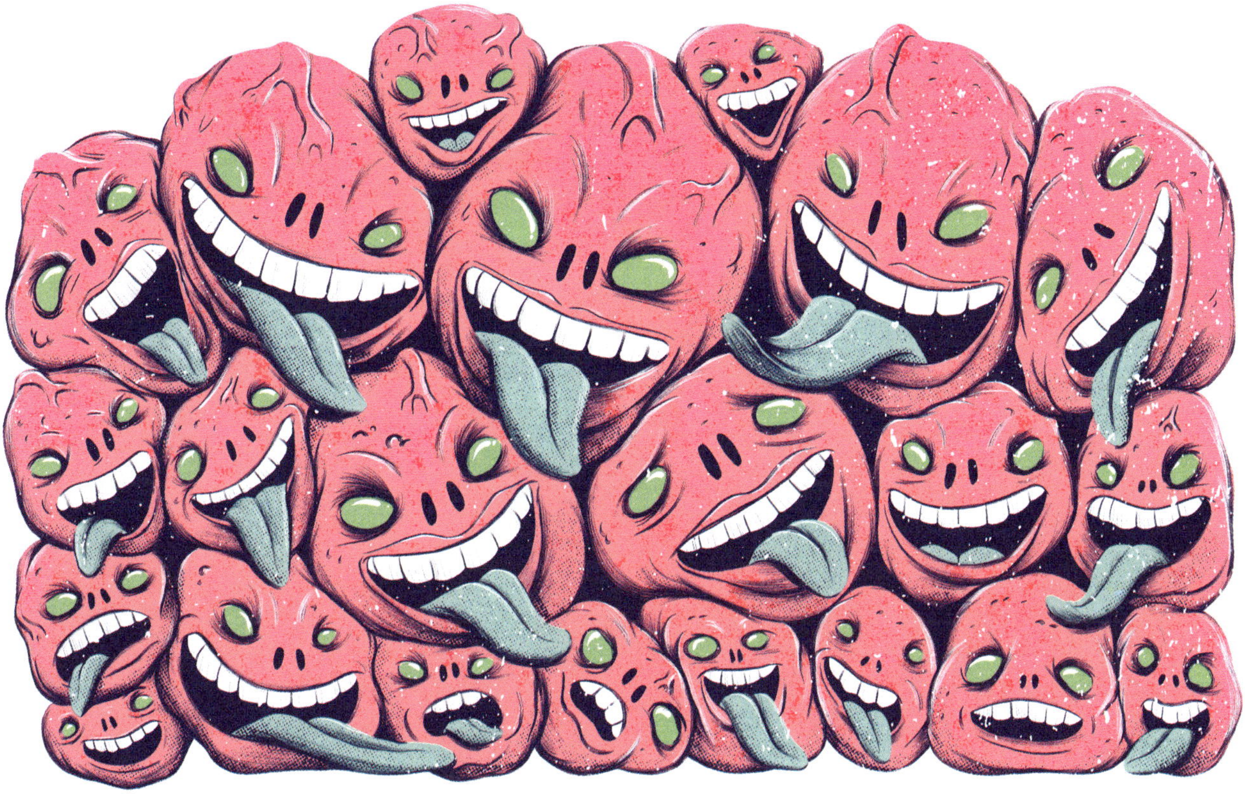

LA PRENSA LLAMÓ a ESTE GRUPO de FUNESTOS MACHITOS «LA JARCA». Y ROSARIO, INDIGNADA, ESCRIBIÓ:

«NUESTRA JUVENTUD MASCULINA NO TIENE NADA de "MACHO". COMO la MAYORÍA son ENGENDROS de un PAR de SAYAS (LA de la MUJER y la del CURA o el FRAILE) y de UNOS SOLOS CALZONES (los del MARIDO o QUERIDO), RESULTAN con DOS PARTES de HEMBRA o, POR lo MENOS, HERMAFRODITAS. [...]

¿QUÉ les QUEDARÍA que HACER a AQUELLAS "POBRES CHICAS"..., DIGO, "POBRES CHICOS"..., SI las MUJERES VAN a las CÁTEDRAS, a las ACADEMIAS, A los ATENEOS, y LLEGAN a SABER OTRA COSA que LIMPIAR los ORINALES, RESTREGARSE CONTRA los CLÉRIGOS y HACER a sus CONSORTES CABRONES y LADRONES, PARA LUCIR ELLAS las ZARANDAJAS de las MODAS?

¡ARREGLADOS QUEDARÍAN ENTONCES TODOS ESTOS MACHIHEMBRAS ESPAÑOLES SI la MUJER ADQUIERE FACULTADES de PERSONA!».

ROSARIO NO ESCRIBIÓ ese TEXTO para la PRENSA ESPAÑOLA. AQUÍ ESE «TONO VARONIL» ERA INDIGERIBLE. LO ENVIÓ a un PERIÓDICO de PARÍS, «EL INTERNACIONAL». PERO, a los POCOS DÍAS, «EL PROGRESO», un DIARIO de BARCELONA del POLÍTICO **ALEJANDRO LERROUX**, lo ROBÓ. LO PUBLICÓ sin PEDIR PERMISO a NADIE... ¡Y se ARMÓ la de SAN QUINTÍN!

HUELGAS en la UNIVERSIDAD, MANIFESTACIONES en los INSTITUTOS, ARTÍCULOS de PRENSA IMPRESOS con SANGRE y BILIS... El ESCRITOR de ZARZUELAS **PEPE JACKSON** ESCRIBIÓ en «MADRID CÓMICO»:

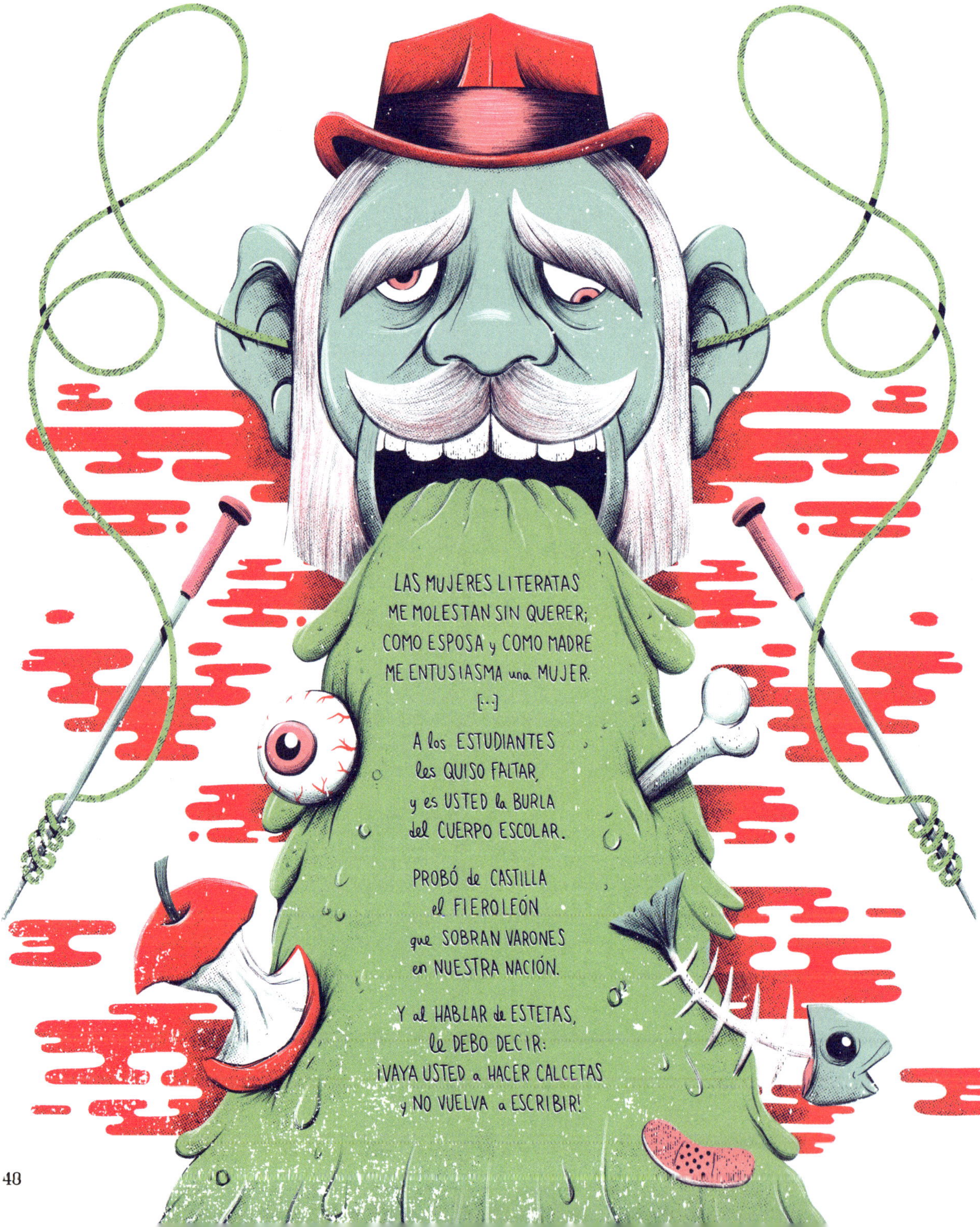

DOS GUARDIAS CIVILES se PRESENTARON en la CASA de la ESCRITORA, en GIJÓN, con UNA ORDEN de CAPTURA. QUERÍAN DETENERLA. PERO ELLA FUE MÁS RÁPIDA y YA ESTABA en PORTUGAL.

ALLÍ PASÓ DOS AÑOS, en el EXILIO, por un REVUELO que TENÍA TODA la PINTA de ENCERRONA POLÍTICA.

«PARECE que las HUESTES DEMÓCRATAS ESTABAN INTERESADAS en ENTREGARME COMO JUDAS a JESÚS, al ESCARNIO y DESPEDAZAMIENTO de las MUCHEDUMBRES IRREFLEXIVAS.»

En 1913, el NUEVO GOBIERNO LIBERAL CONCEDIÓ un INDULTO a «LOS que HUBIEREN SIDO CONDENADOS por DELITOS COMETIDOS por MEDIO de la IMPRENTA, el GRABADO u OTRO MEDIO MECÁNICO de PUBLICACIÓN».

ABATIDA y ARRUINADA, ROSARIO VOLVIÓ a GIJÓN. Y HUYENDO de la PRENSA «CÍNICA, INICUA y BAJUNA» del SEÑOR LERROUX y de los CURIOSOS, DICEN que en la PUERTA de SU CASA COLGÓ un CARTEL: «ES INÚTIL LLAMAR. NO SE ABRE a NADIE».

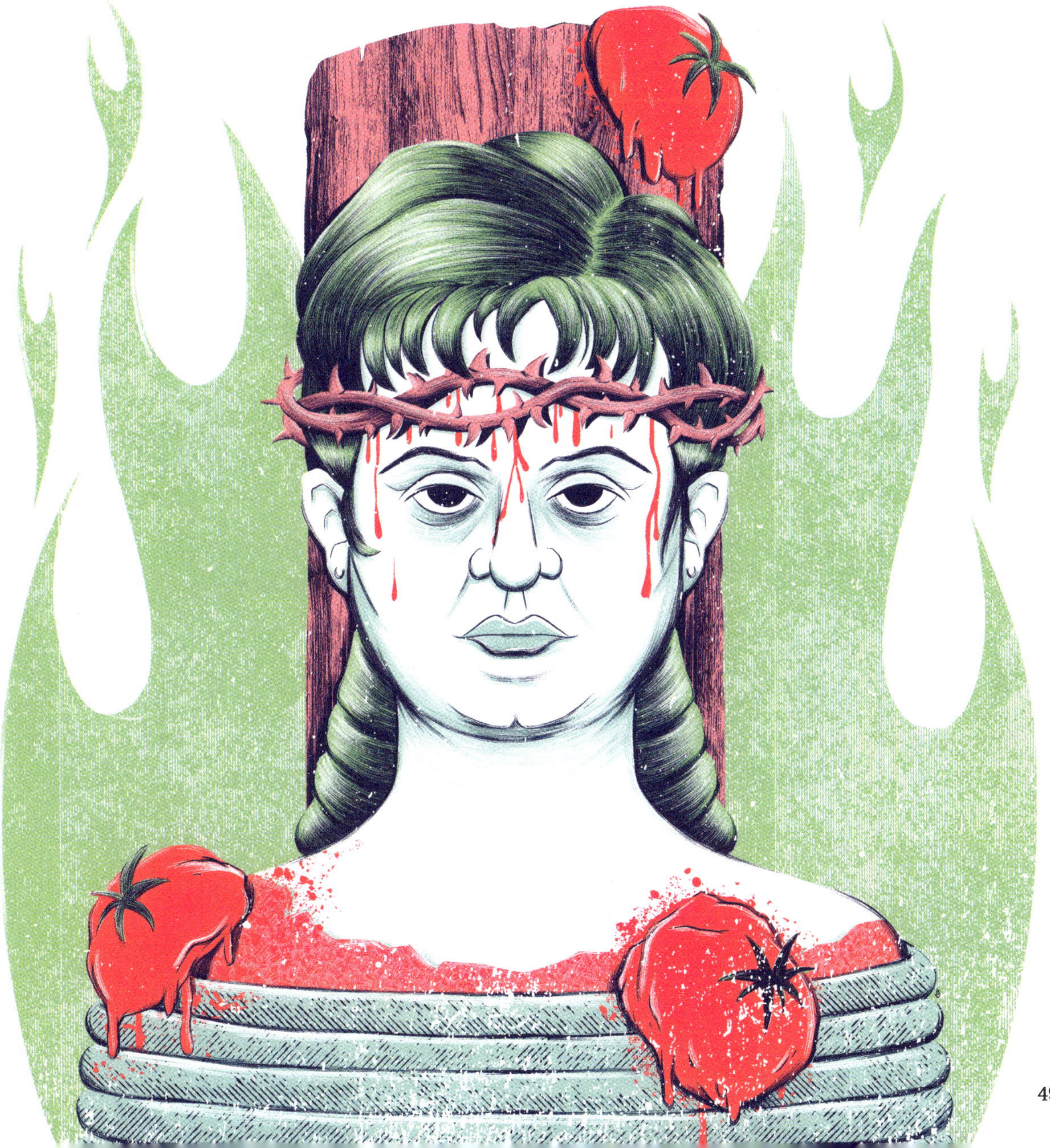

DESCUBRAN UN PASADO ULTRAMODERNO EN ESTA HISTORIA DE...

DOÑA ANGELITA

LA PRECURSORA DEL LIBRO ELECTRÓNICO

ERA ENTONCES, CUANDO la CASA QUEDABA a OSCURAS y en SILENCIO, CUANDO la MAESTRA **ÁNGELA RUIZ ROBLES** ENCENDÍA el CANDIL y EMPEZABA a INVENTAR. DESPUÉS de ACOSTAR a SUS HIJAS, TENDÍA unas CUARTILLAS SOBRE la MESA y TRAZABA ALGO que RESULTABA IMPENSABLE en AQUELLOS AÑOS CUARENTA: UN LIBRO MECÁNICO.

A **DOÑA ANGELITA** (1895-1975) le DOLÍAN los OJOS al VER el SUPLICIO de los CHIQUILLOS por ACARREAR ESAS PESADAS CARTERAS ATIBORRADAS de LIBROS. «YA que TRAEMOS a los NIÑOS a ESTE MUNDO, TENEMOS la OBLIGACIÓN de HACERLES la VIDA MÁS FÁCIL», DECÍA.

EN 1949 REGISTRÓ un «PROCEDIMIENTO MECÁNICO, ELÉCTRICO y a PRESIÓN de AIRE para LECTURA de LIBROS». ERA un SOPORTE para LÁMINAS que NO NECESITABA «MÁS LUZ que SU RESPLANDOR» (la ACTUAL «PANTALLA») y que TENÍA un «SISTEMA de LENTES de AUMENTO que HACE los TEXTOS MÁS GRANDES» (el ACTUAL «ZOOM»).

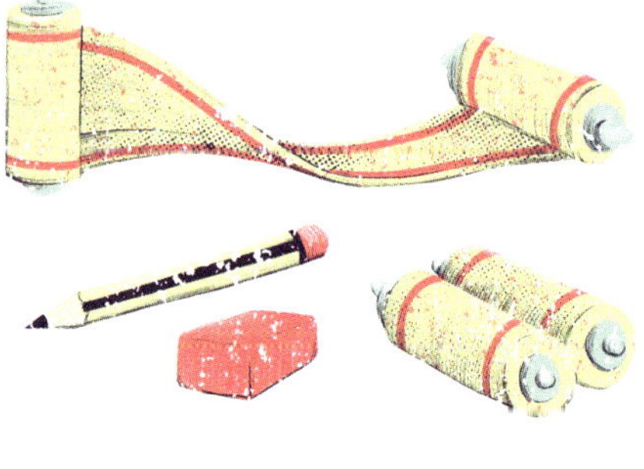

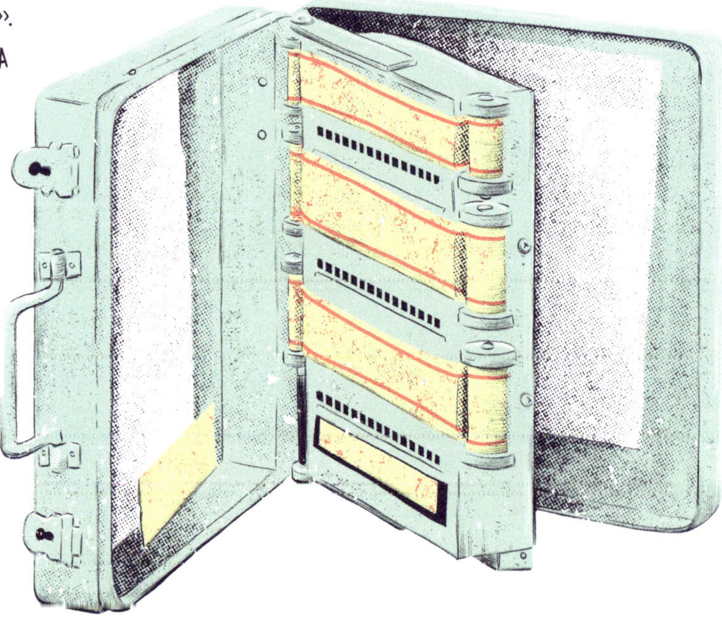

LA MAESTRA, INCANSABLE, SIGUIÓ TRABAJANDO de NOCHE, CUANDO NO HABÍA MÁS LUZ que la de SU ESCRITORIO, para CREAR NUEVOS INVENTOS.

En 1962 REGISTRÓ la PATENTE de un NUEVO DISPOSITIVO: la ENCICLOPEDIA MECÁNICA. LAS LECCIONES, en VEZ de DESPLEGARSE en PÁGINAS, se EXTENDÍAN en unas BOBINAS de PAPEL PARECIDAS a los ROLLOS de las MÁQUINAS de FOTOS. El LIBRO, SIMILAR a un MALETÍN, ENSEÑABA «LOS TEMAS de FORMA INTUITIVA, PRÁCTICA, ATRAYENTE y AMENA», EXPLICÓ DOÑA ANGELITA. ERA un APARATO «IDEOVISUAL» (lo que HOY LLAMARÍAMOS «INTERACTIVO») de «PEDAGOGÍA ULTRAMODERNA».

Un DÍA LLEVÓ los DIBUJOS al PARQUE de ARTILLERÍA de EL FERROL del CAUDILLO y, ALLÍ, unos INGENIEROS MILITARES CONSTRUYERON el PROTOTIPO. DOÑA ANGELITA RECIBIÓ DECENAS de PREMIOS de INVENCIÓN por su ENCICLOPEDIA MECÁNICA, PERO de POCO SIRVIERON TODAS las VISITAS que HIZO a EDITORIALES y MINISTERIOS. NADIE SUPO VER que ESTA MÁQUINA ERA un ANTICIPO del MUNDO DIGITAL que YA SE ESTABA FRAGUANDO en los PAÍSES MÁS AVANZADOS. NADIE ATENDIÓ lo SUFICIENTE a SU ADVERTENCIA:

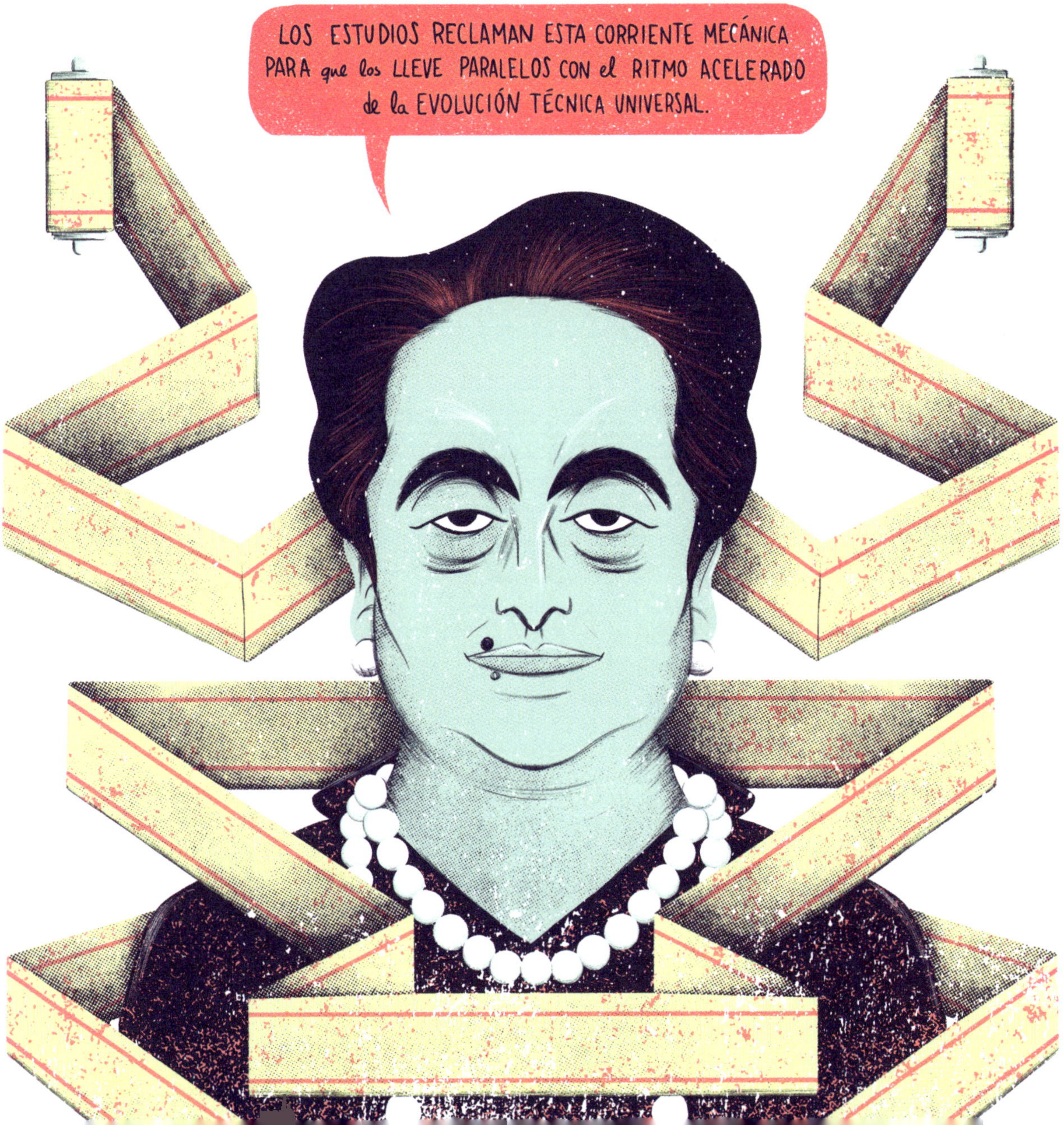

QUÍTENSE LA PAMELA Y ADMIREN A LA SIN PAR...

MARUJA MALLO

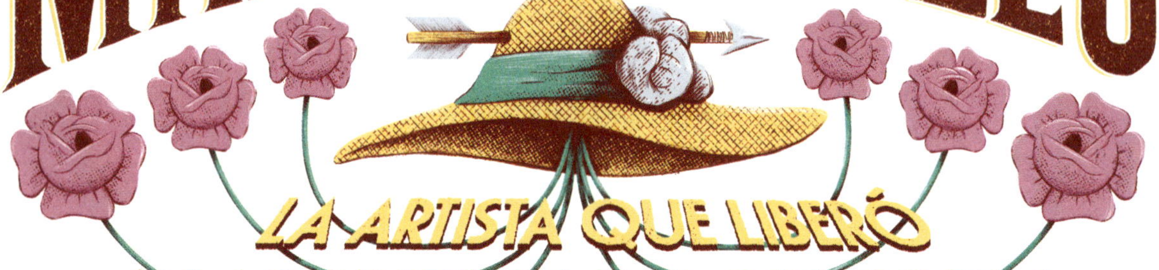

LA ARTISTA QUE LIBERÓ A LAS MUJERES DEL SOMBRERO

ESTE AÑO de 1922 HA ENTRADO una SOLA MUJER en la REAL ACADEMIA de BELLAS ARTES de SAN FERNANDO, la PRESTIGIOSA ESCUELA de ARTE de MADRID. NO ES RARO que en las AULAS SOLO HAYA HOMBRES. LO que EXTRAÑA al MUNDO es que **MARUJA MALLO** PRETENDA SER PINTORA en VEZ de MADRE, ESPOSA y REUNIÓN de TODAS las GRACIAS y BELLEZAS.

A la VEINTEAÑERA le ESTORBAN las CONVENCIONES. Le INTERESA el ARTE; le APASIONA FREUD. TIENE ANSIAS de DESCUBRIR la VIDA que PALPITA en CUALQUIER LUGAR: EN los LIBROS y en las TABERNAS. ACUDE a CONCIERTOS de JAZZ, ESCONDIDA, PORQUE ESTÁ MUY FEO que UNA DAMA FRECUENTE un LOCAL de VARONES.

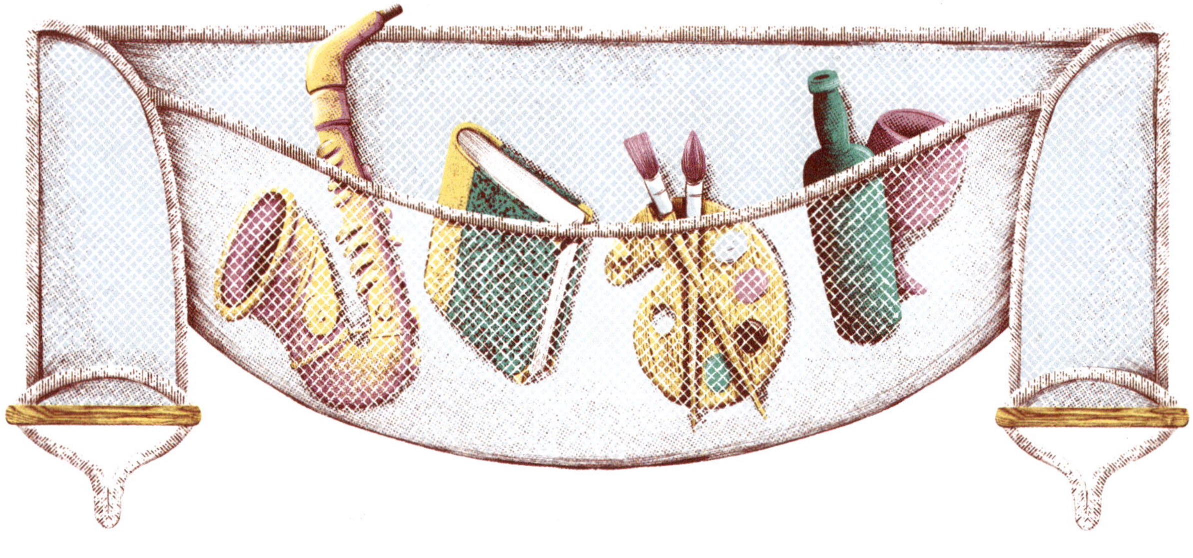

PERO a ELLA le DA IGUAL. Es la AGITADORA de su GRUPO de AMIGOS: POETAS y ARTISTAS de la RESIDENCIA de ESTUDIANTES. Es la que HA ESPABILADO a su AMIGO **SALVADOR DALÍ** desde que LLEGÓ a MADRID, EXCÉNTRICO e INTROVERTIDO, para ESTUDIAR DIBUJO.

A **MARUJA** (1902- 1995) NO le GUSTA LLEVAR la LARGA MELENA FEMENINA que se ESPERA de una SEÑORITA, NI MUCHO MENOS ESCONDERLA DESPUÉS, como es DEBIDO, en un DISCRETO TOCADO. ¡QUÉ DESVERGÜENZA! Ella se HA CORTADO el PELO a lo «GARÇON» (al ESTILO de los CHICOS) y HASTA se VA a ATREVER a QUITARSE el SOMBRERO, PORQUE CREE que le CONGESTIONA las IDEAS.

Un DÍA de 1927 PASEA con MARGARITA MANSO, FEDERICO GARCÍA LORCA y DALÍ por la PUERTA del SOL. ELLAS DECIDEN LIBRARSE del GORRO y, de PRONTO, OYEN GRITAR a su ALREDEDOR:

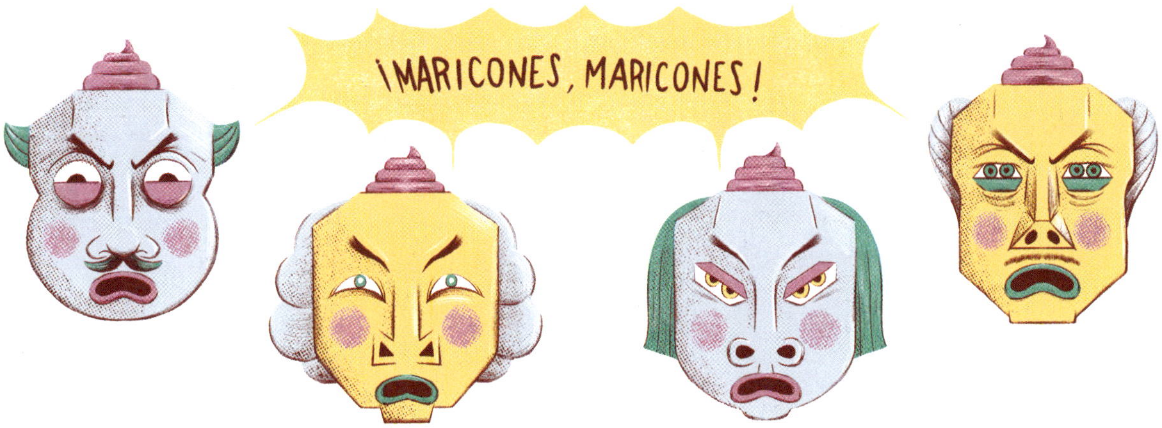

Les LLUEVEN PEDRADAS y, RIÉNDOSE a CARCAJADAS, CORREN HACIA la ESTACIÓN de METRO para ESCAPAR de la IRA de los VIANDANTES.

A MARÚNICA, COMO ELLA SE AUTODENOMINA, le GUSTA la REBELDÍA JUGUETONA. Y de ESTE SUCESO SURGIRÁ DESPUÉS el NOMBRE que TIENEN HOY las MUJERES de la GENERACIÓN del 27: LAS SINSOMBRERO.

La MUJER que PINTA VERBENAS, TIOVIVOS, MEDUSAS y ESTRELLAS de MAR es DUEÑA de su VIDA. TIENE la VALENTÍA de LANZAR al VACÍO lo que se ESPERA de ELLA (ser un «ÁNGEL del HOGAR») y, en su LUGAR, REÍRSE al ESCUCHAR de su QUERIDO AMIGO DALÍ:

«MARUJA, ERES MITAD ÁNGEL, MITAD MARISCO».

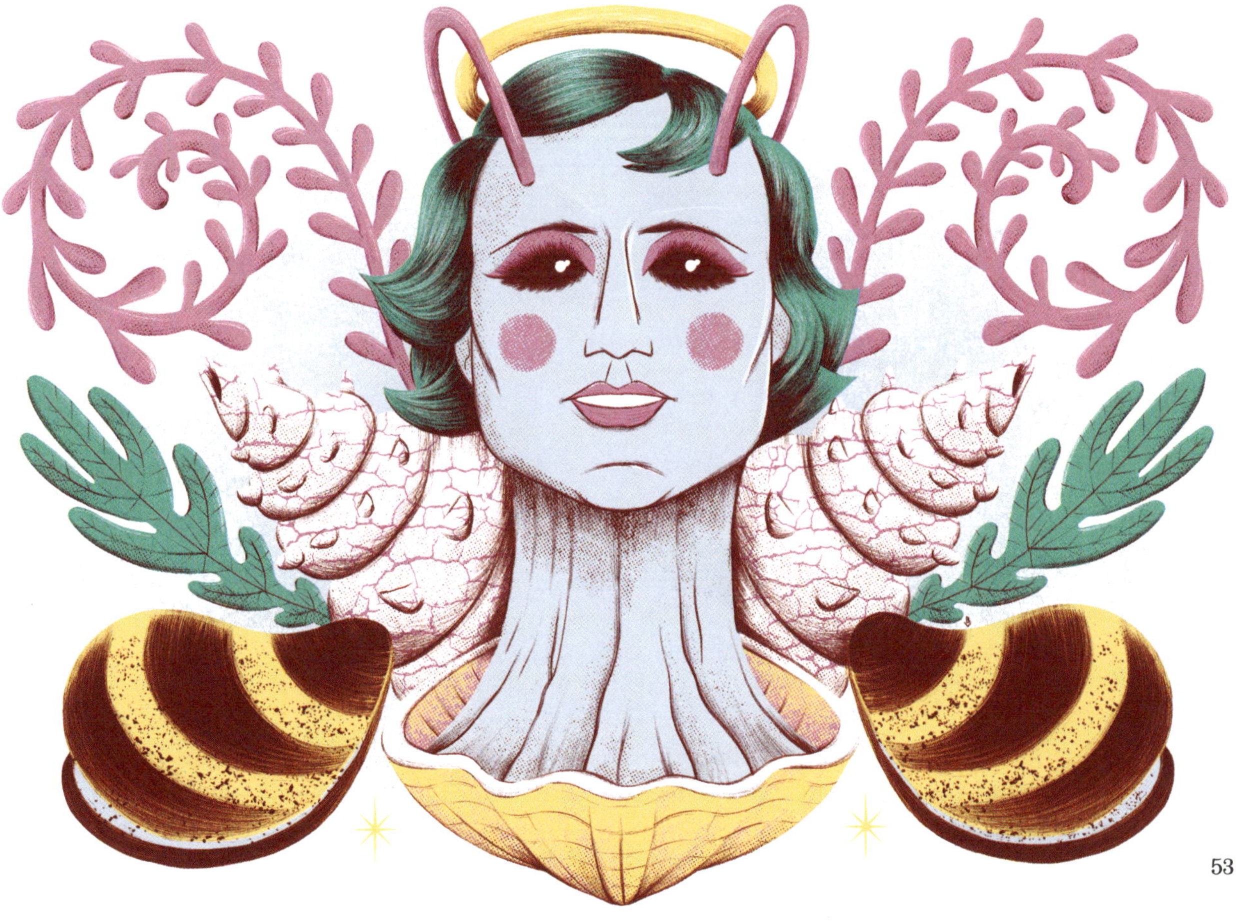

PRESENCIEN LAS ÚLTIMAS Y TRÁGICAS HORAS DE VIDA DEL INMENSO LITERATO

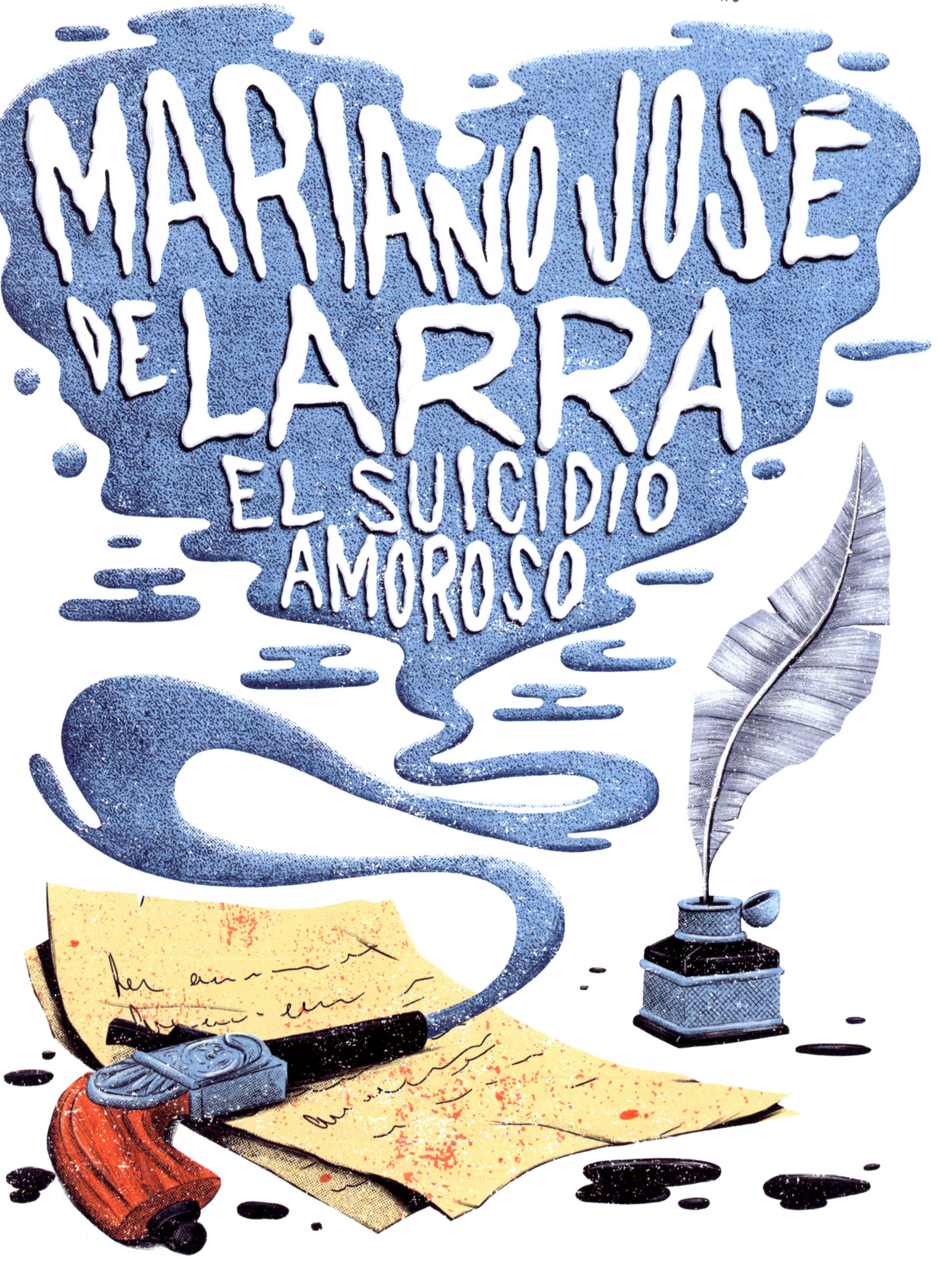

AMANECE en MADRID, FRÍO y GRIS. ESTE 13 de FEBRERO de 1837 MARIANO JOSÉ de LARRA ESTÁ AÚN en la CAMA CUANDO SU CRIADO le ENTREGA UNA CARTA. ¡ES de DOLORES!

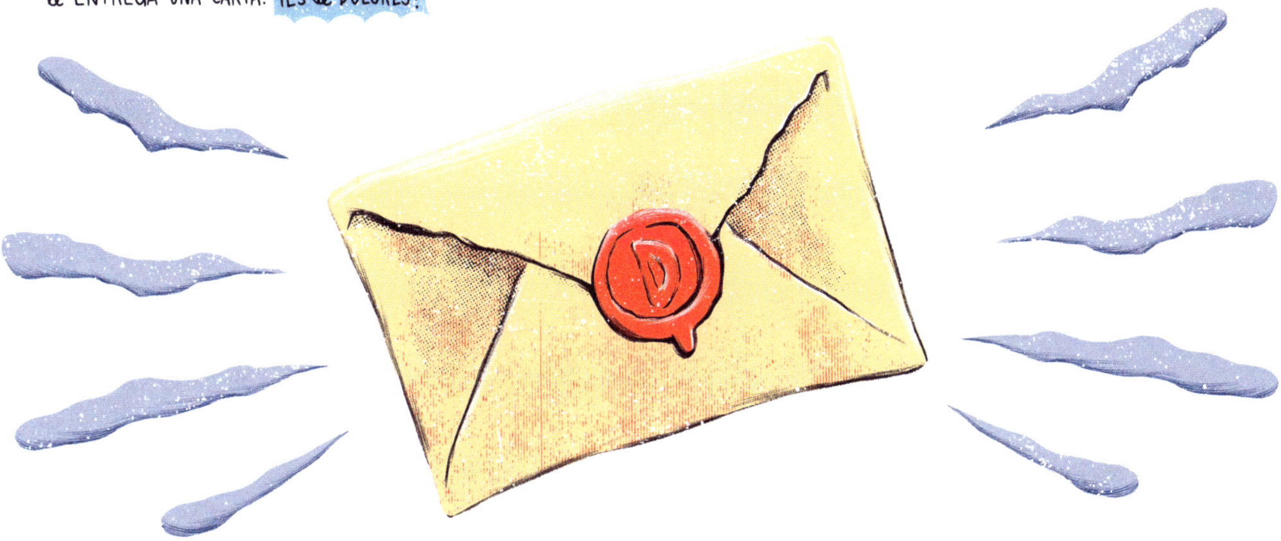

LAS HABLADURÍAS y las CALUMNIAS HAN SEPARADO a ESTOS DOS AMANTES. PERO AHORA, en ESTE PAPEL y en ESTAS LETRAS, LARRA VE un DESTELLO de ESPERANZA.

Ella ANUNCIA que QUIERE VERLO; PRONTO, ESTA MISMA TARDE. Él SALTA del LECHO y ESCRIBE UNA RESPUESTA: SON las ÚNICAS PALABRAS que UNO de los MÁS GRANDES LITERATOS del ROMANTICISMO ESPAÑOL ESCRIBE ESTA MAÑANA.

«GRACIAS: GRACIAS por TODO.
ME PARECE que SI PIENSAN USTEDES VENIR, TU AMIGA y TÚ,
ESTA NOCHE, HABLARÍAMOS y ACASO SERÍA POSIBLE CONVENIRNOS.
EN ESTE MOMENTO NO SÉ qué HACER. ESTOY ABURRIDO
y NO PUEDO RESISTIR a la CALUMNIA y a la INFAMIA.
TUYO.»

LARRA LLAMA a SUS CRIADOS. ES PRECISO ARREGLAR y EMBELLECER la CASA. ORDENA que SE ENCIENDAN TODOS los BRASEROS, que PONGAN FLORES en los BÚCAROS. HAY que VESTIRLO TODO de FIESTA y de ALEGRÍA. ÉL MISMO SE VISTE con ELEGANCIA y LLAMA al PELUQUERO PARA que lo PEINE y le ARREGLE SU BARBA RIZADA.

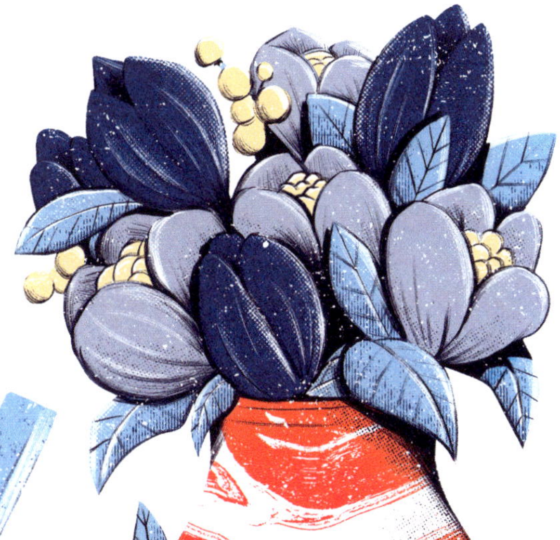

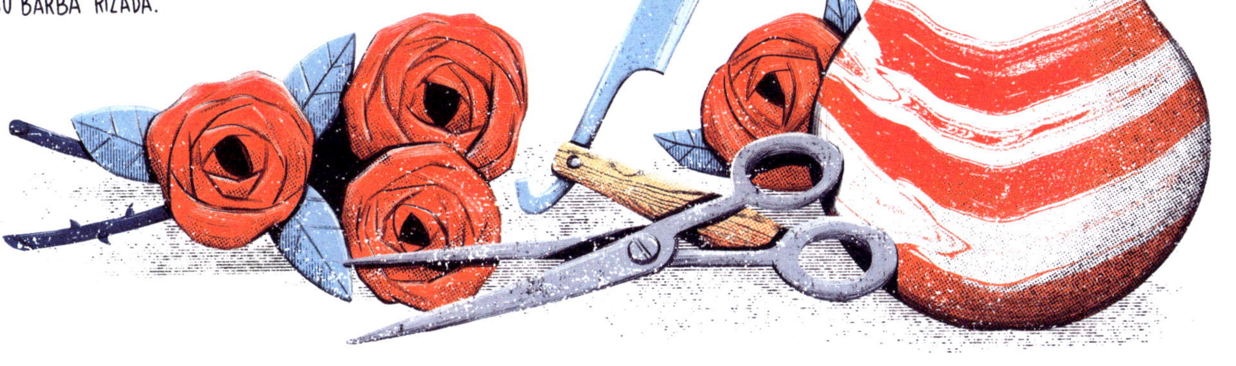

Al CAER la TARDE VA a VER a SU EDITOR. ESTÁ CONTENTO y le PROPONE UNA NUEVA COLABORACIÓN. VUELVE a TENER CONFIANZA en el PORVENIR.

LARRA REGRESA a CASA. TIEMBLA SU CORAZÓN en la ZOZOBRA de la ESPERA, en ESA DUDA CRUEL del AMOR IMPACIENTE. ¿VENDRÁ?

SE ACERCA a la VENTANA, PERO NO QUIERE ABRIR el BALCÓN para que NO ENTRE FRÍO. La COCINERA ENTRETIENE a SU HIJA ADELITA. ESPERA... Y de PRONTO, LLEGA DOLORES. ¡DOLORES! APENAS PUEDE DECIR UNA PALABRA. SOLO TIENE OJOS para MIRARLA y CORAZÓN para QUERERLA.

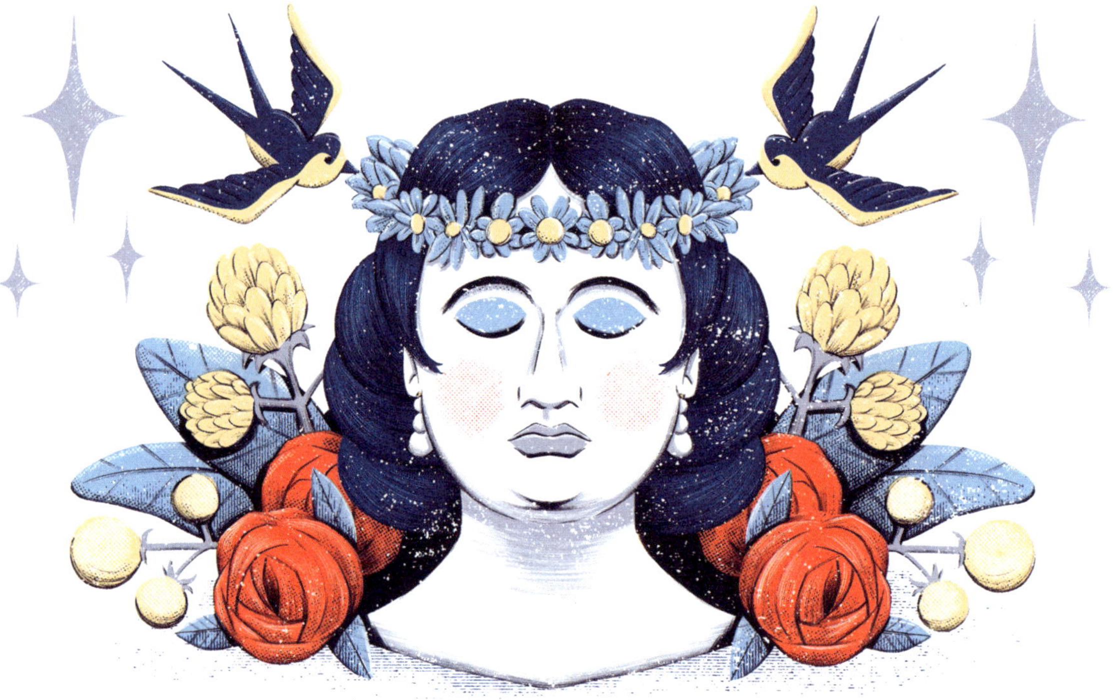

LA AMIGA de DOLORES SE QUEDA en la ANTESALA; ELLA ENTRA en el GABINETE de LARRA. ÉL le DECLARA SU AMOR, SU PADECER. ELLA le RESPONDE con FRIALDAD: HA DECIDIDO VOLVER con SU ESPOSO y NO QUIERE VER al que FUE SU AMANTE NUNCA MÁS.

–¿POR QUÉ HAS VENIDO? –PREGUNTA ÉL.

–QUIERO que ME DEVUELVAS MIS CARTAS. NO DEBE QUEDAR NADA entre NOSOTROS.

LARRA le DA los SOBRES y LLAMA a SU CRIADO.

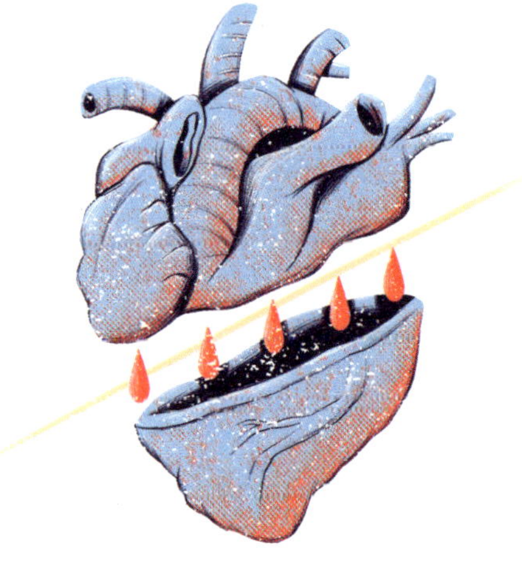

–ACOMPAÑA a ESTAS SEÑORAS a la PUERTA –DICE, y SIENTE ENLOQUECER. YA NO PUEDE ABRAZARLA; NO VOLVERÁ a OLER el PERFUME de ROSA de SU MANTILLA–. ¿ADIÓS? –PREGUNTA, DESESPERADO.

–ADIÓS.

–¿ADIÓS para SIEMPRE?

–SÍ –RESPONDE ELLA FIRME, y SE ALEJA.

¡SE HA IDO! NO QUEDA YA CIELO NI AIRE NI ESPERANZA NI ILUSIÓN. EL MUNDO SE ABRE, CORTADO a PICO por UN HACHAZO, Y NO TIENE DONDE PONER el PIE. ES IMPOSIBLE VIVIR en el VACÍO. ¡LA CAJA AMARILLA! ¡LAS PISTOLAS ESTÁN en la CAJA AMARILLA! AGARRA UNA, la PEGA a SU SIEN y ¡DISPARA!

DOLORES NO HA SALIDO AÚN de la CASA. OYE el DISPARO y SE APRESURA. HUYE. HUYE de AHÍ. TODOS HAN OÍDO el TIRO y UN GOLPE SECO, AUNQUE NADIE PUEDE IMAGINAR lo que HA OCURRIDO en el GABINETE; SOLO DOLORES. PERO, en VEZ de AMOR y DOLOR, SIENTE PÁNICO. NO QUIERE que NADIE SEPA que SE HAN VUELTO a VER. Y con VOZ TEMBLOROSA DICE:

—VUÉLVASE USTED... VUÉLVASE, PEDRO. PUEDEN NECESITARLO...

PERO el CRIADO NO ENTRA; NO PUEDE IMAGINAR lo que HA OCURRIDO. PRONTO SE HACE la HORA en que ADELITA, COMO CADA DÍA, ACUDE a DAR UN BESO de BUENAS NOCHES a SU PADRE. ENTRA en la ESTANCIA y VUELVE CORRIENDO HACIA los CRIADOS.

—PAPÁ ESTÁ DEBAJO de la MESA.

TODOS CORREN a la HABITACIÓN. LARRA YACE PÁLIDO, con los OJOS CERRADOS, INERTE en UNA TERRIBLE EXPRESIÓN de AMARGURA. UN QUINQUÉ ILUMINA el CUADRO FÚNEBRE del INMORTAL ESCRITOR SATÍRICO y COSTUMBRISTA de la ESPAÑA del SIGLO XIX.

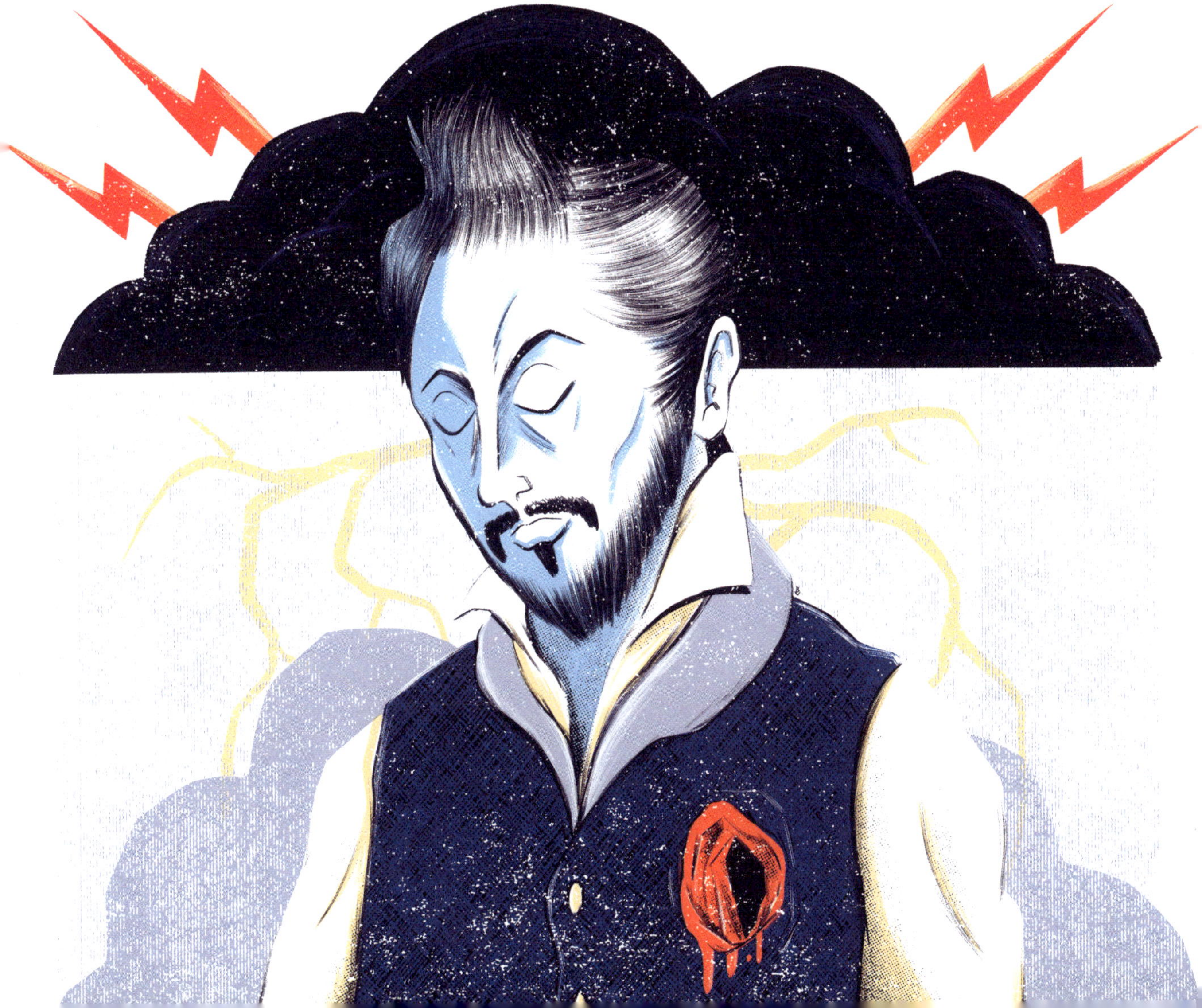

Y AQUÍ LLEGA, CON SUS CASCABELES Y SU ARTE POPULAR, LA INIGUALABLE...

LORETO PRADO

LA MUSA MANOLA

NACIÓ en MADRID UNA NIÑA que a PUNTO ESTUVO de MORIR el DÍA de SU BAUTIZO. El AMA que la LLEVABA en BRAZOS DIO UN TRASPIÉ y ACABÓ ESTAMPADA en el SUELO, SANGRANDO, CON UNA BRECHA en la SIEN. POR FORTUNA, LA MADRINA AGARRÓ el BEBÉ al VUELO y EVITÓ el TROMPAZO MORTAL.

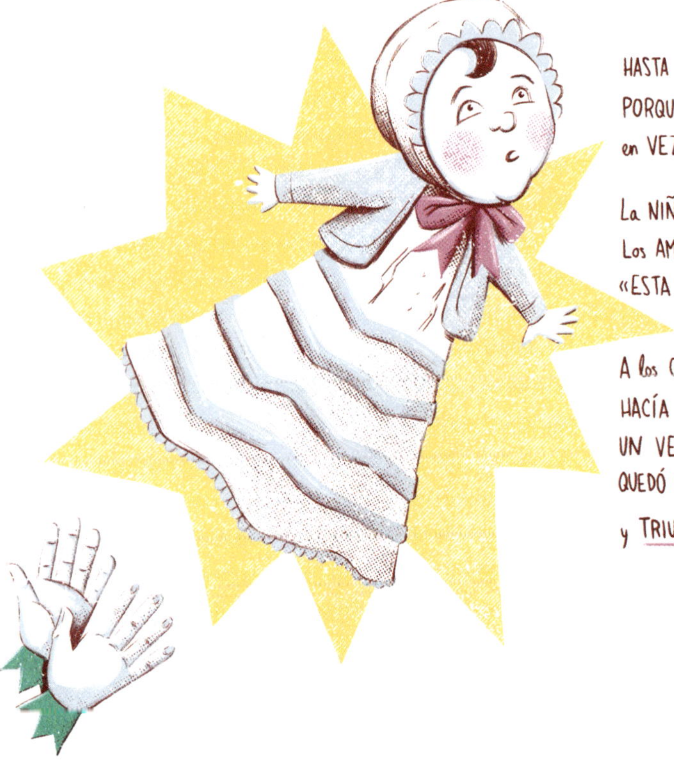

HASTA AHÍ LLEGÓ la SUERTE de **LORETO PRADO** (1863-1943). PORQUE PRONTO la DESGRACIA CAYÓ en SU CASA: MURIÓ SU PADRE y, en VEZ de HERENCIA, DEJÓ MIL DEUDAS.

La NIÑA TENÍA SU GRACIA. CUANDO IBAN de VISITA, HACÍA MONERÍAS. Los AMIGOS de SU MADRE, ENCANTADOS, le DABAN UNA PROPINA: «ESTA NIÑA VALE», DECÍAN.

A los CATORCE AÑOS YA ESTABA en el TEATRO PRÍNCIPE. HACÍA PAPELES de BULTO hasta que, UN DÍA, la TIPLE CÓMICA INGIRIÓ UN VENENO por DISGUSTOS de AMOR. MURIÓ en el ACTO y la OBRA QUEDÓ COJA. ¡URGENTE! ¡UNA SUSTITUTA! HUBO UNA PRUEBA y TRIUNFÓ LORETO.

DESDE ENTONCES NO le FALTÓ FUNCIÓN NI UN DÍA. NADIE HACÍA REÍR COMO ELLA. NADIE TUVO MÁS ÉXITOS en UN SAINETE, UNA REVISTA o UNA OPERETA.

«LORETO es la GRACIA NATURAL y SU CUERPO ESTÁ TODO ÉL AMASADO con el JUGO del CHISTE, GARBO y GARABATO ESPAÑOLÍSIMO», ESCRIBIÓ PARDO BAZÁN.

«SU ARTE, AUNQUE LLAMADO POPULAR, ESTRIBA en el MATIZ, en la INFLEXIÓN de la VOZ, en la RETICENCIA MALICIOSA, en el MIRAR COMO al DESCUIDO y en el CAMBIO INESPERADO de UNA SITUACIÓN a OTRA», DECÍA AZORÍN.

FUE ACTRIZ CÓMICA y EMPRESARIA TEATRAL. ERA, COMO la BAUTIZÓ el POETA EMILIO CARRERE, «LA MUSA MANOLA, la COMEDIANTA MÁS ESPAÑOLA».

CON SU SOCIO LABORAL y COMPAÑERO AMOROSO, **ENRIQUE CHICOTE**, ESCRIBIERON la HISTORIA del GÉNERO CHICO a PRINCIPIOS del SIGLO XX. ERAN TIEMPOS en los que los VECINOS, COGIDOS del BRAZO, en VEZ de «IR al TEATRO» SALÍAN de CASA, ENGALANADOS, DICIENDO:

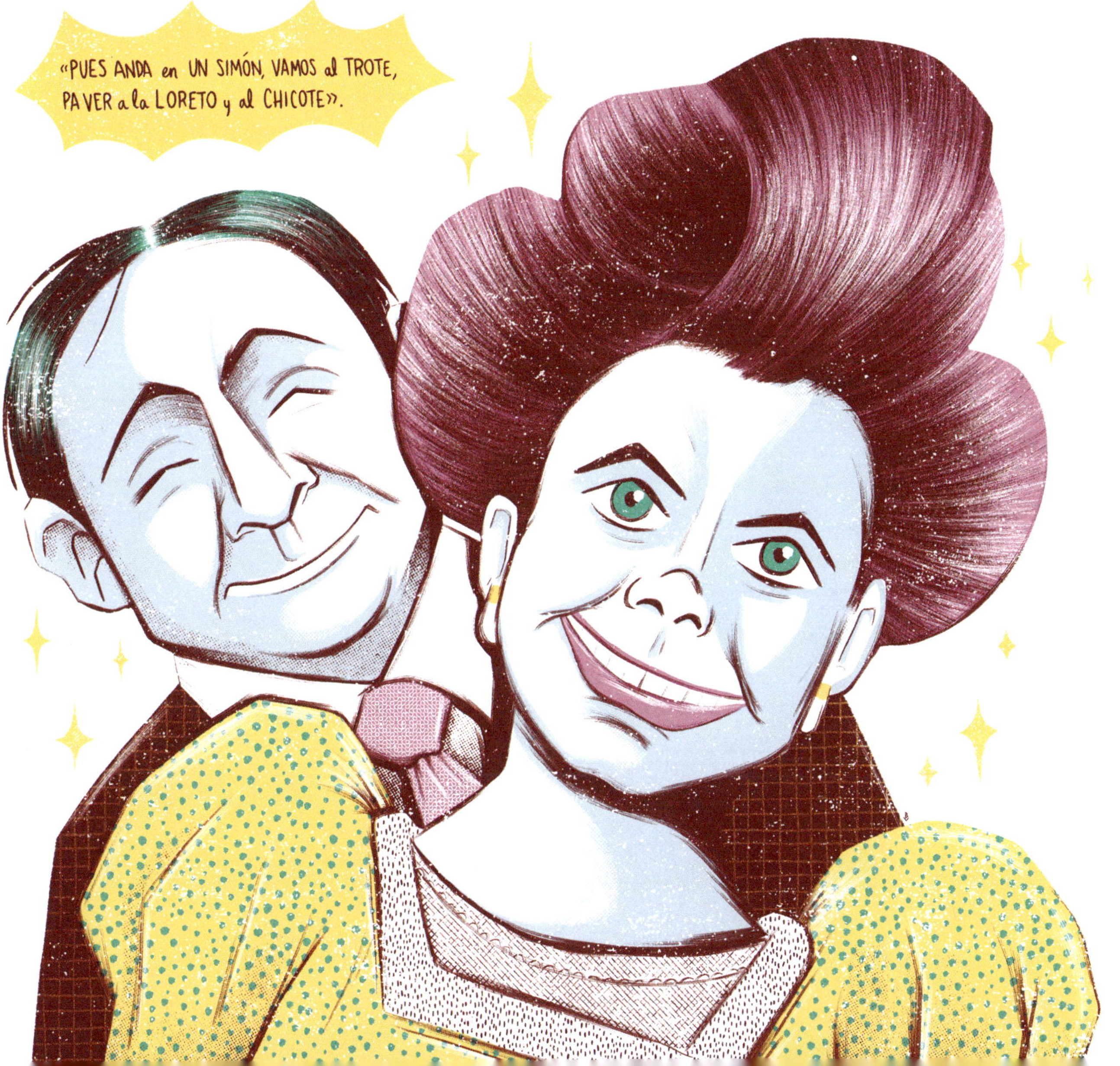

Dio la ruleta de la vida genio y dolor al ejemplar y desconocido...

RAMÓN VEREA

EL INVENTOR DE LA CALCULADORA

El niño iba para cura. A Ramón Silvestre Verea García (1833-1899) lo educó un sacerdote: le enseñó la palabra de Dios y decenas de libros que el resto de los chiquillos de su aldea ni siquiera podían imaginar.

Pero a los diecinueve años su destino de sacerdote pegó un derrape: el gallego perdió la beca que le pagaba el seminario. Lo que parecía una desgracia se convirtió en su «liberación» (así lo describió mucha veces de mayor).

En 1855 embarcó hacia Cuba, y en la isla bella se hizo maestro, escritor e inventor. Empezó ideando una máquina para doblar periódicos. Del Caribe se trasladó a Nueva York, y en la gran manzana creó una «Agencia industrial para la compra de maquinaria y efectos de moderna invención».

Allí fundó la imprenta *El Polígloto* y, en 1878, patentó la calculadora más inteligente de la época. La única capaz de sumar, restar, multiplicar y dividir cifras de hasta nueve dígitos.

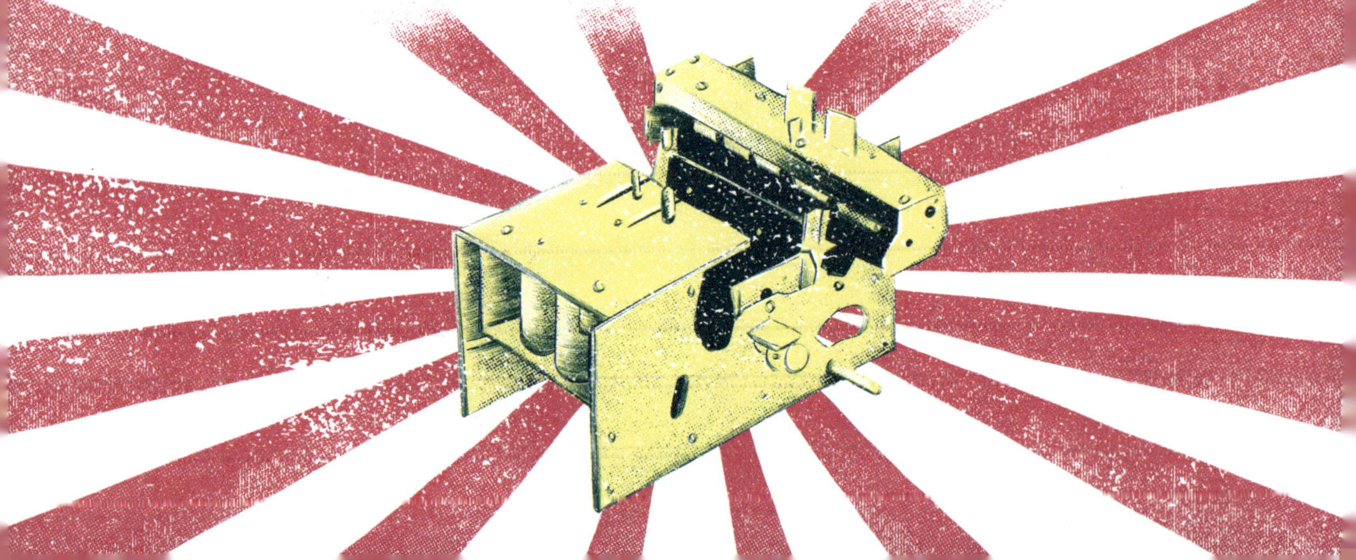

LA VEREA DIRECT MULTIPLIER ERA UNA MÁQUINA AMARILLA de HIERRO y ACERO que PESABA VEINTISÉIS KILOS. TAN APARATOSA COMO EFICAZ. PERO el GALLEGO NO HIZO ESFUERZOS por COMERCIALIZARLA NI OBTENER RÉDITOS. LA INVENTÓ por:

UN POCO de AMOR PROPIO.

MUCHO AMOR NACIONAL (el DESEO de PROBAR que, en GENIO INVENTIVO, un ESPAÑOL PUEDE DEJAR ATRÁS a las EMINENCIAS de las NACIONES MÁS CULTAS).

El AFÁN INNATO de CONTRIBUIR con ALGO al ADELANTO de la CIENCIA.

UN ENTRETENIMIENTO CONFORME a MIS GUSTOS e INCLINACIONES.

LO que de VERDAD le IMPORTABA a RAMÓN ERA el LIBREPENSAMIENTO. DESDE SU INFLUYENTE PERIÓDICO «EL PROGRESO», PUBLICADO en MÁS de VEINTE PAÍSES, DIFUNDÍA la IGUALDAD ENTRE MUJERES y HOMBRES, la LIBERTAD de EXPRESIÓN y la ABOLICIÓN de la ESCLAVITUD.

PERO la PRENSA SIEMPRE FUE UN NEGOCIO MISERABLE. El GRAN PERIODISTA, ESCRITOR e INVENTOR ACABÓ SU VIDA HUNDIDO en la POBREZA. TANTA que lo ÚNICO que DEJÓ al MORIR FUE SU CADÁVER TIRADO en UNA CALLE de BUENOS AIRES.

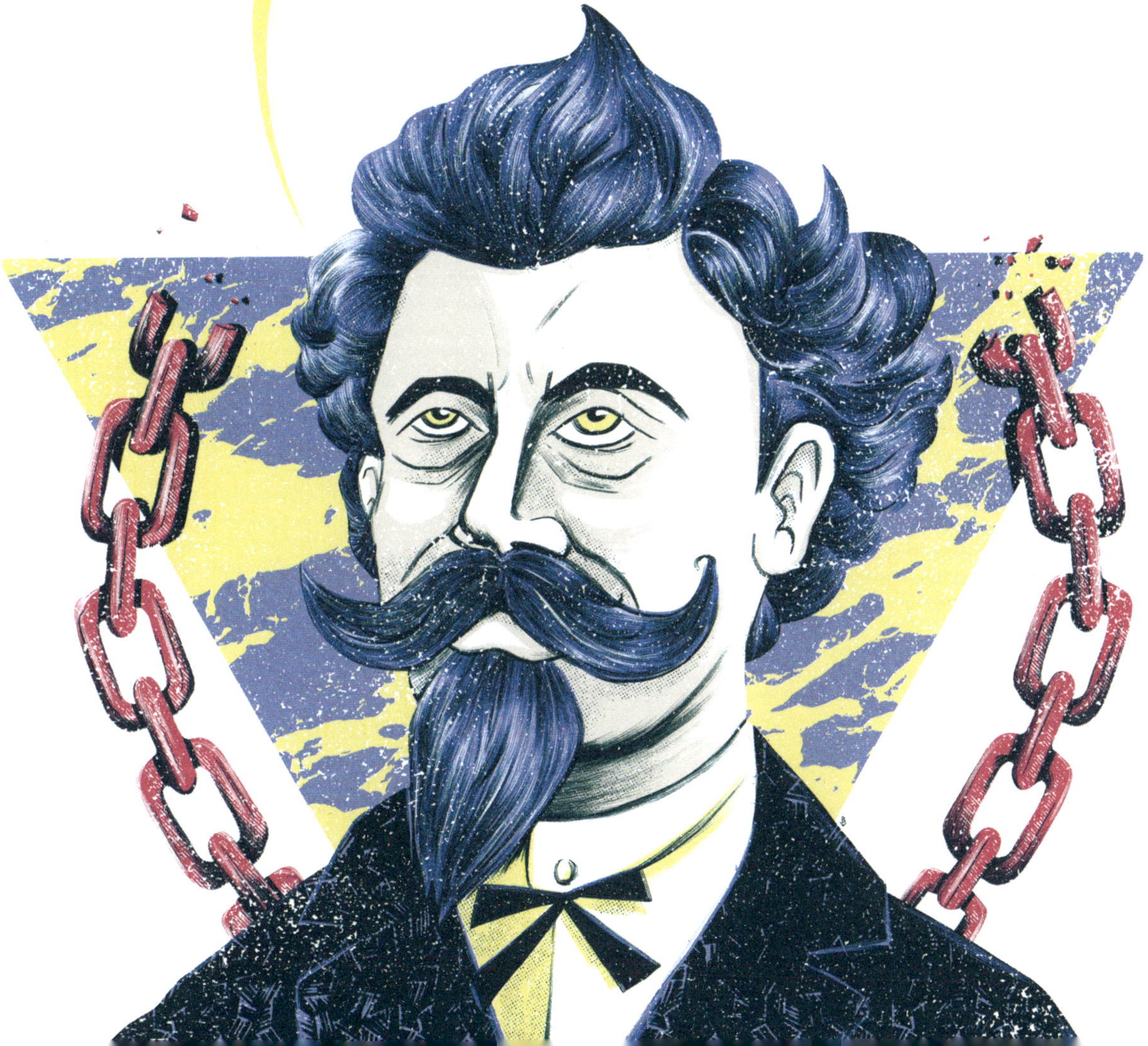

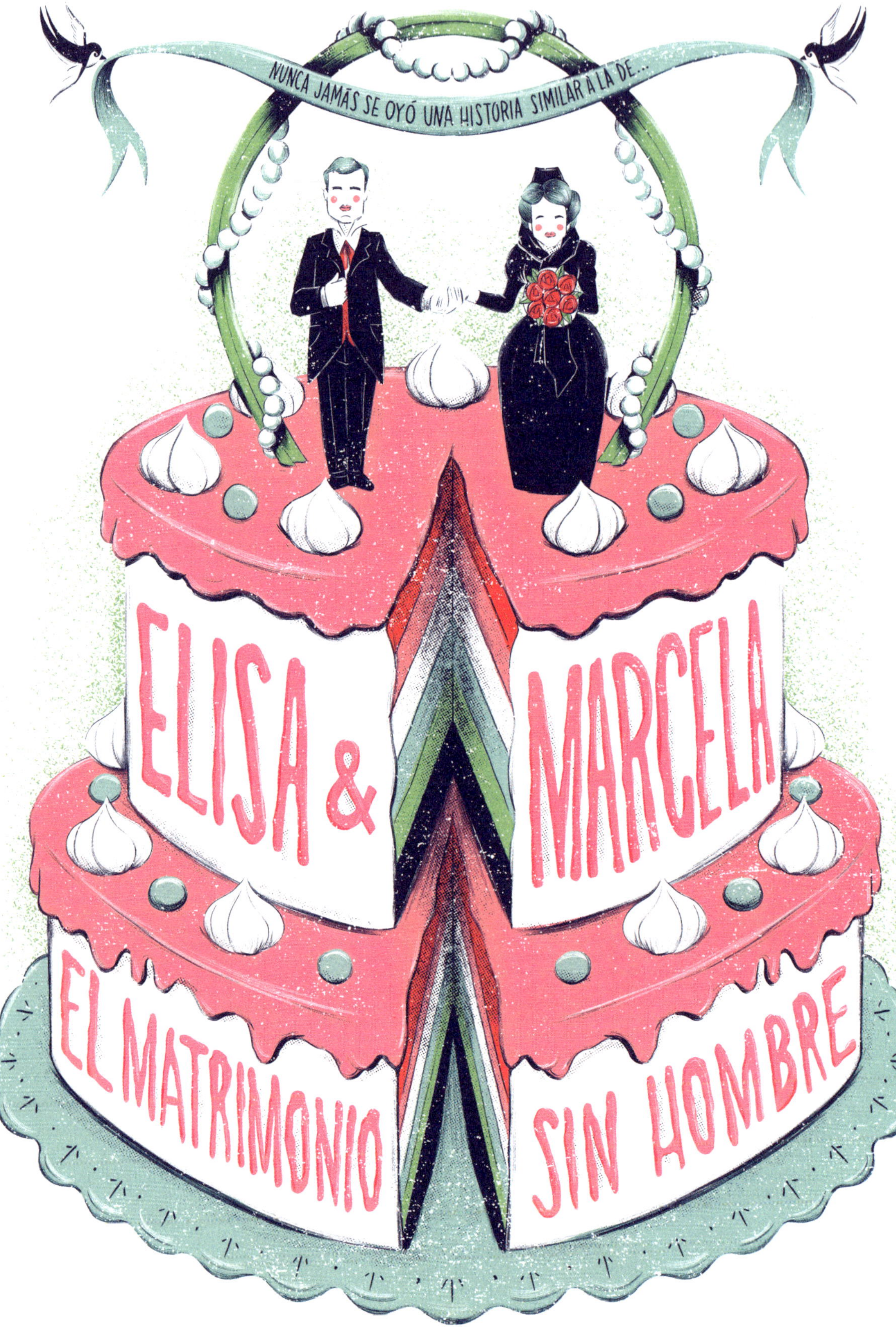
NUNCA JAMÁS SE OYÓ UNA HISTORIA SIMILAR A LA DE...
ELISA & MARCELA
EL MATRIMONIO SIN HOMBRE

El DOMINGO 23 de JUNIO de 1901, en la PRIMERA PÁGINA de «El IMPARCIAL», UNA NOTICIA DICE:

UN FOLLETÍN en ACCIÓN

DOS MUJERES QUE SE CASAN

ACABA de DESCUBRIRSE UN SUCESO EXTRAÑO y FOLLETINESCO que PREOCUPA la ATENCIÓN de las GENTES: UN MATRIMONIO CANÓNICO CONTRAÍDO por DOS MUJERES.

LA HISTORIA

En 1885, la SEÑORITA **MARCELA GRACIA IBEAS**, HIJA de UN CAPITÁN del REGIMIENTO de MURCIA, ESTUDIABA en la ESCUELA NORMAL de MAESTRAS de CORUÑA. UN DÍA la JOVEN LLEGÓ a CASA HABLANDO CON ENTUSIASMO de UNA NUEVA AMIGA, de FINO TRATO: **ELISA SÁNCHEZ LORIGA**.

Las RELACIONES ENTRE las DOS GALLEGAS SE HACÍAN CADA VEZ MÁS ÍNTIMAS. TANTO que EMPEZARON a MOLESTAR a los PADRES de MARCELA: AQUEL NUEVO AFECTO MERMABA el CARIÑO que SU HIJA les PROFESABA.

ENFERMÓ UN DÍA la MADRE y MARCELA SE NEGÓ a CUIDARLA. POR NADA del MUNDO DEJARÍA de IR a la ESCUELA DONDE SU AMIGA la ESPERABA. LOS PADRES la OBLIGARON a QUEDARSE en CASA y ESA MISMA NOCHE APARECIÓ ELISA, CONTRARIADA por la AUSENCIA de la MUCHACHA.

¡HAY que PONER TIERRA de POR MEDIO! LOS PADRES, DISGUSTADÍSIMOS, ANUNCIARON A MARCELA que la ENVIABAN a ESTUDIAR a MADRID. PRESA de UN ATAQUE de NERVIOS, a ESCONDIDAS, ESCRIBIÓ a su AMIGA. ¡NOOO! ELISA CORRIÓ a por MARCELA, PERO el CAPITÁN, FURIBUNDO, BLINDADO en la PUERTA, la ECHÓ a PATADAS.

PASÓ el TIEMPO, PASÓ la DISTANCIA, y MARCELA VOLVIÓ. El ENCUENTRO las LLEVÓ a VIVIR JUNTAS, DURANTE SIETE AÑOS, COMO DOS MAESTRAS, DOS AMIGAS.

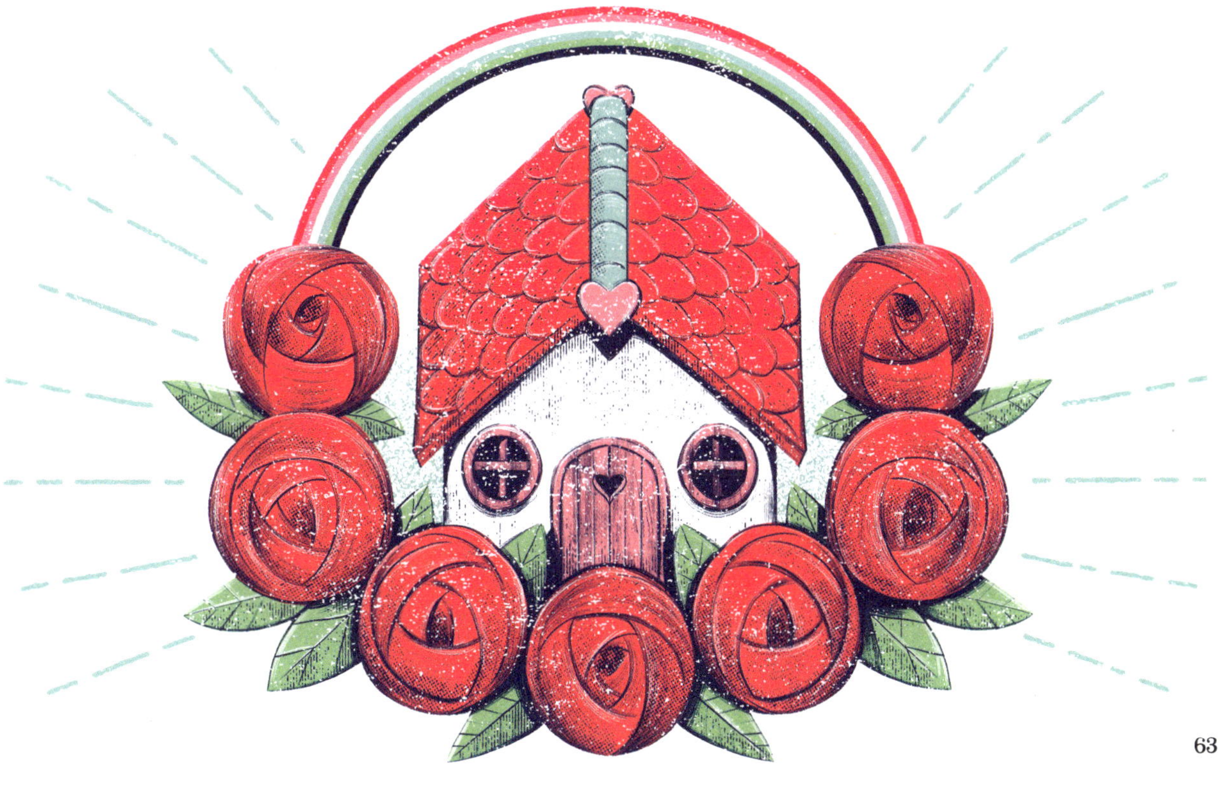

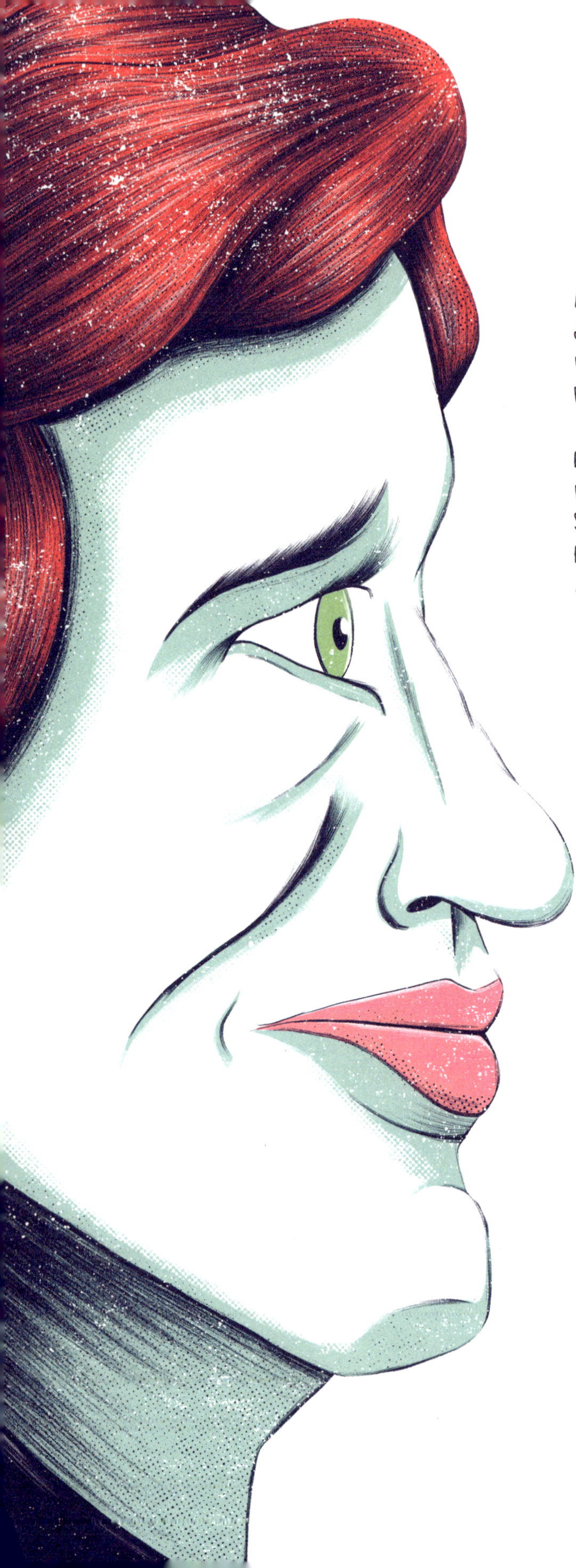

COMIENZA lo INTERESANTE

AHORA VIENE la PARTE GRAVE. ELISA SE MARCHÓ de CORUÑA y, al CABO de UN MES, LLEGÓ UN HOMBRE LLAMADO MARIO SÁNCHEZ LORIGA. VISITÓ al SACERDOTE CORTIELLA y le DIJO que VENÍA de LONDRES. PIDIÓ el BAUTISMO y ANUNCIÓ SU INTENCIÓN de CASARSE.

El 8 de JUNIO de 1901 ELISA y MARIO CONTRAJERON MATRIMONIO. NADIE SOSPECHÓ la SUPERCHERÍA NI ADVIRTIÓ el VERDADERO SEXO BAJO AQUEL TRAJE OSCURO y SOMBRERO BLANCO. El ABUNDANTE PELO de ELISA APARECÍA CORTADO CASI al RAPE en MARIO. SE HABÍA PEINADO SACÁNDOSE la RAYA y DEJÁNDOSE TUPÉ.

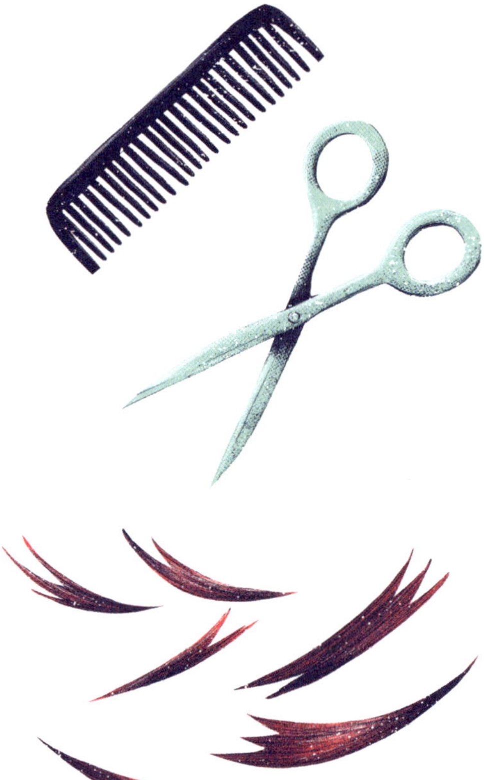

SE DESCUBRE EL ENREDO. EXPLICACIONES INVEROSÍMILES. FINAL DEL FOLLETÍN

LO MÁS INEXPLICABLE es que EL PADRINO CONOCÍA MUY BIEN a ELISA. Y HABLANDO CON SUS AMIGOS, HIZO ESTE RELATO:

«YO HE TRATADO MUCHO a ELISA, PUES SOMOS PARIENTES. SIEMPRE que VENÍA a VISITARME VESTÍA FALDAS de MUJER. PERO en MAYO QUEDEME ABSORTO al PRESENTARSE en TRAJE de HOMBRE, con SOMBRERO CORDOBÉS y el PELO CORTADO. ENTONCES ME CONTÓ UNA LARGA HISTORIA: QUE NO ERA... ELLA, SINO ÉL; QUE SE IBA a CASAR para REPARAR UNA GRAVE FALTA, PUES que la JOVEN CON QUIEN SOSTENÍA RELACIONES AMOROSAS ESTABA ENCINTA. YO lo CREÍ TODO. ME PIDIÓ que APADRINARA SU BODA, FUI DÉBIL y ACCEDÍ».

DESPUÉS del CASORIO LLEGÓ al SACERDOTE UNA CARTA SIN FIRMA:

¡MARIO es UNA MUJER!

LA DENUNCIA LLEGÓ al JUEZ y el JUEZ MANDÓ a UN MÉDICO al HOGAR del MATRIMONIO. MARIO PROTESTÓ, SE REVOLVIÓ, pero el DOCTOR ACABÓ DESCUBRIENDO que, BAJO los PANTALONES, HABÍA UNA HEMBRA.

El JUZGADO de CORCUBIÓN INSTRUYÓ la CAUSA. LOS PERIÓDICOS HABLABAN del «SUCESO DISPARATADO, INVEROSÍMIL, que PARECE ARRANCADO del MÁS DESATINADO de los FOLLETINES». LA HISTORIA SALIÓ a la PRENSA INTERNACIONAL, para COMIDILLA y MOFA de TODO el MUNDO. MIENTRAS, las AMANTES HUÍAN: A PORTUGAL, a BUENOS AIRES..., ALLÁ DONDE PUDIERAN ESCONDER UN AMOR MÁS SOBERBIO que CUALQUIER DESPRECIO.

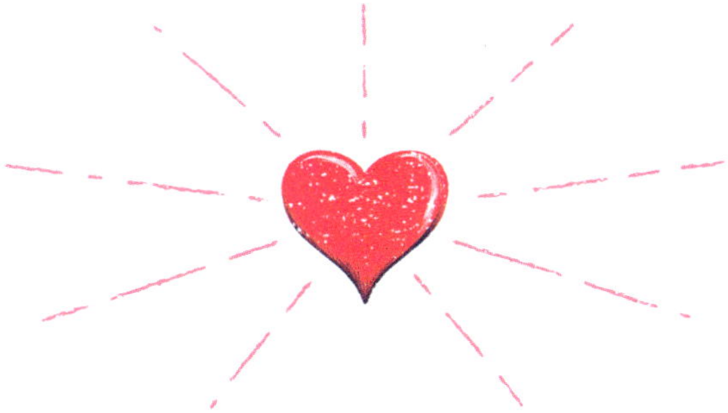

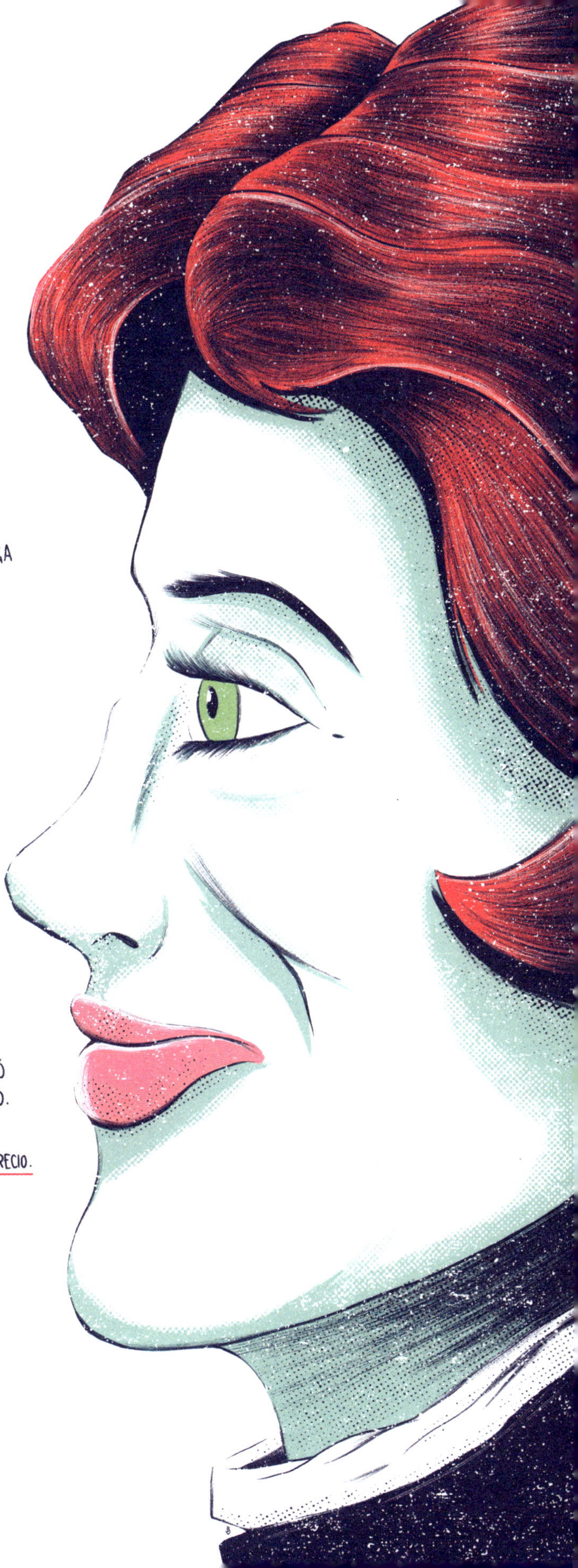

Descubran las semillas del feminismo de hoy de la mano de...

Concepción Gimeno de Flaquer

La periodista feminista

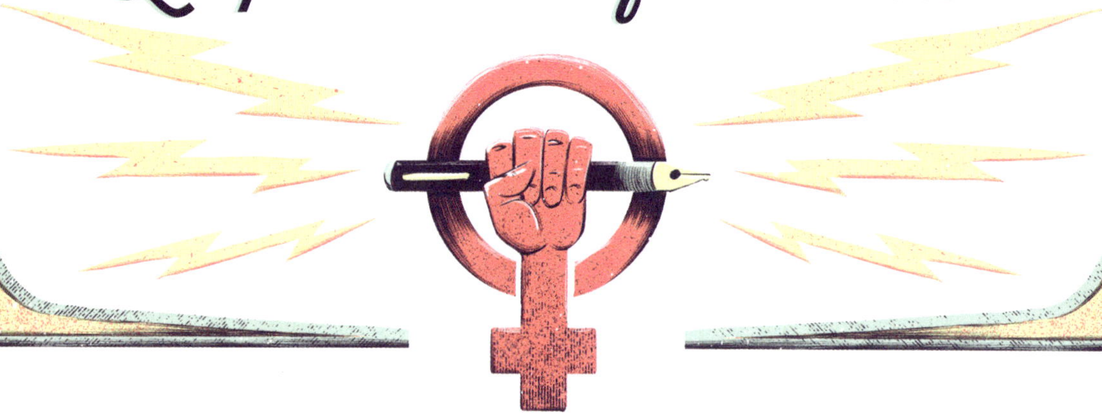

ESCRIBIÓ ARTÍCULOS, FUNDÓ REVISTAS y PUBLICÓ NOVELAS. MARÍA de la CONCEPCIÓN GIMENO de FLAQUER (1850-1919) APUNTALÓ en SUS TEXTOS las BASES de UN FEMINISMO que EN el SIGLO XXI AÚN RESULTA ACTUAL.

VIVIÓ en ESPAÑA, VIVIÓ en AMÉRICA: EN MÉXICO, en BUENOS AIRES... Y A AMBOS LADOS del ATLÁNTICO FUNDÓ REVISTAS. EN MÉXICO CREÓ «El ÁLBUM de la MUJER» y en ESPAÑA lo CONVIRTIÓ en «ÁLBUM IBERO-AMERICANO».

ANTES, JOVENCITA, CON SOLO VEINTISIETE AÑOS, LEYÓ ALGUNOS CAPÍTULOS de SU OBRA INÉDITA «LA MUJER ESPAÑOLA» ANTE el REY ALFONSO XII. TAN GRATA FUE la IMPRESIÓN de los MONARCAS al OÍR SUS PALABRAS que la FAMILIA REAL SIEMPRE le BRINDÓ SU AMISTAD.

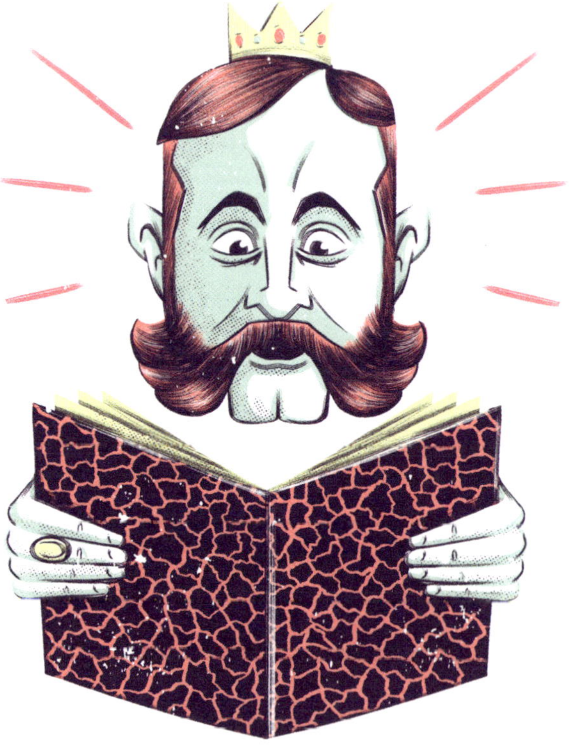

POCO DESPUÉS SE PUBLICÓ el LIBRO. EN «LA MUJER ESPAÑOLA» PEDÍA CONCEPCIÓN UNA «REVOLUCIÓN en el MUNDO de las IDEAS». Los MACHOS DEBÍAN DEJAR de VER a las HEMBRAS COMO ENEMIGAS:

«El HOMBRE NO QUIERE la CULTURA de NUESTRO ESPÍRITU PORQUE TEME que le DISPUTEMOS UNA HOJA de LAUREL para NUESTRAS FRENTES».

AVANZABAN las PÁGINAS y la PERIODISTA ESCRIBÍA:

«El HOMBRE, SIEMPRE EGOÍSTA, en LUGAR de PROTEGER al SEXO que APELLIDA DÉBIL, HA CONSPIRADO de FORMA INFAME CONTRA ÉL. NO SOLO le HA ANATEMATIZADO CRUELMENTE, SINO que le HA USURPADO MUCHAS OCUPACIONES. El HOMBRE HA DESPOJADO GRADUALMENTE a la MUJER de los POCOS MEDIOS CON que CONTABA para DEFENDERSE de la MISERIA.

ES VERGONZOSO, CRIMINAL y HUMILLANTE VER a UN HOMBRE en UN ALMACÉN de MODAS, PLEGANDO y DESPLEGANDO TELAS DELICADÍSIMAS, que OFRECEN EN SUS MANOS el TERRIBLE CONTRASTE que PRESENTA a la VISTA el RASO y la ESTAMEÑA.

ES DEPLORABLE que UN HOMBRE GASTE el VIGOR de SU JUVENTUD en TRENZAR CABELLO, en PEINAR BUCLES y RIZAR SORTIJILLAS y TIRABUZONES. LOS PELUQUEROS NO DEBÍAN EXISTIR. ¿DÓNDE ESTÁ EL SENTIDO COMÚN y la LÓGICA del HOMBRE?».

CONCEPCIÓN, IGUAL que ROSARIO de ACUÑA (OTRA ESCRITORA, OTRA MUJER de 1850, OTRA FEMINISTA), SABÍA que la IGUALDAD ENTRE MUJERES y HOMBRES ERA UN TRABAJO LENTO, ARDUO, COLOSAL.

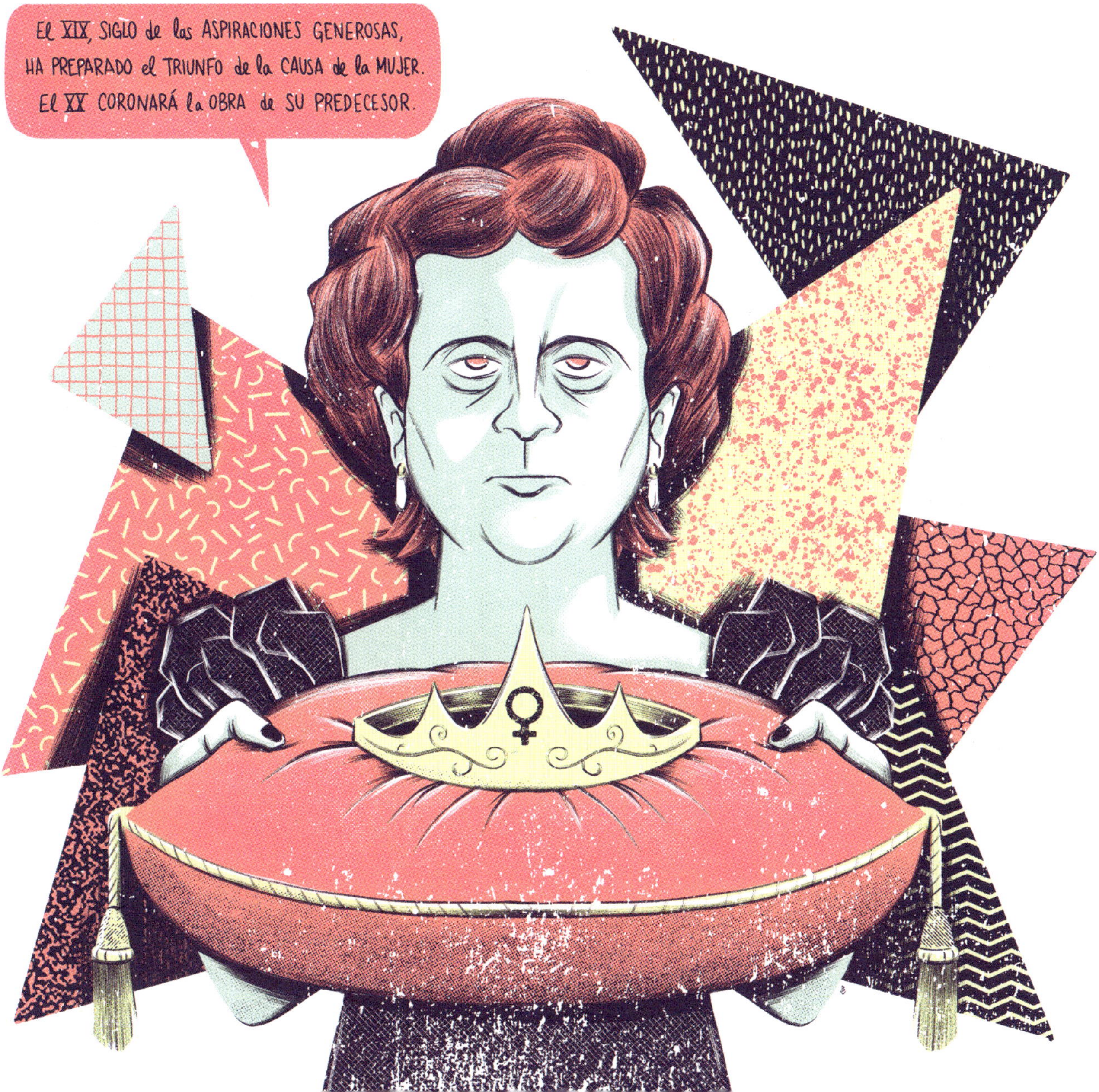

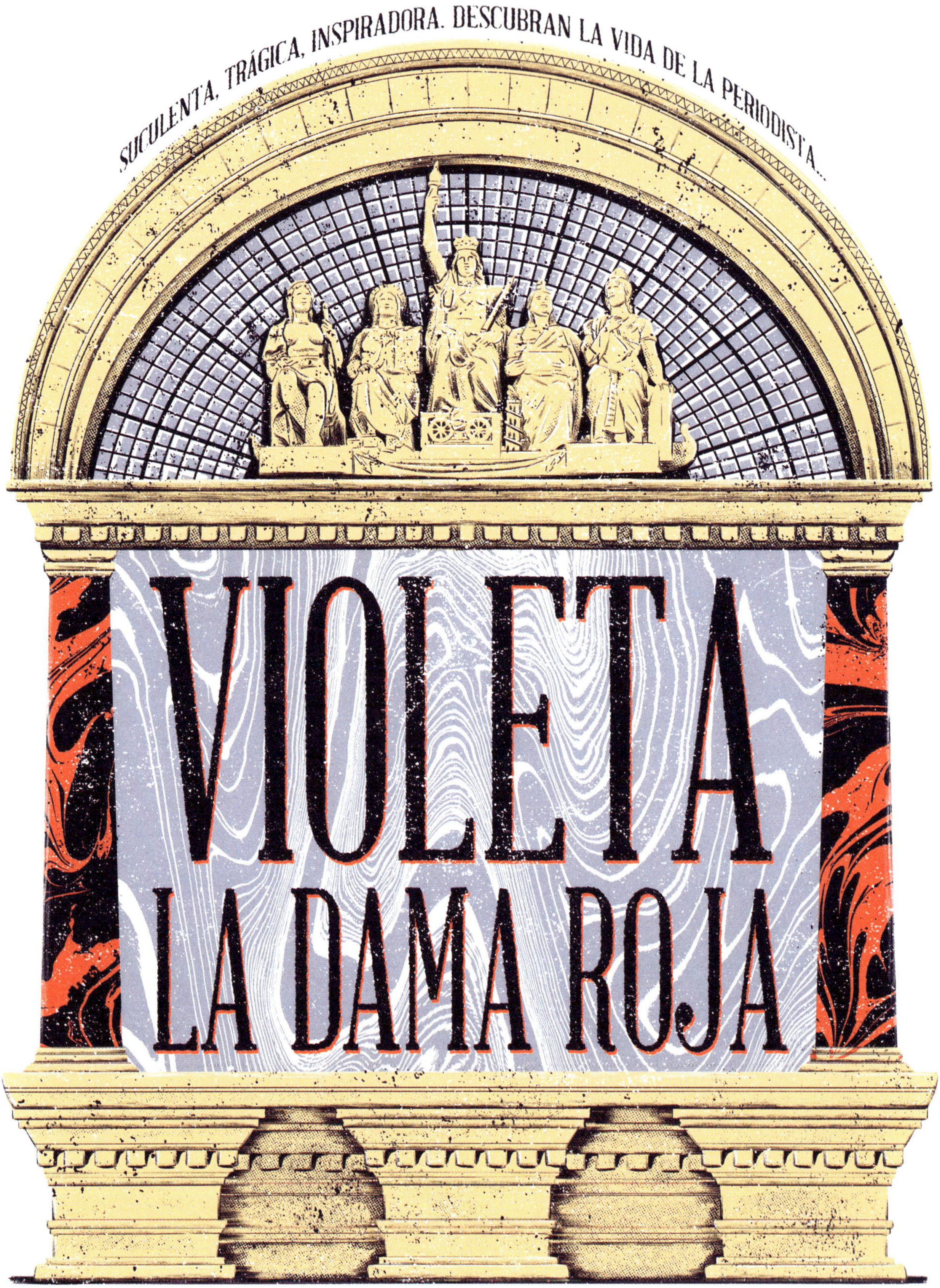
SUCULENTA, TRÁGICA, INSPIRADORA. DESCUBRAN LA VIDA DE LA PERIODISTA...
VIOLETA
LA DAMA ROJA

EN el SIGLO XIX, UN PUÑADO de CABLES ZARANDEÓ el TIEMPO y el ESPACIO. El TELÉGRAFO CONSIGUIÓ lo IMPENSABLE: ALGUIEN PODÍA LEER en AMÉRICA lo que OTRO ESCRIBÍA a la VEZ en la LEJANA EUROPA. EUFORIA.

ESOS MENSAJES LLEGABAN y PARTÍAN desde UN LUGAR FUTURISTA: LA OFICINA de TELÉGRAFOS de MADRID. DECENAS de TRABAJADORES DESCIFRABAN AHÍ el NUEVO LENGUAJE PLANETARIO: el MORSE.

UNA JOVEN de DIECISIETE AÑOS, FALTA de DINERO y LIBERTAD, SE PRESENTÓ a la OPOSICIÓN DESTINADA a MUJERES SOLTERAS y VIUDAS de TELEGRAFISTAS. ¡APROBÓ! A PUNTO de ENTRAR a ESA OFICINA ESTABA **CONSUELO ÁLVAREZ POOL** (1867-1959) CUANDO el DESTINO CORTOCIRCUITÓ.

TOC, TOC

El CARTERO LLAMÓ a SU PUERTA, PERO NADIE ABRIÓ.

CONSUELO NO RECIBIÓ la CARTA que la CITABA COMO AUXILIAR TEMPORERA en TELÉGRAFOS y el DÍA que DEBÍA OCUPAR SU PUESTO NO APARECIÓ.

CORRIÓ la LISTA; PERDIÓ el TRABAJO.

El SUEÑO de TRABAJAR ENTRE MÁQUINAS y VIVIR a SU AIRE ACABÓ ESTAMPADO en lo MÁS RANCIO de la TRADICIÓN. SU MADRE le BUSCÓ UN MARIDO y la OBLIGÓ a CASARSE. DESPUÉS LLEGÓ lo INEVITABLE: PARIR SIN PARAR, PARIR HASTA REVENTAR.

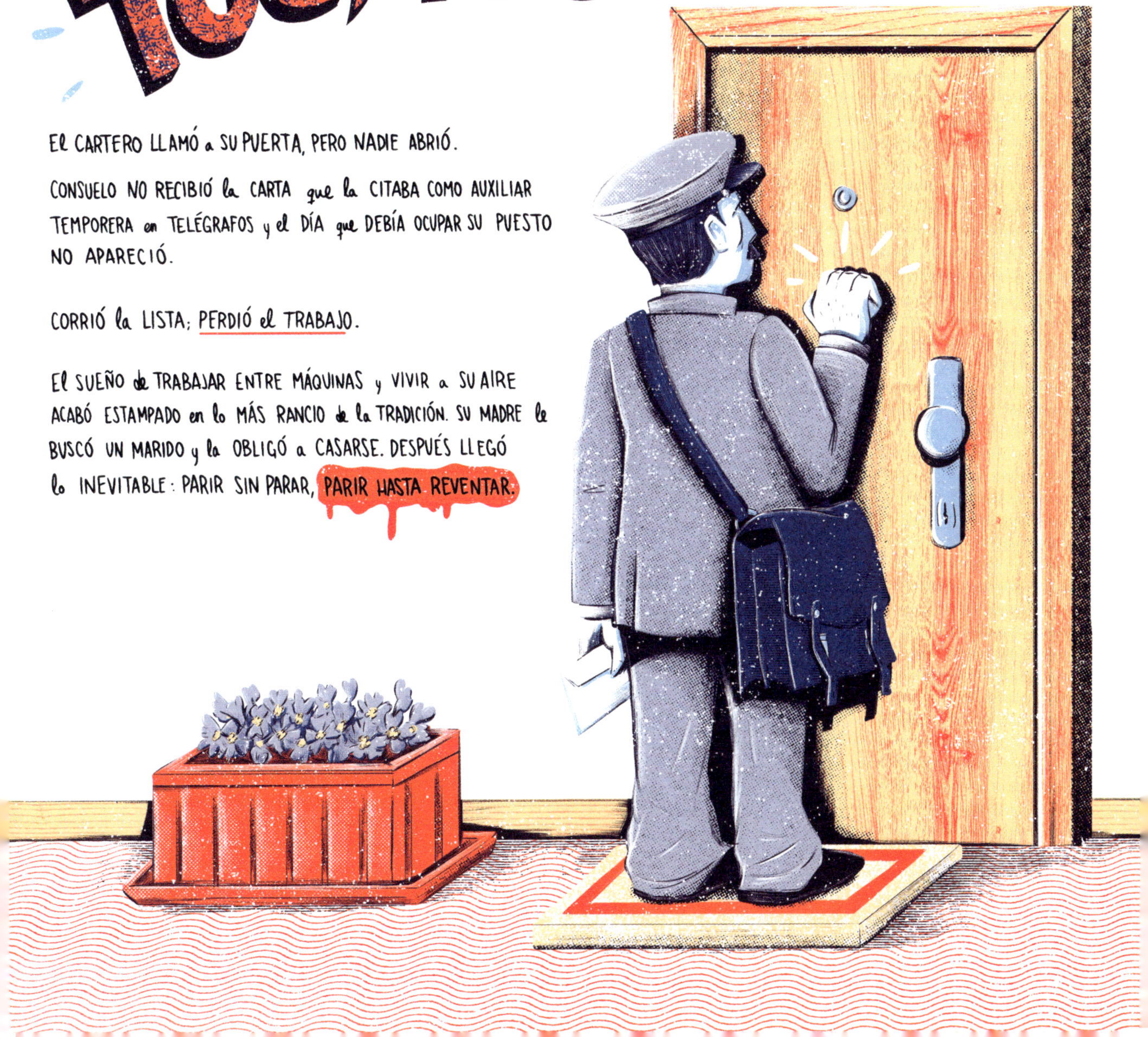

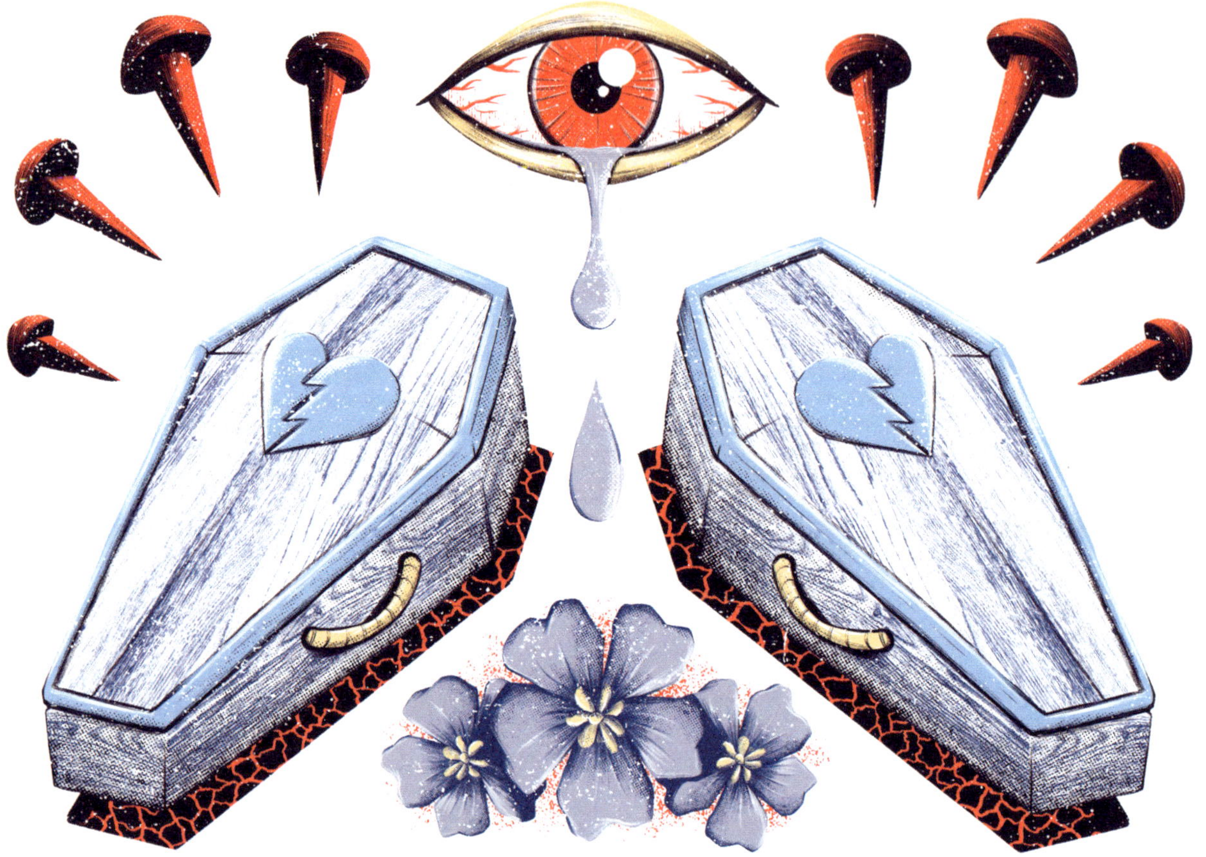

Al PRINCIPIO, la MATERNIDAD le DIO la VIDA: LOS DOS PRIMEROS CRECIERON SANOS. A PARTIR de AHÍ, FUE UNA AGONÍA: la TERCERA SUCUMBIÓ de MENINGITIS y el CUARTO MURIÓ CUANDO INTENTABA NACER.

El DOLOR SOLTÓ UN CHISPAZO: CONSUELO DEJÓ al MARIDO y, DESOYENDO a las COTORRAS, SALIÓ a BUSCAR el DESTINO que le PERTENECÍA.

«MÁS VIRTUD HUIR NOBLEMENTE de UN MARIDO a QUIEN NO SE AMA que ENGAÑARLO a MANSALVA, FINGIR CARICIAS, VENDER PROMESAS y ACEPTAR CON REPUGNANCIA PENOSAS REALIDADES.»

EN MADRID ENCONTRÓ UN TRABAJO de PERIODISTA. UN AMIGO SABÍA que CONSUELO ESCRIBÍA y la RECOMENDÓ en «EL PAÍS». A PARTIR de ENTONCES SE CONVIRTIÓ en VIOLETA, PORQUE ES «LA FLOR de los HUMILDES, la FLOR de la que SUEÑA SU PRIMER AMOR».

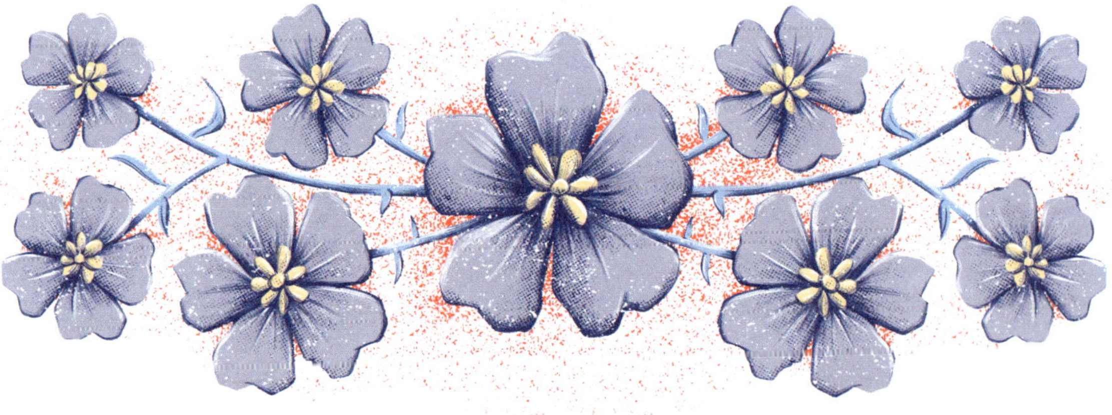

EN AQUEL TIEMPO en que NADIE ESPERABA de UNA MUJER MÁS que UN POTAJE y UN CALCETÍN ZURCIDO, VIOLETA ESCRIBÍA SOBRE la VIDA de LAS OBRERAS, la DESDICHA de la PROSTITUCIÓN, la IMPORTANCIA de la HIGIENE, la DESIGUALDAD ENTRE HOMBRES y MUJERES.

PERO el PERIODISMO APENAS le DIO PARA HABICHUELAS. EN 1908 RECUPERÓ el PUESTO que HABÍA PERDIDO en TELÉGRAFOS. AHÍ TRABAJÓ el RESTO de SU VIDA y AHÍ ESTRENÓ UN CARGO DESCONOCIDO HASTA ENTONCES: FUE JEFA de PRENSA de la INSTITUCIÓN.

TAMBIÉN ESTRENÓ la PRENSA del PORVENIR. EN RADIO ESPAÑA TENÍA UN PROGRAMA SOBRE la MUJER del FUTURO. VIOLETA, DESDE la AGRUPACIÓN de las DAMAS ROJAS, HABÍA DADO DECENAS de CONFERENCIAS por TODO el PAÍS para HABLAR de la REGENERACIÓN, del VOTO FEMENINO y de la NECESIDAD de UNA SOCIEDAD IGUALITARIA.

HASTA que LLEGARON la GUERRA, la POSGUERRA, la PERSECUCIÓN. VIOLETA ERA REPUBLICANA, FEMINISTA y MASONA. Y SOLO SU VEJEZ, GRANDÍSIMA YA, la LIBRÓ de la CÁRCEL. PERO NO ESQUIVÓ el OLVIDO.

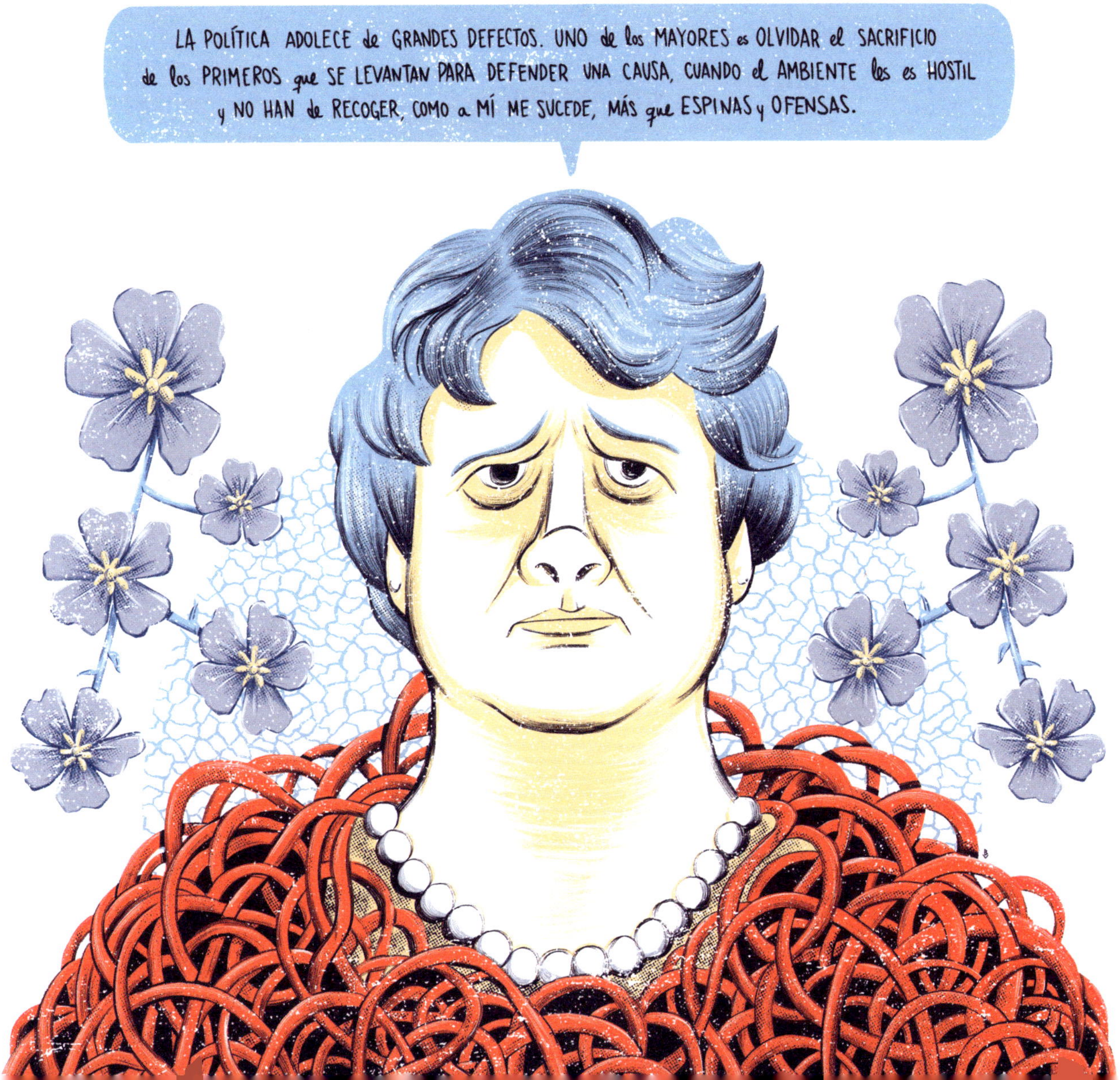

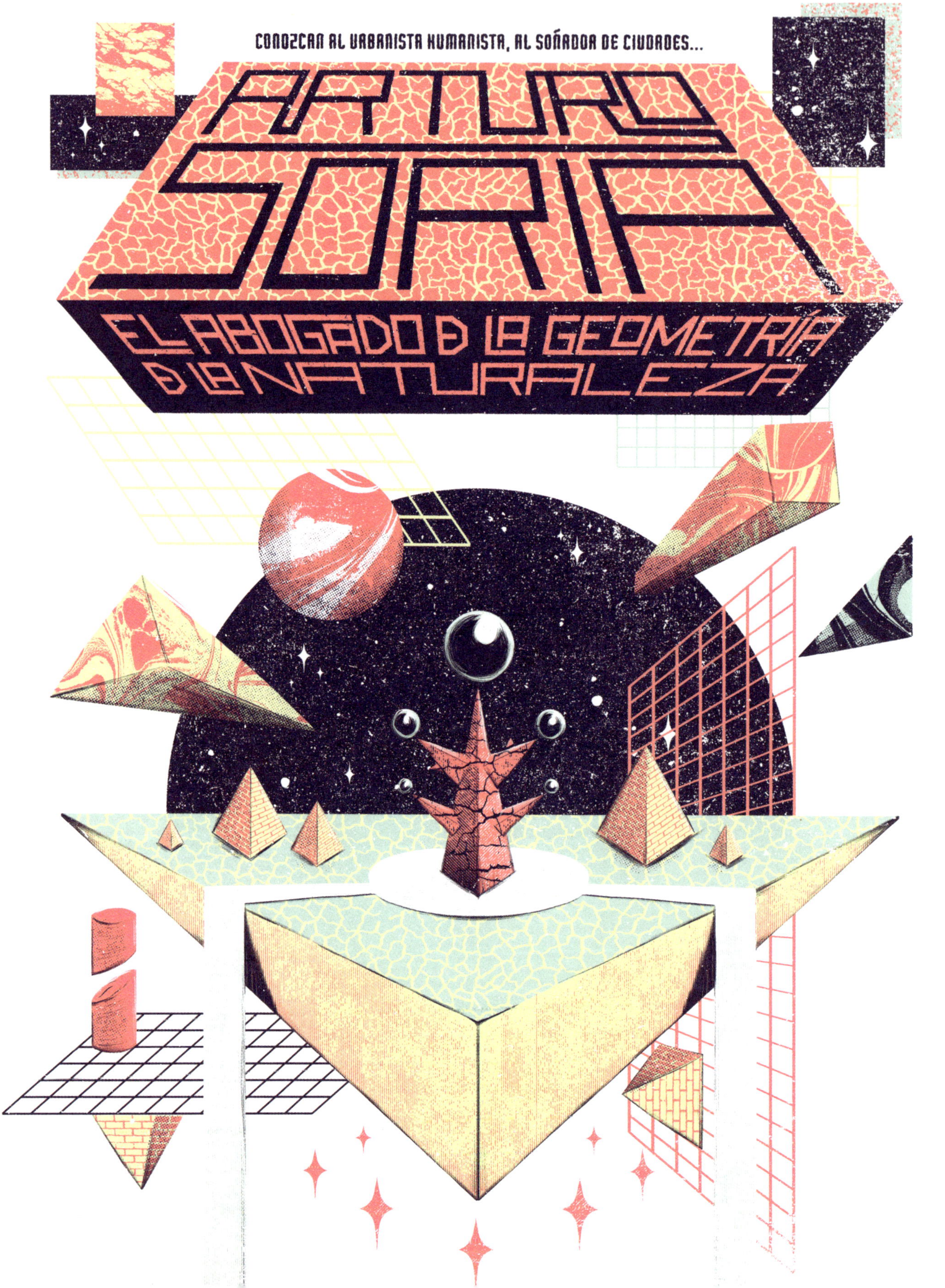
CONOZCAN AL URBANISTA HUMANISTA, AL SOÑADOR DE CIUDADES...
ARTURO SORIA
EL ABOGADO DE LA GEOMETRÍA DE LA NATURALEZA

TAN EXCELENTE FUE de ESTUDIANTE que SU MAESTRO SE BATIÓ en DUELO por ÉL. El MATEMÁTICO MANUEL BECERRA PREPARÓ a ARTURO SORIA (1844-1920) PARA INGRESAR en la ESCUELA de CAMINOS. ERA un ALUMNO BRILLANTE. PERO, en el TRIBUNAL de INGRESO, UN EXAMINADOR lo VETÓ. DECÍA que el JOVEN lo HABÍA RIDICULIZADO, y UN DESAIRE TAL NO SE PODÍA TOLERAR.

A ARTURO le ENTRARON FIEBRES DEPRESIVAS. NO SOPORTÓ SEMEJANTE ATROPELLO. MANUEL BECERRA, PRESO de CÓLERA, RETÓ en DUELO al MIEMBRO del TRIBUNAL. NI ASÍ ENTRÓ el DISCÍPULO en CAMINOS, de MODO que OPTÓ por UN PUESTO de FUNCIONARIO en las OFICINAS de ESTADÍSTICA del FERROCARRIL.

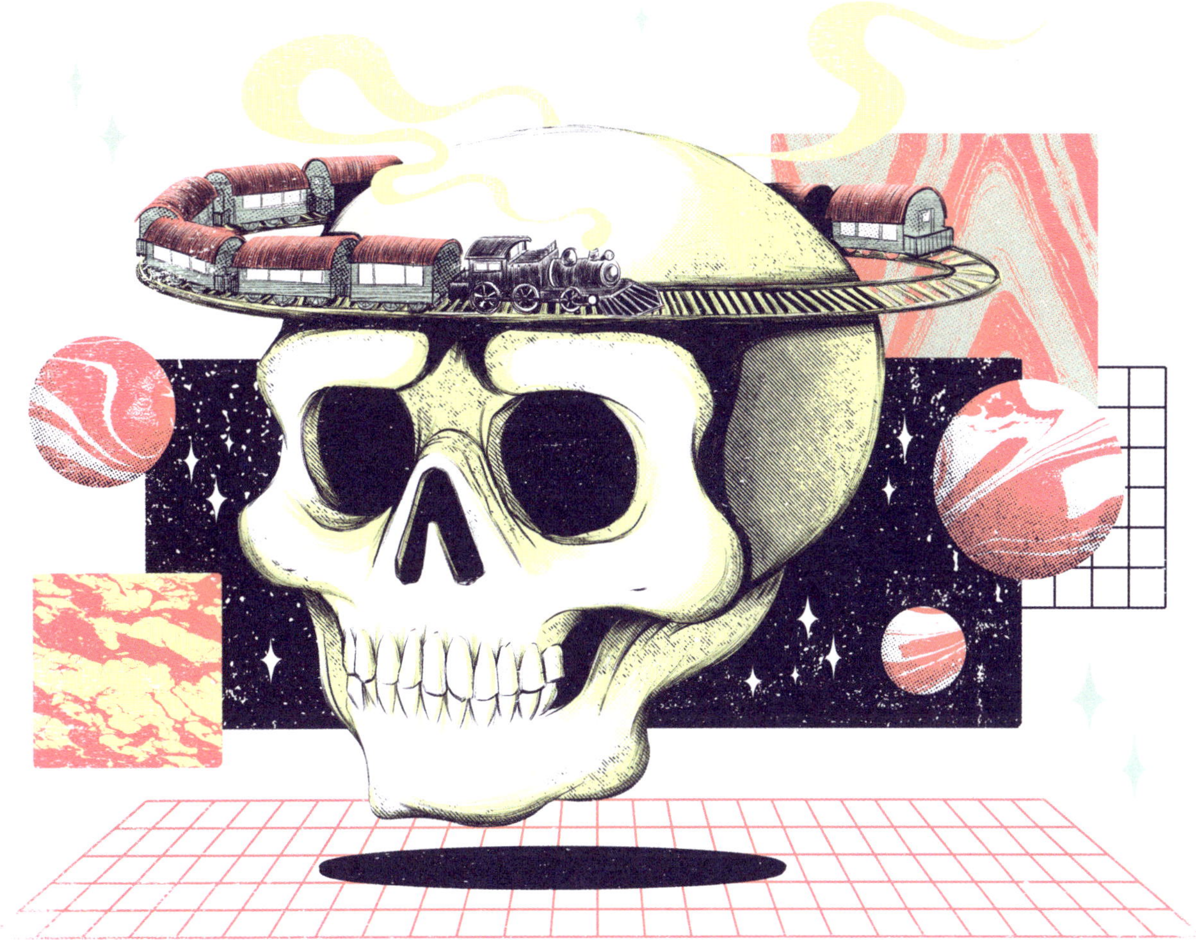

EMPEZARON los TRENES a RONDAR SU CABEZA. DESDE la DIRECCIÓN de TRANVÍAS de ESTACIONES y MERCADOS HABLABA del «SUEÑO TRANVIARIO». ANTES de que EXISTIERA el METRO, IDEÓ UN FERROCARRIL SUBTERRÁNEO PARA RECORRER la CIUDAD. NO PUDO HACERLO REALIDAD.

EN CUANTO OYÓ HABLAR del TELÉFONO, PRESENTÓ UN PLAN al GOBIERNO para CONSTRUIR UNA RED TELEFÓNICA. DE HABÉRSELA CONCEDIDO, HABRÍA SIDO la PRIMERA del PLANETA. NO OCURRIÓ.

El PENSAMIENTO de ARTURO SORIA IBA del NÚMERO RELATIVO a la VERDAD ABSOLUTA. ERA TEÓSOFO:

«HE BUSCADO la VERDAD. NO he TENIDO la INTENCIÓN de HACER NI UNA OBRA PIADOSA, NI MENOS UNA IMPÍA».

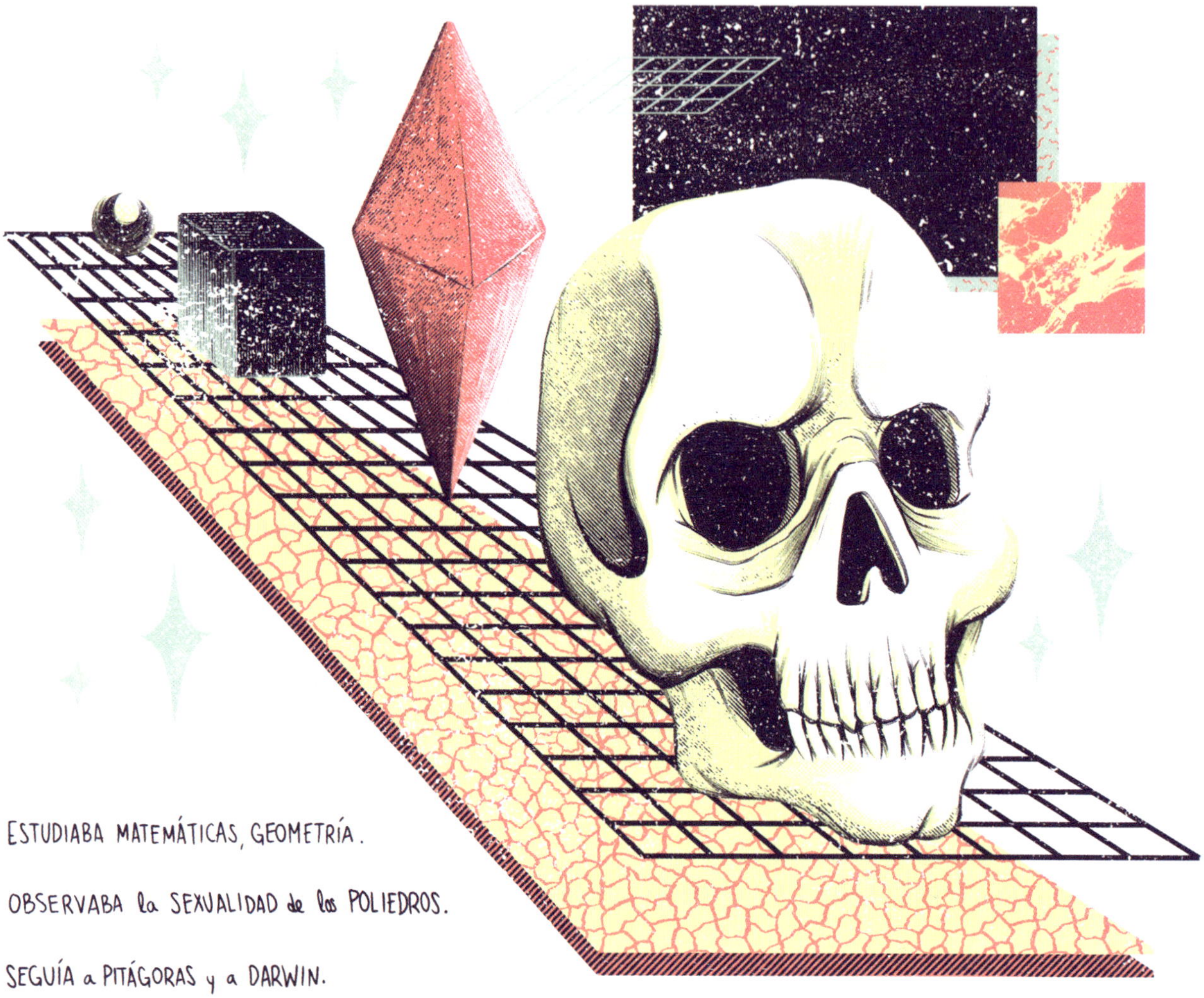

ESTUDIABA MATEMÁTICAS, GEOMETRÍA.

OBSERVABA la SEXUALIDAD de los POLIEDROS.

SEGUÍA a PITÁGORAS y a DARWIN.

LOS NÚMEROS LLEVARÍAN a la ARMONÍA UNIVERSAL; la EVOLUCIÓN de las ESPECIES CONDUCIRÍA al PROGRESO INFINITO.

DIO TANTAS VUELTAS al ASUNTO que lo ACABÓ CONTANDO en el LIBRO «ORIGEN POLIÉDRICO de las ESPECIES»:

«NO HA TENIDO DARWIN la DICHA de VER CON CLARIDAD que el ORIGEN de las ESPECIES VIENE del ORIGEN de las FORMAS; que ESTE es el TETRAEDRO REGULAR, DERIVADO de la ESFERA».

PENSÓ TANTO SOBRE el TEMA que ESCRIBIÓ «El PROGRESO INDEFINIDO»:

«CREEMOS en la APARICIÓN de COSAS NUEVAS MÁS PERFECTAS POTENCIALMENTE CONTENIDAS en las COSAS MENOS PERFECTAS que CONOCEMOS».

A los CINCUENTA AÑOS, CONVENCIDO de que AHÍ DONDE NO PUEDE VIVIR UN ÁRBOL NO DEBEN VIVIR los HUMANOS, CREÓ la COMPAÑÍA MADRILEÑA de URBANIZACIÓN. QUERÍA CONVERTIR los CAMPOS ÁRIDOS del NORDESTE de la CIUDAD en BARRIOS de VIVIENDAS CON VEGETACIÓN:

«PARA CADA FAMILIA, UNA CASA; EN CADA CASA, UNA HUERTA y UN JARDÍN».

ESE ERA SU «SUEÑO LINEAL»; SU PROYECTO de CONSTRUIR la CIUDAD LINEAL. UN LUGAR DONDE NADIE VIVIERA HACINADO en BARRIOS SUCIOS y DESORDENADOS COMO los que SURGÍAN en las AFUERAS de las URBES al CALOR de la REVOLUCIÓN INDUSTRIAL.

ARTURO SORIA QUISO LLEVAR la LUZ de la RAZÓN, del CÁLCULO y de la GEOMETRÍA a las NUEVAS CALLES de MADRID. IGUALDAD y FRATERNIDAD en las POBLACIONES del FUTURO. ASÍ SONABA SU VOZ de MASÓN: de SOLÓN, que FUE el NOMBRE SIMBÓLICO que UTILIZÓ, en HONOR a UNO de los SIETE SABIOS GRIEGOS.

El PROYECTO NAUFRAGÓ en SUS FINANZAS. El PLAN INICIAL NO PUDO LLEVARSE a CABO. PERO QUEDARON SUS IDEAS, SÓLIDAS e INSPIRADORAS, PARA la HISTORIA del URBANISMO.

NO ERA ESTE SU EMPEÑO. A ÉL le HABRÍA GUSTADO TRASCENDER por SUS TEORÍAS de ARITMÉTICA y GEOMETRÍA. POR SU TEOSOFÍA, INCLUSO. NO FUE POSIBLE. TAL COMO INDICÓ en el PRÓLOGO de «ORIGEN POLIÉDRICO de los ESPECIES».

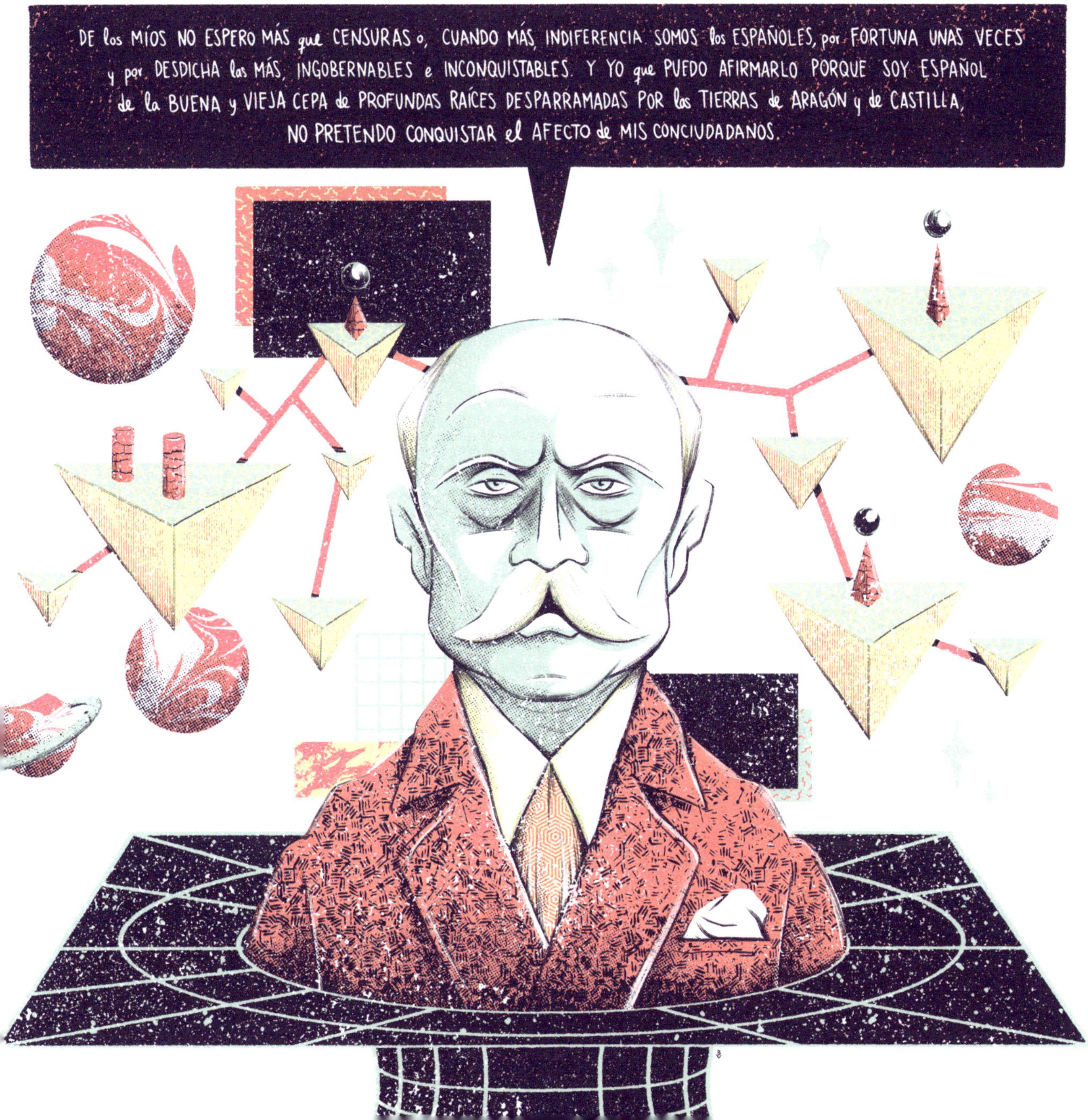

ABRAN SUS OJOS... Y ABRAN SU MENTE... PARA ENCONTRARSE CON...

AURORA BERTRANA

La escritora que defendía el amor libre

DESDE la PROA de un TRANSATLÁNTICO, **AURORA BERTRANA** VE el PARAÍSO. POR FIN. LA ESCRITORA y VIOLONCHELISTA (1892-1974) HA ESPERADO ESTE MOMENTO DESDE que ERA NIÑA: DESDE las TARDES de COLEGIO que PASABA PERDIDA MIRANDO MAPAS.

VIAJA con SU MARIDO, MONSIEUR CHOFFAT, DESPUÉS de CONVENCERLO de que BUSCARA un TRABAJO en la POLINESIA. TIENEN TRES AÑOS por DELANTE para que ÉL MONTE UNA CENTRAL ELÉCTRICA y ELLA RECORRA las ISLAS de OCEANÍA, con SU KODAK al CUELLO y UNA LIBRETA en la MANO.

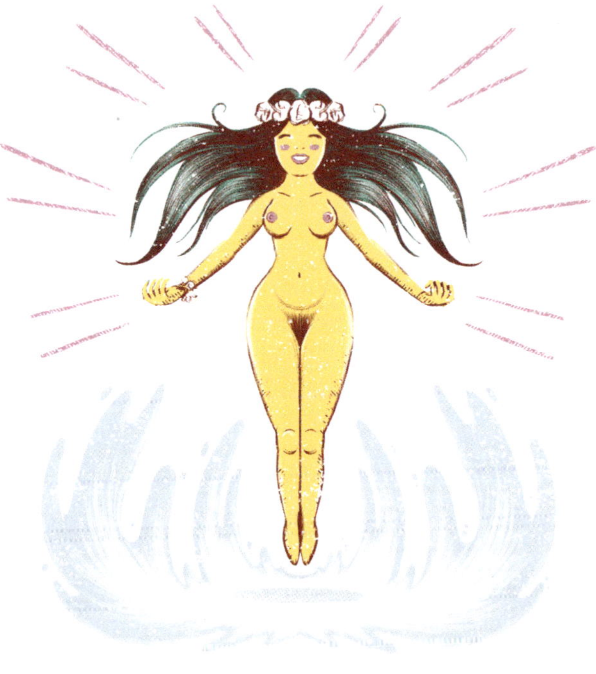

LA PERIODISTA, de TREINTA y CUATRO AÑOS, NUNCA HA VISTO NADA IGUAL. LE MARAVILLA «EL VERDE de la VEGETACIÓN, que PARECE RECIÉN PINTADO, TODAVÍA MOJADO y BRILLANTE de BARNIZ». LE APASIONA el COLOR del CIELO, REFULGENTE, «DE UN AZUL de ESMALTE».

PERO le SORPRENDE MÁS AÚN la LUZ de los POLINESIOS. VIENEN LIBRES de MORALINAS y CASTIGOS de DIOS. AMAN a QUIEN les DA la GANA y HASTA las CORTESANAS (las PROSTITUTAS) SON RESPETADAS COMO NINFAS.

BERTRANA SE ENVALENTONA. ESTO de REVOLCARSE CADA CUAL con QUIEN QUIERA es UN PECADO MARRANO en SU PAÍS de ORIGEN. A ELLA le DA IGUAL. EMPIEZA a CONTARLO (y CON TODO LUJO de DETALLES) en las CRÓNICAS que ENVÍA a VARIOS PERIÓDICOS.

¡¡¡...!!! OJOS COMO PLATOS. ALGUNOS LECTORES GOZAN del EXOTISMO. «¡OOOH!» OTROS SE SANTIGUAN: «¡AAAH!»... AVE MARÍA PURÍSIMA.

«PREGUNTADLE a CUALQUIER MAORÍ SI TUREY HA OBRADO BIEN al HACERSE CORTESANA. NI UNO SOLO OS DIRÁ que NO. ¡NI VOSOTROS NI YO SOMOS NADIE para JUZGAR a ESTA VIEJA RAZA MISTERIOSA! TODO TAHITÍ ADMIRA a SU CORTESANA.»

FRENTE a la ESPAÑA GAZMOÑA de la VIRGINIDAD y los PUDORES, BERTRANA ENCUENTRA un LUGAR DISFRUTÓN DONDE NO SE INSULTA a NADIE por GOZAR del SEXO. LOS ARGUMENTOS MOJIGATOS en los que FUE EDUCADA SE DESPLOMAN. LE ENTUSIASMA que los HOMBRES «NO SE OPONGAN al LIBRE AMOR de las MUJERES CON las que SE JUNTAN y se SEPARAN SIN PASAR NI por el JUZGADO, NI por la VICARÍA. NO TIENEN el INSTINTO de POSESIÓN NI el MISMO CONCEPTO del HONOR que los BLANCOS».

LOS LECTORES DEVORAN los REPORTAJES que ENVÍA desde la POLINESIA. Y en 1930, ya en BARCELONA, BERTRANA PUBLICA ESTAS HISTORIAS, AMPLIADAS, en el LIBRO «PARAÍSOS OCEÁNICOS».

«LA EDICIÓN SE AGOTÓ en QUINCE DÍAS, AUNQUE el EJEMPLAR SE VENDÍA a QUINCE PESETAS -UN PASTIZAL, RECORDÓ SU AUTORA en las MEMORIAS que ESCRIBIÓ al FINAL de SU VIDA-. LA OBRA FUE NO SOLO UN GRAN ÉXITO de VENTAS, SINO un GRAN ÉXITO LITERARIO.»

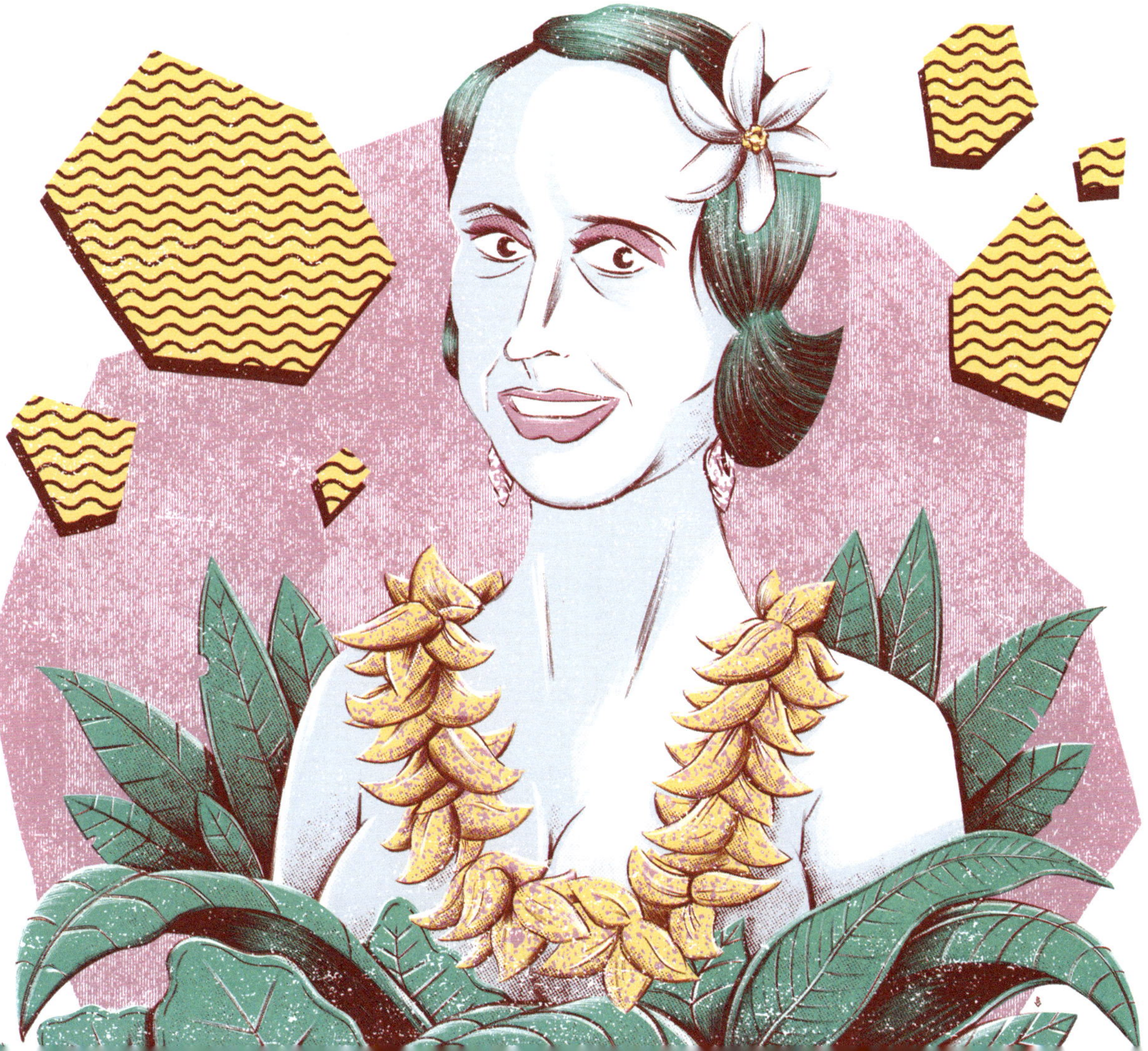

PÓNGANSE SUS MÁS SUCULENTOS LUJOS PARA ASISTIR A ESTA VELADA CON...

EL CABALLERO AUDAZ

EL DIESTRO DE LAS ENTREVISTAS

ERAN CASI DOS METROS de CABALLERO AUDAZ. DOS METROS de PERIODISTA AFAMADO por ENTRAR en los DESPACHOS y CAMERINOS de los GRANDES PERSONAJES de PRINCIPIOS del SIGLO XX y SALIR con UN PAR de NOTAS que CONVERTÍA en BELLÍSIMOS PERFILES. DOS METROS de HOMBRE GALLARDO que le HICIERON VENCER en DOCE DUELOS a ESPADA y PISTOLA.

A JOSÉ **MARÍA** TEODORO **MANUEL VICENTE ANTONIO RAFAEL** del **CORAZÓN** de **JESÚS CARRETERO** y **NOVILLO** (1887-1951) le SOBRABA AMOR de las MUJERES y RECHAZO de los LIBERALES. A ELLAS las CAUTIVÓ con NOVELAS (MUCHAS, ERÓTICAS); a ELLOS los ESPANTÓ por DEFENDER el FASCISMO y las DICTADURAS.

UNA NOCHE de los AÑOS TREINTA, el CABALLERO AUDAZ ANDA por el COMEDOR SEÑORIAL del HOTEL DANUBIO de BUDAPEST. ENTRE el VIBRAR de la CRISTALERÍA, el TINTINEO de los CUBIERTOS y la MÚSICA LÁNGUIDA de UNA ORQUESTA ZÍNGARA, de PRONTO IRRUMPE la MARCHA REAL ESPAÑOLA. LOS COMENSALES SE PONEN en PIE y MIRAN HACIA la PUERTA del COMEDOR.

-«VOILÀ! C'EST le ROI d'ESPAGNE» -DICEN en la MESA de al LADO.

ALFONSO XIII, VESTIDO de ESMOQUIN, IMPECABLE, SALUDA a la ORQUESTA y al PÚBLICO. UNA HORA DESPUÉS, en la TERRAZA, el CABALLERO AUDAZ SE ACERCA al REY DESTERRADO, y ESTE, CABALLEROSO, le TIENDE SU MUSCULOSA MANO de DEPORTISTA:

-¡QUÉ CASUALIDAD ENCONTRARTE TAN LEJOS de NUESTRA ESPAÑA!

-YA, YA, SEÑOR. ¡ESTAR VUESTRA MAJESTAD AQUÍ! -CONTESTA el PERIODISTA, TRATÁNDOLO AÚN COMO SI FUERA el JEFE de ESTADO.

DON ALFONSO de BORBÓN le BRINDA UNA GRAN PITILLERA de ORO y DICE:

-FÚMALO. ES TABACO que me HAN MANDADO de ESPAÑA.

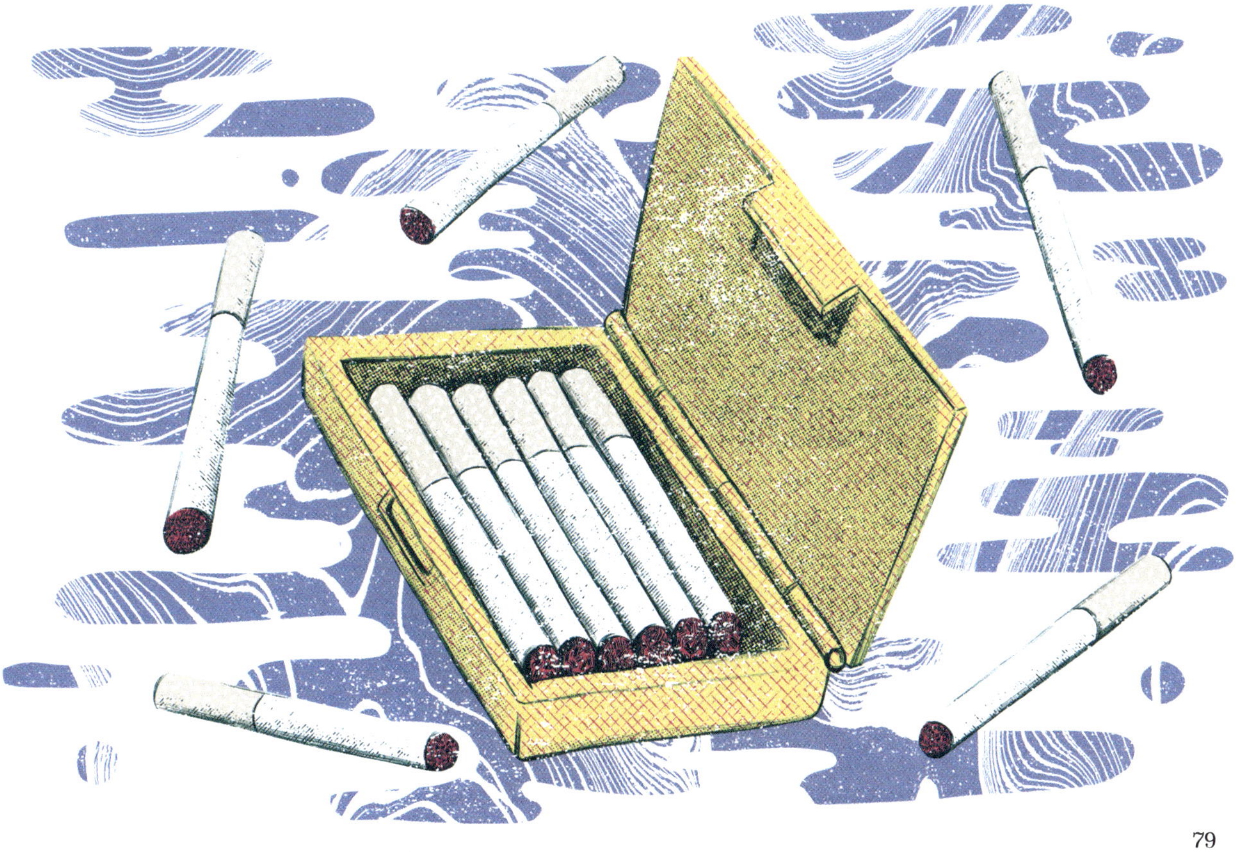

FUMAN, CONVERSAN y, AL FIN, el CABALLERO AUDAZ SE DECIDE:

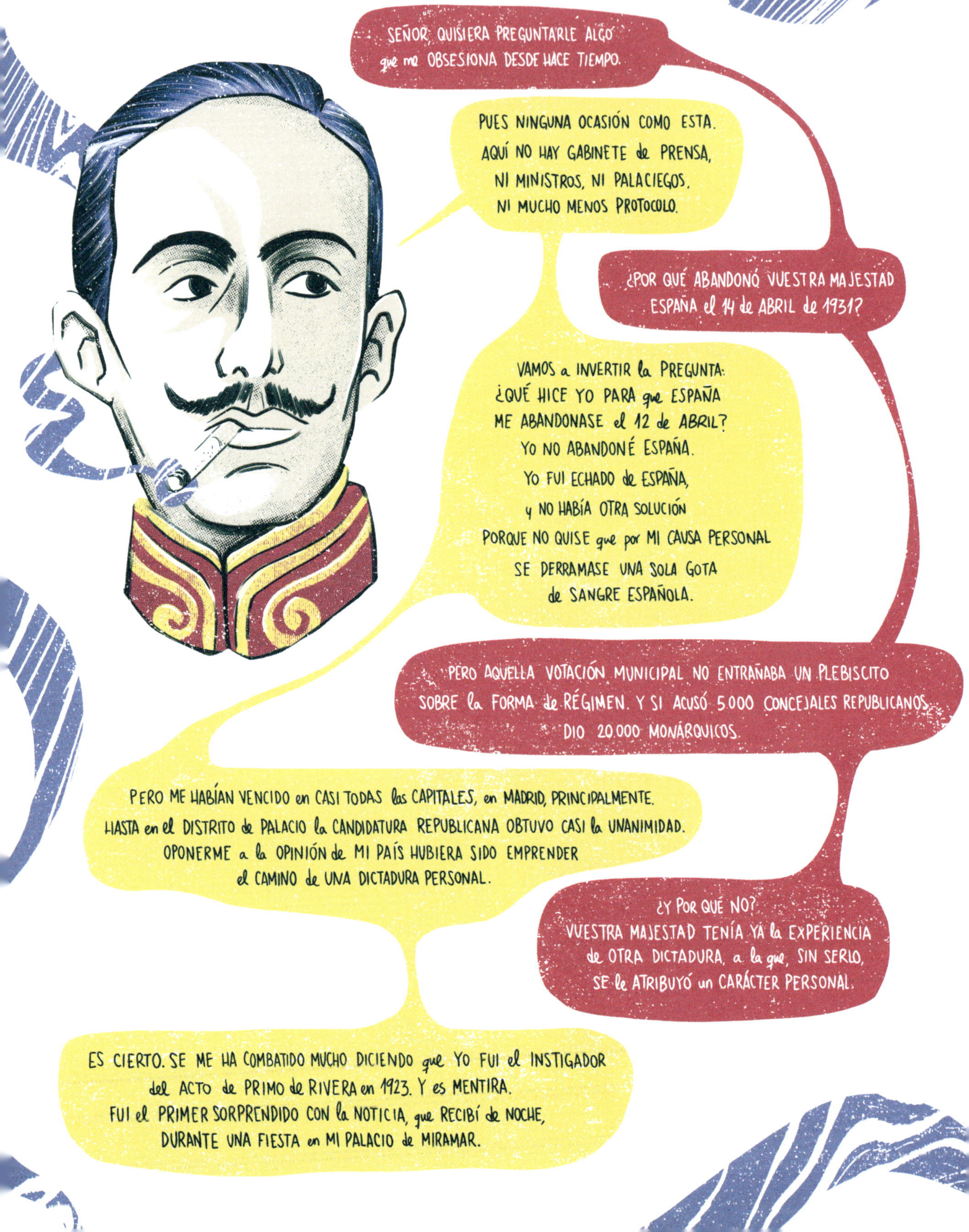

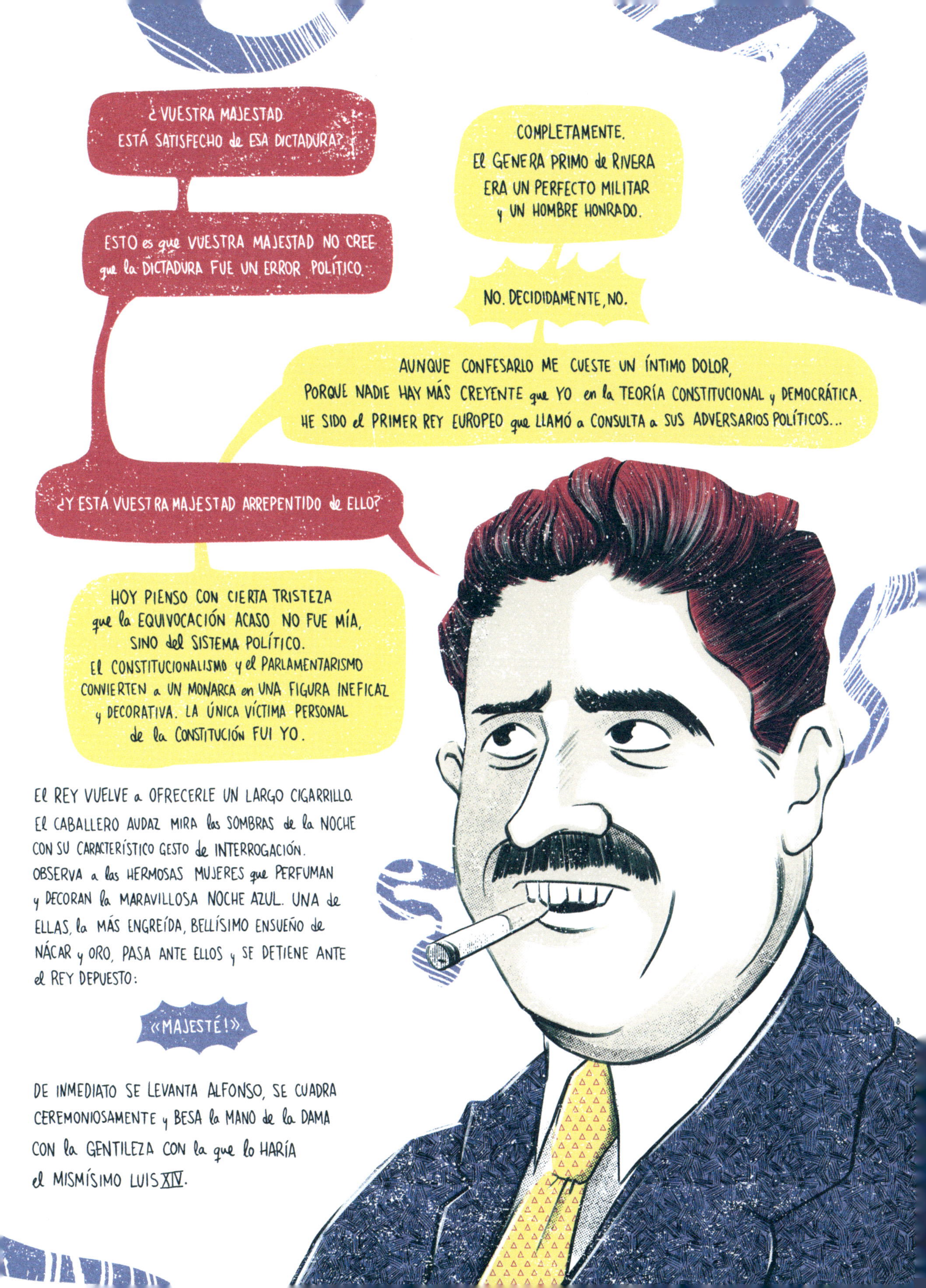
¿VUESTRA MAJESTAD ESTÁ SATISFECHO de ESA DICTADURA?
COMPLETAMENTE. El GENERA PRIMO de RIVERA ERA UN PERFECTO MILITAR y UN HOMBRE HONRADO.
ESTO es que VUESTRA MAJESTAD NO CREE que la DICTADURA FUE UN ERROR POLÍTICO.
NO. DECIDIDAMENTE, NO.
AUNQUE CONFESARLO ME CUESTE UN ÍNTIMO DOLOR, PORQUE NADIE HAY MÁS CREYENTE que YO en la TEORÍA CONSTITUCIONAL y DEMOCRÁTICA. HE SIDO el PRIMER REY EUROPEO que LLAMÓ a CONSULTA a SUS ADVERSARIOS POLÍTICOS...
¿Y ESTÁ VUESTRA MAJESTAD ARREPENTIDO de ELLO?
HOY PIENSO CON CIERTA TRISTEZA que la EQUIVOCACIÓN ACASO NO FUE MÍA, SINO del SISTEMA POLÍTICO. El CONSTITUCIONALISMO y el PARLAMENTARISMO CONVIERTEN a UN MONARCA en UNA FIGURA INEFICAZ y DECORATIVA. LA ÚNICA VÍCTIMA PERSONAL de la CONSTITUCIÓN FUI YO.
El REY VUELVE a OFRECERLE UN LARGO CIGARRILLO. El CABALLERO AUDAZ MIRA las SOMBRAS de la NOCHE CON SU CARACTERÍSTICO GESTO de INTERROGACIÓN. OBSERVA a las HERMOSAS MUJERES que PERFUMAN y DECORAN la MARAVILLOSA NOCHE AZUL. UNA de ELLAS, la MÁS ENGREÍDA, BELLÍSIMO ENSUEÑO de NÁCAR y ORO, PASA ANTE ELLOS y SE DETIENE ANTE el REY DEPUESTO:
«MAJESTÉ!».
DE INMEDIATO SE LEVANTA ALFONSO, SE CUADRA CEREMONIOSAMENTE y BESA la MANO de la DAMA CON la GENTILEZA CON la que lo HARÍA el MISMÍSIMO LUIS XIV.

¡PONGAN EL FLOTADOR EN SUS CINTURAS! NOS TIRAMOS AL RÍO CON...

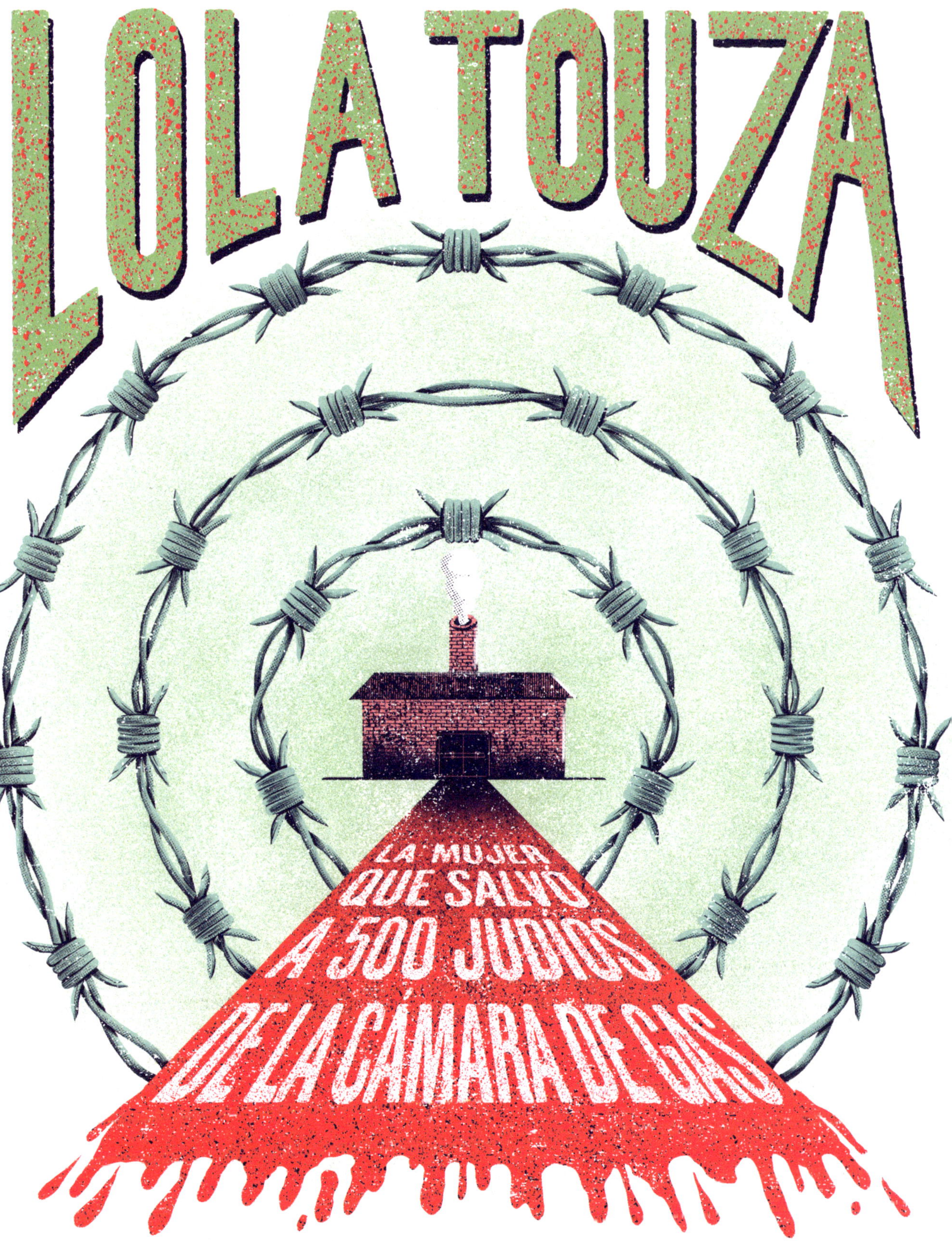

UNA MAÑANA de la POSGUERRA ESPAÑOLA en la ESTACIÓN de TREN de RIBADAVIA. LOLA TOUZA VENDÍA MELINDRES, ROSQUILLAS y LICOR de CAFÉ en SU QUIOSCO hasta que UN HOMBRE ROMPIÓ SU RUTINA.

ERA UN RUBIO FLACO ACURRUCADO en UN BANCO de MADERA. BAJO UN ABRIGO HARAPIENTO y UNA BARBA de NO HABER VISTO CUCHILLA en MUCHO TIEMPO, MIRABA PASAR los TRENES. UNO, OTRO, OTRO...

LOLA SE ACERCÓ a AQUEL POBRE ZARRAPASTROSO. EL HOMBRE NO SABÍA UNA PALABRA de ESPAÑOL, pero, en UN IDIOMA INVISIBLE, ACEPTÓ la AYUDA que le TENDÍA. Ella ERA UNA MUJER BELLÍSIMA, UNA MADRE SOLTERA a la que NO SE CONOCÍA VARÓN. ÉL LLEVABA UN TATUAJE en el BRAZO: «451».

PASARON los MESES y, OTRA MAÑANA de AQUEL 1941, en la que EUROPA ARDÍA en SANGRE y ODIO (¡POR ENÉSIMA VEZ!) LOLA SE ACERCÓ a UN VECINO del PUEBLO: «PACO, ¿CUÁNDO VAIS de PESCA?».

En VOZ BAJA, ella le CONTÓ que ESCONDÍA a un EXTRAJERO y le PIDIÓ que lo LLEVARA de INCÓGNITO a la FRONTERA de PORTUGAL. ESA MADRUGADA, a las CUATRO en PUNTO, el HOMBRE y SU HIJO RECOGIERON al RUBIO FLACO y JUNTOS CAMINARON con UNAS CAÑAS de PESCAR.

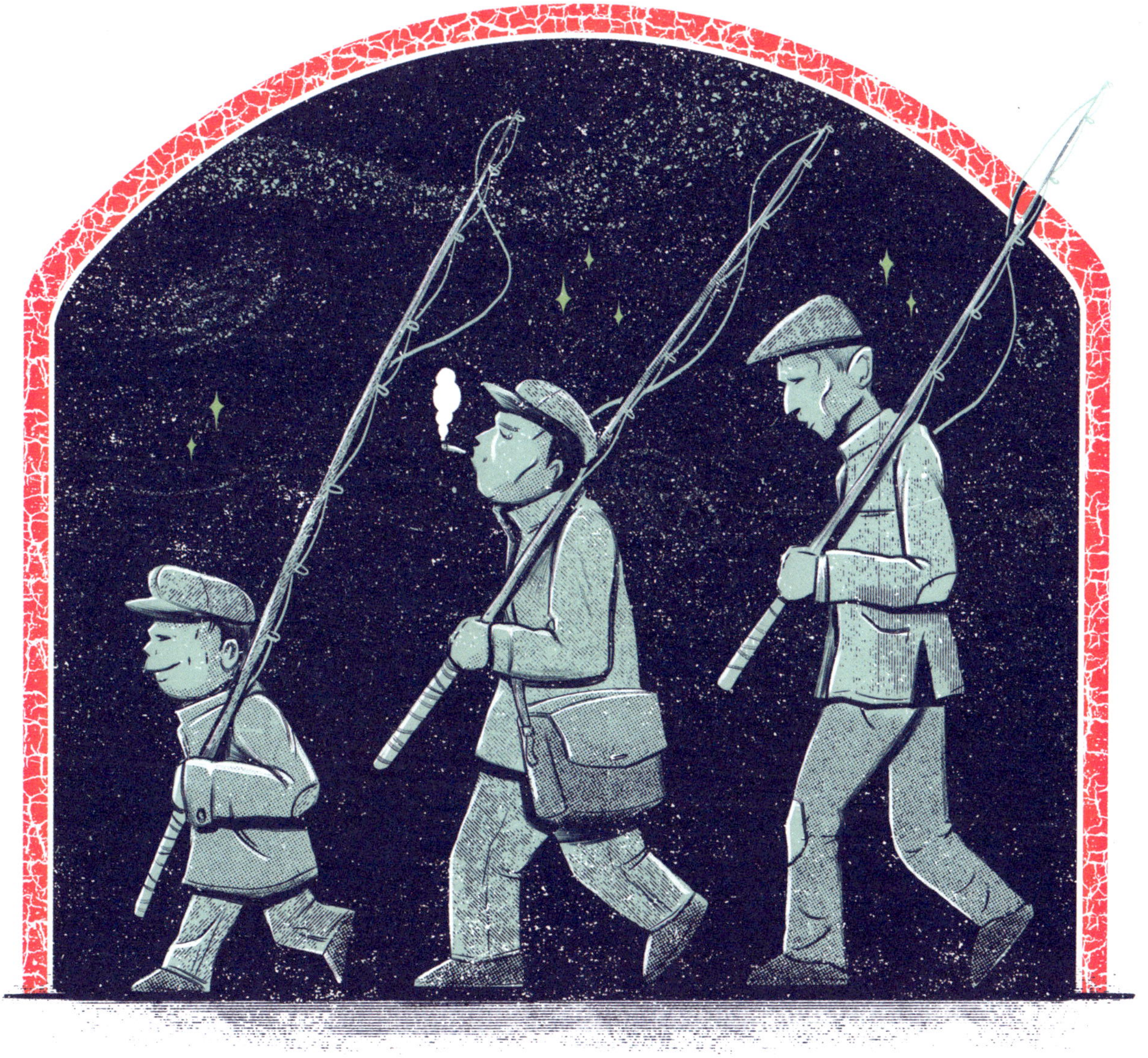

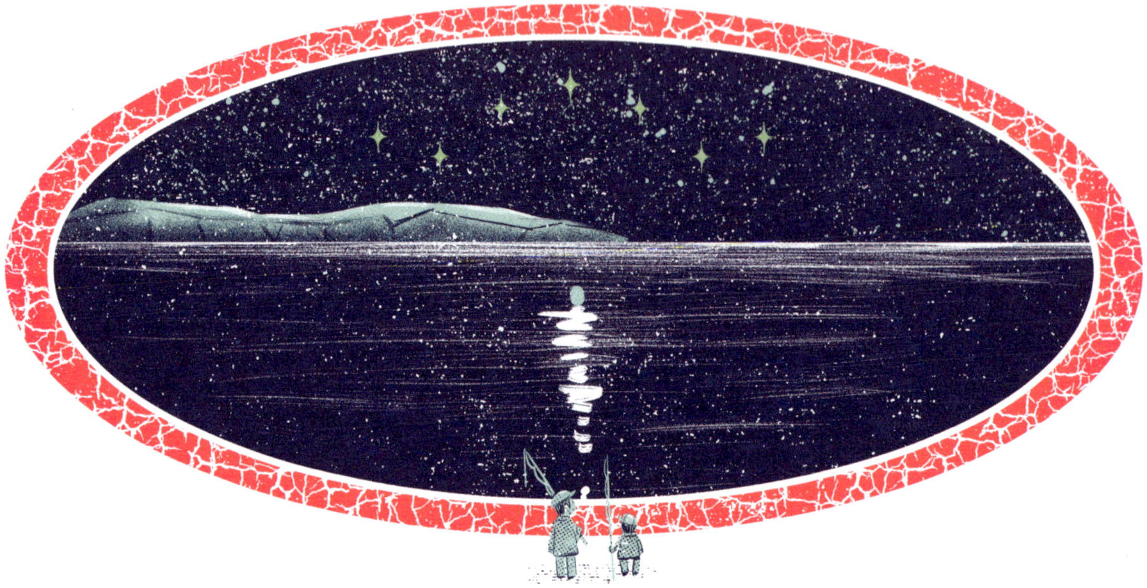

APROVECHARON la OSCURIDAD de la NOCHE SIN LUNA para LLEGAR a UNA ALDEA en la FRONTERA. El EXTRANJERO DIO un DURO de PLATA al NIÑO. En UN ESPAÑOL CHAPURREADO, SE DESPIDIÓ: «TE RECORDARÉ TODA la VIDA, AMIGO», y ECHÓ a NADAR hasta LLEGAR a la ORILLA PORTUGUESA.

AQUEL JUDÍO que ESCAPÓ de la CÁMARA de GAS FUE el PRIMERO de UNA MISIÓN que TENDRÍA OCUPADAS a LOLA y SUS HERMANAS, AMPARO y JULIA, hasta 1945: UNA RED de FUGA SECRETA, ULTRASECRETA, que AYUDABA a los JUDÍOS a HUIR del HOLOCAUSTO. TODO ESTABA ORGANIZADO por las TRES MUJERES, DOS TAXISTAS, UN BARQUERO y un TRADUCTOR.

ENTRE las CESTAS de DULCES, y con GRAN DISIMULO, LOLA RECIBÍA en la ESTACIÓN a JUDÍOS ALEMANES. PREGUNTABAN por «la MADRE» y ELLA los ESCONDÍA entre SU CASA y la CANTINA hasta que, OCULTOS en la NOCHE, SALÍAN por TRES VÍAS: a PIE por SENDEROS, en CARRETERAS de TERCERA y NADANDO el RÍO MIÑO.

RUTAS de NERVIO y MIEDO, porque en GALICIA NO ERA RARO TOPARSE con UN NAZI. DE ESTAS TIERRAS EXTRAÍAN el WOLFRAMIO que TANTO NECESITABAN para HACER MÁS MORTÍFERAS SUS ARMAS de GUERRA.

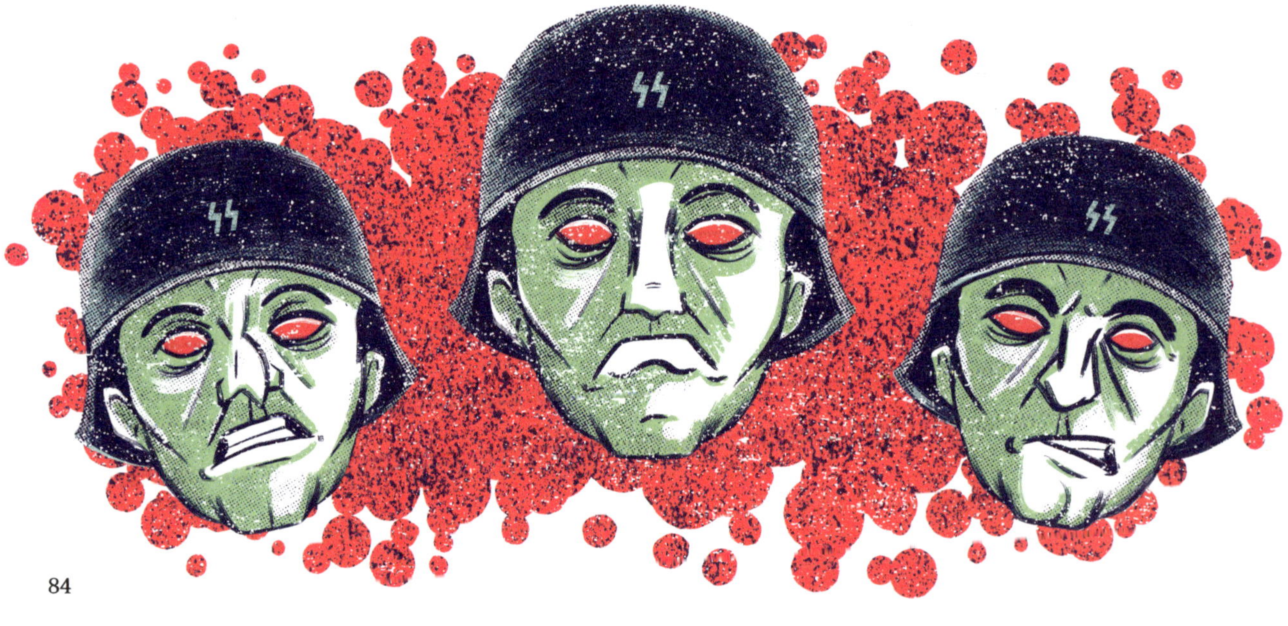

DICEN que PUDO SER el CÓNSUL PORTUGUÉS ARISTIDES de SOUSA QUIEN AVISABA a LOLA, por TELEGRAMA, para que SALIERA al ANDÉN en BUSCA de los JUDÍOS y CUENTAN que ALGUNA VEZ la GESTAPO PASÓ por ALLÍ PREGUNTANDO por «la MADRE».

NUNCA la DESCUBRIERON. NI PODÍAN IMAGINAR que el DINERO que RECAUDABA LOLA en las VELADAS de PASODOBLE y CHACHACHÁ que MONTABA en SU CASA FINANCIABAN el PASADIZO SECRETO que LLEVABA del INFIERNO NAZI al SUEÑO de la LIBERTAD.

AQUELLA MUJER y SUS COMPINCHES ARRIESGARON SU VIDA por SALVAR la de QUINIENTOS DESCONOCIDOS. NUNCA PIDIÓ las GRACIAS. LOLA SE TRAGÓ el SECRETO y HOY NADA SE SABRÍA SI NO FUERA por la CURIOSIDAD de un JUDÍO que CRUZÓ el MIÑO por el PUENTE ESCONDIDO que ELLA TENDIÓ.

El NEOYORQUINO ISAAC RETZMANN PIDIÓ a UN GALLEGO que la BUSCARA. TAN EXTRAÑAS PREGUNTAS de UN RELATO TAN RARO LLEGARON a OÍDOS de UN LIBRERO y, POCO ANTES de CAER en el ESTREPITOSO OLVIDO, esta HISTORIA INVISIBLE al FIN SALIÓ a la LUZ.

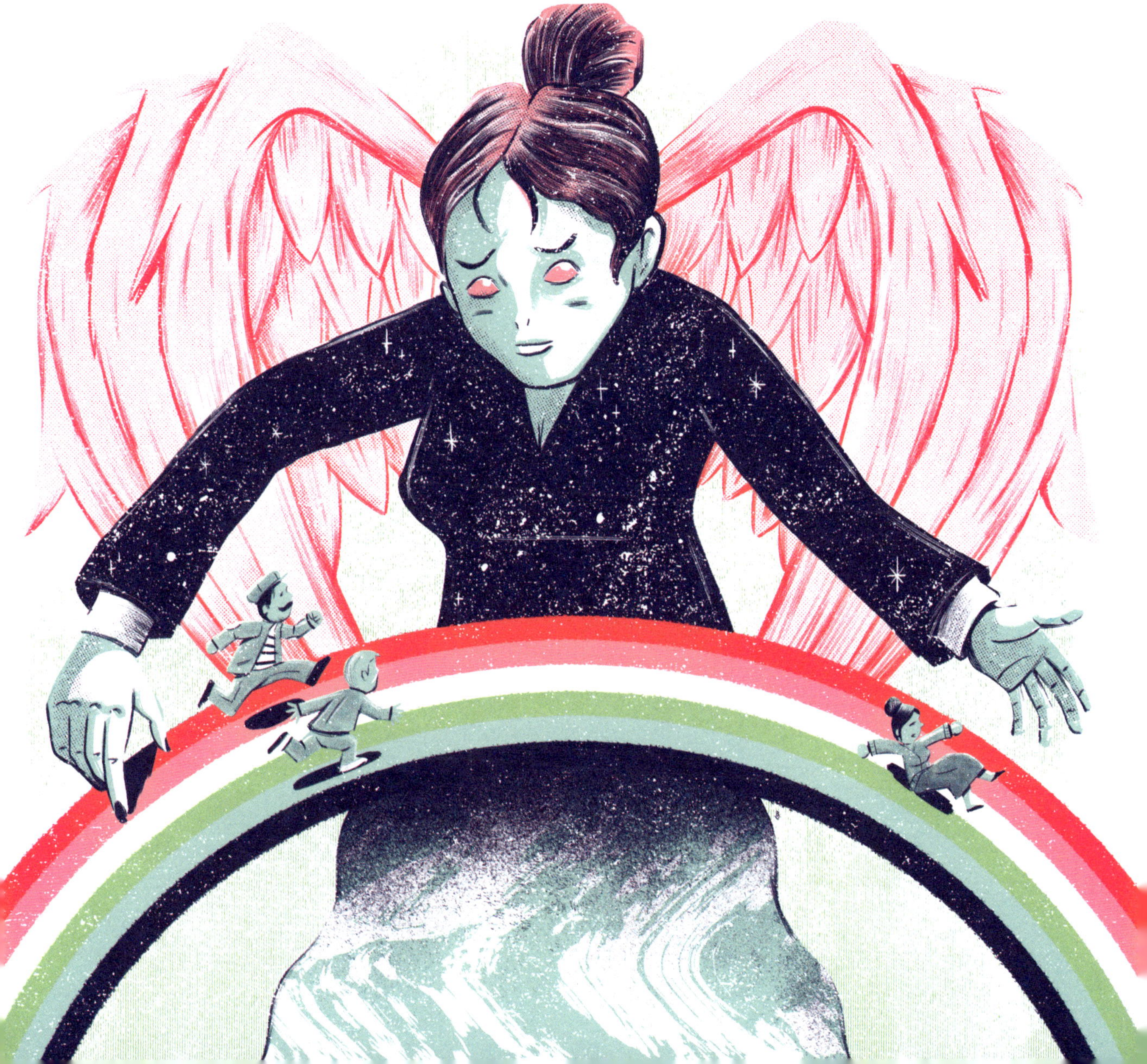

CONTEMPLEN DESDE LA BARRERA, CON UNA BOTA DE VINO, ESTE ESPECTÁCULO IMPREVISTO

¡EL TORO!

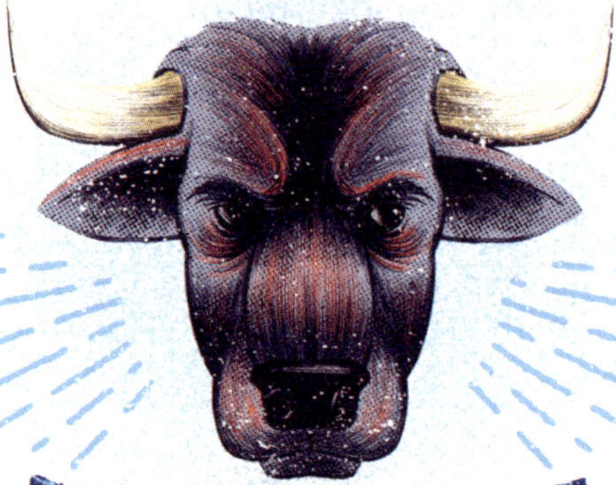

¡QUE VIENE EL TORO!

ES PLÁCIDA ESTA MAÑANA del 23 de ENERO de 1928. El RELOJ MARCA las ONCE en PUNTO y, de REPENTE, APARECE un HERMOSO TORO, de GRAN ROMANA y TAMAÑOS PITONES, CORRIENDO por la RED de SAN LUIS de MADRID.

«¡El TORO! ¡QUE VIENE el TORO!»

LOS VIANDANTES GRITAN de ESPANTO y se ECHAN a la CARRERA. ENTRAN en los PORTALES, SUBEN a los AUTOMÓVILES PARADOS en la AVENIDA. El ASTADO, PATINANDO en los BALDOSINES, TEMBLOROSAS las CARNES, PIDE PELEA. A SU PASO, DEJA HERIDOS y MAGULLADOS.

La CALLE SE HACE COSO. LOS VECINOS ASOMADOS a los BALCONES PONEN los PALCOS. Y las BANDERAS que HOY CUELGAN por el SANTO del REY ALFONSO dan los ROJOS y AMARILLOS a la FIESTA. ¡ESTO PARECE UNA CORRIDA de LEY!

LLEGA el TORO a la PUERTA del CASINO MILITAR y VE ANTE ÉL a UN JOVEN VALEROSO. El HOMBRE le HACE FRENTE. TIRA SU ABRIGO y lo MIRA a los OJOS.

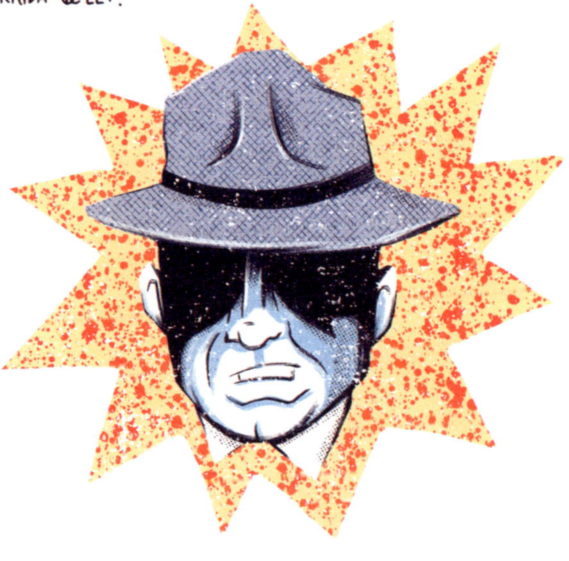

«¡ES FORTUNA! ¡ES el TORERO FORTUNA!», GRITA ALGUIEN, con ALEGRÍA y ALIVIO.

En EFECTO. ES el MATADOR DIEGO MAZQUIARÁN QUIEN INTENTA SUJETAR al TORO FURIOSO.

«¡UN ESTOQUE! ¡TRAEDME UN ESTOQUE!», PIDE a PECHO DESCUBIERTO.

Del CASINO MILITAR SACAN UN SABLE, pero es ENDEBLE. ¡IMPOSIBLE la TORERÍA! ENTONCES ARRANCA un CHÓFER a CASA del DIESTRO a por UN ESTOQUE.

A FORTUNA NO le BASTA con TENER que BANDEAR al TORO MIENTRAS LLEGA la ESPADA. ALGUNOS AFICIONADOS APROVECHAN para ENSAYAR UNOS LANCES y se PONEN ante la RES. BRAVO, el ASTADO se ARRANCA sobre UN MUCHACHITO y lo TIRA en UN PERIQUETE.

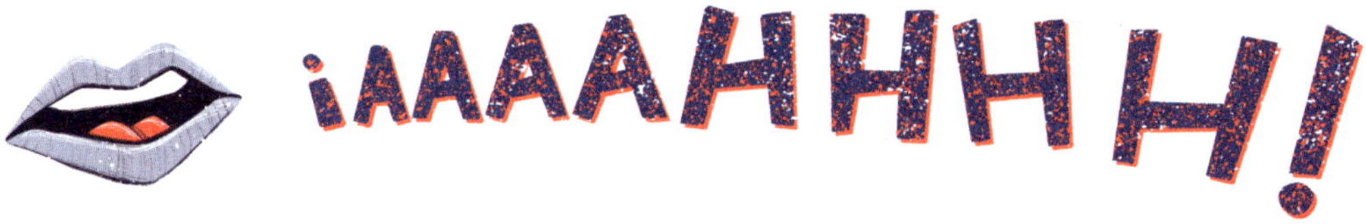

Las MUJERES GRITAN en los BALCONES. Y AHÍ LLEGA FORTUNA para LIBRAR al MUCHACHO de UN PITONAZO.

POR FIN APARECE el CHÓFER CON el ESTOQUE. EL DIESTRO lo DESENVAINA y, con el ABRIGO de MULETA, IGUALA a la RES. ENTRA a MATAR y CLAVA TRES CUARTOS de ESTOQUE.

DESDE las ACERAS, desde los BALCONES, VITOREAN a FORTUNA. LAS DEPENDIENTAS de UNA CASA de MODAS PIDEN al DIESTRO que CORTE UNA OREJA. EL TORERO las COMPLACE y UNA AVALANCHA de HOMBRES lo LEVANTAN y lo PASEAN, TRIUNFANTE, por LA GRAN VÍA.

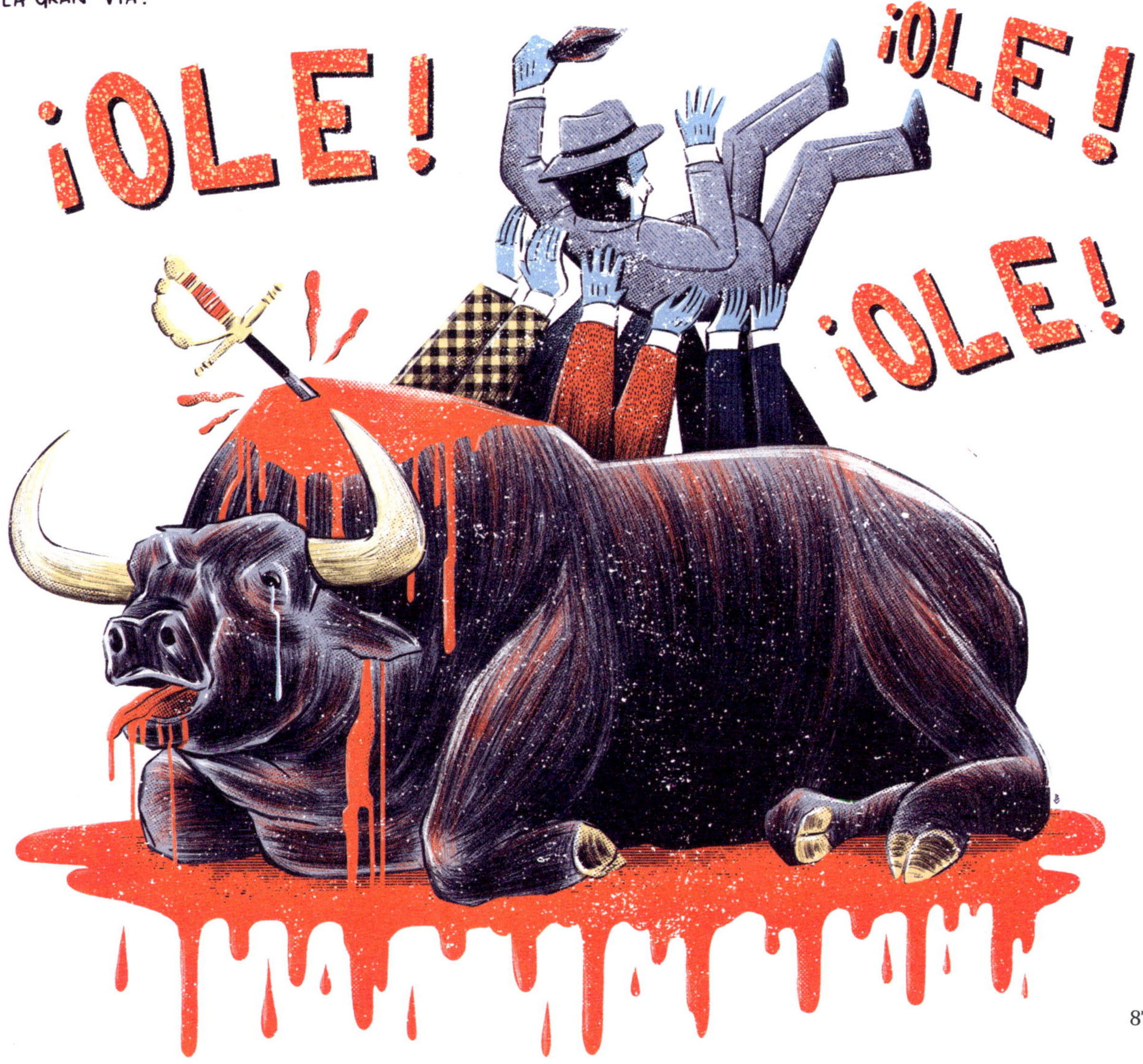

DESLÍCENSE HACIA UN PASADO QUE SE NOS FUE DE LAS MANOS CON...

JERÓNIMO DE AYANZ

EL ESPAÑOL QUE INVENTÓ LA MÁQUINA DE VAPOR

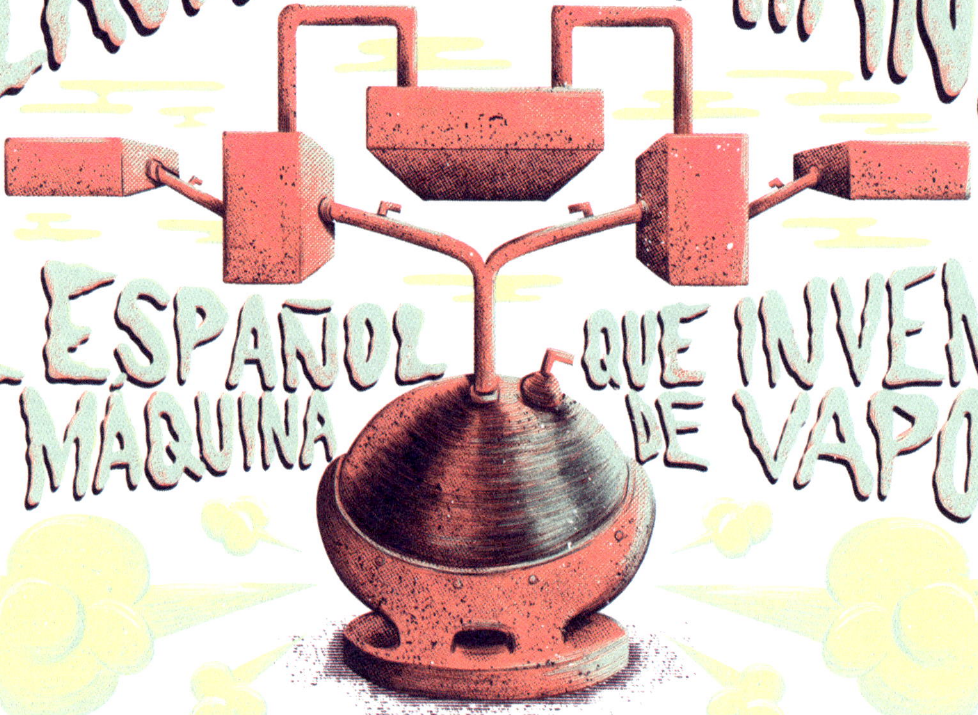

EN los MISMOS AÑOS en que CERVANTES ESCRIBÍA «El QUIJOTE», **JERÓNIMO de AYANZ** INVENTABA una MÁQUINA de VAPOR.

FUE a PRINCIPIOS del SIGLO XVII. AYANZ, ADMINISTRADOR GENERAL de MINAS del REINO de ESPAÑA, IDEÓ un APARATO que BOMBEABA el AGUA con la FUERZA del VAPOR. EN el LIBRO de «PRIVILEGIOS de INVENCIÓN» DONDE QUEDÓ REGISTRADO EXPLICÓ SU FUNCIONAMIENTO:

1. ENCENDER el FUEGO.
2. LLENAR MEDIA CALDERA de AGUA.
3. PONERLA en la LUMBRE hasta que HIERVA.
4. DIRIGIR el VAPOR para que ELEVE el AGUA de un DEPÓSITO de PRESIÓN a un DEPÓSITO de DESCARGA.

POR AQUEL ENTONCES, en 1606, AÚN NO EXISTÍA NADA PARECIDO en EUROPA. FALTABAN CASI CINCUENTA AÑOS para que NACIERA THOMAS SAVERY, el INGLÉS que HA PASADO a la HISTORIA COMO el INVENTOR de la MÁQUINA de VAPOR.

JERÓNIMO de AYANZ REGISTRÓ 48 INVENTOS en SOLO OCHO AÑOS. ARTILUGIOS FUTURISTAS COMO un EQUIPO de BUCEO, una BALANZA de TAL SENSIBILIDAD que PODÍA PESAR la PATA de una MOSCA y un HUMIDIFICADOR para las MINAS que PRECONIZA el ACTUAL AIRE ACONDICIONADO.

ESTE HOMBRE AUTODIDACTA SABÍA de MÚSICA, PINTURA, CIENCIA, TECNOLOGÍA y ESTRATEGIA MILITAR. ERA un RENACENTISTA que DECÍA:

«NINGUNA FILOSOFÍA HAY MÁS CIERTA que la PRUEBA, PORQUE ELLA es la QUE NOS SATISFACE y CONVENCE a NUESTRAS OPINIONES».

En AQUEL TIEMPO TODOS CONOCÍAN a AYANZ por su FUERZA ABISMAL. HASTA **LOPE de VEGA** le DEDICÓ unos VERSOS:

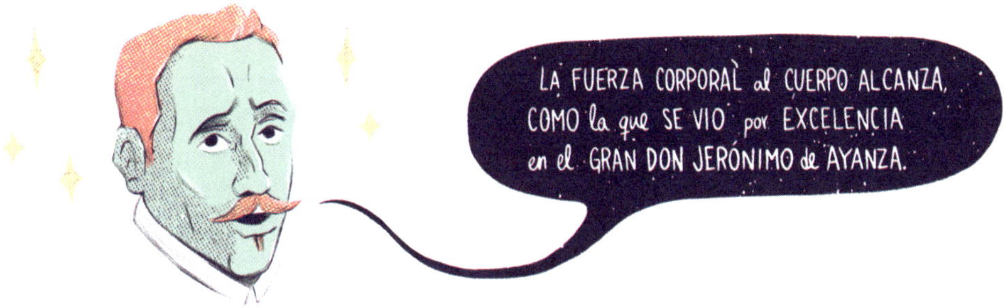

SIN EMBARGO, NI el REY NI NINGÚN POTENTADO SUPO VER el VALOR de un INVENTO que, SEGÚN los INSPECTORES TÉCNICOS, FUNCIONABA a la PERFECCIÓN, IGUAL que el RESTO de los APARATOS.

NADIE INTUYÓ que en ESA MÁQUINA SE JUGABAN los DESIGNIOS del MUNDO: ERA la SEMILLA de la REVOLUCIÓN INDUSTRIAL. LA DESCUBRIERON en INGLATERRA y ESO LLEVÓ a los BRITÁNICOS a CONQUISTAR MEDIO PLANETA a BORDO de SUS TRENES y SUS BARCOS de VAPOR.

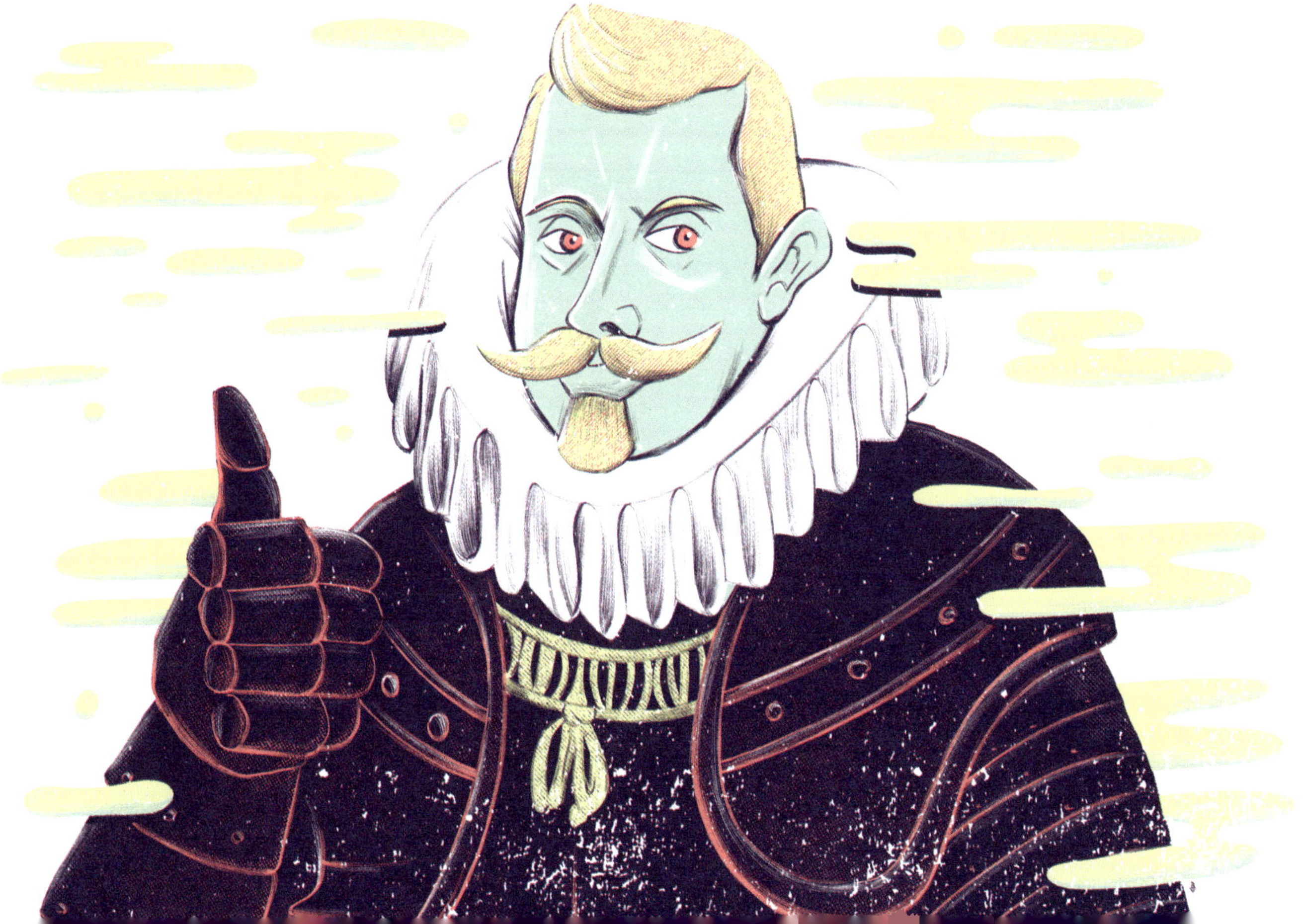

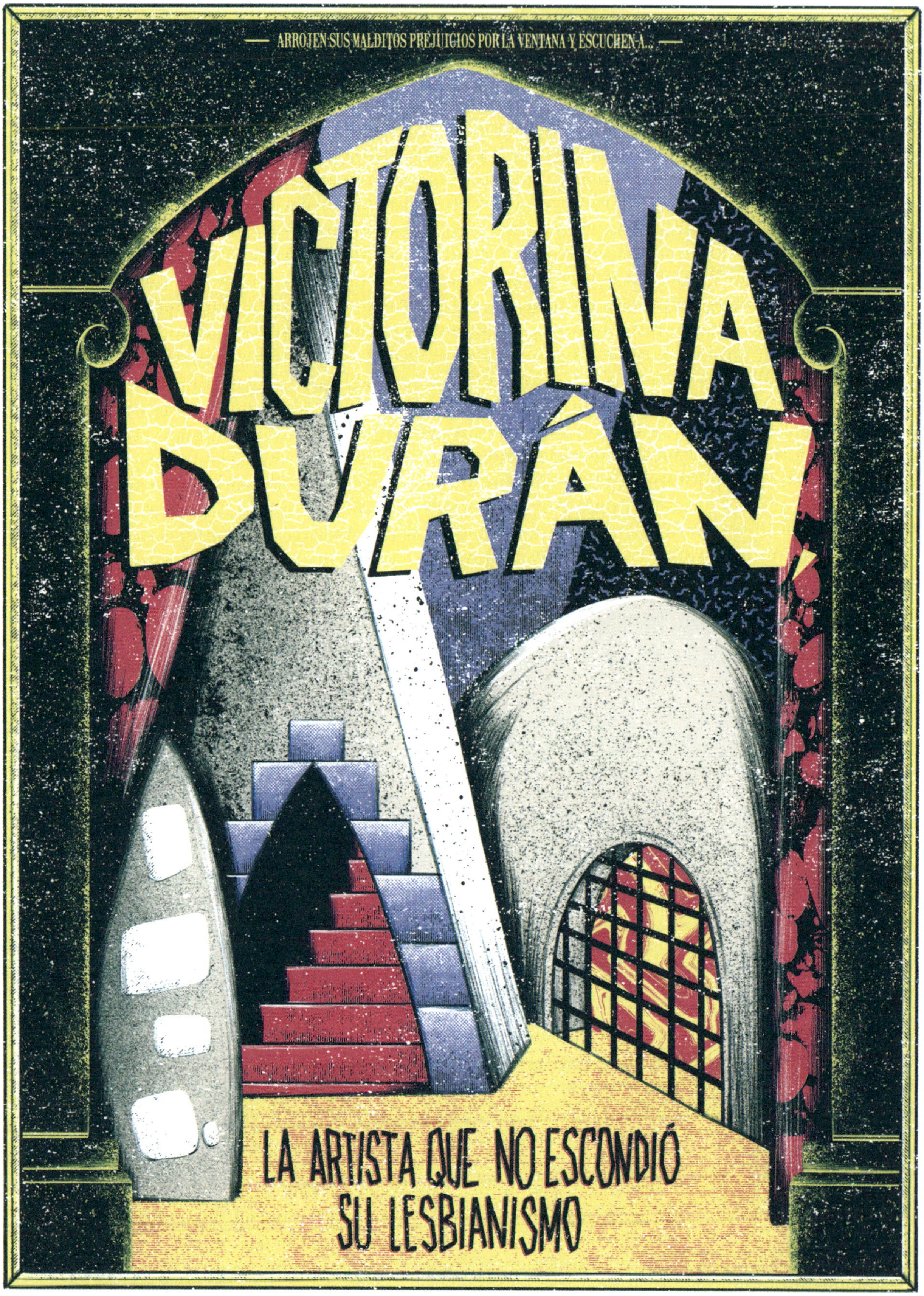
— ARROJEN SUS MALDITOS PREJUICIOS POR LA VENTANA Y ESCUCHEN A... —
VICTORINA DURÁN
LA ARTISTA QUE NO ESCONDIÓ SU LESBIANISMO

«HE VIVIDO el ANGUSTIOSO DRAMA de VERME AISLADA, INCOMPRENDIDA y, lo que ES AÚN PEOR, DESPRECIADA por MULTITUD de SERES "NORMALES".

TODA ESTA GENTE TIENE el "DERECHO SOCIAL" de PERMITIRSE EXCLUIR de SU MUNDO a QUIENES VIVEN UN AMOR "NATURAL" (PUESTO que ESTÁ en la NATURALEZA) y A QUIEN ES CAPAZ de SENTIR, VIBRAR y ENALTECER SU ESPÍRITU CON UNA EMOCIÓN del ALMA que DESCONOCEN la MAYORÍA de QUIENES la JUZGAN.

SI al MÁS IMPERDONABLE de los CRIMINALES la SOCIEDAD, ANTES de JUZGARLE, le DA el DERECHO de UN ABOGADO DEFENSOR, ¿POR QUÉ NO HABÍAN de TENER el SUYO, ANTES de SER JUZGADAS por los DEMÁS, QUIENES SOLO TIENEN el DELITO de AMAR o SENTIR de MODO DIFERENTE?»

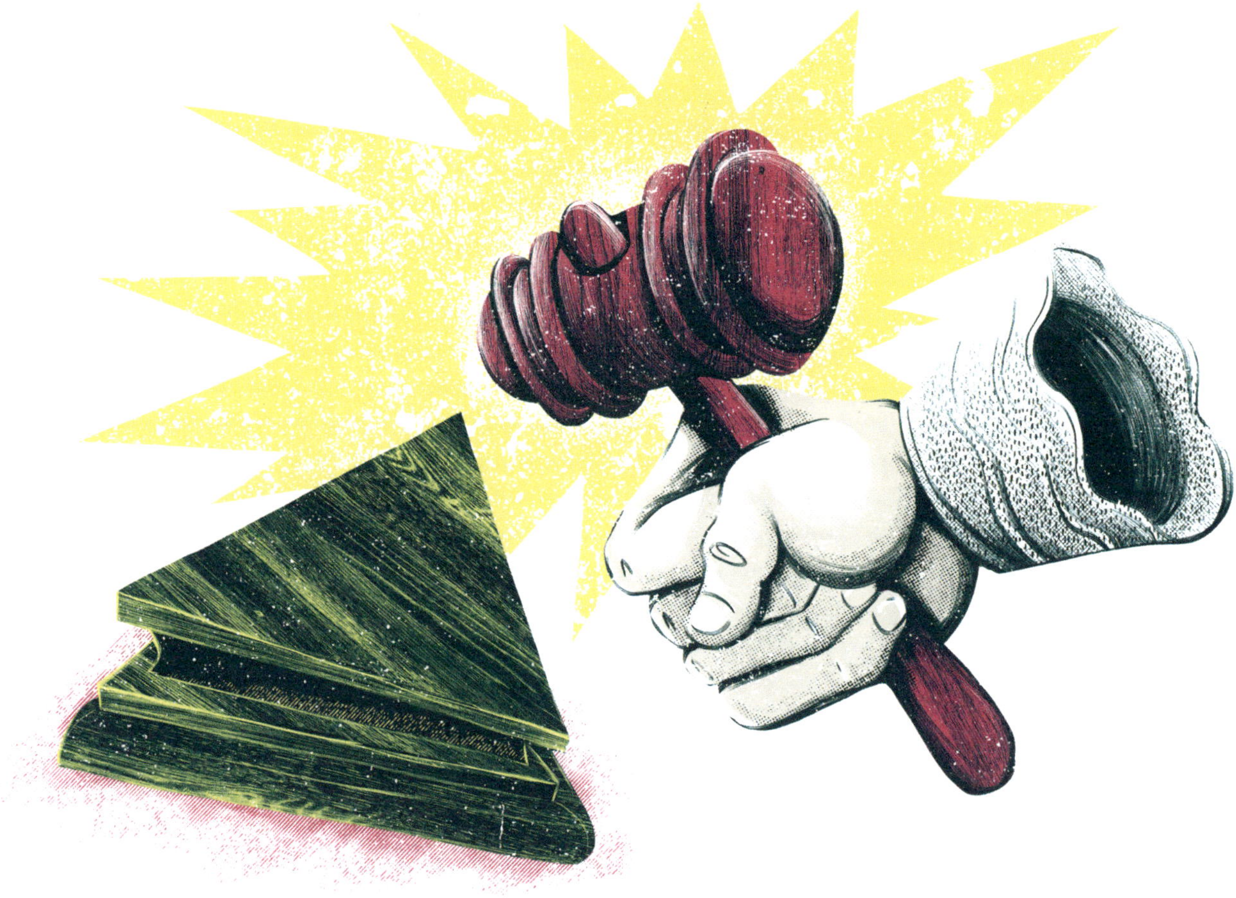

VICTORINA DURÁN (1899-1993) ESCRIBIÓ ESTAS PALBRAS ANTES de MORIR. ALUDÍA a los CHISMORREOS que SE LEVANTABAN a SU PASO CUANDO ERA JOVEN. AUNQUE a ELLA le DIO IGUAL. VIVIÓ COMO QUISO a PESAR de las COMADRES. VIVIÓ «COMO ERA». PORQUE ENTONCES NO SE UTILIZABA la PALABRA «LESBIANA»; SE DECÍA «ES ASÍ».

LA ESCENÓGRAFA y PINTORA NO TUVO MIEDO NI VERGÜENZA de DEJAR ESCRITAS SUS HISTORIAS de AMOR CON VARIAS MUJERES. SIN PUDOR y CON PASIÓN. INCLUSO DESCRIBIÓ el MOMENTO EN que DESCUBRIÓ que «ERA ASÍ». FUE en VALENCIA, UN DÍA de AGOSTO.

«¿INCOMPRENSIBLE?», SE PREGUNTA a SÍ MISMA en SUS MEMORIAS.

«¡¡INEXPLICABLE!!», SE RESPONDE ENTRE UN PAR de EXCLAMACIONES.

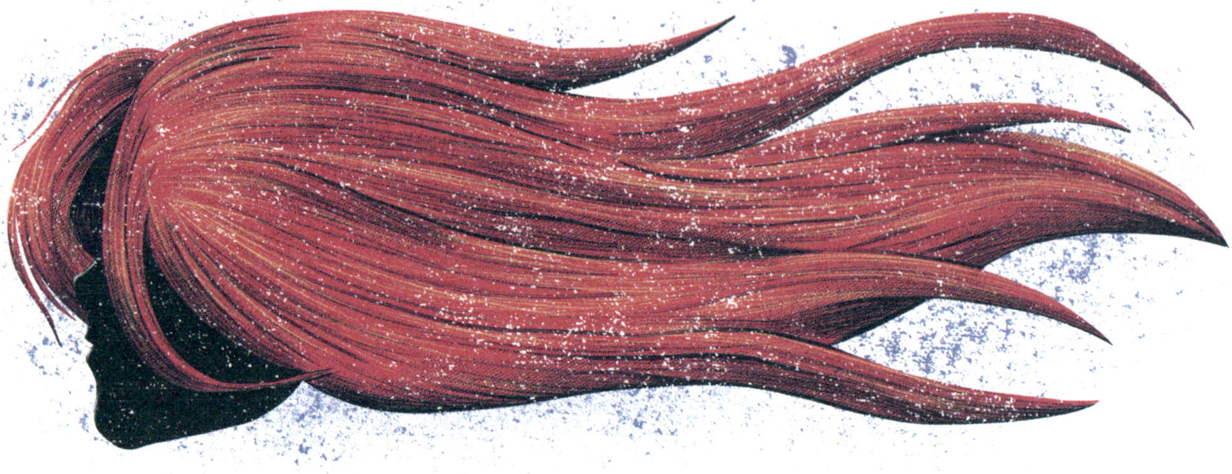

ESTUDIABA en CASA del MAESTRO que la PREPARABA PARA SUS EXÁMENES en la ESCUELA NORMAL. UNA NOCHE, UNA SEÑORA MUY IMPORTANTE, UNA TAL BARONESA M. de L., los INVITÓ a CENAR en UN BALNEARIO. AL LLEGAR al RESTAURANTE, VICTORINA QUEDÓ EXTASIADA por SU BELLEZA, SU ELEGANCIA y SU ATRACTIVO CASI DEMONÍACOS. AQUEL PELO ROJO NO HACÍA MÁS que ACENTUAR SU ESPLENDOR.

«RECONOZCO que SENTÍ UN IMPACTO, MÁS AÚN CUANDO CREÍ que IBA a ENCONTRAR UNA SEÑORA MAYOR, FEA y ABURRIDA.»

DURANTE la CENA, M de L. COQUETEABA y SACABA de QUICIO a los TRES HOMBRES INVITADOS.

«ME PARECIÓ UNA VAMPIRESA de PELÍCULA. TODA MI ATENCIÓN ERA SOLO para ELLA.»

A las CINCO de la MADRUGADA MARCHARON HACIA VALENCIA en DOS COCHES y FUERON a COMER OSTRAS y a VER AMANECER. M de L. les DIJO que NO los LLEVARÍA a CASA: DORMIRÍAN en la SUYA. AL LLEGAR, UNA DONCELLA MEDIO DORMIDA ABRIÓ la PUERTA y DIRIGIÓ al GRUPO a UN CUARTO de HUÉSPEDES.

M. de L. PARÓ a VICTORINA y le INDICÓ:

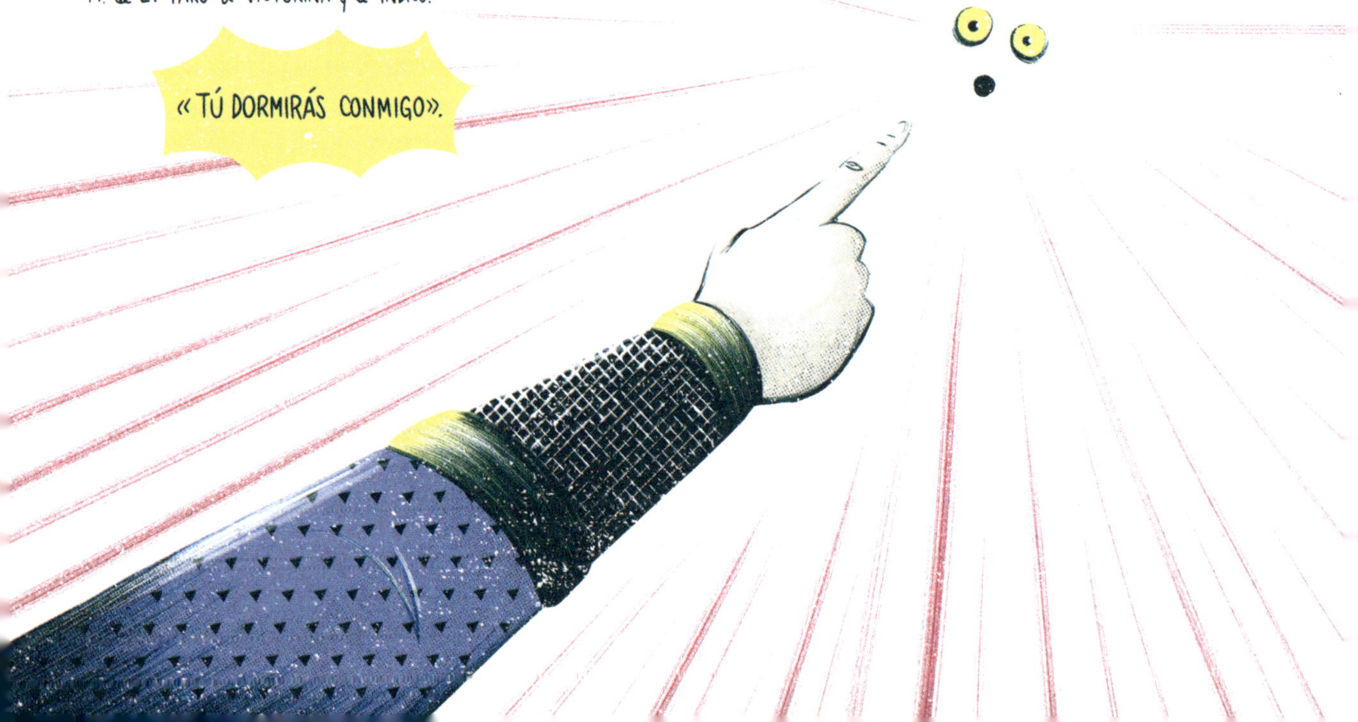

La IDEA de DORMIR CON UNA DESCONOCIDA FASTIDIÓ a VICTORINA. NO ESTABA ACOSTUMBRADA a COMPARTIR CAMA. ENTRÓ la DONCELLA al DORMITORIO y DESNUDÓ a la BARONESA. VICTORINA, SENTADA a los PIES de la CAMA, MIRABA CÓMO la DESPOJABAN de TODO. TODO. HASTA que le PUSIERON UN CAMISÓN TRANSPARENTE.

–VAMOS... ¡ACUÉSTATE! –RECLAMÓ la BARONESA.

–NO TENGO CAMISÓN.

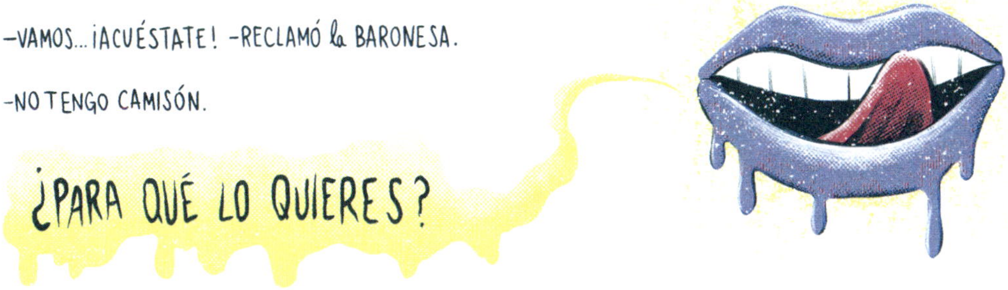

VICTORINA SE DEJÓ el SOSTÉN y las BRAGAS, UNA ESPECIE de BIQUINI IMPROVISADO, y SE METIÓ en la CAMA. CERRÓ los OJOS para DORMIR.

M. de L. SE LEVANTÓ y ENCENDIÓ un VENTILADOR. VICTORINA la MIRÓ y PENSÓ que NINGUNA ESCULTURA de las que VEÍA en la ESCUELA SUPERIOR de BELLAS ARTES ERA COMPARABLE a ESA FIGURA.

EMPEZARON a CHARLAR y VICTORINA SE DIO CUENTA de que, APARTE de ESA CONVERSACIÓN, HABÍA «ALGO ESPECIAL» que HABLABA ENTRE ELLAS. El PELO ROJO ROZÓ a VICTORINA y SINTIÓ UNA DESCARGA ELÉCTRICA. JUNTARON SUS CARAS. VICTORINA VIBRÓ.

–VOY a TENER ENVIDIA de MI PELO, que ASÍ TE HACE SENTIR –SUSURRÓ la BARONESA.

DESPUÉS, UN BESO, OTRO BESO, OTRO, UNO MÁS..., CARICIAS... ¡QUIÉN SABE QUÉ!

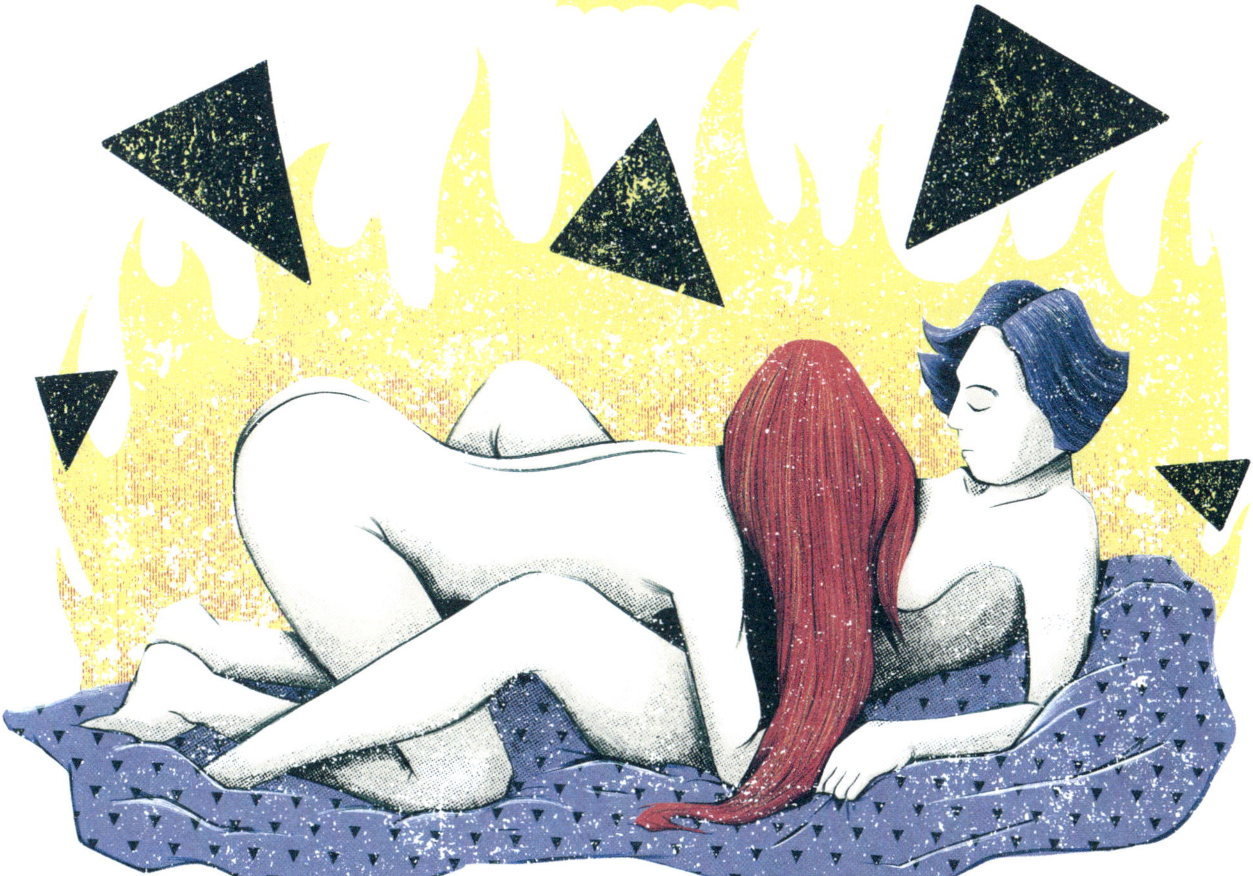

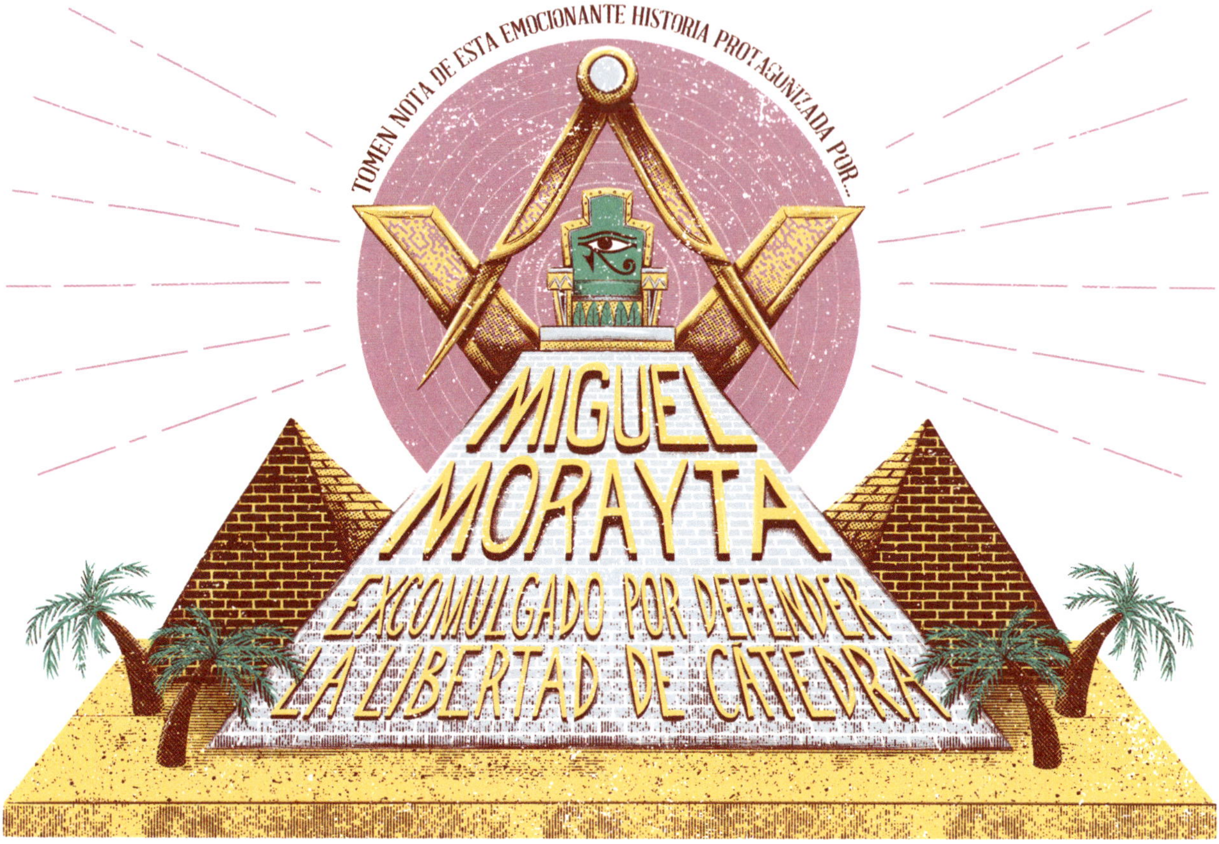

ESTÁ AGITADO el COMIENZO del CURSO 1884-1885. El DISCURSO de INAUGURACIÓN en la UNIVERSIDAD CENTRAL de MADRID HA SULFURADO a la ESPAÑA de SOTANA. ¡HEREJÍA! ¡INSULTO a DIOS!

MIGUEL MORAYTA y SAGRARIO (1834-1917) HA PRONUNCIADO UNA CHARLA SOBRE la HISTORIA y la CIVILIZACIÓN del ANTIGUO EGIPTO. PERO el CATEDRÁTICO NO SE HA CONFORMADO CON HABLAR de las PIRÁMIDES y EL OJO de RA. ENTRE los PÁRRAFOS de SU DIATRIBA, en TAN ALTÍSIMA TRIBUNA, HA COLADO un SACRILEGIO:

«El CATEDRÁTICO, en SU CÁTEDRA, es LIBRE, ABSOLUTAMENTE LIBRE, SIN MÁS LIMITACIÓN que SU CONCIENCIA».

MORAYTA HA OSADO DECIR que UN PROFESOR HA de ENSEÑAR a SU ANTOJO SIN SEGUIR la LEY de DIOS. El MINISTRO ALEJANDRO PIDAL y MON, FERVIENTE DEFENSOR de la UNIDAD CATÓLICA de ESPAÑA, CLAMA:

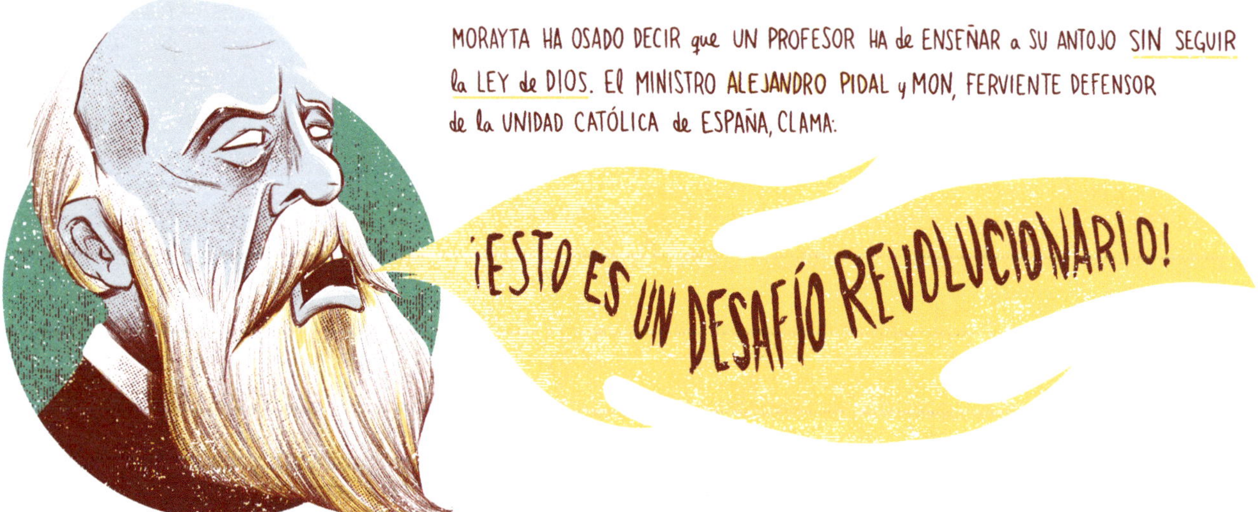

ALGUNOS OBISPOS EXCOMULGAN al PROFESOR. ¡YA VES TÚ! ¡QUÉ DOLOR! MORAYTA es UN LIBREPENSADOR ARDIENTE y ANTICLERICAL. ALGUNAS UNIVERSIDADES APOYAN al CATEDRÁTICO: ENVÍAN DECENAS de CARTAS de PROTESTA al MINISTRO y a la PRENSA.

El 17 de NOVIEMBRE de 1884 las MANIFESTACIONES REVUELVEN MADRID. El 18, los AGENTES SE LÍAN a PALOS con los ESTUDIANTES y REGISTRAN PERIÓDICOS, UNIVERSIDADES y DOMICILIOS de PROFESORES. EMPEZANDO por el de MORAYTA, por SUPUESTO.

El 19, FIESTA de SANTA ISABEL, TRES MIL ESTUDIANTES GRITAN por las CALLES. LAS FUERZAS del ORDEN DETIENEN a UNOS DOSCIENTOS y los MANDAN a PRISIÓN. MUCHOS INTELECTUALES SE DECLARAN a FAVOR de «LA CAUSA» de los JÓVENES en los PERIÓDICOS. ALGUNOS, INCLUSO, PAGAN para que les DEVUELVAN SU LIBERTAD.

DOS AÑOS DESPUÉS, MORAYTA ESCRIBE SU «HISTORIA GENERAL de ESPAÑA», en CUYA DEDICATORIA SE DIRIGE a los ESTUDIANTES:

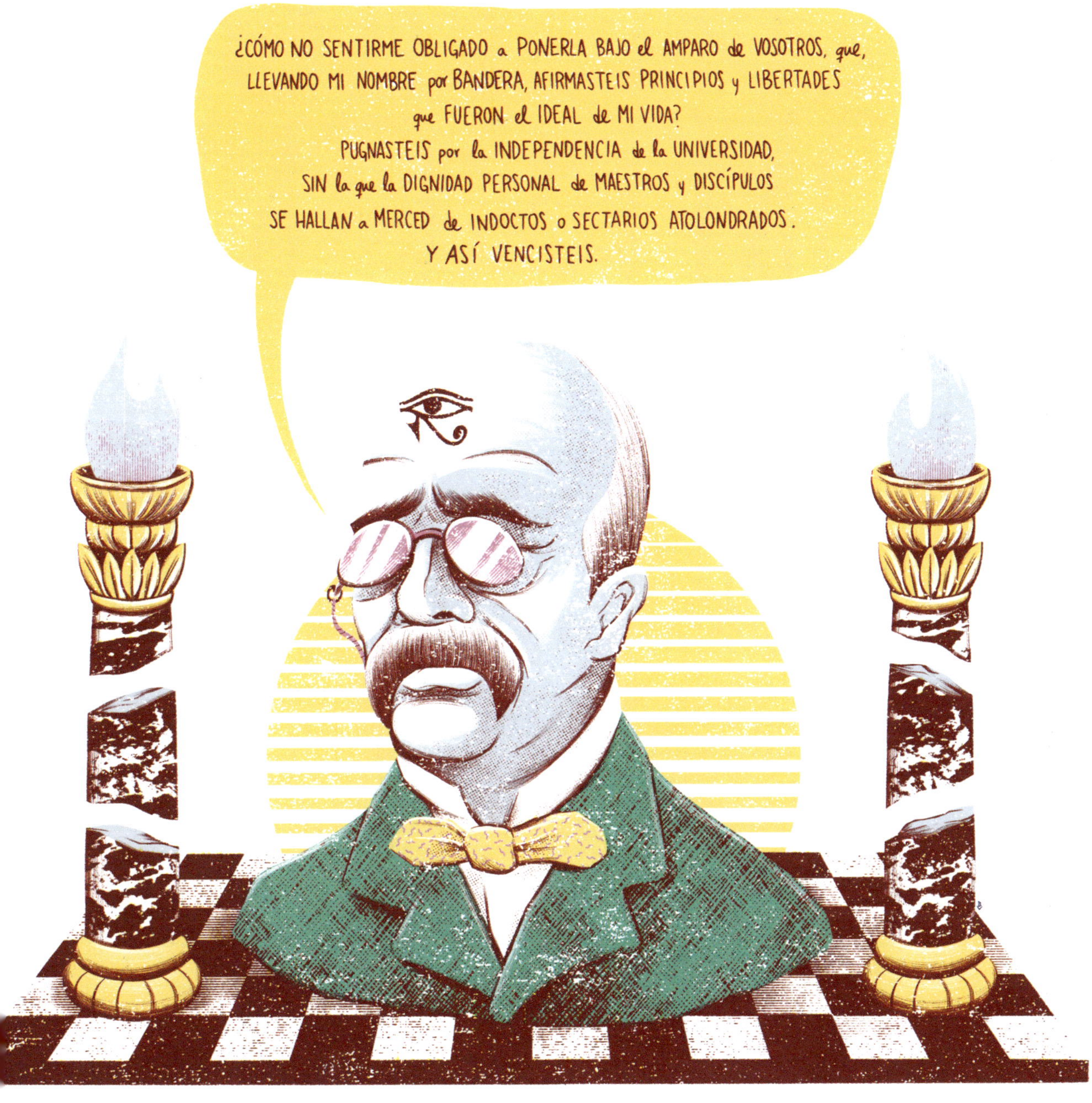

ENTRE EL IDEALISMO Y EL PRAGMATISMO, ENTRE EL QUERER Y EL DEBER, CONTEMPLEN A...

FEDERICA MONTSENY

LA PRIMERA MINISTRA

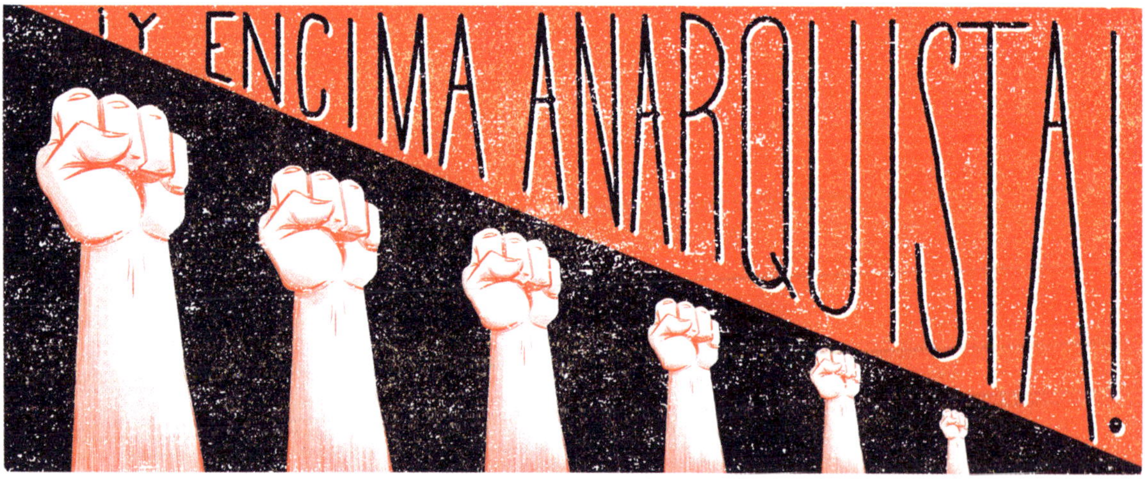

EL DESTINO es SOCARRÓN... GRACIAS a DIOS. FEDERICA MONTSENY (1905-1994) NACIÓ del AMOR y la UNIÓN CIVIL, LIBERTARIA, de DOS GRANDES ANARCAS: TERESA MAÑÉ MIRAVET y JOAN MONTSENY. LA NIÑA MAMÓ el PENSAMIENTO LIBRE desde el DÍA en que NACIÓ. A ello DEDICÓ SU VIDA, hasta que en 1936 ESPAÑA ARDIÓ en LLAMAS y se VIO en la ENCRUCIJADA.

EL PAÍS ESTABA en GUERRA. NO HABÍA LUGAR para la PLURALIDAD. DEBÍAN UNIRSE CONTRA el FASCISMO que QUERÍA IMPONERSE a TIROS. LOS REPUBLICANOS VIERON NECESARIO un GOBIERNO DONDE ENTRARAN hasta los que ODIABAN el ESTADO: LOS ANARQUISTAS.

En el GABINETE de LARGO CABALLERO DIERON CUATRO MINISTERIOS a los ANARQUISTAS. UNO de ELLOS: SANIDAD y ASISTENCIA SOCIAL. NO EXISTÍA hasta ENTONCES, pero los DESASTRES de la GUERRA lo HICIERON IMPRESCINDIBLE. LO OFRECIERON a MONTSENY y ella, DURANTE VEINTICUATRO HORAS, DUDÓ. ¿UNA ANARQUISTA en el GOBIERNO? ¡MALDITA PARADOJA!

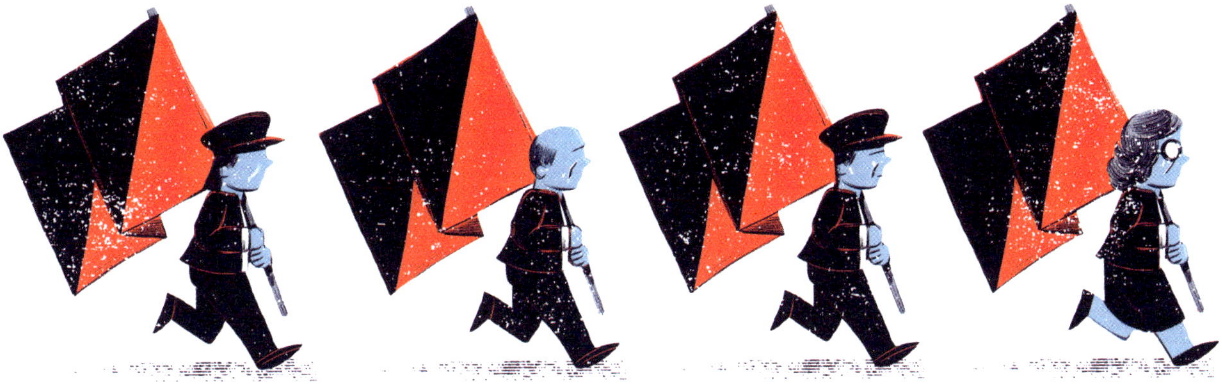

SE OPUSO SU MARIDO, GERMINAL. SE OPUSO SU MADRE: «VAS a DESACREDITARTE a los OJOS de TODOS los COMPAÑEROS». PERO ALGUNOS de SUS FIELES lo VIERON BIEN. SU MANO DERECHA, MATEO BARUTA, la ANIMÓ y le RECORDÓ que ESO de SER MINISTRA ERA UNA EVENTUALIDAD. Ella SEGUÍA SIENDO UNA MILICIANA.

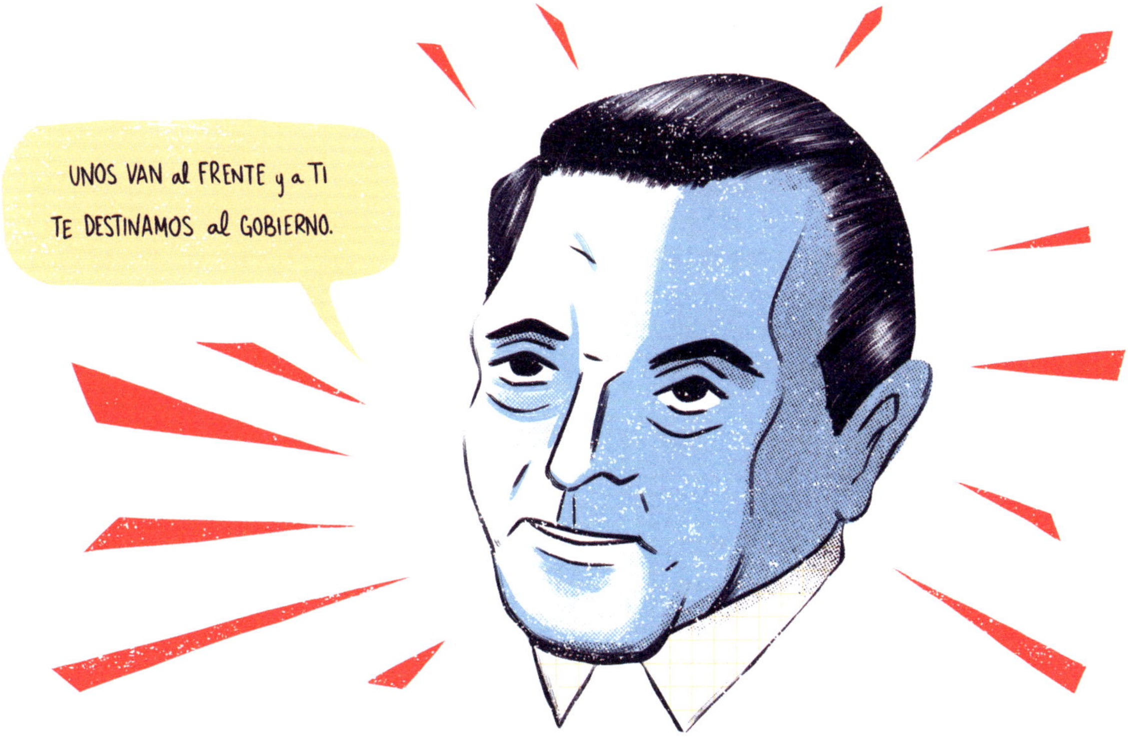

El COMPAÑERO JUAN PEIRÓ, al que OFRECIERON la CARTERA de INDUSTRIA, le DIJO:

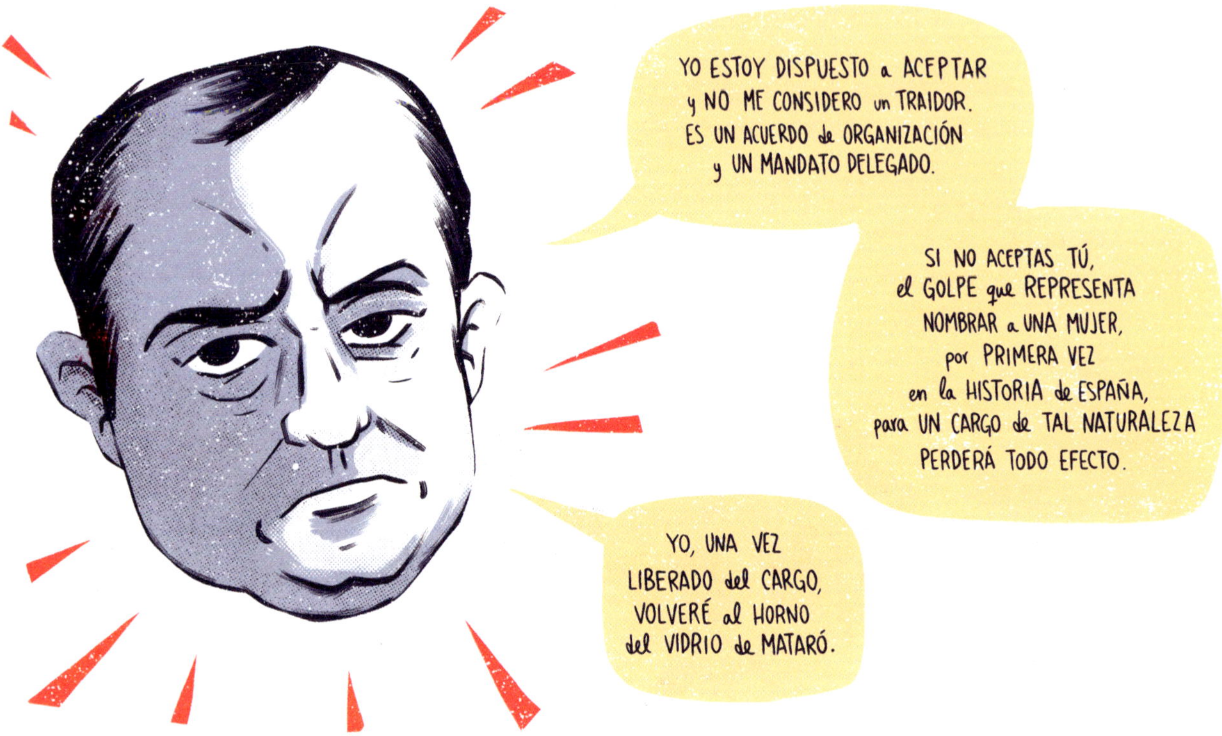

MONTSENY ACEPTÓ el CARGO y el 7 de NOVIEMBRE de 1936 ASISTIÓ a SU PRIMER CONSEJO de MINISTROS. VENÍAN FUERTES los ASUNTOS de DEBATE: los REPUBLICANOS PROPUSIERON TRASLADAR la CAPITAL a VALENCIA PORQUE los FASCISTAS YA ESTABAN en el SUDOESTE de MADRID. PRIMER RIFIRRAFE: los ANARQUISTAS SE OPUSIERON, AUNQUE PRONTO ENTRARON en RAZÓN y la CAPITAL SE FUE al MAR.

FEDERICA VIVÍA en UN PISO de la CONFEDERACIÓN ANARCOSINDICALISTA CNT, pero MUCHAS NOCHES DORMÍA en UNA CAMA de CAMPAÑA, en los SÓTANOS del MINISTERIO de la GUERRA. El SUELDO de MINISTRA IBA al COMITÉ NACIONAL y VIVÍA de SU SALARIO de MILICIANA: DIEZ PESETAS DIARIAS.

El CONSEJO NACIONAL de SANIDAD que DIRIGÍA SE OCUPABA de «HIGIENE y PROFILAXIS, HOSPITALES y SANATORIOS, FARMACIA y SUMINISTROS». El de ASISTENCIA SOCIAL, de «ANORMALES, INVÁLIDOS y DESVALIDOS; PROTECCIÓN a MADRES EMBARAZADAS y LACTANTES; HOGARES de la INFANCIA, GUARDERÍAS y ESCUELAS de CORRECCIÓN y REFORMA».

MONTSENY INTENTÓ ADELANTAR el FUTURO en UN PAÍS DONDE la RELIGIÓN QUERÍA ETERNIZAR la EDAD MEDIA. EN las PRIMERAS SEMANAS COMO MINISTRA DESPENALIZÓ el ABORTO para ACABAR con las CARNICERÍAS que SE HACÍAN a ESCONDIDAS.

REDACTÓ UN DECRETO INSPIRADO en el que CATALUÑA APROBÓ el 25 de DICIEMBRE de 1936 por INICIATIVA del «CONSELLER» ANARQUISTA ANTONIO GARCÍA BIRLÁN.

TAMBIÉN SE OCUPÓ de los REFUGIADOS. A MONTSENY le OBSESIONABAN los NIÑOS SIN PADRES que DEAMBULABAN HAMBRIENTOS por las CALLES.

NO ERA FÁCIL GOBERNAR entre las MIL TENSIONES de UN GOBIERNO de MIL IDEOLOGÍAS, los NERVIOS de VER al «FASCIO» DANDO ESCOPETAZOS, el ALIENTO de la URSS PEGADO al COGOTE... HASTA que, UN DÍA de MAYO de 1937, ESE EQUILIBRIO IMPOSIBLE SALTÓ por los AIRES.

LOS ANARQUISTAS y los REPUBLICANOS SE ENZARZARON en BARCELONA. UNOS QUERÍAN la REVOLUCIÓN; los OTROS, la LEGALIDAD CONSTITUCIONAL. Las JORNADAS de MAYO ACABARON con CIENTOS de MUERTOS y la DESTITUCIÓN del GOBIERNO de LARGO CABALLERO.

FEDERICA VOLVIÓ a BARCELONA. PERO el RECIBIMIENTO NO FUE AMABLE: AL PASAR por la GRAN VIA de LES CORTS CATALANES, DISPARARON a SU COCHE («¡SON los del PARTIDO INDEPENDENTISTA ESTAT CATALÀ!», PENSÓ). ELLA SE LIBRÓ del PLOMO, pero a SU COMPAÑERO BARUTA le ATRAVESARON la PIERNA.

Y SU PADRE, JOAN MONTSENY, NO la ARROPÓ: «CREO que, en BIEN TUYO y en el MÍO, DEBEMOS SEPARARNOS para NO CRUZAR PALABRA ALGUNA y NO SOSTENER OTROS VÍNCULOS que los que PUEDAN UNIR a DOS PERSONAS que SUSTENTAN la MISMA IDEALIDAD».

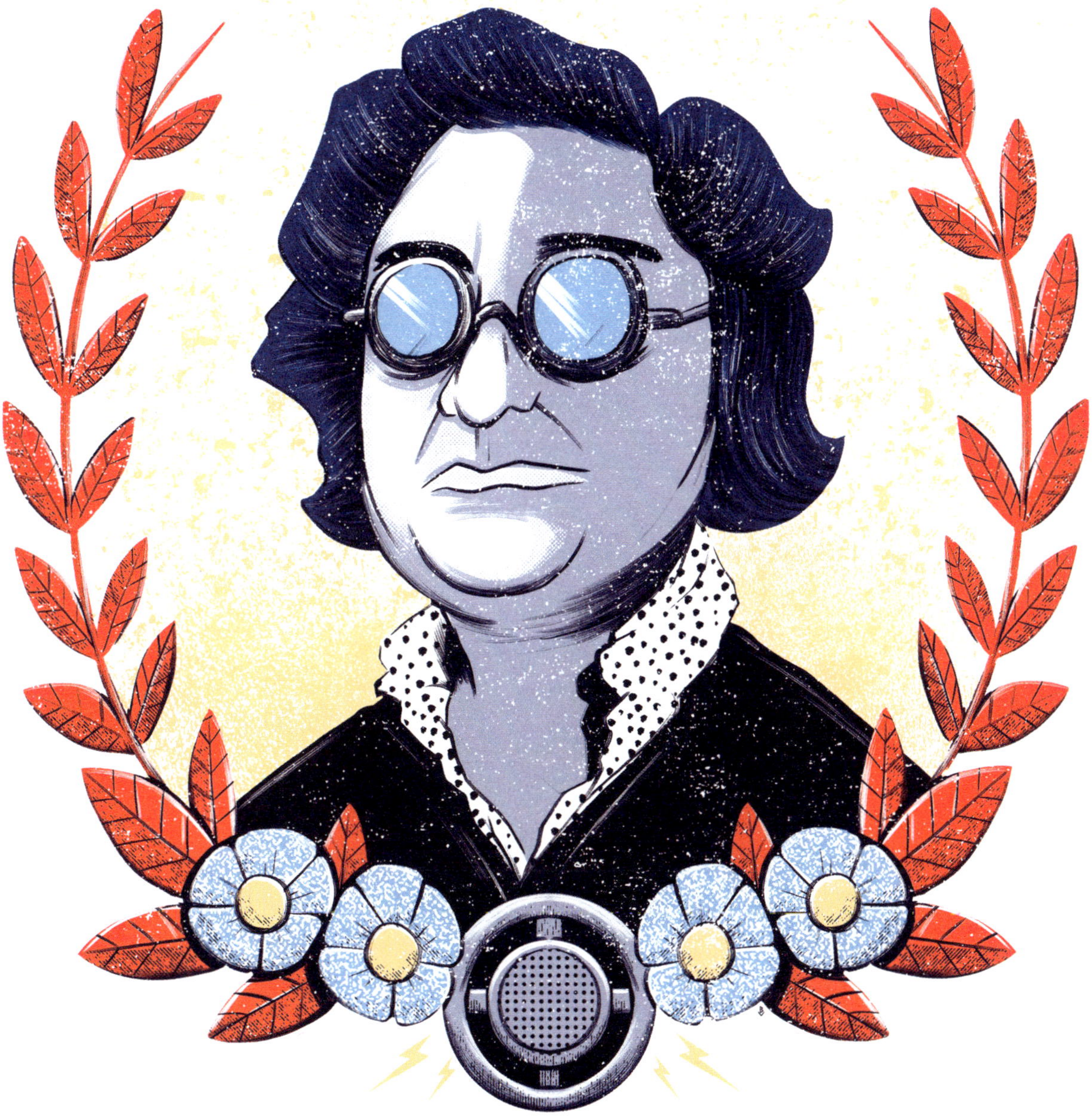

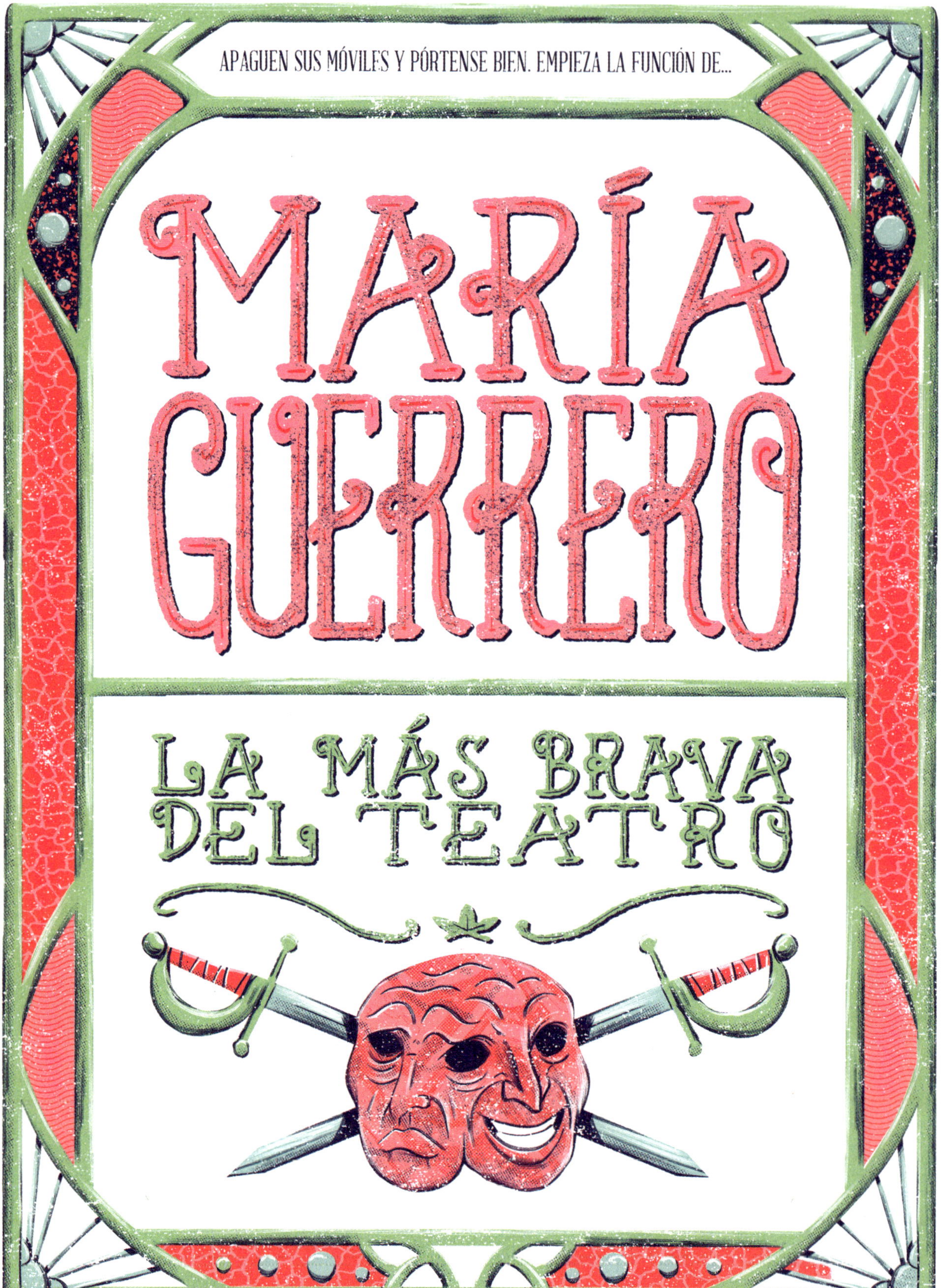
APAGUEN SUS MÓVILES Y PÓRTENSE BIEN. EMPIEZA LA FUNCIÓN DE...
MARÍA GUERRERO
LA MÁS BRAVA DEL TEATRO

A la FAMILIA de UN TAPICERO LLEGÓ UNA NIÑA que NACIÓ como MARÍA GUERRERO y MURIÓ como MARÍA LA BRAVA (1867-1928). PERO el PADRE DEJÓ PRONTO de TAPIZAR las BUTACAS para EMPLEARSE en la GESTIÓN del TEATRO ENTERO, ENTRE..., EJEM..., las RISAS y el PITORREO del MUNDO ESCÉNICO.

AUNQUE la RISOTADA FINAL le CORRESPONDÍA a ÉL, PORQUE SU HIJA, CON APENAS DIECIOCHO AÑOS, DESLUMBRÓ a TODOS en el TEATRO de la COMEDIA de MADRID. EN 1890 MARÍA ERA la PRIMERA ACTRIZ del TEATRO ESPAÑOL y CUATRO AÑOS DESPUÉS CREÓ SU PROPIA COMPAÑÍA.

LOS TAPICES que de NIÑA VIO REMENDAR PASARON a ENALTECER SU PARED CUANDO MATRIMONIÓ con UN GRANDE de ESPAÑA: MARÍA SE HIZO CONDESA de BALAZOTE y de LALAING. SU ESPOSO, FERNANDO DÍAZ de MENDOZA, ADEMÁS de ARISTÓCRATA, ERA ACTOR y DIRECTOR: EL CASORIO FUE REDONDO para los DOS.

ESTRENÓ OBRAS de los MÁS ILUSTRES: BENAVENTE, ECHEGARAY, GALDÓS, MARQUINA, VALLE-INCLÁN... ACTUÓ en EUROPA y AMÉRICA, y ABRIÓ TEATROS AQUÍ y ALLÁ. ERA la MÁS ADMIRADA y, a la VEZ, ARDUA como la ZARZA; FUE la MUJER que OBLIGÓ a SU HIJO a que RENEGARA del SUYO, el FUTURO ACTOR FERNANDO FERNÁN GÓMEZ.

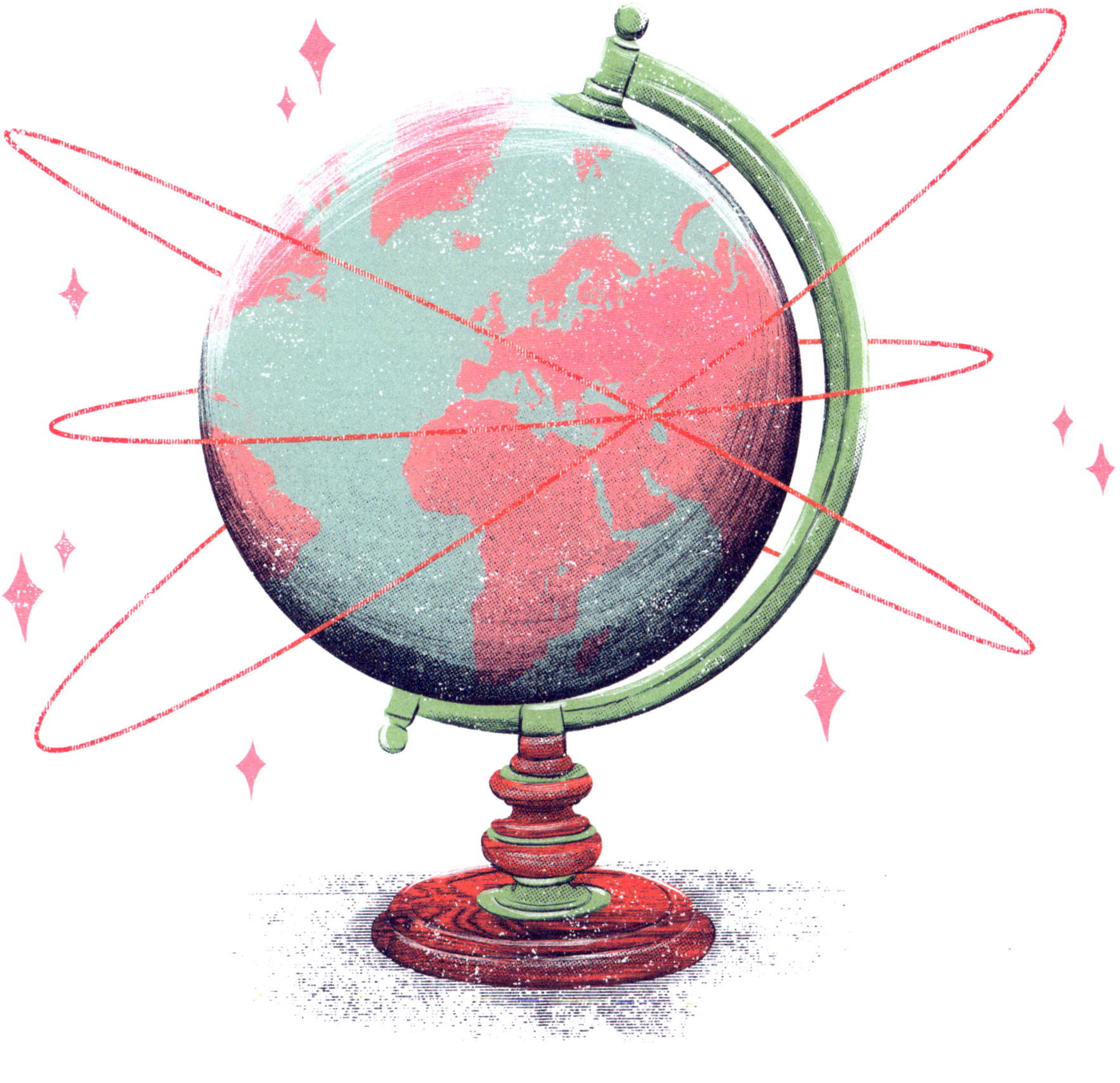

MARÍA ACABABA de VOLVER de AMÉRICA. ERA UNA MAÑANA de 1915. El CABALLERO AUDAZ VISITÓ SU CASA (SU PALACIO, MÁS BIEN). Al MATRIMONIO le GUSTABAN los LUJOS. A RABIAR. El PERIODISTA HACÍA UNA INTERVIÚ al ESPOSO y APARECIÓ ELLA: «TODA ELEGANCIA, GRACIA, MOVILIDAD, NERVIOS y PERFUME». SU PELO, «UN ARTÍSTICO DESORDEN de RIZOS NEGROS COMO la ENDRINA».

—¡OH! NO ME HAGAN USTEDES RETRATOS —PIDIÓ, al VER la CÁMARA FOTOGRÁFICA—. LOS TENGO HECHOS MUY BONITOS. ARRÉGLENSE CON DOS o TRES. SALGO SIEMPRE MUY MAL. ADEMÁS, los ARTISTAS, al LLEGAR a CIERTA EDAD, NO DEBEMOS RETRATARNOS YA, SINO DAR SIEMPRE UNO DONDE SE ESTÉ MEJOR.

El PERIODISTA la CONVENCIÓ. SALIERON al JARDÍN a HACER las FOTOS y ÉL PREGUNTÓ:

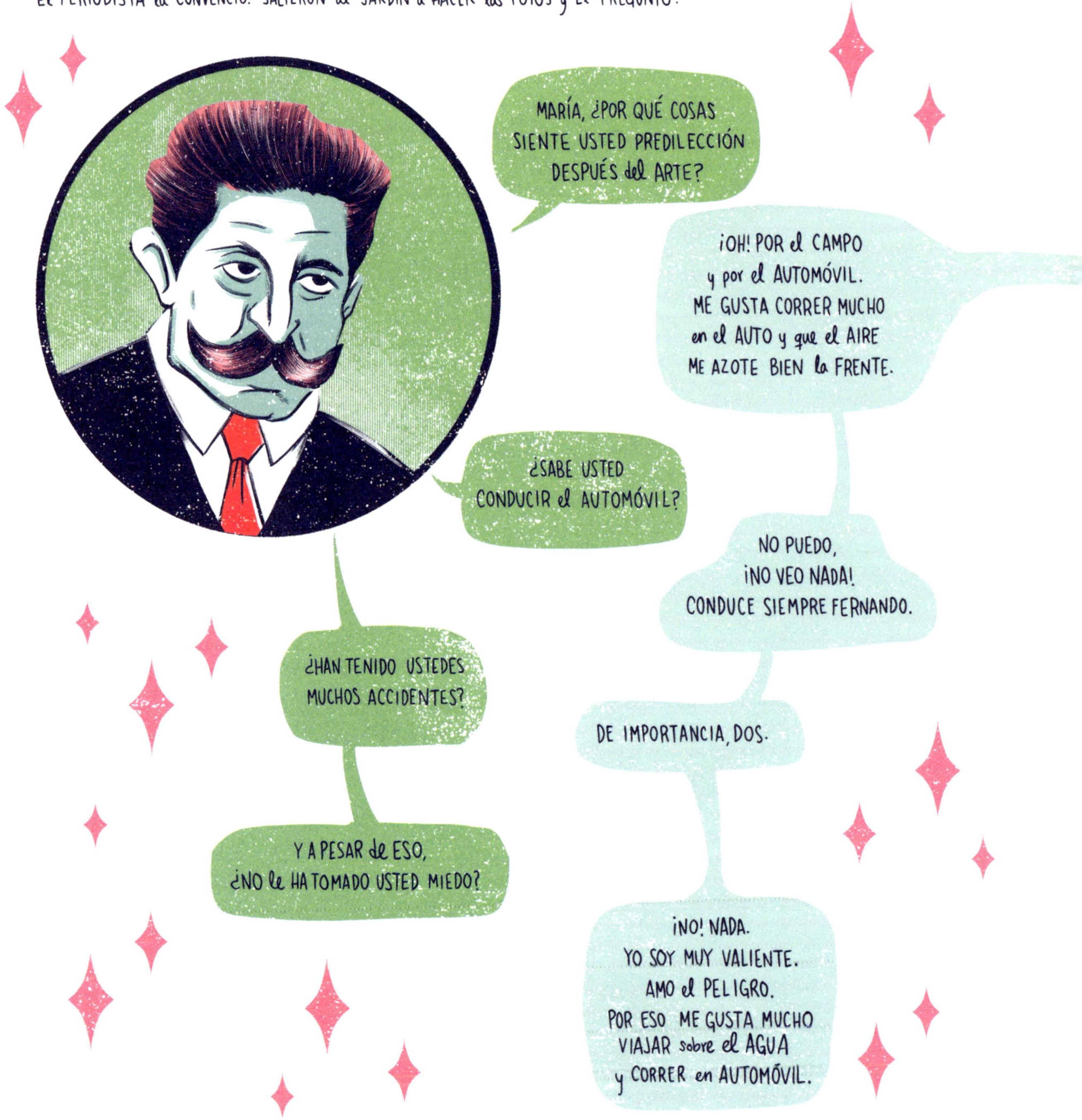

HABLARON en el JARDÍN hasta que el MEDIODÍA SE les FUE ECHANDO ENCIMA. ENTONCES, ella MIRÓ al CIELO CON DELEITE y EXCLAMÓ:

¡QUÉ TARDE MÁS HERMOSA! Y NOSOTROS, AHORA, ¡A METERNOS en las TINIEBLAS del ESCENARIO hasta las SEIS!
¡Y SIEMPRE lo MISMO! ¡ES UNA CONDENACIÓN ESTA VIDA NUESTRA!
Y NO CREA USTED, que HABRÁ MUCHOS ENVIDIOSOS de NUESTRA VIDA Y NUESTRA SUERTE.
¡DIOS MÍO, CON lo que VALE UNA HORA de SOL y AIRE PURO en UN DÍA TAN LINDO COMO ESTE!
EN FIN, YA NOS ESTARÁN ESPERANDO.

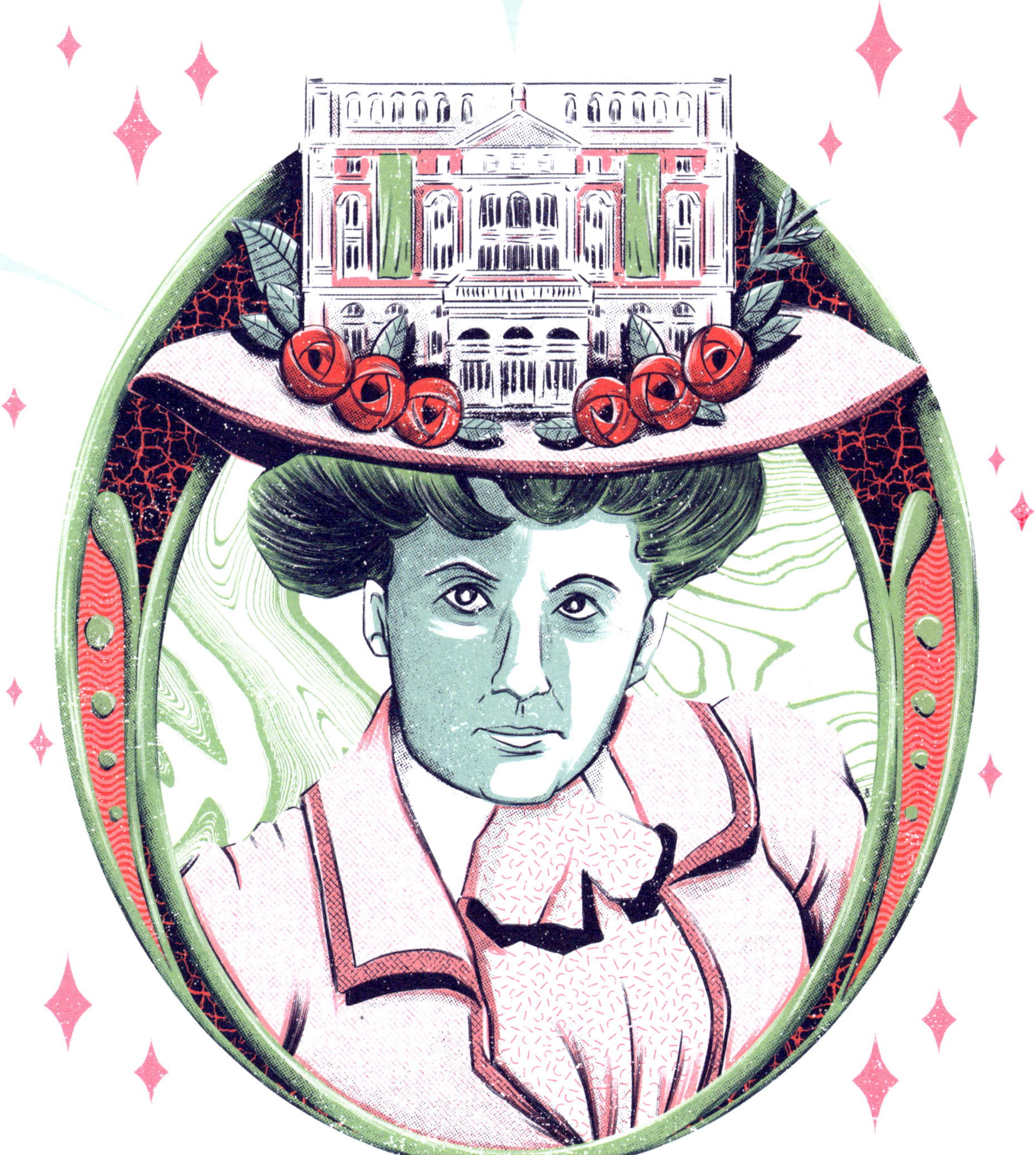

SAQUEN SUS MEJORES GALAS EN ESTE DÍA DE LUTO NACIONAL POR...

JOSÉ CANALEJAS

EL MAGNICIDIO QUE ENSANGRENTÓ LA PUERTA DEL SOL

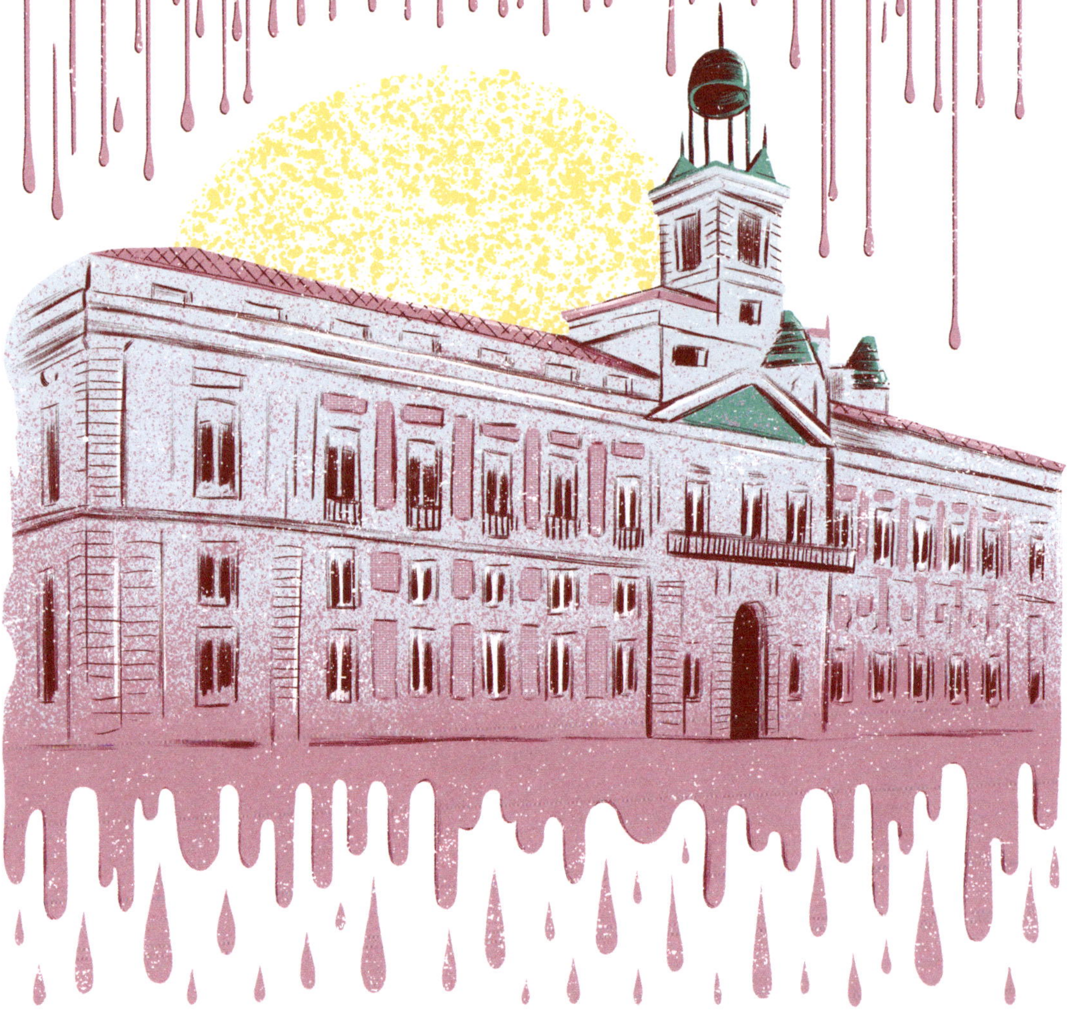

Al SALIR del DESPACHO del REY ALFONSO XIII, UNA RÁFAGA de VIENTO SACUDE a JOSÉ CANALEJAS. «HOY VAMOS a TENER UN MAL DÍA», DICE el PRESIDENTE del GOBIERNO.

A CONTINUACIÓN SE DIRIGE a SU CASA y de AHÍ, a la PUERTA del SOL. AÚN FALTA UN RATO para que EMPIECE el CONSEJO de MINISTROS de ESTA MAÑANA del 12 de NOVIEMBRE de 1912. CANALEJAS (1854-1912) CAMINA SOLO, MEDITABUNDO, DESPREVENIDO. TIENE la DEMOCRÁTICA COSTUMBRE de IR a PIE desde SU CASA HASTA el MINISTERIO de GOBERNACIÓN.

Al PASAR por la LIBRERÍA SAN MARTÍN, DETIENE el PASO y DIRIGE la MIRADA al ESCAPARATE. HAY VARIOS LIBROS que le INTERESAN y UN MAPA de los BALCANES. El PRESIDENTE RECORRE SUS OJOS por ESA EUROPA LEJANA en ESTA MAÑANA TRANQUILA.

UN HOMBRE JOVEN, LIMPIAMENTE VESTIDO CON GABÁN CLARO y TRAJE OSCURO, SE ACERCA a CANALEJAS por la ESPALDA. CASI SE APOYA en SU HOMBRO y, a TODA VELOCIDAD, SACA de SU CHAQUETA UNA PISTOLA BROWNING. El VIAJE MENTAL del PRESIDENTE por los BALCANES ACABA de GOLPE en TRES BALAZOS.

UN PROYECTIL ENTRA por DEBAJO del OÍDO DERECHO, ATRAVIESA el BULBO RAQUÍDEO y SALE por el OÍDO IZQUIERDO. CANALEJAS, ATURDIDO, en UN ÚLTIMO SUSPIRO de VIDA, SE ECHA las MANOS a la CABEZA y EMPIEZA a TAMBALEARSE. EN ESTE TERRIBLE MOMENTO, UN CRIADO del CONDE de VILLAGONZALO CAMINA a SOLO UNOS PASOS y SE APRESURA a SOSTENER en SUS BRAZOS al PRESIDENTE ANTES de que CAIGA DESPLOMADO al SUELO.

LOS GUARDAESPALDAS VEN la ESCENA y ECHAN a CORRER hasta que CONSIGUEN ABALANZARSE SOBRE el CRIMINAL. UN POLICÍA le DA TAL PORRAZO que TUERCE el BASTÓN. EL ASESINO le DISPARA, pero, por FORTUNA, la BALA NO HACE BLANCO.

EN ESTOS RAPIDÍSIMOS FORCEJEOS, en ESTA HUIDA SIN SALIDA, en ESTA ESCENA BÁRBARA y SAGRIENTA que HA ATROPELLADO a la HISTORIA de ESPAÑA, el ASESINO ACABA con DOS BALAS en la CABEZA. (SUICIDIO, DICEN los PERIÓDICOS de ENTONCES. QUIÉN SABE, DICEN los HISTORIADORES UN SIGLO DESPUÉS.)

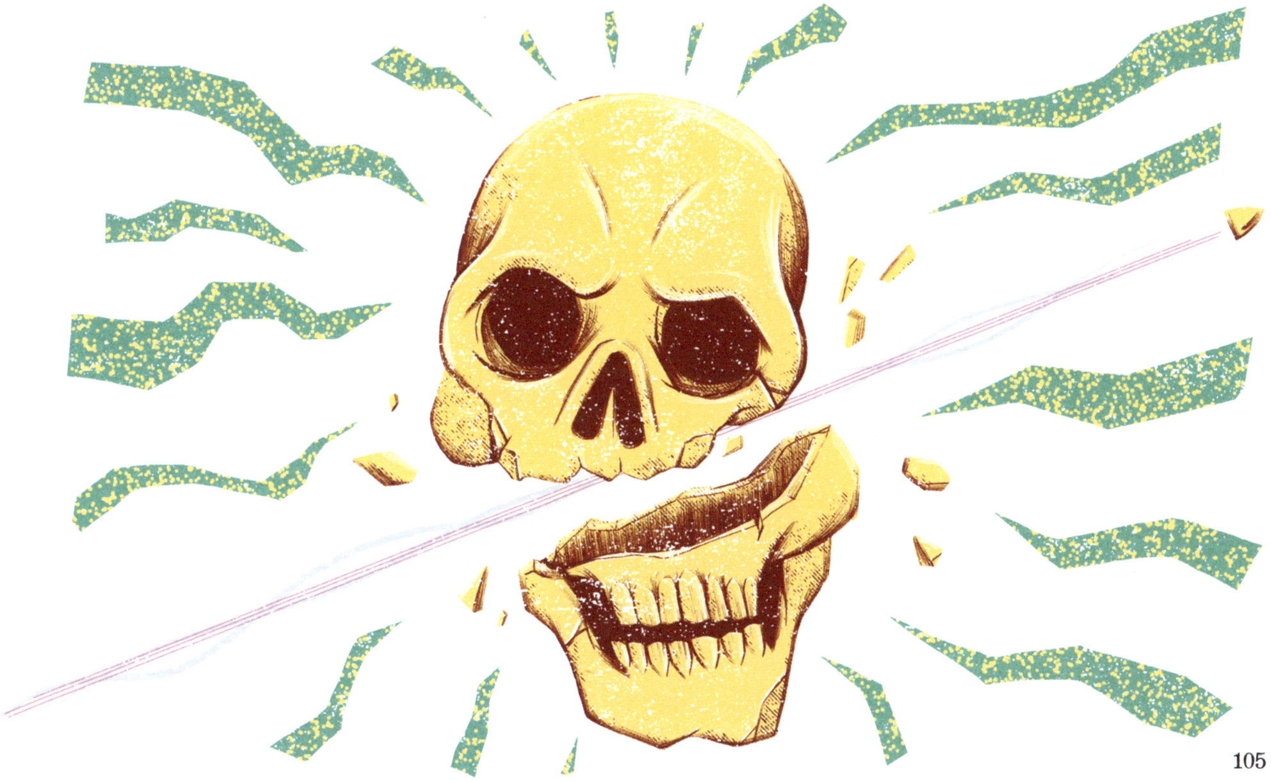

Escenas desgarradoras

La noticia del terrible asesinato se extiende como un reguero de pólvora. Las telefonistas viven una mañana de locura para atender las comunicaciones que se solicitan de todas partes.

Cientos de políticos llegan de inmediato al Salón de Porteros del Ministerio de Gobernación, donde yace el cádaver del presidente. Uno de los primeros es el liberal **Manuel García Prieto**. Al cruzarse con Miguel Moya, el director del periódico «El Liberal», preguntó incrédulo:

-Pero ¿es cierto? ¿Está herido el presidente?

-¡¡¡Muerto!!! -dice una voz, y, ante la horrible noticia, García Prieto sufre un desvanecimiento.

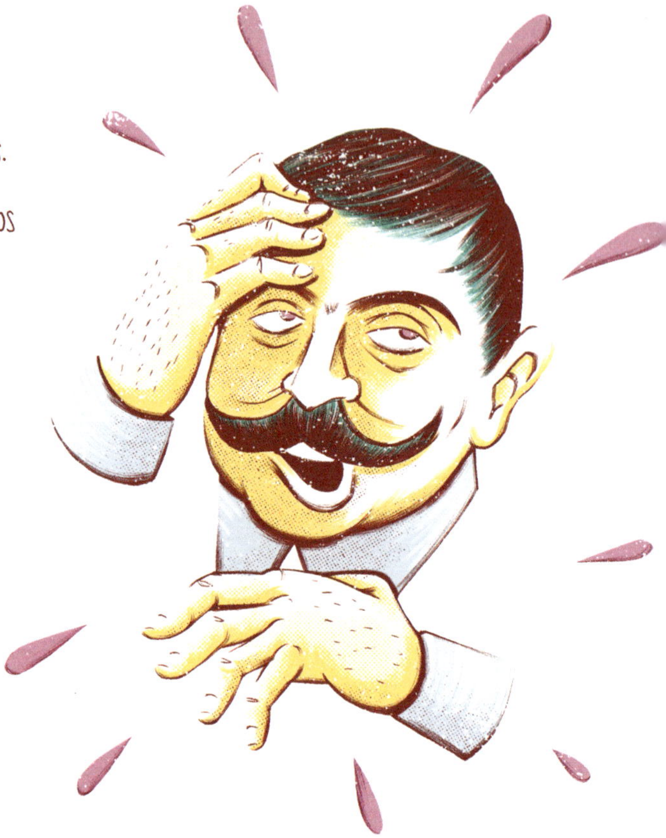

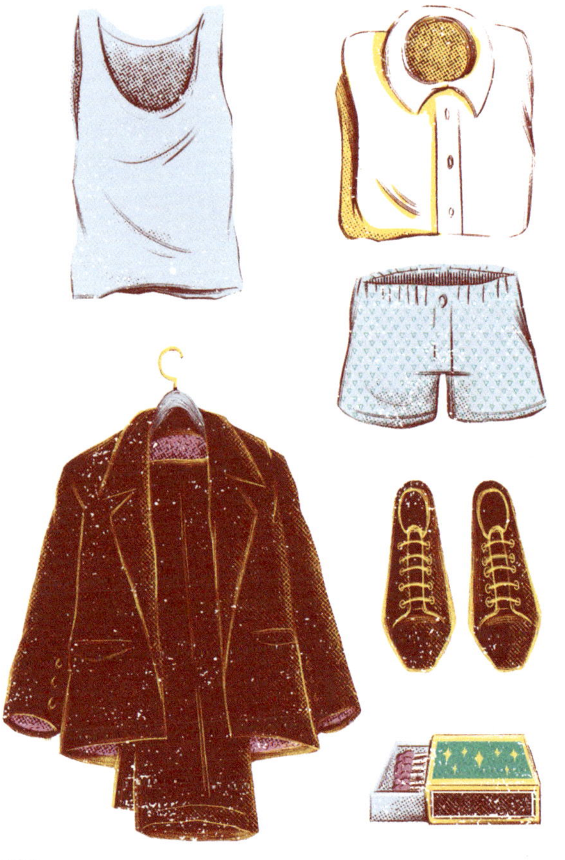

El infame asesino

El juez ordena que registren las ropas del cadáver. Lleva camiseta y calzoncillos de punto celeste, camisa blanca sin almidonar, traje de paño color chocolate y botas que presentan señales de haber sido arregladas con medias suelas.

En los bolsillos encuentran un billete de veinticinco pesetas, una caja de cerillas, un cuaderno con indicaciones médicas, otro que dice «Conflagración internacional. París» y un retrato de una mujer con estas letras: «A mi inolvidable Manuel».

El magnicida es **Manuel Pardiñas**, un hombre fichado en los registros policiales de varios países como «anarquista en acción».

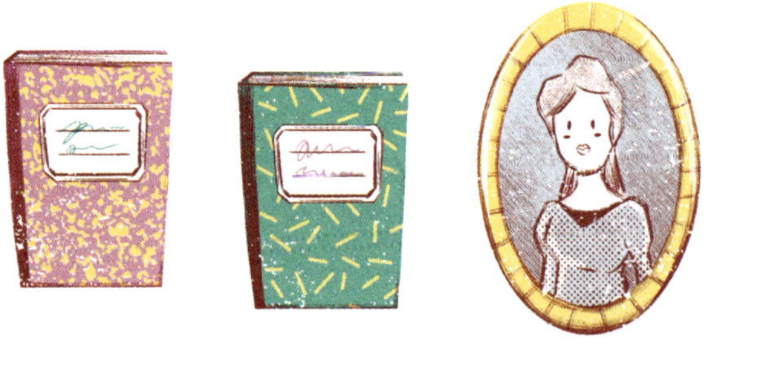

LA GLORIA del PRESIDENTE

«NUNCA SE ha VISTO en MADRID UNA MANIFESTACIÓN de DUELO MÁS GRANDE, MÁS ESPONTÁNEA, MÁS SINCERA, MÁS RESPETUOSA», CUENTA «EL HERALDO» el DÍA del ENTIERRO.

Y HASTA el «ABC» lo DESPIDE CON ESTAS PALABRAS: «UN HOMBRE BUENO, FERVOROSO PROCURADOR de los HUMILDES, INDULGENTE con los EXTRAVÍOS POPULARES, PRUDENTE y SUAVE en las REPRESIONES, que HABÍA SUPRIMIDO, de HECHO, la PENA de MUERTE, y PRETENDÍA BORRARLA del CÓDIGO, que HA SIDO ASESINADO ALEVOSAMENTE CUANDO CAMINABA INDEFENSO y DESCUIDADO, AMPARÁNDOSE en SU NOTORIA BONDAD».

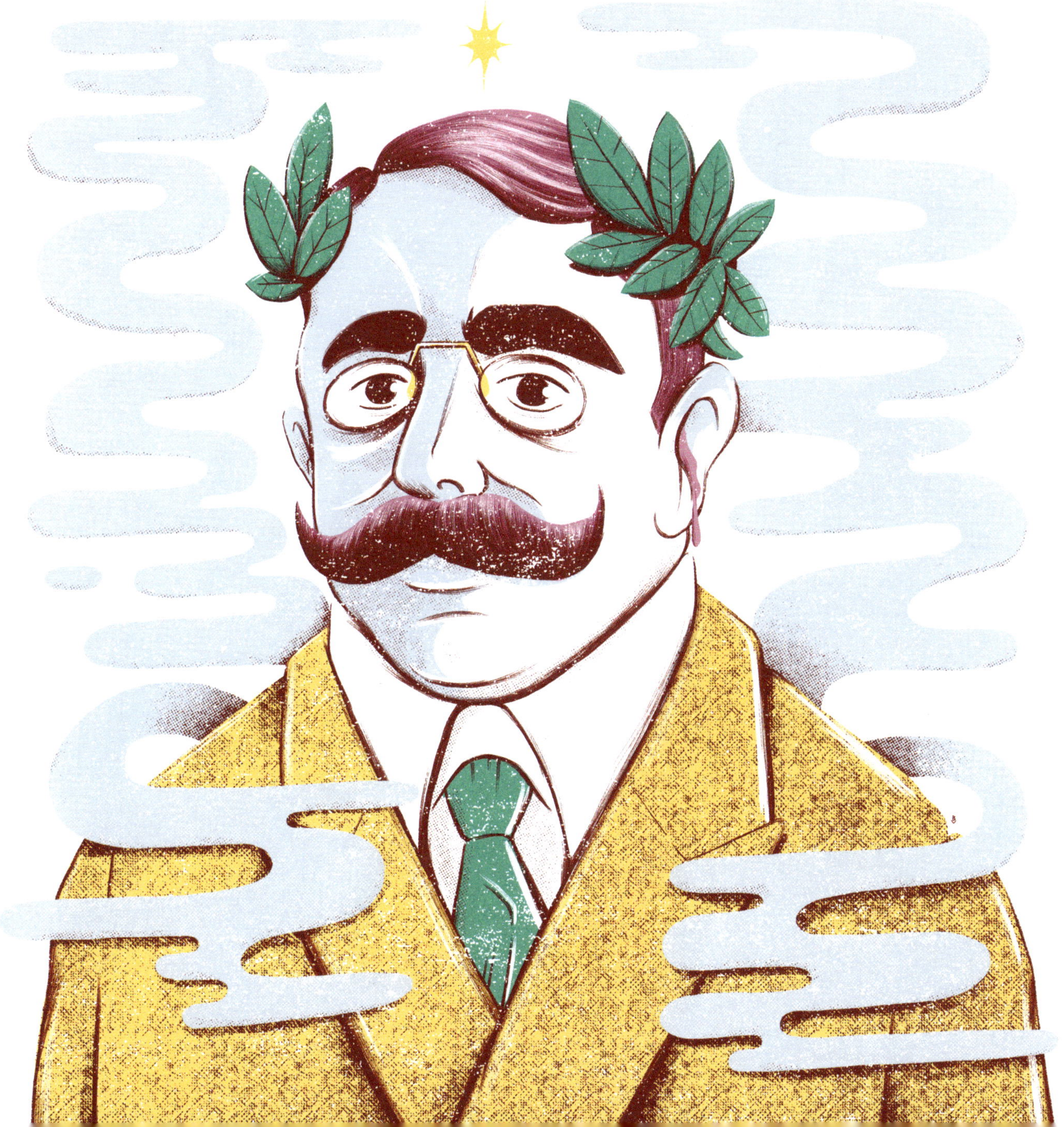

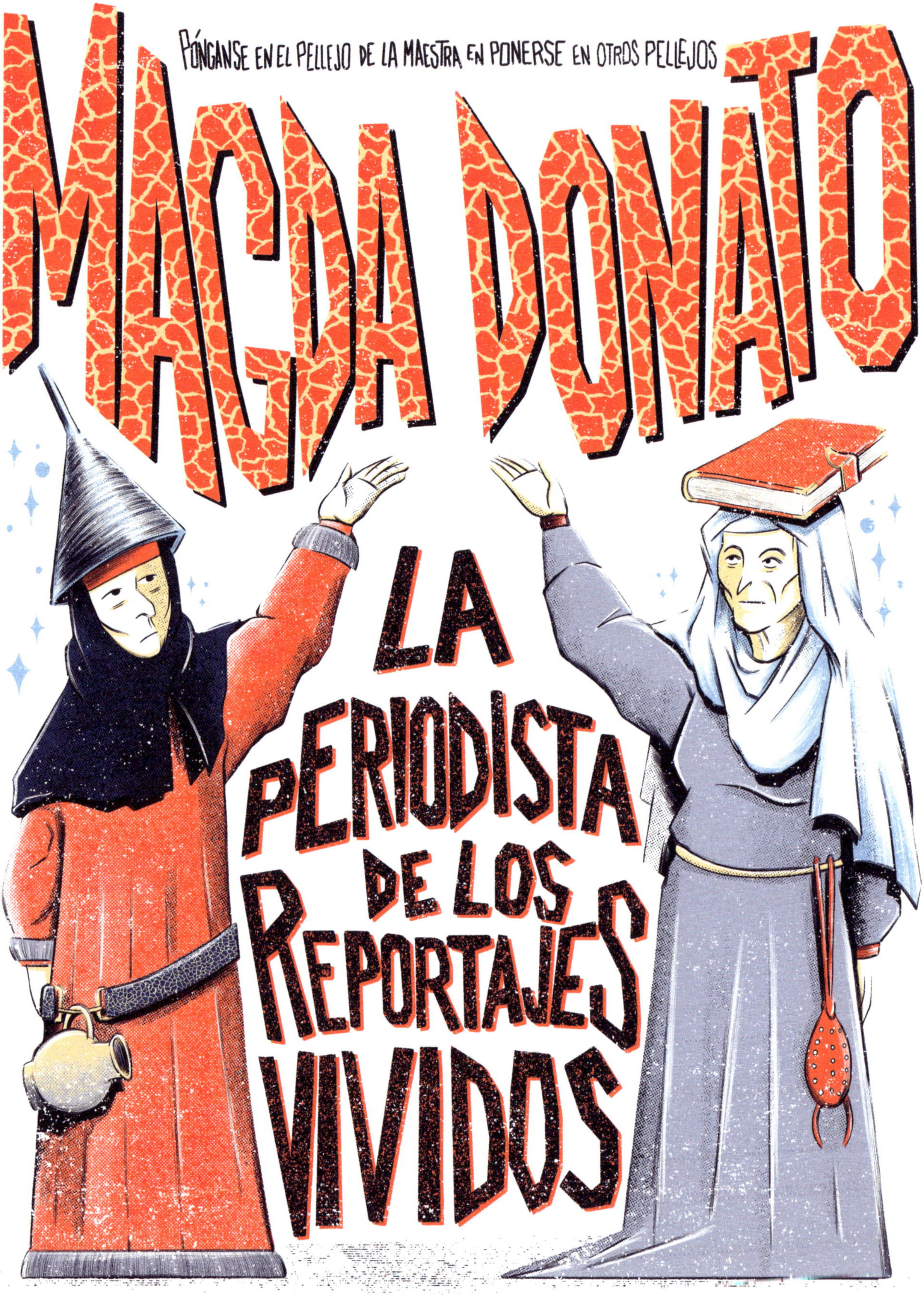
PÓNGANSE EN EL PELLEJO DE LA MAESTRA EN PONERSE EN OTROS PELLEJOS
MAGDA DONATO
LA PERIODISTA DE LOS REPORTAJES VIVIDOS

-DOCTOR AMIGO: YO QUISIERA SER RECLUIDA en UN MANICOMIO.

-¿ACASO ESTÁ USTED LOCA?

-NO, SEÑOR. VAMOS, NO CREO...

-ENTONCES ESTÁ USTED LOCA. QUIERO DECIR que SE NECESITA ESTAR LOCA para QUERER INGRESAR en UN MANICOMIO SIN ESTAR LOCA.

-SOY PERIODISTA y PADEZCO la ENFERMEDAD de la CONCIENCIA PROFESIONAL. Y COMO QUIERO PUBLICAR en «AHORA» UNOS REPORTAJES SOBRE la VIDA de los DEMENTES...

¡ACABÁRAMOS! EN ESTA TARDE de 1932 el MÉDICO le DICE a SU AMIGA, **MAGDA DONATO**, que le PRESENTARÁ a los PSIQUIATRAS MÁS EMINENTES: ELLOS le DARÁN CIENTOS de DATOS y ESTADÍSTICAS, y le CONSEGUIRÁN UN PASE para que VISITE UN MANICOMIO y PUEDA HACER FOTOS.

A la PERIODISTA NO le INTERESA. INSISTE en que NECESITA UN DIAGNÓSTICO de LOCA:

-ASPIRO a que MI REPORTAJE, en LUGAR de ESTAR HECHO «de FUERA ADENTRO», lo ESTÉ «DESDE DENTRO». Y para ELLO es INDISPENSABLE que YO PUEDA PERMANECER en UN MANICOMIO y CONVIVIR con DEMENTES.

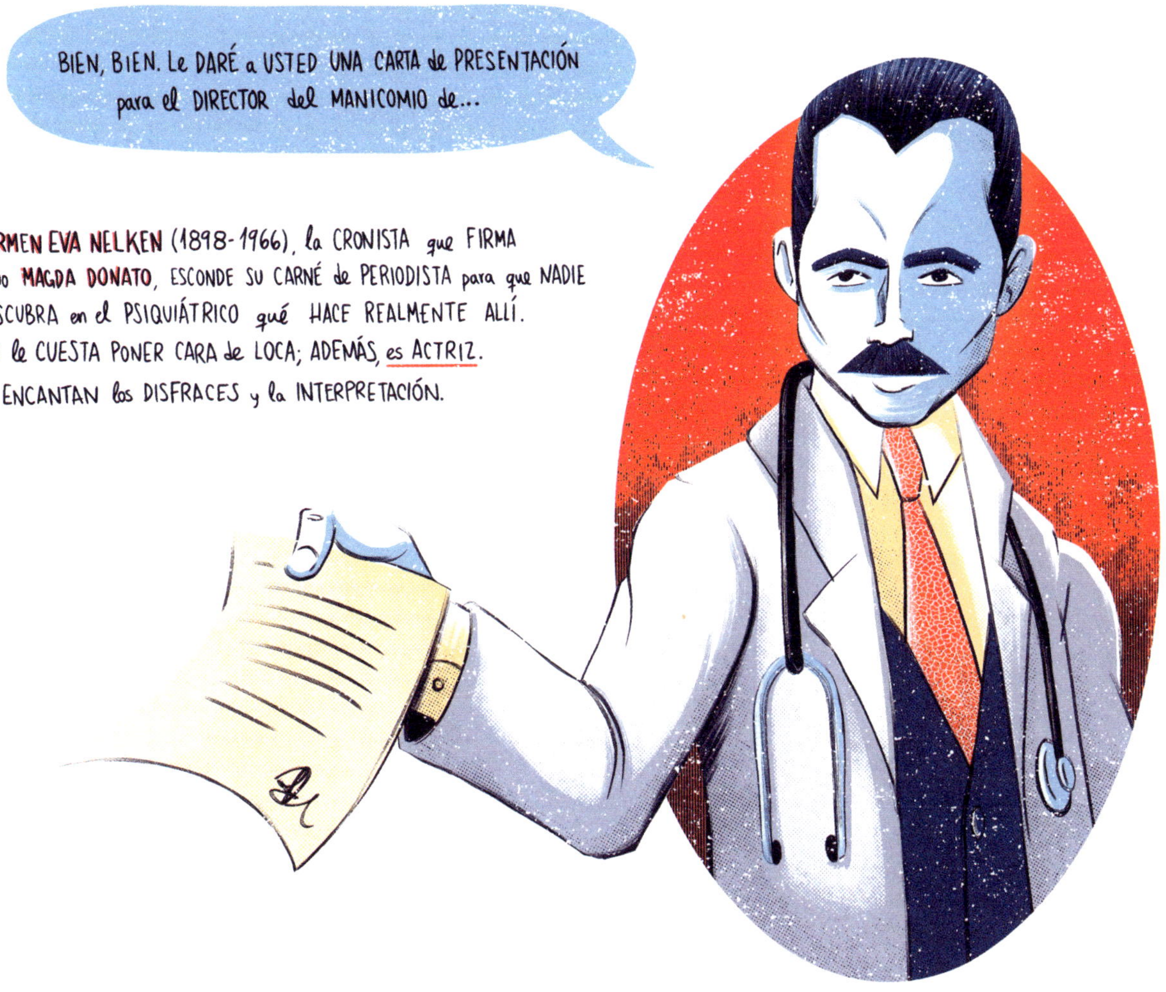

CARMEN EVA NELKEN (1898-1966), la CRONISTA que FIRMA como **MAGDA DONATO**, ESCONDE SU CARNÉ de PERIODISTA para que NADIE DESCUBRA en el PSIQUIÁTRICO qué HACE REALMENTE ALLÍ. NO le CUESTA PONER CARA de LOCA; ADEMÁS, es ACTRIZ. Le ENCANTAN los DISFRACES y la INTERPRETACIÓN.

ESA MAÑANA la INGRESAN en UNA HABITACIÓN SIN ESPEJOS (DICEN que a las ENFERMAS les DIVIERTE ROMPERLOS) y le QUITAN las TIJERAS, las LIMAS y el AFILALÁPICES.

«DUERMA TRANQUILA. SI OYE GRITAR, NO SE ASUSTE. CUALQUIER RUIDO que OIGA, NO SE PREOCUPE.»

A MEDIA NOCHE ENTIENDE el AVISO. DOÑA JUANITA DISCUTE con las VOCES que SOLO ELLA OYE. PELEA y SE DESESPERA hasta LLEGAR al GRITO, a los ACENTOS VULGARES y DESGARRADOS: «¡NO ESCARMIENTA, NO!», «¡QUÉ PEEESTE!».

DOÑA PILAR, UNA JOVEN BELLÍSIMA, SE REMANGA la BATA de FRANELA MARRÓN al VER PASAR al MÉDICO y RÍE. SIEMPRE RÍE. ROMPE UNAS FOTOS de SUS HIJOS en CACHITOS y RÍE con TODA SU ALMA:

«CHICA, ¡MIS HIJOS! ¡QUÉ GRACIA! ¡Y MI MARIDO! ¡QUÉ GRACIA! ¡JA, JA, JA!».

ESTÁ PROHIBIDO HACER FOTOS pero MAGDA APROVECHA «El DESCUIDO de los VIGILANTES para DISPARAR COMO QUIEN CAZA UNA MOSCA al VUELO». EN UN MES YA ha VIVIDO lo que QUIERE CONTAR. ES HORA de IRSE. PODRÍA FUGARSE, pero TIENE OTRO PLAN: PIDE UNA ENTREVISTA con el DIRECTOR del SANATORIO.

-DON J., YO les he ENGAÑADO a USTEDES. ¡YO NO ESTOY LOCA!

El MÉDICO SE QUEDA IMPASIBLE.

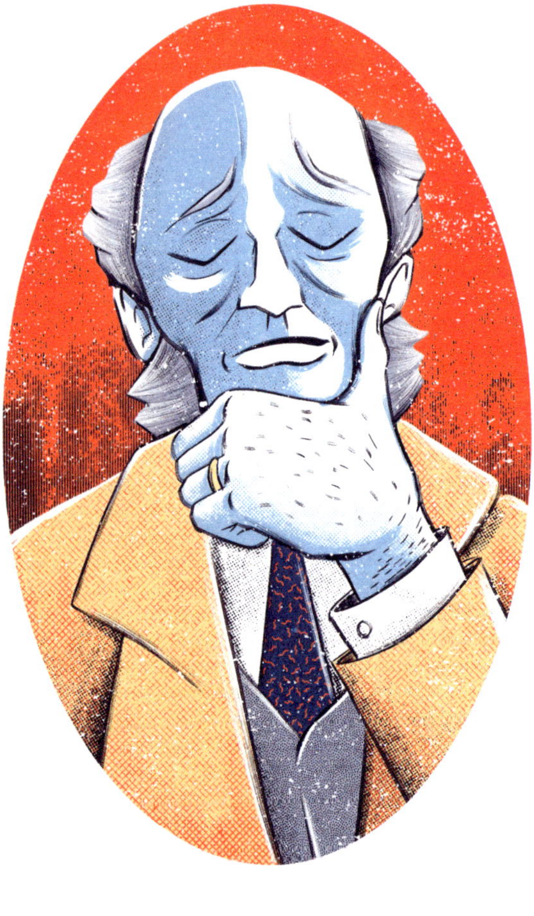

MAGDA BUSCA en SU BOLSILLO el CARNÉ de PERIODISTA, pero NO lo ENCUENTRA. BIEN SE GUARDÓ de NO TRAERLO al MANICOMIO. LLEVARLA a UNA CELDA de RECLUSIÓN HUBIESE SIDO un GRAN BROCHE para ESTE REPORTAJE, pero el PSIQUIATRA, al FINAL, la CREE:

—DOCTOR, LLEVO AQUÍ UN MES. EL TRATO QUE SE ME HA DADO ES EL MISMO QUE A LOS DEMÁS ENFERMOS; ES DECIR, EXCELENTE. PUES BIEN, ESO QUE HE HECHO... NO TENDRÍA VALOR PARA VOLVERLO A HACER.

¿SEGURO? EN CUANTO LA REVISTA «AHORA» PUBLICA «UN MES ENTRE LOS LOCAS», MAGDA HACE QUE LA ENCARCELEN PARA ESCRIBIR OTRO REPORTAJE: «LA VIDA EN LA CÁRCEL DE MUJERES». ES UN PERIODISMO TAN NOVEDOSO Y TAN VALIENTE QUE ALGUNOS NO LA CREEN. ELLA, CONTUNDENTE, LOS RETA Y PUBLICA ESTE ANUNCIO:

«¡5.000 PESETAS PARA LOS LECTORES INCRÉDULOS!

QUIEN DEMUESTRE QUE NO HE VIVIDO COMO RECLUSA PUEDE PASAR POR LA REDACCIÓN DE "AHORA" A RECOGER LAS 5.000 PESETAS».

«LA IDEA DE HACER UN REPORTAJE SINTIÉNDOME LOCA NACIÓ... COMO NACEN ESAS COSAS: PENSANDO, BUSCANDO TEMAS Y PROCEDIMIENTOS QUE ROMPAN EL RITMO DE LO NORMAL, DE LO DIARIO. POR EL AFÁN DE HACER ALGO MÁS PERSONAL, DISTINTO A LO DE SIEMPRE... —EXPLICA AL PERIÓDICO "CRÓNICA"—. ME ENCANTA ESTO DE VIVIR EL REPORTAJE, DE BUSCAR LA VERDAD POR EL CAMINO DE LA SIMULACIÓN.»

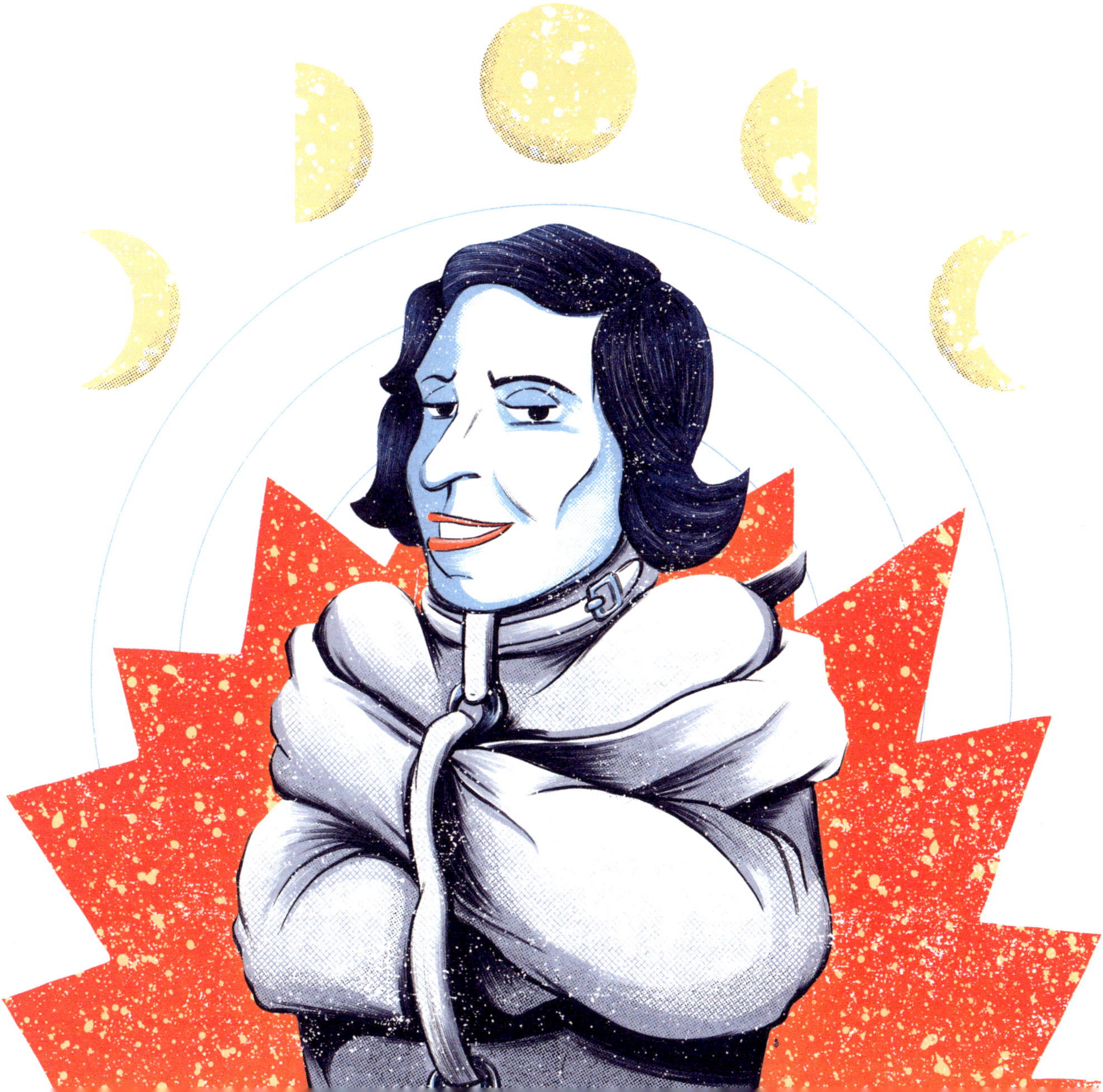

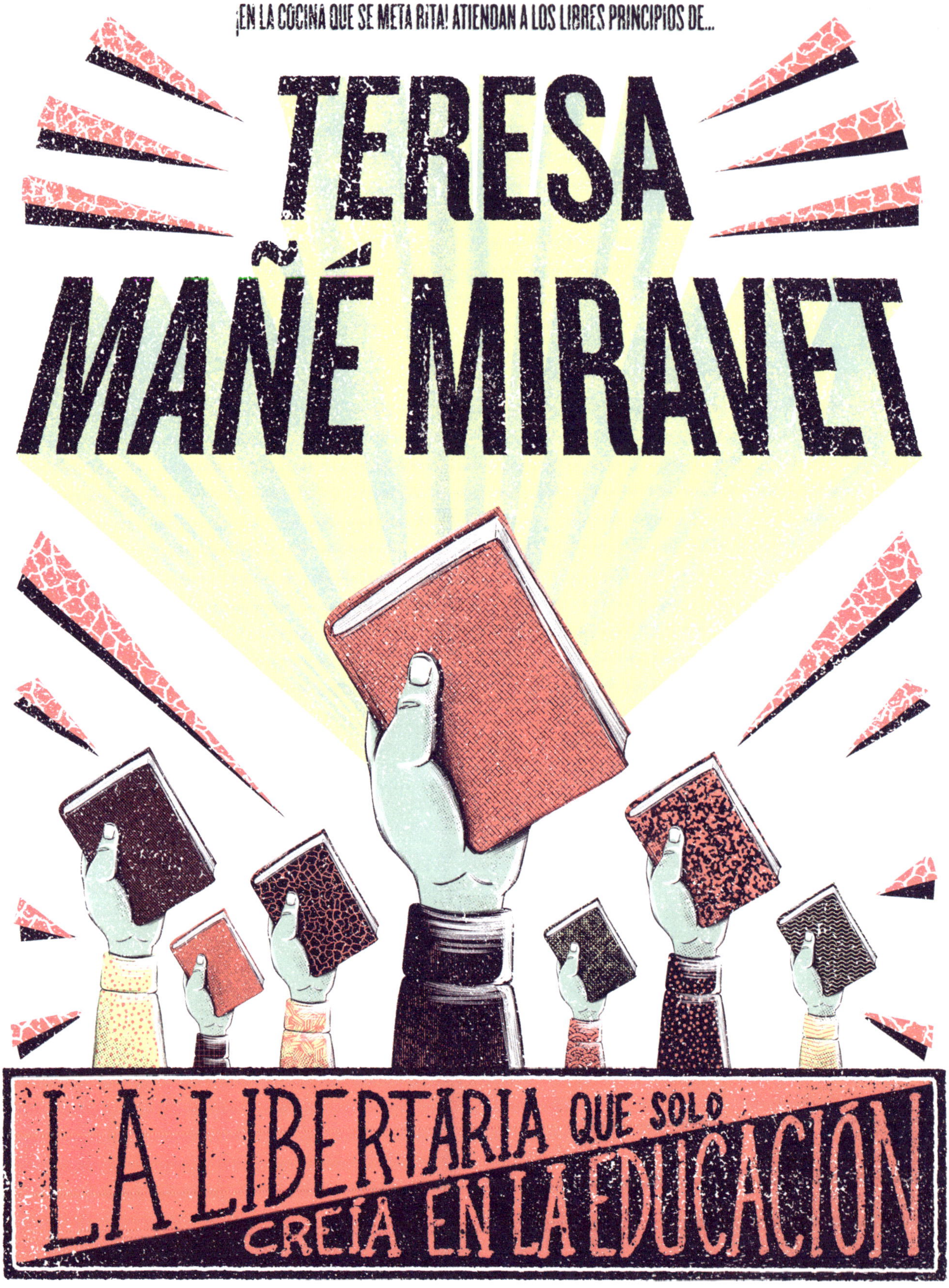
¡EN LA COCINA QUE SE META RITA! ATIENDAN A LOS LIBRES PRINCIPIOS DE...
TERESA MAÑÉ MIRAVET
LA LIBERTARIA QUE SOLO CREÍA EN LA EDUCACIÓN

A TERESA MAÑÉ MIRAVET (1865-1939) le RESBALABA ESA FRASE ESPANTOSA que DIJO UN ESCRITOR: «LA MUJER, en el HOGAR. A COCER GARBANZOS y a HACER CALCETA». ELLA TENÍA OTROS PLANES: QUERÍA SER MAESTRA.

EN 1883 SE MATRICULÓ en la ESCUELA NORMAL de MAGISTERIO de BARCELONA. A la VEZ, ERA AYUDANTE en la ESCUELA PÚBLICA de NIÑAS del SEGUNDO DISTRITO de VILANOVA; y le FUE MUY BIEN: LA JUNTA LOCAL de PRIMERA ENSEÑANZA le CONCEDIÓ los «MAYORES PLÁCEMES».

PERO SE le ATRANCÓ el MAGISTERIO. El PROFESOR de CATECISMO de la DOCTRINA CRISTIANA DEJÓ ESCRITO que NUNCA le APROBARÍA ESTA ASIGNATURA. A TERESA le INTERESABA el PENSAMIENTO LIBRE: AHÍ SE DEBIÓ de PRODUCIR el «¡CRASH!».

EN ESA ÉPOCA EMPEZÓ a ESCRIBIR en PRENSA ANTICLERICAL y LIBREPENSADORA. EN «LA TRONADA», «El VENDAVAL», «LA TRAMONTANA»... DECÍA que, COMO MUJER, SE SENTÍA «UN JUDÍO ERRANTE» SOMETIDO a «la MIRADA SIEMPRE CRUEL y ARTERA de la SOCIEDAD».

«¿QUÉ DEBE HACER la MUJER al CONVENCERSE de que SIRVE para ALGO MÁS de lo que LAS RELIGIONES POSITIVAS ASEGURAN?»

Ella TENÍA la RESPUESTA para SÍ MISMA: SE SACUDIÓ el «ADOCTRINAMIENTO RUTINARIO» de la RELIGIÓN y DECIDIÓ PREDICAR la EDUCACIÓN LAICA: en los COLEGIOS y en los PERIÓDICOS. Y ASÍ...

«LAS RELIGIONES POSITIVAS que HAN SABIDO HACER a la MUJER UNA SIERVA de DIOS y UNA ESCLAVA del HOMBRE DEJARÁN de SUBYUGARLA.»

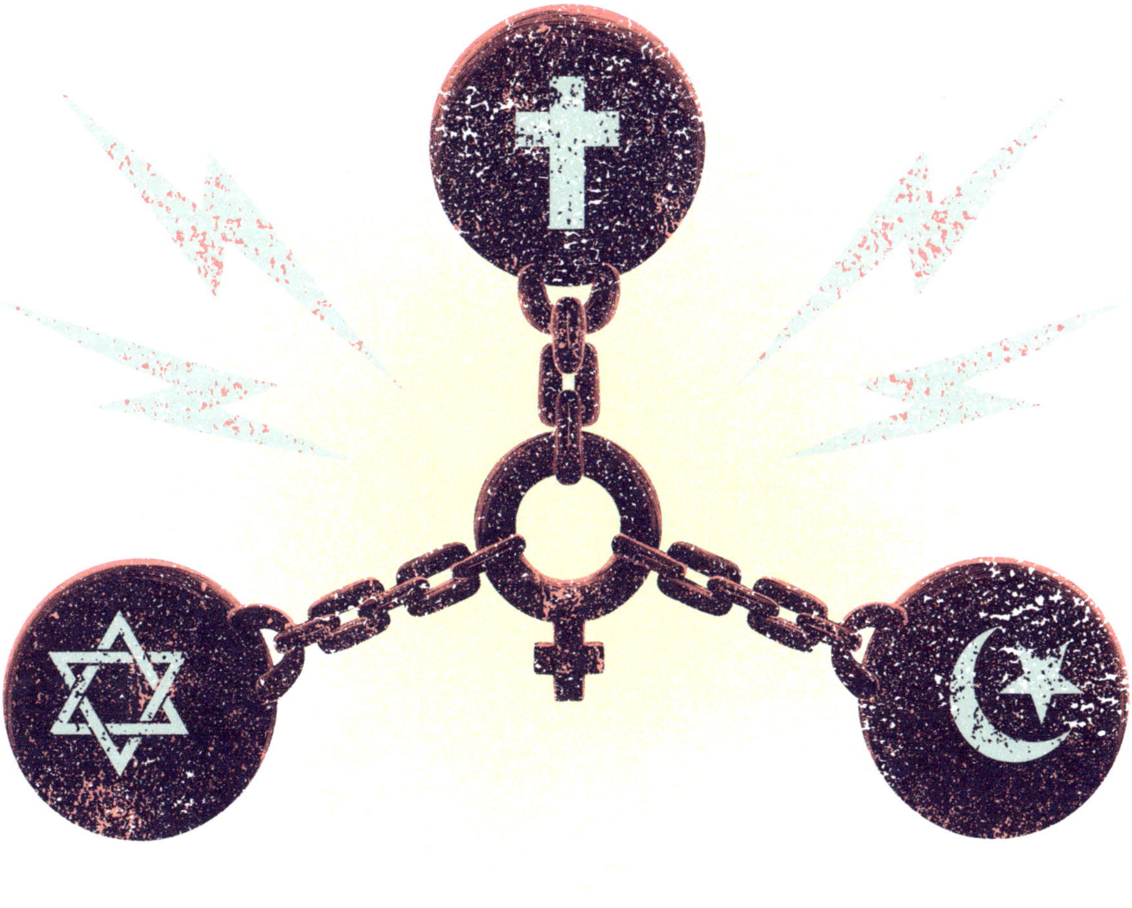

El 1 de MAYO de 1890 SE REUNIERON CIENTOS de LIBREPENSADORES en BARCELONA para REIVINDICAR la JORNADA de OCHO HORAS. ESE DÍA TERESA RECITÓ un POEMA en UN ENTIERRO LAICO. UN HOMBRE QUEDÓ FASCINADO: JOAN MONTSENY. LE ESCRIBIÓ UNA CARTA y ELLA le CONTESTÓ: «(NO SOY) GUAPA, AUNQUE SÍ MUY "EIXERIDETA" (ESPABILADA, VIVARACHA)».

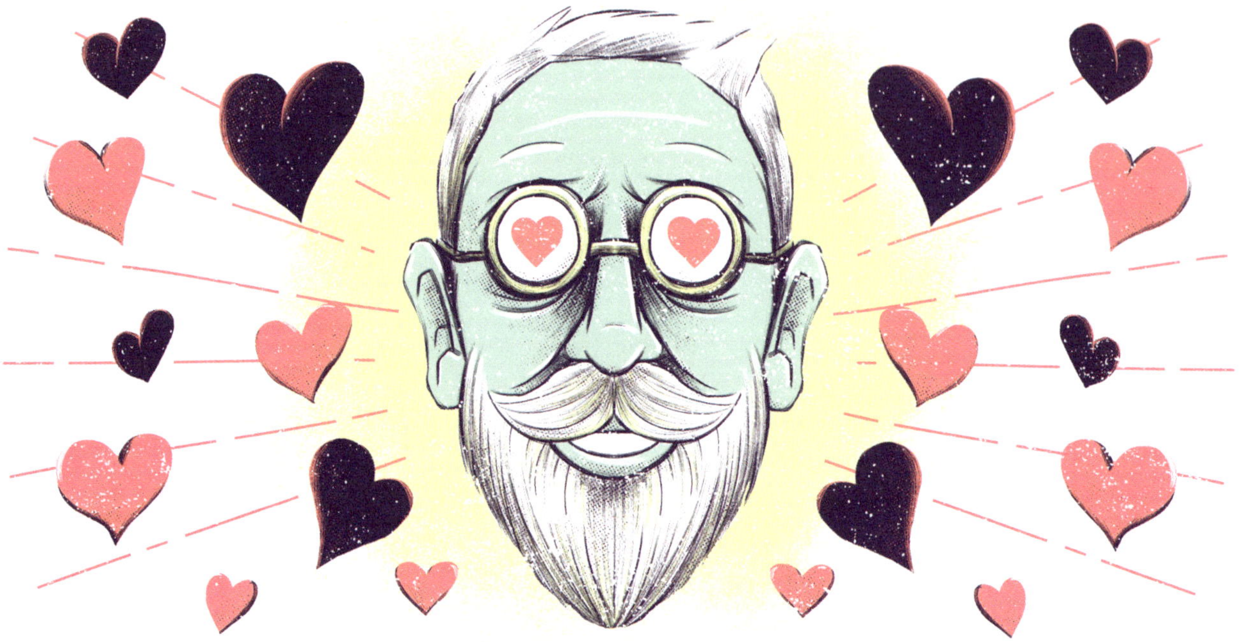

Y ÉL FUE a VILANOVA a CONOCERLA. AL CABO de MENOS de UN AÑO YA ESTABAN CASADOS. PERO, ¡ATENCIÓN!, CASADOS SIN DIOS NI CURA. EN la PRIMAVERA de 1891 CONTRAJERON UN MATRIMONIO CIVIL BASADO en el «AMOR LIBRE» y la «ANARQUÍA SIN RESTRICCIONES».

PARA CONTÁRSELO a SUS AMIGOS, CADA UNO PUBLICÓ UNA CARTA. ÉL ESCRIBIÓ:

«CREO que ESTÁS CONDENADA a AMAR a "UN POBRE HOMBRE". TENDREMOS NECESIDAD de LUCHAR MUCHO, AMADA MÍA, PUES NOS VEREMOS MUY ATACADOS. Y TODO PORQUE NO CREEMOS NI EN los LEYES de los HOMBRES NI en las LEYES de DIOS».

Ella REDACTÓ:

NO PODÍA AMAR al que NO SE IDENTIFICARA CONMIGO.
BUSQUÉ UN CEREBRO que al MÍO SUPERARA.
Y lo QUIERO NO por VANIDAD,
SINO PORQUE NACÍ PARA la LUCHA
y QUIERO UN HOMBRE que VIVE LUCHANDO
por la BONDAD y GRANDEZA de SUS MISMAS CONCEPCIONES.
TE SUPLICO la INSTRUCCIÓN COMO ÚNICA PAGA
al INMENSO AMOR que POR TI SIENTO.

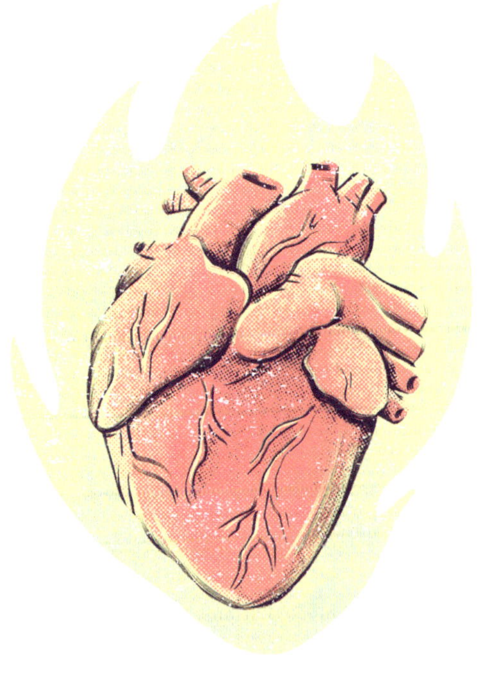

NO SE EQUIVOCÓ NINGUNO de los DOS: SU VIDA FUE UNA LUCHA que PAGÓ CÁRCEL y HOSTIGAMIENTO. AUNQUE NO FALTÓ PASIÓN. ENSEÑARON en ESCUELAS LAICAS y, en 1898, FUNDARON UNA PUBLICACIÓN ANTOLÓGICA: «LA REVISTA BLANCA».

LA DIRIGIÓ SOLEDAD GUSTAVO (la FIRMA de la TERESA ARTICULISTA): Ella ESCRIBÍA, TRADUCÍA, SE OCUPABA de la CORRESPONDENCIA y de la ADMINISTRACIÓN. FEDERICO URALES (El PSEUDÓNIMO de UN MONTSENY que a VECES VIVIÓ ESCONDIDO) ESCRIBÍA y CREABA la RED de RELACIONES CON ARTISTAS, CIENTÍFICOS, SOCIÓLOGOS e «INNOVADORES INTELECTUALES».

LOS PADRES de «LA REVISTA BLANCA» DEJARON SU NOMBRE ESCRITO COMO FUNDADORES de UNA de las GRANDES LECTURAS del ANARQUISMO EUROPEO, E HICIERON ALGO MEJOR: EN 1905 TUVIERON UNA HIJA, FEDERICA MONTSENY: LA PRIMERA MUJER MINISTRA en la HISTORIA de ESPAÑA.

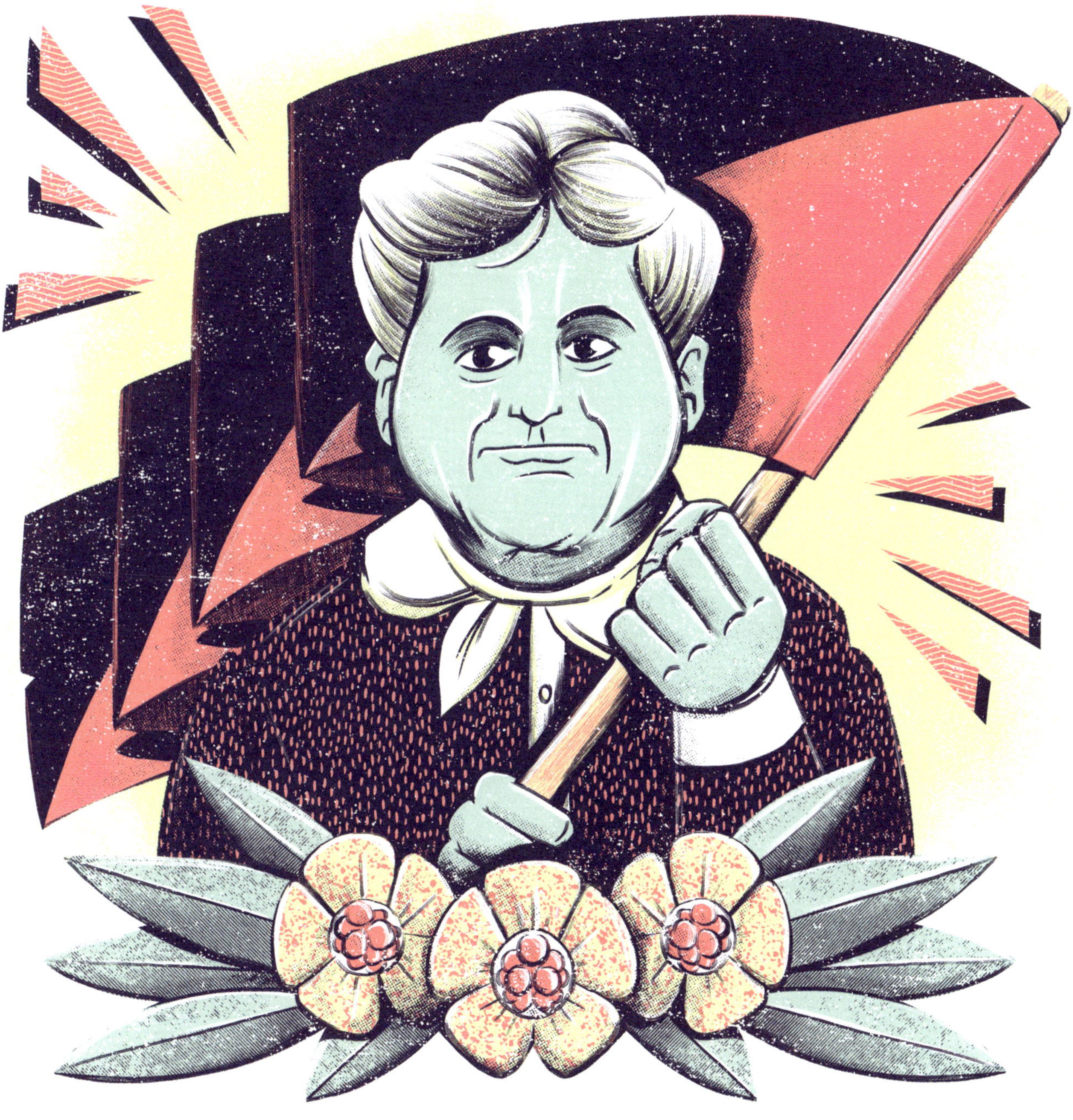

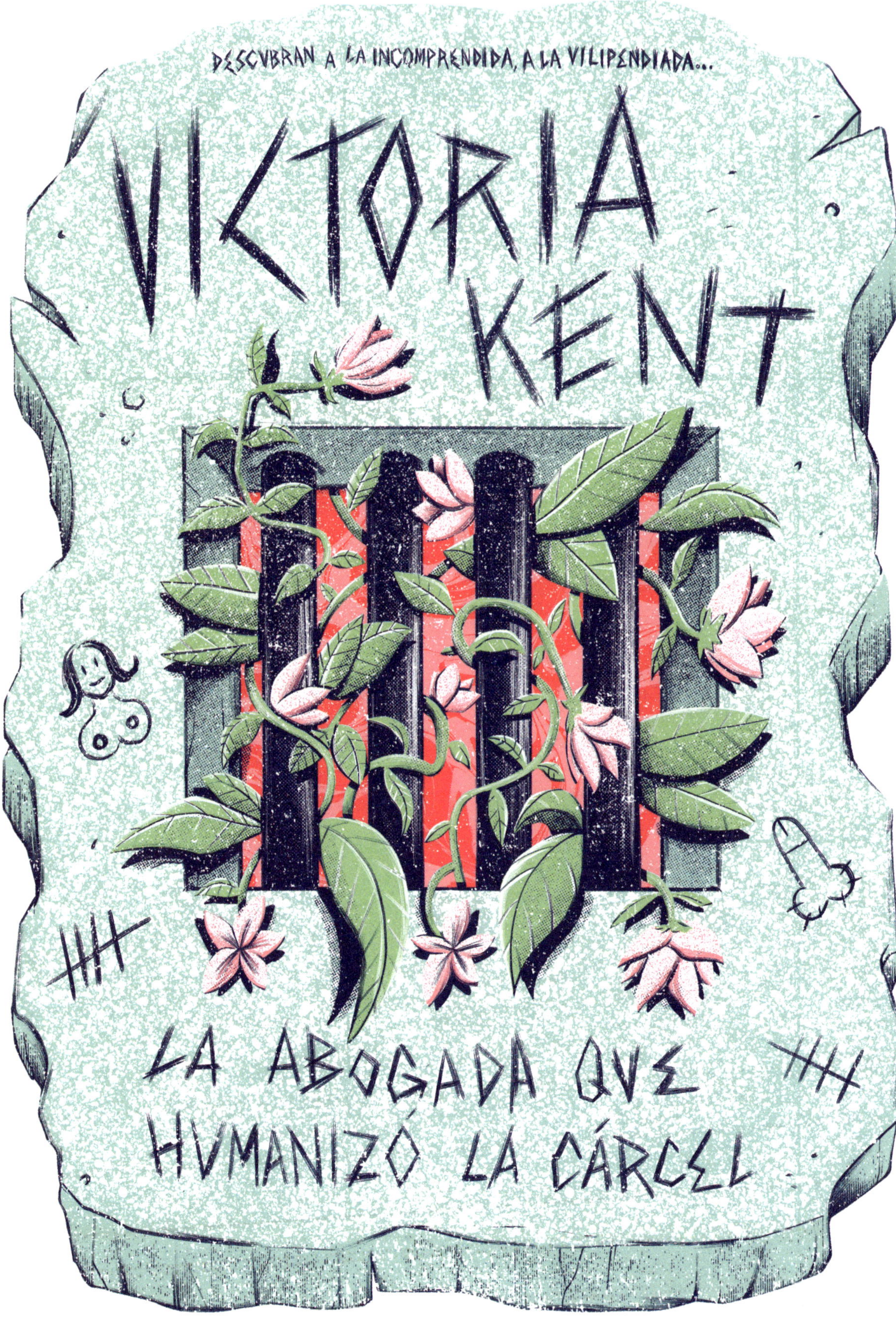
DESCUBRAN A LA INCOMPRENDIDA, A LA VILIPENDIADA...
VICTORIA KENT
LA ABOGADA QUE HUMANIZÓ LA CÁRCEL

En 1925 ACABA la EXCLUSIVIDAD del PANTALÓN en el COLEGIO de ABOGADOS de MADRID. ENTRE TANTO VARÓN, APARECE UNA MUJER: VICTORIA KENT (1891-1987).

ES ENTUSIASTA y DECIDIDA: EN CUATRO AÑOS SE DOCTORA en DERECHO con UNA TESIS SOBRE la REFORMA de la PRISIÓN. Y TIENE IDEALES HERCÚLEOS: PIDE la LIBERTAD de la MUJER, ¡QUE le QUITEN los GRILLETES del PUCHERO y la MORAL!, Y en ELLO PONE SU EMPEÑO desde el LYCEUM CLUB y la ASOCIACIÓN NACIONAL de MUJERES ESPAÑOLAS.

EN el BUFETE de ÁLVARO de ALBORNOZ APRENDE el OFICIO. PERO NO NECESITA MUCHO MAESTRO; PRONTO ABRE UN DESPACHO en UNA HABITACIÓN de SU CASA y DEFIENDE a OBREROS, a FERROVIARIOS, a PESCADORES.

EN los DÍAS que NACE SU REPUTACIÓN de LIBERAL y PROGRESISTA, HAY UN ASALTO al PODER. LOS DEMÓCRATAS ESPERABAN que el PRESIDENTE del GOBIERNO, DÁMASO BERENGUER, RESTABLECIERA la CONSTITUCIÓN, pero el GENERAL NO MUEVE UN DEDO. NO SUELTA el MANDO de SU «DICTABLANDA». ¡GRRR!

UN GRUPO de LIBERALES, HARTICOS, RETAN al GOBIERNO MILITAR de BERENGUER y del REY VIVIDOR, ALFONSO XIII. El GOLPE FRACASA y FUSILAN a los CABECILLAS. A ÁVARO de ALBORNOZ, que TAMBIÉN HA PARTICIPADO, NO lo ATRAVIESAN con PLOMO: LO VAN a JUZGAR, y a VER QUÉ le GUARDA el DESTINO.

¡SU PASANTE! ¡LA ABOGADA BRILLANTE! ¡QUE LLAMEN a VICTORIA!

En el CONSEJO de GUERRA del 20 de MARZO de 1931, la MALAGUEÑA DEFIENDE al «MAESTRO» que le CONTAGIÓ «EL FERVOR de la JUSTICIA». ES la PRIMERA VEZ en la HISTORIA del MUNDO que UNA MUJER ACTÚA COMO ABOGADA ANTE UN TRIBUNAL MILITAR. Y GANA: VICTORIA KENT CONSIGUE la ABSOLUCIÓN de SU DEFENDIDO. LA NOTICIA, en GRANDÍSIMOS TITULARES, en MUCHÍSIMOS PERIÓDICOS, ELEVA AÚN MÁS el PRESTIGIO de la JURISTA.

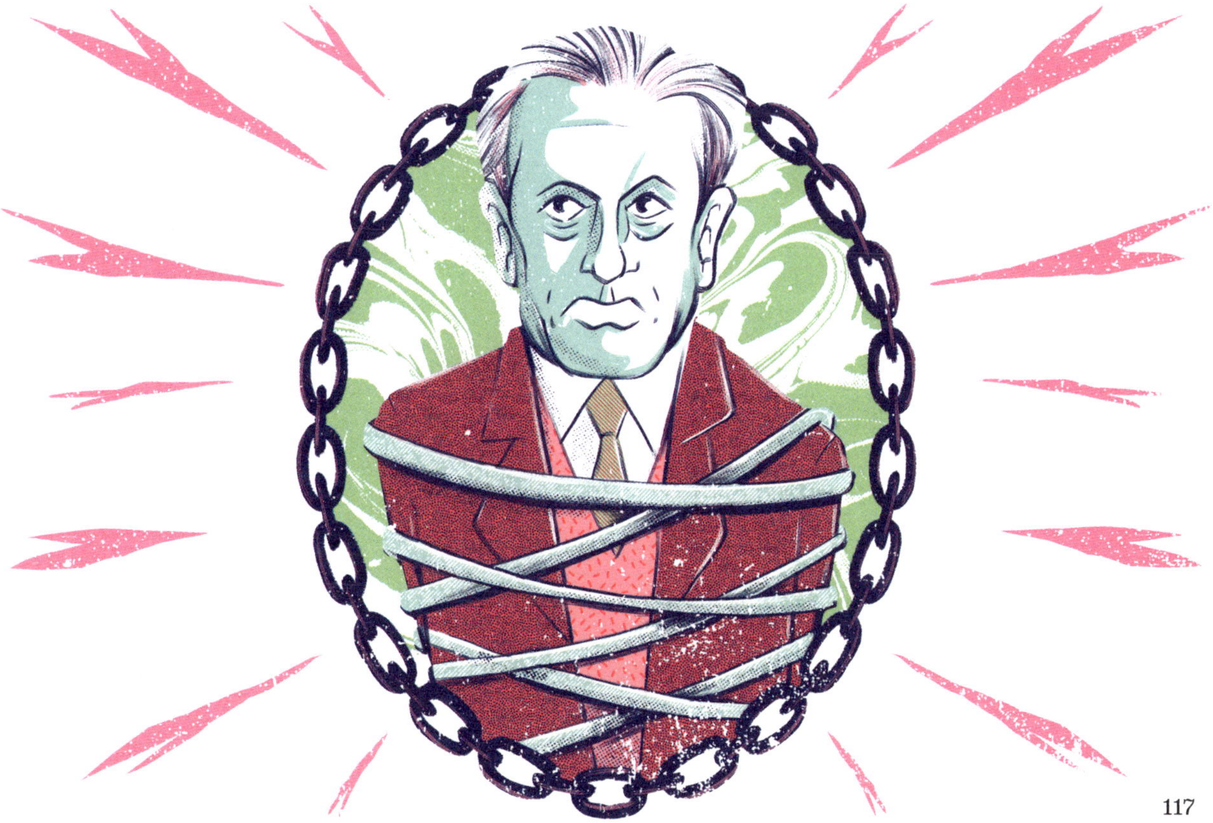

Y POR FIN LLEGA la REPÚBLICA. EN las CORTES CONSTITUYENTES HAY ALGO INSÓLITO: DOS MUJERES, DOS DIPUTADAS (CLARA CAMPOAMOR y VICTORIA KENT). LA PRIMERA PIDE el SUFRAGIO FEMENINO; a la SEGUNDA le ASUSTA. PREFIERE ESPERAR: LA MUJER HA de ESTUDIAR y DESPUÉS VOTAR. AHORA SU PAPELETA PERTENECE al CURA, al CONFESOR, y YA SABEMOS QUÉ QUIERE la IGLESIA: ¡QUE la REPÚBLICA ARDA!

LA POSICIÓN de VICTORIA es IMPOPULAR («HE SIDO DURAMENTE VILIPENDIADA desde el FEMINISMO», DEJÓ ESCRITO). PERO SU TRABAJO es COLOSAL: EL PRESIDENTE, NICETO ALCALÁ ZAMORA, la NOMBRA DIRECTORA GENERAL de PRISIONES por SU EMPEÑO en HUMANIZAR las CÁRCELES (¡ES la PRIMERA MUJER en ESE PUESTO! ¡Y QUÉ MUJER HAY que SER para OCUPAR el LUGAR!).

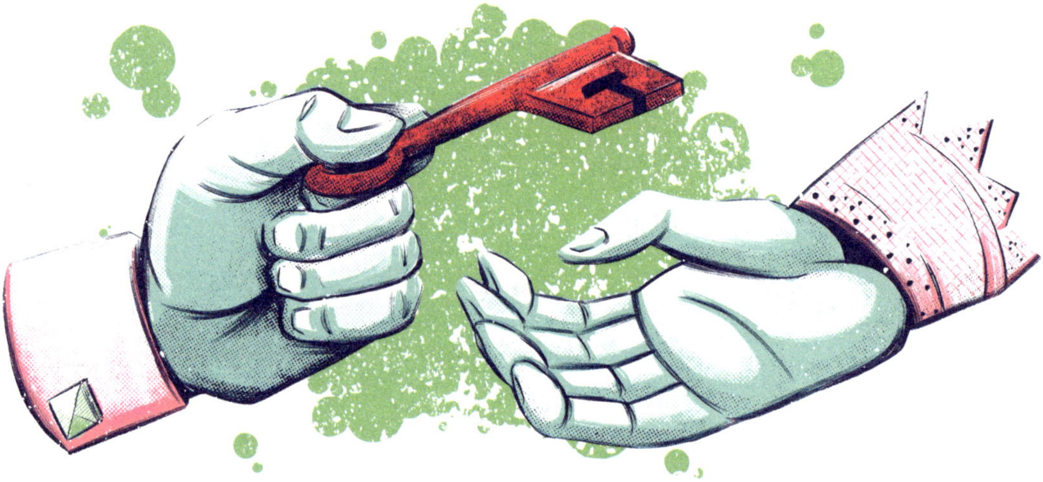

«TENEMOS que MODIFICAR el RÉGIMEN PENITENCIARIO SEGÚN las HUMANAS CORRIENTES CIENTÍFICAS y CORREGIR al DELINCUENTE CON el PROPÓSITO de DEVOLVERLE a la SOCIEDAD como UN HOMBRE ÚTIL.»

LA DIRECTORA PRETENDE UNA REVOLUCIÓN:

- MANDA CERRAR 115 CÁRCELES «INMUNDAS» y CONSTRUIR CÁRCELES DECENTES.
- ELIMINA las CELDAS de CASTIGO, las CADENAS y los GRILLETES, y CON ESE HIERRO CREAN UNA ESTATUA de CONCEPCIÓN ARENAL.
- AUMENTA la RACIÓN de COMIDA para los PRESOS.
- OFRECE a los RECLUSOS un BUZÓN de RECLAMACIONES.
- OTORGA PERMISOS de SALIDA por MOTIVOS FAMILIARES.
- CREA UN INSTITUTO de ESTUDIOS PENALES para que los EMPLEADOS APRENDAN a TRATAR a los PRESOS con DIGNIDAD.

ESCANDALIZADA por el «ESPECTÁCULO de HORROR» que HABÍA ENCONTRADO en las CÁRCELES de MUJERES, MANDÓ CONSTRUIR para ELLAS un EDIFICIO MODÉLICO: la CÁRCEL de VENTAS. NADA de RATONERAS VERGONZANTES. VICTORIA PIDIÓ ESPACIOS AMPLIOS, «BIEN ILUMINADOS por ANCHAS VENTANAS, PATIOS con FUENTES, TERRAZAS para las SALAS de PRESAS MADRES con SUS HIJOS, CELDAS INDIVIDUALES, SALÓN de ACTOS (que NO CAPILLA) y BIBLIOTECA, ADEMÁS de UNA SECCIÓN SEPARADA para PRESAS POLÍTICAS y SOCIALES».

LA DIRECTORA de PRISIONES es YA TAN FAMOSA que HASTA le CANTAN en las VERBENAS. EL FAMOSÍSIMO CHOTIS «EL PICHI» ENTONA:

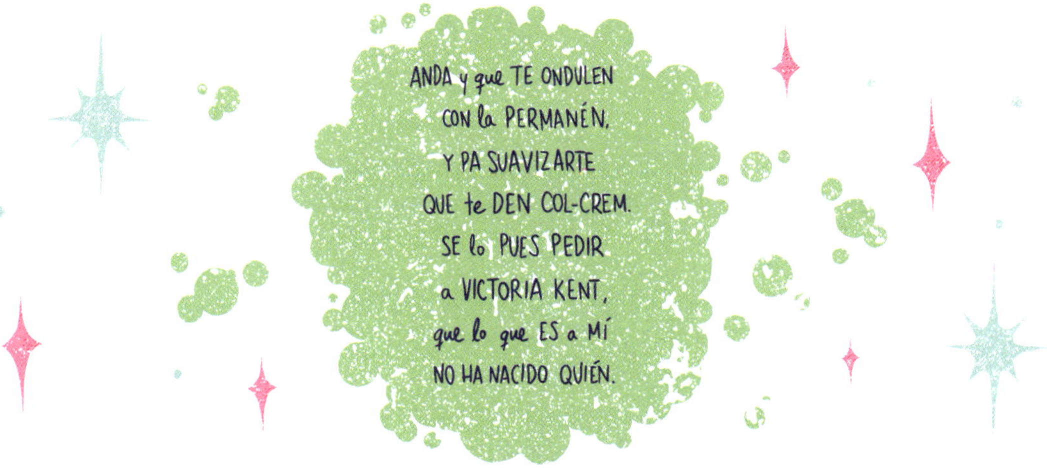

PERO NO SE PUEDE AVANZAR TRES SIGLOS en DOS DÍAS. EL NUEVO MINISTRO de JUSTICIA, ÁLVARO de ALBORNOZ, el HOMBRE al que LIBRÓ de PRISIÓN, CREE que VA MUY LEJOS. LAS MEDIDAS de VICTORIA ESCANDALIZAN a MUCHOS; NO SON POPULARES. Y ELLA, al VER que le PARARÁN los PIES, DIMITE.

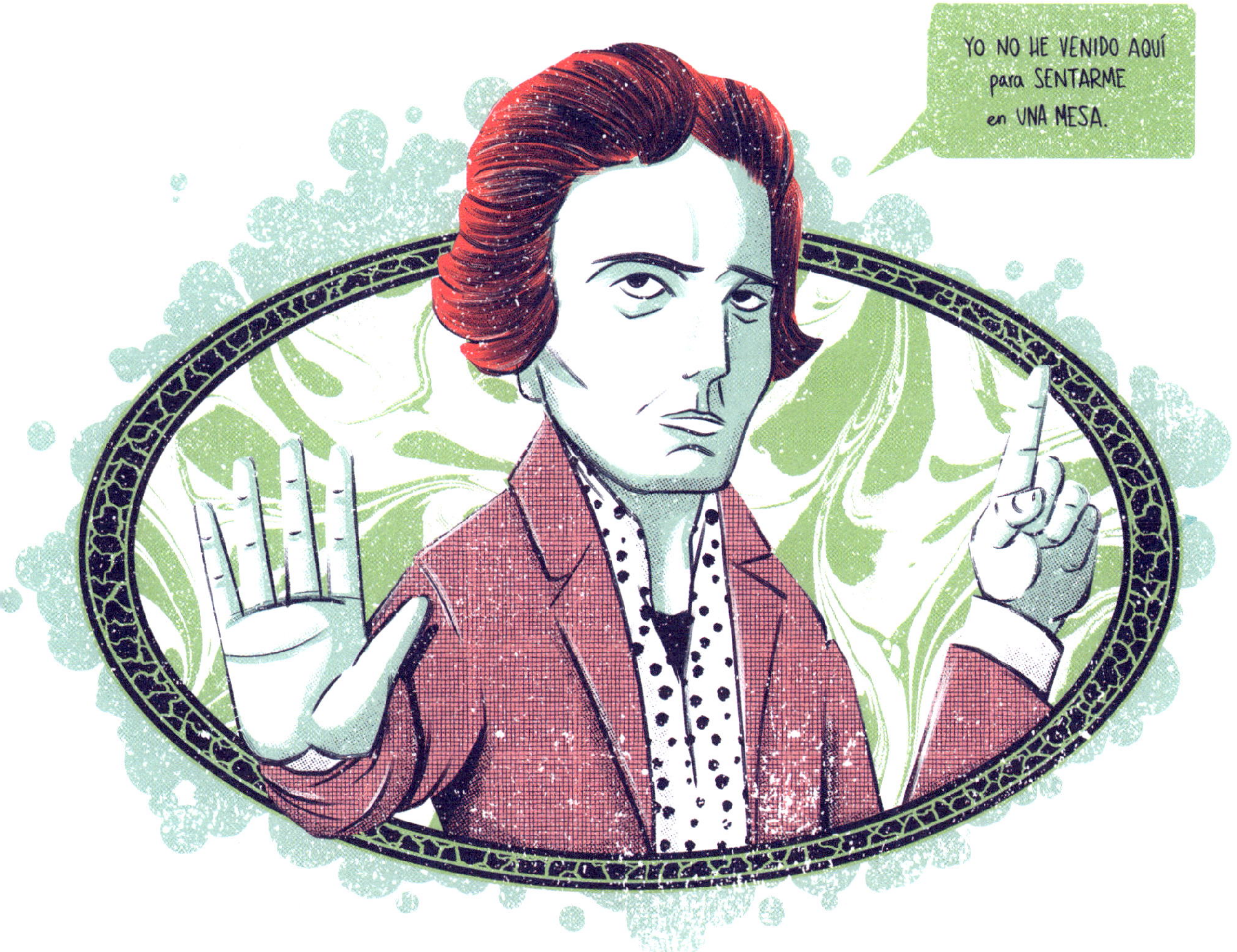

¡QUÉ AMALGAMA! ¡QUÉ MIXTURA! ¡EL PERIODISTA DEMÓCRATA Y EL NAZI PROPAGANDISTA!

MANUEL CHAVES NOGALES

EL MÁS GRANDIOSO PERIODISTA

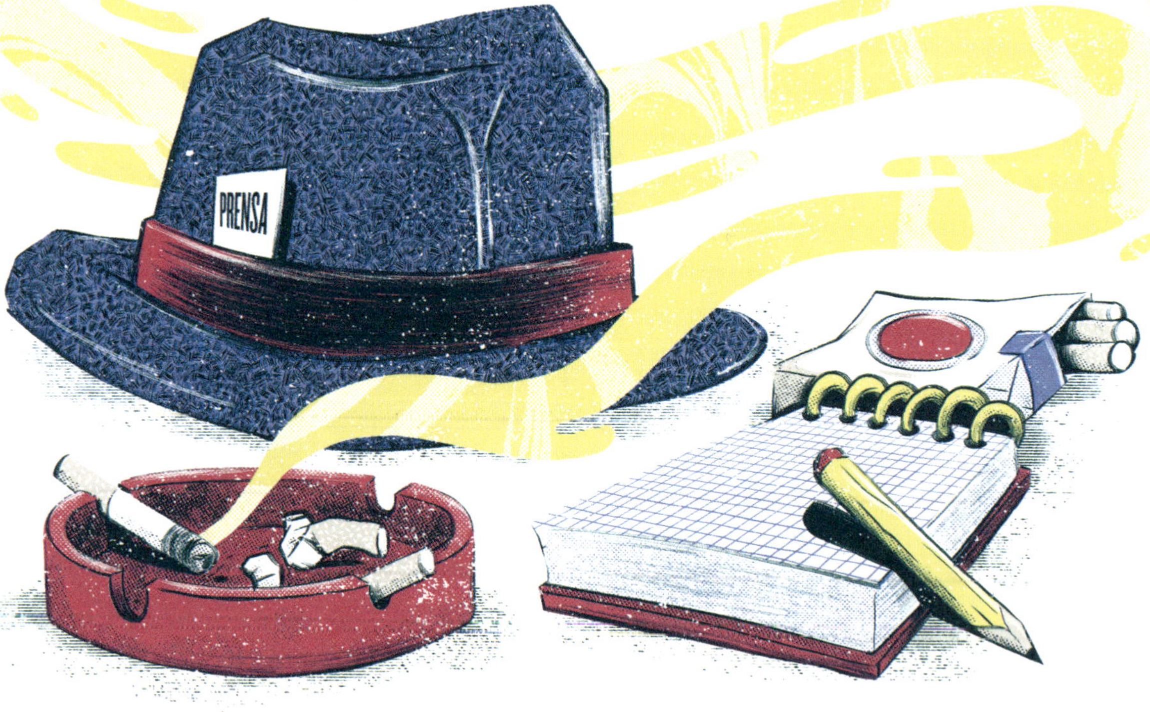

«MI TÉCNICA, la PERIODÍSTICA, NO es UNA TÉCNICA CIENTÍFICA. ANDAR y CONTAR es MI OFICIO», DECÍA el MÁS GRANDE de los GRANDES, MANUEL CHAVES NOGALES (1897-1944).

ANDAR y VOLAR, porque el PERIODISTA RECORRIÓ EUROPA en los PRIMEROS AEROPLANOS, para DESCRIBIR a SUS LECTORES CÓMO ERA la TIERRA desde el FIRMAMENTO.

«TODOS los ESFUERZOS de la HUMANIDAD HAN SIDO para ESTO. PARA que YO AHORA, SIN NINGUNA MOLESTIA NI HEROICIDAD, ME ACOMODE en UN BUTACÓN de la CONFORTABLE CABINA de UNO de ESTOS PAJARRACOS METÁLICOS y SALGA a DAR la VUELTA a EUROPA en UNAS CUANTAS JORNADAS con MI ESTUCHE de ASEO, UNAS CAMISAS, UNOS PIJAMAS y UNOS LIBROS.»

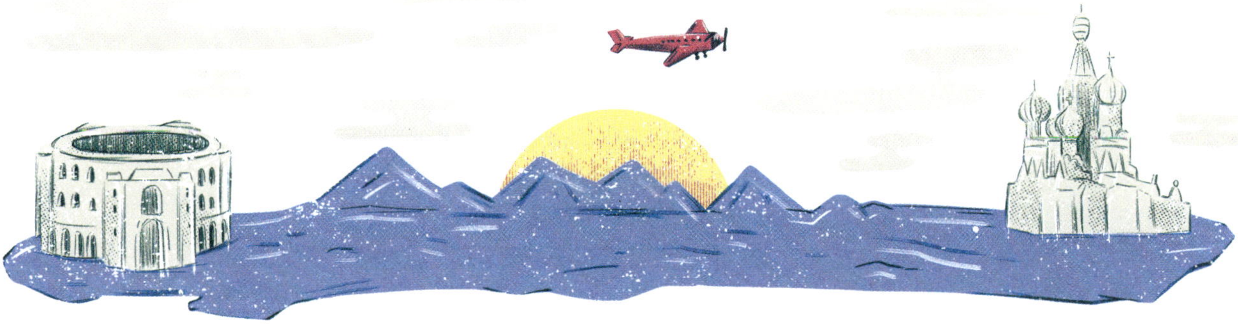

AUNQUE... AQUEL GARBEO ACABÓ SIENDO MÁS ACCIDENTADO de lo que IMAGINABA el REDACTOR JEFE del «HERALDO de MADRID» CUANDO ESCRIBIÓ ESAS PALABRAS en 1928. Del CIELO BAJÓ en PICADO UNA, DOS y hasta TRES VECES. ¡TRES ACCIDENTES de AVIÓN! ¡Y SOBREVIVIÓ a TODOS!

PERO NO es lo PEOR que VIO. El SEVILLANO VIVIÓ y CONTÓ las PEORES GUERRAS del SIGLO XX y CONOCIÓ a MUCHOS de SUS PEORES MONSTRUOS. En 1933 LLEGÓ hasta el DOCTOR GOEBBELS, el MINISTRO de PROPAGANDA ALEMÁN y LUGARTENIENTE de ADOLF HITLER.

«SER CIUDADANO de la REPÚBLICA ESPAÑOLA y PERIODISTA LIBERAL NO es HOY, para los GOBERNANTES ALEMANES, UNA INVITACIÓN a la CONFIANZA.»

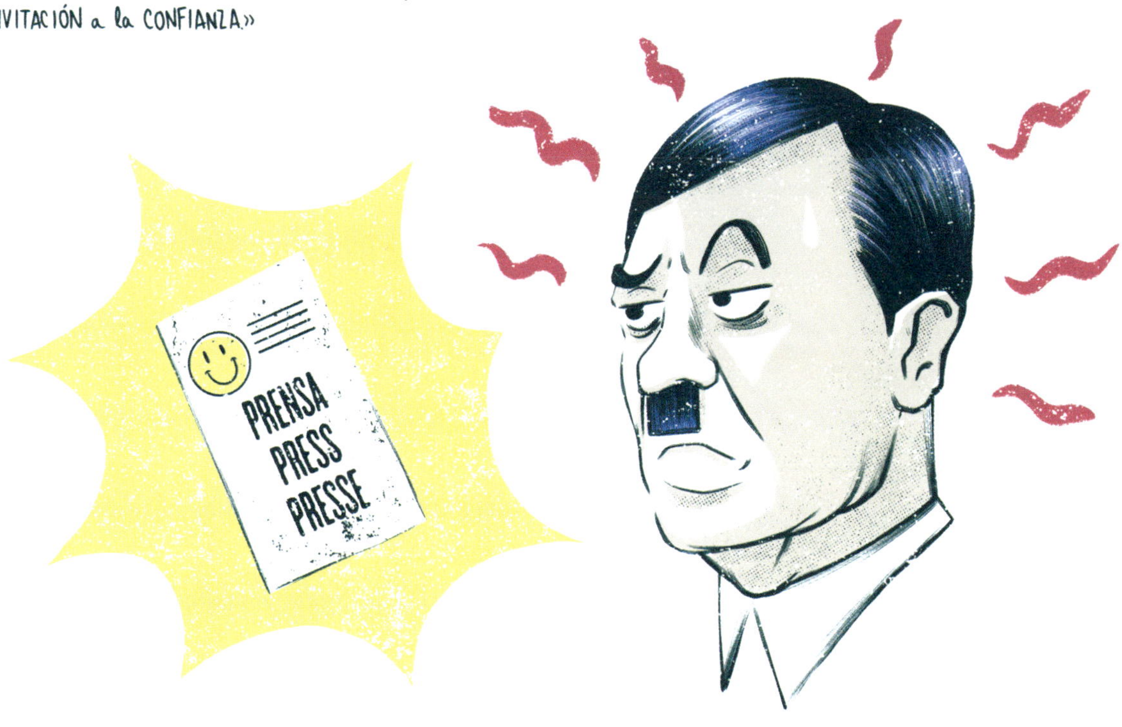

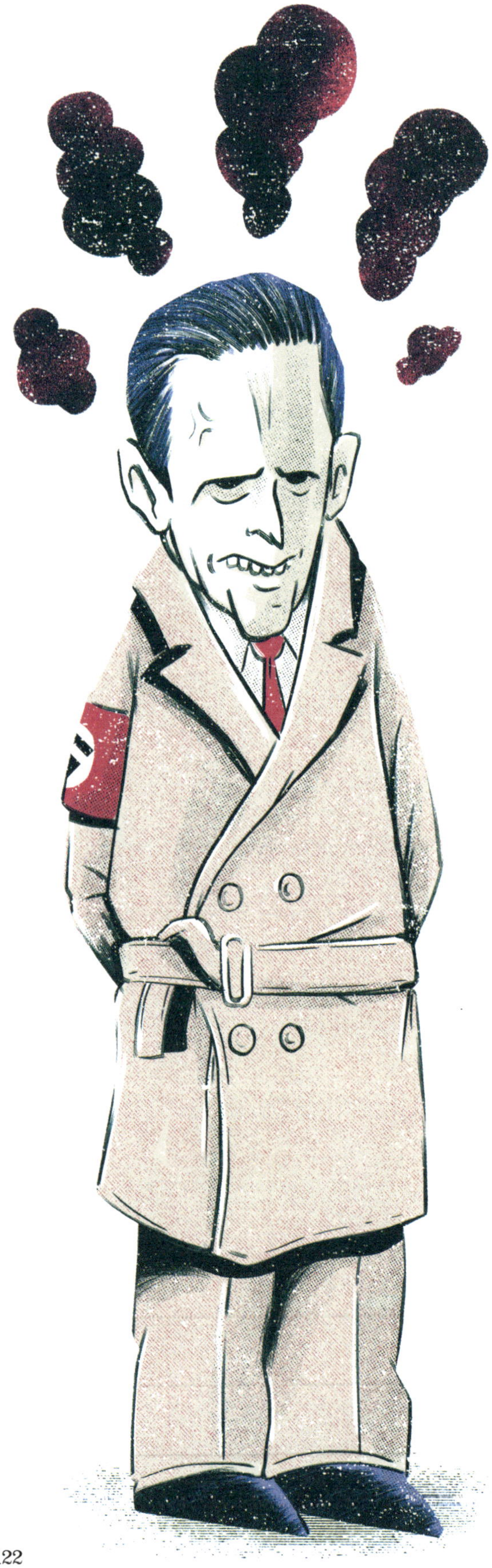

AL FIN LE CONCEDIERON LA INTERVIÚ PARA EL «AHORA», AUNQUE, ¡OJO!, CON CORTAPISAS: TRES PREGUNTAS SOLO Y NADA DE TOCAR UNA COMA A LA RESPUESTA TEXTUAL. NI COMENTARIOS NI INTERPRETACIONES. ACEPTÓ. PERO, ANTES DE LAS CUESTIONES, EXPLICÓ A LOS LECTORES QUIÉN ERA ESE DOCTOR GOEBBELS:

«ES UN TIPO RIDÍCULO, GROTESCO; CON SU GABARDINITA Y SU PATA TORCIDA, SE HA PASADO DIEZ AÑOS SIENDO EL HAZMERREÍR DE LOS PERIODISTAS LIBERALES.

TODOS LOS DÍAS, DESPUÉS DE ANDAR AJETREADO EN MENESTERES REVOLUCIONARIOS, SE ENCERRABA EN EL "ANGRIFF" (EL ÓRGANO EN LA PRENSA DEL NACIONALSOCIALISMO) Y DICTABA A UNA MECANÓGRAFA UN ARTÍCULO DE FONDO MIENTRAS IBA Y VENÍA POR LA REDACCIÓN ARRASTRANDO SU PATA COJA. ESTOS ARTÍCULOS LLEGARON A SER LO QUE TODOS LOS PERIODISTAS QUISIERAN ESCRIBIR: UN VERDADERO SUCESO EN LA CONCIENCIA DEL LECTOR.

GOEBBELS ESCRIBÍA COMO HABLABA: CLARO, SUCINTO, TERMINANTE. ES DE ESA ESTIRPE DURA DE LOS SECTARIOS, DE LOS HOMBRES VOTADOS A UN IDEAL CON EL CUAL FUSILAN A SU PADRE SI SE LES PONE POR DELANTE. EN ESPAÑA NO HAN SIDO ASÍ MÁS QUE ALGUNOS CURAS CARLISTAS, HACE YA MUCHOS AÑOS».

Y ASÍ DISCURRIÓ LA ENTREVISTA:

-¿CÓMO SE PROPONE CONTRARRESTAR LA PROPAGANDA ANTIALEMANA QUE PUEDAN LLEVAR A CABO EN EL EXTRANJERO LOS JUDÍOS EMIGRADOS DE ALEMANIA?

-SEGUIREMOS MANTENIENDO EL PRINCIPIO DE QUE LOS JUDÍOS RESIDENTES EN ALEMANIA TIENEN OBLIGACIÓN DE EVITAR QUE EL PAÍS DONDE VIVEN SEA DIFAMADO.

-¿QUÉ MÉTODOS DE PROPAGANDA PIENSA EMPLEAR EL MINISTERIO FUERA DE LAS FRONTERAS DE ALEMANIA?

-NO HAREMOS NINGUNA PROPAGANDA. NOS LIMITAREMOS a PROCURAR que la VERDAD SEA CONOCIDA en TODO el MUNDO. HEMOS PODIDO COMPROBAR que las IDEAS CORRIENTES en el EXTRANJERO SOBRE la SITUACIÓN de ALEMANIA y SOBRE las CAUSAS ESPIRITUALES de la REVOLUCIÓN ALEMANA SON en EXTREMO CONFUSAS.

-¿CREE el SEÑOR MINISTRO de PROPAGANDA que la DOCTRINA NACIONALSOCIALISTA PUEDE y DEBE ENCONTRAR UN ECO en los DEMÁS PAÍSES?

-PUEDO REPETIR las PALABRAS de MUSSOLINI CUANDO DIJO que el FASCISMO NO ERA ARTÍCULO de EXPORTACIÓN. TAMPOCO lo es el NACIONALSOCIALISMO. PERO TENGO el CONVENCIMIENTO de que la TRANSFORMACIÓN ESPIRITUAL de EUROPA, EXPRESADA en el FASCISMO, el KEMALISMO y el NACIONALSOCIALISMO, SERÁ COMPLETA en UNA o DOS DÉCADAS. CADA PUEBLO DEBERÁ ENCONTRAR en la ESENCIA de SU PROPIA PERSONALIDAD NACIONAL NUEVAS FORMAS para DICHO ESPÍRITU.

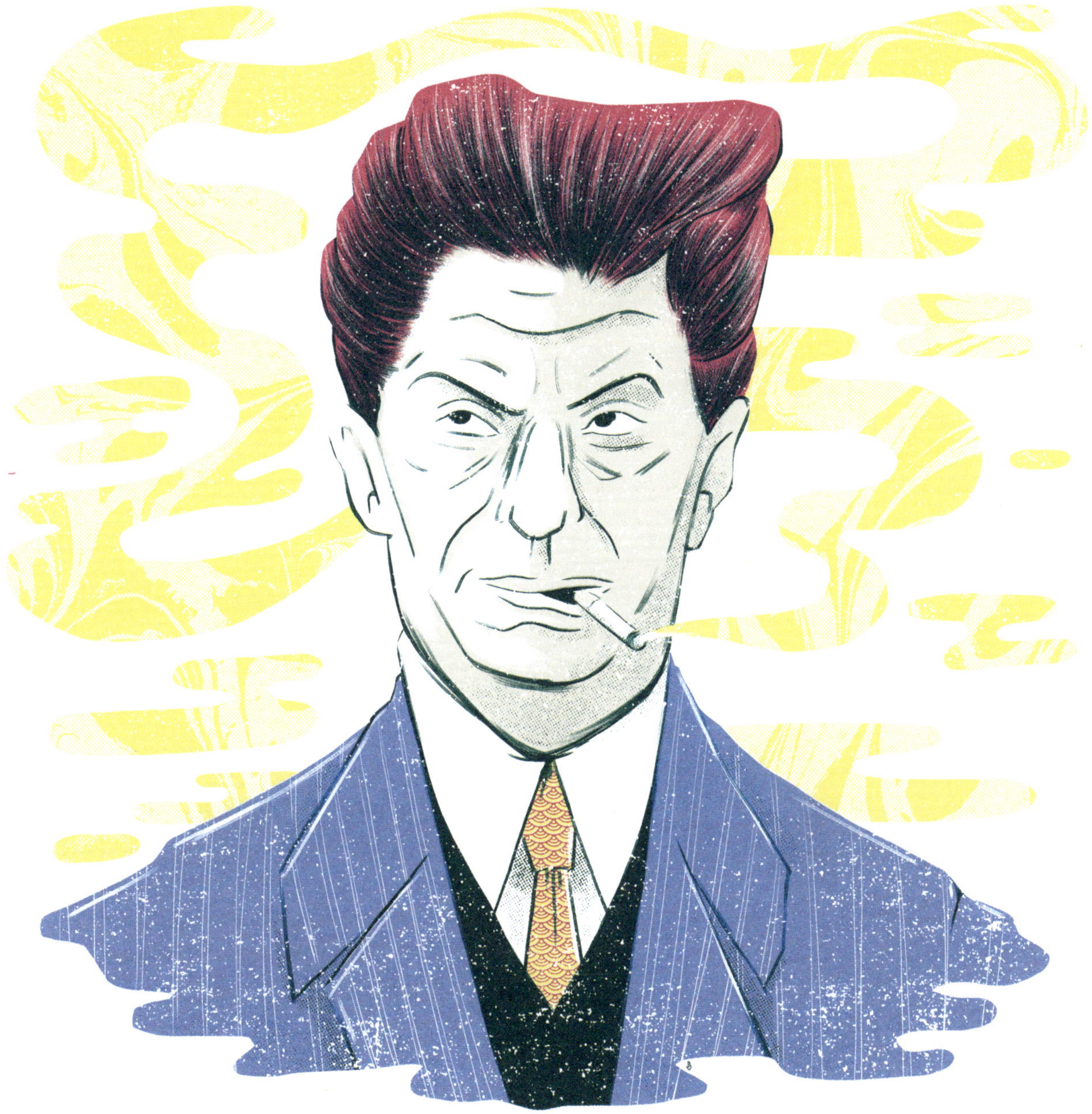

NO DEJEN QUE EL PASADO BORRE EL NOMBRE DE LA EXCELSA...

Gertrudis Gómez de Avellaneda

EL PRIMER ¡NO! DE LA ACADEMIA

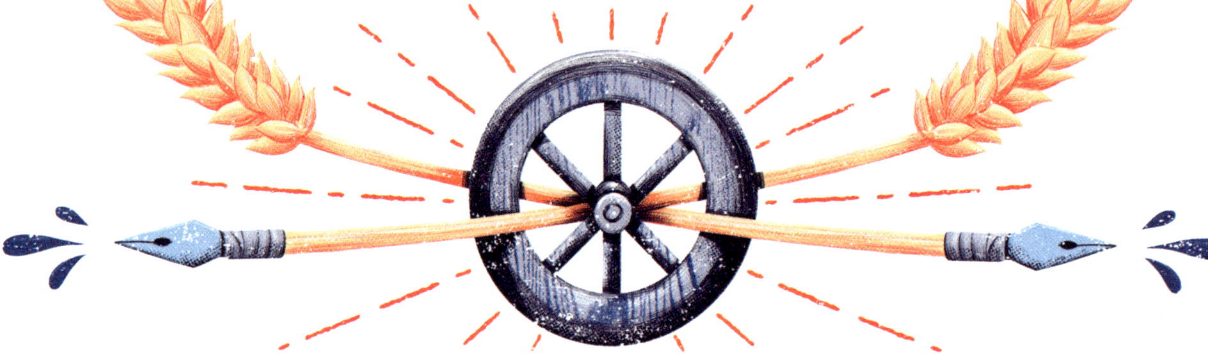

ALTA, ESBELTA y BIEN CONFORMADA. DE UNA COMPLEXIÓN que los CUBANOS LLAMAN «TRIGUEÑO LAVADO»: ESE MORENO CLARO con VISOS ROSADOS, ESA BELLEZA TAN ADMIRADA en la ISLA. DE TEZ SUAVE y TERSA, de VOZ DULCE y MELODIOSA.

GERTRUDIS GÓMEZ de AVELLANEDA (1814-1873) LEÍA con MUCHO DESPEJO, ENTONACIÓN y SENTIMIENTO, y ESTABA DOTADA de AQUELLA MEZCLA de TERNURA y VEHEMENCIA PROPIA de LOS ESPÍRITUS NOBLES, ELEVADOS y GENEROSOS.

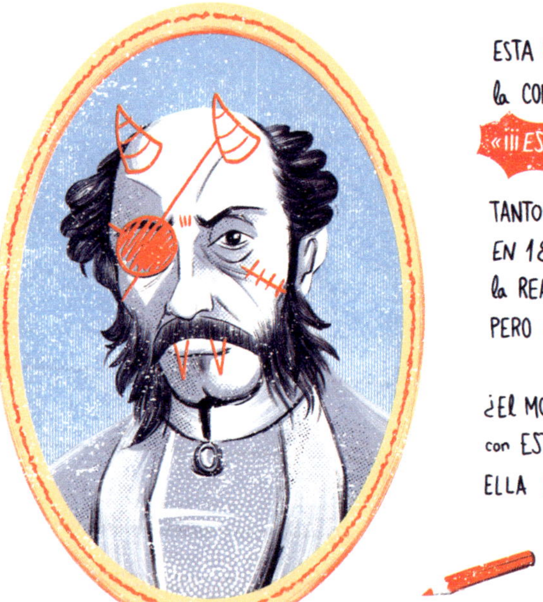

ESTA POETA CUBANA que VINO a VIVIR a ESPAÑA ERA TAN RESPETADA que EN la COMPLETÍSIMA BIOGRAFÍA que PUBLICARON SOBRE ELLA en 1929 DECÍAN: «¡¡¡ES MUCHO HOMBRE ESTA MUJER!!!».

TANTO RECONOCIMIENTO TUVO ESTA ESCRITORA, a la que LLAMABAN TULA, que EN 1853 SE PRESENTÓ a OCUPAR la VACANTE que HABÍA QUEDADO en la REAL ACADEMIA ESPAÑOLA. AMPLIOS CÍRCULOS LITERARIOS la APOYARON, PERO la INSTITUCIÓN DIJO: ¡NO!

¿EL MOTIVO? «LA INCOMPATIBILIDAD de la DIFERENCIA de SEXO con ESTE CARGO.» ¿LOS RESPONSABLES? GERTRUDIS SEÑALÓ a los que ELLA LLAMABA «LA PANDILLA de VENTURILLA VEGA».

En 1889 VOLVIÓ a SONAR el NOMBRE de UNA MUJER para ENTRAR en la ACADEMIA. El PORTAZO VOLVIÓ a SER MAYÚSCULO: ¡NO!

LA INSTITUCIÓN NEGÓ la SILLA a **EMILIA PARDO BAZÁN**, y la CONDESA, AIRADA, PUBLICÓ UNA CARTA en los PERIÓDICOS, DIRIGIDA a la FALLECIDA GERTRUDIS:

CUANDO POSTULABAS el SILLÓN, VACANTE por MUERTE de DON JUAN NICASIO, el ESPÍRITU de la DOCTA CORPORACIÓN ERA MUCHO MENOS HOSTIL que HOY a las MUJERES, y MEDIO SIGLO ANTES TU PRETENSIÓN TENDRÍA AÚN MAYORES PROBABILIDADES de ÉXITO. CON HECHOS VOY a DEMOSTRÁRTELO.

LA ÉPOCA en que ESPAÑA POSEYÓ MAYOR NÚMERO de MUJERES SABIAS FUE la EDAD de ORO de NUESTRAS LETRAS, los SIGLOS XVI y XVII, que VIERON ALZARSE en CÓMPLUTO las CÁTEDRAS de las DOCTORAS y CONSAGRARON el RENOMBRE de la LATINA.

El RESPETO y EQUIDAD para la INTELIGENCIA FEMENINA EMPIEZA a PERDERSE DURANTE NUESTRA LASTIMOSA DECADENCIA del SIGLO XVIII, y YA FEIJOO SE VE en el CASO de ESCRIBIR SU FAMOSA «DEFENSA de las MUJERES», REFUTANDO ARGUMENTOS COMO el de LOS ADMIRABLES FÍSICOS que ATRIBUÍAN a UNA INSUFICIENCIA o DESCUIDO de las FUERZAS NATURALES el NACIMIENTO de MUJERES, PUES la NATURALEZA, en NO COGIÉNDOLA DESCUIDADA, SIEMPRE PRODUCÍA VARONES.

NO OBSTANTE, y a PESAR de ESTOS MALOS VIENTOS que PARA NUESTRO SEXO CORRÍAN, la ACADEMIA ESPAÑOLA TODAVÍA NO lo RECHAZABA de SU SENO, PUESTO que a 2 de NOVIEMBRE de 1784 FUE RECIBIDA COMO ACADÉMICA HONORARIA la MARQUESA de GUADALCÁZAR, DOÑA ISIDRA de GUZMÁN.

VIENE el SIGLO XIX ECHÁNDOLAS de MUY PROGRESISTA, y, CUMPLIDA SU PRIMERA MITAD, PRETENDES TÚ el SILLÓN. NO lo ALCANZAS NI en PROPIEDAD NI HONORARIO, y ESTO INDICA que, LEJOS de ENSANCHARSE, SE HABÍA ESTRECHADO el CRITERIO de la ACADEMIA, PUESTO que NI AUN NOMINALMENTE y por FÓRMULA CONSINTIÓ ADMITIRTE.

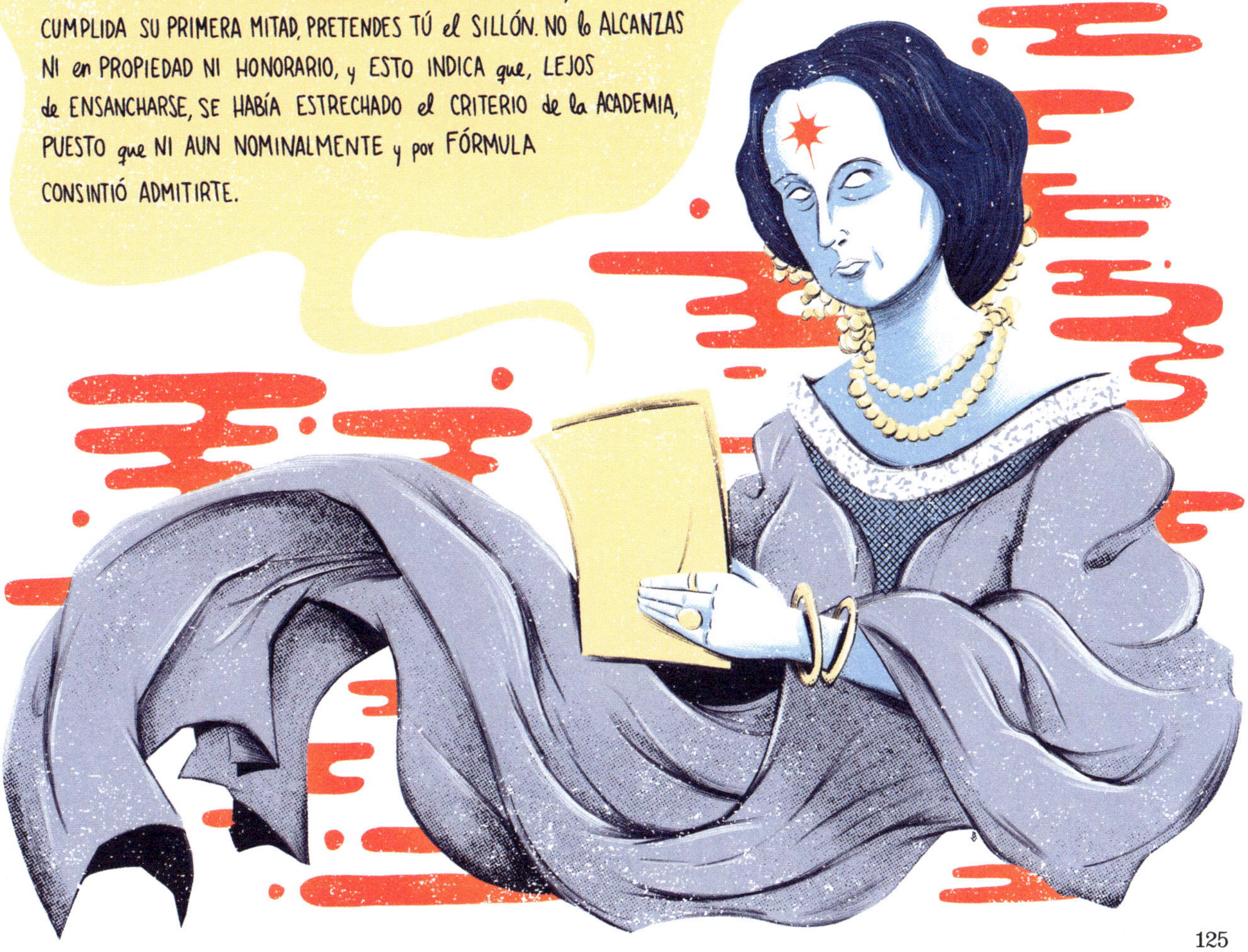

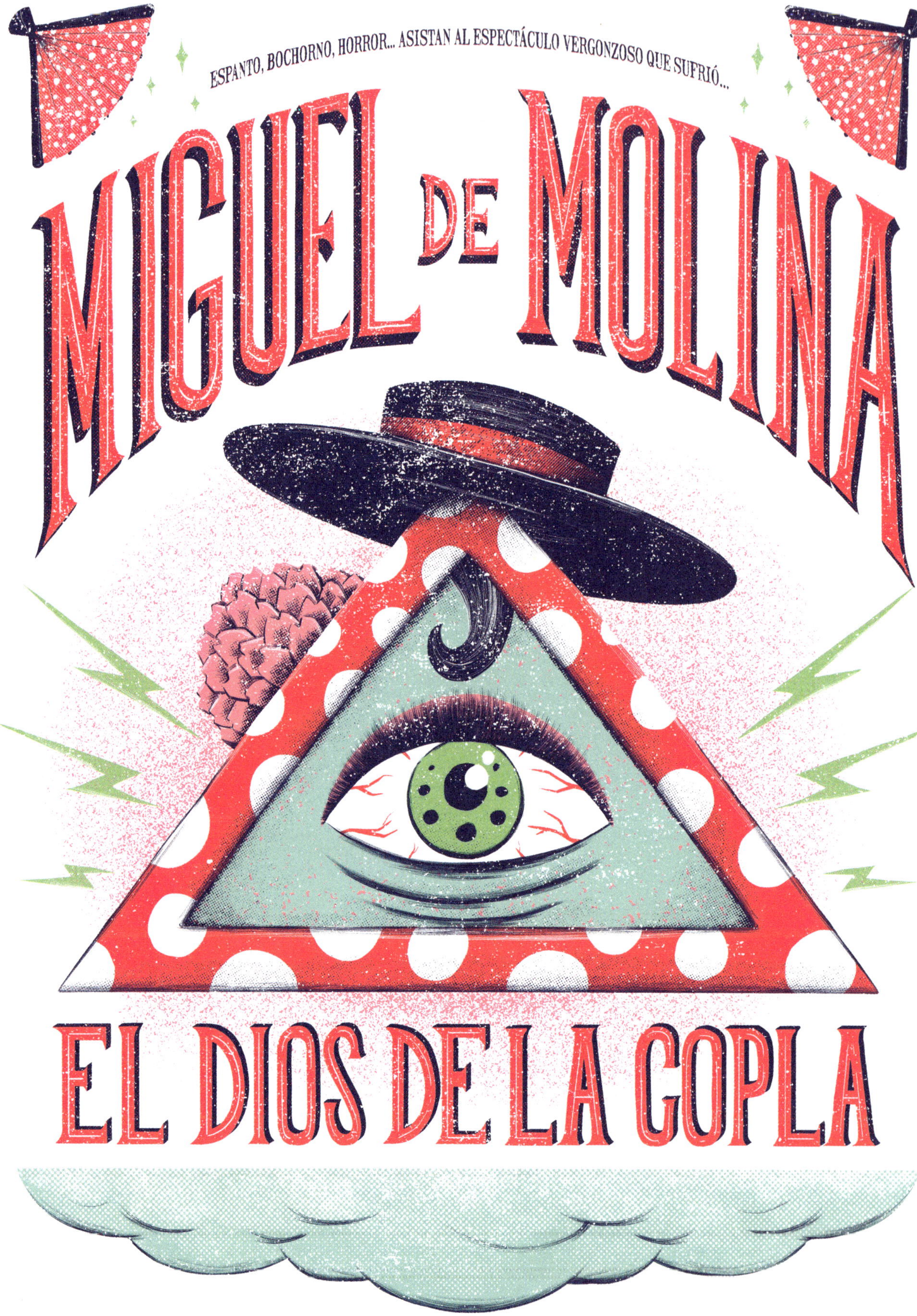
ESPANTO, BOCHORNO, HORROR... ASISTAN AL ESPECTÁCULO VERGONZOSO QUE SUFRIÓ...
MIGUEL DE MOLINA
EL DIOS DE LA COPLA

«Enamoraos» están los tablaos del mejor cantante de copla. Miguel de Molina (1908-1993) pasea su libertad y su arte sin temor al qué dirán. Al escenario sale con flores en el pelo y una blusa «cuajá» de lunares.

«¡La Miguela, la Miguela!», gritan los milicianos del público.

Y a él le gusta. No es un insulto; es así. Él sonríe y les canta:

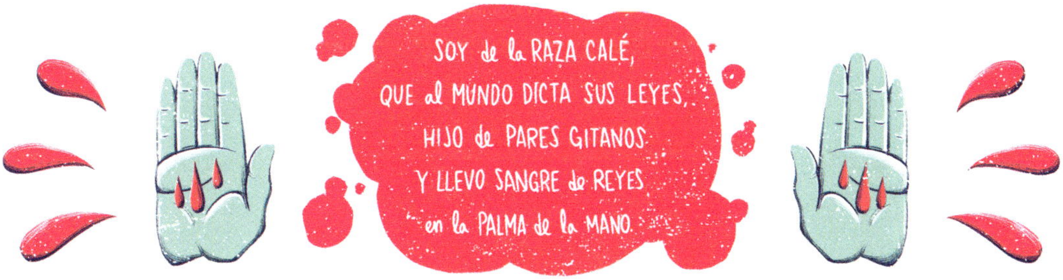

«¿Es que os llamáis así ahora?» se oye un grito y unas risotadas desde las sillas de los espectadores. Y así empiezan a llamar entonces al hombre que no ama mujer: «Ese es de raza calé».

No hay artista en los años treinta a quien paguen mejor. España entera canturrea los «Ojos verdes» de Molina, esa copla que nació en la «madrugá» de un bar barcelonés. Alrededor de una mesa departían Lorca, Miguel y Rafael de León. Este cogió una servilleta y escribió los versos que el cantante hizo copla:

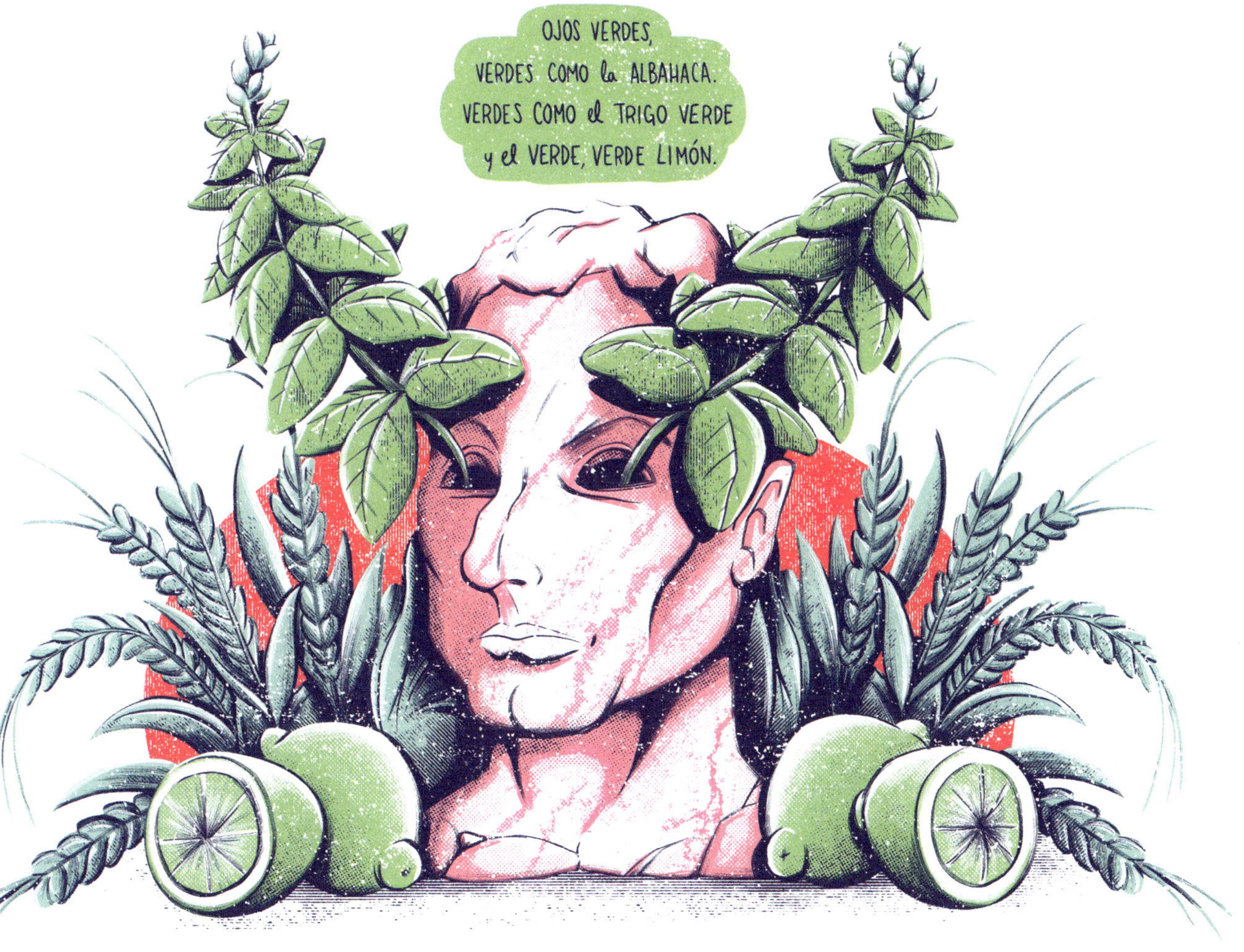

«ENAMORAOS» ESTÁN los TABLAOS hasta que en el VERANO del 36 ACABA la ALEGRÍA: LA HISTORIA del PAÍS SE PARTE en DOS. El CANTANTE SE UNE al BANDO de la LIBERTAD: CANTA ANTE las TROPAS del FRENTE REPUBLICANO, en los HOSPITALES, en los CAMPOS DONDE SUFREN los REFUGIADOS.

TRES AÑOS DESPUÉS, ESPAÑA SE PARTE AÚN MÁS: LOS VENCEDORES y los VENCIDOS. NO HAY PERDÓN para «El BUJARRÓN». AUNQUE ÉL SIGUE CANTANDO y AGUANTANDO el CHAPARRÓN: «¡MARICÓN!».

A SU SUELDO ROBAN UN CERO. LAS 5000 PESETAS que le PAGABAN en la REPÚBLICA SE QUEDAN en 500 por ACTUACIÓN.

PERO lo PEOR LLEGA el 10 de NOVIEMBRE del 39. Al TERMINAR la FUNCIÓN de la TARDE en el TEATRO PAVÓN de MADRID, MIGUEL VA al CAMERINO. ¡PLOF! TRES HOMBRES ABREN la PUERTA de SOPETÓN. VISTEN BOINA BIEN CALADA e IMPERMEABLE BLANCO: LOS TRES IGUAL.

«¡El DIRECTOR GENERAL de SEGURIDAD QUIERE VERLO en SU DESPACHO!»

A MIGUEL le HUELE RARO, PORQUE AHÍ ESTÁ el HOMBRE que CITAN: El DIRECTOR GENERAL de SEGURIDAD, CONDE de MAYALDE.

LEVANTAN a MIGUEL de la SILLA. LO SACAN con el MAQUILLAJE en el ROSTRO y la BRILLANTINA en el PELO. LO EMPUJAN al INTERIOR de UN COCHE. LO LLEVAN RECOLETOS ARRIBA, y en CIBELES, ESCAMADO, MIGUEL PREGUNTA:

–¿NO ÍBAMOS a la DIRECCIÓN GENERAL de SEGURIDAD?

–ADÓNDE VAMOS lo VAS a SABER AHORA –LE ESPETAN CON ASCO y VIOLENCIA.

LO LLEVAN HACIA los ALTOS de la CASTELLANA. A UN DESCAMPADO DONDE NADIE los VE. Le HACEN TRAGAR RICINO hasta HARTARSE, le ARRANCAN el PELO a TIRONES, le GOLPEAN TAN FUERTE con las PISTOLAS que él CREE que SON TIROS.

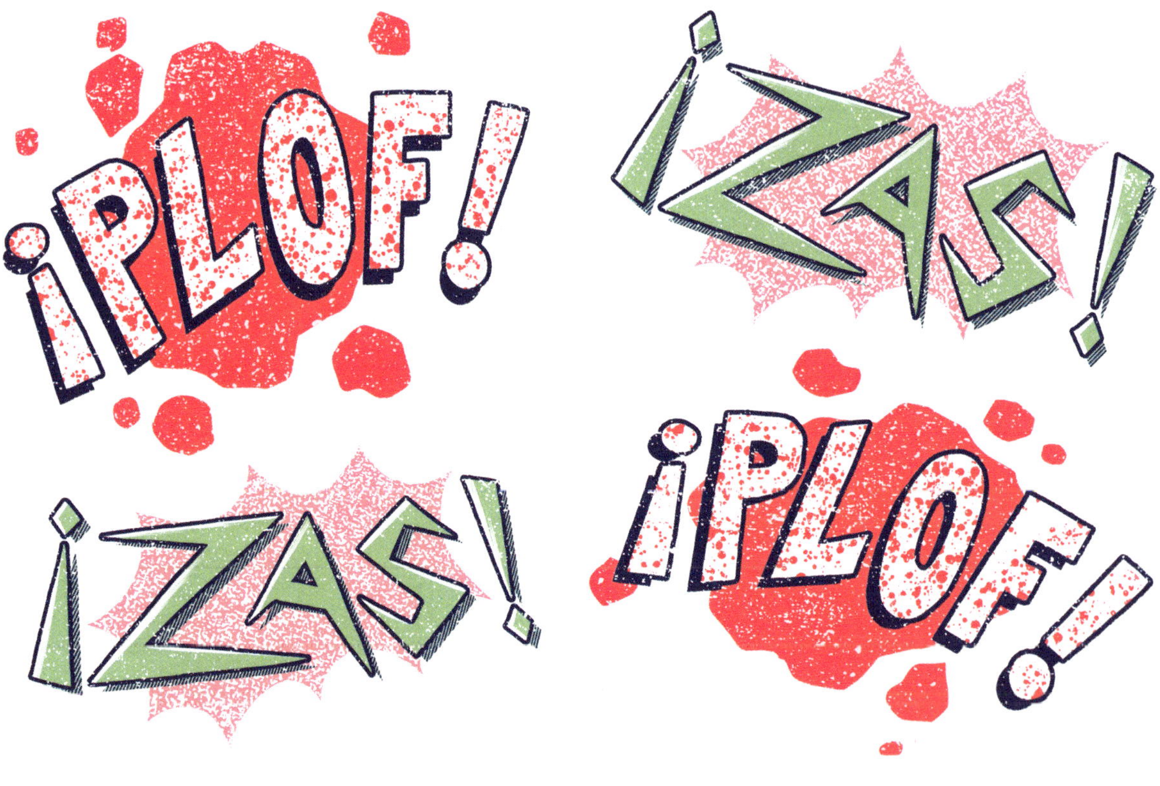

¡ESTO POR ROJO Y MARICÓN!

EL COPLISTA VA PERDIENDO DIENTES en el PALIZÓN. TIENE YA la CARA ROTA, DESENCAJADA, de TANTO MAMPORRO. MIGUEL les VOMITA ENCIMA el RICINO a ESTOS MALDITOS: EL CONDE que DESPUÉS SERÁ ALCALDE de MADRID, el JERARCA de la FALANGE **SANCHO DÁVILA** y UN JEFE de SINDICATOS.

AHORA que FLOTA ENTRE la VIDA y la MUERTE, los TORTURADORES SE APLICAN. AGARRAN los MECHONES de PELO COMO TROFEO y DEJAN al CANTAOR «TIRAO» COMO a UN PERRO.

EN 1942 MIGUEL de MOLINA HUYE a AMÉRICA. ALLÍ, LEJOS del INFIERNO, LLEVA SU COPLA y SU LIBERTAD:

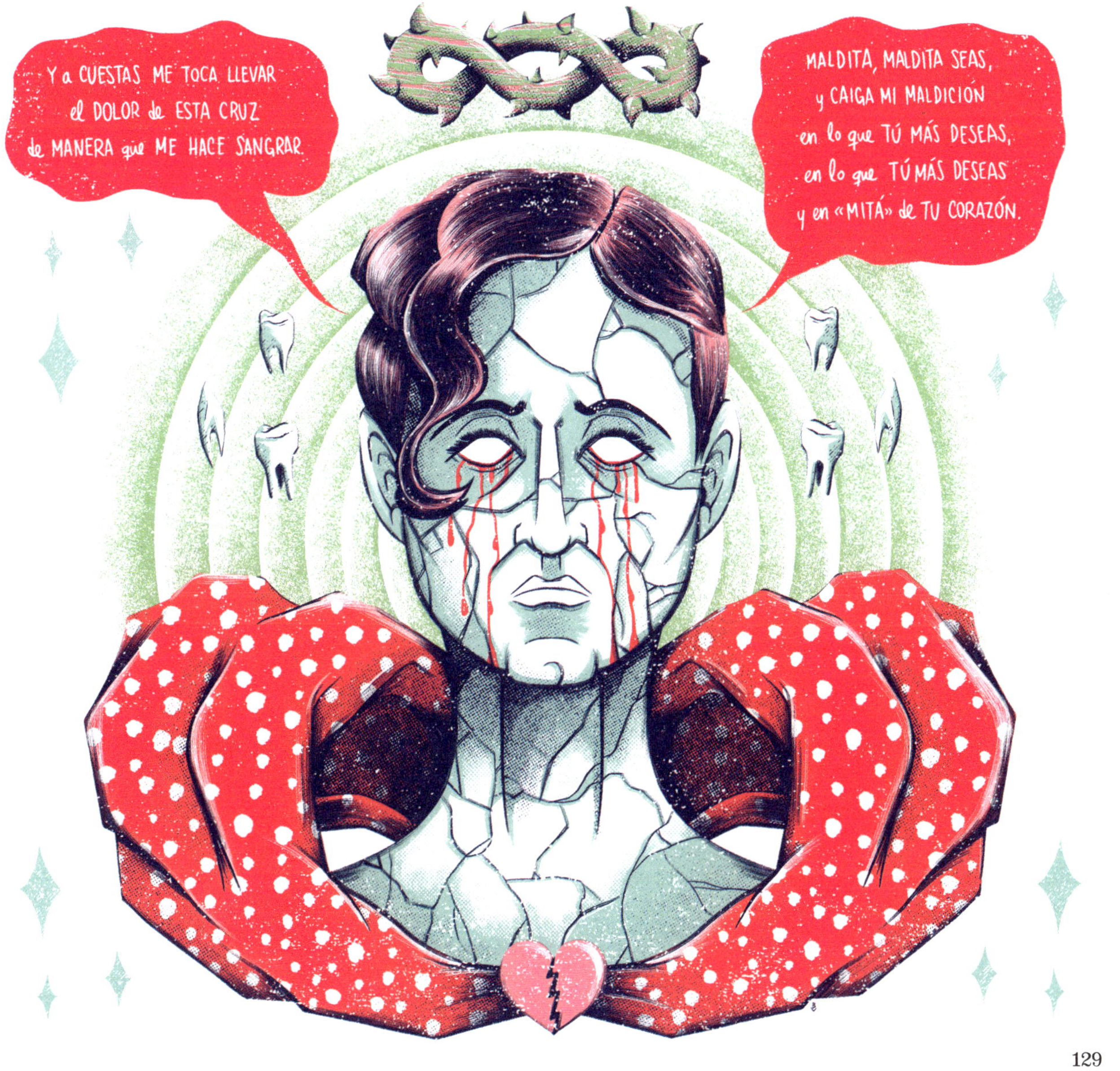

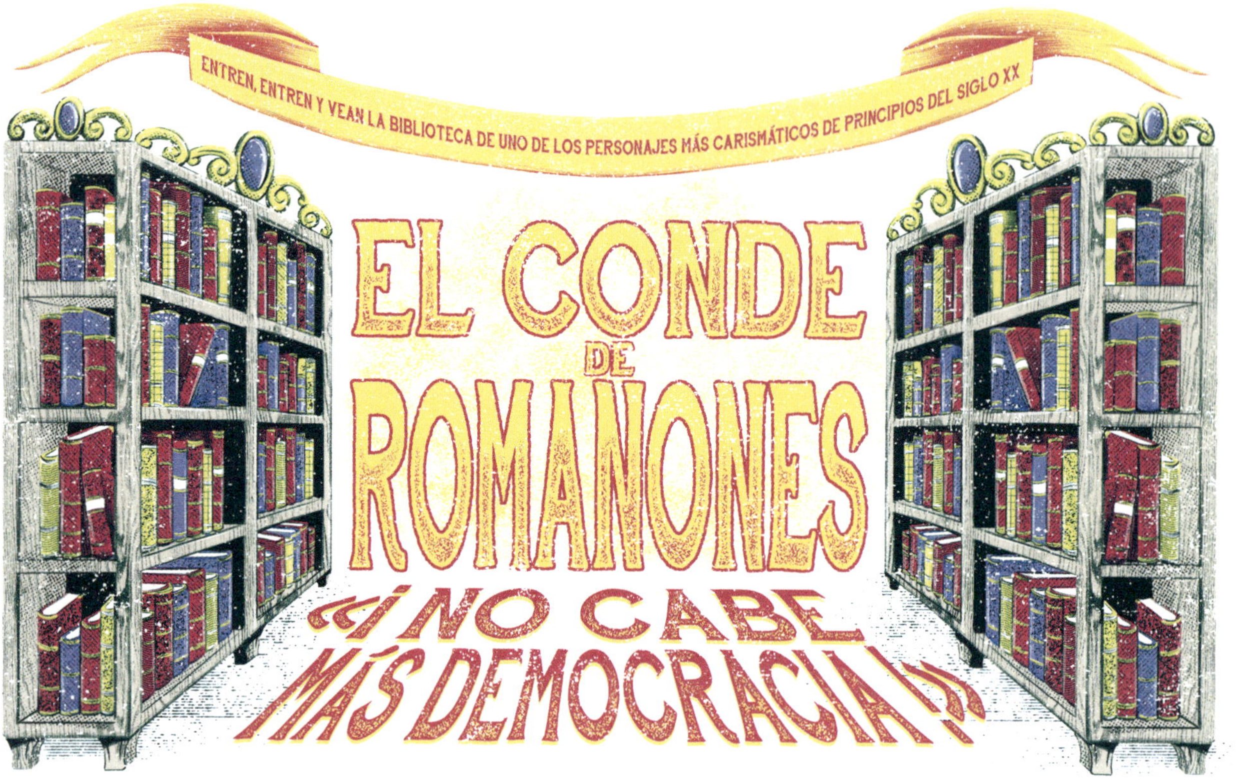

EN ESTA MAÑANA de 1919, EL CABALLERO AUDAZ VA a la CASA del CONDE de ROMANONES. El PERIODISTA ACUDE con el FIRME PROPÓSITO de ENTREVISTAR al PRESIDENTE del CONSEJO de MINISTROS. EN los TIEMPOS que CORREN, ESTAS COSAS NO SE AVISAN. LOS PLUMILLAS VISITAN a los POLÍTICOS con UNA LIBRETA BAJO el BRAZO y UN PUÑADO de PREGUNTAS LLENAS de FORMALISMOS y TRATAMIENTOS POMPOSOS.

El CONDE de ROMANONES, DON ÁLVARO FIGUEROA (1863-1950), INVITA al CABALLERO AUDAZ, JOSÉ MARÍA CARRETERO (1887-1951), a ENTRAR en SU BIBLIOTECA. EN la HABITACIÓN LUCE UN CUADRO de VELÁZQUEZ que MUESTRA a UN PRÍNCIPE ESPAÑOL y UNA FOTOGRAFÍA del CONDE MONTADO en UN AUTO PANHARD: ESTÁ en UNA AVENIDA de PARÍS, y al VOLANTE VA ALFONSO XIII.

EN el CENTRO de la SALA SE ALZA UNA ESTATUILLA del «HÉROE del CASCORRO», y FRENTE al CONDE HAY UNA VITRINA LLENA de JOYAS, BASTONES, PETACAS, PITILLERAS y MIL OBJETOS de ARTE. TODOS, con DEDICATORIAS GRABADAS en el LOMO.

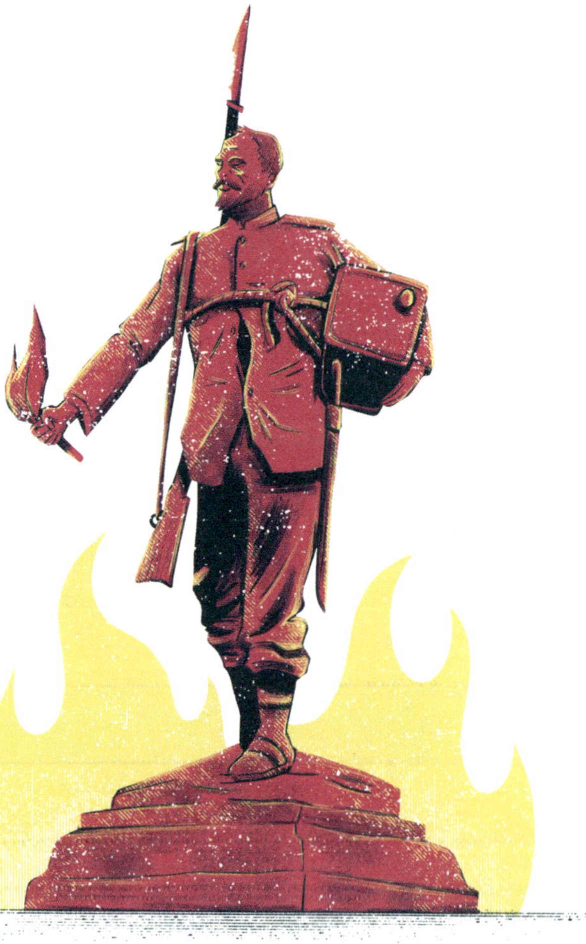

El CONDE VISTE TRAJE de LEVITA. MIENTRAS SOMETEN a INDULGENCIA el OBJETO de la ENTREVISTA, ÉL SE ACARICIA CON la MANO DERECHA las GUÍAS del BIGOTE, RUBIAS y MAL ENGALLADAS. TERMINAN de HABLAR y PONE ESA SONRISA AMABLEMENTE ANCHA, PICARESCA e INSINUANTE. ES UNA EXPRESIÓN HABITUAL de ESTE ILUSTRE POLÍTICO. DESPUÉS, EXCLAMA:

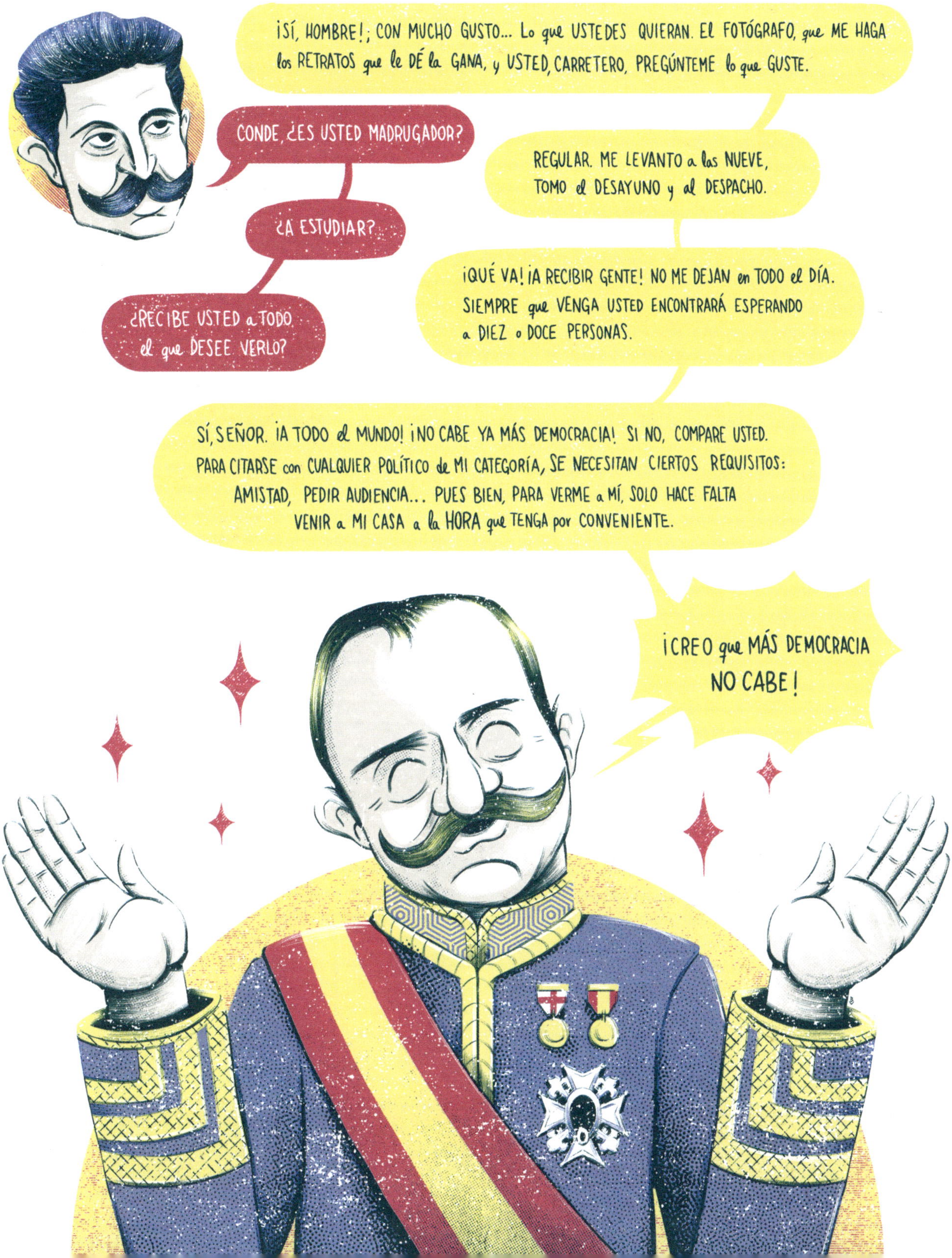

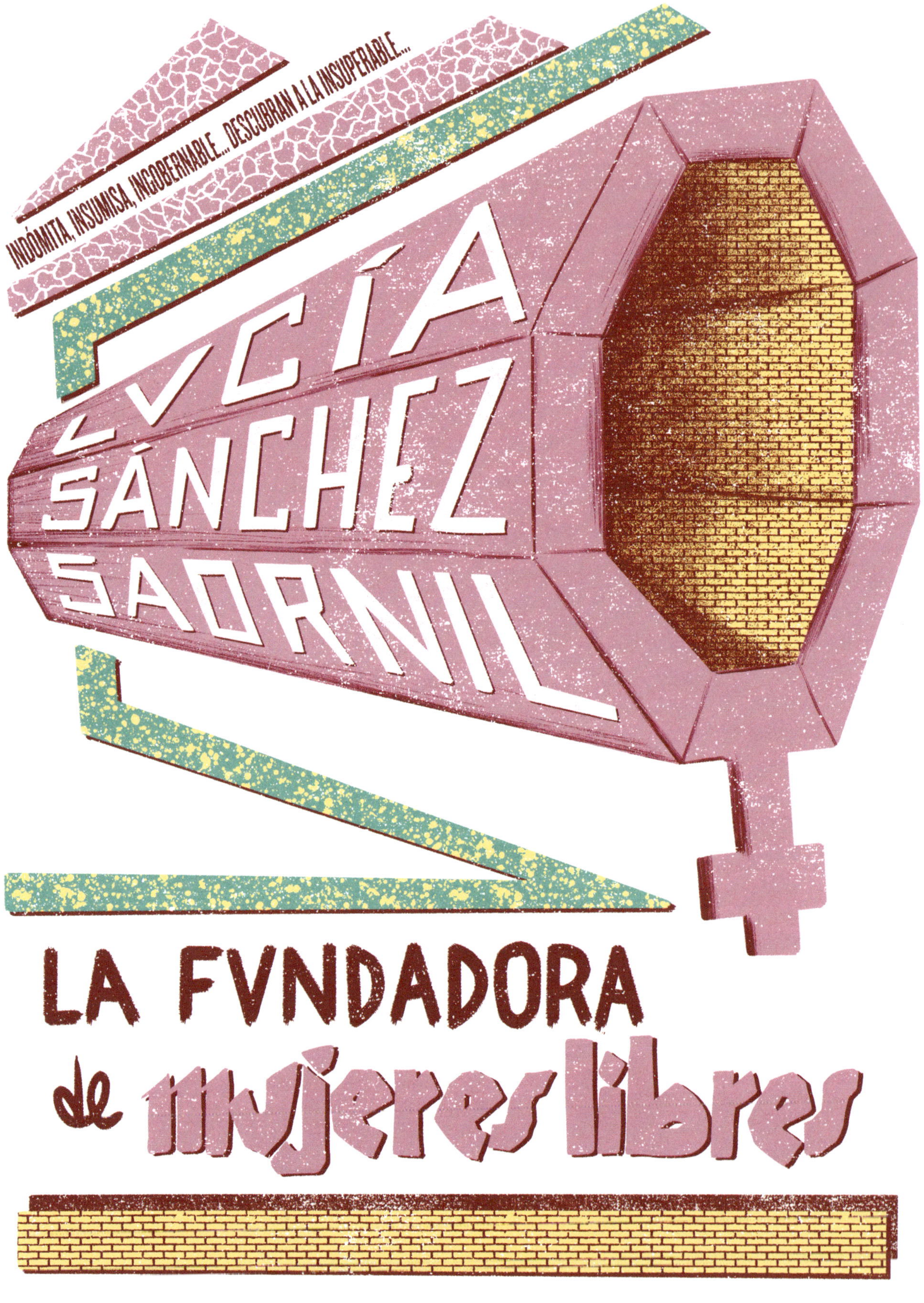
INDÓMITA, INSUMISA, INGOBERNABLE... DESCUBRAN A LA INSUPERABLE...
LUCÍA
SÁNCHEZ
SAORNIL
LA FUNDADORA
de mujeres libres

MENUDA, INQUIETA. TIENE los OJOS NEGROS; COMO SU PELO, COMO SU PIEL. **LUCÍA SÁNCHEZ SAORNIL** (1895-1970) TRABAJA COMO OPERADORA en TELEFÓNICA. BIEN le HA COSTADO LLEGAR HASTA AQUÍ: NACIÓ POBRE y PRONTO QUEDÓ HUÉRFANA.

PINTA y ESCRIBE POESÍA ULTRAÍSTA. MILITA en el ANARQUISMO y ACUSA los ABUSOS que VE en SU EMPRESA o en la CALLE. ESTO le CUESTA que la TRASLADEN por UN TIEMPO de MADRID a VALENCIA.

NI por ESAS CALLA. ESCRIBE en REVISTAS OBRERAS y ANARQUISTAS. Y en UN ARTÍCULO de 1935 en «SOLIDARIDAD OBRERA», DEJA CLARO lo que LLEVA AÑOS DICIENDO en TEXTOS y CONFERENCIAS:

«POR la MADRE QUERÉIS EXCLUIR a la MUJER CUANDO PODÉIS TENER MUJER y MADRE. (...) PARA UN ANARQUISTA, ANTES que el TRABAJADOR ESTÁ el HOMBRE, ANTES que la MADRE DEBE ESTAR la MUJER».

HASTA en el MOVIMIENTO LIBERTARIO el MACHISMO es ATROZ. Y es TAN HONDO que NI ELLOS lo VEN. UN DÍA, LUCÍA PREGUNTA a UN COMPAÑERO en FAVOR de la IGUALDAD por qué NO HABÍA IDO SU COMPAÑERA a la CONFERENCIA:

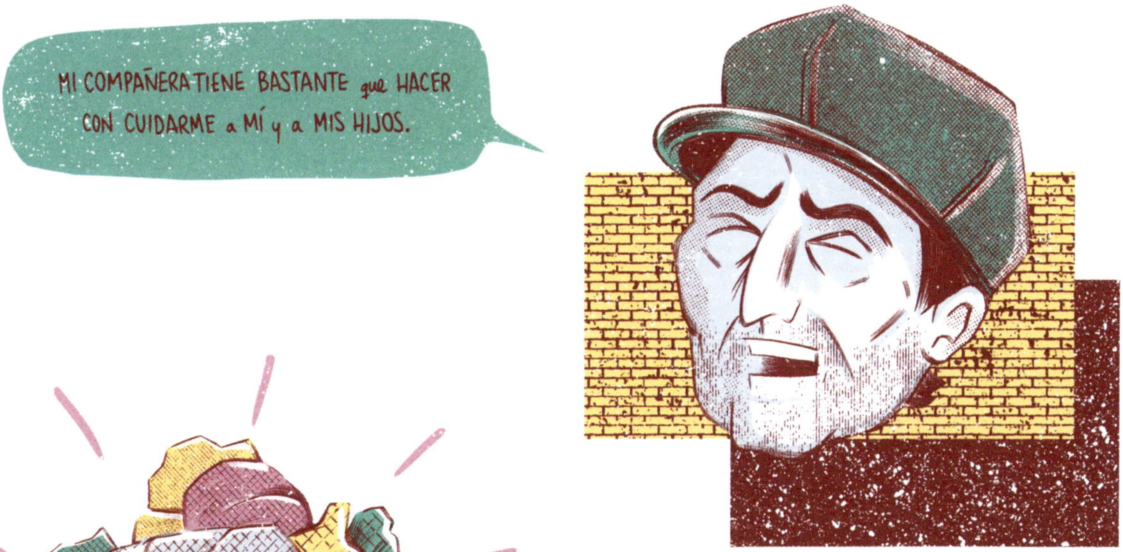

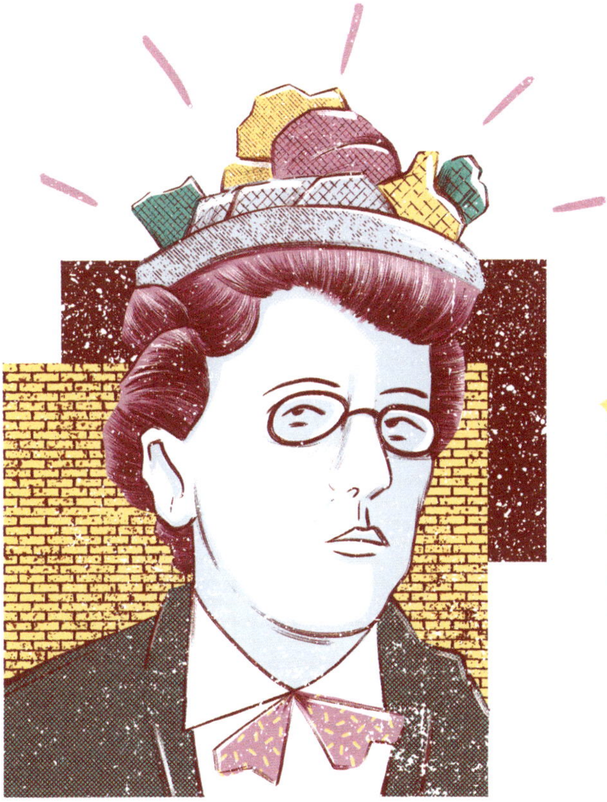

«WHAT?!» ESTÁ CLARO: TENDRÁN que TIRAR ELLAS SIN ELLOS para lo que QUIERAN HACER. Y ASÍ, JUNTO CON **MERCEDES COMAPOSADA** y **AMPARO POCH y GASCÓN**, CREAN UNA ORGANIZACIÓN y UNA REVISTA SIN HOMBRES: «MUJERES LIBRES». EL PRIMER NÚMERO APARECE CON UNA CARTA de SU BUENA AMIGA, la ANARQUISTA UNIVERSAL **EMMA GOLDMAN**, y NI UNA FIRMA MASCULINA.

ES MAYO de 1936 y el HORROR AGUARDA en la ESQUINA. ¡BUM! ESTALLA la GUERRA y LUCÍA, AUDAZ y DILIGENTE, ORGANIZA BRIGADAS FEMENINAS de TRABAJO para SUSTITUIR a los HOMBRES que VAN al FRENTE. En el PERIÓDICO de la CNT, el DRAMATURGO RODOLFO GONZÁLEZ PACHECO la DESCRIBE ASÍ:

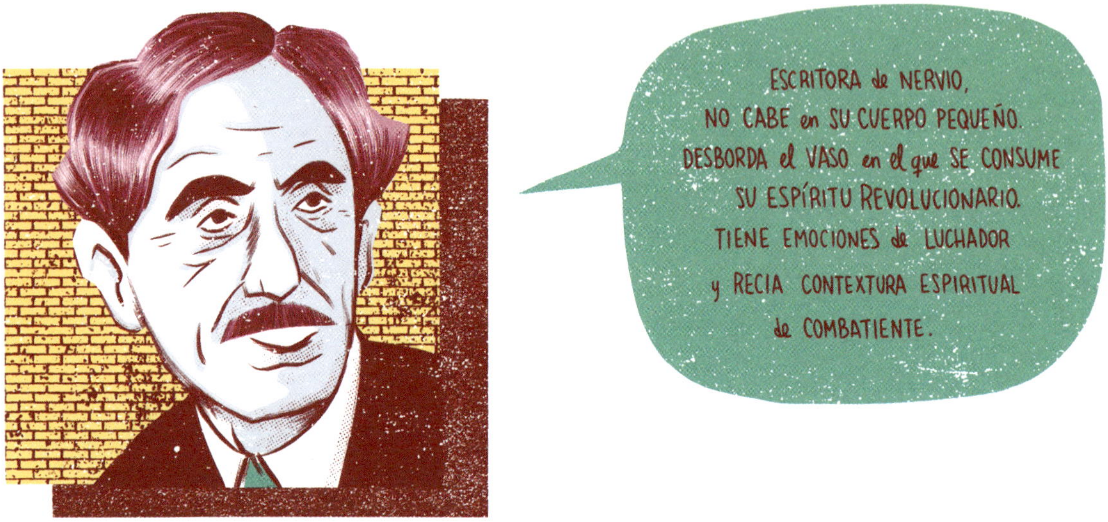

POR MUCHO que le DICEN que ABANDONE MADRID, que ACABARÁ COSIDA a METRALLA, ella SE NIEGA. HAY que RESISTIR. Y lo PIDE en UN POEMA que RECITA por la RADIO:

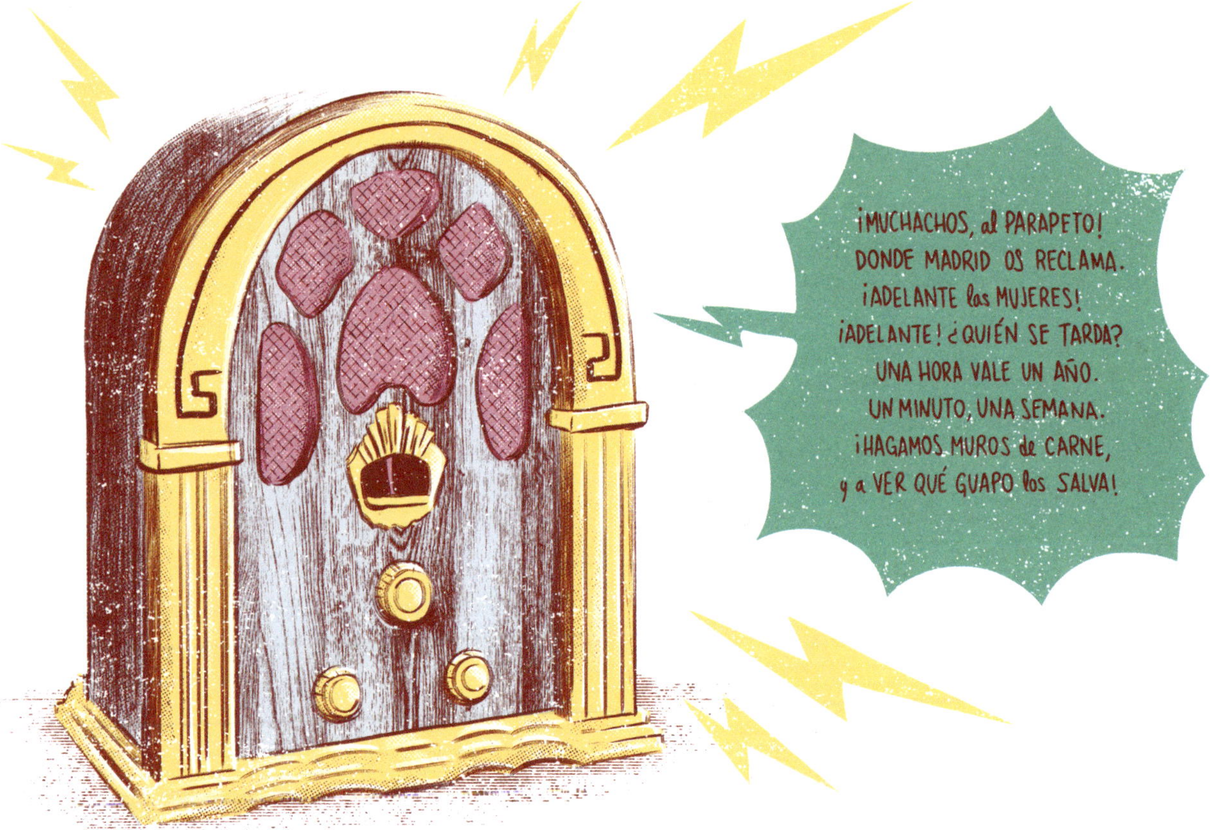

EL ENEMIGO SE IMPONE: A VALENCIA OTRA VEZ. ALLÍ TRABAJA en el SEMANARIO «UMBRAL», pero a UNA JOVEN de la REDACCIÓN NO le ENTRA por el OJO. AMÉRICA BARROSO (MERY) DICE a UNA COMPAÑERA:

-HAY UNA CHIQUITEJA que SE METE en TODO y UN DÍA ME VOY a TENER que DESCARAR CON ELLA, porque, CUANDO SE MARCHA el DIRECTOR, ENTRA en SU DESPACHO, TRAE los PAPELES de la IMPRENTA y EMPIEZA: «ESTO QUIERO, ESTO NO QUIERO...».

-PERO ¿SABES QUIÉN es ESA CHIQUITEJA? ¡LA REDACTORA JEFE!

ESTE PRIMER RECELO SE DISIPA PRONTO, a la VEZ que SE VE el TRIUNFO del EJÉRCITO de FRANCO. Y LUCÍA, ENTRE la RESISTENCIA y la RESIGNACIÓN, en MARZO de 1939 ESCRIBE en «INDOMABLES»:

«POR MUY DERROTADOS que ESTEMOS, NO NOS CONSIDERAMOS VENCIDOS; y desde NUESTRA MISERIA FÍSICA, AÚN PODEMOS MIRAR con DESPRECIO la MISERIA MORAL de UN ULTRADERECHISTA que NI SIQUIERA CONOCE la ELEGANCIA del GESTO y PRETENDE HACER de NUESTRA DERROTA el MULADAR PROPICIO DONDE REGODEAR SUS PEZUÑAS y SU JETA de PUERCO.

NO NOS IMPORTA. EL ANTIFASCISMO ESPAÑOL SIENTE la DIGNIDAD de SU MISIÓN: SABE que ha REALIZADO UNA OBRA; que ha ESCRITO en la HISTORIA, para EJEMPLO del MUNDO, UNA PÁGINA CUYA PROFUNDA y LUMINOSA HUELLA NO PUEDEN BORRAR los INMUNDOS ESCUPITAJOS de la CHUSMA FASCISTA».

LUCÍA PIERDE SU PUESTO en TELEFÓNICA por «DEPURACIÓN». HUYE a FRANCIA, ESCONDIDA, PORQUE SU VIDA NO VALE UNA PERRA. MERY la BUSCA, la AMPARA y la AYUDA a VOLVER (ESCONDIDA OTRA VEZ). DESDE ENTONCES VIVIRÁN JUNTAS. ESCONDIENDO SU VOZ y SU PASADO.

¿SU ASPIRACIÓN? APLASTADA en UN CAJÓN. ¿EL SUEÑO LIBERTARIO? UN RECUERDO ESTRAFALARIO.

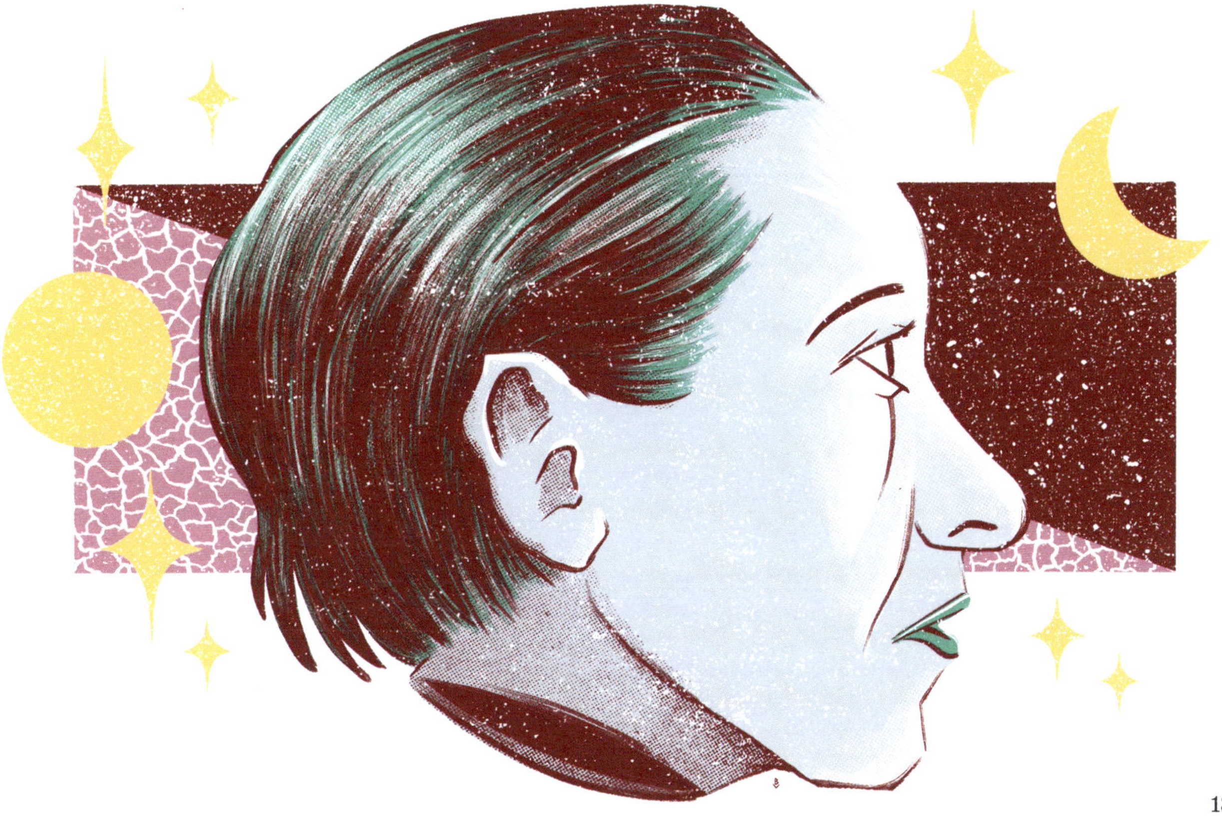

NO LEVANTEN EL COLCHÓN NI REBUSQUEN EN LA ALFORJA... Y GUÁRDENSE BIEN DE...

BALDOMERA LARRA

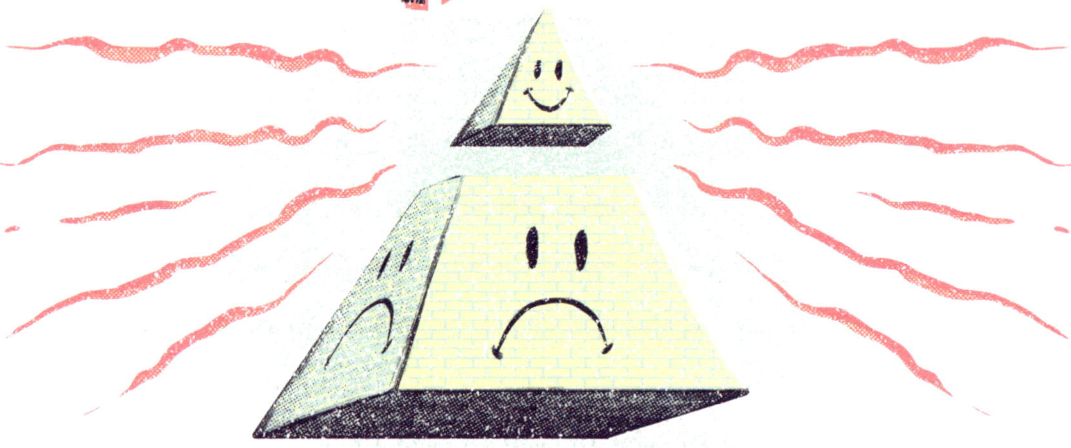

LA INVENTORA DE LA ESTAFA PIRAMIDAL

De PADRE de PLUMA EXCELSA NACIÓ BALDOMERA LARRA WETORET (1833-1915). AUNQUE PRONTO QUEDÓ HUÉRFANA: TENÍA CUATRO AÑOS, MINÚSCULOS E INOCENTES, CUANDO el GRAN MARIANO JOSÉ de LARRA SE MATÓ por AMOR.

El HERMANO MAYOR, LUIS MARIANO, le ECHÓ ARTE a la VIDA. DRAMATURGO y ESCRITOR, DEJÓ un BUEN LEGADO: ZARZUELAS POPULARES y UNA TONADA que AÚN SE CANTA, «El BARBERILLO de LAVAPIÉS».

ADELA y BALDOMERA HICIERON CARRERA del QUERER. LA MAYOR TUVO TRATOS de ACOBA con el REY AMADEO de SABOYA; la MENOR HIZO BODA con CARLOS de MONTEMAYOR, el MÉDICO de la CASA REAL.

PERO CUANDO el MUJERIEGO de AMADEO ABDICÓ, DICIENDO que los ESPAÑOLES ERAN «INGOBERNABLES», el DOCTOR HUYÓ en UN BARCO hasta la ISLA de CUBA. BALDOMERA SE QUEDÓ en MADRID con DOS HIJOS y los BOLSILLOS ROTOS.

La PATILLAS, COMO la LLAMABAN por SUS DOS TIRABUZONES, RECURRIÓ a los PRESTAMISTAS y DICEN que FUE ENTONCES, VIENDO SUS TEJEMANEJES, CUANDO FRAGUÓ el PLAN. EMPEZÓ a PEDIR DINERO, a PRESTARLO y PEDIR MÁS, a PRESTAR MÁS y SEGUIR PIDIENDO hasta que ELLA SE CONVIRTIÓ en la FINANCIERA.

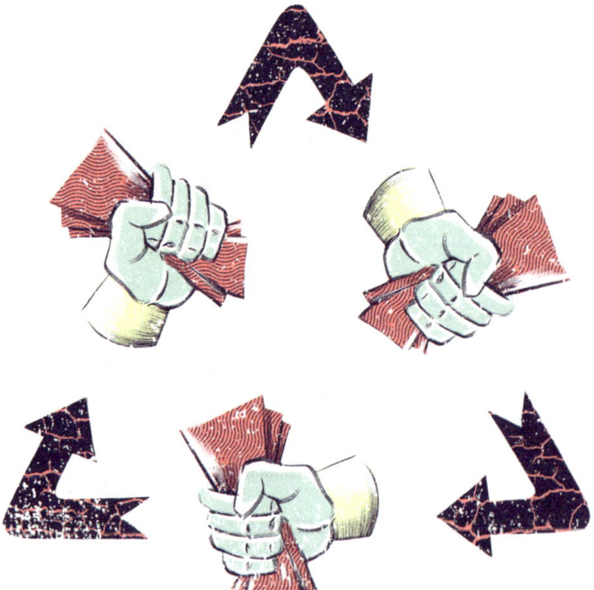

EN 1876 ABRIÓ UN DESPACHO en SU CASA. EL NOMBRE OFICIAL FUE la CAJA de IMPOSICIONES; EL NOMBRE en la CALLE, el BANCO de los POBRES. GENTE de TODA CONDICIÓN INVIRTIÓ ALLÍ SU DINERO: EMPRESARIOS AVEZADOS, LABRADORES MODESTOS, CLÉRIGOS ACAUDALADOS. Y hasta TUVO TRES SEDES: LA ÚLTIMA, de RELUMBRÓN, en el TEATRO ESPAÑOL, en la PLAZA de la PAJA.

Ella MISMA SE ENCARGÓ de DAR FAMA al BANCO. DECÍA que SU MARIDO INVERTÍA el DINERO en MINAS de ORO de LAS AMÉRICAS (lo que NADIE SABÍA es que BALDOMERA, de SU MARIDO, NI UNA CARTA TENÍA). Y CUANDO le PEDÍAN EXPLICACIONES o DETALLES SOBRE el NEGOCIO, Ella SALÍA por PETENERAS: «ES TAN SIMPLE COMO el HUEVO de COLÓN».

TAN POPULAR FUE el BANCO de BALDOMERA que hasta «Le FIGARO», en PARÍS, y «L'INDÉPENDANCE BELGE», en BRUSELAS, HABLARON de ESTOS DINEROS. PERO a «LA MADRE de los POBRES» SE le VINO el CHIRINGUITO ABAJO. DICEN que FUE SU TREN de VIDA SUPERSÓNICO. Y NO HAY DUDA de ALGO MÁS: NO PODÍA ETERNIZARSE UNA EMPRESA CONSTRUIDA SOBRE VIGAS de HUMO y LADRILLOS de MENTIRAS.

A FINALES de AQUEL 1876 HUYÓ en BARCO con los CAUDALES. A los DOS AÑOS la ENCONTRARON y la EXTRADITARON a ESPAÑA. HUBO JUICIO: A SUS CUARENTA y DOS AÑOS, le CAYERON SEIS de PRISIÓN. PERO en la CALLE PIDIERON SU PERDÓN y HASTA le ESCRIBIERON DOS CANCIONES: «DOÑA BALDOMERA» y «EL GRAN CAMELO».

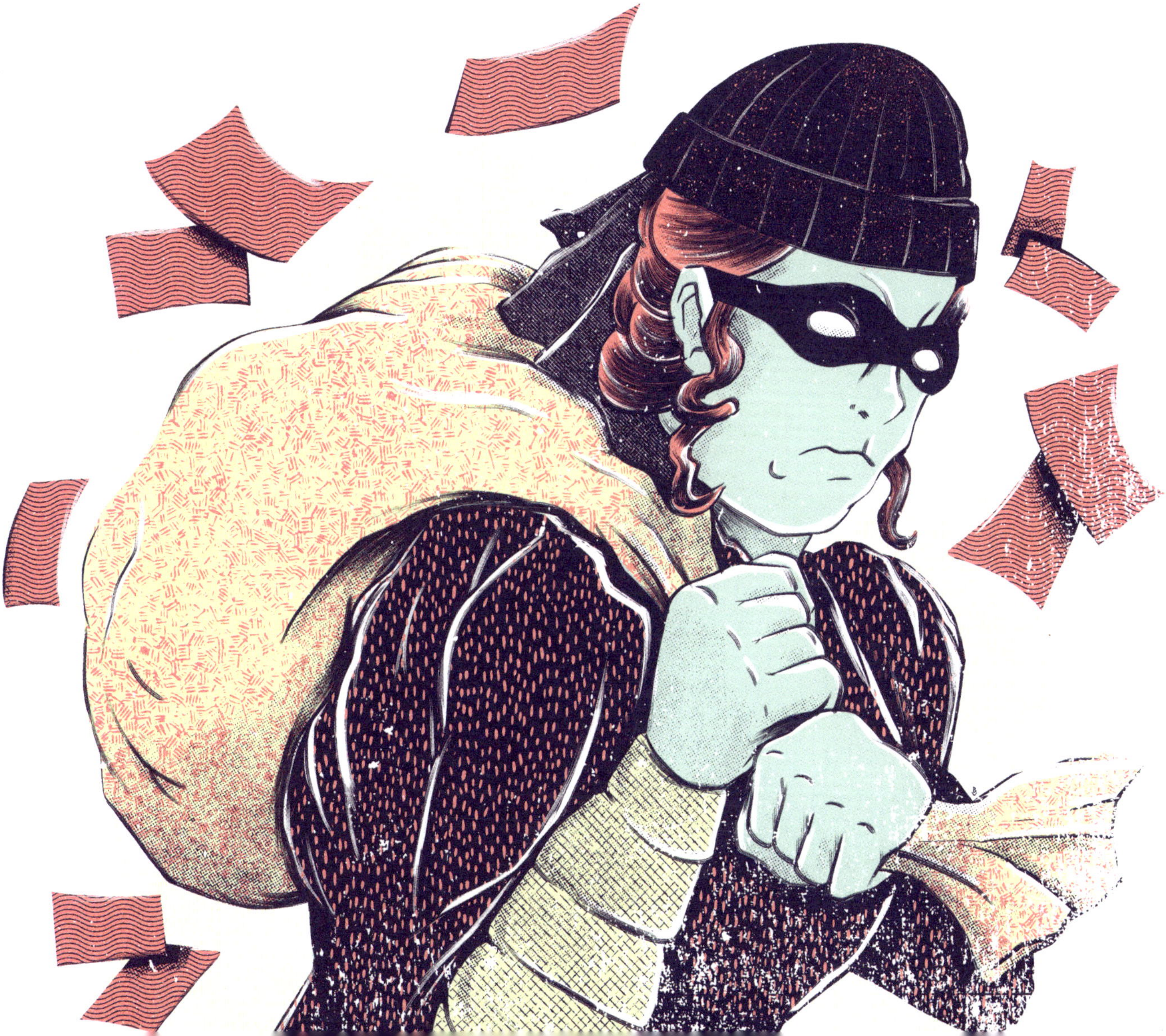

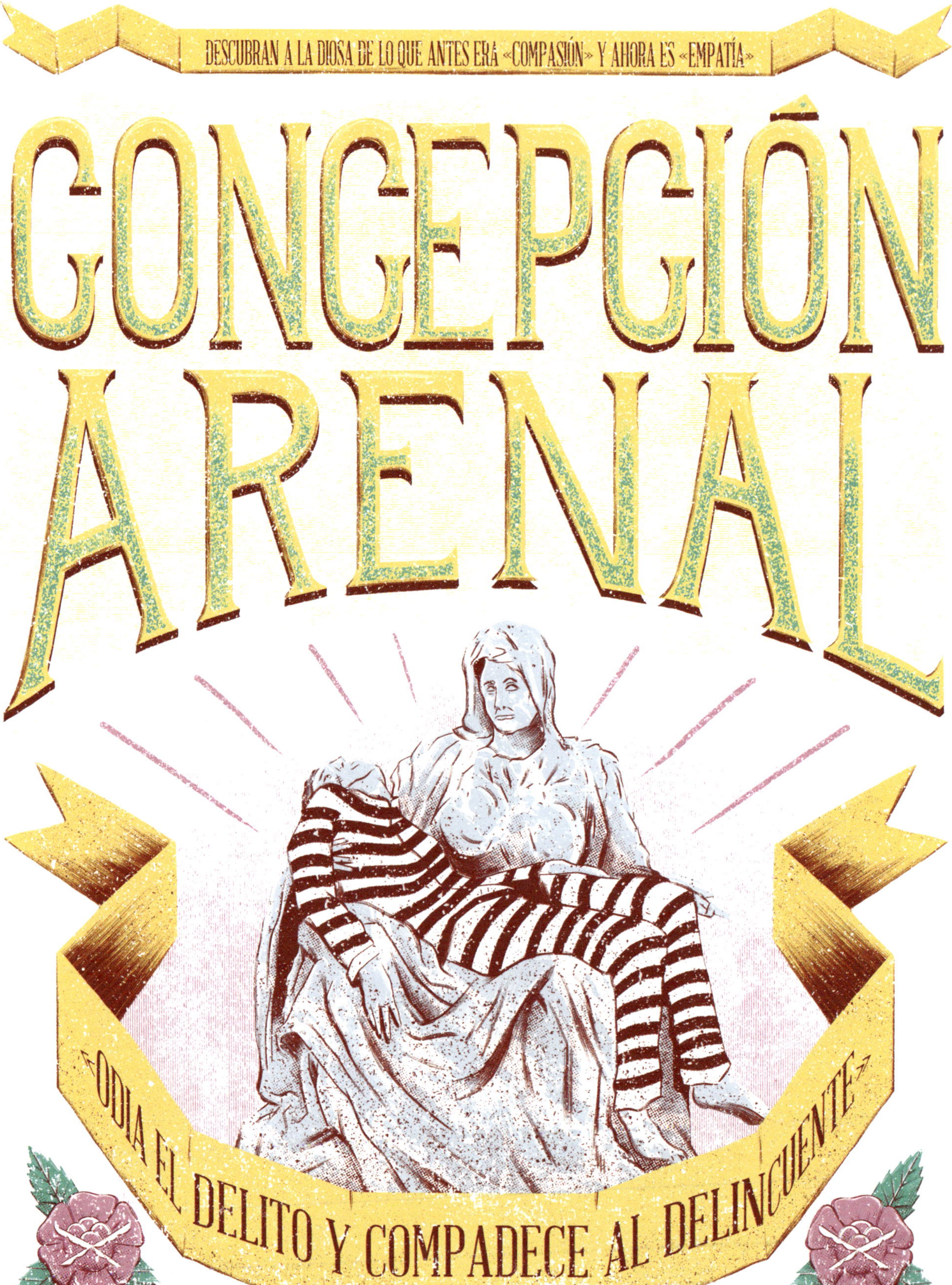
DESCUBRAN A LA DIOSA DE LO QUE ANTES ERA «COMPASIÓN» Y AHORA ES «EMPATÍA»
CONCEPCIÓN ARENAL
«ODIA EL DELITO Y COMPADECE AL DELINCUENTE»

NO FUE NIÑA de COSTURAS NI SUMISIÓN. A CONCEPCIÓN ARENAL (1820-1893) le ENTUSIASMABAN los LIBROS. INCLUSO los de la UNIVERSIDAD, AUNQUE a MITAD del XIX ESTABAN VETADOS para las SEÑORITAS.

ELLA DESAFIÓ la NORMA. ESCONDIDA en ROPAS de HOMBRE, ACUDÍA CADA DÍA a la FACULTAD de DERECHO. HASTA que la DESCUBRIERON y... SIGUIÓ YENDO. PERO, DESDE ENTONCES, ACOMPAÑADA de UN FAMILIAR. ¡PROTEGIDA de los UNIVERSITARIOS! (¿O SERÍA de los BERRACOS?)

CONCEPCIÓN APRENDIÓ la LECCIÓN. EN 1860 HIZO ALGO PARECIDO. AUNQUE ESTA VEZ NO NECESITÓ CAMBIAR de ROPAS; CON SU NOMBRE le BASTÓ. EN UN CONCURSO CONVOCADO por la ACADEMIA de CIENCIAS MORALES y POLÍTICAS, ENTREGÓ un ENSAYO CON la FIRMA de SU HIJO FERNANDO... y, al ABRIR la PLICA, el JURADO DESCUBRIÓ que el VERDADERO AUTOR de «LA BENEFICENCIA, LA FILANTROPÍA y la CARIDAD» NO ERA VARÓN. ¡ERA MUJER!

«Al DAR a la BENEFICENCIA la ORGANIZACIÓN CONVENIENTE,
la RAZÓN DEBE ESTAR REPRESENTADA por el ESTADO.
El SENTIMIENTO, por las ASOCIACIONES FILANTRÓPICAS.
El INSTINTO, por la CARIDAD INDIVIDUAL.»

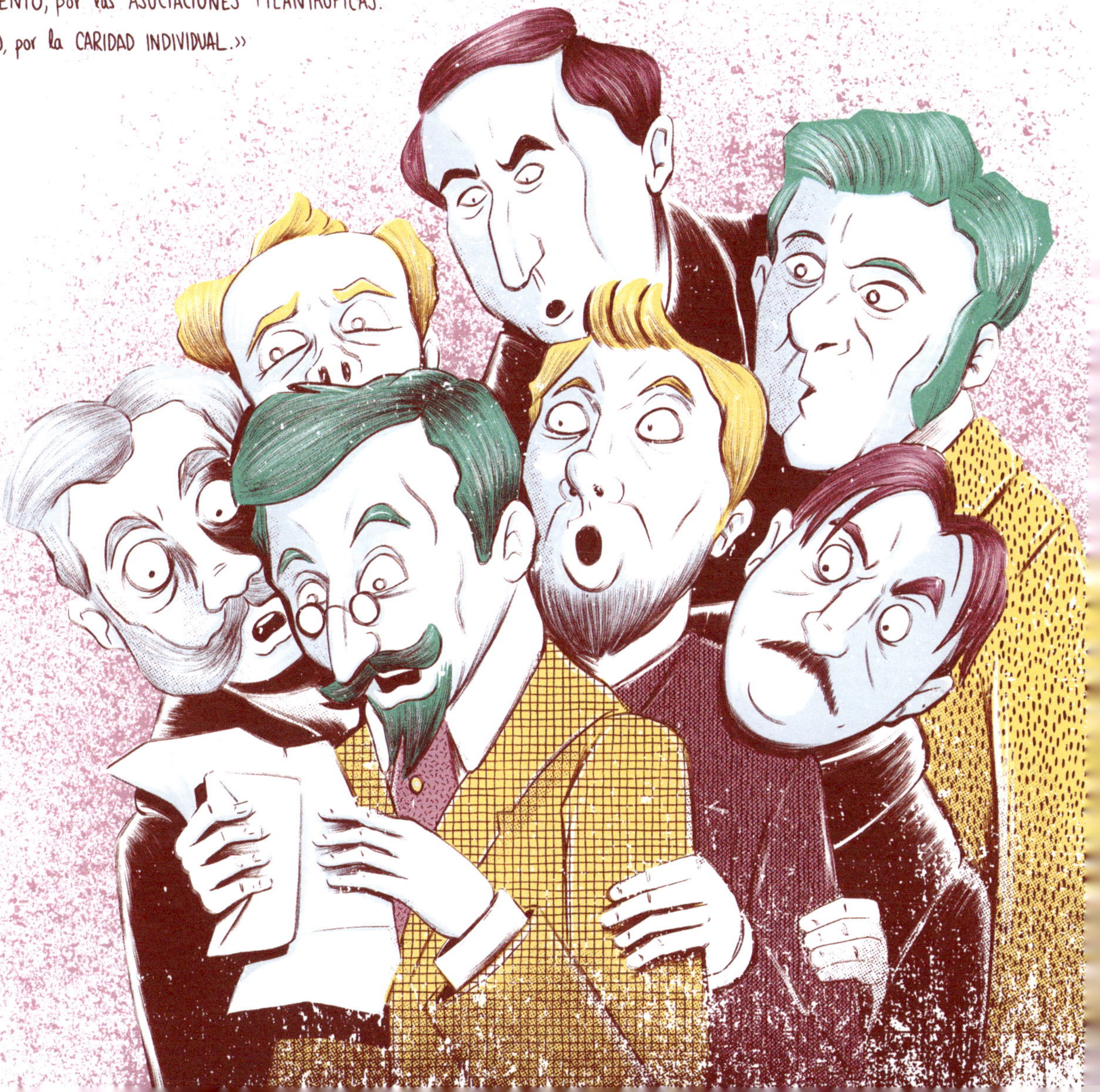

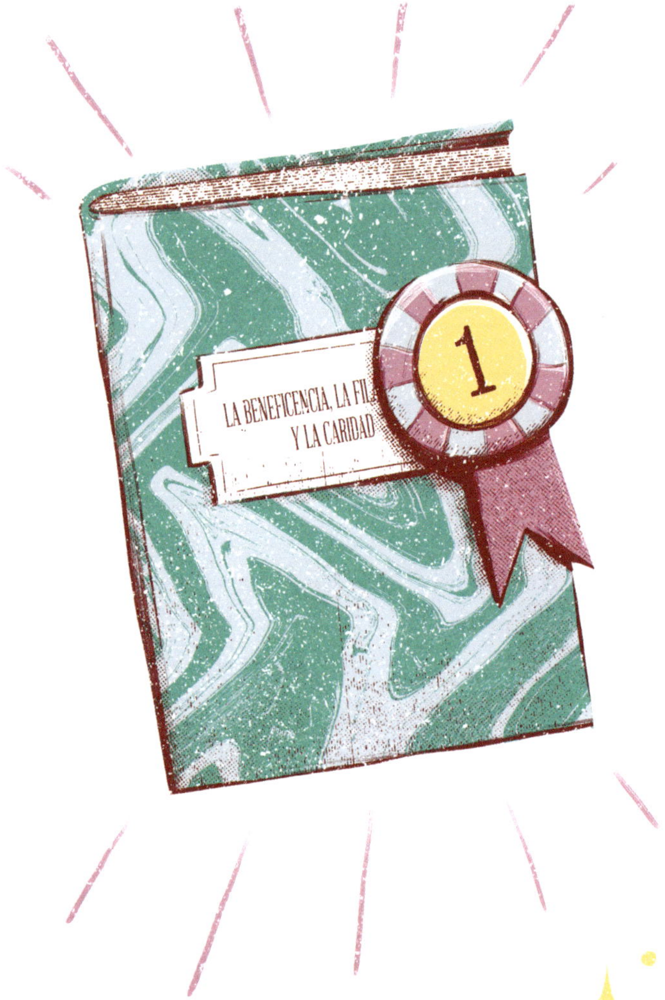

NO HUBO UN TRABAJO MEJOR, PERO la FIRMA, ¡ESA FIRMA!, OCULTABA a UNA MUJER que NO HABÍA SEGUIDO las BASES del CONCURSO al PIE de la LETRA. QUE SÍ, que NO..., HASTA que, al FIN, le CONCEDIERON el PREMIO. FUE la PRIMERA MUJER a la que GALARDONÓ LA ACADEMIA.

PUBLICÓ DESPUÉS el «MANUAL del VISITADOR del POBRE». El DIRECTOR GENERAL de ESTABLECIMIENTOS PENALES, ANTONIO MENA y ZORRILLA, QUEDÓ ADMIRADO (¡OH!) y en 1864 la NOMBRÓ «VISITADORA de CÁRCELES de MUJERES». FUE la PRIMERA MUJER en ESE PUESTO.

EN la PRISIÓN de LA CORUÑA QUEDÓ ATERRADA. ¡VAYA FORMA de TRATAR a las PRESAS! NO VIO UNA MÍNIMA DELICADEZA en la ENFERMERÍA. El PAN que les DABAN ERA COMO PAJA para PASTAR. LOS FUNCIONARIOS las TRATABAN COMO GANADO: SOBREVIVÍAN entre el HAMBRE, el MALTRATO y la SUCIEDAD.

CONCEPCIÓN ORGANIZÓ UNA ASOCIACIÓN de AYUDA a las RECLUSAS FINANCIADA por MUJERES RICAS. LOS CUIDADOS que NO les DABA el ESTADO (y MUCHO MENOS los FUNCIONARIOS) HABRÍAN de LLEGAR de la CARIDAD.

LA VISITADORA EXIGIÓ que TRATARAN a las PRESAS CON RESPETO y que DEJARAN de DARLES PALOS CON la VARA. El DIRECTOR de la PRISIÓN y los GUARDIAS NO PUDIERON SOPORTARLO y MAQUINARON lo INDECIBLE para que la ALEJARAN de ALLÍ. ASÍ OCURRIÓ en 1865, CUANDO el MINISTRO que le HABÍA DADO el PUESTO PERDIÓ el PODER.

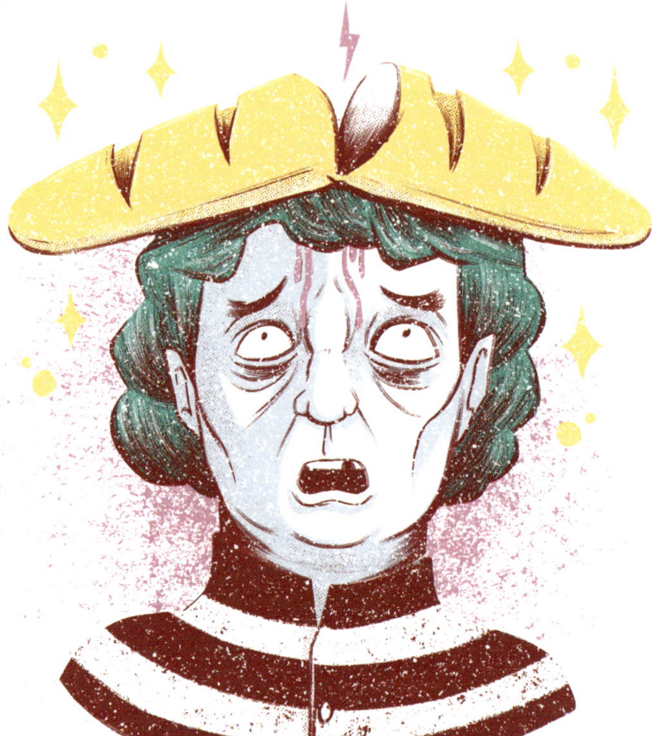

ESE AÑO la PERIODISTA y ESCRITORA PUBLICÓ «CARTAS a los DELINCUENTES»:

«NUESTRA OPINIÓN es que los CRIMINALES SON PERSONAS y NO SON COSAS.

QUE los CRIMINALES ESCUCHAN al que les HABLA INSPIRADO por el DESEO de SU BIEN.

QUE los CRIMINALES COMPRENDEN al que CON CARIDAD les EXPLICA.

QUE los CRIMINALES, SALVO ALGUNAS EXCEPCIONES, NO SON MONSTRUOS FUERA de TODAS las LEYES MORALES.

LAS REGLAS de la MORAL SON APLICABLES en UNA PRISIÓN, COMO las de HIGIENE en UN HOSPITAL.

CREEMOS que HAY ALGUNOS CRIMINALES que PUEDEN CORREGIRSE, y MUCHOS que PUEDEN MODIFICARSE, LLEGANDO, SI NO a SER BUENOS, a NO HACER MAL».

En el INVIERNO en que CONCEPCIÓN SE MARCHÓ de ESTE MUNDO le HICIERON TODO TIPO de HOMENAJES. TANTO en la CALLE COMO en los PERIÓDICOS de EUROPA y de AMÉRICA. NADIE OLVIDARÍA JAMÁS SU FRASE MÁS CÉLEBRE: «ODIA el DELITO y COMPADECE al DELINCUENTE».

En las CÁRCELES DOLIÓ TAMBIÉN SU MUERTE. UN PRESO LLAMADO JOSÉ OTERO GÓMEZ ENVIÓ al AYUNTAMIENTO de VIGO SELLOS por VALOR de 45 CÉNTIMOS (UNA CIFRA GENEROSA para la ÉPOCA) DESTINADOS al PROYECTO de CONSTRUIR UN MAUSOLEO que GUARDARA los RESTOS de CONCEPCIÓN ARENAL.

POR TRES DELITOS de HURTO, OTERO CUMPLÍA UNA CONDENA de VEINTICUATRO AÑOS (¡VEINTICUATRO AÑOS!), UNA BARBARIDAD que ELLA HABÍA DENUNCIADO VARIAS VECES. EN SU CARTA al AYUNTAMIENTO, OTERO ESCRIBIÓ:

«En TODAS las PRISIONES de ESPAÑA, DESPUÉS de DIOS, se VENERA a DOÑA CONCEPCIÓN ARENAL».

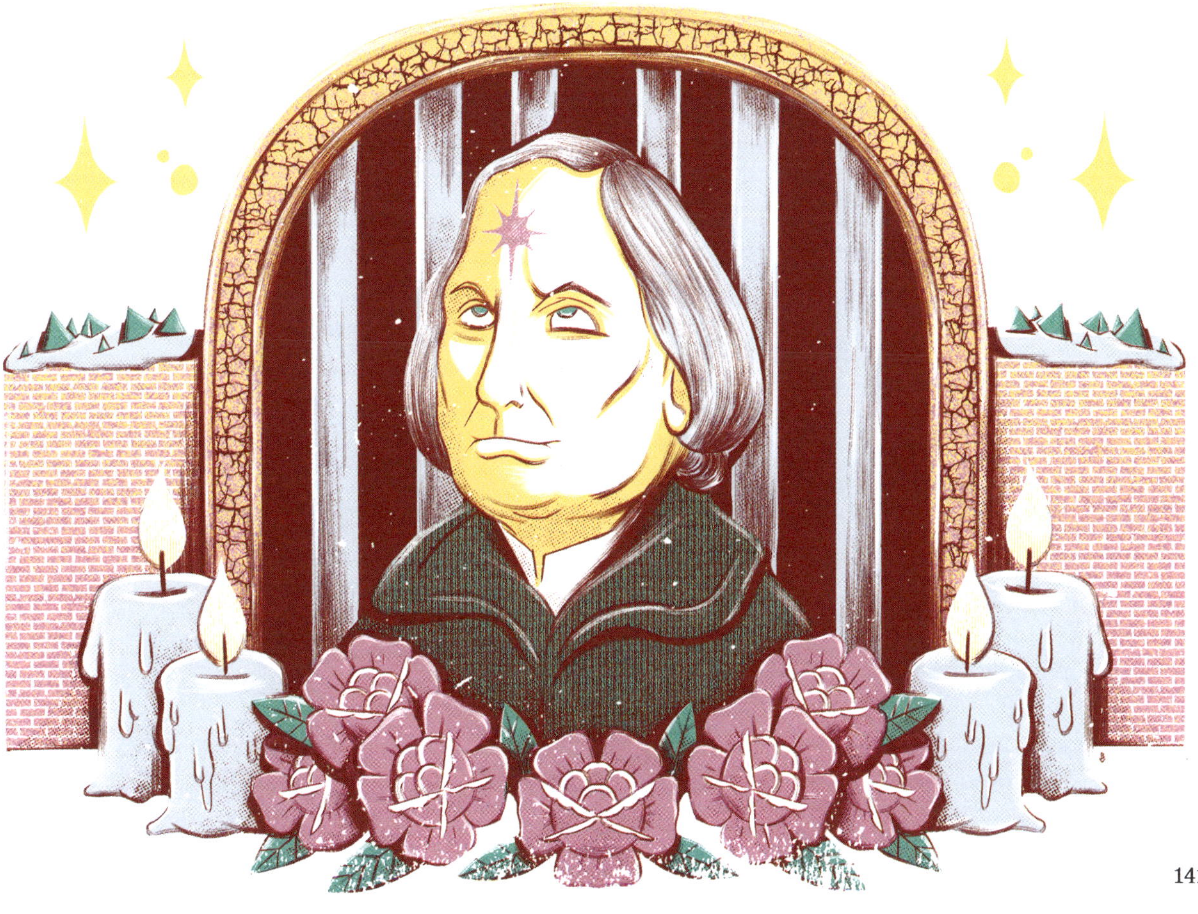

CONOZCAN AL FILÓSOFO QUE DIJO: «LA CIENCIA ES EL PEDESTAL DE LA VERDAD»

NICOLÁS SALMERÓN

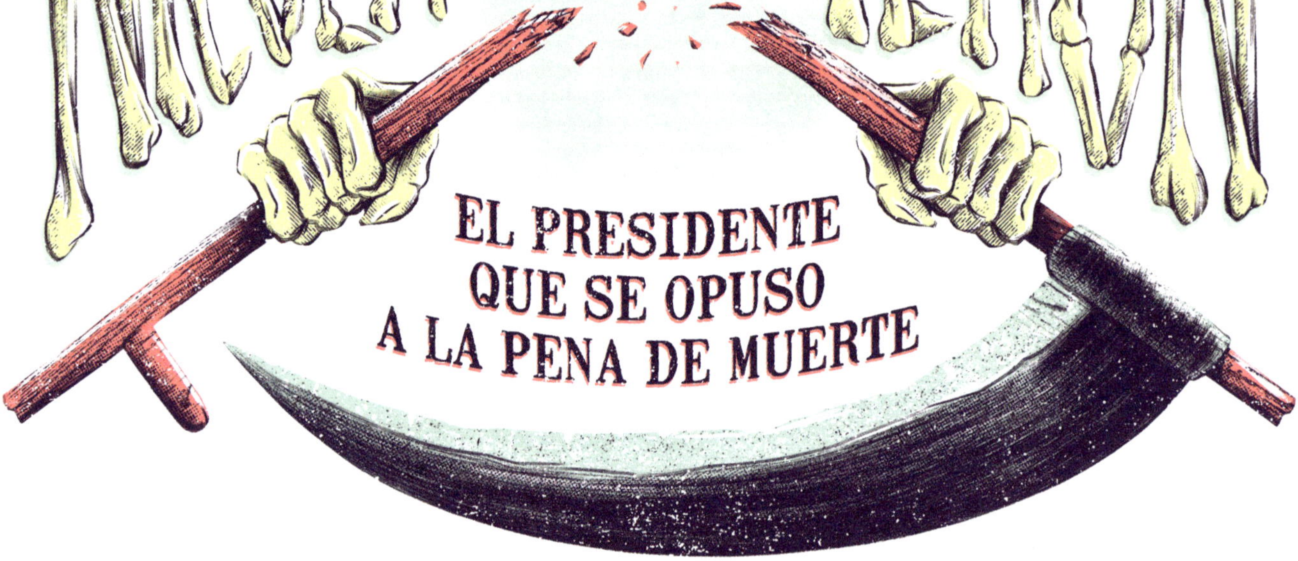

EL PRESIDENTE QUE SE OPUSO A LA PENA DE MUERTE

NO ESTABAN las COSAS para HABLAR con ALEGRÍA. NI SIQUIERA los CATEDRÁTICOS de METAFÍSICA. A NICOLÁS SALMERÓN (1838-1908), PUBLICAR SUS IDEAS en «LA DISCUSIÓN» y «LA DEMOCRACIA» le COSTÓ CINCO MESES de CÁRCEL.

PERO LLEGÓ la GLORIOSA y LEVANTÓ el CASTIGO. ESTA REVOLUCIÓN, que DESTRONÓ a ISABEL II y DIO LUGAR al SEXENIO DEMOCRÁTICO, DEVOLVIÓ la CÁTEDRA a SALMERÓN. ¡Y AÚN MÁS! En 1871 FUE ELEGIDO DIPUTADO en las CORTES GENERALES.

A PRINCIPIOS de 1873 LLEGÓ la NIÑA BONITA (OTRO HITO con NOMBRE FEMENINO). PROCLAMARON la PRIMERA REPÚBLICA ESPAÑOLA y NOMBRARON a SALMERÓN MINISTRO de GRACIA y JUSTICIA. UN MES DESPUÉS, en PLENO VERANO, ASCENDIÓ al PODER MÁXIMO: PRESIDENTE del PODER EJECUTIVO.

PERO el PAÍS ANDABA REVUELTO. HABÍA LEVANTAMIENTOS en VARIAS PROVINCIAS y el EJÉRCITO PIDIÓ que SE APLICARAN las LEYES PENALES con TODA SEVERIDAD. EL CONGRESO, la PRENSA y la OPINIÓN PÚBLICA SE HICIERON ECO de AQUELLAS ANSIAS de MANO DURA.

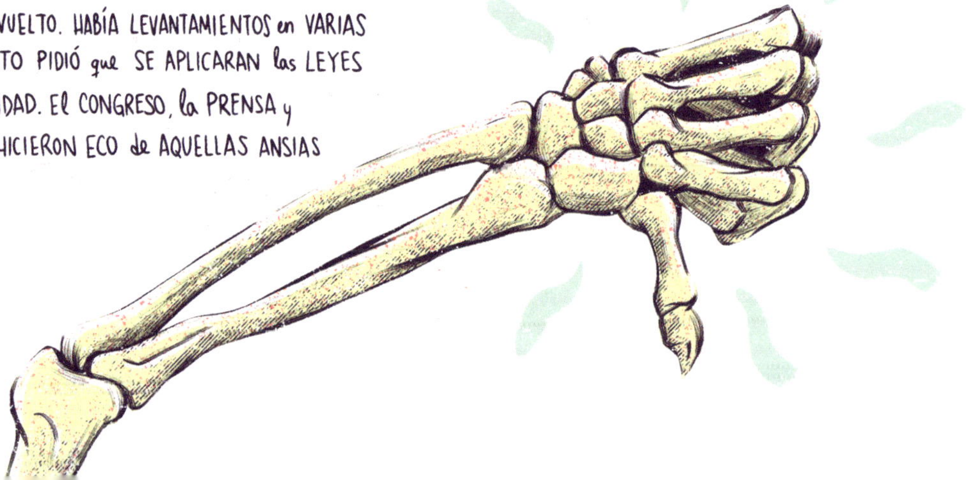

LA NOCHE del SÁBADO 6 de SEPTIEMBRE de 1973, el ORADOR de VERBO GRÁCIL y VOCES RIMBOMBANTES ANUNCIÓ SU DIMISIÓN:

«LA PENA de MUERTE COMO MATERIA de PENALIDAD NO la ADMITIRÉ NUNCA PORQUE es CONTRARIA a MI CONCIENCIA, PORQUE es CONTRARIA a MIS PRINCIPIOS y a los PRINCIPIOS de la DEMOCRACIA».

DOS DÍAS DESPUÉS, «La IBERIA» le DEDICÓ ESTAS PALABRAS:

«El PAÍS lo RECIBIÓ con BENEVOLENCIA SUMA, SU DISCURSO-PROGRAMA LLEVÓ la TRANQUILIDAD a TODAS las CLASES que VIVEN con la PAZ, a TODAS las CLASES que VIVEN del TRABAJO, a TODAS las CLASES, en FIN, AMANTES de la LIBERTAD y del ORDEN.

PERO ¡FATALIDAD de ESTA PATRIA! El SEÑOR SALMERÓN CAE del PUESTO que la ASAMBLEA le CONFIÓ, NO SEGURAMENTE COMO SUS ANTECESORES: SALE por ESCRÚPULOS de CONCIENCIA.

¡BIEN HACE!

NO PODEMOS NI DEBEMOS EXIGIRLE que ACEPTE lo que ALLÁ en el FONDO de SU ALMA MIRA con REPUGNANTE HORROR.

LA HISTORIA le JUZGARÁ en SU DÍA y DESDE LUEGO NOS AVENTURAMOS a PRONOSTICARLE que OCUPARÁ UNA PÁGINA INFINITAMENTE MÁS ENVIDIABLE que la RESERVADA a los DOS COMPAÑEROS (y ANTERIORES PRESIDENTES de La REPÚBLICA), ESTANISLAO FIGUERAS y PI Y MARGALL».

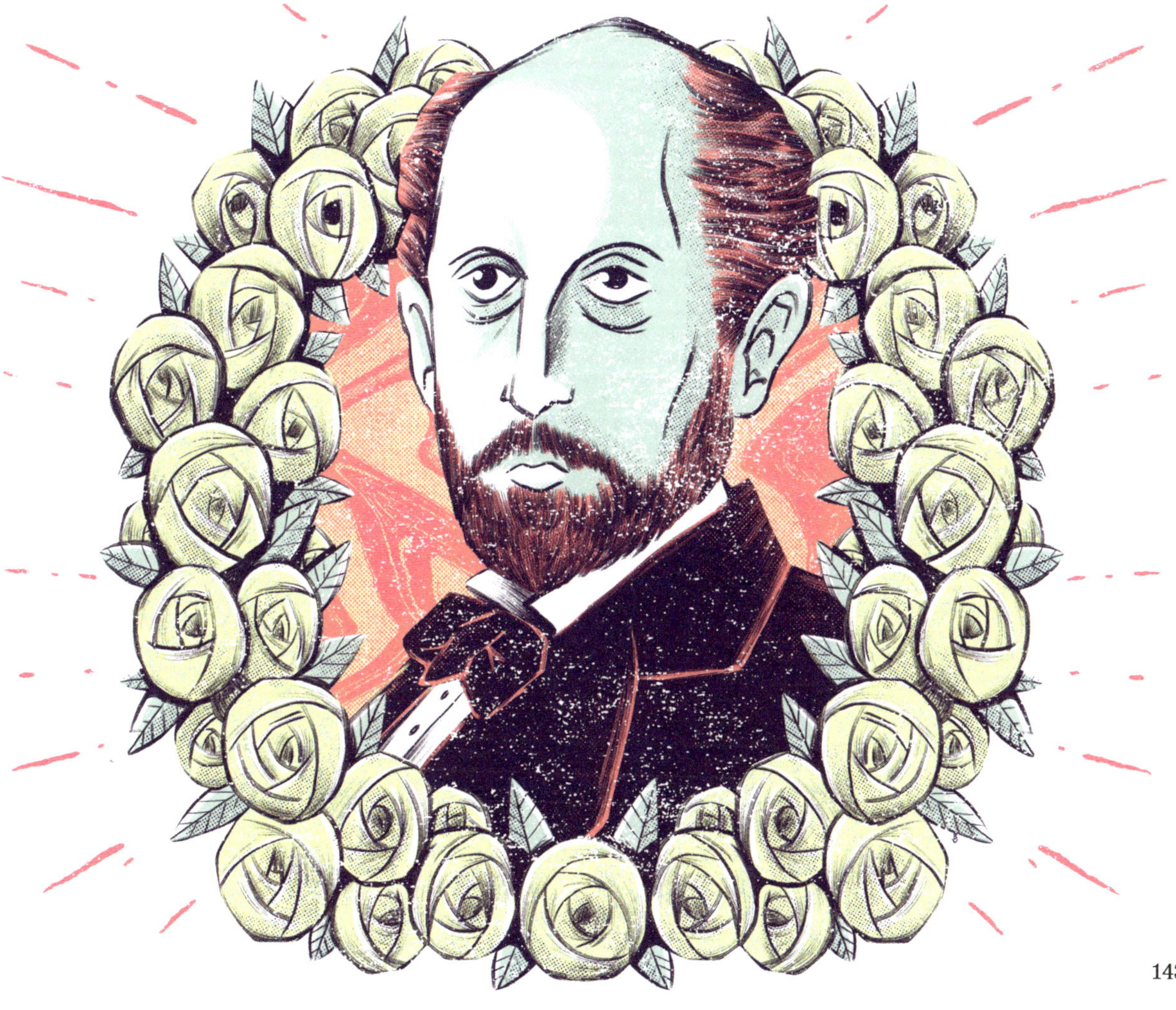

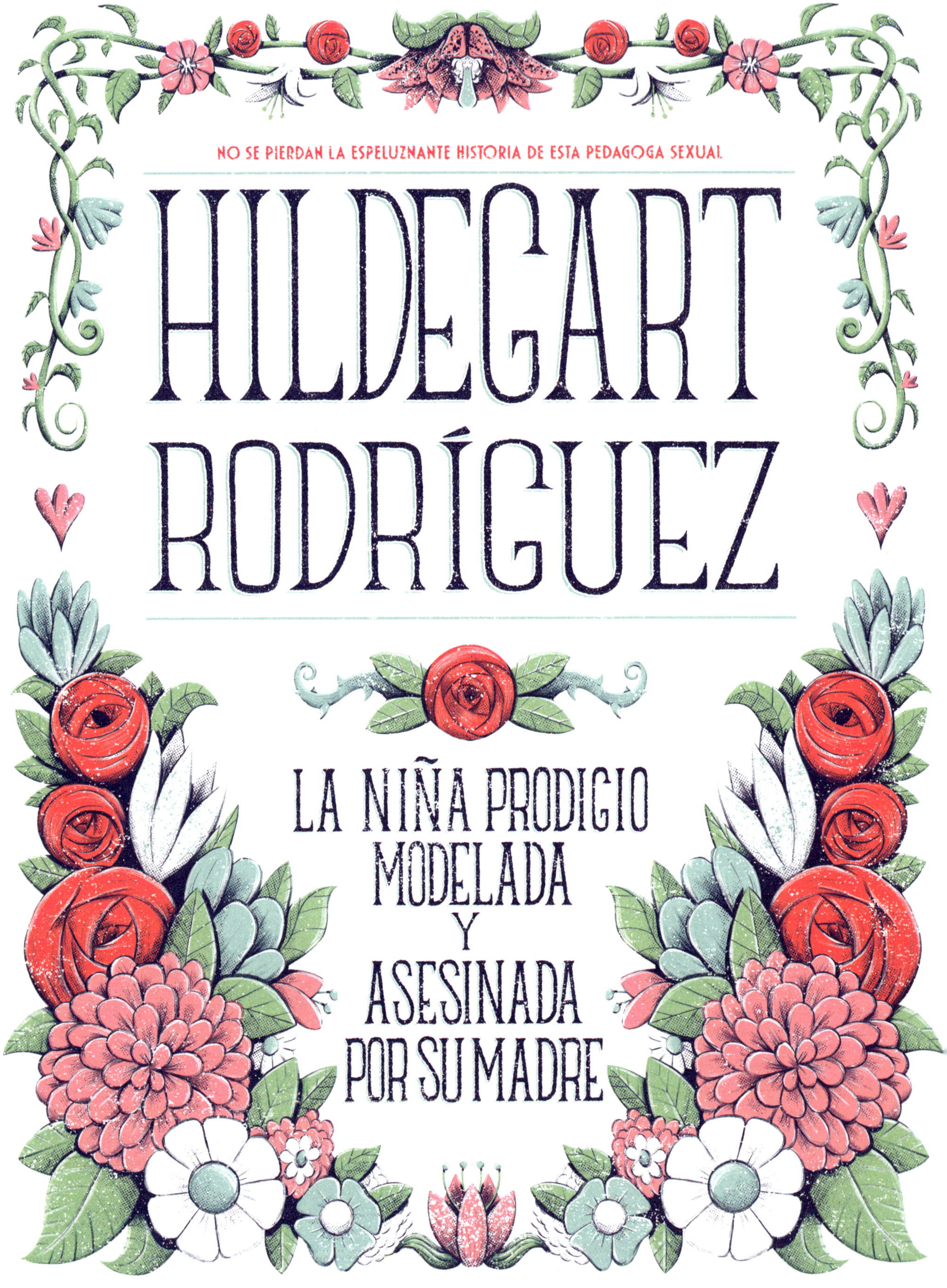
NO SE PIERDAN LA ESPELUZNANTE HISTORIA DE ESTA PEDAGOGA SEXUAL
HILDEGART
RODRÍGUEZ
LA NIÑA PRODIGIO
MODELADA
Y
ASESINADA
POR SU MADRE

AURORA RODRÍGUEZ CARBALLEIRA PLANEABA UNA REVOLUCIÓN FEMINISTA. TENÍA DINERO, TENÍA CULTURA. SOLO le FALTABA UN EJÉRCITO, PERO OPTÓ por UN REDENTOR: TENDRÍA UNA HIJA que LIBERARA a las MUJERES del YUGO VARONIL.

A PRINCIPIOS del SIGLO XX SE DIFUNDIERON, con ALEGRÍA, las TEORÍAS EUGENÉSICAS para MEJORAR la ESPECIE. AURORA las ESTUDIÓ hasta el DELIRIO y ASÍ IDEÓ la FABRICACIÓN de UN SER SOBRENATURAL. En SU CIUDAD, FERROL, BUSCÓ al PADRE IDÓNEO. DIO con UN CURA de FÍSICO ADECUADO e IDEAS CORRECTAS: HABÍA ESCRITO ALGUNOS ARTÍCULOS a FAVOR del PROLETARIADO. Y lo BUSCÓ SACERDOTE para que NO PUDIERA RECLAMAR la PATERNIDAD.

AURORA ERA VIRGEN. TENÍA TREINTA y CINCO AÑOS y NINGÚN INTERÉS por el SEXO. NI BESOS NI CONVERSACIÓN. ¡A lo que VAMOS! Y en CUANTO QUEDÓ EMBARAZADA SE FUE a MADRID.

ALIMENTABA el BOMBO con UNA DIETA CUIDADÍSIMA, SE RODEABA de OBJETOS BONITOS, EVITABA las NOTICIAS DESOLADORAS... Y, por FIN, el 9 de DICIEMBRE de 1914 DIO a LUZ. ¡NIÑA! ¡ERA UNA NIÑA!

A SU HIJA PREFABRICADA le PUSO UN NOMBRE PREFABRICADO: **HILDEGART** («JARDÍN de SABIDURÍA»). Y la EUGENESIA le DIO MÁS de lo que BUSCABA: ADEMÁS de NIÑA, ERA SUPERDOTADA. A los OCHO MESES HABLABA, a los VEINTIDÓS MESES LEÍA. A los CUATRO AÑOS CONSIGUIÓ un TÍTULO de MECANOGRAFÍA, a los DIEZ ENTENDÍA CUATRO IDIOMAS y a los CATORCE EMPEZÓ a ESCRIBIR en PERIÓDICOS y a DAR CONFERENCIAS SOBRE la REVOLUCIÓN SEXUAL.

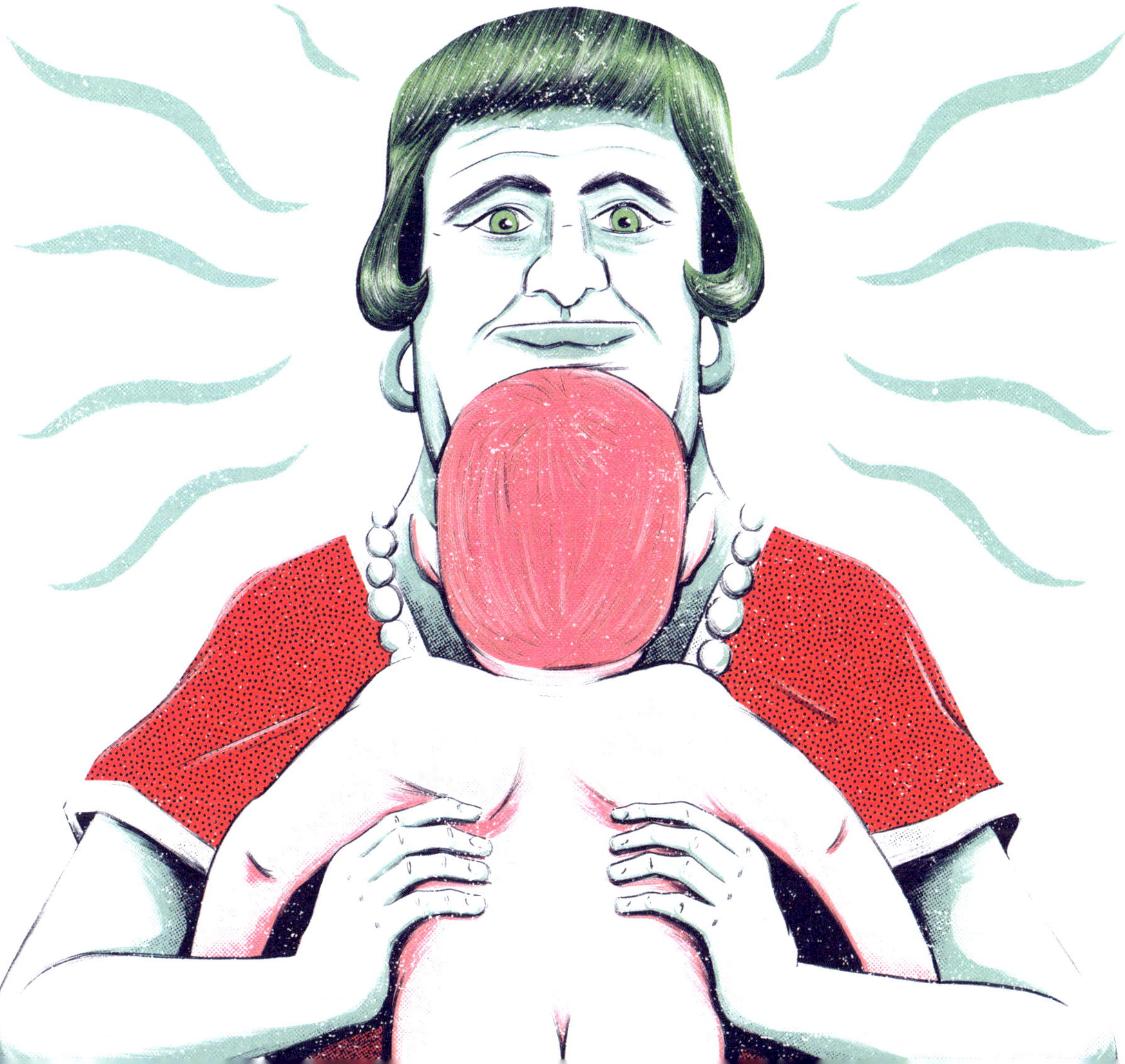

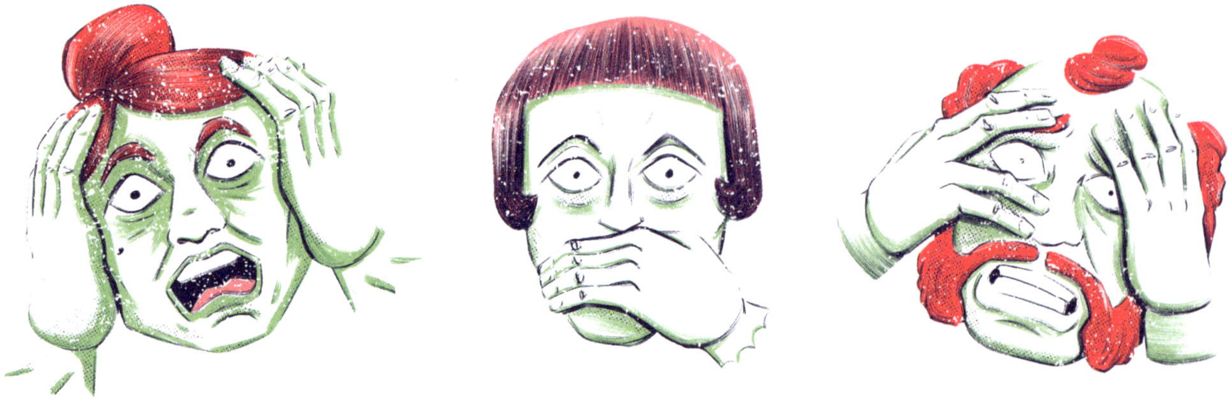

MUCHOS SE ECHARON las MANOS a la CABEZA. ¡UNA NIÑA HABLANDO de SEXO! PERO los LIBERALES la CONVIRTIERON en un REFERENTE de la PEDAGOGÍA SEXUAL y la SALUD PÚBLICA. UNO de SUS LIBROS, «El PROBLEMA SEXUAL TRATADO por UNA MUJER ESPAÑOLA», VENDIÓ NADA MENOS que ¡8.000 EJEMPLARES en UNA SEMANA!

HILDEGART HABLABA con DESPARPAJO de la LIBERTAD SEXUAL, de la POLIGAMIA, de DISTINTOS TIPOS de FAMILIA, de la MATERNIDAD CONSCIENTE en VEZ de la que VENÍA del DESEO de DIOS. ERA la SECRETARIA de la LIGA ESPAÑOLA para la REFORMA SEXUAL SOBRE BASES CIENTÍFICAS que PRESIDÍA GREGORIO MARAÑÓN.

«HILDEGART es TAN ILUSTRE como CONCEPCIÓN ARENAL», DECÍA el DOCTOR.

Los SEXÓLOGOS MÁS REPUTADOS del MUNDO ADMIRABAN SU OBRA. CUANDO H.G. WELLS VISITÓ ESPAÑA, en 1932, PIDIÓ que ELLA FUERA SU AYUDANTE.

DE PUERTAS AFUERA ERA UNA INTELECTUAL y ACTIVISTA POLÍTICA IRREFRENABLE. DE PUERTAS ADENTRO SE LEVANTABA el INFIERNO. La OBRA de INGENIERÍA HUMANA que HABÍA CREADO AURORA EMPEZÓ a RECLAMAR SU LIBERTAD.

«YA NOS QUEDA POCO TIEMPO JUNTAS. PIENSO MARCHARME PRONTO, VIAJAR MUCHO, VIVIR MI VIDA. LIBREMENTE, SIN IMPOSICIONES de NADIE», ADVIRTIÓ a SU MADRE.

AURORA EMPEZÓ a VER CONSPIRACIONES por TODAS PARTES. LA GOTA que COLMÓ el VASO FUE que un POLÍTICO BARCELONÉS, ABEL VELILLA, le PIDIERA MATRIMONIO. ¡IMPOSIBLE! ¡HILDEGART TIENE que CUMPLIR SU MISIÓN! ¡JAMÁS ESTARÁ con UN HOMBRE! A la NIÑA que SE EDUCÓ para PREDICAR la LIBERTAD SEXUAL SE le EXIGÍA la CASTIDAD MÁS ABSOLUTA.

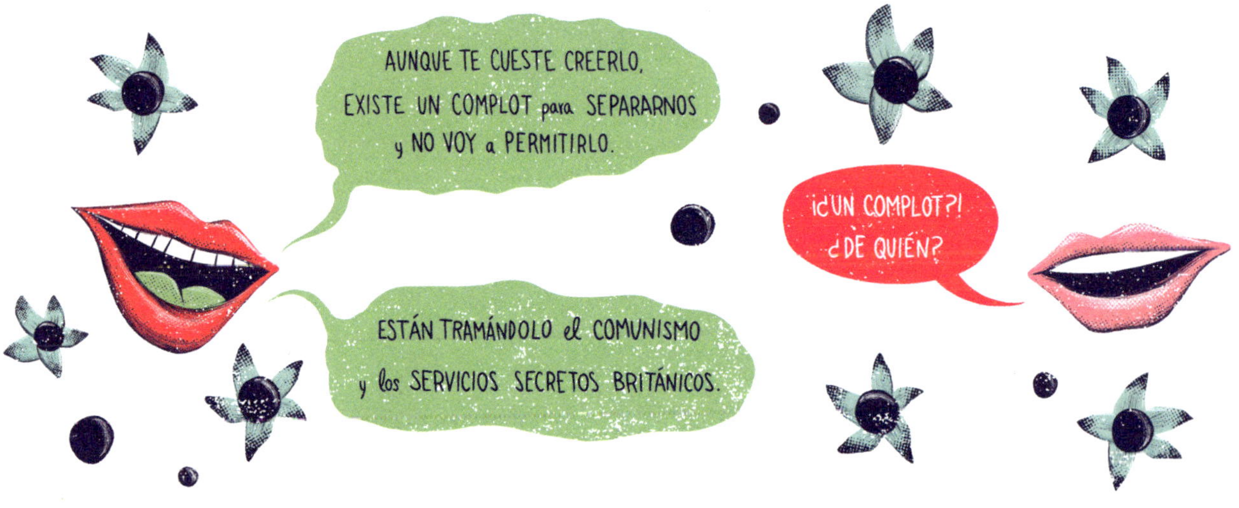

UNA MAÑANA HILDEGART SALIÓ de CASA SIN EL PERMISO de SU MADRE. Al VOLVER, AURORA, ENLOQUECIDA, CERRÓ la PUERTA, BAJÓ las PERSIANAS y CONVIRTIÓ el HOGAR en UNA CÁRCEL.

«¡MAMÁ! ¡RESPÓNDEME! ¿QUÉ ESTÁ PASANDO?»

AURORA, SIN CONTESTAR, ARRANCÓ los CABLES del TELÉFONO y SE METIÓ las LLAVES de CASA en el SOSTÉN.

Al AMANECER del 9 de JUNIO de 1933, AURORA, en BATA, PIDIÓ a la SIRVIENTA que BAJARA a PASEAR a los PERROS. DE UN CAJÓN SACÓ UNA PISTOLA. FUE a la HABITACIÓN de HILDEGART y, en SILENCIO, ABRIÓ la PUERTA.

PUM PUM PUM PUM

CUATRO BALAZOS ASALTARON el SUEÑO de la JOVEN de DIECIOCHO AÑOS. TRES en la CABEZA, UNO en el CORAZÓN.

AURORA DEJÓ la PISTOLA en el TOCADOR, SE PUSO UNOS PENDIENTES de PERLAS y, CON TOTAL SERENIDAD, SE ENTREGÓ a la POLICÍA.

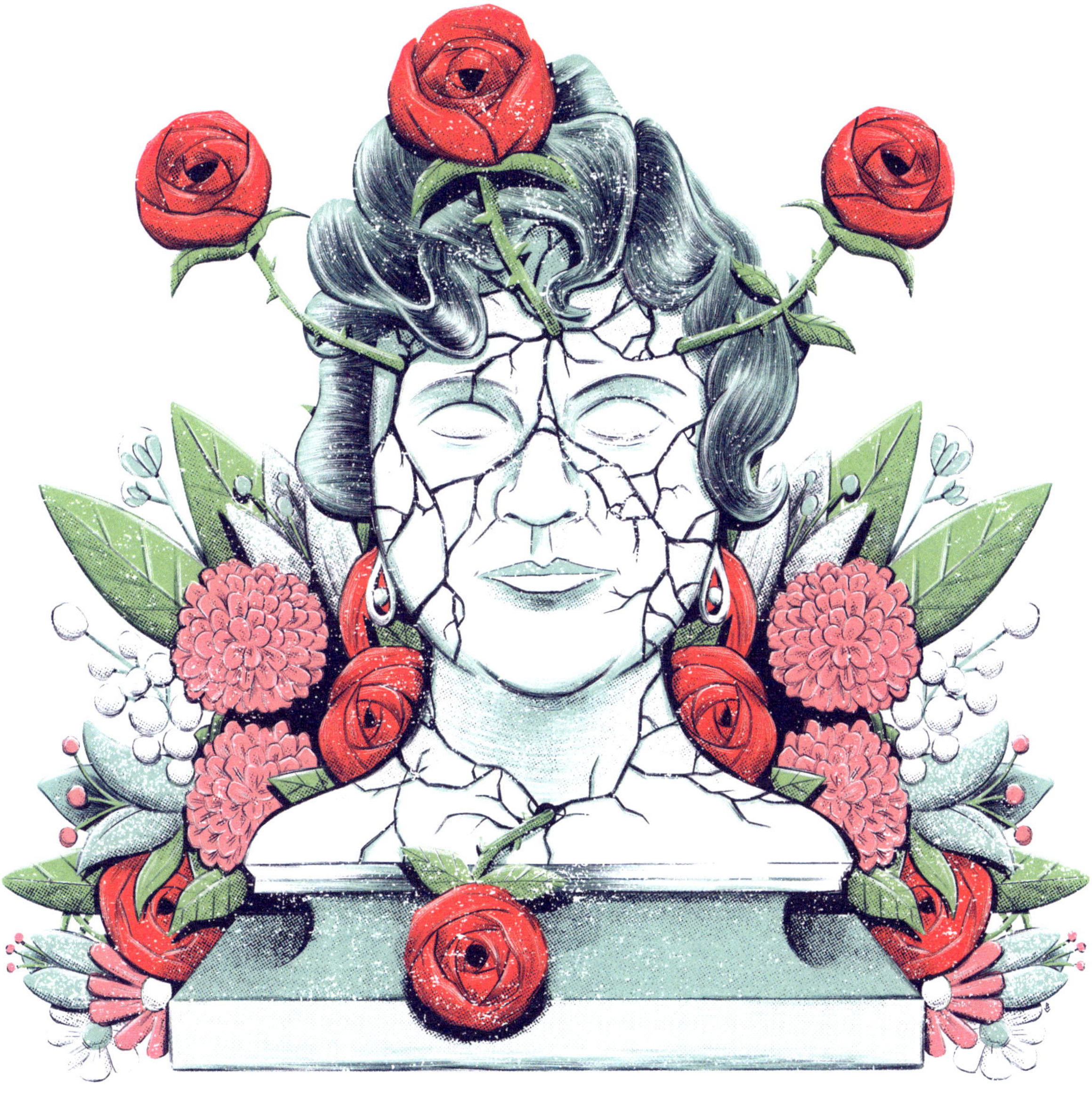

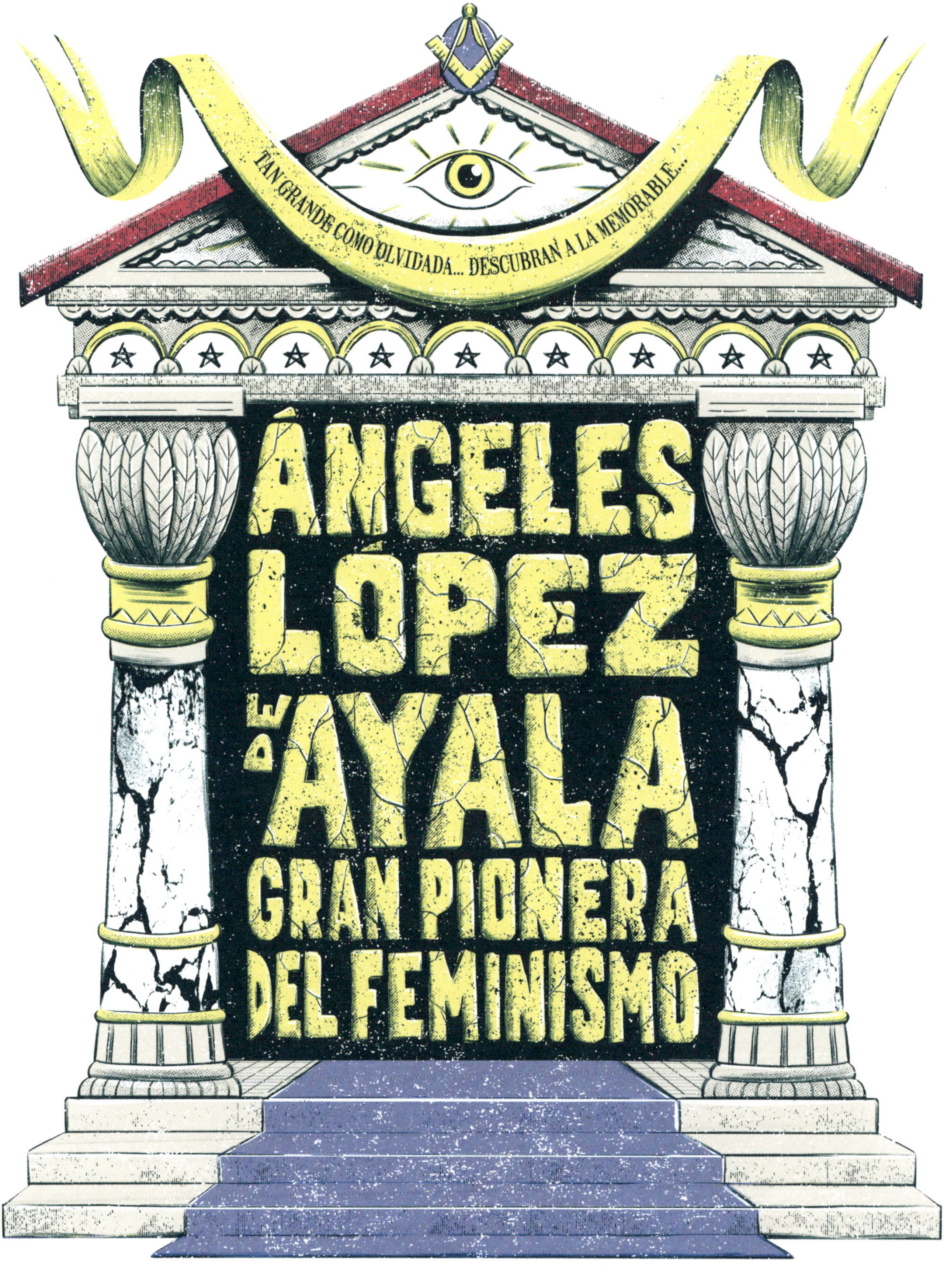
TAN GRANDE COMO OLVIDADA... DESCUBRAN A LA MEMORABLE...
ÁNGELES LÓPEZ DE AYALA
GRAN PIONERA DEL FEMINISMO

ÁNGELES LÓPEZ de AYALA (1859-1926) SE PREGUNTABA QUIÉN HABRÍA SIDO SI SU MADRE NO HUBIERA MUERTO TAN PRONTO. LA ESCRITORA, PERIODISTA, DRAMATURGA y ACTIVISTA QUEDÓ HUÉRFANA a los SIETE AÑOS.

«SI MI MADRE HUBIERA VIVIDO, NO SÉ por qué IDEALES HUBIERA OPTADO MI CRITERIO. PERO MURIÓ y las IDEAS de MI PADRE SE ABRIERON PASO en MI INTELECTUALIDAD y SE EXACERBARON con la LECTURA de VICTOR HUGO.»

A la SEVILLANA le GUSTABA ESCRIBIR. A los DIECISÉIS AÑOS YA HABÍA TERMINADO UNA NOVELA en CUATRO TOMOS: «El TRIUNFO de la VIRTUD».

DESPUÉS PUBLICÓ ARTÍCULOS en «El FÍGARO», «LA EDUCACIÓN», «El HISPALENSE» y «El DISPARATE». HABLABA de lo DURA que ERA la VIDA PARA los OBREROS, para las MUJERES. DENUNCIABA la FALTA de EDUCACIÓN y el FANATISMO RELIGIOSO. PRIMERO, en ARTÍCULOS de PERIÓDICOS de OTROS. DESPUÉS, en los SUYOS PROPIOS.

LÓPEZ de AYALA FUNDÓ «El PROGRESO» (DIFUSOR del PENSAMIENTO REPUBLICANO y ANTICLERICAL), «El GLADIADOR» (VINCULADO a SU ASOCIACIÓN FEMINISTA SOCIEDAD PROGRESIVA FEMENINA), «El LIBERTADOR» (DEFENSOR de la MUJER y los LIBREPENSADORES) y «El GLADIADOR del PENSAMIENTO».

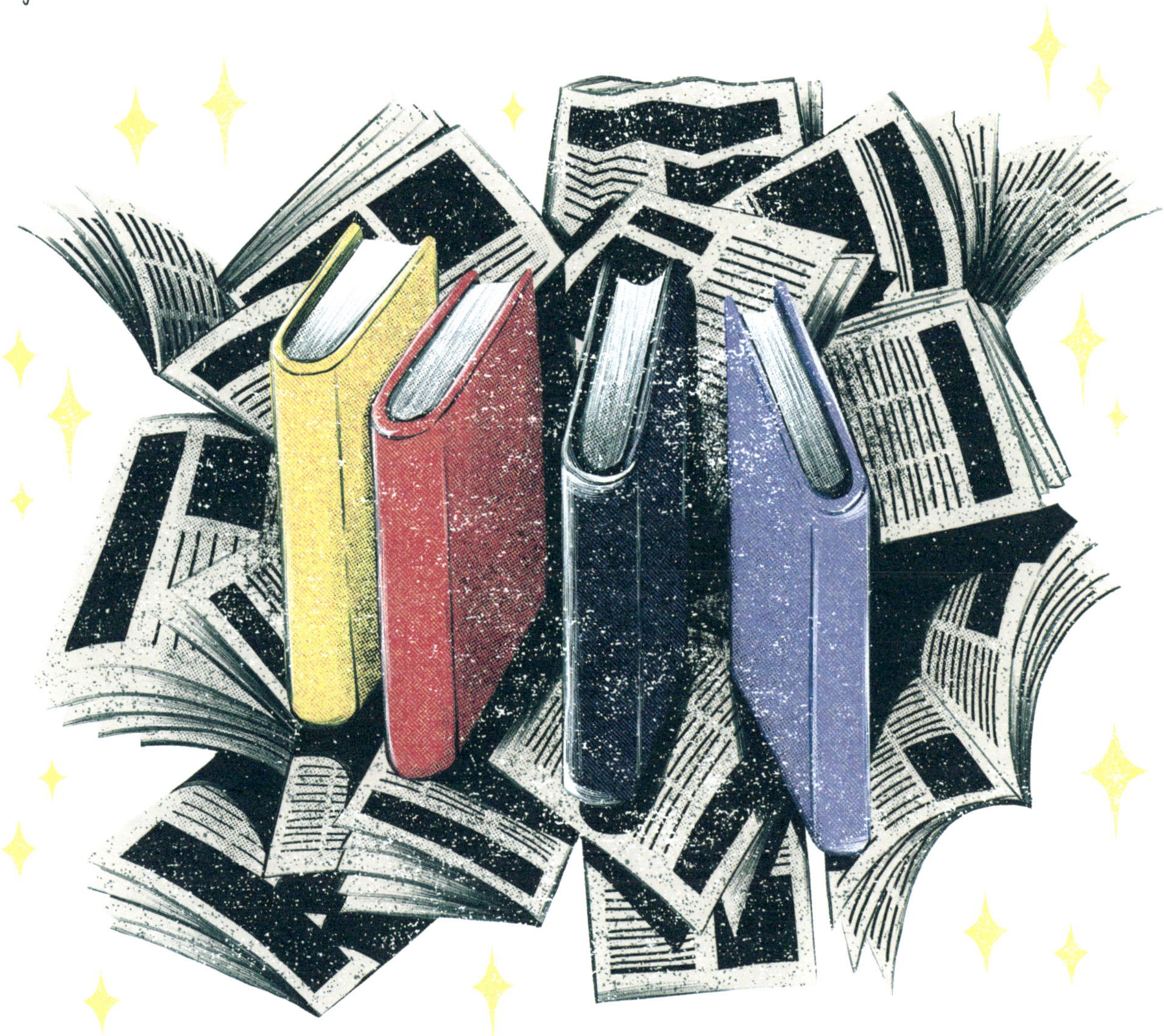

El RIESGO

ATACAR a la MONARQUÍA y la IGLESIA HIZO que ACABARA entre REJAS. VARIAS VECES. UNA, en 1901. DESPUÉS de las HUELGAS GENERALES de BARCELONA, la RECLUYERON en el CASTILLO de MONTJUÏC, porque en UN MITIN CONTRA los JESUITAS TERMINÓ el DISCURSO DICIENDO: «¡VIVA BARCELONA SIN CONVENTOS!».

FUERON OCHO PROCESOS y TRES ENCARCELAMIENTOS para UNA SOLA BIOGRAFÍA.

DEFENDER ESTAS IDEAS PUSO en JUEGO SU VIDA. VARIAS VECES. UNA, la INTENTARON QUEMAR: ALGUIEN PROVOCÓ un INCENDIO en la CASA de SANTANDER DONDE ESTABA con SU MARIDO. ESCAPARON por los PELOS. EN OTRA OCASIÓN INTENTARON ENVENENARLA y en OTRA MÁS... ¡PAM! ¡DISPARARON SIN PIEDAD! RECIBIÓ DOS TIROS en UNA CALLE de BARCELONA, AUNQUE, por SUERTE, las BALAS NO PASARON del VESTIDO.

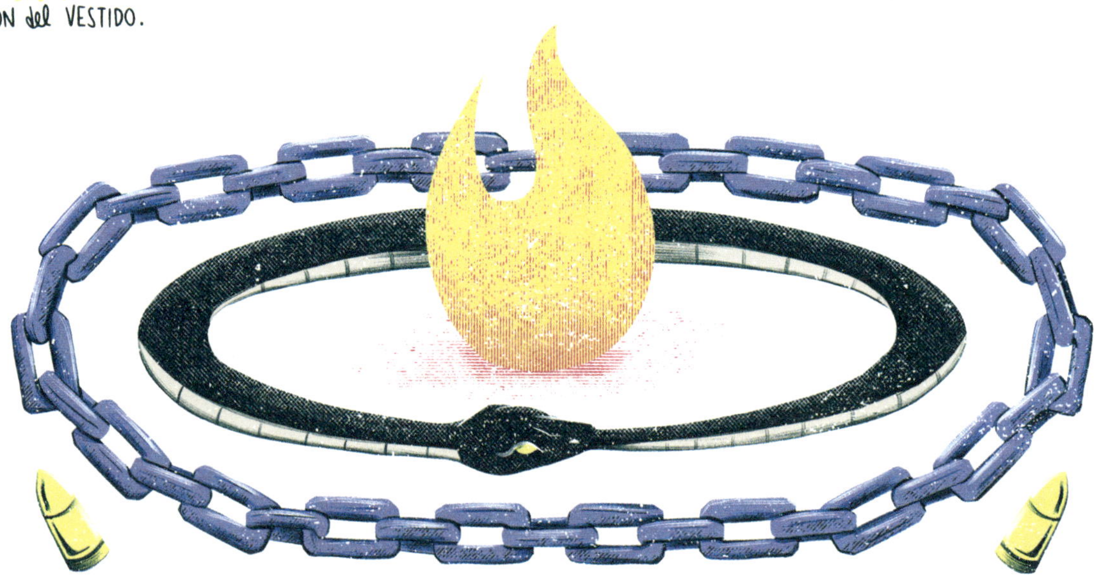

La GRAN MANIFESTACIÓN FEMINISTA

SU VIDA SE RECUERDA, APENAS, por UN DÍA: El 10 de JULIO de 1910. El PRESIDENTE del GOBIERNO, JOSÉ CANALEJAS, DIJO que QUERÍA SEPARAR, de FORMA AMISTOSA, la IGLESIA y el ESTADO. A los CLÉRIGOS les DIERON CONVULSIONES y ORGANIZARON PROTESTAS por TODOS LADOS: «¡QUIEREN DESCATOLIZAR ESPAÑA! ¡ESTÁ a la ORDEN de la MASONERÍA!».

LAS RELIGIOSAS ARMARON ACTOS en CONTRA; las LIBERALES, MÍTINES a FAVOR. En BARCELONA, LÓPEZ de AYALA CONVOCÓ UNA MANIFESTACIÓN. «¡LAS MUJERES por la LIBERTAD!»

«MADRID REÚNE en un IMPORTANTE MITIN, PRESIDIDO por UNA IMPORTANTE ESCRITORA (CARMEN de BURGOS), a MÁS de DOCE MIL SEÑORAS -ESCRIBIÓ en la CONVOCATORIA que PUBLICÓ en "El PROGRESO"-. Y BARCELONA, CUNA de TODAS las DEMOCRACIAS y SAGRADO RECEPTÁCULO de TODAS las JUSTICIAS, MOVILIZA SU LIBERAL EJÉRCITO FEMENINO y ORGANIZA UNA INTERESANTE MANIFESTACIÓN NO VISTA hasta el PRESENTE, que, MODIFICANDO el CONCEPTO en que SE TIENE a la ESPAÑOLA, DEJE ATÓNITOS de PAVOR a los que en ELLA CIFRAN SU ESPERANZA de DOMINACIÓN PERPETUA, de EXPLOTACIÓN y TIRANÍA.»

ESTA LÍDER NATA, MASONA y «REPUBLICANA REVOLUCIONARIA» lo CONSIGUIÓ. NUNCA hasta ENTONCES SE HABÍA VISTO TAL MOVILIZACIÓN de MUJERES.

El OLVIDO y la INGRATITUD

PERO la HISTORIA es DESMEMORIADA; MÁS AÚN, CUANDO QUIERE OLVIDAR. LA VIDA de LÓPEZ de AYALA ESTÁ HOY ESCRITA en TINTA INVISIBLE. NO HA SIDO la PRIMERA VEZ. YA PASÓ ANTES.

EN la PORTADA de «El ATEO» del 4 de ABRIL de 1932, UN TÍTULO DICE: «LUCHADORAS OLVIDADAS». DEBAJO, SU RETRATO, y en el PIE de FOTO:

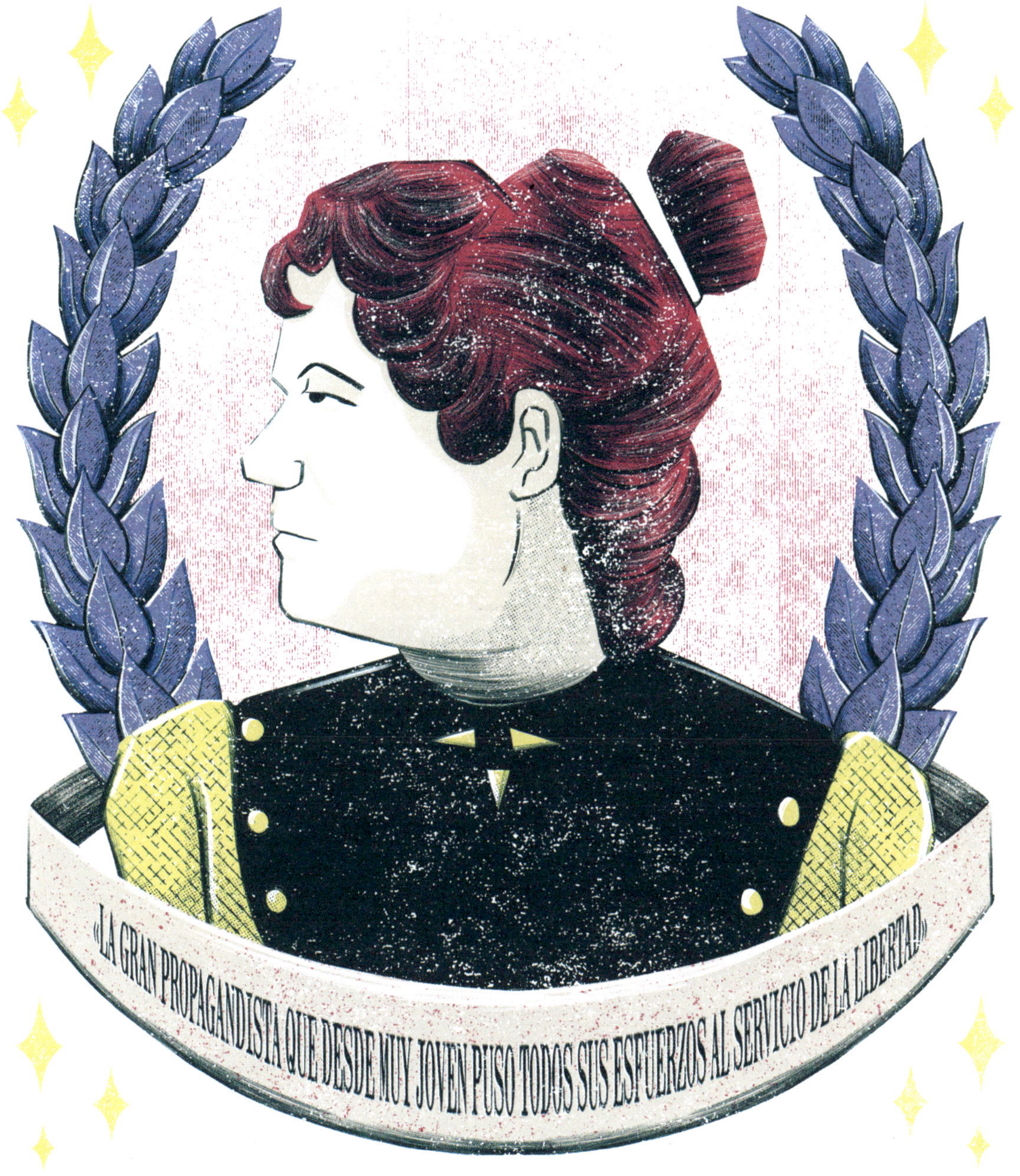

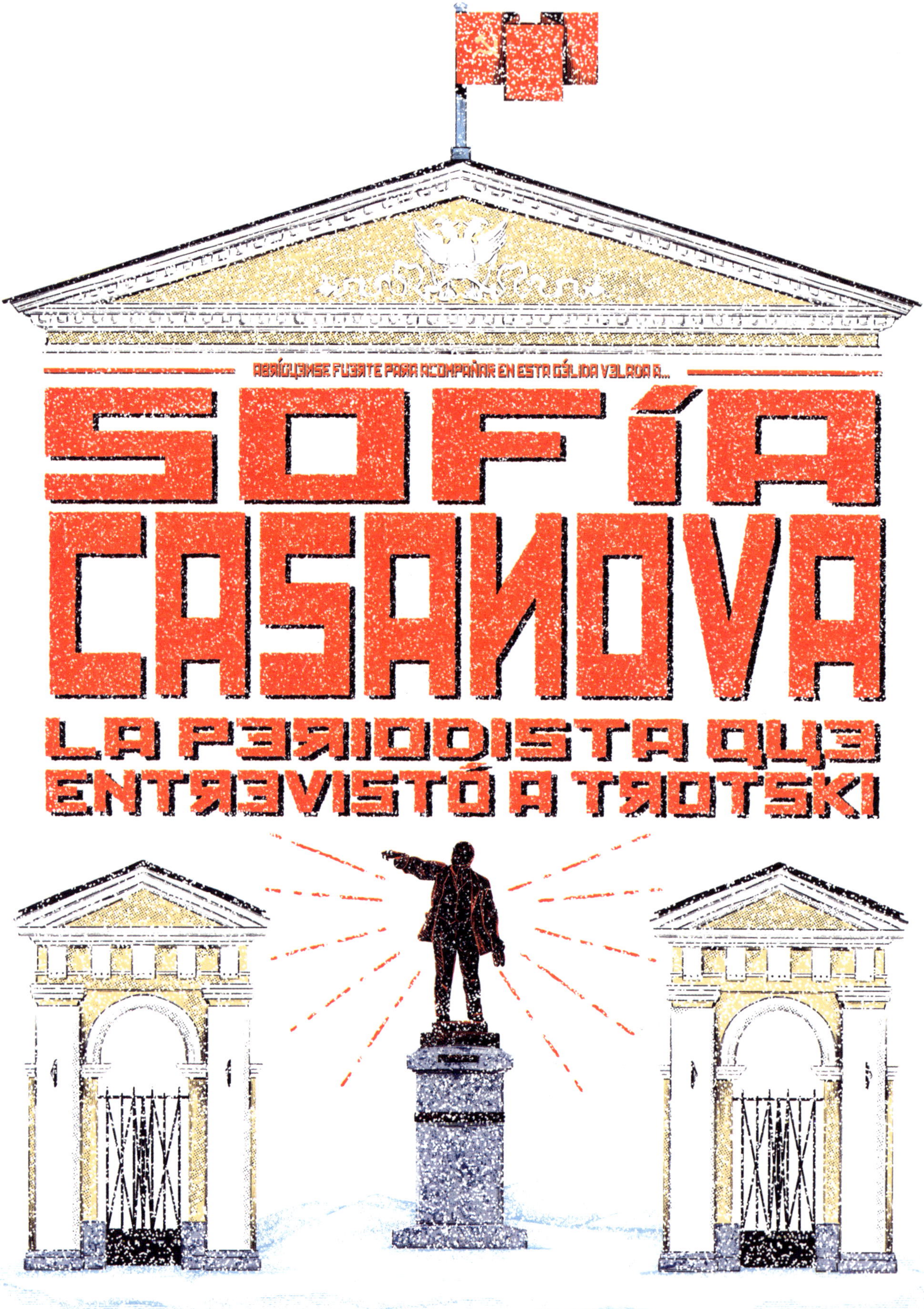
ABRÍGUENSE FUERTE PARA ACOMPAÑAR EN ESTA GÉLIDA VELADA A...
SOFÍA CASANOVA
LA PERIODISTA QUE ENTREVISTÓ A TROTSKI

HIELA en ESTE ENNEGRECIDO DÍA en SAN PETERSBURGO. APENAS HAN PASADO UNAS SEMANAS DESDE que los BOLCHEVIQUES TOMARON la RESIDENCIA OFICIAL de los ZARES y DECLARARON, ENTRE GRITOS de JÚBILO, «¡LA DICTADURA del PROLETARIADO!». LOS RUSOS de BUENA CASA, ATERRORIZADOS, CONTESTARON: «¡ES el FIN de RUSIA, es el FIN del MUNDO!».

EN ESTA TARDE INVERNAL, a la PERIODISTA SOFÍA CASANOVA (1861-1958) le DA el REPENTE de SU VIDA. TIENE CINCUENTA y SEIS AÑOS y los OJOS YA MALHERIDOS, PERO ESO NO la DETIENE. NO DICE a NADIE ADÓNDE VA en ESTE DÍA de BRAVA NIEVE y FRÍO MATÓN. TAN SOLO PIDE a SU CRIADA PEPA que la ACOMPAÑE.

POR la CALLE NO ANDA NI DIOS (de HECHO, ÉL MENOS que NADIE: LO HAN MATADO en la REVOLUCIÓN). NO HAY FORMA de ENCONTRAR a ALGUIEN que las LLEVE en TRINEO a SU DESTINO.

AL FIN DAN CON UN HOMBRE que, ENTRE el VIENTO y la NIEVE, las ACERCA a UN EDIFICIO que SOBRESALE ENTRE UNAS CASUCAS. ES el INSTITUTO SMOLNY. EN la PUERTA HAY UNOS PAISANOS ARMADOS, PEGADOS a UNA HOGUERA para CALENTARSE las MANOS.

-¿ADÓNDE VAN, SEÑORAS? -PREGUNTAN.

-VOY a VER al COMISARIO TROTSKI -CONTESTA SOFÍA.

LOS HOMBRES, CON AMABLE ADEMÁN, le SEÑALAN UNA ESCALINATA. ENTRAN. AL FONDO de ESTE ESPANTABLE EDIFICIO VEN a DOS MARINEROS, TRES SOLDADOS y DOS JÓVENES JUDÍAS ESCRIBIENDO en UNA MESA.

-SEÑORAS, ¿ADÓNDE VAN?

-QUEREMOS VER al MINISTRO de NEGOCIOS EXTRANJEROS -RESPONDE la ESPAÑOLA.

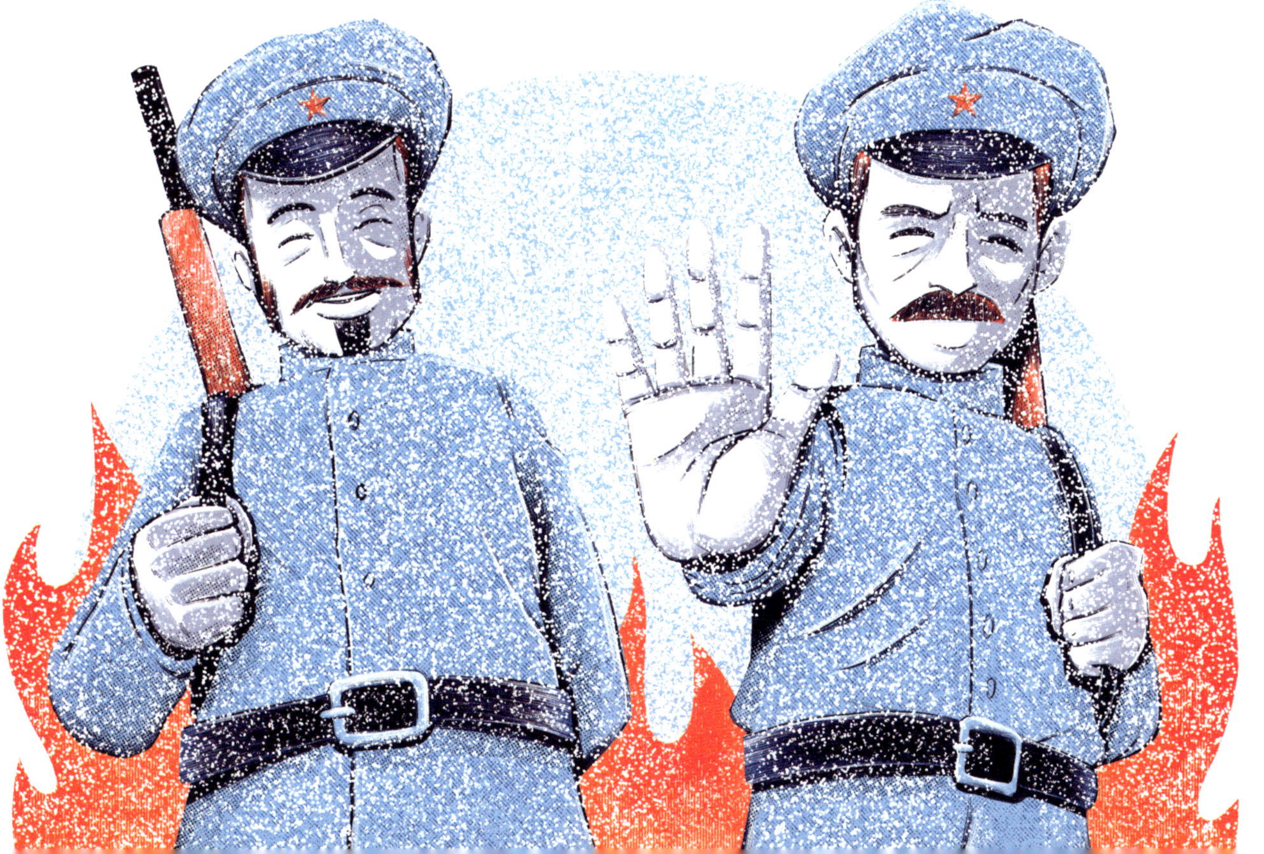

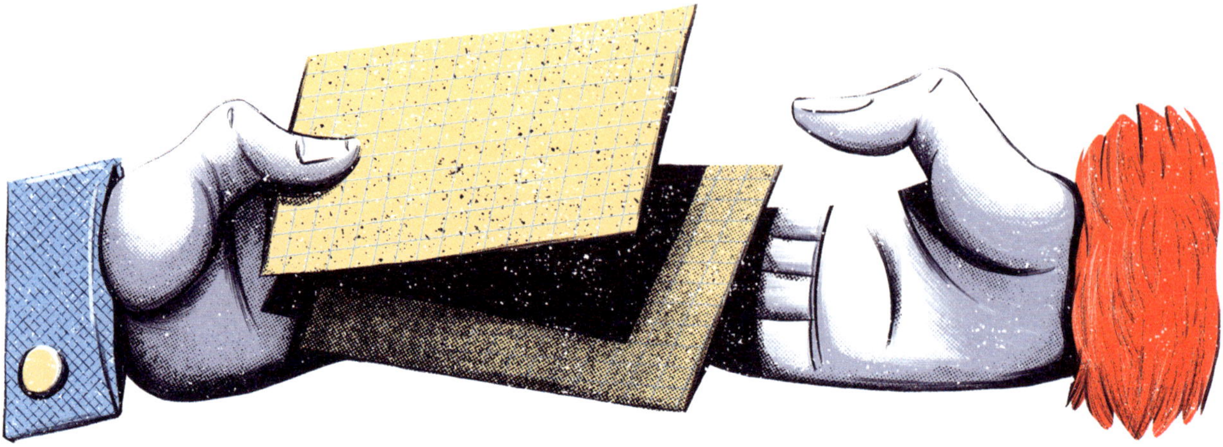

LOS SOLDADOS le ENTREGAN DOS CUARTILLAS de PAPEL TIMBRADO que INDICAN: «PISO TERCERO, PUERTA 67». UNA de las JÓVENES SE LEVANTA y las ACOMPAÑA.

El PÁNICO de PEPA VA ASCENDIENDO con CADA PELDAÑO que SUBEN. ATERRADOS SUS OJOS, CAÍDA SU MANTILLA SOBRE la FRENTE, REPLICA en SU GALLEGO CERRADO:

–¿ADÓNDE ME LEVA, SEÑORA? MIRE que AQUÍ NOS MATAN. A CANALLA ESTÁ MUY ARMADA. A MIN ME TEMBLA O PULSO.

LLEGAN a la PUERTA del DESPACHO de TROTSKI. ESTÁ PROTEGIDO por la GUARDIA ROJA. SOFÍA, MIENTRAS ESPERAN, HABLA CON UN CENTINELA. DE PRONTO... ¡ZAS! ¡NO HAY LUZ! ¡NADIE VE NADA!

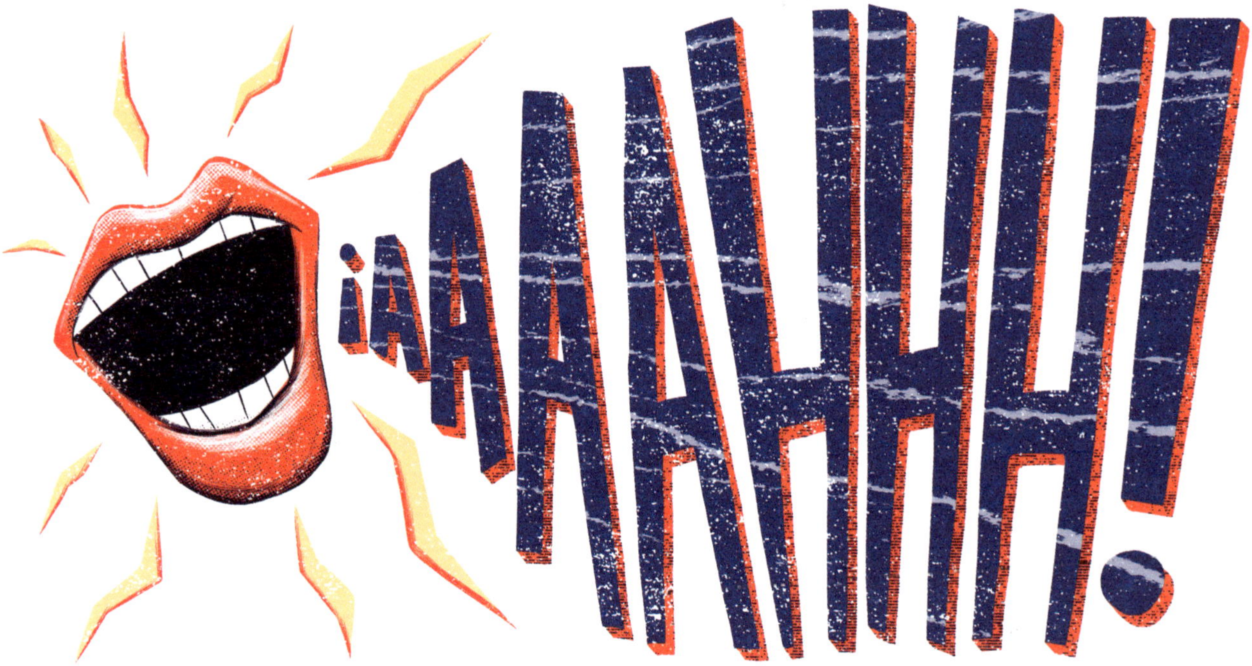

PEPA DA UN GRITO ESCALOFRIANTE y, ATERRORIZADA, SE AGARRA a SU SEÑORA. Al MOMENTO, VUELVE la LUZ. NO HA SIDO MÁS que UN SUSTO; UN CORTE de ELECTRICIDAD en UNA NOCHE de PERROS; «UN MOMENTO de PINTORESCA EMOCIÓN», PIENSA, TRANQUILA, SOFÍA.

–LES RUEGO que PASEN –DICE un SOLDADO.

ATRAVIESAN UNA SALA LLENA de SILLAS y MÁQUINAS de ESCRIBIR. AL FONDO, en UN PEQUEÑO GABINETE, ESPERA TROTSKI. El REVOLUCIONARIO de GAFAS, BIGOTE y PERILLA OFRECE a SOFÍA UN SILLÓN y a PEPA UN SOFÁ. APARTE de UNA MESA y UNA SILLA, en la HABITACIÓN NO HAY MÁS MUEBLES. AMABLEMENTE les DICE en FRANCÉS:

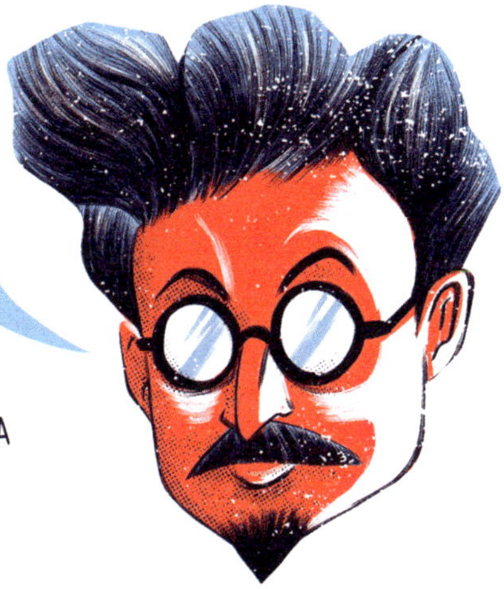

HABLAN de la GUERRA y de la REVOLUCIÓN y, al RATO, se DESPIDEN.

–ME ALEGRO de HABERLA CONOCIDO y, POR SU CONDUCTO, ENVÍO UN SALUDO a ESPAÑA –DICE TROTSKI ANTES de VOLVER a METER SU CABEZA en los CIENTOS de DOCUMENTOS que TIENE ENCIMA de la MESA.

SOFÍA, al LLEGAR a CASA, ESCRIBE en SU DIARIO UNAS PRIMERAS NOTAS: LAS IMPRESIONES INMEDIATAS ANTES de REDACTAR la ENTREVISTA que PUBLICARÁ en el DIARIO «ABC».

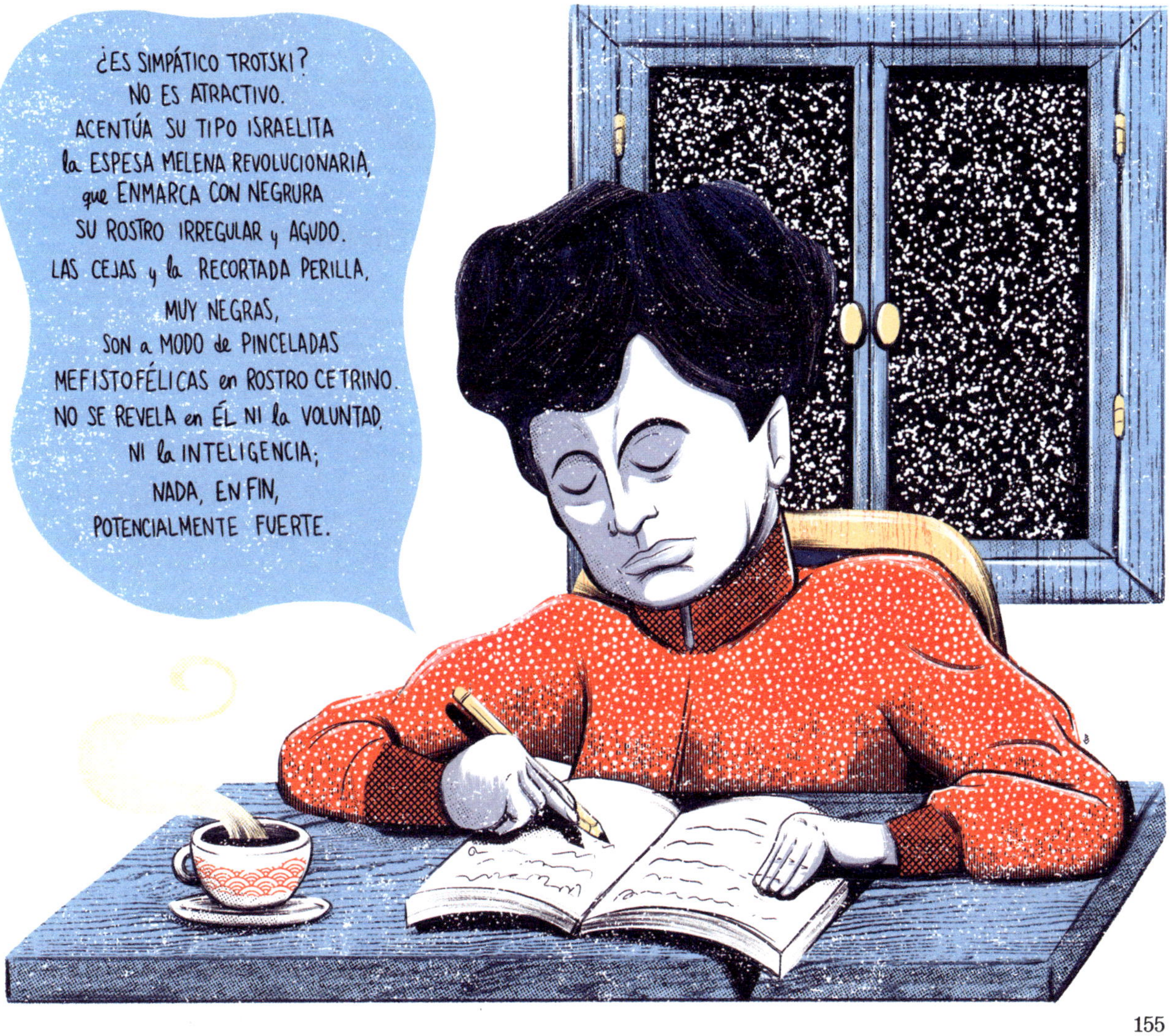

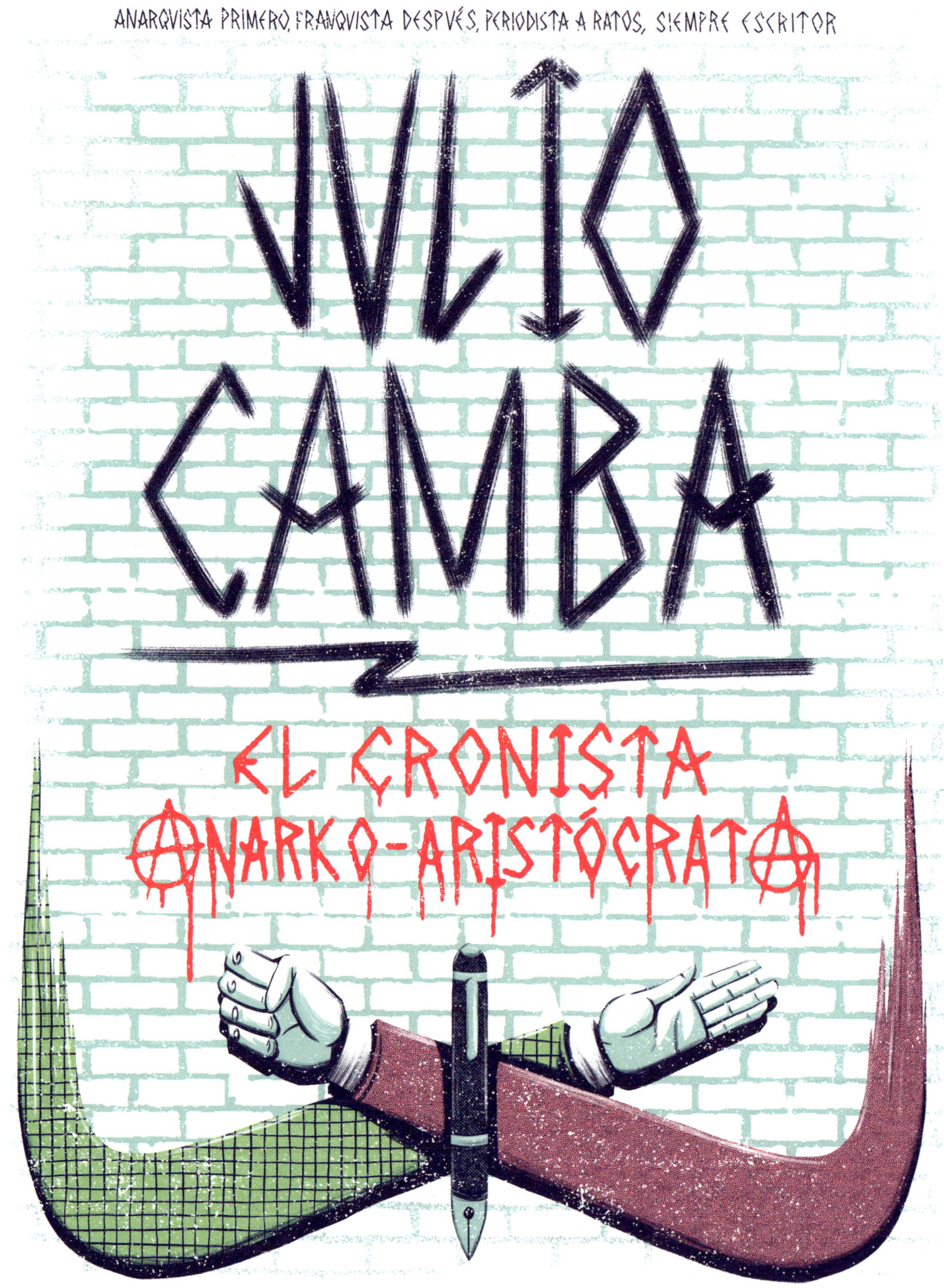
ANARQUISTA PRIMERO, FRANQUISTA DESPUÉS, PERIODISTA A RATOS, SIEMPRE ESCRITOR
JULIO CAMBA
EL CRONISTA ANARKO-ARISTÓCRATA

ESTA MAÑANA de FEBRERO de 1907, los LECTORES del PERIÓDICO «ESPAÑA NUEVA» DESAYUNAN con UN ARTÍCULO INOPINADO. El GOBIERNO HA ANUNCIADO la CONVOCATORIA de ELECCIONES GENERALES y el ESCRITOR CRISTÓBAL de CASTRO, DESCREÍDO de los POLÍTICOS, PROPONE a OTROS CANDIDATOS para REGIR el PAÍS.

EN VEZ de los «NOMBRES PÚTRIDOS» de los DIPUTADOS de OFICIO, da UNA LISTA de ESCRITORES JÓVENES. ENTRE ELLOS, JULIO CAMBA (1884-1962), UN CRONISTA AVISPADO de PLUMA en GUARDIA.

CAMBA es SU CANDIDATO «ANARKO-ARISTÓCRATA». PORQUE, COMO ANARQUISTA, FUNDÓ el PERIÓDICO «EL REBELDE» con SOLO DIECINUEVE AÑOS. PORQUE, en SUS FORMAS, BIEN SE PODRÍA DECIR que ES ARISTÓCRATA (y MÁS lo SERÁ CUANDO, de VIEJO, DECIDA IRSE a VIVIR a UNA HABITACIÓN del HOTEL PALACE y BAJE a ECHAR la SIESTA a la ROTONDA, UNA de SUS SALAS MÁS LUJOSAS).

EL TÍTULO de «ANARKO-ARISTÓCRATA» NO es NUEVO. TIENE un INVENTOR: el DRAMATURGO MARIANO ALARCÓN, que, al LEERLO, SALTA INDIGNADO: «¡ESTO es INTOLERABLE!». FLEMÁTICO, CAMBA RESPONDE: «PARA SER ANARKO-ARISTÓCRATA NO BASTA RIZARSE los BIGOTES con TENACILLAS, QUITARSE las MANCHAS del FRAC y DARSE LUSTRE en los SALONES de LIMPIABOTAS. SE ES o NO SE ES».

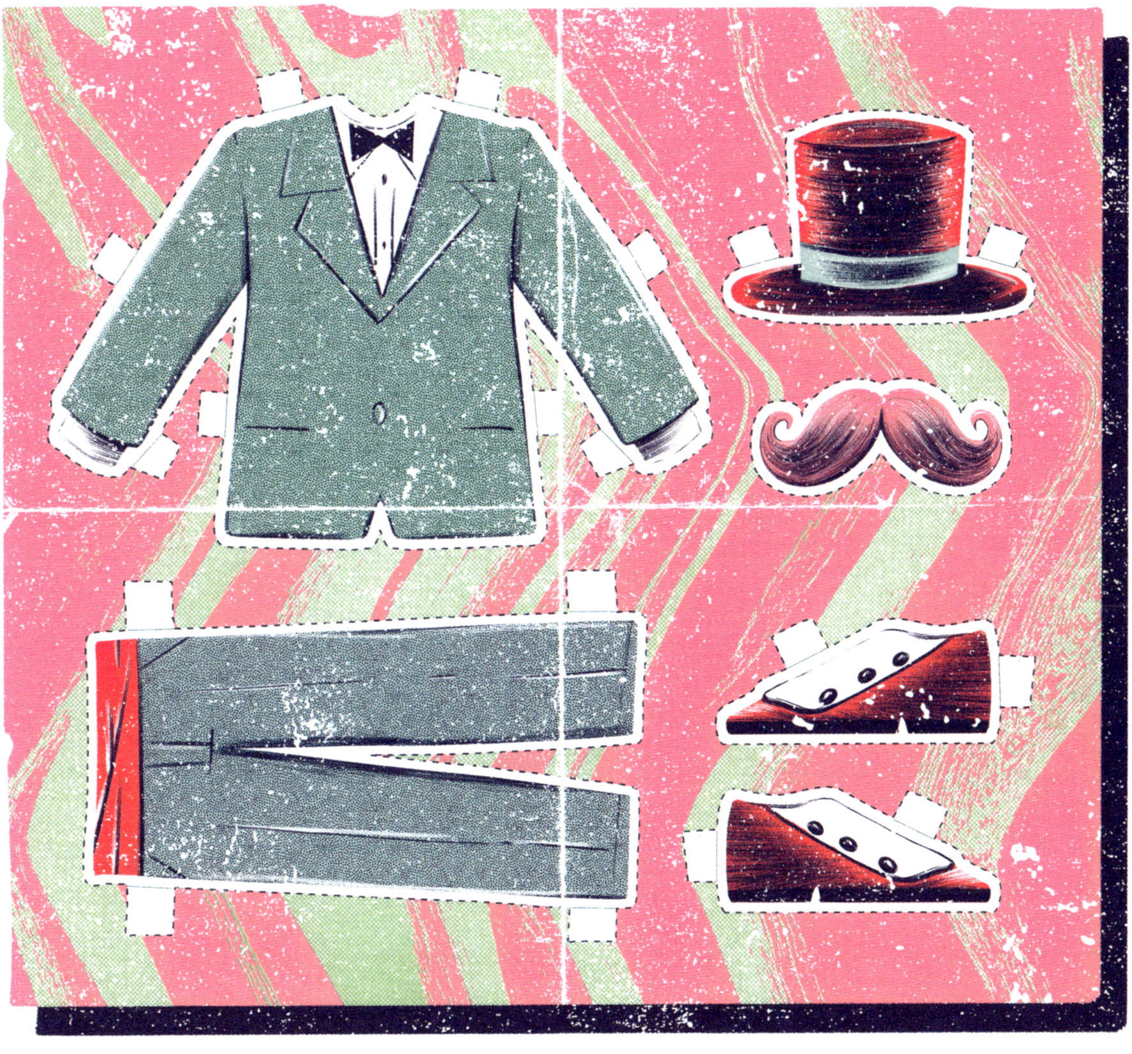

OTRA MAÑANA, TRES MESES DESPUÉS, CAMBA PASEA por los ALREDEDORES del CONGRESO de UNA ESPAÑA que AHORA PRESIDE el CONSERVADOR ANTONIO MAURA. A ESPALDAS del HEMICICLO SE ENCUENTRA con **DON BENITO PÉREZ GALDÓS**, y al DÍA SIGUIENTE, en VEZ de RELATAR los DISCUSIONES PARLAMENTARIAS, CUENTA en «ESPAÑA NUEVA» el DIÁLOGO a PIE de CALLE.

¿QUÉ PRIVILEGIOS TIENE la CARRERA de SAN JERÓNIMO SOBRE la CALLE del TURCO, para que lo QUE SE DICE en la PRIMERA SE RECOJA TAQUIGRÁFICAMENTE y, en CAMBIO, se HAGA OMISIÓN ABSOLUTA de lo que SE DICE en la SEGUNDA?

El AUTOR de los VENERADOS «EPISODIOS NACIONALES» VA DANDO CHUPADAS a la BOQUILLA de SU CIGARRO MIENTRAS HABLA:

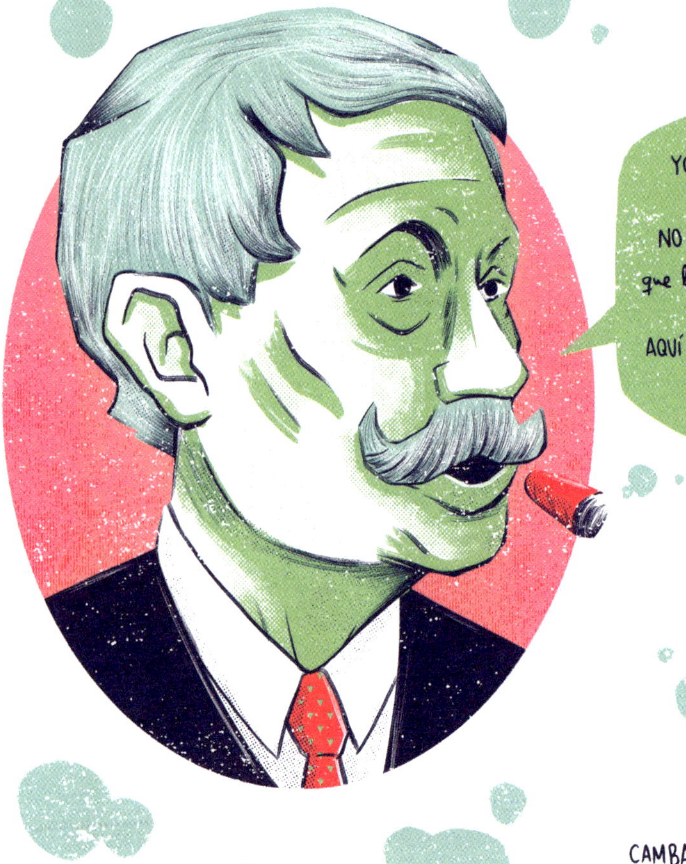

YO HE TOMADO ESTO con MUCHO CALOR, pero YA ESTOY COMPLETAMENTE DESENGAÑADO. ESTO es UNA FARSA. NO HAY NADA MÁS HIPÓCRITA, MÁS FALSO, NI MÁS MISERABLE que la VIDA POLÍTICA de ESPAÑA. El SUFRAGIO UNIVERSAL es, ENTRE NOSOTROS, la MAYOR de las MENTIRAS. AQUÍ HAY UNOS CUANTOS CABALLEROS que DISTRIBUYEN las ACTAS TRES DÍAS ANTES de las ELECCIONES con UN CINISMO ESPANTOSO.

CAMBA ADVIERTE en la VOZ del MAESTRO UNA NOBLE INDIGNACIÓN y UNA INOCENCIA INDIGNADA. PIENSA que HABLA COMO el que ACABA de DESCUBRIR ALGO INSÓLITO.

MIRE USTED, AQUÍ SE HACE un CONCURSO para PREMIAR a UN MAESTRO de MÚSICA. ACUDEN TREINTA OPOSITORES y SE PASAN QUINCE DÍAS TRABAJANDO. AL CABO de los QUINCE DÍAS LLEGA UNA PERSONA BIEN INFORMADA y les DICE: «NO SE MOLESTEN USTEDES. El PREMIO es para FULANO. ESTÁ RESUELTO desde el AÑO PASADO».

DON BENITO DESLIZA la CONVERSACIÓN hacia las CRÓNICAS PARLAMENTARIAS que ESCRIBE CAMBA:

LEO TODOS los DÍAS el «DIARIO de un ESCÉPTICO». ME GUSTÓ el TONO GENERAL que USTED le HA DADO, pero ME PARECE que DEBIERA SER MÁS ESCÉPTICO. ANTE UNA FARSA TAN ODIOSA COMO la PARLAMENTARIA HAY que REVESTIRSE de UN ESCEPTICISMO PROFUNDO y VIOLENTO.

El MAESTRO da la MANO al CRONISTA y ENTRA en la REDACCIÓN de «El LIBERAL». ESA TARDE, CAMBA ESCUCHA a los ELOCUENTES ORADORES que DISCUTEN en el PARLAMENTO, y RECUERDA el MEJOR de los DISCURSOS que HA OÍDO en MUCHO TIEMPO: El de GALDÓS, «UN HOMBRE ILUSTRE, BUENO y HONRADO, que, DESPUÉS de OBSERVAR la VIDA POLÍTICA NACIONAL, SE ESTREMECE de INDIGNACIÓN CONTRA ELLA y DICE: "AQUÍ lo que HACE FALTA es UNA REVOLUCIÓN FORMIDABLE"».

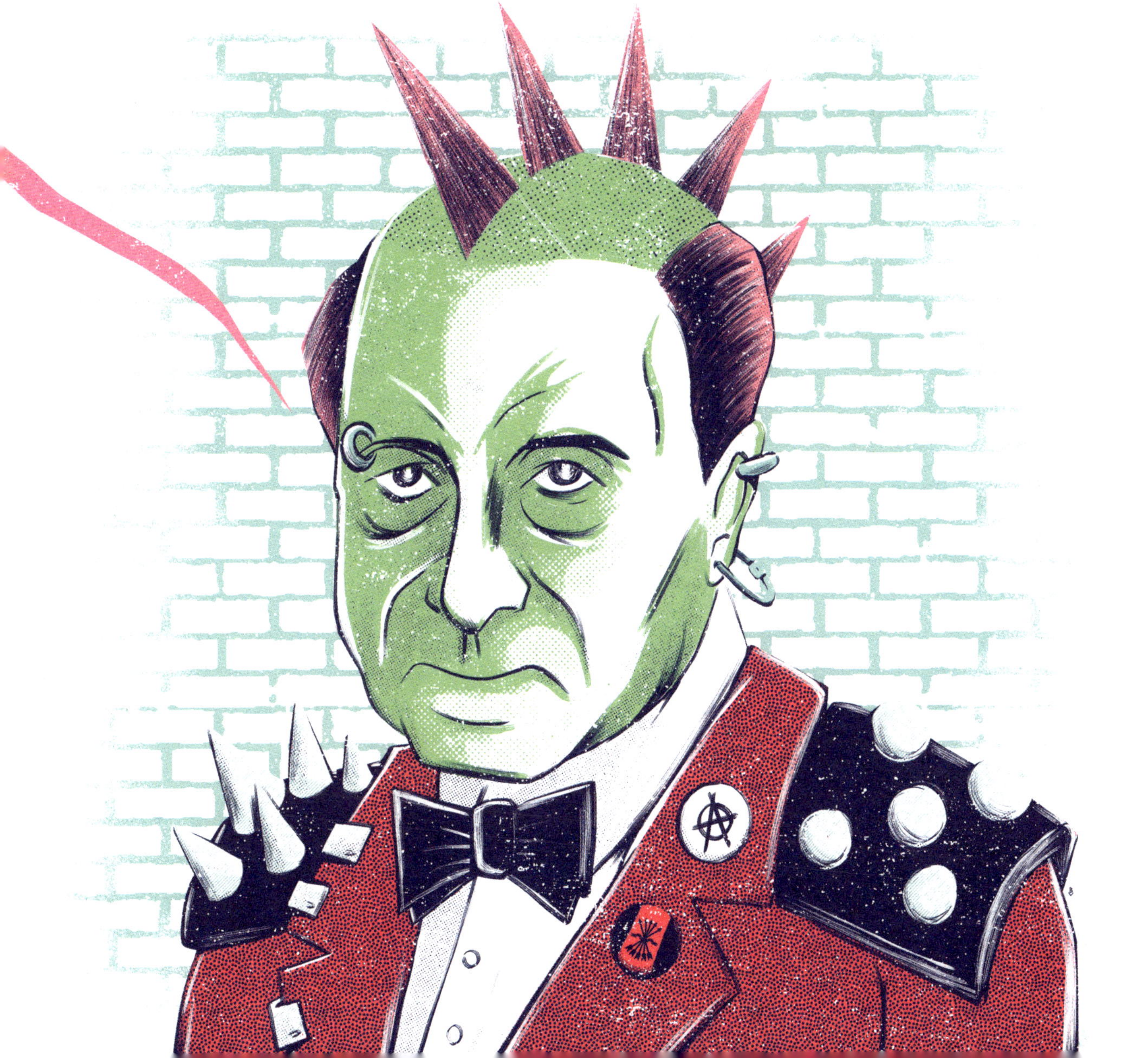

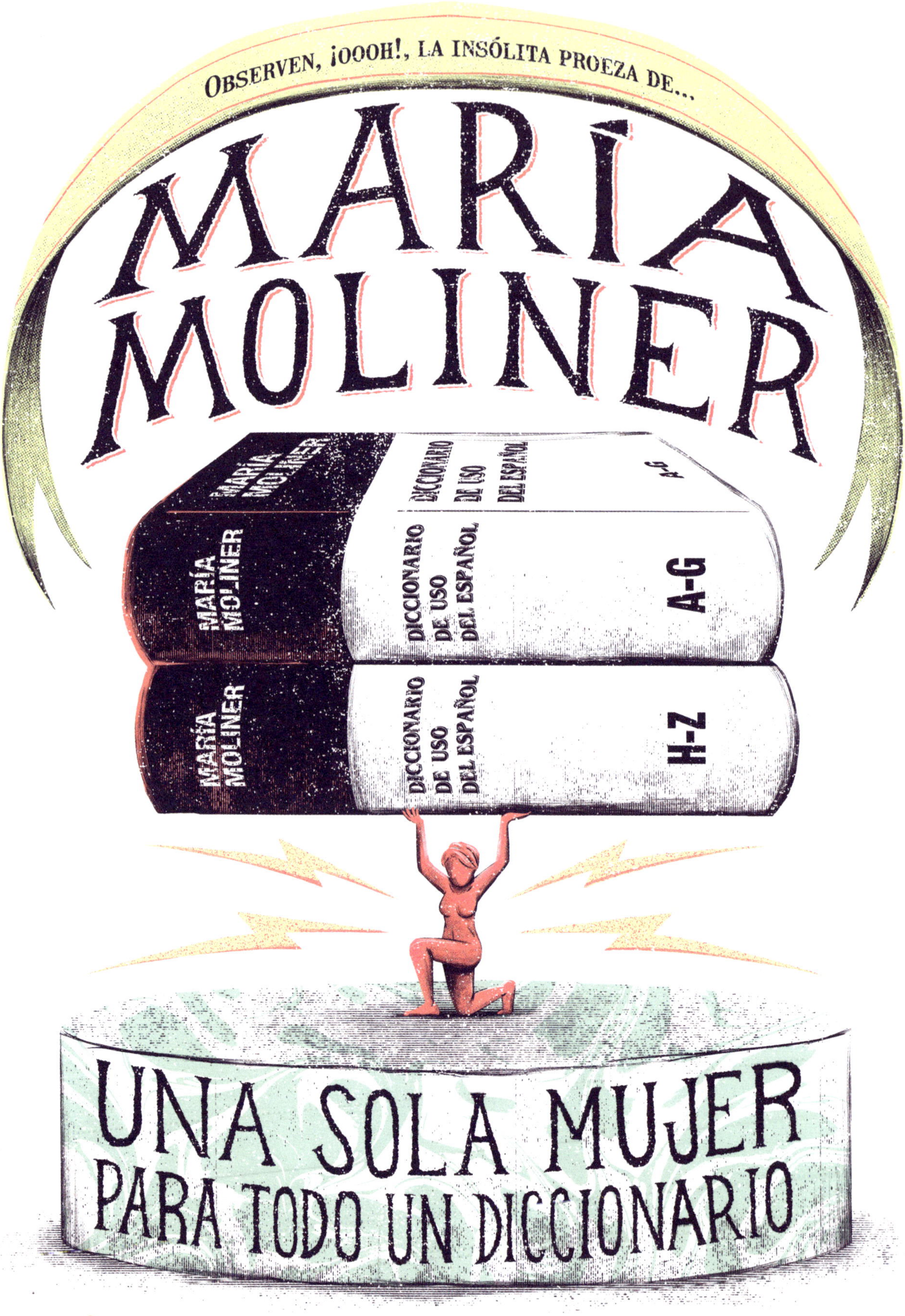
OBSERVEN, ¡OOOH!, LA INSÓLITA PROEZA DE...
MARÍA MOLINER
MARÍA MOLINER
DICCIONARIO DE USO DEL ESPAÑOL
A-G
MARÍA MOLINER
DICCIONARIO DE USO DEL ESPAÑOL
A-G
MARÍA MOLINER
DICCIONARIO DE USO DEL ESPAÑOL
H-Z
UNA SOLA MUJER
PARA TODO UN DICCIONARIO

ERA UNA TARDE PLOMIZA MÁS de la POSGUERRA. AQUEL DÍA de FEBRERO de 1952 ESTABA SOLA en CASA. LOS HIJOS ERAN MAYORES; el MARIDO TRABAJABA LEJOS, en SALAMANCA, CASTIGADO por los VENCEDORES de la GUERRA.

MARÍA MOLINER (1900-1981) EXTENDIÓ UNA CUARTILLA en la MESA del SALÓN y ESBOZÓ el ESQUELETO de UN NUEVO DICCIONARIO de la LENGUA ESPAÑOLA.

DE JOVEN SOÑABA CON CREAR UN COLEGIO. ESTABA CONVENCIDA de que la ÚNICA FORMA de MODERNIZAR ESPAÑA ERA CON EDUCACIÓN Y ASÍ lo HIZO en la SEGUNDA REPÚBLICA: COMO DELEGADA de MISIONES PEDAGÓGICAS, ORGANIZÓ UNA RED de 105 BIBLIOTECAS RURALES en VALENCIA.

PERO en los AÑOS CINCUENTA, DEPURADA por el RÉGIMEN FRANQUISTA, TRABAJABA, APLASTADA, en UNA PEQUEÑA BIBLIOTECA de la ESCUELA de INGENIEROS de MADRID. ALLÍ, la que ALGUNOS LLAMABAN «LA ROJA» POCO PODÍA HACER.

«HABÍA UN PUNTO, el de la TARDE, en que REALMENTE ME SENTÍA VACÍA, SENTÍA que ALGO ME FALTABA, y ENTONCES ME PUSE a TRABAJAR en el DICCIONARIO con TODO ENTUSIASMO», CONTÓ en 1972, en UNA ENTREVISTA con el «HERALDO de ARAGÓN».

FUE en SU HOGAR, SITUADO en la CALLE DON QUIJOTE, DONDE VOLCÓ SU TALENTO. En AQUEL SALÓN CONFLUYERON SU INTELIGENCIA (FUE PREMIO EXTRAORDINARIO de FILOSOFÍA y LETRAS en 1921) y SU DON de ORGANIZACIÓN (FUE la MUJER del JERSEY VERDE que DABA los NÚMEROS en la PANADERÍA, en los AÑOS de GUERRA, PARA que el HAMBRE NO ARMARA UN SINDIÓS).

EN SU DOMICILIO HABÍA UN DESPACHO, pero ERA del MARIDO (COSAS de AQUEL TIEMPO). TOMÓ ENTONCES la MESA del COMEDOR, la MÁS GRANDE de la CASA, y COLOCÓ LARGAS TIRAS de PAPEL, CIENTOS de FICHAS, SU OLIVETTI PLUMA 22 y VARIOS LIBROS de CONSULTA.

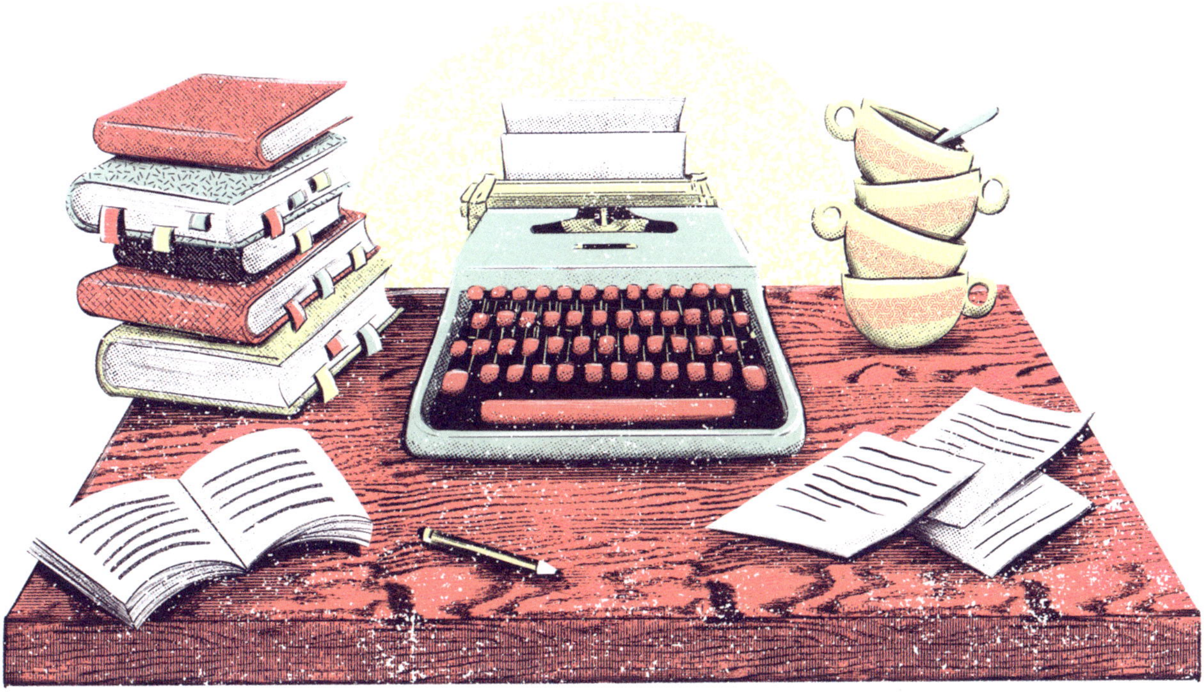

MOLINER EMPEZÓ a ANOTAR las PALABRAS del IDIOMA, UNA a UNA, para DARLES UNA NUEVA DESCRIPCIÓN. PENSABA que las DEFINICIONES del DICCIONARIO de la RAE ERAN ACARTONADAS: COMPLEJAS, LEJANAS, ROCAMBOLESCAS.

ELLA QUERÍA EXPLICAR el SIGNIFICADO de CADA VOZ CON CLARIDAD. Y lo CONSIGUIÓ: «REDACTABA las ACEPCIONES de UN MODO MARAVILLOSO. TENÍA ALMA de LINGÜISTA y las PALABRAS le DEBÍAN de BAILAR en la CABEZA», DECÍA SU EDITOR, JULIO CALONGE.

TAMBIÉN QUERÍA ESTABLECER UNA CLASIFICACIÓN MÁS LÓGICA, MÁS MATEMÁTICA: MOLINER ORGANIZÓ las VOCES por FAMILIAS de PALABRAS y NO SOLO por ORDEN ALFABÉTICO.

POCOS AÑOS DESPUÉS, DÁMASO ALONSO VIO ESAS TARJETAS. ¡OH! El ACADÉMICO de la RAE QUEDÓ ATÓNITO. ESAS FICHAS ERAN el PUNTAL de UNA OBRA FORMIDABLE. ¡CUÁNTA ERUDICIÓN en UNOS PAPELES de ANDAR por CASA! ¡HABÍA que PUBLICAR!

MENUDA HAZAÑA: PUBLICAR UN DICCIONARIO ESCRITO por UNA MUJER y, ¡ENCIMA!, con UN PASADO REPUBLICANO. PERO DÁMASO ALONSO lo CONSIGUIÓ: EN 1955, MARÍA MOLINER FIRMÓ UN CONTRATO CON la EDITORIAL GREDOS.

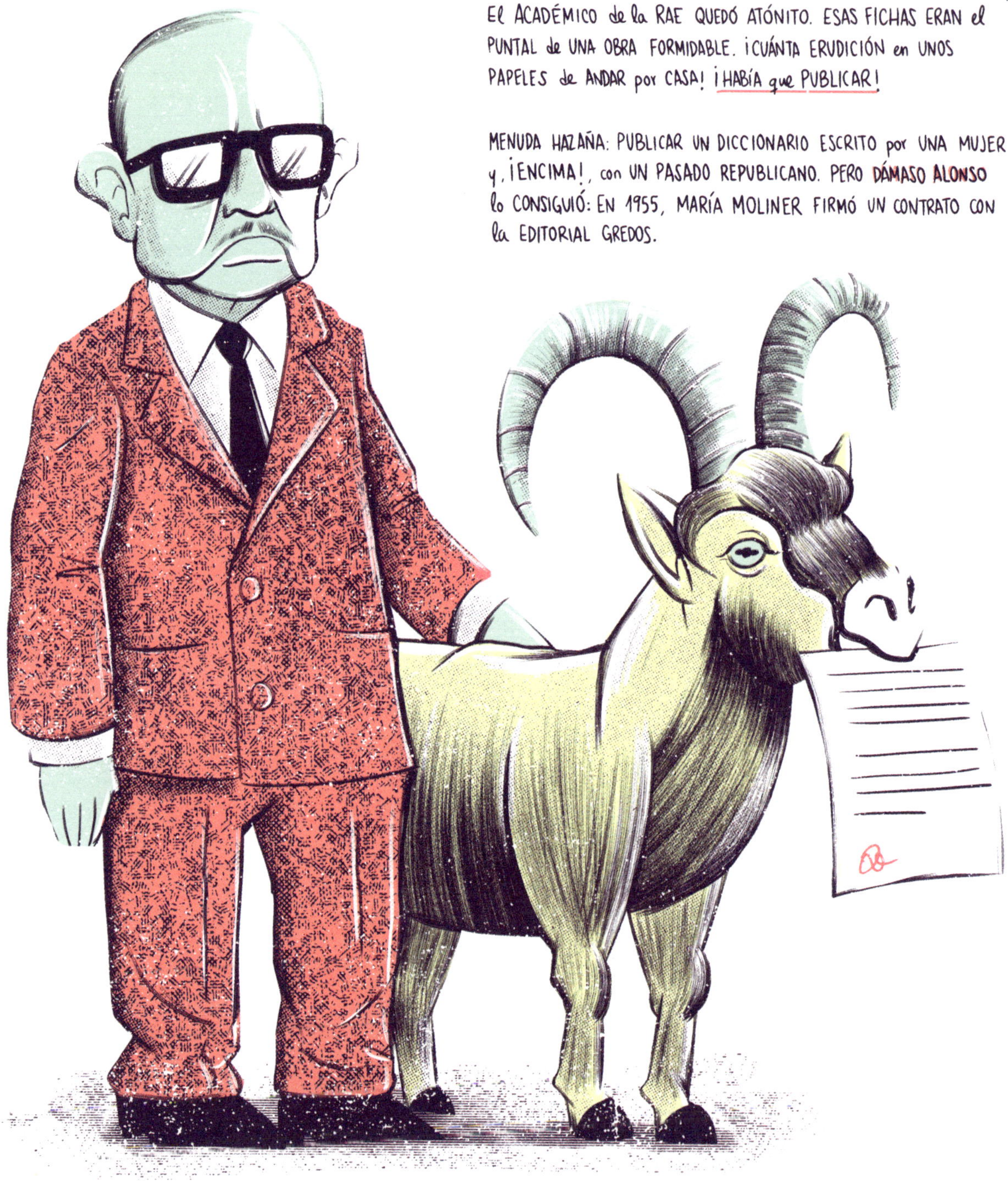

EL PISO de la ARCHIVERA SIGUIÓ LLENÁNDOSE de FICHAS ORDENADAS en CAJAS de ZAPATOS. TUVO que DEJAR CAJONES LIBRES, y MÁS CAJONES LIBRES, para que ENTRARAN las DEFINICIONES. LAS FAMILIAS de PALABRAS OCUPARON CADA RINCÓN de la CASA. TRABAJABA SIN DESCANSO:

«ENTRE las HORAS de la BIBLIOTECA y las HORAS en que YO ESTABA con la CABEZA INCLINADA SOBRE el DICCIONARIO, HABÍA TEMPORADAS de MÁS de QUINCE HORAS DIARIAS», CONTÓ en 1972.

EN 1966 APARECIÓ el PRIMER VOLUMEN del «DICCIONARIO de USO del ESPAÑOL» y UN AÑO DESPUÉS LLEGÓ el SEGUNDO. TODOS QUEDARON ADMIRADOS con el «DICCIONARIO de MARÍA MOLINER». GABRIEL GARCÍA MÁRQUEZ lo DEFINIÓ COMO «EL MAS COMPLETO, MÁS ÚTIL, MÁS ACUCIOSO y MÁS DIVERTIDO de la LENGUA CASTELLANA. ES MÁS de DOS VECES MÁS LARGO que el de la REAL ACADEMIA de la LENGUA y, a MI JUICIO, MÁS de DOS VECES MEJOR».

¿NO MERECÍA la AUTORA de SEMEJANTE OBRA UNA SILLA en la RAE? EN 1972 la PROPUSIERON para la ACADEMIA, pero, OTRA VEZ, CERRARON la PUERTA a UNA SABIA por un PEQUEÑO DETALLE: ERA MUJER. ENTONCES MOLINER DIJO:

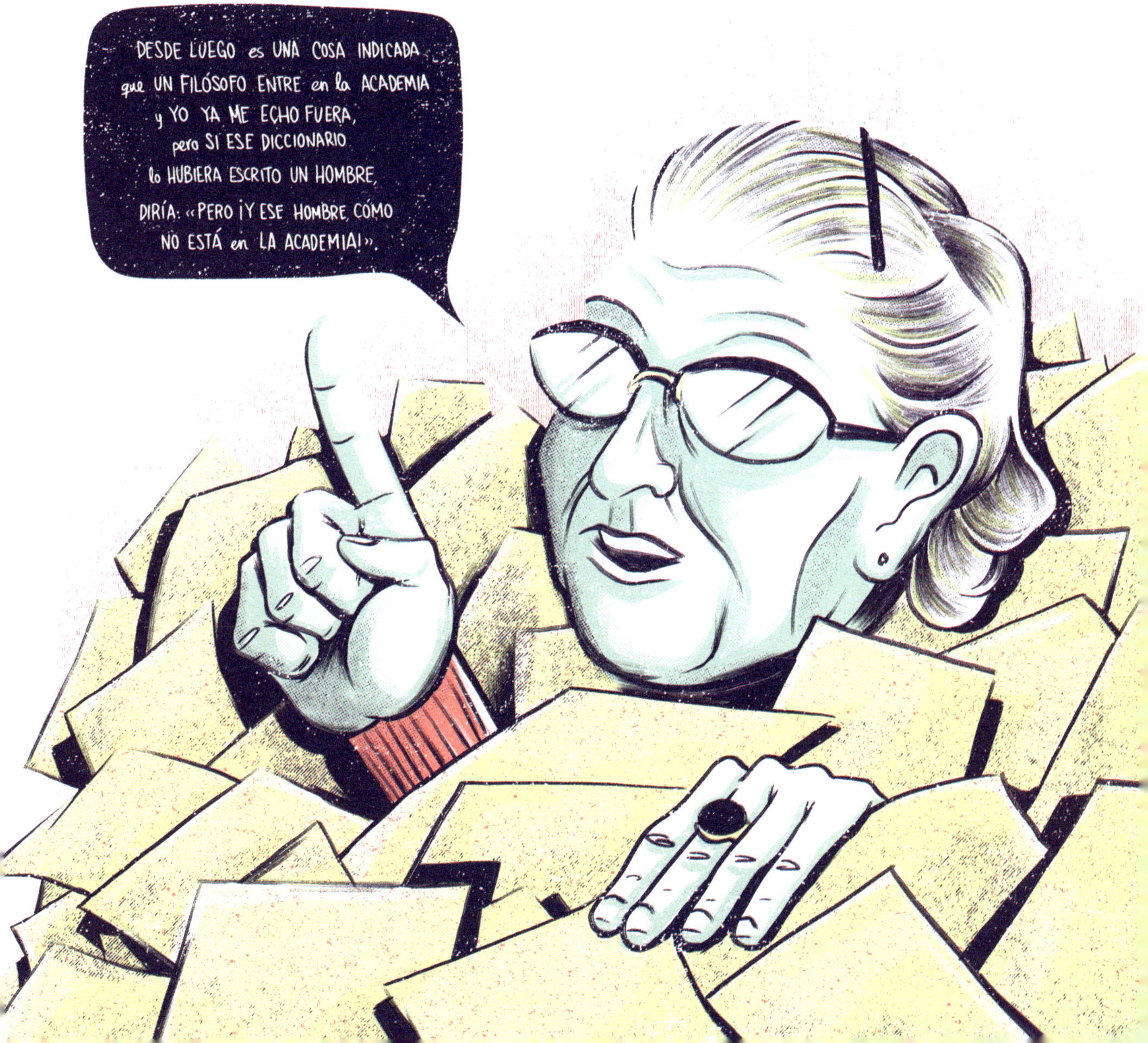

ESTREMECEDORA, ADMIRABLE, MONUMENTAL. CONOZCAN LA VIDA DE...

CANELO

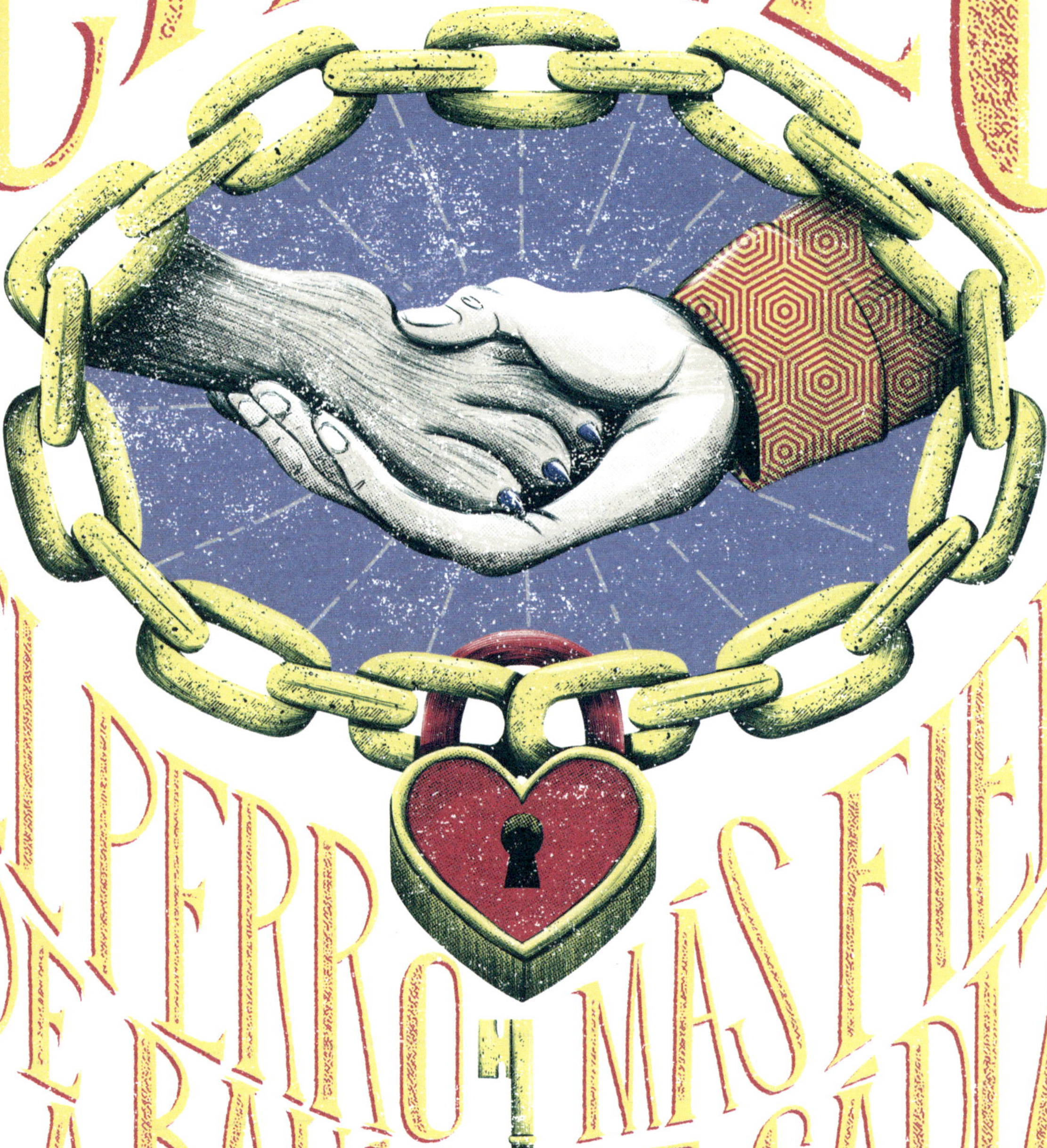

EL PERRO MÁS FIEL DE LA BAHÍA DE CÁDIZ

PASEABAN por CÁDIZ, SIEMPRE JUNTOS, CANELO y SU DUEÑO. El PERRO y el HOMBRE, ENTRE SUS RUTAS, TENÍAN UNA CITA FIJA: EL HOSPITAL PUERTA del MAR. ALLÍ el GADITANO SE HACÍA la DIÁLISIS. CANELO ESPERABA en la PUERTA, OBEDIENTE, SIN MOVERSE UNA CHISPA.

FUE ASÍ la RUTINA de UNOS AÑOS HASTA que UN DÍA ACIAGO de 1990 el AMO DIJO:

«ESPÉRAME AQUÍ, CANELO».

PASÓ la MAÑANA, la TARDE, la NOCHE.

PASÓ el DÍA, el MES, el AÑO.

EL HOMBRE NO VOLVÍA;

CANELO AGUARDABA.

NO HABÍA OTRA IDEA en la CABEZA del PERRO que ESPERAR.
¿CÓMO HACERLE COMPRENDER que SU DUEÑO NO VOLVERÍA NUNCA,
que la ENFERMEDAD FUE MÁS FUERTE que la MEDICINA,
que HABÍA MUERTO de UN INFARTO SIN PODER DECIR ADIÓS?

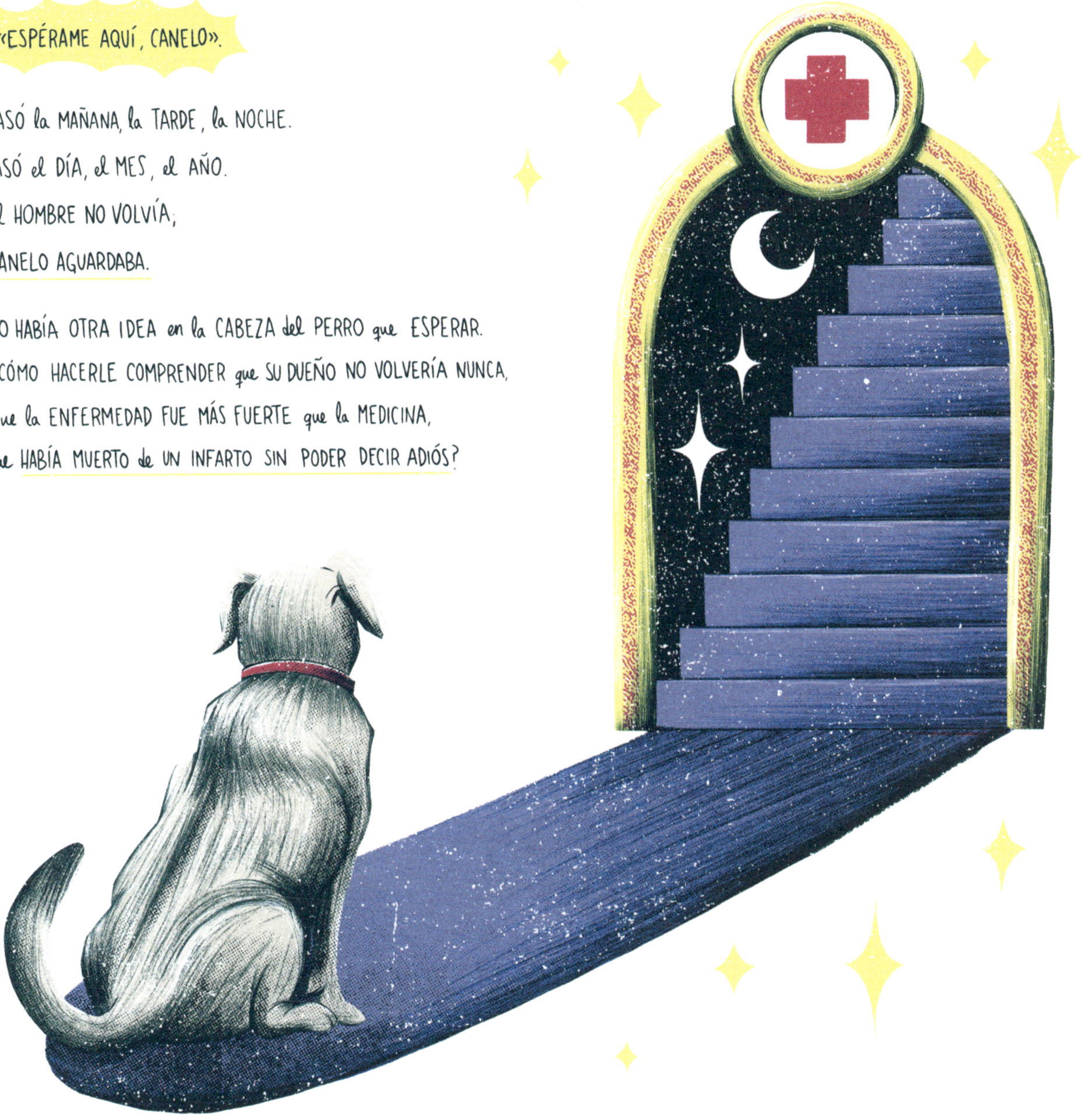

LOS EMPLEADOS del HOSPITAL le DABAN AGUA y COMIDA. EN el RINCÓN DONDE DORMÍA, CON UNOS CARTONES, le HICIERON SU CAMA. LO CUIDABAN TAMBIÉN los VECINOS y, CON los AÑOS, CANELO SE FUE CONVIRTIENDO en el PERRO de TODO CÁDIZ.

PERO HUBO QUIEN lo VIO COMO un CHUCHO INMUNDO y LLAMÓ a la PERRERA. ENTRÓ CANELO en el CENTRO de INTERNAMIENTO y los VECINOS, HORRORIZADOS, RESCATARON al CAN. UNA PROTECTORA de ANIMALES SE ENCARGÓ de SUS VACUNAS, de SUS CUIDADOS y de LLEVARLO de NUEVO al ÚNICO LUGAR DONDE QUERÍA ESTAR: LA PUERTA del HOSPITAL.

VOLVIERON a DENUNCIAR al PERRO. VOLVIÓ a la PERRERA, y ENTONCES el TENIENTE de ALCALDE RESOLVIÓ el ASUNTO para los RESTOS: INDULTÓ a CANELO. ¡QUE DEJEN en PAZ al SER MÁS FIEL de la BAHÍA!

EN SU ETERNA ESPERA ESTABA CANELO UNA TARDE TRÁGICA de 2002. DECÍAN que ANDABA un POCO VIEJO, ALGO SORDO, BASTANTE CIEGO. AL PERRO le GUSTABA ACOMPAÑAR a SUS AMIGOS a CRUZAR el PASO de PEATONES JUNTO al HOSPITAL. IBA, VENÍA; RECIBÍA CARICIAS. PERO ESE DÍA lo que SE LLEVÓ FUE UN RESTREGÓN.

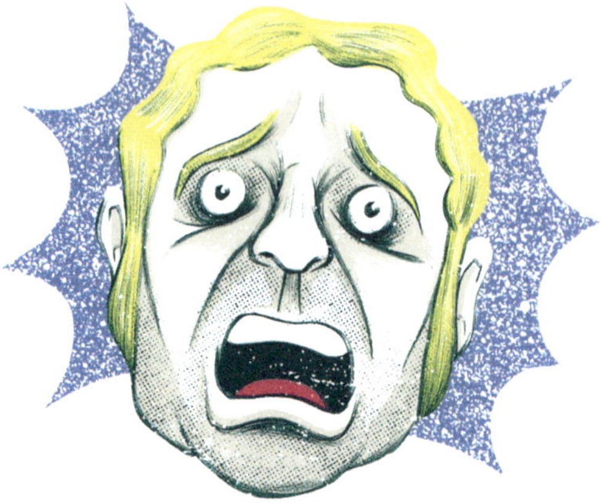

El TAXISTA PEPE «El ALEMÁN» lo SALUDÓ, COMO TODOS los DÍAS.

–¿QUÉ PASA, VIEJO, el PASEÍTO de POR la TARDE? –LE DIJO.

CANELO SE DIRIGÍA al PASO de CEBRA y PEPE, al VER un COCHE, le AVISÓ:

–TEN CUIDADO, CANELO. NO VAYAS a CRUZAR AHORA.

El PERRO CRUZÓ.

–¡QUIETO! –GRITÓ el TAXISTA.

UN VOLVO OSCURO ARROLLÓ al PERRO. LA LARGA ESPERA de CANELO ACABÓ ENTONCES: ASÍ, en UN MOMENTO, de SOPETÓN.

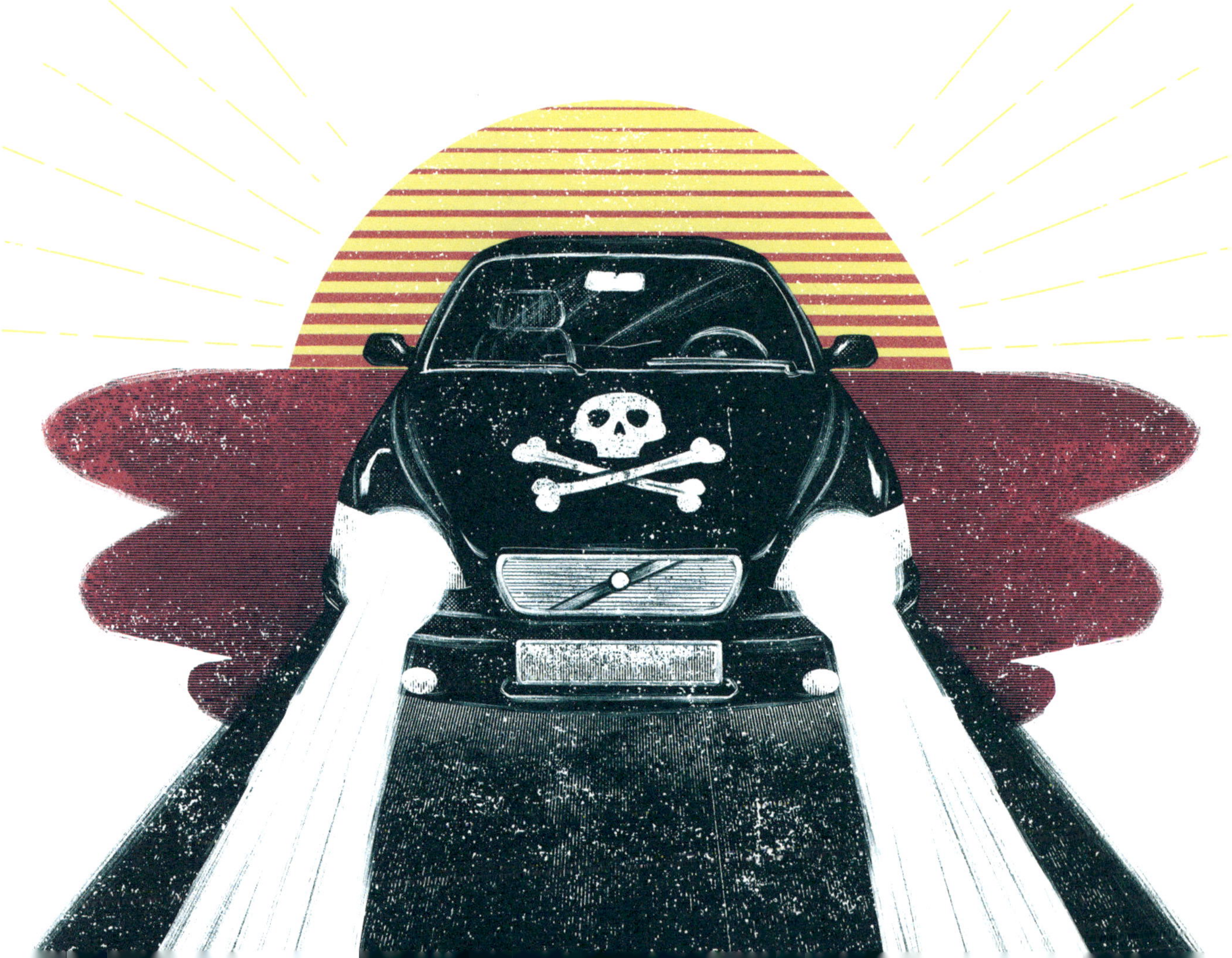

FUE MUERTE de PRIMERA PÁGINA: «CANELO, en el CORAZÓN de TODOS», «EL PERRO MÁS QUERIDO», «MÁS FIEL que MUCHAS PERSONAS», DECÍAN los PERIÓDICOS. «CANELO NUNCA ATACÓ a NADIE. ERA NOBLE, CARIÑOSO y MÁS FIEL que MUCHAS PERSONAS. ANDABA DESPACITO. A VECES SE HACÍA el COJO para ENTERNECER a la GENTE, pero CUANDO OLÍA a UNA PERRITA en CELO CORRÍA a TODA PASTILLA. ERA un PERRO CHULAPÓN, LIGÓN y LISTO COMO el HAMBRE.»

FUE CAN de POSTERIDAD: HACÍA TIEMPO que la CIUDAD QUERÍA un MONUMENTO al PERRO. AHORA, POR FIN, ERA el MOMENTO. La ASOCIACIÓN para la DEFENSA de la NATURALEZA AGADEN ESCRIBIÓ al AYUNTAMIENTO:

«HA ESPERADO DURANTE DOCE AÑOS, a la INTEMPERIE. SE HA NEGADO a IR A UN HOGAR y a VIVIR con UNA FAMILIA. ELLO le GRANJEÓ el CARIÑO y RESPETO de los GADITANOS, y la FAMA en el MUNDO ENTERO, PORQUE CANELO HA SIDO PROTAGONISTA de DOCUMENTALES en CADENAS de TELEVISIÓN de MUCHOS PAÍSES.

HACIÉNDONOS ECO del APOYO de NUMEROSOS CIUDADANOS GADITANOS, TANTO la SOCIEDAD PROTECTORA de ANIMALES de CÁDIZ COMO AGADEN APOYAN que se LEVANTE un MONUMENTO en SU RECUERDO. SERÍA un HOMENAJE a la FIDELIDAD».

HOY, y DESDE 2003, CANELO da NOMBRE a un PASEO PEATONAL en la CIUDAD DONDE es LEYENDA.

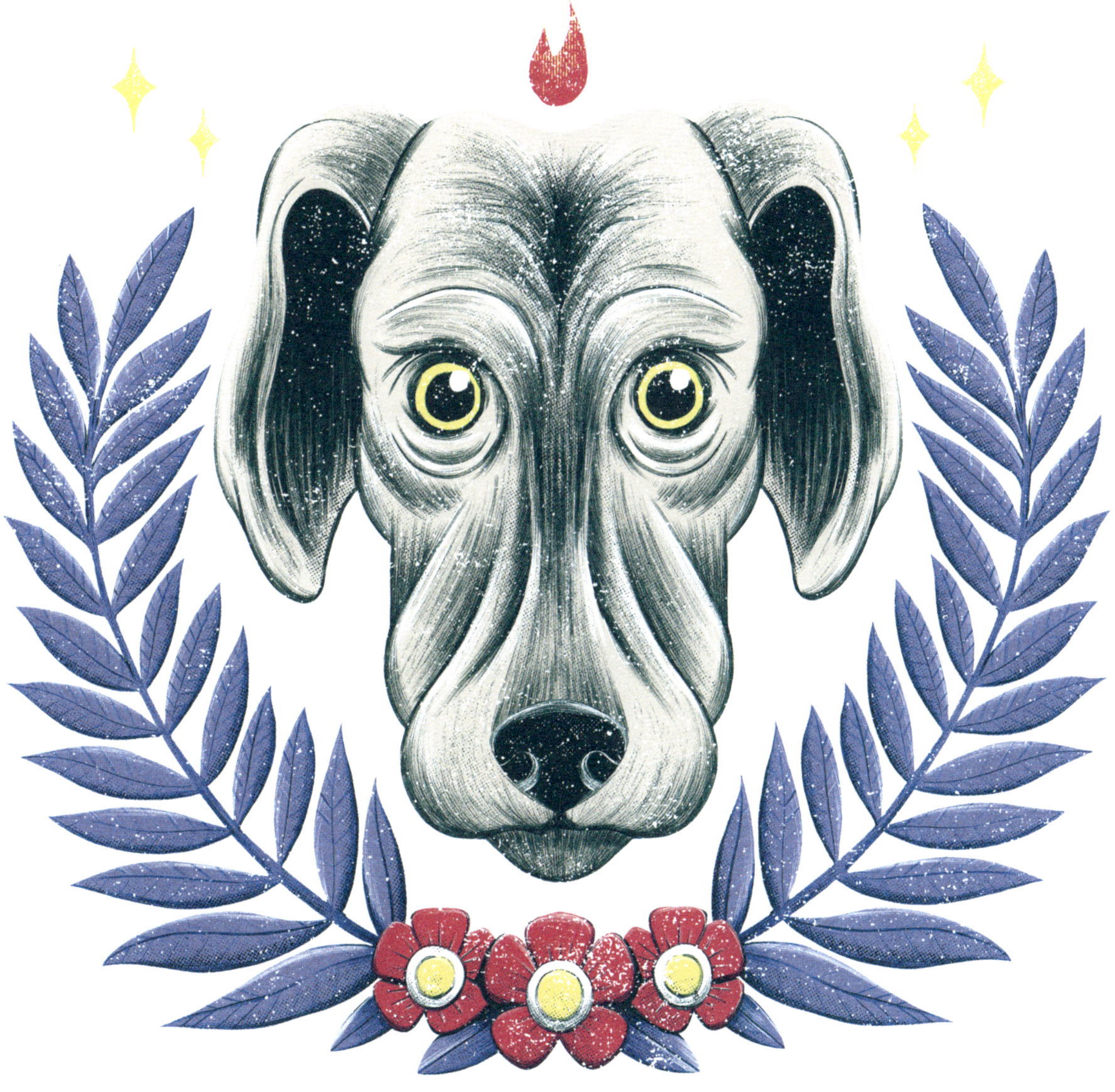

ADMIREN Y APLAUDAN AL GENIAL Y SIN PAR DON...

SANTIAGO RAMÓN Y CAJAL

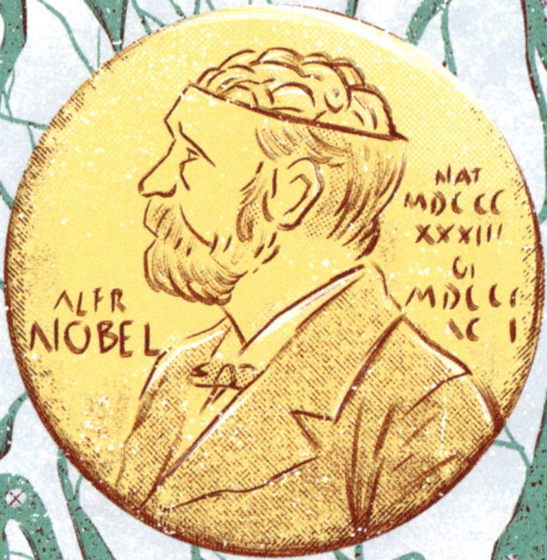

EL PREMIO NOBEL QUE DESCUBRIÓ LOS MISTERIOS DEL CEREBRO

En la PROFUNDIDAD de un MICROSCOPIO, UN MÉDICO ACABA de DESCUBRIR ALGO ASOMBROSO: LAS CÉLULAS del CEREBRO SON INDEPENDIENTES y, ENTRE ELLAS, ENVÍAN y RECIBEN INFORMACIÓN.

El HALLAZGO de SANTIAGO RAMÓN y CAJAL (1852-1934), en el LABORATORIO que HA MONTADO en SU CASA, REVOLUCIONA TODAS las TEORÍAS de los NERVIOS y las NEURONAS DADAS por CIERTAS hasta ESTE AÑO de 1888.

El MÉDICO HUMANISTA SIGUE INVESTIGANDO y DIBUJANDO lo que VE y lo que INTUYE. EN CIENTOS de ILUSTRACIONES y ENSAYOS, en SU SESUDA «HISTORIOLOGÍA del SISTEMA NERVIOSO del HOMBRE y de los VERTEBRADOS», APUNTALA las BASES de la NEUROCIENCIA.

Le LLUEVEN los RECONOCIMIENTOS, INCLUIDO el MAYOR de los MAYÚSCULOS: en 1906 le CONCEDEN el NOBEL de MEDICINA JUNTO al ITALIANO CAMILLO GOLGI. ¡EL PRIMERO que LLEGA a ESPAÑA por UNA APORTACIÓN a la CIENCIA!

DON SANTIAGO SIGUE ESTUDIANDO, PUBLICANDO y, por SUPUESTO, YENDO a TERTULIAS. AHÍ TAMBIÉN APRENDE MUCHO del HUMANO y en 1920 SE ANIMA a PUBLICARLO en UN LIBRO TITULADO «CHÁCHARAS de CAFÉ».

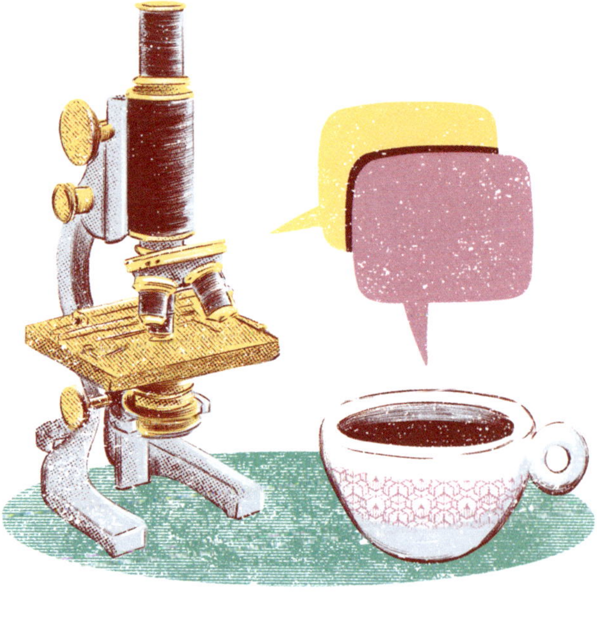

«SON HUMORADAS EXPUESTAS DURANTE CUARENTA AÑOS de ASIDUA ASISTENCIA a las PEÑAS de CAFÉ o de CASINO, DONDE, por MAL de MIS PECADOS, FUI INCANSABLE FANTASEADOR e IRREFRENABLE PARLANCHÍN. Y NO OCULTARÉ que ALGUNAS APRECIACIONES TRADUCEN CONVICCIONES ACTUALES del AUTOR, y DIGO "ACTUALES" PORQUE ME RESERVO el PRECIOSO e INALIENABLE DERECHO de EVOLUCIONAR o RETROGRADAR al COMPÁS de las ENSEÑANZAS de los TIEMPOS.»

En el CAPÍTULO DEDICADO a «El GENIO, el TALENTO y la NECEDAD», DON SANTIAGO ESCRIBE: «DICE el ESPIRITUAL POETA MANUEL MACHADO que, de DIEZ CABEZAS, DOS DISCURREN y OCHO EMBISTEN».

Y da UN CONSEJO al LECTOR: «Las CABEZAS DEBEN JUZGARSE COMO los BOLSILLOS. Al HACERLAS SONAR CON las SACUDIDAS de la CONVERSACIÓN, ADVERTIMOS ENSEGUIDA que UNAS CONTIENEN el ORO de la CIENCIA y del INGENIO, y OTRAS la CALDERILLA de la VULGARIDAD y de la RUTINA».

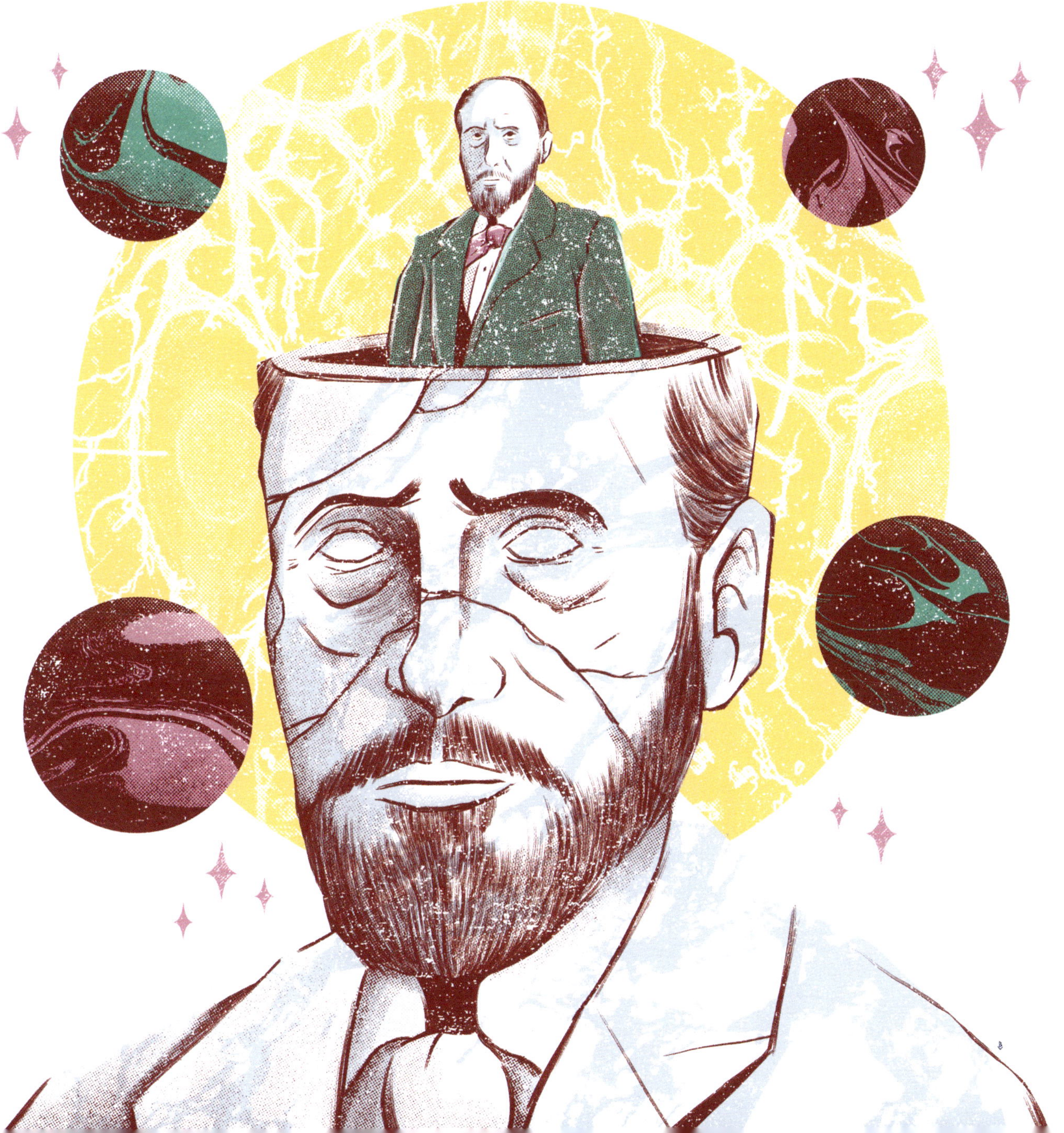

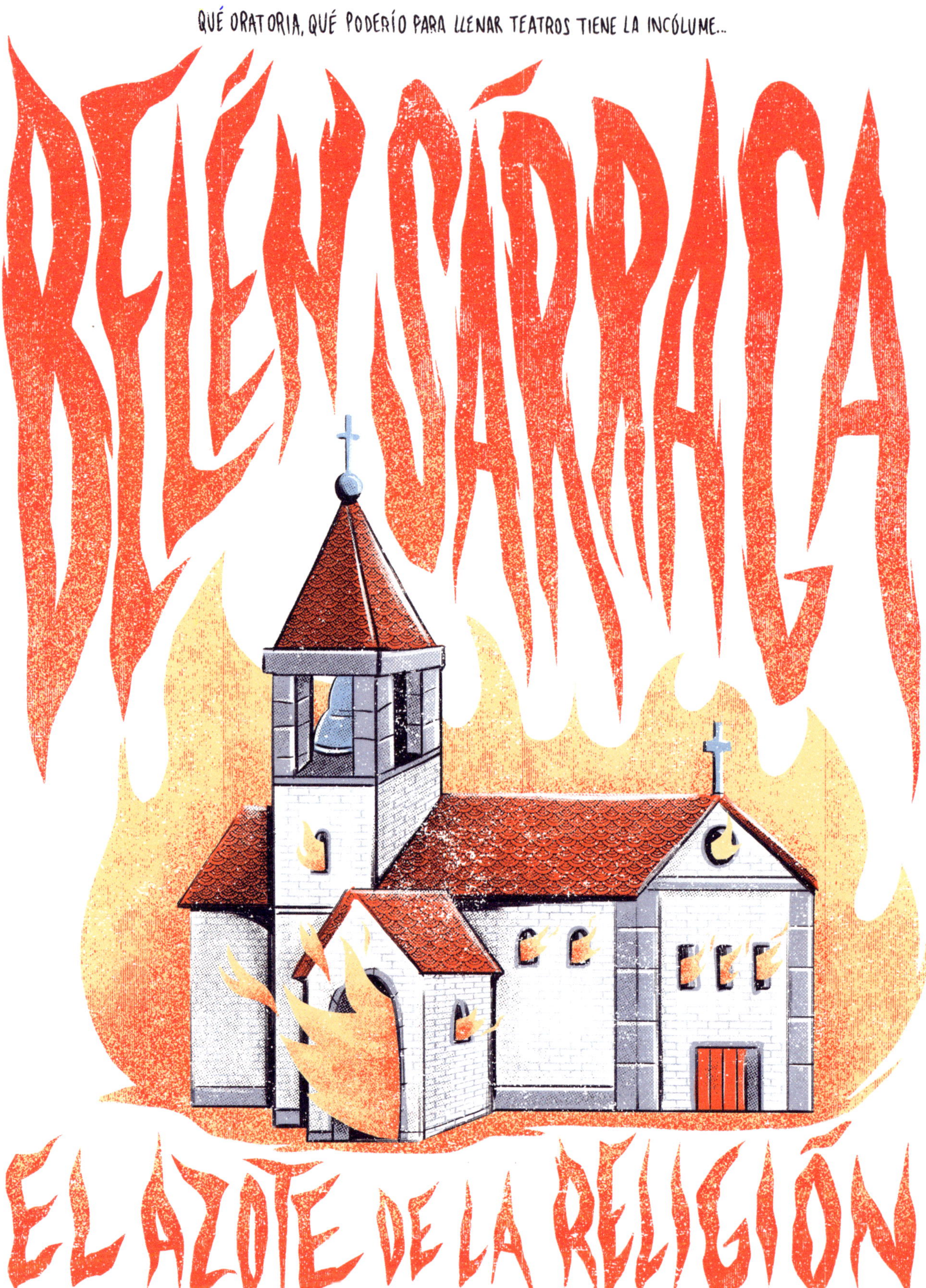
QUÉ ORATORIA, QUÉ PODERÍO PARA LLENAR TEATROS TIENE LA INCÓLUME...
BELÉN SÁRRAGA
EL AZOTE DE LA RELIGIÓN

BELÉN SÁRRAGA (1874-1951) ESTUDIABA MEDICINA en BARCELONA CUANDO TUVO SU PRIMER ENCONTRONAZO con la IGLESIA CATÓLICA. CONTABA DIECINUEVE AÑOS y APENAS HABÍA MUJERES en ESA UNIVERSIDAD. ¡Y QUÉ le IMPORTABA a ELLA! YA ERA INDÓMITA y ROTUNDA.

LA ALUMNA SE PUSO en PRIMERA LÍNEA de UNAS PROTESTAS CONTRA UN OBISPO. El RELIGIOSO HABÍA PEDIDO que QUITARAN la CÁTEDRA al NATURALISTA ODÓN de BUEN y del COS por SUS MANUALES de ZOOLOGÍA, BOTÁNICA y GEOLOGÍA. ¡HEREJE! ¡QUÉ SABRÁ la CIENCIA de los DESIGNIOS del CREADOR!

ESTUDIAR CIENCIA la DISTANCIÓ CADA VEZ MÁS de la IGLESIA. PUEDE que INCLUSO lo LLEVARA en los GENES: SU PADRE ERA REPUBLICANO y MASÓN. ASÍ que, CON el TIEMPO, MÁS que las ENFERMEDADES, le INTERESÓ la LIBERTAD: EN el PENSAMIENTO y en la CALLE.

Y NO HALLÓ MAYOR CADENA que la RELIGIOSA: DECÍA que la CONFESIÓN ERA UNA FORMA de CONTROL; que CONFESARSE ANTE UN CURA ERA lo MÁS INMORAL que UNA MUJER PODÍA HACER. ¿POR QUÉ UNA ESPOSA HA de CONTAR SUS INTIMIDADES a UN CURA y COMPARTIR CON ÉL SUS ASUNTOS PRIVADOS?

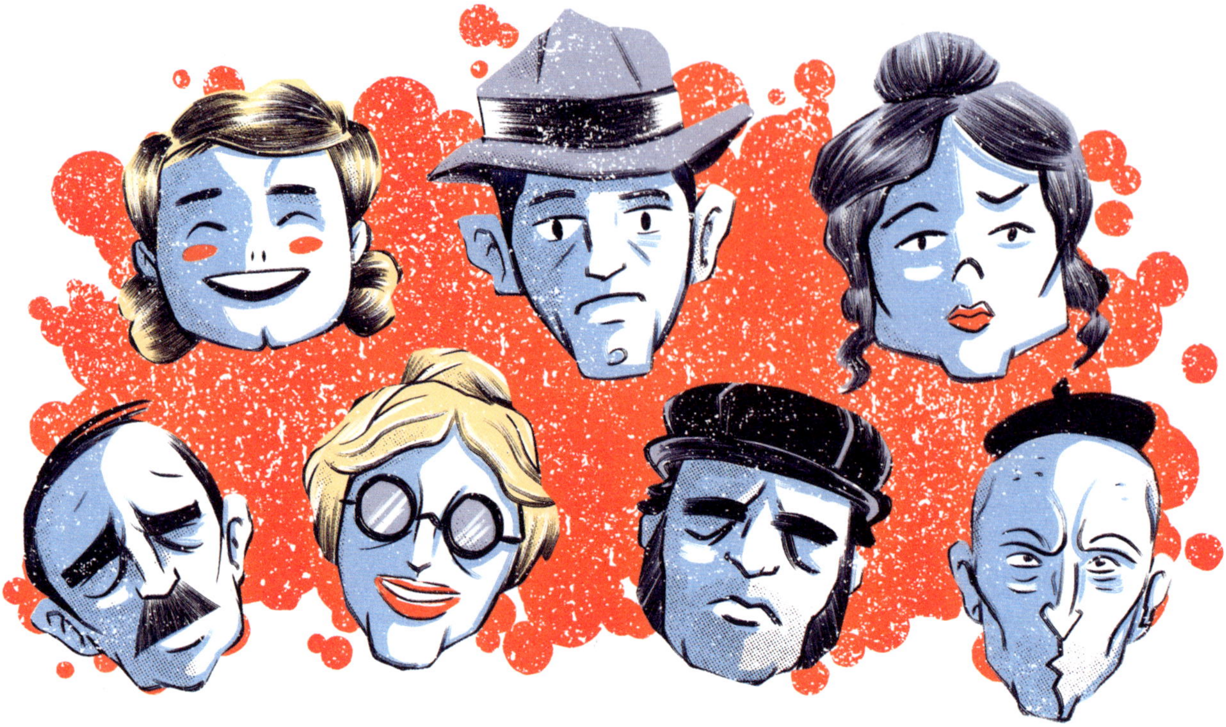

BELÉN DIFUNDÍA SUS IDEAS en «LAS DOMINICALES del LIBREPENSAMIENTO» Y «LA LUZ del PORVENIR». EMPEZÓ a RECORRER CIUDADES, DANDO MÍTINES y LLENANDO TEATROS. ALLÁ DONDE IBA LEVANTABA EXPECTACIÓN: ALGUNOS ACUDÍAN a INSULTARLA (¡MALDITA ATEA!); LA MAYORÍA la APLAUDÍAN y la EXALTABAN.

ABRIÓ ESCUELAS LAICAS y la PRIMERA BIBLIOTECA PÚBLICA RACIONALISTA de VALENCIA. ODIÓ la GUERRA; TANTO, que la ENCERRARON TRES MESES en PRISIÓN ACUSADA de ORGANIZAR UNA MANIFESTACIÓN CONTRA el ENVÍO de SOLDADOS a CUBA. ELLA SE DEFENDIÓ:

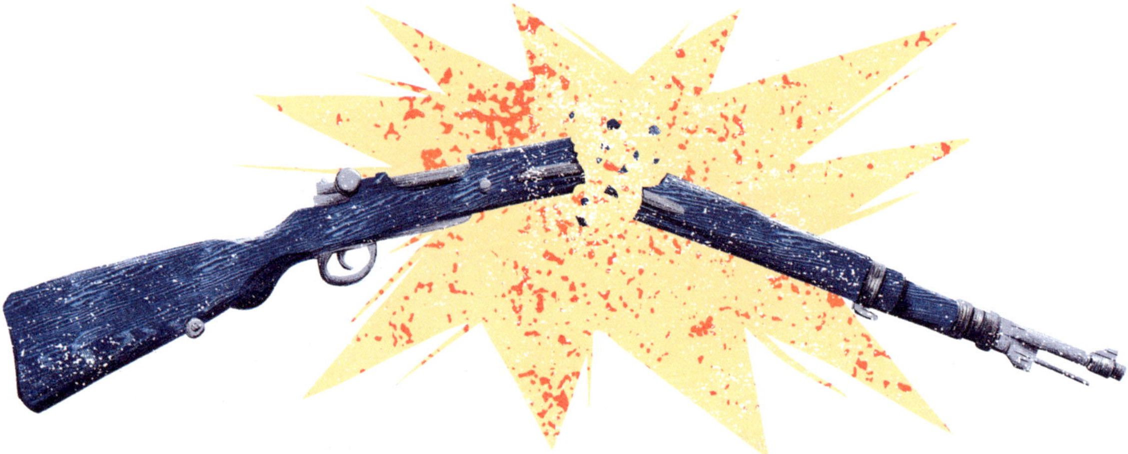

«¿ES DELITO NO AMAR las FRONTERAS? ME DECLARO DELINCUENTE. ¿ES CRIMEN ODIAR las ARMAS de DESTRUCCIÓN? SOY CRIMINAL. PARA MÍ, CUANTO SIGNIFICA INSTRUMENTO de MUERTE es ABORRECIBLE; TANTO ME DA la DINAMITA COMO el CADALSO, el CAÑÓN COMO el PUÑAL».

NI la CÁRCEL la PARÓ. EN 1899 FUE de GIRA MITINERA en PROTESTA por la GUERRA de CUBA, JUNTO con NICOLÁS SALMERÓN, ALEJANDRO LERROUX y BLASCO IBÁÑEZ. LA TENÍAN por UNA ORADORA SIN IGUAL.

A PUNTO ESTABA de TERMINAR el SIGLO XIX CUANDO LLEVÓ SU DISCURSO a SANTANDER. CUANDO YA CASI ACABABAN los CALORES del VERANO, el 31 de AGOSTO, a las NUEVE de la NOCHE, en el TEATRO de la CIUDAD, SE ORGANIZÓ UN MITIN de la LIBREPENSADORA, REPUBLICANA, MASONA, FEMINISTA, ESPIRITISTA y ANTICLERICAL.

EN el PATIO de BUTACAS NO CABÍA UNA MOSCA: EN la CALLE, CIENTOS de PERSONAS PEDÍAN ENTRAR. AL APARECER en el PROSCENIO, le LLUEVEN los APLAUSOS. BELÉN DICE que en ESPAÑA NO HAY SENTIMIENTOS RELIGIOSOS, SINO PURA HIPOCRESÍA. CLAMA que la DECADENCIA del PAÍS SE DEBE a SU CLERICALISMO. PIDE que la MUJER SE LIBERE por FIN y CONTRIBUYA a la OBRA del PROGRESO.

MÁS APLAUSOS. MUCHOS MÁS. PALMAS. PLAS, PLAS, PLAS. LA HIJA de UN OBRERO le ENTREGA UN RAMO de FLORES; LAS ESPOSAS de OTROS OBREROS le REGALAN UNA ESCRIBANÍA de PLATA. Y BELÉN RECITA UNA POESÍA DEDICADA a la LIBERTAD (LA PALABRA que DARÍA NOMBRE a SU HIJA).

SALTABAN CHISPAS de SUS DISCURSOS; ERAN FUEGO y PASIÓN: «EL ACTO RESULTÓ GRANDIOSO. NUNCA HAN VISTO OTRO IGUAL los VECINOS de ESTA INDUSTRIOSA VILLA -PUBLICÓ "EL NOROESTE" DESPUÉS de la CONFERENCIA que DIO en MIERES, en 1899-. EL LOCAL al OBJETO DESTINADO, CON SER MUY ESPACIOSO, RESULTÓ DEFICIENTE para DAR CABIDA a AQUELLAS MULTITUDES que, en ACTITUD HERMOSA y CORRECTA, SE APIÑABAN PARA OÍR la VOZ de DOÑA BELÉN».

A PARTIR de 1907 RECORRIÓ AMÉRICA: ARGENTINA, CHILE, URUGUAY, MÉXICO, COLOMBIA, ECUADOR. LLEVÓ SU CREDO LAICO ALLÁ DONDE ENTENDÍAN SU IDIOMA. FUNDÓ PERIÓDICOS, CREÓ AGRUPACIONES FEMINISTAS Y LIBREPENSADORAS. Y SIEMPRE DISPARÓ el MISMO MENSAJE: EL CLERICALISMO USA a la MUJER COMO el AVENTURERO UTILIZA el ARMA.

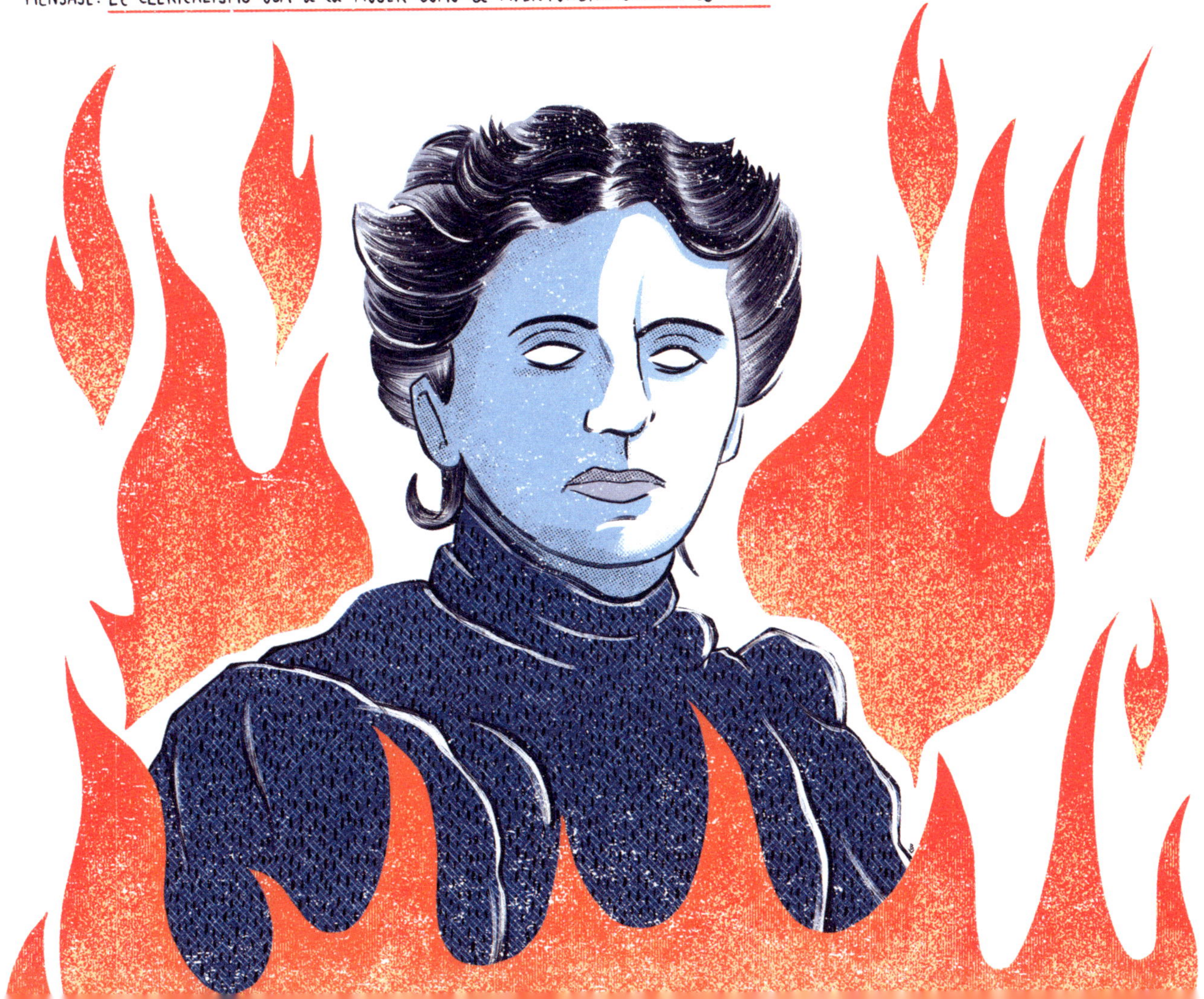

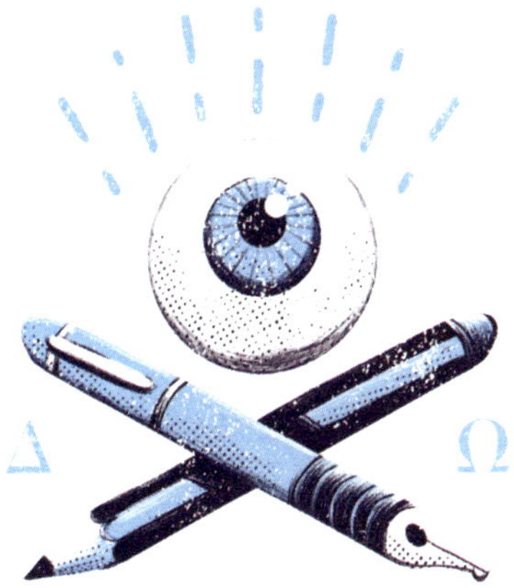